To Vivien

Accounting in the Business Environment

SECOND EDITION

John Watts

Deputy Head, Department of Management Development,
Anglia Business School, Cambridge

London · Hong Kong · Johannesburg · Melbourne · Singapore · Washington DC

PITMAN PUBLISHING
128 Long Acre, London WC2E 9AN

1059

A Division of Pearson Professional Limited

First published in Great Britain in 1993
Second edition published in 1996

© Pearson Professional 1996

The right of John Watts to be identified as Author
of this Work has been asserted by him in accordance
with the Copyright, Designs and Patents Act 1988.

ISBN 0 273 61560 2

British Library Cataloguing in Publication Data
A CIP catalogue record for this book can be obtained from the British Library

10 9 8 7 6 5 4 3 2

Typeset by ⋝ Tek Art, Croydon, Surrey
Printed and bound in Great Britain by Clays Ltd, St Ives plc

The Publishers' policy is to use paper manufactured from sustainable forests

CONTENTS

Ex ante and ex post economic income · Criticisms of economic income · The spectrum of income measures · Replacement cost accounting · Replacement cost accounting – an evaluation · Realisable value accounting · Realisable value accounting – an evaluation · Summary · Reference · Further reading · Test your understanding · Questions

PREFACE TO THE SECOND EDITION

The first edition of *Accounting in the Business Environment* marked a radical departure from traditional accounting texts. From the outset it was concerned to show that accounting was as much about judgements as facts and as much about influencing as informing. In addition, it recognised that contemporary and emerging issues in accounting could only be properly addressed through a conceptual framework underpinned by an awareness of the complexities of modern business organisation.

Particularly gratifying has been the warm reception the first edition received. Its extensive adoption on a wide range of courses at both undergraduate and postgraduate level in so many colleges and universities is not only proof that the text filled a gap in the literature but also that the time was right for a more challenging approach to the teaching of accounting. Many helpful comments and suggestions have been received from lecturers and students concerning the form and content of the book. A large number of these have been incorporated within the second edition.

Also influencing the second edition has been the rapidly developing role of the Accounting Standards Board. Wherever possible, the reader is introduced to the evolving vocabulary of the ASB at the earliest opportunity. For example, the expression 'primary financial statements' is introduced in Chapter 1 as is the idea of cashflow statements. In addition, the American Financial Accounting Standards Board's Statements of Accounting Concepts developed in the first edition have mainly been replaced by the ASB's Statement of Principles. There is also comprehensive coverage of the issues behind the ASB's Financial Reporting Standards up to, and including, FRS 7.

By far the most significant of these – because it affects the format of practically all profit and loss accounts – has been FRS 3, Reporting Financial Performance. Given its pervasive influence, the Statement is discussed in some detail. Chapter 8 outlines the financial reporting implications within a European context. The Statement is then returned to in Chapter 14 when considering the interpretation of published accounts. To highlight the effect of FRS 3 on the interpretation of accounting numbers, Chapter 14 includes a full set of accounts from a well-known quoted company and demonstrates how FRS 3 can be used to help forecast future performance.

Three major changes have been introduced into the second edition as a result of suggestions by readers. The first is the expansion of Chapter 7 on approaches to regulation. This now includes an extensive discussion of the corporate governance debate. Although the chapter describes the major features of the Cadbury Code, that is not the main reason for including the debate within the chapter. Rather it is to provide further insight into why the contents of financial statements are regulated and to allow a European perspective to be introduced into the debate. The second change has been to add a chapter on divisional performance and transfer pricing. The final change has been to introduce a selection of questions at the end of each chapter. Answers to selected questions are to be found at the end of this book. Solutions to questions marked with an asterisk are to be found in the *Lecturer's Guide* which is available to lecturers on request.

Incorporating these changes and the many pronouncements from the Accounting Standards Board within the second edition has resulted in an extensive rewriting of many chapters. In the first edition, for example, SSAP 6 Extraordinary Items and Prior Year Adjustments was discussed in Chapter 13. Although the Statement has been withdrawn, the issues to which it relates are still relevant in explaining the background to FRS 3. Because of that, references to SSAP 6 are now to be found in Chapter 8 which discusses financial reporting in the UK and the European Union. In addition, the opportunity has been taken to make many minor changes aimed at improving both the clarity and flow of the text. Despite this, the structure of the text remains similar to the first edition including the separation of concepts and issues from detailed recording mechanisms – a feature much appreciated by lecturers and students alike.

To all the many lecturers and students who have made comments and suggestions on the first edition, I must say a big thank you. Some of their observations were about content, some about style while others were about detail. Without exception, however, all were helpful. Many of the suggestions have been incorporated within the second edition although it has proven impossible to incorporate all of them in a text of this size.

I also owe a debt of gratitude to Pitman Publishing – and in particular to my editor, Pat Bond – for giving me the freedom in the first edition to challenge the traditional, mechanistic approach to the teaching of accounting and for encouraging me to develop my ideas further in this edition. Thanks are also due to the many students I have come in contact with on the Anglia MBA and the Cranfield MDA. Teaching is very much a two-way process and I have learnt a great deal from discussions with the many senior managers enrolled on those programmes. Many of their ideas have been included in the second edition. My greatest thanks, however, have to be reserved for my wife, Vivien, not just for her emotional support but also for stoically accepting an unfair burden of the everyday, mundane domestic duties which ought to have been more equally shared. As some small compensation, this book is dedicated to her.

John Watts
Cambridge, December 1995

The origins of modern accounting

Accounting is probably more powerful today than it has ever been. Accountants help to run major industrial companies, financial institutions, retail chains, hospitals – even television stations. The fate of many individuals, be they pensioners, employees, shareholders or consumers, hangs on the decisions of accountants. At the same time, rarely has there been more criticism of the role of accounting, with companies reporting apparently healthy profits one minute yet finding themselves in financial difficulties a short while later. To even begin to understand both the power and limitations of accounting involves an awareness of the bases on which accounts are produced.

This chapter:

- Identifies some of the complexities of the modern business world and the changing nature of accounting

- Shows how many of the assumptions of the early years of accounting are still in use today

- Introduces the concepts of money measurement, entity, periodicity, cost attachment

- Develops the idea of duality and recording mechanisms

- Outlines the linkage between profit and balance sheet values

- Explains primary financial statements

- Questions the meaning and uses of accounting information

Open most books on accounting and the chances are that the first page will contain at least one definition of accounting. This might then be followed by a description of what accountants do along with some reference to accounting being the language of business. The image conveyed is that accounting is a well-defined discipline which, if mastered, will enable you to understand and communicate business information with fluency, precision and certainty.

A moment's thought shows this is not necessarily so. The financial history of the UK in recent times is one of companies reporting strong profits one day, only to fall into financial difficulties shortly afterwards. Sometimes it was overstated profits, at other times insolvency, the inability to pay debts as they become due. Often these difficulties occurred despite the businesses being given a clean bill of health shortly beforehand by their auditors, the very people whose role is to examine the financial records of an organisation and form an opinion as to its financial position.

THE CHANGING NATURE OF ACCOUNTING

Definitions are of little help in explaining why companies in financial difficulties have previously shown themselves to be profitable. Even if of use, definitions often only have meaning once the subject has been studied. More importantly, accounting is continuing to evolve, making traditional definitions outmoded even if understandable in the first place. Equally many of today's definitions would be almost unrecognisable to the accountant of yesteryear.

The idea of accounting being the language of business, however, does have more meaning than a mere list of definitions – though not necessarily in the way implied in the original expression. There are similarities with human languages, not only because, like a human language, accounting is continually evolving through time and becoming increasingly complex, but also because it has many different dialects. Meanings not only change through time but also between countries and industries at the same time. What a modern day business person understands by accounting profit is unlikely to be the same as that understood by a nineteenth-century railway company promoter. Profit is unlikely to be measured in the same way in Japan or Germany as it is in the UK. And even in the UK, the elements making up profit in one industry are likely to differ from those in another industry. As if this was not enough, different words are often used to describe the same activity. In the UK for example, goods purchased for resale are called stock while in the USA they are known as inventories.

Despite these many differences, all accounting systems have a common origin and later differences are unlikely to have developed in a totally haphazard way. The possible reasons for the differences are many and varied. They may be technological, with new production methods requiring new ways of recording and reporting organisational activity. They may be societal, as changing values revise ways of looking at accounting. Slavery was abolished stopping the workforce merely being shown as just one other class of chattel while the current concern with environmental pollution may require new methods of reporting in the future. Differences may be due to political systems. Political systems which see a major role for the government in economic affairs will require much greater information about economic activity than a less interventionist political system. Not only will more information be required, the content is likely to be different, reflecting the different needs of government and business. Differences also arise because new thoughts and ideas develop about how business and organisational activity should be reported.

In the early decades of the twentieth century, such differences were of less importance. Much of business organisation was national rather than international in character. In the UK, businesses were overwhelmingly UK owned and based, with overseas activity oriented towards what was then the British Empire. From an accounting view, this posed few difficulties as the accounting environment in the colonies was merely an extension of the one back home. Today, that is no longer so. Even large businesses are now part of even larger groups, and these groups are increasingly international in character. A single group can therefore be operating in several different countries, with each country having its own separate traditions of accounting.

To understand the meaning of financial information in the modern world therefore needs an awareness of these different accounting traditions and why they have taken place. The starting point for this has to be the common origins of accounting. Not only does this provide a framework within which to examine today's accounting information, it will also enable a more meaningful definition and understanding of accounting to be developed.

THE HISTORICAL BACKGROUND

The origins of modern accounting is most closely associated with the name of Luca Pacioli. In 1494 he published a book in Venice called *Summa de Aritmetica, Geometria, Proportioni et Proportionalita* which roughly translated means *Everything about Arithmetic, Geometry and Proportion*. As can be judged from its title, this was a general mathematical work. Within this mathematical work was a section called *De Computis et Scriptures* which described the method used by merchants to record their business activities.

For the first time in print, the text described a more meaningful way of recording financial data than hitherto known – although Pacioli never claimed to be the originator of these new techniques.

It would be wrong, however, to think that no system of recording financial data existed before these times. Examples exist of stock and wages lists, tax assessments and accounts dating back to 4500 BC. It is from the early medieval period, however, that the beginning of modern accounting can be traced. The size of the secular and religious estates existing at that time meant it was impossible for the owners to keep control of activities without appointing stewards or agents to act on their behalf. And because of the complexities even then, problems soon became apparent when information was merely committed to memory. As a result, records began to be kept of what had been entrusted to the steward and how these amounts had been applied.

The logic was simple: the estate property in the hands of the steward at the end of a period should equal the property he was entrusted with at the beginning plus any gains acquired on behalf of the estate less any outgoings. If not, property has either been stolen or lost. This way of controlling the property of an estate became known as the charge/discharge system. Effectively it meant the agent or steward had to account for resources entrusted to him.

Features of modern accounting

To make this work, a way had to be found of aggregating different items of property. Being told that property at the beginning of the period consisted of 100 cows and 30 sheep while property at the end of the period consisted of 70 cows and 80 sheep is not helpful in determining whether property has changed. A common denominator is necessary to add cows to sheep and this was provided by money. *Money measurement* lies at the heart of accounting, enabling physically dissimilar items to be added together.

A second feature of modern accounting also appeared in the charge/discharge system. The property the steward or agent was charged with looking after belonged to the estate. He was *not* charged with looking after the personal property belonging to the abbot, the lord of the manor or whoever happened to own the estate even though in reality the personal property and estate property all belonged to the same person. This separation of personal property from the property of the organisation, even though sometimes *legally* belonging to the same person, is central to the development of modern accounting and is known as the *entity concept*. Even today, the private financial affairs of the individual are kept entirely separate from those of his or her business no matter how artificial this can appear at times. The rationale is a simple one: it was and is *useful* to keep the property of the business separate from the owner's personal property. Mixing the two will simply confuse the issue of what is happening in the organisation.

To demonstrate the workings of the medieval charge/discharge system, consider the following example.

Example 1.1

A person became the steward of the Manor of Berkhamsted on 1 January 1440. He was entrusted with cash of £2,000. During the year, rents received from tenants amounted to £1,500. Wages paid for the maintenance of the estate amounted to £300 and in addition a new building was started and completed costing £700.

At the year end the steward would have had to account for £2,500. This, in turn, would have formed the amount he would have been entrusted with at the beginning of the following year. The make up of this £2,500 is demonstrated in Exhibit 1.1.

Exhibit 1.1 The components of a charge/discharge account

Charge		
Original or opening amount		£2,000
Rents received		£1,500
		£3,500
Discharge		
Wages paid	£300	
New building	£700	£1,000
Closing amount		£2,500

The opening amount to commence next year's activities would then have comprised the *net* charges and discharges of the current year. It would be the *balance* or closing amount of the old year and would have been found by adding the amounts received in the current year to the original amount and then deducting outgoings.

Early record keeping

In all likelihood, the medieval clerk keeping these records would have recorded them in a somewhat different way. He would probably have listed all the resources entrusted to the steward during the year – the rents received as well as the opening amount – in one column on a sheet of paper. He would then have entered in another column the resources used plus any closing amount or balance left over. The two columns would then have equalled one another providing no funds had been lost or misappropriated. To provide additional control, the date of each activity would probably have been recorded along with a short description of what was being recorded. Taken together, the written record would have been a full account of the cash passing through the steward's hands. Because of this the written record became known as an *account*. In all likelihood, it would have appeared similar to the one shown in Exhibit 1.2.

Exhibit 1.2 A medieval charge/discharge account for 1440

Charge and discharge account for the Manor of Berkhamsted year 1440					
1 Jan 1440	Opening balance	£2,000	1 Aug 1440	Wages	£300
1 Sep 1440	Rents	£1,500	1 Oct 1440	Building	£700
			31 Dec 1440	Closing balance	£2,500
Total charge		£3,500	Total discharge		£3,500
Charge and discharge account for the Manor of Berkhamsted year 1441					
1 Jan 1441	Opening balance	£2,500			

As oversimplified as this might be, the charge/discharge type of account had three further features of modern accounting. The first was the regular calling to account. In this particular example the time period was one year, a common period in both medieval times and now. The logic of a twelve-month accounting period, however, was stronger then than now. Then, economic activity was overwhelmingly concerned with survival, the need for warmth in winter and the need for food and drink at all times. The full cycle of economic activity from sowing seed to reaping the harvest was one of four seasons, a twelve-month period. Today, with a more complex and wider range of economic activity most industries face much longer cycles. This need to discover regularly what is happening is known as *periodicity*. Leave it too late and it may be too late to remedy any failings which might have occurred. Report too early and the full picture might not be clear.

There was a second feature of medieval accounting which is still to be found in much of modern accounting information. In the example, £700 was used to construct a new building. This £700 represented how much was *expended*, not how much the building was *worth* at the end of the accounting period. This aspect of the charge/discharge accounting system is still to be found today. The person responsible for the resources was being called to account, to explain what property had been made available and how it had been used. Using financial data for this purpose is known today as *stewardship* accounting and until fairly recently this was believed to be the main purpose behind the production of accounts for even the largest of companies. Even as late as 1952, the Institute of Chartered Accountants in England and Wales were able to state that, 'The primary purpose of the annual accounts of a business is to present information to proprietors showing how their funds were utilised...'[1] An inevitable feature of stewardship accounting is therefore the showing of original costs, not necessarily how much something is *worth*. This emphasis on cost is known as *cost attachment*.

The third feature probably even predates the medieval charge/discharge accounts and is to be found in the nature of the activities being recorded. What is being recorded are *transactions*. Business transactions include activities such as buying and selling, the receipt of money and the payment of money. Transactions have two important elements. They involve an exchange of resources such as the paying out of cash in return for buildings. Secondly, they generate some form of evidence to verify the transaction such as invoices, receipts and bank slips. The data recorded can therefore be viewed as being *objective* in the limited sense that it is verifiable on the basis of the past or historical evidence.

Many of the features of medieval accounts continue to be found in the accounts of today. There is a substantial difference in emphasis, however. The charge/discharge accounts of estates were mainly kept to verify the integrity of the steward or agent. The modern day emphasis on profit and worth of an organisation was not felt to be appropriate to estates.

The origins of modern accounting

Things were very different in the city states of Italy. By the fourteenth century Italian merchants had developed substantial industrial activities with trading branches in many parts of the world. Banking empires based on the city states covered much of the Middle East and merchant venturers were forming partnerships to exploit riches to be found in other lands.

Charge/discharge accounts would have been totally inadequate for this degree of sophistication. They could not easily handle the complexities of many overseas branches within a single organisation nor could they easily provide a way to divide the spoils of the merchant venturers. No one will ever know whether it was the new accounting methods described by Pacioli which enabled more complex business organisations to develop or whether it was the increased complexity of business activity which necessitated the development of the new accounting methods. What is clear, however, is that both evolved over the same period.

So what was this advance which made all this expansion of activity possible? In fact there was no single advance, rather an evolution on several fronts. An awareness developed of different forms of expenditure. Some expenditure was totally consumed during the accounting period (known today as revenue expenditure and covering items such as wages) and some had a life of several years (and now known as capital expenditure, examples of which include ships and buildings). An awareness also developed of the meaning of profit and how all relevant expenses have to be set against income before a profit could be declared. Credit transactions developed along with ways of handling these in the accounts. Evidence even exists in one or two cases of sophisticated systems to handle the reporting complexities of subsidiaries in other countries and the development of costing information by product line.

But underpinning all of this was a new way of looking at the activities of the entity and which was first described in detail by Pacioli in 1494. This new approach recognised that for every business transaction there were two aspects, a gaining or positive aspect and a losing or negative aspect. The cash purchase of a ship would have involved the gaining of one benefit (the ship) and the giving up of another (cash) for an equal amount. The recognition of this relationship, known as *duality* or *double-entry bookkeeping*, considerably enhanced the quality of financial records. Now, there would be more than a single cash account. A new account would be opened whenever it was felt to be useful. In the current example, for instance, there will be both a cash account – recording the history of all cash movements – and a ship account recording the financial history of the ship. That way it would be possible to keep track of changes in all resources in the organisation. More generally, a new account is opened whenever it is felt to be useful and where the benefits outweigh the cost. Some organisations, for example, combine postage expenditure with the cost of telephones within a single account as the total expenditure on both expenses is relatively small. For other organisations, both expenses might involve substantial expenditure and so it might be felt worthwhile to keep separate details.

Pacioli also recognised the need to charge all relevant expenses against sales or turnover before arriving at a figure of profit, a process known as *matching*. Coupled with the inclusion of periodicity, entity, cost attachment and money measurement, a much fuller set of accounting records could be derived which would list the entity's property, its obligations and any profit or loss made. Equally important, the system provided a greater check on the accuracy of the data and so enhanced financial control. This was a great improvement on the charge/discharge system with its emphasis on stewardship and its failure to keep up-to-date records of property acquired in previous periods.

In understanding the duality system, it is critical to differentiate between its inherent logic and the detailed recording and presentation of transactions. The history of accounting appears riddled with prescriptive statements concerning the presentation of financial information. As early as 1494, Pacioli was busy telling his readers, 'at the commencement of each entry... the debtor must always be described first' despite there being no *logical* reason why one aspect of a transaction should be recorded before the other. More recently, the European Union introduced its 4th Directive which, amongst other things, prescribed the way a company's accounts should be presented to members. Whatever the reasons might be for this, there is no *logical* advantage in presenting accounts one way rather than another. What follows is therefore concerned with developing concepts rather than detailed presentation.

DUALITY AND ENTITY

To understand fully the duality system first described by Pacioli and still with us today, it is important to keep in mind the other ideas underpinning accounting information, especially the entity concept. Only events relating to the organisation are to be considered and, in considering each event, there will be two aspects, the gaining or positive aspect and the losing or negative aspect. The application of these two ideas is demonstrated in Example 1.2.

Example 1.2

> Emma Lee has assets of £200,000, made up of a house valued at £130,000, furniture and other household items of £50,000 and cash in her personal bank account of £20,000. On 1 January 19X2 she decides to start a business, Tidy Ties, and transfers £6,000 to a business bank account. On the same day, Mary Anne, a colleague, made an interest free loan to the business of £4,000 repayable in five years' time.
>
> On 10 January she buys goods for resale costing £3,000 cash.
>
> Having bought the goods, the owner of the business next has to find some way of bringing them to the market. She feels the best way is by door-to-door selling and so on 15 January a van is acquired for £3,000 cash. Her next problem is to sell the goods. Because of other business commitments, she arranges for a friend to undertake the selling for a fee of £2,000 which was paid on 28 January. The only other expense was fuel for the van. This came to £1,000 and was paid for on 29 January. Finally, all the goods were sold for £10,000 cash on 31 January 19X2.

The objective of this exercise is to show what is happening to the business of Tidy Ties. This can only be achieved by keeping the affairs of the business totally separate from the owner's personal affairs, however artificial this may appear at times. Consequently, it is only the initial £6,000 transferred to the business which is of relevance and not the rest of the owner's private wealth.

Duality implies two aspects. From the business viewpoint, the gaining or positive part is straightforward: the business has gained cash of £10,000. Less clear is the negative aspect. The business has not lost any asset in gaining the cash. Instead it has incurred two obligations. The easiest one to understand is the loan. There, the business has gained £4,000 but, in turn, it has an obligation to repay that amount at some stage to Mary Anne. Equally, however, the same argument can be applied to the £6,000 cash from the owner, Emma Lee. From the perspective of the *business*, it owes £6,000 to her and £4,000 to Mary Anne. In other words, Emma Lee and Mary Anne have claims totalling £10,000 on the resources in the business of Tidy Ties. This can be explained in terms of stewardship: the business has been entrusted with £10,000 and this is accounted for by the £10,000 in the bank. Put crudely, the good news is that the business has gained £10,000; the bad news is that it belongs to the owner and her colleague.

Returning to Example 1.2, the opening affairs of the business can now be presented in the form of a statement. On 1 January 19X2 the resources of the business stood at £10,000 in the form of cash while its obligations to Emma Lee and Mary Anne who had financed the business also stood at £10,000.

The balance sheet

The resulting statement describing the business is of critical importance in accounting. It shows the *position* of the business, i.e. the resources it possesses and the way those resources have been financed, as being made up of the balances in existence on a *particular* date, in this case 1 January 19X2. Choose another date and it might well be that some of the money would have been used to acquire other benefits, reducing the net amount or balance of money held by the business. Because of this, the statement is known as the *balance sheet* or *position statement* and it always shows the position of the firm *at a particular point in time.*

The positive elements in existence at the balance sheet date are known as *assets*. Assets originate out of past transactions and have financial benefits beyond the balance sheet date.

The obligations, however, are of two forms and *reflect how the business is financed*. There is a qualitative and legal difference between the amount advanced by Emma Lee and the amount advanced by Mary Anne. Because of this, they are recorded under two separate account headings. The loan will have to be repaid at the end of the five years specified in the agreement. This will mean that at some time the asset of cash will be reduced by £4,000 in settlement. In addition, should any aspect of the loan agreement be broken, Mary Anne may well be able to go to court if necessary to enforce the repayment of the loan. Obligations to outsiders which will involve the business having to give up assets are known as *liabilities*.

The obligations to the owner are different. They will continue as long as the business is in being, an indefinite period in most cases if the business is successful. Demanding repayment is equivalent to closing the business. As such, the owner will not demand repayment if the business is to continue. Neither is the owner ever going to go to court as, in law, the owner – Emma Lee – and the business of Tidy Ties are one and the same. Obligations to the owner can take at least two forms. Funds paid into the business are known as *capital*. In addition, the business might make a profit and the owner might decide to keep those profits in the business, perhaps to provide the resources for expansion. These funds go under a variety of names such as *retentions* or *retained profits*. Together, they make up the obligation by the business to the owner and collectively are known as *equity*.

Logically, the balance sheet is just a listing showing the resources of the organisation and the obligations held under the various account headings, in other words, how those resources have been financed: its presentation should be a mere detail. This was certainly the way things were in Renaissance Italy. But even then, Pacioli and others after him were attempting to prescribe the way it should be presented, and this attitude lives on today in UK company law, European Directives and statements and recommendations by professional accountancy bodies. For the moment, these will be ignored. Instead two equally logical balance sheets are shown in Exhibit 1.3 detailing the position of the business on 1 January 19X2.

Exhibit 1.3 Horizontal and vertical balance sheets

(a) Horizontal format				(b) Vertical format	
Balance sheet at 1 January 19X2				**Balance sheet at 1 January 19X2**	
Financed by		*Assets*		*Assets*	
Capital	£6,000	Cash	£10,000	Cash	£10,000
Loan	£4,000				£10,000
	£10,000		£10,000		
				Financed by	
				Capital	£6,000
				Loan	£4,000
					£10,000

Both balance sheets show resources of £10,000 cash being financed by a liability of £4,000 in the form of the loan and £6,000 of equity. Balance sheet (a), with the information spread across the page, is shown in what is known as the horizontal format. A moment's thought will demonstrate that the information could equally logically have been reversed with the assets being shown first followed by the business's obligations. The second presentation, balance sheet (b), shows the position of the entity in the vertical format. Equally, there is no logical reason why the balance sheet should not have been shown with the obligations first and the assets last. The central importance of both approaches is the inevitable balancing of a balance sheet because of the application of duality unless an error has been made.

STARTING TO TRADE: COST ATTACHMENT

Business organisations are not static. They are constantly acquiring resources and then converting them to a form which the customer wishes to purchase, hopefully at a price greater than cost. In manufacturing, this *conversion process* involves taking raw materials and, with help of the workforce and machinery, converting them into a finished product. For traders, the conversion is from bulk purchases in a factory store to individual units at local retail outlets.

In terms of Emma Lee's business, goods are bought for cash of £3,000 on 10 January 19X2. These goods for resale are known as stock in the UK and inventories in the USA. The purchase of stock, like all transactions, has two aspects. In this case it is the gaining of goods costing £3,000 and the giving up of cash of the same amount to pay for them.

Before recording this transaction, it is useful to summarise the understanding of duality so far developed. The gaining of an asset or benefit can be represented by a decrease in another asset or benefit as in the current transaction; in other words the increase in one positive element is associated with a decrease in another positive element.

Alternatively, the gaining of an asset or benefit can be represented by an increase in a liability or obligation. In that case the increase in the positive element is equalled by the increase in a negative aspect – as for example when the owner introduced capital into the business.

This recognition – that each transaction has both a positive and a negative aspect – enables the effect of business transactions to be recorded in a permanent form. There are many methods of recording transactions. What follows simulates the logic in computerised accounting. The gaining aspect will be shown as a positive while the incurring of a liability or the reduction in an asset will be shown as a negative. The results demonstrate the concepts underpinning practically all systems for recording accounting data.

Recording the transactions

Exhibit 1.4 first shows the capital and loan increasing the cash in the business and the loan and capital obligations being recorded. It then shows the stock being purchased. These transactions have different legal and commercial implications and so each has its own separate account. Buying £3,000 of stock will cause the amount of cash to fall to £7,000 and stock to increase by £3,000. After this, it is possible to produce another balance sheet, this time at 10 January 19X2. This is also shown in Exhibit 1.4. There is no need to show the positive and negative signs in the balance sheet. By definition the assets must represent the positive aspects in existence on the balance sheet date while the negative aspects must be the obligations listed under the 'Financed By' heading. This second balance sheet, like the first, is not part of the recording. It is merely a summary statement – or snap shot – of the balances in the accounting records.

Exhibit 1.4 The initial transactions

		Transactions		Balance sheet at 10 January 19X2	
	Capital introduced	*Loan received*	*Stock purchased*	*Assets*	
Cash	+£6	+£4	–£3	Stock	£3
Capital	–£6			Cash	£7
					£10
Loan		–£4		*Financed by*	
Stock			+£3	Capital	£6
				Loan	£4
					£10

The first thing to note about the revised balance sheet is that the totals are the same and that both the capital and the loan have remained constant. Only the *make up* of the assets has changed with the £10,000 entrusted to the business now in the form of £3,000 stock and £7,000 cash.

Secondly, the stock has been recorded at how much it cost – the application of stewardship – rather than how much it is *worth*. This awareness of cost attachment is of importance to the understanding of accounting. The balance sheet does not necessarily reflect the value of the assets shown nor necessarily how much the business is worth. The value of an asset is ultimately based on what it can be sold for, and what an asset can be sold for will depend on circumstances. A forced sale is likely to result in a lower price being achieved than would be achievable in the normal course of events. But even if the balance sheet value was equivalent to what it could be sold for, that does not necessarily mean that the balance sheet shows how much the business is *worth*. How much someone is prepared to pay for a business depends as much on its future profitability as the underlying assets – and future profitability is not shown and cannot be shown on the balance sheet.

Finally there is a linkage between the two balance sheets. The only difference between any two balance sheets of an organisation are the intervening transactions. The opening balance sheet plus the transactions equals the closing balance sheet. Providing therefore that the two balance sheets exist, the intervening transactions can be reproduced in outline even if the transaction data has been lost. This is just one feature of the potential control benefits attributable to duality.

DETERMINING PROFIT

Continuing with the business of Emma Lee, goods costing £3,000 had to be given up in order to obtain the £10,000 cash from sales. This is not the profit, however. Wages of £2,000 and fuel costing £1,000 were also incurred. At the end of the month there is nothing tangible left representing wages and fuel. They were incurred in order to make the sales and were fully consumed during the period. This then gives a clue to what is meant by an expense in accounting. An expense can be viewed as a benefit acquired from a past transaction which has no future financial benefits. (It has to have been derived from a past transaction, otherwise it would not have been recorded in the first place.)

The vehicle still exists and still has plenty of life left in it at the end of the period. Unlike wages and running expenses, its cost has not been fully used up during the period under consideration. It would therefore be wrong to charge the £3,000 cost of the van against the profit for the month. Clearly, if the period chosen had been longer – five years for example – the van might well have been worn out at the period end and so have become a £3,000 charge against profits. The van is only being used up gradually over time. This consuming of an asset over several accounting periods is known as *depreciation* and is a topic in itself. For the moment no depreciation will be calculated as the time period under consideration is so small.

Given this simplifying assumption, the profit for the month of January can now be calculated. This is shown as a statement in Exhibit 1.5. In the UK, this statement is generally known as the *profit and loss account* or the *income statement*. For any particular period of time, it shows what has been achieved by way of trading, both in benefits gained and resources consumed. It therefore shows the *flow* of financial resources entering and leaving the organisation *over a period of time* as a result of trading, with any residual being owed to the owners. This can then be compared with the balance sheet which shows the amount of financial resources and financial obligations in the organisation *at a particular time*.

Having calculated the profit for the month, the problem now is to find a way of recording this information making use of duality.

Exhibit 1.5 Statement of profit for the month of January 19X2

Statement of profit earned in January		
Sales	£10,000	
Expenses		
Stock used	£3,000	
Wages	£2,000	
Fuel	£1,000	
Total expenses	_____	£6,000
Profit		£4,000

First it is necessary to recognise that the business has gained £10,000 of benefits from trading in exchange for giving up benefits or incurring obligations of £6,000. The apparent imbalance of £4,000 can be explained in terms of stewardship. Viewing the business as a separate entity, any gains made by the firm are owed to the owners of the business. Equally, any losses of the business also have to be stood by the owners. Breaking the profit into its component parts and taking the analysis *one stage at a time*, the £10,000 received from the sales are owed to Emma Lee while the using up of stock, wages and fuel totalling £6,000 in making those sales have to be borne by her as well. The net result is that the business owes an additional £4,000 to the owner over and above the initial capital and this represents the profit it has made on her behalf.

Exhibit 1.6 Starting to trade

(£000)	Account balances at 10 January	Van	Wages	Fuel	Sales	Summary total at 31 January *	Sales	Stock	Wages	Fuel	Balance sheet at 31 January 19X2	
		Transactions in January					*Period end adjustments*					
Cash	+7	−3	−2	−1	+10	+11					Assets	
											Van	£3
Capital	−6					−6					Cash	£11
Loan	−4					−4						£14
Stock	+3					+3		−3				
Van		+3				+3					Financed by	
Wages			+2			+2			−2		Capital	£6
Fuel				+1		+1				−1	Retained	
Sales					−10	−10	+10				profit	£4
											Total equity	£10
Profit and loss							−10	+3	+2	+1	Loan	£4
*Optional and outside the recording system												£14

The initial transactions are recorded above in the first part of Exhibit 1.6 which begins with the balances in the accounting records of Tidy Ties at 10 January 19X2. The purchase of the van is similar to the purchase of stock: the firm has gained a van but in so doing has had to give up an equivalent amount of money. For the time being, wages and fuel are similarly shown as benefits which in a limited sense they are. The firm has had the benefits of someone's labour and this is the positive aspect. Similarly the business has had the benefits of the fuel. The dual aspect is that money has been given up in order to gain these benefits and it is this paying out or negative aspect which gives rise to the idea that reducing or eliminating expenses in an organisation is beneficial while the increasing of expenses is not.

Accounting for sales

It is the sales transaction which is the most difficult to understand. The positive aspect, the receipt of cash, is straightforward. It is the negative aspect which is more difficult to comprehend. The key to understanding the negative aspect is to break the business activity down into its component parts *one stage at a time*. Forget just for the moment that stock has had to be given up and other expenses incurred in order to make the sale. Concentrate instead on the receipt of the money. Imagine for a moment that the amount was not a sale but a gift, a donation or a government grant, and assume you are the manager of the business. The good news for you is that the business is better off by £10,000. The bad news is that it is not yours to keep. Yours is merely a stewardship role with an obligation to account for the £10,000 to the owner. Put another way, if the business was to close today, the owner would demand the £10,000 in addition to any capital originally provided. A sales transaction is similar to this. The only difference is that the sale involves a second, parallel set of transactions: the giving up of stock and the incurring of other expenses in exchange for the sale. Combined, the net effect is a profit of £4,000 owing to the owner.

Returning to the £10,000 sales transaction, the negative aspect has to be recorded as ultimately being owed to the owner. Logically, the amount could simply be added to the initial capital but in the real world there will be many sales transactions and it might be useful in the first place to know their total value. In addition, the £10,000 is not all profit. Stock and other expenses were used to obtain this amount and it might be of interest to show this explicitly. Finally, the owner might be interested in knowing how much was originally placed in the business relative to how much profit has been generated. The approach, therefore, is to first collect all the sales transactions together in a single account – in this example there is only one and so appears unnecessary – and then bring this total together with all the expenses of the period in a separate account, the profit and loss account. This is the approach taken in Exhibit 1.6.

The trial balance

After recording sales – or *turnover* as it is more properly called – the next stage is to bring together the sales value and the expenses incurred in making the sales and so determine profit. In the real world, however, especially if a manual accounting system is being used, it is often useful to check on the accuracy of the data so far recorded. Real world situations involve many, many more transactions than recorded here and hence the opportunity for error is greater.

It is therefore useful to check whether duality has been fully applied in the recording of the initial transactions before continuing with the calculation of profit. If it has, the positive balances will equal the negative balances. In Exhibit 1.6 this is shown as the summary total. In manual accounting systems this check is known as the *trial balance*. No matter how described, this check is not part of the accounting records. It lies outside the accounting records and is included within Exhibit 1.6 merely for convenience. Useful as it is, this check is not foolproof. A whole transaction might have been omitted. A positive side of one transaction might have been omitted only to be compensated for by the omission of a negative aspect from another transaction for a similar amount. Even if fully recorded, an amount may have been entered against the wrong heading – for example, the gaining of a van being shown in error as the gaining of more stock.

Period end adjustments

Having checked the accuracy of the recording, it is now possible to complete the exercise and determine profit. As it stands, the summary total accurately reflects the transactions for the month but *not* the final position of the company. The benefits from the use of labour no longer exist nor do the benefits shown as Fuel. To that extent the summary total is overstating the assets of the business. Wages and fuel have been used up in the generation of the sales. And to that extent, the extra £10,000 shown as due to the owners from sales is also an overstatement. Just as the benefit from the sale is due to the owners so the consumption by the business of the resources has to be borne by the owner. Adjustments therefore need to be made at the end of the period to reflect this state of affairs.

This involves bringing the sales and expenses together in the profit and loss account. The mechanics are straightforward and use the duality approach already developed. The first step is therefore to transfer the sales figure to the profit and loss account by using duality. The next stage is to recognise that some of the benefits acquired have been consumed – they have become expenses. A reduction in one benefit will either be reflected in an increase in another one or as a reduction in an obligation. As an obligation is shown initially as a negative amount, any reduction in that obligation will be represented by a positive adjustment.

Stock no longer exists and so the amount shown as stock needs to be eliminated. A similar argument applies to fuel and wages: they have been consumed in making the sales. This consumption of benefits is borne by the proprietor and is recorded under the heading of period end adjustments. Items not eliminated are not eliminated because they still exist at the balance sheet date. Cash still exists as does the van while the obligation to the owner now reflects not just the capital originally introduced but also any profit generated on her behalf and therefore owing to her. To the extent they still exist, these items represent *unexpired balances* and *not* necessarily market values. The balance sheet in Exhibit 1.6 shows these unexpired balances after making all the period end adjustments and determining the profit for the period. There is no stock left: the business's only assets are £11,000 cash and a van costing £3,000. The total owed to the owner is £10,000, made up of £6,000 of capital originally introduced and £4,000 from profits retained in the business but owing to the owner. Finally, there is an amount owing to Mary Anne of £4,000.

The link between profit and balance sheet values

Because the accounting data has been recorded at cost, the balance sheet in Exhibit 1.6 does not necessarily show the current value of the assets. Nor does it show what the business is worth as that depends primarily on its future prospects. However, it does show something more than simply unexpired balances. What it shows is a direct link between the profit for the period and the opening and closing balance sheets.

Consider the bold figures in the profit and loss account. They start with an amount due to the owner of £10,000 from sales (hence the minus). This is then reduced by £3,000 for stock consumed, £2,000 for wages and £1,000 for the fuel. In other words, the account not only shows the overall profit generated in the period but also its detailed make up in a similar way to the earlier profit statement. What is more, it demonstrates a direct relationship between the balance sheet at the beginning of the period and the balance sheet at the end. The equity at the *beginning* of the period plus the profit generated *during* the period equals the equity at the end of the period (assuming, of course, that the owner has neither added more capital nor taken money or other resources out of the business). Emma Lee had invested £6,000 in the business on 1 January. The business made £4,000 profits on her behalf during January and so the business owed £10,000 to the owner at the end of January.

Because of duality, this increase in obligations to the owner from successful trading must be reflected in an increase in resources of the business. Tidy Ties initially had resources of £6,000 from the introduction of capital by Emma. At the end of the period, the business had total assets of £14,000. However, this overstates the assets as there is a £4,000 liability in the form of a loan. The *net* assets – the value of the remaining assets if all liabilities were to be repaid – must be £10,000, a £4,000 increase in resources as a result of profitable trading. The profit and loss account or income statement is therefore a direct link between the opening and closing balance sheets. This linkage is returned to in Chapter 2.

THE FINAL ACCOUNTS

Primary financial statements

In the real world there will be many transactions going through an organisation in any one period. Turnover is likely to comprise a large number of individual sales to customers while outgoings are also likely to be numerous. In addition, there is the added complexity of many more types of expenses being incurred such as rent, insurance and advertising. Nevertheless the principles will be similar to those already developed, with the profit and loss account showing the effect of these transactions on business activity and the balance sheet showing the summary of unexpired benefits and obligations.

Together, the two statements provide a fairly comprehensive financial overview of the firm. As such they might be of use to owners, managers and other bodies such as tax authorities and creditors. Because of this, they are increasingly being known as *primary financial statements*. The profit and loss account will show the accounting profit or loss for the period, the balance sheet and the consequences of this on the net assets of the firm. This change in net assets from trading in turn will be reflected in the change in the obligations of the firm to the owner. The two primary statements form a substantial part of what has become known as the *final accounts* of an organisation.

The cashflow statement

Profit, however, is not the same as the increase in cash. In the case of Tidy Ties, the business started at the very beginning with no cash whatsoever until Emma Lee paid in £6,000 as capital and Mary Anne paid in £4,000 as a loan. At the end of the period, cash totalled £11,000 although the reported profit was £4,000. In the real world, enterprises buy and sell goods on credit. They also buy goods which do not immediately appear fully as an expense in the profit and loss account. Tidy Ties, for instance, purchased a van which was not shown as an expense because it still had future financial benefits. Rarely, therefore, is profit equivalent to the change in cash. Indeed, it is possible for a company to report a profit while showing an ever-decreasing cash balance.

Cash clearly then is critical to the survival of a business. After all, employees are paid with cash not profit! Because of this, a third primary financial statement has evolved in recent years, the *cashflow statement*. The detail of this is discussed in Chapter 11. For the moment, however, the cashflows of Tidy Ties can be determined by summarising the transactions within its cash account.

There are five major types of cash transaction. Two, the payment of business taxes and cashflows paid to the providers of funds such as loan interest, do not apply to the Tidy Ties example. The other three types of transaction, however, can be found in the Tidy Ties accounts. They are cashflows from operations, cashflows from investing and cashflows from financing. A glance at the cash account in Exhibits 1.4 and 1.6 show £10,000 came in from financing – the £6,000 capital introduced and the £4,000 loan – while £3,000 was paid out investing in the van. The rest of the cashflows relate to operations and comprise the cash from sales of £10,000 less the £1,000 from fuel, the £2,000 for wages and the £3,000 for purchases of stock, a net cash inflow of £4,000. This explains the increase in cash from nil to £11,000 and is shown in statement form in Exhibit 1.7. The cashflow statement shows cash generated from operations – trading – of £4,000 but then being reduced by spending £3,000 on the investment in the van. What is interesting is that the cashflow statement shows that despite Tidy Ties having to invest in a van, it was still able to generate positive cashflows even before obtaining finance. Once the financing activities are taken into account, the positive cashflow is increased to £11,000.

Exhibit 1.7 The cashflow statement for January 19X2

(£000)		
Net cash inflow from operations		£4
Investing activities		
Payment to acquire van	£3	
Net cash outflow from investing activities	—	(£3)
Net cash inflow before financing		£1
Financing		
Capital subscribed	£6	
Loan subscribed	£4	
Net cash inflow from financing	—	£10
Increase in cash		£11

THE USES OF ACCOUNTING INFORMATION

Having identified the major primary statements of an organisation, it is useful to pause and consider the implications of what has so far been developed. The method of recording financial data and determining profit, first developed by the Renaissance merchants of the Italian city states and shown above, is still with us today. Before questioning its usefulness in the more complex environment of the modern world, it is worth considering how these merchants would have used their accounting information. Much is conjecture. One thing is clear though: accounts were produced in a particular way because they were of use to the user. And there was little question as to who was the user. The user was the owner who needed the accounts to control the business and make decisions about its future. That is why he was prepared to pay for accounts to be kept. The linkage between the provider and user of accounts therefore was a simple and direct one. The ideas underpinning the accounts depended on one thing and one thing alone: their utility or usefulness to the owner. If new ideas made accounting more meaningful to the owner, they would be incorporated within the reporting system. Few, if any, laws existed to constrain what should be recorded or disclosed.

So what uses might the medieval trader have made of the accounts? The first and foremost use was stewardship. But accounting had other uses. Traders were also interested to know how the business was progressing. Accounts therefore had what was effectively a *scorekeeping* role, letting the owners know what was going on in the business. The accounting results might also have been used to forecast and plan the activities of a subsequent period. The results might even have been used to help the owner make one-off types of decision. For example, a merchant might have used the accounting information to estimate by how much profit would increase if turnover doubled.

Economic aspects to accounting

Accounting therefore probably had a clear role even in the Renaissance world. It was concerned initially with *measuring* and then *recording* transactions in the way outlined in this chapter. Having recorded the data, the results would then have been *communicated* and explained to the user – in this case the owner/trader. These business transactions recorded the acquisition and disposal of financial resources, that is resources *quantifiable* and verifiable in *money* terms. This acquisition and disposal of resources for the benefit of the owner is clearly *economic* activity.

Many definitions of accounting stress this economic aspect of accounting. Accounting has, for example, been defined as 'the measurement, recording and communication of economic data'.[2] This implies an exact role for accounting. It suggests that accounting is value free and benign, that accounting is an unbiased observer and umpire of business events, and that accounting neither influences nor is influenced by its outcomes. Accounting is viewed as merely a dispassionate recording and measuring technique.

Such definitions as the one above stress the economic/resource and the data collection/recording aspects of accounting but there is no mention for whom the accounting information is being produced. In the sixteenth century, there was little need to ask this question. It went almost without saying that accounts were produced for the owner/manager of the business who also happened to be the person paying for the information.

This might still be true today for the small, family-run firm. However, for other types of organisation, this simple relationship no longer holds. Today, the owners of large multinational companies are more likely to be institutions such as pension funds and insurance companies with management totally separated from ownership. There are therefore at least two potential users of accounts and it is not automatic that their needs will be identical. In fact there are other potential users such as governments, employees, consumers and suppliers. Governments can sometimes make their needs felt through the power of law. The same cannot be said for many other groups who rarely have the power or authority to demand information tailored to their own specific needs. Suppliers will primarily be concerned with being paid. They will therefore be concerned with a firm's ability to pay its debts and the *value* of the firm's assets should there be financial difficulties. These are not the same needs as managers. They are more likely to be concerned with *preventing* the firm getting into financial difficulties rather than with security for suppliers in the event of difficulties happening. In the modern world, the simple link between the provider of accounts, the user and whoever pays for the accounts has broken down. Who all the users are and what their needs are is no longer clear. Neither can they be easily determined. What is clear, however, is that it is unlikely all will benefit equally from the same set of accounts because of their differing needs. Given these different needs having to be met from a single set of accounts, the resulting financial information will almost inevitably be a compromise.

Accounting and human behaviour

But even in medieval times, accounts would probably have been used in a more complicated way than suggested by the two modern-day definitions. Actual results of a period would have been compared with expected or planned results and pressure brought to bear on subordinates if the results were adverse. So, even then, accounting was probably being used to influence human behaviour. Indeed, one of the strongest objections to traditional definitions of accounting is their failure to recognise this role for accounting.

> 'To state the matter concisely, the principal purpose of accounting reports is to influence action, that is behaviour. Additionally, it can be hypothesised that the very process of accumulating information, as well as the behaviour of those who do the accounting, will affect the behaviour of others. In short, by its very nature, accounting is a behavioural process.'[3]

Picture the penalties for anyone failing to achieve their budget target in Renaissance Italy! Who could blame an early manager for pushing some of this year's expenditure into next year's accounts and bringing forward some of next year's sales into this year if this showed his performance in a more favourable light.

Not only does this suggest accounting is intimately tied up with human behaviour, increasingly it is being seen to involve judgement. Already in the accounts of Emma Lee, judgement has crept into the definition of profits. We chose not to bother with the depreciation of the van. The argument put forward was that the amount was insignificant. (The reality is that depreciation is a complicated issue and its discussion has to await another chapter!) Judgements like these are forever having to be made in accounting – and what is judgement to one person might be bias to another. In other words:

'Accounting is not solely a matter of recording and classifying. It involves summarisation and interpretation, discretionary tasks requiring the exercise of judgement ... As the volume of information relevant to business activity has become greater, and more complex, the task of providing aggregate statements which reflect, and do not distort the underlying reality has become progressively harder.'[4]

The changing business environment

Accounting is therefore a much more complex discipline than many definitions would have us believe. It is also a changing one. Business environments are continually changing as are ideas about how to represent the financial transactions within those environments. The charge/discharge system could not cope with the complexities of business in Renaissance Italy. The then new idea of duality overcame this. Accounting ideas – theory if you prefer – and accounting practice are therefore never going to be static. Indeed 'the history of accounting reflects the evolutionary pattern of social developments and . . . how much accounting is a product of its environment and at the same time a force for changing it'.[5] Today, business is increasingly capital intensive. Manufacturing has a larger and more complex role. Under these conditions, it is increasingly questionable whether techniques developed for Renaissance traders are adequate for the measurement of activities of complex multinational companies in the modern world.

Values are also changing in society and this in turn may result in new ways of looking at financial activity in organisations. Already new accounting ideas have been and are being floated to deal with issues such as inflation and the impact on the environment of pollution. It is increasingly difficult, for example, to justify the exclusion of environmental damage from the profit statement simply because it cannot be verified by a transaction.

There is therefore a role for new theories in accounting: indeed there always has been. In writing his text, Pacioli was only committing to print the major aspects of a system which had been in common use for many years. The Renaissance merchants of the Italian city states were operating their accounting systems with generally agreed but unstated assumptions. 'They knew no stated theory of accounting, yet the unstated assumptions underlying their accounts constituted a conceptual framework, drawn from the contemporary business environment, within which their accounts were drawn.'[6] The implications of this are clear: no matter how accounting is portrayed as an essentially practical discipline, hidden within it at all times is some implicit, if not explicit, theory.

SUMMARY

Many of the assumptions of accounting have been developed in this chapter, assumptions which – along with others to be developed in Chapter 2 – underpin the production of accounting information today. From this the idea of a balance sheet or position statement has been developed, and connecting the opening and closing balance sheets has been the statement of profit (or loss) or business income. The uses of accounting information have also been outlined. Together, these enabled traditional definitions of accounting to be analysed and questioned. These traditional definitions were found to be lacking because they fail: (a) to recognise explicitly the behavioural elements which permeate both the production and usage of accounting information; (b) to address the thorny issue of just who accounts are produced for and who are the users; (c) to make clear the extent to which values and judgement are involved in the measurement, recording and communicating process.

The use of words such as measurement and recording imply a dispassionate objectivity which may not exist in reality. Indeed 'the ideas of accounting are rooted in the value system of the society in which they operate and are socially determined'.[7] This partly explains why much of the accounting in continental Europe is so different from that found in the UK and USA. But values do not only differ between societies, they also differ within the same society through time. This helps to explain why society, through its legislators, has required more and more accounting information and disclosure over the last hundred years. No longer are accounts produced solely for the owner's benefit. Disclosures now involve information of interest to other parties such as employees. This extension to what is disclosed is paralleled by new ways of measuring what is already disclosed. The answers may not be complete nor, as yet, generally accepted. Nevertheless, it is all evidence of changing values. To take but one example, the definition of profit of use to a shareholder is increasingly being questioned as being too narrow. It is concerned with measuring a financial return and not necessarily with whether there are sufficient resources within the firm to continue in operation. Values are changing in accounting, of that there can be little doubt. The validity of the restrictive assumptions developed in this chapter and their meaning in the technically complicated, socially diverse modern world have therefore to be constantly questioned. The process has begun already as the limitations of existing assumptions and ideas have become apparent. It is being spurred on by the rapid internationalisation of both production and organisations and the consequent exposure to different accounting systems based on different values. To understand accounting in the modern world therefore involves an understanding of values and their changes. Only by understanding values can meaning be attributable to accounting techniques and concepts. This is the rationale of this text.

REFERENCES

1 Institute of Chartered Accountants in England and Wales (1952) *Accounting in Relation to Changes in the Purchasing Power of Money*.
2 Hindmarch, A., Atchison, M. and Marke, R. (1984) *Accounting, an Introduction*, p. 3, Macmillan.
3 American Accounting Association (1971) *Report of the Committee on the Behavioural Science Content of the Accounting Curriculum*.
4 Sidebotham, R. (1973) *Introduction to the Theory and Context of Accounting*, 2nd edn, p. 32, Pergamon Press.
5 Glautier, M.W.E. and Underdown, B. (1994) *Accounting Theory and Practice*, 5th edn, Pitman.
6 Sidebotham, op. cit.
7 Glautier and Underdown, op. cit.

FURTHER READING

Carsberg, B. and Hope, T. (1881) *Current Issues in Accounting*, Philip Allan.
Carsberg, B. and Dev, S. (1984) *External Financial Reporting*, Prentice Hall.
Chatfield, M. (1974) *A History of Accounting Thought*, The Dryden Press.
Parker, R. and Yamey, B. (1994) *Accounting History*, Oxford University Press.
Walton, P. (1994) *History of Accounting in Western Europe*, Academic Press.

TEST YOUR UNDERSTANDING

1 Identify six concepts or ideas which influence the preparation of accounts.

2 With what idea do you associate the name of Luca Pacioli and what was its importance.

3 Identify which of the following statements is true:
  (a) a balance sheet shows the value of the assets of a business;
  (b) a balance sheet shows the value of the business;
  (c) a balance sheet shows the unexpired cost of resources acquired by the business;
  (d) a balance sheet shows the cost of resources consumed by the enterprise.

4 Explain the difference between an asset and an expense.

5 Why does a balance sheet balance?

6 Explain the difference between equity and liabilities.

7 A person begins a business with £20,000 of capital. At the end of the period, there are no liabilities and assets total £26,000. The owner has not introduced any further capital nor taken anything out of the business. Is the profit for the period (a) £4,000, (b) £6,000 or (c) £8,000?

8 List three primary financial statements.

9 What is meant by the term 'net assets'?

10 An enterprise has made £50,000 profit for the period. Which of the following statements are true:
  (a) the cash balance at the end of the period is £50,000;
  (b) the increase in cash for the period is £50,000;
  (c) the cash position of an enterprise cannot be determined from the profit figure alone.

11 Identify five possible uses of accounting information.

QUESTIONS

1 On 1 April, Roger Jones began a business with £60,000 cash. The next day he purchased shop premises for £40,000 cash. All his subsequent transactions were also for cash.

On 3 April, he purchased stock costing £12,000. Sales over the next week totalled £20,000. The following week a further £10,000 of sales took place. He then purchased additional stock costing £6,000 and this was then sold for £15,000 by the end of the month. His only other expense was £4,000 for wages. There was no stock left at the end of the month.

Using the above information prepare the profit and loss account, the balance sheet and the cashflow statement for the business of Roger Jones for the month of April.

2 Rachel Adams commenced business on 1 August. All her transactions were for cash. On that day she introduced £20,000 capital into the business. During the month she paid out £3,000 as one month's rent for the premises she was trading from. Afterwards,

she purchased stock for £6,000 and this was later all sold for £9,000. Her only other expense was £4,000 for wages.

Required: prepare three primary financial statements for Rachel's business for the month of August.

3* Peter Thomson started in business on 1 January by opening a business bank account on that date with £10,000 cash and employing Jane Williams as a sales manager at a salary of £1,000 per month. He planned to sell a single product, the Danpark and so on 10 January he purchased 20 units of these, paying £2,000 by cheque. He purchased a further 40 units of Danpark on 12 January at a cost of £4,000, again paying by cheque.

On 20 January he sold all the goods, receiving a cheque for £9,000 in exchange. No other transactions took place during the month other than the payment of Jane's salary by cheque. On 1 February, Peter Thomson bought 20 units of Danpark for £2,000. In addition he acquired a van on the same date which cost £3,000 although it was worth £4,500. On 10 February, he purchased a further 20 units of Danpark for £3,000. All of the stock was sold by the end of February for £5,000 to George Jones who paid for them by cheque. He also informs Peter that he will want to buy 10 units in March at a unit price of £250 although this good news is tempered by a complaint from a neighbour who feels Peter should be paying £100 per month for parking the van on the neighbour's ground. At the end of the month, Peter issued a cheque for £1,000 as Jane's salary.

(a) Record the above transactions and produce a profit and loss account and balance sheet for each of the two months, justifying your treatment of the planned sales to George Jones, the valuation of the van and the possible parking charge. (Depreciation on the van can be ignored.)

(b) Explain why the profit generated over the period is not fully reflected in the change in the bank account.

CHAPTER 2

Accounting profit – the basic issues

In its early years, accounting served a relatively simple world. As that world became more complex, however, accounting had to evolve to keep pace. Not only did technology become more sophisticated, there was also a move away from the owner-manager towards limited companies and the breakdown of ownership from control. If accounting was to reflect this increased complexity, additional concepts and rules would be necessary.

This chapter:

- Extends the relationship between profit and balance sheet values via the income equation

- Introduces the concept of capital maintenance

- Develops the concepts of matching, revenue recognition, continuity and prudence

- Discusses the validity of the accounting concepts

- Demonstrates the composition of the final accounts

- Identifies the elements included in the balance sheet equation

Other things being equal, successful trading results in a net increase in assets equivalent to the profit for the period and this is reflected in an equivalent increase in the owners' equity. Assuming no further funds have been introduced or withdrawn by the owner, profit generated can therefore be measured in three ways: as the profit calculated in the profit and loss account, as the increase in net assets or as the increase in equity.

Greater detail will be shown in the profit and loss account. The full profit and loss account shows the activities of the business *during a period of time* whereas a single balance sheet shows the position of the entity *at a particular point in time*. Both balance sheet approaches – via the net assets or the equity – therefore work by freeze-framing the business at two separate moments and comparing the changes in the balance sheets between the two dates. The profit and loss account approach, however, arrives at profit by looking at the detailed transactions making up those balance sheet changes. As such it concentrates on the *financial flows* affecting the business whereas both balance sheet approaches look at changes in the *stock* of financial resources. In the case of Tidy Ties in Chapter 1, the opening equity after day one was £6,000 and this was represented by net assets of the same amount. At the end of the month, the equity had increased to £10,000 represented by £10,000 of net assets. Whichever balance sheet approach is taken, the increase is £4,000 and this is equivalent to the profit for the period.

THE INCOME EQUATION

Some transactions – such as the purchase of land for cash – do not directly affect trading activity. The only outcome is a *rearranging* of the firm's assets with less held in the form of cash and more in the form of land. Most non-trading activity therefore simply *changes the composition* of a firm's assets and obligations rather than their total. There is at least one major exception to this. The introduction of new funds by the owners will result in both the net assets and equity increasing by similar amounts. Owners introducing more cash into the business will see an increase in the asset of cash and a corresponding increase in the equity of the business. Sometimes the reverse will happen. Rather than keeping profits within the business, the owners may withdraw them for their personal use. The effect of these *drawings* will be to reduce cash and at the same time reduce the indebtedness of the firm to the owners by reducing equity.

This enables the link between profit and the balance sheet to be revised. The resources or wealth owing to the owners by a business can either be measured by the net assets of that business or alternatively by the equity – the owners' claims on those assets. No matter whether measured from the net assets perspective or the equity perspective, any change in that wealth will either be due to the generation of trading profits or losses or the introduction or withdrawal of equity. Letting W_0 represent the wealth at the beginning of the period, W_1 the wealth at the end of the period, Y_1 the profit generated in that period and D_1 the addition or withdrawal of equity, this can be expressed in the form of an equation.

$$W_0 + Y_1 \pm D_1 = W_1 \qquad (2.1)$$

All that equation 2.1 is saying is that the closing wealth – whether measured as net assets or equity – will equal the wealth at the beginning of the period plus any profits plus any capital introduced (a positive value for D_1) less any capital withdrawn (a negative value for D_1). Using the data from Tidy Ties in the previous chapter, the opening wealth was £6,000, the profit or income was £4,000 and with no change to the capital paid in, the wealth at the end of the period is £10,000.

This is not necessarily how much Emma Lee would receive should the business be closed. It is merely the figure derived using cost attachment to value items which have not expired at the balance sheet date.

Equation 2.1 can be revised. Deducting W_0 from both sides and adding D_1 to both sides of equation 2.1 results in equation 2.2:

$$Y_1 = W_1 - W_0 \pm D_1 \qquad (2.2)$$

Assuming there are no drawings or capital injections, equation 2.2 is simply saying that income is no more than the change in the owners' wealth or capital in the business. Put another way, if the closing capital W_1 is less than the opening capital of W_0 there is no profit – indeed there is a loss. Consequently there can only be profit provided the capital of the business has been maintained. This need to maintain capital before declaring a profit is central to accounting. To demonstrate the problem consider Example 2.1 which continues the trading of Emma Lee from the previous chapter. The opening balances in the accounts of the business at the beginning of February will be the same as those at the end of January in the same way that the closing balance of one's own bank statement equals the opening balance of the next period.

Example 2.1

Assume Emma Lee bought some more stock in February for £3,000 which was then sold for £10,000 by the end of the month. Wages for the month came to £2,000 while fuel used totalled £1,000. (Assume all transactions were for cash.)

The van was destroyed by fire at the end of the month and was found to be worthless.

This problem is similar to the first month of trading except for the loss of the van. As in the first month, the issue of van depreciation is ignored. The resulting profit of £4,000 is shown in Exhibit 2.1. Sales are shown under the more general description of turnover and from this has been deducted the expenses incurred in making those sales.

Exhibit 2.1 shows the gain from operating or trading. What it does not show is the expense of the van destroyed. The loss of the van does not arise from normal operations or trading and so is not an expense incurred in making the sales of the period. It is analogous to an individual having a monthly salary of £1,000 and monthly outgoings of £700 but who in one particular month is fined £200 for speeding. To suggest a net surplus for that month of £100 may well be correct. It does not, however, give a fair or representative figure of normal (or operating) income and expenses.

Exhibit 2.1 Statement of profit for the month of February 19X2

Statement of profit earned in February		
Turnover		£10,000
Expenses		
Stock used	£3,000	
Wages	£2,000	
Fuel used	£1,000	
Total expenses	————	£6,000
Profit		£4,000

Consider now the balance sheet approach to profit determination and in particular the assets of the business. At the end of the month the firm had cash of £15,000 comprising the opening balance of £11,000 plus cash received from sales of £10,000 less the payment of £6,000 for stock, wages and fuel consumed. The van no longer exists and so the total of the firm's assets will be limited to the cash of £15,000. Deducting the loan of £4,000 gives net assets of £11,000 and so the owner's equity at the month end must also equal this. With net assets and equity at the beginning of the month of £10,000, profit, being the difference between capital at the beginning and end of the period, must equal £1,000.

The income statement versus position statements

There is a conflict between the profit and loss account and balance sheet analysis as a result of the destruction of the van. Ultimately there exists only an extra £1,000 of assets on 28 February as at the beginning of the month.

But many people feel uneasy with this balance sheet calculation of profit. The amended profit of £1,000 is not a fair representation of the trading activity for the month because of the serious influence of an abnormal and non-recurring expense. The original profit and loss account figure of £4,000 was trying to convey the results of business activity during the period – in other words it was a representative or *scorekeeping* figure. The balance sheet approach, however, appears to be more concerned with stewardship. Whether or not these differences can be resolved is a matter for later chapters. For the moment the month end balance sheet must show the reality of the loss of the van and hence profit for February is reduced to £1,000. Exhibit 2.2 demonstrates this. As before, the elements of the transactions making up the profit and loss account have been highlighted. The retained profit in the balance sheet of £5,000 comprises the £4,000 retained profit for January plus the £1,000 retained profit for February after writing off the cost of the van.

As a result of showing the profit for the month as £4,000 in the profit and loss account, the essential link between the profit and loss account and balance sheet has been broken. *The income equation is a useful way of identifying if this link has been broken.* In the case of Tidy Ties, despite no changes to the capital of Tidy Ties, the equity and net assets have only increased by £1,000. Expressed in terms of the income equation, W_1 equals £11,000, W_0 equals £10,000 and so profit appears to be only £1,000 despite a profit of £4,000 reported in the profit and loss account.

Exhibit 2.2 The second month of trading

(£000)	Account balances at 1 February	Stock	Wages	Fuel	Sales	Summary total at 28 February*	Sales	Stock	Wages	Fuel	Van
		Transactions					*Period end adjustments*				
Cash	+11	−3	−2	−1	+10	+15					
Capital	−6					−6					
Loan	−4					−4					
Retained profits	−4					−4					
Van	+3					+3					−3
Stock		+3				+3		−3			
Wages			+2			+2			−2−		
Expenses				+1		+1				−1	
Sales					−10	−10	+10				
Profit and loss account							−10	+3	+2	+1	+3

Balance sheet at 28 February 19X2

Assets		
Cash		£15
		£15
Financed by		
Capital		£6
Retained profits		£5
Total equity		£11
Loan		£4
		£15

* Optional and outside the recording system

In effect, by showing the reported profit as £4,000 in the profit and loss statement, the expense of the van has been charged to equity in general rather than specifically to this period's profit and loss account, a process known as reserve accounting. (Reserves are explained in Chapter 3.) Whatever the rights and wrongs of showing profit as either £4,000 or £1,000, there is a danger, by simply concentrating on the profit and loss account, that the user of the accounts would not be aware of the real loss from the destruction of the van – after all, resources of £3,000 have permanently left the business. It therefore seems reasonable to highlight this issue to the user. As will be seen later, since 1993, UK companies have been required to do just this by producing a further primary financial statement, along with the profit and loss account, balance sheet and cashflow statement. This they do by producing a statement of total recognised gains and losses. An example related to Tidy Ties is shown as Exhibit 2.3.

Exhibit 2.3 Statement of total recognised gains and losses

Profit for the month of February	£4,000
Loss on destruction of van	£3,000
Total gains and losses recognised in February	£1,000

THE NEED FOR MEASUREMENT RULES

The linkage between the profit and loss account and balance sheet values was not of any great import for a long time. Accounting was a purely practical discipline concerned with the need to keep a permanent record of financial activity. Its driving force was unambiguously based on the utility to the owners of the business who were more often than not the managers and this is how it remained for a long time. Indeed, 'accounting remained relatively stagnant from the sixteenth century to the early nineteenth'.[1] Any developments were of a technical nature, involving improvements to the recording of data. The primary purpose remained stewardship or control with the accounts being perceived as merely a historical record.

For many organisations, this was sufficient. Much of business activity related to agriculture, with well-established relationships based on the seasons. Costs would be incurred in spring for the planting of seeds with the benefits from the harvest being reaped later that same year. No further information would be required as the results would be plain to see. Other organisational activity mainly took the form of one-off joint ventures between traders with a single, well-defined objective. On achieving that objective, the joint venture would come to an end. Accounts would then be produced for the period of the joint venture showing the amounts originally subscribed plus revenues received less any outgoings. Profits would then be divided, capital returned and the venture terminated.

Accounting and the Industrial Revolution

By the second half of the nineteenth century, these simple trading structures were being replaced. Until then, much of manufacturing tended to be home-based with the owner being the employee as well as the manager. Most products would have involved the simple conversion of raw materials into a basic finished product such as a chair with the major input being provided by the human skills of the owner/employee aided by a few basic tools. The Industrial Revolution changed all that. Complex and expensive machines were developed which in turn required large factories and huge workforces to operate them. Both products and production processes became more complex and this was met by breaking manufacture and assembly into its component parts.

Information now became critical. In the past, a manufacturer would have known the cost of any component because it would have been bought in from self-employed outworkers at a specific price. With the growth of factories, however, employees were paid wages and these wages were not always dependent on immediate output. Manufacturers therefore needed a way of calculating the cost of each aspect of production, a cost which was self-evident before the Industrial Revolution in the form of the price charged by the outworker.

Other changes were also taking place. The cost of large factories and complex machinery and the time lags between production and sale resulting from the new production methods meant that the finance required multiplied many-fold and certainly beyond the reach of many individuals. The answer was for investors to come together in groups. But this now meant there was a breakdown between the ownership and management of the business. As a result, it became imperative for the owners to bring the management to account from time to time.

The growth of limited liability

Around the same time it became obvious that the volume of investors required to support the application of these new inventions would be insufficient without providing them with some form of protection. As the law stood, they would have been in exactly the same position as other owners of businesses if the entity fell into difficulties. The law was clear. The business was merely an extension of the activities of the individuals who happened to own it no matter how it was treated in accounting. If the business fell into difficulties – if it could not pay its way – then anyone owed money by the business was effectively owed money by the individuals and could simply call on the owners as individuals for the amount due. This is still the position today for sole traders and partnerships. To overcome this problem, the law was changed to allow individuals to come together to form companies and for their obligation to the company to be limited to either the amount they had invested in the business or the amount they had agreed to invest, whichever was the larger.

Having overcome the reticence of investors to invest by limiting their liabilities to the company, a further problem developed. Creditors, people who are owed money by the company, were no longer as well protected. Previously, the activities of the business were of little importance to creditors as they could always call on the owners as individuals for repayment. This was no longer possible and so the law attempted to provide some form of protection for them by requiring any capital subscribed to remain in the business. In other words, the owners could not simply invest a sum of money in the business one day and demand its return the next. The only way the owners could take funds out of the business other than closing the company down was from profits generated – and as was developed in equation 2.2 earlier, it is only possible to report a profit once capital has been maintained. Unfortunately, the law was mainly silent as to how businesses should value assets and hence how capital should be measured.

CONCEPTS, POSTULATES, ASSUMPTIONS AND CONVENTIONS

Coupled with these major changes to the business environment was a change in the focus of accounts. Until then, accounting had been predominantly based on its utility to owner/managers as a form of control or stewardship. The emphasis now changed towards the needs of the investors who owned but did not manage the company. Their concern was less with day-to-day operating data and more with the overall performance and security of the firm. Unfortunately, the greater complexity of industry made the measurement of profitability more difficult while the lack of guidance either from the law or any other source over how to value assets gave nineteenth – and even twentieth – century management a wide area of discretion. As will be seen in a later chapter, attempts have been and continue to be made to remedy this problem.

An attempt to limit this discretion was provided by the appointment of auditors on behalf of the investors in a company and certainly by the turn of the century they were a recognised body of expertise. From amongst these auditors evolved 'ways of treating' accounting transactions. These tended to be practical solutions to practical problems derived from unwritten and certainly uncodified assumptions mainly passed on by word of mouth. Indeed it was only during the twentieth century that these assumptions and solutions began to be actively classified and developed by authors and authorities to provide a framework within which accounts should be produced. Even today there is some confusion over the terminology, extent and classification of these ideas and assumptions. Nevertheless, they are worth considering because of their influence in valuing the assets of a business and hence in determining reported profit.

Some authors break down the ideas of accounting into concepts, postulates, assumptions and conventions. Others use these terms interchangeably. Some feel that one or two of these ideas are more fundamental than others or that certain of the ideas are merely derivatives of the fundamental ones. This only serves to confuse. From now on, only the term concepts will be used. Concepts are therefore those generally accepted ideas and assumptions which (often implicitly) provide the parameters and constraints within which the overwhelming majority of accounting reports are produced.

Entity and duality concepts

Some of these concepts have been met already. The entity concept has been shown to be one of the earliest ideas applied to accounting. It restricts financial records to those relating to the organisation. Although not universal, most accounting systems and reports also make use of the duality concept. Generally it provides a fuller view of the entity than other approaches such as the medieval charge/discharge system or the quick monthly check of the bank statement undertaken by most families. The benefits from the application of duality increases as organisations become larger and more complex. The owner of a small business might be able to recall from memory all of its assets and liabilities. This becomes less and less practical as an organisation grows and hence a formal system providing such a listing is extremely useful. This duality does.

Periodicity concept

Periodicity has its origin in the need to call managers to account. This would have been at the end of the joint venture for the merchants of Renaissance Italy. Any profits generated would have been unambiguous, being the difference between the initial amount invested and the amounts returned to the partners on completion. Modern business activities, however, are rarely formed for a single object and limited life. Investors need to know at regular intervals how the firm is performing, not just for control or stewardship purposes but also for reassurance or comfort – the so-called *scorekeeping* use of financial information. The overall profit therefore has to be broken down into convenient periods. But this poses special difficulties as part of the overall anticipated profit relates to unknown and unknowable future periods. For example, a business might be building a bridge over the next five years. Only at the end of year five will it be possible to determine with certainty the success or otherwise of the operation and yet owners will not be prepared to wait that long for financial statements. Consequently the reported profit for any single period is almost inevitably based on implicit assumptions about the business's future and its profitability.

Money measurement and cost attachment

The money measurement and cost attachment concepts are linked. The supreme advantage of money measurement is that it allows disparate items to be aggregated. Lorries can be added to computers to form a total by expressing both in terms of money. Unfortunately, the corollary of this is that some significant features of an organisation such as the quality and value of its workforce are excluded from the financial accounts.

The use of cost to value and record transactions has its origins in stewardship, a function it at least partially performs even today. Because the cost of a transaction is measurable and generally supported by evidence in the form of an invoice, it can be described as being objective. It might, however, only be objective in the limited form of being verifiable. The original cost of an asset may be less objective from a decisional view-point. In their decision making, managers might be more concerned with a variety of other costs such as how much an asset would cost to replace or how much it could be sold for if disposed of today. Only by accident would the original or historical cost pro-vide this information and yet this is the valuation base most often used in balance sheets.

Implicit in the use of the cost attachment and money measurement concepts is a fur-ther assumption, namely that the monetary unit is stable. The expenditure of a pound of thirty years ago is assumed to convey the same message about resources acquired and given up as the same monetary amount today. In times of rising prices this is blatantly not so. Because of inflation, the pound of thirty years ago would purchase far more resources than the pound today. Adding assets measured in pounds of yester-year to assets purchased in pounds today therefore has little real meaning. Money as a measur-ing and additive device becomes distorted with rising prices. Despite this evident diffi-culty, most accounts still happily show the aggregation of asset costs from several different time periods without considering the intervening ravages of inflation and the eventual meaning of the aggregate total.

Matching and accruals

In the accounts of Tidy Ties, profit was only derived after charging all expenses – the resources consumed – against the turnover for the period. This is what is meant by match-ing. Although it appears straightforward, it does beg the question as to what is meant by resources consumed.

Consider a business which has bought stock for £1,000, three-quarters of which was sold in a particular period. Costs consumed by a business become an expense of the peri-od. Costs not consumed remain as an asset at the period end. In this case therefore only £750 is charged as an expense against revenue generated. This approach is applied to all of the costs incurred by a firm, even if the costs are intangible. A company might, for exam-ple, purchase twelve months' insurance for £1,400 cash at the beginning of a six-month accounting period. At the end of the first period, only half of the insurance will have been consumed; the balance of £700 will therefore be a benefit yet to be consumed, i.e. an asset. It is effectively a payment in advance, a payment made in one period but which relates to activities of a subsequent period. This type of asset is known as a *prepayment*.

So far it has been assumed that all purchases have been made for cash. This is unreal-istic and so the time has now come to relax that assumption. Matching involves the charg-ing against revenue of *all* expenses incurred in generating that revenue. Failure to charge costs consumed simply because they have not been paid would overstate profitability in one period at the expense of the period when the costs were paid. When a benefit is received but not immediately paid, the supplier becomes a creditor of the business, i.e. the firm has taken on an obligation to pay the amount at some future date. The firm has therefore gained an asset and, instead of reducing the asset of cash to pay for it, has incurred an obligation or liability to pay the amount in the future. Recognising transac-tions at the stage where there is an obligation to pay cash rather than at the time the cash is paid is part of the *accruals* concept.

By way of example, consider a firm which buys stock for £3,000 on credit. Two-thirds of the stock is sold in the current accounting period although the creditor is not paid until the following accounting period. The £2,000 of stock consumed is an expense of the period in which it is offset against turnover even though it is not yet paid. Exhibit 2.4 shows the recording of these transactions.

Exhibit 2.4 Dealing with credit purchases

	This period		Next period
	Stock purchased (£000)	Stock consumed (£000)	Creditor paid (£000)
Cash			–3
Stock	+3	–2	
Creditor	–3		+3
Profit and loss account		+2	

The gaining of stock is shown in the normal way but because it was not immediately paid for, it cannot be shown as a reduction in cash. Instead it is shown as an increase in an obligation by the business to the creditor. Stock consumed is then charged to the profit and loss account in the normal way. At the end of the period, the balance sheet would show stock unused as an asset of £1,000 and the creditor of £3,000 as a liability of the business. The payment in the next period eliminates this obligation by the organisation while at the same time reducing the cash balance. Amalgamating the first and third transactions simplifies to the gaining of stock and the giving up of cash – the normal way of handling a purchase – with the creditor merely being a temporary heading or account which is reduced to zero as soon as the creditor is paid.

This need to match *all* expenses against revenue extends even beyond credit purchases to situations where the benefits may have been consumed but no invoice received from the supplier. Electricity is continually being used by a business, for example, and yet invoices will often only be issued by the supply company at the end of each quarter. Consider a company which has received three invoices totalling £9,000 for electricity consumed over the first nine months of trading. At the end of twelve months it will need to determine profit for the year. Charging only £9,000 will understate the true expenses and hence overstate profits. The only option available to the firm is to *estimate* the electricity for the final quarter. Inevitably, estimates are unlikely to be exact but are preferred to the alternative of ignoring a very real element of expense for the period.

It seems reasonable to estimate electricity expenses for the final quarter at £1,000 per month – the average for the preceding nine months – unless there is evidence to the contrary such as the final quarter usage being different from other quarters. This estimating of an expense is known as an *accrual* and is just one further example of the general accrual concept which permeates the matching concept. The recording of an accrual is similar to that for a creditor except it cannot be shown as a creditor because *legally* it is not a proven debt until the invoice is received. In the subsequent period the accrual is paid.

This results in £3,000 being charged to the profit and loss account to which it relates even though the actual invoice is not received until a later period. Exhibit 2.5 shows the recording involved on the assumption that after the period end the actual invoiced electricity for the three months was £3,000 which was immediately paid. The amount outstanding, the accrual, will be eliminated in exchange for a reduction in the cash held within the business.

Exhibit 2.5 Accrual accounting

| | **This period** | | | **Next period** |
	Invoices received (£000)	Accrual (£000)	Electricity consumed (£000)	Invoice received (£000)
Cash	−9			−3
Electricity	+9	+3	−12	
Accrual		−3		+3
Profit and loss account			+12	

What though if the £3,000 accrual proved to be different from the actual amount finally invoiced – a common occurrence whenever an estimate is made? In Exhibit 2.6 the actual charge is assumed to be £4,000. One possibility would be to go back and recalculate the previous period's accounts. By then though it is too late. There is little alternative but to charge the difference as an expense to the second period along with other electricity expenses for that period. This will overstate electricity used in the second period but this is almost inevitable when estimating. Had no accrual been made at all, the whole of the £3,000 relating to the previous period would have been charged to the second period. On the basis that it is better to be approximately right than perfectly wrong, the estimating element in accruals can be justified. However, having said that, an important aspect of accounting has been compromised, namely the verifiability of accounting

Exhibit 2.6 Accrual accounting and estimating

| | **This period** | | | **Next period** | |
	Invoices received (£000)	Accrual (£000)	Electricity consumed (£000)	Invoice received (£000)	Clear accrual (£000)
Cash	−9			−4	
Electricity	+9	+3	−12		+1
Accrual		−3		+4	−1
Profit and loss account			+12		

information by transactions and supporting documentation. As will be seen later, this is merely one example among many of judgements entering into accounting. In Exhibit 2.6 the matching of the invoice in the second period against the accrual leaves a balance outstanding of £1,000. This is cleared by charging the balance to the expense of electricity for the second period and this will ultimately be charged to the profit and loss account for that period along with other electricity invoices received and any subsequent accrual necessary.

Revenue recognition

In order to determine profit, costs consumed have to be matched with revenue or turnover. However, no guidance has been given as to the meaning of revenue. The issue so far has been side-tracked by assuming all sales were for cash. But just as purchases can be made on credit, so can sales. There are therefore at least two points at which it is possible to record and report the sale: when the sale is actually made or, assuming a credit sale, when the cash is received. Waiting for the cash to be paid before recognising an expense has been shown to be inappropriate. A similar argument might equally be applied to revenue. In fact this is merely a further aspect of the accruals concept introduced in the previous section. The accruals concept would suggest that a sales transaction should be recognised at the stage when there is a right to receive cash rather than waiting for the cash itself.

Recognising revenue as soon as the business obtains a *right* to money rather than waiting until the cash is received is likely to be a more realistic measure of activity and hence profit for the period. This emphasis on the right to money rather than its receipt will still be supported by a transaction, namely an invoice. This right is clearly a benefit and, as such, an asset of the firm. The customer now becomes a *debtor* of the firm. The invoice is tangible legal evidence that the customer owes the amount; in other words, it is objective in the limited sense of being verifiable. The right to money, however, is only an effective right if the amount is likely to be paid. Most organisations therefore recognise revenue as soon as it is capable of being objectively measured subject only to the ultimate receipt of cash or its equivalent being reasonably certain. Only at this stage is there sufficient evidence of a sale being made and, hopefully, a profit realised. Because of this, the concept is sometimes called the *realisation concept*.

By way of example, assume a firm sells goods on credit for £6,000 in one period which are only paid for in a subsequent period. The sale will form part of the turnover of the first period even though the cash is not received until the second period. These transactions are recorded in Exhibit 2.7. At the end of the first period there is an asset of £6,000 which would appear on the balance sheet under debtors. In the subsequent period there will be a rearranging of the assets to reflect the payment by the debtor.

Recognising turnover as soon as it can be objectively measured, subject only to confidence that the debt will be honoured, is intuitively attractive and consistent with common sense. Ask anyone who has had to sell a property in a depressed housing market. Their relief comes as soon as contracts are exchanged – the legal stage when the sale is enforceable in law. This is the point at which they would recognise a sale has been made. Unfortunately, revenue recognition in the business world is not always as clear. There are occasions when a sale might not be recognised until the cash or its equivalent is

Exhibit 2.7 Dealing with credit sales

	This period		**Next period**
	Sale recorded	*Profit calculated*	*Receipt from debtor*
	(£000)	*(£000)*	*(£000)*
Cash			+6
Debtors	+6		−6
Sales	−6	+6	
Profit and loss account		−6	

received even though an invoice might have been issued. Recognising a sale only when the cash has been received is likely to apply whenever the contract is not enforceable at law. In the UK this would apply to revenue generated by a bookmaker from gambling. At the other extreme, there are examples when revenue is recognised even before a sale is made! Gold production is an obvious example. With gold still playing an important role in the world monetary system, the holding of (unsold) stocks of gold is as good if not better than money in the bank. In that sense, unsold stocks are as good as cash and hence can be recognised as turnover before actually being sold.

Continuity

Implicit in the revenue recognition, cost attachment and matching concepts has been an assumption about the future of the firm. The matching concept was introduced by considering stock of £1,000, three-quarters of which had been sold in a particular period. The application of the concept resulted in £750 being charged as an expense and £250 being carried forward as an asset. For this to be valid, the company must be assumed to have a continuing existence to enable the £250 of stock to be sold in a subsequent period. This is a big assumption but one which is implied in all accounting reports unless the opposite is specified. The assumption that a firm has a continuing existence is known as the 'going concern' or continuity concept.

Consider a motorist who takes out twelve months' car insurance on 1 January at a cost of £600. Asked to calculate the cost of insurance per month, he would simply divide the total cost by 12 to derive £50 per month. The cost of six months' insurance would therefore be £300. There is, however, a hidden assumption in this answer – namely that the motorist has a continuing existence as a motorist. Now assume he is banned from driving for six months on 1 July. If he has any sense, he will surrender what is left of the policy to the insurer and claim a refund. The insurer, however, is likely to repay less than half the original amount because of administrative costs. Assuming the surrender value is £100, the insurance cost for the first six months will be £500 with a closing asset of only £100. Only if the motorist has a continuing existence as a motorist can it be said that the insurance is £300 for six months. The continuity concept therefore can be seen to modify the traditional treatment of expenses developed in the matching and cost attachment concepts when the business is no longer viewed as a going concern.

Other concepts

The concepts so far developed still leave a great deal of discretion or judgement with the individual accountant. However, other concepts have evolved to interpret this freedom. The four additional concepts which help to interpret the concepts already developed are: conservatism, consistency, materiality and substance over form.

Conservatism or prudence

Continuity is not the only factor which modifies the concepts so far developed. Consider the stock problem outlined earlier and its closing value assuming continuity of £250. What would be the implication if the government passed new quality regulations which the stock did not meet? The firm is still a going concern and so there is no need to write down the value of closing stock to satisfy that concept. The revenue recognition concept might be of help. That suggested turnover should only be recognised when revenue was capable of being objectively measured. Given that the regulations have yet to impinge on the firm, it would seem reasonable to recognise the difficulty on the same basis as revenue, that is when the stock comes to be sold or realised. Secondly, if the problem was reversed, if the stock was worth much more than its recorded cost, no profit would be taken until a sale was realised. Strong as these arguments are, it is not the way a nineteenth-century auditor would have seen the issue. He would have argued that this was an overvaluing of assets and, via duality, the overvaluing of the funds belonging to the owners. Reducing the stock to what it was worth would give a more realistic measure of the capital in the business and hence the degree of creditor protection. This is the argument which is used even today despite it distorting the cost attachment, matching and revenue recognition concepts.

Today, the conservatism or prudence concept is summed up by the phrase, 'anticipate losses, not profits'. If a loss is on the horizon, this should be reflected in the current period's accounts and not left until the loss is realised. Although applicable to most assets, it is of particular importance when valuing stock. Returning once more to the stock problem, if as a result of the government regulations it was felt that the stock could only be sold for £100, this is the amount that would be shown in the balance sheet. Consequently, £900 would be the amount charged against income for the period with profits being reduced by the £150 loss in the value of the unsold stock.

The £100 is how much the stock could be sold for: it is therefore its realisable value. This gives rise to a phrase often seen when describing balance sheet stock values, 'the lower of cost or net realisable value'. The cost of the stock was £250 but as it was likely only to realise £100, the lower figure has been used to value the stock. Realisable value does not have to be the selling price: it can be even lower. Net realisable value is the worth of the stock in its present state. Assume that in order to sell the stock for even £100, £20 of remedial work was necessary in order to get the stock in a marketable state. The net realisable value of the stock – its value at the balance sheet date if less than cost – would be only £80 and hence £920 would be the amount charged to the profit and loss account for stock consumed.

Consistency

Where more than one way of treating a transaction exists, the accounting information would have little meaning if the actual treatment depended on the whim of the person doing the recording. Without some form of constraint, one sale transaction in the gold mining company might be recorded as soon as the metal was extracted, another when the cash was received. The overall turnover for the year would therefore have little meaning. To overcome this, accountants have tended to apply the concept of consistency to the individual business, that is treating similar transactions in a similar way both within accounting periods and between accounting periods. In other words, all sales by the gold mining company would be recognised at the same point not only throughout the current account period but also in other accounting periods. Having said that, (a) there is no reason why a one-off change cannot take place if it is felt to provide more meaningful information and (b), the consistency only applies to the specific organisation. It does not extend across different firms in the same sector.

Materiality

Accounting has evolved out of the practical concerns of practical people. Their need to have information was not an all-embracing one. Insignificant items are unlikely to affect decision making or control and yet their detailed treatment might involve a great deal of time and effort. Because of this, some transactions might be treated in a different way to that suggested by the concepts so far developed. Assets with a life of several time periods such as plant and machinery are not written off immediately as an expense of a single time period. A doormat meets the same criteria as plant and machinery and yet, because it is not a significant or material item, it is likely to be written off as a simple trading expense of the period in which it was acquired.

Although a simple enough idea, materiality as an order of magnitude has not been defined. What may be material to one firm may not be material to another. One privatised UK company, for example, writes off as an immediate expense all assets below a cost of £5,000! It is highly unlikely that a small shopkeeper would take that approach. Materiality therefore has to be related to the size of a firm. But size can be measured in at least three ways: by a firm's asset base, by its turnover or by its profitability. And between these three measures there might be conflict. Consider a firm which treats all assets costing below £5,000 as a simple trading expense and assume it acquired 100 desktop computers for £4,000 each. Now assume its turnover was £1,000 million and its assets £800 million. Writing off as an expense the £400,000 cost might not be viewed as being material on these bases. What though if its reported profit for the year was only £200,000? Had the company not written off the machines as an expense, the reported profit would have been £600,000 prior to charging any depreciation. The writing off of the £400,000 in this case could hardly be described as immaterial. Clearly there is no a priori logical way of determining materiality. Once more, the measurement of materiality involves judgement.

Substance over form

In law, there is no difference between a sole trader's business and the sole trader as an individual. Despite this, the business accounts are produced as though they are totally separate. This application of the entity concept recognises the economic substance or reality rather than the legal form. In matching expenses against income, all expenses were included including accruals. Legally an accrual is not a creditor as no invoice has yet been issued by the creditor. Once again, accounting emphasises the underlying reality rather than the technical or legal position. This is what is meant by substance over form. If in doubt as to how to record a transaction, the underlying reality should be recorded. This concept will be returned to from time to time as greater complexities are introduced. For the moment though it is worth considering the validity of the concepts when applied to the financial reports of organisations.

THE VALIDITY OF ACCOUNTING CONCEPTS

Accounting concepts are open to criticism on two counts: their relevance to today's financial complexities and their internal consistency. The relevance of some concepts has already been questioned. In particular the adherence to (historical) cost may not be appropriate. There is, however, a more general criticism – that concepts relate to a business world which no longer exists. It can be argued that concepts emphasise traditional stewardship values based on the needs of a single user or user group. Such a focus may be inappropriate today. These criticisms will be returned to in Chapter 6. Of more immediate concern is whether the concepts make accounting information more meaningful and the extent to which some concepts might be in conflict with others.

Difficulties of application

The major cause of difficulties – and hence the need for judgement – is the need periodically to report the results of a continuing activity. If the activity had a finite life and if it was possible to wait until its end before producing accounts then few difficulties would exist. By the end of the activity's life all of the revenues from sales would have been received and all of the costs consumed. Any remaining assets would have been sold, leaving only cash to be repaid to the owners. Revenue recognition would not be a problem as all revenues would have been received. Similarly all costs would have been accounted for, eliminating any problems from matching. Prudence, continuity, consistency and all the other concepts would have no role. Problems in applying concepts are therefore problems derived from the need for periodicity and because the organisation has a continuing existence.

Concepts have been defined as those generally accepted ideas and assumptions which act as parameters or constraints on the production of accounting reports. Some concepts are clear and specific, for example those relating to duality and entity. Others are more vague or capable of a variety of interpretations. In a recession, judging that a firm is a going concern might well involve a whole range of subsidiary judgements such as whether the debtors of the firm are still able to pay their way or whether banks will continue to finance the business by way of existing overdrafts. The reality of going concern is therefore not as clear as first thought.

The conditions for recognising revenue are clear. What is less clear is their interpretation. In terms of the gold mining example, the stages at which revenue can be recognised can be expanded to five: when the gold is extracted, when the sale is agreed, when the invoice is raised, when the gold is delivered or when the cash is received. Deciding which option to take involves judgement and different firms might exercise that judgement differently.

A similar problem exists when matching expenses with revenue. As will be seen in Chapter 3, there can be a variety of ways of measuring certain costs and hence determining expenses and profit. The conclusion is that some concepts allow a variety of applications and so limit their effectiveness as constraints on financial reporting. There is, however, a further set of problems involved in the application of concepts, namely that some concepts are in conflict with others.

Internal inconsistency

There is a whole range of potential pairings of concepts which might produce conflict. Matching and prudence can often suggest different treatment of transactions. Consider a company which has spent a large sum of money on the development of a new product, as yet to be marketed. Matching suggests these costs should be carried forward for eventual offsetting against subsequent revenue. Prudence, however, might argue for the costs to be written off in the current period because the future revenue is insufficiently certain.

Prudence can also conflict with cost attachment. Having agreed that items will appear at their historical cost, this ruling is abandoned if the realisable value is less. This anticipation of losses sits uneasily with the revenue recognition concept which denies the business the opportunity of anticipating profits. As another example, consider materiality which can often be used to override other concepts. A failure to fully accrue an expense may be excused on the grounds that the adjustment would have been insignificant. Unfortunately, materiality does not easily lend itself to logical quantification. Materiality is a concept similar to sin: the problem is everyone attaches different meanings to the word. Likewise with materiality: although intuitively sensible, problems of judgement arise as soon as it comes to be applied.

Some argue that the way to resolve these problems is to recognise the prudence concept as being superior to all others, that if in doubt, apply the prudence or conservatism concept. But even this is difficult to apply consistently. Taken to its extreme, prudence would mean the abandonment of the going concern concept as that involves a view about the future and the future is always uncertain.

There is no simple resolution to these quirks which make life difficult for both the producer and user of accounts. For the producer, it involves making judgements about the values and significance of transactions and their implication for the continuing life of the business. These judgements, however, will not necessarily have been disclosed to the user. The danger therefore is for users to accept accounting reports at face value, not fully aware of the detailed assumptions made in their production. Because of this, it is worthwhile examining the application of concepts to accounting reports and considering the implications for the user.

THE APPLICATION OF CONCEPTS

The amount of reported profit and the valuation of the assets and liabilities in the final accounts of the business will depend partly at least on how accounting concepts have been applied. Some concepts are continually being used whenever transactions are recorded – duality and entity for example. Others such as the continuity concept may only have to be explicitly considered at the period end when calculating profits. Some concepts allow only one application: there is basically only one way to apply the concept of duality. Other concepts allow a choice in their application. These choices are known as *accounting bases* and from these the firm will have to choose one as its *accounting policy*. A firm will therefore have several accounting policies, each one reflecting the application of the various concepts to its accounts. And once chosen, the consistency concept suggests that these should not change unless there is good reason.

Example 2.2 demonstrates the application of accounting concepts. Some of the concepts such as duality, entity and matching are automatically applied. Others will need an accounting policy to be determined before recording transactions. Revenue recognition is probably the most important policy of this form. In the example, revenue is recognised as soon as an invoice has been issued.

Example 2.2

Ron Marshall is in business selling electrical pumps to a variety of customers. His sole source of supply is the MegaPump Corporation in the United States. The balance sheet of his business on 31 December 19X5 is reproduced below:

Assets	(£)
Shop premises	20,000
Stock	4,000
Cash	56,000
	80,000
Liabilities	
Capital	20,000
Retained profits	60,000
	80,000

Ron believes there is a growing market for electrical pumps but to meet this will involve him considerably expanding his business. Consequently the business borrows £40,000 cash on 1 January 19X6 – transaction (a) below – while at the same time negotiating a bank overdraft facility of £30,000. The interest payable on the loan is 10% per annum, and on the bank overdraft 20%. His transactions during 19X6 are given below. Unless otherwise specified, all transactions can be assumed to be for cash and depreciation can be ignored.

		(£)
(a)	Obtains the loan from colleague	40,000
(b)	Purchase stock, paying cash	30,000
(c)	Purchase stock on credit	50,000
(d)	Cash sales during the year	80,000
(e)	Sales on credit	90,000

▶

(f)	Employee wages (cash)	20,000
(g)	Electricity paid	3,000
(h)	Business rates paid	6,000
(i)	Wages paid to self	20,000
(j)	Purchase van for business use	25,000
(k)	Paid own income tax	7,000
(l)	Paid interest on loan	1,000
(m)	Paid van insurance and road tax	4,000
(n)	Fuel and other van expenses paid	5,000
(o)	Sundry expenses paid	8,000
(p)	Consultancy fees paid	15,000
(q)	Tow bar fitted to van (cash)	1,000
(r)	Paid creditors	30,000
(s)	Received from debtors	70,000

The van was purchased on 1 July 19X6 and twelve months' insurance and road tax were also paid on that date. The rates paid related to the first eight months of the accounting year. Since receiving the invoice for electricity consumed, Ron believes he has used a further £1,000 of electricity. Stock unsold at the end of the period is estimated by Ron to have cost £20,000. However, because his supplier has recently reduced prices, buying the unsold stock now would only cost £14,000 although it is still thought that the stock could be sold next year for £25,000.

The treatment of loans

The balance sheet at the end of business at 31 December 19X5 shows the assets and equity faced by the firm at the start of business on 1 January 19X6. At this stage there are no liabilities. Exhibit 2.8 incorporates this along with the recording of the subsequent transactions. The loan results in an increase in cash to the entity of £40,000. The negative aspect is that the business owes the amount to the lender and will have to repay the loan at some stage. The provider of the loan is therefore a creditor. The amount is not shown as a creditor, however, as this would be misleading. Creditors arising from the purchase of stock require payment in a matter of weeks. The provider of the loan is making a long term commitment to the firm which presumably will continue, providing the terms of the loan are not breached by, for example, failing to pay the interest when due. It is therefore part of the long term funding of the organisation in a similar way to the owner's equity. There are, however, differences between a loan and equity. The owner obtains his reward by making profits; a lender obtains his reward by receiving interest. Interest is payable irrespective of whether profits are made and so is treated like any other expense which has to be provided for before declaring a profit. Secondly, the provider of a loan remains a creditor of the business and can demand the loan's repayment if its terms are breached – irrespective of the needs of the owner.

Exhibit 2.8 Recording the transactions

	Account balances 1 January 19X6	(a)	(b)	(c)	(d)	(e)	(f)	(g)	(h)	(i)	(j)	(k)	(l)	(m)	(n)	(o)	(p)	(q)	(r)	(s)	Summary total at 31 December 19X6
Transaction (£000)																					
Shop	+20																				+20
Stock	+4		+30	+50																	+84
Cash	+56	+40	–30		+80		–20	–3	–6	–20	–25	–7	–1	–4	–5	–8	–15	–1	–30	+70	+71
Capital	–20																				–20
Retained profits	–60																				–60
Loan		–40																			–40
Creditors				–50															+30		–20
Sales					–80	–90															–170
Debtors						+90														–70	+20
Wages							+20														+20
Electricity								+3													+3
Rates									+6												+6
Drawings										+20		+7									+27
Van											+25										+25
Loan interest													+1								+1
Van expenses														+4	+5			+1			+10
Sundry expenses																	+8				+8
Consultancy																+15					+15

Credit transactions

Transaction (b), the purchase of stock for cash, is straightforward with the positive aspect being the gaining of the stock and the negative aspect the giving up of cash. This can then be compared with transaction (c) which involves credit purchases. Here the negative aspect is not the giving up of cash but the incurring of an obligation or liability to pay cash at some future date. This liability is recorded under the heading of creditors.

The next two transactions involve sales. The first, sales for cash, shows the benefit as being the cash received but as this does not belong to the business, the negative aspect is shown as an obligation to the owner in the sales account. The second sales transaction, transaction (e), involves sales on credit. This is a little more complicated. There is no cash being gained. Instead the positive aspect is the gaining of a right to cash and this is shown as a debtor. Although it might not be as practical as cash, there is little argument that it is a benefit to the entity. Once more, however, the benefit does not belong to the business but is merely held on behalf of the owner to whom it is due. It is therefore recorded in the sales account in a similar way to a cash sale as the accounting policy of the firm is to recognise sales as soon as the invoice is issued.

Drawings

The employees' wages, electricity paid and business rates paid are all benefits received in exchange for the giving up of money and are recorded in the normal way. On the face of it, transaction (i), the payment of wages by Ron to himself, should also be recorded as the receiving of a benefit in exchange for the payment of cash. Its recording, however, is totally different to the previous – apparently similar – transactions. All of the previous transactions were verifiable by a transaction and evidenced by some form of documentation – there can be little question that an electricity invoice represents electricity used. The payment of wages to the owner by the business lacks this verifiability.

There is, however, a wider issue. The total return due to Ron Marshall is partly due to his physical effort, partly due to the amount of capital introduced and partly due to his entrepreneurial skills. These are inevitably interlinked. Breaking his total return down into its component parts is therefore not feasible in any objective way. Because of this, the explanation given for Ron taking funds out of the firm is irrelevant. Instead the simple, objective reality is recorded, namely that money has been taken out of the business by the owner and as a result the business owes that amount less to him. In effect it is a return of capital – no matter how described. In outline therefore cash should be reduced and the owner's capital account reduced by a similar amount.

The owner, however, might wish to know at the end of the accounting period how much has been withdrawn during the period. If the drawings were immediately recorded as a reduction in the capital account, it would involve an extensive and time consuming analysis of that account to find the information. It is useful therefore to collect all of the drawings together in a temporary account which will immediately show the total figure. At the end of the period, this total can then be netted off against his equity. The drawings are a benefit to the business in the limited sense that the business's indebtedness to Ron has been reduced. As such they are the positive aspect of the transaction, the paying out of cash being the negative aspect.

Transaction (j), the purchase of the van for cash, is straightforward. It is the next transaction, transaction (k), which requires a little thought. In the UK, as in many other countries, the Inland Revenue choose to ignore the accounting concept of entity when dealing with unincorporated bodies such as sole traders and partnerships. No matter how useful it is to accounting, they view the individual and his business (unless it is a limited liability company) as one and the same. The tax is raised on the individual with any profits from the business merely being one component of the overall income of the individual. All that has happened in transaction (k) is that the owner has decided to pay his personal tax demand from the business's cash account. Effectively, this represents the owner withdrawing money from the firm: the reasons are irrelevant.

Judgement in recording accounting transactions

The next five transactions should pose no recording difficulties – although the payment of interest sometimes causes difficulty in deciding what benefit has been received. The benefit has been the use by the business of someone else's money and this benefit is represented by interest in a similar way to wages being the benefit of someone's labour. The negative aspect is that the interest involves the paying out of cash.

Two of the transactions, (m) and (n), have been combined. However, whether they should be merged for recording purposes within a combined van expenses account or shown separately involves judgement – judgement about the benefits and the cost of separately reporting the items.

The reason for incurring consultancy fees, transaction (p), has not at this stage been made explicit. For recording purposes this does not matter; the benefit has been the gaining of someone's services, the negative aspect, the paying out of cash. The only decision involved in recording the transaction is whether to open a new account or to include it in an existing one. Again, the choice depends on the utility and cost of the information to the owner/user. In this particular case, the transaction has been judged of sufficient importance for it to be recorded in its own separate account. This treatment can be compared with the treatment of transaction (q), the fitting of a tow bar to the van. Logically this is the acquisition of another asset, the tow bar, or at least the enhancement of an existing asset, the van. As such the benefit should be shown as an increase in the value of the van account or as the acquisition of a separate asset. This is not, however, the way the transaction has been treated in Exhibit 2.8. Instead the materiality concept has been invoked. The amount expended on the tow bar has been viewed as insignificant and so treated as just another van expense. This decision to invoke the materiality concept is not based on any firm argument. Judgement has once more been used to determine how to record the transaction – and judgement is essentially subjective.

The completion of credit transactions

The final two transactions involve the (partial) completion of the earlier credit transactions. Creditors are paid and this involves the business giving up cash in exchange for an equivalent reduction in the obligation to creditors. Likewise, cash is received from customers and so cash is increased but at the expense of an equivalent decrease in the asset of debtors.

Having completed the recording of the transactions and checked their accuracy via the optional summary total (or trial balance), it is now possible to determine the profitability of the business. This involves the matching of all relevant expenses against revenue generated and is demonstrated in Exhibit 2.9.

Exhibit 2.9 Period end adjustments

Adjustments (£000)	Summary total	(a)	(b)	(c)	(d)	(e)	(f)	(g)	(h)	(i)	(j)	(k)	(l)	Account balances at 31December 19X6	(m)	(n)	Revised balances
Shop	+20													+20			+20
Stock	+84						−64							+20			+20
Cash	+71													+71			+71
Capital	−20													−20			−20
Retained profits	−60													−60	−38	+27	−71
Loan	−40													−40			−40
Creditors	−20													−20			−20
Sales	−170				+170												
Debtors	+20													+20			+20
Wages	+20							−20									
Electricity	+3		+1						−4								
Rates	+6	+3								−9							
Drawings	+27													+27		−27	
Van	+25													+25			+25
Loan interest	+1			+3							−4						
Van expenses	+10					−8								+2			+2
Sundry expenses	+8											−8					
Consultancy	+15												−15				
Accruals		−3	−1	−3										−7			−7
Profit and loss account					−170	+8	+64	+20	+4	+9	+4	+8	+15	−38	+38		

Accruals

Some of the costs incurred understate the real expenses of the period. The rates paid of £6,000 relate only to the first eight months of trading. As this is the equivalent of £750 per month, it seems reasonable to estimate the cost for the full twelve months at £9,000 unless there is evidence to the contrary. An accrual of £3,000 is therefore required. A similar accrual for £1,000 is required for electricity estimated as consumed but not invoiced. In fact there is a third accrual necessary even though it has not been explicitly specified. A loan of £40,000 was taken out on 1 January 19X6 at a 10 per cent rate of interest. Only £1,000 has been recorded as being paid and yet the interest on a £40,000 loan is £4,000. An accrual of £3,000 is therefore needed to reflect the true interest charge for the period.

Prepayments

Having completed all of the accruals, two further adjustments are necessary. The insurance and road tax of £4,000 was for a twelve-month period beginning 1 July 19X6. At the end of 19X6 only half of this has been consumed. On the assumption that the firm has a continuing existence, £2,000 should be charged to the period as an expense and £2,000 shown as an asset representing benefits paid but not yet consumed. The insurance was charged to the van expenses account which totals £10,000. Of this, £2,000 represents the prepayment of van insurance and road tax and hence the van expenses charged to the profit and loss account are £8,000.

The valuation of stock

The second adjustment concerns the stock. Cost attachment suggests stock should be valued at its cost, not what it is worth. This would give a value of £20,000 for the stock. Prudence, however, overrides this when the value of the stock is less than its cost. The cost of replacing the stock is now only £14,000 and initially it appears that this is the value to be applied to the unsold or closing stock. If this lower stock value is carried forward as an asset, the loss in the value of the stock would automatically be charged against profits for the period by charging a higher cost of sales. In fact there is no need to amend the value of the closing stock at all. According to the owner, the stock can still be sold for £25,000 and so its realisable value is still higher than cost.

Research and development expenditure

Before determining the profit of the business the reason for the consultancy fees needs to be found. Assume they relate to development work on a new improved pump. The matching concept would suggest that this cost is carried forward as an asset to be offset against revenues generated from sales of the new pump in future periods. The prudence concept, however, offers conflicting advice. If there is uncertainty about the revenues likely to be generated, the costs should be written off immediately against profits. To make a decision in these circumstances involves judgement – there can be no clear cut right or wrong answer. Given this, the prudence option is taken with the costs being written off against the current year's profits. In the real world, research and development can be a significant part of the costs for a company. With no hard and fast logical rule, almost any treatment can be defended and criticised. This would not matter except for the effect on profit from choosing different policies.

Other adjustments

Having clarified the issue of the consultancy fee and the calculation of the accruals and prepayments, profit can now be derived by matching expenditure against revenue. Adjustments (a), (b) and (c) represent the accruals made for rates, electricity and loan interest.

The transferring of the sales revenue to the profit and loss account is shown as adjustment (d). All expenses of the year should then be matched against this to derive the annual profit. Adjustment (e) shows £8,000 of van expenses being charged against sales for the period with the £2,000 prepaid insurance and road tax being carried forward. The stock consumed and charged to the profit and loss account is recorded in adjustment (f) while adjustments (g) to (l) represent straightforward expenses written off in the normal way.

The make up of the profit for the year is represented by the bold figures in the profit and loss account. To complete the final accounts, two further adjustments are necessary. The owner's retained profits (or retentions) need to be updated to show the effect of profits generated on his behalf by the business in the current year and to reflect the amounts withdrawn from the business by Ron over the same period. Amendments (m) and (n) record these adjustments. The original retentions of £60,000 has been increased by the profits generated of £38,000 and then reduced by the £27,000 of drawings made during the period.

THE PRESENTATION OF ACCOUNTS

Included within Exhibits 2.8 and 2.9 is sufficient data to produce the final accounts of Ron Marshall's business for the year ended 31 December 19X6. The cashflow statement can be determined from analysing the cash account in Exhibit 2.8, the profit for the year from analysing the bold figures in the profit and loss account in Exhibit 2.9, while the data in the revised balances column of Exhibit 2.9 contains all the necessary elements to produce a year end balance sheet. Exhibits 2.8 and 2.9 also show in a convenient form the essential linkage between the opening and closing balance sheets via the recorded transactions and how the closing equity is made up of the opening amount plus the profit generated plus any new capital – none in the case of Ron Marshall – less any amounts withdrawn.

The approach used in Exhibit 2.9, however, suffers from two disadvantages. It becomes impractical when the number of transactions becomes large. Other methods of recording need to be found which still apply the same logic but are capable of handling larger volumes of data. This problem is addressed in Chapters 4 and 5. The second problem concerns the presentation of the final accounts. In the form in which they are presented in Exhibit 2.9, a knowledge of accounting logic is required to make meaning of all of the data.

Overcoming this involves reproducing the primary financial statements as separate reports and in a form which a user will find both more meaningful and more useful.

Expense classifications

This, however, involves making yet further judgements about who are the users and what are their information needs. For the moment this will be ignored. The assumption made is that users will find accounts useful if the accounts help them in decision making. Unfortunately, decision making covers a whole range of issues. Consider a car manufacturer. He might be interested in knowing the cost of running the paint spraying department. This would require the profit and loss account expenses being broken down by department. He might wish to know the cost of producing a particular model of a car. In this case the expenses need to be broken down not by department but by product. At other times he might be concerned to know the expenses broken down by expenditure type, for example the total cost of labour or materials. Finally he might at times be concerned with making decisions which relate to changes in business activity. What would happen to costs if sales volume increased by, say, 20 per cent? To answer this requires expenses to be classified by how they behave. Some expenses increase as business activity increases. Increases in sales volume, for example, involve increases in the consumption of stock. Costs which change as volume changes are known as *variable* or *marginal costs*. Other costs are unlikely to change immediately when activity changes. Business rent and rates, for example, have to be paid irrespective of the sales level achieved. Because these costs (within reason) do not vary with changes in activity, they are known as *fixed costs*. Exactly how expenses are classified in the profit and loss account will involve a judgement as to which form of expense presentation is the most relevant to the user.

Fixed and current assets

So far, the balance sheet has merely been presented as a listing of assets, liabilities, and equity without any attempt at classification. It might help the user if this was remedied. Consider first all the assets remaining at the year end. Some are unlikely to change from one period to the next. They are held for long term use by the business to help generate sales – the shop premises and the van for example. Other assets are likely to be constantly changing as trading takes place. Debtors will pay their accounts. Stock will be constantly changing as existing stock is sold and replaced by new stock. Prepayments will be used up and new prepayments calculated at the end of the next accounting period. Finally cash will be constantly changing as debtors pay their accounts, creditors are paid in turn and Ron takes out drawings for his own use.

It is useful to classify separately these two types of assets. Those which are intended to be kept for long term use in the business are known as *fixed assets*. Those which by their very nature are constantly changing as a result of trading are known as *current assets*. Within the two classifications there is no hard, logical breakdown. However, it has been found helpful and useful to show the individual assets in order of liquidity, that is the ease with which they can be turned into cash. In the UK, each listing generally begins with the least liquid asset. Within current assets, cash will be the most liquid, followed by debtors and then stock.

Equity, debt and current liabilities

A similar analysis is possible when analysing how the business has been financed. Already, the conceptual and legal differences between equity and other liabilities have been identified in Chapter 1. With the introduction of loans, creditors and accruals, it is now possible to classify liabilities into two groupings. Loans, in general, are essentially long term in nature in a similar way to a mortgage on a house. Depending on the exact terms of the loan, the immediate concern of the loan creditor – the provider of the funds – is with receiving interest on the amount advanced to the business rather than the immediate repayment of the loan. This financing of the business by long term borrowings is often known as *debt finance* or *debt capital*. Trade creditors – those suppliers of goods and services that ultimately make up the expenses incurred in making sales – will want fully repaying in the near future. Similarly with accruals. In a short while, invoices will be received for the amounts represented by accruals and so accruals will, in turn, be converted into creditors. Creditors then require paying fairly quickly, resulting in an outflow of cash which becomes a mirror image to debtors on the asset side of the balance sheet. Because of this, creditors and accruals along with other liabilities which will currently require payment are known as *current liabilities* to differentiate them from *long term liabilities* such as loans.

ANALYSING THE PROFIT AND LOSS ACCOUNT

Businesses which trade often find it useful to divide the profit and loss account into two parts. The first part, known as the *trading account*, shows the difference between turnover and those expenses uniquely identifiable with that turnover. For a trader, by far the most important expense will be the cost of the stock consumed in making those sales although other expenses such as carriage inwards – the cost of delivering the goods to the trader – should also be included. Together, these expenses are known as the *cost of sales*. Deducting the cost of sales from turnover produces a kind of profit. It represents how much profit the business has generated from trading before deducting expenses such as rates, wages and loan interest which, although essential for the running of the business, cannot be uniquely identified with business activity in the form of turnover. This profit is known as the *gross profit*. Expenses which cannot be uniquely identified with the generation of turnover are known as *overheads*. They represent the cost of running the business. Deducting these expenses from the gross profit results in the *net profit*, the amount ultimately due to the owners. This is how Ron Marshall's profit and loss account in Exhibit 2.10 has been prepared. To make the profit and loss account a little more informative, expenses have also been classified by function.

Many overheads remain the same irrespective of the sales volume of the business. Expenses such as rates which do not change as business activity changes are known as *fixed costs*. There is, however, a second type of *cost behaviour*. Some expenses, known as *variable* or *marginal costs*, vary as business activity varies. For a trader, the major variable cost will be the stock consumed in making sales. Double the volume of sales and the volume of stock consumed will double.

Exhibit 2.10 The year end profit and loss account and balance sheet

Trading and profit and loss account for the year ended 31 December 19X6		(£)	Balance sheet at 31 December 19X6		(£)
Turnover		170,000	**Assets**		
Cost of Sales		64,000	*Fixed assets*		
Gross profit		106,000	Shop premises		20,000
			Van		25,000
					45,000
Property expenses					
Rates	9,000		*Current assets*		
Electricity	4,000	13,000	Stock	20,000	
Administration			Debtors	20,000	
Wages	20,000		Prepayments (van expenses)	2,000	
Sundry expenses	8,000	28,000	Cash	71,000	113,000
Distribution expenses					158,000
Van expenses		8,000	**Financed by**		
Financial expenses			*Owner's funds*		
Loan interest		4,000	Capital		20,000
Other expenses			Retentions		71,000
Research and development	15,000	68,000			91,000
Net profit		38,000	*Long term liabilities*		
Less drawings		27,000	Loan		40,000
Retained profits for the year		11,000			
			Current liabilities		
			Creditors	20,000	
			Accruals	7,000	27,000
					158,000

Forecasting profits

This awareness of cost behaviour makes it possible to forecast the effect on profit of changes in business activity. Ron Marshall's business simply involves the buying and selling of pumps. The only clear variable (or marginal) cost will therefore be the cost of sales. All other expenses are likely to be fixed. Interest, for example, is payable even if sales fall to zero, and it is assumed that wages will have to be paid irrespective of activity. Possibly the only savings from overheads if activity falls would be in van expenses but even here the road tax and insurance are fixed elements. On the assumption that all overheads are fixed, it is now possible to forecast the effect of changes in sales activity on profit.

Consider the possibility of increasing sales by 50 per cent. Assuming no need to reduce prices to achieve this increased level of sales, turnover will increase by £85,000. To estimate the effect on profit, however, requires an awareness of cost behaviour. Stock used will also increase by 50 per cent, assuming no quantity discounts, resulting in an increase in expense of £32,000. As all other costs are assumed fixed, there will be no further increase in expenses. Overall therefore profit will increase by £53,000, the difference between the extra sales and the extra stock consumed. In other words, a 50 per cent increase in sales activity results in a 140 per cent increase in profitability.

An analysis of the expenses provides a further insight into likely profitability. Most of the overheads are inevitable if the business is to continue trading – wages have to be met and rates paid. There is, however, one out-of-the-ordinary expense. This is the research and development expenditure into the possibility of a new pump. Even if nothing ever comes of the proposal, it is unlikely that the research expense will recur in subsequent years. It is therefore possible to forecast that, other things being equal, next year's profits will be increased by £15,000 – even if there is no change in the level of sales – because of the expense saved in not having to pay for further consultancy.

THE CASHFLOW STATEMENT

Groupings within the cashflow statement

Before moving on to consider the revised presentation of the balance sheet, it is worth comparing the reported profit with the change in the cash position within the business. Chapter 1 has already identified the major types of transactions which affect the cash account. Cash can change because of operating activities, i.e. trading; because of increases or decreases in long term sources of finance such as capital or loans; because of payments to the providers of finance; because of investments in fixed assets; and because of tax payments to the Inland Revenue. Apart from taxation, which is excluded from the example of Ron Marshall, Exhibit 2.11 shows totals for all these groupings. These totals

Exhibit 2.11 The cashflow statement

Cashflow statement for the year ended 31 December 19X6		
	(£000)	*(£000)*
Net cash inflow from operating activities[1]		28
Interest paid	(1)	
Drawings	(27)	
Net cash outflow from servicing finance[2]		(28)
Payment to acquire van	(25)	
Net cash outflow from investing activities[3]		(25)
Net cashflow before financing		(25)
Financing – loan	40	
Net cashflow from financing[4]		40
Increase in cash		15
Analysis of changes in cash during the year		
Balance at 1 January 19X6		56
Net cash inflow		15
Balance at 31 December 19X6		71

Workings:
1. Transactions (b) –30, (d) +80, (f) –20, (g) –3, (h) –6, (m) –4, (n) –5, (o) –8, (p) –15, (q) –1, (r) –30, (s) +70
2. Transactions (i) –20, (k) –7, (l) –1
3. Transaction (j) –25
4. Transaction (a) +40

have been derived by analysing the transactions found within the cash account for the year. At the commencement of trading, the cash balance was £56,000. By the end of the period, this had increased to £71,000, a net increase of £15,000. Profit, however, was reported as £38,000. Profit is therefore not the same as the change in cash.

Rarely will they equal one another. Sales are sold on credit and so not all turnover manifests itself in the form of cash within the accounting period. On the other hand, not all purchases are paid immediately and so some expenses will not cause a corresponding outflow of cash. Some cash inflows and outflows do not affect the profit and loss account. Raising more capital or the obtaining of a loan will result in a cash inflow. Similarly the withdrawal of funds or the purchase of a fixed asset will result in a cash outflow although neither of these will immediately appear as an expense in the income statement.

From Exhibit 2.11 it can be seen that the cashflow generated from trading was only just enough to cover the payments to the providers of finance – the £27,000 of drawings to Ron Marshall, the owner and the £1,000 of interest to the colleague who provided the loan. After making the investment in the van, the cashflow for the year is negative. Should this trend continue into the future, the business would run out of cash without further finance being provided. A critical lesson therefore is to recognise that profit is not the same as the change in cash. Without cash, creditors and employees cannot be paid nor can a return be given to the providers of finance.

Cashflow versus the profit and loss account

Given this importance of cash generation, it might be felt that users should concentrate on the cashflow statement rather than the profit and loss account. After all, profit is based on accounting judgements such as when to recognise revenue while cash is unambiguous. You have either received cash or you have not. You have either paid a creditor or you have not.

As appealing as this might be, it is too simplistic. Cashflow can be manipulated. Consider a domestic household faced with a cashflow problem. Probably the first thing they would do would be to start using up the food in the freezer rather than going to the supermarket. Next, they might delay paying the newspaper bill and the window cleaner – in other words, their creditors. If this is insufficient, they might try asking people who owe them money – debtors – to pay up early. Finally, if all else fails, they might start selling off the family assets such as the television, the car and even the home. The result is an increase in cashflow but a decrease in stock from the freezer which will have to be replenished some day, an increase in liabilities in the form of creditors and a decrease in some essential assets such as the car and home.

Business enterprises can manipulate their cashflows in a similar way. It would seem, therefore, that it is less a case of choosing between the cashflow statement and the profit and loss account, and more a case of using both intelligently. The profit and loss account shows the net flow of *resources* entering the business as a result of operations, the gaining of assets in the form of debtors or cash from making sales less the giving up of resources such as stock and the incurring of expenses such as wages in exchange. As such, profit can be viewed as a measure of business performance or economic activity. Other things being equal, an increase in resources as a result of trading – i.e. making a profit – represents a better performance than a decrease in resources from making a loss. The cashflow statement, on the other hand, emphasises a single resource – cash – because of its critical importance in an organisation's short term survival. Without immediate cash or access to cash, creditors cannot be paid and this might well lead to the demise of the business. Equally, without long term profits, cashflow will eventually dry up as more resources will be leaving the organisation than entering it via sales and eventually this must be reflected in a deteriorating cash position. Both statements, therefore, are measuring an entity's activities – but from different perspectives and so the need is to read and understand both.

THE BALANCE SHEET

The balance sheet shown in Exhibit 2.10 has merely taken the year end balances derived in Exhibit 2.9 and put them into groupings. Fixed assets have been brought together and subtotalled, as have current assets and current liabilities.

Dividing the balance sheet into its component parts of fixed assets, current assets, current liabilities, equity (or owner's funds) and long term liabilities enables the balance sheet to be expressed as an equation. Given that total assets equals total liabilities, it follows that:

Fixed assets + Current assets = Current liabilities + Long term liabilities + Equity   (2.3)

This is known as the *balance sheet equation*. It has been logically derived and, as with all equations, it will still balance even if adjustments are made, provided the adjustment applies equally to both sides. Consider the balance sheet in Exhibit 2.10. Superficially the business appears to have £158,000 of assets. A moments thought, however, shows this to be an overstatement. Consider what would happen to the assets and liabilities of the business if it stopped trading for a few weeks. On the assets side, debtors will eventually pay their accounts causing the value of debtors to fall and cash to increase by an equivalent amount. This, however, does not change the overall level of current assets, merely their composition. The same is not true when suppliers are paid. If all of the creditors and accruals are paid, current liabilities will fall to zero and cash will fall by an equivalent amount. There is therefore a direct link between current liabilities and current assets. Indeed the current assets of £113,000 in Exhibit 2.10 only stand at that figure because suppliers have yet to insist on payment. As soon as they are paid, current assets will fall by £27,000 to £86,000. Because of this it seems more realistic to deduct current liabilities from current assets to reflect the underlying assets of the firm. This result is shown in equation 2.4:

Fixed assets + Current assets – Current liabilities = Long term liabilities + Equity   (2.4)

The balance sheet derived from this equation is shown as balance sheet (a) in Exhibit 2.12. Before considering the meaning of this balance sheet, however, there is one further revision possible to the balance sheet equation. It is possible to deduct the long term liabilities from both sides. The amended equation is shown as equation 2.5 and results in balance sheet (b) in Exhibit 2.12:

Fixed assets + Current assets – Current liabilities – Long term liabilities = Equity   (2.5)

Exhibit 2.12 The entity and proprietorial balance sheets

Balance sheet (a) at 31 December 19X6			*(£)*	**Balance sheet (b) at 31 December 19X6**			*(£)*
Assets				**Assets**			
Fixed assets				*Fixed assets*			
Shop premises			20,000	Shop premises			20,000
Van			25,000	Van			25,000
			45,000				45,000
Current assets				*Current assets*			
Stock	20,000			Stock	20,000		
Debtors	20,000			Debtors	20,000		
Prepayments	2,000			Prepayments	2,000		
Cash	71,000	113,000		Cash	71,000	113,000	
Current liabilities				*Current liabilities*			
Creditors	20,000			Creditors	20,000		
Accruals	7,000	27,000	86,000	Accruals	7,000	27,000	86,000
			131,000				131,000
				Less long term liabilities			
Financed by				Loan			40,000
Owner's funds							91,000
Capital			20,000				
				Financed by			
Retentions			71,000	*Owner's funds*			
			91,000	Capital			20,000
Long term liabilities				Retentions			71,000
Loan			40,000				91,000
			131,000				

There are now three equations and three balance sheets all purporting to show the final position of Ron Marshall's business at 31 December 19X6. To break through the confusion, it is first necessary to recognise that each balance sheet and each equation reflects identical data. Any apparent differences arise from basic algebraic manipulation. In choosing which balance sheet and which equation is to be preferred, it is necessary to consider their relative worth to the user.

Consider a manager who needs to know the level of resources within the business. There are three potential asset totals, each one representing one of the three balance sheets developed: the £158,000 shown in Exhibit 2.10 and the £131,000 and £91,000 figures shown in Exhibit 2.12. Given that the £27,000 represented by the current liabilities will soon have to be paid, it seems the original balance sheet is an overstatement of the assets available to management. The resources over which management have control are the £131,000 net assets shown in balance sheet (a) of Exhibit 2.12. These are not susceptible to short term demands from creditors but represent assets available long term in the business subject only to the loan conditions continuing to be met.

Consider now balance sheet (b) with an asset total of £91,000. This is of less meaning to management who presumably require £131,000 of assets to run the business at its current level of operations. Instead it shows how the owner's funds have been used in the business and what assets are reflected by those funds. Effectively, the owner *controls*

£131,000 of assets of which £40,000 are financed by loans leaving the net assets of £91,000 to represent the use of the owner's funds.

It is possible therefore that both balance sheets might be of use – albeit for different purposes. Balance sheet (a) looks at the business from the wider perspective of management or the business itself. How it is financed between debt and equity is viewed as a separate issue. Because of this concern with the business, such a view is known as the *entity* approach to accounts. Balance sheet (b), however, is more concerned with explaining how the owner's investment in the business has been used. This emphasis on the owner has resulted in the approach being called the *proprietorial* approach. Intuitively it seems that both the management and the workforce will primarily be concerned with the assets held within the business, viewing as secondary how they have been financed. Equity investors, however, are more likely to focus their attentions on their particular investment. This difference in attitudes is represented by the two balance sheets in Exhibit 2.12.

Before leaving the balance sheet of Ron Marshall's business, there is one source of finance given in the original example which is not reflected in the final accounts – the £30,000 bank overdraft facility. This is inevitable given the nature of an overdraft. A loan involves the immediate receipt of cash and the immediate incurring of an obligation. Even if not used immediately, the cash is within the business and hence a loan is immediately recorded in the accounts. An overdraft is different. An overdraft facility is an agreement by a bank to a client to allow cheques to be issued even when there are insufficient funds in the account to meet the cheques. If the facility is activated, the cash (or more accurately, the bank) balance will ultimately have a negative value and, rather than being shown as a current asset, it will be shown as a current liability. Until that time, however, the facility will have no affect on the reported assets and liabilities of a firm. Logically, it cannot be shown on the balance sheet because no transaction has taken place. This is the reality despite the potential advantage to a firm holding such a facility.

THE INCOME EQUATION REVISITED

The introduction of the balance sheet equation and the development of the entity approach enables the income equation developed at the beginning of this chapter to be revised. Originally equation 2.2 expressed income as:

$$Y_1 = W_1 - W_0 \pm D_1 \tag{2.2}$$

where Y_1 represented income for period 1, W_1 represented equity or net assets at the end of the period, W_0 the equity or net assets at the beginning of the period and D_1 the equity introduced or withdrawn within the period.

Two perspectives of the balance sheet have been developed, that of the entity and that of the proprietor. Income equation 2.2 can handle both approaches. Consider first the proprietorial approach. The original equity in the business was £80,000, the closing equity was £91,000 and the only other transaction concerning the owner was the withdrawal of funds for his personal use of £27,000. Keeping in mind that all of these values are 'book' values based on accounting conventions such as cost or net realisable value, whichever is the lower, the income for the period, Y_1, is as follows:

$$Y_1 = £91,000 - £80,000 + £27,000 = £38,000$$

In other words, Y_1 is equal to the profit for the period calculated in the traditional way. Consider now the approach where all the elements are expressed in terms of the business. Here the closing capital represents the net assets viewed from an entity perspective. The closing assets of £131,000 are represented by the owner's closing investment in the firm plus the balance sheet value of any long term loans. The opening assets or wealth were £80,000 and the only other transactions were the drawings of £27,000 and the loan introduced of £40,000. Expressing this as an equation once more shows income for the period of £38,000:

$$Y_1 = £131,000 - £80,000 + (£27,000 - £40,000) = £38,000$$

The importance of the income equation is that it ties income firmly into wealth measures – as measured by the accounting concepts and balance sheet values developed in this chapter. This relationship is critical when it comes to the analysis and interpretation of the underlying profitability of a business. As was shown in the earlier example of Tidy Ties, it is possible to report some expenses via previous retentions rather than the current profit and loss account, the effect of which is to boost the current reported profit figure.

SUMMARY

This chapter began and ended with a discussion of the income equation. It demonstrated the central relationship between income and owner's funds or equity. How income is measured therefore affects the value of assets and hence the value of equity. Because of this, there followed an extensive discussion of the role accounting concepts play in assigning values to transactions. What became clear was the extent of judgement in accounting, both in deciding how to value assets and in deciding how information should be presented. Using the balance sheet equation, three equally logical balance sheets were developed. As a result it was suggested that deducting current liabilities from current assets had greater meaning than showing current liabilities as a source of finance. Whether the financing side of the balance sheet should show merely the equity stake in the business or whether it should be extended to show the debt finance as well depended on the perspective from which the business was viewed. The proprietorial approach is predominantly concerned with the interest of the owner(s) while the entity approach is more concerned with reflecting the wider business perspective. Armed with this understanding, it is now possible to move on to more realistic issues in the measurement and valuation of income.

REFERENCE

1 Lee, G.A. (1986) *Modern Financial Accounting*, 4th edn, p. 10, Van Nostrand Reinhold (UK).

TEST YOUR UNDERSTANDING

1 A business starts the year with net assets of £100,000. It reported profits for the year of £40,000. No additional capital was introduced and no drawings took place during the period. Assuming no other complications, should the equity at the year end be (a) £60,000, (b) £140,000, (c) £100,000?

2 Assuming the owners of a business introduce no further capital nor make any drawings, identify which of the following statements is true. Capital maintenance refers to:
   (a) the paying in of cash by the owner(s) of a business;
   (b) the regular payments by the business to the owner(s) to maintain their income;
   (c) only declaring a profit if the opening value of equity is maintained.

3 What is meant by reserve accounting?

4 The balance sheet, the profit and loss account and the cashflow statement are all primary financial statements. Identify a further primary statement to be found in the accounts of UK companies.

5 The concept of matching refers to:
   (a) charging all expenses for a period, including invoices not yet paid or received, against revenue;
   (b) identifying goods and services purchased with their respective invoices;
   (c) recording revenues and expenses in the same currency;
   (d) the value of net assets equalling the value of an enterprise's equity.

6 When is revenue recognised in the accounts of a business?

7 What is meant by the expression 'going concern'?

8 A business paid £100,000 for 100 units of stock of which 50 units were sold. At the end of the period, the purchase price of the stock had fallen to £800 per unit. The business believes it can sell the remaining stock for £1,400 per unit once it has paid an extra £300 per unit to make the stock marketable. At the period end, the stock will be valued at: (a) £40,000; (b) £50,000; (c) £70,000; (d) £60,000.

9 Differentiate between accounting bases and accounting policies.

10 A sole trader has a turnover of £100,000 in one month. During the period, stock consumed totalled £40,000. The only other transactions were three months rent paid of £45,000 and wages for the month of £10,000. The wages comprised £1,000 to a sales assistant and £9,000 wages to the owner. The profit for the period was: (a) £5,000; (b) £35,000; (c) £14,000; (d) £44,000.

11 Explain the following terms: fixed assets; current assets; current liabilities.

12 During a four-week period, a retailer achieved a turnover of £50,000. The cost of sales comprised stock consumed of £30,000. The only other expenses related to wages of £1,000 per week and rent of £3,000 per four weeks. The retailer believes the sales volume in the next four-week period will increase by 20 per cent without any change to the selling price. The estimated profit next period is: (a) £13,000; (b) £17,000; (c) £16,000; (d) £15,600.

QUESTIONS

1 Jane Greenwood is the owner of Quick Factors, a wholesale business supplying equipment to garages. The business operates out of two premises, one owned by the business and the other rented at £200 per week. The balance sheet of Quick Factors on 1 March 19X7 is shown below.

Fixed assets			(£)
Premises			30,000
Vehicles			20,000
			50,000
Current assets			
Stock	2,400		
Debtors	2,900		
Prepayment of rent	600		
Cash and bank balances	3,800	9,700	
Current liabilities			
Creditors	4,200		
Accruals – electricity	700	4,900	4,800
			54,800
Financed by			
Capital			28,000
Retentions			26,800
			54,800

Over the next four weeks, the following transactions took place:

(a)	Credit sales	£4,100
(b)	Cash and cheques received from debtors	£1,800
(c)	Payment to creditors	£700
(d)	Purchase of stock on credit	£1,900
(e)	Payment of rent	£1,200
(f)	Invoice for electricity consumed to 14 March received and paid	£1,400
(g)	Credit sales	£4,400
(h)	Purchase of stock on credit	£1,200
(i)	Wages paid for the four weeks	£2,700
(j)	Cash received from debtors	£6,200
(k)	Payment to creditors	£5,100

On 28 March, Jane estimated that the business had consumed £300 of electricity since receiving and paying the original invoice and that the cost of stock unsold at the end of the period was £2,400.

Making use of the above data, prepare the profit and loss account and balance sheet of Quick Factors at 28 March 19X7. (Depreciation can be ignored.)

2 On 1 July, the assets in the balance sheet of Kevin's Hardware Shop comprised premises of £80,000, fixtures and fittings of £30,000, stock of £65,000, debtors of £34,000 and cash of £4,500. The business's only liabilities related to creditors and totalled £51,000.

Six months later, Kevin left all the accounting records with his accountant. Unfortunately, there was a fire at the accountant's premises which destroyed all of Kevin's accounts. During the six-month period, no fixed assets had been sold. Kevin, however, was able to verify that additional fixtures and fittings had been purchased for £14,000 cash and this was subsequently confirmed by the supplier.

A check of his storeroom showed that stock on 31 December totalled £73,000. Enquiries to customers showed that debtors owed the business £42,000 while creditors were able to demonstrate that the business owed them £13,500. Cash on the premises and at the bank totalled £6,000.

Kevin is particularly worried by this state of affairs as during the period he had paid in £40,000 additional capital in the form of cash and yet the cash balance had only increased by £1,500, suggesting to him that the business was no longer as profitable as it used to be.

Estimate the profit of Kevin's Hardware Shop for the six-month period and suggest why profit may not be the same as the increase in a business's cash. (Depreciation can be ignored.)

3* Anne Preston is the owner of a small printing business, partly financed by a £50,000, 10 per cent loan. The business's balance sheet at 31 December showed the following assets: premises, £30,000; plant and machinery, £40,000; stocks, £20,000; debtors, £35,000; and cash and bank, £5,000. Apart from the loan, the only other amount owing related to trade creditors of £10,000. During the following 12 months, the following transactions took place.

(a)	purchased additional stock on credit	£30,000
(b)	sales to customers – all on credit	£90,000
(c)	cash received from debtors	£85,000
(d)	payments to creditors	£35,000
(e)	wages actually paid	£12,000
(f)	payment of tax charge	£8,000
(g)	payment of general expenses	£9,000
(h)	payment of business rates	£7,000
(i)	payment for replacement of major part in machine	£3,000

At the year end, Anne estimates that electricity used but not invoiced – included within general expenses – totalled £3,000 and that £3,000 of the rates paid relate to the following year. Closing stock with a retail value of £13,000 was on hand at the year end. Although this had cost £10,000, its current wholesale cost was only £9,000. (Depreciation can be ignored.)

Record the above transactions and produce a profit and loss account and balance sheet suitable for the needs of Anne Preston, making clear any assumptions made.

CHAPTER 3

Accounting profit – application and implications

A major objective of business activity is to generate profits. Not only is profit a measure of a business's performance, it is also a source of income for the owners. For modern enterprises, with production taking place in advance of sales and with assets having lives of several years, periodic profit measurement becomes increasingly difficult. Equally, with the growth of limited liability, how profit is measured affects the security of creditors.

This chapter:

- Describes the recording and sharing of profit in partnerships

- Discusses the concept of limited liability and the implications for capital maintenance

- Differentiates reserves from provisions and shows the implications of these for profit measurement

- Examines the components of stocks, their valuation and the effect on reported profit

- Introduces the cost flows involved in manufacturing organisations

- Identifies the difficulties of revenue recognition where sales relate to more than one period

Profit is one of the most important measures of business performance. In many organisations it forms the basis on which rewards are made. Chief executives may have their remuneration tied to the level of profits achieved while some companies provide for profit sharing with their employees. Investors tend to look on profit as a measure of a company's success and as a source from which they can take their rewards in the form of dividends and capital growth. This concern with the sharing of profit is not confined to large companies. It applies equally to unincorporated entities such as partnerships whenever there is more than one owner.

The image conveyed is that profit is an exact and unambiguous figure. Certainly this is the way it tends to be reported in the media. In one sense profit is exact. It is the difference between revenues and expenses. However, hidden in those figures are assumptions and judgements about how transactions should be recorded and assumptions and judgements about the future viability of the company. Change just one assumption and the likelihood is that the profit figure would also change. How profit is calculated therefore takes on a new importance as it at least partially affects the division of profit between potentially competing claimants.

PARTNERSHIPS

The division of profit is not an issue for a sole trader. All the profit belongs to the single owner. This clearly is not the case where two or more people are in business together. Partners are free to choose how they share the profits and although it is sensible to have a written partnership agreement, equally they are free to keep such agreements informal. Exactly how the profits are divided will be agreed by negotiation amongst the partners. Nevertheless there are features common to most agreements. A partner who does more work or brings in more business or provides more capital will presumably want this to be recognised. The partnership agreement might express this in terms of paying one or more partner a 'salary' in recognition of the extra work undertaken and the payment of interest on capital to partners who have brought in capital. Partners who withdraw money from the business might be asked to pay interest on those amounts taken out of the business. Any profit left over will then have to be shared in the proportions agreed amongst the partners.

Although straightforward, the language used in partnership agreements is confusing. The agreement relates to the sharing out or *appropriation* of profit. A partner's salary therefore is *not* an expense of the business, unlike the salary of an employee. It is merely a way of dividing the profit to reflect the extra work by some of the partners. Treating such 'salaries' as a share or appropriation of profit rather than an expense is consistent with the treatment of 'salaries' paid by sole traders to themselves. Using similar arguments, apportioning part of the profits to reflect the relative capital investments of partners, even if *called* interest, is no more than a division or apportionment of profit. This is demonstrated in Example 3.1.

Sharing the £55,000 profit between the partners results in Smith receiving £42,000 and Weston receiving £13,000. The calculation of this appropriation is shown in Exhibit 3.1 where the salary and interest on capital are shown merely to be ways of dividing the profit.

Example 3.1

> Smith and Weston are in business buying and selling cars. The capital of Smith is £10,000 and that of Weston £20,000. Their partnership agreement provides for interest on capital at 10 per cent and a salary to Smith of £30,000 per annum. Profits are to be divided equally. In the year ended 31 December 19X1, the profit of the business was £55,000.

Exhibit 3.1 The division of profit: partnerships

	Profit	Appropriation	
		Smith	*Weston*
Profit for the year	£55,000		
Less salary	(£30,000)	£30,000	
	£25,000		
10% interest on capital	(£3,000)	£1,000	£2,000
	£22,000		
Division of profit (50:50)	(£22,000)	£11,000	£11,000
TOTAL	nil	**£42,000**	**£13,000**

Common sense suggests it would be useful to keep a separate capital account for each partner otherwise calculations such as interest on capital become more difficult. Partners would then have to decide whether to add their share of profits to the balance in the capital accounts or keep profits and capital separate. Certainly if profits (and drawings) are kept separate from the capital accounts, it is easier to see the extent to which the business is being financed by the original capital rather than profits retained in the business. It also makes the calculation of any interest on capital provided in the agreement much easier.

In England and Wales there is an additional reason why it might be prudent to keep the capital and profits separate. On the ending of the partnership, it is possible that losses will have been so large that the overall capital of one or more of the partners will be negative. Should the partner not be able to finance the loss, it will have to be borne by the other partners. Without limited liability, they are fully responsible for all of the debts of the business. This was the problem faced by a partnership in 1904. To resolve the matter, the partners took the case to law. In a famous but perhaps illogical ruling, the case of *Garner* v *Murray* held that the remaining partners should finance the deficiency themselves in proportion to their 'last agreed capital' and *not* their profit-sharing ratios. Keeping separate capital accounts makes clear to the partners the extent of their obligation should a similar difficulty recur. Having said that, the ruling does not apply to Scotland which has its own separate legal system, nor does it apply to partnerships where the agreement specifies some other way of treating such losses.

Partnerships and the law

The problem of partnership agreements not covering all eventualities was long ago recognised by governments. In the UK, the Partnership Act was passed in 1890. If the partnership agreement was silent, this Act provided for profits to be divided equally, no interest to be allowed on capital nor charged on drawings, no salaries to be paid to partners and for interest to be paid at 5 per cent per annum on any funds provided by partners in excess of their agreed capital.

Such legislation was not required for a sole trader as he would only be arguing with himself about how profits were to be apportioned. Similarly, there is no meaningful way a sole trader can make a long term loan to his own business. Even if described as such, it would still effectively be capital as being a creditor to oneself is not a particularly meaningful concept. Loans to a partnership are a different matter, however. One partner making a loan to the business will personally benefit by receiving interest, with the overall cost being an *expense* borne by *all* of the partners.

Current accounts

Most partnerships choose to keep capital accounts separate from profits and drawings. The common name for the account where each partner's profit is recorded is the *current account*. This account will record the share of the profit due to a partner less any drawings made over the accounting period. Logically, the way the partnership profits are shared or appropriated between partners could be calculated outside the accounting system in a similar way to Example 3.1. Only the net effect would then be recorded in the accounts. Many partnerships, however, prefer to show the division as transactions within the accounts. If this is the case, a second, temporary account has to be opened known as an *appropriation account*. This is the approach developed in Example 3.2.

Example 3.2

> Alan and Barry agree to start a business on 1 January. Alan introduces £30,000 capital in the form of cash and Barry introduces £60,000. Their partnership agreement provides for 10 per cent interest on capital, 10 per cent interest on drawings and for Alan to receive a salary of £20,000 p.a. In addition, Alan makes a loan to the business of £20,000 at an annual interest rate of 15 per cent. The interest on this was paid to him at the end of the year. Sales during the year came to £65,000; purchases totalled £40,000 and rent and rates paid for the year came to £7,000. All transactions were for cash. At the end of the year the stock unsold was valued at £25,000. On 1 July, Barry had taken out drawings of £20,000.

The profit for the year can easily be calculated as £40,000, made up of the turnover of £65,000 less cost of sales £15,000, expenses of £7,000 and loan interest of £3,000. The partnership agreement, however, is silent as to how this profit should be divided and so the provisions of the Partnership Act will come into force. This is the approach taken in Exhibit 3.2 where the profits are divided equally in accordance with the Act.

Exhibit 3.2 The division of profit with interest on drawings

	Profit	Appropriation	
		Alan	*Barry*
Profit for the year	£40,000		
Less salary	(£20,000)	£20,000	
	£20,000		
10% interest on capital	(£9,000)	£3,000	£6,000
	£11,000		
Add interest on drawings	£1,000		(£1,000)
	£12,000		
Division of profit (50:50)	(£12,000)	£6,000	£6,000
TOTAL	nil	**£29,000**	**£11,000**

Before sharing the balance of profits, however, provision has to be made for the salary of Alan, the interest on capital to both partners and an adjustment to allow for the effect of the drawings. As the drawings only took place half way through the year, only half of the full year interest rate of 10 per cent has been applied, i.e. £20,000 × 10 per cent × ½ year.

Having calculated the apportionment of the profit, all that remains is to record the transactions. Only at the stage of apportioning the profit does the recording of transactions differ from a sole trader. Exhibit 3.3 records all of the data immediately after the partners have introduced the £90,000 of capital and the £30,000 loan. Because of the simplified nature of this example, no trial balance has been extracted prior to the calculation of profit. The £40,000 profit could have simply been shared between the partners with £29,000 being recorded in Alan's current account and £11,000 in Barry's current account.

Exhibit 3.3 Partnerships – detailed appropriation

(£000)	Opening balances	Stock	Rent	Sales	Interest	Drawings	Sales	Stock	Rent	Interest	Salary	Interest on capital	Interest on drawings	Division of profit	Drawings	Closing balances
Cash	+120	−40	−7	+65	−3	−20										+115
Capital – Alan	−30															−30
Capital – Barry	−60															−60
Loan – Alan	−30															−30
Stock		+40						−15								+25
Rent and rates			+7						−7							
Sales				−65			+65									
Loan interest					+3					−3						
Drawings – Barry						+20									−20	
Profit and loss account							−65	+15	+7	+3	+40					
Appropriation account											−40	+20	+3 +6	−1	+6 +6	
Current account – Alan												−20	−3		−6	−29
Current account – Barry													−6	+1	−6 +20	+9

(Table headers: "Period end adjustments" spans Sales Stock Rent Interest; "Appropriation" spans Interest on capital, Interest on drawings, Division of profit, Drawings.)

The alternative treatment is to record fully all the adjustments making up the division of the profits within an appropriation account. This is the approach taken in Exhibit 3.3. The profit of £40,000 is transferred to the appropriation account simply because it is easier to work from a new account rather than the cluttered profit and loss account. Each element making up the division of profit is then transferred to the current account of the relevant partner. Finally, the drawings of Barry are netted off against his division of the profits. There is now a permanent record within the accounts. All that remains is for the final accounts to be developed from the data in Exhibit 3.3. These, with the exception of the cashflow statement, are reproduced in Exhibit 3.4 where a proprietorial balance sheet has been chosen.

Exhibit 3.4 The final accounts:partnerships

Trading and profit and loss account for the year ended 31 December		(£)	Balance sheet at 31 December		(£)
Turnover		65,000	**Assets**		
Cost of sales		15,000	*Fixed assets*		nil
Gross profit		50,000			
Property expenses					
Rates	7,000		*Current assets*		
Finance expenses			Stock	25,000	
Loan interest	3,000	10,000	Cash	115,000	
Net profit		40,000		140,000	
			Current liabilities	nil	140,000
Appropriation					140,000
Interest on drawings – Barry		1,000	*Less long term liabilities*		
		41,000	Loan from Alan		30,000
Salary – Alan	20,000				110,000
Interest on capital:			**Financed by**		
Alan	3,000		*Owners' capital*		
Barry	6,000	9,000	Alan	30,000	
Division of profits:			Barry	60,000	90,000
Alan	6,000		*Current accounts*		
Barry	6,000	12,000 41,000	Alan	29,000	
			Less Barry	9,000	20,000
					110,000

The final accounts are similar to those of a sole trader except for the appropriation account in the profit and loss statement and the more detailed breakdown of the sources of finance in the balance sheet. The appropriation account shows the profit split between the partners. As with a sole trader, profits retained in the business, less any drawings, serve to increase the equity of the business. Most partnerships prefer to keep the division of the profits in separate current accounts, partly because this is useful and more informative and partly because it prevents any possible future legal difficulties. Despite this separation, the reality is that Alan's total equity in the business is £59,000 made up of the £30,000 original capital introduced plus the £29,000 of profits less, in his case, nil drawings, while Barry's equity at the year end is £51,000. In his case, the £60,000 originally introduced into the business has been reduced by taking out £9,000 more than his eventual profit share.

LIMITED COMPANIES

The use of an appropriation account is not restricted to partnerships. It is equally applicable to limited companies. Limited companies have certain advantages over partnerships. With one or two exceptions, partnerships can have no more than 20 members. Limited companies have no such restriction.

The main advantage, however, is that the liabilities of the members of a limited liability company are restricted to the amount agreed as their respective capitals or, in the case of companies limited by guarantee, to amounts guaranteed – unlike members of a partnership whose liabilities are unlimited. (Companies limited by guarantee are rarely found in business and are not considered further.) If the capital has been fully paid to the company, there are no further financial obligations, even if the company was to become insolvent. The only possible exception to this might be if fraudulent trading has taken place. On the face of it, therefore, creditors are less well protected when dealing with a limited company rather than an unincorporated body. To minimise this lack of protection, the law views the capital of the company as a permanent source of funds, returnable to the owners only on a liquidation – and only then after all the creditors have been paid.

There is, however, another substantial difference between limited companies and unincorporated businesses such as sole traders and partnerships. Despite the accounting convenience of viewing the unincorporated business as being separate from the owner(s), *in law* they are one and the same. Limited companies, however, have a legal existence totally separate from their owners. Legally they are a separate entity which can sue – and be sued – in their own right. They can even face criminal prosecution and be fined, although clearly, not being human, they cannot face imprisonment.

Types of limited company

There are at least two reasons why a limited company is formed. The first is to provide the protection of limited liability and continuity for the small to medium – often family controlled – company which would otherwise have probably been a partnership. The second reason is to provide a vehicle for the general public to participate in a much more substantial type of business. In the first case, investors are likely to know the business in detail and might easily be playing an active part in its management. In the second case, investors are likely to be many and varied with no day-to-day awareness of what is happening in the enterprise.

The informational needs of investors are therefore likely to differ according to the type of company. For a member of a small family company, there is less need for the law to protect them by forcing the company to publish accounting information to members as they are likely already to have a good working knowledge of the company and access to the accounting information by way of their management role in the business. Secondly, the case for making the accounting information of a small family business publicly available to all and sundry is not self-evident.

The share capital of a company

Irrespective of the reasons for forming a company, its capital needs to be broken down into convenient parts to enable investors to acquire as much or as little as they desire. These parts are known as shares. In some ways, the number of shares is a mere detail. Take, for example, a company which is formed by raising £100,000. It could divide this capital into 100,000 parts of £1 each, into 50,000 parts of £2 each or two parts of £50,000 each. An investor desiring 50 per cent of the company would be indifferent between 50,000 shares of £1 each, 25,000 shares of £2 each or one share of £50,000. In each case, the investor owns half of the company.

There is, however, a wider issue. In the latter case, it is impossible for a shareholder to own only one-tenth of the company because the capital has not been broken down into sufficiently small parts. Such a structure denies an investor the opportunity of acquiring his or her ideal proportion. Equally important, it denies the company the opportunity of having small investors as members and in that sense makes the shares less marketable.

There are two types of capital found in companies limited by shares. The *nominal* or *authorised* capital is the maximum amount of capital the directors have authority from the shareholders to raise, broken down by the type or class of shares, their number and their *nominal* or *face* value. By way of example, a company might be authorised to issue £2,000,000 of capital made up of 1,000,000 shares. The nominal or face value will therefore be £2. How much capital the company will *issue* will depend on its needs. There can therefore be a difference between the authorised and *issued* capital. From an accounting aspect, the important element is the issued capital. The authorised capital is primarily a public declaration of the limit to which a company *can* issue capital. It is not that significant, however, as members can vote to change this amount whenever they wish.

The legal format of companies

In law there is a range of different types of limited companies in the UK, only two of which, the private limited company and the public limited company, are regularly used by business. Unfortunately, these do not exactly mirror the two classes identified above although from an accounting perspective, both are very similar. Both are formed by individuals known as promoters who create a company by lodging various documents with a government official known as the Registrar of Companies. The essential difference between the two is that public limited companies are allowed to raise funds from the general public whereas private limited companies must restrict the right to buy and sell shares.

Given the power of limited companies, legislatures all over the world have sought to tie the company in with individuals who can be held ultimately responsible for the company's actions. In the UK this initially involves the promoter supplying to the registrar the names and addresses of the first directors and the company secretary. In addition the legal abode, known as the registered office, needs to be stated to enable communications to be sent to the company. And because the company is not a human person but only a legal person, the registrar needs to know its constitution and the rules for its internal working.

The constitution is contained in a document called the *memorandum of association*. In here will be found details of the company name, whether it is a private or public company, the country under whose jurisdiction it falls (basically England and Wales or

Scotland), what the company has been formed to do (known as its objects clause), a statement that the liabilities of members is limited, the amount of the nominal or authorised capital (including the nominal value of the shares) and a formal declaration that the subscribers to the request to form the company agree to its formation and are prepared to pay in or *subscribe* the capital agreed. The internal rules of the company are known as the *articles of association* and govern such matters as how directors are appointed and the extent of their powers, the appointment of auditors and the rights, including the voting rights, of the subscribers to the capital.

In the UK, a private limited company is not defined in detail. Instead the 1985 Companies Act sets out the conditions which make up a public limited company. Failure to meet these conditions automatically makes a company a private one and hence prevents it from allowing the general public to subscribe for shares. To be a public limited company, the memorandum must state it is one and its name should also include the phrase 'Public Limited Company' or its abbreviation of 'plc'. In addition, the minimum capital agreed to be taken up – or subscribed – by the members must be £50,000. Finally, the company must have been correctly registered as a plc. Companies not meeting these conditions are private companies and have to include the phrase 'Limited' as the final part of their name although this can be abbreviated to 'Ltd'.

Private, public and quoted companies

Before discussing the various types of shares and loans a company can issue, it is useful to bring out the difference between private companies, public companies and those with a stock exchange quotation. The danger is to think of private limited companies as only being vehicles for small family businesses. Although this is often the case, it is not automatically so. What is a private limited company is dependent on the legal definition explained earlier. Some of the UK's most famous names are only limited companies – B and Q and Superdrug, for example, are private limited companies owned in turn by Kingfisher plc.

In many people's minds, the terms 'plc' and 'quoted' are synonymous. This is an understandable mistake as the phrase 'going public' is often used to describe a company seeking a stock exchange quotation. In fact there is a very real difference. A public company is able, if it so wishes, to offer its shares to the general public.

A stock exchange quotation is more than this. It is a facility whereby the company's shares can be bought and sold on a recognised stock exchange. A stock exchange is a formal market to bring together buyers and sellers. Before allowing its securities to be traded on the market, the company will have to meet all of the requirements of that stock exchange over and above the requirements laid down by company law. All quoted companies therefore have to be public companies but not all public companies meet the conditions for a stock exchange quotation.

As an aside, some relatively small companies play on this confusion, believing that 'plc' has a higher status than a mere limited company. As can be seen, the capital requirements are not particularly onerous. Indeed, it is even less onerous than appears, because the £50,000 relates to the capital to be issued but the 1985 Companies Act only requires a minimum of 25 per cent of the capital to be paid in full, the balance being paid when the company deems it necessary.[1]

CAPITAL INSTRUMENTS

Just as sole traders and partnerships do not have to rely entirely on their own funds to fully finance the business, so limited companies have a choice of sources of finance. The only difference is that, for companies, there is a bewildering array of forms of finance. No longer is it a simple case of choosing between loans (i.e. debt finance) and equity. Instead there is a whole range of hybrid or *mezzanine* finance which is neither straight debt nor straight equity. Together, the various forms of finance which can be issued by a company are known as securities or *capital instruments*.

This would be of little importance but for the relationship between borrowings and risk. Interest on borrowings has to be paid irrespective of whether or not there is profit or cash. Other things being equal, the higher the level of borrowings, the greater the risk to the ultimate owners from the unavoidable interest charges. Whether a source of finance is classified as debt or equity therefore takes on a special significance in the eyes of existing and potential shareholders in the company.

Types of shares

When a company first offers shares, it is free to attach whatever rights it sees fit to them and to call them by almost any name it thinks suitable provided only that the information is the same as that contained in the memorandum and articles of association. This information will be repeated in the offer document known as the *prospectus* and so an investor is then free to choose whether these terms and conditions are acceptable. A company can offer more than one class of share and only within each class would the rights and obligations be identical. Some classes of shares might have full voting rights, others none or only limited rights.

The holders of shares with voting rights will have elected directors to manage the company on their behalf. As owners, the shareholders can only obtain their reward from an appropriation of profit. It is the directors who recommend how much of the profits can be returned to the shareholders, generally in the form of cash payments known as *dividends*. This is how the shareholders obtain their rewards from the company. Dividends, however, can only be paid out of profits. Paying a dividend when the company has no profits is effectively returning capital to the shareholders and, as was shown in Chapter 2, is illegal because of the reduction in the security to the creditors.

Ordinary shares

Ordinary shares are by far the most popular form of capital in companies. The holders of ordinary shares are the ultimate risk-takers and the ultimate owners. Only after all other claims have been met is it possible for them to obtain their reward. Their reward, however, is not just the residual profits distributed by way of ordinary share dividends but also any surplus should the company decide to close down or liquidate itself. Because of this ultimate right to all residual amounts, ordinary share capital is known as equity capital.

Some companies divide their ordinary shares into more than one class, often based on voting rights. In the past it was not uncommon for the original owners of a business to hold on to power by issuing new ordinary shares, identical in every other way to those pre-existing except for voting rights. This might mean that the new issue would carry no voting rights whatsoever. More likely, the original shares would have greater voting rights.

When a company wishes to issue *extra* shares, it does not have to issue them to the general public. Instead it can offer them to existing shareholders in proportion to the shares held. A holder of 10 per cent of the ordinary shares, for example, would have the right to subscribe for 10 per cent of the new capital being raised. Where an issue is offered to existing shareholders it is known as a *rights issue*.

Preference shares

Preference shares can provide another source of finance for a company. The funds provided from preference shares are still part of the share capital of a company and the preference shareholders are still part of its ownership in a legal sense. Their preferential treatment comes from their position in the order of distributions. Only after the preference shareholders have received their dividend can the ordinary shareholders be rewarded – and only then if there are sufficient profits available for distribution. To that extent the preference shareholders are taking a lower risk and this is reflected by their dividend being limited to a fixed rate per share and, in most cases, the absence of voting rights. In addition, they will not participate in any surplus over and beyond the return of the nominal value of the preference share capital on a liquidation unless other conditions have been explicitly attached to the shares. The preference shareholders have no legal right, however, to their dividend. Directors, for example, have the power to recommend that no dividend of any form be paid. The preference shareholders' only comfort is that they have to receive their dividend before any can be paid to the ordinary shareholders. Given the limited rights of preference shareholders, although part owners of the business in a legal sense, they are not part of the equity of the company. The term 'equity' is restricted to those shareholders who are entitled to what remains after all other claims on profits or surpluses have been met – the ultimate owners.

As with ordinary shares, the rights attached to preference shares can vary. The preference shares might be *cumulative* or *non-cumulative*. A cumulative preference share has the advantage that any failure to pay a dividend has ultimately to be made good in future years before a dividend can be paid to the ordinary shareholder. No such benefit accrues to the holder of a non-cumulative preference share. Some preference shares are known as *participating* preference shares. This right entitles them to dividends beyond that specified on the share once certain conditions such as a particular level of profit have been met.

Loans and debentures

A company can borrow money rather than raise it from a share issue providing it has the power to do so within its articles of association. Legally, loans to a company are not part of its capital even though they are often referred to as debt capital. The providers of such loans are creditors who can demand payment in the form of interest irrespective of a company's profitability.

Sometimes a company will offer the lender security on the loan in the form of a charge on the company's assets. Such loans are often called debentures or debenture stock. The security can be either fixed or floating. A fixed charge is similar to a domestic mortgage on a house with the company security often being specific land or buildings. As a result, the company cannot dispose of the asset unless the debenture holder releases the charge. A floating charge is a general charge on all the assets of the company but the creditor has no legal rights over the assets until an event specified in the deeds to the mortgage – such as a failure to pay interest when due – occurs. Clearly, debentures are less risky than unsecured loans. As a consequence, they will normally offer a lower rate of interest.

As with shares, the detailed conditions attached to the debt finance can vary greatly. The loans can be irredeemable or redeemable. Irredeemable loans never have to be repaid provided the conditions of the loan are not breached while redeemable loans may specify a range of dates for redemption. A debenture described with a date such as 2000/2010 implies that it can be redeemed, at the company's option, at any date between 1 January 2000 and 31 December 2010.

Hybrid securities

Redeemable preference shares

Hybrid securities are many and varied. They encompass the range between equity and straightforward debt. The preference shares described earlier are just one example. Although part of the ownership and receiving their reward from dividends, they are not part of the equity. A more complex example is redeemable preference shares. As their name implies, these are shares which will be repaid at a specified date or within a specified time period. On the face of it, this appears to be illegal as the capital of the company – those funds maintained permanently in the company to protect creditors – will be reduced. Despite this, it is legally possible to redeem *any* class of shares provided the resulting reduction is made good either by a further issue of shares – not necessarily of the same class – or by reclassifying profits retained in the company as permanent capital.

Deed discounted loans and premiums on redemption

Loans can also have greater complexities than outlined earlier. Deep discounted loans are characterised by having extremely low nominal interest rates, sometimes even zero, and which are offered for sale to investors at a price substantially below their nominal value. Although the mathematics of such instruments are complex, the concept is straightforward and implication clear. Consider a company which issues a loan with a nominal value of £100 at a zero rate of interest for £80 and which matures in four years' time. The reality is that the company has borrowed £80 and will pay £20 interest over those four years. Until recently, the £100 would have been shown as a liability but the treatment of the 'discount' of £20 could have been recorded in a variety of ways. One way would be to write it off against part of the total amount owing to the ordinary shareholders and known as the share premium account. (The share premium account is discussed below.) The effect of this would have been for the interest to be excluded from the profit and loss account thereby boosting reported profits – another example of reserve accounting introduced in Chapter 2. Another option would have been to report the interest as £5 per year for each of the four years. As reasonable as this sounds, anyone who has bought a house on a mortgage would realise that interest is not as simple as this treatment suggests. In the case of the house, interest payments are greatest in the early years.

Issuing a loan with a premium on redemption is not dissimilar. Consider a company which issues a loan for £100 at a 4 per cent rate of interest but which will repay to the lender £110 in five years' time when the loan matures. Presumably investors would only offer to buy such a low interest bearing loan because of the premium of £10 in five years' time. As such, the premium is, in reality, part of the interest. As with the deep discounted loan, this raises a number of issues. Should the loan be recorded at £100 or £110 in the balance sheet? And how should the premium be treated? One possibility is to again write it off to the share premium account and again avoid it being charged to the profit and loss account. Such issues as these are concerned with (economic) substance over (legal) form and have recently been addressed by the accounting profession. They are discussed more fully in Chapter 8.

Convertible securities

A further complexity relates to securities such as loans or preference shares which in their terms and conditions allow the user to convert the security into ordinary shares. In exchange for this benefit, the holders would be prepared to sacrifice part of their immediate return. The question then arises, should the convertible preference shares and convertible loans be counted as equity? How they are treated has to await the discussion in Chapter 8 but what is already clear is the issue: if the securities are classified as equity, the proportion of debt in the capital structure – with all its inherent risk – will appear to be reduced.

Warrants

Although there are many other types of hybrid securities, it is sufficient to give a flavour of the conceptual difficulties to consider just one more. Warrants are options granted by a company to subscribe for new shares at a given price – the 'exercise price' – generally within a specified time in the future. Sometimes these are issued on their own as an alternative to paying a dividend. More often they are attached to new issues of loans. The holder will anticipate the market price of the shares being greater than the exercise price and so the warrants will have a value reflecting this difference. In exchange, the holder will be prepared to accept a lower rate of interest on the loans. The result is that the interest charge in the profit and loss account will be lower than had there been no warrants attached to the loans. Yet again, the issue is whether the profit and loss account should reflect the 'real' interest charge, that is, after taking account of the value of the warrants.

CAPITAL, PROFIT AND DISTRIBUTIONS

There are at least three major differences between companies and other forms of business organisation. Because the activities of the business are legally separate from the activities of its members as shareholders, the company will pay tax in its own right –

unlike a partnership or sole trader where the *individual* is taxed on *all* of his or her individual earnings irrespective of where they are derived from. In the UK this tax is known as *corporation tax*.

The second difference arising from a company being a separate legal entity relates to the legal position of directors. The directors, acting as directors, are technically employees of the company even though in reality they might also be the major shareholders. Because of this, payments to them *as directors* – such as salaries and directors' fees – are an expense of the business and not an appropriation. Only payments due to them in their role as *shareholders* such as dividends are an appropriation.

The final difference relates to the treatment of profits retained in the business. For a sole trader or partnership, there was no legal difference between capital or retentions. For companies, capital is viewed as a permanent source of protection for creditors, a source which can only be legally reduced by making losses or with the consent of the courts. Paying a dividend out of capital would reduce creditors' security and be illegal. Retained profits therefore have to be kept totally separate from issued share capital if the directors wish to make them available to shareholders at some later stage.

THE ACCOUNTING TREATMENT OF LIMITED COMPANIES

Starting a company

Example 3.3 demonstrates the difference between a limited company and a partnership. To enable the final accounts to be produced, some simplified trading transactions have been introduced. In the example, the business is started by the potential owners buying an 'off-the-shelf' ready-formed company. This is by far the most popular way of starting a limited liability business. Ready-made companies are formed by a variety of firms and can easily be bought for less than £200. This saves the new owners having to go through all of the procedures themselves.

Example 3.3

George and Jerry decide to start a business on 1 January 19X3. Rather than enter into a partnership they buy a ready-made limited company for £200 and issue a total of 20,000 £1 ordinary shares which are fully taken up in equal proportions by George and Jerry. In addition George lends the business £10,000 in the form of a 10 per cent debenture secured on a floating charge while Jerry subscribed for all of the 20,000 £1 15 per cent preference shares agreed to be issued.

During the year they buy some land and buildings costing £25,000. Sales totalled £100,000 while trading expenses such as wages and stock consumed totalled £40,000. In addition, George was paid a salary of £20,000. Corporation tax assessed and paid totalled £13,000. The interest on the debenture was also paid. At the end of the year they propose paying a 10 per cent dividend on the ordinary shares. Apart from the dividends, all transactions were for cash.

The company will not have traded but it will be complete with a model set of articles and all of the other trappings required of a company, including a name. Once purchased, the new owners will call a formal meeting to elect new directors and a company secretary, change the objects clause if required and most likely change the company's name to something more appropriate.

The trading transactions of Example 3.3 are recorded in the normal way in Exhibit 3.5. However, the salary and loan interest payable to George is now shown as an expense of the company because of the separate legal entity of the company. Similarly, the company is responsible for paying its own corporation tax.

Exhibit 3.5 Limited company appropriations

(£000)	Transactions									Adjustments				Appropriation	Closing balances
Cash	+20	+10	+20	−25	+100	−40	−20	−13	−1						+51
Ordinary shares	−20														−20
Debentures		−10													−10
Preference shares			−20												−20
Land & buildings				+25											+25
Sales					−100					+100					
Expenses						+40					−40				
Salary							+20					−20			
Corporation tax								+13						−13	
Interest									+1				−1		
Profit and loss										**−100**	**+40**	**+20**	**+1**	**+39**	
Appropriation														−39 +13 +3 +2	−21
Creditor preference shares														−3	−3
Creditor ordinary shares														−2	−2

After charging all the expenses against the turnover of £100,000, the profit will be £39,000. This, however, is before charging corporation tax. In effect corporation tax is another expense. As a result, the £39,000 pre-tax profit is reduced by £13,000 in the appropriation section to give an after-tax profit of £26,000. Of this, £3,000 is due to the preference shareholder(s) – who happens to be Jerry – £2,000 is due to the ordinary shareholders and £21,000 is retained in the company. As none of the dividends have yet been paid, they are recorded as creditors.

The profit and loss account within the accounting records is highlighted in bold figures while the closing balances are represented by the final column of Exhibit 3.5. One transaction is missing from the profit and loss account, the initial payment for the company. This has been deliberately excluded as it was not an expense of the company as an entity. Given this, all that remains is to show the final accounts in a more presentable form.

Exhibit 3.6 reproduces the accounts using the proprietorial form of balance sheet with the long term obligations of the company deducted from the net assets of the company. The undistributed profits are shown separately from the issued share capital as the latter is a permanent source of funds whereas the retentions might wish to be distributed in the future. Until then, the retentions represent a further investment in the company by the shareholders. The total of all amounts ultimately due to the shareholders in a company – whether issued capital or retentions and no matter how described – is known as *shareholders' funds*.

Exhibit 3.6 The final accounts for a limited company

Profit and loss account year ended 31 December 19X3			Balance sheet at 31 December 19X3			
			Assets			
Turnover		£100,000	*Fixed assets*			
Trading expenses		£40,000	Land and buildings			£25,000
Gross profit		£60,000	*Current assets*			
Other expenses			Cash		£51,000	
Salary	£20,000		*Less current liabilities*			
Debenture interest	£1,000	£21,000	Preference share dividend	£3,000		
Net profit before tax		£39,000	Ordinary share dividend	£2,000	£5,000	£46,000
Corporation tax		£13,000				£71,000
Net profit after tax		£26,000	*Less debentures*			£10,000
Less appropriations						£61,000
Preference share dividend	£3,000		**Financed by**			
Ordinary share dividend	£2,000	£5,000	*Authorised and issued share capital*			
Retained profits carried forward		£21,000	20,000 £1 ordinary shares			£20,000
			20,000 £1 15% preference shares			£20,000
						£40,000
			Retained profits			£21,000
			Shareholders' funds			£61,000

RESERVES IN COMPANY ACCOUNTS

Revenue reserves

In ordinary language a reserve is something which is put aside or kept back. To the extent they have not been distributed, the retained profits of £21,000 are a reserve. The shareholders are free to do what they want with these reserves and to describe them in any way thought suitable. Part could be earmarked for long term retentions, part made available for distributions. Amounts set aside might be called a general reserve or some other name. The name is not important. All the shareholders are doing is making a public and voluntary demonstration of their intent. Assume George and Jerry's company agreed to set aside £10,000 of the profits as a general reserve. No significant change has happened. Instead of shareholders' funds comprising issued share capital of £40,000 and retentions of £21,000, they would now comprise the same issued capital, a general reserve of £10,000 and retentions of £11,000. Such reserves are known as *revenue reserves* because they have been created out of the profits or net revenues held back in the business. Logically there is no difference between them. They merely reflect a statement of intent, and this is the way the law in the UK sees them.

Capital reserves

There is, however, a second type of reserve known as a *capital reserve*. Capital reserves are non-distributable; that is, they cannot be used to pay out dividends. It is possible for a company's articles of association to specify that part of its revenue reserves are non-distributable although in doing so, it is denying itself flexibility. More likely, capital reserves will have been created in one of the three ways specified by UK law.

The share premium account

One form of capital reserve is formed when shares are issued for more than their nominal value. Consider the formation of a company which raises £100,000 by the issue of share capital. This could be raised by issuing 100,000 £1 ordinary shares or 50,000 £2 ordinary shares or any other combination. If 100,000 £1 shares are issued, the opening balance sheet will be similar to that in part (a) of Exhibit 3.7. An alternative, however, is to issue only 50,000 £1 shares but to charge investors £2 for each share. The business would still receive £100,000 but legally the issued capital would now only be £50,000 with the balance being a reserve. This is shown in part (b) of Exhibit 3.7.

Exhibit 3.7 Issue of shares at a premium

Balance sheet (a)		Balance sheet (b)	
Net assets		*Net assets*	
Cash	£100,000	Cash	£100,000
	£100,000		£100,000
Issued share capital		*Issued share capital*	
100,000 £1 ordinary shares	£100,000	50,000 £1 ordinary shares	£50,000
		Reserves	£50,000
	£100,000		£100,000

Financially, investors would be indifferent between the two treatments: either way their *investment* in the business would be £100,000. Creditors, however, would perceive things differently. Company (a) has £100,000 of permanent protection in the form of issued share capital while company (b) could refund the reserve to its shareholders, leaving only £50,000 of capital to protect creditors. Because of this, the law in many countries, including the UK, prevents such reserves being distributed. The reserve, known as a *share premium reserve* or *share premium account*, represents the excess or premium paid over the nominal price of the share.

More generally, a share premium arises when *extra* shares are being issued in an existing company. Just as a balance sheet does not necessarily reflect the *value* of a business, so the nominal value of a share does not necessarily reflect its (market) price. Both depend on future prospects for their value. Through time, the market price of a share is likely to exceed its nominal value. Consequently, a company raising extra funds would be foolish to ask only the nominal value for the new shares as, once issued, the new shares would be identical to the existing ones.

In Exhibit 3.8 a company with issued share capital of 200,000 £1 shares wishes to raise £100,000 additional funds for expansion. Because of its reputation and future prospects, it believes its £1 shares are *worth* £4. Consequently, it need only issue 25,000 £1 shares to raise the £100,000. The £75,000 difference is the share premium. The effect of this on the balance sheet is demonstrated in the first three columns of Exhibit 3.8.

Exhibit 3.8 The share premium account and bonus shares

	Original balance sheet	Issue shares	Closing balance sheet	Bonus shares	Closing balance sheet
Fixed assets	£300,000		£300,000		£300,000
Current assets – cash	£100,000	+£100,000	£200,000		£200,000
	£400,000		£500,000		£500,000
Issued share capital	£200,000	–£25,000	£225,000	–£75,000	£300,000
Share premium account		–£75,000	£75,000	+£75,000	
Profit and loss account	£200,000		£200,000		£200,000
Shareholders' funds	£400,000		£500,000		£500,000

Uses of the share premium account

Although the share premium account cannot be used for distributions, the law does allow it to be used for certain restricted purposes. When shares or debentures are issued there is bound to be expenses resulting from the issue of a prospectus and the meeting of legal fees for example. If a share premium account exists, these issue expenses can be written off against the share premium account rather than charged to the profit and loss account. Similarly any expenses incurred when originally forming the company can also be written off against the share premium account. A moment's thought shows the effect of this is to reduce the permanent capital of the company. Despite that, it is legally allowable.

Bonus shares

A further allowable use for the account is to issue bonus shares. The term bonus shares is a total misnomer. In the initial closing balance sheet of Exhibit 3.8 the revised shareholders' funds total £500,000, made up of the issued share capital of £225,000, the share premium account of £75,000 and the profit and loss account balance of £200,000. Assuming the assets could be sold for their book values, the total of £500,000 is the amount returnable to shareholders on a liquidation. This is the only way the £75,000 could be returned to them. In effect, the share premium account is similar to share capital, a permanent source of funding within the company.

Bonus shares recognise this reality by eliminating the share premium account and transferring the amount to share capital. There is neither a gain nor a loss, but simply the recognition that the share premium ultimately belongs to the ordinary shareholders. However, the only way they can have access to it is on a liquidation and so transferring it to the share capital merely recognises this reality. The result is that for every three shares currently held, a shareholder will now receive an extra one. The effect of this on the balance sheet is shown in the final two columns of Exhibit 3.8.

There will, however, be neither a financial gain nor a loss to shareholders. Consider a holder of half the shares. Before the bonus issue, he would have owned 112,500 shares which entitled him to assets of £250,000. Afterwards, he owns 150,000 which still entitles him to £250,000 of assets. Although the number of shares have increased, he is neither better nor worse off. The asset backing per share has fallen but this has been compensated by an increase in the number of shares.

Premium on redemption

There is one final use which can be made of a share premium account under UK law. A company has a great deal of freedom in establishing the benefits and conditions attached to any shares, debentures or loan stock they might issue. Collectively known as a company's securities, the exact conditions attached to the shares and loans will depend on market conditions at the time of issue.

Debentures are often redeemable and it is even possible for shares to be redeemable under certain circumstances. To make such securities more attractive at the time of issue, it is possible for the company to agree a premium upon redemption. The holder of such a security will receive more than its nominal value when redeemed. This premium is an extra cost for the company in the year of redemption and, as was shown in the earlier discussion on hybrid securities, would normally be charged at some stage to the profit and loss account. Where a share premium account exists, however, UK law allows the premium to be charged against the share premium account. This is demonstrated in Exhibit 3.9 where the debentures are redeemed at 105, that is £105 is repaid for every £100 of debenture.

Exhibit 3.9 Redemption at a premium

Balance sheet (a)				Balance sheet (b)			
(£000)				*(£000)*			
Net assets				*Net assets*			
Cash	425	−105	320	Cash	425	−105	300
Less debenture	100	+100		Less debenture	100	−100	
	325		320		325		320
Financed by				*Financed by*			
Issued share capital				Issued share capital			
100,000 £1 shares	100		100	100,000 £1 shares	100		100
Share premium account	25	+5	20	Share premium account	25		25
Profit and loss reserve	200		200	Profit and loss reserve	200	+5	195
	325		320		325		320

Both balance sheets show £100,000 of debentures being redeemed for £105,000 with the cash being decreased by £105,000 and the obligation to the debenture holders being eliminated. The only difference is the way the premium on redemption is treated. Balance sheet (b) has effectively charged the cost against the current year's profits which are included within the profits retained in the business. Balance sheet (a), however, has made use of UK company law provisions and reduced the value of the share premium account. In both cases the shareholders' funds fall by the £5,000 premium on redemption. Charging the £5,000 to the share premium account, however, ensures the *distributable* reserves are not reduced and in so doing, reduces the security of the creditors.

Capital redemption reserve fund

Despite this anomaly, the protection of creditors by preventing capital being returned to the shareholders is central to the idea of limited liability. This does not prevent a company redeeming part or all of a class of shares. The law, however, requires the resulting reduction in the amount of capital to be filled. This can be achieved by simply issuing additional shares – not necessarily of the same class – to fill the void. Preference shares for instance could be redeemed and their place in the capital structure filled by a further issue of ordinary shares. This way creditors are not disadvantaged.

There is, however, a second way of meeting this legal requirement to maintain capital as far as possible. Legally, revenue reserves can be returned to the shareholders at any time. Transferring an amount equivalent to the capital redeemed from the revenue reserves to the permanent part of the shareholders' funds achieves the same objective as a new issue of shares. A bonus issue of shares out of the *revenue* reserves is one way of bringing this about although a transfer from the share premium account would *not* be acceptable as it is already part of those permanent funds. Another way is simply to transfer an amount from the revenue reserves into a permanent or capital reserve without issuing bonus shares. Such a reserve is known as a *capital redemption reserve account* and is the second of the capital reserves establishable by law.

Exhibit 3.10 Capital redemption reserve fund

(£000)		Redeem shares	Replace void	
Net assets				
Cash	510	−100		410
	510			410
Financed by				
Issued share capital				
100,000 £1 ordinary shares	100			100
100,000 £1 redeemable preference shares	100	+100		
Capital redemption reserve			−100	100
Share premium account	60			60
	260			260
Profit and loss reserve	250		+100	150
	510			410

In Exhibit 3.10, the preference shares are redeemed, causing both cash and the permanent share capital to decrease by £100,000. The creation of a capital redemption reserve for an equivalent amount remedies this by transferring part of the revenue reserves to the company's permanent capital.

Asset revaluation reserve

There is one final capital reserve recognised by law. Although straightforward in application, its creation questions the whole validity of traditional accounting concepts. One major accounting concept is cost attachment. Assets are to be shown in the balance sheet at their (historical) cost unless prudence dictates a lower amount. Recording an asset at its *value* is unacceptable as there is no *transaction* as evidence to support it.

Implicit in the historical cost concept is a stable unit of measurement and yet even modest inflation can cause original cost to lose its meaning. At an inflation rate of only 4 per cent p.a. the value of money halves in under 18 years. Inflation therefore distorts the meaning conveyed by historical costs. Showing an 18-year-old asset in the accounts at its original cost therefore considerably understates the financial resources originally required to acquire it.

A variety of complex solutions are available to reflect the effect of changing prices on a business and they are returned to at a later stage. One simple approach is to revalue some or all of the assets of a company, a remedy available in Britain since the 1948 Companies Act. The major danger of such an approach is the taking of profits on an unrealised transaction. To overcome this, the law in the UK and many other states requires the increase in value to be taken to a capital reserve where it cannot be distributed to shareholders as profit.

Exhibit 3.11 shows a company with fixed assets of £300,000 which it believes have a value of £420,000. The assets are increased to reflect this and a capital reserve, *the revaluation reserve*, is created. The alternative treatment, had it been allowed by law, would

Exhibit 3.11 The revaluation of assets

(£000)		Revaluation	
Net assets			
Fixed assets	300	+120	420
Current assets	200		200
	500		620
Financed by			
Issued share capital			
250,000 £1 ordinary shares	250		250
Share premium account	100		100
	350		350
Profit and loss reserve	150		150
Revaluation reserve		−120	120
	500		620

have been to take the revaluation to the current year's profit and loss account hence not only enhancing the company's profits for the period but also making the amount available for distribution.

However sensible revaluation might be as a way of reflecting the 'true' value of the company's assets, it has two severe disadvantages. First, it has broken the link with historical cost resulting in an amalgam of asset values, some at cost and some at valuation. Secondly, it has introduced two further areas of judgement: (a) should a firm revalue its assets and (b), what should that value be?

PROVISIONS

All reserves involve the setting aside of resources although none of them affect reported profit. The capital reserves – the share premium account, the capital redemption reserve fund and the asset revaluation reserve – are all created outside the profit and loss account. Similarly, revenue reserves are a division or appropriation of that profit rather than a reduction in it.

A similar setting aside of resources takes place *within* the profit and loss account. Most expenses can either be evidenced by an invoice or estimated and an accrual made. Some expenses, however, are so uncertain that they cannot be estimated with any degree of accuracy even though they are known to exist. These are known as *provisions*. How much to charge to the profit and loss account becomes a question of judgement.

Unlike reserves which essentially relate to incorporated bodies, provisions are a feature of all types of business entity. Provisions are therefore similar to reserves in that they involve the setting aside of resources – the amount of which often involves considerable judgement – but equally they are similar to expenses in that they represent a charge to the profit and loss account.

Provisions – an example

Should a company suddenly find it has been producing a faulty product, compensation claims are likely to follow. Profit will be adversely affected and prudence suggests this should be recognised immediately. Unlike accruals, however, there is no clear base on which to estimate the liability. Extreme judgement is required in *providing* for the expense.

Because of this, any charge will be shown separately as a provision although its mechanical recording is similar to that for an accrual. The amount will be charged to the profit and loss account as an expense and will appear as a form of creditor in the accounts. It cannot be shown as an actual creditor, however, because neither the individuals nor the amounts are known. It will therefore be recorded as a provision and shown as such in the balance sheet.

Not all provisions are of this form. Sometimes they will relate to a fall in the value of an asset rather than an increase in a liability. There are two important examples of this, the provision for bad or doubtful debts and the provision for depreciation of a fixed asset.

The provision for bad or doubtful debts

From time to time, a firm will sell goods on credit only to find that the customer is unable to pay. This in itself involves judgement in deciding when this stage has been reached. Does the business wait until the customer is formally declared bankrupt before recognising the debt as being bad or does it take a commercial judgement at an earlier stage? Whatever the stage chosen, it will be necessary to reflect the reality in the accounts of the business otherwise the assets will be overvalued.

For a recognised bad debt, the procedure is straightforward. The asset of debtors needs to be reduced and the cost of this – like all expenses – borne by the owners of the business. This writing down of an asset is therefore no different in principle to any other expense and its treatment is shown in Exhibit 3.12(a) where debtor A has been declared bankrupt. The bad debt is shown as an expense of the period which is ultimately charged to the profit and loss account.

Exhibit 3.12 Bad debts and the provision for bad debts

(a) Bad debts				(b) Provision for bad debts		
	Balances	Expense created	Charge to P & L		Balances	Provision created	Charge to P & L
Debtor A	£200	–£200		Debtor A	£200		
Debtor B	£300			Debtor B	£300		
Debtor C	£400			Debtor C	£400		
Bad debts		+£200	–£200	Bad debts		+£300	–£300
				Provision for bad debts		–£300	
Profit and loss account			+£200	Profit and loss account			+£300

Sometimes, however, a business believes that some of its debtors are likely to prove bad but is unable to identify any individual debtor. The only option is to create a general provision. This is shown in part (b) of Exhibit 3.12 where it is assumed that one-third of debtors will eventually prove bad. The amount is ultimately charged to the profit and loss account as prudence dictates but as neither the exact amount nor the individual debtors can be identified, a general provision has had to be created.

Technically this provision should appear as a liability on the balance sheet and that is the way it is treated in some continental countries. Logically, however, there has been an overall reduction in the value of debtors and so the normal UK treatment is to deduct the provision from the gross amount of the debtors for reporting purposes.

The provision for depreciation

The second major provision faced by most organisations concerns depreciation. For most people, depreciation is viewed as the loss in value of a (fixed) asset through time either because of obsolescence resulting from the introduction of improved technology or because of physical deterioration. Such a view, however, begs the question as to what is meant by value. Everyone knows a new motor car loses relatively more value in its earlier years.

The original cost of the car is easily ascertained but what value should be used at the end of the year to determine its depreciation? Immediately there are two values: what the car could be sold for and how much it would cost to buy an identical, one-year-old car. Depreciation therefore is not as simple a matter as first thought even where a ready market exists – as with motor cars.

For companies with expensive, specific plant, there may not be a readily ascertainable market price. Professional estimates are possible. However, this involves cost, time and the making of many assumptions and judgements, not least of which will be whether there is a continuing demand for the output of the plant. And given the intention of long term use when buying a fixed asset, the relevance of such a valuation is questionable. Motorists, for example, do not constantly check the market value of their cars. Value only has relevance when a car is about to be sold. Until that point, no matter how interesting, vehicle values – and hence depreciation – do not enter the day-to-day decision making of motorists.

Because of this, accountants developed a different approach to depreciation. The basic difference between a fixed asset and any other expense such as labour or materials is that a fixed asset has a longer life. If the accounting period is equal to the life of the asset, the asset would simply be written off as an expense to the profit and loss account along with all the other expenses.

Cost allocation

Imagine a business acquiring a £10,000 asset with a life of five years and sales and other expenses over that same period of £70,000 and £20,000 respectively. Over five years the profit will be £40,000 after charging for the asset consumed. Waiting for five years before determining profit, however, is likely to be unacceptable for most users. From an accounting point of view therefore, the problem of depreciation arises from the need to report profits regularly rather than waiting to the end of an asset's life. A way has to be found of charging the expense to individual accounting periods. Given this, accounting depreciation becomes a process of *cost allocation* rather than valuation, a definition which is consistent with the historical cost valuation to be found in most balance sheets.

Although this avoids the cost and judgement involved in using *values* to determine depreciation, it does not totally avoid the need for judgement. Often an asset will have a residual value at the end of its life and this residual value inevitably has to be an estimate. Equally the life of an asset is an estimate and with rapid technological change, an increasingly difficult one to make. Technological change can easily make equipment obsolete before it is physically worn out and so the estimate may be based on an asset's *economic* life rather than its physical life.

For some firms, the life of an asset and its associated residual or terminal value may be less a question of technical estimation and more one of policy. For example, an airline may, as a matter of policy, change its aircraft every ten years as part of its image even though their technical life may be twenty years or more. For other firms and other assets, their estimated life may mainly be based on physical usage. Lorries working on unmade roads carrying stone or coal are likely to have shorter lives than similar lorries working on good roads and carrying computer equipment. The life of an asset therefore will be the lesser of its physical life and its economic life.

Determining original cost

Before choosing how to charge depreciation to accounting periods, one further piece of information is required, the original cost. For many firms this will not be an issue. For others, the purchase price of an asset may only be one part of the overall cost of acquisition. Many fixed assets involve substantial costs over and above the purchase price of the asset itself. The cost of transporting a piece of heavy equipment from the manufacturer to the customer is but one instance. Such costs are as much a part of the overall asset cost as the initial purchase price. Further difficulties can occur when the fixed asset is not purchased from an outside supplier but is instead manufactured internally. How the costs of manufacture are built up will be returned to at a later stage. For the moment consider an easier example.

A hotel chain can acquire new hotels either by purchasing them ready-built or by appointing architects, surveyors and contractors and building them itself. Clearly the cost of the materials and labour expended on its building will form part of the cost of the fixed asset. Such costs are there for all to see in the final product. But what of interest on funds borrowed by the hotel chain? Physically – and financially – interest charges are less clearly traceable to the final completed hotels and the argument for including such expenses within the cost of the asset are less clear. Despite this, several large quoted companies in the UK choose to include interest in the cost of some of their fixed assets while others take a more prudent approach and write off the interest to the profit and loss account in the year the interest is incurred. Estimating even the cost of a fixed asset is therefore less objective than at first thought.

Straight line depreciation

Having identified in principle the cost of an asset and estimated its residual value and life, there is a final stage to consider – the charging of depreciation to individual accounting periods. By far the easiest approach is to charge depreciation in equal amounts per period by deducting the terminal or residual value from the original cost and dividing the result by the estimated life of the asset. This is known as the *straight line* method and is demonstrated in Example 3.4.

Example 3.4

A firm buys a piece of machinery for £50,000. Its estimated life is four years after which its estimated selling price is £6,480.

The depreciation charge each and every year will be:

$$\text{Depreciation provision} = \frac{\text{Original cost} - \text{Residual value}}{\text{Estimated life}} = \frac{£50,000 - £6,480}{4} = £10,880$$

£10,880 will be charged as an expense to the profit and loss account in each of the four years. Because the life is estimated at four years, this is the same as saying that the depreciation charge is 25 per cent p.a. At the end of the first year, the cost of the asset will be reduced by £10,880 to £39,120 reflecting that part of the original cost allocated as depreciation to the current year's profit and loss account.

The figure of £39,120 is known as the *net book value*. It does *not* necessarily represent the current market value of the asset. Rather it represents the original expenditure less a charging of part of that as an expense to the current accounting period. In the second accounting period, this net book value will be reduced by a further £10,880 to £28,240 as a further year's accounting depreciation is charged to the profit and loss account. By the end of year four the net book value will have been reduced to the asset's residual value after which, providing the estimate is accurate, it can be sold for that amount.

Reducing balance depreciation

There is, however, more than one way to allocate depreciation between the different years. Other approaches charge more depreciation in the earlier years. Two examples of this are the *sum of the digits* method found mainly in the United States and the *reducing balance* method. Both are very similar but as the sum of the digits method is rarely found outside the USA it will not be considered further as a method of depreciation although it is returned to in another context later in this chapter.

The reducing balance method achieves its objective of charging more depreciation in earlier years by calculating depreciation as a constant *percentage* of the net book value – unlike the straight line method which charges a constant *amount* based on cost less residual value. Because the net book value is falling year by year, the percentage depreciation rate will have to be higher than that chosen for the straight line method.

Unfortunately, estimating the percentage rate is not as simple as for the straight line method. One approach is to use a 'trial and error' approach. Exhibit 3.13 demonstrates this. Arbitrary rates have been chosen until one is found which reduces the original amount to the residual value.

Exhibit 3.13 The reducing balance method of depreciation

Depreciation rate	20%	60%	40%
Original cost	£50,000	£50,000	£50,000
Depreciation year 1	£10,000	£30,000	£20,000
Net book value	£40,000	£20,000	£30,000
Depreciation year 2	£8,000	£12,000	£12,000
Net book value	£32,000	£8,000	£18,000
Depreciation year 3	£6,400	£4,800	£7,200
Net book value	£25,600	£3,200	£10,800
Depreciation year 4	£5,120	£1,920	£4,320
Residual value	£20,480	£1,280	£6,480

The 20 per cent rate is insufficient to reduce the book residual value to the estimated residual value. Equally, the 60 per cent rate is too high. It produces a book residual value far below the estimate residual value and hence charges too much depreciation to the accounts over the life of the asset. The required rate is therefore somewhere between 20 per cent and 60 per cent. In this instance it is found by guesswork to be 40 per cent. Normally several trials may be necessary to derive the required rate. An alternative to the trial and error approach is to make use of the following formula where r is the required depreciation rate, n is the life of the asset, s is the residual value and c is the initial cost:

$$r = (1 - \sqrt[n]{s/c}) \times 100\% = (1 - \sqrt[4]{6{,}480/50{,}000}) \times 100\% = 40\%$$

Depreciation methods compared

It is sometimes argued that the reducing balance method is more representative of the real world by charging higher depreciation in earlier years. In addition, as maintenance tends to increase with age, the combined costs of depreciation and maintenance will tend to be equal in each and every period. This is demonstrated in Exhibit 3.14 where the vertical axes represent costs and the horizontal axes represent years. The decreasing depreciation charge through time under the reducing balance method is balanced by the increasing maintenance charge. Superficially attractive as this might be, accounting depreciation is still an allocation of cost, *not* a measurement of value lost and is still based on subjective judgements concerning the asset's life and residual value.

Exhibit 3.14 Reducing balance depreciation and maintenance

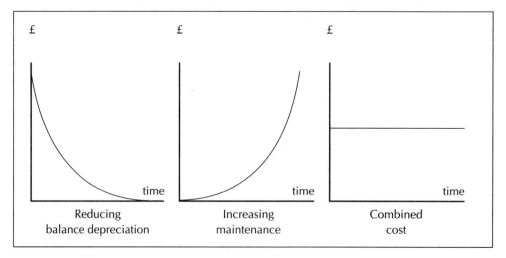

Accounting for depreciation

Irrespective of the method of depreciation, the amount allocated needs to be recorded in the accounts as both an expense of the period and as a reduction in the net book value. Logically the asset cost could simply be reduced and the profit and loss account charged with the depreciation. However, in the real world, there might be several assets to depreciate and so it is convenient to record the charges in a temporary expense account prior to charging the depreciation to the profit and loss. This is the approach chosen in Exhibit 3.15 which uses the reducing balance data from Example 3.4.

A second problem occurs when the asset is directly reduced by the depreciation charge. Part (a) of Exhibit 3.15 demonstrates this. In subsequent periods, the original cost will have been lost from the accounts. Only by a detailed searching of the records would it be found. The alternative, more informative approach, shown in part (b), is to record the reduction in the asset's value separately from the asset itself in the explicit form of a provision for depreciation. In subsequent periods, this provision will increase as further depreciation is charged to the profit and loss account.

Exhibit 3.15 *Providing for depreciation*

	Depreciation (a)				Depreciation (b)		
	Asset cost	Depreciation provision	Charge to P&L		Asset cost	Depreciation provision	Charge to P&L
Fixed asset	+£50,000	–£20,000		Fixed asset	+£50,000		
Cash	–£50,000			Cash	–£50,000		
				Provision for depreciation		–£20,000	
Depreciation		+£20,000	–£20,000	Depreciation		+£20,000	–£20,000
Profit and loss			+£20,000	Profit and loss			+£20,000

For year 1, the balance sheet, using method (a), will simply show an asset with a net book value of £30,000. The balance sheet showing method (b) is more informative. It will show the asset at its original cost of £50,000 but then with the provision for depreciation deducted to give the same net book value of £30,000. This is the way depreciation is reflected in UK balance sheets.

Disposal of fixed assets

Sometimes a fixed asset may be disposed of before the end of its estimated life, either because the estimate was wrong or because of changed market conditions. The asset will be recorded in the accounts at its cost less accumulated depreciation. But how much an asset can be sold for depends on market conditions rather than its net book value. As a result, a profit or loss can arise on the disposal of the asset. The recording is straightforward. A mini profit and loss account – often called a sale of asset account – is opened to handle the transactions relating to the disposal, with any balance being either a profit or a loss.

Of more importance than the recording, however, is the meaning of any subsequent profit or loss. A profit or loss on disposal can arise in three ways: the asset's life was incorrectly forecast, the residual value was inaccurately estimated or the market value of the partly used asset could have substantially changed. If the profit or loss on disposal is due to inaccuracies in the original estimates then any gain or loss really relates to previous years' activities. Depreciation will have been under- or over-provided in previous periods and profit over- or under-stated. To the extent they have not been distributed, previous year's profits are contained within the retained profits reserve. There is therefore a strong case for associating any profit or loss on disposal directly with retained profits from previous years. Equally, any gain or loss arising from a change in market values is a capital gain or loss which does not arise from trading.

Including such gains or losses within the profit and loss account is likely to distort the profit figure reported. Despite this, the normal treatment is to record the gain or loss in the profit and loss account. From a balance sheet perspective, there is no difference between the approaches: the total of shareholders' funds will be identical. The issue though is whether the gain or loss should be channelled through the current year's profit and loss account or accounted for via reserves in the form of previous years' profits retained in the business. Both approaches are demonstrated in Example 3.5. To emphasise the asset disposal, trading activity has been restricted to cash sales and the using up of existing stock.

Example 3.5

> Bennett Marketing Ltd has a machine which cost £80,000 and whose life is estimated at four years. Its residual value is estimated to be nil and it is being depreciated using the straight line method. At the end of two years, the company's only other assets are stocks of £60,000 and cash of £20,000. The business is financed by ordinary share capital of £90,000 and retentions of £30,000. The company has no liabilities. During the following year, half the stock was sold for £80,000 cash and the machine was disposed of for £30,000, also for cash. There were no other transactions during the year.

Before deriving the profit for the year, it is first necessary to verify that there is full data. The shareholders' funds total £120,000 and these are represented by stocks of £60,000 and cash of £20,000, leaving other assets of £40,000. The machine cost £80,000 but as this was two years old, its net book value would be £40,000, the balance of the other assets.

The asset was sold after three years. The total depreciation provided will therefore equal £60,000 made up of £40,000 for the first two years plus £20,000 for the current year. With a net book value of £20,000 and a disposal price of £30,000, the gain on disposal will be £10,000. The effect on the opening balances of this and other transactions is demonstrated in Exhibit 3.16.

Exhibit 3.16 The disposal of an asset

(£000)		Trading transactions				Gain treated as profit			Reserve accounting			
Fixed asset	+£80			−80								
Provision for depreciation	−£40		−20		+60							
Stock	+£60	−30				£30			£30	£30			£30
Cash	+£20	+80			+30	£130			£130	£130			£130
Depreciation			+20	−20								
	£120					£160			£160	£160			£160
Ordinary share capital	−£90					£90			£90	£90			£90
Reserves	−£30					£30	−40		£70	£30	−10	−30	£70
Sales		−80	+80										
Profit and loss account		−80	+30	+20		£30	−10	+40		£30		+30	
Sale of asset				+80	− 60	−30	£10	+10		£10	+10		
	£120					£160			£160	£160			£160

Under the heading *Trading transactions* are recorded cash sales for the year of £80,000 less stock consumed of £30,000 and less depreciation for the year of £20,000. (As there is only one depreciation transaction, it is not strictly necessary for the depreciation to have first been posted to a depreciation account. The amount could simply have been written straight to the profit and loss account.) Next the book value of the asset less accumulated depreciation (£80,000 less £60,000) is transferred to the sale of asset account where it is matched with the sales proceeds of £30,000 to give a profit of £10,000.

In the columns headed *Gains treated as profit*, this profit is added to the trading profit to produce an overall profit of £40,000 for the year. As there are no dividends proposed, this combined total is then added to profits retained from previous years in the reserves. In the *Reserve accounting* columns, the alternative treatment is presented where the gain on the disposal of the asset is immediately transferred to reserves. This has the advantage of not distorting the trading profit for the period but at the expense of hiding a significant transaction within the reserves. In both approaches, the final column represents the balance sheet at the year end. These are identical, demonstrating that the only argument is whether to treat the gain on disposal as profit for the year – the normal treatment – or to account for it via the reserves.

Had the gain been accounted for via reserves, knowledge of the income equation developed in Chapter 2 would have immediately identified the subterfuge – although, as also identified in Chapter 2, this is less critical now that a further primary statement identifying all gains and losses has been introduced. With an opening wealth or shareholders' funds of £120,000, profits of £30,000 and no dividends, the closing wealth or shareholders' funds should equal £150,000. That they equal £160,000 highlights that an adjustment via the reserves has taken place.

THE VALUATION OF STOCK

How organisations value fixed assets affects both reported profit and the state of the balance sheet. Despite this, the calculation of depreciation is riddled with assumptions and judgements concerning an asset's life, estimated residual value and the depreciation method selected.

Similar issues apply to the valuation of stock. How stocks are valued directly affects the cost of sales and hence the reported profit. A business may have stocks left over from a previous period of trading. To these will be added purchases of more stock for the current period. Together the value of opening stock plus purchases form a 'pool' of resources available to be sold. From this will be deducted the value of stock remaining at the period end to give the cost of stock used in the period or, as it is usually called, the cost of sales. This can be expressed as an equation:

Opening stock + Purchases – Closing stock = Cost of sales

The higher the value of closing stock, the lower the cost of sales and hence the higher the reported profit for the period. How stock is valued therefore is as critical to reported profit as the choice of the depreciation method. So far, stock has been valued at its (historical) cost unless this has been greater than its realisable value in which case prudence dictates the use of the lower value. Nothing, however, has been said about how the closing stock value has been derived. Consider Example 3.6 which relates to a simple retailing situation where all the stocks are purchased in a completed state ready for sale. Manufacturing involves additional complexities and is returned to later.

Example 3.6

> Sue Sings starts a business with £1,000 cash which she uses to buy 100 units of stock for £1,000. A second 100 units is later purchased for £1,200. At the end of the accounting period, 100 units had been sold for £1,200. All transactions are for cash.

FIFO stock valuation

Sue Sings' total purchases are 200 units at a cost of £2,200. With sales of 100 units, closing stock must be 100 units. What is less clear is the *value* of that closing stock. Physically, it makes sense to sell the earliest stock first otherwise stock with a limited life might be ruined. There is, however, a choice of methods for valuing closing stock. One method is to use the costs which relate to the physical units unsold. For Sue, the *value* of the closing stock would be £1,200 representing the cost of the last 100 purchased. The cost of sales therefore would be the £2,200 value of the purchases less the £1,200 value of the closing stock. In other words, the cost of sales comprises the earliest values incurred. This association of the earliest stock costs with the cost of sales, replicating the physical usage of stock, is known as the *First In, First Out* or FIFO method of stock valuation.

Although superficially attractive, there is one major objection to this approach. In times of increasing costs, it can overstate real profits. On the face of it, Sue has sold goods for £1,200 which cost £1,000 suggesting she could withdraw the £200 profit and continue trading. Given the data in the question, however, all of the revenue needs to be retained within the business in order to finance the replacement stock.

The accounting implications of this are demonstrated in Exhibit 3.17 where, for demonstration purposes only, the second tranche of stock purchases has been shown to be bought after the sales have been made. Balance sheet A shows the £1,000 capital introduced into

Exhibit 3.17 The valuation of stock

Balance sheet Transactions	A	Purchase stock	B	Sale of stock	C	Purchase stock	D
Cash	£1,000	−1,000		+1,200	£1,200	−1,200	
Stock		+1,000	£1,000	−1,000		+1,200	£1,200
	£1,000		£1,000		£1,200		£1,200
Capital	£1,000		£1,000		£1,000		£1,000
Profit and loss				−1,200 +1,000	£200		£200
	£1,000		£1,000		£1,200		£1,200

the business being represented by cash. Stock is then purchased and the position of the business is represented by balance sheet B. After the stock is sold, the position of the business is represented by balance sheet C. (As there are so few transactions, sales have been taken directly to the profit and loss account rather than via the intermediate sales account.) Finally the replacement stock is purchased and this is shown in balance sheet D. Balance sheets B and D both reflect the same physical position of a single asset comprising 100 units of stock. Only the values have changed. Had Sue withdrawn the £200 'profit', she would have had insufficient funds in the business to continue at the same level of operations – and yet continuity or 'going concern' is one of the fundamental concepts of accounting.

The £200 gain is due to price increases and not trading. Sue would have been as well off holding on to the stock and not trading. Only if she was to stop trading might the £200 be a real profit. Whether it is or not is returned to in a later chapter. One way of reducing the problem of FIFO is to reverse the stock valuation method by progressively using the most current values of stock for the units sold. This method is known as *Last In, First Out* or LIFO.

LIFO stock valuation

Physically, stock will continue to be issued on a First In, First Out basis. Under LIFO though, the latest values will be used to calculate the cost of units sold. In terms of Example 3.6, the 100 units sold will be valued at the cost of the latest 100 bought. The cost of sales will therefore be £1,200, leaving closing stock of £1,000 and a reported profit of nil. Using LIFO to value stocks appears to give a more realistic profit figure for a business, given the assumption of continuity. It is far from perfect, however.

The improvement in the cost of sales calculation has been achieved at the cost of an out-of-date value for the closing stock in the final balance sheet. Secondly, LIFO uses the latest price paid only to the extent of the latest number of units purchased. If units sold are greater than the latest number of units purchased then part of the cost of sales will relate to earlier purchases. Not all of the units sold will therefore be valued at the latest price paid. Thirdly, the cost of sales will not necessarily be 'accurate' if there have been price changes since the last stocks were purchased. Finally, if a business runs down its stocks, the resulting cost of sales might bear little relationship to reality because of the out-of-date values in stocks now being consumed. In Example 3.6, if the closing stocks were sold without being replaced, the cost of sales would be £1,000 even though their current cost is £1,200.

Weighted average stock valuation

There are many other ways of valuing stock. A traditional compromise between LIFO and FIFO is the use of the *weighted average* method. The total cost of stocks available to be sold in a period, including any purchases, is divided by the number of units available. Closing stocks and cost of sales will therefore be valued on a similar basis. Using the data from Example 3.6, the total costs came to £2,200, the units were 200 and so the unit cost was £11. As 100 units were sold and 100 units remained as stock, both the cost of sales and closing stocks would have been £1,100. Example 3.7 demonstrates the use of the weighted average method and compares it with FIFO and LIFO. Not only are different levels of profit possible under the different methods but also profit can be manipulated when using the LIFO and weighted average methods.

Example 3.7

Norwich Ltd retails a particular brand of computer. The selling price is £1,100. During a three-month period it made the following purchases: 1 January, 100 computers at £500, 1 February 200 at £400 and 1 March 200 at £600. By the end of March, 250 computers had been sold. Towards the end of the period, the manufacturer advises the company that the new units will be available at £400 each. This is not likely to affect selling prices.

The top section of Exhibit 3.18 shows the differing reported profits as the stock valuation base changes. Under FIFO, the values used to derive cost of sales comprise the value of the first 100 units purchased plus 150 of the second tranche. The closing stock is made up of the balance of the second tranche plus all of the third tranche of stock. LIFO reverses this process with the cost of sales containing the cost of the latest 200 purchased plus 50 from the previous delivery. The weighted average cost is found by calculating the unit cost (£250,000/500) and multiplying by the number sold to derive the cost of sales and by the number still in stock to derive the value of the closing stock.

Exhibit 3.18 Stock manipulation and reported profits

Profit and stock values without additional stock purchases

Stock purchases			FIFO cost of sales			LIFO cost of sales			Weighted average		
Units	Price	Cost	Units	Price	Cost	Units	Price	Cost	Units	Price	Cost
100	£500	£50,000	100	£500	£50,000	200	£600	£120,000	250	£500	£125,000
200	£400	£80,000	150	£400	£60,000	50	£400	£20,000			
200	£600	£120,000									
		£250,000			£110,000			£140,000			£125,000
Sales					£275,000			£275,000			£275,000
Profit					**£165,000**			**£135,000**			**£150,000**
Closing stock					**£140,000**			**£110,000**			**£125,000**

Profit and stock values with additional stock purchases

Stock purchases			FIFO cost of sales			LIFO cost of sales			Weighted average		
Units	Price	Cost	Units	Price	Cost	Units	Price	Cost	Units	Price	Cost
100	£500	£50,000	100	£500	£50,000	250	£400	£100,000	250	£467	£116,750
200	£400	£80,000	150	£400	£60,000						
200	£600	£120,000									
250	£400	£100,000									
		£350,000			£110,000			£100,000			£116,750
Sales					£275,000			£275,000			£275,000
Profit					**£165,000**			**£175,000**			**£158,250**
Closing stock					**£240,000**			**£250,000**			**£233,250**

The bottom section demonstrates how both the LIFO and weighted average methods can be manipulated. The only assumption made is that a delivery of 250 extra units of stock takes place before the end of the accounting period. No extra sales are involved. This results in revised costs of sales for both the LIFO and weighted average stock valuation methods. Because an extra delivery of 250 units is assumed, this is the 'last in' figure for the commencement of the cost of sales calculation under LIFO. As prices have fallen, this revised cost boosts the apparent reported profit. A similar argument applies to the weighted average computation. The prudence argument of the lower of cost or net realisable value is irrelevant in this particular case because the selling price (the net realisable value) is still above the cost. Both the LIFO and weighted average techniques therefore are capable of being manipulated short term to give the appearance of improved profitability. Only under FIFO does the reported profit remain the same, with the additional purchases simply increasing the size of the closing stock.

Choosing whether to value stocks using FIFO, LIFO, the weighted average or some other method involves judgement – a judgement which has been shown to influence the reported profit for any given year. But over and above these issues are further stock valuation problems whenever a firm makes products to sell rather than purchasing them complete and ready-made. These problems arise directly from the manufacturing process.

MANUFACTURING AND THE VALUATION OF STOCK

Most large firms are not traders selling ready-made goods. Rather they are manufacturers which buy raw materials or semi-finished goods to convert to a final product with the help of labour, machinery and other expenses. Exactly how this is done varies from industry to industry dependent on its technology. Nevertheless there are similarities in all manufacturing processes. The cost of the inputs – the raw materials, the labour and the manufacturing overheads – are brought together to form the cost of the finished outputs. This cost is known as the *cost of production*. In essence it is equivalent to the purchases made by a trader, the crucial difference being that a manufacturer separately buys the component parts making up the final product whereas a trader buys them already combined as a finished product. And just as a trader might find it useful to have several stock accounts for each product marketed, so a manufacturer might maintain a separate cost of production for each item manufactured.

By way of example, a business might purchase raw materials for £3,000, employ labour at a cost of £4,000, pay £2,000 for rent and rates and incur £1,000 of depreciation on manufacturing equipment. Assuming all the raw materials are issued to production and that production is fully completed during the period, the cost of production, the equivalent of purchases for a trader, would be £10,000. In the real world it is unlikely to be this simple.

Not all raw materials are likely to have been issued to production. At the end of the period, there is likely to be a stock of *raw materials*. Similarly it is possible that not all of the production commenced during the period will have been fully completed at the period end. Unfinished production forms another type of stock known as *work in progress*. Some of the completed production may not have been sold, giving rise to a third type of stock equivalent to the closing stock of a trader and known as *finished stock*. It is therefore possible for a manufacturer to have at least three types of stock, all of which have to be valued at the period end to derive the cost of production and the cost of sales. Exhibit 3.19 shows in a diagrammatic form the financial flows making up the income statement of a manufacturer.

Exhibit 3.19 Financial flows in manufacturing

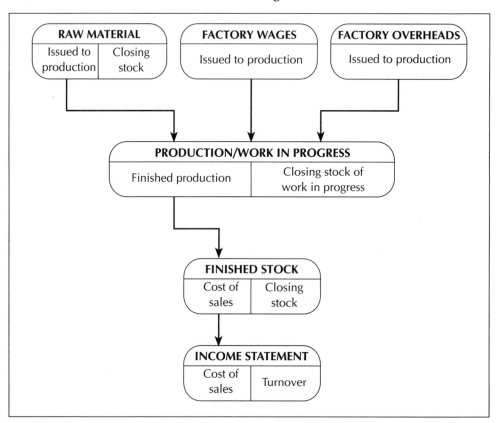

Financial flows in production

Some of the raw materials will be issued to production. At the same time wages and overheads will be incurred which will ultimately convert the raw materials into completed production. However, not all of the production will be completed at the period end. Some will remain as a stock of work in progress at the period end and this will need to be recorded as an asset in the accounts.

Completed production will be available for sale. This generally involves the physical transfer of the completed production to a finished goods store. Financially the value will also need to be transferred to a finished stock account. This is the equivalent to the stock account of a trader, and from there onwards the process is similar to the financial recording of a trader with any finished stock consumed forming the cost of sales for the manufacturer. Example 3.8 and Exhibit 3.20 demonstrate how these flows are recorded in the accounts.

Example 3.8

Wilmslow Ltd was established on 1 January 19X8 with 400,000 £1 ordinary shares issued at par. It entered into an agreement to rent a factory for £50,000 p.a. and separate offices for £20,000 p.a. Both rents were paid on 1 January. On the same day the company bought £40,000 of machinery for use in the factory, office equipment costing £20,000 and raw materials costing £60,000, leaving a bank balance of £210,000.

During the year the following transactions took place: Factory wages paid, £80,000; Factory electricity, £10,000; Office salaries, £30,000; Electricity for the offices, £6,000; Material issued to production, £40,000. Depreciation is to be charged at 25 per cent p.a. straight line on all fixed assets. The closing work in progress was valued at £70,000 while the closing finished stock was valued at £50,000. Sales during the year came to £200,000 and no credit transactions of any form took place.

Recording the data

The first column of Exhibit 3.20 represents the initial data. This is then followed by the recording of expenses incurred. Once these have been recorded in the normal way, items relating to production are all brought together in the production or work-in-progress account, including the depreciation of the factory machinery as this is also an expense of manufacturing. To derive the cost of finished production, the £70,000 value of the incompleted work – the closing work in progress – must be deducted from the £190,000 cost of inputs. (Had there been opening work-in-progress, this would have simply been added to the production expenses of the current period.)

Exhibit 3.20 Transaction flows in manufacturing

(£000)	Expenses					Production							Trading						
Share capital	−400																		−400
Bank	+210	−80	−10	−30	−6							+200							+284
Factory rent	+50						−50												
Office rent	+20													−20					
Machinery	+40																		+40
Equipment	+20																		+20
Raw material	+60					−40													+20
Factory wages		+80				−80													
Factory electricity			+10			−10													
Office salaries				+30										−30					
Office electricity					+6										−6				
Depreciation provision – machinery							−10												−10
Production/WIP						+40	+80	+10	+50	+10	−120								+70
Finished stock											+120			−70					+50
Sales												−200	+200						
Profit and loss														−200	+70	+20	+30	+6	+5 −69
Depreciation provision – equipment																		−5	−5

The resulting £120,000 of finished production is the equivalent of purchases for a trader. £50,000 remained unsold at the period end and so the cost of sales must be £70,000. All other expenses – including the depreciation of the office equipment – are expenses of running the business. They are similar to the overheads of a trader and are charged to the profit and loss account in the normal way.

The result shown in bold in Exhibit 3.20 is a normal profit and loss account, identical in all respects to the statements produced for a trader. Manufacturers, however, are extensively involved in the making of the products and so it is helpful to supplement the traditional profit and loss account with a *manufacturing account*, detailing the cost of production and represented by the production/work in progress account in Exhibit 3.20. Although the detailed presentation can vary, all manufacturing accounts will contain information similar to that shown in Exhibit 3.21 where the final accounts for Wilmslow are reproduced.

Exhibit 3.21 The final accounts for a manufacturer

Manufacturing, trading and profit and loss account for the year ended 31 December 19X8			Balance sheet at 31 December 19X8			
Turnover		£200,000	*Fixed assets*			
Manufacturing account				*Cost*	*Depreciation*	*Net*
Raw material purchased	£60,000		Machinery	£40,000	£10,000	£30,000
Less closing stock	£20,000		Equipment	£20,000	£5,000	£15,000
Raw material issued to production	£40,000			£60,000	£15,000	£45,000
Direct wages	£80,000					
Direct cost	£120,000		*Current assets*			
Factory overhead			Stocks:			
Electricity	£10,000		Raw materials	£20,000		
Rent	£50,000		Work in progress	£70,000		
Depreciation of machinery	£10,000	£70,000	Finished stock	£50,000		
		£190,000		£140,000		
Less closing work in progress		£70,000	Cash/bank	£284,000		
Cost of production		£120,000		£424,000		
Less closing finished stock		£50,000	*Current liabilities*	nil	£424,000	
Cost of sales		£70,000			£469,000	
Gross profit		£130,000				
Other expenses:			*Financed by:*			
Office rent	£20,000		Shareholders' funds			
Office salaries	£30,000		400,000 £1 Ordinary shares		£400,000	
Office electricity	£6,000		Profit and loss reserve		£69,000	
Depreciation of office equipment	£5,000	£61,000			£469,000	
Net profit		£69,000				

Direct and indirect costs

The final accounts for a manufacturer are made more complex by the need to determine the cost of production. There is, however, a further complexity in valuing the cost of production – and other activities for that matter – whenever resources are shared between more than one business activity. Charging all of an expense to production would overstate that cost if other activities such as marketing and finance also make use of and benefit from the expense. Some method of sharing or *apportioning* the cost between the various beneficiaries has to be found. When an expense is unique to an activity, it is known as a *direct cost;* when shared between two or more activities, it is known as an *indirect cost.* An expense therefore can only be classified as a direct or indirect expense when related to an activity and not by an analysis of the expense in isolation.

Consider a company with three factories, each of which makes four products. The salary of the chief executive is an overhead at all times. From a *company viewpoint,* the salary is a direct expense. It is not shared by any other organisation such as another company. From a factory viewpoint, however, the salary is indirect as it is shared between the three factories. The ultimate test of a direct cost is to ask whether the expense would be eliminated if the *activity* was eliminated. Closing down the company would mean that the chief executive's services were no longer required. At that level, his salary is a direct expense. Closing only one of the factories, however, will still leave a need for a chief executive to oversee the remaining factories. At this lower level of activity therefore his salary is an indirect expense.

Assume now that each factory has a factory manager. Not only are these direct costs of the company which would be saved if the company stopped trading, they are also direct to the individual factory. Eliminate one factory and the need for that factory's manager no longer exists. Move to the level of individual products, however, and the factory manager now becomes an indirect cost of each product although a product line manager will be a direct cost of the particular product. A factory manager is still required even if the product range is reduced by one. Only at the level of individual production units will the product line manager become an indirect cost. At that level, direct costs will include expenses such as material, labour (if paid by results) and (electricity) power used to make the individual units.

This is the way materials and labour have been treated in Exhibit 3.21 although electricity has been treated as an indirect overhead because no breakdown is available between power used for machines – a direct cost – and power used for other purposes. Although not strictly accurate, such treatment of electricity can be justified on the grounds that the cost of the increased accuracy might outweigh the benefits and on the grounds of materiality. To verify that labour and material are direct costs, the test once more is to ascertain what would happen if one less item was produced. Both material and labour are assumed to be uniquely identifiable with units of output with all other expenses assumed to remain constant – at least in the short term.

Fixed and variable costs

At this level of individual units direct costs are also variable or marginal costs; that is, a change in output by one results in a *pro rata* change in costs. All other costs – the overheads – are fixed costs, fixed in the sense that their total cost does not change as output varies. This is true whether they are direct to the product such as the product line manager's salary or whether they are an apportionment shared between several activities such as the factory rent or the chief executive's salary. Technically, it is possible that some overheads are variable. For the most part though overhead costs are fixed and this is the meaning generally attached to overheads in normal speech. It is these fixed costs or overheads, especially the apportioned ones, which make the valuation of manufacturing stocks both difficult and, at times, subjective.

The problem relates to the nature of fixed costs. Consider for a moment the variable costs of material and labour. To the extent that production is unsold, it is physically possible to see the raw material element in closing stocks. And to the extent that the raw material has now been converted into a finished product, it is equally possible to trace the labour used. Financially it is also possible to trace these costs. Increase production by one unit and costs will increase by the extra material and labour involved – assuming of course labour is paid by results. Because of this, the physical and financial identification of variable costs in closing stock is relatively straightforward.

However, no similar relationship exists for fixed costs. It is just not possible physically to identify the rent, for example, in units of production let alone other manufacturing overheads such as the personnel function or the factory manager's salary. Nor is it possible to identify cost changes with production changes. Change production by one unit or even ten units, for instance, and there is likely to be no change in the fixed costs. Fixed costs therefore do not vary with activity; they vary with time. Ignoring price rises, rent for six months will be double the rent for three months. The yearly cost of the factory manager will be twice that for a six-month period. On the other hand, variable costs are not influenced by time. They are influenced by activity. To estimate the material element in production cost requires information about the number of units produced, not the length of the production period.

Absorption and marginal costing

Because of this, one way to treat production fixed costs is to recognise them as being time based and to charge them as an expense of the period when they were incurred. The effect of this is to value both closing work-in-progress and finished stocks at their marginal or variable costs. There is, however, a counter argument. Production is effectively impossible without fixed costs such as the rent of a factory and a manager to supervise that factory. Using this argument, fixed costs are as much a part of production as variable costs. Including overheads in the cost of production (and hence stocks) is known as *absorption costing*. The alternative, the charging of overheads as an expense of the period when incurred, is known as *marginal costing*. Both approaches are demonstrated in Example 3.9 and Exhibit 3.22.

Example 3.9

Garforth Ltd manufactures a single product. It plans to sell 4,000 units in each of the next three years. Units produced are planned to be 5,000 in year 1, 4,000 in year 2 and 3,000 in year 3. The product will sell for £90 each. Labour is estimated at £10 per unit and material at £30 per unit. Annual fixed overheads comprise rent of £10,000, the production manager's salary of £30,000, electricity for lighting, heating and running the machines (known as light, heat and power) of £20,000 and supervisors' salaries of £40,000. No work-in-progress is planned.

Exhibit 3.22 Absorption vs. marginal costing

Absorption costing				Marginal costing			
(£000)	Year 1	Year 2	Year 3	(£000)	Year 1	Year 2	Year 3
Variable or direct costs	£200	£160	£120	Variable or direct costs	£200	£160	£120
Fixed costs or overheads	£100	£100	£100	Variable cost of production	£200	£160	£120
Cost of production	£300	£260	£220	Less closing stock	–£40	–£40	nil
Less closing stock	–£60	–£65	nil	Plus opening stock	nil	+£40	+£40
Plus opening stock	nil	+£60	+£65	Variable cost of sales	£160	£160	£160
Cost of sales	£240	£255	£285	Add overheads	£100	£100	£100
Turnover	£360	£360	£360	Total cost	£260	£260	£260
				Turnover	£360	£360	£360
PROFIT	£120	£105	£75	PROFIT	£100	£100	£100

This question is deliberately oversimplified to bring out the consequences of different valuation methods on reported profits. The variable costs are £40 per unit and the fixed costs £100,000 each year. In practice, these variable costs are often called direct costs, the implicit assumption being that units produced is the activity under consideration. The salaries of the supervisors, included in the overheads, are therefore indirect labour.

The cost of sales figures have been calculated in the normal way by adding any opening stocks to production completed before deducting any closing stocks. The variable cost of production comprises the unit variable cost of £40 multiplied by the number produced in the year. Fixed costs are added to this when calculating the absorption cost of production.

Exhibit 3.22 uses the FIFO valuation technique whenever necessary. In the first year, 5,000 units are produced even though sales volume is only 4,000 units. Closing stock therefore is valued at 1,000/5,000 of the production cost and this then forms the opening stock for year 2. Year 2's production equals the sales volume but, assuming a FIFO system, the stock values brought forward from year 1 are assumed to be sold first. The result therefore is that 1,000 units of year 2's production is carried forward to year 3. As production in year 2 is 4,000 units, the value of this closing stock will be 1,000/4,000 of the cost of production. This logic applies to both absorption and marginal costing. The differences in value arise because of the way the fixed costs are treated with the marginal costing approach treating them as a time-based expense to be written off in each period and the absorption approach treating them as part of the cost of production.

Marginal and absorption costing compared

Given the same costs, revenues and other data in both approaches, any differences in reported profits must be due entirely to the way overheads have been treated. With identical sales and no change in costs, it would seem reasonable to assume profits would also be constant in each of the three years. It would also seem reasonable to assume that 1,000 units of stock at the end of the first year would have the same cost as 1,000 units of stock one year later. Marginal costing does just that. Irrespective of when the goods were *made,* the unit cost when sold remains at £40 and so, given identical sales volumes in each year, the (marginal) cost of sales will also be identical. Such symmetry is unlikely to be found with absorption costing if sales volume and production volume differ.

Under an absorption costing approach, profits will vary between £120,000 and £75,000. The value of 1,000 units of stock at the end of year 1 will be £60,000 but the same number of units at the end of year 2 will be valued at £65,000. The reason for this has to lie with the treatment of fixed costs. The greater the production, the lower the fixed cost per unit. The overall cost per unit is therefore going to vary with the numbers produced. Consequently, the closing stock at the end of a high-production period will be valued at a lower unit cost. At the same time, if production volume is greater than sales volume, some of the fixed expenses are carried forward in the closing stock resulting in the overall cost for the *current period* falling and hence reporting a higher profit than under marginal costing. This is exactly what has happened in year 1 where, with production at 5,000 units and sales at 4,000 units, only 4,000/5,000 of the fixed costs have been treated as an expense within the cost of sales.

Absorption costing lends itself to manipulation. Consider year 3, where currently there is no closing stock. Now assume production increases to 5,000 units but sales volume remains the same. Under a marginal costing regime, the variable cost of production will increase by 2,000 units at a unit cost of £40, a total of £80,000. Closing stock, however, will also increase by 2,000 units at £40 and so there will be no effect on the variable cost of sales and hence profit. With absorption costing, the increase in variable costs will also be £80,000 to give a revised cost of production of £300,000 in a similar way to year 1. With sales in year 3 of 4,000 units, a revised production of 5,000 units and an opening stock of 1,000 units, the closing stock will be 2,000 units of the revised production. Its value will be 2,000/5,000 × £300,000 or £120,000. The revised cost of sales will therefore comprise the opening stock of £65,000 plus the cost of production of £300,000 less the closing stock of £120,000, a revised cost of sales for year 3 of £245,000. The result is a £15,000 decrease in the cost of sales and hence a £15,000 increase in the reported profit for year 3 without having to sell a single extra unit!

Absorption costing and published accounts

Despite this, in many parts of the world, including the UK, the published accounts of quoted companies will have used absorption costing in deriving their profit. Through time both approaches will tend to give a similar result. In Exhibit 3.22, for example, the total profit over the three years is £300,000 in both cases and, in fairness, Example 3.9 is an extreme example to develop a point.

In addition, most companies base the overhead per unit on some form of 'normalised' annual production rather than simply each year's production. In the case of Garforth Ltd this would presumably be an output of 4,000 units per annum as this is the average over the three years. The overhead per unit in finished stock would therefore be £100,000/4,000 or £25 at all times and, given a marginal cost of £40, each unit of closing stock would be valued at £65. This would value the 1,000 units of closing stock in each of years 1 and 2 at the same figure of £65,000. This at least brings some consistency to the valuing of identical stock volumes on the balance sheet. Unfortunately, however, it does little to improve the consistency in the profit and loss account. Deducting the revised closing stock of £65,000 from year 1's cost of production will now give a cost of sales for that year of £235,000. With the value and units of opening and closing stock being identical for year 2, the cost of sales for that year will be £260,000. With year 2's closing stock of £65,000 forming the opening stock of year 3, the cost of sales for year 3 will be £285,000. Deducting these costs of sales from the turnover of £360,000 in each year gives revised profits of £125,000, £100,000 and £75,000.

The implication is clear: for any one year, substantial differences can occur in reported profit when using absorption costing. Why then is it still so extensively used? Arguments in favour of absorption costing when valuing stocks revolve around fairness and equity. Production cannot take place without incurring overheads and so it would be unfair and misleading to exclude them from the cost of production.

Unfortunately concepts such as equity and fairness do not lend themselves to objective measurement and so the extent of overheads included in closing stocks will still be a measure of judgement. This is particularly true when the production fixed costs are shared with other functions. A firm's factory and office block might share the same site, for example. How to share that cost between the factory – and hence production – and the administrative function will inevitably involve judgement. Floor area might be one obvious way but despite the initial appeal of this, it is fraught with judgements. What if part of the area is worth more than another? Area abutting the main road might be more valuable than area towards the back of the site. And what if part of the area is used for neither production nor administration? How should that be split between the two functions? Such problems will be returned to when looking at financial information for management. For the moment though it might be useful to consider a further extreme example which may show absorption costing in a better light.

In defence of absorption costing

Imagine a company which only makes one product, Christmas Crackers, which are produced in the first 10 months of the year but only sold in the last two months. At the end of the first six months, the variable cost of paper, fancy hats, etc. and labour totals £400,000 while the fixed overheads such as rent and heat, light and power total £600,000. At the end of the first six months there would be no sales. With no sales, absorption costing would value the closing stock at £1,000,000. Marginal costing, however, would value the closing stock at £400,000 and report a loss for the first six months of £600,000, the overheads for the period. For many people, reporting a loss in these circumstances is felt to be misleading. Losses imply something is wrong with the business and yet there is nothing obviously wrong with this particular business. It is merely that its sales are seasonal. Examples such as this lend support to the fairness and equity argument for including overheads within the cost of production.

RECOGNISING REVENUE

The valuation of stock and the depreciation of assets are not the only areas of judgement likely to affect reported profits. Problems can also exist when attempting to apply strictly the accruals concept. This suggested that revenues and expenses should generally be recognised as they are *earned* or *incurred* and not when monies are received or paid. But such concepts have evolved from a time when much of production was started and completed within a single accounting period. For many firms this is no longer the case. Production of a turbine generator for a power station or the building of an airport might take several years. Prudence suggests that profit on such activities should only be taken once all expenses and revenues can be matched. That has to be at the completion stage at the earliest. Logic, however, suggests that profit is not all earned in the final year and recognising revenue when earned and expenses when incurred is part of the accruals concept.

Long term contracts and the matching and prudence concepts

There is therefore a conflict. Adherence to prudence requires profit only to be reported on completion. Adherence to the accruals concept, however, requires profit to be recognised as earned, that is over the life of the project. Such a conflict cannot be reconciled. There is a straight choice between accruals and prudence. In the UK – although not necessarily elsewhere – it has been resolved by appealing to utility or practical usefulness.

A single profit on completion is felt to distort business activity and mislead users of accounts. Showing profits over the project's life is felt to avoid these difficulties. There is, however, a price to be paid for any possible utility and that is the lack of any hard logic to help apportion the profit to individual accounting periods. This difficulty applies particularly to firms undertaking long term contracts such as shipbuilders, defence manufacturers and civil engineering businesses, all of which undertake work which often takes several accounting periods to complete.

Common to most of the activities will be a contract specifying the timing and the amounts of monies due, quality standards and a production schedule. Some contracts are divided into stages and provide for payments as each stage is completed. The normal method is for an agent of the client such as an engineer or architect to issue a document certifying that the work has been satisfactorily completed up to the agreed stage and for a value to be put on it. This *work certified* is a proportion of the sales value of the contract and triggers the stage payment. From an accounting aspect, the difficulty lies in relating the expenses and the contract price to specific periods to determine profit. This difficulty is addressed in Example 3.10 where, to simplify matters, the planned data is also assumed to be the actual data.

Example 3.10

West and Bromwich plc are awarded a £9 million contract to construct a new theatre over two years. The contract is broken down into two stages, the first, lasting for nine months, results in a value of work certified of £3 million while the second stage, to be finished by the end of the contract period, is for £6 million.

Costs are estimated at £3 million in each of the two years. The cost of the work certified at the end of stage one is £2.5 million.

The overall profit from the contract is £3 million, made up of the contract turnover of £9 million less expenses over the two years of £6 million. Apportioning this to individual years cannot be other than arbitrary as the contract itself is the source of the profit, not individual accounting periods. Taking all of the profit at the beginning of the contract, though, appears rash, while taking all of the profit at the contract end might be misleading. It therefore seems both reasonable and prudent to relate profit to the degree of completion. Unfortunately there are at least three ways profit can be apportioned over time.

The first involves apportioning the contract value and expenses (and hence profit) on the basis of the proportion of work completed in a period, the second uses the proportion of turnover in the form of work certified to estimate activity while the third attempts to match work certified in a period to the expenses incurred in the work certified.

In the first case the cost of the work completed in year 1 is £3 million out of a total cost of £6 million and so 50 per cent of the turnover, expenses and profit will be reported in the first year. In the second case, sales value rather than costs are used to apportion activity between years and with work certified in year one of £3 million out of a total contact price of £9 million, one-third of turnover, expenses and profit will be taken into year 1. The final case involves the matching of the value of the work certified with the expenses involved in generating that value. The turnover for year 1 will be the work certified of £3 million, the expenses will be £2.5 million and so reported profit will be £0.5 million. It is therefore possible to have three totally different ways of reporting the profitability of the same project. These are summarised in Exhibit 3.23.

Exhibit 3.23 Revenues, expenses and profits for contracts

Activity base	(1) Work completed			(2) Work certified			(3) Matching		
	Year 1	Year 2	Total	Year 1	Year 2	Total	Year 1	Year 2	Total
Turnover	£4.5m	£4.5m	£9.0m	£3.0m	£6.0m	£9.0m	£3.0m	£6.0m	£9.0m
Expenses	£3.0m	£3.0m	£6.0m	£2.0m	£4.0m	£6.0m	£2.5m	£3.5m	£6.0m
Profit	£1.5m	£1.5m	£3.0m	£1.0m	£2.0m	£3.0m	£0.5m	£2.5m	£3.0m

In each case the total profit over the two years is identical. The problem relates to how the activities are reported in individual years and to what is known as *attributable profit*. It is therefore a problem of periodicity. Logically there is nothing to choose between the three methods: all are equally arbitrary. Superficially, the matching approach might appear more attractive as expenses are directly related to revenues receivable. There are, however, two objections to this approach. Given the question, the revenues and expenses only relate to nine months' activity. Secondly the profit is generated from the successful completion of the contact. Trying to determine how much profit is generated by one stage rather than another is therefore not particularly meaningful. A similar argument might be applied to the reporting of turnover using the work certified method. This leaves the work completed method. Unfortunately such a method is open to abuse. By increasing the proportion of work completed in any single period, it is possible to increase the reported profits of that period even though the client might not be willing to accept the project earlier than the specified completion date.

Balance sheet implications

The choice of method for reporting profit will have ramifications for the assets and liabilities disclosed in the balance sheet. Whichever method is chosen, the expenses of £3 million for year 1 will have to be recorded in the accounts like any other transaction. This is demonstrated in Exhibit 3.24 where the expenses are recorded as work-in-progress and are assumed to have been paid for in cash. The amount recognised as turnover is shown directly in the profit and loss account and recorded as a debtor. To determine the attributable profit, the work-in-progress is then reduced by the expenses. The values of work-in-progress and debtors which will appear as assets on the balance sheet appear as bold figures in the final column.

Exhibit 3.24 Asset values for contracts

	(1) Work completed			(2) Work certified			(3) Matching		
Cash	−3.0		−3.0	−3.0		−3.0	−3.0		
Work-in-progress	+3.0	−3.0	**nil**	+3.0	−2.0	**+1.0**	+3.0	−2.5	**+0.5**
Debtor		+4.5	**+4.5**	+3.0		**+3.0**	+3.0		**+3.0**
Profit and loss		−4.5 +3.0	−1.5		−3.0 +2.0	−1.0		−3.0 +2.5	−0.5

The result is that methods which show higher profits also show higher asset values. This follows inevitably from the duality concept. Showing a higher turnover has to be reflected in a higher level of debtors for sales on credit. This finding is of importance when measuring the performance of a business. Because of this and the discretion implied, debtors and stocks arising from contracts are shown separately in UK published accounts. Stocks are identified as *long term contract balances* while debtors are shown as *amounts recoverable on contracts*.

It is sometimes suggested that the calculated profit should be further reduced to take account of the problems involved in apportioning profits to accounting periods other than the final period. No hard logic supports such treatments. Despite that, some authors still suggest that reported profit should be reduced to two-thirds of the calculated profit and/or the proportion of cash received to work certified. However prudent these adjustments might be there is no logical justification for them nor any legal obligation to make such adjustments. Firms are free to choose the basis on which to *pro rata* contract profits.

The treatment of losses

Such freedom is not, however, without constraints. Profits in any single period cannot be greater than the overall profit of the contract less any profit already taken in previous periods. Secondly, no profit should be taken if the overall profit cannot be forecast with reasonable certainty. Thirdly, if an overall loss is foreseeable, prudence dictates that all of the loss is reported in the current period. The treatment of a loss and other complications is considered in Example 3.11.

The loss for the year is £10,000, being the difference between the value of the work certified and its cost. Overall though the actual costs to date plus forecast future costs total

Example 3.11

> Leeds and York entered into a contract for £290,000 to build a swimming pool for a local authority. After 12 months the costs incurred totalled £180,000 and the estimated further costs to completion were £140,000. The work certified at the end of the first 12 months was valued at £50,000 although the contract provided for the client making a stage payment for £80,000 which had been paid by the year end. The cost of the work certified came to £60,000.

£320,000 resulting in a loss on the contract of £30,000. Prudence therefore demands an immediate provision for future losses of £20,000. These and other transactions are recorded in Exhibit 3.25 where expenses are assumed to have been paid by cash.

Exhibit 3.25 The treatment of loss in contracts

(£000)					Summary 1			Summary 2
Cash	−180			+80	−100			−100
Work-in-progress	+180		−60		+120	−20	−30	+70
Debtor		+50		−80	−30		+30	nil
Profit and loss		−50	+60	+20	+30			+30
Provision for contract loss				−20	−20	+20		nil

At the summary 1 stage, the work in progress is shown as £120,000. This, however, is an overstatement. Prudence suggests stock should be valued at the lower of its cost or net realisable value. The work-in-progress (together with further work) will be delivered to the client at a price below cost and this loss is the loss shown in the provision for contract loss. It therefore seems both reasonable and prudent to reduce the work in progress by the contract loss provision as far as possible. This is its realisable value.

There is, however, a further issue. The client has paid more than the work certified, the amount recognised in turnover for the current period. Because of this, the client appears as a creditor. But this is rather artificial as the payment results directly from the contract work undertaken for him and shown as work in progress. And unlike any other creditor, the client will not demand payment but rather that the contract be completed. It therefore seems sensible to show this reality by relating the prepayment to the associated work-in-progress and reducing that figure by the extent of the prepayment.

Complexities in other industries

Contracts are not the only area where there are complications in recognising revenue. Whisky production is a multi-million pound industry but, like contracting, production stretches over several accounting periods. It faces a similar problem. Should distillers store whisky for twelve years and then report a single large profit when sold or should that profit be taken over the production period of the whisky? There is, however, one critical difference from contracting. A contractor has a legally enforceable agreement with the client. A whisky producer only has the belief that there will still be a demand for his product at maturity. This makes the taking of profit over the maturing period somewhat more problematic than taking profits over a contract's life. It involves *forecasting* not only demand but also prices many years ahead in order to estimate the profits from whisky distillation.

Despite this, the practice is common even amongst large quoted companies of taking profits as the whisky matures rather than waiting until sold. Each year, not only are the costs of maintaining whisky added to the stock value, rather than being charged as an expense to the profit and loss account, but a proportion of the overall profit is also added to the stock value even though not realised.

Credit sales and hire purchase

Difficulties in determining revenue will exist whenever the revenue from a sale covers more than one accounting period. As a final example consider sales made on long term credit or hire-purchase. Technically there is a difference between the two. Both usually involve a deposit being made by the customer followed by an agreed number of instalments. With a hire purchase transaction, the legal ownership stays with the seller and is only transferred to the buyer on the payment of a notional fee once all the instalments have been made. A credit sale, however, involves the immediate transfer of title to the buyer. If accounting followed the strict letter of the law, an asset acquired under a credit sale would immediately appear in a business's balance sheet while the identical asset purchased under a hire purchase agreement would not. Not only would this be misleading, it would also be nonsense. The commercial substance of the two transactions are identical even if the legal form is different and it is the substance argument which is preferred in UK accounting.

Recognising profit

For a business providing hire purchase or credit sale facilities, there is the problem of determining the periods to which the profit relates. Normally the hire purchase or credit instalment price will be greater than the cash price. Consequently there will be two elements of profit: the profit on the sale of the goods and the 'profit' or interest implicit in the credit charge. As the interest element results from the deferred payments by the buyer, it is consistent with matching to recognise the interest element of profit over the life of the agreement. The question though is whether the normal trading profit should also be spread over the life of the agreement or whether that should be recognised in total at the time the sale is made. Both methods can be found in practice. Taking all of the trading profit in the initial period might well be consistent with matching. Whether it is prudent is another matter, especially if the second-hand value on a repossession is low and the cost of enforcing the agreement high.

Apportioning interest

There is a second issue concerning the apportioning of the interest over the agreement period. Effectively the seller is loaning funds to the buyer and so the amount outstanding – and hence interest – will be greater at the beginning of the period than at the end. Matching demands that this is reflected in the accounts. The most accurate way of handling this has to wait until Chapter 20. There is though an acceptable approximation which makes use of the 'sum of the digits' technique to be found in the USA and elsewhere for calculating depreciation. This involves identifying the number of periods over which the payments are to be made.

For a six-month period, for example, the first month will recognise six times the interest of the final month, the second month will recognise five times the final month's interest, the third month will recognise four times the final month's interest and so on. Starting from period one, each period will be identified by a digit representing one more than the previous period. These are then added to give the 'sum of the digits'. For an agreement covering six monthly payments, the sum of the digits will be 21, made up of $1 + 2 + 3 + 4 + 5 + 6$ and so the first month will show interest as being 6/21 of the total, the second month 5/21, the third month 4/21, etc. Had the credit period been twelve instalments the sum of the digits would have totalled 78. Because of this, the method is often called the rule of 78. Example 3.12 demonstrates this sum of the digits or 'rule of 78' method. A short, four-month credit period has been taken not because such a period is realistic but simply to reduce the tedium of calculation.

Example 3.12

> Hoylake plc sells industrial plant and machinery. On 1 November, it sold equipment costing £8,000 on extended credit terms for £11,000. The cash price would have been £10,000. The agreement provided for four equal monthly instalments, payable at the end of each month. Hoylake's accounting year end is 31 December.

The sum of the digits, $1 + 2 + 3 + 4$, totals 10. Shown in the accounts to December will be 7/10 of the £1,000 interest, 4/10 in respect of November and 3/10 in respect of December. Rather than deriving the sum of the digits by adding all the digits, use can be made of the formula, $n(n + 1)/2$ where n is the number of periods. Ignoring the fact that the 'rule of 78' is merely one way of apportioning the interest, the greater issue is whether the rule should also apply to the profit on the sale or whether the total mark-up should be shown as part of the current year's profits.

Both approaches will be found in company accounts in the UK which makes for difficulties in attempting to evaluate, for any single accounting period, the performance of businesses involved in these type of transactions. Logically there are three possible ways of recording the sale in Example 3.12: to take all of the sales and profit into the current year, to take only part of the sales and profit into account, or to take into account all of the sales but only part of the profit. The reality is that the second option is rarely if ever used despite its approximation to the treatment of long term contracts.

The valuation of debtors

A further difficulty concerns the valuation of the debtor in the accounts. On the one hand, a credit transaction for £11,000 has taken place and on that basis the full amount of the debt should be shown. This is the legal position. On the other hand, interest is not due immediately and so showing the full amount of the debt would overstate the reality of debtors resulting from trading. A variety of ways are available to record this but probably the fullest method would be to record the total amount of the debt and then reduce this by the amount of the interest not yet due in a similar way to providing for bad debts. This is the way the transaction has been recorded in Exhibit 3.26.

Exhibit 3.26 Accounting for credit sales

				Summary 1		Summary 2
Stocks			−£8,000	−£8,000		£−8,000
Debtor	+£11,000			+£11,000		+£11,000
Provision for interest		−£1,000	+£700	−£300		−£300
Provision for unrealised profit					−£600	−£600
Profit and loss	−£11,000 +£1,000 +£8,000 −£700			−£2,700	+£600	−£2,100

The sale on 1 November is initially recorded at its full value of £11,000 but because £1,000 of this is not due at that stage, both the sales value in the profit and loss account and the debt in the debtor's account are reduced by the £1,000. The reduction in the debtor is achieved by the creation of a provision in an identical manner to the creation of a doubtful debt provision. Stock is then deducted from turnover in the normal manner within the profit and loss account to produce a trading profit of £2,000. At the end of the year though, £700 of the interest is due and owing by the debtor. The profit is therefore increased by £700 while the amount owing by the debtor is also increased by a similar amount, albeit by reducing the provision.

Summary 1 shows the position of the business at the year end on the assumption that all of the mark-up is taken into account at the time of the sale while interest accrues over the period of the agreement. On the balance sheet, the debtor will be shown with a value of £10,700 reflecting the fact that £300 of the interest is not yet due. The profit for the period will be £2,700, made up of the trading profit of £2,000 plus the interest earned of £700. Should the firm prefer to recognise profit over the life of the agreement then, using the sum of the digits approach, 3/10 has yet to be earned. The profit is therefore reduced by £600 and effectively the debt is also reduced by this amount, not by reducing the debtor but by the creation of a further provision. The balance sheet will, as a result, show debtors of £10,100, made up of the original amount of £11,000 less the provision for interest not yet earned less the provision for profit not yet earned.

SUMMARY

This chapter has explored the critical role of profit in different forms of business organisation. It has introduced some of the complexities such as reserves and provisions which are to be found in limited companies – by far the most significant business organisation in the modern world.

Three specific areas have been examined in detail because of their effect on reported profit: the calculation of depreciation, the valuation of stock and the recognition of revenue. All have been shown to depend on assumptions and judgements, a knowledge of which is essential to the understanding and interpretation of business information.

With so much judgement involved, it is little wonder that there are increasing attempts to regulate the contents of accounting reports by governments and other authorities. This chapter has gone some way to explaining the need for regulation of accounting data. The framework of regulation and its legitimacy is returned to in later chapters. Before so doing, however, it is useful to consider the practical ways accounting data is recorded in business organisations. This is the subject of the next two chapters.

REFERENCE

1 Companies Act 1985, Section 193.

TEST YOUR UNDERSTANDING

1 Partnerships are governed by the Partnership Act of 1890. Is this statement true or false?

2 A current account records:
  (a) details of current assets;
  (b) items of current expenditure;
  (c) the detailed division of profit between partners;
  (d) the amount in the current account at a bank.

3 A company is formed with an authorised share capital of 100,000 £1 ordinary shares and an issued share capital of £60,000. An investor has acquired half of the shares. The book value of the shareholding is (a) £50,000 or (b) £30,000, (c) unknown.

4 A public limited company is one which:
  (a) has a quotation on any recognised stock exchange;
  (b) has a quotation on the London stock exchange;
  (c) has informed the public that it has limited liability;
  (d) has an authorised share capital of more than £50,000;
  (e) has an issued share capital of more than £50,000;
  (f) allows the public to subscribe for its shares.

5 A capital instrument refers to
  (a) a share issued on the London stock exchange;
  (b) any security which provides long term finance for a company;
  (c) an asset acquired for long term use in a company;
  (d) a hybrid security.

6 Capital maintenance is a concept which prevents ordinary shares or loans from being redeemed except on a liquidation. Is this statement true or false?

7 Identify three differences between the accounting treatment of a limited company and an unincorporated business.

8 What is the difference between a reserve and a provision?

9 What is the legal definition of a revenue reserve and what are the financial implications?

10 List three capital reserves and explain how they differ from a revenue reserve.

11 Depreciation is the loss in value of an asset and the expression 'net book value' represents how much an asset is worth in its current state. Is this statement true or false?

12 In times of inflation, the FIFO method of stock valuation:
   (a) overstates profit and understates the stock value in the balance sheet;
   (b) overstates profit and overstates the stock value in the balance sheet;
   (c) overstates profit and shows stock values at the cost of the latest purchases;
   (d) understates profit and shows stock values at the cost of the latest purchases;
   (e) understates profits and shows stock values at the cost of earlier purchases.

13 Differentiate absorption costing from marginal costing.

14 In long term contracts, there is potential conflict between two fundamental concepts. What are these concepts and why might there be a conflict?

QUESTIONS

1 Amanda and Barry are in partnership. Their partnership agreement provides for Amanda to receive 8 per cent interest on the loan she has made to the business and for Barry to receive a salary of £17,000 per annum. Interest on the loan is to be credited directly to Amanda's current account at the end of each year. Each partner is entitled to 10 per cent interest on their capital. The same rate is also charged or credited on the opening balances of the partners' current accounts. Any remaining profits are then to be divided equally. The balance sheet of the business on 1 July 19X6 was as follows:

Premises		£65,000
Fixtures and fittings		£15,000
		£80,000
Current assets:		
Stocks	£18,000	
Debtors	£19,000	
Prepayments	£2,000	
Cash/bank	£36,000	
	£75,000	
Less current liabilities		
Creditors	£10,000	
Accruals	£5,000	
Net current assets		£60,000
		£140,000
Less loan from Amanda		£50,000
		£90,000
Financed by:		
Capital Amanda	£50,000	
Barry	£30,000	£80,000
Current accounts Amanda	£20,000	
Barry	(£10,000)	£10,000
		£90,000

The prepayment related to rates paid in advance while the accrual was an estimate of electricity used but not invoiced.

During the following year purchases of stock totalled £60,000 and sales came to £90,000. All purchases and sales were on credit. Cash received from debtors came to £60,000 while payments to creditors totalled £51,000. Over the 12 months, Amanda withdrew £8,000 and Barry £12,000. Other invoices received and paid during the year were £15,000 for electricity and £9,000 for rates. At the year end, closing stock was estimated at £31,000, rates prepaid at £4,000 while electricity used since the last invoice received was estimated at £6,000. (Ignore depreciation.)

Record the above transactions and produce the trading and profit and loss account and balance sheet for the year ended 30 June 19X7.

2* Turner Fine Art Ltd manufactures reproduction sculptures which it sells through department stores. Its balance sheet on 31 March last year was as follows:

Fixed assets		£200,000
Current assets		
Stocks	£60,000	
Debtors	£40,000	
Cash/bank	£120,000	
	£220,000	
Current liabilities		
Trade creditors	£10,000	£210,000
		£410,000
Long term liabilities		
5% debentures		£40,000
		£370,000
Financed by:		
Authorised and issued share capital		
100,000 £1 ordinary shares		£100,000
50,000 8% £1 preference shares		£50,000
General reserve		£80,000
Profit and loss reserve		£140,000
		£370,000

During the following year, purchases and sales on credit were £90,000 and £240,000 respectively. Cash received from debtors totalled £250,000 and that paid to creditors, £70,000. During the year, the following payments were also made: debenture interest, £2,000; preference dividend, £4,000; ordinary dividend, £6,000; administration expenses, £30,000; and directors' fees, £12,000.

At the year end, closing stock was estimated at £50,000 and the corporation tax liability at £40,000. In addition, the directors proposed a final ordinary share dividend of 10% and that £20,000 of profits be transferred to the general reserve. (Ignore depreciation.)

Record the above information in the accounts of Turner Fine Art Ltd and produce the trading and profit and loss account and the balance sheet at the year end.

3 Swindon plc's balance sheet at 31 December is as follows:

Fixed assets	£200,000
Net current assets	£600,000
	£800,000
Financed by:	
200,000 £1 ordinary shares	£200,000
100,000 6% redeemable preference shares	£100,000
Retentions	£500,000
	£800,000

On 1 January, it redeemed the preference shares at par. Three months later, it raised £200,000 cash by issuing ordinary shares at £2 each. At the same time, it revalued its fixed assets to £500,000.

Show the effect of all these transactions on the balance sheet of Swindon plc.

4 Jonathan Knowles is a manager with Porter's Chains Ltd. On reading the company's latest set of accounts, he notices that the plant and machinery is almost fully depreciated and has asked for approval to replace them within the next 12 months as they will then be fully depreciated. The reply from the financial director suggests they cannot be replaced for another three years as the funds are not available.

He has asked you for advice and argues that not only must the financial director know that the equipment has to be replaced – 'otherwise, why will he be showing their net value as zero in next year's accounts' – but that the cash must be available as full depreciation has been charged over the previous years.

5 Porter's Chains Ltd has also recently purchased a new computer for £10,000. Its estimated life is four years after which it is likely to have a residual value of £625. Using the straight line and reducing balance methods of depreciation, estimate the depreciation charge for each of the four years of the asset's life.

6* Lilac plc commenced work on a £430,000 contract exactly one year ago. Expenses incurred to date are: wages, £75,000; materials, £40,000; consumables £6,000; hire of plant, £5,000; head-office overheads, £7,000. Estimated future expenditures to complete the contract are as follows: wages, £30,000; materials, £35,000; consumables, £2,000; hire of plant, £6,000; head-office overheads, £5,000. In addition, the directors believe it is prudent to provide an extra £4,000 for unforeseen contingencies.

Cash received from the client for work certified was £160,000. Twenty per cent of work certified is withheld by the client until the contract is completed. Work costing £20,000 had been completed but not certified at the year end.

Estimate the possible profits which Lilac plc can report on the contract for the year just ended and show how these policies will affect the balance sheet.

7* Mogul Manufacturing Ltd's balance sheet on 30 September last year is reproduced below.

Fixed assets

Plant and machinery			£600,000
Less depreciation to date			£240,000
			£360,000

Current assets

Stocks			
Raw materials	£20,000		
Work-in-progress	£30,000		
Finished goods	£30,000	£80,000	
Debtors		£60,000	
Prepayments		£4,000	
Cash/bank		£100,000	
		£244,000	

Current liabilities

Trade creditors	£50,000		
Accruals	£6,000	£56,000	£188,000
			£548,000

Financed by			
Authorised and issued share capital			
20,000 £10 ordinary shares			£200,000
Retained earnings			£348,000
			£548,000

The prepayments relate to factory rent while the accruals are in respect of factory electricity. In the following year, sales were £250,000 and purchases of raw materials, £60,000. All sales and purchases of raw materials take place on credit.

Cash received from debtors during the year came to £280,000 while payments made to creditors were £90,000. Other payments made were £40,000 factory wages, £30,000 office salaries, £20,000 factory rent, £6,000 office rent, £24,000 factory electricity and £7,000 office electricity.

At the subsequent year end, there was a closing stock of raw materials of £30,000. Work-in-progress was valued at £22,000 and finished stock at £50,000. There were no accruals or prepayments but the plant and machinery was to be depreciated at 10 per cent per annum on cost.

Using the above information, record the transactions and prepare the manufacturing, trading and profit and loss account for the year.

CHAPTER 4

The generation and recording of financial data

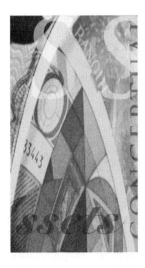

The concept of duality allows accounting transactions to be recorded and the profit and loss account and balance sheet to be produced. The detailed application of duality can take a variety of forms. One of the earliest and most popular manual applications is known as double-entry bookkeeping.

This chapter:

- Describes the mechanics of double-entry bookkeeping

- Discusses the need for verification and develops the idea of the audit trail

- Examines the use of the trial balance

- Demonstrates the division of the accounting system into ledgers

- Introduces the use of daybooks

- Shows how final accounts can be produced from the trial balance

Most accounting concepts attempt to constrain the wilder excesses of financial reporting. Duality, however, serves a different purpose. It is concerned with the way data is recorded rather than how it is valued and measured. Its development so far, of listing all the accounts and the transactions in a single table, has the advantage of transparency. Immediately, the effect of any transaction on the profit and loss account and balance sheet is identified. However, it is not particularly practical for use in a real business with a high volume of transactions and a large number of accounts.

A variety of techniques have been developed to overcome this difficulty, all with differing degrees of sophistication, depending on the complexity and volume of the data. Despite this variety, all are *logically identical* to the duality approach already developed and differ only in detail. This chapter is primarily concerned with the traditional manual recording mechanism known as double-entry bookkeeping first developed in medieval Venice.

DEBITS, CREDITS AND BOOKKEEPING

Allocating each account heading a single line has only limited practicality. To overcome this, one option would be to use a whole page for each account heading. And rather than recording a transaction in terms of a plus and a minus, the page could be divided into two with one side showing positive elements and the other side negative elements. The approach would be similar to that used in the medieval charge/discharge accounts outlined in Chapter 1.

Consider the case of a person starting a business with £1,000 cash on 1 January 19X9. From the *business's* point of view the positive aspect is the gaining of cash while the negative aspect is the incurring of an obligation to the owner for a similar amount. As with the tabular approach already developed, a new account will be opened whenever this is felt to be desirable. In this example, the need is for a capital account and a cash account.

Debits and credits

It is totally arbitrary whether the positive aspect is shown on the left-hand side or the right-hand side of the account. By convention, however, the positive aspect is recorded on the left-hand or *debit* side and the negative aspect on the right-hand or *credit* side. The terms debit and credit date back to Pacioli's Venice and are often abbreviated to 'Dr' and 'Cr'. Debit simply relates to value received and credit to value given: neither term has any moral or ethical connotations.

To record the introduction of £1,000 of capital will therefore involve the debiting of the cash account (reflecting the receipt of cash) and the crediting of the capital account (reflecting the amount owed by the business to the owner). But because each account will now be on a separate page, the detail of the transaction will no longer be transparent. To overcome this, each account will include a narrative explaining the reason for the transaction along with the transaction date. This is demonstrated in Exhibit 4.1 which shows the recording of capital of £1,000 being introduced into the business.

Within the *cash account*, cash received is shown as a gain by being recorded on the left-hand or debit side of the account, the side specified as the gaining side. The full transaction is made clear within that single account by the use of the narrative which describes why the cash has increased by £1,000. In so doing, it also explains where the corresponding entry is to be found. By allocating a full page to each account, many more transactions are possible, although at the cost of not immediately seeing the full transaction. The narrative serves to overcome this limitation.

Exhibit 4.1 Double-entry bookkeeping

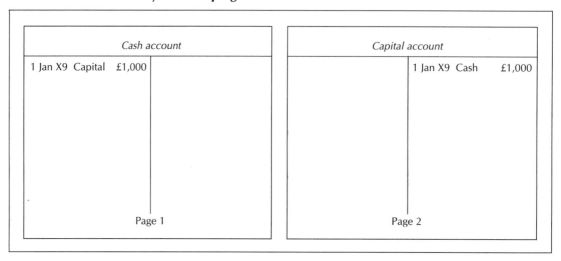

Cash account		
1 Jan X9 Capital £1,000		
	Page 1	

Capital account		
		1 Jan X9 Cash £1,000
	Page 2	

A similar argument applies to the capital account which, in practice, would appear on a separate page. Because the item is recorded on the right-hand or credit side, it is instantly clear that the amount is an obligation. Together, the debit to the cash account and the credit to the capital account records the same information as the tabular approach developed in the previous three chapters.

'Credit' – a source of confusion

Before developing a fuller example of double-entry bookkeeping, it is useful to consider what would have happened if the £1,000 cash had been paid into a bank account. Instead of the cash account being debited with £1,000, a bank account would have been debited. This sounds strange! If people deposit money with a bank they are in credit and their bank statements show credit balances. Why then should the accounts of the business show this as a debit?

The reason is straightforward. When money is deposited at the bank, cash will increase in the accounts of the bank. From the *bank's perspective*, this is the positive or debit aspect of the transaction. At the same time the bank now owes the amount to the customer. The customer is therefore a *creditor of the bank* and so the bank has to show this in its books as the negative or credit aspect of the transaction. A bank statement is simply a copy of the customer's account in the bank's books and so if a person has money in the bank, that person is a creditor of the bank and the account will show a credit balance. In that person's *own accounts* though, the amount will be shown as a debit balance.

DOUBLE-ENTRY BOOKKEEPING – A WORKED EXAMPLE

It is now possible to show how transactions in general are recorded. For convenience, several accounts will be recorded on the same page although in practice each account would take up a full page to allow many debits and credits to be recorded in a single account. Example 4.1 and Exhibit 4.2 demonstrate the recording of transactions making use of the more practical approach of double-entry bookkeeping.

Example 4.1

Tony Arnold starts a business on 1 April 19X1 by depositing £10,000 with the Mudling Bank. On 4 April, he buys stock on credit from Richard Field costing £4,000. On 6 April he sells goods on credit to John Brown for £6,000. Further goods costing £6,000 are purchased on credit on 8 April, also from Richard Field. Sales on credit on 12 April comprise £4,000 to John Brown and £3,000 to Bryan Hill. On 18 April, goods costing £5,000 are purchased on credit from Ace plc. On 20 April credit purchases from Ford Suppliers Limited total £4,000. Credit sales on 26 April comprise £6,000 sold to John Brown, £7,000 sold to Bryan Hill and £4,000 sold to George Dale. At the end of the month, Tony pays £1,000 to an assistant, £1,500 to his landlord for the use of the premises and withdraws £2,000 as his own wages. On 30 April he receives a cheque for £10,000 from John Brown and pays £4,000 to Richard Field. At the end of the month goods costing £4,000 remain unsold.

Exhibit 4.2 The recording of transactions

Capital account							Bank account					
			1/4 Bank	R1	10,000	1/4 Capital	R1	10,000	30/4 Wages	C1	1,000	
						30/4 Brown	R2	10,000	30/4 Rent	C2	1,500	
									30/4 Drawings	C3	2,000	
									30/4 Field	C4	4,000	
									30/4 Balance	cf	11,500	
								20,000			20,000	
						1/5 Balance	bf	11,500				

Stock account							Richard Field – creditor account					
4/4 Field	P1	4,000	30/4 **Trading a/c**		15,000	30/4 Bank	C4	4,000	4/4 Stock	P1	4,000	
8/4 Field	P2	6,000	30/4 Balance	cf	4,000	30/4 Balance	cf	6,000	8/4 Stock	P2	6,000	
18/4 Ace	P3	5,000						10,000			10,000	
20/4 Ford	P4	4,000							1/5 Balance	bf	6,000	
		19,000			19,000							
1/5 Balance bf		4,000										

Exhibit 4.2 (Continued)

Sales account								John Brown – debtor account				
30/4 **Trading a/c**	30,000	6/4 Brown	S1	6,000	6/4 Sales	S1	6,000	30/4 Bank	R2	10,000		
		12/4 Brown	S2	4,000	12/4 Sales	S2	4,000	30/4 Balance	cf	6,000		
		12/4 Hill	S3	3,000	26/4 Sales	S4	6,000					
		26/4 Brown	S4	6,000			16,000			16,000		
		26/4 Hill	S5	7,000	1/5 Balance bf		6,000					
		26/4 Dale	S6	4,000								
	30,000			30,000								

Wages account						Bryan Hill – debtor account			
30/4 Bank	C1	1,000	30/4 **P & L a/c**	1,000	12/4 Sales	S3	3,000		
		1,000		1,000	26/4 Sales	S5	7,000		

Rent account						Ace plc – creditor account			
30/4 Bank	C2	1,500	30/4 **P & L a/c**	1,500	18/4 Stock	P3	5,000		
		1,500		1,500					

Drawings						Ford Suppliers – creditor account			
30/4 Bank	C3	2,000	30/4 **P & L a/c**	2,000	20/4 Stock	P4	4,000		
		2,000		2,000					

Trading and profit & loss a/c for April				George Dale – debtor account			
Cost of sales	15,000	**Sales**	30,000	26/4 Sales	S6	4,000	
Gross profit cf	15,000						
	30,000		30,000				
Wages	1,000	**Gross profit** bf	15,000				
Rent	1,500						
Net profit cf	12,500						
	15,000		15,000				
Drawings	2,000	**Net profit** bf	12,500				
Balance cf	10,500						
	12,500		12,500				
		Balance bf	10,500				

As with the tabular form of recording developed in the previous chapters, all sales are collected together in a temporary sales account. That way, the total of sales for the period is immediately identified. These are then brought together in the trading and profit and loss account.

The need for verification

There is, however, more to bookkeeping than recording. Of equal importance is the ability to verify the data. Documentary evidence should exist for most, if not all, of the transactions in Example 4.1. For sales, this might include sales invoices signed by the customer. For purchases, it might include agreed purchase orders and invoices from the suppliers. In order to verify that the transactions are real, some procedure is necessary whereby the recorded transactions can be identified with the documents proving the transaction. Such a procedure forms part of what is known as the *audit trail*. In terms of this example it can be met by introducing a further column which will uniquely reference the documents with the recorded transaction.

The audit trail

Sales invoices, the invoices sent to customers whenever a sale is made, are generally consecutively numbered. A copy of an invoice signed by the customer, or alternatively a copy of an invoice matched with a goods received note signed by the customer, will be sufficient documentary evidence of the sale. If these copy invoices are filed away in consecutive order, it will be sufficient to record their sales invoice number in the reference column. A direct link between the accounting records and the original document will then be established.

A similar procedure is possible for purchase invoices received from suppliers. The only difference is that there is no automatic, unique ordering system. The supplier's invoice number is for the supplier's benefit, not the customer's, and so it will be necessary to add a reference to each supplier's invoice. The purchases from Richard Field on 4 April might be coded as *purchase invoice number 1*, for example, with the purchases from him on 8 April being identified as purchase invoice number 2. The invoice from Ace would then be purchase invoice number 3 and that from Ford purchase invoice number 4.

This is the approach taken in Exhibit 4.2 where P represents a purchase invoice and S a sales invoice. Similarly the reference whenever an amount is paid might be the cheque number – here shown as C followed by the cheque number – while amounts received might be referenced by a consecutive number attached to each bank paying in slip and identified by the letter R.

Recording the transactions

Ignore for the moment transactions in bold type, transactions affecting the trading and profit and loss account. Instead concentrate on the individual transactions of Tony Arnold's business. The capital paid into the bank is recorded on the left or debit side of the bank account, representing the positive aspect of the opening transaction. The negative aspect, the obligation of the business to Tony, is recorded on the right or credit side of the capital account. (Had it been of benefit, a balance sheet could have been extracted at this stage showing the £10,000 cash in the bank as an asset and the capital as an obligation of the same amount.)

The next transaction involves the gaining of stock and the incurring of an obligation to Richard Field, a creditor. Once more, the logic is identical to the duality concept developed in previous chapters. The increase in the asset of stock reflects the positive aspect of the transaction while the gaining of a creditor reflects the negative aspect. Consequently, the stock account is debited and the creditor's account is credited.

The sale to John Brown represents the gaining of a debtor by the business. The negative aspect means that this amount (less any expenses) is now owed by the business to Tony Arnold, the owner. Temporarily, the amount owing to Tony is held in another account called *sales*. This allows sales data to be instantly accessible and also eliminates a great deal of unnecessary detail within the trading and profit and loss account.

Following further purchases and sales on credit, wages and rent are then paid. Wages and rent represent benefits derived from the hire of labour and the use of premises. The amounts involved are recorded as benefits received in exchange for giving up cash.

Finally a creditor is partially paid while a debtor pays part of his account. The amount received from John Brown involves an increase in cash but a corresponding reduction in the amount he still owes while the decrease in cash from paying Richard Field is compensated by a decrease in the liability outstanding to him. The cash received from John Brown will be recorded as a debit or benefit to the bank account and a credit to the debtor's account. He originally owed £16,000 to the business. Having paid £10,000, the net amount owed is now only £6,000. Similarly with the creditor, Richard Field. The business originally owed him £10,000 but having paid him £4,000, the amount outstanding is now only £6,000.

PERIOD END PROCEDURES

One disadvantage with the double-entry, 'T' account recording mechanism is that it is not easy to see if duality has been applied all the way through the recording of the transactions. This was much less of a problem with the tabular format where each transaction was shown as a positive and a negative figure in a single column. It therefore makes the need for a summary check or trial balance all the greater.

If duality has been correctly applied, the total value of the debits must equal the total value of the credits as each individual transaction comprises an identical debit and credit. Where there are both debit and credit transactions in a single account, it is not clear from a visual inspection whether the net amount is a debit or credit. Before producing a trial balance therefore it is necessary to calculate the net figure.

Balancing the accounts

The method used to calculate the net figure on an account appears archaic and cumbersome although it is both accurate and consistent with duality. Consider the bank account. A total of £20,000 has been deposited and £8,500 withdrawn, leaving a net amount of £11,500 in the bank. In terms of the charge/discharge accounts introduced in Chapter 1, £20,000 has been entrusted to the business and so £20,000 has to be accounted for. The amount entrusted to the business has to equal the amount used plus the amount remaining and this amount remaining forms the balance available for the next period. This was the approach used by the medieval traders who first used duality in accounts and is still with us today when manually recording transactions using double-entry book-keeping.

Returning to the bank account, the £20,000 of deposits is accounted for by withdrawals of £8,500 and £11,500 of unspent cash represented by the balance carried forward. In other words, the 'charge' equals the 'discharge'.

However, all of the transactions within the bank account, other than the balance carried forward, have adhered to duality by being recorded twice, once in the bank account and once elsewhere. To maintain duality, the balance of £11,500 also needs to be recorded twice. This is achieved by showing the corresponding debit aspect as the balance brought forward. As convoluted as this might seem today, it does work. The bank account figure at the beginning of the next month *is* £11,500.

The remainder of the individual accounts are balanced in a similar way at the end of a period. In addition, balancing can be used whenever a page of an account is fully used, thus enabling an account to be as large as needed by carrying the account balance to another page.

The trial balance

Having recorded the transactions and balanced the other accounts, it is now possible to produce a trial balance. This is extracted prior to producing the income statement and before adjusting the owner's capital for any profit made or amounts withdrawn. The trial balance is only a prima facie check. It does not guarantee accuracy nor is it part of the accounts. It is merely a memorandum or working paper outside of the accounts which demonstrates that the accounts appear to be in order.

Exhibit 4.3 shows the resulting trial balance. The trial balance has been taken after recording the data relating to the trading activities of Tony Arnold but before any period end adjustments. On the basis that it balances, there is sufficient confidence to continue with the exercise and produce the final accounts for the period. In the accounts shown in Exhibit 4.2, figures relating to period end adjustments and the production of the trading and profit and loss account are shown in a bold type face.

Exhibit 4.3 The trial balance

Bank	£11,500	Capital	£10,000
Stock	£19,000	Richard Field – creditor	£6,000
John Brown – debtor	£6,000	Sales	£30,000
Bryan Hill – debtor	£10,000	Ace plc – creditor	£5,000
George Dale – debtor	£4,000	Ford Suppliers – creditor	£4,000
Wages	£1,000		
Rent	£1,500		
Drawings	£2,000		
	£55,000		£55,000

Calculating the gross profit

The income statement is divided into two parts. The first part is the trading account – the difference between sales and the cost of those sales. This enables the gross profit to be shown within the final accounts. Sales for the period totalled £30,000. By debiting the sales account and crediting the trading account, the sales value is effectively transferred to the trading account.

Similarly with stock. Of the £19,000 of stock purchases, £4,000 remains unsold and so the cost of sales must be £15,000. The £15,000 has been consumed in making the sales. It is no longer an asset. Consequently it must be charged as an expense to the trading account. The logic is identical to that of the earlier tabular approach. The stock must be reduced by the amount consumed and offset against the turnover for the period. With sales and cost of sales together in the one account, the difference must be the gross profit. This is simply the balance on the trading account and, like all balances, is carried forward thus ensuring duality.

Calculating the net profit

The gross profit balance, however, is not the final profit. Other expenses – overheads – have been incurred and these need to be deducted before deriving the net profit. This is the purpose of the profit and loss account, the second part of the income statement. Expenses consumed during the period are transferred to the profit and loss account where they are offset against the gross profit balance.

The mechanical recording required to achieve this is similar to the recording of sales and cost of sales in the trading account. Any balance on the profit and loss account must either be a net profit or a net loss. In the case of Tony Arnold's business, there is a net profit of £12,500 which is represented by the excess of credit values over debit values.

This, however, is not the total of retentions as Tony has made drawings of £2,000 during the period. A third section has therefore been added to the income statement, netting off these drawings against the profit earned to give retentions of £10,500. The choice then – for any unincorporated business – is to either leave that figure as retentions or to transfer it to the capital account. Both approaches can be met in practice. In Exhibit 4.2, the retentions have been kept separate from the initial capital.

THE FINAL ACCOUNTS

Having completed the transactions, the final stage involves presenting the accounts in a form suitable to the user. The trading and profit and loss account is as much an integral part of double-entry bookkeeping as the bank or capital accounts. A copy of this will be made available to the owner when the final accounts are prepared. The balance sheet, however, is merely a listing of the balances remaining on accounts at the end of the period. Exhibit 4.4 shows the final accounts – excluding a cashflow statement – in a form suitable for presentation to the user.

Exhibit 4.4 The final accounts

Trading and profit and loss account for one month ended 30 April 19X1			Balance sheet at 30 April 19X1			
Sales		£30,000	*Fixed assets*			nil
Cost of sales		£15,000				
Gross profit		£15,000	*Current assets*			
Expenses:			Stock		£4,000	
Wages	£1,000		Debtors[1]		£20,000	
Rent	£1,500	£2,500	Bank		£11,500	£35,500
Net profit		£12,500	*Less current liabilities*			
			Creditors[2]			£15,000
Notes to the accounts						£20,500
1. Debtors	Brown	£6,000	*Less long term liabilities*			nil
	Dale	£4,000				£20,500
	Hill	£10,000				
			Financed by			
2. Creditors	Ace	£5,000	Owner's capital			£10,000
	Field	£6,000	Retentions			£10,500
	Ford	£4,000	*Owner's equity*			£20,500

LEDGERS, DAY BOOKS AND THE JOURNAL

Ledgers

The use of the manual system of bookkeeping outlined above enables the number and size of accounts to be limitless. To reduce the risk of records being lost and to reduce the risk of fraud, the individual accounts of a business used to be kept in bound books known as *ledgers*. Even though accounts today are more likely to be stored on computer disks, the term is still used to describe a collection of individual accounts.

With a high volume of transactions and a large number of accounts, a single ledger might be insufficient as, no matter how many accounting staff are employed, only one person can have access to the ledger at any one time. For many firms there will be three types of transactions which involve either a large volume of transactions or a large number of accounts; these relate to debtors, to creditors and to cash. Consequently it is often useful to record these transactions in separate ledgers.

Details of individual debtors accounts will be kept in a ledger known as the *debtors ledger* or *sales ledger*. For the business of Tony Arnold in Example 4.1, this ledger would contain the accounts of Brown, Dale and Hill. The accounts of creditors will be kept in a second ledger known as the *creditor ledger* or *purchases ledger* while a separate ledger, known as the *cash book*, will be used to record transactions involving money. There is a final ledger where the remaining accounts need to be kept. This is often known as the *nominal* or *general* ledger. No new concept is involved in this breakdown. It is merely a physical division of the accounts to make the recording of transactions more effective.

Day books

Even this subdivision, however, is not particularly practical. Having to enter a transaction as soon as a sale is made, stock is acquired or wages paid would soon result in more time being used to record transactions than running the business. This was a problem faced by Pacioli and the medieval traders. A way had to be found of separating business activities such as serving customers from the detailed recording of the transactions.

Their solution was the keeping of a diary or *rough book* from which the transactions could be entered into the ledgers or books of account at a more suitable time. Through time this evolved into lists of sales, lists of purchases, lists of cash transactions and a final list for any other type of transaction. Originally these were produced on a daily basis and became known as day books – a term which is still with us today even though the lists might be produced on a weekly or monthly basis! Such lists or day books had the advantage of divorcing the activities of the business from their recording. Not only did this make for a more efficient running of the business, it also introduced an important element of control or verification into the accounts.

Consider the data in Example 4.1. Rather than recording the sales and purchases of stock in the accounts as they happen, a monthly day book could be kept instead. These *day books* could then be used to enter the transactions in the accounts at the period end. As a sale takes place, details will be entered in the sales day book, probably by the sales assistant. An example, using data from Example 4.1, is shown in Exhibit 4.5.

Exhibit 4.5 A sales day book

	SALES DAY BOOK		Page 1
Date	*Customer name*	*Invoice number*	*Amount*
6 April 'X1	John Brown	S001	£6,000.00
12 April 'X1	John Brown	S002	£4,000.00
12 April 'X1	Bryan Hill	S003	£3,000.00
26 April 'X1	John Brown	S004	£6,000.00
26 April 'X1	Bryan Hill	S005	£7,000.00
26 April 'X1	George Dale	S006	£4,000.00
			£30,000.00

Day books, audit trails and accounting controls

Some sales day books show additional information such as the customer's own reference, the code given to his account, where applicable, and details of the sale. Not only does this assist the audit trail, it is also part of the wider control function of accounting.

The first check is to ensure that the invoice numbers are in consecutive order to reduce fraud. The likelihood is that at least three copies will be made of the day book: one to remain with the sales department, one to go to the nominal or general ledger section and one to go to the sales or debtor ledger section. The nominal ledger will contain the sales account and so the £30,000 total from the sales day book list will simply be entered in that account. To complete the audit trail, the reference will be to the relevant page of the sales day book from where individual transactions can then be traced. In the sales ledger, the individual debtors' accounts will be debited with the amount owing and, again, the audit trail will be completed by reference to the relevant page of the sales day book.

The outcome is that the sales account will have been credited with £30,000 and the individual debtors' accounts also debited with £30,000. Not only has this made for an efficient division of labour within the accounts function, it has also reduced the amount of administration required of the sales personnel.

A similar but opposite approach is required of the purchases day book where a listing of purchases will be made. One copy will then go to the nominal ledger section to record the total as stock purchased and a second copy will go to the purchase ledger section where the individual suppliers' accounts will be credited.

Reducing fraud

There is, however, a third advantage to this use of day books. They reduce the risk of fraud by making collusion necessary. Imagine a dishonest accounts employee being related to one of the debtors. Under the original system, the employee could have omitted to record the entire transaction and yet the accounts would still have balanced. Now, unless there is collusion, the employee will only be responsible for one aspect of the transaction. A failure to record one side of the transaction will be discovered because, if the other side has been recorded, the accounts will not balance.

The handling of money

The handling of money by a business is one of the most sensitive areas of control. For many companies, cash in the form of cheques will arrive in the post. Ideally a listing of all monies received should be made under supervision. The list will be similar to the outline sales day book already discussed and will record the name of the debtor and the amount enclosed along with other relevant information.

A copy of this list will then be sent to the person responsible for maintaining the cash book who needs only enter the total plus a reference to the *cash received list*. A second copy will then be delivered to the sales ledger section who will enter the details from the list to the individual debtors accounts. This results in both the debit and credit transactions being recorded but by separate staff who in turn are separate from those originally itemising the amounts received. As a result, the possibility of fraud is reduced.

The journal

There is one set of transactions which will not be captured by the use of lists and day books. Examples include the writing off of bad debts, the payment of dividends and the charging of depreciation. By their very nature these are irregular events which cannot be captured by the day book/list system nor are they likely to have supporting documents such as purchase or sales invoices.

The only possible control is to ensure the transaction has been agreed by an official of the firm who possesses sufficient authority and that there is permanent evidence of the agreement. This is the modern-day role of the *journal*. The journal is simply a permanent list explaining the accounting adjustment made, its reason and the authority. Exhibit 4.6 gives an example relating to a bad debt.

Exhibit 4.6 The journal

Date	Narrative		Debit	Credit
1 January 19X2	Bad debts account	Dr	£10,000	
1 January 19X2	Don Tanner – debtor			£10,000
	Don Tanner declared bankrupt, Cambridge Court 31 December 19X1. Authorised by J. Stittle, Financial Controller			

The journal entry shows that the bad debts account should be debited with the amount outstanding on the individual debtor's account and the debtor's account credited, clearing that account. Without the need for, and evidence of, authority, fraud is possible. A member of staff could otherwise be in collusion with a dishonest debtor and arrange for the debt to be written off, to the benefit of the debtor but to the disadvantage of the firm. The journal entry in Exhibit 4.6 is shown in a traditional form.

By convention, the debit element is recorded first along with a confirmation that this is indeed the debit item. Traditionally the credit item has also been indented. As quaint as this might be, there is no hard logical reason for the presentation. Of far more importance are the reasons for the use of the journal.

PRODUCING ACCOUNTS FROM THE TRIAL BALANCE

By definition, a trial balance is a listing of all the balances making up the accounts. Each account within the trial balance will be made up of its opening balance plus any transactions recorded during the period. The trial balance is therefore a summary of the books of account. Because of this, it is possible to produce a set of final accounts from the trial balance provided any period end adjustments such as the level of closing stock and any depreciation charges for the period are given.

The trial balance of Tony Arnold's business, for example, showed sales of £30,000 and stocks of £19,000. With the knowledge that stock unsold at the period end is £4,000, it is possible to derive the gross profit. And given the expenses listed in the trial balance, it is possible to derive the net profit and the period end balance sheet.

Example 4.2 shows the trial balance of a limited company. From this data, it is possible to produce a set of final accounts. These are shown later in Exhibit 4.9. Most of the accounts will either appear in the trading and profit and loss account or the balance sheet and these are identified by the codes P&L and B/S. One or two balances might be divided between the two statements. Stock is one example, part of which will have been consumed during the period and part remaining unsold at the period end.

Example 4.2

The trial balance of Knowall plc for the year ended 31 March 19X5 is reproduced below along with all necessary year end adjustments.

	(£000)		*(£000)*
Freehold land (B/S)	200	Sales (P&L)	710
Plant and machinery (B/S)	200	Rents receivable (P&L)	10
Motor vehicles (B/S)	160	£1 ordinary shares (B/S)	250
Opening stock (P&L)	30	£1 15% preference shares (B/S)	200
Purchases (B/S and P&L)	320	Share premium account (B/S)	50
Salespersons' salaries (P&L)	50	General reserve (B/S)	60
Administration wages and salaries (P&L)	60	Profit and loss account balance (B/S)	80
General distribution expenses (P&L)	20	Provision for depreciation on plant (B/S)	80
General administration expenses (P&L)	30	Provision for depreciation on vehicles (B/S)	40
Directors' remuneration (P&L)	40	10% debentures (B/S)	100
Trade debtors (B/S)	300	Trade creditors (B/S)	70
Cash and bank (B/S)	240		
	1,650		1,650

The stock unsold at the end of the period was valued at £50,000. Included in general administration expenses was £3,000 of rent which related to the subsequent period. Corporation tax was estimated at £43,000 for the year. No dividends or interest on debentures had been paid during the year although a 20 per cent dividend on the ordinary shares was proposed. Depreciation was 20 per cent p.a. straight line on plant and machinery and 25 per cent on the reducing balance for motor vehicles.

Choice in the method of recording data

In the trial balance, the opening stock for the period has been recorded separately from subsequent additions in the form of purchases. Merging these two accounts would produce the form of stock account developed in previous chapters. Logically there is no difference between showing purchases separate from opening stock or merging both figures. The choice is based on its usefulness to the user: whether it is more useful to identify purchases separate from stocks brought forward from a previous period or more useful to merge them together from the very beginning.

This choice, however, opens up a wider issue in recording. Often it will be possible to record a particular transaction in a variety of ways. Because the result will be the same whichever approach is taken, the way the transaction is recorded will be a mere detail. Nevertheless it only serves to confuse when seemingly similar transactions are recorded in different ways. The solution is first to identify the underlying reality and then choose a method which will reflect this reality in the accounts.

Consider the cost of sales for Knowall plc. The opening stock is valued at £30,000, the purchases during the period are £320,000 and so with closing stock of £50,000, the cost of sales must be £300,000. Ultimately this £300,000 has to appear as cost of sales in the trading section of the trading and profit and loss account while the £50,000 must appear in the nominal ledger as an unexpired debit balance and reflected in the balance sheet as an asset.

There are at least two ways of recording this data which will give the same result. The first involves most of the adjustments being recorded in the stock account while the second sees the adjustments taking place within the trading account. Both are demonstrated in Exhibit 4.7.

Exhibit 4.7 Alternative approaches to recording data

Method (a)				Method (b)			
Purchases				**Purchases**			
Balance b/d	320,000	Stock	320,000	Balance b/d	320,000	Trading a/c	320,000
	320,000		320,000		320,000		320,000
Stock				**Stock**			
Balance b/d	30,000	Trading a/c	300,000	Balance b/d	30,000	Trading a/c	30,000
Purchases	320,000	Balance c/d	50,000		30,000		30,000
	350,000		350,000	Trading a/c	50,000		
Balance b/d	50,000						
Trading account				**Trading account**			
Cost of sales	300,000			Opening stock	30,000	Closing stock	50,000
				Purchases	320,000		

Method (a) is similar to the treatment of stocks developed for the columnar approach of earlier chapters. The opening stock and purchases are combined to form a 'pool' of goods available for resale. £50,000 of this is as yet unsold and so £300,000 of stock must have been consumed during the period. The double-entry transactions are therefore to credit the stock account with the cost of the stock sold and to debit the trading account by the same amount. The balance carried forward within the stock account then appears as the balance brought forward.

Method (b) is much more convoluted. It first involves the 'pool' of goods being transferred to the trading account. This initially results in £350,000 being debited to that account and the appearance of zero stock in the stock account. To correct this, the trading account is then credited with £50,000 and the stock account debited by the same amount. The result, in both cases, is a cost of sales of £300,000 and a stock unsold at period end of £50,000.

Accruals and prepayments

Other adjustments are necessary to the trial balance of Knowall plc before the final accounts can be produced. The amount charged as general administration expenses needs to be reduced by £3,000. In terms of double-entry bookkeeping, the easiest approach involves a treatment similar to method (a) in Exhibit 4.7. Of the £30,000 debited to general administration expenses, only £27,000 have been consumed. That account has been credited with £27,000 and the profit and loss account debited to leave a balance on the general administration expenses account of £3,000 representing the prepayment.

An equal but opposite argument can be applied to accruals. The corporation tax, for example, needs to be debited to the profit and loss account and an account for the Inland Revenue credited. Given that an ordinary dividend is proposed, it will also be necessary to accrue not only this dividend but also the preference share dividend.

Finally depreciation needs to be charged to the profit and loss account. Again, there is more than one way of recording this but the easiest approach is to debit the profit and loss account and credit the provision for depreciation account. The result will see the net book value of the assets being reduced by the charge to the profit and loss account. Perhaps an even easier approach is to apply the columnar form of the earlier chapters as the trial balance is no more than the summary totals used in that approach. This is the approach taken in Exhibit 4.8. Transactions (a) and (b) are the revenues generated from sales and

Exhibit 4.8 Period end adjustments and the final accounts

	Original balances £000	(a)	(b)	(c)	(d)	(e)	(f)	(g)	(h)	(i)	(j)	(k)	(l)	(m)	(n)	(o)	(p)	Final balances
Land	+200																	+200
Plant	+200																	+200
Motor vehicles	+160																	+160
Opening stock	+30			−30														
Purchases	+320			−270														+50
Sales salaries	+50				−50													
Administration wages	+60					−60												
Distribution expenses	+20						−20											
Administration expenses	+30							−27										+3
Directors' remuneration	+40								−40									
Trade debtors	+300																	+300
Cash and bank	+240																	+240
Sales	−710	+710																
Rents receivable	−10		+10															
Ordinary shares	−250																	−250
Preference shares	−200																	−200
Share premium	−50																	−50
General reserve	−60															−10		−70
Profit and loss account balance	−80																−10	−90
Depreciation provision – plant	−80									−40								−120
Depreciation provision – vehicles	−40										−30							−70
Debentures	−100																	−100
Trade creditors	−70																	−70
Profit and loss – this year		−710	−10	+300	+50	+60	+20	+27	+40	+40	+30	+10	+43	+30	+50	+10	+10	
Debenture interest accrued												−10						−10
Corporation tax accrued													−43					−43
Preference dividend proposed														−30				−30
Ordinary dividend proposed															−50			−50

rentals. Transaction (c) is the stock consumed, comprising the opening stock plus part of the purchases sold. Transactions (d) to (h) are the expenses already recorded being written off to the profit and loss account while (i) and (j) are the recording of this year's depreciation. The accrual of debenture interest is represented by (k), (l) is the corporation tax accrued while (m) and (n) represent the recording of the proposed dividends. The transfer of £10,000 to the general reserve is represented by (o) and, finally, the balance of £10,000 of undistributed profits is transferred to the accumulated retentions. Once all these adjustments have been made, the final accounts – excluding the cashflow statement – can be derived in the normal way and these are shown in Exhibit 4.9.

Exhibit 4.9 The final accounts

Trading and profit and loss account for the year to 31 March 19X5

	(£000)	(£000)
Sales		710
Opening stock	30	
Purchases	320	
	350	
Less closing stock	50	
Cost of sales		300
Gross profit		410
Selling & distribution costs		
Salespersons' salaries	50	
General distribution expenses	20	
Depreciation – cars	30 100	
Administration expenses		
Administration wages and salaries	60	
General administration expenses	27	
Depreciation – plant	40	
Directors' remuneration	40 167	267
Operating profit before tax		143
Other income		
Rents receivable		10
		153
Debenture interest		10
Net profit before tax		143
Provision for corporation tax		43
Net profit after tax		100
Add undistributed profits 1 April 19X4		80
		180
Appropriations		
Proposed preference share dividend	30	
Proposed ordinary share dividend	50	
Transfer to general reserve	10	90
Undistributed profits 31 March 19X5		90

Balance sheet as at 31 March 19X5

	(£000)	(£000)	(£000)
Fixed assets	Cost	Depreciation	Net
Freehold land	200	nil	200
Plant & machinery	200	120	80
Motor vehicles	160	70	90
	560	190	370
Current assets			
Stocks	50		
Trade debtors	300		
Prepayments	3		
Cash and bank	240	593	
Current liabilities			
Trade creditors	70		
Other creditors			
Debenture interest	10		
Corporation tax	43		
Preference dividend	30		
Ordinary dividend	50	203	390
			760
Less long term liabilities			
10% debentures			100
			660
Financed by			
250,000 £1 ordinary shares			250
200,000 £1 15% preference shares			200
Share premium reserve			50
General reserve			70
Profit and loss account balance			90
			660

SUMMARY

No new concepts were introduced in this chapter. Instead, it merely developed one particular application of duality in the form of double-entry bookkeeping. Its mechanical application used the traditional 'T' accounts, with each transaction being entered twice, once as a debit and once as a credit. Day books were also introduced to show how the system could be made both operational and secure. From these records it was shown how it was possible to produce the final accounts of a business.

Although many texts still use traditional double-entry bookkeeping to explain accounting matters, its use elsewhere is only limited. Today, the overwhelming majority of companies use computerised accounting systems. These are discussed in the next chapter.

TEST YOUR UNDERSTANDING

1 Explain the meaning of debit and credit in accounting.
2 Why is a debit balance on a company's bank account shown as a credit balance in the bank statement?
3 What is the purpose of a trial balance and what does it prove?
4 What are day books?
5 Why is it necessary to have a journal in an accounting system?

QUESTIONS

1* Making use of the data given in Example 2.2 of Chapter 2, record the transactions making use of double-entry bookkeeping and prepare a trading and profit and loss account and balance sheet suitable for presentation to Ron Marshall.

2* The Aberdeen Motor Supply Company Ltd keeps its accounts using a purchase ledger, sales ledger, a separate cash book and a nominal ledger. Control accounts are kept in the nominal ledger which represent total debtors and creditors. Transactions are first recorded in sale and purchase day books and then transferred to the actual books of account. Cash received and paid is initially recorded on summary sheets and then entered into the accounts. The company's balance sheet at the beginning of May 19X2 is reproduced below, along with the individual balances in the sales and purchase ledgers.

Plant and machinery		£10,000
Stock	£5,428	
Debtors	£2,811	
Cash/bank	£8,549	
	£16,788	
Less creditors	£4,388	£12,400
		£22,400
Financed by		
Ordinary share capital		£18,000
Retentions		£4,400
		£22,400

Debtors' balances in sales ledger		**Creditors' balances in purchase ledger**	
Robert Smith	£645	Motafacta plc	£2,457
Harold Jones	£720	Karpart Supplies Ltd	£1,362
Jane Jolly	£300	Speediparts Ltd	£569
Mota Kars Ltd	£215		
Burnup Fuels Ltd	£378		
Eldor Street plc	£553		

During the month of May, the following transactions took place.

1 May	Cash received from Jane Jolly	£300
1 May	Cash received from Eldor Street plc	£553
1 May	Sales to Robert Smith	£245
2 May	Purchases from Motafacta plc	£789
2 May	Cash paid to Speediparts Ltd	£569
2 May	Sales to Harold Jones	£745
5 May	Sales to Jane Jolly	£523
6 May	Cash received from Robert Smith	£645
8 May	Purchases from Karpart Supplies	£370
9 May	Sales to Mota Kars Ltd	£950
13 May	Purchases from Motafacta plc	£579
14 May	Sales to Jane Jolly	£630
15 May	Cash received from Jane Jolly	£523
16 May	Cash paid to Motafacta plc	£700
17 May	Purchases from Motafacta plc	£845
19 May	Sales to Burnup Fuels Ltd	£745
22 May	Sales to Robert Smith	£370
24 May	Sales to Eldor Street plc	£949
24 May	Cash received from Harold Jones	£1,465
24 May	Sales to Jane Jolly	£327
24 May	Purchases from Karpart Supplies	£452
25 May	Cash received from Jane Jolly	£630
26 May	Purchases from Speediparts plc	£643
27 May	Sale to Robert Smith	£486
29 May	Sale to Harold Jones	£328
30 May	Purchases from Motafacta plc	£471

The only other transactions during the period related to the payment of wages for £2,100 cash and the providing of £200 as one month's depreciation. Closing stock at the end of the month was £6,472.

(a) Record the above transactions in the books of the Aberdeen Motor Supply Company Ltd, making use of,wherever possible, journals and day books.

(b) Prepare a trading and profit and loss account and balance sheet for the company at the end of May in a form suitable for presentation to the company's directors.

3 The trial balance of Acorn Mills Ltd at 30 September 19X5 was as follows:

	(£)	(£)
Purchases and sales for the year	610,000	900,000
Vehicles at cost	160,000	
Provision for vehicle depreciation		48,000
Opening stock	160,000	
Trade debtors and creditors	80,000	52,000
8 per cent loan stock		100,000
Directors' fees	12,000	
Bad debts written off	2,000	
Loan interest paid	4,000	
Share premium account		40,000
Profit and loss account balance		57,000
Wages	35,000	
Rates	3,000	
Heating and lighting	6,000	
Office salaries	48,000	
Administration expenses	38,000	
Freehold property	350,000	
Ordinary share capital		400,000
Furniture and fittings	30,000	
Provision for depreciation of fixtures and fittings		6,000
Provision for bad debts		3,000
Bank	68,000	
	1,606,000	1,606,000

Robert Henley, the financial director, has estimated that since last receiving the invoice for heating and lighting, an additional £2,000 of power has been used. He also estimates that £1,000 of rates and £2,000 of administration expenses represent payments in advance.

The vehicles are to be depreciated at 20 per cent on cost while furniture and fittings are to be depreciated at 10 per cent on cost. In addition, the provision for bad debts should be maintained at 5 per cent of the current value of debtors. Closing stocks were valued at £140,000.

Using the above information, prepare the profit and loss account and balance sheet of Acorn Mills Ltd for the year ended 30 September 19X5.

4 Carol Evans has the sole UK marketing and selling rights to the KareTaker, a revolutionary cleaning machine. A condition of the agreement is that the product is sold at a price fixed by the manufacturer. Currently this is cost plus 50 per cent.

One month ago, on 1 October, Carol decided to return to full-time education and so she agreed to employ Alan Jones to run the company. On that date the balance sheet was as follows:

Fixed assets

Cost		£600
Less depreciation		£100
		£500

Current assets

Stock	£400	
Debtors	£300	
Bank/cash	£100	
	£800	

Less current liabilities

Creditors	£200	£600
		£1,100

Financed by:

Owner's capital		£1,100
		£1,100

One month later, Alan sent a profit and loss account and balance sheet to Carol. The result of one month's trading was a profit of £800 detailed below.

Trading and profit and loss account month ended 31 October

Sales		£5,500
Less cost of sales		£4,500
Gross profit		£1,000
Expenses		
Wages	£100	
Depreciation	£100	£200
Net profit		£800

Balance sheet at 31 October

Fixed assets

Cost		£600
Less depreciation		£200
		£400

Current assets

Stocks	£200	
Debtors	£200	
Bank	£1,600	
	£2,000	

Current liabilities

Creditors	£500	£1,500
		£1,900

Financed by

Capital 1 October		£1,100
add profits for month		£800
		£1,900

Carol decided to visit Alan after receiving these good results but, on the day of the meeting she received a phone call to say that Alan had left in a hurry and would not be coming back. As a result, Carol checked the figures and satisfied herself that all of those in the balance sheet were accurate. She particularly verified the bank balance back to the bank statements. In summary, the statements showed an opening bank balance of £100 at the beginning of the period, £5,100 received from debtors, £3,500 paid to creditors and £100 used to pay wages. As all purchases were made from the same supplier, she again quickly verified their accuracy.

Making use of the above data and applying duality, estimate how much cash is missing.

CHAPTER 5

Introduction to computerised accounting

Although accounting was one of the first areas of business activity to be computerised, its growth was originally restricted to larger organisations because of the high initial costs involved. Today, with the rapid fall in prices of personal computers and the equally impressive increase in their power, it is possible to buy a complete computerised system for under £1,000. As a result, it is not unusual to find even small businesses keeping their accounts on a computer.

This chapter:

- Discusses the difference between software and hardware
- Develops the outline structure of accounting programs and the use of account codes
- Demonstrates the input of financial data
- Identifies areas where transactions can be automatically generated
- Highlights the uses and limitations of computerised accounting

Designing an accounting system involves judgement. Sometimes this relates to the design of company-wide accounting policies such as the treatment of depreciation. At other times it may be more detailed. Decisions, for example, have to be made as to whether or not two or more expenses should be combined within the one account heading. Once made, these judgements are likely to be incorporated within the organisation's detailed procedures to ensure uniformity of treatment.

By comparison, bookkeeping is a mechanical task which involves the recording and processing of accounting data in accordance with a pre-established set of rules and instructions. No matter how complex bookkeeping may appear at times, the scope for judgement is extremely limited, provided procedures have been agreed and duality is applied. Once it has been agreed that all vehicle expenses are to be recorded in a single account then any operator aware of this and aware of duality will always enter a paid fuel bill by debiting the vehicle expenses account and crediting the cash account. Employ a new bookkeeper and, provided the procedures have been understood, the same transaction will be recorded in an identical way.

It is this mechanical but complex nature of bookkeeping which makes it an ideal candidate for computerisation. To call such an application 'computerised accounting' though is something of a misnomer. Much of computerised accounting is concerned with mechanical recording, the domain of bookkeeping. Nevertheless, the term has entered the language and because of that, this chapter will continue to use the term 'computerised accounting' to discuss ways of recording transactions held on a computer.

COMPUTER SYSTEMS

Hardware and software

All computer systems share certain similarities. There will be the hardware (the physical equipment such as the machine itself) and the software – the program or set of instructions represented or stored magnetically in the machine and which enables it to perform specific tasks. Some software – known as the operating system – is used to run the computer system and allow it to communicate with its different parts. Other software performs specific tasks required by the user and is known as applications software. An accounting program or package is but one such example. Others include spreadsheets, word processors and databases. Physically, computer installations can range from a mainframe computer costing many hundreds of thousands of pounds through to an IBM compatible personal computer, the size of a notebook and costing less than a thousand pounds.

Whatever the size and whatever the cost, all machines will have a central processing unit or CPU, which, amongst other things, acts as a short term memory store by holding data electronically and which carries out the instructions of the program. Even today this kind of store – known as random access memory or RAM – is relatively expensive. More than that, it is volatile. Turn off the power supply and the electronically held data will be lost from RAM. A secondary or backing store is therefore required and this is provided by magnetic tape or disks which can hold data and instructions permanently.

The applications software is likely to have been installed on a hard disk if the hardware is a personal computer. This ensures the software is permanently stored. To load this into the CPU and make it available to the user, however, requires an instruction. This normally involves entering a predefined word, set by the manufacturer of the software, via the keyboard. Once the program has finished its task, the results have to be communicated to the user. If not required immediately, the results can be stored in a magnetic form on either disk or tape, to be recalled when convenient. Alternatively, they can be displayed immediately either on a monitor (known as a video display unit or VDU) or, if a permanent record is required, sent to a printer.

Data processing

Data is the raw material for producing information. Data processing is concerned with the screening, collation, arranging, summarising and reporting of that data. The output is information – data or facts processed such that they are now meaningful and relevant to the recipient's needs. Computers are ideal for this task, particularly where the volume of data is large and the processing is repetitive.

Bookkeeping is no more than a specific application of data processing. Under both manual and computerised systems, there is raw data which has to be transformed into accounting reports such as the trial balance, the profit and loss account, the balance sheet and the cashflow statement. Exhibit 5.1 shows in outline the process applicable to both systems.

Exhibit 5.1 Data processing

SYSTEM	INPUT	PROCESS	OUTPUT
MANUAL	Transactions written into day books and ledgers	Accounts manually totalled and balanced using agreed procedures	Final accounts
COMPUTERISED	Operator keys in transactions and other data	Stored data processed by software to programmed rules	Final accounts

Source documents

The inputs will be the sales and purchase invoices, the cash summaries and the journal entries outlined in Chapter 4. These are the *source documents*, the evidence which initiates the recording of the transaction. The process which transforms these into outputs will involve the *classifying* of transactions into expenses types, the *calculation* of totals and their *summary* in the form of a trial balance or a set of final accounts. The outputs will then be filed data in the form of up-to-date ledgers and accounts and reports such as the trial balance and balance sheet.

Transforming data into information

In a manual accounting system the transformation of data is undertaken by human beings. In a computerised system the transformation is achieved by the set of instructions called a program. The common feature of both is the large amounts of data input and output and the repetitive and routine nature of the transformation process. No matter how complex a manual system appears to be, it mainly involves the debiting of one account and the crediting of another with some totalling and summarising included towards the end. For people, not only is this one of the most boring activities possible, its mundane and repetitive nature can easily lead to errors such as the failure to record both aspects of a transaction or the incorrect balancing of an individual account. It is because of this that bookkeeping is so suitable for computerisation. Once the data has been entered, the speed of calculation is extraordinary by human standards. With access to backing store in the form of disks and tape, the amount and speed of access to data is far in excess of that found in manual systems. And because computer programs do not forget nor suffer from fatigue, computerised accounting systems are extremely reliable.

Despite the advantages of computerised accounting, there are certain limitations. Computers carry out instructions exactly as requested – no matter how silly the instructions might be. They apply no perception, reasoning or intelligence to instructions. If £10,000 is entered as the cost of a pair of shoes, a human operator would use common sense and spot this as being unreasonable. No such ability is available within a computer program unless a specific instruction has been written to guard against such silly figures. Care is therefore necessary when appraising the suitability of accounting software to ensure such checking procedures have been built into the program.

ACCOUNTING SOFTWARE

Some firms will have accounting software specially written for the business. Although costly and time consuming, this does allow the software to be specifically tailored to the firm's needs. Most firms, however, cannot afford the luxury of bespoke software. For them, there is no alternative but to buy commercial software which, although less expensive, is unlikely to satisfy completely their requirements. Irrespective of the source of the software, all commercially available programs have certain common features.

What follows is an overview of some of the common features to be found in many commercial software packages for the IBM personal computer or PC compatible desktop computer. Data entry is therefore assumed to be via a keyboard with the help of a monitor while output will be channelled either to the monitor or to a printer should 'hard copy' be required. Permanent storage of both data and programs is assumed to be on disk.

Account codes

Computers only have limited volatile memory or RAM. There may also be practical limitations on the amount of backing store available in the form of disks. Because of this, programmers will attempt to use as little memory and as little disk space as possible when writing the accounting software. One way to achieve this is by using codes instead of names for accounts. The code 1234 for instance takes up less disk space and less memory than 'Provision for Depreciation of Motor Vehicles Account'. However, to help the user, the program may well show the name of the account as well as the number whenever the code is called up. Often this will be by the simple expedient of a computer file matching codes to account names. This then enables the account name to be shown whenever there is a machine/human interface while allowing the more convenient codes to be used for processing data when away from the human eye.

There is, however, a second reason for using numbers to identify accounts. A hierarchical coding structure is possible. A company manufacturing furniture, for example, might use a four-digit code in its accounting system with codes within the range 3000–3999 being used for various purchases. The range 3100–3199 might represent purchases of wood, the range 3200–3299 might represent paints and varnishes and the range 3300–3399 might represent furniture fittings. Given that any account beginning with the digits 31 must relate to wood purchases, the third digit might be used to break down the coding further into different types of wood while the fourth digit might relate to specific departments or products.

Purchases could then be shown as a global figure by totalling the balances on all accounts beginning with 3 or as more detailed subdivisions within the coding structure. In principle, this degree of sophistication was possible using a manual system. However, time and cost would rarely have made it feasible. With a computer package, the most time consuming aspect is the actual inputting of the data. Once entered, re-sorting is a relatively speedy and straightforward matter.

Check digits

One problem with using digits to describe accounts is the possibility of numbers being transposed so that the code 3421 is entered as 4321, for example. The use of check digits can reduce this type of error. A check digit is an extra digit added to the code which bears a unique mathematical relationship to the digits comprising the 'real' code.

Consider an account code of 5812. Each digit of the code will be given a weighting and the sum of these forms the basis for the check digit. For example, the first digit might be multiplied by 4, the second by 3, the third by 2 and the fourth by 1. The sum of this is 47, made up of $(5 \times 4) + (8 \times 3) + (1 \times 2) + (2 \times 1)$. To derive the check digit, this total of 47 is deducted from a calculable higher figure. Often the calculable figure is the next highest multiple of a selected base or modulus. Using modulus 11, the next highest multiple will be 55. The check digit will then be 8, equalling the difference between 55 and 47. Part of the program will check for this relationship whenever an account code is entered and will reject input where the first four digits do not have this unique relationship with the final digit.

THE STRUCTURE OF ACCOUNTING PROGRAMS

The fewer instructions contained within a program, the less RAM it will use and the faster it will run. Despite the huge *amount* of data passing through the modern large business, much of that data will be very similar in nature. Put another way, there will only be a small number of transaction *types*. This is a further reason why computerised accounting is so popular and to be found in all but the smallest of businesses.

Types of accounting transaction

To simplify matters, assume there are no cash transactions, all payments and receipts being via a bank account, and that the business being considered is a simple retailer. The *types* of transactions will be limited to seven, irrespective of the *number* of transactions. These will be:

1 sales on credit and subsequent payment
2 cash sales where payment is by cheque
3 purchases on credit and subsequent payment
4 cash purchases paid by cheque
5 other receipts
6 other payments
7 journal entries.

The recording of transactions will be by far the largest accounting task faced by the business. Other tasks required to maintain a set of accounts will involve the opening and naming of accounts, the production of reports (including a trial balance and the final accounts) and what is often described as utility routines. Utility routines might include the ability to change tax rates such as VAT, the opening of accounts where entries are to be made automatically by the program and the wiping clean of all data other than period end balances when commencing a new period. Having previously made a copy on a spare floppy disk of the full data, this last facility both saves hard disk space and tidies up individual accounts ready for the recording of the next period's transactions. At the same time, the saving to a floppy disk ensures all the data can be recreated, if necessary, at any time in the future.

Automatic generation of transactions

It is the automatic recording of certain entries within computerised accounting which not only ensures the 'books' will always balance but also reduces the possibility of error. Consider an owner introducing capital into the business in the form of money. This is a receipt of money and so is an example of a Type 5 transaction above. Calling up that particular routine, the program will automatically recognise that money is being received. Without any prompting from the operator, the bank account will automatically be debited. All the operator has to input is the code for the other account involved, the amount and any desired narrative. Upon completion of the entry, the program will then verify that the account exists and automatically post the amount as a credit item.

Customising the software

Before recording transactions, it will be necessary to customise the software to suit the user's own purpose by specifying the number of accounts in each ledger. Allowing the user to choose the number of accounts in each ledger enables disk space to be used more efficiently by only allocating sufficient disk space to meet the user's needs. It will also be necessary to establish tax rates for VAT purposes should this apply. Finally the accounts such as the bank account and the VAT account, where entries are automatically recorded, need to be identified.

In many accounting packages, these facilities will be found within the utilities routines of the software. Exhibit 5.2 shows the opening menu of one particular software package, Sage's Sterling Financial Controller suite of programs, where utilities are accessed from the opening menu. Although the detail will vary from package to package, the information shown is representative of many of the more popular packages available in the UK today.

Calling up the utilities menu will enable the number of accounts for each ledger to be specified. The account numbers to be used for the bank account and VAT account would also be input by the user. Any code is acceptable but given that most of the entries to those accounts will be generated automatically, it seems sensible to choose codes which are less likely to be keyed in accidentally. For example, the coding structure might start with purchases in the 3000 series, sales in the 4000 series, fixed assets in the 6000 series and so on. Choosing codes outside this range – 0079 for instance – will reduce the possibility of data accidentally being entered in the bank and VAT accounts. Once this has been completed, the final stage before being able to record transactions is the opening of all necessary accounts in the ledgers.

Opening an account

The routine for opening individual accounts from the main menu in Exhibit 5.2 will be similar, whether they relate to debtors and creditors in the sales and purchases ledgers or the opening of the capital, stock, sales and expense accounts in the nominal ledger. Accounts for each ledger can be opened by choosing the 'Open Accounts' option avail-

Exhibit 5.2 Computerised accounting – the opening menu

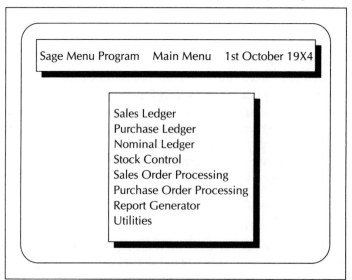

Sage Menu Program   Main Menu   1st October 19X4

Sales Ledger
Purchase Ledger
Nominal Ledger
Stock Control
Sales Order Processing
Purchase Order Processing
Report Generator
Utilities

able under the various postings modules of the main menu. All accounts will require a code plus a name. In addition, the sales and purchase ledger routines will have the additional facility of incorporating extra data such as an address and telephone number. These can then be used to send statements to customers and suppliers.

Calling up any posting routine will give the user at least two options: to open up an account by keying in a code and description or to record a transaction within a pre-existing account. Providing the code is a valid code and has not been previously allocated, no further action is required to open an account other than instructing the program to accept the keyed-in data. This is the equivalent of writing account names at the top of each page of a ledger in a manual system.

Recording transactions

Assuming sufficient accounts have been opened, it will then be possible to record the transactions. Consider a company starting business with £10,000 cash in the form of share capital. Bank receipts will be accessed from within one of the modules available from the main menu. In the Sage software, this is found within the nominal ledger module.

Calling up the bank receipts option will cause an input screen to appear on the monitor, similar to the one shown in Exhibit 5.3. Depending on the particular software, the

Exhibit 5.3 Computerised accounting – bank transactions

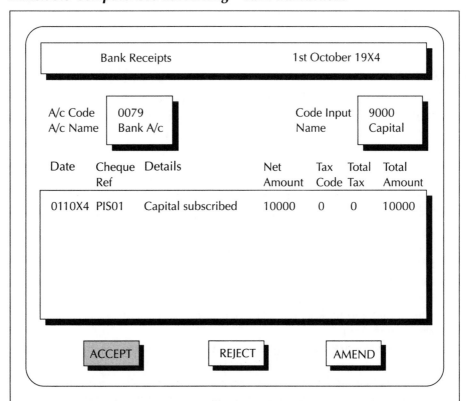

Bank Receipts					1st October 19X4		

| A/c Code | 0079 | | | | Code Input | 9000 | |
| A/c Name | Bank A/c | | | | Name | Capital | |

Date	Cheque Ref	Details		Net Amount	Tax Code	Total Tax	Total Amount
0110X4	PIS01	Capital subscribed		10000	0	0	10000

ACCEPT	REJECT	AMEND

account code and name to be debited will be automatically shown as a result of calling up the bank receipts option without any assistance from the user. In Exhibit 5.3 the account code chosen for the bank account is 0079 and this appears along with the account name as a confirmation.

As the bank receipts routine has been chosen, the program will automatically know that the account code entered by the user in the right-hand box must be credited with the value of the transaction. More than that, as soon as the code is entered, the name of the account will appear, confirming to the user that the correct account has been called. Details of the transaction can then be entered in the body of the input screen. The exact details will vary from package to package. Nevertheless many will automatically show the current date, taken from the computer's own internal clock, eliminating the need to enter the date. (Should the date not be the valid one, it will be possible to overwrite this with the required date.) Some systems will also provide for an automatic reference. The reference PIS01 refers to paying-in slip number 1. It is possible for programs automatically to increment this by one for each extra transaction so that the next time the bank receipts module is called up, the reference will automatically be PIS02.

The detail column is optional. It merely provides a facility for the operator to record a note about the transaction. Another automatic facility often found is the calculation and recording of any tax implications. There are no tax implications for this transaction and so this will be signified to the program by keying in the appropriate code – 0 in this example – within the tax code column. From this, the total, tax-inclusive amount of the transaction will automatically be calculated. Finally, there is a choice of recording the transaction, amending it prior to recording if an error is noted or abandoning the recording of the transaction.

Storing records

Accepting the data will cause the bank account to be debited and the capital account to be credited by entering this data on disk. There will be two *records* created, the one relating to capital and the other relating to money paid into the bank account. Within each record will be several pieces of data such as the date, the reference and the amount. In computing, these are known as *fields*. A collection of similar records is known as a *file*.

In a manual system, each ledger is the equivalent of a file. Exhibit 5.4 shows the manual recording of the earlier bank transaction. Two records are shown, the capital account and bank account with similar fields for date, details, reference and debits and credits. In this simplified example, the two records constitute the file of accounting transactions.

Unlike a manual system, detailed program instructions will not be expressed in terms of debits and credits. Rather, the program will instruct amounts to be added to an account for a debit and deducted from an account for a credit in a similar way to the pluses and minuses used in the tabular approach to bookkeeping developed in Chapters 1 to 3. If it was possible to look inside a file held on disk, the contents would be similar to those shown in Exhibit 5.5.

Two records are demonstrated in Exhibit 5.5. In each case, the first field will have been automatically generated by the software and signifies that this record is part of the first transaction entered. Subsequent entries of data will see this figure incrementing by one. The second field identifies the particular account, the third field the date and the fourth

Exhibit 5.4 Manual storage of accounting data

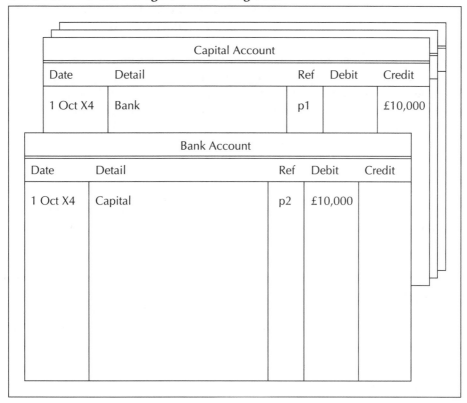

Exhibit 5.5 Data held on file

00001 0079 1204X3 PIS01 'Capital Subscribed' +10000 +0 /00001 9000 1204X3 PIS01 'Capital Subscribed' −10000 −0

and fifth fields, the references input by the user. The final two fields show the net amount of the transaction and the tax. (There is no need to store the gross amount as the program can be instructed to add these two amounts together should the total be required.) The crucial difference is that the first record, relating to code 0079, the Bank Account, shows the £10,000 as a positive, while the second record, account 9000, the Capital Account, shows the amount as a negative. In effect the combined records are a trial balance showing assets of £10,000 and obligations of £10,000.

The generation of sales and purchase transactions

This automatic generation of transactions applies equally to sales and purchases except that even greater degrees of sophistication are possible. Take for instance a sales transaction. For some software, calling up the sales ledger postings module from the main menu might well offer the option of sales invoice production. The resulting screen will probably only require the customer's account code to be input, a code for the product being sold and the quantity. From this limited data, the program will add the customer's name and address. At the same time it will check the stock account to see if sufficient units are available and, if so, also check the current selling price. This information will then be added to the invoice along with a description of the goods based on the product code. The VAT will then be automatically calculated and the invoice totalled. Having issued the invoice, the program will automatically debit the customer's account and credit the sales and VAT accounts while also reducing the stock figure by the cost of the units sold. Similar procedures will apply to purchases.

Journal entries

The one type of transaction where the opportunity for reducing manual inputs is limited is the journal. By their nature, journal transactions such as depreciation and the writing-off of a bad debt are both irregular and specific. As a result the input screen will be very similar to a manual system. Information about the accounts to be debited and credited will be requested by that part of the program. About the only help available from the program will be checks to verify the accounts exist and that the total value of the debit entries equals the value of the credits. Once accepted, the program will then create further records to be added to the files, the debit amounts shown as pluses and the credit amounts as minuses.

Accounting reports

Equally as impressive as the assistance accounting software provides when recording data are the reports available. At a moment's notice it is possible either to print out or show on the screen details of any individual account as well as summaries of total sales-to-date or purchases-to-date broken down by customer, supplier or product type for instance. Other reports might show details of accounts where the customer has failed to pay within a specified time. Probably the most impressive reports though are instantaneous trial balances or – after the normal period end adjustments for stock unsold, accruals and prepayments – a full set of final accounts, all found by simply calling up one of the report routines.

These are just some of the facilities provided by commercially available software running on microcomputers. There is, however, a limit to what can be achieved by using a single, stand-alone machine. Only one person can have access to the computer at any one time and the speed with which the accounts can be updated will be limited by the speed with which data can be entered by the single keyboard. Where this is a problem, the solutions are many and varied, ranging from a network of microcomputers to the use of a full-blown mainframe computer with many input devices. The range of input devices is also much greater with larger systems, ranging from bar code readers found in many of the larger retail chains to 'hole in the wall' cash dispensers at banks. Nevertheless, all will enable accounting transactions to be recorded in a way not dissimilar to that of the system outlined above for a stand-alone microcomputer.

ACCOUNTING CONTROL AND COMPUTERS

Computer errors

Despite the advantages of speed, accuracy, consistency and reliability found with computerised accounting systems, new control problems follow in their wake. Machines have no judgement. They will not, of their own volition, recognise that a monthly salary of £50,000 to a works employee should at least be questioned before being recorded. Such difficulties can be overcome, however, by writing into the program 'reasonableness' checks. This involves specifying a range within which data will be accepted for a particular field.

Other errors derive from the technology involved. Faulty hardware can cause records to be lost. Back-ups are therefore essential to reduce this problem. Software problems can also occur. One popular piece of accounting software still being marketed allows the total of the debtors and creditors to be different from the sum of the individual account balances by use of a journal entry!

More likely, the software will be too rigid for the user. Manual systems can easily accommodate individual changes to the system. Software packages might require an expensive rewriting of the program.

Human errors

Many of the problems do not relate to the machine as such but to the human/machine interface. Some human errors, although possible using manual systems, are much more likely when using computer systems. Calling up the wrong routine by, for example, entering data in the sales ledger rather than the purchase ledger, is much more likely with a computer system. Such an error in a manual system would involve physically choosing the wrong ledger. With a computer system it merely involves the wrong selection from a screen menu.

In a manual system, the breakdown of responsibilities to reduce fraud was relatively easy. Certainly with accounting software held on a single machine, this may no longer be possible. There might only be one single security code to access the package and one operator might be responsible for entering all of the data. On the more expensive packages and in software specifically written for the firm, this is less likely. Operators will then be given their own unique access code and this will limit their access to particular parts of the accounts. Any entries made will also identify the operator responsible.

Security will also be a greater practical problem with a computerised system. The sheer speed of a computer means that the size of fraud possible is greater. With a manual system, there is a physical time constraint on the number of fraudulent entries possible. The concentrated information on a disk means it is both far easier to copy or destroy compared with a manual system. It only takes a few seconds to copy data from one floppy disk to another and even less to instruct the computer to erase all the files. Because of this, security is a much greater issue than for manual systems.

SUMMARY

Computerised accounting systems are many and varied reflecting the size and complexity of business organisations. Deliberately, this chapter has concentrated on commercial software for microcomputers. Such packages are relatively cheap and widely available whereas tailor-made packages will be unique to a particular organisation.

The recording of accounting transactions was shown to involve only a few routines but a great deal of data. Because of this, bookkeeping is ideally suited to computerisation. The automatic generation of records not only saves time but also reduces errors. And once data has been input, it can then be processed much faster than an equivalent manual system.

There is, however, a price to be paid for this improved speed and accuracy. Commercial software may not be able to cater fully for all the user's needs whereas bespoke software may be too expensive. Hardware and software problems can occur, often with serious consequences.

The separation of duties, part of the controls used to reduce fraud, is more difficult to achieve when accounts are kept magnetically.

The technology also brings with it its own problems. The wrong routine might be called up, leading to incorrect posting of transactions. Magnetic data is more susceptible to corruption and its accidental erasure is more likely than under a manual system.

Although called computerised accounting, the software has been shown to be more akin to computerised bookkeeping. Even packages which provide for the production of final accounts still require human inputs and judgements to estimate depreciation charges, closing values of stock and bad debts. As important as recording mechanisms are, to understand the meaning of accounts requires an understanding of the values and assumptions contained within those accounts. This is the subject matter of subsequent chapters.

FURTHER READING

Bhaskar, K. N. and Housden, R. J. W. (1986) *Accounting Information Systems and Data Processing,* Heinemann.

Havard, M. and McBride, P. K. (1987) *Using Accountancy Software in Business,* Heinemann.

Muggeridge, L. and Trott, F. (1994) *A Guide to Accounting Software,* Kogan Page.

Page, J. and Hooper, P. (1987) *Accounting and Information Systems,* Prentice Hall International.

Rahman, M. and Halladay, M. (1988) *Accounting Information Systems,* Prentice Hall International.

Wilkinson J. W. (1993) *Accounting and Information Systems,* John Wiley and Sons.

TEST YOUR UNDERSTANDING

1 Distinguish between hardware and software.

2 Differentiate data from information.

3 What are source documents?

4 List two advantages of account codes.

5 A company uses a five digit coding system plus a check digit derived from the modulus 11 base. The first digit is multiplied by 5, the second by 4, the third by 3, the fourth by 2 and the fifth by 1. The sixth digit of the code is then the check digit. Code 673411 refers to purchases of material B for the manufacturing department at the Paris site of a multi-national company. An operator accidentally transposes the first two digits and types in 763411. Verify that the accounting system will prevent the transaction from being entered.

6 Explain what is meant by a 'reasonableness' check.

QUESTIONS

1 Compare and contrast manual and computerised accounting systems.

2 Identify why accounting software packages are increasingly popular.

CHAPTER 6

Measuring profit – different assumptions, different conclusions

Central to all accounting systems is the measurement of income and the maintenance of capital. However, all accounting reports are based on concepts and assumptions which have evolved through time. Adding to this are the judgements about a business's future and the life of its assets which have to be made whenever a report is prepared. Both the legitimacy of those assumptions and the validity of the judgements are increasingly being questioned.

This chapter:

■ Identifies the desirable qualities of accounting systems

■ Discusses who are the users of accounting reports

■ Examines whether accounting reports are possible without having to make assumptions and judgements

■ Develops the concept of economic income as a standard against which to judge other income and capital maintenance measures

■ Introduces the use of current values as an alternative to historical cost

The early users of accounting lived in a simple world with only low level technology, little expensive capital equipment and simple trading patterns. Historical accounting, with its emphasis on stewardship, was more than adequate for them. The complexities of modern business organisations, with the separation of ownership from management, the heavy dependence on expensive capital equipment and trading patterns spreading over several years, could never have been envisaged. The problems arising from different methods of depreciation, stock valuation and income recognition are problems of this greater business complexity as is the division of profits between managers in the form of salaries and bonuses and shareholders in the form of dividends.

Over the years, solutions to these difficulties have tended to develop in a pragmatic, piecemeal fashion with little coherent thought supporting them, as evidenced by the methods outlined in Chapter 3. Perhaps a better way of tackling these problems would be to go back to basics and ask what the objectives of accounting are and from this develop a suitable theory or set of theories. One approach is to recognise that accounting has many of the attributes found in other systems.

CHARACTERISTICS OF SYSTEMS

A physical system can be defined as 'a set of elements which operate together to accomplish an objective'.[1] The elements of an accounting system will be records (such as invoices), procedures (duality), rules (matching and prudence, for example), a unit of measurement (historical cost, current values, etc.) and reports (such as the primary financial statements). The purpose or objective of the system will be financial information and so the elements will not be randomly assembled but rather identified as belonging together because of this common goal.

Put more generally, a system is composed of three elements: inputs, process and outputs. All systems will have a *boundary* which delineates itself from other systems. Viewing an individual person as a biological system, the boundary is easy to identify: the skin, the hair and nails. Inside this boundary is the system; outside is what is known as the *environment*. Accounting systems, however, are abstract and the boundary is not as easy to define. Clearly the books of account are within the boundary, as are accounting reports. But what of sales forecasts? To the extent that the forecast is used to form a view on the value of closing stock or the business's continuing existence, it would appear part of the system. To the extent that the forecast merely shows a different set of customers it might more meaningfully be viewed as being outside the boundary.

Open and closed systems

Systems can be open or closed. A *closed system* is totally self-contained; it does not exchange information or energy in any way with its environment. Evidence from the physical sciences suggests that closed systems will run down through loss of energy or become disorganised – a condition known as *entropy*. Imagine an accounting department trying to record all the transactions of a modern multinational business with no more than the medieval clerk's parchment and quill pen. Only by being aware of changes in the environment in the form of the power and availability of computers and adapting to them would it be possible to survive the task of processing all the documents. By adapting to its environment, the accounting department has become an *open system*. An open system is able to interact with the environment by exchanging information, material or energy. It is able to adapt to changes in its environment in such a way as to continue its existence.

Feedback

There is a second feature which differentiates systems: the presence or absence of *feedback*. Systems are goal seeking. It therefore seems sensible to check if the system is achieving its goal – and this applies whether the system is open or closed. With feedback, outputs from the system are compared with a desired state or standard and a message is sent back to the input device. Feedback which seeks to reduce the difference between actual and planned output is known as *negative feedback*, whereas *positive feedback* causes the system to amplify the difference. Negative feedback, by closing the gap between actual and planned output, attempts to keep a system operating within prescribed limits. This it does by use of a sensor and a control device to generate corrective action at the input stage. Where this feedback is automatic, it is known as a *closed loop*. Exhibit 6.1 shows in diagrammatic form such a system.

The system bounded by the double lines in Exhibit 6.1 has general applicability. Before considering its application to accounting, it might be useful to demonstrate its working by relating it to a central heating system. Most central heating systems are closed loops with negative feedbacks which do not interact with their environments. In terms of the diagram in Exhibit 6.1, the power supply is the input which, through the process of a boiler, converts the power to output in the form of heat. Most central heating systems have a thermostat which enables the user to establish the desired heat. This is equivalent to the desired standard of the system. The control device will also be in the thermostat which measures the actual temperature against the standard set.

Exhibit 6.1 Diagrammatic representation of a system

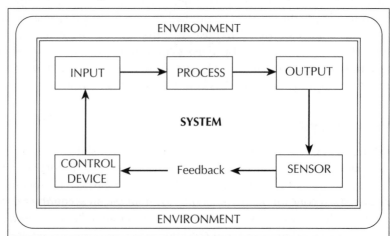

If the actual temperature is below the standard, the message is sent to generate more heat by applying more power. This will have the effect of closing the gap between desired and actual output. Similarly, if the actual temperature had been above the desired temperature, the message would have been to produce no more heat. This is negative feedback taking place.

One difficulty is that heating systems do not interact with their environment in any sophisticated way. Assume the heating system is installed in a block of flats. Its boundary will be the walls, floor and ceiling of that flat, its environment the flats above, below and on either side. Now consider what would happen if the flat above had been left unoccupied in freezing weather and a water pipe suddenly bursts. The system is insufficiently sophisticated to recognise this. If the system were able to interact with its environment, the least it should do is shut down to reduce the risk of electrical faults and gas escapes if the water extinguishes the flame. Instead, freezing water, dripping down from the floor above, cools the temperature in the flat with the result that the closed system demands even more heat to warm the flat to the desired standard, aggravating the problem further by warming the otherwise frozen burst pipe.

Accounting and systems

Applying the systems approach to accounting is more difficult because of uncertainty as to where the boundary lies and the extent to which it is a closed or open system, even though it is clear that accounting involves inputs, a process and outputs. But this very difficulty is helpful in identifying the issues thrown up by trying to superimpose an accounting system evolved from medieval times on a modern business organisation.

In designing a central heating system two considerations would be uppermost: the desired temperatures for the owners and its cost – in other words, their needs and resources. From this would follow the outputs required and consequently the necessary inputs. Accounting systems also should be driven by the needs of the users. The difficulty, in terms of Exhibit 6.1, is knowing where the user is positioned. The medieval trader would have clearly been within the boundary of the system as the sensor, paying the accountant and demanding a change to the inputs and the process if the output information was not suited to his needs. In the modern world, however, it is not always easy to identify the user or, more likely, the users. Even if possible, they might not be in a position automatically to influence the form and content of the financial output.

The role of directors

Just who the users might be is returned to later. But in terms of a large, modern business organisation with many shareholders, the needs of managers and shareholders will not necessarily be identical. There will therefore be at least two user groups. In the UK and most other countries, it is the directors of a company who are legally responsible for the recording of transactions and the production of the final accounts and they may have a natural in-built bias against disclosing more information than strictly necessary for fear of alerting competitors. Although auditors are appointed by the members of a company, with a widely dispersed shareholding and no dominant shareholder, the directors have considerable influence in recommending the choice of auditor. As such, they are in a very strong position to determine what is disclosed in those final accounts.

If this is an accurate description of accounting systems, then it is the directors who act as the sensor, with the shareholders being at least partially outside the system's boundary. The extent to which the information needs of shareholders, or indeed other users, are satisfied will therefore depend on the extent to which the accounting system is an open system, able to exchange information with its environment about the needs of users. This requires a mechanism whereby shareholders and other users are able to make their information needs known and the extent to which managers are able to articulate and support those needs. Without such a mechanism, the only effective sanction open to shareholders would be to sell their holdings if dissatisfied with the level of financial disclosure.

ACCOUNTING AND ACCOUNTING THEORY

If it is possible to identify users and their needs, then it should be possible to design an accounting framework which satisfies those needs. Not only would it help resolve issues already raised, such as the valuation of stock, the depreciation of assets and the recognition of revenue, it would also give guidance to other controversies as they arise. Such a framework would provide a sound theoretical base both to explain current accounting treatments and aid the analysis of evolving issues.

The role of theory

Whatever the discipline, theory has two purposes: to explain and predict. In accounting, early theory was concerned with identifying what accountants do. Observations were made and analysed in order to identify consistent patterns of behaviour. This *inductive* approach to theory is identified with the concepts and applications developed in earlier chapters. From these practices, new theories could then be developed. Such an approach has provided only limited success. First, in many cases there were no consistent patterns. Several methods of stock valuation can hardly be described as a consistent pattern. Secondly, it did not provide a strong base from which to mount improvements or address evolving accounting issues. Crudely, it suggested that what is, ought to be.

Because of this, an alternative approach to theory developed, a *normative* approach concerned with the information users should have available to make rational decisions. Aimed directly at improving accounting practice, normative theory attempts to derive a logical set of accounting rules and procedures derived from a basic set of assumptions. It is both deductive in developing a logical argument from basic principles and inductive in attempting to identify the basic needs of users. As a result, it is less concerned with the classification and analysis of accounting practices than in changing those practices. Accounting theory can therefore be defined as 'logical reasoning in the form of a set of broad principles that (i) provide a general frame of reference by which accounting practice can be evaluated and (ii) guide the development of new practices and procedures'.[2]

THE SEARCH FOR A CONCEPTUAL FRAMEWORK

At its most extreme, normative theory has involved a search for the holy grail of accounting, an all-encompassing conceptual framework by identifying users and then discovering their needs. This has manifested itself in the publication of many substantial reports originating from the accounting profession both in the UK and North America over the last twenty-five years.

In 1973, the Trueblood Report, *Objectives of Financial Statements*, was published by the American Institute of Certified Public Accountants and this was followed by the Financial Accounting Standards Board's search for a detailed conceptual framework. (The FASB is a powerful body in the USA with extensive power over, *inter alia*, the contents and presentation of published accounts.) In the UK, the combined accountancy bodies produced a document entitled *The Corporate Report* in 1975. In Canada, Professor Edward Stamp produced *Corporate Reporting: Its Future Evolution* in 1980 for the Canadian Institute of Chartered Accountants. This was followed by a discussion document, *Making Corporate Reports Valuable*, published by the Institute of Chartered Accountants of Scotland in 1988 and *Framework for the Preparation and Presentation of Financial Statements*, published by the International Accounting Standards Committee in 1989. More recently in late 1994, the UK Accounting Standards Board completed seven draft chapters which will form the basis for its Statement of Principles.

Although the detailed content of these reports varied, all had similar objectives: the identification of users and their needs. This so-called *user decision oriented* approach is concerned with the ability of alternative accounting methods to provide useful information for decision making by users. All of the reports require the identification of:

1 *objectives:* why financial reports such as the final accounts are published;
2 *users and their needs:* who are the main groups of users of financial reports and what do they require from the reports;
3 *choice of accounting method:* the establishment of criteria for choosing the required content, disclosure and layout of financial reports.

IDENTIFYING THE USERS

Several attempts have been made to identify the users of financial reports. Exhibit 6.2 shows the users identified by just three reports.

Exhibit 6.2 Identification of users of financial reports

Corporate Report	Stamp Report	FASB
Equity investor group	Shareholders	Investors
Loan creditor group	Creditors, long and short term	Creditors
Employee group	Analysts and advisers	Other users
Analyst-adviser group	Employees	
Business contact group	Non-executive directors	
Government	Customers	
Public	Suppliers	
	Industry groups	
	Trade unions	
	Government departments	
	Public	
	Regulatory agencies	
	Other companies	
	Standard setters and academics	

Financial reporting

The first glaring omission is any reference to management as a user group. This is because management has full access to all the information available within an accounting system and is able to influence its design. Most other users do not have this access and so the term *financial reporting* has been coined to refer to the 'informational needs of external users who lack the authority to prescribe the financial information they want from an enterprise and therefore must use the information that management communicates to them'.[3]

For the most part, the user groups identified in Exhibit 6.2 are self-explanatory. Within the analyst-adviser group would be found financial analysts, journalists, credit rating agencies and trade union researchers amongst others. Included within the business contact group would be found trade creditors, customers and competitors, while the government user group is interpreted widely to include the tax authorities and other agencies.

Loan creditors

Common to all three classifications are the needs of shareholders and other providers of finance. Short term loan creditors require payment in the very near future. Their primary concern will therefore be with the business's liquidity – the availability of cash when the loan is due for repayment. Suppliers of long term loans will also share this concern but in addition they will be interested in the longer term viability of the company to ensure future repayments. Equally important perhaps will be a second, fall-back position: that should the business fail, the *value* of its assets will be sufficient to repay those loans.

Investors

Existing and prospective equity investors are looking for a return on their investment, both in the form of dividends and capital gains from an increase in the price of their shares. This growth in the share price depends on many factors. Some factors, such as interest rates, are outside the control of the company. Other things being equal, an increase in interest rates makes bank and other deposits more attractive relative to shares. Many factors, however, are under the long term control of the company. A share can be made more attractive to investors in at least two ways – and if it is made more attractive, there is likely to be an increased demand which is reflected in an increased share price. One way is to improve the quality of its earnings by reducing the amount of risk. Another way is to improve growth by successfully developing new products and new markets. This suggests that investors are interested in knowing; (a) where current profits come from and the extent to which they generate positive cash flows; and (b) where future profits are likely to come from. Future profits result from current activities such as the level of research and development, the acquisition of new businesses and expenditure on fixed assets such as plant and machinery. They also depend on future plans such as the markets the company wishes to be in and the products they plan to produce, and the way these are to be achieved; in other words, the company's strategy.

Employees

Employees or their representatives are concerned with the ability of the business to meet the demands from wage negotiations and with current and future job security. This suggests that they share some of the informational needs of investors. Investors, however, are concerned with the broader picture. Employees are more likely to need more detailed, localised information about the quality of current profits and the planned strategy for their part of the business, supplemented by additional non-financial information such as future staffing levels.

The business contact group

Within the business contact group, suppliers will require similar information to that required by short term loan creditors. In addition though, their future prospects might well be tied up with the future prospects of the business. Suppliers will therefore be concerned not only with the future viability of the business but also its future production plans and from where purchases are likely to be sourced.

Similarly customers might also be concerned with the business's future plans and viability if they in turn are dependent on the business for supplies, after-sales service or the enforcement of any guarantees given by the enterprise. The future plans and viability of the business are also likely to be of more than passing interest to competitors. Their concern will extend to how efficiently the business is being run and, should they be considering making a takeover bid, details of major shareholders as well as the strengths of the existing management.

The government and the public

The government, through its various agencies, will be concerned with reported turnover and profit for VAT and corporation tax purposes. In addition, much more detailed information may be required for national statistics. The future plans of businesses are also of significance even in today's 'hands-off' environment. Surveys of whether businesses plan to build up stocks or take on more employees may well influence interest rate changes or the choosing of the date for a general election!

Lastly, there is the catch-all group, the public. Much of the information desired by the public will be of a non-financial nature – that is, non-financial in the traditional sense developed in earlier chapters. Levels of pollution, health and safety records, proposed employment levels and political and charitable donations are all examples of information which may well be of interest to the public.

The information needs of the users

What is clear from this outline of assumed users and their assumed needs is that (a) much of it is forward looking; (b) different users have different needs; (c) different users will possess different levels of financial skills; and finally (d) a great deal of the information is not currently fully provided in the published financial statements of companies.

Only under the most restrictive of assumptions would it be possible for a system of accounting to satisfy all the needs of all users, if for no other reason than the potential conflict between the demands of different groups. What is also clear is the substantial differences between the user groups identified by the FASB and the other listings. The most notable omission is government. Governments, however, have the power, through legislation, to force disclosures and ways of recording expenses and enforce reporting practices. In that sense, they are not external users, who were defined by the FASB as lacking authority to demand financial information.

The rights of users

This still leaves a substantial difference between the FASB groupings and those identified by other reports. The FASB listing, however, takes on a rationale of its own if, instead of asking what are the *needs* of users, the *rights* of users in a free market are considered. Defining rights in economic or power terms, shareholders as a group can demand a significant say in both the design and the contents of the outputs from the business's accounting system – although for this to be an effective demand requires a majority of the shareholders acting in concert. Similarly with providers of debt finance: they can make the offer of a loan conditional on the supply of sufficient, suitable accounting information.

This view, that it is the shareholders – and to a lesser extent other providers of finance – who have the main interest in a company is predominantly an Anglo-American view. Their interest is a property right from owning the shares. Others, such as employees and suppliers, also have an interest in the company. But in the UK and USA that interest is defined in contractual terms. For an employee, it is a contract of employment; for a customer it is a contract to supply goods. The implication is that these interests are little more than inputs to the production and selling process.

There is, however, another way of looking at companies and organisations in general which recognises that employees, customers and suppliers have a greater stake in the organisation than as mere factors of production. Employees who have invested long hours and much expense developing skills of relevance to an organisation have made a long term commitment to that organisation. Equally, suppliers who incur specialised capital expenditure, the output from which can only be taken up by one customer, have also entered into a long term commitment. To describe these as mere inputs is an inadequate description of their role in the organisation.

An alternative approach is to view employees, customers and suppliers as having a wider interest as *stakeholders*. From this perspective, they have made just as much a commitment to the organisation as providers of finance. Particularly in the case of employees, this stakeholder role has been recognised and enshrined in legislation in many countries. The result is greater disclosure of financial information. For example, German law gives employees a stake in the running of companies, including access to more detailed financial information. This suggests that it is only by introducing regulations or legislation that the informational needs of other users will be addressed by companies.

The authors of several of the conceptual framework reports would disagree with this suggestion. They argue that a great deal of the information needs is common to all users and that in providing information which meets the needs of the investor group, other groups' information requirements will also be satisfied.

DEVELOPING A CONCEPTUAL FRAMEWORK

The most recent attempt to develop a conceptual framework was completed in draft form in late 1994 by the UK Accounting Standards Board (ASB). Although not actually called a conceptual framework, the Board's *Statement of Principles* covers most of the areas associated with previous frameworks. The Statement of Principles aims to improve the understanding of, and comparability between, financial statements by developing a logical set of concepts to guide accounting practice and future developments. Users of accounts will then be aware of the bases on which accounts have been prepared and this will help them interpret financial statements in a more meaningful way. Users are defined as including existing and potential investors, lenders, suppliers and other trade creditors, customers, employees, governments and their agencies and the public. Within this, the ASB has identified the investor user group as the primary group.

The Statement of Principles contains seven Chapters. Chapter 1, *The objectives of financial statements*, considers the purpose of financial statements. Chapter 2, *The qualitative characteristics of financial information*, looks at the desirable features of financial statements. The components of financial statements and how they should be defined and recognised are then covered in the next two chapters. Chapter 3, *Elements of financial statements* and Chapter 4, *The recognition of items in financial statements* are therefore interlinked. The value attached to elements in the final accounts – cost or current value, for instance – is then considered in Chapter 5, *Measurement in financial statements*. Chapter 6, *Presentation of financial information*, is concerned with how the information developed in earlier chapters should be shown in order to meet the identified objectives of financial statements. Finally, Chapter 7, *The reporting entity*, looks at the issues when one company owns or has rights over another company.

Chapter 1 The objectives of financial statements

According to the ASB, the objective of financial statements is 'to provide information about the financial position, performance and financial adaptability of an enterprise that is useful to a wide range of users in making economic decisions'. Information about an entity's financial position, both the resources it controls and how it is financed, is found in its balance sheet. Although the measurement of its financial performance is primarily provided by the profit and loss account, an understanding of how this converts to cash and the general liquidity and solvency position is also important. This understanding can be derived from the cashflow statement and the cash and net current assets position on the balance sheet.

These financial position and performance objectives are familiar ones and have been developed in earlier chapters of this book. It is the financial adaptability objective which is new. In terms of the systems model introduced earlier, it is concerned with the ability of the organisation to adapt to changes in its environment and survive. An insight into financial adaptability can be gathered from all three accounting statements. The cashflow statement helps identify how cash is generated and absorbed, enabling the user to estimate how this might change as a result of any change to the business's operations. The profit and loss account can give some indication of the breakdown of costs – for example, between fixed and variable costs or recurring and non-recurring expenses – and so help a user to forecast changes in profits as a result of changes in the environment. Lastly, the balance sheet, by classifying assets and sources of finance, can give some idea of the flexibility within the enterprise. A company with fixed assets predominantly made up of motor cars is likely to have greater flexibility than a company whose fixed assets are specific to an industry and where there is little marketability. A similar argument applies when comparing the amount of debt finance in a company's capital structure. Other things being equal, the greater the debt, the less the financial adaptability.

In evaluating the enterprise's financial position, performance and adaptability, it is necessary to consider all the financial statements, along with any notes to the accounts. They are interrelated as they merely reflect different aspects of the same transactions.

Chapter 2 Qualitative characteristics of financial information

Having identified the objectives of financial statements, the Accounting Standards Board then considered the qualities which make accounting information useful. Rather than simply listing these qualities, the ASB made a deliberate attempt to rank them by introducing a threshold quality and then primary and secondary characteristics. These are shown in detail in Exhibit 6.3.

Materiality – a threshold quality

Before considering the desirable qualities of accounting information, the ASB introduced a test or threshold quality of materiality. Information is material if its omission or misstatement could influence the economic decisions of users. Failure to meet the test of materiality means that information is insignificant, cannot be of help to users and so should not be considered further.

Relevance and reliability

Having past the test of materiality, the ASB then identified the primary characteristics of accounting information as relevance and reliability. Relevant information is information

Exhibit 6.3 Qualitative characteristics of accounting information

(*Source*: Accounting Standards Board, 1994)

which influences the economic decisions of users. This it does in two ways. First, the information enables a user to *confirm* or correct previously held beliefs. This is the feedback or scorekeeping role of accounting information. Secondly, the information can have predictive value by helping the user to make forecasts about future levels of profitability, liquidity, resources, financial structure and financial adaptability. Relevant information also depends on what the ASB calls the choice of aspect, that is, the perspective from which a transaction or event is recorded. For example, a property might be recorded in the balance sheet at its cost or current valuation. Both represent faithfully the transaction but from different perspectives or aspects.

Reliable information is information which is free from material error or bias. It will faithfully represent – be a valid description and measurement of – the transaction or event. This suggests that the transaction should be both verifiable and shown under the appropriate account heading. To be reliable, the substance or economic reality of a transaction needs to be shown rather than some (artificial) legal form. For example, under a hire purchase agreement, the legal title to an asset only passes to the purchaser once all payments have been made. In substance, however, the purchaser is also the owner of the asset from the beginning with a liability to the finance company for the amount outstanding.

To be reliable, information should also be neutral. By neutral, the ASB meant that information should not unduly influence or distort a user's decision making. For example, a company might have reported a lower than expected profit, not because of poorer trading than expected but because of a one-off expense such as substantial damages in a law case. Failure to disclose this would not be neutral as it is sending out the (untrue) message that future profits are also likely to be at this lower figure. Within the constraints of materiality and cost, information also needs to be complete. Any significant omission is likely to be misleading and hence unreliable. Finally the ASB included prudence as a desirable attribute of reliability although the Board recognised that deliberate over- and understatements would not be neutral and hence would not be reliable.

Comparability and understandability

Having identified relevance and reliability as the primary characteristics of useful accounting information, the ASB then looked at other qualities which, if lacking, would limit the usefulness of the information. They identified two secondary qualities, comparability and understandability.

Information in isolation is often of only limited meaning. Being told that a person's salary in Ruritania is 3,000 monetary units per annum carries little or no meaning without some standard against which to measure it. Because of this, it is desirable that users should be able to compare an entity's performance and position both at different times and between similar organisations in order to establish trends. Consistency of treatment helps in the former case, compliance with accounting standards – by reducing the range of possible treatments – might help in the latter while disclosure of policies and other information will help in both cases.

None of this will be of much use, however, if the user cannot understand the financial statements. Whether or not users can understand financial statements depends partly on their abilities and partly on the way the information is presented.

Trade-offs

In the real world, there will be trade-offs between all four characteristics and these will be constrained by both timeliness and cost. Other things being equal, the longer the delay between the end of an accounting period and the reporting date, the less uncertainty there will be in any assumptions made. For example, the position of a debtor on the balance sheet date might well have been resolved by delaying the reporting of the accounts by three months. However, there is a price to pay for this increased reliability and that is the decreased relevance of the statements as a result of the delay – old news is no news. Equally there is often a financial cost to pay for improving any of the characteristics, be they primary or secondary. This involves weighing the financial cost against the potential benefits.

Difficulties in making the chapter operational

What is clear from the ASB's identification of the qualitative characteristics of accounting information is that there is a deliberate ranking as a result of classifying some characteristics as primary and others as secondary. However reasonable this might be, a different ranking could easily be sustained. For example, understandability might be viewed as a threshold quality. If the financial statements cannot be understood by anyone then they would not be relevant and so understandability might be viewed as a prerequisite for relevance.

In attempting to apply these qualitative criteria, there is also the potential for conflict. Future cashflows might score high on relevance but fail on reliability. For historical cost accounting based primarily on past transactions, the reverse applies. Indeed, given that historical costs tend to overstate profits in times of rising prices, it could be argued that such a system is not neutral as it distorts decision making. Equally, comparability and consistency may be inconsistent with other characteristics. Applying the same depreciation rates to different industries may well be consistent but is unlikely to be reliable or relevant. Consider, for example, a vehicle making local deliveries from a Knightsbridge store. The vehicle may well have a life of ten years. Now consider the same vehicle but being used to move rock in a quarry. Being consistent, by applying the same depreciation rates to both vehicles is likely to reduce relevance. Similarly, comparability between years may be impossible when a company has made significant changes to its business operations – perhaps by moving out of brewing and into fast food outlets.

Because of the essentially qualitative nature of the exercise, there are difficulties when it comes to making it operational. Take as an example, the secondary characteristic of understandability and in particular the users' abilities. The ASB interprets this as '... users are assumed to have a reasonable knowledge of business and economic activities and accounting and a willingness to study the information with reasonable diligence ... Information about complex matters that should be included in the financial statements because of its relevance ... should not be excluded merely on the grounds that it might be too difficult for certain users to understand'.[4] To date, there appears to be no objective way of measuring reasonable knowledge or reasonable diligence.

Attempting to apply the cost/benefit test is also not without difficulties. Costs are often relatively easy to identify. It is the benefits which are most difficult to quantify. More than that, the beneficiaries may not be the same group as the one footing the bill. For example, the beneficiaries of additional disclosure may be competitors while both the explicit cost of paying for the information to be provided plus the implicit cost of giving away confidential information is borne by the existing shareholders. Because of all these issues, no matter how beneficial the analysis, making it operational involves value judgements.

Chapter 3 Elements of financial statements

The ASB views Chapters 3 and 4 as the core of the Statement of Principles. Chapter 3 identifies seven components or *elements* which comprise the financial accounts, all of which are interrelated. These are assets, liabilities, equity, gains, losses, contribution from owners and distributions to owners. As the income equation developed in Chapter 2 of this text demonstrated, these elements are all linked. With no contributions from or distributions to owners, gains or losses for a period manifest themselves in a change in net assets over the period which, in turn, is reflected in an identical change in equity. How assets and liabilities are measured are therefore of significance and it has been the previous lack of *definitions* which has allowed items to be excluded or included in balance sheets – often to the advantage of managers. The Accounting Standards Board's Chapter 3 recognises this and attempts to define the essential attributes each of the seven elements must have to be included in financial statements. Guiding any definition will be the primary and secondary characteristics of relevance, reliability, comparability and understandability.

Assets and liabilities

Assets are defined as 'rights or other access to future economic benefits controlled by an entity as a result of a past transaction or event'. Without rights – and these rights imply the entity has control of a resource to the exclusion of others – it is not possible to share in future benefits and so there can be no value. Equally rights but no future benefits also have no value. With no future value, the element cannot be an asset: it must be an expense.

An asset, to be an asset, also has to be acquired. By far the most common way of acquiring an asset is to undertake a transaction, by giving up another asset or acquiring an obligation such as a creditor. However, it is also possible to recognise an asset gained by other means and this is what is meant by the term 'event'. Examples would include a government grant to acquire an asset or the gaining of damages. To pass the test of reliability in the form of evidence, both transactions and events must have occurred, i.e. they must be based in the past. From this definition, it is clear that the ASB is concerned with the substance rather than the legal form of an asset as nowhere does the definition mention ownership.

Having defined assets, the definition of liabilities is almost a mirror image of the definition of an asset. Liabilities are 'an entity's obligations to transfer economic benefits as a result of past transactions or events'. This does not necessarily mean that the liability itself is a past event but rather that it arises from a past event. For example, a corporation tax liability will be shown as a liability in the year end accounts as it arises from past trading even though it is not a legal liability until the Inland Revenue assesses the amount some time later.

Equity, gains and losses

The definition of equity follows on from the analysis of the balance sheet developed in Chapter 2 of this text where, in equation (2.5), equity was defined as total assets less total liabilities. It is 'the ownership interest in the entity, ... the residual amount found by deducting all liabilities of the entity from all of the entity's assets'.

Gains are then described as 'increases in equity, other than those relating to contributions from owners' while losses are 'decreases in equity, other than those relating to distributions to owners'. Gains can therefore include not only gains recognised in the profit and loss account – what are sometimes called revenue gains – but also gains as a result of changes in market value such as when property is revalued. Likewise, losses are more than 'revenue losses' – i.e. expenses. They can also include decreases in market values such as when stock is valued at its realisable value if below cost.

Contributions from owners are 'increases in equity resulting from investments by owners in their capacity as owners'. This will normally be in the form of cash although it is possible for an owner to bring in other resources to the business, to accept equity in exchange for giving up a liability claim against the organisation or to accept equity in exchange for services provided. Distribution to owners are 'decreases in equity resulting from transfers made to owners in their capacity as owners'. By far the most popular distribution is through cash dividends although it could include the purchase by the company of its own shares or any other return of capital.

Chapter 4 The recognition of items in financial statements

Chapter 4 was issued at the same time as Chapter 3 and both need to be read together. Recognition means being included in the primary financial statements. To be recognised, an item should meet one of the definitions of an element outlined above. In addition, there are two further conditions. First, there should be sufficient evidence that the change in the asset/liability inherent in the item has occurred. Secondly, the item can be measured as a monetary amount with sufficient reliability. By way of an example, consider research expenditure. It has the qualities of an asset defined earlier. There has been a change in assets/liabilities. Cash has decreased and the benefits of research gained. Where the definition of research as an asset falls down is in the final criteria of insufficient evidence to measure the future benefits in monetary terms.

The recognition process is constantly taking place in accounting, whenever a past event indicates there has been a measurable change in assets or liabilities. This process falls into three stages: (i) the initial recognition as when an asset is purchased; (ii) a subsequent remeasurement such as a revaluation; and (iii) a derecognition as when an asset is sold or destroyed.

This still leaves the issue of how to report the recognition of a gain or loss. The profit and loss is of major importance in measuring an entity's performance. Profit also determines the maximum funds available for distribution and so clear criteria need to be established for determining whether or not gains or losses are recognised in the profit and loss account. To be included in the profit and loss account, gains and losses have not only to be earned – i.e. recognised as an increase in equity by meeting the earlier criteria – but also realised. Realised means that conversion to cash or cash equivalents has already occurred or is reasonably certain to occur in the near future as in the case of sales on credit. If a gain meets the earned condition but not the realised condition, it still meets the general recognition criteria. Often such gains are transferred directly to reserves as when freehold property is revalued. The ASB, however, believe this is inadequate and so they propose a further primary financial statement, a *Statement of Total Recognised Gains and Losses*. This statement is returned to when discussing the ASB's Chapter 6.

Chapter 5 Measurement in financial statements

Although having identified the elements making up the final accounts, no mention has been made of how they should be measured. In the UK, balance sheets are an amalgam of historical costs and *ad hoc* revaluations. Exactly what this makes the balance sheet is unclear. Indeed Sir David Tweedie, the Chairman of the Accounting Standards Board has been quoted as saying that 'the British balance sheet, is quite frankly, a mess. There is no logic behind the summation of assets valued on the basis of historical costs, revaluations of several years ago and current valuations. Despite this we cheerfully add these numbers together as if they mean something.'[5]

Historical cost and current cost values

One answer would be to measure all assets and liabilities in the balance sheet at their historical cost unless prudence demands a lower figure. The alternative is to show them at some form of current value or current cost. (The implications of this are discussed later.) Although recognising that some form of current cost value is more relevant to users than historical costs, Chapter 5 failed to recommend either approach as such. Instead it proposed 'an evolutionary development of eclectic valuation methods in response to developing user needs'.[6] At the initial stage of recognition, the valuation method will be the traditional historical cost base although the chapter stated that the 'soundest method of valuing assets at the second (remeasurement) stage of recognition' is one based on current costs. Three current-cost bases are identified in the chapter, entry values, exit values and value to the business. Replacement costs – how much it would cost today to replace the net assets – is an example of entry values while an example of exit values is realisable values, how much the net assets could be *sold* for today. Although all have advantages, the chapter prefers 'value to the business'. This is a hybrid form of current cost and is discussed in a later chapter of this text when considering accounting for inflation.

Capital maintenance

If equity is the difference between assets and liabilities, then how you measure assets and liabilities will determine the value of that equity. Within equity is capital and only after capital has been maintained is it possible to make a distribution. How you measure assets and liabilities will therefore influence the value of capital to be maintained and the funds available for distribution. Chapter 5 of the Statement of Principles identified three approaches to capital maintenance. The first was the traditional historical cost based concept of maintaining the original money or nominal amount of the capital in order to protect creditors. The second, current purchasing power, is a modification of this to take account of any changes in the purchasing power of money resulting from inflation. (This is also discussed further in Chapter 12 in the context of inflation accounting.) Finally, capital maintenance can be viewed as maintaining the physical or operating capacity of the enterprise. This issue has already been touched on when considering the FIFO and LIFO stock valuation methods and is expanded below. Under this definition, a profit can only be declared once the entity has provided for the replacement of its operating assets. Unfortunately, having discussed the three approaches to capital maintenance, the ASB was unable to come to a firm conclusion as to which approach should be used. This is particularly regrettable as different users are likely to prefer different definitions of capital maintenance. Investors are likely to prefer the traditional definition of capital maintenance in money terms as this gives them greatest freedom to distribute reserves. Employees, on the other hand, are more likely to prefer an operating definition of capital maintenance as this is concerned with sustaining the business.

Chapter 6 Presentation of financial information

Chapter 6 is concerned with applying the principles previously developed in order to meet the objective of financial statements determined in Chapter 1 of the Statement of Principles. Financial information can either take place within the primary financial statements or in supporting notes.

The four primary financial statements

The chapter identifies four primary financial statements: (i) the balance sheet; (ii) the profit and loss account; (iii) the cashflow statement; and (iv) the statement of total recognised gains and losses.

The first three have been extensively discussed throughout this text and even the fourth one has been alluded to from time to time. The need for an explicit primary statement reflecting the total recognised gains and losses of an entity has become necessary because significant gains and losses in accounts have often been reported via the reserves rather than the profit and loss account. No matter what the justification for this, users tend to focus on the profit and loss account and so there is a danger that they might miss other significant gains and losses such as asset revaluations which affect the total equity of a company. The introduction of a fourth primary financial statement is an attempt to overcome this difficulty.

Presentation and disclosure

Because financial statements involve the processing of large volumes of data, there is a need to aggregate, classify and structure the data to allow the wider picture to be seen. Aggregation involves the condensing and simplifying of data while classifying involves the placing of transactions or events into reasonably homogeneous groups within the accounts. Structuring is then concerned with giving items and groups appropriate prominence. For the user to assess the primary financial statements requires accounting policies to be disclosed while any notes to the financial statements need to amplify or explain the items in those primary statements.

Of particular interest was the section in the chapter relating to good presentation. Some aspects identified are obvious good practice such as reporting separately items that have been unusual in amount or incidence judged by the experience of previous periods. Others, such as distinguishing between the performance of different business segments, are already incorporated in existing UK standards or law. What is more significant is identifying as good practice the need to distinguish amounts that are affected in different ways by changes in economic conditions or business activity. This marks a significant departure from normal practice. It implies that turnover and expenses should not be given as a single figure as has been the norm but rather be broken down between continuing, acquired and discontinued activities. Clearly this helps make accounting information more relevant by identifying the financial implications of activities likely to continue into the future.

Chapter 7   The reporting entity

In the modern world, even small companies often own other companies known as subsidiaries. The company owning the subsidiary is known as the parent. Taking a narrow approach, the parent company could simply show the subsidiary as an investment in its accounts. This, however, disguises the underlying reality that the parent controls all the assets of the subsidiary. To show the economic substance, UK companies with subsidiaries have had to produce consolidated accounts since the introduction of the 1948 Companies Act. In effect, consolidated accounts aggregate the assets and liabilities of the parent with those of the subsidiary. How this is done is discussed in Chapter 9 of this text.

There is, however, an intermediate stage between owning shares in another company as a simple investment and owning them for control. This intermediate stage may well mean a company having influence over another even though it does not have legal control. Chapter 7 of the Statement of Principles sets out the conditions that determine whether or not entities should produce individual and consolidated accounts. The chapter focuses on the circumstances in which one business is deemed to control another and how to account for situations where there is influence but not full control.

THE PROSPECTS FOR A CONCEPTUAL FRAMEWORK

A conceptual framework can be defined as a comprehensive set of generally accepted beliefs and values which provide a reference point to identify how events and transactions should be measured and disclosed to others. Such a framework would help standard setters when developing new standards or resolving accounting problems, improve comparability by reducing the range of accounting policies, limit personal bias and political pressures, reduce the expense of clarifying accounting problems and increase user understanding and confidence.

That there have been so many attempts over the last 25 years to develop an accounting framework, the latest of which has been outlined above, suggests the scale of the problem and the fundamental difficulties being encountered. Indeed it has been suggested that all projects of this type are fatally flawed because 'an accounting framework which serves all, or even a favoured sector of the community . . . irrespective of their preferences, their beliefs and their endowments, is at present an impossible dream.'[7]

The reason for this somewhat depressing conclusion is that there is no single practical method of accounting which equally helps all users. Partly this is because different users have different ideas about what is relevant information and the trade-off between relevance and reliability. Partly, it is also because there is often a difference between the user group that pays for the information and the user group that benefits.

Despite this, the ASB's dogged view is that 'as investors are the providers of risk capital to an enterprise, the provision of financial statements that meet their needs will also meet most of the needs of other users'. The limitation of the ASB approach is reinforced when it is recognised that their Statement of Principles is of more relevance to the Anglo-American form of private enterprise with its separation of managers from investors and the predominant role for stock exchanges. Other countries often take a different approach. For example, the banks in Germany not only provide debt finance, they are also significant shareholders and play an active role in the strategic management of the company. Because of this, the type of framework developed by the Accounting Standards Board may be less relevant to other countries.

The wider issues

In a rather perverse way, some good has come out of the search for a conceptual framework. It has brought to a head the thorny question of who are the users of accounting reports and what are their needs and rights. It has also identified some useful qualities associated with information for decision making although so far it has not been possible to make these operational. (That there are inconsistencies within these qualities should not trouble accountants too greatly as inconsistencies abound even between the traditional concepts.) But perhaps the most important thing is that it has destroyed the myth that accounting is a value-free, dispassionate activity. Supporting any figure appearing in a financial report will be, often implicit, assumptions, be they concerned with when to recognise profits or how to value assets. Users unaware of these assumptions may well be put at a disadvantage.

At the same time, the search for a conceptual framework has opened up the glaring difference between the forward-looking needs of most of the identifiable users of accounts and the backward-looking results they are given in financial reports. At the centre of all this is a debate about valuation and income measurement.

What follows is an outline of attempts to make accounting information more meaningful to at least some of the user groups. As such, the proposals relate to that part of theory concerned with 'what ought to be', rather than what is. However, in doing so, it opens up a separate debate. Users may be technically unaware of the finer details of existing financial reporting let alone any alternative. This begs the question – which will remain unanswered at this stage – as to how to handle a situation where there is a difference between what users perceive as their needs and what information accountants or others believe they should receive.

CRITICISM OF HISTORICAL COSTS

In its early days there is little question that accounting was driven by the needs of users, users who could enforce their will by being owner/managers and whose main need was for stewardship. The later development of limited companies and the increasing complexity of production technology saw ownership being divorced from management control and shareholders having less influence over the quality and quantity of financial information.

At the same time the relative needs of users moved towards information for decision making rather than stewardship. Despite this, the basis for much of financial reporting is historical cost. The main advantage of historical cost accounting is that, being based on transactions, data is verifiable. Because of this, a further advantage is the relative ease in obtaining the data in the first place. Unfortunately, historical cost is of least benefit in the two areas where it is needed most, the calculation of depreciation and the valuation of stock. Historical cost is therefore not as objective as it might first appear. In times of rising prices, it can overstate the underlying profit from activities by understating the cost of stock consumed – especially if valued on a FIFO basis – and understating the depreciation charge necessary for the replacement of assets. Equally, the information contained on the balance sheet will convey less and less meaning with changing prices. But perhaps its greatest criticism is that its focus on the past does not help users plan for the future. Because of this, a variety of proposals have been put forward to overcome at least partly these limitations.

INTRODUCTION TO ECONOMIC INCOME

The relationship between the income and wealth of a business has already been established in Chapter 2 where the income equation for an entity was developed. Provided there has been neither injections of extra funds such as additional capital subscribed nor leakages from the business by way of dividends or drawings, the value of net assets at the end of a period less the value at the beginning of the period will equal the profit for the period. And because of duality, the equity at the end of a period less the equity at the beginning of the period will also be equivalent to that profit.

This relationship has concerned economists from the days of Adam Smith onwards although the major debate is centred on the first half of the twentieth century. As early as 1919, Irving Fisher[8] had identified income as a flow and wealth as a stock. Although primarily writing about personal income, this is not dissimilar to the idea of the balance sheet showing a stock of assets with the profit and loss account acting as a flow linking the opening and closing balance sheets.

Where he differed from accounting was in the measurement of income. Income for him was the 'psychic experiences' or pleasure derived from the consumption of goods made possible by money income – what would be called today in another context the *feel good* factor. Put crudely, a person could have the same money income as a previous period but if the pleasure derived from the second period's consumption of income was less than that in the first, income would be less. Fisher did recognise the impossibility of measuring income in this way. The principle, however, is of some importance. Today, for example, most people are likely to prefer an income derived from activities involving less risk to an identical money income derived from much riskier and uncertain means.

The Hicksian approach to income

A later economist, Sir John Hicks, moved the economic debate forward by emphasising the capacity to consume rather than consumption itself. For him, income was the most a person *can* consume during a period and still remain as well off at the end of the period as at the beginning.[9] Income is therefore made up of two elements, consumption (dividends?) and savings (retentions?) which can only be recognised once capital has been maintained. Superficially this is similar to the accountant's measure of profit, with profit equalling the increase in net assets or, equivalently, the increase in equity, assuming no injections or leakages of funds.

There are, however, two major differences: the valuation of that wealth or 'well-offness' and the relationship of wealth to income. For the accountant, wealth is measured at the historical cost of the assets (less adjustments for items such as depreciation) with income being generated from the original assets and flowing into the period end valuation of wealth.

Economic income is measured differently. Wealth or capital is viewed as a stock of future benefits (or income generating capacity) with income being the balance or residue flowing from that stock. To appreciate this needs an understanding of why assets have value. Assets only have value because benefits will flow from their acquisition and ultimately these benefits will be an increased command over resources – in other words, money. The more benefits flowing from an asset, the greater its worth. In money terms, income will then be what is left over once this value has been maintained. The relationship of (money) benefits to value can be expressed quantitatively through an understanding of compounding and discounting.

Compounding

The mathematics of compounding are relatively straightforward. If an investment is made which pays interest and that interest is not withdrawn then in subsequent periods the interest receivable will not only be based on the original investment but also on the interest retained from previous periods. This is demonstrated in Example 6.1.

Example 6.1

An opportunity arises to invest money in a government saving scheme. The interest receivable is 25 per cent per annum although it will not be possible to withdraw any monies until the end of the third year. An individual decides to invest £1,000,000 in the scheme.

At the end of the first year the government will owe to the investor the original amount plus 25 per cent interest. At the beginning of the second year therefore the total amount invested will be £1,250,000 and so at the end of the second year the government will have to pay interest not only on the original amount but also the interest from year one which has not been withdrawn. The interest on this will be 25 per cent of £1,250,000, a total of £312,500. This is added to the amount already owing to make the total amount invested at the beginning of the third year £1,562,500. Finally, at the end of the third year, the investor will be repaid this amount plus 25 per cent interest of £390,625, a total of £1,953,125.

Within this computation is a pattern. The value of the investment at the end of each year is 100 per cent of the value at the beginning of the year plus the interest earned. In this example, the amount owing at the end of any single year can be calculated by simply multiplying the amount owed at the beginning of the year by 125 per cent or equivalently by 1.25. This is demonstrated in Exhibit 6.4 where the start of year 1 is identified as the end of year 0 in a similar way to the closing balance of one year being identified as the opening balance of the next.

Exhibit 6.4 Compounding

End of year	Detail	Amount	Computation
0	Investment	£1,000,000	
1	25% interest	£250,000	
1	Balance	£1,250,000	= £1,000,000 × (1.25)
2	25% interest	£312,500	
2	Balance	£1,562,500	= £1,250,000 × (1.25) = £1,000,000 × (1.25) × (1.25) = £1,000,000 × (1.25)²
3	25% interest	£390,625	
3	Balance	£1,953,125	= £1,562,500 × (1.25) = £1,000,000 × (1.25) × (1.25) × (1.25) = £1,000,000 × (1.25)³

The process of compounding can be simplified further. The amount at the end of year 2 has been shown to equal 1.25 the amount at the beginning of that year. In its turn the balance at the beginning of year 2 is the balance at the end of year 1 and this is equivalent to 1.25 of the opening balance of year 1. The balance at the end of year 2 is therefore £1,000,000 multiplied by 1.25 twice or 1.25^2. Similarly the balance at the end of year 3 is £1,000,000 multiplied by 1.25^3.

Developing a formula

This approach can be generalised. To find how much any amount will grow to simply involves the original amount being multiplied by $(1 + r)^n$, where r is the interest rate and n is the number of periods over which the investment is made. For example, if interest rates are 10 per cent per annum and an investment of £100,000 is made for four years, the terminal value will be £100,000 × $(1.1)^4$ or £146,410 by the end of year 4.

The conclusion from Example 6.1 is that the investor will be better off by £953,125 and in the second example the improvement will be £46,410. For this to have any real meaning to the user, at least three important assumptions have to be made.

First, no inflation is assumed over the period (or at least the inflation rate is known for certain), otherwise the result will have little meaning to the user because of the distortion arising from inflation. Without inflation, the assumption is that the investor in the first example will end up with £953,125 more purchasing power or resources than at the beginning.

The second major assumption is that there will be no change in the rate of interest over the time period of the investment otherwise the calculated terminal amount may not be realised. In terms of Example 6.1, if the interest rate were to fall to 10 per cent in the final year, the amount of interest for that year would fall to £156,250 preventing the planned terminal amount from being realised.

Finally, an assumption has to be made about the riskiness of the investment. Intuitively, lending money to a well-established firm with a strong asset structure and quality products will be less risky than lending to a company with few resources and poor prospects. For the moment this and the other real-world problems will be ignored in order to allow the idea of discounting to be developed.

Discounting

With the assumptions of no risk, no inflation and a constant rate of interest, it is possible to reverse the logic of compounding. Instead of asking by how much an investment of £1,000,000 will grow at 25 per cent p.a. over three years, the argument can be reversed by asking how much £1,953,125 receivable in three years' time is worth today if interest rates are 25 per cent per annum. Money in the future has less value than money today – even without inflation and risk – simply because money *now* gives an immediate command over resources which could be invested to grow in the way demonstrated in Example 6.1. This awareness of compounding provides the answer to evaluating money receivable or payable in the future.

At 25 per cent p.a., £1,953,125 at the end of year 3 is equivalent to £1,000,000 now as an investment of £1,000,000 becomes an investment of £1,953,125 in three years at 25 per cent p.a. This process of converting future cashflows to their present-day equivalent is known as *discounting*. One immediate objection to this is the uncertainty of future events – the 'bird in the hand is worth two in the bush' syndrome – but for the moment this can be ignored as the assumption has been made that there is no risk. The process of discounting is therefore similar to converting foreign currency to its equivalent in the local currency.

Consider a company which holds UK funds of £1,000 and 2,000 Ruritanian dollars. Simply adding the two amounts together would be meaningless. Assuming the exchange rate is 2 Ruritanian dollars to the pound sterling, converting allows the total to be expressed as £2,000 or 4,000 dollars. The process of converting to a common base has enabled the two amounts to be added. Logically, either base is acceptable. Practically, however, a UK user will be more familiar with the UK currency and its purchasing power and so the pound sterling computation is likely to convey more meaning. Discounting is a similar process. Amounts receivable at several different times in the future can be converted to their equivalent in today's currency or any other year's currency but, by showing these amounts as equivalent values *today*, meaning can be conveyed.

Developing a formula

As with compounding, a formula can be developed to speed the discounting calculation. With compounding, the original value was given and from that the terminal value was derived. With discounting, the problem is reversed with the terminal value given and its present day equivalent value unknown. In terms of compounding, the unknown factor X was the terminal value. With discounting, the unknown factor X is the value today. Mathematically, these two statements can be expressed in terms of the data in Example 6.1 as:

$$£1,000,000 \times (1.25)^3 = X \qquad \text{(Compounding equation)}$$

and

$$X \times (1.25)^3 = £1,953,125 \qquad \text{(Discounting equation 1)}$$

Dividing both sides of the discounting equation by $(1.25)^3$ enables X to be solved:

$$X = \frac{£1,953,125}{(1.25)^3} \qquad \text{(Discounting equation 2)}$$

To complete the development of the discounting equation, the term on the right-hand side can be expanded. Dividing any sum by $(1.25)^3$ is the same as multiplying that sum by $1/(1.25)^3$ and this is how the formula is shown in discounting equation 3.

$$X = £1,953,125 \times \frac{1}{(1.25)^3} = £1,953,125 \times 0.512 = £100,000 \quad \text{(Discounting equation 3)}$$

More generally, the formula for calculating the value today, or *present value* as it has become known, is

$$PV = NCF \times \frac{1}{(1+r)^n}$$

where *NCF* is the net cashflow, the net amount of cash receivable in a particular time period, r the rate of interest applicable, n the period when the cashflow is received and *PV* the value today of that cashflow. When used to calculate a present value of a future income stream, the interest rate is known as the discount rate.

With this understanding of discounting it is now possible to derive the value today of any future income stream provided the amounts involved and the interest rate are known – and given the assumption of no risk, the result will be unambiguous. Example 6.2 demonstrates the calculation of the *present value* of such a stream of future cashflows.

Example 6.2

> An opportunity exists to buy an asset. Its cost is £1,000 and it will enable cashflows to be generated of £800 in year 1 and £600 in year 2. Interest rates are 10 per cent p.a.

The normal simplifying assumption in this sort of calculation is to assume that cashflows – the command over resources – occur at year ends. Accepting this, it is then possible to derive the value of the asset and hence develop the idea of economic income. The present value of the income stream is shown in Exhibit 6.5. The cashflow at the end of year 1 will be multiplied by $1/(1.1)^1$ or 0.9091 and the year 2 cashflow by $1/(1.1)^2$ or 0.8264 to derive their values today.

An investor making this investment will be exchanging an immediate outlay of £1,000 for a future inflow which has a value *equivalent* to £1,223 today. The difference, known as the *net present value*, measures the gain from the investment. Had the net present value been negative, the investor would not undertake the proposal as to do so would result in a loss.

Exhibit 6.5 Calculation of present value

End of year	Cashflow	Discount factor	Present value
1	£800	0.9091	£727
2	£600	0.8264	£496
			£1,223

IDEAL ECONOMIC INCOME

The value of the proposal in Exhibit 6.5 is £1,223. This is its worth to an investor. It is the value today of that future income stream comprising £800 at the end of year 1 and £600 at the end of year 2. This is how Hicks and others saw wealth or capital: as the present value of a future income stream. For an economist, it is the income stream which causes the capital value whereas for an accountant the argument is reversed with capital in the form of assets enabling income to be generated.

The economic argument has a strong theoretical appeal, not least because it is consistent with the belief that users evaluate information about the future before making decisions and the greater the future benefits, the greater their worth today. There are, however, major assumptions underpinning the economist's model of capital and income. These are the assumptions of perfect competition and include perfect knowledge, no transaction costs, no market barriers restricting entry or exit, no government taxes and a homogeneous product.

Implications of the assumptions

The assumption of perfect knowledge means there is no risk either to the timing or the amount of future cashflows and so investors will not demand different returns to compensate for different levels of risk. The return they demand will be the one they are able to obtain elsewhere, which will be the market rate of interest. With the assumption of no transaction costs, there will be no administrative expenses in bringing borrowers and lenders together and hence the borrowing and lending rate will be identical. Coupled with no barriers to entry or exit, there will be no constraints preventing anyone from participating in the market. With these assumptions it is possible to derive ideal economic income, ideal in the sense that, however unrealistic, everything is known in advance and with total certainty. The concepts involved are developed by making use of the information given in Example 6.3.

Example 6.3

Cardiff Ltd begins business by purchasing a machine for £18,000. This is its only asset. Market interest rates are 25 per cent p.a. and it can be assumed for simplicity that the cashflows are receivable and payable at the end of each year. At the end of year 3 the

▶

machine will have no residual value. Any surpluses made will be paid out as dividends. The revenue and expenses are all for cash and are as follows:

Year	Revenue	Expenses	Net cashflow
1	£8,000	£3,000	£5,000
2	£20,000	£10,625	£9,375
3	£30,000	£14,375	£15,625

Present value of the proposal

To determine the value of resources generated from this proposal, it is first necessary to deduct the expenses from the revenue for each year to form the yearly net cashflows. The emphasis is on cashflows as the cash represents an unambiguous command over resources. Accounting profits, however, are influenced by concepts and judgements. Secondly, it is necessary to derive the value today of the proposal as this forms the economist's idea of capital. This requires that net cashflows be reduced to their present values and summed. The first year's net cashflow will be multiplied by $1/(1.25)^1$, the second by $1/(1.25)^2$ and the third by $1/(1.25)^3$ to give factors of 0.8000, 0.6400 and 0.5120 respectively. The present value of these cashflows will equal £18,000 which, by coincidence, happens also to be the initial cost of the proposal.

At the end of year 1, the capital value of this income stream will be reduced because year 1's net cashflow will have been received and partly paid out as a dividend. It will therefore no longer form part of the future income stream. As partial compensation, the future amounts will have higher present values because the date when they will be realised is one year nearer. Similarly at the end of year 2, the capital value will be simply based on the single future net cashflow for year 3 while at the end of year 3, the future income stream will be nil and hence so will its present value. The capital values of the proposal at the end of year 0 (i.e. now), and at the end of the subsequent years are shown in Exhibit 6.6.

Exhibit 6.6 Year end values of wealth

	Present value end of year 0			Present value end of year 1			Present value end of year 2			Present value end of year 3		
NCF	Factor	PV	NCF	Factor	PV	NCF	Factor	PV	NCF	Factor	PV
£5,000	0.8000	£4,000	£9,375	0.8000	£7,500	£15,625	0.8000	£12,500	nil	nil	nil
£9,375	0.6400	£6,000	£15,625	0.6400	£10,000						
£15,625	0.5120	£8,000									
		£18,000			£17,500			£12,500			nil

Developing economic income

At the commencement of the business, the asset – made up of the present value of its future benefits in the form of cash – is worth £18,000. One year later, the cashflow for year 1 will have been realised and so the value of the asset will have fallen. Its present value of £17,500 will comprise the present value of the final two years of cashflows. This loss in the value of an asset arising from a decrease in future benefits is *economic depreciation*.

As in traditional historical cost accounting, this loss in value has to be made good before declaring a profit otherwise any distribution will partially include a return of capital. In other words, capital has to be maintained. Consequently economic income for year 1 will be the net cashflow of £5,000 less the economic depreciation of £500 and so the maximum dividend payable without reducing capital will be £4,500.

In year 2, the value of the asset will have fallen by a further £5,000 with the result that the net cashflow of year 2 has to be reduced by this amount to form the profit of £4,375. Finally, at the end of year 3 the asset will be worthless because no further benefits exist. Given an opening capital value for year 3 of £12,500 and a closing value of nil, economic depreciation will be £12,500. Deducting this from the net cashflow for year 3 of £15,625, the economic income or profit will be £3,125.

At the end of the three years, funds retained in the business to provide for depreciation will be £18,000, made up of £500 retained from year 1, £5,000 from year 2 and £12,500 from year 3, and so capital will have been maintained. The total income, however, will be rather more than the figures so far calculated as the assumption of the model is that there is but a single borrowing and lending rate. Given this, a rational organisation will invest any retentions to generate extra income in the form of interest received. The funds withheld at the end of year 1 to cover economic depreciation for that year will generate £500 × 25 per cent or £125 by the end of year 2 and so enable dividends to be increased by that amount. Similarly, at the beginning of year 3, the accumulated funds retained to cover depreciation will be £5,500, made up of the £500 from year 1 and the £5,000 from year 2. At 25 per cent p.a., this will generate interest of £1,375 by the end of year 3. Total dividends possible will therefore comprise the original operating profit plus any interest generated. The full implications of this are shown in Exhibit 6.7.

Exhibit 6.7 Ideal income

Year	Opening wealth	Closing wealth	Economic depreciation	Net cash-flow	Operating profit	Add interest	Net profit
1	£18,000	£17,500	£500	£5,000	£4,500	nil	£4,500
2	£17,500	£12,500	£5,000	£9,375	£4,375	£125	£4,500
3	£12,500	£0	£12,500	£15,625	£3,125	£1,375	£4,500

Economic income as interest

By including the interest received on the funds retained to cover economic depreciation, ideal income becomes a constant, in this case, £4,500 p.a. This is no more than a 25 per cent return in each and every year on the original £18,000 value. In that sense, ideal income is simply interest and so the firm can continue its existence into the indefinite future by investing its £18,000 year three cash balance at 25 per cent p.a. to produce profits of £4,500 in all subsequent years. Should it be necessary, these values can be recorded in the traditional format of a profit and loss account and balance sheet. The result is shown in Exhibit 6.8.

Exhibit 6.8 Ideal income final accounts

Income statement year:		1	2	3
Turnover		£8,000	£20,000	£30,000
Expenses		–£3,000	–£10,625	–£14,375
Economic depreciation		–£500	–£5,000	–£12,500
Operating profit		£4,500	£4,375	£3,125
Interest received		nil	£125	£1,375
Net income		£4,500	£4,500	£4,500
Less dividends		£4,500	£4,500	£4,500
Balance sheet end of year:	0	1	2	3
Fixed assets	£18,000	£18,000	£18,000	£18,000
Less depreciation	nil	£500	£5,500	£18,000
Net	£18,000	£17,500	£12,500	nil
Cash	nil	£500	£5,500	£18,000
	£18,000	£18,000	£18,000	£18,000
Financed by capital	£18,000	£18,000	£18,000	£18,000
	£18,000	£18,000	£18,000	£18,000

Ideal income and the conceptual framework

The search for a value-free and neutral conceptual framework has been shown to be an impossible dream. To produce financial reports involves the satisfying of one user group's needs in preference to others. The ideal income model, however, provides the one exception to this difficulty. In this economist's world, it will not matter how the accounting information is presented, as the model's major assumption is perfect knowledge available to all. Users will therefore be able to see through any distortions within the financial reports and replace the perceived distorted data with corrected data of their own. Problems such as accounting depreciation, stock values and the apportionment of contract profits to individual periods – all involving judgement – will no longer be issues. Secondly, given the assumptions of the ideal income model, the dividend needs of individual shareholders within the investor user group will be of no importance. Given the ability to borrow and lend funds at a single, market-determined rate of interest, shareholders can arrange their own preferences independent of the firm's dividend policy.

At its simplest, an investor preferring capital growth to dividends can merely take the dividends of earlier years and reinvest them at 25 per cent p.a. until such time as funds are required. Equally, an investor requiring funds prior to the receipt of a dividend can sell the rights to those dividends in the market at no penalty as the model assumes a single interest rate. Assume the firm in Example 6.3 is owned by a single investor and the investor requires additional funds at the end of year 2 over and above the £4,500 dividend receivable in that year. The right to the £4,500 dividend in year 3 can be sold in the market without difficulty. There will be no risk to the buyer because uncertainty about the future has been assumed not to exist. Given a market rate of interest of 25 per cent p.a., the £4,500 due at the end of year 3 can be exchanged for £3,600 at the end of year 2 as this amount is simply the present value of £4,500 receivable in one year's time at a 25 per cent discount rate, i.e. £4,500 × $1/(1.25)^1$.

EX ANTE AND EX POST ECONOMIC INCOME

Before discussing the validity of economic income, it is possible to develop the model a stage further and allow for the forecasting of cashflows to be less than ideal. This will involve the cashflow data being changed at some stage after the commencement of the investment to incorporate revised, originally unforeseen information. The implications of this will differ, depending on the time perspective taken.

One approach is to use the data available at the *beginning* of a period to calculate the income for the forthcoming period, the equivalent of planning or forecasting in traditional accounting. This is known as *ex ante income*. A second approach, known as *ex post income*, calculates income using data available at the *end* of a period and is analogous to the traditional historical cost profit and loss account produced for stewardship purposes. Ex post income therefore uses hindsight whereas ex ante income uses foresight.

In both cases, as a result of revising the cashflows part way through the project, the closing balance of wealth for one period will not automatically form the opening wealth for the next period. This difference arises from the need to revise the value of the wealth to incorporate the financial implications of the new information. Both the ex ante and ex post approach are developed in Example 6.4.

Example 6.4

Using the same data as in Example 6.3, assume that at the end of period 1/beginning of period 2 the forecast of net cashflows for year 3 changes to £16,000.

Ex ante income

Ex ante income measures income with information available at the beginning of the period. As the new information only becomes available at the end of year 1/beginning of year 2, it will not affect the measurement of ex ante income for year 1. Year 1's ex ante income will be identical to ideal income for that year. The opening balance for year 2, however, has to be amended to take account of the new information available at that stage and this will affect all subsequent yearly wealth calculations. From there on, the calculation of economic income is similar to the calculation of ideal income. Exhibit 6.9 shows the calculations of ex ante wealth.

Exhibit 6.9 Wealth values – ex ante income

Present value end of year 0			Present value end of year 1			Present value start of year 2			Present value end of year 2		
NCF	Factor	PV	NCF	Factor	PV	NCF	Factor	PV	NCF	Factor	PV
£5,000	0.8000	£4,000	£9,375	0.8000	£7,500	£9,375	0.8000	£7,500	£16,000	0.8000	£12,800
£9,375	0.6400	£6,000	£15,625	0.6400	£10,000	£16,000	0.6400	£10,240			
£15,625	0.5120	£8,000									
		£18,000			£17,500			£17,740			£12,800

The present value at the end of year 3 has been omitted as, given the question, it will be zero with no cashflows beyond that year. The opening and closing wealth values for year 1 are the same as for ideal income because ex ante income calculates wealth with information available at the beginning of the period and the revised expectation is not known at that stage. The information will be available though when calculating economic income for years 2 and 3. At the beginning of year 2, there is an increase in the value of the capital of £240. Effectively this is a capital gain although in the economic literature it has become known as a *windfall* gain. Before discussing the treatment of this windfall gain, it is useful to compare the figures of wealth using the ex post approach.

Ex post income

Using an ex post approach, economic income is calculated using information available at the end of a period. Consequently, the change in circumstances will be recognised one year earlier and the net cashflows used for the year will be the actual ones received rather than those forecast. The implication of this is shown in Exhibit 6.10.

Exhibit 6.10 Wealth values – ex post income

Present value end of year 0			Present value end of year 1			Present value end of year 2			Present value end of year 3		
NCF	Factor	PV	NCF	Factor	PV	NCF	Factor	PV	NCF	Factor	PV
£5,000	0.8000	£4,000	£9,375	0.8000	£7,500	£16,000	0.8000	£12,800	nil	nil	nil
£9,375	0.6400	£6,000	£16,000	0.6400	£10,240						
£16,000	0.5120	£8,192									
		£18,192			£17,740			£12,800			nil

The assumption of ex post income brings the capital gain forward one period to £192 at the beginning of year 1. Effectively this shows the same capital gain as the ex ante wealth measures as a gain of £192 at the beginning of year 1 grows to £240 by the beginning of year 2 at 25 per cent interest per annum.

Windfall gains and losses

A significant issue for accounting is how to treat windfall gains and losses. If a rigorous and unambiguous value-free treatment can be developed within this model, there are likely to be implications for the reporting of historical cost profits. The issues are similar whether considering ex ante or ex post income. To avoid partial repetition therefore, only ex post income will be considered. Using ex post measures, the cashflow will be the actual cashflow of the year and the closing wealth will be the most up-to-date available information at that time. The difficulty lies in determining the opening balance. Should it be the original value or the revised value, to give what Bromwich[10] calls *ex post income I* and *ex post income II*? Put another way, the central issue is whether any capital gain should be included with profit and, equally, whether any capital loss should first be made good before declaring a profit – an issue of equal importance in determining traditional accounting income.

Assuming all windfall gains are available for distribution and all windfall losses have first to be made good, i.e. the ex post income I concept, income for year 1 will be £4,740. This is made up of the net cashflow of £5,000 less economic depreciation of £260. (Economic depreciation is the difference between the opening wealth before the revised information of £18,000 and the ex post wealth of £17,740 at the year end.) The alternative approach – ex post income II – produces economic income of £4,548 made up of the same net cashflow of £5,000 and the same year end wealth of £17,740 but with the opening wealth valued at the ex post revised figure of £18,192. Choosing between the income values is of much more than academic interest. It will give guidance as to whether companies in the real world should include capital gains and losses in their reported profits.

Analysing windfalls

Probably the easiest way forward is to recognise that the capital gain has occurred because of a failure to forecast with total accuracy. Had the new information been available from the beginning, a revised ideal income could have been calculated for each year. With perfect foresight, it would have been recognised from the beginning that the income for year 3 would have been £16,000. This then provides a standard or ideal against which to measure the two ex post income statements. The wealth values for this revised ideal income, comprising cashflows of £5,000, £9,375 and £16,000 in years 1 to 3, will be identical to those shown in Exhibit 6.10. The resulting ideal economic income for each year is shown in Exhibit 6.11 where interest has been calculated as before at 25 per cent p.a. on the accumulated economic depreciation.

Exhibit 6.11 Revised ideal income

Year	Opening wealth	Closing wealth	Economic depreciation	Net cash-flow	Operating profit	Add interest	Net profit
1	£18,192	£17,740	£452	£5,000	£4,548	nil	£4,548
2	£17,740	£12,800	£4,940	£9,375	£4,435	£113	£4,548
3	£12,800	£0	£12,800	£16,000	£3,200	£1,348	£4,548

This analysis suggests that recognising capital gains as profits overstates income in the year of recognition and what should be recognised is the enhanced income in all future years flowing from the capital gain. The suggestion therefore is that ex post income II is a more appropriate measure. In fact, within the model, distributing the capital gain as profit would not affect shareholders because of the assumption of perfect certainty. With this quality, they would be able to see through the overstated profits of ex post income I and invest part of the dividends to give the income stream in Exhibit 6.11. Of more importance is the implications for real-world measures of income. Without the assumption of perfect certainty, distributing capital gains (or fully making good capital losses) may provide investors with a distorted measure of income when viewed on a yearly basis.

Not recognising capital gains as income nor fully making good capital losses is consistent with observed behaviour. Consider, a family winning £1 million in a lottery and assume their normal after-tax income from employment is £30,000 per annum. Common sense suggests they are unlikely to view income in the year of the win as £1,030,000 and in subsequent years as £30,000. More likely they will perceive the win as enhancing their income in all future years – in other words recognising the interest as the income rather than the initial amount. Similarly, a household faced with a sudden need to carry out an unforeseen structural fault to their home at a cost of £50,000 are unlikely to view that as a deduction from the household income in that year. Rather, they are likely to obtain a loan which effectively reduces their ability to consume in future years.

There is a second argument. In the real world of risk and uncertainty, investors will recognise risks attached to an investment and demand a higher return as compensation. Capital losses are in that sense expected and so making good the loss before recognising income would be double counting.

CRITICISMS OF ECONOMIC INCOME

A clear advantage of economic income is its close association with human behaviour. Assets are valued by individuals and corporations because of the future benefits attached to them. A second advantage of economic income is that it provides a framework and insight into the treatment of capital gains and losses, a not inconsiderable factor in the real world. There are, however, severe difficulties with the model when it is related to the real world.

Lifting the assumptions

The real world is full of technical imperfections and uncertainties. Borrowing rates are higher than lending rates and taxes exist. Investors cannot simply borrow forward to satisfy any need for earlier cashflows without incurring these extra costs. Under these circumstances therefore, economic income is no longer value free. The timing of dividends becomes important and the desire for these will vary from individual to individual. Worse, in the real world future benefits are uncertain and so lending institutions such as banks may not be prepared to provide funds simply on the security of future beliefs.

Applied to the real world, economic income is essentially subjective. It centres on figures which exist only as beliefs in the decision maker's mind and with its emphasis on future cashflows for calculating economic depreciation, even ex post profit becomes an amalgam of current and future data. Effectively, economic income is merely interest. Unlike accounting income which builds from an existing capital base and matches revenues against expenses, economic income incorporates gains in the form of cashflows as soon as they are known – even though they may not happen for several periods. In other words, economic income is determined not by production and selling but at least partly by the accrual of information about the future. And this concern with the value of future information means that realised and unrealised capital gains and losses are not differentiated. In Example 6.4 for instance, the capital gain is recognised prior to its realisation by both the ex ante and ex post measures.

Inability to monitor performance

Because of this concern with future values, economic income cannot be audited in any meaningful sense and, consequently, it is unable to fulfil the stewardship role of accounting. And given that accounting is concerned with aiding decision making and evaluating past decisions, a measure of profit based on the assumption that decisions have already been *made* is unlikely to be appropriate. This inability to monitor the recent past because of its emphasis on the future severely limits the role of economic income.

It views the need for company liquidity as a detail. Lack of funds is not a major problem as, given the assumptions, borrowing or lending is possible on the basis of the assumed perfect knowledge. Similarly, it is silent about the efficiencies and inefficiencies of management. To the extent that managers are considered at all, they will simply be reflected as part of future expenses. Again, this is inevitable given the assumption of perfect knowledge which restricts their role to a mechanistic one of bringing production to the market-place without any need for judgement or discretion.

Balance sheet values

In a similar way, the value of individual assets are of little importance. The value of the business is dependent simply on its future income stream and its discount rate. This cashflow results from the bringing together of several assets with the skills of the workforce and the entrepreneurial abilities of the managers in making sales. As a result, identifying cashflows and hence economic value with individual assets is impossible except under the simplest of scenarios. Consequently any balance sheet values based on economic income can change as a result of changes in future prospects or discount rates rather than because of changes in the asset values supporting that income.

Given the model's assumption of perfect knowledge, the need for fall-back values of individual assets to protect creditors is a total irrelevance. With perfect knowledge there is no risk and so there is no need to be concerned with the security of creditors.

This contamination of economic income with the future severely limits its usefulness as a way of determining prudent behaviour for deriving income. Before leaving the subject, however, it is worth remembering that incorporating views about the future in measures of income is not a criticism of economic income alone. In historical cost financial reporting the future also plays a major role, in determining depreciation, valuing stocks and apportioning profits, whenever the life of the trading activity is longer than the accounting period. And underpinning all values in financial accounting is the assumption of 'going concern', the belief that the business has a life into the indefinite future.

THE SPECTRUM OF INCOME MEASURES

Traditional historical cost accounting and economic income based on future values are two extremes of the same spectrum. Both are concerned with the measurement and valuation of income and the maintenance of capital. Historical cost accounting is backward looking and predominantly concerned with *input* or *entry* values – how much an asset or benefit originally cost. Economic income, however, emphasises future *output* or *exit* values, the (market) worth of assets or benefits based on prospective cashflows.

In terms of the primary qualities identified by the conceptual framework project, there is little doubt that economic income is high on relevance. Equally there is little doubt it is low on the other primary quality of reliability because of the essential subjectivity of economic wealth. Historical cost accounting tends to be the reverse of this although the reliability argument based on transactions can be overstated especially when items such as depreciation and stock valuation are considered.

The issues

At the heart of the debate on income measurement are those fundamental issues: what is to be measured, how is it to be valued and what capital is to be maintained. Historical cost accounting measures past transactions valued in the main at past purchase costs and with the emphasis on maintaining the owners' money capital. Its firm foundation, based on transactions, is its greatest strength but at times it can result in misleading information. This is particularly so when prices are changing. Two identical assets purchased at different times at different prices will simply be aggregated for balance sheet purposes. At the time of sale, the lower cost asset will appear to show a greater profit even though much of this might simply be due to inflation rather than entrepreneurial activity.

There is a more serious conceptual difficulty. Depreciation has been shown to be an allocation of cost. Over the life of a fixed asset, its total cost should be charged against revenues to avoid the overstating of profits. Effectively, this ensures sufficient resources (although not necessarily cash) are retained in the organisation to cover the original cost and hence maintain capital. In times of rising prices though, this is unlikely to be sufficient to provide for the asset's replacement. For the medieval merchants undertaking a joint venture, this would not have mattered. The accounting system would have fulfilled their needs by unambiguously determining the profits available for distribution at the end of the venture. Most modern businesses are not formed merely for a limited period with a limited objective. They are assumed to be going concerns with a continuing indefinite existence. But to have a continuing existence at the same level of operations requires assets to be replaced as they are used up in the production process.

Given that profit indicates the maximum amount which can be consumed without impoverishing the business, traditional accounting will not provide sufficient resources in the form of the accumulated depreciation provision to maintain operations when prices are rising. Profits will effectively be overstated. Under such circumstances, the application of traditional accounting is inconsistent with its fundamental assumption of going concern.

Despite this, historical cost accounting may still have a role to play in the modern world. Its stewardship role must not be understated. In addition it does clearly record the legal rights and obligations created by the underlying transactions. Amounts owed, for example, are clearly stated. Nevertheless it often provides misleading information for decision makers because of its adherence to historical cost.

Current values

The fact is many users believe that accounts show current values. That this is based on their ignorance of traditional accounting concepts is immaterial *if* it is accepted – as all attempts to develop a conceptual framework have suggested – that accounting should be concerned with fulfilling user needs. If users believe that accounts show current values, and on the assumption that current values would help decision makers, then current values *should* be provided. Any resulting accounting system would still be transaction based but with the use of current rather than historical costs.

There are two forms of current values dependent on whether buying or selling prices are considered. *Replacement cost accounting* emphasises input or entry values, the cost of purchasing a replacement asset at the time of the financial report. *Realisable value accounting* is concerned with output or exit prices, the disposal value of an asset. Neither system depends on inflation for its justification as even without general inflation there can be changes in buying and selling prices which reflect changes in market conditions.

Both systems accept the impossibility of measuring future net cashflows and the impossibility of associating net cashflows with individual assets. Instead they concentrate on valuing the individual assets as a measure of their future worth. Given that an asset will generally be worth more the greater the financial benefits it is likely to generate, current values can be viewed as a surrogate for the present value of cashflows found in economic income. Indeed, in the economist's perfectly competitive world, entry and exit current values would not only equal one another, they would also equal the present value of the future benefits generated from holding those assets.

REPLACEMENT COST ACCOUNTING

All accounting systems are concerned with the maintenance of capital prior to declaring a profit. Where they differ is in how that capital is defined, measured and valued. Hicks defined profit as the most which can be consumed while remaining as well off at the end of a period as at the beginning. With replacement cost accounting, this 'well-offness' is measured in terms of the physical or operating capacity of the firm and not the money values or present values of traditional accounting or economic income.

If a firm has the capacity to produce 400 units over each of the next four years, then only if it still has that same capacity at the end of its first year can it be said to have made a profit. Anything less and capital or 'well-offness' will not have been maintained. If capacity at the end of the first year is limited to only producing 400 units annually over the following *three* years then some capital has been consumed and this has to be made good before a profit can be declared.

Replacement cost profits

Replacement cost accounting requires a firm to be in a position to replace assets consumed before a profit can be declared. In that sense it is making operational the 'going concern' concept of traditional accounting by only declaring a profit after sufficient resources have been set aside to ensure continuity at the existing level of operations. To demonstrate this, consider Example 6.5.

Example 6.5

A sole trader starts business with a fixed asset costing £2,000 with a one-year life and 200 units of stock costing £100 each. By the end of the year these are all sold for cash for £150 each. By then the replacement cost of the stock is £120 each and the fixed asset £3,000.

At the end of the year, the £22,000 of assets comprising the stock of £20,000 and the fixed asset of £2,000 will have transformed themselves into the single asset of cash of £30,000 because the fixed asset has a life of only one year. This increase in assets will then be reflected in an increase in obligations by the business to the owner, in other words, a historical cost profit of £8,000. Withdrawing this profit from the business will reduce the owner's funds to £22,000, the original amount, and so capital in money terms will have been maintained.

However, withdrawing the historical cost profit of £8,000 from the business would leave insufficient resources to fully replace the assets. To start the second year with the same physical level of assets requires the acquisition of a new fixed asset costing £3,000 and 100 units of stock costing £24,000. £27,000 therefore needs to be retained in the business for it to be capable of being in the same physical position as at the beginning of the year. Effectively the £8,000 historical cost profit needs to be reduced by providing for extra resources of £5,000 to replace assets, making the replacement cost profit £3,000.

Holding gains

Had the owner not traded in the year, the closing balance sheet would have shown the same physical assets as at the beginning of the year. Using replacement costs, these would have been valued at £27,000. With an opening value of £22,000, the trader would have effectively made a profit of £5,000 simply from holding the assets. Because of this, the £5,000 resulting from changing prices is referred to as a *holding gain*. Technically this £5,000 is retained to provide for the replacement of assets.

It is an essential provision if the business wishes to continue operating. It is a provision unavailable for distribution, similar to the provision for bad debts or the provision for depreciation, although with one significant difference. A provision for bad debts will, if accurately estimated, be associated with a real and permanent loss of resources should the actual debtors fail to pay. The £5,000, however, will only need to be retained in the business while trading continues. Should the business cease trading, this amount will be returnable to the owner along with the original capital subscribed and any profits retained within the business. Looked at in that way, the £5,000 becomes an appropriation of the retained historical cost profit, in other words a reserve similar to the general and other reserves discussed in Chapter 3.

To record this, the profit will be reduced by the £5,000 and a replacement reserve for an identical amount created. This is how it is treated in Exhibit 6.12 where the historical cost final accounts are shown along with the resulting replacement cost accounts.

Exhibit 6.12 Historical cost and replacement cost profit

Historical cost final accounts		Replacement cost final accounts	
Sales	£30,000	Sales	£30,000
Cost of sales	£20,000	Historical cost of sales	£20,000
Gross profit	£10,000	Gross profit	£10,000
Depreciation	£2,000	Depreciation	£2,000
Net Profit	£8,000	Historical cost profit	£8,000
		Replacement cost reserve	£5,000
		Operating profit	£3,000
Assets:		Assets:	
Cash	£30,000	Cash	£30,000
	£30,000		£30,000
Financed by:		Financed by:	
Owner's capital	£22,000	Owner's capital	£22,000
Profits	£8,000	Operating profit	£3,000
Owner's funds	£30,000	Replacement cost reserve	£5,000
		Owner's funds	£30,000

Replacement cost accounting and long term debt

Example 6.5 has concentrated on what to measure and how it should be valued. Without long term debt in the business, it did not have to differentiate between the proprietorial and entity concepts of capital. In an all-equity business they are one and the same. Allowing a business to have long term debt produces an interesting result using replacement cost accounting. Consider again Example 6.5 but instead of the business being totally equity financed, assume it is 50 per cent financed by a loan. For simplicity, the loan can be assumed to be interest free. The revised capital structure at the beginning of the first year will now be £11,000 of owner's funds and £11,000 of long term debt while the closing historical cost balance sheet will show the business being financed by the original capital of £11,000, the loan of £11,000 and retained profits of £8,000. Of this £8,000, only £3,000 is available for distribution and currently the replacement reserve is being totally financed by the owner.

Once more it is worthwhile remembering the idea of income developed by Hicks and developing his concept of 'well-offness' a little. Put another way, income is the maximum amount which can be distributed while leaving the business in the same position at the end of a period as at the beginning. The position of the business at the beginning of the period was not just that it had one fixed asset and 200 units of stock but that these were financed 50 per cent by debt. The partial financing of a business by borrowing is known as gearing and the greater the proportion of debt finance, the greater the gearing.

To reproduce the identical scenario at the end of the period therefore requires not only an identical array of assets but also identical gearing. Anything less and it cannot be argued that the situations are the same. Accepting this, the £27,000 replacement cost of assets should continue to be financed by 50 per cent debt. This will involve borrowing an additional £2,500 to make the total borrowings £13,500. In other words, part of the extra cost of replacement will be borne by additional debt, reducing the amount required to be financed by equity. With £13,500 being financed by debt, only £13,500 needs to be financed by equity and so the replacement cost reserve can be reduced by the £2,500 financed by the extra debt. The result is a replacement cost operating profit available for distribution of £5,500.

Replacement cost accounting – a worked example

In replacement cost accounting, there are three major adjustments: the gearing adjustment where the business is partly financed by debt, the adjustment to the fixed assets and the adjustment to the stocks. Taking account of these three areas will substantially ensure an entity can continue into the future and profits will not be overstated. The effect on fixed assets and stocks is brought out in Example 6.6.

Example 6.6

A company started business with fixed assets of £200,000, 1,000 units of stock at a unit cost of £100 and cash of £50,000 financed by 350,000 £1 ordinary shares. Depreciation is to be calculated using the straight line method on the assumption that the asset has a life of 10 years and a zero residual value.

During its first year of operations it sells 900 units of stock for cash at a price of £160 per unit. The unit replacement cost of the stock at the end of the year is £120 and the replacement cost of a new machine is £240,000. At the beginning of the second year, 1,000 units of stock were purchased for cash at a unit price of £120. Their replacement price at the year end was £140 and the replacement cost of a new machine at that stage was £300,000. 800 units were sold during the year for cash at a selling price of £200.

Exhibit 6.13 shows the recording of these transactions using both historical cost and replacement cost assumptions. Items making up the profit and loss account are once again shown in bold type.

Exhibit 6.13 Historical and replacement cost accounting

Historical Cost Accounting

(£000s)	Balance sheet 0	Recording year 1			Balance sheet 1	Recording year 2				Balance sheet 2
Fixed asset	200				+200					+200
Depreciation				-20	-20				-20	-40
Net book value					+180					+160
Stock	100		-90		+10	+120		-94		+36
Cash	50	+144			+194	-120	+160			+234
	350				384					430
Capital	350				-350					-350
Year 1 profit		-144	+90	+20	-34					-34
Year 2 profit							-160	+94	+20	-46
	350				384					430

Replacement Cost Accounting

(£000s)	Balance sheet 0	Recording year 1			Balance sheet 1	Recording year 2				Balance sheet 2
Fixed asset	+200		+40		+240		+60			+300
Depreciation				-24	-24			-30	-6	-60
Net book value					+216					+240
Stock	+100		+20	-108	+12	+120	+22	-112		+42
Cash	+50	+144			+194	-120	+160			+234
	350				422					516
Capital	-350				-350					-350
RCA reserve		-40	-20		-60		-22	-60	+6	-136
Year 1 profit		-144	+108	+24	-12					-12
Year 2 profit							-160	+112	+30	-18
	350				422					516

The historical cost accounts

The first year's historical cost income statement comprises the 900 units sold for £144,000 less their original cost of £100 per unit to give a cost of sales of £900,000. The only other expense is the depreciation charge of £20,000 based on the ten-year assumed life of the asset. The balance sheet at the end of that year shows the fixed asset at its original cost less depreciation to give a net book value of £180,000, the stock at cost (100 units multiplied by £100) and the cash balance of £194,000. Whether using historical cost or replacement cost accounting (RCA), the initial transactions are recorded in an identical. Before producing the RCA profit and loss account though it is necessary to recognise the replacement values of assets.

The replacement cost accounts

The fixed asset has a replacement cost of £240,000 at the end of the first year and so its value in the RC accounts is increased to reflect this change. Following the normal convention that any gains in a business belong to the owners, the corresponding entry is as a charge to the replacement cost reserve. Although not available as a distribution if the business wishes to continue its existing level of operations, the replacement cost reserve has been shown to be available for distribution on a liquidation and hence, ultimately, it is part of shareholders' funds. Secondly, the replacement cost of the stock held at the beginning has increased to £120,000. To show the replacement cost in the accounts therefore requires the stock being increased by £20,000 and the replacement cost reserve also being increased by this amount. Had there been any expenses such as wages and rents during the year, no adjustment would have been necessary. Even in the RC accounts, they would have appeared simply at their original monetary value because they are only expenses and do not appear as assets within the capital to be maintained.

To complete the profit and loss account, 900 units of stock were sold out of the original 1,000 units and so 900/1000 of the £120,000 of stock must be charged to the income statement. Similarly with the depreciation charge, with a ten-year life and straight line depreciation, one-tenth of the replacement cost is charged to the profit and loss account for year 1. In fact this treatment is theoretically incorrect. As has already been shown, straight line depreciation does not attempt to reflect loss of value but merely an (arbitrary?) allocation of cost. Ideally depreciation should have been based on the difference between the £240,000 replacement cost of a new asset and the current cost of acquiring a one-year-old asset – the meaning given to depreciation in ordinary speech. As will be seen below, this is often difficult if not impossible to calculate for specific commercial assets with a limited market and so the less pure treatment can be justified. It will after all provide fully for the asset's replacement at the end of its life and that presumably is the major objective.

The calculation of year 2's profits follow an identical logic to that for year 1. The historical cost income statement has valued stock on a first in, first out basis. Given a sales volume of 800 units, the cost of sales will be made up of the original 100 units remaining from year 1 plus 700 of the 1,000 units purchased in year 2. The cost of sales will therefore be £94,000 comprising the opening stock value of £10,000 plus 700/1,000 of the £120,000 of purchases, a total of £84,000.

Asset values

For replacement cost purposes, the cost of the fixed asset has now risen to £300,000 and so its RC value in the accounts has increased by £60,000. Similarly with stock: the total stock at the beginning of the year was 1,100 units including the 1,000 units purchased at the beginning of the year. With a year end unit replacement cost of £140, their RC value will be £154,000 which represents an increase over book values of £22,000. From the 1,100 units of stock, 800 were sold and so the replacement cost of sales is £112,000.

Back-log depreciation

With a ten-year life, the depreciation charge for year 2 will be £30,000 representing the consumption of one-tenth of the fixed asset's current replacement cost of £300,000. Given the data in the question, this is perfectly accurate within the confines of straight line depreciation. There is, however, a problem when it comes to showing the value of the asset in the balance sheet. The balance sheet will accurately show a fixed asset with a replacement cost of £300,000. With only eight of its ten years' life remaining, its net book value should be £240,000. The total depreciation accumulated from the two years of trading though only totals £54,000. Effectively, the depreciation for the first year has been undercharged.

Had it been known that the ultimate replacement cost was going to be £300,000, £30,000 depreciation would have been charged to year 1 rather than only £24,000. The provision of this extra depreciation is known as *back-log depreciation*. The problem is identical to the problem of all accruals. Estimates will rarely be accurate. The normal treatment would therefore be to correct this error by charging the amount of the mis-estimation against the current year's income. Despite this, it is generally recommended that the back-log depreciation should be effected via the replacement cost reserve rather than the profit and loss account balance and this is the way it has been shown in Exhibit 6.13.

Such treatment is justified on the basis that the increase in the replacement cost has increased the replacement cost reserve and the back-log depreciation is merely a consequence of this. In practice it does not greatly matter which treatment is adopted provided sufficient profits are retained within the business. The underprovision has been corrected. However, by charging the back-log depreciation against the replacement cost reserve, there would not be sufficient resources within the entity to fully provide for its eventual replacement if all retentions were to be distributed.

REPLACEMENT COST ACCOUNTING – AN EVALUATION

The separation of holding gains and losses

Replacement cost accounting, by separating holding gains from operating gains, not only gives a more meaningful definition of profit for organisations with a continuing existence, it also results in a more meaningful balance sheet with assets shown at current values. The £46,000 historical cost profit of year 2, for example, is made up of a true operating profit of £18,000 plus realised holding gains resulting from the £10,000 underprovision of depreciation and £18,000 from the stock consumed. Breaking historical cost profit down in this way enables shareholders to evaluate dividend proposals amongst other items while the use of current values in the balance sheet gives a better guide to the future than original costs. Equally important it reduces the need for certain judgements such as choosing between LIFO and FIFO for stock purposes and, in theory, eliminates the need to choose the bases for depreciation – although the solution to Example 6.6 showed the limits to this. For many observers, the major advantage of replacement cost accounting is in its adherence to historical cost transactions for recording data. This maintains the integrity of legal rights and obligations. In that sense it can be viewed as an evolution of traditional accounting rather than an alternative. Equally, by differentiating between operating gains and holding gains, it gives full force to the concept of prudence.

Holding gains and distributable profit

The treatment of holding gains, however, is not without controversy. For year 2, there was a holding gain of £22,000 from stock. To the extent that part of this stock has been sold, £18,000 of that amount is a realised holding gain with the balance an unrealised holding gain represented by the unsold closing stock of 200 units multiplied by the £20 increase in their replacement cost. Two early proponents of replacement cost accounting[11] suggested that all gains, both operating and holding, should be included in the profit figure irrespective of whether realised or not. Presumably the logic for this is that by distributing all gains, the shareholders could then decide whether to reinvest those same distributions back into the company and allow it to continue.

Such an empowerment of the owners sounds fine but in the real world there are practical difficulties with such an approach. Taxes exist on dividends preventing such simple symmetry. Secondly, how much an asset will realise on a liquidation is not necessarily related to its replacement cost as will be demonstrated below. The reality is that there is a hierarchy of distributions possible under replacement cost accounting. Operating profits can clearly be distributed without impoverishing the firm, although even some of these may need to be kept back if the firm plans to grow without raising additional external finance. Below this are realised gains which are represented by additional resources within the firm, generally as a result of sales. Historical cost accounting makes these available for distribution by default in the traditional profit figure, by only calculating the cost of sales at the stock's original cost and depreciation at original cost.

Distributing these realised gains and then returning to shareholders at a later date for extra funds to continue the business when assets need to be replaced might be viewed as giving more choice to the shareholders – although institutional difficulties in the real world such as taxes might make this less than ideal. The real objection to distributing holding gains is when they are unrealised. Traditional accounting avoids this by emphasising the realisation concept, that is by bringing in these capital gains only when an asset is sold. Prudence therefore makes the suggestion that unrealised gains should be distributed a suspect proposal.

The measurement and meaning of replacement cost

A further difficulty with replacement cost accounting is its alleged subjectivity in determining replacement values. Certainly this can pose difficulties. Ideally, replacement cost and depreciation should be calculated by reference to market values. This presupposes market information is obtainable which is not necessarily the case for highly specific industrial plant and equipment. Even where traded, there might still be difficulties because of different prices for different quantities, though having said that, the same difficulty applies equally to balance sheet values using historical costs. Approximations to replacement cost, however, can be determined by reference to suppliers lists and governmental and other statistical indices. And even if this does not provide for the calculation of market driven depreciation, the traditional methods such as straight line depreciation will ensure sufficient resources are retained in the business to enable continuity without the requirement for additional outside financing. That replacement costs can be relatively easily approximated is evidenced by many of the privatised UK utilities which, having used replacement costs while in the public sector, continue to use them despite having very specific, non-marketable assets.

Where difficulties do exist is if an asset is not going to be replaced or where a replacement is no longer available because of obsolescence or other technological change. If the asset is not going to be replaced because the firm is moving out of a particular industry, then replacement costs are irrelevant and replacement cost accounting is no longer appropriate for prudently measuring profit. A greater difficulty occurs when there is technological change.

Guidance can be found by going back to basics and remembering that replacement cost 'well-offness' is concerned with having the same operating capacity at the end of a period as at the beginning. If an existing asset is capable of producing, say, 30,000 units per annum and it is replaced by a machine capable of 60,000 units each year at the same cost, then it might be appropriate to take as the replacement cost half of the price of the new machine. Taking its full price might be inappropriate as it gives the firm a higher production capability than with the existing machine at the beginning of the period. Adjustments to the resulting figure may be necessary if the new machine also provides cost savings. These will be based on the value today of the future cost savings using an approach similar to that for finding the value of a future income stream when discussing economic income.

REALISABLE VALUE ACCOUNTING

There is another way of looking at current values known as *realisable value accounting*. Instead of considering the *entry* values of replacement cost accounting, *exit* values are used. There is a simple logic to this for users: most people, if asked to value their assets, would estimate how much their assets could be sold for and use this as their answer. In other words, they would measure their capital or wealth using current exit values or selling prices.

This begs the question as to the form of selling prices. It is unlikely to be the price agreed on a forced sale. More likely it is the price achievable in the normal course of events. Such a price is measuring the next best alternative to the holding of the assets. Given a motorist owns a car, there are a variety of options available. The car could be given away or sold. If those are the only choices open to the motorist then the next best alternative to keeping the car is to sell it for the best possible price. By keeping the car, the motorist is being denied the use of the cash available on a sale. In terms of economics, the opportunity cost of keeping the car – the real cost to the motorist – is the foregoing of the benefits derivable from the cash. Put crudely, the real value of an asset is what it can be sold for, not how much it cost. To see the implications of this, consider Example 6.7.

Example 6.7

> Using the data from Example 6.6, assume that at the end of the first year the stock could be sold for its current market price of £160 and the asset could be sold for £170,000, while at the end of the second year the selling price of the stock remains at £200 but that the asset can only be sold for £150,000.

Determining expenses

In the normal course of events the closing stock at the end of year 1 will be sold for £160 per unit. That they were actually sold for £200 would not have been known at the end of the first year. The realisable value will therefore be £16,000. With this figure as the closing stock and original purchases of £100,000, the cost of sales will be £84,000. The only other expense is depreciation. Given that the fixed asset can be sold for £170,000 the real- isable value depreciation will be £30,000. Had there been any other expenses such as wages or rent, the cash value would have simply been charged to the profit and loss account, although had there been prepayments, logically these should also have been reported at their realisable value. The calculation of year 2's realisable value income state- ment follows the identical logic to that of year 1 and both years' final accounts are shown in Exhibit 6.14.

Exhibit 6.14 Realisable value accounting

(£000)	Balance sheet 0	Recording year 1	Balance sheet 1	Recording year 2	Balance sheet 2
Fixed asset	200		+200		+200
Depreciation		−30	−30	−20	−50
Net book value			+170		+150
Stock	100	−84	+16	+120 −76	+60
Cash	50	+144	+194	−120 +160	+234
	350		380		444
Capital	−350		−350		−350
Year 1 profit		−144 +84 +30	−30		−30
Year 2 profit				−160 +76 +20	−64
	350		380		444

As can be seen from Exhibit 6.14, the basis for realisable value accounting is still the transaction and so it shares that aspect of objectivity with both historical cost and replace- ment cost accounting.

The treatment of holding gains

The realisable value profit figure will not only have a different valuation base to other methods of accounting, it will also have a different composition. Replacement cost account- ing in its pure form excludes all holding gains and losses, emphasising instead operat- ing income based on the concept of realisation. Historical cost, without making it explicit, automatically brings in realised holding gains and losses by only charging historical cost of sales against turnover. (Showing a total lack of symmetry, it will show unrealised hold- ing losses where, for example, the cost of stock is greater than its realisable value.) Realisable value accounting, however, by valuing assets at their exit prices, incorporates both unrealised and realised holding gains and losses.

REALISABLE VALUE ACCOUNTING – AN EVALUATION

If user needs are important – and if this is interpreted as actually providing what users *think* accounting information shows – then there is a strong case for realisable value accounting. Confusion exists in the minds of users when a company forced to cease trading is unable to realise the historical cost values in its balance sheet. Realisable values overcome this. Creditors, for example, are not only concerned with the ability of a firm to pay its debts but also in their security should it meet trading difficulties.

Investor decisions

More than that, realisable values provide shareholders with information to make an informed choice. By showing the current cash value of the assets, investors can decide whether there are better opportunities elsewhere. For example, if a business is able to generate annual profits of £10,000 from assets with a realisable value of £200,000, this 5 per cent return can be compared with returns available elsewhere on those £200,000 of funds. By constantly evaluating the business in those terms, investors are able to make informed choices as to whether the business *should* continue in its present form. Replacement cost accounting by comparison ignores this choice by starting from the premise that existing operations are to continue.

Realisable values and economic income

As with replacement cost accounting, using realisable values overcomes problems of stock valuation and the estimation of depreciation which haunt traditional accounting. There is a final advantage of realisable values. In general, the greater the future benefits, the greater the realisable value. In the sense that realisable values are based on future expectations, they might be a close approximation to the present value wealth calculations of economic income.

Limitations of realisable values

Many of the arguments in favour of realisable values are based on the disposal value of the assets. This in turn, however, limits the usefulness of the technique for income measurement purposes. Despite what has been said, there may well be a high degree of subjectivity in the estimation of realisable values especially where there is only a narrow market.

With specialised assets, their realisable value will effectively be their scrap value. Consider, for example, the building of a railway siding to transport bulky goods from a factory. This will only have value as a siding to the existing owner's current operations. To anyone else, its worth – its realisable value – will be extremely low. Its value to the owners, however, based on the discounted present value of its future benefits, might be extremely high if it saves the business other transport costs.

Perhaps the strongest argument against realisable values though is its denial of the going concern assumption. Paying out realisable value profits will include both realised and unrealised holding gains, not only anticipating income but also, in the long term, preventing a business from continuing its existing level of operations. As soon as it is accepted that the business is a going concern, the realisable values will have far less meaning as most businesses hold assets to use, not to sell.

SUMMARY

This chapter has been about user needs. Viewing accounting as a system demonstrated how, in modern, complex organisations, the needs of owners would not automatically be met. The role of theory was then discussed and from the normative approach developed the idea of a conceptual framework. From this, a range of users were identified but what became clear is that producers of financial reports have to choose between the, at times, conflicting needs of user groups. In that sense, accounting cannot be value free except under the most limited of conditions within economic income.

The notion of economic income met one of the major qualities identified in conceptual frameworks namely relevance. This is where traditional historical cost accounting is at its weakest. The subjective nature of economic income, however, has caused it to be rejected as a practical measure of financial reporting. Of equal concern was the assumption in economic income that decisions about the future had already been made. This limited the role of accounting to the evaluation and presentation of information whereas most observers would view accounting as being an aid to making those decisions.

A way of merging the best of economic income and historical cost income was found in current value accounting. Two approaches were developed: replacement cost accounting based on current entry values and realisable value accounting based on current exit values. With different emphases and perspectives, it is less a case of choosing which is the 'correct' approach and more an awareness that both can be of use in different circumstances. In a later chapter a third approach will be developed when considering how to account for inflation. Before considering further models, however, it is useful to consider how governments and other regulatory bodies have influenced accounting systems. That is the subject of Chapter 7.

REFERENCES

1 Davis, G. B. and Olson, M. H. (1985) *Management Information Systems*, p. 270, McGraw-Hill.
2 Hendriksen, E. S. (1992) Accounting Theory, 5th edn, p. 1, Irwin.
3 Financial Accounting Standards Board (1978) *Statement of Financial Accounting Concepts No. 1*, 'Objectives of financial reporting by business enterprises', para. 28.
4 ASB draft Chapter 2 paragraph 38.
5 *Management Accounting*, November 1991.
6 ASB draft Chapter 5 paragraph 61.
7 Bromwich, M. (1991) *Financial Reporting, Information and Capital Markets*, p. 294, Pitman.
8 Fisher, I. (1919) *Elementary Principles of Economics*.
9 Hicks, J. R. (1946) *Value and Capital*, 2nd edn, p. 172, Oxford University Press.
10 Bromwich, op. cit., pp. 58–9.
11 Edwards, E. and Bell, P. (1961) *The Theory and Measurement of Business Income*, University of California Press.

FURTHER READING

Accounting Standards Board (1994), *Draft Statement of Principles*.

Belkaoui A. R. (1992) *Accounting Theory*, 3rd edn, Academic Press.

Bromwich, M. (1991) *Financial Reporting, Information and Capital Markets*, Pitman.

Davis, G. B. and Olson, M. (1988) *Management Information Systems*, 2nd edn, McGraw-Hill.

Financial Accounting Standards Board (1974–1985) *Statements of Financial Accounting Concepts*.

Hendriksen, E. S. (1992) *Accounting Theory*, 5th edn, Irwin.

Kam V. (1990) *Accounting Theory*, 2nd edn, John Wiley and Sons.

Lee, T. A. (1986) *Income and Value Measurement*, 3nd edn, Chapman and Hall.

McMonnies, P. N. (ed.) (1988) *Making Corporate Reports Valuable*, Institute of Chartered Accountants of Scotland/Kogan Page, London.

Parker, R. H. and Harcourt, G. C. (1969) *Readings in the Concept and Measurement of Income*, Cambridge University Press.

Schoderbek, C., Schoderbek, P. and Kefalas, A. (1980) *Management Systems*, Business Publications.

Solomons, D. (June 1986) 'The FASB's Conceptual Framework: An Evaluation', *Journal of Accountancy*.

Sterling, R. R. (1970) *Theory and Measurement of Enterprise Income*, University of Kansas Press.

TEST YOUR UNDERSTANDING

1 What is meant by the term 'conceptual framework'?

2 According to the Accounting Standards Board, what is the objective of financial statements?

3 From the following list, identify (a) a threshold quality, (b) primary characteristics and (c) secondary characteristics of useful accounting information.

- **(i)** timeliness;
- **(ii)** comparability;
- **(iii)** materiality;
- **(iv)** reliability;
- **(v)** understandability;
- **(vi)** relevance;
- **(vii)** the relationship of benefits to cost.

4 In accounting, assets are resources owned by the business. Is this statement true or false?

5 Why was it necessary for the Accounting Standards Board to introduce a fourth primary financial statement other than the profit and loss account, balance sheet and cash-flow statement and what is the statement called?

6 What are the essential similarities and differences between historical accounting income and economic income?

7 In economic income, how should a windfall gain be recognised and what are the implications for historical accounting income?

8 What is meant by (a) input or entry values and (b) output or exit values?

9 Differentiate between replacement cost accounting and realisable cost accounting.

10 What is meant by back-log depreciation?

QUESTIONS

1 Identify the users of financial reports and their needs. Discuss the extent to which traditional financial accounting satisfies those needs.

2 On 1 January 19X4 the balance sheet of Huntingdon Ltd comprised fixed assets of £160,000 which had been acquired on that day, stocks at cost of £64,000 and cash of £40,000. The stocks related to a single finished product and on 1 January the company held 800 units. The assets were financed by 150,000 £1 ordinary shares and retained profits of £114,000.

During that year 600 units were sold and turnover totalled £84,000. At the beginning of 19X5, a further 800 units of stock were purchased at a unit cost of £90. Sales during 19X5 totalled 700 units at a selling price of £150 per unit. The only other expense in either year was depreciation of 20 per cent per annum straight line.

Further details relating to the fixed assets and stock are:

	Fixed assets	Stock
Replacement cost end 19X4	£180,000	£90 per unit
Replacement cost end 19X5	£200,000	£100 per unit
Realisable value end 19X4	£110,000	£130 per unit
Realisable value end 19X5	£80,000	£140 per unit

The replacement cost of the fixed assets relate to new equipment.

Making use of the above information, calculate the profit for Huntingdon in each of the years and prepare the balance sheet at the end of the second year assuming (a) historical costs; (b) replacement costs; and (c) realisable values.

3 Hoylake Mersey Holidays was established on 1 January this year with a capital of £240,000 invested in fixed assets. These assets have a life of three years with no residual value and will be depreciated by equal amounts over their useful life.

Sales are forecast to be £530,000 in each of the three years and labour, material and administration costs are estimated at £200,000 per annum. Interest or discount rates are 25 per cent per annum. Where applicable, interest received is to be based on surplus cash at the beginning of the year. No dividends are proposed during the three years and surplus cash within the company will be invested on short term deposit.

The company believes that the assets could be sold for £100,000 at the end of year 1 and £10,000 at the end of year 2. Their value at the end of year 3 will be nil. At the end of year 3, the company will be liquidated.

There are no stocks and all sales and purchases will be for cash. Where necessary, year end rests may be assumed.

Using the above data, estimate income for each of the three years assuming:

(a) Economists' ideal income;
(b) Accountants' historical income; and
(c) Realisable values.

4* Dudley Rhodes acquired all of the share capital in Huyton Electrical Lathes Limited for £800,000 on 1 January last year. The business consists of importing a single lath from the small kingdom of San Serif and selling to the UK market. On the date of acquisition, the stock consisted of 100 lathes at cost. Other information relevant to the company is contained within the balance sheet outlined below.

Huyton Electrical Lathes Ltd balance sheet at 31 December

Net assets	(£000)	(£000)
Fixed assets at cost		1,300
Less accumulated depreciation		900
		400
Current assets		
Stock	300	
Cash	60	
	360	
Less current liabilities		
Creditors	60	300
		700
Financed by:		
100,000 £5 ordinary shares		500
Retained profits		200
		700

The fixed assets have been depreciated at 25 per cent per annum straight line on the assumption that their residual value would be £100,000 although Dudley believes that the reducing balance method of depreciation is more appropriate. At the time of the purchase, Dudley valued the business at £900,000. The fixed assets would have cost £2 million to replace if new or £600,000 to replace with equipment of a similar age and condition although he believed their realisable value was only £200,000.

During the subsequent 12 months, the company purchased 100 extra lathes for £400,000 cash and also sold 100 lathes for £800,000 cash. In addition, at the beginning of the year it paid the outstanding creditors. These were the only transactions.

At the year end, all the fixed assets were worn out and realised £50,000 cash. The company is also informed by the supplier that the unit cost of the lathes will be changing to £5,000 although selling prices are not likely to change. In addition, the supplier plans to establish a separate selling organisation in the UK in four years' time and will no longer be prepared to sell to Huyton Electrical Lathes Ltd beyond that date. Because of this, Dudley will close the business at the end of the fourth year. During those four years, the unit cost, selling price and sales volume of the lathes are unlikely to change. Stock levels will be kept to 100 lathes except for the final year and it can be assumed that purchases take place on the 1st January each year while sales take place on the 31 December.

Bank overdraft facilities are available to Huyton Electrical Lathes Limited at 10 per cent per annum – the current borrowing and lending rate in the market.

Using the above information and making any assumptions necessary, estimate the profit for Huyton Electrical Lathes for the year using: (a) historical cost values; (b) realisable values; (c) replacement costs; and (d) economic income.

Financial reporting – approaches to regulation

Governments are increasingly leaving the provision of most goods and services to market forces. One exception to this appears to be the provision of financial information where the trend is for greater and more detailed control over the shape and contents of financial reports. Sometimes this is through legislation, sometimes by the encouragement of private-sector, quasi-legal bodies and sometimes through an agency of government.

This chapter:

- Identifies the similarities between accounting information and public goods

- Introduces the corporate governance debate and the need for regulation

- Outlines the increasing legal regulation of financial reports in the UK

- Discusses the role and legitimacy of the accounting profession in determining accounting standards

- Critically evaluates the effectiveness of three private sector accounting standards

- Explains the role and authority of the Accounting Standards Board

The search for an accounting framework – value free, neutral and of equal benefit to all users – is an impossible search. Partly this is because the trade-offs between relevance and reliability will vary between users but partly it is because the meaning of relevance and reliability differs between users. Creditors who are concerned with security are likely to find realisable values more relevant. Employees, on the other hand, are more likely to prefer replacement costs as these emphasise the need to maintain operating capacity before determining profit. In a similar way, the relative importance of the attributes making up reliability is likely to differ between different groups. Conflict can also arise in determining the *extent* of accounting disclosure. Extending the disclosure requirements may help some groups such as creditors and competitors but may disadvantage other groups such as employees and shareholders if the disclosure reduces the enterprise's competitive advantage.

Choosing who to favour with accounting information therefore cannot be resolved by technical arguments. Instead it involves making political choices. At first then it might seem self-evident why governments and other authorities should try to control and shape the contents of financial reports. Such choices, however, do not *explain why* users or consumers of financial information should be protected. In many ways, the demand for financial information is no different from the demand for information about other goods or services such as housing and yet the law does not intervene to force the seller of a house to disclose information. If information is required, the buyer (as the user of information), has to acquire the services of a solicitor or surveyor. The question then is why, if information about a house can be left to market forces, there is a need for regulation when it comes to information about companies.

ACCOUNTING INFORMATION AS A PUBLIC GOOD

Public goods

One answer is that accounting information has many of the qualities of a *public good*. Public goods are goods and services such as prisons and police forces which either would not be supplied or would be inadequately supplied if left solely to market forces. These public goods have qualities different from other goods and services. First, supplying a public good to one person in effect supplies that good to all others at little or no extra cost. Secondly, the consumption of part of that good by one person does not reduce its availability to others. Finally there is a 'lumpiness' in the supply of public goods.

To demonstrate this, consider a shipping company that builds a lighthouse. In making its own voyages safer, it automatically supplies that safety to other shipowners at no cost to them. More than that, the consumption of the benefits of the lighthouse by the others does not deprive the original shipping company of any benefits. There is then the 'lumpiness' argument. If the company came together with another company to build the lighthouse and one preferred a different design to the other, there is no way that both companies' preferences could be sensibly accommodated. Building one design precludes the building of the other. This leads to a further issue, that of the 'free-rider' who, although wanting the lighthouse to be built, will refrain from disclosing this in the hope that others will pay for the service. Because of these insurmountable problems, effective provision may only be possible when undertaken by a public agency.

Most goods are not of this form. If you have a garage built, you are not also providing garaging for your neighbours – unlike when building a lighthouse. Similarly, the size of your garage does not influence in any way the size of garages desired by your neighbours. Should your neighbours want garages, they are forced to *reveal their preferences* by offering to pay the price to have them built, otherwise no garages will be constructed.

The features of accounting information

Accounting information has many of the features of a public good. The cost of an audit for a large quoted company can be in excess of £2 million. This would be the cost faced by a single shareholder demanding the information privately. Once produced, the cost to a second investor would be effectively nil if any extra printing costs are ignored. It is therefore in the second investor's interests to remain silent – not to reveal his or her preferences – in the hope that someone else will pay for the supply of information. The second condition for a public good – that consumption by one person does not reduce the availability to others – equally applies. The original amount of information is still available after it has been used by a second or third person. Finally the 'lumpiness' argument is also applicable. Different users have different needs in terms of presentation, extent of disclosure and values used. Choosing, for example, one level of disclosure suitable for one user group makes it impossible to choose another level of disclosure for any other user group.

Despite these similarities to a public good, accounting reports could logically be controlled by market forces if any information obtained could be kept private. This would enable only the purchaser of the accounting report to benefit from the contents. Ignoring the fact that this is perilously close to 'insider dealing' which is illegal in the UK and several other countries, there is a problem in keeping the information private. A supplier would have at least to give an indication of the contents of the reports. With many goods this does not matter. Disclosing information about a car's performance does not supply the potential purchaser with part of the car. When information is the end product though, the slightest disclosure involves giving away part of the product. Equally, there will be a tendency for free riders to benefit from private information simply by watching the behaviour of the original purchaser.

The need for intervention

The difficulties of excluding free riders and the problem of the joint supply of information to all users combine together to limit the supply of accounting information below what it would otherwise be in a free market. Because of this, there is a strong argument for regulation to minimise this underprovision by enforcing disclosure. In the main this is achieved by forcing companies to provide audited accounts and for these to be lodged with a public official, the Registrar of Companies in the UK. Effectively the audit fee is similar to a lump sum tax on the company which ultimately has to be borne by shareholders, consumers (if it results in increased prices) or the taxpayer if the audit fee is tax allowable. Because of this there may be little incentive in supplying anything other than the minimum information required which, in its turn, only reinforces the need for regulation.

There is, however, a counter argument. Some players in financial markets are able to demand additional information. Banks demand information over and above that to be found in the published accounts when arranging loans or overdrafts. Tax authorities also demand additional information as do trade unions if they are sufficiently strong. Equally, there is evidence of the voluntary disclosure and auditing of company financial information long before legislation made it mandatory.[1]

Companies volunteering additional information may provide added value to investors in the form of comfort and security and, as a consequence, improve their share price. With no legal obligation to produce audited final accounts, firms failing to volunteer the information would attract less investors just as organisations failing to 'volunteer' information to banks in the current climate might find those banks declining to advance loans and overdrafts. This argument suggests that markets themselves could be the regulator. If companies were to provide inadequate information, shareholders would either sell their shares, causing the price to fall, or act directly on the directors by demanding that the quality of accounting information be improved. Either way, the market would ensure that the quality of information improved.

THE LINK BETWEEN OWNERSHIP AND CONTROL

All this presupposes that markets are sufficiently efficient and powerful for shareholders to be able to force directors to act in the best interests of the owners and to satisfy their accounting needs. If markets have imperfections which prevent the owners being sovereign then there is a second reason, over and above the public good argument, why accounting information may need to be regulated. And even if markets can satisfy those owners' needs, market efficiency says nothing about satisfying the financial information needs of other stakeholders.

Legally, directors are appointed by the shareholders to run a company in the best interests of those shareholders. But, with widely dispersed shareholdings, the link between ownership and control begins to break down, giving the directors greater power. In terms of the system diagram of Exhibit 6.1, it is the directors who act as the sensor in determining (at least in part) the accounting policies and disclosures. The shareholders are outside the system. Only if the interests of the directors and the shareholders coincide or if there is some mechanism to make their interests the same would there be no problem. The issue is as old as humankind – *quis custodiet ipsos custodes* – who is to guard the guards?

Organisations and goals

An organisation without members is inanimate. It needs members – be they shareholders, managers, employees, customers or suppliers – to give it direction and make things happen. As such, an organisation cannot have goals separate from those of its members.[2] But with individuals and groupings within the organisation having their own separate goals, there is likely to be both conflict and for those goals to be constantly changing as the external environment changes. The goals of the organisation will therefore be the goals of the grouping(s) with the greatest power – what is known as the dominant coalition.

Senior management's role includes balancing these tensions between members to allow the organisation to survive and succeed. This they do by offering members inducements in exchange for subsuming individual or group goals in favour of the organisation's goals. For employees this might be in the form of remuneration and/or conditions of service. For shareholders, it might be increasing dividends and a rising share price. For suppliers, it might be regular orders and prompt payment. Failure to satisfy the objectives of members may ultimately cause them to sever links with the organisation.

This places a lot of power in the hands of senior managers such as directors. Senior managers, however, are not merely disinterested umpires: they are a grouping themselves. And with dissipated shareholdings, the link between ownership and control is weakened, leaving even greater power in the hands of the senior managers. Without action from shareholders, the running of the organisation will be in the hands of the directors. The directors – or at least some of them – will have become the dominant coalition, able to determine the objectives of the organisation and how members should be rewarded. The danger is that the directors and other senior management are able to pursue their own interests at the expense of other groupings such as shareholders and employees.

Agency theory

This is the problem addressed by agency theory. Although the development of agency theory is complex[3], the issues are straightforward. Agency theory recognises there are many barriers preventing markets being an adequate regulator. One barrier is the breakdown of ownership from control. Another arises from economic barriers preventing competitors entering markets which would otherwise force directors to behave in the best interests of shareholders.

Agency theory considers what happens when one person or grouping known as the principal delegates decision making to another (the agent). Applying this to shareholders and directors, two problems can be identified. The first is that agents – the directors – are assumed to be motivated by self interest and there can be a conflict between this and the interests of the organisation. The second is that the principals – the shareholders – are not in a position to monitor and control the detailed actions of the agents.

The solution to these problems lies in either giving incentives to the agent to act in the best interests of the principal through the reward system or improving the information system by improving the monitoring of the agent's performance. Whichever approach is taken, it is necessary to introduce binding contracts between the principal and the agent which specify the actions to be undertaken by the agent and the rewards which will result.

Performance related remuneration

Tying in the agent's reward system to the interests of the owners suggests some form of performance-related remuneration rather than a fixed salary. Any scheme to encourage the agent to act in the best interests of the owners has to be based on performance rather than effort as, given the legal nature of the contracts, an agreed performance benchmark has to be measurable. Effort will not have that quality.

Remuneration schemes should reward managerial efficiency rather than luck and reflect the contribution of the managers to the financial well being of the shareholders. Schemes should be clearly defined, easy but inexpensive to operate and incapable of management manipulation. This suggests that a performance measure based on profit may be inadequate. First, profit can be manipulated by such techniques as changing the depreciation policies, an example of a technique known as creative accounting. Secondly, profit may be partly due to macro-economic factors such as the levels of interest rates rather than the effort of managers. Thirdly, profit can be increased by taking on extra risk rather than improved performance and this may not be in the best interests of the shareholders.

One way of overcoming these difficulties is to tie in remuneration to the level of share prices. Profits bought at the cost of increased risk are unlikely to cause a share price to increase. Reward packages based on share price performance may even overcome the manipulation of profits problem *if* investors can see through such tricks. If investors recognise that any improvement in profitability is fictitious, they are unlikely to pay more for the shares. Unfortunately, share prices do not simply reflect management performance. They also reflect the macro-economic factors identified earlier.

A popular way of rewarding senior management for performance is to issue share options. One scheme, executive share options, allows managers to acquire a given number of shares over a given time period at a fixed price. As the price at the time of issue is normally fixed substantially below the current market price, managers have to perform sufficiently well to drive the share price up if the option is to have any value.

Unfortunately, this may not be entirely under management's control because of macro-economic factors. Because of this, some companies prefer a performance share incentive scheme. These schemes allot shares in the company to executives on attaining targets such as profit after tax or profit per share. Although such a scheme excludes the vagaries of stock exchange values from managers' rewards, it replaces them by the other difficulties involved in measuring accounting profit.

Monitoring

There is another way of addressing the issues raised by agency theory and that is by incurring what are known as *agency costs*. In theory, one agency cost would be for the principals – the shareholders – to take out an insurance policy which would recompense them if the directors acted against the owners' interests. A more practical example of an agency cost would be the cost of introducing a policing regime to monitor the activities and performance of the directors. This might involve increasing the disclosure requirements in the accounts or by setting up management audits to specifically address the performance and activities of senior managers.

CORPORATE GOVERNANCE – THE UK EXPERIENCE

If agency theory was the *theory*, the UK in the 1980s and 1990s was the laboratory to test the issues raised by the theory. By far the most notable example of the conflict between the interests of directors and the interests of shareholders related to the late Robert Maxwell. Maxwell fraudulently misused the pension funds of Mirror Group Newspapers in order to finance an illegal scheme to support the share price of another of his companies, the Maxwell Communications Corporation.

Although less extreme, there are many other examples of potential conflicts between shareholders and directors, including the remuneration of some directors appearing to be on an ever-increasing spiral irrespective of company performance. Also being questioned in the mid 1990s was the rapid increase in the remuneration packages of the directors of privatised industries despite the same individuals having been quite content to accept much lower remuneration when their industries were in the public sector and despite some very poor investments into other areas. For example, a report by S G Warburg[4] identified Britain's privatised water and electricity companies as having made outside investments totalling £1.6 billion between 1989 and 1994. Of this amount, £1 billion had to be written off while the results from those diversifications for the year 1993/4 totalled £51 million of losses. Another cause for concern was directors taking on rolling contracts, often extending for several years. The result has been to give them a measure of job protection unavailable to others and for large compensation payments to be made when they were ultimately dismissed.

Finally, there has been instances where shareholders have felt they have not been kept fully informed of activities. One notable example concerned Aerostructures Hamble plc. The company was formed in 1990 after a £46.7 million management buy-out from British Aerospace. In 1994, Aerostructures Hamble went public with a market value of approximately £70 million. On the basis of a profits forecast issued at the time, the shareholders paid 120p per share. Within 15 weeks of the issue of the shares, the company had to issue a profits warning and the shares crashed to 73p.

Corporate governance is the term used to describe how companies are run and their relationships with their stakeholders. In the UK and USA, it is primarily concerned with the long term relationship between managers and shareholders and includes the checks and balances on power and authority, incentives for managers and the communications – including disclosure of information – between the managers and investors. What is clear is that corporate governance in some UK companies has been less than satisfactory.

Four issues can be identified. The first concerns dominant personalities in charge of major companies who have too much authority. Such overpowering individuals have been known to keep information and accounting controls to themselves and to force their views on weaker board members. The second concerns the relationship of auditors to the company. The third issue is the lack of an independent test against which to justify the large remuneration packages being earned by some directors while the fourth anxiety relates to the lack of disclosure by directors – especially of information relating to their own rewards and conditions of service.

The Cadbury Report

It was issues such as these which caused the accountancy profession, the Stock Exchange and the Financial Reporting Council to establish a committee chaired by Sir Adrian Cadbury. (The role of the Financial Reporting Council is discussed below.) The committee produced a report in December 1992 entitled 'The Financial Aspects of Corporate Governance', otherwise known as the Cadbury Report. The task of the committee was to examine, and to make recommendations on, the role of directors and auditors in quoted companies. The committee identified two areas of concern, (a) the relationship between the company, its directors and its auditors, and (b) the need for a code of best practice for company directors.

The audit recommendations

In addressing the role of auditors, the committee stressed the need for a 'professional and objective' relationship to exist between the auditors and the management of a company. With a dominant personality running the company, auditors might have to depend on that person for a great deal of information. There is also the danger that an auditor could become too close to such a personality. Although in law it is the shareholders who elect the auditors, the committee recognised that it is the directors who make the appointment where there are widely dispersed shareholdings. Because of this, there is no longer any direct link between the auditors and the shareholders. Adding to this problem, audit firms compete with one another on price which may be at the expense of meeting shareholders' needs. The committee also recognised that companies 'are likely to have a clear view as to the figures they wish' to present to shareholders while, at the same time, wishing to minimise audit costs.

To overcome these difficulties, the Cadbury Report made a number of recommendations. The first was that more effective accounting standards should be developed to reduce the freedom of directors in choosing policies and making disclosures. Secondly, the report recommended that quoted companies should establish audit committees to reduce the power of any dominant personality to influence the content of financial statements and the accounting controls which underpin them. Thirdly, the extent to which the auditors are financially dependent on the company should be made transparent by separately disclosing fees paid to them for audit and non-audit work. Finally, the Cadbury Committee recommended that there should be a periodic change of audit partner.

The code of best practice

The second task of the Cadbury Committee was to draw up a code of best practice for directors and their boards. Since June 1993, the Stock Exchange has required the annual reports of quoted companies to carry a statement saying they have complied with the code or to explain any non-compliance. In the UK, many boards of directors include both senior managers with responsibilities for the detailed operations of the enterprise and other persons without such responsibilities. The former are known as executive directors, the latter as non-executive directors.

Non-executive directors

The code sees a major role for these non-executive directors. Their role is to bring an independent judgement into the boardroom. To perform this role, non-executive directors should be free from any business or financial connection with the company apart from their fees and shareholdings and any fees should reflect the time which they commit to the company. Equally, their calibre and number should be such that their views carry significant weight in the board's decisions. Non-executive directors should be selected for specific periods through a formal process and their nomination should be a matter for the board as a whole. In effect, the Cadbury Report sees the role of the non-executive directors as being an independent counterweight to any overpowering chief executive or group of executive directors.

Executive directors

This concern with the power of executive directors is also addressed in other ways. The code recommends that the service contracts of executive directors should not exceed three years without shareholder approval. The total emoluments and those of the chairman and highest paid UK director should be fully disclosed including the identification of salaries and any performance-related element. The basis on which performance is measured should also be explained. Probably more significantly, the code recommends that directors' pay should be determined by a remuneration committee made up wholly or mainly of non-executive directors.

The board of directors

The code requires a board to meet regularly and to monitor the executive managers. In addition, the board should identify a formal schedule of matters on which the board alone can make decisions. This places the direction and control of the company firmly in the hands of the board and this is reinforced by the code requiring a clearly accepted division of responsibilities at the head of the company. The purpose of this latter requirement is to ensure a balance of power and authority such that no single person has 'unfettered powers of decision'. Normally this will require the roles of chairman and chief executive being split but where the roles are combined, it is essential that there is a strong independent element on the board with an appointed leader.

Best practice will also require the board to concern itself with financial controls. In particular, the Cadbury Committee recommended that audit committees be made compulsory under Stock Exchange rules. An audit committee acts as a bridge between the company and its auditors and reinforces the independence of auditors by taking issues such as their appointment and remuneration away from the executive directors. Because of this, its membership should be restricted to non-executive directors.

The role of shareholders

The corporate governance debate in the UK has been concerned with the relationship between shareholders and directors. It ignores all other stakeholders. The idealised picture presented is one of shareholders exercising their proprietorial rights by, *inter alia*, attending the annual general meeting (AGM) to approve the accounts, appoint the auditors and elect the directors who run the company in between the annual meetings. Non-executive directors are then appointed to bridge the gap between ownership and control and prevent abuses by the directors. These non-executive directors, allegedly elected for their wisdom, experience and contacts, are independent of the detailed operations of the company. Their role is to bring a dispassionate view to the proceedings and to monitor the executive directors.

The reality is that few shareholders attend the AGM, most preferring to vote by proxy, and even when it comes to appointing the directors, most shareholders merely confirm the recommendations of the board. For small, private investors this is understandable as their concern is mainly with short term gains rather than with the detailed strategic and operational issues facing the company. Most shares, however, are held by financial institutions such as pension funds, unit trusts and insurance companies and managed by fund managers. But even here there is a tendency for the fund managers to be less interested in the day-to-day running of companies than in developing a balanced portfolio of investments for their fund. This concentrates power in the hands of the directors.

The role of the institutions

Why is it that the institutional investors – the real owners – choose not to use their power? One reason is the perspective of the institutions. They see themselves as investors rather than owners. The interest of fund managers is in their funds and the performance of those funds, not the companies they have invested in. Because fund managers are likely to be judged and rewarded on their funds performance, their answer to a problem tends to be to sell the shares rather than revamp the management. A second reason is that the institutional investors do not have the technical, managerial or financial experience to act as owners. This puts them at a disadvantage against an expert and entrenched management. Finally the institutions may not wish to become too close to the day-to-day running of the company for fear of being a shadow director – that is a person recognised as a director in law by their influence over the direction of a company even though not a director in name. The UK answer, as proposed by the Cadbury Report, is to promote the role of the non-executive director.

The role of the non-executive director

The role of the non-executive director, however, is not without conflict. While monitoring the full-time directors and remaining independent of them, non-executive directors are supposed to play a full role in all board matters. But UK law does not recognise these different roles. The law is clear: the board of directors is a unitary board, where all members have equal obligations. And despite having the same legal obligations as other directors, non-executive directors are generally paid substantially less than full-time directors. This then raises a further issue: can non-executives gain sufficient knowledge about the company to perform their role effectively by making perhaps no more than 12 visits to the company per year.

It is also possible to question the independence of non-executive directors in some companies. The impression given is that they are directly elected by the shareholders at the annual general meeting. The reality is that they are likely to be selected by the chairman and the board with the support of proxy voting. A similar concern relates to their role on remuneration committees. Given the disinterest shown by many shareholders, once again the reality is that it is the executive directors who fix the pay of the non-executive directors. In turn, the non-executive directors then fix the pay of the executive directors. The potential for conflict, however, is worse than that. Many non-executive directors are themselves executive directors of other companies and so are unlikely to be impartial observers of levels of executive remuneration.

CORPORATE GOVERNANCE – AN ALTERNATIVE APPROACH

There is another model of corporate governance which begins to address some of these difficulties. According to one recent study by Sheridan and Kendall,[5] good corporate governance consists of structuring, operating and controlling a company to: (i) fulfil the long term strategic goals of the owners; (ii) consider and care for the interests of past, present and future employees, including their recruitment, training, working environment and retirement procedures; (iii) take account of the needs of the environment and the local community; (iv) maintain excellent relations with both customers and suppliers and (v) comply with all applicable legal and other regulations.

Examples of this wider perspective of corporate governance can particularly be found in Germany. There, the Cadbury-style approach to corporate governance is hardly known. This may be because there are far fewer quoted companies than in the UK but it may also be because there is explicit recognition of other stakeholders in companies and of the responsibilities of ownership. German companies have traditionally depended more on banks than stock exchanges for their long term finance, banks that play an active role in the strategic management of the enterprise. In addition, there is also a business culture, enshrined in law, which views a company as more than the property of the providers of finance. In particular, the law provides for a more active role for employees in the affairs of companies.

The two-tier approach to governance

One way this happens is through a two-tier structure of management rather than the unitary board found in the UK. In effect there are two boards; the management board or *vorstand* and the supervisory council or *aufsichrat*. The management board, comprising full-time professional managers, has total responsibility for managing the company both in its day-to-day operations and when considering policy. The supervisory council has responsibility for appointing and controlling the members of the management board – although company articles can often enhance this role.

In some ways, the supervisory council appears to fulfil a similar role to the non-executive directors in the UK. However, there is a substantial difference both in terms of focus and composition. First, according to Sheridan and Kendall[6], the focus of German supervisory boards is on strategic issues, with remuneration and audit rarely mentioned – almost the opposite role to that of UK non-executive directors. Secondly, directors representing the employees must be on the supervisory council. Thirdly, it tends to be the investors – particularly the banks – who place the other directors on the supervisory board and these directors act as representatives of their organisation rather than in their own right.

The labour laws in Germany view employees as legitimate stakeholders in a company and provide for both representation and a say in the decision-making process, a process known as co-determination. The right to seats on the supervisory council comes from the *Betriebsverfassungsgesetz* (BetrVG) or Works Constitution Act. For any *Aktiengesellschaft* (AG) or public company and for any *Gesellschaft mit beschranker Haftung* (GmbH) or private limited company with over 500 employees, one-third of the members of the supervisory council must be elected by the employees. Further, for companies with over 2,000 employees the proportion of employee representatives increases to 50 per cent as a result of the *Mitbestimmungsgesetz* (MitbestG) or Co-determination Act.

Employee information

Corporate governance also extends to the shop floor level. The Works Constitution Act provides for the formation of a works council or *betriebsrat* at all plants with over five employees. The works council has various powers including access to information and co-determination in such areas as general working conditions. Works councils with more than 20 employees have to be consulted in advance where there are substantial changes in the operations of the business such as a relocation, merger or the introduction of new working methods.

THE NEED FOR REGULATION

There are three clear reasons emerging to explain why accounting information should be regulated. First, accounting information has many of the qualities of a public good. Secondly, there is the difficulty of getting directors to act in the best interest of the shareholders at all times. Accepting for the moment the Cadbury Committee's favourable view of the non-executive directors' role, on their own, non-executive directors are not the total answer. In their report, the Committee argued for an improvement in accounting standards as a way of reducing the potential conflict between directors and shareholders – and this can only come from some form of regulator. Lastly, there is a need to consider the interests of other stakeholders, a need which cannot find expression when financial reporting is dictated by the property rights of the equity shareholders.

Despite these strong arguments, it does not *automatically* follow that regulation leads to an improvement in financial reporting. Nor does it give any guidance as to whether regulation should be through the law or through some other agency. All that regulation does is transfer the question of the scope and type of information to be provided from the directors and the market-place to the regulator. It does not overcome the issue of judgement and the choice of which groups to benefit and which groups to penalise. Having said that, the regulation of financial reporting is a feature of most countries as has been the increasing demand through time for more and more financial disclosure. Nowhere is this pattern more clear than in the United Kingdom.

THE LEGAL REGULATION OF UK FINANCIAL REPORTS

The origins of the limited liability company

Since the passing of the Joint Stock Companies Act in 1844, it has been possible to form a limited company by a simple process of registration with the Registrar of Companies. Before then, it was much more expensive and difficult to form a company as an Act of Parliament or the granting of a Royal Charter was normally required. The primary concern of the 1844 Act was to protect the shareholders by the annual production of a 'full and fair' balance sheet signed by the directors and audited by one or more shareholders.

With no definition of the term 'full and fair', no requirement to produce a profit and loss account, no established body of accountants and little or no power in the hands of the Registrar of Companies, there was a great deal of abuse. In particular, the creditors were disadvantaged, not only because of the effect of limited liability on their security but also because they had no automatic right to see the balance sheet and because no rules existed to determine when dividends could be paid. This was addressed by the Joint Stock Companies Consolidation Act in 1862 which only allowed dividends to be paid out of profits.

The influence of the accounting profession

In addition, Parliament began to address the need for more detailed accounting requirements of the emerging large companies, particularly in the railway and banking sectors. In 1868, for example, the Regulation of Railways Act laid down proper accounting methods and standard forms of published accounts. By far the greatest change, however, was taking effect outside of Parliament. The 1870s onwards saw the increasing growth of accounting as a profession although the origins of the profession predate this by several decades. The origins of the Institute of Chartered Accountants of Scotland can be traced back to 1853 while the Institute of Chartered Accountants in England and Wales was formed in 1880.

This building up of a profession and the development of accounting concepts such as prudence and matching made accounting a powerful influence on subsequent UK legislation and, for much of the twentieth century, legislation tended to follow the best practices of the profession. By 1900, with the profession firmly established, it was possible for Parliament to pass the Companies Act of that year which required the compulsory annual audit of companies. This was followed by a 1907 Act (consolidated in 1908) requiring a *public* company to file audited balance sheets with the Registrar of Companies. Up until then, only shareholders and debentureholders were entitled to a copy of the balance sheet. For the first time creditors now had open and automatic access to company balance sheets although private companies were still excluded.

Extending the contents of published accounts

The accounting history of the twentieth century has seen a move away from the belief that company activities are a private affair between itself and its shareholders and towards more disclosure and regulation. The Companies Acts of 1928 and 1929 required fixed assets to be differentiated from current assets and for a profit and loss account to be submitted to shareholders, albeit not audited and not submitted to the Registrar of Companies. So began the movement away from simply considering the security of creditors towards the informational needs of shareholders and other users.

The beginnings of modern accounting

The features of modern-day accounting began to emerge following the passing of the 1948 Companies Act. This Act required every company to be audited by professionally qualified auditors and for a copy of the company's *audited* profit and loss account, balance sheet, auditors' report and directors' report to be presented annually to shareholders. In addition, where a company owned others, consolidated accounts had to be produced. In the balance sheet this involves replacing the original asset of the shares with the underlying assets controlled as a result of owning those shares. The balance sheet will therefore show the combined assets of all the companies. A similar process takes place within the profit and loss account. The result is to show the economic substance of the transaction over its legal form.

The 1948 Act was followed by a further one in 1967 which addressed some of the limitations in the earlier Act. The 1967 Act forced companies to disclose their turnover in their published profit and loss account and for the overall figure of profit to be broken down into significant classes of business undertaken by the company. In addition, politico-social factors began to appear. The level of exports had to be specified as did the average number of employees and any political and charitable donations made.

True and fair

Perhaps the most significant requirement of the 1948 Act was for the accounts to show a 'true and fair' view. Unfortunately neither that Act nor any subsequent Act ever defined the term despite its significance in being the central and overriding objective. A recent legal opinion has attempted to define the concept of 'true and fair'.[7] This suggests that 'true and fair', although a question of law, cannot be interpreted without evidence of the practices and views of accountants. More than that, the opinion believes 'true and fair' to be a dynamic concept. To be 'true and fair' the financial statements will normally have to comply with accounting standards. (These are discussed below.) Within this, they should be free of intentional bias; they should disclose all material facts and they should show the substance or economic reality of transactions rather than merely their legal form.

Increasing intervention

Further major Companies Acts were introduced in the UK during the 1980s which took away from accountants a great deal of discretion in the way accounts are presented and the extent of disclosure The driving force behind these Acts were European-wide Directives originating from the European Union. Because of this it is useful to defer their consideration until the wider aspects of continental accounting have been developed.

Pressure against the traditional freedom of accountants to use their professional judgement when preparing financial statements was also coming from another source. A series of scandals in the late 1960s brought home to the general public that all was not well in the accounting profession. The problems centred on the wide range of different possible accounting policies and their effect on reported profits. Although the problem had been recognised as early as 1942 when the English Institute started to issue recommendations to members, these generally only restated current good practice, often allowed a wide number of possible solutions and were for guidance only.

ACCOUNTING STANDARDS AND REGULATION BY THE PROFESSION

This lack of both rigour and enforcement powers along with the lack of detail in UK company law left a great deal of discretion to managements. Even today it is the directors of a company who are responsible for the production of company accounts. They were therefore in a position to select policies and to that extent partially manipulate the information contained in the financial reports.

Matters came to a well-publicised head in 1967 when GEC made a bid for AEI, a competitor. With only two months to go to the year end, AEI produced a profit forecast of £10 million. Following the takeover, the actual results from AEI became a loss of £4.5 million. Of the difference of £14.5 million, £5 million related to 'matters substantially of fact' and £9.5 million related to 'adjustments which remain matters substantially of judgement'. In other words, the forecast profit figure of £10 million could have been reduced to £0.5 million simply by making different assumptions. It will come as little surprise that much of this difference arose because of different methods of valuing stock!

In the light of subsequent events, perhaps the most significant example of management's discretion to choose policies related to the sale of Pergamon Press Ltd to Leasco Ltd. The *audited* accounts for 1968 showed a profit of £2.1 million but became a loss of £495,000 when recalculated by Leasco. The owner of Pergamon, a Mr Robert Maxwell, offered as an explanation that 'accounting is not the exact science which some of us once thought it was'.

The Accounting Standards Committee

The subsequent outcry left the accounting profession with little alternative but to put its house in order if government regulation was to be avoided. In 1969 therefore the Institute of Chartered Accountants in England and Wales announced the formation of what was to become the Accounting Standards Committee (ASC) and by 1976 all the recognised accounting bodies in the UK had become members. The aims of the Committee were to:

(a) narrow the areas of difference and variety in accounting practice;
(b) require the disclosure of accounting bases (policies) in financial reports;
(c) require the disclosure of departures from agreed standards;
(d) ensure wider exposure for major proposals of accounting standards;
(e) continue to encourage improved accounting standards in legal and regulatory measures.

The first three aims were concerned with improving the quality of financial information, the last two with achieving acceptance and legitimacy. In principle, standards can relate to four aspects of accounting: the provision of additional information about existing accounting elements such as the disclosure of accounting policies, the disclosure of new areas of accounting information such as an additional primary financial statement, the choice of a particular valuation method such as FIFO or LIFO and the uniform presentation of financial information.

The work of the Accounting Standards Committee concentrated on the first three types of standard although current company law reflects a standard of the fourth kind.

THE STANDARD SETTING PROCESS

Up to 1982 the Accounting Standards Committee comprised 23 part-time, unpaid members, all accountants and all representing their particular professional bodies. Originally there was an imbalance in favour of the auditing profession but this imbalance and the lack of user representation was addressed in 1982 when the ASC was restructured with users plus accountants in industry and commerce and the public sector forming the majority.

The working of the ASC

Having identified an issue, the Committee would organise basic research and set up a planning subcommittee. Appropriate interest groups would then be consulted. Following this a detailed technical paper known as an Exposure Draft would then be issued to allow further consultations to take place. Once accepted by the ASC, the final proposals would then be forwarded to the Councils of the six accounting bodies making up the ASC and only if *all* six approved the recommendations would the proposals form a Statement of Standard Accounting Practice.

By the end of its life, the Accounting Standards Committee had produced 25 Statements of Standard Accounting Practice. Of these, several had to be revised or amended, some were withdrawn and some have subsequently been replaced by its successor body, the Accounting Standards Board. To the extent they have not been superseded, the SSAPs issued by the ASC remain in force.

In order to evaluate the work of the Committee it might be useful to look in some detail at three standards which relate to areas of accounting already introduced. These are SSAP 9 Stocks and Long Term Contracts, SSAP 12 Accounting for Depreciation and SSAP 13 Accounting for Research and Development. Most standards are to be applied to all companies, although some are only applicable to quoted companies. In addition, standards can be overridden where this is necessary to give a true and fair view.

SSAP 9 STOCK AND LONG TERM CONTRACTS

There are three aspects to stock valuation: how it should be valued, how it should be measured and whether profit should be taken before the final transfer of that stock to the customer. The valuation issue involves choosing whether to use FIFO, LIFO or some other method of pricing stock. The measurement issue is concerned with identifying the components of stock to be included in that valuation. Essentially the choice is between marginal and absorption costing, and if using absorption costing, the basis for charging overheads to production and hence stock. Finally, the issue of whether or not to include profit relates to the valuation of long term contracts not yet completed. Overriding all this is the need for prudence and the need to value stock at the lower of cost or net realisable value.

One immediate problem in trying to understand SSAP 9 Stocks and Long Term Contracts is knowing exactly where the standard begins and ends. It contains five parts, an explanatory foreword, a definition of terms, the standard itself and two parts relating to UK and Irish law. This is then followed by three appendices which are explicitly stated as not forming part of the standard. Despite this, they run for 12 pages even though the standard itself is condensed into a single page.

The Standard Accounting Practice

Ignoring for the moment the problem of long term contracts, Part 3, the Standard Accounting Practice itself, simply states that stocks should be stated at *the lower of cost and net realisable value*, that this should be applied to each item or grouping rather than the overall total stock figure and that the stocks should be classified in the balance sheet in the way required by current law. The statement also requires the accounting policies applied to stock to be stated and applied consistently within the business from year to year.

The explanatory foreword specifies that stocks should 'comprise that expenditure which has been incurred in the normal course of business in bringing the product or service to its present location and condition. Such costs will include *all related production overheads*, even though they might accrue on a time basis.' In other words, the standard requires an absorption costing approach to stock valuation although little or no guidance is given as to how overheads are to be apportioned other than suggesting that the method chosen should provide the 'fairest possible approximation to the expenditure actually incurred in bringing the product to its present location and condition'. Apart from a reference in the part of the statement dealing with the definition of terms which defines production overhead as 'overhead incurred...for production, based on the normal level of activity, taking one year with another', all other guidance is to be found in the appendices which do not form part of the statement!

'Normal activity' and the components of overheads

This emphasis on normal activity prevents all production overheads being charged to a few units of output when the low volume is due to some abnormal and unforeseen event. It recognises, for example, that if a company with production overheads of £100,000 normally produces 1,000 units, the overhead per unit should be £100 and that if production fell to a single unit because of some misfortune, it would be wrong to value that single unit with overheads of £100,000. Instead, presumably the single unit of stock should show overheads of £100 with the balance being written off as a loss to the profit and loss account. What the statement does not give is any detailed instructions as to how normal activity should be calculated other than to consider actual levels of activity for the current and previous years and budgeted levels for the current and subsequent years.

Equally, it is vague about the make up of the total of overheads to be included in stock. While emphasising production overheads, Appendix 1 suggests that overheads relating to 'design, and marketing and selling costs incurred before manufacture may be included...where firm sales contracts have been entered into'. Similarly the appendix allows part of the cost of management to be allocated to production where management is partly involved in production. This logic is even extended to that part of the accounts department which relates to production such as the payroll section and any section which produces production reports.

Finally Appendix 1 comes down against LIFO and other similar methods because '...they often result in stocks being stated in the balance sheet at amounts which bear little relationship to recent cost levels'. However true this may be, an equivalent effect is possible within the profit and loss account when using FIFO!

Long term contracts

Long term contracts have already been outlined in Chapter 3 where the conflict between the realisation and prudence concepts and the need for information were developed. In terms of the language of the 1948 Act, waiting until the end of a contract before reporting profits might be true but it is unlikely to be fair. SSAP 9 recognised this by emphasising the matching rather than the prudence concept. Indeed it went further and made the recognition of profit through time mandatory, effectively banning the more prudent policy of waiting until project completion before recognising profit.

Unfortunately, having proposed that profit should be recognised through the life of the contract, the standard offers little advice on calculating the revenue and expenses for any period to determine the 'attributable' profit. The only guidance given is that each long term contract 'should be assessed individually and reflected in the profit and loss account by recording turnover and related costs as contract activity progresses. Turnover is (to be) ascertained in a manner appropriate to the stage of completion of the contract, the business and the industry in which it operates.' No further guidance is offered in the standard itself other than the need for prudence spelt out in clause 29. This requires that where the outcome of a long term contract can be assessable 'with reasonable certainty before its conclusion, the prudently calculated attributable profit should be recognised in the profit and loss account'. It therefore appears that the three different methods for determining profit demonstrated in Example 10 of Chapter 3 are all equally acceptable.

Reporting contract work-in-progress in the final accounts

The rest of the standard is concerned with how the information is recorded in the balance sheet. Effectively it follows the approach of Example 3.10 although it is expressed in the most convoluted of language. The recognition of turnover from a contract results in a debtor for an identical amount. The standard requires that this be shown in the balance sheet within debtors as 'amounts recoverable on contracts'.

Some of the costs of the work-in-progress on the contract will have been charged as expenses against this turnover, allowing the attributable profit to be calculated and reducing the work-in-progress as a consequence. Any balance of contract work in progress should be shown under stock as 'long term contract balances' in the balance sheet. Any payments on account received from the client will cause the amount shown as a debtor to fall. Should payments on account be greater than the amount charged as turnover to the debtor, then the balance will first be used to reduce the 'amounts recoverable on contracts' with any remainder being shown as a creditor.

The primacy of matching

Running through SSAP 9 are two dominant themes, the need for matching and the need for disclosure. The dominance of matching caused the ASC to require production overheads to be included in stocks despite the dangers of distortion outlined in Chapter 3 and despite the argument that a marginal costing approach might be more prudent. The statement does not address these issues other than suggesting in the non-mandatory appendix that prudence should not be applied by omitting production overheads but by the determination of net realisable value. Taken as a whole, the statement in parts is dogmatic, vague and, at times, misleading. It is dogmatic in its requirements that production overheads should be included in stock valuations and that profit should be recognised over the life of long term contracts without offering any hard logic as to why this should be. It is vague when it comes to the application of its preferred methods of treatment in that there remains discretion in the choice of the components of production overheads and the measurement of activity. And it is misleading in that its rejection of LIFO is contained in an appendix which explicitly does not form part of the statement.

SSAP 12 ACCOUNTING FOR DEPRECIATION

Some of these difficulties are also to be found in SSAP 12 Accounting for Depreciation which was originally issued in December 1977 and amended in 1981 before being completely revised in January 1987. One reason for the changes was the inability to find a suitable definition of depreciation. By the time of the revised standard, depreciation had become 'the measure of wearing out, consumption or other reduction in the useful economic life of a fixed asset whether arising from use, effluxion of time or obsolescence through technological or market changes'. The original 1977 definition had used the phrase 'other loss of value of a fixed asset' rather than the current phrase 'other reduction in the useful economic life of a fixed asset' which would have allowed depreciation to be a process of valuation (with all the difficulties that entails) rather than an allocation of cost.

The Standard Accounting Practice

That depreciation is an allocation of cost is now made clear in paragraph 15 of the revised statement which states, 'Provision for depreciation of fixed assets having a finite useful economic life should be made by allocating the cost (or revalued amount) less estimated residual value of the assets as fairly as possible to the periods expected to benefit from their use. The depreciation methods used should be the ones which are most appropriate having regard to the types of asset and their use in the business.' Unfortunately, no guidance is given as to the most appropriate method of depreciation. Part 1 of the Statement, Explanatory Note, suggests, 'There is a range of acceptable depreciation methods. Management should select the method regarded as most appropriate to the type of asset and its use in the business so as to allocate depreciation as fairly as possible to the periods expected to benefit from the asset's use. Although the straight line method is the simplest to apply, it may not always be the most appropriate.'

The depreciation of buildings

Prior to the original standard in 1977, many organisations did not provide for depreciation of their properties. SSAP 12 addressed this from the beginning although immediately there were objections from property companies who would have seen their reported profits fall as a result of the depreciation charge. The ASC responded by exempting property companies from the standard and by designing a standard, SSAP 19, for such organisations which detailed the circumstances in which property companies do not have to depreciate their assets.

As a result, the revised standard is now applicable to all fixed assets other than (a) those fixed assets which have their own specific standards, namely investment properties, goodwill and development costs, and (b) investments such as shareholdings in other companies. All other fixed assets are subject to the standard which explicitly states that 'buildings are no different from other fixed assets' although any 'freehold land does not normally require a provision for depreciation, unless it is subject to depletion by, for example, the extraction of minerals'. Despite this, many retail chains and hoteliers have chosen to ignore the standard, arguing instead that by regular maintenance there is no need to provide depreciation on such buildings. Indeed, this argument seems to have found favour with a subcommittee of the ASC's successor as it supported the failure of a major hotel chain to depreciate its buildings.

The cost basis for depreciation

Although the standard gives no guidance as to an appropriate method of depreciation, it does give clear guidance as to the process involved. Depreciation should be based upon the asset's historical cost unless it has been revalued, in which case the latter figure should form the basis for calculating the depreciation charge.

Of particular concern to the standard setters was the habit of some companies to underestimate asset lives or to charge extra depreciation in the profit and loss account, perhaps to provide for a more realistic depreciation charge or to effectively build up a (secret) reserve for replacement. No matter how prudent this might be, the standard firmly addressed both issues by specifying that 'it is essential that asset lives are estimated on a realistic basis' and that 'the accounting treatment in the profit and loss account should be consistent with that used in the balance sheet'. In other words, if an asset has been depreciated by £1,000 in the profit and loss account, its value in the balance sheet should also have been reduced by this amount. Should additional depreciation be felt necessary, this should be achieved by first revaluing the asset and then charging depreciation on that amount or by the creation of a reserve for the replacement of the asset out of after-tax profits. Finally, guidance is also given on the estimation of any residual value. This should be based on prices prevailing at the date of acquisition or revaluation and not the estimated value obtainable at the end of the asset's life.

The depreciation charge on revalued assets

One other major issue is addressed in the standard. Changes are possible in the depreciation charge as a result of revaluations or revised estimates of assets lives. Consider an asset costing £140,000 with an original estimated life of ten years but which, during its third year, is felt to only have a seven-year life in total. Assuming straight line depreciation and a zero residual value, the asset will have been depreciated by £28,000 at the end of year 2 to give a net book value of £112,000. Effectively, the original asset life was miscalculated. Given a life of only seven years, the depreciation should have been £20,000 p.a. and not the original £14,000 p.a.

One option would be to charge £20,000 in each of the subsequent years plus an extra £12,000 in year 3 to make up for the earlier underprovision. A second approach would be to also charge £20,000 in all subsequent years but to match the earlier underprovision against previous years' profits by reducing the reserves. Yet a third option would be to accept the net book value at the beginning of year 3 of £112,000 and depreciate this amount over the remaining estimated life of five years to give a subsequent depreciation charge of £22,400 p.a.

In years gone by, most firms would have chosen the second option as this would have considerably reduced the effect on current and future profits. The original SSAP 12 took the third approach, using the net book value and depreciating that balance over the rest of the asset's life. The revised standard though, while maintaining the original recommendation, now allows the first approach when 'future results would be materially distorted'.

Implications of the statement

Apart from the obligation to depreciate properties – and even a failure to do so has subsequently been condoned – and the treatment of depreciation when an asset's value or estimated life changes, the statement contained few specific requirements. Its emphasis has been on identifying the assets to be depreciated, the elements making up the depreciation charge and how this should be reported rather than giving guidance as to depreciation rates for specific assets. Even the disclosure requirements of (a) method used, (b) economic life or depreciation rate, (c) depreciation for the period and (d) accumulated depreciation for each major group adds very little to existing practice. Consequently it is no surprise that there still exists a great deal of discretion in choosing asset lives and with many of the disclosure requirements being interpreted broadly in published accounts. One major quoted company, for example, recently declared that assets within one particular grouping are depreciated over the range from five to 30 years! Any real standardisation in SSAP 12 therefore relates to methods of recording and reporting rather than the equally important issue of valuation.

SSAP 13 ACCOUNTING FOR RESEARCH AND DEVELOPMENT

Stock values and the size of the depreciation charge are not the only significant factors influencing the profit reported in financial reports. In the modern world, firms are increasingly spending large amounts of money on research and development in the hope of developing new or improved products which will contribute to future profitability. Sometimes this research and development effort will be aborted even before product development while on other occasions, products with varying degrees of success will result.

Conflict between prudence and matching

Traditionally, matching suggests that revenues should be offset by all the expenses incurred in generating those revenues while prudence requires all expenses to be immediately charged to the profit and loss account unless future benefits related to those expenses are sufficiently certain. There is therefore a clear conflict when relating these two concepts to research and development. Given the large amounts involved, whether R & D is written off as an expense or carried forward as an intangible asset for later matching against future revenues will be critical to the level of reported profit. Despite this importance, probably in more than any other area of accounting, the decision involves a great deal of specialised technical and commercial judgement on the part of the directors responsible for the final accounts, judgement which because of its specialised nature makes it difficult for accountants and auditors to question.

Approaches to the problem

One approach would be to accept the primacy of prudence and write off all research and development expenditure in the year incurred. This, however, would be to treat unsuccessful R & D in the same way as successful R & D, although it would presumably not prevent the successful company from publishing its success outside the narrow confines of the final accounts and allowing users to make their own judgement.

Another approach would be to consider whether research and development has the properties of an asset. Using the Accounting Standards Board's Statement of Principles as a guide, R & D appears to meet the requirements of an asset under Chapter 3. In that chapter, assets were defined as 'rights or other access to future benefits controlled by an entity as a result of a past transaction or event'. Research and development will have involved cash being given up in exchange for the intellectual rights to the results of that R & D and these will reside with the company. Where there is a greater problem is in meeting the two recognition criteria of Chapter 4. There is little problem with the first condition, that a change in the asset/liability has occurred. Cash has decreased and the benefit of R & D has been gained. It is in the second condition, that the item can be measured as a monetary amount with sufficient reliability, that there is a problem.

The Standard Accounting Practice

This was the issue faced by the Accounting Standards Committee. SSAP 13 Accounting for Research and Development differentiates between pure research, applied research and development. Pure research is defined as 'experimental or theoretical work undertaken...for its own sake rather than directed towards any specific aim or application' whereas applied research is 'directed towards a specific aim or objective'. Development is essentially different. It involves the 'use of scientific or technical knowledge to produce new or substantially improved...products or services'.

The view of SSAP 13 is that both forms of research are insufficiently identifiable with future economic benefits to be an asset and so should be written off as expenditure as incurred. The statement then permits, but does not demand, the capitalisation of development expenditure which then must be matched against the (future) revenues to which it relates.

This permissive approach leaves it to the directors to decide whether any development expenditure should be treated as an asset in the balance sheet. To reduce this discretion, the standard requires certain conditions to be met before the expenditure can be capitalised. These are that (a) there is a clearly defined project; (b) the related expenditure is separately identifiable; (c) the outcome of the project has been assessed with reasonable certainty as to its technical feasibility and commercial viability; (d) the total of existing and future development costs plus the subsequent production, selling and administration costs are reasonably expected to be less than the future revenues from the project, in other words, the project is likely to be profitable; and (e) adequate resources exist or will exist to enable the project to be completed. Providing these conditions are met, the development expenditure may be capitalised.

The rest of the standard is concerned with disclosure. It requires a clear explanation of accounting policies relating to development in the notes to the accounts and disclosure of movements within the asset of deferred development expenditure. In addition, the total research and development expenditure in the profit and loss account must be broken down between current year's expenditure and expenditure from previous years now being amortised (written off).

Implications of the statement

SSAP 13 is dominated by the need for prudence but with matching allowable in certain circumstances. By denying the opportunity of capitalising pure and applied research, it may reasonably be viewed as narrowing the range of possible treatments. But what is disturbing in a statement is the allowance of two diametrically opposite policies for development expenditure. Equally worrying is the lack of detailed examples where capitalisation would or would not be valid. Other things being equal, development expenditure relating to a pre-existing product with an established market is more likely to be matchable with future revenues than development expenditure on a totally new product. Despite this, the standard offers no guidance even though in its explanatory notes it was able to differentiate between activities which would normally be viewed as research and activities which would normally be viewed as development.

Perhaps part of the reason for its vagueness and reliance on judgement to interpret what guidance is given can be explained by the lobbying which took place at the exposure draft stage. The original exposure draft leading to SSAP 13 required *all* expenditure to be written off in the year it was incurred – a treatment required in the USA today. This would at least have been an unambiguous standard applicable to all. Following intense lobbying – mainly from the aerospace and defence industries – this was revised. Had the standard demanded that development expenditure be immediately written off, the net assets, and hence capital employed, in affected companies would have fallen. This would have immediately affected the profitability of such firms as many government contracts specify a price based on cost plus a percentage of the capital employed. A revised exposure draft then suggested that all development expenditure meeting certain conditions must be capitalised and this, in turn, was objected to by other companies. The final outcome was SSAP 13, a compromise which allowed but did not require development expenditure to be capitalised.

A REVIEW OF THE ASC STANDARD SETTING PROCESS

That the Accounting Standards Committee was replaced by the more powerful Accounting Standards Board in August 1990 suggests that all was not well with the ASC standard setting process. Criticism of the process has focused on two related aspects, the effectiveness of the ASC and its legitimacy.

The effectiveness of the ASC

In terms of its original objectives, the ASC did manage to narrow some of the areas of difference in financial reporting. SSAP 13, for example, now requires all research expenditure be written off rather than treated as an asset. And where the ASC was unable to narrow areas of difference, it did attempt to ensure disclosure to allow users to make a more informed judgement.

Unfortunately, some standards were only achieved after giving in to particular interest groups or by allowing more than one treatment – the very antithesis of what most people would understand by the word 'standard' – while other standards had either to be amended or withdrawn.

Lack of an agreed framework

Part of the reason for failing to get matters right first time was because the ASC never had a framework within which to develop its standards. Not only was the committee formed as a knee-jerk reaction to the scandals of the 1960s but even its first standard, SSAP 1 Accounting for Associate Companies, was a fire-fighting response to a technical problem.

It was only with the publication of SSAP 2 Disclosure of Accounting Policies that the ASC made its one formal contribution to the development of a conceptual framework. In that statement, the ASC identified four fundamental accounting concepts which underlie the periodic financial accounts of business enterprises. These are: (a) going concern; (b) accruals, i.e. the matching of revenue earned against expenses incurred rather than revenues received against expenses paid; (c) consistency; and (d) prudence. These broad basic assumptions have already been developed in earlier chapters along with other assumptions on which modern financial reporting is founded.

Within the framework of these fundamental concepts the statement identified accounting bases as those methods developed to enable concepts to be applied to individual financial transactions. The 'straight line' or 'reducing balance' methods, for example, are two bases by which depreciation can be calculated, while choosing to carry forward development expenditure or writing it off immediately are alternative bases for the treatment of development costs. From within these bases the standard requires an enterprise to choose a particular accounting policy which is 'in the opinion of management, appropriate to its circumstances and best suited to present fairly its results and financial position'. Choosing straight line depreciation therefore might be one firm's accounting policy on depreciation.

Only if the accounts are produced on assumptions which differ from the four fundamental concepts – as, for example, when it is no longer possible to view the firm as a going concern – need the assumptions be stated. Finally, in its definition of terms, SSAP 2 explicitly states that where 'the accruals concept is inconsistent with the prudence concept,...the latter prevails'.

Lack of consistency between standards

The effectiveness of the standard setting process was probably flawed from the start, simply because it was originally viewed as a vehicle for resolving technical matters rather than as a forum for developing a wider framework. This failure to provide a full rationale has resulted in, at times, a lack of consistency between standards, allowed more than one treatment within a single statement, and sometimes left unclear the detailed practice demanded.

To give but one example, SSAP 2 requires prudence to override other concepts if there is a conflict. Despite this, SSAP 9, with its clash between matching and prudence in long term contracts, appears to favour matching when reporting the results of those long term contracts.

The only rationale for the Statements of Standard Accounting Practice are the concepts identified in SSAP 2 and even here the Explanatory Foreword to the Statements makes it clear that standards are subject to the 'true and fair' override.

The legitimacy of the ASC

There is though a wider criticism of the ASC standard setting process which relates to its authority and legitimacy. Until the 1989 Companies Act, UK legislation made no mention of accounting standards. Logically any organisation can impose rules on its members as a condition of being a member; this applies as much to social clubs as to accountancy bodies. What no organisation can do is impose rules on non-members – and this was the problem faced by the ASC. In law, it is the *directors* who are responsible for the contents of published accounts and the accounting profession has no control over their activities. Directors are only bound by the law of the land and, until 1989, UK legislation did not acknowledge the existence of accounting standards.

This therefore placed accountants in an invidious position. On the one hand their professional bodies were telling them to apply accounting standards. On the other, their clients were not party to these regulations. Legally, the clients are the shareholders but the directors are in a powerful position to influence the appointment and remuneration of auditors. This may well explain two phenomena of the ASC's existence: its influence by pressure groups – as when developing SSAP 13 – and its singular failure to enforce accounting standards on companies and auditors who breached those standards.

THE GOVERNMENTAL REGULATION OF ACCOUNTING

Accepting that accounting information has many of the properties of a public good and that there is a potential conflict between directors and shareholders begins to explain why its provision is not simply left to market forces. What it does not explain is why some legislatures play an active role in the provision of financial information while others leave it mainly to the private sector. At the one extreme is the situation which existed in the UK until 1981 whereby the government laid down a very general company law framework and left it to the private sector in the form of the accounting profession's ASC to fill in the detail. At the other extreme are countries such as France and Germany whose governments dominate the regulation of accounting, even to the extent of specifying allowable accounting policies and valuation rules.

Governmental regulation

There are benefits and limitations to both approaches. Given that the provision of accounting information involves making judgements about what to disclose and how to value transactions, some users will gain while others inevitably will lose. Forcing firms to immediately write off research expenditure, for example, deflates not only the profits of firms carrying out a great deal of research, it may actually cause them to cut back on the amount of research undertaken. As a result, such firms would be penalised relative to firms undertaking very little research. Choosing who to favour and who to penalise in this way is essentially a political judgement based on values. It might therefore be argued that resolution of such issues that cannot be resolved by the market should be by the democratically elected legislature rather than some unelected or self-appointed body.

Enforcement problems are then minimised because of the legitimacy of Parliament and the authority of the law and this is reinforced by the law providing a full and formal appeals procedure. The legislature is also able to consider the wider, welfare implications of its policies. If, for example, the introduction of an accounting standard causes reported profits to fall, the legislature could consider the ramifications of this by, for example, amending tax laws or any other relevant legislation – something outside the powers of a private regulator.

Although not immune from pressure groups, parliamentarians are drawn from a wider cross-section of the community and are less susceptible to such single issue pressure groups as those faced by the ASC when considering research and development. The great danger of a private sector regulatory body is that it can be 'captured' by those with a sectional interest. Firms of auditors, for example, might be able to dominate the regulatory body and agree on common treatments which otherwise would appear as collusion and to question their independence.

Limitations of governmental regulation

There are disadvantages to the governmental regulation of accounting. Technical issues might be decided on party political grounds as, for instance, when the Labour government's 1967 Companies Act required companies to disclose political donations.

Government legislative timetables are often full and have to consider many other matters than just accounting. As a result, regulations concerning the contents of financial reports might be given a low priority within that timetable or passed without sufficient consideration of the issues. Equally, with a packed legislative programme, laws once passed may be difficult to change.

Private sector regulation

Private sector regulation tends to be a mirror image of the advantages and disadvantages of public sector regulation. By far the major issue is determining the authority of a private sector regulator to impose 'quasi laws' on the financial community. Until the passing of the 1989 Companies Act and the establishment of the Accounting Standards Board one year later, the authority in the UK was mainly implicit.

The support of informed opinion

To make their statements as authoritative as possible, private regulators attempt to obtain the backing of informed opinion, generally in the form of the accounting profession and the stock exchange. Certainly this was the approach of the ASC and helps to explain why all six of the recognised UK accounting bodies had to agree any standard before it could be issued. Likewise, the Council of the Stock Exchange require all quoted companies to abide by accounting standards.

Limited powers of enforcement

Where the ASC fell down was in having only limited powers of enforcement. For less serious failures by a company, the auditors would merely note the non-compliance in their audit report, while for more serious cases they could qualify the audit report. Rarely, however, were these powers ever used despite several well-known examples of companies failing to comply with standards.

Consultation

A second way to increase the authority of private sector standard setting is to carry out as wide ranging a consultation process as possible to encourage general acceptance and reduce the likelihood of non-compliance. Without sufficient enforcement powers, private sector regulators need compliance to demonstrate their authority and justify their existence.

Any strong objections to a proposal or threat of non-compliance would deny the standard setting body its role and hence threaten its survival. Such was the case of SSAP 16 Current Cost Accounting, an attempt to come to terms with high levels of inflation then current in the UK. Issued first in March 1980, the statement was made non-mandatory in June 1985 and finally withdrawn in April 1988 after having seen extensive lobbying from individual members of the English Institute and the failure of many quoted companies to apply its provisions. It is probably no coincidence that in the same year that SSAP 16 was withdrawn, the Dearing Report, a report sponsored by the UK accounting bodies, recommended the replacement of the ASC by the more powerful Accounting Standards Board.

Consensus

To reduce the threat of non-compliance, private sector regulatory bodies attempt to find a consensus. However, this sometimes means that subsequent standards tend to fudge the issues or settle for a compromise. This poses the danger that recommendations will be vague, provide a variety of treatments or favour those with the greatest power. An unfortunate by-product of this process is the considerable lengthening of the standard setting process and hence a reduction in its immediate effectiveness. For example, what became SSAP 16 started life as Exposure Draft 18 in November 1976, although this, in itself, was the result of a government committee established earlier in January 1974. Following the rejection of compulsory current cost accounting by the individual membership of the English Institute in July 1977, revised guidelines were published in November 1987. This was then followed by a revised Exposure Draft, ED 24, published in April 1979, until finally, in March 1980, the original SSAP 16 was published.

THE REGULATION OF ACCOUNTING – A MIDDLE WAY

There is a third way to regulate accounting which combines the authority of state control with the flexibility of a private sector regulator. This involves governments forming or supporting an agency to regulate accounting standards. Such an agency would have a proper mandate from Parliament and the backing of the courts. It would probably be more effective than straightforward central control by government, partly because of the expertise of its staff, partly because it can take a wider view than the narrow technical aspects to standard setting and partly because it can react faster to emerging issues than any legislature. Equally important, it will have greater independence and greater authority than a self-regulating body. Such advantages though do have a cost. The framework within which such agencies operate needs to be made clear otherwise there is a danger of it taking on a life of its own, making promulgations not necessarily to help users but to justify its own existence. There is also the possibility of political pressure by elected representatives pursuing their own areas of interest, be it a favourite hobby horse or the protecting of industries particular to their own constituency.

The American experience

For historical reasons, there are many accounting similarities between the USA and Great Britain. Both countries share a common emphasis on the accruals and true and fair approaches and many of the major accounting firms have joint UK–USA roots. There is, however, a substantial difference. The USA is a federation of 50 states each with its own separate company legislation. Because of this, the legal financial reporting framework has developed differently from the UK. State company law has never included any significant accounting regulations and until the Wall Street crash of 1929, financial reporting for most companies was almost completely unregulated.

The Securities and Exchange Commission

The federal government identified this lack of regulation as a contributory cause of the 1929 crash. Their reaction was to pass the Securities Exchange Act of 1934 which established the Securities and Exchange Commission to administer the regulation of securities such as shares and debentures.

The Commission is an agency of the federal government comprising five members appointed by the President and with quasi-judicial powers. It is an independent regulatory body with power to prescribe valuation rules and the form and content of financial reports. Any company wanting its securities to be marketable – the equivalent of a public company in the UK – must register with the SEC and comply with its audit and accounting rules.

From its beginning, the Commission has tended to maintain only a supervisory role over accounting standards, preferring to leave the detail to the private sector. Originally this was via the Committee on Accounting Procedures, established by the American Institute of Certified Public Accountants in the 1930s, and then by its replacement in 1959, the Accounting Principles Board.

The Financial Accounting Standards Board

As in the UK many years later, there was increasing dissatisfaction with the standard setting process, its domination by the accounting profession and its limited progress in identifying fundamental concepts on which to build further developments. This led to the formation of three new bodies: the Financial Accounting Standards Board with responsibility for setting standards; the Financial Accounting Foundation to oversee the FASB and raise funding; and an advisory body, the Financial Accounting Standards Advisory Council. Since 1973, the Financial Accounting Standards Board has been the organisation recognised by the SEC for the establishment of financial reporting standards within the USA.

The Financial Accounting Standards Board is financed by voluntary donations from industry, accounting firms and investor organisations and supports a technical staff working directly with the Board. Not only does it issue statements, it also created a committee, the Emerging Issues Task Force, to address newly discovered problems and issue speedy guidance.

Apart from its position as the SEC designated body for developing accounting standards, the FASB is also required to reinforce its authority by carrying out the 'due process' of extensive consultation. Initially this involves the appointment of a task force representing preparers, auditors and users of financial information. Following a study of the literature concerning the issue under consideration and the commissioning of any necessary additional research, it then publishes a comprehensive discussion document and conducts a public debate. Only after the subsequent issue of an Exposure Draft and the analysis of the resulting comments is the standard issued.

THE CURRENT UK REGULATORY REGIME

The Dearing Committee

The American model of accounting regulation may have been in the minds of the members of the Consultative Committee of Accounting Bodies (CCAB) – the co-ordinating body for all the recognised UK accounting bodies – when it set up the Dearing Committee in response to growing criticism of UK accounting standards. The findings of the Dearing Committee were published as a report entitled *The Making of Accounting Standards* in September 1988. It identified a number of weaknesses with the regulatory regime of the old Accounting Standards Committee; the lack of compliance, the absence of a conceptual framework, excessive flexibility in many standards, a failure to sufficiently involve non-accountants, delays in introducing standards and no mechanism to deal with emerging issues. In addressing these weaknesses, a number of recommendations were made, the most notable of which was that accounting standards should have legal backing.

The Dearing Committee also recommended the establishment of a new body, the *Financial Reporting Council* (FRC) to oversee two other entities, the *Accounting Standards*

Board (ASB) and the *Review Panel*. The proposal was for the Financial Reporting Council to have overall responsibility for the standard setting process including (i) giving guidance on work programmes and broad policy issues, (ii) ensuring sufficient funding for the standard setting process and (iii) the appointing of members to its associated bodies. The Accounting Standards Board was then to be charged with the development of new accounting standards under a full-time chairman and technical director while the Review Panel was to have a policing role monitoring the accounts of large companies and enforcing compliance with standards.

The 1989 Companies Act and the Financial Reporting Council

The vehicle for implementing many of these proposals was the 1989 Companies Act. For the first time, this Act provided statutory recognition for accounting standards. Directors of companies now have to state whether or not their accounts have been prepared in accordance with applicable accounting standards and to provide details and reasons for any departure.

In addition, the Act also provided for the creation of the Financial Reporting Council, a company limited by guarantee which was formed in 1990 with 25 members. Membership is drawn from a much wider grouping than the earlier ASC. Apart from representatives of the accounting profession, there are also representatives from the City, industry and academia as well as observers from the Treasury and the Bank of England. The funding for the Council's work comes from its sponsors such as the Department of Trade and Industry, the London Stock Exchange, the banking community as well as the accounting profession in the form of the CCAB while its powers are derived from powers delegated to it from the Secretary of State for Trade and Industry.

The Accounting Standards Board

A subsidiary company of the Financial Reporting Council, the Accounting Standards Board has been prescribed as the standard setting body for the purposes of Section 256(1) of the Companies Act 1985.[8] From 1 August 1990, the Accounting Standards Board replaced the ASC as the body responsible for accounting standards. The board comprises no more than nine members under a full-time chairman and technical director but is supported by a full-time staff of qualified accountants.

Initially, the ASB took on all the existing Statements of Standard Accounting Practice but gradually these are being replaced by its own standards which are known as Financial Reporting Standards. The process normally begins by the board becoming aware of an area of accounting where a standard is thought necessary. It then either commissions research or conducts its own investigations. This is followed by a discussion draft or discussion paper outlining the issues identified and inviting submissions from interested parties. After considering these representations, the board issues what is known as a Financial Reporting Exposure Draft (FRED) and, once more, comments are invited from users. Finally, the ASB reviews and, if necessary, revises the document before issuing it as a Financial Reporting Standard (FRS). No longer is it necessary for the six professional bodies to endorse a standard unanimously before it is accepted. Instead, the ASB issues standards in its own right providing it achieves a two-thirds majority of its own board.

Already the increased power of the ASB is making itself felt. By the end of 1994, it had completed, in draft form, its Statement of Principles, the conceptual framework requested by the Dearing Committee. In addition, it had issued seven standards of its own and these are outlined in subsequent chapters. The ASB has learnt the lesson of the vague, at times, discretionary standards of its predecessor. Financial Reporting Standards are now longer and more detailed, often expressed in quasi-legalistic language and prescriptive in nature. The result has been to reduce the discretion of the preparers of financial statements. The list of standards currently in existence from both the ASB and the ASC are shown in Exhibit 7.1.

Exhibit 7.1 Current accounting standards

	Title	*Issued*
SSAP 1	Accounting for Associated Companies (amended August 1974, revised April 1982) *	January 1971
SSAP 2	Disclosure of Accounting Policies	November 1971
SSAP 3	Earnings per Share (revised August 1974 and amended by FRS3)	February 1972
SSAP 4	The Accounting Treatment of Government Grants	April 1974
SSAP 5	Accounting for Value Added Tax	April 1974
SSAP 8	The Treatment of Taxation Under the Imputation System in the Accounts of Companies (revised December 1977, addendum March 1988)	August 1974
SSAP 9	Stocks and Long Term Contracts (revised September 1988)	May 1975
SSAP 12	Accounting for Depreciation (amended November 1981, revised January 1987)	December 1977
SSAP 13	Accounting for Research and Development (revised January 1989)	December 1977
SSAP 15	Accounting for Deferred Taxation (revised May 1985)	October 1978
SSAP 17	Accounting for Post Balance Sheet Events	August 1980
SSAP 18	Accounting for Contingencies	August 1980
SSAP 19	Accounting for Investment Properties	November 1981
SSAP 20	Foreign Currency Translation	April 1983
SSAP 21	Accounting for Leases and Hire Purchase Agreements	August 1984
SSAP 22	Accounting for Goodwill (revised July 1989)	December 1984
SSAP 24	Accounting for Pension Costs	May 1988
SSAP 25	Segmental Reporting	June 1990
FRS 1	Cashflow Statements	March 1992
FRS 2	Accounting for Subsidiary Undertakings	December 1992
FRS 3	Reporting Financial Performance	June 1993
FRS 4	Capital Instruments	June 1994
FRS 5	Reporting the Substance of Transactions	September 1994
FRS 6	Acquisitions and Mergers	December 1994
FRS 7	Fair Value in Acquisition Accounting	December 1994

* Updated by the ASB's *Interim Statement on Consolidated Accounts*

The Review Panel

The Dearing Committee also identified the need for a review panel if standards are to be enforced. This was also addressed in the 1989 Act which gave power to the Secretary of State for Trade and Industry or persons authorised by him to ask the Courts to determine whether annual accounts comply with the true and fair requirement. According to the ASB, compliance with accounting standards will normally be necessary for financial statements to give a true and fair view. In special circumstances, the need to give a true and fair view will require a departure from accounting standards, but the Board envisages that only in 'exceptional circumstances will departure ... be necessary...'[9]

For public and large private companies, these powers have been delegated to the Review Panel, a subsidiary of the FRC, with the Department of Trade and Industry exercising its powers in other cases. If necessary, the Review Panel can ask the Courts to compel corrective action – even if this involves a revised set of accounts – although, so far, this has not proven necessary.

The Panel can act on its own initiative or in response to information received from sources such as qualified audit reports and press comment. One of its earliest and most spectacular interventions concerned Trafalgar House plc where the company was forced to restate its 1991 profit of £122m as a loss of £38m. Another example concerned Forte plc which failed to apply SSAP 12 by not depreciating its hotel properties. Despite this failure to apply the standard,the Panel found in favour of the company.

UITF

Sometimes an issue will appear which is not covered by an existing standard but which is sufficiently important that it must be urgently addressed. To cover such situations, the ASB established a subcommittee known as the Urgent Issues Task Force (UITF). Its pronouncements – known as 'abstracts' – are as authoritative as if they were standards themselves. Indeed, many are later superseded by Financial Reporting Standards.

Many of the pronouncements of the UITF are extremely technical. Nevertheless some idea of its tasks can be gleaned by considering UITF Abstract 4. Under the Companies Act, liabilities falling due after more than one year require separate disclosure on the face of the balance sheet but *all* debtors have to be shown as current assets. There is therefore a lack of symmetry between long term creditors and long term debtors. The Abstract requires that debtors due after one year be disclosed separately within current assets on the face of the balance sheet rather than by way of a note if they are material in the context of net assets.

The future regulation of UK accounting

As a result of the implementation of the Dearing proposals, the UK now has a conceptual framework to guide accounting developments; accounting standards have been given legal backing; and an effective enforcement mechanism has been put in place in the form of the Review Panel. In some ways, the model chosen by Dearing follows that of the USA. The Financial Reporting Council is a company limited by guarantee and so technically is a private sector regulator. It is also self-regulating in that it is supported by the accounting profession but is not legally controlled by government. The Accounting Standards Board has been prescribed as the standard setting body just as the USA's Financial Accounting Standards Board was the chosen vehicle of the Securities and Exchange Commission. The ASB has even copied the FASB's task force to tackle emerging issues.

Unlike the FASB, however, the Financial Reporting Council and the Accounting Standards Board owe their position directly to an Act of Parliament. In other words, they are statute based even though not statute controlled. This deriving of authority directly from statute, coupled with the more legalistic and prescriptive approach to standards, is getting closer to the accounting models found in many continental European countries. There, it is often the norm for the state to lay down detailed and prescribed regulations concerning the format and content of financial statements.

This trend towards more specific Financial Reporting Standards, backed by legal remedies where companies fail to comply, is being reinforced from another quarter, the European Union (EU). Not only is there a history of statute-driven accounting in many European countries, there is also an EU requirement to harmonise financial reporting across member states – and to ensure harmonisation requires legislation by member countries.

From this, it appears there are two forces moving UK accounting away from its traditional base of individual professional judgement towards a more prescriptive, legally enforceable regulatory framework. One is the Accounting Standards Board which owes its origin to the failures of the previous, professionally regulated regime; the other is the European Union with its emphasis on compatibility between the financial statements of member states. Both forces are moving towards a similar goal, that of greater consistency between financial statements and improved levels of disclosure, and backed by legal sanctions.

SUMMARY

Company accounts do not necessarily satisfy the needs of all users. First, even within one user group, there are unlikely to be identical needs. Secondly, as accounting has many of the features of a public good, users may prefer to be free-riders and not reveal their preferences. Thirdly, there is the corporate governance debate and the difficulty of making directors act in the best interest of shareholders. Fourthly, some stakeholders may not have their informational needs met as their relationship with the company is simply a contractual one. Because of this, there is a role for a regulator.

The work of the Accounting Standards Committee as a regulator has been considered and three Statements of Standard Accounting Practice examined in detail. From this study, two weaknesses in the ASC approach became apparent: the effectiveness of its standards and the committee's legitimacy.

Two further models of regulation were then considered: direct control by government and the use of an agency set up by, but independent of, the government. The current regulator in the UK, the Accounting Standards Board, has many similarities to the Financial Accounting Standards Board in the USA. Unlike the USA, however, UK financial reporting is now also controlled by extensive legislation as a result of European directives. This forms the subject of Chapter 8.

REFERENCES

1 See Watts, R. L. (April 1977) 'Corporate Financial Statements: A Product of the Market and Political Processes', *Australian Journal of Management*, and Leftwich, R. (January 1983) 'Accounting Information in Private Markets: Evidence from Private Lending Agreements', *The Accounting Review*, Vol. 58.

2 For a development of this approach see Cohen, K. J. and Cyert, R. M. (1965) *Theory of the Firm: Resource Allocation in a Market Economy*, Prentice Hall.

3 See Ashton, D. (1991) 'Agency theory and contracts of employment', in Ashton, D., Hopper, T. and Scapens, R. (eds) *Issues in Management Accounting*, Prentice Hall.

4 See *The Sunday Times* 15 May 1994 for further details.

5 Sheridan, T. and Kendall N. (1992) *Corporate Governance*, Financial Times/Pitman Publishing, p. 27.

6 Ibid., p.40.

7 Arden, M. (1993) Appendix to *Foreword to Accounting Standards*, Accounting Standards Board.

8 Under the Accounting Standards (Prescribed Body) Regulations 1990 (Statutory instrument 1990 No 1667).

9 Accounting Standards Board (1993) *Foreword to Accounting Standards*, para. 17.

FURTHER READING

Accounting Standards Board (1991ff) *Financial Reporting Standards*.

Blake, J. (1993) *Accounting Standards*, Pitman Publishing.

Bromwich, M. (1991) *Financial Reporting, Information and Capital Markets*, Pitman.

Davies, M., Paterson, R. and Wilson, A. (1994) *UK GAAP*, Macmillan.

Dimsdale, N. and Prevezer, M. (1994) *Capital Markets and Corporate Governance*, Oxford University Press.

Freear, J. (1981) 'Historical Background to Accounting', in Carsberg, B. and Hope, T. P. A. (eds) *Current Issues in Accounting*.

Institute of Chartered Accountants in England and Wales (1971–1990) *Statements of Standard Accounting Practice*.

Monks, R. and Minow N. (1994), *Corporate Governance*, Blackwell Publishers.

Prentice, D. D. and Holland P. (1993) *Contemporary Issues in Corporate Governance*, Oxford University Press.

TEST YOUR UNDERSTANDING

1 A public good is one which (a) the general public can buy; (b) is provided by a public limited company; (c) is not adequately provided by private markets.

2 List the features of a public good which are found in the provision of accounting information.

3 What is meant by the term corporate governance?

4 Outline two approaches to corporate governance.

5 Give three reasons why accounting information is increasingly regulated.

6 The phrase true and fair:

(a) is a legal concept defined in the 1948 Companies Act;
(b) requires that auditors should verify the accuracy of accounting statements;
(c) is a way of presenting accounts such that they are fair to all stakeholders;
(d) none of these.

7 Identify four types of accounting standard.

8 Since the passing of the 1989 Companies Act UK company accounts have to abide by accounting standards. True or false?

9 SSAP 9 is concerned with the treatment of:

   (a) stocks and long term contracts;
   (b) depreciation;
   (c) research and development.

10 Depreciation is:

   (a) the loss in value of an asset in a period;
   (b) an allocation of part of the net cost of an asset to a period based on the asset's life;
   (c) the difference between an asset's replacement cost and its realisable value.
   (d) resources retained in the business to provide for the replacement of an asset at the end of its life;
   (e) cash held back to provide for an asset's replacement at the end of its life;
   (f) none of these.

11 Research and development is charged as an expense in the period incurred. True or false?

12 List the weaknesses of the Accounting Standards Committee regime identified by the Dearing Committee.

13 Accounting standards in the UK are developed and issued by:

   (a) the accounting profession;
   (b) the Review Panel;
   (c) the Financial Reporting Council;
   (d) the Financial Accounting Standards Board;
   (e) none of these.

QUESTIONS

1 Preston Ltd acquired a machine for £300,000 which it is depreciating by equal annual amounts. When purchased, the asset was believed to have a five year life and no residual value. Part way through the second year, it became clear that the asset would only have a four year life in total.

   Advise the company as to its options when charging depreciation to the accounts for the second year.

2* Explain the difference between research and development and how both are treated in the accounts of UK companies.

3* 'Let the buyer beware' is a maxim which governs the buying and selling of many goods and services in the UK. Despite this, the history of accounting is one of increasing regulation.

   (a) Explain why the demand and supply of accounting information is not left entirely to markets.
   (b) Identify three possible models of regulation and comment on their strengths and weaknesses.

CHAPTER 8

Financial reporting – the UK and the European Union

Superficially, accounting reports appear very similar, irrespective of their country of origin. A more detailed investigation, however, shows substantial differences between countries both in terms of the regulation of accounting and the detailed contents of the reports. Considerable differences still exist between member states of the European Union despite the implementation of harmonising legislation.

This chapter:

- Identifies the main reasons why accounting systems differ between states

- Outlines the regulation of accounting in Germany and France

- Discusses the implementation of the EU's Fourth Directive relating to financial statements

- Details the effect of the Fourth Directive on the form and content of UK published accounts

- Shows how the Accounting Standards Board is changing the format and content of UK financial statements

The many different approaches to accounting and its regulation found in member states of the European Union was the problem faced by the Commission of the European Parliament when it began to look at means of harmonising financial reports in order to break down barriers and develop the single market. At the one extreme were countries like the UK and Ireland where much of accounting had evolved through time to satisfy market needs, where an important role was left to judgement and the determination of true and fair, and which were primarily driven by private sector standards and regulations within a general legal framework. At the other extreme were accounting systems such as those found in Germany and France which were essentially state driven, which required uniform or identical treatment of similar transactions by all entities and which required accounts to show that these rules had been truthfully obeyed rather than showing a fair view of the entity's commercial activities.

To give full consideration to the richness and diversity of accounting practices throughout Europe – yet alone the rest of the world – would require a whole series of texts rather than a small section of a single text. Nevertheless with the UK and the USA as models of market/commercially driven accounting and France and Germany as examples of government/uniform driven accounting, it is possible to develop an insight into the difficulties not only of harmonisation but also of inter-country interpretation of financial reports.

REASONS FOR DIFFERENT ACCOUNTING SYSTEMS

Such major differences in accounting will only rarely originate by accident. There is a whole range of reasons why countries adopt a particular form of accounting. Some are historical such as the similarities between UK accounting and that of many countries in the Commonwealth where the link is the historical connection with Great Britain. Other reasons may relate to the stage of economic development or the influence of religion as in the Islamic world. For Western Europe, however, there appear to be six major factors which have influenced the nature of accounting and financial reporting. These are: legal systems, methods of finance, taxation, the size and influence of the accounting profession, the role of theory and, on rare occasions, accidents of history.

The legal system

The USA, Ireland and England and Wales, unlike much of continental Europe, have legal systems based on common law. Statute law provides a framework but this is then supplemented by judgements based on the findings of individual cases. Common law rules are concerned with providing a solution to a particular case, taking account of all the circumstances, rather than with finding a universal set of rules for future use. Such a framework of law allows a great deal of flexibility.

The 1981 Companies Act was the first UK statute to incorporate a European Directive on company law and accounting. Until then, UK company law had never included a great deal of detailed rules to regulate company behaviour and financial reporting. Even though the history of UK company legislation has shown an increasing pattern of regulation and disclosure, a great deal of discretion had traditionally still been left for the accounting profession to apply its collective and individual judgement. Nowhere was this clearer than the failure of UK statute law to define what was meant by the central requirement of true and fair in the 1948 Act.

Much of continental Europe has a totally different system of law based on the Roman *jus civile*, with Scotland having elements of both systems. Roman law, based on ideas of justice and morality, requires a detailed codification of rules covering all eventualities and this applies equally to accounting and financial reporting. Under such a system, accounting is likely to be a branch of company law rather than a discipline in its own right. Such a system, being based on detailed, prescriptive codes, will, by its very nature, be much more difficult to change.

Methods of finance

Legal systems are not the only feature which differentiate the countries of Europe. From the early days of the Industrial Revolution, UK companies have depended to a large extent on outside shareholders, separate from the original owners, to finance business activity and this has manifested itself in a large and active stock exchange. Public companies have therefore played a major role in the economic life of the UK – as they also have in the Netherlands which, despite having a much smaller stock exchange, nevertheless has many multinational companies such as Royal Dutch-Shell, Philips and Unilever quoted on its exchange.

In other European countries, different patterns of ownership emerged. In France and Italy, a significant amount of capital has traditionally been provided by the state or by banks while the smaller, family-controlled business was, for a long time, a noticeable feature of the French economy. In Germany, the banks were important owners of companies as well as providers of loan capital. In the latter case, this dominant role by the banks arose partly out of the economic crises of the 1930s when bank intervention, in the form of loans, prevented many business failures and partly by the wide use of bearer shares by public companies. Unlike the UK where shareholders have to register their shares by name, companies with bearer shares do not keep a share register. Effectively shareholders are anonymous with shareholder rights conveyed by possession of the share certificate. To ensure security therefore, shareholders generally lodge such shares with banks for safekeeping and often give the same bank the power of proxy to vote as it sees fit. With shares both owned in their own right and held on trust for other shareholders, banks have often been able to play a significant role in many German companies.

From this brief outline, two distinct approaches to finance can be identified: the shareholder group and the bank/state/family group, with the UK emerging as by far the most important member of the shareholder group. In the UK, for example, approximately 2,000 domestic companies are quoted on the stock exchange while Germany and France only have between a third and a quarter of this number quoted on their exchanges.

Countries with a major tradition of private shareholders – including institutions such as pension funds – will tend to require a great deal of audited information as individual shareholders are denied access to the detailed internal information of the company. Although stewardship plays a part, the major reason for demanding this information will be to compare performance both between years and between firms – and this suggests a need for matching and accruals which involves judgement and which in turn involves experts.

In the bank/state/family group there is less likely to be such demands. As major shareholders, they are able to access internal information whenever required and make their own judgements about its contents. Any external reporting will largely be to serve the needs of the state as tax collectors or compilers of government statistics and, given the influence of banks as owners and creditors, any reporting is likely to be identified with extreme conservatism in the choice of values. Having said that, over the last 30 years there have been moves in most continental countries to require public companies to publish more detailed, audited statements. In Germany this resulted from the passing in 1965 of the *Aktiengesetz* law on public companies while France established the *Commission des Opérations de Bourse* (COB) in 1968 to improve the quality of published information and encourage the growth of the exchange. And overriding all of this has been the development of European law laying down detailed financial reporting procedures in member states.

The role of taxation

A third element determining the type of financial reporting has been taxation. By the time company taxation became important in the UK and the Netherlands, accounting reports and auditing were already well established. Consequently the practice grew up for the tax authorities to start with the financial or *commercial* results produced for reporting purposes and to adjust these to derive the profit figure for tax purposes as laid down by law.

Consider, for example, a company which has reported an accounting profit of £60,000 after charging straight line depreciation of 25 per cent on a machine purchased that year for £40,000 and after charging £5,000 entertaining expenses. Now assume that the tax laws do not allow a company to claim entertainment expenses but does allow a company to claim the full cost of any asset purchased in the year of acquisition. For tax purposes, the profit will be £35,000 made up of the original profit of £60,000 less the £30,000 written down value of the asset not charged against the financial accounts but allowable for tax plus the £5,000 of entertaining shown as an expense in the financial or commercial accounts but disallowable for tax purposes. Assuming an identical £60,000 result the following year, the taxable profit will be £75,000 made up of the £60,000 reported profit plus the disallowed £5,000 of entertaining expenses plus the £10,000 of depreciation already allowed in the previous year's computation of taxable profit.

Such complexities often do not exist in other European countries. To a large extent, the rules for taxation are the rules for financial reporting, resulting in the accounts for shareholders, the commercial accounts, being similar to the tax accounts.

The importance of the accounting profession

A fourth identifiable feature differentiating countries is the size and age of the accounting profession. Countries with a large number of private shareholders, a large number of public companies and which strive to achieve a true and fair view are likely to need a large number of accountants and auditors capable of exercising the necessary judgement to form opinions. This makes for a very powerful accounting profession which in turn enables the profession to influence further the form and content of accounting practices.

It could be argued that the real reason for the large number of accountants in the UK has been the statutory requirement until recently for all companies, private as well as public, to be audited by qualified auditors since the 1948 Act. But this would not explain why there are so many accountants in the USA where the influence of the SEC's requirements only extend to those companies listed with the SEC.

Care has to be taken in using the statistics on the number of accountants in different countries. Of the approximately 150,000 accountants in the UK belonging to professional bodies with the power to audit, many members do not carry out that role either because they specialise in some other area of accounting such as taxation or because they work in industry or commerce, for example, rather than in professional practice.

Comparing this with Germany, an accountant only remains a member of the *Institut der Wirtschaftsprüfer*, the German professional accounting body founded in 1931, while in practice. Secondly, there is a separate profession of tax experts actually larger than the accounting body. Thirdly, the German training programme is much longer so that many of the students of the German body would have been included in the total of qualified accountants had they been in the UK.

Nevertheless with only 6,000 members of the German *Institut* and 11,000 of its French equivalent, the *Ordre des Experts Comptables et des Comptables Agréés* founded in 1942, there still remains a significant difference in size. The accounting profession on much of the continent is therefore not only much smaller than in the Anglo countries, it also developed much later. Consequently it was less able to influence the shape of financial reporting at the earlier stages of the evolution of accounting. This may partly explain another feature differentiating accounting in France and Germany from the UK and the USA.

Auditing in the UK and USA is a private sector activity. Passing the examinations and meeting the regulations of the respective accounting bodies is the way to qualify as an auditor. In France and Germany, matters are somewhat different. There, the professional bodies set examinations and lay down codes of ethics but members then have to apply for membership of a second, state-controlled body to practise as an auditor. In France this is the *Compagnie Nationale des Commissaires aux Comptes* reporting to the French Ministry of Justice while in Germany it is the *Wirtschaftsprüferkammer* which is responsible to the Federal Ministry of Economics.

The role of theory

The two final factors identifiable as influencing the development of European accounting has been the role of theory and accidents. The clearest example of theory influencing the practice of accounting has been in the Netherlands. This has manifested itself in one or two major companies using for many years a form of replacement cost accounting in their external financial reports. Probably more important than this is the 'combination of almost extreme permissiveness with high professional standards' although this permissiveness has been moderated as a result of introducing European Directives on company law and reporting.[1]

There is a standard setting body, the *Raad voor de Jaarverslaggeving* or Council for Annual Reporting, but it has far less power than the UK Accounting Standards Board or the American FASB and companies are not obliged to follow its guidelines nor need accounts be qualified for any such failure. This reflects the important academic influence within

Dutch accounting where the concern is to show business economic reality or fairness. Of interest is the unique control over the quality of Dutch financial reports via the *Ondernemingskamer*, the Enterprise Chamber or accounting court of the Court of Justice, which allows interested parties – shareholders, employees, trade unions but *not* auditors – to lodge complaints if they feel the financial reports do not comply with the law.

Accidents of history

Accident of history is the final major identifiable factor influencing the form of accounting to be found in different countries. The clearest example of this has been the, often whole-sale, adoption of UK laws by members of the British Commonwealth. As will be seen, it was the German occupation of France in the Second World War which caused the latter to develop an accounting plan as a way of imposing uniformity on French accounting.

FINANCIAL REPORTING IN GERMANY

Germany has a much wider range of business organisations than the UK. Sole traders *(Einzelkaufmann)* and partnerships *(Offene Handelsgesellschaft* or OHG) exist as do public limited companies *(Aktiengesellschaft* or AG) and private limited companies *(Gesellschaft mit beschränkter Haftung* or GmbH). Beyond this though are other forms of organisation such as the *Kommanditgesellschaft auf Aktien* (KGaA), a modified form of public company having one partner with unlimited liability.

Origins of uniform accounting

Influencing all these many different forms of business organisation is the *Handelsgesetzbuch* (HGB) or Commercial Code which lays down uniform ways of treating transactions. This is part of a long history of accounting uniformity in Germany dating back to before the First World War when originally the codes were developed by firms for internal, cost accounting purposes. Not only did these help management by providing costing data, they also aided the making of inter-firm comparisons between members of the kartels which were a feature of the German business landscape for many years. This was rein-forced in the 1930s by the National Socialists who needed uniform or standardised finan-cial information to control the economy and who were concerned about profiteering as the country moved towards a war footing. In 1937 this led to the first ever national chart of accounts, known as the Goering Plan, to be applied throughout the private sector.

The German Commercial Code

Today, all businesses are subject to the accounting requirements of the Commercial Code, unlike in the UK where there are no statutory accounting requirements of any form for unincorporated entities such as sole traders and partnerships. Amongst other things, the HGB requires all businesses to keep books of account and prepare annual financial state-ments in accordance with the accounting principles laid down in the code and other leg-islation.

The form and content of the legislation varies depending on the form of incorporation. This is therefore a second difference from the UK where the same Companies Acts apply to all types of limited company. In Germany, public companies are subject to the law governing public companies known as the *Aktiengesetz* or AktG while the law relating to private companies is contained within the *Gesetz über Gesellschaften mit beschränkter Haftung* or GmbHG. And with the passing of the *Bilanzrichliniengesetz* or Accounting Directives Law in 1985, companies are now also subject to two major European Union Directives, the Fourth Directive which is outlined below, and the Seventh Directive which is covered in Chapter 9.

Within this detailed legal framework, there has been little scope yet alone inclination for the relatively small number of German accountants to take on the wider role of their Anglo-American colleagues. The influence of the German profession on the format and content of financial reports has been weak with their role mainly restricted to checking and confirming the compliance of companies with the legal and other statutory requirements. And until the passing into German law of the European Directives in 1985, only public companies plus certain other types of large business organisation had to be audited. Even now with the passing of the Accounting Directives Law, what are technically known as *small* companies do not have to be audited even though these are by far the most important in terms of numbers.

Impact of tax laws

Of far more importance than the role of the accounting profession in the development of German accounting principles has been the impact of the tax laws. Expenses are only allowable in the tax accounts *(Steuerbilanz)* if the commercial or final accounts *(Handelsbilanz)* produced for shareholders contain the same figures. This concept, that the accounts for tax purposes are based on the accounts produced for commercial or reporting purposes, is known as the *Massgeblichkeitsprinzip*, the 'authoritative or binding' principle.

Developments in accounting are therefore more likely to be traceable to the findings of the Federal Fiscal Court rather than recommendations of the accounting profession. Nowhere is this clearer than in the treatment of depreciation. In the UK, SSAP 12 is the authority for determining how depreciation should be reported in the final accounts of limited companies. Not only are its requirements general in nature, they are also totally independent of any depreciation rates allowable for tax purposes. In Germany, however, the tax regulations lay down specific depreciation rates to be used for particular assets – and for certain industries or for certain geographical locations, these can be extremely generous. However, for these depreciation allowances to be claimed against tax, they also have to appear in the financial or commercial accounts. The effect of *Massgeblichkeitsprinzip* is to reduce the role of matching and accruals in financial reporting.

Legal and correct vs. true and fair

From a UK perspective, the depreciation charge in the German financial accounts is certainly correct and reflects the legal realities but it can hardly be viewed as fair or representative. Such generous treatment of depreciation – and other items such as bad debt provisions – over and above that required for matching purposes is symptomatic of another feature of much of continental accounting. Effectively, by charging a greater amount of depreciation, a hidden reserve has been created by understating asset values and understating profits in the year of the charge. In subsequent years, the profits are then overstated as a result of this earlier accelerated depreciation. The financial implications of legal and correct vs. true and fair was highlighted in Daimler-Benz's first half-year's profit figures for 1993. Under German commercial and tax law, the company reported a net profit of DM168 million. Under American financial reporting standards, this was converted to a loss of DM949 million!

This concern with a 'legal and correct' view of accounts rather than 'true and fair' inevitably results from the detailed provisions of the Commercial and Tax Codes and the influence of *Massgeblichkeitsprinzip*. This has posed particular difficulties in many continental countries when trying to implement European Directives. One requirement of these Directives, mainly as a result of UK and Dutch influence, is that all accounts subject to the Directives should show a true and fair view.

In Germany this has been met by making additional disclosures rather than changing the basis of accounting away from the uniformity requirements of the Commercial and Tax Codes. Accounting is therefore still to a large extent an 'exercise in accurate bookkeeping ... to satisfy detailed rules and the scrutiny of the tax inspector'.[2] This emphasis on detailed legal rules and *Massgeblichkeitsprinzip* provides little scope for flexibility or judgement. The role of auditors is mainly to determine whether the law has been obeyed and any tax demand is correct. Given this lack of flexibility it comes as no surprise to discover the only allowable method of depreciation is strictly historical cost while the presentation of accounts is influenced more by detailed bookkeeping and legal considerations than the information needs of users.

Materiality for instance appears to have little or no role in German accounting. Only if an asset costs below DM800 – about £350 – can it be written off as an expense in the year of acquisition. Similarly, no matter how small an asset, liability or expense, it has to be reported if a heading for that classification is provided by the code.

An example of the strictly legal nature of German accounting is provided by the treatment of dividends proposed. In the UK it is normal for the directors to propose a dividend and for this to be recorded by deducting the amount from retained profits and creating a current liability, a form of creditor, shown in the balance sheet as dividends proposed. Legally, for these to be payable, shareholders have to agree the dividend at the company's annual general meeting. Because this will not have taken place at the time of the balance sheet, legally there is not a creditor and so it will not be included in German final accounts.

The final accounts

The German concern with final accounts reflecting the detailed bookkeeping manifests itself not only in the presentation of the balance sheet but also in its make up. As was demonstrated in Chapter 1, logically there is no difference between the vertical and horizontal formats. Despite this, the law in Germany requires balance sheets to be of the horizontal form, with all of the assets on the left-hand side and all of the liabilities on the right-hand side. Such treatment reflects the respective debit and credit balances in the books of account rather than the shareholder orientation of Anglo-Dutch accounting with its emphasis on net assets and shareholders' funds.

This concern with reflecting the records in the books of account resulted in the 1965 *Aktiengesetz* or public company law requiring profit to be shown as the final item on the liabilities side of the balance sheet and any loss as the final item on the assets side. Similarly, accounts such as the provision for bad debts were shown as liabilities rather than as deduction from the value of the debtors. Many of these difficulties have been eliminated following the adoption of the EU Directives on company law although the treatment of unpaid capital still follows this concern to reflect the recording of transactions.

Assume a company issues £100,000 of shares but only requires 50 per cent of the amount to be paid immediately. In terms of bookkeeping, the share capital has increased by £100,000 and this is reflected in cash increasing by £50,000 and a form of debtor, the amount yet to be paid by the shareholders or *uncalled capital,* increasing also by £50,000. From a shareholder's point of view, it seems sensible to show in the balance sheet the net funds employed in the company by deducting the £50,000 uncalled capital from the gross figure of £100,000. The assets side of the balance sheet would then show how the funds actually introduced into the business have been used. Not only is this not the way it is shown in Germany, it is not the way it can be shown in any other member state of the European Union. Just as the UK influenced the company law Directives by introducing the concept of true and fair, so Germany influenced the Directives by introducing prescriptive formats for final accounts. As a result, a balance sheet would now reflect the legal position by showing the capital of £100,000 as an obligation and the unpaid capital of £50,000 as an asset.

FINANCIAL REPORTING IN FRANCE

Although French law requiring businesses to keep accounts can be traced back to the *Code de Commerce* of 1808 and beyond, the modern-day features of French accounting originated in one of those accidents of history, the occupation of France by Germany in the Second World War.

An accident of history

The Industrial Revolution came late to France and was less extensive than in many other countries. Even until quite recently most French businesses were closely controlled, often family-owned affairs. Consequently the need for a major stock exchange and a large accounting profession never existed. With the German occupation, however, came the need for increased production for the war effort, increased financial controls and the idea of uniform accounting.

An inter-ministerial commission was charged with its development and by 1941 had completed its work. The commission recommended the introduction of uniform accounting by way of a detailed chart or plan of accounts to be applied to all business organisations. Not only would this provide consistency between firms, it would also enable aggregate national data to be produced. Needless to say, although not identical, it had many of the features of the Goering Plan introduced in Germany in 1937. The Plan was to have been implemented through a structure of industrial committees but because of opposition and other factors, it was only taken up by the aircraft industry.

The idea of an accounting plan, however, was resurrected by the post war French government. Influential civil servants were keen to develop a national accounting code both to improve the quality of national statistics and to assist in the national planning process. In addition, the government was concerned to embark on a programme of nationalising the basic industries but recognised the severe shortage of professional accountants. Not only was the size of the accounting profession in the form of the *Ordre des Experts Comptables et des Comptables Agréés* small, it had only been formed in 1942.

Origins of French uniform accounting

In 1946, the government established a commission to consider accounting standardisation. As a result of the commission's findings, the government established in 1947 the *Conseil National de la Comptabilité* attached to the Ministry of Finance. The Conseil had responsibility for the development of the *Plan Comptable Général* which the commission had proposed, a responsibility it has even today. The main difference between the 1947 Plan and the earlier one was that the management accounting section was made optional.

Initially the Plan was only mandatory for nationalised industries and companies receiving public subsidies. However, it soon became adopted by the private sector because (a) a 1959 decree required the Conseil to adapt the plan for all recognised industries, (b) it was increasingly being used as a standard by the accounting profession and (c) a 1965 decree related business taxation to the chart of accounts and model reports within the Plan. Today, the plan is enforced by a company law passed in 1983 and applies to all businesses, including unincorporated ones to which the *Code de Commerce* applies.

The code now incorporates the two major EU Directives on company law and accounting disclosure. Although these Directives were only intended to apply to incorporated bodies, by including them in the code they have effectively been extended to other forms of business – unlike the UK and Germany which restricts them to limited companies.

As in Germany, France has a wider range of business organisations than the UK. Not only are there public companies *(Société Anonyme* or SA), and private limited companies, *(Société à Responsabilité Limitée* or SARL) but in addition other forms of organisation, such as the limited liability partnership known as *Société en Commandite par Actions* are more significant than in the UK. Similarly accounting law has been influenced greatly by tax law. But of more interest is that France has introduced uniformity in a different way to Germany, by the *Plan Comptable Général* rather than through specific statutes.

The contents of the Accounting Plan

The current version of the Plan (*Plan Comptable Révisé*, 1982) applies to all businesses registered in France. In many ways it is similar to the detailed accounting manuals issued within large, modern companies to ensure consistency of treatment throughout the organisation. Company accounting manuals generally require a common treatment of similar transactions by all units within the group. Identical depreciation and stock valuation policies, for example, might be established for all parts of the organisation and a common coding structure established. Sharing the same account codes not only makes aggregation of group data that much easier, it also allows comparisons to be made between units within the group. Examples of coding structures were given in Chapter 5.

The French Accounting Plan is in three parts. The first part deals with the detailed recording procedures, the structure of the accounting system and terminology. Subjects covered include the organisation of the accounting system, the processing of transactions and the detailed code of accounts and their standard definitions. Part 2 deals with financial accounting and includes such matters as valuation and measurement rules, the determination of periodic income and the format of annual accounts, including consolidated accounts. The final part is the optional section on management accounting and contains details of the bases and methods for determining product costs.

There are many variants to the Plan covering adaptations for specific industries and an abridged version for businesses below a certain size. Common to all though are the uniform charts of accounts, broken down into eight classifications. These major headings for the financial accounts are reproduced in Exhibit 8.1.

Exhibit 8.1 The outline chart of accounts

1. Capital Accounts and related Loans and Debts
2. Long Term Assets (mainly fixed assets)
3. Stocks and Work in Progress
4. Accounts with Third Parties (debtors and creditors)
5. Financial Assets and Liabilities (such as Investments)
6. Expenses
7. Sales Revenue and Other Income
8. Special Accounts not Included Above (such as adjustments relating to previous periods)

Within each code there are further subclassifications down to five digits. Within Class 1, for example, will be found code 10 relating to capital and reserves, code 11 showing the profit and loss account figure brought forward and code 12 showing the current year's profit or loss. Similarly, Class 6 is broken down into nine subclasses and includes code 60 for purchases and stock movements, code 61 for purchases from subcontractors, code 64 for staff costs and code 68 for depreciation. This in turn is broken down further such that code 601 relates to purchases of raw materials and code 602 relates to purchases of other forms of stock. Further breakdown is provided for within these three digits. Code 6022, for example, relates to consumable supplies and within that code 60225 relates to office supplies while code 60226 relates to motor vehicle fuel.

Benefits and limitations of the Accounting Plan

The all-pervading nature of the Plan, backed by the law, has many advantages. It simplifies the work of auditors and tax inspectors. It also reduces the need for accountants by limiting the variety of accounting systems and eliminating accounting expertise and judgement in many areas. This latter point has been reinforced by the wide availability at reasonable cost of microcomputers and inexpensive standard software packages. It also aids the collection of national statistics by allowing a civil servant to collect detailed information simply by aggregating the amounts recorded by firms under any particular code.

However, it is not without disadvantages. Standardisation does not automatically improve the quality of financial data. Forcing all firms to use the same depreciation rates, for example, has been shown to be misleading when wear and tear varies depending on the way an asset has been used. Standardised charts of accounts may well give a legal and true picture of an enterprise's business activity; they may not necessarily give a fair one to external users of accounts.

INTERNATIONAL STANDARDS AND EUROPEAN DIRECTIVES

What is clear from this brief summary of accounting in different countries is the increasing standardisation of financial reporting within national boundaries. But if standardisation is so beneficial within each country, how much greater might be the benefits if standards applied across those boundaries? Modern industry in the form of multinational enterprises striving for economies of scale is, after all, no respecter of national frontiers. Similarly, capital markets are increasingly international in outlook with companies no longer looking to their indigenous stock exchanges and financial institutions as the sole source of finance. Given this, the need for international comparability becomes imperative not only for investors and managers but also for governments in their role as tax collectors.

The International Accounting Standards Committee

An attempt to address this issue was begun in June 1973 with the formation of the *International Accounting Standards Committee*. Founded by the professional accounting bodies of Australia, Canada, France, Germany, Ireland, Japan, Mexico, the Netherlands, the UK and the USA, it has since been joined by representatives of accounting bodies from more than 70 countries. The IASC is therefore essentially a private sector body and within this lies its major weakness.

Although it provides a ready-made set of standards for countries as yet to have developed their own, the standards tend to reflect a flexible, investor-oriented approach and this may not be ideal for countries with an insignificant number of public companies or where the objectives of accounting are government oriented. But their greatest limitation is the lack of any mechanism to enforce the standards. As far as possible, UK standards are supposed to incorporate the requirements of the international ones but the standards themselves have no authoritative standing in the UK. Companies are not required to comply with them nor are auditors required to note departures from them in their audit report.

European Union harmonisation

Similar issues were faced by the European Union as it strove towards harmonising company law across member states. Its difficulties were both conceptual and structural. As shown in Chapter 6, the search for a single, value-free conceptual framework is an impossible dream. Any proposals would therefore involve choosing one set of values over another, in particular choosing between the investor orientation of UK and Dutch financial reporting and the more creditor/tax orientation of countries such as Germany and France.

In fact, the problems were even more deep-seated than that. Accounting had developed under two totally different legal systems and with two totally different objectives. Uniform accounting, with its main purpose of satisfying the needs of government and with its base in Roman law, sat uneasily with the individual investor needs of Anglo-Dutch accounting. And even within these two groups there were substantial differences in emphasis. The Dutch with their concern for accounting theory and a business economics approach faced different issues to the Irish and British with systems pragmatically evolved through time. Similarly with systems of uniform accounting: France addressed this primarily through its codified charts of accounts whereas the German system operated mainly through company and tax law.

Directives and regulations

Two main mechanisms exist for implementing Community legislation: Directives which have to be incorporated into national laws, and Regulations which become the law throughout the Community without passing through the legislature of individual states. Of the many Directives issued, four are of particular importance to accounting.

The Second Directive was concerned with separately identifying public companies, defining the minimum capital requirements of public companies and determining distributable profit. In the UK this Directive was implemented in the 1980 Companies Act. Public companies had to include the term 'public limited company' or the initials plc in their name. It also introduced another feature common on the continent but not in the UK, that public companies should have a minimum issued share capital. In the UK this was set at £50,000. No such minimum capital requirement was contained in the Directive for private limited companies. Despite that, the German private company law of 1980, the *Gesetz über Gesellschaften mit beschränkter Haftung* or GmbHG, extended the requirement to private companies registered in Germany.

Until the incorporation of the Second Directive in UK company law, no statutory definition of distributable profits existed. Any legal guidance came from individual cases. Now, as a result of the Second Directive, a private company can only pay a dividend if its balance of realised profits exceed its realised losses, while for a public company this has to be reduced further, by the *excess of unrealised losses over unrealised profits*.

The Eighth Directive concerned itself with the qualification and work of auditors and was incorporated in the UK Companies Act of 1989. The Directive requires persons carrying out statutory audits to be approved by the authorities of EU member states and for there to be mutual recognition of auditing qualifications between member states. This involves member states identifying 'recognised qualifying bodies'. For Germany and France there already existed state run auditing bodies. The UK, however, chose to take the private sector route even for this by delegating the powers to the main UK accounting bodies. Predominantly these were the English, Scottish and Irish Institutes of Chartered Accountants plus the Chartered Association of Certified Accountants. The two Directives of most importance to financial reporting, however, were the Fourth, dealing with the format and rules of accounting, and the Seventh, dealing with consolidated accounts. Consideration of the Seventh Directive is deferred until Chapter 9. Of far more significance for the UK was the Fourth Directive.

THE FOURTH DIRECTIVE

Resolving the deep-seated accounting differences between member states was the task faced by the European Union in drafting the Fourth Directive. It involved much more than the resolution of different legal systems and different approaches to financial reporting. Two further issues were of equal importance. Some member states imposed detailed, legally enforceable accounting procedures such as charts and codes on all business entities, incorporated and unincorporated. Secondly, many continental countries partially or totally exempted private limited companies from having to publish and have audited their final accounts. From the beginning therefore the Directive was concerned with three issues: the valuation rules to be applied; the format or presentation of the final accounts; and the extent of disclosure.

The first draft of the Fourth Directive was published in 1971, before the UK and Ireland had joined the Community, and was very much influenced by the German public companies Act, the *Aktiengesetz*, of 1965. The original proposal, for example, required by law that the final item on the liabilities side of the balance sheet should be the accumulated profit retained in the company, broken down between the amount for the year and the balance from previous years. Should these be losses rather than profits, they were to be shown as the final items on the assets side of the balance sheet, reflecting the German emphasis on bookkeeping. Even now the Directive retains many of the prescriptive features of German accounting. These, however, have been tempered by the influence of Anglo-Dutch accounting and the need for compromise to meet the needs of individual member states.

The valuation rules

Now, the overriding objective of the Directive is to show a true and fair view, although given the alien nature of this concept for some countries, it has mainly been achieved by additional disclosure rather than changing the monetary values within the accounts.

Reflecting the Accounting Standards Committee's SSAP 2, five concepts are invoked to guide the production of accounts: going concern, accruals, consistency, prudence and the separate valuation of elements. This last requirement – undertaken as a matter of course by most UK accountants – reflects the conservatism within the *Aktiengesetz* which *by statute* required the lower of cost or net realisable value rule to be applied separately in accounts rather than to groupings. Effectively it prevents unrealised gains being used to offset unrealised losses. The inclusion of the going concern and accruals concepts, omitted from the first draft of the Directive, reflected the influence of Anglo-Dutch accounting and the difficulty of harmonising two essentially different accounting traditions.

Nowhere was this difficulty more apparent than in determining the valuation rules to apply to final accounts, with the Dutch permitting replacement costs, the British *ad hoc* revaluations and the Germans adhering strictly to historical cost. The outcome was that the Directive gave member states the right to permit *or* require companies to use any of the three valuation methods either as the main accounts or as a supplement. However, the historical cost tradition dominates the Directive. Where revaluations or replacement costs are allowed, extensive notes are required showing such matters as (a) the year of valuation, (b) the name or qualification of the valuer if valued this year, and (c) sufficient data to enable the historical cost result to be calculated.

The format of the final accounts

For UK accountants, the most noticeable influence of the *Aktiengesetz* on the Fourth Directive was a prescribed format and content for the published final accounts. Logically, a balance sheet is merely a listing of unexpired balances at the balance sheet date. Its presentation for a UK accountant was to be decided on the basis of user needs. Chapter 2 demonstrated three possible balance sheets: a basic one which merely listed the balances of the assets and liabilities; an entity approach with current liabilities deducted from current assets to show net assets and their financing by long term funds; and a proprietary balance sheet showing how shareholders' funds had been used. Within these balance sheets, the detailed contents were organised according to current best practice.

The German tradition was different. It emphasised the need for a *correct and sure view*. German law required the balance sheet to reflect accurately the books of account by making the balance sheet a summary of these balances – the basic balance sheet outlined above – with prescribed subheadings and contents. The *Aktiengesetz* even went as far as demanding a horizontal balance sheet with assets on the left and liabilities on the right, reflecting the debits and credits of the original books of account.

This German tradition runs throughout the Fourth Directive. To accommodate this within the Anglo-Dutch tradition has meant further compromise. In its final form, the Directive allows two balance sheet formats and four profit and loss account formats. The balance sheet can either be presented horizontally or vertically. In its horizontal format, it very much follows the German approach, that the balance sheet should be a truthful representation of unexpired balances as they appear in the accounts. In its vertical format, it represents the proprietorial balance sheet of UK accounting.

The allowable profit and loss formats follow similar reasoning. In its horizontal format, it appears similar to the 'T' account presentation of double-entry bookkeeping while in its vertical format it is similar to the user-oriented statement developed in Chapter 2. Within these two prescribed presentations of the profit and loss account, two classifications are allowed. One classification breaks down the expenses by three prescribed functional headings of cost of sales, distribution and administrative expenses. The other breaks down expenses by their nature or type such as raw materials, staff costs and depreciation.

Member states are allowed to prescribe a particular format or to leave the choice to individual companies. Whichever format is chosen, the contents have to be those laid down in the Fourth Directive and in the *order* prescribed by the Directive. The UK and the Netherlands have interpreted the requirements broadly and allow all formats, although the vertical format is by far the most popular, with companies mainly choosing to break down expenses by function. With a totally different accounting tradition, it may come as no surprise to know that France and Germany are much more prescriptive, allowing for instance only the horizontal format for the balance sheet.

Disclosure

There were, however, other areas of difference which the Fourth Directive had to accommodate. Many countries had a tradition of partially or fully exempting private companies from the need to audit and publish annual accounts. The Directive allows, but does not require, member states to continue that tradition. To harmonise this across member states needed some common measure to define such companies. This it chose to do by defining *small* and *medium* sized companies using three criteria: turnover, number of employees and balance sheet total. To qualify, a company has to meet two out of the three criteria, with lower levels being set for the small company qualification.

Member states may exempt small companies from publishing their profit and loss account and from being audited while medium companies may be allowed to publish an abridged profit and loss account and be exempted from disclosing other information. Germany and the Netherlands have made full use of this provision by exempting small companies from being audited. The UK took advantage of the small and medium companies publishing exemptions from the beginning but it was only from August 1994 onwards that the UK allowed certain small companies to be exempted from the need for an audit.

THE UK AND THE FOURTH DIRECTIVE

The 1981 Companies Act originally implemented the Fourth Directive in the UK although this has subsequently been consolidated within the 1985 Companies Act. The Fourth Schedule to the 1985 Act is mainly concerned with financial reporting matters. Part I specifies the general rules and allowable formats. It allows a company to choose any of the formats originally specified in the Fourth Directive. Once specified, a company is required to adhere to its choice unless there are grounds for change.

Part II, headed Accounting Principles and Rules, is divided into three sections. Section A incorporates the five accounting concepts of the Fourth Directive. Section B deals in detail with the historical accounting rules while Section C effectively specifies a number of options up to full replacement cost accounting. Should a company take advantage of these alternative accounting rules, supplementary information must be provided to enable the historical cost accounting information to be calculated, emphasising the primacy of historical cost values within the Fourth Directive.

The allowable balance sheet formats are shown in detail as Appendices 1 and 2 to this chapter along with Appendix 3 which shows the two prescribed cost classifications of the profit and loss account in a vertical format. (The horizontal format has been omitted to avoid repetition.) The prescribed formats are also shown in outline in Exhibit 8.2.

Small and medium companies

Not all companies have to file the extensive disclosures required by the Act with the Registrar of Companies. The UK has taken advantage of the small and medium company provisions granted within the Fourth Directive although all companies must provide

Exhibit 8.2 **The major prescribed headings in company accounts**

Format 1 Profit and loss account		Format 2 Profit and loss account		
	(£)		(£)	(£)
1. Turnover	X	1. Turnover		X
2. Cost of sales	(X)	2. Changes in stocks of finished goods		
3. Gross profit or loss	X	and work in progress		(X)
4. Distribution costs	(X)	4. Other operating income		X
5. Administration costs	(X)	5. (a) Raw materials	(X)	
6. Other operating income	X	(b) Other external charges	(X)	(X)
10. Other interest receivable		6. Staff costs		
and similar income	X	(a) Wages and salaries	(X)	
11. Amounts written off investments	(X)	(b) Social security costs	(X)	
12. Interest payable and similar charges	(X)	(c) Other pension costs	(X)	(X)
13. Tax on profit or loss on ordinary activities	(X)	7. (a) Depreciation etc. written off		
14. Profit or loss on ordinary activities		fixed assets	(X)	
after taxation	X	(b) Exceptional amounts written off		
		current assets	(X)	(X)
		8. Other operating charges		(X)
		12. Other interest receivable		
		and similar income		X
		13. Amounts written off investments		(X)
		14. Interest payable and similar charges		(X)
		15. Tax on profit or loss		
		on ordinary activities		(X)
		16. Profit or loss on ordinary activities		
		after taxation		X

Format 1 Balance sheet

		(£)	(£)
B.	**Fixed assets**		
	I Intangible assets (trade marks, development costs)	X	
	II Tangible assets (land and buildings, plant and machinery)	X	
	III Investments (shares in other companies)	X	X
C.	**Current assets**		
	I Stock (raw materials, finished goods)	X	
	II Debtors	X	
	III Investments (shares in other companies)	X	
	V Cash at bank and in hand	X	
		X	
D.	**Prepayments and accrued income**	X	
		X	
E.	**Creditors: amounts falling due within one year** (trade creditors, bank overdrafts)	(X)	
F.	**Net current assets**		X
G.	**Total assets less current liabilities**		X
H.	**Creditors: amounts falling due after more than one year** (debentures)		(X)
			X
K.	**Capital and reserves**		
	I Called-up share capital		X
	II Share premium account		X
	III Revaluation reserve		X
	IV Other reserves		X
	V Profit and loss		X
			X

shareholders with a full set of accounts. The main advantage of the provisions is therefore the lack of publicity. To qualify, a company has to meet two out of the three conditions detailed in Exhibit 8.3 for the current and immediately preceding year.

Exhibit 8.3 Small and medium company exemption limits

	Small	Medium
Turnover: not more than	£2,800,000	£11,200,000
Assets (items A-D on each format): not more than	£1,400,000	£5,600,000
Average number of employees: not more than	50	250

If a company qualifies as a small company, it does not have to file a profit and loss account nor a directors report while its balance sheet is limited to the items which are assigned a letter or a Roman numeral. In addition, it does not have to file all the notes which go with the accounts nor does it have to file information about directors' salaries. For a medium company, no modification to the balance sheet is permissible although a modified profit and loss account is allowed which effectively starts with the gross profit by combining items 1, 2, 3 and 6 in Format 1 and items 1 to 5 in Format 2. In addition, it is excused filing the analysis of turnover and profit by class of business and geographical market outlined below.

From 11 August 1994, certain companies are no longer required to have their accounts audited. To qualify for the exemption, a company must have an annual turnover of £90,000 or less and gross assets of less than £1.4 million. Public companies, banking and insurance companies, trade unions, employers' associations and subsidiaries of larger companies cannot claim this exemption. Equally, the exemptions are not mandatory. A company which would otherwise qualify must still have an audit if 10 per cent or more of its shareholders request one. For companies with a turnover above £90,000 but below £350,000 (£250,000 for charities), there is still relief from a full audit. Instead, they have to produce a reporting accountant's report. For both types of small company, all the other provisions of the Companies Act still applies.

Effect on UK financial reporting

Implementing the Fourth Directive was a significant event in the history of UK accounting. For the first time, the law was prescribing the form and content of final accounts. Not only must accounts show the exact headings and subheadings, they must also follow the prescribed sequence. Only if the current and comparative figures are zero can the headings be omitted. They cannot be excluded on the grounds of not being material.

The only discretion relates to headings with Roman numerals. Paragraph 3(4) of the 4th Schedule to the 1985 Act effectively allows items with Roman numerals to be shown in the form of notes rather than on the face of the accounts. The balance sheet headings affected by this are to be found in Appendices 1 and 2. Perhaps of more significance is that legally much of the profit and loss account can be shown by notes although in practice this is not done!

The profit and loss account

The analysis of expenditure

Format 1 of the profit and loss account analyses costs by function. Although the cost of sales is likely to include some fixed costs and the distribution and administration costs are likely to include some variable costs, nevertheless, *as an approximation*, the headings tend to reflect cost behaviour. As such they are more user-oriented than the alternative. One weakness within Format 1 is that the Act does not define the composition of the three main expense headings.

Format 2, by identifying the costs incurred, is more concerned with reflecting the original bookkeeping entries. Not all the costs, however, will have been consumed in making sales. Some will remain in the firm in the form of closing stock. An adjustment is therefore necessary to turn costs incurred into expenses consumed. The cost of an expense consumed can be expressed as:

Expenses consumed in a period = Opening stocks + Costs incurred – Closing stocks

and this simplifies to:

Expenses consumed in a period = Costs incurred + (Opening stocks – Closing stocks)

or:

Expenses consumed in a period = Costs incurred + Change in stocks.

Item 2 on the second format serves to turn the costs incurred into the expenses consumed. For both formats, the Act also requires the profit and loss account to show the profit or loss before taxation, the total dividends paid and proposed and any movement on reserves such as the transfer of part of retentions to a general reserve.

The analysis of turnover

In both formats, turnover is exclusive of VAT or any other form of sales tax. If a company carries on more than one class of business, both the turnover attributable to each class and any profit or loss before tax must be disclosed. In addition, a geographical breakdown of turnover is required unless this would seriously prejudice the interests of the company. Income from listed and unlisted investments has to be shown separately.

Disclosure of other costs

The staff costs and depreciation, already disclosed in Format 2, also have to be disclosed – generally by way of a note – if Format 1 is chosen. And in both cases, the average number of employees has to be given. Whichever format is chosen, other expenses have also to be disclosed, generally by way of a note. Interest payable must be analysed between bank loans and overdrafts, loans repayable within five years, loans repayable beyond five years, and other loans. The total of directors' emoluments (including pension contributions) broken down between directors' fees and other payments has to be disclosed along with the amount and the number of directors who waive their emoluments. Emoluments excluding pension contributions have to be shown for the chairman (plus the highest paid director if paid more than the chairman) and an analysis of the remuneration provided to other directors showing their number within £5,000 remuneration bands is also required.

The two other major expenses which have to be disclosed are charges for the hire of plant and machinery and auditors' remuneration. As a result of the 1989 Companies Act, the latter has now to be broken down between fees in their capacity as auditors and fees relating to other services provided.

The balance sheet

Turning to the balance sheet formats, both contain very similar data although Format 2, the horizontal format, is very much a summary of the balances in the books of account with all the debit balances on one side and all the credit balances on the other. Format 1 is similar to the proprietorial balance sheet developed earlier with the net assets equalling shareholders' funds.

The treatment of creditors

One difference reflects the legalistic and creditor orientation to accounting found in many continental countries. No mention is made of long term debt within the major headings identified by letters in Format 1. Instead, loans and debentures are defined in terms of their legal reality, as creditors rather than by their function. The Act therefore differentiates between creditors falling due within one year and those falling due after more than one year.

Although in most cases traditional current liabilities will be found under amounts falling due within one year and long term loans and debentures will be found under amounts falling due after more than one year, nevertheless, it is possible for these to be reversed. This might happen for instance when debentures are due to be redeemed within the next twelve months and so represent creditors due within one year even though it might be the company's intention to replace them by a fresh issue.

This need to differentiate between short term and long term creditors based on a 12-month horizon also extends to Format 2 even though there is only a single heading provided in the Act. Normally this will be disclosed by way of a note. For both formats, an additional note is required identifying creditors not due for repayment in less than five years time and those creditors repayable by instalments, part of which falls due for repayment in excess of five years' time. These requirements are in addition to the statutory disclosure shown by arabic numerals.

The treatment of assets

Extensive disclosure is also required amongst the assets. Under intangible fixed assets, development costs are particularly identified. The Act is quite clear: development costs can only be included in a company's balance sheet *in special circumstances*. Unfortunately the phrase is not developed and so the only guidance in the UK is that given by SSAP 13. Movements on fixed assets and depreciation have to be disclosed, showing opening values, any acquisitions and disposals during the year, any transfers and the closing balance.

Amongst the current assets, the treatment of stock within the Act is of particular significance. Not only does it specifically allow FIFO and weighted average, it also allows

LIFO or 'any other method' similar to the three identified. There is therefore a conflict between the 1985 Act and SSAP 9 although the Act's overriding requirement to show a true and fair view may possibly be interpreted as supporting the standard. Finally, within the heading of debtors, the Act requires the amount to be split between those falling due within one year and those falling due after more than one year. In the UK, this has subsequently been clarified. Under the Urgent Issues Task Force's Abstract 4, this breakdown should be shown on the face of the balance sheet within current assets.

Accounting policies and contingencies

Over and above the detailed disclosure required in the balance sheet and profit and loss account, the 1985 Companies Act requires the accounting policies adopted by the company and any contingent liabilities to be disclosed. The accounting policies to be disclosed are those which are material to the profit and loss account and balance sheet such as the policies on revenue recognition and depreciation and the valuation of stock.

Since the 1989 Companies Act this has been extended and it is now mandatory to state 'whether the accounts have been prepared in accordance with the applicable accounting standards' and to disclose 'particulars of any material departure from those standards and the reasons for it'.

Contingent liabilities are liabilities which will only arise if a particular, uncertain event takes place. Examples include pending law suits where the liability will only exist if the case goes against the company and guarantees given by the company which will only have to be honoured if agreed conditions are not met. The Act requires the (estimated) amount, its legal nature and any security provided to be disclosed, normally by way of a note. SSAP 18 Accounting for Contingencies goes beyond this and recognises contingent gains. Following prudence, it requires a probable contingent loss to be charged as an expense and any contingent gain to be shown by way of a note. If a contingent loss is only possible, it should be disclosed by way of a note although any contingent gain should be ignored. Should either a gain or a loss be only considered remote, both can be totally ignored.

UK PUBLISHED ACCOUNTS

As a result of the implementation of the Fourth Directive and the requirement of the 1989 Act that accounts should normally be produced using accounting standards, the form and content of UK published accounts are now much more detailed. Although this may make for more meaningful interpretation, one major problem when comparing different firms is the choice of profit and loss account formats open to them. Example 8.1 addresses this difficulty and demonstrates the two possible vertical profit and loss account formats. The example shows the trial balance of Bender plc after recording all transactions for the year, other than any necessary year end adjustments, and enables the profit and loss account to be produced in those two formats.

As the Act does not specify the detailed contents of each heading, certain judgements have to be made. The directors, for example, have been classified as an administration expense although logically, had one been designated as the sales director, the appropriate emoluments would have appeared within the distribution costs.

Example 8.1

Bender plc has an authorised share capital of 3 million £1 ordinary shares, of which 2 million have been issued. It is also financed by £1 million of 10 per cent debentures redeemable in seven years' time and a 12½ per cent bank loan repayable in nine months' time. The company manufactures and sells a single product range. The trial balance for the year ended 31 December 19X9 is given below.

	(£000)		(£000)
Raw material stock	75	Sales	3,000
Stock of work in progress	120	Trade creditors	100
Finished stock	90	10% debentures	1,000
Raw material purchases	525	Bank loan	2,000
Factory wages	700	Provision for depreciation – buildings	80
Factory National Insurance	50	Provision for depreciation – plant etc.	160
Factory pension	100	Provision for depreciation – cars	25
Office salaries	140	Royalties received	35
Office National Insurance	25	Ordinary share capital	2,000
Office pensions	35	Share premium account	200
Sales department salaries	120	Profit and loss reserve	600
Sales department National Insurance	20		
Sales department pensions	30		
Directors' fees	50		
Directors' salaries	160		
Directors' pensions	40		
Rates	600		
Light and heat	200		
Car expenses – sales staff	30		
Freehold land and buildings	2,000		
Factory plant and machinery	500		
Cars	100		
Debtors	1,000		
Cash	1,300		
Rent	200		
Debenture interest	100		
Loan interest	250		
Overdraft interest	40		
Capitalised development expenses	400		
Trade marks	200		
	£9,200		£9,200

The freehold land and buildings are used entirely by the factory. Buildings are depreciated at 1 per cent p.a., plant and machinery at 20 per cent p.a. and cars at 25 per cent p.a. – all straight line and with no residual values. £400,000 of the rates and £100,000 of the light and heat relate to the factory. The balance on both accounts is split equally between the sales and administration departments which also share the rent in equal proportions. Plant and machinery includes £100,000 purchased this year. Closing stocks are: raw materials, £100,000; work in progress, £690,000; and finished stock, £140,000.

▶

Corporation tax is estimated at £30,000, payable in nine months' time. The auditors' fee is estimated at £10,000 and a dividend is proposed of £50,000. None of these have been recorded in the accounts.

Details of the emoluments paid to the directors are:

	Directors' fees	Salaries	Pension contributions
Chairperson	£20,000	£40,000	£20,000
Ms Exe	£20,000	£70,000	£10,000
Mr Wye	£10,000	£20,000	£5,000
Mrs Wye	nil	£30,000	£5,000
	£50,000	£160,000	£40,000

Apart from period end adjustments for depreciation, the provision for corporation tax, dividends and the audit fee, the major difficulty is in analysing the expenses between the prescribed headings required by the Companies Act. For Format 1, this will involve a mini manufacturing account to derive the cost of sales and then the grouping of the remaining expenses within the distribution and administration classifications. Format 2 requires the analysis to be undertaken by expenditure type and poses less difficulty. The analysis for both formats is shown in Exhibit 8.4. With this analysis it is then possible to produce both formats of the profit and loss account. The only other judgement required is deciding how to treat the royalties paid. In both cases, this has been shown under the heading of other operating income.

Exhibit 8.4 The building up of cost headings

Cost of sales	(£000)	Distribution costs	(£000)
Opening raw material stock	75	Sales employment costs including pensions	170
Add purchases	525	Car expenses	30
Less closing raw material stock	–100	Car depreciation	25
Raw material issued to production	500	Rent	100
Factory employment costs including pensions	850	Rates	100
Factory depreciation	20	Light and heat	50
Plant and machinery depreciation	100		475
Rates	400		
Light and heat	100	**Administration costs**	(£000)
Add opening work in progress	120	Office employment costs including pensions	200
Less closing work in progress	–690	Rates	100
Transfer to finished stock	1,400	Light and heat	50
Add opening finished stock	90	Rent	100
Less closing finished stock	–140	Auditors fee	10
Cost of sales	1,350	Directors' emoluments	250
			710

Exhibit 8.4 (Continued)

Interest payable	(£000)	Raw materials and consumables	(£000)
Debenture interest	100	Opening raw material stock	75
Loan interest	250	Add purchases	525
Overdraft interest	40	Less closing raw material stock	–100
	390		500

Depreciation	(£000)	Other external charges	(£000)
Buildings	20	Audit fee	10
Plant and machinery	100	Directors' fees	50
Cars	25	Rates	600
	145	Light and heat	200
		Car expenses	30
		Rent	200
			1,090

Staff costs

	Wages & salaries (£000)	Social security (£000)	Pensions (£000)
Factory	700	50	100
Office	140	25	35
Sales	120	20	30
Directors	160	nil	40
	1120	95	205

Change in stocks

	Opening stock (£000)	Closing stock (£000)	Change (£000)
Work in progress	120	690	570
Finished stock	90	140	50
			620

Having analysed the expenses, the next stage is to put the information in the prescribed format and extend this by the use of notes where necessary. The resulting final accounts and relevant notes are shown in Exhibit 8.5. Both profit and loss accounts are shown for demonstration purposes although only one will be required to satisfy publication and filing needs.

Exhibit 8.5 The published final accounts

Profit and loss account 12 months ended 31 December 19X9

Format 1

	(£000)
Turnover	3,000
Cost of sales	(1,350)
Gross profit	1,650
Distribution costs	(475)
Administration costs	(710)
Other operating income	35
Interest payable and similar charges	(390)
Profit on ordinary activities before taxation	110

Format 2

		(£000)
Turnover		3,000
Change in stocks and work in progress		620
Other operating income		35
Raw materials and consumables	(500)	
Other external charges	(1,090)	(1,590)
Staff costs: Wages and salaries	(1,120)	
Social security	(95)	
Pension costs	(205)	(1,420)

Exhibit 8.5 (Continued)

Format 1	(£000)	Format 2	(£000)
Tax on profit on ordinary activities	(30)	Depreciation	(145)
Profit for the financial year	80	Interest payable and similar charges	(390)
Dividends proposed	(50)	Profit on ordinary activities before taxation	110
Retained profit for the year	30	Tax on profits on ordinary activities	(30)
Profit retained 1 January 19X9	600	Profit for the financial year	80
Profit retained 31 December 19X9	630	Dividends proposed	(50)
		Retained profit for the year	30
		Profit retained 1 January 19X9	600
		Profit retained 31 December 19X9	630

Balance sheet at 31 December 19X9

	(£000)	(£000)	(£000)
Fixed assets			
Intangible assets			600
Tangible assets			2,190
			2,790
Current assets			
Stocks		930	
Debtors		1,000	
Cash at bank and in hand		1,300	
		3,230	
Creditors: amounts falling due within one year			
12½ bank loan	2,000		
Trade creditors	100		
Other creditors including taxation and social security	90	2,190	
Net current assets			1,040
Total assets less current liabilities			3,830
Creditors: amounts falling due after more than one year			
10% debentures repayable 2,000			1,000
			2,830
Capital and reserves			
Called-up share capital			2,000
Share premium account			200
			2,200
Other reserves: profit and loss account			630
			2,830

Notes to the accounts:

1. Accounting policies
   (i)   The accounts have been prepared under the historical cost concept.
   (ii) Depreciation is provided on fixed assets at rates estimated to write off their cost over their useful lives. Freehold properties are depreciated at 1 per cent per annum, equipment and vehicles at 20–25 per cent per annum.
   (iii) Stocks are valued at the lower of cost or net realisable value and include an appropriate proportion of production overheads.
   (iv) Turnover represents amounts invoiced, net of VAT, for goods supplied.

Exhibit 8.5 (Continued)

2. Interest payable

On bank loans, overdrafts and borrowings repayable wholly within 5 years	£290,000
On loans repayable wholly or partly after 5 years	£100,000

3. Profit on ordinary activities before taxation is after charging:

Staff costs: Wages and salaries	£1,120,000	
Social security costs	£95,000	
Pensions	£205,000	£1,420,000
Depreciation		£145,000
Auditors' remuneration		£10,000
Directors emoluments: Fees as directors	£50,000	
Other emoluments	£200,000	£250,000

The chairman's emoluments were £50,000. The emoluments of the highest paid director were £80,000. Two other directors received emoluments within the band £25,001–£30,000.

4. Taxation

UK corporation tax at 35 per cent on the profits for the year	£30,000

5. Dividends

Ordinary: proposed 2,000,000 at 2½ per cent	£50,000

6. Fixed assets

Cost	Freehold land and buildings	Plant and machinery	Vehicles	Total
At 1 January 19X9	£2,000,000	£400,000	£100,000	£2,500,000
Additions during the year		£100,000		£100,000
At 31 December 19X9	£2,000,000	£500,000	£100,000	£2,600,000
Depreciation				
At 1 January 19X9	£80,000	£160,000	£25,000	£265,000
Charge for Year	£20,000	£100,000	£25,000	£145,000
At 31 December 19X9	£100,000	£260,000	£50,000	£410,000
Net book values				
At 1 January 19X9	£1,920,000	£260,000	£75,000	£2,255,000
At 31 December 19X9	£1,900,000	£240,000	£50,000	£2,190,000

7. Stocks

Raw materials and consumables	£100,000	
Work in progress	£690,000	
Finished goods and goods for resale	£140,000	£930,000

8. Debtors

Trade debtors	£1,000,000

9. Other creditors including taxation

Dividends proposed	£50,000	
Corporation tax	£30,000	
Audit fee	£10,000	£90,000

10. Called-up share capital

Authorised: 3,000,000 £1 ordinary shares	
Issued: 2,000,000 £1 ordinary shares fully paid	£2,000,000

ACCOUNTING STANDARDS AND THE FORMAT OF REPORTED PROFIT

Directives of the European Union have not been the only influence shaping the format and contents of UK published accounts in recent years. Another influence has been accounting standards issued by the Accounting Standards Board and its predecessor, the Accounting Standards Committee.

One issue tackled by both bodies was how to present accounting profit in the accounts of companies. Accounting profit is not the simple figure many users think it is. Formally, it is defined as revenue less expenses but apart from how to value expenses such as depreciation and stock consumed, there is a further complexity. Some expenses inevitably result from trading: the stock consumed, the wages paid and the rent incurred. Other expenses are different in nature: they are unlikely to recur. Examples include the payment of a speeding fine and the cost of refurbishment following a fire. If users want to apply current profits to the forecasting of future profits, it is essential that these 'one-off' or irregular expenses are identified. Equally, non-recurring revenues also need to be highlighted.

This was the problem facing the Accounting Standards Committee. Reporting a profit of £8 million when £7 million of that came from the sale of a property rather than from trading may be true but it is hardly fair. The issue is similar to that identified as windfall gains and losses in economic income. Economic income suggested that 'one-off' gains or losses were best treated as additions or reductions to capital. After all, common sense suggests that a person earning £20,000 p.a. who wins £5 million in the National Lottery would not consider income for that year as £5,020,000. More likely, income for all years will be revised to the £20,000 salary plus the returns available from investing the £5 million. Theory therefore suggests that one-off or unusual transactions should be accounted for via the reserves or capital rather than shown within the income for the year.

SSAP 6 Extraordinary Items and Prior Year Adjustments

Until this problem was formally addressed by the ASC, the practice of some companies was to take 'good news' transactions to the profit and loss account and 'bad news' ones straight to the reserves. It was in attempting to overcome this sort of abuse that the ASC rejected the solution proposed by economic income. Instead they proposed in SSAP 6 an 'all inclusive' approach whereby practically all transactions went through the profit and loss account but with separate disclosure of unusual items.

In the statement, they attempted to separate those regular, normal activities – what the standard called *ordinary* activities – from one-off or unusual transactions. Two types of irregular activity were identified. *Exceptional items* were normal activities but of an abnormal size or incidence. For example, bad debts are a normal result of trading but these might be so abnormally large in one period that they need to be disclosed separately to give a true and fair view. *Extraordinary items* were supposed to be the real one-offs. Formally they were defined as, 'material items which derive from events or transactions that fall outside the ordinary activities of the company and which are therefore expected not to recur frequently or regularly'. Examples included the expropriation of assets and the the sale of an investment not acquired with the intention of resale.

The treatment of extraordinary and exceptional items

What was particularly significant was the different treatments of exceptional and extraordinary items in the profit and loss account. Exceptional items, being ordinary transactions of abnormal size, were included as income or expenditure within the profit on ordinary activities before taxation and normally only disclosed by way of a note. Extraordinary items, however, were deducted after the profit on ordinary activities after taxation. This different treatment was critical because the profit on ordinary activities after taxation was treated as the headline figure by the financial community both in calculating earnings per share and when reporting profits in the media. In effect, profit on ordinary activities after tax was viewed as an indication of the normalised or sustainable profit of the business. By emphasising this measure of profit, the statement was treating exceptional items as part of 'normal' profit and extraordinary items as windfall gains or losses 'below the line' of profit on ordinary activities after tax.

However useful this may have been as a concept, the breakdown between exceptional and extraordinary items became increasingly abused by directors wanting to show their own performance in a favourable light. One-off 'bad news' transactions tended to be reported as extraordinary items 'below the line' while one-off 'good news' tended to be reported as exceptional items within profit on ordinary activities and only disclosed in the detailed notes. Probably the most common abuses were to show losses on the termination or sale of an operation and the cost of fundamental restructuring of the company as extraordinary items. Directors were able to do this because of the failure of SSAP 6 to specify exactly which transactions were exceptional and which were extraordinary. Indeed, one of the few specific examples given in the standard – the disposal of fixed assets – could be reported as either an extraordinary or exceptional item!

FRS 3 Reporting Financial Performance

It was because of the abuses of SSAP 6 that the Accounting Standards Board introduced in June 1993 Financial Reporting Standard 3, Reporting Financial Performance. This standard has severely restricted the range of transactions which can be viewed as being extraordinary by redefining exceptional items. In addition, the Board recognised that the performance of a company is made up of several components which 'differ in stability, risk and predictability'. Companies, for example, can acquire and dispose of operations in the course of a year. The result of these cannot be adequately summarised in a single profit figure and so there is a need for the separate disclosure of the components making up the overall profit or loss.

The format of the FRS 3 profit and loss account

FRS 3 extends the disclosure requirements of the Fourth Directive/Companies Act. As a result of the standard, a company's profit and loss account now has to show:

(i) an analysis between continuing operations, acquisitions and disposals to the level of operating profit with turnover and operating profit being the minimum disclosure on the *face* of the profit and loss account;

(ii) all exceptional items, other than in (iii) below, within their statutory (Fourth Directive) headings, with disclosure by way of a note or on the face of the profit and loss account if this is necessary to give a true and fair view;

(iii) profits or losses on the sale or termination of an operation, the costs of a fundamental reorganisation or restructuring, and profits or losses on the disposal of fixed assets as separate items on the face of the balance sheet after operating profit but before interest;

(iv) extraordinary items.

Definitions

Certain activities have been explicitly identified in (iii) above as only being exceptional items. The opportunity to classify transactions or events as extraordinary has been further reduced by rigorous definitions of the terms used in the standard. Ordinary activities are widely defined and include the effects on the company arising from its 'political, economic and geographical environments, irrespective of the frequency or unusual nature of the events'. Discontinued activities can only be discontinued if (i) the sale or termination is completed by the earlier of three months after the period end or the date on which the final accounts are approved; (ii) if a termination, the activities cease completely; (iii) the sale or termination has a material effect on the nature and focus of the company's operations; and (iv) the assets, liabilities and results are clearly distinguishable, physically, operationally and for financial reporting purposes.

Exceptional items are defined in a similar way to that found in SSAP 6 while extraordinary items possess 'a high degree of abnormality which arises from events or transactions that fall outside ... ordinary activities ... and are not expected to recur'. According to the Explanation section of the standard, extraordinary items are 'extremely rare'. Reinforcing this reduced role for extraordinary items, the headline figure of earnings per share is to be calculated *after* extraordinary items – unlike in SSAP 6. As a result, the standard has significantly reduced the motivation for classifying items as extraordinary.

Prior year adjustments

SSAP 6 was not only concerned with extraordinary items; it was also concerned with prior year adjustments, an issue also addressed by FRS 3. The problem of prior year adjustments relates to transactions or events happening in the current period which ideally should have been matched against a previous period. By prior year adjustments, neither SSAP 6 nor FRS 3 were concerned with the normal adjustments and corrections which result when estimates such as accruals and prepayments are not accurate. Rather, they were concerned with something more substantial.

The issue concerns how a prior year adjustment should be reported. As the transaction or event belongs to a previous period, reporting it in the current period would distort the current period's profit as a measure of performance. Logically, a prior year adjustment needs to be matched against the income to which it relates and this will be found subsumed within the reserves brought forward at the beginning of the period.

However logical this treatment of prior year adjustments is, there is a danger in all forms of reserve accounting. Given the importance of the profit and loss account, a major item affecting profits will not have been reported in that statement. In unscrupulous hands, this could be abused with 'bad news' transactions attempting to be classified as a prior year adjustment. Because of this, both SSAP 6 and FRS 3 narrowly defined the types of activity which could be classified as a prior year adjustment. Formally, both statements classified a prior year adjustment as 'material adjustments applicable to prior years arising from changes in accounting policies or from the correction of fundamental errors'. Deciding to write off development expenditure rather than capitalising it as an intangible asset would be an example of a change in accounting policies. An example of a fundamental error would be if the previous year's closing stock – this year's opening stock – had been incorrectly calculated.

The published profit and loss account contains not only information relating to the current period but also comparative figures for the preceding period. FRS 3 and its predecessor SSAP 6 requires prior year adjustments to be accounted for by restating the comparative figures in the primary statements and notes and adjusting the opening balance of reserves for the cumulative effect.

Additional disclosure

The usefulness of the requirement, however, is open to question given the modern-day emphasis on current profitability. Effectively a major transaction has been downgraded. To counter the effect of this and other permissible forms of reserve accounting, FRS 3 has introduced a new primary financial statement, the statement of total recognised gains and losses, which is on par with the balance sheet, the profit and loss account and the cashflow statement. This statement comprises not only the profit or loss for the period but also all other movements on reserves which reflect gains and losses attributable to the shareholders. As a result, prior year adjustments are now highlighted in a major financial statement. Other transactions and events found in that statement are foreign exchange translation gains and losses which are discussed in Chapter 10 and gains and losses on the revaluation of assets.

That the statement of total recognised gains and losses is viewed by the Accounting Standards Board as a primary financial statement shows the increasing need to look at more than a single figure when evaluating a company's performance. This has been reinforced by two further requirements of FRS 3. The first additional requirement reinforces the statement of total recognised gains and losses. Companies must now include in the published accounts a note reconciling the movement on shareholders funds. This comprises not just the items identified as total recognised gains and losses but also includes changes in share capital, dividends paid and any writing-off of goodwill direct to reserves. The writing-off of goodwill to reserves is explained in the next chapter where groups are discussed.

There is a further disclosure required by FRS 3 if companies operate a modified historical cost system. The simplest example of this is where a company reports a revised depreciation charge as a result of revaluing assets. For such companies, the standard requires a note of what the historical cost profits would have been had no revaluation taken place. This note must be shown either immediately after the profit and loss account or after the statement of total recognised gains and losses.

FRS 3 – an example

The effect of FRS 3 on the traditional profit and loss account is demonstrated in Example 8.2 and Exhibit 8.6.

Example 8.2

An extract from the accounts of Jenkins plc for the year 19X9 is reproduced below. The opening shareholders' funds were £400 million but during the year, the company raised an additional £100 million of ordinary share capital. During the year freehold industrial buildings were revalued from a book value of £35 million to £41 million. The remaining useful life of the buildings is six years.

Jenkins plc profit and loss account	*19X9*	*19X8*
	(£m)	*(£m)*
Turnover	350	320
Cost of sales	(240)	(224)
Gross profit	110	96
Distribution costs	(33)	(28)
Administration expenses	(46)	(42)
Operating profit	31	26
Interest payable	(4)	(5)
Profit on ordinary activities before taxation	27	21
Tax on profit on ordinary activities	(10)	(8)
Profit for the financial year	17	13
Dividends	(6)	(4)
Retained profit for the financial year	11	9

During the year, the company made a loss of £3 million on the disposal of its Welsh division where the operating loss for the year to the date of disposal was £5 million. However this was compensated for by the acquisition during the year of all the assets, brand names and activities of Aberdeen Ltd to form the Scottish division of Jenkins plc. Information relating to both divisions is as follows:

	Welsh Division		**Scottish Division**
	19X9	*19X8*	*19X9*
	(£m)	*(£m)*	*(£m)*
Turnover	34	41	29
Cost of sales	(28)	(32)	13
Gross profit	6	9	16
Distribution costs	(5)	(7)	(2)
Administration expenses	(6)	(6)	(3)
Operating profit/(loss)	(5)	(4)	11

FRS 3 identifies two ways of showing the performance of continuing, acquired and disposed operations within the profit and loss account. The first way breaks down turnover into the three classes, with acquisitions being a subtotal within continuing activities. Operating profit is also broken down between continuing operations, acquisitions and disposals, leaving the detailed make up of their operating expenses to a note to the profit and loss account. This is the approach taken in Exhibit 8.6. The alternative approach, not shown in Exhibit 8.6, involves the three types of operation being shown in a columnar form on the profit and loss account, starting with turnover and then deducting the cost of sales and other operating expenses. Also shown within the profit and loss account is the loss on closing down the Welsh division. This has been assumed to have been originally recorded within Jenkins plc's administration expenses. Now, because of FRS 3, it has to be separately identified as an exceptional item on the face of the balance sheet.

Exhibit 8.6 also shows the other additional disclosure requirements of FRS 3. The statement of total recognised gains and losses identifies the surplus on revaluation of the industrial buildings as a further gain belonging to the shareholders. The note of historical cost profit and loss shows that the reported profit would have been £1 million greater had the accounts been prepared on a strict historical cost basis. This is because the

Exhibit 8.6 The FRS 3 statements and notes

Profit and loss account for the year ended 19X9

	19X9 (£m)	19X9 (£m)	19X8 as restated (£m)	(£m)
Turnover				
Continuing operations[1]	287		279	
Acquisitions	29			
	316		279	
Discontinued operations	34	350	41	320
Cost of sales		240		224
Gross profit		110		96
Distribution costs		(33)		(28)
Administration expenses[2]		(43)		(42)
Operating profit				
Continuing operations[3]	28		30	
Acquisitions	11			
	39		30	
Discontinued operations	(5)	34	(4)	26
Exceptional item[4]		(3)		
Profit on ordinary activities before interest		31		26
Interest payable		(4)		(5)
Profit on ordinary activities before taxation		27		21
Tax on profit on ordinary activities		(10)		(8)
Profit for the financial year		17		13
Dividends		(6)		(4)
Retained profit for the year		11		9

Exhibit 8.6 (Continued)

Note to the profit and loss account

	Continuing operations 19X9 (£m)	Discontinued operations 19X9 (£m)	Total 19X9 (£m)	Continuing operations 19X8 (£m)	Discontinued operations 19X8 (£m)	Total 19X8 (£m)
Cost of sales	212	28	240	192	32	224
Net operating expenses						
Distribution costs	28	5	33	21	7	28
Administration expenses	37	6	43	36	6	42
	65	11	76	57	13	70

The total figure for continuing operations in 19X9 includes the following amounts relating to acquisitions: cost of sales £13 million, distribution costs of £2 million and administration expenses of £3 million.

Statement of total recognised gains and losses

	19X9 (£m)	19X8 (£m)
Profit for the financial year	17	13
Unrealised surplus on revaluation of properties	6	–
Total gains and losses recognised since the last annual report	23	13

Note of historical cost profits and loss

	19X9 (£m)	19X8 (£m)
Reported profits on ordinary activities before taxation	27	21
Difference between historical cost depreciation charge and the actual depreciation charge of the year calculated on the revalued amount[5]	1	–
Historical cost profit for the year on ordinary activities before taxation	28	21

Reconciliation of movements in shareholders' funds

	19X9 (£m)	19X8 (£m)
Profit for the financial year	17	13
Dividends	(6)	(4)
	11	9
Other recognised gains and losses relating to the year	6	–
New share capital subscribed	100	–
Net addition to shareholders' funds	117	9
Opening shareholders' funds	400	391
Closing shareholders' funds	517	400

Workings

1. Total turnover of £350 million less £34 million and £29 million relating to acquisitions and disposals.
2. Administration expenses of £46 million less £3 million loss on disposal.
3. Balancing figure after eliminating operating profit and losses on acquisitions and disposals.
4. Loss on disposal.
5. Increase in net book value of £6 million and six year remaining life to give an extra charge of £1 million.

buildings with a remaining life of six years have been revalued by £6 million to give an increased depreciation charge of £1 million per annum. Finally, there is the note reconciling the movement in shareholders' funds.

Implications of FRS 3

FRS 3 attempts to move users away from a single figure of profit in measuring performance and to severely limit the use of reserve accounting. Where reserve accounting is still permissible, it attempts to make users aware of this by making the statement of total recognised gains and losses a primary financial statement. The effect is to make pre-tax profits more volatile because they will include one-offs such as factory closures. In effect, it leaves investors to decide which items really matter. According to County NatWest Securities[3] two earnings concepts will gain prominence, normalised earnings found by adjusting for extraordinary items, and maintainable earnings, i.e. those attributable to the on-going business. Unfortunately, this increased information has been bought at the cost of making the profit and loss account a more detailed and complex document, requiring the user to use judgement in determining what is useful and what is not.

DEBT AND EQUITY IN THE BALANCE SHEET

The reporting of profits in UK accounts is not the only issue where the Accounting Standards Board has extended the requirements of the Fourth Directive and UK company law. In FRS 4 Capital Instruments, it addressed the financial reporting problems arising from the wide range of securities that companies can issue. In between ordinary shares and straightforward debt such as a 10-year, 12 per cent loan is a whole array of other forms of finance known as hybrid securities. One example is a convertible debenture which contains the option of being converted to a specific number of (generally) ordinary shares as an alternative to being redeemed. Common to all these hybrid securities are that they have qualities of both debt and equity. As a result, until the introduction of FRS 4 in June 1994, directors had a choice of how they should be classified in the balance sheet. For a company with excessive debt, the temptation was to classify the hybrid security as equity to give the appearance of less risk.

This not only affected the balance sheet: it could also give a misleading impression in the profit and loss account. A debenture, for instance, could have been issued at a very low rate of interest but with a large premium payable on redemption. Until the date of redemption, the profit and loss account would benefit by the low interest charge. In reality, the premium is no more than delayed interest to compensate for the low nominal rate and so the reported profits prior to redemption would have been overstated. In addition, some short term borrowings were able to be classified as long term borrowings where there was some form of contractual agreement to allow one set of short term borrowings to be replaced by another set on maturity. The effect was to show what were essentially current liabilities as long term liabilities.

FRS 4 Capital Instruments

This was the problem faced by the Accounting Standards Board and the reason it issued FRS 4. The standard tries to stop directors showing what is essentially debt as equity and what is essentially short term debt as long term debt. In addition, it requires that their respective costs are properly disclosed in the profit and loss account.

Definitions

The standard defines capital instruments as all 'instruments that are issued ... as a means of raising finance including shares, debentures, loans ...'. Because capital instruments are so numerous and varied and because new ones continue to evolve, the standard could not consider every single form of hybrid finance. Instead, it applies a general test based on an instrument's legal status. Capital instruments (other than shares) are liabilities 'if they carry an obligation to transfer economic benefits'. The fact that investors might waive that obligation in exchange for shares – as in the case of convertible debentures – is irrelevant. Until conversion, convertible debt should be recorded as a liability. Likewise, capital instruments that do not contain an obligation to transfer economic benefits should be reported within shareholders' funds.

The balance sheet

Capital instruments must be recorded in the balance sheet as either liabilities or shareholders' funds by applying the test outlined above. However, to avoid misleading users, convertible debt should be separately identified under liabilities and disclose the redemption date, the amount, the conversion period and the number and class of shares into which the debt will be converted. The note should also state whether the conversion is at the option of the company or the holder.

An analysis of the maturity of any debt finance should be presented showing amounts falling due:

(a) in one year or less, or on demand
(b) between one and two years
(c) between two and five years
(d) in five years or more

The term of the debt is the earlier of (a) the date on which the issuer could redeem the debt and (b) the lender could force the redemption. If the debt is short term, it needs to meet certain stringent conditions before it can be classified as long term debt. To classify short term debt as long term debt requires that the refinancing facilities are committed by the balance sheet date; the debt and the facility are part of a single agreement with the same lender; the finance costs are not significantly higher than that of the current debt; the lender's obligations are firm and cannot be avoided; and the lender is expected to be able to fulfil its obligations under the facility.

In addressing shareholders' funds, FRS 4 recognises that preference shares and similar securities are more like debt than equity in that their owners are only entitled to a limited, specified return and do not share in the distribution of residual values on a liquidation.

Because of this, the standard differentiates between equity and non-equity interests. Equity interests belong to the ultimate owners of the company, the ordinary shareholders, and these interests should be shown separately from the non-equity interests within shareholders' funds.

The profit and loss account

Within the profit and loss account, FRS 4 gives a more meaningful charge to interest where loans are either issued at a discount or are redeemable at a premium in exchange for a low nominal interest rate. The reality is that the initial discount on the face value of the loan or the premium payable on redemption merely represents disguised interest. Equally, if a loan has apparently low interest rates for part of its term and higher interest rates for the balance, then the higher rates are merely compensation for the lower rates and should be reported accordingly.

FRS 4 forces these non-standard forms of loan to be shown in a more meaningful way. Unfortunately, the language used in FRS 4 is convoluted. For example, the instructions for the profit and loss account specify that 'the finance costs of debt should be allocated to periods over the term of the debt at a constant rate on the carrying amount. All finance costs should be charged to the profit and loss account'. Presumably relating to the balance sheet, the standard then states that 'the carrying amount of debt should be increased by the finance cost in respect of the reporting period and reduced by payments made in respect of the debt in that period'. Finally, immediately after issue, the standard requires debt to be stated at the amount of the net proceeds. What this really means is that the 'true' interest should be charged to the profit and loss account and any difference between this 'true' figure and the interest paid or payable should be added or deducted from the amount of the loan to give the 'true' value of the loan. In effect, FRS 4 is about applying the accruals concept by considering the interest consumed rather than just paid.

FRS 4 – a worked example

Another problem when considering FRS 4 is that there are so many different types of capital instrument that detailed treatment cannot be specified in advance. To partially overcome this, the standard includes application notes to demonstrate some of the more popular but complex financial instruments. Rather than considering all these, the general concept behind FRS 4 can be developed. Example 8.3 considers the effect of obtaining a loan with issue costs and a premium on redemption.

Example 8.3

Trafford and Smith Ltd require to borrow £100,000 in order to acquire a new machine. Two options are available to them. The first is a three-year loan of £100,000 at a 25 per cent interest rate and no issue costs. The second is for £130,000 over the same period but with issue expenses of £30,000. The latter facility offers an interest rate of 10 per cent but involves a premium on redemption of £15,750.

For the first option, the real cost of borrowing is clearly 25 per cent p.a. The sum advanced is £100,000. This is then followed by the £25,000 interest in each of the three years plus the £100,000 repayment at the end of year 3. Together, these payments to the lender extinguish the debt. The interest rate can be more formally developed by making use of the discounting technique introduced in Chapter 6. Although the lender receives interest of £75,000 in total, this is only paid in subsequent years and so its value today will be less. If the interest rate *is* 25 per cent then the value today of all the repayments to the lender will just equal the amount initially advanced. This is demonstrated as option 1 in Exhibit 8.7. To the right of the discounted cashflow calculation is a summary of the loan account. At the beginning, there is a loan of £100,000 to which £25,000 interest is accrued. This £25,000 is 'the finance cost in respect of the reporting period'. The interest 'payments made in respect of the debt in that period' are also £25,000 and so the balance outstanding at the end of year 1 remains at £100,000. This is the year end carrying amount and is the amount which will appear in the balance sheet. A similar pattern is identifiable in subsequent years until the loan is repaid at the end of year 3. The charge to the profit and loss account is a constant rate of 25 per cent p.a. of the carrying amount as required by the standard.

Exhibit 8.7 *Interest charges and balance sheet values under FRS 4*

Option 1

End of year	Payments	25% factor	DCF	Opening debt	Interest accrued	Interest paid	Closing debt
1	£25,000	0.8000	£20,000	£100,000	£25,000	£25,000	£100,000
2	£25,000	0.6400	£16,000	£100,000	£25,000	£25,000	£100,000
3	£125,000	0.5120	£64,000	£100,000	£25,000	£25,000	£100,000
			£100,000			Loan repaid	£100,000
						Balance	nil

Option 2

End of year	Payments	25% factor	DCF	Opening debt	Interest accrued	Interest paid	Closing debt
1	£13,000	0.8000	£10,400	£100,000	£25,000	£13,000	£112,000
2	£13,000	0.6400	£8,320	£112,000	£28,000	£13,000	£127,000
3	£158,750	0.5120	£81,280	£127,000	£31,750	£13,000	£145,750
			£100,000			Loan repaid	£145,750
						Balance	nil

This approach allows the second option to be analysed. Although borrowing a notional £130,000, the issue costs reduce this to only £100,000. In exchange for receiving this £100,000, Trafford and Smith Ltd have to pay the lender interest of 10 per cent on the £130,000 in each year plus, at the end of year 3, the repayment of the £130,000 advanced and the £15,750 premium. Exhibit 8.7 shows this is equivalent to borrowing at 25 per cent

p. a. Prior to FRS 4, the interest charged to the profit and loss account would have been £13,000 while the balance sheet would have shown a debt of £130,000. Now, FRS 4 recognises that the real or effective rate of interest is 25 per cent p.a. as a result of the heavy issue costs and the premium on redemption. The amount charged to the profit and loss account will therefore be the figure shown under the heading of interest accrued. To the extent that the interest paid is less than this, the amount outstanding – the carrying amount – will increase, causing interest to increase in subsequent years. Once more, there is a constant rate on the carrying amount with the interest charged to the profit and loss account always being equal to 25 per cent of the opening debt.

The validity of FRS 4

FRS 4 was introduced to stop directors showing debt as equity by developing sophisticated forms of capital instruments. To make certain this will be achieved, the standard is both long, complex and legalistic. This legalistic approach – however necessary – appears to be inconsistent with the Accounting Standards Board's preference for economic substance over legal form. Consider, for example, convertible loan stock issued many years ago in £100 units which can either be exchanged for 20 ordinary shares or redeemed at par in two years' time. Now assume the ordinary shares are currently quoted at £15 each. If conversion was possible today, the loan stock would be worth £300 as this is the value of the underlying shares. No one would take the cash option as that would only realise £100. Put another way, the closer the date of conversion, the more investors will view the stock as another way of acquiring ordinary shares. This is the underlying reality even though it has been rejected by the ASB.

Another issue arising from the ASB approach to capital instruments concerns how they are presented on the balance sheet. It can be argued that breaking down complex financial instruments into two groupings is simplistic and possibly even misleading as hybrid securities are not simple ordinary shares nor simple loan stock. In the United States, a different approach has been taken. There, a third category of finance has been introduced. Known as mezzanine finance, it recognises the complexities of hybrid securities and so records them in between debt and equity on the balance sheet. Yet another approach would be to recognise that hybrid securities have qualities of both debt and equity and for these to be analysed into their component parts. This is known as 'split accounting' and is the route proposed by both the International Accounting Standards Committee and the Canadian Institute of Chartered Accountants.

SUMMARY

Two forms of regulation currently dominate UK financial reporting. For the first time in the UK, the state is playing an active role in the detailed format and content of financial reports as a result of the implementation of European Directives. Parallel with this has been the active intervention of the Accounting Standards Board. Compared with its predecessor, it has much greater power and independence and is beginning to use these powers.

Which will have the greater influence on the shape of UK accounting is difficult to say. Two pointers, however, suggest that the legalistic influence will be of increasing importance. First, the law has for the first time concerned itself with the monitoring of accounting standards as a result of the 1989 Companies Act. Secondly, and perhaps more importantly, there are still substantial differences between the accounts of the member countries making up the European Union. Despite the implementation of the Fourth Directive, identical accounting data are still likely to be shown differently in member states. This is partly due to different traditions and partly because the directives themselves are compromises.

Having accepted the legitimacy of the state influencing the detail of financial reports, it will make it more difficult to object to future directives which seek to further close the gap between standards in different member states.

REFERENCES

1 Parker, R. (1991) 'Financial Reporting in the Netherlands', in Nobes, C. and Parker, R. (eds) *Comparative International Accounting*, 3rd edn, p. 229, Prentice Hall.
2 Nobes, C. (1989) *Interpreting European Financial Statements*, p. 16, Butterworths.
3 Reported in *The Sunday Times*, November 1992.

FURTHER READING

Alexander, D. and Archer, S (1991) *European Accounting Guide*, Academic Press.
Alexander, D. (ed.) (1995) *Comparative International Accounting*, The Dryden Press.
Blake, J. and Amat, O. (1993) *European Accounting*, Pitman Publishing.
Gordon, P. and Gray, S. (1994) *European Financial Reporting: United Kingdom*, Routledge.
Hopwood, A. (1989) *International Pressures for Accounting Change*, Prentice Hall.
Nobes, C. and Parker, R. (1991) *Comparative International Accounting*, 3rd edn, Prentice Hall.
Nobes, C. (1989) *Interpreting European Financial Statements*, Butterworths.
Nobes, C. (1992) *Accounting Harmonisation in Europe*, F-T Management Reports.
Nobes, C. (1994) *International Guide to Interpreting Company Accounts*, F-T Management Reports.
Ordelheide, D. and Pfaff, D. (1994) *European Financial Reporting: Germany*, Routledge.

TEST YOUR UNDERSTANDING

1 List the possible reasons for different accounting systems in the European Union.

2 What are the essential differences between accounting in the UK and accounting in France and Germany?

3 Identify the advantages and limitations of French accounting.

4 The European Union's Fourth Directive was concerned with:

   (a) the training and qualifications of auditors;
   (b) the format and content of financial statements;
   (c) the accounts of groups of companies;
   (d) the preparation of published accounts in more than one language;
   (e) the definition of a public company.

5 In Germany, unlike the UK, some companies neither have to be audited nor publish a profit and loss account. True or false?

6 Outline the two ways that expenditure can be analysed in a profit and loss account which meet EU requirements.

7 British balance sheets no longer differentiate between short term and long term liabilities. Why is this and how are they now summarised?

8 What was SSAP 6 attempting to do and why was it replaced?

9 Identify the two major changes in UK financial reporting which have resulted from the introduction of FRS 3.

10 FRS 4 deals with capital instruments. What are these and why was it necessary to introduce the Standard?

QUESTIONS

1 Beldam plc has an authorised share capital of 5,000,000 £1 ordinary shares. In addition, it is financed by an 8 per cent debenture repayable in 370 days' time and a bank loan repayable 10 days earlier. The company's trial balance is given below. The directors estimate that half of the rent, rates, light and heat relates to the factory with the balance being shared equally between the selling and administration functions.

Six months ago, on 1 July 19X8, the company acquired £800,000 of additional factory plant and machinery. As with existing plant and machinery, this is to be depreciated at 20 per cent p.a. on cost. The company's fleet of cars are depreciated at 25 per cent p.a. while the office equipment is depreciated at 10 per cent p.a. Both the cars and the office equipment use the straight line method of depreciation and any residual values are thought to be negligible. Corporation tax for the year is estimated to be £800,000 and the directors are recommending a 20 per cent dividend for the year. At the year end the stocks were valued at £100,000 for raw materials, £862,000 for work-in-progress and £1,088,000 for finished stocks unsold. None of these adjustments have been recorded in the trial balance.

The directors of the company are Jane Greenwood, Paul Moran and Denys Jackson. Jane Greenwood is the chairperson of the company and received director's fees of £40,000, a salary of £70,000 and pension contributions of £22,000. Paul Moran received fees of £30,000, a salary of £100,000 and pension contributions of £36,000 while Denys Jackson received fees of £10,000, a salary of £44,000 and pension contributions of £20,000.

	(£000)		*(£000)*
Factory machinery	2,800	Sales	7,482
Office equipment	400	Share premium account	500
Cars	84	Trade creditors	362
Debtors	2,127	General reserve	840
Cash/bank	819	8% debentures	1,000
Capitalised expenditure	500	Capital redemption reserve fund	700
Patents	790	Bank loan	248
Raw material stock	300	Provision for depreciation – machinery	200
Work-in-progress	460	Provision for depreciation – equipment	160
Finished stock	420	Provision for depreciation – cars	52
Raw material purchases	1,500	Profit and loss account balance	621
Factory wages	2,000	Royalties received	47
Factory pensions	240	Ordinary share capital	2,000
Factory national insurance	35		
Office salaries	80		

	(£000)		*(£000)*
Office pensions	15		
Office national insurance	10		
Sales department salaries	120		
Sales department pensions	15		
Sales department national insurance	12		
Directors' fees	80		
Directors' salaries	214		
Directors' pensions	78		
Rent and rates	480		
Light and heat	360		
Car expenses	63		
Debenture interest	80		
Loan interest	32		
Audit fee	98		
	14,212		14,212

Using the above information, prepare in a vertical format a profit and loss account and balance sheet for Beldam plc for the year to 31 December 19X8 in accordance with the European Community's Fourth Directive as implemented by the UK's 1985 Companies Act.

2 Gransden plc is a multiple retailer and its results for the year ended 31 December 19X6, along with comparative figures for the preceding year, are shown as follows:

	19X6 *(£m)*	19X5 *(£m)*
Turnover	400	370
Cost of sales	310	281
Gross profit	90	89
Distribution costs	12	10
Administration expenses	18	20
Operating profit	60	59
Interest payable	12	12
Profit on ordinary activities before taxation	48	47
Taxation on profit of ordinary activities	16	17
Profit for the financial year	32	30
Dividends	12	8
Retained profit for the financial year	20	22

During the year, Gransden made a profit of £6 million on the disposal of its Southern division. This has been recorded under administration expenses. In addition, it acquired the trading activities of Major Minor Retailers. This was financed by the issue of 40 million £1 ordinary shares at a price of £3. Early in 19X6, Gransden revalued its freehold premises from £200 million to £300 million. These are being depreciated over 50 years and, at the time of revaluation, their average age was 30 years. Details of the Southern division and the revenues and expenses generated from the acquisition of Major Minor are given below.

	Disposal 19X6 (£m)	Disposal 19X5 (£m)	Acquisition 19X6 (£m)
Turnover	20	24	40
Cost of sales	14	15	18
Gross profit	6	9	22
Distribution costs	2	2	5
Administration expenses	3	2	7
Operating profit	1	5	10

Making use of the above information, prepare the profit and loss account and other statements in accordance with FRS3 on the assumption that Gransden's shareholders' funds at the commencement of 19X6 totalled £600 million.

3* On 1 January, a company issued a £100,000 debenture at 5 per cent with a premium payable on redemption of £30,526 at the end of five years. Interest is payable on 31 December each year.

Making use of the following discount factors, verify that the effective interest rate is 10 per cent and show how the interest and the carrying amount will be reported in the published accounts of the company under the provisions of FRS4.

End of year	10 per cent discount factors
1	0.90909
2	0.82645
3	0.75131
4	0.68301
5	0.62092

APPENDIX 1

COMPANIES ACT 1985 VERTICAL BALANCE SHEET (FORMAT 1)

	£	£	£
A Called-up share capital not paid *			X
B Fixed assets			
I Intangible assets			
1 Development costs	X		
2 Concessions, patents, trade marks and similar rights and assets	X		
3 Goodwill	X		
4 Payments on account	X̲	X	
II Tangible assets			
1 Land and buildings	X		
2 Plant and machinery	X		
3 Fixtures, fittings, tools and equipment	X		
4 Payments on account and assets in course of construction	X̲	X	
III Investments			
1 Shares in group undertakings	X		
2 Loans to group undertakings	X		
3 Participating interests	X		
4 Loans to undertakings in which the company has a participating interest	X		
5 Other investments other than loans	X		
6 Other loans	X		
7 Own shares	X̲	X̲	X
C Current assets			
I Stocks			
1 Raw materials and consumables	X		
2 Work in progress	X		
3 Finished goods and goods for resale	X		
4 Payments on account	X̲	X	
II Debtors			
1 Trade debtors	X		
2 Amounts owed by group undertakings	X		
3 Amounts owed by undertakings in which the company has a participating interest	X		
4 Other debtors	X		
5 Called-up share capital not paid *	X		
6 Payments and accrued income *	X̲	X	
III Investments			
1 Shares in group undertakings	X		
2 Own shares	X		
3 Other investments	X̲	X	
IV Cash at bank and in hand		X̲	
[Total of C]		X	
D Prepayments and accrued income		X̲	
		X	

	£	£	£

E Creditors: Amounts falling due within one year

		£	£	£
1	Debenture loans	X		
2	Bank loans and overdrafts	X		
3	Payments received on account	X		
4	Trade creditors	X		
5	Bills of exchange payable	X		
6	Amounts owed to group undertakings	X		
7	Amounts owed to undertakings in which the company has a participating interest	X		
8	Other creditors including taxation and social security	X		
9	Accruals and deferred income *	X̲	(X)	

F Net current assets (liabilities) [C + D – E]   –   X

G Total assets less current liabilities [A + B + F]   X

H Creditors: Amounts falling due after more than one year

		£	£	£
1	Debenture loans	X		
2	Bank loans and overdrafts	X		
3	Payments received on account	X		
4	Trade creditors	X		
5	Bills of exchange payable	X		
6	Amounts owed to group undertakings	X		
7	Amounts owed to undertakings in which the company has a participating interest	X		
8	Other creditors including taxation and social security	X		
9	Accruals and deferred income *	X̲		(X)

I Provision for liabilities and charges

		£	£	£
1	Pensions and similar obligations	X		
2	Taxation, including deferred taxation	X		
3	Other provisions	X̲		(X)

J Accruals and deferred income *   (X̲)

     X̲

K Capital and reserves

		£	£	£
I	Called-up share capital			X
II	Share premium account			X
III	Revaluation reserve			X
IV	Other reserves			
	1 Capital redemption reserve	X		
	2 Reserve for own shares	X		
	3 Reserves provided for by the articles of association	X		
	4 Other reserves	X̲		X
V	Profit and loss account			X̲
				X̲

* allowable alternative positions

APPENDIX 2

COMPANIES ACT 1985 HORIZONTAL BALANCE SHEET (FORMAT 2)

ASSETS

ASSETS	£	£	£
A Called-up share capital not paid *			X
B Fixed assets			
I Intangible assets			
1 Development costs	X		
2 Concessions, patents, trade marks and similar rights and assets	X		
3 Goodwill	X		
4 Payments on account	X	X	
II Tangible assets			
1 Land and buildings	X		
2 Plant and machinery	X		
3 Fixtures, fittings, tools and equipment	X		
4 Payments on account and assets in course of construction	X	X	
III Investments			
1 Shares in group undertakings	X		
2 Loans to group undertakings	X		
3 Participating interests	X		
4 Loans to undertakings in which the company has a participating interest	X		
5 Other interests other than loans	X		
6 Other loans	X		
7 Own shares	X	X	X
C Current assets			
I Stocks			
1 Raw materials and consumables	X		
2 Work in progress	X		
3 Finished goods and goods for resale	X		
4 Payments on account	X	X	
II Debtors			
1 Trade debtors	X		
2 Amounts owed by group undertakings	X		
3 Amounts owed by undertakings in which the company has a participating interest	X		
4 Other debtors	X		
5 Called-up share capital not paid *	X		
6 Prepayments and accrued income *	X	X	
III Investments			
1 Shares in group undertakings	X		
2 Own shares	X		
3 Other investments	X	X	
IV Cash at bank and in hand		X	X
D Prepayments and accrued income *			X
			X

LIABILITIES

LIABILITIES	£	£
A Capital and reserves		
I Called-up share capital		X
II Share premium account		X
III Revaluation reserve		X
IV Other reserves		
1 Capital redemption reserve fund	X	
2 Reserve for own shares	X	
3 Reserves provided by articles of association	X	
4 Other reserves	X	X
V Profit and loss account		X
		X
B Provision for liabilities and charges		
1 Pensions and similar obligations	X	
2 Taxation, including deferred taxation	X	
3 Other provisions	X	X
C Creditors		
1 Debenture loans	X	
2 Bank loans and overdrafts	X	
3 Payments received on account	X	
4 Trade creditors	X	
5 Bills of exchange payable	X	
6 Amounts owed to group undertakings	X	
7 Amounts owed to undertakings in which the company has a participating interest	X	
8 Other creditors including taxation and social security	X	
9 Accruals and deferred income*	X	X
D Accruals and deferred income*		X
		X

* allowable alternative positions

APPENDIX 3

COMPANIES ACT 1985 PROFIT AND LOSS ACCOUNTS

Format 1	£	£	Format 2	£	£
1 Turnover		X	1 Turnover		X
2 Cost of sales		(X)	2 Change in stocks of finished goods		
3 Gross profit (or loss)		X	and work in progress		(X)
4 Distribution costs		(X)	3 Own work capitalised		X
5 Administration expenses		(X)	4 Other operating income		X
6 Other operating income		X	5 (a) Raw materials and consumables	(X)	
7 Income from shares in			(b) Other external charges	(X)	(X)
group undertakings		X	6 Staff costs		
8 Income from participating interests		X	(a) Wages and salaries	(X)	
9 Income from other fixed			(b) Social security costs	(X)	
asset investments		X	(c) Other pension costs	(X)	(X)
10 Other interest receivable			7 (a) Depreciation and other amounts		
and similar income		X	written off tangible and		
11 Amounts written off investments		(X)	intangible fixed assets	(X)	
12 Interest payable and similar charges		(X)	(b) Exceptional amounts written off		
13 Tax on profit or loss			current assets	(X)	(X)
on ordinary activities		(X)	8 Other operating charges		(X)
14 Profit or loss on ordinary			9 Income from shares in group undertakings		X
activities after taxation		X	10 Income from participating interests		X
15 Extraordinary income	X		11 Income from other fixed asset investments		X
16 Extraordinary charges	X		12 Other interest receivable and similar income		X
17 Extraordinary profit or loss	X	X	13 Amounts written off investments		(X)
18 Tax on extraordinary profit or loss		(X)	14 Interest payable and similar charges		(X)
19 Other taxes not shown			15 Tax on profit or loss		
under the above items		(X)	on ordinary activities		(X)
20 Profit or loss for the financial year		X	16 Profit or loss on ordinary		
			activities after taxation		X
			17 Extraordinary income	X	
			18 Extraordinary charges	(X)	
			19 Extraordinary profit or loss	—	X
			20 Tax on extraordinary profit or loss		(X)
			21 Other taxes not shown		
			under the above items		(X)
			22 Profit or loss for the financial year		X

Notes relating to the 4th Schedule of the Companies Act 1985

(a) All the items identified by letters or Roman numerals must be stated in sequence, using the exact headings given by the Act.

(b) The letters and numerals do not have to be used.

(c) The chosen formats shall be used consistently.

(d) Any item can be shown in greater details than specified.

(e) The items detailed by arabic numerals can be shown by way of notes.

(f) Any item can be omitted if the value for the current and preceding year is zero.

(g) The profit and loss account must also show:

(1) the profit or loss before taxation;

(2) the total of dividends paid and proposed;

(3) proposed and actual movements on the reserves.

(h) Preliminary expenses, research costs and expenses relating to the issue of shares and debentures may not be treated as assets in a company's balance sheet.

CHAPTER 9

Financial reporting – group activities

Most quoted companies own other companies known as subsidiaries. To reflect this reality, there evolved the accounting concept known as a group. To begin to understand the published accounts of most quoted companies therefore requires an understanding of how the financial reports of all the companies in a group are brought together to form the group accounts, a process known as consolidation.

This chapter:

- Develops the mechanics of consolidation
- Differentiates between merger and acquisition accounting
- Demonstrates the treatment of associated undertakings
- Analyses the effect of the relevant accounting standards on financial reporting
- Considers the implications of the European Union's Seventh Directive on group structures

A significant feature of the modern business world is the coming together of companies to form a group. The reasons are many and varied. Sometimes it is to achieve economies of scale, to minimise competition or reduce the risk and uncertainties faced by the management of the business. At other times, it may be to achieve control over sources of supply or gain access to outlets. A variety of terms are used to describe such business combinations; amalgamation, merger, takeover and acquisition are just some of the more popular terms used.

Whatever the terminology and whatever the reason for their formation, groups are increasingly significant and increasingly powerful especially as many cross national boundaries. It was therefore perhaps inevitable that the European Union should address the issue of financial reporting for such groups in its Seventh Directive. Fortunately, many of the issues were already well rehearsed. Accounting for groups had long been a feature of USA – and to a lesser extent UK – accounting. This was partly because the group as a structure first came to prominence in the States in the early 1900s and partly because, with few statutory accounting rules existing at that stage, there was the opportunity to experiment with new ways of reporting group financial activities.

GROUP STRUCTURES

A group consists of more than one legal entity. Purchasing only the *assets* of another business is conceptually no different from the purchasing of any other individual assets and so would not create a group. The legal entities therefore have to continue to exist after the formation of a group but with some form of interlocking relationship such that either one enterprise controls another or there is joint control. This is the first condition necessary for a group to be recognised. The obvious way to achieve the relationship is for one company, known as the *parent*, to acquire the shares of another, the *subsidiary*. Alternatively a third company could be formed – the *holding company* – to acquire the shares in the other two. These relationships are demonstrated in Exhibit 9.1.

Exhibit 9.1 Group and non-group relationships

Group relationships			Absence of a group	
Company A	Company B	Company C	Company A	Company B
acquires shares of	acquires shares of	formed to acquire shares of both	buys net assets of	buys net assets of
Company B	Company A	Companies A and B	Company B	Company A

In all five options shown in Exhibit 9.1, the end result will be the same: a business made up of the assets of companies A and B. Where the assets are purchased, these will immediately be added to the acquiring company's existing assets and the combined amounts reported on any future balance sheet. However, where a group exists, legally it is the shares which have been acquired and it is these which will appear on any subsequent balance sheet. Such a balance sheet will show the legal form rather than the economic or business substance. As such, it is potentially misleading. It may well give a legal and correct view; it is unlikely to give a true and fair one.

Group accounts attempt to overcome this conflict between form and substance. By far the most popular method is to aggregate or merge the accounts of the entities concerned, a process known as *consolidation*. The end result will be a balance sheet showing the group's combined assets as though each asset had been purchased individually rather than through the acquisition of shares.

This gives rise to a second condition for a group. Showing the result of the individual enterprises as though they were a single business needs to be meaningful. Aggregating two companies within a group which undertake similar activities is likely to meet that criteria. It will show not only the turnover controlled by the group and its underlying market strength but also its asset make up, the extent of fixed assets, the level of debtors or stock and its long term borrowings. Aggregating two totally dissimilar companies, such as an airline and a bank, even though one might own the other, is equivalent to trying to add chalk to cheese. Any consolidated information is likely to convey very little meaning. Consolidated accounting therefore assumes a group of enterprises can be viewed as a unified, accounting entity in their own right.

CONSOLIDATION – THE BASIC MECHANICS

Now that a group has been identified, it is possible to show how a group balance sheet is developed. Consider Example 9.1 where, to simplify matters, only the value of the main balance sheet headings have been given. Pluses and minuses have been included in workings as a reminder of which items are assets and which items are obligations.

Example 9.1

The balance sheet of Haven Ltd on 31 December 19X3 comprised fixed assets of £50,000 and current assets less current liabilities of £40,000. This was financed by ordinary share capital of £70,000 and retentions of £20,000. On that date it agreed to buy the business of Safe Ltd for £20,000 cash. The assets of Safe comprise fixed assets of £20,000 entirely financed by issued and fully paid ordinary share capital.

Haven can buy the business in at least two ways: it can acquire the net assets, leaving Safe with the task of distributing the cash received amongst its shareholders before closing the company down, or it can acquire all of the shares in Safe by giving the cash directly to the shareholders. Whichever approach is taken, Haven ends up with the net assets of Safe and Safe's shareholders end up with £20,000 cash.

The purchase of assets

The transactions necessary to record *the purchase of the net assets* is shown in Exhibit 9.2 where Haven's fixed assets increase to reflect the purchase of Safe's fixed assets and where net current assets fall to show the cash payment for those assets. Also shown in Exhibit 9.2 is the elimination of the fixed assets in Safe's accounts and the increase in cash resulting from the sale. When finally paid out, the obligation of Safe to its shareholders is eliminated and the company liquidated. Purchasing Safe's business therefore leaves Haven with fixed assets of £70,000 and net current assets of £20,000.

Exhibit 9.2 The purchase of a business

(£000)	Haven Ltd				Safe Ltd			
Fixed assets	+£50	+£20	+£70	Fixed assets	+£20	−£20		
Net current assets	+£40	−£20	+£20	Cash		+£20	−£20	£0
	£90		£90		£20			£0
Ordinary share capital	−£70		−£70	Ordinary share capital	£20		+£20	£0
Reserves	−£20		−£20					
	£90		£90		£20			£0

The purchase of shares

If the accounts are to show a true and fair view, this same business reality needs to be recorded when a business is acquired through the purchase of shares. Exhibit 9.3 shows the balance sheet of Haven both immediately before and immediately after the acquisition of Safe's share capital. Such a balance sheet is both legal and correct, showing the asset of shares in Safe as an investment. But it is hardly likely to be true and fair as it hides the fact that Haven owns and controls the assets of Safe. To correct this, the group balance sheet needs to show what lies behind the investment.

This can be achieved in one of two ways. Duality allows the net assets of a company to be calculated by either summing the individual assets less liabilities or totalling the shareholders' funds. Recognising this, the extent of the parent's investment in a subsidiary can be calculated by determining the net assets it effectively owns in that subsidiary or by calculating the obligations of that subsidiary to the parent. Having purchased the entire share capital of Safe, Haven has effectively acquired the £20,000 of fixed assets. This is the same as saying the obligation of Safe to Haven is represented by the shareholders' funds of £20,000 ordinary share capital.

Exhibit 9.3 Basic consolidation

(£000)	Haven Ltd			Safe Ltd	Consolidation		
Fixed assets	+£50		+£50	+£20	+£70		+£70
Investment in Safe		+£20	+£20		+£20	−£20	
Net current assets	+£40	−£20	+£20		+£20		+£20
	£90		£90	£20	£110		£90
Ordinary share capital	−£70		−£70	−£20	−£90	+£20	−£70
Reserves	−£20		−£20		−£20		−£20
	£90		£90	£20	£110		£90

Merging the balance sheets

In Example 9.1, the £20,000 asset of investment in the parent company's accounts really represents the £20,000 of fixed assets in the subsidiary. A simple substitution would therefore suffice. However, for situations of greater complexity, a more logical approach is required which recognises the parent's investment as a claim to the shareholders' funds in the subsidiary. These need to be netted out on consolidation. Perhaps the easiest approach is initially to merge the two balance sheets. Exhibit 9.3 shows the result of this in the first column under the Consolidation heading.

Simply merging the two sets of accounts, however, results in a partial double counting. Haven has an asset of the investment in its subsidiary. Similarly the subsidiary owes to Haven, its shareholder, the shareholders' funds represented by the ordinary share capital. Effectively they are a mirror image of each other. Coming together as a group, these cancel one another out. It is the same principle in any family. One partner may owe the other partner an amount of money. Individually, the one partner is a creditor, the other a debtor. But from a family perspective, the *family* neither owes nor is owed any money. Bringing inter-group indebtedness together has the same effect. This is the purpose of the transaction shown in the second column of the consolidation where the inter-group indebtedness is cancelled out. The net result is a consolidated balance sheet showing the business reality of Haven owning and controlling £70,000 of fixed assets and £20,000 of net current assets – exactly as if the assets had been directly purchased.

Shareholders' funds

Effectively the net assets of the subsidiary are being acquired indirectly via the purchase of all the shares in the subsidiary rather than directly. The obligation of the subsidiary to account for these assets to the owners is represented by the shareholders' funds. These obligations will normally be more than the book value of the ordinary shares: they will also include any share premium account, any general reserves and any profit and loss account balance – indeed any amount to which the shareholder is ultimately entitled. It is claims to these amounts which have effectively been bought when the parent acquired the shares in the subsidiary and so it is these amounts which have to be netted off against the parent's asset of investment in subsidiary.

This is demonstrated in Example 9.2 where Major Ltd has acquired all the shares in Minor Ltd. In the subsidiary's books this obligation to the shareholder is represented by all the

Example 9.2

Major Ltd has today acquired all the shares in another private limited company, Minor. The net assets of Major total £80,000 made up of fixed assets of £30,000, an investment in all the shares in Minor for £40,000 and net current assets of £10,000. Major is financed by £30,000 ordinary share capital, £20,000 share premium account and £30,000 retentions. Minor's balance sheet comprises fixed assets of £25,000 and net current assets of £15,000 which are financed by £10,000 of ordinary share capital, £8,000 of share premium and £22,000 retained profits.

elements making up the shareholders' funds no matter how described. Netting these off against the investment in the parent's accounts will result in the business reality of the group being shown. The workings to this are shown in Exhibit 9.4 where buying all the shares in Minor gives Major access to the assets financed by the total of the shareholders' funds.

Exhibit 9.4 Consolidation with reserves

(£000)	Major Ltd	Minor Ltd	Consolidation			
Fixed assets	+£30	+£25	+£55			+£55
Investment in Minor	+£40	+£40		−£40		
Net current assets	+£10	+£15	+£25			+£25
	£80	£40	£120			£80
Ordinary share capital	−£30	−£10	−£40	+£10		−£30
Share premium account	−£20	−£8	−£28	+£8		−£20
Retentions	−£30	−£22	−£52	+£22		−£30
	£80	£40	£120			£80

The effect of these adjustments is to replace Major's £40,000 investment in the subsidiary by the underlying net assets in Minor. Fixed assets, current assets and any current liabilities are combined line by line.

What is important to realise is the shareholders' funds are *not* ultimately combined on the acquisition of a subsidiary. The consolidated balance sheet will simply show the shareholders' funds relating to the parent. Intuitively this is because consolidation seeks to replace the asset of investment in the subsidiary by its underlying assets. Technically it is because the asset of investment represents a claim on the shareholders' funds and the two are netted out on consolidation.

This raises a further issue. The process of consolidation is a paper exercise. No records of any adjustments are made in the books of account for any group member as these are separate legal entities. Consolidation is merely a process of making the final accounts of the parent more meaningful by incorporating the activities of subsidiaries.

GOODWILL

The purpose of group accounts is to show the underlying assets and liabilities represented by the investment in subsidiaries. Logically, the alternative to buying the shares of a subsidiary is to acquire the individual net assets. Had these been bought individually, it is unlikely that the price would have been their cost in the subsidiary's balance sheet. Rather it will be the amount the subsidiary is prepared to sell them for, in other words their market value.

Consistency demands a similar process of asset valuation when acquiring the business through the purchase of shares. The revised amount is known as the fair value of the assets. Only when this has been determined will it be possible to estimate if the price paid is greater than the value of the underlying assets.

Almost inevitably the price paid *will* be greater than the revised asset values simply because what is being acquired is more than the business assets: it is the gaining of a ready-made business with existing customers, suppliers, workforce and profits. This excess over the value of the net assets is known as *goodwill.*

Goodwill as an asset

Having identified what is meant by goodwill, the next problem is to determine whether it is an asset or an expense. In their Statement of Principles, the Accounting Standards Board identified three qualities necessary before an asset could be recognised. First there must exist a right to future economic benefits and these should be controlled by the entity as a result of a past transaction or event. Secondly, there must be sufficient evidence of a change in an asset or liability. Thirdly, the item should be capable of being measured as a monetary amount with sufficient reliability.

A company acquires another by giving up cash or, as will be seen later, by issuing shares. The second condition is therefore met. What is less clear is the extent of future benefits and whether these can be measured with sufficient reliability. Depending on the answer to these last two conditions, goodwill can either be shown in the balance sheet as an asset or written off as an expense.

Goodwill on consolidation

Whether or not to write off goodwill is returned to later after further complexities in group accounts have been discussed. For the moment, assume that goodwill is treated as an asset. This enables any difference between the purchase price of the subsidiary and the fair value of its underlying assets to be recorded in the balance sheet. Example 9.3 demonstrates the issues involved.

Example 9.3

Parent plc's balance sheet on 30 June 19X4 comprised fixed assets of £40 million, current assets of £30 million and current liabilities of £10 million. It was financed by £30 million of ordinary share capital, £10 million share premium account and £20 million retained profits. On that date it acquired all the ordinary shares in Child Ltd for £15 million.

Child's balance sheet comprised fixed assets of £8 million, current assets of £5 million and current liabilities of £2 million. These were financed by £5 million issued share capital, £1 million share premium account, £2 million revaluation reserve and £3 million retentions. The open market value of Child's fixed assets was £11 million.

Revaluation of assets

The recording of these transactions is shown in Exhibit 9.5. The purchase of the shares in Child Ltd, shown as transaction (a) in Exhibit 9.5, is a proper and legitimate accounting transaction and will be recorded as such in the actual books of account of Parent plc.

Exhibit 9.5 Goodwill and revaluation of acquired assets

(£m)	Parent plc (a)			Child Ltd (b)			Consolidation (c)	(d)	
Goodwill							+£1		+£1
Tangible fixed assets	+£40		+£40	+£8	+£3	+£11	+£51		+£51
Investment in Child		+£15	+£15				+£15	−£1	−£14
Net current assets	+£20	−£15	+£5	+£3		+£3	+£8		+£8
	£60		£60	£11		£14	£74		£60
Ordinary share capital	−£30		−£30	−£5		−£5	−£35	+£5	−£30
Share premium account	−£10		−£10	−£1		−£1	−£11	+£1	−£10
Revaluation reserve				−£2	−£3	−£5	−£5	+£5	
Retentions	−£20		−£20	−£3		−£3	−£23	+£3	−£20
	£60		£60	£11		£14	£74		£60

The next stage, amending Child's fixed asset values to £11 million, arises only because of the consolidation exercise and no record will be made in the accounts of Child Ltd. The necessary adjustment is shown as transaction (b) where the fixed asset value is increased by £3 million, with a corresponding increase in shareholders' funds. The result is that Parent, in taking over Child Ltd, has acquired £14 million of net assets and this claim is represented by the shareholders' funds in the subsidiary comprising the ordinary share capital, the share premium, the increased revaluation reserve and the retentions. Having revalued the assets, it is then possible to begin the process of consolidation by first aggregating the two revised balance sheets.

Parent plc, however, has paid £15 million for the £14 million of assets in Child. The difference is goodwill. Transaction (c) records the goodwill within the investment as a separate asset, leaving the £14 million balance within the investment account as Parent's claim on the shareholders' funds within Child. These now equal one another and transaction (d) nets them out. The result is a final balance sheet showing tangible fixed assets of £51 million, net current assets of £8 million and an intangible asset of £1 million comprising the goodwill on consolidation.

PRE-ACQUISITION AND POST-ACQUISITION RESERVES

Pre-acquisition profits

Immediately a group is formed, the shareholders' funds in the subsidiary take on a new meaning. As far as the *group* is concerned, they simply represent the claims by the parent on the subsidiary's assets and this claim is netted off against the parent's investment on consolidation. In terms of the *group* balance sheet the subsidiary's shareholders' funds will no longer exist. Any reserves included within the subsidiary's shareholders' funds – known as pre-acquisition reserves – cannot therefore be distributed as a profit.

Should they be so used, by paying a cash dividend for example, the overall effect will be zero. The net assets in the subsidiary will fall as the cash is paid out but this will be balanced by the receipt of that cash by the parent. The result is no overall change to the group balance sheet. Any such cash received by the parent is effectively a partial refunding of the purchase price and as such would be used to reduce the cost of the investment.

Post-acquisition profits

The treatment of post-acquisition profits is totally different. They represent a return from the investment. As such they can quite legitimately be included as part of the group's profits. This is demonstrated in Example 9.4 which shows the balance sheets of Parent and Child, originally developed in Example 9.3, one year later.

Example 9.4

> On 30 June 19X5, the balance sheet of Parent plc included tangible fixed assets of £42 million, net current assets of £6 million and the investment in Child Ltd, £15 million. Child's balance sheet on the same day showed tangible fixed assets of £9 million and net current assets of £4 million. No further capital had been raised, no dividends paid and no further revaluations made in either company.

As no dividends have been paid, the profit for the period can be found by calculating either the net increase in assets or the net increase in retentions. This is the approach shown in Exhibit 9.6 where the profit for the year of Parent must be £3 million as both reserves in the form of retentions and net assets have increased by this amount. Using similar reasoning, Child's profit for the year must be £2 million. As a whole, the group must have made £5 million profit and so group reserves must increase by this amount upon consolidation.

To derive the group balance sheet showing this information it is first necessary to record once more the revision to Child's asset values for consolidation purposes as no entry was ever made in the individual books of account. This is shown as transaction (a) in Exhibit 9.6. Once this has been done, it is then necessary to identify the value of the assets acquired by Parent *on the date of acquisition* to establish any payment made for goodwill. (This is merely a repetition of the exercise undertaken earlier in Example 9.3 except the data on the respective balance sheets have moved on one year.) Once this has been completed, the group balance sheet can be derived.

Exhibit 9.6 Pre-aquisition and post-acquisition reserves

(£m)	Parent plc	Child Ltd (a)			Consolidation		
Goodwill					+£1		+£1
Tangible fixed assets	+£42	+£9	+£3	+£12	+£54		+£54
Investment in Child	+£15				+£15	−£1	−£14
Net current assets	+£6	+£4		+£4	+£10		+£10
	£63	£13		£16	£79		£65
Ordinary share capital	−£30	−£5		−£5	−£35	+£5	−£30
Share premium account	−£10	−£1		−£1	−£11	+£1	−£10
Revaluation reserve		−£2	−£3	−£5	−£5	+£5	
Retentions	−£23	−£5		−£5	−£28	+£3	−£25
	£63	£13		£16	£79		£65

At the date of acquisition, Parent gained control of £14 million assets in Child. This is the same as saying that the subsidiary's share capital, share premium, revaluation reserve and retentions at the acquisition date also equalled £14 million. Taking this approach, the shareholders' funds in the subsidiary due to Parent plc will need to be netted off against the investment, again to leave goodwill of £1 million. This exercise is shown under the heading of consolidation. The result is a group balance sheet combining not only the group net assets but also its combined *post-acquisition* profits.

ACQUISITION BY SHARES OR OTHER SECURITIES

When acquiring a subsidiary, the purchase price does not have to be in the form of cash. As with any other purchase in a free market, the determination of price and the choice of form and method of payment is left to the parties concerned. Rather than offering cash, a bidding company might prefer to offer its own shares, debentures or other securities in exchange for the shares in the subsidiary.

Advantages of a share-for-share exchange

For the shareholder in the subsidiary one major advantage of such a share-for-share exchange is that no tax is payable on any capital profit made. Had the consideration been for cash, the Inland Revenue would have recognised this as a realised capital gain and hence any profit would have been taxable. A second possible advantage of a share-for-share exchange exists where the bidding company is more successful than the company being acquired. Exchanging shares enables the subsidiary's shareholders to acquire a continuing interest in the wider, more successful group and given that the shares are likely to be in a quoted company, shareholders have the added security of being able to sell their shares whenever necessary.

The valuation of shares

Although the exact details of any offer will vary, one thing is for certain. The shareholders in the company being acquired will not want to suffer a loss as a result of the exchange of shares. The value of their new shareholding will therefore have to be at least as much as their existing shareholding. How much an individual share is worth depends on a variety of factors: future profitability, future risk, interest rates and other factors.

Rarely will the market price of a share equal its nominal price. A company, for example, could have issued its shares at a face or nominal value of £1 many years ago. The current market price is likely to be rather more than this. For the sake of argument, assume it is £4. A company bidding for these shares will have to offer at least that amount.

With a cash exchange, there can be little argument. An offer of £6 cash is a clear capital gain of £2. An offer of two shares in the bidding company in exchange for each share in the company being bid for is more difficult to evaluate. The holder of one share has an existing investment worth £4. Any share exchange will only be profitable if the value of the replacement shares are worth at least as much. If the bidder's shares are currently priced at £2.50 each on the stock market, then the shareholder has the opportunity of giving up a single share in the existing company worth £4 for two in the bidding company worth a total of £5. This is the logic used in Example 9.5 where a group is formed not by a cash payment but by a share exchange.

Example 9.5

> Bach plc is considering the acquisition of all the share capital in Elgar plc. Bach is funded by 15 million £1 ordinary shares and £20 million of retentions. The fair value of its net assets is £50 million. Currently the market price of its shares are £4. Elgar is financed by 10 million £1 shares and £30 million of retentions. Its net assets are valued at £45 million and its share price is currently £5.

Duality enables the value of the net assets for each company to be found by calculating the total of shareholders' funds. To develop the group balance sheet, it is then necessary to estimate how much Bach should pay for Elgar, the number of shares to issue and the cost of any goodwill.

With 10 million shares issued, each worth £5, the value of Elgar plc is at least £50 million. In the real world, a bidder needs to offer in excess of this to entice existing Elgar shareholders to accept the offer. Ignoring this extra complexity, Bach, with a share value of £4, should offer 12.5 million of its own shares – £50 million ÷ £4 – for the 10 million shares in Elgar. The new shareholders recognise Bach shares are worth more than their face value and so are prepared to accept this exchange.

Share premium account

Receiving assets – consideration – of £50 million in exchange for shares with a nominal value of £12.5 million must mean the shares have been issued at a premium of £37.5 million. A share premium account therefore has to be opened. This is shown as transaction (a) in Exhibit 9.7.

Exhibit 9.7 Payment by shares – Bach acquires Elgar

(£m)	Bach plc			Elgar plc			Consolidation		
		(a)			(b)			(c)	(d)
Goodwill								+£5.0	+£5.0
Tangible net assets	+£35.0		+£35.0	+£40.0	+£5.0	+£45.0	+£80.0		+£80.0
Investment in Elgar		+£50.0	+£50.0				+£50.0	–£5.0 –£45.0	
	£35.0		£85.0	£40.0		£45.0	£130.0		£85.0
Ordinary share capital	–£15.0	–£12.5	–£27.5	–£10.0		–£10.0	–£37.5	+£10.0	–£27.5
Share premium account		–£37.5	–£37.5				–£37.5		–£37.5
Other reserves	–£20.0		–£20.0	–£30.0	–£5.0	–£35.0	–£55.0	+£35.0	–£20.0
	£35.0		£85.0	£40.0		£45.0	£130.0		£85.0

Completing the group balance sheet

The revaluation of the assets in Elgar to their fair value is shown as transaction (b). Bach will be paying £50 million for net assets of £45 million. The goodwill on consolidation will therefore be £5 million and this is shown as (c). Having calculated and transferred the goodwill out of the investment, the balance must represent Bach's interest in the shareholders' funds of Elgar which are netted out as transaction (d). The end result of the consolidation is a balance sheet showing net assets/shareholders' funds of £85 million if the goodwill is capitalised.

Reverse takeover

Logically, instead of Bach bidding for Elgar, their roles could be reversed. There can often be sound reasons why the smaller company bids for the larger one even though the smaller company's investors become a minority within the enlarged group. One practical reason might be the smaller company already having a stock exchange quotation. If the larger company does not have a quote, allowing the smaller one to make the bid effectively obtains a quote for the larger company without having to invest the time and expense of formally applying to be listed. This is known as a reverse takeover.

Whatever the reasons, it might be useful to see the final balance sheet if Elgar made a bid for Bach. With a current market price of £4 and 15 million shares in issue, Bach is capitalised at £60 million. As Elgar's shares are quoted at £5, it would have to issue 12 million shares to acquire Bach. The difference between the £12 million of share capital issued and the consideration received of £60 million worth of shares is the share premium.

Similarly, goodwill will be the difference between the £60 million price paid and the £50 million valuation placed on the assets acquired. The effect of these transactions are shown in Exhibit 9.8 where the effect of Elgar acquiring Bach is to produce a balance sheet showing net assets and shareholders' funds of £100 million.

Exhibit 9.8 Payment by shares – Elgar acquires Bach

(£m)	Elgar plc	(a)	Bach plc	(b)	Consolidation (c)	(d)
Goodwill					+£10.0	+£10.0
Tangible net assets	+£40.0	+£40.0	+£35.0+£15.0	+£50.0	+£90.0	+£90.0
Investment in Bach	+£60.0	+£60.0			+£60.0–£10.0–£50.0	
	£40.0	£100.0	£35.0	£50.0	£150.0	£100.0
Ordinary share capital	–£10.0 –£12.0	–£22.0	–£15.0	–£15.0	–£37.0	+£15.0 –£22.0
Share premium account		–£48.0			–£48.0	–£48.0
Other reserves	–£30.0	–£30.0	–£20.0–£15.0	–£35.0	–£65.0	+£35.0 –£30.0
	£40.0	£100.0	£35.0	£50.0	£150.0	£100.0

The takeover paradox

There is therefore a choice of two balance sheet values to describe the same phenomenon of Bach and Elgar becoming a group! Why then does the group balance sheet total £100 million if Elgar acquires Bach but only £85 million when it is the other way round? And why do other reserves total £30 million if Elgar acquires Bach but only £20 million if the roles are reversed?

There is but a single cause for the anomaly, the concern with historical costs as witnessed by a transaction. The final group balance sheet is made up of an amalgam of historical book values relating to the parent and fair or current values for the subsidiary as evidenced by the revaluation of its assets. Reversing which company is the parent also reverses which current asset values are brought into the group balance sheet. Secondly, both have goodwill as measured by the difference between their current market values and the historical book values of their net assets. Only one, however, brings this goodwill into the group accounts, the one being acquired. Change the company being acquired and the amount of recorded goodwill also changes. Mathematically, consolidation allows $a + b$ to equal c but $b + a$ to equal d!

GOODWILL AND FAIR VALUATIONS

The problem of goodwill and fair values are interlinked. There is also the problem of how to account for goodwill – as an asset or an expense? These issues were originally addressed by the Accounting Standards Committee in SSAP 22, Accounting for Goodwill, a standard which, with certain adjustments, is still current. In paragraph 2 of that standard, the ASC recognised that goodwill was not a normal type of asset as it is 'incapable of realisation separately from the business as a whole'. In the same paragraph, the ASC also recognised that there was no clear link between costs incurred and the value of goodwill; that the individual intangible factors such as image and brand loyalty which contribute to goodwill cannot be separately valued; that the value of goodwill may fluctuate wildly and that the value of goodwill is highly subjective. These are strong arguments to suggest that goodwill should be recorded as an expense rather than an asset. But there is an even stronger objection to capitalising goodwill as an asset: goodwill arising from *within* the parent will not have been capitalised, simply because it will have been built up over time and not acquired via a transaction. There is therefore a basic inconsistency of treatment between two parts of the same group.

The treatment of goodwill in the accounts

SSAP 22 was at least clear about one thing: *non-purchased* goodwill should not appear in the balance sheet of any company or group. Paragraphs 38 and 39 initially appeared at least as clear: 'Purchased goodwill should not be carried in the balance sheet of a company or a group as a permanent item...' and 'Purchased goodwill...should normally be eliminated from the accounts immediately on acquisition...' Unfortunately the effect of this was totally destroyed a few paragraphs later when not only was goodwill allowed to be capitalised and written off over its useful economic life but both methods of accounting for goodwill were explicitly allowed within the same group for different acquisitions!

To make matters even more confusing, when goodwill is immediately written off, it is not to be charged against the profit for the period but against reserves. No justification was given for this although the obvious benefit to the group from charging goodwill immediately against reserves is that future reported profits will appear higher than they otherwise would be. Logically, it appears inconsistent for the same goodwill to be an expense against profits when being amortised over a period of years and yet not appearing to be an expense when written off immediately.

Reasons for different goodwill policies

Whether or not a company writes off goodwill in its consolidated accounts will depend on a variety of factors. Leaving goodwill in the balance sheet increases net assets and hence increases the equity in the group. This may be important if a company has a high level of debt in its total capital structure. A company might have entered into legal covenants with its lenders restricting the amount of debt to a certain proportion of equity. If there is a danger of this covenant being breached on an acquisition, capitalising goodwill may avoid the breach. A derivative of this is to attempt to identify and value the intangible components within goodwill and show these components separately. By far the most popular example of this is brand accounting where an attempt is made to put a value on brands on the balance sheet. By way of an example, when Elgar acquired Bach, it could have valued Bach's brands at £6 million. These would have appeared as a separate intangible asset on the balance sheet, leaving the balance of £4 million to either be capitalised as goodwill on the balance sheet or written off against reserves.

Other companies which may be more concerned with showing greater profitability may prefer to write off the goodwill. Not only will this eliminate the amortisation or depreciation change of the goodwill in future years, it will also make relative profit appear higher. This will be the case when investors compare profits with the net assets of the group in order to determine profit per pound of assets employed. The effect of writing off the goodwill to reserves on the group accounts of Bach and Elgar are shown in Exhibit 9.9.

Exhibit 9.9 The effect of writing off goodwill on the consolidated balance sheet

	Bach acquires Elgar			Elgar acquires Bach		
Goodwill	+£5.0	−£5.0		+£10.0	−£10.0	
Tangible net assets	+£80.0		+£80.0	+£90.0		+£90.0
	£85.0		£80.0	£100.0		£90.0
Ordinary share capital	−£27.5		−£27.5	−£22.0		−£22.0
Share premium account	−£37.5		−£37.5	−£48.0		−£48.0
Other reserves	−£20.0	+£5.0	−£15.0	−£30.0	+£10.0	−£20.0
	£85.0		£80.0	£100.0		£90.0

Goodwill and the Accounting Standards Board

The problems of goodwill have been identified in a discussion paper issued by the Accounting Standards Board in March 1994. In the paper, the ASB considered two matters, what the appropriate treatment of intangibles such as brands should be when the practice is to write off purchased goodwill against reserves, and the potential inconsistency of treatment between purchased and internally generated goodwill.

The discussion paper proposed that there should be no separate treatment for purchased intangibles: they should be subsumed within purchased goodwill as they cannot be measured with sufficient reliability. Unfortunately, as valid as this might be, it introduces an anomaly. Had the company directly purchased an intangible asset by, for instance, buying the right to a brand name, this could still be recorded in the balance sheet as an asset.

The discussion paper then identified six possible methods of accounting for goodwill. Conceptually these can be reduced to three; (a) retain goodwill subject to an annual review of any impairment, (b) capitalise goodwill and amortise it over its useful life, and (c) write off goodwill immediately against reserves. Although superficially attractive, the first option is difficult to sustain as purchased goodwill will be gradually replaced by internally generated goodwill through time. Option (b) can be arbitrary when deciding the period over which the goodwill is amortised while both options (a) and (b) suffer from an inconsistent treatment when compared with internally generated goodwill. Until these issues are resolved, the choice available under SSAP 22 will continue.

Pre-acquisition write downs

Separate from the problem of how to account for goodwill is another difficulty; how to derive the fair value of assets and liabilities acquired. SSAP 22 defined fair value as 'the amount for which an asset (or liability) could be exchanged in an arm's length transaction'. In paragraph 14, it also stated that anticipated future losses or costs of reorganisation may need to be taken into account and included in the liabilities at the time of the acquisition. This meant that the fair value of the assets acquired was effectively reduced by providing for any liabilities which the acquiring company may incur in transforming those assets to a form suitable for its own use. This is an example of a pre-acquisition write down. Another is the reduction in the value of stock. To justify this treatment, the analogy is often made of a house purchase for, say, £100,000, which requires an extra £50,000 of work being undertaken to make it habitable. A purchaser has two options; to buy the house for £100,000 and incur £50,000 of extra *capital* expenditure or to buy the house in a good state of repair for £150,000. Whichever approach is taken, so the argument goes, the purchaser has a £150,000 asset. Example 9.6 relates this to a business example.

Example 9.6

> On 1 April 19X8, the balance sheet of Berlin plc comprised fixed assets of £500 million, stock of £80 million, debtors of £20 million and cash of £300 million. This was financed by £300 million issued ordinary share capital and £600 million reserves. On that day it acquired all the shares in Munich plc, paying £240 million in cash. The balance sheet of Munich comprised fixed assets of £70 million, stock of £60 million, debtors of £40 million and cash of £10 million. This was financed by £60 million ordinary share capital and £120 million reserves. Berlin estimated that the fair value of the fixed assets was £40 million and the fair value of the stock was £20 million. The fair value of Munich's other assets equalled their book values. In addition, Berlin believes there will be reorganisation costs of £30 million.

The cash in the opening balance sheet of Berlin plc will be reduced by the £240 million purchase price. This is shown as transaction (a) in Exhibit 9.10. Transaction (b) shows the reduction of Munich's assets to their fair value. The fair value of assets taken over totals

Exhibit 9.10 Acquisition of a company and provisions

(£m)	Berlin plc (a)			Munich plc (b)	(c)		Consolidation (d)	(e)	
Goodwill							+£160	+£160	
Fixed assets	+£500		+£500	+£70	–£30	+£40	+£540		+£540
Investment in Munich		+£240	+£240				+£240	–£160	–£80
Stock	+£80		+£80	+£60	–£40	+£20	£100		+£100
Debtors	+£20		+£20	+£40		+£40	+£60		+£60
Cash	+£300	–£240	+£60	+£10		+£10	+£70		+£70
	£900		£900	£180		£110	£1,010		£930
Ordinary share capital	–£300		–£300	–£60		–£60	–£360	+£60	–£300
Reserves	–£600		–£600	–£120	+£70 +£30	–£20	–£620	+£20	–£600
Reorganisation provision					–£30	–£30	–£30		–£30
	£900		£900	£180		£110	£1,010		£930

£110 million. However, there needs to be a further £30 million expended to put these in a form suitable for Berlin. This is reflected in the consolidation within Exhibit 9.10 by transaction (c) where reserves are reduced by £30 million and a provision for a similar amount created. The overall fair value of the net assets is therefore only £80 million. With a purchase price of £240 million, goodwill must be £160 million. Transaction (d) shows this being recorded as an asset. The final stage is to net out the shareholders' funds acquired of £80 million after the creation of the provision. This is recorded as transaction (e). Mechanically, the provision is a kind of creditor. When the £30 million reorganisation expenditure is eventually incurred, cash will be reduced by that amount and the provision eliminated.

FRS 7 Fair Values in Acquisition Accounting

As valid as the provision for reorganisation and the writing down of the other assets might be, they lend themselves to abuse. By creating a provision on acquisition, £30 million of what would otherwise have been revenue expenditure will not be charged to any subsequent profit and loss account. Further, the reduction in stock values will reduce any future cost of sales while the reduction in the value of fixed assets will reduce future depreciation charges in the profit and loss account. As a consequence, future profits will be boosted. The most extreme example of this was when Coloroll plc acquired John Crowther for £213 million in shares and cash. By undertaking so many fair value adjustments and provisions Coloroll wrote off £224 million – £11 million more than the initial cost!

In an attempt to stamp out this sort of abuse, the Accounting Standards Board introduced FRS 7 Fair Values in Acquisition Accounting. Although a complex and prescriptive document, the central issue is clear. In determining fair values, the valuation of assets and liabilities should be seen through the eyes of the seller and not take account of what the buyers intend to do with those elements. In particular, any planned post-acquisition provisions for reorganisation costs, restructuring expenses or foreseeable losses are to be reported as post-acquisition expenses *through the profit and loss account* and not as liabilities of the business being acquired. As a result of FRS 7, Berlin, is no longer able to create the pre-acquisition provision. Instead, it must recognise the fair value of the net assets acquired as £110 million, not the £80 million in Exhibit 9.10. Any subsequent reorganisation costs will then be charged to the profit and loss account.

MERGER ACCOUNTING

So far, groups have been considered from the perspective of a takeover; where one company purchases another, takes over its operations and has overall control of the subsidiary. For takeovers, the *acquisition* or *purchase* method of consolidation described above might well be valid. However, it is questionable whether the consolidated accounts would show a true and fair view if the group comprised enterprises of roughly similar size which had joined together as a genuine marriage of interests and where no one undertaking was the dominant partner.

Effect of merger accounting

To counter this criticism there evolved in the USA an alternative way of looking at a consolidation known as the *merger* or *pooling of interest* method and which became increasingly popular in the UK during the 1980s. The method recognises that if enterprises come together to pool their resources then the combined assets should equal the individual assets of the businesses forming the group. The assets and liabilities are simply added together. No revaluation of any form takes place. And because it is only a pooling of interests rather than the purchase of one business by another, no goodwill is created nor any share premium recognised in the group accounts. The effect of merger accounting on the group balance sheet of Bach and Elgar outlined earlier in Example 9.5 is shown in Exhibit 9.11 where it is assumed that Bach initiates the merger.

Exhibit 9.11 Merger accounting

(£m)	Bach plc (a)			Elgar plc (b)	Consolidation (c)	(d)		
Tangible net assets	+£35.0		+£35.0	+£40.0	+£75.0			+£75.0
Investment in Elgar		+£12.5	+£12.5		+£12.5	−£10.0	−£2.5	
	£35.0		£47.5	£40.0	£87.5			£75.0
Ordinary share capital	−£15.0	−£12.5	−£27.5	−£10.0	−£37.5	+£10.0		−£27.5
Retentions	−£20.0		−£20.0	−£30.0	−£50.0		+£2.5	−£47.5
	£35.0		£47.5	£40.0	£87.5			£75.0

As before, the market value of Elgar's shares is £50 million and so with Bach's share price at £4, 12.5 million £1 shares will have to be issued in exchange for Elgar's shares. Under merger accounting, however, no sale has taken place and so no share premium will be raised. The investment in Elgar will therefore be recorded in transaction (a) at the value of the ordinary shares issued. With no revaluation of assets, the balance sheets will then be combined and the share-for-share exchange netted out without reference to the reserves.

Often, the cost of the investment will not equal the ordinary share capital of the other enterprise and so any outstanding balance will have to be accounted for via the reserves. In this particular example, £12.5 million of shares were issued to acquire £10.0 million of share capital and so reserves will have to be reduced by the difference. Had Elgar been the vehicle for the merger rather than Bach, the reverse would have occurred. Net assets would have been the same at £75 million, as would the total of shareholders' funds. Within the shareholders' funds though, Elgar would have only issued £12 million of shares to acquire £15 million in Bach and so a capital reserve of £3 million would have been created instead.

Implications of merger accounting

Merger accounting is certainly simpler. It effectively involves the simple aggregation of balance sheet data. Some would argue it is more meaningful by not mixing the current and historical values to be found under acquisition accounting. However, this presupposes that historical costs relating to different time periods have meaning for investors.

One clear advantage to the merger method of acquisition accounting is its transitive nature, that $a + b$ equals $b + a$ even though the elements making up the shareholders' funds may differ slightly. Its major advantage from a group management perspective, however, is that the reserves are simply combined, making them available for distribution – unlike pre-acquisition reserves under acquisition accounting. In addition, where fair values are above book values, the depreciation charge in the profit and loss account will be less as merger accounting does not require that assets and liabilities be revalued. A cynic might argue that these are the major reasons for the popularity of merger accounting amongst managers. Certainly, the possible abuses of merger accounting was of concern to the Accounting Standards Board when it introduced FRS 6 Acquisitions and Mergers. This standard is discussed below in the context of the regulation of group accounts in the UK.

MINORITY INTERESTS

Whichever method is used for consolidation, from time to time some shareholders may choose not to sell their shares to the group. This poses a problem for the reporting of group activities. One way to tackle this would be to consolidate the proportion of the subsidiary owned by the parent. The alternative approach emphasises *control* rather than ownership. If the parent owns more than 50 per cent of the subsidiary, it actually controls 100 per cent of it. The alternative treatment is therefore to consolidate the whole of the subsidiary but then show that part of the subsidiary not belonging to the group is a form of creditor known as the minority interest. Both approaches are developed from the information contained in Example 9.7.

Example 9.7

> Shop plc acquired 75 per cent of the issued share capital of Branch Ltd 12 months ago when Branch's reserves stood at £8 million. Today, the balance sheet of Branch shows fixed assets of £40 million, current assets of £30 million and current liabilities of £10 million financed by ordinary share capital of £36 million and reserves of £24 million. There has been no change to the capital structure over the last year, no dividends have been paid and the asset values of one year ago were also their fair values.
>
> Shop's net assets today comprise fixed assets of £30 million, current assets of £25 million, current liabilities of £15 million and investment in Branch, £45 million. Shareholders' funds are made up of £50 million ordinary share capital and £35 million of reserves.

Calculating goodwill

Because the acquisition took place 12 months ago, the value of the assets acquired at that date need to be derived in order to calculate the value of any goodwill. One year ago, the reserves of Branch stood at £8 million and the ordinary share capital at £36 million and so net assets would have been £44 million which was also the fair value. Shop paid £45 million for ¾ of the net assets and so it gained ¾ of the issued share capital (£27 million) and ¾ of the £8 million reserves existing at that time (£6 million). Goodwill attributable to the purchase by Shop is therefore £12 million.

Proportional consolidation

Exhibit 9.12 demonstrates both ways of showing the consolidated balance sheets. Bringing in only the proportion of the subsidiary owned is shown in the first part of Exhibit 9.12. Three-quarters of each element making up Branch's balance sheet is added to the full balance sheet of Shop in transaction (a). Eliminating the goodwill from the investment in Branch Ltd, transaction (b), leaves the £33 million invested in Branch's shareholders' funds at the date of acquisition. Transaction (c) matches the balance of the investment against the share capital and reserves acquired, eliminating both totals from the consolidated balance sheet.

Exhibit 9.12 The treatment of the minority interest

(£m)	Shop	Branch (a)	Consolidation (b)	(c)	Shop	Branch	Consolidation (d)	(e)	(f)
Goodwill			+£12	+£12			+£12		+£12
Tangible fixed assets	+£30	+£30	+£60	+60	+£30	+£40	+£70		+£70
Net current assets	+£10	+£15	+£25	+£25	+£10	+£20	+£30		+£30
Investment in Branch	+£45	—	+£45 −£12	−£33 —	+£45	—	+£45 −£12	−£33	—
	£85	£45	£130	£97	£85	£60	£145		£112
Ordinary share capital	−£50	−£27	−£77	+£27 −£50	−£50	−£36	−£86	+£27 +£9	−£50
Retentions	−£35	−£18	−£53	+£6 −£47	−£35	−£24	−£59	+£6 +£6	−£47
Minority interest								−£15	−£15
	£85	£45	£130	£97	£85	£60	£145		£112

The adjustment does not fully eliminate all of Branch's reserves. The amount outstanding represents post-acquisition profits attributable to the group and hence is a legitimate element on the consolidated balance sheet. The final result shows shareholders' funds of £97 million matched by the same amount of net assets.

Full consolidation

However useful such an approach is, it does not fully show the assets *controlled* by Shop plc. The alternative approach is shown in the second part of Exhibit 9.12 where both balance sheets are fully amalgamated. The goodwill adjustment (d) follows identical logic to the partial consolidation as does the netting out of the investment (e). This still leaves a quarter of the share capital and reserves in Branch not yet eliminated. This is because those funds were not acquired by Shop but belong to the minority of shareholders who chose not to sell their shares.

For consolidation purposes, the minority interest can be viewed as a form of a creditor and this is the way it has been treated in transaction (f). Effectively, transactions (e) and (f) have divided Branch's shareholders' funds between those belonging to Shop and those belonging to the minority shareholders in Branch. Within those belonging to Shop, a further split has been made between those funds representing claims to assets acquired and those relating to subsequent profits generated.

The end result is a balance sheet with shareholders' funds of £97 million as before but now showing the group *controlling* £112 million of net assets due to the partial financing of the subsidiary by the minority shareholders. Because of the additional insight provided by showing the net assets *controlled* by the group, the full consolidation approach has traditionally been the way minority shareholdings have been treated and indeed is the only way allowable under current accounting standards. Before discussing the legal and regulatory constraints on group accounts, however, there is one final situation to be covered, where a parent has influence but not control.

ASSOCIATED UNDERTAKINGS

A business can invest in another for two reasons, control or as a simple investment. If a business invests to obtain control then, within the constraint of historical cost, consolidated accounts are more likely to share a true and fair view. If the investment is merely to obtain a dividend return, then it can most fairly be described by showing the investment at cost on the balance sheet – perhaps with its market value disclosed by way of a note – and any dividends received as income separate from the trading profit within the profit and loss account. However, there is a third possibility: that a business invests in another to influence actively its policies even though it does not have formal control.

A company might acquire a sufficiently large stake in another to appoint a director to the board and so influence policy. This may well make commercial sense if the other company is a major customer or a critical supplier. Alternatively, several companies might come together to undertake a particular task in the form of a joint venture. Such schemes are popular in the construction industry for multi-million pound projects. By forming a separate company to undertake the joint venture, the assets of the founding businesses are protected by the limited liability of the joint venture should the project fail. Whatever the reasons, the relationship is much more than that of a simple investor concerned with dividends and yet because no one company has control, it is not possible to incorporate the substance of the relationship by simple consolidation. The issue then is how to account for a business over which there is influence but not control.

Such businesses are known as *associated undertakings*. One solution to the difficulty would be to include the associate's proportion of assets and liabilities in the form of a proportional consolidation as considered earlier in Example 9.7. However, if the associate is a limited company, it is the directors of the associate who have immediate and direct control over its assets and liabilities. The group as a shareholder will only be a minority within the associate company and have no automatic right to its net assets – unlike the position of a subsidiary where the group has that control. The group cannot, for instance, agree to sell or acquire new assets in the associated company without the agreement of the other shareholders. A proportional consolidation would therefore give a misleading impression of the group's net assets over which it had control, and yet merely showing the investment in the balance sheet and dividends received in the profit and loss account might be equally misleading.

Accounting for associate undertakings

The solution proposed by the Accounting Standards Committee in its SSAP 1 Accounting for Associated Companies is in effect a 'one-line' form of consolidation, bringing in the group's proportion of assets in the associate not by aggregating them with the group's assets but by showing the amount as a separate item within the group balance sheet. Such an approach is known as *equity accounting*. If the associate is not a company, SSAP 1 allows proportional consolidation because of the different legal relationship between the group and the associate. In a partnership, for instance, the assets directly belong to the partners and not to any separate legal entity. Including the partner's proportion within the group's accounts would therefore be quite legitimate. Whichever approach is taken the total of net assets and the level of shareholders' funds will be identical as Example 9.8 demonstrates.

Example 9.8

The group balance sheet of DC Power plc immediately before incorporating its associate, AC Power Ltd, showed fixed assets of £40 million, net current assets of £30 million and a 25 per cent investment in AC Power at cost of £15 million. These were financed by 40 million £1 ordinary shares and £45 million of retained profits.

On the same day AC Power's balance sheet showed fixed assets of £48 million and current assets less current liabilities of £12 million being financed by 20 million £1 ordinary shares and £40 million of reserves, although when DC Power acquired its stake these reserves stood at only £16 million. There has been no change in AC Power's capital structure since DC Power acquired its stake.

Given that the reserves of AC Power stood at £16 million and its ordinary share capital at £20 million when the stake was acquired, DC Power acquired 25 per cent or £9 million of AC's shareholders' funds and so had a claim to £9 million of its net assets. Having paid £15 million for the stake, the goodwill – or the premium on acquisition as it is sometimes called – is found to be £6 million.

Proportional consolidation

In the first section of Exhibit 9.13, the proportional consolidation is shown. Twenty-five per cent of AC's balance sheet, shown as (a), is merged with DC's balance sheet. The £6 million of goodwill within the investment is then shown separately under transaction

(b) to leave a balance of £9 million. This represents 25 per cent or £5 million of the share capital and 25 per cent or £4 million of the reserves originally acquired and so transaction (c) nets these out. The result is a consolidated balance sheet merging the net assets and showing the reserves of DC as having increased by the 25 per cent of post-acquisition reserves attributable from within the associated company.

Exhibit 9.13 Associated undertakings

(£m)	DC	AC (a)	Proportional consolidation		Equity accounting	
			Consolidation		DC	
			(b)	(c)		(d)
Goodwill			+£6	+£6		
Tangible fixed assets	+£40	+£12	+£52	+£52	+£40	+£40
Net current assets	+£30	+£3	+£33	+£33	+£30	+£30
Investment in AC	+£15		+£15 −£6 −£9		+£15 +£6	+£21
	£85	£15	£100	£91	£85	£91
Ordinary share capital	−£40	−£5	−£45	+£5 −£40	−£40	−£40
Retentions	−£45	−£10	−£55	+£4 −£51	−£45 −£6	−£51
	£85	£15	£100	£91	£85	£91

Equity accounting

The second part of Exhibit 9.13 shows the alternative equity accounting approach. The net assets and shareholders' funds of AC Power when DC acquired its stake were £36 million. Currently they stand at £60 million. Given that there has been no additional funds introduced into the business, this increase in assets of £24 million must have occurred because of profit generated between the two dates. As 25 per cent of AC belongs to DC, 25 per cent of the increase in the assets and reserves (all post-acquisition by definition) need to be brought into DC's balance sheet. Transaction (d) shows this £6 million increase being added to both the investment in subsidiary account and the group reserves.

The net result is that both equity accounting and proportional consolidation show the same total of shareholders' funds and the same overall level of net assets. The essential difference is that proportional consolidation adds the associate's proportion of assets and liabilities to the group data line by line whereas equity accounting adds them as a single amount. Exhibit 9.14 explains why. By definition, the cost of the investment in an asso-

Exhibit 9.14 The composition of the investment in associated undertakings

Investment in associate + Increase in attributable net assets

= (Goodwill + Proportion of attributable net assets at acquisition date) + Increase in attributable net assets

= Goodwill + (Proportion of attributable net assets at acquisition date + Increase in attributable net assets)

= Goodwill + (Proportion of attributable net assets at current balance sheet date)

ciate comprises the underlying value of the assets attributable to the investing company at the acquisition date plus any goodwill. To this is later added any increase in the net assets attributable to the investing company since the acquisition. The final total must therefore equal the proportion of the net assets currently attributable to the investing company plus any goodwill.

Disclosure in the final accounts

The rules requiring a subsidiary's assets to be shown at fair values and the required treatment of goodwill under SSAP 22 apply equally to associated undertakings. In addition, because of its 'one line' consolidation, SSAP 1 requires the composition of the investment in the associated company to be shown. This must differentiate the investing group's share of the associate's net assets from any goodwill or premium paid on the acquisition, in effect the bottom line of Exhibit 9.14. To comply with this, a note to the accounts would show the £21 million investment in Exhibit 9.13 as being made up of £15 million as the group's proportion of the associate's net assets plus £6 million goodwill or premium on acquisition.

THE CONSOLIDATED PROFIT AND LOSS ACCOUNT

Throughout the many complexities affecting group accounts, little has been said explicitly about the consolidated profit and loss account. In fact the treatment of the group profit and loss account has already been developed when consolidating balance sheets. With no changes to the structure of shareholders' funds and no dividends declared, any change in the reserves between one period and the next must be due to profits retained in the group and so must equal the profit for the period. This is demonstrated in Example 9.9.

Example 9.9

Kennedy Ltd acquired all the shares in Mutter Ltd exactly one year ago. The outline final accounts for both companies are given below. No dividends were paid during the year and there had been no changes in the capital subscribed for either company.

Balance sheet at year end			Trading and profit and loss account for the year		
Company	Kennedy	Mutter		Kennedy	Mutter
	(£000)	(£000)		(£000)	(£000)
Fixed assets	500	350	Turnover	600	500
Investment in Mutter	300		Cost of sales	150	200
Net current assets	100	50	Gross profit	450	300
	900	400	Distribution costs	50	30
Financed by			Administration costs	250	70
£1 ordinary shares	550	100	Profit before taxation	150	200
Reserves	350	300	Tax on profit on ordinary activities	50	80
	900	400	Profit for the year	100	120

Although the question does not give the level of reserves in Mutter at the time of acquisition, these can be determined from the data given. The net assets/shareholders' funds in Mutter currently stand at £400,000. But these are after retaining the profit for the year of £120,000. Therefore the shareholders' funds in Mutter at the beginning of the year must have been £280,000. These are the resources acquired by Kennedy one year previously for £300,000 and so the goodwill must have been £20,000. The £280,000 balance of Kennedy's investment represents the shareholders' funds originally acquired in Mutter and so both are eliminated on consolidation in the normal way. This is reproduced in Exhibit 9.15 along with the group profit and loss account.

Exhibit 9.15 The group profit and loss account

(£000)	Group balance sheet at year end					Profit statement for the year			
	K	M	Consolidation		Group		K	M	Group
Goodwill			+£20		+£20	Turnover	−£600	−£500	−£1,100
Tangible fixed assets	+£500	+£350	+£850		+£850	Cost of sales	+£150	+£200	+£350
Investment in Mutter	+£300		+£300 −£20	−£280		Gross profit	−£450	−£300	−£750
Net current assets	+£100	+£50	+£150		+£150	Distribution costs	+£50	+£30	+£80
	£900	£400	£1,300		£1,020	Administration costs	+£250	+£70	+£320
						Profit before taxation	−£150	−£200	−£350
Ordinary share capital	−£550	−£100	−£650	+£100	−£550	Tax on ordinary activities	+ £50	+ £80	+£130
Retentions	−£350	−£300	−£650	+£180	−£470	Profit for the year	−£100	−£120	−£220
	£900	£400	£1,300		£1,020				

Developing the profit and loss account

At the beginning of the year, the group reserves would have consisted solely of those within Kennedy. Mutter's reserves at that date were entirely pre-acquisition and are eliminated from the group balance sheet upon consolidation. As Kennedy's reserves at the year end were £350,000 and the retained profit for the year was £100,000, the group opening reserves must have been £250,000. Group closing reserves are shown to be £470,000 and so the group profit for the year, assuming no dividends and transfers from the reserves, must be £220,000. This is the answer given by amalgamating the two profit and loss accounts. The group profit and loss account therefore is mainly a more detailed explanation of the movement on reserves.

Before looking at the exceptions to this, it might be beneficial to rework the Kennedy–Mutter exercise but assuming the investment was for only 75 per cent of the shares in Mutter. The opening net assets of Mutter will still be £280,000 except that only £210,000 will now relate to Kennedy, causing the goodwill on consolidation to increase to £90,000. Twenty-five per cent of the share capital and 25 per cent of the reserves in Mutter belong to the minority interest and this is the composition of the minority interest element in the balance sheet shown in Exhibit 9.16. Similarly, 75 per cent of the share capital and 75 per cent of the pre-acquisition reserves are netted out against the investment by Kennedy. This leaves 75 per cent of the post-acquisition reserves of Mutter to be added to group reserves. As the group was only formed one year ago, this is equivalent to the group taking 75 per cent of Mutter's current year's profits. The reworking of the example is shown in Exhibit 9.16.

Exhibit 9.16 The group profit and loss account

(£000)	\[Group balance sheet at year end\] K	M	Consolidation			Group		\[Profit statement for the year\]	K	M	Group
Goodwill			+£90			+£90		Turnover	−£600	−£500	−£1,100
Tangible fixed assets	+£500	+£350	+£850			+£850		Cost of sales	+£150	+£200	+£350
Investment in Mutter	+£300		+£300	−£90	−£210			Gross profit	−£450	−£300	−£750
Net current assets	+£100	+£50	+£150			+£150		Distribution costs	+£50	+£30	+£80
	£900	£400	£1,300			£1,090		Administration costs	+£250	+£70	+£320
								Profit before taxation	−£150	−£200	−£350
Ordinary share capital	−£550	−£100	−£650	+£75	+£25	−£550		Tax on ordinary activities	+£50	+£80	+£130
Retentions	−£350	−£300	−£650	+£135	+£75	−£440		Profit after taxation	−£100	−£120	−£220
Shareholder's funds	£900	£400	£1,300			£990		Minority interest (25%)		+£30	+£30
Minority interest					−£100	−£100		Group profit for the year	−£100	−£90	−£190
	£900	£400	£1,300			£1,090					

Once again, the group profit and loss account only confirms in detail what is shown in outline in the balance sheet. Of interest is the make up of the profit and loss account which follows the philosophy of the balance sheet by showing the profit *controlled* by the group before deducting the minority interest at the end.

Implications for merger accounting

The profit and loss account under merger accounting is not dissimilar to the one under acquisition accounting although, if it is a genuine merger, the minority interest is likely to be small if it exists at all. However, in the first year the profit figure may be significantly different depending on which method has been used.

Under acquisition accounting, the group profit will only include that proportion of the subsidiary's profit earned since acquisition, the pre-acquisition profit having been matched against the investment in the parent company's accounts. Merger accounting, however, allows the reserves – and hence profits – simply to be aggregated. Therefore if a company joins a group half way through its accounting year, only half of that year's profit will appear as group income if the group was formed from an acquisition while all of the profit will be combined if it was formed from a merger.

Inter-group transactions

One danger to be avoided when consolidating accounts is that of double counting. For this reason the stake acquired in the subsidiary's shareholders' funds is netted off against the investment made when producing the consolidated balance sheet. Equally any other form of inter-group indebtedness also has to be eliminated.

A similar problem occurs in the profit and loss account when there are inter-group sales and purchases. Once more the easiest way to explain the problem is to consider a domestic analogy. Assume a person sells to their partner a motor car for £1,000. The partner then resells the car to a total stranger for £2,000. The problem is determining the level of sales turnover. The first partner has sales of £1,000; the second, sales of £2,000. Taken as a *family unit*, however, only one car has been sold and the reality is the family is better off by turnover of £2,000. That is the amount which has come into the family from outside.

A similar issue relates to measuring profitability. Assume a person sells to their partner a computer for £800 which had originally cost £600. A profit of £200 has been made on the sale. But viewing the partners as a *family*, there is no profit. At the start, the first partner had a computer and the second partner had cash of £800. After the sale, the first partner now has £800 and the second partner an asset of one computer. Taken as a group, no profit has been realised. Only when something is sold to a third party is it possible to recognise profit as having been made. These issues are considered in Example 9.10.

Example 9.10

> P plc makes a single product which has a market price of £200. In a particular period it sells one unit but produces two units. The total cost of production is £60. It can either sell the product direct to the customer or alternatively sell all its production to a wholly owned marketing subsidiary, M Ltd, for £100 which would then make the sale.

Revising the group profit and loss account

If the company decides to make the sale itself, its turnover will be £200, its cost of sales will be £30 – half the production cost – and its profit will be £170. With a closing stock of one unit, the value on the balance sheet will be £30. This is the reality. Should P plc decide to make the sale through its marketing subsidiary, the consolidated profit and loss account must also show the same reality. Exhibit 9.17 demonstrates the recording in each company's accounts and the adjustments necessary to the group profit and loss account.

The profit and loss account of P plc demonstrates the two units sold to M Ltd for £100 at a cost of £60, leaving no stock within P. Half of these are sold by M to give a cost of sales for M of £50 and closing stock of the same amount. With a selling price of £200, the one unit sold generates a profit of £150 for M Ltd.

Exhibit 9.17 Inter-group transactions and profits

	P	M	P&M	(a)	(b)	(c)
Turnover	–£100	–£200	–£300	+£100		–£200
Cost of sales	+£60	+£50	+£110	–£100	+£20	+£30
Gross profit	–£40	–£150	–£190			–£170
Closing stock	nil	+£50	+£50		–£20	+£30

Aggregating the two profit and loss accounts, however, overstates turnover, profit and the value of the stock. The reality is one unit has been sold for £200, its cost was £30 and so group profit should be £170. Adjustment (a) eliminates the 'internal' sale to reveal the external sale. This still leaves the profit and stock overstated. Stock should be valued at the lower of cost or net realisable value. From a group perspective, valuing it at £50 includes an unrealised profit of £20. The stock value therefore has to be written down by this amount and the write down charged as an expense to the consolidated profit and loss account. Transaction (b) records this. The result is the group profit and loss account shown as (c) which agrees with the reality established earlier. To complete any group profit and loss account therefore, inter-company sales and purchases always have to be excluded to eliminate double counting although any inter-group profits only have to be eliminated to the extent that they have not been realised.

THE REGULATION OF GROUP ACCOUNTS IN THE UK

The need for regulation

Groups can be powerful economic entities. It is therefore not surprising that regulators should want a say in how their activities are reported. Without regulation, groups might choose to show their legal form rather than their economic reality. Recording only the investments on the balance sheet rather than the underlying assets and showing only dividends received rather than actual profits has been shown to be misleading.

Even a regulation simply requiring consolidation would leave the method of consolidation open to choice, if not abuse. Most groups would prefer merger accounting as this allows all the reserves to be distributable while not requiring the revaluation of assets to their fair values. Future reported profits would therefore be higher as a result of the lower depreciation charge relative to the revalued assets of acquisition accounting. Such a simple regulation would also be open to abuse. An unscrupulous group might claim a business as a subsidiary when useful to the group but deny the relationship when detrimental by manipulating the rules or temporarily reducing its shareholding so that it appeared not to have control of the subsidiary.

Statements of Standard Accounting Practice

Although the 1948 Companies Act required group accounts to be produced, in keeping with those times it did not specify the detailed procedures. For a long time the dominant method of consolidation practised by the accounting profession was acquisition accounting. Merger accounting was not allowed because of a clause in the 1948 Act which appeared to make illegal the issue of shares for their face value when their fair value was greater. Only after the passing of the 1981 Companies Act was this amended, allowing merger accounting to be used.

The Accounting Standards Committee also addressed the issue of groups in three standards, SSAP 1 Accounting for Associated Companies, SSAP 14 Group Accounts and SSAP 23 Accounting for Acquisitions and Mergers. Of these, only SSAP 1 is still current. That statement required an equity accounting approach to associated undertakings except for partnerships or other non-corporate joint ventures where proportional consolidation was allowed. SSAP 14 offered no detailed guidance on the mechanics of consolidation. Instead it mainly concerned itself with achieving uniform accounting periods and policies for group members and defining the circumstances and treatment under which subsidiaries did not have to be consolidated. Finally, SSAP 23 laid down the circumstances and conditions where merger accounting might be applied.

By far the most controversial aspects of the standards concerned definitions: in what way is an acquisition different from a merger, what conditions make for a subsidiary rather than an associate and when is a shareholding an associate rather than a simple investment. It was the flexibility in definitions – and the consequent abuse by directors – which has led the Accounting Standards Board to either replace or make proposals for the revision of all three standards.

Defining an associate

The 1971 version of SSAP 1, for instance, defined an associate in one of two ways. An undertaking was an associate if the relationship was (a)...'a partner in a joint venture or consortium' or (b)...'long-term and substantial (i.e. not less than 20 per cent of the equity voting rights) and...(able) to exercise a significant influence...' By the time the 1982 version had been published part (a) had been amended to include the ability to exert significant influence while part (b) had dropped the 20 per cent rule. The presumption was that 20 per cent would still give influence but the standard could now be rebutted.

In May 1991 this was further revised when the Accounting Standards Board published its *Consolidated accounts – interim statement*. By December 1992, most requirements of the interim statement had been withdrawn as a result of the Accounting Standards Board issuing Financial Reporting Standard No. 2, *Accounting for Subsidiary Undertakings*. Nevertheless the part relating to associate undertakings is still current. The interim statement excludes the whole of part (a) from its definition of an associate and the word 'substantial' from part (b). Throughout all these changes, the single objective has been to tighten the standard and prevent avoidance by, for example, a company choosing to hold only 19 per cent in what would otherwise have been an associate or, equally distorting, claiming a share of another company's profits where there was insignificant influence.

Associates and joint ventures

In July 1994, the ASB issued a discussion paper on associates and joint ventures which is likely to form the basis for a replacement to SSAP 1. This was partly in recognition of the increasing importance of joint ventures. It was also partly in recognition that some companies had been abusing the conditions of SSAP 1 by including profits from associated undertakings where there was little real influence.

The discussion paper is concerned to restrict equity accounting to 'strategic alliances', that is, where the investor is effectively a partner. This is a narrower category than is currently recognised under SSAP 1. Failure to meet this definition will mean the investment being viewed as a simple investment. Under the ASB's proposals, three conditions will have to be met before 'significant influence' can be established and equity accounting applied. The first is that 'the investor must exercise influence over the operating and financial policies of the investee .. sufficient for it to fulfil its role as a partner'. The second condition is that 'the investor must reasonably expect to benefit ... from the economic benefits ... of the investee ... [and] ... have the ability to secure access ... to its share of ... [the investee's] cashflows. Finally, 'the investor's interest must provide it with some protection from changes in the ... policies of the investee'. All of these conditions reinforce the idea of an active partnership and so are more restrictive than the conditions found within SSAP 1.

If these proposals go ahead, it will be more difficult for a company to claim an investment in another as an associate. This will certainly reduce the boosting of profit figures by bringing in profits from other companies where there is no real associate relationship. Unfortunately, it will make another abuse, the exclusion of a loss-making associate from the profit and loss account by claiming insufficient influence, more likely. Before going ahead with these proposals, the ASB also has to overcome a legal difficulty. The UK persuaded the other members of the European Union to adopt the equity accounting of SSAP 1 in the EU's Seventh Directive and, as will be seen below, this was incorporated into UK law with the passing of the 1989 Companies Act.

Defining a merger

In preparing the way for merger accounting, the 1981 Companies Act allowed the issue of equity shares in exchange for other shares in a business combination without having to raise a share premium provided that 90 per cent of the shares had been acquired. Within this framework, SSAP 23 Accounting for Mergers and Acquisitions had to develop rules within which merger accounting might be allowed. Given the advantages of merger accounting on the subsequent reported performance of the group, SSAP 23 was concerned to establish that a genuine merger had taken place. This it did by applying certain conditions such as (a) immediately prior to the offer the company making the offer held less than 20 per cent of the equity shares and voting rights in the other; (b) the combination resulted from an offer to the holders of all the equity/voting shares in the company being acquired and that 90 per cent of these shares had agreed to take up the offer and (c) at least 90 per cent of the fair value consideration payable to the holders was in the form of equity capital. Only if these conditions were met might merger accounting be used.

Clearly a cash offer could not be viewed as a merger as it involves the shareholders in the offeree company leaving the group. What was interesting about these conditions though was the absence of any reference to relative size. Equally significant was the way companies stuck to the letter of the standard but broke its spirit in order to obtain the benefits of merger accounting.

In 1994, the Accounting Standards Board replaced SSAP 23 by FRS 6 Acquisitions and Mergers in order to tackle these omissions and abuses. This it did by laying down criteria for the use of merger accounting. These are:

1 No party to the combination is portrayed as either acquirer or acquired either by its own board or management or by that of another party to the combination;
2 All parties to the combination, as represented by the board of directors or their appointees, participate in establishing the management structure for the combined entity and in selecting the management personnel, and such decisions are made on the basis of a consensus between the parties to the combination rather than purely by exercise of voting rights;

3 The relative sizes of the combining entities are not so disparate that one party dominates the combined entity by virtue of its relative size;

4 The consideration received by the equity shareholders primarily comprises equity shares in the combined entity and any non-equity consideration represents an immaterial proportion of the fair value of the consideration received by the equity shareholders. The consideration for any equity shareholding acquired within the previous two years by one of the entities in another should be taken into account in determining whether this criterion has been met;

5 No equity shareholders of any of the combining entities retain any material interest in the future performance of only part of the combined entity.

If a business combination meets these specific criteria and if the use of merger accounting for the combination is not prohibited by companies' legislation then merger accounting should be used. Acquisition accounting – which involves the establishment of fair values within the acquired company – should be used for practically all other business combinations.

FRS 6 takes a different approach to its predecessor SSAP 23. Rather than setting down quantifiable parameters which can be easily manipulated, FRS 6 specifies the conditions for merger accounting in qualitative terms. As these are so widely drawn, the vast majority of combinations will be treated as acquisitions in the future – a position acknowledged in paragraph 44 of the standard which states that 'a merger is a rare type of business combination'.

Off balance sheet finance

Although not strictly related to groups, the Accounting Standards Board's FRS 5 Reporting the Substance of Transactions has implications for group accounting. Despite the refusal of the standard to use the term, it is really about off balance sheet finance. It is about companies showing the true extent of their liabilities and the assets and activities financed by those liabilities. The standard has been described as a 'daunting document for any reader to grapple with and ... it is by no means certain that the ASB's intentions will be clearly understood by the accounting profession'.[1] This is inevitable given the wide range of schemes available. Nevertheless, as its title states, the standard is concerned with showing the substance of transactions and not just their legal form. The standard requires that a 'group or series of transactions that achieves or is designed to achieve an overall commercial affect should be viewed as a whole'. In addition, the criteria for asset and liability recognition identified in the Statement of Principles are also brought into play.

Transactions or events which require particular analysis include ones where (a) the party that gains the principal benefits generated by an asset is not the legal owner; (b) a transaction is linked to others such that its commercial effect can only be understood by considering the series as a whole; (c) an option is included that makes its exercise extremely likely.

One example of such a transaction is a sale with a repurchase option. This type of transaction is often found in the transactions of whisky distilleries. A good whisky takes many years to mature. Despite this, some distilleries 'sell' immature whisky to a bank or other financial institution. In fact, the whisky never leaves the distillery's bonded warehouse although its legal title has passed to the financial institution. The distillery then has a contract with the bank allowing the distillery to buy the whisky in, say, four years' time at a price above the original selling price but below the value of a four-year-old whisky. Looking only at the first transaction, there has clearly been a sale even though the spirit is still in the bonded warehouse. Looking at the last transaction, it is equally clear that there has been a purchase. Taken together, however, it is clear that there has simply been a loan with the difference between the original selling price and the buy-back price being interest. Rather than recognising the original transaction as a sale, FRS 5 requires the 'sale proceeds' to be accounted for on the balance sheet as borrowings.

Off balance sheet finance and groups

There is a particular form of off balance sheet finance which has, in the past, particularly affected groups. Prior to FRS 5, it was possible for a company to use another entity – what the standard calls a 'vehicle' – to house certain assets and liabilities but where the 'vehicle' did not meet the legal definition of a subsidiary. As a result, the entity would not be consolidated within the group accounts. This was particularly useful if a company's debt could be transferred to the vehicle. Queens Moat Houses plc – a hotel chain – for instance arranged what is known as a sale and leaseback agreement of its properties. As a result, £41 million of debt was kept out of the group balance sheet and £18 million added to the reported profit in the company's 1991 accounts.

FRS 5 tackles this issue by viewing the entity as a quasi-subsidiary to be consolidated in the normal way if the commercial affect of the transaction is no different from that which would result were the vehicle a subsidiary. In addition, disclosure is required, in summary form, of the financial statements of the quasi-subsidiaries.

THE EUROPEAN UNION AND THE SEVENTH DIRECTIVE

The concept of the group as an accounting entity is relatively new to Europe. Although it first appeared in UK legislation as early as 1948, it was not until 1965 that reference was made to groups in German statutes while its first mention in French law was not to appear until 1985. Apart from the UK, Germany had probably the most developed group accounting prior to the introduction of the EU's Seventh Directive on group accounts. But even in Germany, only public and other large companies were required to consolidate their financial statements. And within that requirement were other exemptions. Overseas subsidiaries were often excluded while neither the equity method nor proportional consolidation were permitted.

If the Fourth Directive's prescriptive disclosures were predominantly influenced by German ideas, the Seventh Directive's valuation rules were predominantly influenced by the experience of the UK. All four forms of consolidation found in the UK are to be found in the Seventh Directive: acquisitions or purchase accounting, mergers or pooling of interests accounting, proportional consolidation and the equity method of accounting for associates.

Definition of a subsidiary

But just as the UK influenced the Fourth Directive with the introduction of the true and fair view, so continental Europe and Germany in particular influenced the definition of a group. The now defunct SSAP 14 had defined a subsidiary in terms of legal rights. According to SSAP 14, a company was a subsidiary if (a) another company was a member of it and controlled its board of directors or (b) another company held more than half of the equity share capital. The Seventh Directive took a wider view. Consolidation is required where there is:

(a) a majority of the share voting rights; or
(b) a shareholding plus a right to appoint or remove a majority of the directors; or
(c) a dominant influence pursuant to a control contract (not necessarily with a shareholding); or
(d) a shareholding plus a majority of the voting rights.

In addition, consolidation *may* be imposed by member states where there is:

(e) a participating interest plus an actual dominant influence or unified management.

Without entering into the meaning of all the terms, it is clear that the definition of a group is being extended beyond its formal legal definition of a majority of votes / shares to include effective control.

Continental Europe has a wider range of business organisations than the UK as Chapter 7 outlined. As a consequence, consolidation of business *undertakings* is required even though the undertakings might not be limited companies. (This is why the term 'undertakings' is now used rather than 'companies'.)

Exemptions

Certain exemptions were given, mainly to accommodate the lack of accounting resources amongst some member states. The Directive allows member states to grant exemptions to financial holding companies and small groups, the latter again being defined in terms of turnover, balance sheet total and number of employees. In addition, subsidiaries may be excluded from the group accounts on the grounds of:

(a) materiality; or
(b) severe long-term restrictions; or
(c) information unobtainable without disproportionate expense or undue delay; or
(d) shares held exclusively with a view to subsequent resale; or
(e) different activities (with exclusion obligatory if required to show a true and fair view).

The Directive requires full consolidation for subsidiaries with merger accounting as an option. Associates are to be recorded in group accounts using equity accounting with proportional consolidation possible for joint ventures. Goodwill – often referred to as the *consolidation difference* in continental Europe – follows the UK approach and is required to be calculated by reference to the value of the assets acquired on the date of acquisition. For France and Germany this has meant a significant change as they were used to calculating goodwill by reference to the book value of the assets at the *balance sheet* date, resulting in calculated goodwill varying from year to year.

Although no formal format was specified for group accounts, the Directive requires that the minority interest be shown as separate figures on both the balance sheet and profit and loss account. From an accounting aspect, much of the remainder of the Directive is concerned with detail such as using the same valuation rules within group companies and requiring all inter-company debts, transactions and profits to be eliminated. The overall effect of the Seventh Directive therefore was to bring continental Europe more in line with Anglo-American reporting.

THE SEVENTH DIRECTIVE AND THE UK

The Seventh Directive was incorporated into UK law by the 1989 Companies Act inserting new sections into the 1985 Companies Act. Given the UK influence on that Directive, the most noticeable change was in the use of the wider term 'undertaking' to replace 'companies'. Previously a subsidiary had to be a company and would only have existed as a subsidiary if some other company held more than half of the equity share capital or was a shareholder and controlled the board of directors. The 1989 Act accepted totally the wider definition, based on control and laid down by the Seventh Directive. Now, an undertaking is a parent undertaking in relation to another undertaking if:

(a) it holds a majority of the voting rights in that undertaking; or
(b) it is a member of that undertaking and has the right to appoint or remove a majority of its directors; or
(c) it has the right to exercise a dominant influence over the undertaking:
    (i) by virtue of provisions contained in the undertaking's memorandum or articles; or
    (ii) by virtue of a control contract; or
(d) it is a member of the undertaking and controls alone, pursuant to an agreement with other shareholders or members, a majority of the voting rights in the undertaking; or
(e) it has a participating interest and it either:
    (i) actually exercises a dominant influence over the other undertakings; or
    (ii) is managed on a united basis with the other undertaking.

By 'participating interest', the Act meant 'an interest held by an undertaking in the shares of another undertaking which it holds on a long-term basis for the purpose of securing a contribution to its activities by the exercise of control or influence arising from or related to that interest'.

Financial Reporting Standards and company law

FRS 2 Accounting for Subsidiary Undertakings, which has superseded SSAP 14, has extended this definition. A holding of 20 per cent or more is presumed to be a participating interest. In addition, a participating interest includes where an undertaking has an interest which can be converted into an interest in shares or where shares are held by others on behalf of the (parent) undertaking.[2]

The 1989 Act went on to require associated undertakings to be consolidated using the equity method except for unincorporated joint ventures where proportional consolidation is permitted. The Act also permitted merger accounting although its conditions for use differed slightly from the conditions required under the now defunct SSAP 23. No maximum shareholding immediately prior to the merger proposal was specified. It was though more restrictive when determining the allowable non-equity proportion of the purchase consideration. Now, the fair value of any non-equity consideration cannot exceed 10 per cent of the *nominal* value of the shares issued rather than the fair value of SSAP 23. In addition, adoption of merger accounting by an undertaking must accord with 'generally accepted accounting principles and practice'. Because of this last condition, it appears that the requirements of FRS 6 override the technical requirements of the Act.

As a result of the 1989 Act, group accounts must be consolidated accounts. The technical exemptions permitted are identical to those laid down in the Directive: materiality, severe long term restrictions, disproportionate expense or delay, shares held for resale or different activities. In addition an *unlisted* company is exempt from the preparation of group accounts provided its parent is established under the law of another EU member state and it is either a wholly owned subsidiary or its minority shareholders agree to the exemption, while relief from the provision of group accounts is also available for 'small' and 'medium' groups.

It seems likely, however, that companies in the UK will rarely be allowed to exclude subsidiary undertakings. FRS 2 Accounting for Subsidiary Undertakings takes the view that a subsidiary should only be excluded under exceptional circumstances. It takes the view that most special circumstances are better dealt with by additional disclosure rather than exclusion from consolidation. For example, in discussing the disproportionate expense and undue delay exemption, the FRS 2 considers 'neither expense nor delay can justify excluding from the consolidated accounts of the group a subsidiary undertaking that is material in the context of the group'. The Reporting Standard also goes further than the 1989 Act by requiring (not permitting) subsidiaries to be excluded where there are severe long term restrictions, where they are held exclusively with a view to resale or where their activities are substantially different from the group. In the latter case, however, the standard believes it is 'exceptional for such circumstances to arise and it is not possible to identify any particular contrast of activities where the incompatibility with the true and fair view generally occurs. It would therefore seem that FRS 2 is attempting to reduce the manipulation of group accounting by severely restricting the grounds on which a subsidiary can be excluded.

SUMMARY

Both the conceptual and regulatory issues involved in group accounting have been discussed in this chapter. A feature common to both is the adherence to historical cost even though there is no reason why an enterprise cannot make use of the alternative accounting rule provided under the Fourth Directive. The concern with historical costs has a long legal tradition in continental Europe and may possibly be justified in terms of stewardship with its emphasis on transactions and verifiability. It is, however, more difficult to justify when considering the needs of users.

Without reopening the issue of who are the users and what are their needs, it is unlikely that a system which allows five different sets of balance sheet values to describe the same event will be of much benefit to anyone. The culprit is historical cost based on transactions. Because historical costs are used, the assets of a prospective subsidiary are not at current values and because the parent is effectively purchasing the subsidiary a transaction takes place which requires the cost to the parent to be identified. As will be seen in the next chapter, this concern with historical costs brings further difficulties for groups where subsidiaries reside in a foreign country.

A second issue relates to the role of regulation. Only with the passing of the Seventh Directive into state law have many continental countries had to report group activities. This has been less of a problem for the UK where the law first recognised group structures in the 1948 Companies Act. Even so, there have been difficulties in the recent past with UK companies taking advantage of limitations in the law and accounting standards. The Accounting Standards Board has rigorously tackled these abuses in the short time it is has been in existence. In so doing it has gone well beyond the requirements of the EU's Seventh Directive. It has addressed when subsidiaries can be excluded in group accounts in FRS 2 and FRS 5. It has severely restricted the use of merger accounting in FRS 6 while in FRS 7 it has attempted to reduce the choice of fair values in acquisitions. Given these extensive developments by the Accounting Standards Board, there must be a question mark over the continuing adequacy of the Seventh Directive to act as a guide to group accounts.

REFERENCES

1 Davies M., Paterson R. and Wilson A. (1994) *UK GAAP*, 4th edn, Macmillan.
2 Accounting Standards Board (1992) FRS 2 *Accounting for Subsidiary Undertakings,* para. 15.

FURTHER READING

Accounting Standards Board (1992) *Accounting for Subsidiary Undertakings.*
Accounting Standards Board (1994) *Acquisitions and Mergers.*
Accounting Standards Board (1991) *Consolidated Accounts – Interim Statement.*
Accounting Standards Board (1994) *Fair Values in Acquisition Accounting.*
Accounting Standards Board (1994) *Reporting the Substance of Transactions.*
Alexander, D. and Archer, S. (1991) *European Accounting Guide,* Academic Press.
Davies, M., Paterson, R. and Wilson A. (1994) *UK GAAP,* Macmillan.
Fédération des Experts Comptables Européens (1993) *Seventh Directive Options and their Implementation,* Routledge.
KATO Communications (1993) *Accounting for Brands,* F-T Management Reports.
Lewis, R. and Pendrill, D. (1994) *Advanced Financial Accounting,* 4th edn, Pitman.
Nobes, C. and Parker, R. (1991) *Comparative International Accounting,* 3rd edn, Prentice Hall.
Paterson, R. (1993) *Off Balance Sheet Finance,* Macmillan.

TEST YOUR UNDERSTANDING

1 Consolidation refers to:
   (a) the accounts of the parent company;
   (b) the accounts of the holding company;
   (c) the aggregating of the elements in the accounts of all entities within a group after allowing for inter-company balances;
   (d) none of these.

2 Goodwill is:
   (a) the difference between the consideration paid for an entity and the book value of its net assets;
   (b) the fair value of an acquired entity's net assets less the purchase consideration;
   (c) the value of the purchasing entity's intangible assets;
   (d) the difference between the fair value of a group's assets and their underlying book values.

3 Differentiate between pre-acquisition and post-acquisition reserves.

4 Goodwill arising on acquisition is:
   (a) immediately written off against reserves;
   (b) capitalised and amortised over its useful life;
   (c) added to the goodwill arising from the parent company's trading;
   (d) written off as an expense against profits in the year of acquisition.

5 What is a pre-acquisition write down and how does FRS 7, Fair Values in Acquisition Accounting, treat it?

6 Explain the difference between merger and acquisition accounting.

7 A minority interest is:
   (a) the amount of profit and equity within a group belonging to shareholders in subsidiaries;
   (b) dividends paid to shareholders who individually own less than 2.5 per cent of the issued share capital;
   (c) dividends paid to shareholders aged under 18 years;
   (d) interest paid to those shareholders who do not have control;
   (e) the profit and equity attributable to outside shareholders within a group's subsidiaries;
   (f) the profit and equity attributable to outside shareholders within the parent company.

8 What is an associated undertaking and how is it reported in the profit and loss account of a company?

9 What is the purpose of FRS 6?

10 What is meant by off balance sheet finance?

11 The European Union's Seventh Directive addresses:
   (a) group accounting within member states;
   (b) ways of protecting minority interests against oppressive shareholdings;
   (c) the qualifications of auditors for group accounts;
   (d) standard terminology in group accounts quoted on a stock exchange within member states of the European Union.

12 The 1989 Companies Act inserted new sections into the 1985 Companies Act allowing subsidiaries to be excluded from group accounts *inter alia* if there is (a) disproportionate expense or undue delay or (b) severe long term restrictions. Is this still the legal position?

QUESTIONS

1 On 1 July, Peacock plc made a cash offer for all the shares in Wiseman plc at £2 per share. The fair value of Wiseman's fixed assets was £100,000. All other assets already reflect their fair values. The balance sheets of the two companies before the offer and before any revisions to Wiseman's asset values are reproduced below.

Peacock plc's balance sheet			**Wiseman plc's balance sheet**		
		(£000)			(£000)
Fixed assets		290	Fixed assets		80
Stock	40		Stock	14	
Debtors	25		Debtors	18	
Cash	240		Cash	44	
		305			76
Creditors	(40)	265	Creditors	(16)	60
		555			140
Financed by			Financed by		
£1 ordinary shares		340	£1 ordinary shares		100
Reserves		215	Reserves		40
		555			140

Show the balance sheet of the group on 1 July immediately after the acquisition of Wiseman plc using acquisition accounting and assuming:

(a) Peacock plc acquired all the shares of Wiseman plc;

(b) Peacock plc was only successful in acquiring 75 per cent of Wiseman plc's shares.

2 On 31 March, Devon plc acquired 90 per cent of the ordinary shares in Kingsbridge Ltd. The balance sheets of the two companies are reproduced below after the acquisition has taken place but before revaluing Kingsbridge's fixed assets to a fair value of £110,000.

Devon plc			**Kingsbridge Ltd**		
		(£000)			(£000)
Fixed assets		150	Fixed assets		80
Investment in Kingsbridge Ltd		120			
Stock	10		Stock	27	
Debtors	25		Debtors	14	
Cash	15		Cash	20	
Creditors	(10)	40	Creditors	(11)	50
		310			130
£1 ordinary shares		140	£1 ordinary shares		60
Reserves		70	Reserves		20
£1 preference shares		100	£1 preference shares		50
		310			130

Using the above information, produce the consolidated balance sheet of the group on 31 March using acquisition accounting.

3* Hockney plc and Sisley plc are considering combining their operations by a share-for-share exchange. The outline balance sheets of the two companies on 1 September 19X2 are as follows:

Hockney plc	(£000)	**Sisley plc**	(£000)
Net assets	1,800	Net assets	1,400
	1,800		1,400
Financed by		Financed by	
£1 ordinary shares	1,000	£1 ordinary shares	900
Retained profit	800	Retained profit	500
	1,800		1,400

The current market price of a Hockney share is £6 and that for a Sisley is £4. These are the values applicable should the companies join forces. The fair value of each company's net assets are: Hockney, £2,000,000; Sisley £1,700,000.

Before agreeing to combine, the directors of both companies have asked for your advice concerning the resulting group balance sheet. You are therefore required to produce the prospective balance sheet:

(a) using the acquisition or purchase method assuming
   (i) Hockney bids for Sisley
   (ii) Sisley bids for Hockney;
(b) using the merger or pooling of interest method assuming Hockney is used as the vehicle for the merger.

CHAPTER 10

Financial reporting – multinational enterprises

Groups of companies are becoming increasingly international. Partly this arises from trading in foreign markets and partly from the acquisition of foreign subsidiaries. This poses particular difficulties for financial reporting as data measured in different currencies have to be aggregated.

This chapter:

■ Differentiates between currency conversion and currency translation

■ Discusses the implications for groups where subsidiaries are located abroad

■ Identifies and evaluates the use of the temporal and closing rate methods of currency translation

■ Critically debates the implications of the relevant Statement of Standard Accounting Practice and the European Union's Seventh Directive

Groups of companies are becoming increasingly international, with subsidiaries established in many different parts of the world. This may be due to modern complex technology which requires world markets to achieve efficient production levels. It may be because of marketing strategies concerned with the development of global brands or it may simply be an attempt to reduce risk by spreading the area of operations. Whatever the reasons for the growth of multinational enterprises, there are implications for financial reporting.

CHOICE OF REPORTING CURRENCY

To produce group accounts, data has to be additive. Simply adding pounds sterling to US dollars without some form of translation will be meaningless. A common unit of currency is needed for reporting purposes and this will normally be the currency of the country where the parent or holding company resides.

Using the currency of the country where the parent resides may be less than ideal. Consider a parent company which resides in the UK but entirely trades through subsidiaries in the United States. For all intents and purposes, the group has become an American company. The dominant currency will be the dollar and so reporting in dollars is likely to convey more meaning.

A case could be made for converting to pounds sterling if the majority of shareholders were UK based. It would after all give them information in a familiar unit of currency. However, with the composition of shareholders increasingly cosmopolitan, the strength of the argument is lessened. With fixed exchange rates this is not a major problem; with fluctuating exchange rates, the location of the group can become significant.

Implications of floating exchange rates

Consider a company which does not trade. Its only assets are cash deposits of £100,000 held in the UK and $100,000 held in the USA. Assuming an exchange rate of $2 to £1, the wealth can be measured in dollars as $300,000 or in pounds as £150,000. One year later, provided the exchange rate has not altered, the total wealth will be identical. There will neither have been a profit nor a loss. More than that, an investor would be indifferent as to how the wealth was expressed. $300,000 is the equivalent of £150,000 and it would simply be a matter of investor choice which currency was used to measure the wealth.

Assume now that at the end of the year the exchange rate has fallen to $1 to £1. Exhibit 10.1 shows the opening and closing wealth in both US dollars and pounds sterling.

Exhibit 10.1 Wealth measurement – fluctuating exchange rates

Opening wealth	$	£	Closing wealth	$	£
£100,000	200,000	100,000	£100,000	100,000	100,000
$100,000	100,000	50,000	$100,000	100,000	100,000
	300,000	150,000		200,000	200,000

If the company was based in the USA it would be reporting a loss of $100,000. If, however, the company was based in the UK it would be reporting a profit of £50,000! Even worse, assume all the shareholders were based in the USA but that the company was based in the UK. There is a danger of the US shareholders simply taking the UK 'profit' and translating it into its $50,000 equivalent at the current rate of exchange. Whether the shareholders have made a real profit will depend on a variety of factors, not least the relative purchasing powers of the currencies. Of more concern at this stage is an awareness of the difficulties of incorporating profit and asset values within group accounts when the subsidiaries are spread across more than one country under a fluctuating exchange rates regime.

The Seventh Directive

What is clear from this introduction is that the merging of financial information measured in different currencies is much more than a simple technical exercise. It involves the fundamental question of what is being measured. Until the implementation of the Seventh Directive, this was not a significant problem for many member states of the European Union. Several states had not required groups to publish consolidated accounts and even where they were obligatory, as in Germany, state law often did not extend to the full consolidation of foreign subsidiaries.

Now, all member states require undertakings to produce consolidated accounts including the full consolidation of foreign subsidiaries. Despite this, the Seventh Directive offers little in the way of guidance as to how this should be done. Authoritative statements, however, do exist for both the UK and the USA. In America, the Financial Accounting Standards Board initially issued Statement of Financial Accounting Standards No. 8 in 1975. Following objections to its main thrust by a large number of companies, this was withdrawn and replaced by FAS 52 in 1981. In the UK, the Accounting Standards Committee issued SSAP 20 Foreign Currency Translation in 1983 which proposed a similar treatment to the one suggested in FAS 52.

TRADING TRANSACTIONS

Some insight into the difficulties can be gleaned by developing rules for the treatment of foreign exchange gains and losses when a business undertakes otherwise straightforward transactions across national boundaries. Example 10.1 considers three such basic transactions: a sale, a purchase of stock and the taking out of a loan.

At an exchange rate of $2 to £1, Everest has received £90,000 and this is the amount of the loan on 1 December. The stock received has cost £8,930 and a creditor now exists for the same amount. Finally, the sales to Germany are equivalent to £8,265 and this is represented by a debtor for the identical amount. These are recorded in the first part of Exhibit 10.2.

Example 10.1

Everest Sports Gear plc, based in Glasgow, distributes leisure wear throughout Europe. Its year end is 31 December.

On 1 December it obtained a loan for $180,000 from a bank in the USA. On the same day it purchased mountaineering garments from France for 85,728 French francs and sold leisure clothing to a customer in Germany for 24,795 Deutschmarks. On 18 January the German customer paid the amount owing and Everest paid its French supplier.

Details of exchange rates are as follows:	(DM)	(US $)	(FF)
1 December	3.00	2.00	9.60
31 December	2.90	1.80	9.50
18 January	2.85	1.90	9.40

Exhibit 10.2 Currency conversion

		This year		Year end adjustments			Summary	Next year	
	Loan	Purchases	Sales	Loss	Loss	Gain	Balances	Receipt	Payment
Cash	+£90,000							+£8,700	–£9,120
Stock		+£8,930							
Debtor			+£8,265			+£285	+£8,550	–£8,850	
Loan	–£90,000			–£10,000			–£100,000		
Creditor		–£8,930			–£94		–£9,024		+£9,024
Sales			–£8,265						
Profit or Loss on exchange				+£10,000	+£94	–£285		–£150	+£96

Currency gains and losses

At the year end, Everest owes the same foreign currency to the loan holder and the trade creditor. However, because the rates have increased, the amounts owed in sterling have increased. Prudence requires these amounts to be restated. However, the opposite has happened to the debtor. Although prudence legitimately argues that the losses should be recognised, it is less clear why the gain should be accepted as profits should only be taken when realised.

However, given the Accounting Standards Board's definitions of elements outlined in Chapter 6 of this text and the criteria for recognition developed in Chapter 4 of the ASB's Statement of Principles, there is objective evidence of both the currency gain and loss in the form of market-derived exchange rates. Secondly, the debtor is reasonably certain to pay. The currency gain therefore meets the two criteria established and so is a legitimate source of income. The effect of these currency changes are recorded as year end adjustments in Exhibit 10.2 with the revised values to be recorded in the year end balance sheet being shown in the summary column.

The alternative might have been to recast the original transaction rather than accounting for the difference via the profit and loss account. But this would have overstated the sale made, the stock acquired and the loan received. At the *date of the transaction*, Everest acquired stock of £8,930. The subsequent £285 arose simply because of changes in exchange rates and the delay in payment. It should therefore be recognised as a profit on exchange rather than as an increase in the value of the stock acquired. Accepting this, an argument can still be made for the gain or loss being shown separately from the operating profit, perhaps by an adjustment to reserves, rather than distorting the profit from trading. SSAP 20 rejects this though.

The accounting treatment

SSAP 20 Foreign Currency Translation takes the view that currency gains or losses are a normal feature of operations when trading with foreign countries. As such they should be accounted for via the profit and loss account like any other income or expense although, if their size is exceptional, the amount might need to be disclosed separately to give a true and fair view.

Effectively SSAP 20 is applying the accruals concept of SSAP 2. Foreign exchange gains and losses exist at the year end and the extent of these are recorded even though the subsequent gains or losses might be different. Any subsequent gains and losses occur because of a failure to pay or receive monies at the balance sheet date. As such, they should be accounted for when they arise. This is the way they are treated in Exhibit 10.2. When the debtor finally pays, the pound will have fallen further against the Deutschmark and so a further exchange gain will then be reported in the following year's accounts along with the additional loss incurred on the French currency by delaying payment until 18 January.

SSAP 20 and the 1985 Companies Act

In one sense SSAP 20 treats currency gains on long term borrowings differently. The 1985 Companies Act requires only profits realised at the balance sheet date be included in the profit and loss account. SSAP 20 by contrast views exchange gains on long term liabilities as being unrealised.

Despite that, the Statement requires any gain to be recorded in the profit and loss account – presumably making use of the true and fair override. For *distribution purposes*, however, SSAP 20 views any gain as being unrealised. Nevertheless it is clear that SSAP 20 has contravened the requirement of SSAP 2 that prudence should prevail when in conflict with the accruals concept.

Not all accounts will include exchange gains and losses in their income statement. Businesses can often avoid the complications of foreign exchange gains and losses by the use of market mechanisms. One way would be to agree a single rate at the outset between the parties. No gains or losses will then exist because no change in the exchange rate will have occurred. Where such a rate is agreed, SSAP 20 requires it be used. Another option would be to cover against the risk by buying currency forward. Under these circumstances SSAP 20 *permits* that forward rate be used to eliminate any exchange rate differences in the accounts.

FOREIGN SUBSIDIARIES

Currency conversion and translation

Accounting for foreign subsidiaries is not the same as accounting for cross border individual transactions. Individual transactions involve *currency conversion*, the exchange of one currency for another as a result of a transaction. No such transaction nor exchange of currency takes place when group accounts are consolidated. Instead the subsidiary's accounts are merely re-expressed in terms of the group's currency, allowing consolidation to take place. This process is known as *currency translation*. Nevertheless, the treatment of individual transactions provides a useful insight into accounting for foreign subsidiaries. Consider the simplified information given in Example 10.2.

Example 10.2

A UK company's balance sheet comprised fixed assets of £80,000 and cash of £120,000 which was financed by ordinary share capital of £160,000 and reserves of £40,000. It formed a subsidiary in Erehwon by investing £100,000 of its cash balance. The subsidiary was formed with a share capital of $200,000 which it used to acquire $180,000 of fixed assets, leaving the balance as cash. At the time of formation the exchange rate was two Erehwon dollars to the pound sterling. No trading took place in either company but by the end of the year the exchange rate had moved to $4 to £1.

At the end of the year the subsidiary's financial data can be translated using the original exchange rate, the year end or closing rate or a mixture of both. Exhibit 10.3 shows the application of these to the subsidiary's assets at the year end.

The historical rate

Using the original exchange rate to translate the Erehwon subsidiary's accounts into their UK equivalent shows the real resources given up by the UK company when making the investment. This is known as the historic rate method. It is therefore consistent with the stewardship basis of accounting. It also shows clearly that no goodwill has been paid on the acquisition, allowing the assets to be simply substituted for the investment in the parent's books on consolidation. The translation, however, is using an exchange rate which no longer exists.

Exhibit 10.3 Possible translation values

(000) Parent	Subsidiary	Cost	Historic rate		Closing rate		Temporal rate	
			Rate	*Amount*	*Rate*	*Amount*	*Rate*	*Amount*
Investment in subsidiary £100	Fixed assets	$180	$2	£90	$4	£45	$2	£90
	Cash	$20	$2	£10	$4	£5	$4	£5

The closing rate method

Using the closing rate overcomes this and, superficially at least, is consistent with intuitive logic by showing at the year end the $200,000 in Erehwon being equivalent to £50,000 in the UK. A further advantage is that it shows the real value of the cash held in Erehwon has fallen in terms of pounds sterling because of the exchange rate differences.

Unfortunately, applying that same logic to the fixed assets produces a figure with little meaning. The £45,000 of fixed assets is neither a measure of the original resources given up nor the current value of the assets in either the UK or the foreign country. Had the fixed assets been purchased for $180,000 but then immediately shipped to the UK, they would have been recorded at their UK equivalent cost of £90,000. Ignoring customs duties and transportation costs, in principle this could even be done at the year end, in which case the parent would have acquired a late delivered asset of £90,000.

The temporal method

Accepting this argument, the only loss made as a result of establishing the subsidiary is the real loss in pounds sterling of the cash balance which is now only worth £5,000. Logically therefore it is necessary to apply the current rate to assets such as debtors and cash which are fixed in monetary terms and where genuine exchange gains and losses are possible but to apply the historic rate to all other (non-monetary) assets. To complete this logic, similar rules are necessary for monetary liabilities. This process is known as the temporal method.

The only other complexity occurs when a non-monetary asset is revalued but even there it is possible to develop a logical rule. Had the asset been transferred to the parent on revaluation date, it would have been transferred at the rate existing at the time. The rule therefore is to measure monetary assets and liabilities at the closing rate and all other assets at the rate existing at the time of acquisition or revaluation.

The result is a translation method consistent with traditional accounting values, that assets are valued at cost or net realisable value, whichever is the lower. There is no evidence that the value of the fixed assets have fallen below their original equivalent cost of £90,000 and so this is the amount which will be shown in the consolidated accounts. The original $20,000 'cost' of cash held abroad, however, has fallen in sterling to £5,000. Using the lower of cost or realisable value rule, this loss has to be shown in the group profit and loss account and the £5,000 recorded in the balance sheet.

The treatment of gains and losses on translation

On translation, the £100,000 investment in the subsidiary will be represented by the £95,000 translated value of its net assets. No adjustment is made to the share capital of the subsidiary to reflect the change in exchange rates. Instead, the full extent of the loss is shown where it belongs – in the profit or loss for the period as negative retentions owed to the owners.

An alternative would involve showing shareholders' funds acquired of only £95,000, hiding the loss for the period and showing goodwill on acquisition as being equal to the loss. Such a treatment, however, would not be consistent with the facts in the example.

£100,000 was the cost of the investment and £100,000 was the value of the assets originally acquired.

The necessary entries to produce the consolidated accounts are shown in Exhibit 10.4. As is to be expected, consolidation eliminates the subsidiary's capital from the group accounts, leaving only the capital of the parent. The group reserves are then reduced by the translation loss caused by consolidating the foreign subsidiary.

Exhibit 10.4 The temporal method of consolidation

(000s)	Parent			Subsidiary translation			Consolidation	
Fixed assets	+£80		+£80	+$180	$2	+£90	+£170	+£170
Investment in subsidiary		+£100	+£100				+£100	−£100
Cash	+£120	−£100	+£20	+$20	$4	+£5	+£25	+£25
	£200		£200	$200		£95	£295	£195
Ordinary share capital	−£160		−£160	−$200		−£100	−£260 +£100	−£160
Retentions	−£40		−£40			+£5	−£35	−£35
	£200		£200	$200		£95	£295	£195

THE TEMPORAL METHOD OF TRANSLATION

Features of the temporal method

The temporal method of currency translation is consistent with the traditional stewardship accounting assumption of the lower of cost or net realisable value. Consequently, the process of translation produces subsidiary accounts based on the same valuation methods as the parent's accounts. The temporal method therefore at least has the advantage of consistency – unlike the closing rate method which produces values for non-monetary assets which have little meaning in terms of historical cost or current values.

Perhaps more important than this is its universal applicability. Financial reports reflecting replacement costs or realisable values can equally be translated using the temporal method's rules. Assets revalued on the balance sheet date will simply be translated at the relevant historical rate at the date of revaluation which, in this instance, will be the closing rate. It was for such reasons that the US Financial Accounting Standards Board made the temporal method mandatory in FAS 8 published in 1975.

Unfortunately the temporal method can, at times, produce apparently perverse results. More than that, if a subsidiary includes heavy borrowings in its capital structure, extensive exchange losses are likely when the home currency weakens. It was this as much as anything else which led large sections of American business to object to the temporal approach of FAS 8. These issues are explored in Example 10.3.

Example 10.3

A UK company established a wholly owned subsidiary in Ruritania with an issued share capital of 200,000 Ruritanian dollars. At the time, the exchange rate was four dollars to the pound sterling. Details of the subsidiary's opening and closing balance sheets for the current year along with its profit and loss account are as follows:

Opening balance sheet	($000)	($000)	Closing balance sheet	($000)	($000)	Profit and loss account	($000)
Fixed assets		800	Fixed assets		800	Turnover	600
Depreciation		160	Depreciation		320	Depreciation	(160)
		640			480	Other expenses	(450)
Debtors and cash	300		Debtors and cash	500		Loss for year	(10)
Creditors	150	150	Creditors	200	300		
		790			780		
Long term loan		450	Long term loan		450		
		340			330		
Ordinary share capital		200	Ordinary share capital		200		
Retentions		140	Retentions		130		
		340			330		

The fixed assets were all acquired when the subsidiary was formed. At the commencement of the year the exchange rate was $3.75:£1, the weighted average for the year was $3.00:£1 while at the year end it had fallen to $2.50:£1.

The profit and loss account

The temporal method's requirement that non-monetary elements should be translated at their relevant historical rates extends to the profit and loss account. Strict adherence to this, however, would require each sale and each purchase to be translated at the rate in existence at the time of each individual transaction, a practical impossibility for most firms. This difficulty can be overcome by using a weighted average rate.

In the profit and loss account this approximation will apply to all sales and most expenses. Two items of expense, however, will need adjustment. The cost of sales comprises opening stock consumed plus purchases made less closing stock carried forward. To measure the sacrifice in sterling involved in consuming the opening stocks requires the use of the rate current at the time of their purchase. Similarly, in translating the value of the closing stock into the home currency, the appropriate rate is the one in existence at the time of their purchase. Perhaps more significant than this is the translation rate for depreciation. Depreciation is an allocation of cost and hence the appropriate rate to use is the one used in translating the particular fixed assets in the balance sheet, in other words the rate existing when the assets were acquired.

Calculating translation gains and losses

With this in mind, it is possible to translate the subsidiary's activities into pounds sterling ready for consolidation. Part of the exercise is to calculate the translation gain or loss for *the current year*. This requires the position at the start of the year to be known in order to differentiate between current and previous year differences on exchange.

In Exhibit 10.5 the opening assets and liabilities are translated at their relevant rates. For non-monetary assets and liabilities, this will be their historic rate. For monetary assets and liabilities, it will be the rate current at the time of the opening balance sheet. Given that shareholders' funds equals net assets less long term liabilities, the level of retentions – including the whole amalgam of previous exchange gains or losses – can be found by deducting the share capital from the net assets. In essence the UK value of the foreign subsidiary's reserves is the balancing figure of £30,000.

Having calculated the sterling value of the opening retentions in the subsidiary, the next stage is to translate the elements making up the profit and loss account. For the Ruritanian subsidiary, the weighted average rate for the year is used for all elements except the depreciation charge which is merely an apportionment of the sterling cost of the fixed assets. The result is a translated profit of £10,000. As is the norm, this profit is then added to the opening retentions of £30,000 to give retentions of £40,000 at the year end. The other assets and liabilities are then translated using the appropriate rates for the year end to give net assets attributable to the shareholders of £60,000 when expressed in sterling.

Exhibit 10.5 *The temporal method and difference on exchange*

Opening balance sheet				Profit and loss account				Closing balance sheet				
		Rate				Rate					Rate	
	($000)	($)	(£000)		($000)	($)	(£000)		($000)		($)	(£000)
Fixed assets	800			Turnover	600	3.00	200	Fixed assets		800		
Depreciation	160			Depreciation	160	4.00	40	Depreciation		320		
	640	4.00	160	Other expenses	450	3.00	150			480	4.00	120
				Profit/(loss)	(10)		10					
Debtors and cash	300							Debtors and cash	500			
Less creditors	150	150 3.75	40					Less creditors	200	300	2.50	120
		790	200							780		240
Long term loan		450 3.75	120					Long term loan		450	2.50	180
		340	80							330		60
Ordinary share capital		200 4.00	50					Ordinary share capital		200	4.00	50
Retentions		140 (a)	30					Previous retentions		140	(b)	30
		340	80					Profit this period		(10)	(c)	10
								Exchange difference			(d)	(30)
										330		60

Notes:

(a) The balancing figure after the net assets have been translated into the home currency.
(b) The sterling value of the previous year's retentions calculated in (a).
(c) The sterling profit for the year.
(d) The balancing figure using the same logic as for (a).

However, with ordinary share capital of £50,000 and the year end reserves of £40,000 (including the profit of £10,000), there is an imbalance of £30,000. This is the difference on exchange. Consequently the original translated profit of £10,000 from operations is reduced to a net loss of £20,000 as a result of the £30,000 loss on exchange.

Verifying the loss

This £30,000 difference on exchange can be verified by recognising it is only monetary assets and liabilities which are affected by the temporal translation method. The net monetary assets comprise the debtors plus cash less the creditors. At the beginning of the year they stood at $150,000 but by the year end had grown to $300,000. The year end figure effectively comprises the year beginning figure plus changes resulting from trading. The value of the original net monetary assets will therefore have increased as a result of the change in exchange rates. A similar but opposite argument can be made for the long term borrowings, the cost of which will have increased because of the exchange rate changes. Finally the increase in the monetary assets, assumed to have been received on average when the exchange rate was $3 to £1, will also have increased in value. The effect of this is shown in Exhibit 10.6.

Exhibit 10.6 Analysis of exchange losses

	Ruritania ($)	Rate ($)	UK (£)
Sterling value of opening net monetary assets at the beginning of the year	150,000	3.75	40,000
Sterling value of opening net monetary assets at the end of the year	150,000	2.50	60,000
GAIN			20,000
Sterling value of loan at the beginning of the year	450,000	3.75	120,000
Sterling value of loan at the end of the year	450,000	2.50	180,000
LOSS			60,000
Sterling value of additional monetary assets during the year	150,000	3.00	50,000
Sterling value of additional monetary assets at end of the year	150,000	2.50	60,000
GAIN			10,000
Net loss on exchange			**30,000**

Profitability and the temporal method

Some strange things have happened to the subsidiary's accounts upon translation into sterling. The reported operating loss of $10,000 has suddenly become an operating profit of £10,000. Secondly, the relationships between the various elements within the accounts have also changed. In terms of Ruritanian dollars, the $780,000 of year end assets were financed by $450,000 of debt capital and $330,000 of equity, a ratio of 1.36:1. On conversion, however, the long term loan becomes £180,000 and the equity only £60,000 to give a ratio of 3:1 implying a much greater reliance on debt with all the risk which that entails.

The reason for these changes appears to lie in using the historical rate to translate some elements but the closing rate to translate others. In fact the reason is deeper than that. The differences arise from the use of historical cost accounting. Had replacement cost or realisable value accounting been used, the rate would have been the closing one for all elements and such apparent inconsistencies would not occur. What particularly worried American business about FAS 8 was less the reasons and more the reality. Many US companies were reporting large losses on translation arising from their large overseas borrowings from the then weakening dollar. Before looking at the validity of the criticisms it is useful to have an awareness of the temporal method's replacement.

THE CLOSING RATE METHOD OF TRANSLATION

Economic logic

The reaction of the US Financial Accounting Standards Board to these criticisms was to replace FAS 8 by FAS 52 although the vote to do this was won by the narrowest of margins. FAS 52 was concerned that consolidated accounts should provide information which is consistent with expected economic effects following an exchange rate change and that the results of individual subsidiaries should be reflected in those accounts.

The latter point was concerned with avoiding the 'loss into profit' paradox. The first point recognises that, other things being equal, an overseas investment should be worth more after a devaluation of the home currency. To achieve these objectives, the closing rate method was proposed. By using the same rate for all items making up the profit and loss account, proportionality would be maintained and the 'loss into profit' paradox avoided. In addition, an overseas subsidiary's balance sheet would show higher asset values after a devaluation and this agrees with economic logic. Example 10.4 demonstrates these points.

Example 10.4

A UK company establishes an overseas subsidiary by investing $6,000 and borrowing $2,000 locally. The funds were used to acquire fixed assets. At the time of the subsidiary's creation the exchange rate was $2 to £1. No trading took place but by the end of the year the exchange rate had fallen to $1 to £1.

The closing rate and temporal rate compared

The subsidiary's balance sheet translated at the time of its formation is shown in Exhibit 10.7 along with the year end balance sheet translated using both the temporal and closing rate methods.

Given that the UK company has a net investment of $6,000 in the overseas subsidiary, logic would suggest that this investment would be worth more after a devaluation and this conclusion is reflected by the closing rate mechanism. What is questionable, however, is the meaning of the £3,000 gain on translation.

Exhibit 10.7 The temporal and closing rate methods of translation

| | At acquisition | | | Temporal | | Closing rate | |
| | | Rate | | | Rate | | Rate | |
	($)	($)	(£)	($)	(£)	($)	(£)
Fixed assets	8,000	2	4,000	2	4,000	1	8,000
	8,000		4,000		4,000		8,000
Financed by							
Ordinary share capital	6,000	2	3,000	2	3,000	2	3,000
Loan	2,000	2	1,000	1	2,000	1	2,000
Gain or (loss)					(1,000)		3,000
	8,000		4,000		4,000		8,000

The closing rate mechanism agrees with the temporal method that the real amount of foreign borrowings is £2,000. Other things being equal, this is the amount the UK company would have to pay to surrender the loan. Similarly, the original capital is also £3,000 under both methods. The validity of the closing rate mechanism therefore centres on the value attached to the non-monetary assets. It is difficult to say what the £8,000 value represents under the closing rate method. It is neither the resources given up by the parent nor the current value of those assets in either the home or foreign currency.

Calculating translation gains and losses

Before discussing this further, Exhibit 10.8 shows the result of translating the Ruritanian data of Example 10.3 using the closing rate method. Some of the confusion associated with the closing rate method is to be found in the recommended treatment of the profit and loss account. FAS 8 specified the exchange rate applicable to profit and loss transactions at the time of the transaction but, aware of the impracticality of this, allowed the use of a weighted average rate. In the UK SSAP 20 showed even greater confusion by permitting either the average or closing rate. That there should be such confusion is inevitable given the lack of rigorous logic supporting the closing rate approach.

To simplify matters, Exhibit 10.8 converts the profit and loss account using the closing rate. As before, the UK value of retentions at the beginning of the year have to be calculated to allow any loss or gain on translation for the current accounting period to be derived.

Using the closing rate method ensures that the $10,000 loss in the Ruritanian subsidiary remains a loss when translated. The loss of £4,000 is simply the $10,000 loss converted at the closing rate of $2.50 to the pound. As with the temporal method, the exchange difference is found by deducting the value of the ordinary share capital from the net assets less long term loans. The only difference is that using the closing rate method produces a profit on currency translation of £45,000.

Exhibit 10.8 The closing rate method and difference on exchange

Opening balance sheet				Profit and loss account				Closing balance sheet			
		Rate				Rate				Rate	
	($000)	($)	(£000)		($000)	($)	(£000)		($000)	($)	(£000)
Fixed assets	800			Turnover	600	2.50	240	Fixed assets	800		
Depreciation	160			Depreciation	160	2.50	64	Depreciation	320		
	640	3.75	171	Other expenses	450	2.50	180		480	2.50	192
Debtors and cash	300			Profit/(loss)	(10)		(4)	Debtors and cash	500		
Less creditors	150 150	3.75	40					Less creditors	200 300	2.50	120
	790		211						780		312
Long term loan	450	3.75	120					Long term loan	450	2.50	180
	340		91						330		132
Ordinary share capital	200	4.00	50					Ordinary share capital	200	4.00	50
Retentions	140	(a)	41					Previous retentions	140	(b)	41
	340		91					Loss this period	(10)	(c)	(4)
								Exchange difference		(d)	45
									330		132

Notes:
(a) The balancing figure after the net assets have been translated into the home currency.
(b) The sterling value of the previous year's retentions calculated in (a).
(c) The sterling profit for the year.
(d) The balancing figure using the same logic as for (a).

Verifying the gain

The exchange rate difference can be verified by analysing the individual components. The workings are shown in Exhibit 10.9. Because the closing rate was chosen to translate the profit and loss account, the whole of the £45,000 gain can be explained in terms of the opening net assets. As the closing rate is applied to all of the net assets of the subsidiary, any analysis has to recognise this by expressing the gain or loss in terms of the opening values of the net assets.

Exhibit 10.9 Analysis of exchange gain

	Ruritania ($)	Rate ($)	UK (£)
Sterling value of opening net assets at the beginning of the year	790,000	3.75	211,000
Sterling value of opening net assets at the end of the year	790,000	2.50	316,000
GAIN			105,000
Sterling value of loan at the beginning of the year	450,000	3.75	120,000
Sterling value of loan at the end of the year	450,000	2.50	180,000
LOSS			60,000
Net gains on exchange			**45,000**

Had the average rate for the year been used, the reported UK loss would have been £3,000 ($10,000/£3). Whichever rate is used, proportionality with the subsidiary's accounts expressed in the local currency is maintained. That two separate rates are allowable by SSAP 20, however, points to the poverty of thought which went into the promotion of the closing rate method and this is only reinforced by the statement's requirement that any gains or losses on translation should be accounted for via the reserves and not brought into the current period's profit and loss account.

THE FOREIGN CURRENCY TRANSLATION DEBATE

Consistency of treatment

With the closing rate method showing a profit on translation of £45,000 and the temporal method showing a loss of £30,000, both cannot be correct. The essence of the temporal method is that the valuations used in the subsidiary are consistent with the valuations used in the parent. Both valuations measure the historical resources given up in acquiring an asset, subject only to prudence and the use of the lower of cost or net realisable value rule. This applies even after several years have lapsed since the parent resourced a foreign subsidiary.

At all times the alternative to a subsidiary purchasing a new asset is the remittance of those funds to the parent. Therefore whenever a subsidiary does purchase an asset, there is an opportunity cost to the parent expressed in the exchange rate applicable had those funds been remitted. When translating overseas accounts therefore, the historical rate at the time of the transaction appears to be the valid one to use.

Resolving the 'loss into profit' paradox

This still leaves the thorny problem of the 'loss into a profit' paradox and the distortion of ratios and relationships within the foreign subsidiary on consolidation. What has to be considered is the purpose of the accounts and for whom they are prepared. Group accounts are *not* prepared for the minority interest or creditors in the foreign subsidiary. They have access to the subsidiary's individual accounts in the local currency.

Group accounts are prepared for the shareholders of the group primarily on the basis of stewardship and this is the reason for the translation. That it is wrong to produce group accounts on the basis of stewardship may or may not be a valid criticism. It is also irrelevant to this particular problem. Instead of investing in an overseas subsidiary, the parent could have acquired the assets itself but financed them by a foreign loan. The cost attachment concept would have shown the assets at their acquisition price irrespective of what might have happened to the value of the loan. Had the exchange rate moved unfavourably, prudence would have required the loss on the loan to have been shown as an expense, independent of and separate from the valuation of the asset. That the asset is held abroad in a subsidiary should not distort this reality.

The problem of the translated book value of a subsidiary falling on devaluation because of the presence of debt finance is merely an extension of this argument. Despite the introductory comments of FAS 52, accounts are not currently prepared to reflect expected economic effects. *They are based on measuring reality as evidenced by the past if using historical costs or the present if using replacement cost or realisable values.* On that basis, the fall in book values due to anticipating the loss on the loan is consistent with prudence. Equally, not recognising the increase in asset values is consistent with cost attachment.

Even the 'loss into profit' paradox can be resolved. The adjustment to the depreciation charge by translating at the historical rate reflects the wisdom from investing when exchange rates were more favourable. Using the profit and loss data of the Ruritanian subsidiary in Example 10.3, assume the subsidiary leased the fixed asset for $160 per annum rather than purchasing it. Assume further the lease could either be with a UK company at a fixed exchange rate of $4 to £1 or with a local firm. Upon the exchange rate falling to $3 to £1, the charge will only be £40 in sterling if leased from the UK but $160/£3 or £53 if leased locally. Effectively the temporal method is reflecting the same concept. The profit on translation reflects the advantageous exchange rate at the time of acquisition. It is therefore possible that the subsidiary with its loss and the group translation with its profit are both showing a 'true and fair' view, albeit from different perspectives.

SSAP 20 FOREIGN CURRENCY TRANSLATION

The concept of the net investment

SSAP 20 recognised the strength of these arguments. Despite that, it requires the closing rate method to be applied to most subsidiaries. In order to reach this conclusion it identified the concept of the *net investment*. The net investment concept views overseas subsidiaries as having a considerable degree of autonomy, often with local finance and operating mainly within the confines of the foreign business environment. The assumption is that the parent is not interested in the detailed assets but rather the return from the investment in the form of dividends. The investment is therefore viewed as being in the business as a whole rather than its individual assets and liabilities and this is measured by the total of the net investment using closing rates.

The logic is similar to an individual in the UK investing in a foreign company. To make the accounts more informative, the investor might translate the information into its pounds sterling equivalent. On these grounds SSAP 20 justified what it chose to call the closing rate/net investment method. The statement requires the closing rate to be applied to the balance sheet and either the closing rate or the average rate to the profit and loss account. Although many would not disagree with this approach, what is questionable is whether such a foreign company is a subsidiary for group accounting purposes.

SSAP 14 defined consolidated financial statements as 'one form of group accounts which present the information contained in the separate financial statements of a holding company as if they were the financial statements of a single entity'. Critical to the definition of a group for consolidation purposes then is the idea of a single entity and yet SSAP 20 describes the closing rate method for consolidation in terms of relatively independent subsidiaries!

Despite this, SSAP 20 requires the closing rate/net investment method to 'normally be used'. Only in those circumstances 'where the trade of the foreign enterprise is more dependent on the economic environment of the investing company's currency' should the temporal method be used. Put another way, where the parent and the subsidiary act as though they are a single entity, the temporal method should be used.

Treatment of exchange differences

Perhaps the uncertainty over the respectability of the closing rate mechanism can best be gleaned by the statement's requirement that any exchange differences on translation using the closing rate/net investment method should be recorded as a movement on reserves. Only if the temporal method is used should the difference on exchange be recorded via the profit and loss account.

The justification for accounting for exchange differences via the reserves under the closing rate method was given in paragraph 19 of SSAP 20 where it was felt that the differences 'may result from many factors unrelated to . . . trading performance . . . (and) . . . in particular they do not represent or measure changes in actual or prospective cash flows'. More meaning might have been derived from this statement if it had spelt out exactly what the differences do represent. Duality requires each transaction to have two aspects and the other side of the gain or loss on exchange has certainly been recorded as a change in asset values. If it is unclear what the gain or loss on exchange represents, it is equally unclear what the change in asset values causing those differences represents. More than that, accounting for transactions via the reserves can run counter to prudence with losses being hidden from the income statement as will be seen later.

Foreign subsidiaries and foreign loans

SSAP 20 contained one more provision of interest to groups. A group might raise a foreign loan to pay for an overseas investment. Showing any loss on exchange from the loan while keeping the cost of the overseas investment at its original amount was felt to be unfair, particularly as the loss would have to be accounted for via the profit and loss account – no matter that it was consistent with the prudence concept of anticipating losses but not gains. SSAP 20 recognised this and permits, although does not require, the *equity* investment also to be translated at the closing rate.

If the loan had been for the full price of the investment and they were both in the same foreign currency, the effect will be to change the book value of the investment by an equal but opposite amount to the change in the value of the loan with no net affect on reserves or the profit and loss account. This offset may not be equal when the loan and the investment are for different amounts or in different currencies with different exchange rate movements. In that case, the exchange difference on the investment should be taken to reserves where it is available for offset up to the value of the exchange difference on the loan. If the exchange gains or losses on the borrowings are greater than those on the investment, the difference must be accounted for in the profit and loss account.

Availability of offset

This offset is available in two distinct ways: in the parent's individual accounts and the group accounts providing the closing rate is used. This is not double counting. Rather it is recognition that the individual investment is eliminated on consolidation. It is therefore only the exchange gain or loss on translation which is available to be offset against the loan gain or loss. This is demonstrated in Example 10.5.

Example 10.5

Verygood plc acquired Tresbon SA 12 months ago for 2,850,000 French francs financed by a loan of 855,000 Deutschmarks. The balance sheet of Verygood plc at the year end before adjusting for any exchange rate differences comprised the investment in the subsidiary, other assets of £615,000, the loan, ordinary share capital of £300,000, retentions brought forward from the beginning of the year of £200,000 plus the profit for the year of £115,000.

The assets of Tresbon SA at the year end consisted of net assets of FF2,280,000 financed by ordinary share capital of FF1,000,000, retentions brought forward of FF900,000 and FF380,000 profit for the year.

At the beginning of the year the exchange rate was FF10 to the pound and DM3 to the pound whilst at the end of the year, the rates had fallen to 9.5 and 2.5 respectively. It is the policy of Verygood plc to account for foreign subsidiary profits using the closing rate.

Company offset

From this information, the individual or company balance sheet of Verygood plc can be calculated. This is shown in Exhibit 10.10. In the original balance sheet the investment and the loan are shown at their cost in pounds sterling at the date of the transactions. The investment in the subsidiary is the acquisition price of FF2,850,000 translated at the exchange rate at the time of FF10 to the pound while the loan represents the original DM855,000 translated at DM3 to the pound.

Exhibit 10.10 SSAP 20 and offset – the individual company

Balance sheet (£000)	Original	Offset	Revised
Investment in subsidiary	+285	+15	+300
Other assets	+615		+615
	900		915
Ordinary share capital	−300		−300
Opening reserves	−200		−200
Profit for the year	−115	+42	−73
Shareholders' funds	−615		−573
Loan	−285	−57	−342
	900		915

At the end of the year, the pound has fallen in value against the Deutschmark and this loss needs to be brought into the accounts. At a year end rate of DM2.5 to the £1, the loan of DM855,000 is now the equivalent of £342,000, a loss on exchange of £57,000. Using the offset arrangement of SSAP 20, however, not all of this needs to be charged against profits for the period. Because of the parallel fall in the value of the £1 against the French franc, the investment of FF2,850,000 can now be translated at 9.5 to give a revised UK value of £300,000, a gain of £15,000. Consequently this is the value the investment will be shown at in the parent's individual accounts. This gain is available to partially offset the loss on the loan with the difference being charged to the profit for the year. Whatever the strength of the argument in allowing the offset, it does produce a revised figure for the investment which is very difficult to interpret being neither the original cost of the investment nor its current value.

Group offset

A similar process of offset is allowable when consolidating the group accounts except that any gain or loss on the loan is available for offset against the currency translation gain or loss of the subsidiary. Using the data in Example 10.5, Exhibit 10.11 shows the offset allowable and the resulting group accounts for Verygood plc.

Exhibit 10.11 SSAP 20 and group offset

Balance sheet (000)	Subsidiary (FF)	Rate	(£)	Parent (£)	Combined (£)	Adjustments (£)	(£)	(£)	(£)
Goodwill							+95		+95
Investment in subsidiary				+285	+285	−190	−95		
Other assets	+2,280	9.5	+240	+615	+855				+855
	2,280		240	900	1,140				950
Ordinary share capital	−1,000	10.0	−100	−300	−400	+100			−300
Opening reserves	−900	10.0	−90	−200	−290	+90			−200
Profit for the year	−380	9.5	−40	−115	−155			+47	−108
Shareholders' funds	−2,280		−230	−615	−845				−608
Loan				−285	−285			−57	−342
Gain on exchange			−10		−10			+10	
	2,280		240	900	1,140				950

The subsidiary's net assets and profit for the year are translated using the closing rate method. In this particular case there is no need to calculate the exchange difference at the end of the previous year as it was not part of the group at that stage. Consequently any gains or losses on exchange must relate to this year.

Having translated the foreign subsidiary's accounts and established the gain on exchange, the accounts are then combined. Verygood paid £285,000 to acquire Tresbon. At the end of the first year, the net assets in the French subsidiary totalled FF2,280,000. Having made a profit of FF380,000, the net assets at the beginning of the year must have been FF1,900,000 assuming no dividends have been paid. At an exchange rate of FF10:£1, the sterling value of these net assets (and hence shareholders' funds) was £190,000. Goodwill therefore must have been £95,000.

The separating of the investment between the value of the shareholders' funds acquired and the goodwill is shown in the first two adjustments to the combined accounts. Finally, the amount outstanding on the loan is now £342,000 as a result of exchange rate movements. Prudence requires that this increase of £57,000 should be reflected in the final accounts. SSAP 20, however, does not require all of this to be accounted for as a reduction in reserves. It can be partly offset by the exchange gain and so group reserves are reduced by £47,000.

THE CLOSING RATE METHOD AND MONETARY ASSETS

The closing rate method can distort group profitability when a foreign subsidiary is used to make investments. Investors look for a return which will not only cover inflation but also give, in addition, a real return.

The effect of inflation

Inflation also affects exchange rates. Other things being equal, a country with a high inflation rate will see its currency weaken relative to the currency of a country with low inflation. A company in an inflation-free country investing in a country with 20 per cent annual inflation will need to see its foreign investment increase by 20 per cent just to ensure no loss. To achieve a real profit therefore will require a return in excess of 20 per cent. The consequences of this when the closing rate method is used for reporting the results of a foreign subsidiary is demonstrated in Example 10.6.

Example 10.6

Two countries are identical in all respects except for the rate of inflation. The home country has zero inflation but the foreign one is expected to have 25 per cent inflation into the foreseeable future. A company in the home country is considering investing £100,000 as a short term deposit over the next 12 months. Interest rates in the home country are 20 per cent p.a. while the current exchange rate is £1 in the home country to $1 in the foreign country.

Real and nominal interest rates

In terms of purchasing power, £1 in the home country will originally buy a similar basket of goods as $1 in the foreign country. With 25 per cent annual inflation, $1.25 will be needed at the end of the year to buy the same basket of goods which could still be bought for £1 in the home country. Free markets will therefore ensure the exchange rate at the end of the year becomes $1.25 to £1 as otherwise speculators could make profits by buying in one country and selling in another.

An investment by the home company in the foreign company of £100,000 at the beginning of the year will therefore need to grow to £125,000 just to avoid making a loss as the exchange rate will then be $1.25 to £1. In addition, if real interest rates – independent of inflation – are 20 per cent p.a. then this return will also be required to make the foreign investment worthwhile. To find the nominal or market interest rate in the foreign country needs both inflation rates and real interest rates to be considered.

In the home country with zero inflation, the value of the investment at the year end would be:

$$£100,000 \times 1.20 = £120,000$$

In the foreign country, the original investment of $100,000 would need to grow by an additional 25 per cent to cover inflation, i.e.:

$$\$100,000 \times 1.2 \times 1.25 = \$150,000$$

With a year end exchange rate of $1.25 equalling £1, the $150,000 translates to £120,000. In other words, there is no advantage in investing in one country rather than another. Both investments give a profit of £20,000. The apparent high interest rate of 50 per cent in the foreign country is due entirely to its prospective rate of inflation.

With this conclusion, it is now possible to show how the closing rate method of accounting would report the result. At the end of the year, the subsidiary's sole asset will be the funds of $150,000 to give a profit of $50,000 on the opening amount. The year end balance sheet plus the calculation of exchange loss on translation is shown in Exhibit 10.12.

Exhibit 10.12 The treatment of exchange loss in group accounts

	($)	Rate	(£)
Asset	150,000	1.25	120,000
	150,000		120,000
Capital	100,000		100,000
Profit	50,000	1.25	40,000
Exchange loss			(20,000)
	150,000		120,000

On consolidation, the £40,000 of profit will be recorded as part of group profitability. The exchange loss, however, is required by SSAP 20 to be treated via the reserves. This causes the real operating profit to be overstated. Any excess profit within the £40,000 is due to the home value of the investment falling and this is represented by the exchange loss. Only if the exchange loss was to be charged directly against profits – as required by the temporal method – would the subsidiary's contribution to overall group profitability be accurately stated.

Given the importance investors place on profitability, the closing rate method is misleading. And mislead it certainly does. Polly Peck plc, a major UK company much favoured by investors for its phenomenal growth of profits until its recent collapse, used exactly this technique. So-called sophisticated investors, however, concentrated on the profit and loss account figure to the exclusion of the movement on reserves where a different story would have been told.

SUMMARY

The inclusion of foreign subsidiaries within group accounts is a relatively new departure for many European countries although there is a considerable history of their inclusion within UK-based accounts. Only since the incorporation of the Seventh Directive into state law has it become a statutory obligation in all member states. What is particularly worrying is that the Directive contained little or no directions as to how the foreign subsidiaries should be treated.

Two approaches have been discussed, the temporal and the closing rate methods. Despite the temporal method being consistent with accounting values used elsewhere, it was shown to have quirks such as changing the relative importance of elements in the subsidiary's final accounts – especially the debt to equity ratio – and the turning of subsidiary profits into losses and vice versa. The closing rate/net investment method appears to overcome these difficulties although at the cost of questionable figures in the final accounts. But even this method is not immune from distorting the results of groups. Only where replacement costs or net realisable values are used are these difficulties avoided. The fault therefore lies as much with the traditional emphasis on historical accounting data as any particular translation method.

Until this issue is addressed, companies in the UK and USA will continue mainly to incorporate foreign subsidiaries using the closing rate method despite its limitations. As for the rest of Europe, it is too early to say, although given the importance of the US and UK stock markets it seems likely that the closing rate method will dominate their reports as well.

FURTHER READING

Lewis, R. and Pendrill, D. (1994) *Advanced Financial Accounting*, 4th edn, Pitman.
Lorensen, L. (1972) *Reporting Foreign Operations of US Companies in US Dollars*, Accounting Research Study No. 12, AICPA.
Nobes, C. (Autumn 1980) 'A review of the translation debate', *Accounting and Business Research*, No. 40, ICAEW.
Westwick, C. A. (1986) *Accounting for Overseas Operations*, Gower.

TEST YOUR UNDERSTANDING

1 Complications exist when measuring the performance of entities located in a foreign country as a result of (a) fixed exchange rates; (b) floating exchange rates.

2 Guidance on the consolidating of foreign subsidiaries for UK parent companies is to be found in:
   (a) the Seventh Directive of the European Union;
   (b) SSAP 12;
   (c) SSAP 20;
   (d) FAS 52.

3 A UK company sells £120,000 of goods to a customer in Ruritania where the currency is the dollar. The invoice was stated in Ruritanian dollars. On the day of the sale, the exchange rate was $3:£1. At the year end, the exchange rate was $2.4:£1. Shortly after the year end, when the exchange rate stood at $2:£1, the customer paid the full invoice amount. At the year end, this is shown in the accounts as:

(a) Turnover £40,000 and debtor £40,000;
(b) Turnover £50,000, debtor £40,000, profit and loss expense £10,000;
(c) Turnover £40,000, debtor £50,000, increase in reserves £10,000;
(d) Turnover £40,000, debtor £50,000, increase in profit and loss £10,000.

4 Charlemont Ltd is a UK company. It has no overseas subsidiaries but it is partly financed by a loan denominated in Italian lira which is repayable in six year's time. At the year end there was a currency gain of £20,000 on the loan. Charlemont reported profits of £200,000 for the year and wishes to pay all profits as a dividend. Ignoring taxation, the maximum dividend it can pay is:
(a) £180,000;
(b) £200,000;
(c) £220,000;
(d) none of these.

5 Differentiate between currency conversion and currency translation.

6 How does the temporal method of currency conversion differ from the closing rate method?

7 What is meant by the term 'net investment'?

8 In UK accounts, how is the exchange difference on translation recorded?

9 Where a group has raised loans abroad to finance the acquisition of a subsidiary, any adverse movement in currencies affecting the loan is able to be at least partially offset if the group uses:
(a) the temporal method of exchange translation;
(b) the closing rate/net investment method of exchange translation.

QUESTIONS

1 Guildhall plc purchased a small French company exactly one year ago when the exchange rate was 10FF:£1. To partially finance the acquisition, Guildhall obtained a loan of DM150,000. At the time the exchange rate stood at DM3:£1. One year later, the exchange rates had changed to FF9 and DM2.5 to the £1 and the balance sheets of the two companies prior to consolidation were as follows:

Guildhall	*(£)*	**Subsidiary**	*(FF)*
Investment in French subsidiary	90,000	Net assets	1,170,000
Other assets (net)	4,500,000		
	4,590,000		1,170,000
Financed by			
Ordinary share capital	2,000,000	Ordinary share capital	400,000
Retained profits to date	2,540,000	Previous year's retentions	320,000
Loan	50,000	Current year's retentions	450,000
	4,590,000		1,170,000

The subsidiary had made no distributions during the year nor were any planned.

Using the above data, show the balance sheets for the company and the group at the year end, identifying the treatment of any exchange rate differences.

2 Three years ago, Master plc acquired all the share capital in Servant Inc, a company registered in San Serif. At the time, the reserves of Servant Inc stood at $300,000 and the exchange rate at $10 to £1. The current year, however, has seen a consistent fall in the value of the pound sterling against the San Serif dollar. At the beginning of the year, the exchange rate was $9:£1. At the year end, this had changed to $7:£1 although the average rate of exchange during the year had been $8:£1.

The balance sheets and profit and loss accounts of both companies for the current year are outlined below. Since the takeover, there have been no acquisitions or disposals of fixed assets within Servant Inc nor have there been any change to its capital structure.

Servant Inc balance sheet		($)	Master plc balance sheet		(£)
Net fixed assets		630,000	Net fixed assets		87,000
Debtors	252,000		Investment in Servant		110,000
Cash	126,000		Debtors	34,000	
	378,000		Cash	2,000	
less creditors	189,000	189,000		36,000	
		819,000	less creditors	3,000	33,000
less loan stock		44,100			230,000
		774,900	less loan stock		13,700
					216,300
Financed by			Financed by		
Issued ordinary share capital		200,000	Issued ordinary share capital		100,000
Retentions		574,900	Retentions		116,300
		774,900			216,300

Servant profit and loss account		($)	Master profit and loss account		(£)
Turnover		616,000	Turnover		130,000
Cost of sales		336,000	Cost of sales		78,000
Gross profit		280,000	Gross profit		52,000
Depreciation	126,000		Depreciation	5,000	
Other expenses	28,000	154,000	Other expenses	7,400	12,400
Net profit		126,000	Net profit		39,600

Using the above information, produce a consolidated balance sheet and profit and loss account assuming that Servant is treated as an acquisition:

(a) using the temporal method of currency conversion, and

(b) using the closing rate/net investment method and applying the year end rate.

3* Heavens plc acquired 80 per cent of the issued share capital of Star Ltd, a company registered in Rainbowland. At the time, the reserves of Star stood at $2,700,000 and the exchange rate was $9:£1. Three years ago, Star purchased additional fixed assets with a current net book value of $3,600,000. At that time, the exchange rate was $6:£1. There have been no other purchases or disposals of fixed assets since Star was acquired by Heavens and only the additional fixed assets are being depreciated.

The balance sheet of Heavens and Star at the current year end are detailed below along with the profit and loss account of Star.

Balance sheets	Star		Heavens		Star's Profit and loss account for the year		
	($000)		(£000)				($000)
Net fixed assets		10,800		1,400	Turnover		45,000
Shares in Star Ltd				600	Opening stock	1,200	
Stock	750		450		Purchases	37,050	
Debtors	1,200		500		Closing stock	750	37,500
Cash	740		120		Gross profit		7,500
	2,690		1,070		Distribution costs	600	
Trade creditors	400	2,290	300	770	Administration expenses	1,890	2,490
		13,090		2,770	Net profit before taxation		5,010
Long term loans		2,000		2,000	Corporation tax		1,680
		11,090		770	Net profit after taxation		3,330
					Dividends		1,092
Financed by					Retentions for the year		2,238
Issued share capital		1,800		370			
Retentions/reserves		9,290		400			
		11,090		770			

At the beginning of the accounting year, the exchange rate had been $4:£1 although the opening stock had been purchased when the rate was $5:£1. The average exchange rate for the current year had been $3:£1 although by the year end this had fallen to $2:£1. At the time the closing stock was purchased the exchange rate was $2.5:£1 and at the time the tax and dividends were paid it had been $2.8:£1.

Depreciation on the additional fixed assets acquired totalled $720,000 for the year and had been accounted for within administration expenses. The creditors repayable beyond 12 months represent long term loans in the businesses. Included within the retentions of Heavens plc are retained profits for the current year of £100,000. At the time of the acquisition of the shares in Star Ltd, the subsidiary's book values were also felt to be its fair value. Heavens plc accounts for Star Ltd by way of the acquisition method of consolidation. Any goodwill on consolidation is written off against reserves.

Using the above data, produce the consolidated balance sheet of Heavens plc using both the temporal and closing rate methods of currency conversion on the assumption that the average rate for the year is used in the latter case.

CHAPTER 11

Financial reporting – funds and cashflow

Profit rarely equals the increase in cash as financial reports are produced by matching income with expenses rather than receipts with payments. In modern, complex organisations, this may involve substantial judgements being made about asset lives, the capitalisation of expenses and when to recognise revenue. More than that, it is not accounting profit which pays suppliers and the workforce but cash. The availability of cash is therefore critical to the survival of the enterprise.

This chapter:

■ Examines the concept of funds

■ Develops the logic of funds flow and cashflow statements

■ Introduces Financial Reporting Standard No. 1

■ Provides worked examples of FRS 1

■ Evaluates the strengths and weaknesses of cashflow statements

Profit is rarely the same as the increase in cash. This was shown in the cashflow statements outlined in Chapters 1 and 2. At its simplest, this is because sales and purchases often take place on credit terms. But there are other reasons. Depreciation is an expense although not a cash outflow. Any outflow would be at the time of a fixed asset's acquisition, not when it is apportioned to accounting periods, and only then if acquired for cash. On the other hand, some costs – the capitalisation of expenses, for example – involve cash outflows but do not appear as expenses of the current period. Yet other costs, such as the writing off of goodwill, are not handled via the profit and loss account at all but indirectly through the reserves.

As early as July 1975, the old Accounting Standards Committee recognised the need for a supplementary statement to the accounts addressing these differences when it issued SSAP 10 Statements of Source and Application of Funds. Subsequently, this has been replaced by a more powerful standard, FRS 1 Cashflow Statements issued by the Accounting Standards Board. The ASB attaches sufficient importance to the cashflow statement for the Board to identify it as a primary financial statement along with the balance sheet, the profit and loss account and the statement of total recognised gains and losses. Despite this, and despite the added insight such statements can bring to the understanding of an enterprise's financial affairs, there is currently no European Union legislation requiring such statements to be prepared by member states.

THE DEFINITION OF FUNDS

One major difficulty is determining exactly what such a supplementary statement should be measuring. There are three possible definitions of funds going through an organisation.

Cash

The first is cash – cash after all gives control over resources in a market economy. Transactions which increase the amount of cash will be shown as sources of funds while transactions involving cash outflows will be shown as uses or applications of funds. One limitation of defining funds as cash is its ability to be manipulated. A business can delay payment to creditors or pressurise debtors into paying more quickly, either of which will increase the size of the cash balance.

Working capital

To overcome this problem, a wider definition of funds has sometimes been suggested. Chapter 2 introduced the idea of current assets and current liabilities and their netting off to produce net current assets. The components of net current assets are part of a cycle which, in the normal course of events, quickly convert to cash. Stock is purchased, giving rise to a creditor. The stock is then sold on credit and creates a debtor. In turn the debtor pays, increasing the amount of cash, enabling the creditor to be paid and so the cycle commences all over again. For this reason, net current assets used to be known as *circulating capital* although today the term *working capital* is more widely used. Working capital is therefore not only a wider definition of funds, it is also a wider definition of liquidity than cash alone.

Explaining changes in funds using the working capital definition overcomes the manipulation difficulties of using cash. Putting pressure on debtors to make early payment might well increase the amount of cash. It will, however, also decrease the amount of debtors, resulting in no overall change in the level of working capital, merely a change in its composition. Only those transactions which change the amount of working capital will be shown as increasing or decreasing the amount of funds in the enterprise.

Using this second definition of funds, a purchase of fixed assets will be shown as an application or outflow of funds irrespective of whether the assets were acquired for a cash payment or by the creation of a creditor. Had the fixed asset been acquired by the issue of a new long term loan, however, the transaction would have simply been the gaining of a fixed asset in exchange for the incurring of a long term liability. Neither transaction would have involved working capital and so both the raising of the loan and its use would have been outside the statement of source and application of funds using either the cash or working capital measures.

General financial resources

A third possibility is therefore to define funds in an even broader sense as financial resources in general. Such a definition would capture the increase in funds made available to the business by the granting of the loan and the parallel decrease in funds from purchasing the fixed assets.

THE LOGIC OF THE FUNDS STATEMENT

The flow of funds passing through an enterprise will vary depending on which definition of funds is used. Taking the information provided in Example 11.1 it is possible to produce the final accounts of a business plus all three different funds flow statements.

Example 11.1

Ashridge Ltd was formed on 1 January. On that day it raised £50,000 cash by issuing 50,000 £1 shares payable at par. During the year it purchased £60,000 of fixed assets, £20,000 of which were paid for by cash and the balance by the supplier sourcing a long term loan. Stock purchased on credit totalled £18,000 and credit sales were £70,000. Wages for the year totalled £17,000 and these were paid for in cash. During the year £11,000 was paid to creditors and cash received from debtors came to £25,000. Part way through the year, an interim dividend of £5,000 was paid and the directors recommended a further dividend of £8,000 although this had not been paid at the year end. Closing stocks were estimated at £8,000 and depreciation of 25 per cent is to be provided on the fixed assets. Interest on the loan can be ignored.

Recording the transactions

The recording of these entries is shown in Exhibit 11.1. Benefits received are shown as a plus and obligations as a minus.

Exhibit 11.1 The accounting transactions

(£000)	Shares issued	Fixed assets Cash	Loan	Stock	Sales	Wages paid	Creditors paid	Cash from debtors	Interim dividend	Final dividend	Sales to P & L	Cost of sales	Wages to P & L	Depre-ciation	Divid-ends	Closing balances
Cash	+50	−20				−17	−11	+25	−5							+22
Ordinary share capital	−50															−50
Fixed assets		+20	+40													+60
Loan		−40														−40
Stock				+18									−10			+8
Trade creditors				−18			+11									−7
Sales					−70						+70					
Debtor					+70			−25								+45
Wages						+17							−17			
Dividends									+5	+8					−13	
Other creditors										−8						−8
Profit and loss											−70	+10	+17	+15	+13	−15
Provision for depreciation														−15		−15

With a closing stock of £8,000 and purchases of £18,000, the cost of sales must equal £10,000. From this must be deducted the wages paid of £17,000. The only other expense is depreciation. At the end of the period, the depreciation of £15,000 is charged as an expense in the normal way, even though no cash is involved. The result is a net profit for the period of £28,000. From this must be deducted the dividends of £13,000, including the dividend proposed of £8,000 which is recorded as a non-trade creditor. In effect, dividends are a partial return of shareholders' funds to the owners, leaving £15,000 of the period's profits within the company.

The final accounts

Exhibit 11.1 includes a full set of final accounts. The profit and loss account, including any distributions, is shown as the penultimate line while all the information necessary to reproduce a balance sheet is to be found in the final column. These are reproduced in a more meaningful form in Exhibit 11.2.

At the very beginning of the year, before the shares were issued, the company was no more than a hollow shell with no profits and no funds of any form. One year later, retained profits had increased to £15,000, the amount of cash in the business had increased to £22,000 and the working capital had increased to £60,000.

The reason for the change in the cash position can be explained by simply analysing the cash line of Exhibit 11.1 while the change in the working capital can be explained by summing the transactions which relate to working capital. Both of these are reproduced in Exhibit 11.3.

Exhibit 11.2 The final accounts

Profit and loss account for the year		Balance sheet at year end			
Turnover	£70,000	Fixed assets at cost			£60,000
Less cost of sales	£10,000	Depreciation			£15,000
Gross profit	£60,000				£45,000
Wages	£17,000	Current assets			
Depreciation	£15,000	Stock	£8,000		
Net profit	£28,000	Debtors	£45,000		
Dividends	£13,000	Cash	£22,000	£75,000	
Retentions for the year	£15,000	Current liabilities			
		Trade creditors	£7,000		
		Other creditors	£8,000	£15,000	£60,000
					£105,000
		Long term loan			£40,000
					£65,000
		Financed by			
		Ordinary share capital			£50,000
		Retentions			£15,000
					£65,000

Exhibit 11.3 Cash and working capital movements

Summary of cash transactions

(£000)	Capital introduced	Fixed assets	Wages paid	Creditors paid	Debtors paid	Dividend paid	Total
Cash	+50	−20	−17	−11	+25	−5	+22

Summary of working capital transactions

(£000)	Capital introduced	Fixed assets	Stock bought	Sales on credit	Wages paid	Creditors paid	Debtors paid	Dividend paid	Dividend proposed	Cost of sales	Total
Cash	+50	−20			−17	−11	+25	−5			+22
Stock			+18							−10	+8
Debtor				+70			−25				+45
Trade creditor			−18			+11					−7
Other creditors									−8		−8
Net movements	+50	−20	nil	+70	−17	nil	nil	−5	−8	−10	+60

Cash and working capital movements

The cash line is effectively the cash account, showing every item of cash paid in and out of the business. It therefore explains in detail how the opening cash balance of nil moved to a closing cash balance of £22,000.

The second part of Exhibit 11.3 is a little more complex. The detailed transactions for every working capital account are reproduced and the overall effect summarised under the heading of net movements. It shows working capital having increased from its zero base by the introduction of £50,000 cash from the issue of shares and its reduction through the *cash* expenditure of £20,000 on fixed assets. The £18,000 stock purchase has no effect on the working capital total as the increase in stocks is balanced by an equivalent increase in creditors. The sales on credit, however, have unambiguously increased working capital by creating debtors of £70,000. Likewise, the payment of wages has seen working capital in the form of cash reduced by £17,000. The payment of the creditor and the receipt of cash from the debtor will have no affect on working capital as both simply involve the exchange of one element of working capital for another. Unlike the cash funds analysis, *both* the dividend items appear as an outflow even though the proposed dividends have yet to be paid. Finally the cost of sales reflects stock leaving the working capital and is therefore an application of working capital funds.

THE DEVELOPMENT OF THE FUNDS FLOW STATEMENT

The essential difference between the two approaches is that the cash measurement of funds only recognises a movement when cash is directly involved whereas the working capital definition recognises a movement as soon as the obligation is acknowledged. The working capital concept of funds flow is therefore accruals based. The workings for both types of funds flow can be incorporated into a statement. Examples of these are shown in Exhibit 11.4. To make both statements more meaningful, the source and application of funds have been broken down to show funds generated from trading (which are likely to be more representative of general activity) and funds relating to other discrete sources and applications.

Exhibit 11.4 The source and application of funds statement

Source and application of funds (cash)			Source and application of funds (working capital)		
Funds generated from operations			Funds generated from operations		
Cash from debtors		£25,000	Sales		£70,000
Cash paid to creditors		(£11,000)	Cost of sales		(£10,000)
Wages paid		(£17,000)	Wages		(£17,000)
		(£3,000)			£43,000
Other sources of funds			Other sources of funds		
Capital introduced		£50,000	Capital introduced		£50,000
		£47,000			£93,000
Application of funds			Application of funds		
Purchase of fixed assets	£20,000		Purchase of fixed assets	£20,000	
Dividends paid	£5,000		Dividends paid	£5,000	
		£25,000	Dividends proposed	£8,000	£33,000
Change in funds		£22,000	Change in funds		£60,000

Cash funds and working capital funds compared

Although both statements include similarities, of more interest are the differences between the two statements. Certainly the working capital definition of funds shows a much healthier position, implying that the £20,000 purchase of fixed assets plus the dividends of £13,000 could easily be met from the funds generated from operations. Analysis of the cash funds statement, however, shows this is not the case. Cash generated from operations was negative and certainly not sufficient to pay for the fixed assets let alone the dividends as well.

A limitation of both statements is that neither includes the £40,000 of assets financed by the loan provided by the supplier. Had the loan been an independent transaction, separate from the acquisition of assets, both statements would have reported the inflow of cash and the outflow when the assets were subsequently purchased.

Deriving the data – a short cut

Leaving these issues aside for a moment, there is a more important practical problem. In the real world, it is not feasible to analyse every cash or working capital transaction whenever a source and application of funds statement is prepared. Some other method needs to be found. The solution lies in the application of duality. The cash implications of any transaction can be determined in one of two ways: either directly via the cash account or indirectly by analysing the other side of the transaction.

Consider first a company which only has cash sales. The cash generated from sales can simply be found by taking the turnover figure. Now consider a business which sells for cash and credit and has a £30,000 opening balance of debtors. Assuming sales of £100,000 for the period and a closing balance of debtors of £50,000, cash received must be £80,000. The cash received can be identified directly from the cash account or indirectly by recognising that:

$$\text{Opening debtors} + \text{Sales} - \text{Cash received} = \text{Closing debtors}$$

Using this equation, there is no need to separately identify credit sales as cash sales will be included in both the overall figure for sales and in the overall figure for cash received. The effect of cash sales is therefore cancelled out when calculating closing debtors. Rearranging this equation enables the cash received to be indirectly calculated as

$$\text{Cash received} = \text{Opening debtors} + \text{Sales} - \text{Closing debtors}$$

or:

$$\text{Cash received} = \text{Sales} + (\text{Opening debtors} - \text{Closing debtors})$$

With sales of £100,000 and a net increase in debtors of £20,000, cash received must be £80,000. This particular example concerns the cash element of sales although the approach is equally valid for all other account headings. The balance on any account after adjusting for the accruals or non-cash elements must represent the effect of the total cash transactions.

There is one activity which is a little more complex, the cost of sales. Again, it is useful to make use of duality and to express the relationships in the form of an equation. The equation for the cost of sales is:

Opening stock + Purchases – Closing stock = Cost of sales

Rearranging the equation it is possible to derive a formula for purchases:

Purchases = Cost of sales + (Closing stock – Opening stock)

This, however, says nothing about cash paid. To calculate *cash* paid as a result of purchasing stock requires an analysis of the creditors account. Showing this in the form of an equation gives:

Opening creditors + Purchases – Cash paid = Closing creditors

and rearranging this equation enables the cash paid for purchases to be calculated:

Cash paid = Purchases + (Opening creditors – Closing creditors)

This now enables the cash paid to suppliers to be derived by a process of substitution. Purchases had earlier been defined as Cost of sales plus the change in the stocks and so the cash paid for purchases equals:

Cost of sales + (Closing stock – Opening stock)
+ (Opening creditors – Closing creditors)

With the general rule of adjusting each account heading for the change in the non-cash element, it is possible to produce a source and application of cash statement without having access to the detailed movements in the cash account. Effectively, this involves reversing all non-cash changes to leave only the effect of cash transactions on each account.

Building up the funds flow statement

The source and application of funds statement is concerned with changes in funds over the accounting period. Chapters 1 and 2 demonstrated that the difference between two balance sheets must represent the change in *resources* from trading plus any additional sources of funds obtained in the period less any outflows such as dividends or tax payments. The first stage therefore is to calculate the difference between the opening and closing balances for the accounts on the balance sheet. As a result, certain key figures will be disclosed such as the change in debtors, the change in the creditors and the change in the stock.

The next stage is to reverse all transactions not involving cash at the balance sheet date by applying duality. This will then reveal the underlying cash consequences of each account heading.

There is no need to adjust the individual elements making up the profit and loss account to derive funds generated from operations. If there have been no dividends paid and no transfers between reserves, the change in the retentions between the two balance sheet dates will represent the profit (or loss) for the year. The profit for the year is merely the net figure of sales less expenses and so adjusting the single profit figure – the change in retentions – for all the non-cash elements applicable to turnover and expenses will identify the funds generated from operations. If there have been appropriations, as in the case of Ashridge in Example 11.1, these must first be corrected, again by applying duality. The end result will show, under the retentions heading, the *cash* effects of trading along with the funds generated and used elsewhere.

The source and applications of cash statement

Exhibit 11.5 demonstrates the steps involves in producing a source and applications of cash statement by making use of the information derived from the accounts of Ashridge Ltd.

Exhibit 11.5 The source and applications of cash statement – workings

(£000)	Balance sheet Opening	Closing	Difference	Dividend reversals	Depreciation reversal	Adjustments Debtors	Creditors	Stock	Fixed asset/ Loan	Total
Cash	+0	+22	+22							+22
Fixed assets	+0	+60	+60						−40	+20
Provision for depreciation	+0	−15	−15		+15					
Stock	+0	+8	+8					−8		
Debtor	+0	+45	+45			−45				
	0	120	120							42
Ordinary share capital	−0	−50	−50							−50
Loan	−0	−40	−40						+40	
Trade creditors	−0	−7	−7				+7			
Other creditors	−0	−8	−8	+8						
Dividends	−0	−0	−0	+13 −8						+5
Retentions	−0	−15	−15	−13	−15	+45	−7	+8		+3
	0	120	120							42

The first step is to calculate the difference between the opening and closing balance sheets to reproduce, amongst other things, the retentions for the period. This is then followed by the disaggregation of the profit and loss account represented by those retentions.

The dividend would ultimately have been recorded as both an appropriation of the profit and loss account and a cash outflow or the creation of a creditor. The first adjustment therefore reverses this, increasing the profit figure to give the net profit before dividends for the period of £28,000 and showing dividends paid or payable as a separate item. This still overstates dividends *paid* by the extent of the dividends proposed of £8,000. The accrual 'other creditor' relates to this proposed dividend. As this accrual did not involve cash, reversing the transaction will show dividends actually *paid* of £5,000.

The same logic applies to depreciation. The depreciation of £15,000 involved no cash and so this also has to be reversed.

The increase in Ashridge's debtors of £45,000 means that cash has yet to be received from them. As a consequence, the balance on retentions is overstated in cash *terms* by this amount. Reversing the increase in debtors puts the turnover figure within retentions on a cash basis. A similar argument applies to the treatment of creditors and stock. Reversing these changes eliminates the unpaid element within the cost of sales subsumed within the balance on retentions. The end result is a negative cash generated from operations value of £3,000 which agrees with the detailed analysis of the cash account where £25,000 cash was generated from debtors but cash paid to creditors and employees totalled £28,000.

The final adjustment relates to the loan and the associated fixed assets acquired. Reversing this eliminates the only other non-cash transaction of the period.

The result is the values contained in the individual headings of the earlier source and application of cash but without accessing the detailed cash account. Operations consumed £3,000 of cash; the issue of ordinary share capital generated £50,000 and this was applied by purchasing £20,000 of fixed assets and paying a dividend of £5,000. The result is an increase in cash for the period of £22,000.

One technical difference between the workings of Exhibit 11.5 and the direct examination of the cash account is the reversal of the signs. In the cash account the capital introduced was shown in the familiar way as a plus and the fixed assets purchased as a negative. In Exhibit 11.5, however, the capital introduced is shown as a minus while the acquisition of the fixed assets is shown as a plus. The reason for this sudden change is that the transactions are being analysed *not* from the cash book but from the other side of the transactions. The signs are therefore reversed.

Source and applications of working capital

Using working capital as the definition of funds does not materially change the logical development of a funds flow statement except to reverse transactions involving *working capital* rather than cash. Once again, the first stage is to calculate the differences between the balance sheet elements and then to disaggregate the profit and loss account. After that has been achieved, it is merely necessary to reverse those transactions which do not involve working capital. These are shown in Exhibit 11.6.

Exhibit 11.6 The source and application of working capital statement – workings

(£000)	Balance sheet			Dividend reversal	Depreciation reversal	Fixed asset/ Loan	Total
	Opening	Closing	Difference				
Cash	+0	+22	+22				+22
Fixed assets	+0	+60	+60			−40	+20
Provision for depreciation	+0	−15	−15		+15		
Stock	+0	+8	+8				+8
Debtor	+0	+45	+45				+45
	0	120	120				95
Ordinary share capital	−0	−50	−50				−50
Loan	−0	−40	−40			+40	
Trade creditors	−0	−7	−7				−7
Other creditors	−0	−8	−8				−8
Dividends	−0	−0	−0	+13			+13
Retentions	−0	−15	−15	−13	−15		−43
	0	120	120				95

Unlike the cash analysis, the working capital funds flow recognises changes in funds on an accruals basis. Consequently, the workings are less complex. The increase in retentions of £15,000 represents retentions for the year. As before, dividends are added back to reflect funds generated from operations and to show dividends as a separate application. No further adjustment is required, however, as the working capital concept of funds recognises an outflow as soon as the obligation is recognised rather than waiting for the cash payment.

Because of this accruals emphasis, no further adjustments are required to the profit and loss account other than the depreciation adjustment which does not involve working capital. Finally, the reversal of the loan and the associated fixed assets takes place, again because no working capital was involved in the original transaction.

The wider definition of funds

Had the general resources definition of funds been used, the reversal of the loan/fixed assets adjustment would not have been necessary. Using that wider definition of funds, the loan would have been shown as a source and the fixed assets as an application. As it is, concentrating on the narrower working capital definition, the sources of funds comprise £43,000 from operations and £50,000 from the issue of ordinary share capital. The applications relate to the acquisition of fixed assets of £20,000 and the dividends paid or payable of £13,000. All other account balances relate to working capital. As a result, the net increase in funds of £60,000 can be explained by the increase in cash of £22,000, the increase in stocks of £8,000 and the increase in debtors of £45,000 less the increase in trade creditors of £7,000 and less the increase in non-trade creditors of £8,000.

THE ACCOUNTING STANDARDS COMMITTEE AND FUNDS FLOW

Funds flow and profit

One advantage of both the working capital and total resources definitions of funds is that it is possible to identify the profit for the period within the funds flow statement. In that sense the statement provides a useful link with the profit and loss account and balance sheet. In Exhibit 11.6, for instance, the funds generated from operations is simply the profit before appropriations of £28,000 with the non-fund item of depreciation added back to give a figure of £43,000. This link was probably in the minds of the members of the Accounting Standards Committee when they introduced SSAP 10, Statements of Source and Application of Funds.

SSAP 10, however, suffered from two general weaknesses. The first was its failure to define what is meant by funds. The second related to the design of the Statement. In effect it was a cannibalised version of a funds flow statement, taking ideas from both the cash and working capital approaches to funds. The result was the statement neither explained the movement of cash nor the change in working capital identified from the balance sheet.

In addition, there was a further weakness specific to groups in a year when an acquisition was made. In the appendix to SSAP 10, two possibilities were considered. The first, consistent with the group profit and loss account and balance sheet, would show the source and application of funds for the group as a whole. The second, however, effectively excluded the subsidiary from the funds flow statement and replaced it by the outlay of funds by the parent when acquiring the subsidiary. With such limited guidance offering two totally different approaches to recording funds flow, it was perhaps inevitable that groups tended to do what they pleased when producing source and application of funds statements. There was little surprise therefore to find the Accounting Standards Board making this area of reporting the subject of its first Financial Reporting Standard.

THE ACCOUNTING STANDARDS BOARD AND CASHFLOW STATEMENTS

Financial Reporting Standard Number 1 Cashflow Statements became effective from 23 March 1992. It totally rejected the modified working capital concept of funds found in SSAP 10 in favour of cashflows. Four limitations of working capital funds flow were identified in the standard.

Limitations of working capital funds flow

First, funds flow based on working capital can obscure movements relevant to the liquidity and viability of an enterprise by, for example, masking a shortage of cash through the building up of stock or debtors within the overall working capital total. Secondly, the ASB argued that cashflow is more widely understood than working capital funds flow. Thirdly, it argued that historical cashflows can be used as a direct input to a business valuation model. By this, the Board probably had in mind the forecasting of the present value of enterprises by using past cashflows to forecast future (discounted) cashflows. Finally the ASB believed that the SSAP 10 approach did not provide new data but simply reorganised existing data by adding back depreciation and other such adjustments, the values for which already existed in the profit and loss account or balance sheet.

Users' needs

The ASB takes the view that users of financial statements need information on the 'liquidity, viability and financial adaptability' of enterprises. The profit and loss account and balance sheet based on accruals should still be viewed as the primary basis for making projections about a company's future. However, the standard recognises that accrual accounting may fail to reveal the 'leads and lags' in historical cashflows caused by, for example, depreciation and the capitalisation of expenses. Because of this, FRS 1 requires most entities to report cash generated and absorbed in a standardised form for each accounting period, one of the few exemptions from this requirement being 'small' companies.

Cashflow defined

To make this effective, the ASB has avoided the failing of SSAP 10 and clearly defined what it means by cashflow. Cashflow is to consist of cash plus cash equivalents. By cash, it means cash in hand plus deposits repayable on demand with any bank or other financial institution. Cash equivalents relate to short term, highly liquid investments which are readily convertible into known amounts of cash without notice and which were within three months of maturity when acquired, less advances from banks repayable within three months from the date of the advance. Cash and cash equivalents are therefore tightly defined.

The three-month condition, although in some ways arbitrary, reflects a concern for the intention of a transaction rather than its legal definition. It avoids the distorting problems encountered in the Fourth Directive whereby a long term loan on the balance sheet becomes a current liability simply because it is due for redemption within 12 months. One problem with emphasising cash, however, is that it is still possible to omit major transactions which do not involve cash such as the issue of shares directly to acquire a fixed asset. Had the two events been independent, both would have appeared on the cashflow statement. The standard implicitly accepts this difficulty by requiring major transactions not resulting in movements of cash or cash equivalents to be disclosed in the notes to the cashflow statement where disclosure is necessary for an understanding of the underlying transactions.

The treatment of subsidiaries

The standard also addressed another failing of SSAP 10 by specifying the treatment of an acquisition or disposal of a subsidiary. Where a group acquires or disposes of a subsidiary, the amount of cash and cash equivalents paid or received should be shown net of any cash or cash equivalents transferred as a result of the acquisitions and disposals. The result is to show strictly the cash implications for the group.

For example, a group might issue shares of £2 million plus cash of £100,000 to acquire a subsidiary with, amongst other assets, cash of £500,000. The reality is that the group has gained cash of £400,000 as a result of the acquisition and this is the figure which must appear in the cashflow statement. In addition, a note to the cashflow statement should show a summary of the effects of the acquisition or disposal, indicating how much of the consideration comprised cash and cash equivalents and the amount of the cash and cash equivalents transferred as a result of the acquisition or disposal.

The analysis of cashflows

Common sense suggests there are only six general reasons why cashflows occur in a company. Cashflows result from trading, from the payment of corporation tax, from the purchase and disposal of fixed assets, from the raising and redeeming of long term sources of finance, from the receipt of dividends and interest as a result of previous investments and from the payment of dividends and interest to existing providers of finance.

FRS 1 recognises this logic, although it merges the last two headings and specifies a more logical ordering. In addition it requires particular cashflows to be separately reported under the five general headings as well as a subtotal showing the net cash inflow or outflow before cashflows from financing. An outline format of the standard is reproduced in Exhibit 11.7 complete with examples of particular cashflows to be reported under the general headings.

Exhibit 11.7 FRS 1 the cashflow statement

Cashflow statement for the year ended ...		
Net cash inflow from operating activities		£x
Returns on investments and servicing of finance		
Interest received	£x	
Interest paid	(£x)	
Dividends paid	(£x)	
Net cash inflow from returns on investment and servicing of finance		£x
Taxation		
Corporation tax paid	(£x)	
Tax paid		(£x)
Investment activities		
Payment to acquire intangible fixed assets	(£x)	
Payment to acquire tangible fixed assets	(£x)	
Receipt from sale of tangible fixed assets	£x	
Net cash outflow from investing activities		(£x)
Net cashflow before financing		£x
Financing		
Issue of ordinary share capital	£x	
Repurchase of debenture loan	(£x)	
Expenses paid in connection with share issues	(£x)	
Net cash inflow from financing		£x
Increase in cash and cash equivalents		£x

Notes to the cashflow statement:

1 Reconciliation of operating profit to net cash inflow from operating activities

Operating profit	£x
Depreciation charges	£x
Increase in stocks	(£x)
Increase in debtors	(£x)
Increase in creditors	£x
Net cash inflow from operating activities	£x

2 Analysis of changes in cash and cash equivalents during the year

Balance at beginning of the year	£x
Net cash inflow	£x
Balance at end of year	£x

3 Analysis of the balances of cash and cash equivalents as shown in the balance sheet

	This year	Last year	Change in year
Cash at bank and in hand	£x	£x	£x
Short term investments	£x	£x	£x
Bank overdrafts	(£x)	(£x)	(£x)
	£x	£x	£x

Exhibit 11.7 (Continued)

4 Analysis of changes in financing during the year	*Share capital*	*Debenture*
Balance at beginning of the year	£x	£x
Cash inflow/(outflow) from financing	£x	(£x)
Balance at end of year	£x	£x

In addition to the detailed cashflows, the standard also requires a note to the statement reconciling the operating profit reported in the profit and loss account to the net cashflows from operations. The statement must show separately movements in stock, debtors, creditors and any other operating differences between the cashflow and profits. Complementing this is a further note reconciling the financing section of the cashflow statement to the opening and closing balance sheet figures.

One issue the ASB considered but did not resolve was the presentation of the cashflow from operations. One approach would be to show the actual cash received from customers and cash paid to suppliers and employees, in other words, the summarised cash account developed earlier. This is known as the *gross* or *direct* basis. The other, the *net* or *indirect* method, adjusts the operating profit for the changes in working capital to derive cash generated. Although preferring the gross method, the standard allows either approach. Given that much of the data for the net method is readily available, it is this method which is more likely to be found in practice.

THE FRS 1 CASHFLOW STATEMENT

The mechanics of cashflow statements have already been covered, particularly the net or indirect method where cash generated from operations is derived by adjusting for the change in debtors, stock and creditors. Where FRS 1 is different is in specifying a standard format and requiring the acquisition or disposal of a subsidiary to be accounted from a cash perspective. The presentation of the standard format is developed in Example 11.2.

This example contains the opening and closing balance sheets for Saffron plc plus its profit and loss account for the year. Although more detailed than the earlier example, a similar logic applies when developing the FRS 1 Cashflow Statement. Reversing all transactions not involving cash will highlight the effect of cash on the elements within the final accounts.

Four additional complexities are introduced into the question. The first involves taxation. To show the cash implications of taxation – how much tax was actually paid – requires the same type of adjustments as for dividends developed in the earlier example. The second complexity, the introduction of interest, has also to be treated in a similar way.

The third is an increase in the general reserve by a transfer of part of the current year's profits. No cash has left the business as a result of this transaction; it is simply an appropriation of profit. As such, it needs to be reversed when developing cashflow.

Example 11.2

Saffron plc's accounts for the last year are reproduced below. During the year, the original loan was retired at par and a new one issued. Assets, originally costing £260,000 and with accumulated depreciation of £60,000 were sold for £50,000 while depreciation charged for the year totalled £120,000. No acquisitions or disposals were made during the year. The item 'Other creditors' relates to interest accrued but not yet paid at the balance sheet dates.

Balance sheet	Last year (£000)	Last year (£000)	This year (£000)	This year (£000)	Profit and loss account for the year	(£000)
Fixed assets at cost		840		860	Turnover	800
Less depreciation		220		280	Cost of sales	240
		620		580	Gross profit	560
Current assets					Administration costs	390
Stock	130		90		Operating profit	170
Debtors	250		350		Interest payable	20
Cash	100		75		Profit on ordinary activities before tax	150
	480		515		Taxation	70
Current liabilities					Profit on ordinary activities after tax	80
Trade creditors	95		105		Proposed dividend	50
Other creditors	15		10		Retentions for the year	30
Taxation	50		80		Add opening retentions	170
Dividends	20		50			200
	180		245		Transfer to general reserve	100
Net current assets		300		270	Closing retentions	100
		920		850		
Loan		300		200		
		620		650		
Ordinary share capital		200		200		
Share premium		50		50		
General reserve		200		300		
Retentions		170		100		
		620		650		

The final complexity relates to the sale of fixed assets at a loss. Profit for the year will include this loss on disposal of fixed assets. What has to be shown, however, is the *cash received*. Given that the loss (or profit for that matter) was calculated by deducting the after-depreciation cost of the asset sold from the consideration received, it follows that *cash received* is equivalent to the net book value of the disposal less the loss or plus the profit. Exhibit 11.8 shows the workings necessary to reproduce the cashflow statement for Saffron plc.

As before, the starting position is to deduct the opening balance sheet data from that of the closing balance sheet.

Exhibit 11.8 Developing the cashflow statement for Saffron plc

	Last year	This year	Difference	Transfer	Dividend	Tax	Interest	Depreciation	Asset sale Loss	Cost	New loan	Other	Summary
Net fixed assets	+620	+580	−40					+120		+200			+280
Stock	+130	+90	−40									+40	0
Debtors	+250	+350	+100									−100	0
Cash	+100	+75	−25										−25
	1,100	1,095											
Trade creditors	−95	−105	−10									+10	0
Other creditors	−15	−10	+5				+20						+25
Taxation	−50	−80	−30			+70							+40
Dividends	−20	−50	−30		+50								+20
Loan	−300	−200	+100								+200		+300
Ordinary share capital	−200	−200	0										0
Share premium	−50	−50	0										0
General reserve	−200	−300	−100	+100									0
Retentions	−170	−100	+70	−100	−50	−70	−20	−120	−150			+50	−390
Sales of asset									+150	−200			−50
New loan											−200		−200
	−1,100	−1,095											

The first adjustment is simply reversing the transfer to the general reserve as this has no cashflow implications. The next three adjustments disaggregate the dividends, tax and interest payable from profit, enabling them to be shown as separate applications. Although these three adjustments could be shown as separate items in the workings as in the earlier example, this is not strictly necessary when dealing with cash as the respective accounts are already uniquely identified on the balance sheet as creditors. At the beginning of the year, for example, £20,000 was owing to the shareholders by way of dividends proposed but not yet paid. Despite the shareholders being given a further proposed dividend of £50,000, at the year end the balance had only increased to £50,000. Cash paid during the year must therefore equal £20,000. By reversing the non-cash transactions in the dividend account, this £20,000 cash paid out is highlighted. A similar argument applies to the treatment of the taxation and interest.

At this stage, the balance on the retentions totals £170,000, the operating profit for the year. This is then followed by the now familiar depreciation adjustment as no cash is involved in that transaction.

Included in the profit for the period is the loss from the sale of the assets. Assets with a net book value of £200,000 have been sold for £50,000, a loss of £150,000. This loss is removed from the retentions and shown separately in order not to distort cash generated from operations. Assets with a net book value of £200,000 have been given up in this transaction but that £200,000 did not involve cash in the current period and so the transaction has to be reversed to derive the cash implications. The result is the showing of £50,000 of cash received from the sale of the asset.

Next, the new loan brought funds into the business. Recording this as a minus (as signs are reversed when developing any kind of funds statement) effectively disaggregates the net change on the loan account of £100,000 to show the £200,000 of new funds and the retirement of the old loan of £300,000. Finally, to show the *cash* generated from operations requires the change in debtors, stocks and creditors to be offset against the balance on retentions in recognition that sales and operating expenses were not all for cash.

The end result is a summary in the final column of the cashflow effects of Saffron's activities for the year. These are presented in the format required by FRS 1 in Exhibit 11.9.

Exhibit 11.9 The FRS 1 cashflow statement for Saffron plc

Cashflow statement for the year ended . . .		
	(£000)	*(£000)*
Net cash inflow from operating activities		390
Returns on investments and servicing of finance		
Interest paid	(25)	
Dividends paid	(20)	
Net cash outflow from servicing of finance	——	(45)
Taxation		
Corporation tax paid	(40)	
Tax paid	——	(40)
Investment activities		
Payment to acquire tangible fixed assets	(280)	
Receipt from sale of tangible fixed assets	50	
Net cash outflow from investing activities	——	(230)
Net cashflow before financing		75
Financing		
Retirement of loan	(300)	
Issue of loan	200	
Net cash outflow from financing	——	(100)
Decrease in cash and cash equivalents		25
Notes to the cashflow statement:		
1 Reconciliation of operating profit to net cash inflow from operating activities		
Operating profit		170
Depreciation charges		120
Loss on sale of tangible fixed assets		150
Decrease in stocks		40
Increase in debtors		(100)
Increase in creditors		10
Net cash inflow from operating activities		390

Exhibit 11.9 (Continued)

2 Analysis of changes in cash and cash equivalents during the year

Balance at beginning of the year	100
Net cash outflow	25
Balance at end of year	75

3 Analysis of the balances of cash and cash equivalents as shown in the balance sheet

	This year	Last year	Change in year
Cash at bank and in hand	100	75	(25)
Short term investments	nil	nil	nil
Bank overdrafts	nil	nil	nil
	100	75	(25)

4 Analysis of changes in financing during the year	*Share capital*	*Loans*
Balance at beginning of the year	200	300
Cash outflow from financing	nil	(100)
Balance at end of year	200	200

FRS 1 AND SUBSIDIARIES ACQUIRED

FRS 1 not only laid down a prescriptive format for the presentation of the cashflow statement and a tight definition of the meaning of cash, it also explicitly addressed the problems arising when a company acquires or disposes of a subsidiary in an accounting period. What has to be shown is the cash implications of the acquisition or disposal. The process involved can be shown by making use of the information contained in Example 11.3.

Although appearing more complex than previous examples, the logic is identical. All non-cash items have to be reversed to show the effect on the company of *cash* transactions. As before, a new heading is introduced if one does not already exist to enable this reversal to take place. Exhibit 11.10 shows the opening differences between the balance sheets and all subsequent adjustments.

Example 11.3

The opening and closing group balance sheets of Dublin Bay Scientific plc are reproduced below along with its profit and loss account for the year.

Balance sheet	Last year (£m)	(£m)	This year (£m)	(£m)	Profit and loss account for the year	(£m)	(£m)
Fixed assets							
Intangible				550	Turnover		800
Tangible		500		500	Cost of sales		(240)
Investments				100	Gross profit		560
		500		1,150	Distribution costs	(150)	
Current assets					Administration expenses	(160)	(310)
Stock	200		290		Group operating profit		250
Debtors	120		240		Dividends receivable	10	
Cash	170		50		Interest payable	(40)	(30)
	490		580		Group profit before tax		220
Creditors: within one year					Group taxation		(70)
Trade creditors	80		150		Group profit after tax		150
Corporation tax	50		80		Appropriations		
Dividends	30		50		Dividends	(50)	
	160		280		Transfer to general reserve	(20)	(70)
Net current assets		330		300	Retained profit		80
		830		1,450			
Creditors: more than one year							
Loan		200		550			
		630		900			
Capital and reserves							
Ordinary shares		300		400			
Share premium		60		160			
General reserve		30		50			
Profit and loss reserve		240		290			
		630		900			

Depreciation for the year totalled £130 million. During the year, a loss of £20 million was made on the disposal of fixed assets with a net book value of £140 million. The intangible fixed asset relates to development costs capitalised during the year. It is the company's policy to write off any goodwill in the year of acquisition. No loans or shares were redeemed but the company paid £250 million to acquire all the £100 million share capital of Galway Bay Scientific Ltd. The consideration was in the form of £100 million of shares plus £50 million cash. Net assets acquired as a result of the takeover comprised fixed assets of £100 million, stock of £10 million, debtors of £20 million and cash of £140 million less creditors of £50 million.

Exhibit 11.10 FRS 1 group cashflow – workings

(£m)	Balance sheets Opening	Closing	Change	Goodwill	Share capital	Share premium	Non-cash assets	Summary
Goodwill				+30			−30	
Intangible fixed assets	+550	+550					+550	
Tangible fixed assets	+500	+500	+0				−100	−100
Investments		+100	+100					+100
Stock	+200	+290	+90				−10	+80
Debtors	+120	+240	+120				−20	+100
Cash	+170	+50	−120					−120
Trade creditors	−80	−150	−70				+50	−20
Corporation tax	−50	−80	−30					−30
Dividends	−30	−50	−20					−20
Loan	−200	−550	−350					−350
Share capital	−300	−400	−100		+100			
Share premium	−60	−160	−100			+100		
General reserve	−30	−50	−20					−20
Profit and loss	−240	−290	−50	−30				−80
Subsidiary purchased					−100	−100	+110	−90

(£m)	Summary	General reserve	Dividend, tax and interest payable	Dividend received	Capitalised expenses	Sale of asset Loss	NBV	Depreciation	Reversal of accruals	Summary
Intangible fixed assets	+550				−550					
Tangible fixed assets	−100						+140	+130		+170
Investments	+100									+100
Stock	+80								−80	
Debtors	+100								−100	
Cash	−120									−120
Trade creditors	−20								+20	
Corporation tax	−30		+70							+40
Dividends	−20		+50							+30
Loan	−350									−350
General reserve	−20	+20								
Profit and loss	−80	−20	−50 −70 −40	+10	+550	−20		−130	+160	+310
Subsidiary purchased	−90									−90
Interest paid			+40							+40
Dividend received				−10						−10
Sale of fixed asset						+20	−140			−120

Acquisition, goodwill and the effect on cash

The first point to note is that the increase in retentions on the balance sheet of £50 million does not agree with the £80 million stated on the profit and loss account. During the
year Dublin Bay acquired £220 million of assets within Galway Bay for a consideration

of £250 million. The difference is goodwill which has been written off against reserves. Reversing this non-cash transaction reconciles the balance sheet increase to the amount shown in the profit and loss account.

The only new factor introduced into this question is the purchase of an acquisition during the year. FRS 1 requires the cashflow statement to show the *cash* implications of this. In order to produce the statement therefore, details of the acquisition must be available. A casual glance at the data shows what the end result must be. The parent company paid out only £50 million cash but in so doing acquired £140 million within the subsidiary. The net effect was therefore a cash inflow resulting from the acquisition of £90 million. This can more rigorously be found by applying the logic of reversing all non-cash transactions.

Adjusting to a cash basis

The £250 million purchase price for the subsidiary was satisfied by £50 million of cash and £100 million of shares. The (market) value of the shares must therefore have been £200 million and so a share premium of £100 million must have been paid. Neither the shares nor the share premium involved cash, however, and so these transactions need to be reversed.

Similarly no *cash* was involved in acquiring the subsidiary's fixed assets, goodwill, stock, debtors and creditors. Reversing these eliminates all the non-cash transactions making up the consolidation, leaving only the net cash effect shown in the first part of Exhibit 11.10.

Having identified the cash effect of acquiring the subsidiary, the second part of Exhibit 11.10 is relatively straightforward. It simply involves reversing the transfer to the general reserve since no cash was involved and the disaggregation of the profit and loss account to show the separate cashflows represented by the dividends, interest and tax.

The capitalised expenses are equivalent to negative depreciation. They represent a cash outflow not shown as an expense and so also have to be reversed. As before, the loss on the sale of the fixed assets is combined with their net book value to show the cash received and finally the debtors, stock and creditors are adjusted to show cash rather than funds generated from operations. From these workings, the cashflow statement shown in Exhibit 11.11 can be produced.

Exhibit 11.11 *The completed cashflow statement for a group*

Cashflow statement for the year ended . . .		
	(£m)	(£m)
Net cash outflow from operating activities		(310)
Returns on investments and servicing of finance		
Dividend received	10	
Interest paid	(40)	
Dividends paid	(30)	
Net cash outflow from returns on investment and servicing of finance		(60)

Exhibit 11.11 (Continued)

	(£m)	(£m)
Taxation		
Corporation tax paid	(40)	
Tax paid	——	(40)
Investment activities		
Payment to acquire shares in X plc	(100)	
Payment to acquire tangible fixed assets	(170)	
Receipt from sale of tangible fixed assets	120	
Purchase of subsidiary net of cash and cash equivalents acquired	90	
Net cash outflow from investing activities	——	(60)
Net cashflow before financing		(470)
Financing		
Issue of loan stock	350	
Net cash inflow from financing	——	350
Decrease in cash and cash equivalents		120

Notes to the cashflow statement: *(£m)*

1 Reconciliation of operating profit to net cash inflow from operating activities

Operating profit	250
Depreciation charges	130
Capitalised expenses	(550)
Loss on sale of fixed asset	20
Increase in stocks	(80)
Increase in debtors	(100)
Increase in creditors	20
Net cash outflows from operating activities	(310)

2 Analysis of changes in cash and cash equivalents during the year

Balance at beginning of the year	170
Net cash inflow	(120)
Balance at end of year	50

3 Analysis of the balances of cash and cash equivalents as shown in the balance sheet

	This year	Last year	Change in year
Cash at bank and in hand	50	170	(120)

4 Analysis of changes in financing during the year

	Debenture
Balance at beginning of the year	200
Cash inflow from financing	350
Balance at end of year	550

CRITICISMS OF FRS 1

FRS 1 states that the purpose of the cashflow statement is to 'assist users of the financial statements in their assessment of the reporting entity's liquidity, viability and financial adaptability'. The success of the statement has therefore to be judged in the light of these objectives.

Liquidity

Liquidity is concerned with the extent to which assets are held in the form of cash or assets readily convertible into cash. As such, it is essentially a balance sheet measure. One problem with the Standard is the rigid and narrow definition of cash and cash equivalents with the latter being defined as highly liquid investments

The Accounting Standards Board's definition of liquidity is cash plus cash equivalents. Cash equivalents were defined as short term, highly liquid investments which are readily convertible into known amounts of cash without notice and which were within three months of maturity when acquired, less advances from banks repayable within three months from the date of the advance. It is this narrow definition which has raised the most objections. Partly because of these objections, the ASB announced a review of FRS 1 in 1994.

Modern day cash management is an extremely complex activity and this complexity is not reflected in the narrow definition adopted by the ASB. For instance, if a company has surplus cash over, say, the next six months, it would be foolish to leave those funds idle in a bank account. Far better to invest it over that period in some form of relatively risk-free security such as government stocks which will mature at the end of the period. The question then arises as to whether this is an investment similar to the purchase of a fixed asset or merely a more efficient way of holding cash.

If the statement is primarily concerned with liquidity, then liquidity should be the determining factor in identifying whether a particular investment is a cash equivalent. This would require a redefinition of cash equivalents to include all financial investments – that is, investments other than in physical or intangible assets – which can be readily convertible into known amounts with insignificant risk of changes in their value. Consider, for example, the possibility of investing in a savings bank where a higher rate of interest is offered in exchange for, say, a six-month notice of any withdrawal. Such accounts rarely prevent investors from obtaining their cash. Rather, a penalty is imposed in the form of a reduced interest rate if the notice given is less than six months. For many investors, the access to the original cash, despite the interest rate penalty, would be included in a definition of liquidity.

As another example, consider a financial investment in government stocks or some other equally risk-free security made 22 months ago and assume the investment had a two-year term. With repayment in two months' time, many investors would view this as part of their liquidity – probably more so than a financial investment made today and maturing in three months' time. Despite this, none of the examples described would be considered as cash equivalents under FRS 1.

Viability and financial adaptability

If the primary objectives of the standard are viability and financial adaptability, then the argument about definitions is less important. Instead, the emphasis will be on showing the quality of the profit earned by identifying the extent to which the business generates and absorbs cashflow in making its profits; in other words, the ability of profit to turn itself into cash.

Through time, assets will need to be replaced merely to maintain current levels of operations. Because of this, a case can be made out for differentiating between those investing activities which merely replace existing assets and those investing activities which increase operating capacity. The suggestion is that those investing activities required to maintain the current levels of operations should be shown as part of the *operating* cashflow. This concept is known as *free cashflow*. Formally free cashflow is the cashflow after interest, taxation and on-going capital expenditure but before strategic acquisitions and disposals. As such, it is a measure of the company's ability to be self-financing.

One possible objection to this approach is that it might fail the reliability test identified in the ASB's Statement of Principles. Replacement assets, by virtue of being more modern, will rarely be exactly the same as the original ones. To that extent, there might be an element of enhancement in the replacement. Nevertheless, some companies find it meaningful to differentiate between replacement and enhancement. Guinness plc, for example, provided a supplementary statement showing free cashflow at the foot of its cashflow statement in its 1993 accounts.

SUMMARY

Measuring business activity only by the value of cash transactions can be distorting. Waiting until cash is received or paid would give no real measure of either the sales level achieved or the level of production. Because of this, traditional accounting developed rules to identify profits based on the accruals concept of matching income with expenditure. However beneficial this might be, it both allows judgement to creep in when determining profit and underplays the importance of cash in a business. Cash is the life blood of a business. Without it, creditors cannot be paid nor stocks acquired. Merely showing the cash balance at the year end on the balance sheet is inadequate.

Year end cash can easily be manipulated by encouraging debtors to pay earlier than usual and delaying payments to creditors. A single figure also does not identify the sources of the cash. Providing cash is available in the business, a company can continue in existence at least for the short term, even though profitability may be low or even negative. An apparently profitable company with few cash resources, however, is likely to face difficulties.

It was because of this that the Accounting Standards Committee first addressed the issue of a supplementary statement to the profit and loss account and balance sheet to show what was happening to funds within an enterprise. Unfortunately, not only did its resulting SSAP 10 fail to define funds, it also approached the issue from a (modified) working capital approach. Perhaps even worse, it fudged the issue of the acquisition and disposal of subsidiaries.

FRS 1, the first Financial Reporting Standard issued by the more powerful Accounting Standards Board, has grasped this nettle. It firmly favours cashflow reporting with additional notes to the statement to cover other major funds flows. In terms of Example 11.3 for instance, a note would be required showing the net assets and the consideration given in acquiring the subsidiary. Certainly FRS 1 requires more information than appears on the face of the profit and loss account and balance sheet. Cash received from the sale of assets has to be disclosed as must the cash implications of the acquisition. Nowhere is this brought out more clearly than in the cashflow statement to accompany the balance sheet and profit and loss account of Example 11.3. From a casual glance of both documents, it is not clear that operations are responsible for a sizeable cash outflow nor that matters would have been much worse had it not been for the acquisition of a large cash balance by taking over the subsidiary. Certainly, with its standardised format, the FRS 1 cashflow statement is more easily understood by the user. Unfortunately, the standard's greatest strength – the reduction in directors' freedom to choose the presentation and extent of disclosure – is also its weakness. Objections can legitimately be made about the definition of cash and cash equivalents. Equally, there is a strong argument to be made for differentiating between investing activities which merely replace operating capacity and activities which enhance that capacity.

FURTHER READING

Lee, T. A. (1984) *Cash Flow Accounting*, Van Nostrand Reinhold.
Lewis, R. and Pendrill, D. (1994) *Advanced Financial Accounting*, 4th edn, Pitman.
Loveday, G. (1992) 'Cash Flow: When the Fiddling Has to Stop', *Accountancy* (June).

TEST YOUR UNDERSTANDING

1 Cashflow statements in the UK have to be prepared in a format determined by:
  (a) FRS 1;
  (b) FRS 3;
  (c) SSAP 6;
  (d) SSAP 10;
  (e) The European Union's Fourth Directive;
  (f) The European Union's Seventh Directive.

2 Identify three possible definitions of funds.

3 A cashflow statement can be prepared by analysing and summarising the detailed transactions in the cash account. Identify an alternative method of deriving similar data.

4 How does the ASB define cashflow?

5 Park plc acquired Foreman Ltd by issuing 200,000 £1 shares and paying cash of £100,000. The market value of the shares were £3 each. At the time of acquisition, the balance sheet of Foreman showed cash of £150,000. In Park's cashflow statement at the year end, this part of the transaction would be recorded as:
  (a) cash outflow £700,000;
  (b) cash inflow £150,000;

(c) cash outflow £300,000;

(d) cash inflow £50,000.

6 Differentiate between the gross or direct method and the net or indirect method for determining cashflows.

7 Identify the headings making up a cashflow statement.

8 What is meant by the expression 'free cashflow'?

QUESTIONS

1 Nimrod Ltd is a small company based in Malvern. Its balance sheet for the year just ended is reproduced below along with the previous year's balance sheet. Also enclosed is a summary of the company's profit and loss account for the year. There have been no disposals of assets during the year.

Balance sheet	Last year (£000)	This year (£000)	Profit and loss account for the year	(£000)
Fixed assets at cost	600	1,000	Profit on ordinary activities before tax	270
Less depreciation	200	240	Taxation	70
	400	760	Profit after tax	200
Current assets			Dividends	80
Stocks	400	350	Retentions for the year	120
Debtors	120	320	Add retentions brought forward	540
Cash and bank	400	360	Retentions carried forward	660
	920	1,030		
Current liabilities				
Trade creditors	300	180		
Corporation tax	50	70		
Dividends payable	30	80		
	380	330		
Net current assets	540	700		
	940	1,460		
Less loans		400		
	940	1,060		
Financed by				
Ordinary share capital	400	400		
Retentions	540	660		
	940	1,060		

Using the above information, prepare a cashflow statement which meets the requirements of FRS 1. (Loan interest can be ignored.)

2 The accounts of James Sound Systems Ltd for the year just ended are reproduced below. During the year, the fixed assets were revalued by £110,000 while assets originally costing £240,000 and with accumulated depreciation of £50,000 were sold for £230,000.

Depreciation for the year, charged to the profit and loss account and included within administration costs, came to £90,000.

During the year, the loan outstanding at the beginning of the year was retired and replaced by a new one. Interest of 10 per cent per annum had been paid on the new loan during the year and accounted for within administration costs. In addition, the company had issued some new ordinary shares. Issue costs, again accounted for within administration costs, totalled £60,000.

Balance sheet	Last year (£000)		This year (£000)		Profit and loss account for the year	(£000)
Fixed assets at cost		400		900	Turnover	950
Less depreciation		120		160	Cost of sales	300
		280		740	Gross profit	650
Current assets					Administration costs	415
Stocks	120		200		Net profit before taxation	235
Debtors	200		300		Corporation Tax	70
Cash and bank	800		350		Net profit after tax	165
	1,120		850		Dividends proposed	20
Current liabilities					Retentions for the year	145
Trade creditors	180		140		Add opening retentions	360
Corporation tax	60		80			505
Dividends payable	10		20		Transfer to capital reserve	30
	250		240		Closing retentions	475
Net current assets		870		610		
		1,150		1,350		
Less loans		400		220		
		750		1,130		
Financed by						
Ordinary share capital		200		300		
Share premium account		50		75		
Capital reserve		140		280		
Retentions		360		475		
		750		1,130		

Produce a cashflow statement for James Sound Systems Ltd for the year.

3*   On 1 July 19X7, Alpen Aggregates plc acquired all the share capital of Cambridge Concrete plc. The purchase consideration was £280 million which was satisfied by the issue of 90 million £1 shares plus £100 million cash. The group balance sheet and profit and loss account at the year ended 31 December 19X7, along with the assets and liabilities of Cambridge Concrete at the time of acquisition, are reproduced below. The book values of Cambridge Concrete were also considered to be the fair values.

Balance sheets	Group at 31.12 19X6 (£ m)	Group at 31.12 19X7 (£ m)	Subsidiary at 1.7.19X7 (£ m)	**Group profit and loss account for 19X7**	(£ m)
Tangible fixed assets	850	950	80	Operating profit	300
Stocks	180	290	20	Dividends receivable	20
Debtors	100	80	10	Interest payable	(50)
Cash	30	20	170	Group profit for the year	270
Trade creditors	(90)	(120)	(40)	Group taxation	(100)
Other creditors	(60)	(140)		Group profit after tax	170
	1,010	1,080	240	Dividends	(40)
Debentures	(300)	(100)		Transfer to general reserve	(30)
	710	980	240	Retained profit	100
Financed by					
£1 ordinary shares	310	400	140		
Share premium	80	170	40		
General reserve	40	70			
Retained profit	280	340	60		
	710	980	240		

Other creditors within the group at the year end comprise £100 million corporation tax and £40 million dividends (£40 million and £20 million respectively for 19X6). Group depreciation for the year totalled £160 million. In addition, tangible fixed assets with a net book value of £220 million were sold for a profit of £40 million.

Prepare a group cashflow statement for the year end 31 December 19X7.

CHAPTER 12

Financial reporting – the impact of inflation

The traditional assumption of accounting has been that the unit of currency is stable. With inflation, however, data are distorted and consequently accounting is not even fulfilling its basic stewardship role, as adding pounds of different years in a depreciation currency is not particularly meaningful. Two major methods have been proposed to tackle the issue of inflation, namely the use of current purchasing power and the use of current costs.

This chapter:

- Identifies the major issue as being that of capital maintenance

- Demonstrates the logic of current purchasing power and identifies the critical difference between monetary and non-monetary items

- Develops the argument in favour of current cost accounting and discusses the concept of deprival value

- Provides worked examples of both methods

- Critically appraises both methods of adjusting for inflation

Financial reports have traditionally been based on the accruals concept. Charging the historical cost of expenses consumed against turnover maintained the money value of capital. Any profit could then be distributed without impoverishing the security of creditors.

CAPITAL MAINTENANCE AND RISING PRICES

Specific price changes

Distributing all the profit as a dividend – although maintaining the *money* value of capital – may prevent a company from continuing its current levels of operations. The cost of a fixed asset, for example, may have increased. Consequently, depreciation based on historical costs will retain insufficient resources in the business to provide for the asset's ultimate replacement. This difficulty has never concerned the law. All that mattered was for the creditors to be protected to the extent of the money value of the capital. That the payment of the dividend might not maintain the operating capacity of the business was felt to be a shareholder choice, of no consequence to others.

Such a view may be appropriate for the owner-managed type of company where shareholders have access to the detailed financial records of the company. They, after all, can form their own judgement on the level of retentions required to maintain operating capacity. For other types of company, where ownership and control are separated, it is arguably less appropriate. But even accepting the narrow concept of money capital maintenance, there is a further problem.

General price changes

Implicit within all accounting reports has been the assumption of a stable unit of currency, enabling transactions to be added. However, inflation – generally rising prices – destroys much of the meaning from such additions. Little sense can be made from adding a pound of assets today to a pound of assets of yesteryear as a measure of total resources. It is the equivalent of adding a pound to a dollar without translating them into a common currency. By maintaining only the money value of capital, its real value falls in periods of inflation, to the disadvantage of creditors.

Inflation and UK financial reports

In principle, there are two ways of accounting for inflation. The good news is that the Accounting Standards Committee has addressed both approaches by the issue of Statements of Standard Accounting Practice. The bad news is that both statements have been withdrawn. It could be argued that the withdrawal of the ASC from the debate is because inflation has fallen considerably in the UK. Even a modest annual inflation rate of 4 per cent, however, is equivalent to 22 per cent over five years or 48 per cent over ten years. With many assets having a life considerably in excess of this, inflation can still distort balance sheet values. The reasons for the failure of the accountancy profession to address the issue therefore have to be found elsewhere.

Certainly viewing company directors as patrons might offer some insight. Just as the temporal method of foreign currency translation was abandoned in the USA following concern about its effect on reported profits, so adjusting for inflation reduced the reported profits of a large number of companies.

To be fair, the issue is more complex than this. The two possible methods of adjusting for inflation have such different fundamental assumptions about the purpose of accounts that conflict was perhaps inevitable. The one simply involves adjusting the historical values in the final accounts to their equivalent in pounds today; the other asks more fundamental questions about what resources have been consumed and what resources are required to maintain the business. Both approaches are considered below.

CURRENT PURCHASING POWER

In the absence of inflation, the historical cost of an asset measures the resources given up at the time of its acquisition. Inflation, however, distorts this information. The purchase of a fixed asset twelve months ago at a cost of £40,000, for example, is equivalent to £80,000 today if annual inflation is 100 per cent. Consequently, the £40,000 cost in the year end balance sheet will need amending if the distorting effects of inflation are to be neutralised.

The translation process

Current purchasing power accounting does this by translating the original cost into its current day equivalent of £80,000. Had there been no inflation, no adjustment would have been necessary. Current purchasing power accounting is therefore purely concerned with eliminating the distortion resulting from inflation by showing costs re-expressed in pounds today. Pounds today are used because a user understands the resources they will buy – which is why the technique is called current purchasing power. As such it is a process of translation from one value of currency into another and makes no attempt to show current values.

To demonstrate the workings of current purchasing power accounting, consider the balance sheets in Exhibit 12.1 which show the financial position of four companies exactly one year ago. To simplify matters, assume no trading has taken place over the current year but that there has been 20 per cent inflation.

Exhibit 12.1 Current purchasing power outlined

Company A		Company B		Company C		Company D	
Fixed assets	£1,000	Cash	£1,000	Debtors	£1,000	Fixed assets	£1,000
	£1,000		£1,000		£1,000		£1,000
Financed by:		Financed by:		Financed by:		Financed by:	
Ordinary shares	£600	Ordinary shares	£600	Ordinary shares	£600	Ordinary shares	£200
Retentions	£400	Retentions	£400	Retentions	£400	Retentions	£300
						Loan	£500
	£1,000		£1,000		£1,000		£1,000

With no trading, the year end historical cost balance sheets will be the same as those at the beginning of the year and profit in each case will be zero. There has, however, been 20 per cent inflation. Consequently paying out £1 a year ago was equivalent to paying out £1.20 today.

The treatment of fixed assets

For company A, the £1,000 cost of the fixed assets in the opening balance sheet is equivalent to £1,200 expressed in today's pounds. Similarly the share capital can be re-expressed as the equivalent of £720 in pounds today while the retentions can likewise be adjusted to £480. The result is an opening balance sheet re-expressed in terms of current purchasing power. This is not to say that the fixed assets are currently worth £1,200. Rather the adjustment is measuring the real resources given up in acquiring those assets by expressing their cost in the familiar form of pounds today.

The year end balance sheet can also be expressed in CPP terms. Nothing has changed and so the fixed asset with an historical cost of £1,000 is still equivalent to £1,200 in today's pounds.

The treatment of shareholders' funds

At the beginning of the year the capital was the equivalent of £720 today and this needs to be maintained not only to maintain the same real protection to creditors but also to determine if a profit has been made. Using a balance sheet analysis, profit is represented by the change in retentions. With year end fixed assets of £1,200 and share capital of £720, the difference is retentions of £480 and so there has neither been a profit nor a loss. The only change has been to translate elements expressed in pounds of yesteryear into pounds today, in much the same way that foreign currencies are translated into the home currency.

The treatment of cash

Company B is similar to company A except its £1,000 of assets are all in the form of cash. The opening balance sheet expressed in current purchasing power terms will also show assets of £1,200, capital of £720 and retentions of £480. There is, however, a difference in the year end CPP balance sheet.

Because company B held its opening £1,000 of assets in the form of cash, one year later it will still be only holding £1,000 of cash. There has been a genuine loss. At the beginning of the year, the £1,000 of cash would have bought a basketful of goods which today would cost £1,200. By the year end it would only buy goods costing £1,000, a loss of £200 through holding cash.

Inflation has whittled away the real value of the money. Like all other losses, this will reduce retentions. The lower of cost or net realisable value rule forces the year end CPP balance sheet to show the reality of only £1,000 of assets. Maintaining the real value of capital at £720 leaves retentions as the difference of £280 and so the CPP shareholders' funds have fallen by £200 as a result of holding money.

The treatment of debtors

Company C's only asset is a debtor of £1,000. Once again, its opening CPP balance sheet will be similar to companies A and B both in terms of asset values and shareholders' funds expressed in pounds today. By the year end, however, the debtor has not paid and still owes £1,000. The debt is fixed in monetary terms at £1,000 and so company C has lost £200 of purchasing power over the year in the same way as if it had held cash.

The treatment of creditors

This logic applies in reverse when a company has creditors. With 20 per cent inflation, company D's opening CPP balance sheet will show fixed assets equivalent to £1,200 today. Adjusting the sources of finance also by 20 per cent to show their present-day equivalents, capital will be £240, retentions £360 and the loan £600. With no trading, the closing CPP balance sheet will still show fixed assets of £1,200 and capital maintained at £240. The loan, however, is an obligation fixed in monetary terms at £500. This is the limit of the company's liability and so CPP retentions at the year end will total £460, an increase of £100 reflecting the gain from owing £100 less loan in real terms.

MONETARY AND NON-MONETARY ITEMS

Developing the current purchasing power balance sheet

The mechanics of current purchasing power accounting can be demonstrated by using two of the four companies as examples. The first stage is simply to translate all elements of the opening balance sheet into current purchasing power to express the opening balance sheet in terms of pounds today.

The next stage is to produce the year end balance sheet in the same unit of currency, enabling like to be measured with like. Any difference in the reserves will reflect the profit or loss for the period. With no trading, any profit or loss can only occur because of inflation. However, if the same fixed assets exist at both the beginning and end of a period, their values will be identical whether measured in historical cost or current purchasing power terms. Gains and losses from inflation can therefore only occur because of changes in the value of monetary items such as debtors, creditors and cash which are fixed in monetary terms.

The effect of this on companies B and D is shown in Exhibit 12.2 where pluses and minuses are once again used to identify assets and liabilities. Company A has been excluded as it exhibits neither a gain nor a loss while company C has been excluded as it merely replicates company B.

From an analysis of company B's opening and closing CPP balance sheets, £200 of current purchasing power has been lost because it chose to keep all its assets in the form of cash and this is reflected in the decrease in CPP retentions.

Company D has kept all of its assets in a non-monetary form and so has suffered neither a gain nor a loss as a result. However, at the beginning of the year, the loan was equivalent to £600 today and as this is fixed in monetary terms, there has been a gain from this source of £100. Losses or gains from inflation can therefore only happen if a business has either net monetary assets or net monetary liabilities.

Exhibit 12.2 Adjusting to current purchasing power

		Company B						Company D		
	Historic cost	Opening CPP	Loss	Closing CPP			Historic cost	Opening CPP	Gain	Closing CPP
Cash	+£1,000	+£1,200	–£200	£1,000	Fixed assets		£1,000	£1,200	nil	£1,200
	£1,000	£1,200		£1,000			£1,000	£1,200		£1,200
Financed by:					Financed by:					
Share capital	–£600	–£720		–£720	Share capital		–£200	–£240		–£240
Retentions	–£400	–£480	+£200	–£280	Retentions		–£300	–£360	–£100	–£460
					Loan		–£500	–£600	+£100	–£500
	£1,000	£1,200		£1,000			£1,000	£1,200		£1,200

Choice of index

Converting to current purchasing power requires an index of changing prices. Because CPP accounting is trying to eliminate the effects of inflation in general, the index should be one of general price changes rather than a narrower, more specific index.

In the UK, the Index of Retail Prices has normally been used. If the index twelve months ago stood at 120 but now stands at 150, goods in general are $^{30}/_{120}$ or 25 per cent more expensive and the index to translate expenditure of one year ago into its equivalent today is $^{150}/_{120}$ or 1.25.

To translate non-monetary assets and liabilities originating a year ago into their CPP equivalent involves multiplying the amount by 150 to represent current-day pounds and dividing by 120, the value of the pound when the transaction took place. This logic applies to both the opening and closing balance sheets.

Monetary items, however, are treated differently. The $^{150}/_{120}$ rate will be used to translate the opening monetary items into their year end equivalents as the 120 index is the pound's value at that date. At the year end, the relevant index will be 150 and so the rate to be used is $^{150}/_{150}$ or unity. Put simply, when converting monetary items at the year end, a pound today is worth a pound today and so no adjustments are necessary.

This process of translation is similar to that involved in the temporal method of currency translation in so far as the denominators in the index are concerned. The numerator will always be the current index of prices. For non-monetary assets and liabilities, the denominator will be the historical rate, the rate in existence at the time of the transaction. For monetary items, the relevant denominator will be the closing rate, the rate existing at the balance sheet date.

CURRENT PURCHASING POWER AND TRADING

Having established how to treat monetary and non-monetary items and how to develop an inflation index, it is now possible to show how these are used in a simplified set of final accounts by making use of the data given in Example 12.1.

Example 12.1

A company was formed 12 months ago with fixed assets of £50,000, stock costing £30,000 and a cash balance of £20,000. These were financed by ordinary share capital of £100,000. Two-thirds of the stock was sold in the year for £70,000 cash. In calculating the annual profit, depreciation of 20 per cent is to be provided. No other transactions took place.

An index of prices stood at 687.5 on 1 January, 750 on 1 July and 825 on 31 December.

The historical cost final accounts

In order to show inflation adjusted accounts using current purchasing power, it is first necessary to calculate the historical annual profit and derive the opening and closing historical cost balance sheets. These are shown in Exhibit 12.3 where the profit and loss account is represented by the bold figures.

Exhibit 12.3 The historical cost final accounts

(£000)	Opening balance sheet	Sales	Cost of sales	Depreciation	Closing balance sheet
Fixed assets	+50			−10	+40
Stock	+30		−20		+10
Cash	+20	+70			+90
	100				140
Ordinary capital	−100				−100
Profit and loss		**−70**	**+20**	**+10**	**−40**
	100				140

The CPP balance sheet

As with historical accounts, CPP profit can be calculated by analysing revenues and expenses or by comparing the difference between the opening and closing values on the balance sheets. The balance sheet analysis is shown in Exhibit 12.4 where the opening balance sheet is first converted to year end CPP pounds and then compared with the closing balance sheet produced on a similar basis.

With both balance sheets expressed in current purchasing power and opening retentions of nil, the closing retentions of £30,000 – found by deducting the share capital from the closing net assets – must equal the profit for the period.

Exhibit 12.4 The opening and closing CPP balance sheets

(£000)	Opening HC balance sheet	Index	Opening CPP balance sheet	Closing HC balance sheet	Index	Closing CPP balance sheet
Fixed assets	+50	825/687.5	60	+40	825/687.5	48
Stock	+30	825/687.5	36	+10	825/687.5	12
Cash	+20	825/687.5	24	+90	825/825	90
	100		120	140		150
Ordinary capital	−100	825/687.5	120	−100	825/687.5	120
Retentions	nil	825/687.5	nil	−40	Balance	30
	100		120	140		150

The CPP profit and loss account

The CPP can be confirmed from an analysis of the profit and loss account expressed in current purchasing power terms. The numerator for each profit and loss account entry will again be 825 to express the values in year end pounds but the denominator must be the price index at the time the transactions took place. To determine the CPP profit therefore requires information about when the sales and expenses were incurred. Whenever there is inflation, receiving £1 at the beginning of the year is going to be worth more than receiving the same amount at the year end.

Initially assume the sale took place at the year end. This will involve no adjustment to the sales value as it will already be in current purchasing power terms at 31 December. The £30,000 of stock, however, was acquired when the price index stood at 687.5 to give a CPP value of £36,000. With two-thirds sold, the cost to the profit and loss account must be £24,000. Alternatively this could have been calculated directly by simply uprating the historical cost of sales to take account of the change in the price index in the way shown in Exhibit 12.5.

Depreciation follows a similar argument and can be calculated by taking 20 per cent of the original CPP cost or uprating the cost in the historical profit and loss account.

Exhibit 12.5 The CPP profit and loss account – sales at the year end

(£000)	Historic cost	Index	Current purchasing power
Turnover	70	825/825	70
Cost of sales	20	825/687.5	24
Gross profit	50		46
Depreciation	10	825/687.5	12
Net profit	40		34

There is one slight problem. The profit figure according to the profit and loss account does not agree with the profit figure according to the balance sheet. As the historical cost figures are in agreement, the difference has to lie with the CPP adjustments.

Adjusting for monetary assets and liabilities

The only way CPP adjustments can affect profit is through holding monetary assets or liabilities. At the beginning of the year, the company had £20,000 of cash. It held this amount throughout the year, unlike the £70,000 from sales which were only originated at the year end. The £90,000 cash in the closing balance sheet can therefore be analysed further.

The £20,000 cash held since the beginning of the year was worth the equivalent of £24,000 in today's pounds as demonstrated in the CPP opening balance sheet. At the end of the year it was still being held but with a current value equal to its cash amount of £20,000. There has therefore been a loss from holding monetary assets of £4,000. No loss occurred on the other £70,000 cash as this was only received at the year end and so is already expressed in CPP pounds. Consequently the net CPP profit to be reported is £30,000 made up of the £34,000 CPP profit from operations less the £4,000 loss on holding net monetary assets.

The timing of monetary transactions

Had the sales taken place at the beginning of the year, the opening historical cash balance would have been £90,000 which would have translated to £108,000 in today's pounds. By holding this as cash, the year end CPP balance sheet would still only show cash of £90,000 with a consequent loss on monetary assets of £18,000. Exactly when transactions involving monetary items such as debtors, creditors or cash takes place is therefore critical to the computation of the loss or gain from monetary items.

To demonstrate this, assume that the £70,000 sales in Example 12.1 took place on average half way through the year. The resulting profit and loss account before any loss or gain on monetary items is shown in Exhibit 12.6.

Exhibit 12.6 The CPP profit and loss account – sales half way through the year

(£000)	Historic cost	Index	Current purchasing power
Turnover	70	825/750	77
Cost of sales	20	825/687.5	24
Gross profit	50		53
Depreciation	10	825/687.5	12
Net profit	40		41

The only difference between the profit and loss accounts is due to the different timings of the sales. With sales taking place on average half way through the year, this was equivalent to receiving £77,000 at the year end. The result is an increase in CPP net profit from £34,000 to £41,000. There will, however, be no change in the year end CPP balance sheet as identical assets and liabilities are being held. The balance sheet profit will still be £30,000 and so the loss on monetary items must be £11,000 to reconcile with the profit and loss account figure.

This can be verified by analysing the movement on monetary items – only cash in this example – and translating them into CPP terms. At the beginning of the year the net monetary items comprised cash of £20,000 with a CPP value of £24,000. Half way through the year, £70,000 was received with a value today of £77,000. In terms of CPP, year end cash should therefore equal £101,000. The actual cash, however, is only £90,000 and so there has been a loss of £11,000 as a result of holding monetary assets. With this adjustment, the CPP profit and loss account reconciles to the closing balance sheet.

CPP ACCOUNTS – A FULL EXAMPLE

To produce a full set of inflation adjusted accounts using current purchasing power requires the profit and loss account and both the opening and closing balance sheets to be expressed in current pounds. From this it will be possible to derive not only the CPP operating profit but also any gain or loss from holding monetary items. With this in mind, a full set of CPP accounts can be prepared using the data given in Example 12.2.

Example 12.2

The opening and closing balance sheets of Albertville plc are given below along with the profit and loss account for the current year. The company's fixed assets were purchased at the time of incorporation when a general price index stood at 240. The index stood at 288 when the opening stocks were purchased and at 342.86 when the closing stocks were acquired. At the beginning of the year the index stood at 300 and this had increased to 360 by the year end although the average for the year was 333.33. Sales, purchases, other expenses and the loan interest can be assumed to have occurred on average throughout the year.

Balance Sheet	Last year (£000)	This year (£000)	Profit and loss account this year	(£000)	(£000)
Fixed assets	300	300	Turnover		400
Less Depreciation	120	180	Opening stock	60	
	180	120	Purchases	200	
Stocks	60	160	Less closing stock	–160	
Debtors	30	40	Cost of sales		100
Cash	5	60	Gross profit		300
	275	380	Depreciation	60	
			Loan interest	25	
Ordinary share capital	120	120	Other expenses	200	285
Retentions	45	60	Net profit for the year		15
Loan	100	100			
Trade creditors	10	100			
	275	380			

Deriving the opening and closing CPP balance sheets

The first step is to recalculate the opening and closing balance sheets in terms of current purchasing power. The numerator in all cases will be 360 to convert balance sheet amounts to current pounds. In the opening balance sheet the fixed assets and capital will use 240 as the denominator, the price index when those transactions took place. The stock in the opening balance sheet will use 288 as its denominator, representing the price level when the stocks were purchased, while all of the monetary items will use the denominator applicable to the date of the opening balance sheet.

A similar process is required to produce the closing balance sheet except the original stocks have since been sold. When the closing stocks were purchased the price index stood at 342.86 and so this will be the denominator necessary to translate their value to current purchasing power. The revised balance sheets for Albertville are shown in Exhibit 12.7.

Exhibit 12.7 The opening and closing CPP balance sheets

(£000s)	Opening HC balance sheet	Index	Opening CPP balance sheet	Closing HC balance sheet	Index	Closing CPP balance sheet
Fixed assets	+180	360/240	+270	+120	360/240	+180
Stock	+60	360/288	+75	+160	360/342.86	+168
Debtors	+30	360/300	+36	+40	360/360	+40
Cash	+5	360/300	+6	+60	360/360	+60
	275		387	380		448
Ordinary capital	−120	360/240	−180	−120	360/240	−180
Retentions	−45	Balance	−75	−60	Balance	−68
Loan	−100	360/300	−120	−100	360/360	−100
Trade creditors	−10	360/300	−12	−100	360/360	−100
	275		387	380		448

The opening retentions of £75,000 is the balancing figure after all other assets and liabilities have been expressed in CPP terms. Using similar logic, the reserves had fallen to £68,000 by the end of the year, implying a CPP loss of £7,000.

The CPP profit and loss account

The current purchasing power profit and loss account shown in Exhibit 12.8 though suggests a loss of £24,000. The difference of £17,000 therefore must be the gain from having net monetary liabilities. Exhibit 12.8 verifies this gain and shows its composition.

The net monetary liabilities at the beginning of the year, comprising the debtors, cash, creditors and the loan, totalled £75,000 in historical cost terms or £90,000 in CPP terms and this can be verified from the opening balance sheet. By the end of the year this had increased to £100,000. The £100,000 comprises two elements, the £75,000 of net monetary liabilities effectively held throughout the year plus the £25,000 increase during the year.

On the assumption that this increase occurred on average half way through the year, the increase would have been £27,000 in CPP terms. As these net monetary liabilities are fixed in money terms, the amount owed at the year end remains at only £100,000 and so there has been a gain from net monetary liabilities of £17,000.

Exhibit 12.8 The CPP profit and loss account

(£000)		HC	Index		CPP
Turnover		400	360/333.33		432
Opening stock	60		360/288	75	
Purchases	200		360/333.33	216	
Less closing stock	−160		360/342.86	−168	
Cost of sales		100			123
Gross profit		300			309
Depreciation	60		360/240	90	
Loan interest	25		360/333.33	27	
Other expenses	200	285	360/333.33	216	333
Profit/loss		15			−24
Net monetary liabilities		HC	Index		
at beginning of the year		75	360/300	90	
Increase during the year		25	360/333.33	27	
				117	
Money value of monetary liabilities				100	
Gain from net monetary liabilities					17
Net loss as per balance sheet					−7

THE VALIDITY OF CURRENT PURCHASING POWER

The limited objective of CPP accounting

This approach to tackling the effect of inflation on financial reports is similar to the recommendations of the now withdrawn SSAP 7 Accounting for Changes in the Purchasing Power of Money. In evaluating current purchasing power adjustments, it is essential to keep in mind what is being attempted. The objective is simply to eliminate general inflation from the traditional historical cost financial reports. With zero inflation, there would be no adjustments and so both CPP and historical cost final accounts would be identical.

The purpose of the adjustments is to show the cost in today's currency of resources given up or acquired by an entity, a task fulfilled by historical cost accounts only when there is no inflation. The emphasis of CPP accounting is therefore on maintaining the *real* financial or money capital of the entity, similar to historical cost accounting when there is no inflation.

As with traditional accounting, CPP accounting makes no attempt to show current values other than through the application of the lower of cost or net realisable rule. Neither does it show whether the entity has maintained its operating potential. It would be unfair to criticise CPP accounting for these limitations. They are real limitations but they flow from historical cost accounting, not from current purchasing power adjustments as such.

Choice of index

A great deal of the criticism of current purchasing power focuses on the choice of the price index. SSAP 7 suggested the Index of Retail Prices or RPI. In the narrow sense of being verifiable, this has the advantage of being objective. To the extent that the underlying historical accounts are also objective, the result is a verifiable set of CPP accounts.

It has been argued, however, that the RPI with its base centred on 'middle income' households is inapplicable to business enterprises which purchase only a relatively narrow range of goods. Companies, it is argued, do not hold general purchasing power but rather specific purchasing power relevant to the relatively few items they wish to purchase.

However valid this might be for the company in terms of operating performance, it ignores the focus of traditional accounts. What is of concern is the consumption opportunities of shareholders and this is best measured by a general price index.

The effect on highly geared companies

A further criticism is that companies viewed as most risky by investors, those with excessive levels of borrowings and parallel obligations to pay out large amounts of interest irrespective of profitability, will appear to be more successful under a CPP regime.

Gains from net monetary liabilities do not reveal themselves as increases in cash. Nevertheless, high inflation does reduce the real amount borrowed as any home buyer in the UK throughout the middle 1980s will verify. With a loan at the beginning of the year of £1,000 in current purchasing power and at the end of the year of, say, £800, the loan has been reduced by £200. In effect there has been a hidden repayment. In a sophisticated economy, lenders will realise this and demand higher interest rates as compensation. It could therefore be argued that high interest rates as a result of inflation equally distort operating profits and by including the gains from net monetary liabilities, this distortion is reduced.

CPP's rejection in the UK

Why then was the CPP method of adjusting for inflation rejected? Certainly it did not find universal favour with all company directors, especially those who could see their reported profits being reduced by its introduction.

Secondly, the Accounting Standards Committee required CPP accounts to be produced in addition to the historical accounts and this was felt to be confusing.

The major reason, however, was a lack of confidence that CPP accounting was the best way of tackling the problem of inflation. Even before the publication of SSAP 7, the government had established a committee, known as the Sandilands Committee, to enquire into inflation accounting and from its early days, it was clear the Committee was looking at a totally different approach to inflation accounting. Perhaps because of this, the ASC made SSAP 7 only a provisional standard and not a mandatory one.

CURRENT COST ACCOUNTING

The Sandilands Committee rejected the idea of accounting for inflation using current purchasing power. Instead, it proposed a system based on the *specific price changes faced by an individual business enterprise* and which emphasised the need to maintain the specific purchasing power of that business rather than general purchasing power. It was also concerned that ordinary money should form the unit of account rather than the 'funny money' of CPP accounting. These proposals were taken up by the Accounting Standards Committee and formed the foundation for the subsequent SSAP 16 Current Cost Accounting.

The maintenance of operating capacity

Maintaining the purchasing power of the individual business is the same as maintaining operating capacity and this implies replacement cost accounting. However, strict adherence to the replacement cost accounting outlined in Chapter 6 may not always be valid. There may, for example, be occasions when a firm will not wish to replace a particular asset even though it wishes to remain in the same kind of business. Current cost accounting attempts to address this issue. It does so by developing a rule for valuing assets based on how badly off a business would be if deprived of any particular asset.

Deprival value

This idea of valuing an asset by its *deprival value* was first suggested by Bonbright[1] in assessing legal damages on the loss of an asset. It was then developed by Baxter[2] in relationship to depreciation and has since been extensively applied in other areas of accounting. Ignoring any intrinsic value, there are three possible values which can be attached to an individual asset: (a) its replacement cost, (b) its realisable value (or what it can be sold for), and (c) its economic value to the business. If a business were deprived of an asset through theft, destruction or whatever, the greatest expense faced would be the cost of replacing the asset. By an insurance company replacing the asset, the firm is as well off as it was before the loss, always providing there were no losses from any delay in replacing the asset.

There are, however, occasions when the replacement cost would overstate the loss. This will occur whenever the asset is not sufficiently profitable to be replaced. This is best demonstrated by a simple example.

Assume a family buys a tin of paint for £20 to redecorate a room. At that stage, being deprived of the paint would involve them having to replenish it at a cost of £20. Its deprival value is therefore £20, its replacement cost. Now assume that having bought the paint, the family decide it is the wrong colour but are unable to exchange it for some reason.

The family is faced with only three options: to sell the paint second-hand, to keep it in case it can be used elsewhere or to throw it away. If they choose to throw it away, the deprival value is nil. They are simply recognising it as being worthless, the £20 loss being a consequence of their original mistake rather than from being deprived of the paint. Two other options are possible, however: a neighbour might offer to buy the paint from them for £15; alternatively, they could use it in some other way such as painting a fence, saving the £8 cost of fence paint.

The family is now faced with three costs, the replacement cost of £20, the net realisable value of £15 by selling it to the neighbour or the value if used elsewhere within the family – its economic value – of £8. The replacement cost is irrelevant as there is no intention of replacing the original paint. But if deprived of the paint, they will be forced either to pay out £8 to paint the fence or lose the opportunity of gaining £15 from the sale to the neighbour. Clearly if the family were rational, they would sell the paint to the neighbour as this brings in £15 which is more than the saving from using it within the household. £15 is therefore its deprival value, the amount by which the family would be worse off by no longer having the asset.

Had the neighbour only offered £4 then the family would have been better off using the paint on the fence. Being deprived of the paint in those circumstances would involve additional expenditure of £8 to paint the fence and so the deprival value would be £8.

The deprival value rule

This simple example demonstrates the rule for determining deprival value. First, derive the economic value and the realisable value and choose whichever is the higher. Secondly, compare this figure with replacement cost and choose whichever is the lower. Exhibit 12.9 shows the rule in a diagrammatic form. The deprival value can never be greater than the replacement cost even if the economic value and realisable value are greater as, by replacing the asset, the entity is as well off as before the loss.

Exhibit 12.9 The deprival value rule

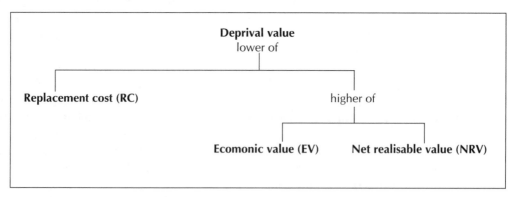

Probably the greatest difficulty for a business is determining the economic value. One approach would be to estimate the future cashflows from the asset and, by discounting, estimate their present value today. Fortunately, a company will rarely be in this situation. Logically, there are six permutations of the three values. These are shown in the table on p.389.

Of the six possible outcomes, only one involves the economic value as the deprival value. Four use replacement cost. This even understates the importance of replacement cost. Most assets will presumably be being used profitably. If this is the case, then the present value – the worth to the business in terms of cashflows generated – will be greater than the replacement cost. In most cases therefore an asset's deprival value will be its replacement cost.

Possible asset values			Deprival value
NRV > EV > RC			RC
NRV > RC > EV			RC
EV > RC > NRV			RC
EV > NRV > RC			RC
RC > EV > NRV			EV
RC > NRV > EV			NRV

THE CURRENT COST FINAL ACCOUNTS

Valuing assets and liabilities

Logically a current cost balance sheet should show assets and liabilities at their deprival value or *the value to the business* as it is sometimes called. In the majority of cases, this will involve fixed assets being stated at their replacement cost.

The treatment of current assets, however, will vary. Stock will need to be adjusted to show its current cost at the balance sheet date in a similar way to fixed assets while cash, being cash, is already at its value to the business. Debtors and creditors represent cash receivable and payable in the future. Applying the principle of discounted cashflow, technically their value to the business *today* will be less than their book value. Rarely if ever is any adjustment made to cover this timing difference – presumably because it would not be material.

The same immateriality argument, however, cannot apply to long term liabilities. Consider an irredeemable loan of £100,000 issued many years ago with a 5 per cent interest rate, and assume that current and future interest rates are going to be at least 10 per cent. Investors will not be prepared to pay £1 for each £1 unit of the loan to derive interest of 5p. By investing £1 elsewhere, a 10p return is obtainable. Market forces will drive down the stock exchange value of the loan to a total of £50,000, as only at that value would the £5,000 of interest give investors the 10 per cent return available elsewhere. Consequently the company could buy back the loan from the market at a cost of £50,000 rather than redeeming it. £50,000 is therefore the current cost of the loan to the company. Despite this no such adjustment is ever made in practice.

Values in the profit and loss account

Similar complexities apply when determining the values within the profit and loss account. Using the Hicksian idea of 'well-offness', a firm needs to have the same operating capacity at both the beginning and end of a period in order to declare a profit. This operating capital maintenance measure is by far the most popular although there are alternatives taking the narrower shareholder perspective of financial capital maintenance.

The maintaining of operating capacity is usually interpreted as maintaining the net operating assets of the business. However, difficulties arise in defining just what is included under this heading. Clearly fixed assets are part of the operating capacity. If their cost has increased, depreciation needs to be based on this revised amount in order to retain sufficient funds to provide for their replacement. Stock is also necessary to run a business and so this also must be based on replacement cost in order to maintain operating capacity.

Debtors, creditors and cash

The argument becomes more complicated when extended to debtors, creditors and cash. Other elements of working capital will increase as a result of rising prices. Increased costs of production are bound to increase selling prices in the long term. This is how inflation works its way through the system. If goods are sold on credit the money value of debtors will increase as a result of the price rises even though the physical volume of sales might remain the same. These have to be financed. (Strictly it is not the full amount of the debtors which need to be financed but only the debtors less the profit element.) An equal but opposite line of reasoning applies to creditors.

What is less clear is the extent to which this argument applies to other elements of working capital such as cash. After all, a retailer might need to keep a higher cash balance the higher the money value of sales. Indeed cash will fluctuate as the level of stock, debtors and creditors fluctuate. Some cash therefore is likely to be directly related to maintaining operating capacity.

Long term debt

Finally there is the argument that in a geared company, the shareholders do not have to bear all the increased cost of maintaining operating capacity. If a company is normally financed by 50 per cent borrowings, then it is likely to be financed in that proportion in the future. Arguably only that part of the increased cost of maintaining operating capacity financed by equity needs to be taken into account when determining operating profit.

Preparing the current cost accounts

There are four possible adjustments necessary to produce the current cost profit and loss account. The current cost profit and loss account will commence with the actual turnover for the year as current cost accounting uses the actual currency as the unit of measurement. From this must be deducted the expenses at their current cost *at the time the revenue was recognised*. A sale half way through the year will be matched with the current cost of the stock consumed at that time while a sale at the year end will be matched with the current cost of stock given up at the year end. The total cost of sales in the profit and loss account will therefore be an amalgam of earlier and later current costs.

The second adjustment will normally involve charging depreciation on the full replacement cost of the asset. The third adjustment will reflect the necessary additional funding of debtors and cash less creditors. Finally, the total of these adjustments needs to be reduced to the extent they are normally financed by loans and other long term borrowings.

The resulting current cost accounts can be prepared in one of two ways. Transactions can be converted to their current costs as they occur so that the final accounts are automatically in current cost form. This approach was used for replacement cost accounting in Chapter 6. Alternatively, historical cost accounts can be prepared and adjustments then made to show the current cost values – the treatment favoured by SSAP 16. Although the standard has now been withdrawn and no longer has any authority, the second treatment is shown below to give an insight into the alternative presentation.

THE FULL COST OF SALES ADJUSTMENT

The cost of sales adjustment is the difference between the historical cost of goods sold and the current cost. Deducting this adjustment from the historical cost profit or loss will give the profit based on the current cost of sales. Where sufficient records have been kept, it is possible to identify uniquely any single sale with the *current cost* of the resources given up in making that sale. This is demonstrated in Example 12.3.

Example 12.3

> Aberdeen Ltd uses a FIFO system for valuing stock. At the beginning of the year its only asset comprised 40 units of stock which had cost £5 each. This was also its current cost at that stage. On 1 March, 30 units were sold for £8 each and replaced by 20 units costing £5.50 each. Twenty units were sold on 1 July for the same price of £8 although the current cost had risen to £6. No other transactions took place before the end of the year by which time the current cost of the stock had risen to £6.50 per unit. All transactions were for cash.

The historical cost of sales

The recording of these transactions using historical cost is reproduced in Exhibit 12.10. The historical cost of the stock sold in the first sale relates to 30 units of the opening stock at £5 each. The FIFO cost of the next 20 units sold total £105. This comprises the final ten units of opening stock at £5 and ten units of the stock purchased at £5.50 each. The historical cost transactions of Aberdeen are shown in Exhibit 12.10 with the profit and loss account being shown in bold type. From this, the historical cost of sales can be identified as £255.

Exhibit 12.10 The historical cost final accounts

	Opening balance sheet	First sale	Cost of sales	Purchases	Second sale	Cost of of sales	Closing balance sheet
Stock	+£200		−£150	+£110		−£105	+£55
Cash		+£240		−£110	+£160		+£290
	£200						£345
Capital	−£200						−£200
Profit and loss		−£240	+£150		−£160	+£105	−£145
	£200						£345

Identifying the current cost adjustment

To translate the historical cost profit of £145 into its current cost equivalent requires some way of identifying price changes. Most organisations keep detailed records of stock movements for day-to-day control and these can easily be amended to incorporate current costs in a form similar to that shown in Exhibit 12.11 for the stock transactions of Aberdeen.

Exhibit 12.11 Historical and current cost stock movements

Date	Detail	Units	Historical cost	Current cost
1 January	Opening balance	40	£200	£200
1 March	Current cost adjustment	—	—	£20
		40	£200	£220
1 March	Sale	30	£150	£165
		10	£50	£55
1 March	Purchase	20	£110	£110
		30	£160	£165
1 July	Current cost adjustment	—		£15
		30	£160	£180
1 July	Sale 10 @ £5.00 £50			
	10 @ £5.50 £55	20	£105	£120
		10	£55	£60
31 December	Current cost adjustment	—		£5
		10	£55	£65

The historical cost stock receipts and issues are supplemented by current cost data. Before the first sale for example, the stock values are uprated to their current cost, enabling the cost of sales to be identified in both historical and current cost terms.

From this it can be seen that the cost of sales were understated by £15 in both cases while the closing value of stock is understated by £10. The historical cost profit therefore needs to be reduced by £30 to reflect current costs while the balance sheet stock value needs to be increased by £10. These adjustments create a current cost reserve of £40 as the other side to the transactions. The resulting current cost accounts of Aberdeen are shown in Exhibit 12.12.

Exhibit 12.12 The cost of sales adjustment and the final accounts

Profit and loss account		Balance sheet	
Turnover	£400	Stock	£65
Cost of sales	£255	Cash	£290
Historical cost profit	£145		£355
Current cost adjustment			
Cost of sales adjustment	£30	Capital	£200
Current cost profit	£115	Current cost reserve	£40
		Retentions	£115
			£355

APPROXIMATING THE COST OF SALES ADJUSTMENT

Average current costs

Current cost accounting matches sales in actual pounds with the current cost of those sales at the date of sale. With inflation, current costs matched with sales at the beginning of the year are likely to be lower than current costs matched with year end sales. But if sales take place *evenly throughout the year*, the lower current costs of earlier months will be compensated by the higher current costs of later months. Consequently, the approximate current cost of sales for the year can be found by multiplying the number of units sold by the average unit current cost for the year.

Recognising this enables a further approximation to be developed which eliminates the need for detailed current cost record keeping. The cost of sales – however valued – comprises opening stocks brought forward plus purchases for the year less closing stocks unsold. If purchases also *take place evenly throughout the year*, the earlier purchases will be at lower prices and the later purchases at higher prices. The total value of purchases will therefore already be at their average current cost for the year. If the opening and closing stocks can be expressed in similar current cost terms by the use of indices of stock prices, it is possible to estimate the current cost of sales. This is demonstrated in Example 12.4.

Example 12.4

The opening stock for Bromley Builders was £75,000. The stock had been purchased on average over the three previous months of the year. In addition, the company purchased £400,000 of additional stock evenly throughout the current year. Closing stocks, which were acquired on average over the last three months of the year, were valued at £90,000.

An index of building stock costs suggests the average for the fourth quarter of last year was 150, the average for the current year was 160 and the average for the final quarter of the current year was 180.

The replacement cost of sales using indices

Bromley Builders' cost of sales using both historical and current costs is shown in Exhibit 12.13. Because the purchases took place evenly throughout the year, they are already at their average current cost for the year. As the average stock index for the year was 160 and the opening stock was purchased when the index stood at only 150, the opening stock needs to be multiplied by $^{160}/_{150}$ to show its cost on the same current cost basis as purchases. Similarly, the closing stock was purchased when the index stood at 180 while the average index for the year was 160. It therefore needs to be multiplied by $^{160}/_{180}$ to show its value in average current costs for the year. With both stocks and purchases measured in the same average current costs, the current cost of sales will be £400,000. Consequently, the cost of sales adjustment, the adjustment required to bring the historical cost of sales up to its current cost, will be £15,000.

Exhibit 12.13 The cost of sales adjustment

	Historical cost	Index	Current cost
Opening stock	£75,000	160/150	£80,000
Purchases	£400,000	160/160	£400,000
Closing stock	−£90,000	160/180	−£80,000
Cost of sales	£385,000		£400,000

In fact there is no need to calculate the full current cost of sales to derive the cost of sales adjustment. Purchases are already at their average current cost for the year and require no adjustment. The difference between the two cost of sales figures arises solely from adjustments to the opening and closing stocks of £5,000 and £10,000 respectively. This is demonstrated in Exhibit 12.14.

Exhibit 12.14 The cost of sales adjustment

	Historical cost	Current cost	Adjustment
Opening stock	£75,000	£80,000	+£5,000
Purchases	£400,000	£400,000	nil
Closing stock	–£90,000	–£80,000	+£10,000
Cost of sales	£385,000	£400,000	£15,000

The opening stock needs to be increased by £5,000 to show it in terms of the average current cost for the year. The closing stock, however, needs to be reduced by £10,000 to value it on a similar base. Despite that the adjustment is shown as a plus. This is because closing stock is deducted from the total of opening stock plus purchases to derive the cost of sales and so £5,000 – (–£10,000) equals + £15,000.

THE MONETARY WORKING CAPITAL ADJUSTMENT

The problem of definition

Adjusting for changes in the monetary working capital requirements of a business is one of the more controversial areas of current cost accounting, partly because there is no single objective definition, unlike the cost of sales adjustment. Logically, if prices increase and volume stays the same then a company will have to finance a higher monetary level of debtors unless they can be encouraged to pay more quickly. Equally logically, part of this increased finance will be offset by an increased money amount of creditors.

Some firms might restrict their definition of monetary working capital within net operating assets to debtors less creditors. Others might include part of their cash balance on the basis that a higher monetary level of sales requires a higher cash float. Whether or not to include cash is made all the more difficult if it is remembered that there is a direct relationship between at least some of the cash balance and debtors, creditors and stock. Allow the level of debtors to increase and cash falls. Build up stocks and cash also falls. Pay creditors more quickly than usual and cash falls yet again. Cash – or at least part of cash – is therefore not a simple residual.

SSAP 16 recognised the difficulties of identifying in an objective way those monetary assets and liabilities which form part of the net operating assets of the business. It defined monetary working capital as (a) trade debtors, prepayments and trade bills receivable, plus (b) stock not subject to the cost of sales adjustment, less (c) trade creditors, accruals and trade bills payable *in so far as they arise from the day-to-day operating activities of the business* as distinct from transactions of a capital nature. However, it then went on to recognise fluctuations in bank balances and overdrafts resulting from changes in debtors, creditors and stock and allowed these to be included in monetary working capital.

Calculating the adjustment

For demonstration purposes, monetary working capital will be restricted to debtors less creditors. The issue then becomes one of identifying how much of the change in these balances is due to changing prices – and hence is part of the maintenance of existing operating capacity – and how much represents a real change resulting from higher volumes.

The solution follows the same logic as the cost of sales adjustment. The opening and closing balances for both debtors and creditors are recalculated using the average current costs for the year. To do this requires relevant indices. Creditors arise from purchasing raw materials and so an index based on the particular raw material will normally prove suitable for estimating creditors in current cost terms. Debtors, however, are associated with sales and involve the business financing the cost of the finished goods sold. To measure debtors in current cost terms therefore requires an index based on finished goods. With opening and closing balances being measured in the same unit of current costs, any difference must then represent a 'real' change separate from any change caused by price movements. This 'real' change can then be deducted from the historical cost change to show the change due to price movements. This is demonstrated in Example 12.5.

Example 12.5

At the beginning of the year Grantham Ltd had debtors of £55,000 and creditors of £40,000. By the end of the year these had risen to £97,500 and £60,000 respectively.

Raw material and finished goods indices for the period were as follows:

Index	Raw material	Finished goods
Beginning of the year	160	110
Average for the year	168	120
End of the year	180	130

The £55,000 of debtors at the beginning of the year is equivalent to £60,000 when expressed in average current costs for the year. With a finished goods price index of 130 at the end of the year, the closing debtors of £97,500 are equivalent to £90,000 in terms of mid-year current costs. The 'real' increase in debtors is therefore £30,000 and not £42,500 as shown using historical cost data. Consequently the £12,500 difference must reflect the increase in the value of debtors caused by increased prices. A similar argument applies to the creditors where the increase of £6,000 is due to price movements.

The £12,500 increase in the money value of debtors is being partly financed by the £6,000 increased money value of the creditors. As a result, the company needs to retain a net extra £6,500 within the business just to keep the same real level of debtors less creditors and hence maintain operating capacity. This it will do by reducing the historical cost profit by the £6,500 monetary working capital adjustment and increasing the current cost reserve by a similar amount. The detailed workings are shown in Exhibit 12.15.

Exhibit 12.15 The monetary working capital adjustment

Debtors	Historical cost	Index	Current cost	Adjustment
Opening balance	£55,000	120/110	£60,000	£5,000
Closing balance	£97,500	120/130	£90,000	£7,500
Difference	£42,500		£30,000	£12,500
Creditors				
Opening balance	£40,000	168/160	£42,000	£2,000
Closing balance	£60,000	168/180	£56,000	£4,000
Difference	£20,000		£14,000	£6,000

Monetary working capital adjustment: £12,500 – £6,000 = £6,500

THE DEPRECIATION ADJUSTMENT

As with all other expenses, current cost depreciation can either be calculated by using up-to-date current costs or indices. Using indices will certainly save time and expenses if fixed assets are highly specific and with a limited market. Whichever method of valuation is chosen, at the year end, fixed assets will be shown in the balance sheet at their current cost on that date.

The need for backlog depreciation

In the profit and loss account, however, expenses – including depreciation – will be shown at their *average current cost* for the year. The increase in depreciation for the year reported in the balance sheet will therefore not be the same as the depreciation charged to the profit and loss account. To overcome this problem, backlog depreciation similar to that required in replacement cost accounting will need to be provided. The implications of this are brought out in Example 12.6.

Example 12.6

A fixed asset was purchased one year ago for £160,000 when a relevant fixed asset index stood at 96. The asset is to be depreciated at 20 per cent per annum.

At the year end the index stood at 105 while the average for the year was 102.

The depreciation adjustment is the extra depreciation necessary to bring the historical depreciation up to its current cost equivalent based on average year values. With a historical cost of £160,000, 20 per cent depreciation will be £32,000. The current cost of the asset – using mid-year values – is £170,000 and so current cost depreciation will be £34,000. Adjusting the profit and loss account by the difference in depreciation will lower profits by £2,000 and therefore show depreciation on the same average valuation basis as cost of sales and the monetary working capital adjustment. The workings for this are shown in Exhibit 12.16.

Exhibit 12.16 The depreciation adjustment

	Historical costs	Mid-year index	Mid-year current costs	Year end index	Year end current costs
Cost	£160,000	102/96	£170,000	105/96	£175,000
Depreciation	£32,000	102/96	£34,000	105/96	£35,000
Net book value	£128,000		£136,000		£140,000

Recording the adjustments

Parallel with the depreciation adjustment will be a further adjustment reflecting the increase in the asset's value. The asset value will have been increased to reflect its current cost and the current cost reserve similarly increased. Depreciation is only an allocation of this (revised) cost and so, unlike other adjustments, it will not be recorded in the current cost reserve. Instead, the provision for depreciation will simply be increased to reflect the allocation of the increased current cost of the asset.

At the *year end*, however, the fixed asset's current cost is £175,000 and so the 20 per cent depreciation in year end current costs needs to be £35,000. Additional depreciation of £1,000 – backlog depreciation – therefore needs to be provided. Charging this to the current cost profit and loss account would destroy its valuation base of average current costs for the year. The only alternative is to account for the backlog depreciation via shareholders' funds and, in particular, the current cost reserve. The result will be a balance sheet reflecting current costs at the balance sheet date and a profit and loss account matching current costs of sales with the turnover generated throughout the year. The recording of the necessary adjustments are shown in Exhibit 12.17 where it is assumed the asset was purchased for cash.

Having recorded the historical cost transactions, the asset is then revalued. The provision for depreciation is then increased to show the average current cost for the year. Finally, back-log depreciation is provided to enable the balance sheet to fully reflect current costs at the balance sheet date.

Exhibit 12.17 The recording of the depreciation adjustment

(£000)	Historical cost purchase	Historical cost depreciation	Current cost adjustment	Depreciation adjustment	Back-log depreciation	
Fixed asset	+160		+15			+175
Provision for depreciation		−32		−2	−1	−35
NBV						+140
Cash	−160					−160
Profit and loss account		+32		+2		+34
Current cost reserve			−15		+1	−14

THE GEARING ADJUSTMENT

Justifying the gearing adjustment

Using the Hicksian idea of income, income is defined as the maximum that can be consumed while remaining in the same position at the end of a period as at the beginning. If a company financed its operating capacity by 50 per cent borrowings at the beginning of the year then to be in the same position, it needs to finance that same year end operating capacity by 50 per cent as well. Anything else and like is not being compared with like.

Current cost accounting is concerned with maintaining operating capacity and so if additional finance is required to maintain capacity, that is also likely to be partly financed by borrowings. Consequently the equity shareholders will not have to finance all of the current cost adjustments. This is the logic of the gearing adjustment. It seeks to show the current cost profit attributable to the ordinary shareholders.

The problem of definition

Conceptually there is a strong justification for making the gearing adjustment when income is viewed in its classical Hicksian sense. Where difficulties arise is in the definition of borrowings and equity.

Logically equity should be the shareholders' funds used to finance the current cost of the operating assets. Non-operating assets such as investments would then be excluded from the calculation. But one objection to this is that current costs will include the revalued fixed assets and these represent unrealised holding gains. To overcome this, the shareholders' funds in the historical accounts might be used.

The second difficulty is in choosing whether to use the opening or closing levels of equity and debt. Again the Hicksian definition of income is helpful. This relates income to the maintenance of the opening position, implying that the opening gearing should be maintained.

Finally there is the thorny issue of how to measure the value of borrowings. As has already been shown, the current cost of debt is its open-market value and with high market interest rates relative to the rate associated with the loans, the current value of the debt is likely to be below its book value.

SSAP 16 required a gearing adjustment to be made where finance was partly provided by borrowings. Net borrowings were defined as the aggregate of all liabilities and provisions (including convertible debentures and deferred tax but excluding dividends) other than those included within monetary working capital less the aggregate of all current assets other than those subject to a cost of sales adjustment and those included within monetary working capital.

Calculating the gearing adjustment

This convoluted expression is a catch-all phrase. Effectively it means net borrowings comprise items such as loans and debentures less any cash which is not viewed as being part of monetary working capital. The gearing was to be calculated using the data from both the opening and closing current cost accounts, in other words an average for the year, presumably because the gearing adjustment reduces the amounts of the other current cost adjustments and those were based on average current costs for the year. Formally, the gearing ratio was defined as:

$$\text{Gearing ratio} = \frac{L}{L + S}$$

where L is average *net* borrowings and S the average of the ordinary shareholders' interests. Together L + S is equivalent to the net operating assets in the entity. The effect of this is demonstrated in Example 12.7.

Example 12.7

The opening and closing current cost balance sheets of Plymouth plc before adjusting for gearing were as follows:

(£000)	Last year		This year	
Net fixed assets		850		1,000
Stock	250		340	
Debtors	210		230	
Bank	100		200	
	560		770	
Creditors	80	480	100	670
Net assets		1,330		1,670
Loan		300		300
		1,030		1,370
Financed by				
Ordinary share capital		500		500
Current cost reserve		290		380
Retentions		240		490
		1,030		1,370

Using the data in Example 12.7, it is assumed that the cash balance does not form any part of the company's monetary working capital. Consequently *net* borrowings in the opening balance sheet will be the loan of £300,000 less the bank of £100,000, a total of £200,000. At the year end, net borrowings will have fallen to £100,000 as a result of the increase in the cash balance. Consequently, average net borrowings for the year will be £150,000.

Having established the value of L, S can be found in one of two ways: by identifying the operating assets financed by shareholders or identifying the funds which finance those assets. The cash in this example is not part of the monetary working capital and so has to be deducted from net assets to derive net operating assets. From these operating assets have to be deducted the net borrowings to give the operating assets financed by the ordinary shareholders. This is equal to shareholders' funds as demonstrated in Exhibit 12.18.

Exhibit 12.18 The equity interest

(£000)	Last year	This year
Net assets	£1,330	£1,670
Less Bank	−£100	−£200
Net operating assets	£1,230	£1,470
Less *Net* borrowings	−£200	−£100
Shareholders' funds	£1,030	£1,370

Shareholders' funds were £1,030,000 at the beginning of the year and £1,370,000 at the end, giving an average for the year of £1,200,000. With both L and S defined in average terms, the gearing ratio will be:

$$\text{Gearing ratio} = \frac{L}{L + S} = \frac{£150,000}{£150,000 + £1,200,000} = 0.1111$$

Had the current cost adjustments affecting the profit and loss account totalled £100,000 only 89 per cent would be borne by the ordinary shareholders. The full current cost adjustments therefore would be reduced by £11,000 along with a reduction in the current cost reserve by a similar amount.

CURRENT COST ACCOUNTING – A FULL EXAMPLE

The cost of sales, depreciation and monetary working capital adjustments

Example 12.8 uses the historical cost accounting data of Albertville plc outlined in Example 12.2. By making the simplifying assumption that the company is a retailer, the stock indices can be used not only for the cost of sales adjustment but also for the monetary working capital adjustment.

Example 12.8

Specific indices relating to Albertville plc are reproduced below:

	Stock	Fixed assets
End of year	280.0	201.6
Date closing stock acquired	268.8	
Average for the year	252.0	189.0
Start of year	210.0	176.4
Date opening stock acquired	201.6	
Date fixed asset acquired		126.0

The adjustments necessary to produce the current cost profit and loss account are shown in Exhibit 12.19 and follow the logic developed earlier.

Exhibit 12.19 The current cost adjustments

(£000)	Historical cost	Index	Current cost		Historical cost	Index	Current cost
Cost of sales adjustment				**Depreciation adjustment**			
Opening stock	60	252/201.6	75	Depreciation for year	60	189/126	90
Purchases	200		200				
Closing stock	−160	252/268.8	−150				
Cost of sales	100		125				
Cost of sales adjustment			25	**Depreciation adjustment**			30

Monetary working capital: debtors	Historical cost	Index	Current cost	**Monetary working capital: creditors**	Historical cost	Index	Current cost
Opening balance	30	252/210	36	Opening balance	10	252/210	12
Closing balance	40	252/280	36	Closing balance	100	252/280	90
Increase	10		0		90		78

Net monetary working capital adjustment 10 − 12 = −2

The balance sheet adjustments

Exhibit 12.20 shows a single amount for retentions of £60,000 in the historical cost balance sheet. Within this must be the historical cost profit for the year. Consequently, the £60,000 needs amending to show the effect of the current cost adjustments relating to the cost of sales, depreciation and monetary working capital. These are recorded as the first three adjustments in Exhibit 12.20.

Exhibit 12.20 Deriving the year-end current

(£000)	Historic cost balance	Cost of sales adjustment	Depreciation adjustment	Monetary working capital adjustment	Current cost revaluations Stock	Current cost revaluations Fixed asset	Back-log depreciation	Current cost balance sheet
Fixed assets	+300					+180		+480
Depreciation	−180		−30				−78	−288
Stocks	+160				+7			+167
Debtors	+40							+40
Cash	+60							+60
	380							459
Share capital	−120							−120
Retentions	−60	+25	+30	−2				−7
Current cost reserve		−25		+2	−7	−180	+78	−132
Loan	−100							−100
Creditors	−100							−100
	380							459

The adjustments, however, only relate to expenses consumed in the period. To complete the exercise, the balance sheet values need to incorporate current costs. At the time of purchase, the index for the closing stock stood at 268.8. By the year end it had increased to 280.0 and so the year end current cost was £167,000, an increase of £7,000. As a result, the stock and the current cost reserve is increased by this amount.

A similar argument applies to the cost of the fixed asset. With a year end index of 201.6 and an index of 126.0 at the time of acquisition, the year end current cost of the fixed assets was £480,000. To reflect this in the balance sheet, both the value of the fixed assets and the current cost reserve will be increased by £180,000.

However, £480,000 is not the book value of the fixed assets. The historical cost depreciation also needs to be restated. Using the same index values, the current cost, year end depreciation should be £288,000. With only £210,000 actually provided – including the current cost adjustment in the profit and loss account – back-log depreciation totals £78,000 including any amounts relating to previous years.

The gearing adjustment

If this was an ungeared company, no further adjustments would be necessary. With gearing, however, not all the adjustments have to be borne by the shareholders. Determining the gearing adjustment involves valuing the opening and closing shareholders' funds.

Shareholders' funds at the year end comprise £120,000 share capital, £7,000 retentions and the £132,000 current cost reserve, a total of £259,000. Using the gearing adjustment specified in SSAP 16, however, also requires the opening current cost shareholders' funds. If the company was already preparing accounts using current costs, this information would be readily available from the previous year's accounts. In the case of Albertville, however, it is necessary to calculate their value.

A glance at Exhibit 12.20 shows that the cost of sales adjustment and the net monetary working capital adjustment do not affect *total* shareholders' funds. They are merely transfers between retentions and the current cost reserve. To derive the opening shareholders' funds therefore merely requires the current cost of the assets and liabilities at the beginning of the year.

Creditors, debtors and cash are already at their current cost and so the only adjustments apply to fixed assets and stock.

The opening stock was acquired when the stock index stood at 201.6. The index at the beginning of the year stood at 210.0 and so the current cost stock value at the beginning of the year was £62,500, an increase of £2,500.

The opening net fixed assets of £180,000 were acquired when the fixed asset index stood at 126.0. (The net figure can be used as the original cost and the accumulated depreciation share the same indices.) With an index of 176.4 at the beginning of the year, the opening current cost of the fixed assets, net of depreciation, must be £252,000. An adjustment of £72,000 is therefore required in both the fixed asset account and the current cost reserve.

The opening current cost reserve will therefore comprise the net £72,000 relating to the fixed assets plus the £2,500 relating to the stock. With historical opening shareholders' funds of £165,000, the opening current cost shareholders' funds will be £239,500. The average shareholders funds can now be calculated, enabling the gearing adjustment to be made. The necessary workings are shown in Exhibit 12.21.

Exhibit 12.21 **The gearing ratio**

(£000)		Net borrowings		Shareholders' funds
	Loan	Cash	Net	
Opening value	100	5	95.00	239.50
Closing value	100	60	40.00	259.00
Average			67.50	249.25

$$\text{Gearing ratio} = \frac{L}{L+S} \quad \frac{67.50}{67.50 + 249.25} = 21\%$$

Of the £53,000 of current cost adjustments, 21 per cent or £11,000 will not have to be financed by the shareholders. To complete the year end balance sheet therefore, £11,000 needs to be transferred from the current cost reserve back to the profit and loss account because of the gearing adjustment. This allows the current cost accounts to be prepared in a form similar to that shown in Exhibit 12.22.

Exhibit 12.22 **The year end current cost final accounts**

Current cost profit and loss account		*(£000)*	**Current cost year end balance sheet**		*(£000)*
Turnover		400	Fixed assets at cost		480
Cost of sales		100	Depreciation to date		288
Gross profit		300			192
Depreciation	60		Stock	167	
Loan interest	25		Debtors	40	
Other expenses	200	285	Cash	60	
Historical cost operating profit		15		267	
Current cost adjustments			Creditors	100	167
Cost of sales	25				359
Monetary working capital	–2		Loan		100
Depreciation	30				259
	53		Financed by		
Gearing adjustment	–11	42	Ordinary share capital		120
Current cost operating loss		27	Retentions		18
			Current cost reserve		121
					259

CURRENT COST ACCOUNTING – AN APPRAISAL

Current cost accounting is radically different from current purchasing power accounting. Current cost accounting concerns itself with maintaining physical capacity or operating capital rather than the maintenance of financial capital. As such it would appear to be of more relevance to users. Both the profit and loss account and balance sheet are likely to be closer to what many users consider them to be with the balance sheet in particular being transformed from a statement of historical unexpired balances into a document showing current costs.

Some, however, would argue that it is *not* a system of inflation accounting. Inflation is generally rising prices. But current cost accounting addresses the issue of *specific* price changes while ignoring any gains or losses from holding monetary assets and liabilities. There might therefore be specific price changes and hence changes in the current cost values even though inflation was zero. The counter argument to this is that it is *more* than a system of inflation accounting. The adjustments take account not only of inflation but also specific price changes. It is also possible to extend the analysis to consider gains and losses on monetary items. In some ways, the debate as to whether or not it is a system of inflation accounting is sterile. The wider issue, of which inflation is only a part, is whether it provides a more meaningful definition of income for users.

There are, however, some very real technical limitations with current cost accounting, not least of which is the problem of identifying the components of monetary working capital. A second problem is the subjectivity in the use of indices while a third area of difficulty is the treatment of assets which are not going to be replaced or where there has been extensive technological change. These difficulties may all have contributed to the demise of SSAP 16 in the UK. The explanation least often put forward, however, was the adverse effect of current cost accounting on reported profits.

SUMMARY

Two models for handling the impact of inflation on company reports have been reviewed. Current purchasing power takes as its base traditional historical cost accounts and then adjusts the figures for changes in purchasing power since the date of the transaction. Without inflation there would be no adjustments. Current cost accounting takes a radically different perspective by redefining the capital to be maintained as operating capacity rather than financial capital. Where current cost data is not available, specific indices can be used as an approximation.

With both SSAP 7 and SSAP 16 withdrawn, no company in the UK is obliged to take explicit account of inflation. The Fourth Directive, however, does allow for this under its alternative accounting rules. In a narrow legal sense therefore, current cost accounting passes the objectivity test for financial data. Many of the newly privatised companies in the UK take advantage of the alternative accounting rules and produce their main accounts on a current cost basis. British Gas, for instance, in its accounts for 1991 reported a current cost profit of £1,556 million after allowing for a £41 million gearing adjustment. By comparison, the historical cost equivalent was £1,849 million, a reduction of 16 per cent.

It is perhaps unfortunate that current cost accounting has become so closely identified with inflation accounting. It is much more than a technical adjustment to neutralise rising prices; rather it is a new way of looking at income based on maintaining capacity. In some ways therefore it is an alternative to traditional cost accounting rather than to current purchasing power accounting. Whether it is superior involves judgements about who are the users and what are their needs. The suspicion though is the debate will not go away.

REFERENCES

1 Bonbright, J.C. (1937) *The Valuation of Property*, McGraw-Hill.
2 Baxter, W.T. (1971) *Depreciation*, Sweet and Maxwell.

FURTHER READING

Accounting Standards Committee (1986) *Accounting for the Effects of Changing Prices: A Handbook.*
Baxter, W.T. (1984) *Inflation Accounting*, Philip Allan.
Carsberg, B.V. and Page, M.J. (1984) *Current Cost Accounting: The Benefits and the Costs*, ICAE&W.
Myddleton, D.R. (1984) *On a Cloth Untrue*, Woodhead-Faulkner.
Tweedie, D. and Whittington, G. (1984) *The Debate on Inflation Accounting*, Cambridge University Press.

TEST YOUR UNDERSTANDING

1 Current purchasing power accounting shows:
 (a) the replacement cost of assets in the balance sheet;
 (b) the realisable value of assets in the balance sheet;
 (c) the historical cost of assets measured in pounds of today;
 (d) the historical cost of assets less an adjustment for inflation.

2 At the beginning of a period, a company has fixed assets costing £100,000. There were no other assets or liabilities and no trading takes place but there is inflation of 20 per cent. Ignoring depreciation, the current purchasing power results for the period will be:
 (a) neither a profit nor a loss;
 (b) profit of £20,000;
 (c) loss of £20,000;
 (d) none of these.

3 At the beginning of a period, a company has cash of £100,000. There were no other assets or liabilities and no trading takes place but there is inflation of 20 per cent. Ignoring depreciation, the current purchasing power results for the period will be:
 (a) neither a profit nor a loss;
 (b) profit of £20,000;
 (c) loss of £20,000;
 (d) none of these.

4 Current purchasing power overstates the profitability of highly geared companies compared with all equity financed ones. True or false?

5 Before recognising a profit, current cost accounting is concerned to maintain:
 (a) money capital;
 (b) money shareholders' funds;
 (c) the 'real' cost of shareholders' funds;
 (d) operating capacity.

6 Define what is meant by deprival value.

7 A company has a machine which originally cost £50,000 although it is now fully depreciated. Because of changing consumer tastes, it is no longer of any use for its original purpose. Its replacement cost is £40,000. The machine could either be sold for £10,000

or kept in the business and used to make a new product. If used to make a new product, the company would save the £20,000 cost of buying a machine to make the new product. The deprival value is:

(a) £50,000;

(b) nil;

(c) £40,000;

(d) £10,000;

(e) £20,000.

8 List the adjustments to historical cost accounts found in replacement cost accounts.

9 What is meant by back-log depreciation?

QUESTIONS

1 Potton Ltd is a retailer buying stock for resale through its two stores. Its opening and closing balance sheets for the year to 31 December 19X3 are reproduced below along with its profit and loss account for the year. The fixed assets were acquired when the company was formed. At that time an index of general prices was at 70. The opening stocks were purchased when the index stood at 110 while the index stood at 130 when the closing stocks were acquired. At the commencement of the year, the index was 120. This had increased to 140 by the year end although the average for the year was only 126.

Balance sheet	19X2	19X3	Profit and loss account for 19X3	
	(£000)	(£000)		(£000)
Fixed assets	600	600	Turnover	195
Depreciation	300	330	Cost of sales	130
	300	270	Gross profit	65
Stock	40	50	Depreciation	30
Debtors	60	70	Other expenses	15
Cash	20	70	Net profit	20
Creditors	(50)	(70)		
	370	390		
Financed by				
Ordinary share capital	300	300		
Retentions	70	90		
	370	390		

Making use of the above data, prepare the current purchasing power profit and loss account and balance sheet for Potton for 19X3. (All workings should be to the nearest £000.)

2 Retailer Ltd's balance sheet and profit and loss account for the year ended 30 September 19X8 are reproduced below. The opening stock was purchased on 30 August 19X7 while the closing stock was purchased on 24 August 19X8. The fixed assets were purchased on 1 February 19X4.

Using the information provided, produce current cost accounts for the year on the assumption that all sales and purchases took place evenly throughout the year and that the stock index provided is an adequate measure for calculating the monetary working capital adjustments. All calculations should be to the nearest £100.

Retailers Ltd balance sheets one year ended 30 September

	19X7 (£000)		19X8 (£000)	
Fixed assets		800		800
Less depreciation		160		240
		640		560
Current assets				
Stock	60		100	
Debtors	60		110	
Cash	200		275	
	320		485	
Less creditors	30	290	55	430
		930		990
Less loan		400		400
		530		590
Financed by				
Ordinary share capital		300		300
Retentions		230		290
		530		590

Profit and loss account for the year ended 30 September 19X8

	(£000)	
Turnover		800
Opening stock	60	
Purchases	500	
Closing stock	(100)	460
Gross profit		340
Depreciation	80	
Other expenses	200	280
Net profit		60

The following indices are felt to be appropriate to the business.

Date	Stocks	Fixed assets
30 September 19X8	687.5	540.0
24 August 19X8	625.0	539.0
Average for year to 30 September 19X8	600.0	500.0
1 October 19X7	500.0	400.0
30 August 19X7	480.0	395.0
1 February 19X4	310.0	250.0

3* Lime Street Stationers Ltd was formed exactly two years ago with a capital of £2,000. Its balance sheet at the end of the first year along with the balance sheet and profit and loss account for the current year is detailed below.

Balance sheet		Last year		This year	Trading and profit and loss account		
Fixed assets		£2,000		£2,000	Turnover		£2,000
Less depreciation		£200		£400	Opening stock	£200	
		£1,800		£1,600	Purchases	£1,000	
					Closing stock	(£400)	£800
Current assets:					Gross profit		£1,200
Stock	£200		£400				
Debtors	£300		£600		Overheads:		
Cash	£500		£800		Depreciation	£200	
	£1,000		£1,800		Other expenses	£100	£300
Less creditors	£400	£600	£100	£1,700	Net profit		£900
		£2,400		£3,300			
Financed by:							
Ordinary share capital		£2,000		£2,000			
Retentions		£400		£1,300			
		£2,400		£3,300			

Sales and purchases took place evenly throughout the year. The fixed assets were purchased two years ago while the year end stocks shown in both balance sheets had, on average, been purchased three months before. A general index of prices covering the two years showed the following inflation:

Index	Value
Now	180
Last quarter, year just ended	160
Average for year just ended	150
One year ago	125
Closing quarter, previous year	120
Two years ago	100

Produce a current purchasing power profit and loss account and balance sheet for the current year and a statement verifying any monetary gains or losses.

CHAPTER 13

Financial reporting – detailed issues

Previous chapters have concentrated on developing the framework within which published accounts are prepared and on discussing its validity. However, several detailed issues remain to be discussed before it is possible to interpret the information contained in published accounts.

This chapter:

■ Considers the effect on financial reporting of events after the balance sheet date

■ Discusses the treatment of contingencies

■ Analyses the treatment of taxation in published accounts

■ Demonstrates the accounting treatment of financial leases in the UK

■ Outlines the treatment of pensions in UK accounts

Previous chapters have concentrated on the wider accounting issues facing modern business. This chapter is different. It brings together several detailed topics which complement the wider and more general perspective of earlier chapters. Combining these topics with the issues previously developed will provide a framework within which the contents of financial reports can be appraised.

POST BALANCE SHEET EVENTS

Published financial statements are primarily backward looking. They are prepared on the basis of conditions existing at the balance sheet date. Nevertheless they have to include judgements about the future in order to determine depreciation and value assets such as stock.

Once published, there is little that can be done if new information comes to light which would have amended those judgements. But this begs the question of how to treat new information discovered after the balance sheet date but before publication of the accounts. This was the issue addressed by SSAP 17 Accounting for Post Balance Sheet Events, the findings of which have partly been incorporated within Schedule 7 of the 1985 Companies Act.

Adjusting events

SSAP 17 recognised two forms of new information which might colour a user's interpretation of the accounts. One form might give a new insight into events which existed at the balance sheet date such as a debtor being found to be insolvent after the year end. Other examples would include an insurance claim outstanding at the year being resolved or the profitability of a long term contract being revised after the year end. These are known as *adjusting events*.

Non-adjusting events

The second form of new information relates to conditions which never even existed at the balance sheet date such as the issue of new shares, the acquisition of a subsidiary or a disaster occurring in the subsequent period. These are known as *non-adjusting events* and are totally independent of the previous year's trading.

The effect on financial reports

Having established the two types of event which might affect the final accounts, the statement then had to consider the time period to which they should relate. The activity which triggers the publication of the accounts is their approval by the board of directors. This is the cut-off point used by SSAP 17.

Any material *adjusting event* which takes place before then needs to be incorporated into the accounts. Adjusting events simply represent revised judgements about the year end values and so the accounts have to be revised to reflect this new information. In addition, the accounts would need to be amended if a non-adjusting event such as a major disaster after the balance sheet date cast doubt on the company as a going concern.

Non-adjusting events occurring between the balance sheet date and the approval of the accounts by the directors should merely be noted in the financial statements along with an estimate of their financial implications.

Similar disclosure requirements extend to transactions undertaken before the year end, the purpose of which is to alter the appearance of the company's balance sheet. This so-called *window dressing* might involve a company borrowing money shortly before the year end and repaying it shortly afterwards to make its liquidity look healthier in the final accounts. Given that window dressing can take many forms, however, it is doubtful if this requirement will totally eliminate the phenomenon.

CONTINGENT LIABILITIES

Another area of difficulty concerns contingent liabilities. A contingent liability is a potential liability which will only become an actual liability on the occurrence or non-occurrence of one or more uncertain events. One example would be a warranty or guarantee on goods sold which would only have to be met if their delivery or performance failed to meet the agreed contractual conditions. Another example would be court action against a company, the outcome of which cannot reasonably be estimated.

The Fourth Schedule of the 1985 Companies Act requires companies to show three types of contingent liability: (a) any arrears of cumulative dividends; (b) particulars of any charge on the assets of the company to secure the liabilities of any other person; and (c) the legal nature of any other contingent liabilities not provided for, the estimated amount and any security given.

Relationship to post balance sheet events

Contingent liabilities (or gains) are closely related to post balance sheet events. Should a contingent liability at the year end become an actual liability before the accounts are signed by the directors then it would be an adjusting event and the accounts would have to be adjusted to reflect the new information. Anything less and it is a non-adjusting event. SSAP 18, Accounting for Contingencies, formalised the treatment of contingencies. Its requirements can be best summarised in a diagrammatic form. Exhibit 13.1 shows the possible treatments.

Exhibit 13.1 Contingent gains and losses

	Contingent loss	Contingent gain
Where event is probable and quantifiable	Accrue	Note to the accounts
Where event is possible	Note to the accounts	Ignore
Where event is remote	Ignore	Ignore

Where a note is required, this should disclose '(a) the nature of the contingency; and (b) the uncertainties which are expected to affect the ultimate outcome; and (c) a prudent estimate of the financial effect...or a statement that it is not practicable to make such a statement'.

Lack of guidance

What is clear from this treatment is the emphasis on prudence in requiring a different treatment for losses in most cases. Of more significance is the lack of guidance in determining what is meant by probable, possible or remote. Given the effect on reported profit, there is a real temptation for directors to judge contingent liabilities as being possible rather than probable and allow them to be tucked away as a footnote in the body of the accounts where they can be described using the blandest of language.

For example, the 1989 accounts of Coloroll plc stated in the notes that there was a contingent liability in connection with '...the sales with recourse of £7,500,000 of redeemable preference shares and £14,250,000 senior and subordinated loan notes in Response Group Ltd which were received as part consideration for the sale of the clothing interests of John Crowther Group plc...' Only in February 1990, when the Response Group called in the receivers, did the full implications of this contingent liability become clear. As a result shortly afterwards Coloroll were also forced to call in the receivers.

TAXATION IN COMPANY ACCOUNTS

Operating profit after tax has already been identified as one of the most significant figures in the final accounts. Only by deducting tax can the amount available to the owners from current trading be determined. In effect, tax is being viewed as another expense of the business rather than a division or appropriation of the profit.

The tax accounts

In all countries, the tax on company profits is calculated by following detailed and complex rules laid down by the state. How this tax is then reported in financial statements will vary from country to country although two distinct and separate approaches can be identified.

Countries which emphasise the 'legal and correct' view of accounting prepare their final accounts in accordance with strict legal regulations. As a result, their financial or commercial accounts are very similar, if not identical, to their taxation accounts with any tax charge shown in the financial accounts likely to be the legally owed amount.

Accounting in countries such as the USA and UK, however, evolved from a different tradition. The 'true and fair' concept was concerned with economic substance rather than legal form. Accounting profit will be concerned with matching income with expenditure and that involves judgement. Taxation profit, on the other hand, is concerned with facts and rules laid down by law. Consequently there is likely to be a substantial difference between the profit figure for tax purposes and the profit figure for reporting purposes.

Permanent and timing differences

In the UK, companies pay *corporation tax* on their taxable profits. Differences between accounting profit and profit for corporation tax purposes can arise in one of two ways.

Permanent differences occur when an item of income or expenditure is recognised in one profit figure but not the other. In the UK, the cost of entertaining UK clients will appear as an expense in the accounting profit but is a disallowed expense for tax purposes. Equally, dividends received from another company, although part of the accounting profit, will be excluded from the taxable profit as corporation tax has already been borne by the originating company.

The second way a difference can arise between the financial and taxation profit is through *timing differences*, where the same income or expenditure is recognised in both profit computations but in different accounting periods.

Financial accounts are prepared using the accruals or matching concept. They show revenue *earned* rather than received and expenses *incurred* rather than paid. However valid that might be for reporting purposes, it lends itself open to abuse if used for tax purposes, with companies possibly accruing extra expenses in order to reduce taxable profit.

To overcome this, taxation agencies such as the Inland Revenue in the UK have developed precise rules and regulations. Their definition of profit is more closely related to revenue *received* and expenses *paid* both of which are unambiguously verifiable. For example, a company might take out a 12-month loan half way through its accounting year with interest payable at the end of the 12 months of, say, £100,000. On an accruals basis, £50,000 of this interest would be charged to the first year and £50,000 to the second year. For tax purposes, however, the £50,000 in the first year would be disallowed as the expense had not been paid although £100,000 would be allowable for tax in the second year when the amount was actually *paid*.

This timing difference of £50,000 disallowed in the first year is *reversed* by allowing £100,000 in the tax computation of the second year. Taking both years together, £100,000 would have been allowed. This reversal of any initial difference between the tax and accounting profit is the central feature of timing differences. Some timing differences, however, take rather longer to reverse than one year. Probably the most important of these is depreciation.

Capital allowances

Because of the degree of judgement involved in estimating depreciation, the Inland Revenue disallows the depreciation charged in the financial accounts, replacing it by an amount laid down by law and known as a *capital allowance.*

Not all assets are entitled to a capital allowance. Commercial buildings – other than those in enterprise zones – do not attract any form of capital allowance. As a consequence there will be a permanent difference between accounting and taxable profit for as long as the buildings are being depreciated. At the other extreme, both commercial and industrial buildings in an enterprise zone are entitled to a capital allowance of up to 100 per cent of their cost in the year acquired, causing the initial year's taxable profit to be substantially below the accounting profit. Industrial buildings outside an enterprise zone and hotels attract a capital allowance each and every year of 4 per cent on cost until the asset has been fully depreciated while for plant and machinery and aircraft the capital allowance is 25 per cent on the reducing balance.

Often the annual capital allowance will be different from the depreciation charge. Through time, however, these differences will balance one another out, resulting in total depreciation and total capital allowances ultimately being the same. The question then is not only how this should be reported but how timing differences in general should be reported.

INTRODUCTION TO DEFERRED TAXATION

Before looking at the complexities of depreciation and capital allowances on reported after-tax profits, the issues involved can be identified by considering a much shorter timing difference caused by loan interest. The details are given in Example 13.1.

Example 13.1

> Grimsby Ltd makes an annual pre-tax operating profit of £100,000 in its first two years of trading before receiving loan interest. Half way through its first year it invests £600,000 as a loan, repayable 12 months later with interest at 10 per cent p.a. Corporation tax is 50 per cent.

The accounting and taxable profit

In the financial accounts, the £60,000 of interest will be spread equally over the two years to give a net profit before tax of £130,000 in each of the two years. This seems reasonable as, given the data, there is no difference between the two years. Both have a profit of £100,000 before interest receivable and tax and, using the matching concept, both years earn six months interest of £30,000 as a result of making the loan.

Exhibit 13.2 Accounting and taxation profit

Taxable profit computation	Year 1	Year 2
Accounting profit before tax	£130,000	£130,000
Less interest accrued	£30,000	£30,000
	£100,000	£100,000
Add interest received	nil	£60,000
Taxable profit	£100,000	£160,000
Tax at 50%	£50,000	£80,000
Accounting profit before tax	£130,000	£130,000
Taxation	£50,000	£80,000
Accounting profit after tax	£80,000	£50,000

This, however, is not the way the Inland Revenue sees the accounts. It will not recognise interest accrued but will recognise interest receivable to give taxable profits of £100,000 in the first year and £160,000 in the second year. Tax will therefore be £50,000 and £80,000. Deducting these values from the pre-tax accounting profits of £130,000 in each year gives after-tax profits of £80,000 for year 1 and £50,000 in year 2. The detailed workings are shown in Exhibit 13.2.

Legal and correct vs. true and fair

Grimsby's after-tax profits of £80,000 and £50,000 are legally correct. Whether or not they are true and fair is another matter. Certainly showing such different results when nothing has really changed is confusing if not misleading. Without further information, a user viewing the accounts at the end of year 1 would probably have forecast a similar after-tax profit for year 2.

One way to resolve the issue is to go back to basics. The Inland Revenue is not ignoring the interest in year 1 for all time; rather it is delaying its inclusion in profit until actually *received*. The difference in taxation is merely a timing difference as a result of the two different treatments of interest. In other words, the tax has simply been *deferred*.

Because of this, paying out the £80,000 after-tax profits as a dividend in year 1 would be foolhardy as some of the second year's tax charge really relates to part of year 1's accounting profit. Had the first six months interest been *received* during the first year then the taxable profit would have been £130,000 in each year, the same as the financial profit, with tax being £65,000 in each of the two years. It therefore seems sensible to *accrue* for the extra tax due even though not legally payable at the end of year 1. This is the essence of *deferred taxation*.

Calculating the deferred taxation

The only difference between year 1 and year 2 is the timing difference relating to the different treatment of interest in the two profit computations. Part of the tax paid in year 2 therefore has to be accrued for in year 1, increasing the tax charge in year 1 and reducing it in year 2. The necessary adjustments are shown in Exhibit 13.3.

Exhibit 13.3 *Analysis of timing differences*

Year	Interest accrued	Interest receivable	Timing difference	Cumulative difference	Tax on timing difference
1	£30,000	nil	£30,000	£30,000	£15,000
2	£30,000	£60,000	–£30,000	nil	–£15,000

The initial timing difference of year 1 – known as the *originating difference* – shows taxable profit being £30,000 less than accounting profit because of the treatment of the interest. The second timing difference – known as the *reversal* – shows taxable profit being

£30,000 more than accounting profit. At the end of the two years, the cumulative effect is nil.

By calculating the tax as an accrual, based on the difference between the amount allowed for interest in the financial accounts and the amount in the tax computation, the tax charge is matched more evenly with accounting profit. The resulting revised after-tax accounting profit is shown in Exhibit 13.4.

Exhibit 13.4 Deferred taxation

		Year 1		Year 2
Operating profit before taxation		£130,000		£130,000
Corporation tax	£50,000		£80,000	
Deferred tax	£15,000	£65,000	–£15,000	£65,000
Operating profit after tax		£65,000		£65,000

In the balance sheet, deferred tax will be shown as a liability. This liability will then gradually be reduced as the amount is charged as tax to the profit and loss account.

Deferred tax and capital allowances

A similar logic applies where capital allowances do not equal the depreciation charged in the financial accounts. Timing differences, however, are often much longer and the amounts involved more substantial. This is demonstrated in Example 13.2.

Example 13.2

> A company commences business with a single asset which cost £300 and which attracts a 100 per cent capital allowance. The asset has a life of three years with no residual value and is depreciated in equal amounts each year. Profits generated after depreciation but before tax are £300 in each year. Corporation tax is 50 per cent.

The calculation of taxable profit and the subsequent profit and loss account *without* providing for deferred tax is shown in Exhibit 13.5. As the asset cost £300 and depreciation is straight line, depreciation will be £100 per annum although this will be disallowed for tax purposes and replaced by the capital allowance.

High capital allowances have the effect of accelerating the depreciation charge allowable for taxation purposes. With a 100 per cent capital allowance, all the depreciation is taken into year 1 for taxation purposes rather than spread over the asset's life. Over the life of the asset, however, the capital allowances and the total depreciation charge will equal one another as can be verified from the total column of Exhibit 13.5.

Exhibit 13.5 Capital allowances and taxable profit

	Year 1	Year 2	Year 3	Total
Operating profit before tax	£300	£300	£300	£900
Add back disallowed depreciation	£100	£100	£100	£300
	£400	£400	£400	£1,200
Less capital allowance	£300	nil	nil	£300
Taxable profit	£100	£400	£400	£900
Corporation tax at 50%	£50	£200	£200	£450
Operating profit before taxation	£300	£300	£300	£900
Corporation tax	£50	£200	£200	£450
Operating profit after taxation	£250	£100	£100	£450

Similarly, with no permanent differences, accounting and taxable profit will also equal one another by the end of the asset's life. With total depreciation equalling total capital allowances and total accounting profit equalling total taxable profit, the total tax will be 50 per cent of both taxable and accounting profit. Any difference between accounting and taxable profit for any particular year must therefore be due to timing differences resulting from the different treatment of the asset cost.

With identical accounting profits and identical tax rates in each year, both the matching principle and common sense suggest that after-tax income should also be identical. Establishing a deferred taxation account allows this to happen. The amount to be provided for deferred taxation – both positive and negative – is simply the difference between the expense in the financial accounts and the expense allowable for taxation, multiplied by the relevant tax rate. This provision is shown under the column headed tax on timing difference in Exhibit 13.6.

Exhibit 13.6 Capital allowances and timing differences

Year	Capital allowance	Depreciation	Timing difference	Cumulative difference	Tax on timing difference
1	£300	£100	£200	£200	£100
2	nil	£100	–£100	£100	–£50
3	nil	£100	–£100	nil	–£50

Exhibit 13.6 shows that charging an extra £100 as deferred tax in year 1's accounts and £50 less in the two subsequent years will make the after-tax profit figure consistent with the pre-tax profit figure. The profit and loss account including deferred taxation is shown in Exhibit 13.7 along with an extract from the balance sheet showing the treatment of deferred taxation.

Exhibit 13.7 Capital allowances and operating profit

Profit and loss account extract		Year 1		Year 2		Year 3		Total
Operating profit before taxation		£300		£300		£300		£900
Corporation tax at 50%	£50		£200		£200		£450	
Deferred taxation	£100	£150	–£50	£150	–£50	£150	nil	£450
Operating profit after tax		£150		£150		£150		£450
Balance sheet extract								
Provision for liabilities and charges								
Deferred taxation provided in the accounts								
Accelerated capital allowances		£100		£50		nil		

Balancing allowances and charges

Had the asset in Example 13.2 had a residual value, the Inland Revenue would have allowed too great a capital allowance in the first year. To compensate, a balancing charge would have been imposed in the year of disposal. On the other hand, where total capital allowances are less than total depreciation, a balancing allowance will be granted by the Inland Revenue on disposal of the asset.

Example 13.3 demonstrates how a balancing allowance occurs and how it is treated for deferred taxation purposes. By the end of year 5 the asset is fully depreciated. However, £31,640 of the asset's value has yet to be allowable for taxation. As the asset has come to the end of its life, there is a balancing allowance of £31,640 in year 5. The calculations and necessary adjustments for deferred tax are shown in Exhibit 13.8.

Example 13.3

An asset costs £100,000. It has a five-year life, no residual value and is depreciated in equal annual amounts. Corporation tax is 40 per cent and the asset attracts an annual 25 per cent capital allowance on the reducing balance.

In the first year, deferred tax of £2,000 will be charged to the profit and loss account in recognition that the capital allowance is greater than the accounting depreciation. This will then be used to reduce the tax charge in subsequent years below the amount *paid* to the Inland Revenue. In this particular case there will be an imbalance until the final balancing allowance of year 5 although in reality this is less likely to happen when there are many assets within a company, all at different stages of their lives.

Exhibit 13.8 Deferred taxation with a balancing allowance

Year	Detail	Capital allowance	Depreciation	Timing difference	Cumulative difference	Tax on timing difference
0	Original cost	£100,000	£100,000			
1	Capital allowance/depreciation	£25,000	£20,000	£5,000	£5,000	£2,000
	Balance	£75,000	£80,000			
2	Capital allowance/depreciation	£18,750	£20,000	–£1,250	£3,750	–£500
	Balance	£56,250	£60,000			
3	Capital allowance/depreciation	£14,063	£20,000	–£5,937	–£2,187	–£2,375
	Balance	£42,187	£40,000			
4	Capital allowance/depreciation	£10,547	£20,000	–£9,453	–£11,640	–£3,781
	Balance	£31,640	£20,000			
5	Balancing allowance/depreciation	£31,640	£20,000	£11,640	nil	£4,656
	Balance	nil	nil			nil

Changes in the rate of corporation tax

One complexity which has been overlooked is how to treat the effect of changes in the rate of corporation tax on the deferred taxation provision. Two possibilities exist. The *deferral method* views deferred taxation as a benefit (or charge) in the year of the originating timing difference which is reported in subsequent years. Consequently, its reversal in future years is independent of any subsequent changes in tax rates. The alternative approach, the *liability method*, views the deferral as amounts ultimately payable at the rate of tax when the reversal takes place. Viewed in this light, the deferred tax account should be maintained at the rate applicable to the year of reversal – in effect the current rate. The original standard on deferred taxation, SSAP 11, allowed either approach!

DEFERRED TAXATION IN COMPANY ACCOUNTS

SSAP 11, however, was never made operational. Before it could be implemented, there was a great outcry from industry as the implications of deferred taxation became clear. Many companies do not simply buy a single asset. Where a company regularly purchases assets, the *total* of its capital allowances will often be in excess of its *total* depreciation charge for all foreseeable years. This is particularly true if a company is growing and expanding its asset base or if the replacement costs of its assets are increasing. The implications for a company are brought out in Example 13.4. To simplify matters, a 100 per cent capital allowance is assumed although the same logic applies equally to lower rates of capital allowances.

Exhibit 13.9 shows the effect on reported profit and the balance sheet of providing for deferred taxation. The 100 per cent capital allowance is claimed in the first year of each asset's life but the depreciation is spread evenly over the life of the asset. If the company continues replacing assets with ones which cost more – a not unreasonable assumption with even low rates of inflation – or continues to expand its fixed asset base, it will always be faced with net originating differences.

Example 13.4

A company depreciates its fixed assets at 25 per cent p.a. straight line. None of its assets have a residual value. Corporation tax is assumed to be 40 per cent over all relevant years. Details of assets purchased over five years are

Year	Asset	Amount
1	A	£100
2	B	£120
3	C	£140
4	D	£160
5	E	£180

Exhibit 13.9 Continuing investment and deferred taxation

	Year 1	Year 2	Year 3	Year 4	Year 5
Capital allowance	£100	£120	£140	£160	£180
Depreciation asset A	£25	£25	£25	£25	
Depreciation asset B		£30	£30	£30	£30
Depreciation asset C			£35	£35	£35
Depreciation asset D				£40	£40
Depreciation asset E	£25	£55	£90	£130	£45 £150
Net originating difference	£75	£65	£50	£30	£30
Deferred taxation at 40%	£30	£26	£20	£12	£12
Deferred taxation account	£30	£56	£76	£88	£100

Looking at assets in *total* rather than individual assets, there will be no reversals of the timing differences. The liability for deferred taxation will simply grow larger and larger.

The meaning of deferred taxation

The first problem faced was one of interpretation. Legally, deferred taxation is certainly not a current liability as it does not reverse within 12 months. But most long term liabilities consist of loans and debentures. Was deferred taxation part of the long term funding of the business, and if so, would it affect the gearing of the company?

Gearing normally results from a deliberate *financing* policy decision of management to acquire additional funding by long term loans. The deferred taxation, however, arises from an *accounting* policy. Treating it as a long term liability was also politically dangerous with its suggestion that an increasing proportion of the business was being financed by the Inland Revenue.

The second problem was one of definition. With a scenario of increasing replacement costs, even without an expansion of the fixed asset base, the deferred taxation might never be reversed. Only if the monetary cost of new fixed assets were to fall or if there was to be a change in the system of capital allowances would any reversal take place. This begs the question of what is meant by a liability.

Formally, the Accounting Standards Board, in its Statement of Principles, defined a liability as 'an entity's obligations to transfer economic benefits as a result of past transactions or events'. Informally, it is an amount payable in the future. Whichever definition is used, it is clear that deferred taxation is not a liability if the total of capital allowances continue to exceed the aggregate depreciation in the future.

With increasing originating timing differences and no change to the system of capital allowances, reversal would only take place if the company was to liquidate itself. Accounts, however, are produced on the basis of a going concern and so this possibility is irrelevant. Using the language of the subsequent standard, the liability would not crystallise. At the most therefore the deferred taxation is a contingent liability.

Full provision and partial provision

These were the issues faced by the Accounting Standards Committee in trying to salvage the remains of SSAP 11. Its replacement, SSAP 15 Accounting for Deferred Taxation, rejected the idea that deferred taxation should include all originating differences, the so-called full provision of SSAP 11. Instead it required only partial provision. In its original form, the standard required full provision unless it could be shown that the event would not crystallise. In a revision to the standard, this burden of proof was watered down to only providing if the event would *probably* crystallise.

The implications of SSAP 15 (Revised) are two-fold. The full provision approach of SSAP 11 meant that the deferred taxation could be precisely calculated as it equalled the reversal of the original timing differences. SSAP 15 (Revised), however, introduced an additional area of judgement. In order to determine whether an originating difference would reverse and crystallise requires a forecast of future fixed asset purchases in order to estimate future capital allowances. Secondly, by emphasising whether reversals would crystallise, it was concerned with *future liabilities*. As such the liability method rather than the deferral method of accounting for deferred taxation is the only appropriate treatment.

For a company which will continue to have an excess of capital allowances over depreciation into the foreseeable future, there will be no need to provide deferred taxation to cover the resulting timing differences. The only deferred taxation likely to be provided will relate to the short term timing differences caused by elements such as loan interest receivable and payable. For other companies, the deferred taxation relating to capital allowances will be limited to the total of reversals forecast. The implications of this are demonstrated in Example 13.5.

With capital allowances of £90 in the current year, depreciation of £40 and a tax rate of 50 per cent, deferred tax of £25 would normally be provided on the timing difference of £50. A forecast of future capital allowances and depreciation charges, however, shows this reversal will never fully take place. From the workings shown in Exhibit 13.10, the maximum likely reversal will be £30 as a result of the excess of depreciation over capital allowances in the following two years. Beyond that, no further reversals are forecast. With a 50 per cent corporation tax rate, only deferred tax of £15 relating to the total of these reversals needs to be provided in the current year. This will then be used to reduce the tax charge in the profit and loss account by £5 for year 1 and £10 for year 2.

Example 13.5

For the current year, a company has capital allowances of £90 and a depreciation charge of £40. Based on forecast capital expenditure, it estimates its capital allowances and depreciation charges over the next four years as being:

Year	Capital allowances	Depreciation	Year	Capital allowances	Depreciation
1	£40	£50	3	£85	£60
2	£30	£50	4	£95	£75

In all subsequent years, capital allowances are expected to be greater than the depreciation charge. Corporation tax can be assumed to be 50 per cent.

Exhibit 13.10 Deferred taxation and partial provision

Year	Capital allowance	Depreciation	Timing difference	Cumulative difference
Current	£90	£40	£50	£50
1	£40	£50	–£10	£40
2	£30	£50	–£20	£20
3	£85	£60	£25	£45
4	£95	£75	£20	£65

The reporting of deferred taxation in company accounts

The reporting of deferred taxation in UK financial reports is governed by both SSAP 15 (Revised) and the 1985 Companies Act. The standard requires deferred taxation to be shown separately in the profit and loss account as a component of the total tax charge with deferred tax on any extraordinary items being shown separately as part of the tax on extraordinary items. In the balance sheet, the balance on deferred taxation should be analysed into its major components.

What is important is that the statement also requires by way of a note the amount of *unprovided* deferred taxation relevant to both the profit and loss account and balance sheet figures. In other words, unprovided deferred taxation is treated as a contingent liability. These requirements are supported by the 1985 Companies Act which requires provisions for taxation, including deferred taxation, to be included in the balance sheet under the heading, 'provision for liabilities and charges'.

TAXATION SYSTEMS

International comparisons

The effect of SSAP 15 (Revised) is to allow two companies with otherwise identical profits to report different after-tax operating profits *if* their future capital expenditure is planned to be different. This complication becomes even greater when comparing companies from different countries. First, the taxation regime may actually influence what is reported as accounting profit. Chapter 7 has already highlighted the dominant role of taxation in determining the values to be found in German financial reports. Secondly, the tax *base* – what is income and expenditure for taxation purposes – can vary considerably from country to country. Most countries other than the UK provide the equivalent of capital allowances on commercial property while the USA and Japan allow LIFO stock valuation when computing taxable profits provided it has been used in the financial accounts. Thirdly taxation *systems* vary between countries.

The classical system

In principle there are two approaches to company taxation, the classical and the imputation systems. The classical system existed in the UK from 1965 to 1973 and is still to be found today in countries such as the USA. It involves companies being taxed on their taxable profits and then shareholders further being taxed on any dividends received.

The company would normally withhold an amount equivalent to the basic rate of income tax from the dividend payment but this is merely an administrative convenience. In effect the company is acting as a tax collector for the taxation authorities. The cost to the company is the full cost of the dividend. Should a shareholder not have to pay tax, the tax withheld can be reclaimed while additional tax is payable if the shareholder is a higher rate taxpayer.

The workings of the classical system are demonstrated in Example 13.6. The example is concerned with showing the logic of the classical system. Because of this, it does not relate to any specific country. To simplify matters, the accounting profit is assumed to be also the taxable profit.

Example 13.6

Newcastle Ltd's profit for the current year is £100,000. It pays a dividend of £20,000 to its shareholders. Corporation tax is 50 per cent and the basic rate of income tax is 25 per cent.

With profits of £100,000 and corporation tax of 50 per cent, corporation tax payable will be £50,000. The company will then pay out £20,000 as a dividend, £15,000 to the shareholders and £5,000 to the tax authorities. Had the company not paid the dividend, it would have had additional retentions of £20,000.

If the shareholders do not pay tax, the £5,000 paid to the tax authorities can be reclaimed. The reporting and recording of this, together with the effect on retentions had the dividend not been paid, is shown in Exhibit 13.11.

Exhibit 13.11 The classical system of taxation

Profit and loss account extract			No dividends	Dividends
Profit for the year before taxation			£100,000	£100,000
Corporation tax at 50%			£50,000	£50,000
Dividends				£20,000
Retentions for the year			£50,000	£30,000

Transactions	Profit	Corporation tax	Dividends Payable	Paid
Profit and loss account	−£100	+£50	+£20	
Creditor: corporation tax		−£50		
Dividends payable			−£20	+£20
Cash				−£15
Creditor: tax authority				−£5

For a *basic rate taxpayer* the amount received will only be £15,000. To pay this £15,000 has therefore cost the company £20,000 in reduced retentions and this distortion is the alleged weakness of the classical system. Not only has it introduced double taxation, it also introduced a bias in favour of retentions. Put another way, it only costs the shareholders £15,000 to invest £20,000 in the company if this is done by refraining from a dividend rather than by making a direct investment.

The imputation system

To mitigate the effects of double taxation and the bias in favour of retentions, many European countries, including the UK, France and Germany, have introduced an imputation system of taxation. This views the amount withheld from the dividend – £5,000 in the above example – in a different light.

No longer is the tax simply *collected* by the company and *paid* by the shareholder. Instead, it becomes an advance payment of corporation tax. Using the data of Newcastle Ltd in Example 13.6, if £15,000 is received by shareholders, the £5,000 withheld becomes an advance payment of the total corporation tax charge. Any shareholder who does not pay tax will, as before, be able to make a claim for a refund while higher rate taxpayers will have to pay an additional amount. For the company, however, the £5,000 is paid to the tax authorities as an advance on its ultimate corporation tax liability and so, in the case of Newcastle, only an *additional* £45,000 will be required to satisfy its corporation tax obligation.

If Newcastle Ltd pays no dividends, its corporation tax charge will be £50,000 to leave retentions of £50,000 as before. If a dividend is paid, however, it only costs the company £15,000 to give shareholders £15,000 net of basic rate tax as the extra £5,000 is *advance cor-*

poration tax (ACT). This ACT is used to offset the final amount of corporation tax due. With a total corporation tax of £50,000 and a dividend costing the company £15,000, retentions will be £35,000.

Paying the shareholders £15,000 net of basic rate tax has only cost Newcastle £15,000 in reduced retentions whereas under the classical system, it would have cost the company £20,000. As a result, the bias against distributions has been, in this case, totally eliminated. The only loser has been the tax authorities. They are worse off by £5,000. On a changeover from a classical to an imputation system therefore, governments normally increase the rate of corporation tax to ensure tax revenue does not fall.

FINANCIAL REPORTING UNDER THE IMPUTATION SYSTEM

Originally, the imputation system in the UK was firmly tied in to the basic rate of income tax. Dividends received from UK companies were originally treated as though they had already borne income tax at the basic rate. The Inland Revenue would have assessed dividends in the hands of shareholders as a net payment from which it would have *imputed* that the basic rate tax has already been withheld. Using the data in Example 13.6, the dividend of £15,000 would have been equivalent to a gross amount of £20,000 where the basic rate of tax is 25 per cent. The £5,000 difference in the hands of the shareholder is known as the *tax credit* and was originally sufficient to offset any basic rate tax liability of an investor. Had the investor no taxable income, the amount of the tax credit would have been repayable. Equally, had the investor sufficient income to pay higher rate tax, additional tax equivalent to the difference between the basic and higher rates would have been payable.

Tax credits and advance corporation tax

The link between the tax credit and the basic rate of tax has been broken in the UK in recent years. For instance, the basic rate of income tax was 25 per cent for the year 1995/96 but the value of the tax credit on UK dividends was only 20 per cent. This is not the only complication. This 20 per cent tax credit can be reclaimed by shareholders who have insufficient funds to pay income tax. Likewise, if the shareholder pays higher rate income tax – 40 per cent for 1995/96 – tax equivalent to an extra 20 per cent of the gross amount has to be paid. For basic rate taxpayers, however, the 20 per cent tax credit is treated as satisfying their full 25 per cent tax liability arising from the dividends!

The tax credit for any dividend can be calculated providing the tax rate applicable to the tax credit is known. Letting G represent the gross amount, N the net amount, TC the amount of the tax credit and R the applicable rate of income tax, the net amount will be:

$$N = G \times (1 - R) \tag{13.1}$$

and the tax credit will be:

$$TC = G \times R \tag{13.2}$$

Rearranging equation 13.1 gives:

$$G = \frac{N}{(1-R)}$$

and substituting into equation 13.2 gives:

$$TC = \frac{N}{(1-R)} \times R \quad = N \times \frac{R}{(1-R)}$$

In Example 13.6, the net amount was £15,000 and with a tax rate of 25 per cent, $(1-R)$ equals 75 per cent to give a tax credit of £15,000 × 25%/75% or £5,000. Had the tax rate applicable to tax credits been 20 per cent then the net amount of £15,000 would have been multiplied by 20 per cent/80 per cent to give a tax credit of £3,750 and a gross equivalent of £18,750.

Whenever a UK company makes a dividend payment it also has to pay ACT equivalent to the amount of the tax credit imputed by the Inland Revenue to the shareholders. If the value of the tax credit is 20 per cent, then the advanced corporation tax is 20 per cent/80 per cent or ¼ of any dividend payment. The ACT paid is then available for offset against the total corporation tax, leaving only the net amount – known as *mainstream corporation tax* – payable at the year end.

Restrictions on use of ACT

On occasions, the ACT will not be offset against the corporation tax charge for the year. Where a company receives dividends from another company, the tax credit imputed to those dividends can be used to offset any ACT payable.

On the other hand, the Inland Revenue restricts the amount of ACT available to be offset against corporation tax. The maximum amount of ACT which can be set off against corporation tax is limited to the amount of ACT which would have been payable if dividends plus ACT equalled the company's taxable profits. The implications of this are brought out in Example 13.7.

Example 13.7

Eltisley plc made a dividend payment of £2 million in 19X5. Taxable profits for the year came to £1.5 million. Corporation tax is 33 per cent and advanced corporation tax is ¼ of any dividend payment.

With taxable profits of £1.5 million, this amount is the most that can be paid out in dividends and advance corporation tax combined if the ACT is to be allowable against the corporation tax charge for the period. The maximum allowable ACT will therefore be 20 per cent of the £1.5 million, in other words £300,000. The ACT paid on the distribution of the dividends, however, was £500,000 to give £200,000 of ACT disallowed in the period. Exhibit 13.12 shows the detailed workings.

Where there is surplus ACT, the Inland Revenue offers two major reliefs. Any ACT not available for offset against current UK taxable profits can be carried back six years against previous UK taxable profits or carried forward indefinitely. However, what is of equal importance is how this unrelieved ACT should be reported in the annual accounts.

Exhibit 13.12 The maximum ACT allowable

	(£000)
Taxable profit	1,500
Maximum ACT off-set allowable = 20%	300
ACT on dividend = £2 million × 1/4	500
Surplus ACT	200
Corporation tax = £1.5 million × 33%	495
Less ACT	300
Mainstream corporation tax	195

The imputation taxation system and published accounts

The Accounting Standards Committee considered the imputation system in SSAP 8, The Treatment of Taxation under the Imputation System in the Accounts of Companies. Logically the advance corporation tax can be reported in one of two ways, as a cost of the dividend or as its name implies, as an advance on the total corporation tax payable. Using the data in Example 13.6, Exhibit 13.13 shows the two presentations.

The retentions will be the same whichever method is used. Alternative B, however, is the treatment required by SSAP 8. Its justification is based on taxation law. In the introduction to SSAP 8 for instance it states that 'corporation tax is charged at a single rate on a company's income whether distributed or undistributed...When...a company makes a distribution...it does not withhold income tax from the payment, but is required to make an advance payment of corporation tax...The charge for corporation tax therefore comprises the mainstream corporation tax and the ACT.' To reinforce this, the statement goes on to say that 'from the paying company's point of view the concept of "gross" dividends and the deduction of income tax at source therefrom has disappeared'. Later, the introduction provides further support for the treatment by explaining that 'the right of the company to deduct income tax from dividends no longer applies...The fact that the dividend will carry a tax credit is a matter affecting the recipient rather than the company's method of accounting for the dividend.'

Exhibit 13.13 Alternative treatments of tax under an imputation system

Profit and loss account extract	Alternative A		Alternative B	
Profit for the year before taxation		£100,000		£100,000
Corporation tax at 50%	£50,000		£50,000	
Less ACT	£5,000	£45,000		£50,000
Profit after tax		£55,000		£50,000
Dividends	£15,000		£15,000	
Add ACT	£5,000	£20,000		£15,000
Retentions for the year		£35,000		£35,000

Franked investment income

A sceptic might well ask, however, since when has UK financial reporting been based on legal form and is it just a coincidence that alternative B also shows a higher tax charge and a lower dividend payment? This scepticism is only reinforced when the issue of franked investment income is considered.

Franked investment income mainly comprises dividends from other UK companies. These have already borne corporation tax in the originating company and so will not comprise part of the profit for corporation tax purposes in the recipient company. They do, however, carry with them a tax credit although, if the company has other taxable profit, this will normally not be reclaimable. Despite that, SSAP 8 requires franked investment income to be grossed up and for the increase then to be shown as part of the total tax charge for the year even though such treatment lacks symmetry with dividends paid.

Unrelieved ACT

The only other factor affecting the tax charge as a result of the imputation system is the treatment of unrelieved ACT. Although unrelieved ACT remains available indefinitely, its value is questionable if it cannot be used to reduce the mainstream corporation tax charge in the near future.

The standard requires that where its recoverability is not reasonably certain and foreseeable, it should be treated as an addition to the tax charge. The statement then suggests that if unrelieved ACT is viewed as being recoverable within the next accounting period, it can be carried forward as a deferred asset. However, if a company has a deferred taxation account, this represents future tax obligations and so the asset of recoverable ACT – even if not recoverable within the next accounting period – can be offset against this liability.

Implications of SSAP 8

Users of accounts are often concerned with measuring the relative performance of two similar companies in different countries. A UK investor might, for example, be interested in the performance of a UK telecommunications company relative to its American equivalent. The different treatment of taxation makes this complicated. To compare dividends requires either the UK dividend to be grossed up or the American dividend to be netted down to show their worth in the hands of shareholders.

A further difficulty concerns the three different treatments of unrelieved ACT. Without a deferred taxation account, a company would show unrelieved ACT as an additional tax charge unless it was recoverable within the next accounting period. In that case it would be shown as a deferred asset, strengthening the net assets on the balance sheet and showing an increased after-tax profit. Judging whether unrelieved ACT is recoverable is not always easy and so it is possible once again for two otherwise identical companies to treat its recovery in different ways for reporting purposes.

The third way of treating unrelieved ACT also avoids the extra charge to taxation shown in the profit and loss account. Where a company maintains a deferred taxation account, unrelieved ACT can be offset against this on the grounds that the deferred taxation refers to a liability from which ACT can be offset.

THE PRESENTATION OF TAXATION IN UK COMPANY ACCOUNTS

Because of the effects of the imputation system and the treatment of deferred taxation, an awareness of how taxation is reported in UK company accounts is essential if meaning is to be attributable to the critical figure of operating profit after taxation. The detailed make up of the taxation charge is considered in Example 13.8.

Example 13.8

The annual operating profit of Kippax plc before taxation and before taking account of any franked investment income is £280,000 although the taxable profit is only £100,000 as a result of accelerated capital allowances.

During the year it received a dividend of £16,000 and paid one of £120,000. Corporation tax is chargeable at 33 per cent while advanced corporation tax is ¼.

Recording the transactions

The recording of these transactions is shown in Exhibit 13.14. On paying the dividend of £120,000, the company also creates a liability to the Inland Revenue of £30,000 advance corporation tax payable. As this can later be offset against the total corporation tax charge, the effect is to create at the same time both a creditor and a debtor for the ACT.

Exhibit 13.14 The recording of taxation

(£000)	Profit	Dividends Paid	Received	Mainstream corporation tax	ACT recovered	Dividends grossed	Summary
Operating profit	−280						−280
Corporation tax				+13	+20	+4	+37
Dividend received			−16			−4	−20
Dividend paid		+120					+120
ACT payable		−30	+4				−26
ACT recoverable		+30	−4		−20		+6
Creditor Inland Revenue				−13			−13
Cash		−120	+16				−104

The full £30,000, however, does not have to be paid to the Inland Revenue. The £16,000 dividend received carries with it an associated tax credit of £4,000. This can be offset against both the ACT payable and receivable, reducing the net amount due to the Inland Revenue as an advance payment to £26,000.

With taxable profits of £100,000 and a corporation tax rate of 33 per cent, the total corporation tax charge will be £33,000. The maximum allowable ACT, however, is restricted to 20 per cent of the £100,000 taxable profits and so the mainstream payment will be £13,000. With only £20,000 of the ACT recoverable capable of being used in the current year, there is a closing balance on that account of £6,000. Finally SSAP 8 requires dividends received to be shown at their gross amount with the difference being shown as part of the overall tax charge. This is the purpose of the final transaction in Exhibit 13.14.

The final accounts

How these transactions are finally reported in the annual accounts involves judgement about the future. If the difference between the taxable and accounting profits caused by the accelerated capital allowances is likely to be reversed then deferred taxation needs to be provided, increasing the tax charge for the current year. The timing of the ACT recoverable also has to be considered. If it is unlikely to be recoverable in the next period then it should be charged to the profit and loss account as part of the total tax charge unless there is a sufficiently large provision for deferred taxation.

On the assumption that the timing differences due to capital allowances being greater than the depreciation charge will not reverse, no deferred tax will be provided. Assuming further that the ACT will not be recoverable in the next accounting year, the relevant parts of the final accounts will be as shown in Exhibit 13.15.

Exhibit 13.15 Taxation in the final accounts

Extract from the profit and loss account			Extract from the balance sheet	
Trading profit before tax		£280,000	Creditors due within one year:	
Franked investment income		£20,000	Mainstream corporation tax	£13,000
Operating profit before taxation		£300,000	ACT payable	£26,000
Tax on ordinary activities				
Corporation tax at 33%	£33,000			
Tax on franked investment income	£4,000			
Irrecoverable ACT	£6,000	£43,000		
Operating profit after taxation		£257,000		
Dividends paid		£120,000		
Retentions for the year		£137,000		

LEASING

FRS 3 recognised that the performance of a company is made up of several components which 'differ in stability, risk and predictability'. In order to begin to measure risk and predict future performance, the extent of any fixed costs and the degree to which the business is financed by borrowings need to be known.

As an approximation, depreciation tends to be a fixed cost as does loan interest, especially long term loans. Such fixed costs are incurred irrespective of the level of sales activity. Other things being equal, changes in profits will be disproportionate to changes in turnover. With heavy fixed costs, a small decrease in turnover will result in a much larger decrease in profit and similarly vice versa. Because of this, the company law of most countries, including the UK, requires disclosure of items such as depreciation and interest payable along with details of the loans and their repayment schedule.

Operating leases

The law, however, often lags behind the subtlety of commercial practice and no better example exists than that of leases. Rather than acquire an asset, a company might instead rent or *lease* the asset. There are two forms of lease. *Operating leases* traditionally involve the short term hiring of an asset as when a firm rents a van for a few days to move machinery from one site to another. More formally, the hire period is normally substantially less than the asset's economic life with the lessor (the person who legally owns the asset) retaining most of the risks and rewards of ownership of the asset. Repairs, for example, will normally be borne by the lessor who will also be responsible for finding enough customers to ensure sufficient rental income to make a profit.

Operating leases pose no major accounting problems. In the books of the lessor, the asset is recorded in the normal way, as a fixed asset and depreciated over its useful life. Rentals earned then form part of the turnover for the year. In the accounts of the company using the asset (the lessee) the cost of the hire will be charged to the profit and loss account in a similar way to any other expense.

Financial leases

There is, however, another form of lease known as a *financial lease*. Financial leases grew in popularity throughout the 1970s in the UK partly because of the unique circumstances of that time. Capital allowances for plant and machinery stood at a very favourable 100 per cent. But to take full advantage of this a company had to have sufficient taxable income against which to offset any capital allowance.

Many industrial companies found they had insufficient taxable profits to make use of the allowances. Banks and other financial institutions on the other hand had large taxable profits but few purchases of plant and machinery and hence few capital allowances. It therefore made sense for a financial institution to buy the asset, claim the capital allowance and then hire the asset on a long term basis to the industrial company. The financial institution was then able to reduce its own corporation tax and pass on some of these savings in the form of a reduced rental to the company. More than that, it avoided an industrial company having to raise additional funds to make an outright purchase.

Off balance sheet finance

At the time, the normal accounting treatment was to treat such leases as operating leases, in other words as a simple expense in the lessee's accounts and as an asset which generated rental income in the lessor's books. This was certainly the legal form. However, where the rental agreement substantially covered the life of the asset, the reality was that the lessee had acquired for all practical purposes a fixed asset financed by a loan from the institution. This, after all, would have been the alternative open to the industrial company.

Treating the transaction as an ordinary operating lease hid this effective loan. Because of that, financial leases became known as *off balance sheet* finance. Had the asset been acquired by taking out a loan, this information would have been available for users to interpret. It would have appeared in the balance sheet as a liability and in the profit and loss account as interest payments along with the depreciation charge on the asset. By using a financial lease, the only possible disclosure would have been the hire charge. Treating financial leases in this way therefore not only distorted the composition of operating profit but also hid an effective change in a company's gearing.

Hire purchase

Showing the substance of a fixed asset acquisition when financed by hire purchase was already common practice in the UK even though legal title did not pass until the final payment had been made. Indeed this was even recognised in tax law with the capital allowance being claimable by the company having possession rather than legal ownership of the asset. The financial reporting of an asset acquired on hire purchase is demonstrated in Example 13.9.

Example 13.9

> Chigwell Ltd acquires a fixed asset under a hire purchase agreement. Its cash price is £1,000 and is paid for in two equal annual instalments of £600. The asset is to be depreciated at 20 per cent p.a. on cost.

With a cash price of £1,000 and a total hire purchase price of £1,200, total interest is £200 on an effective loan of £1,000. In reality, interest will be greater in the earlier years reflecting the larger amount owing. For simplicity, however, interest is assumed to be £100 in each of the two years of the agreement.

Exhibit 13.16 shows the substance of the transaction from the beginning, that an asset costing £1,000 has been acquired on credit. If this was not repayable within 12 months the creditor would be shown as a long term liability in the balance sheet. Interest accrues through time and so, using the simplifying assumption of equal amounts in each year, there is an expense of £100 at the end of the first year owing to the finance house. The payment of £600, however, reduces the net amount owing to £500. A similar set of transactions take place in the following year to leave the company with an asset at cost of £1,000 less accumulated depreciation of £400 and total interest charged over the two years of £200.

Exhibit 13.16 Accounting for hire purchase

	Acquisition	Interest	Depreciation	Payment	Summary	Interest	Depreciation	Payment	Summary
Fixed asset	+£1,000				+£1,000				+£1,000
Depreciation provision			–£200		–£200		–£200		–£400
Creditor	–£1,000	–£100		+£600	–£500	–£100		+£600	
Profit and loss a/c		+£100	+£200		+£300	+£100	+£200		+£600
Cash				–£600	–£600			–£600	–£1,200

Accounting for finance leases

The only difference between a hire purchase agreement and a financial lease is that under a hire purchase agreement the legal title to the asset ultimately passes to the company possessing the asset. With a financial lease, the title remains with the lessor and this fact was used to justify the different treatment of finance leases. With financial leases extending over the effective life of an asset, however, such different treatments became increasingly untenable.

The problem was first identified in the United States as far back as 1949 when lessees were required to disclose the amount and timing of annual rental payments and to assess whether they should be capitalised in a similar way to hire purchase transactions. It was not, however, until 1976 that the United States' Financial Accounting Standards Board issued its Statement No. 13 Accounting for Leases and not until 1982 that the statement became fully operational. This was followed by the UK Accounting Standards Committee issuing in 1984 SSAP 21 Accounting for Leases and Hire Purchase Contracts. SSAP 21 is extremely complex, requiring the ASC to issue guidance notes. Because of that, its detailed requirements and terminology will not be considered. Nevertheless, its principles are relatively straightforward.

The concern with substance

SSAP 21 is concerned with the substance of transactions. In the user's (or lessee's) books, the asset should be shown as a fixed asset and the financing as a liability. In the provider's (or lessor's) books, the asset should be treated as a sale and replaced by the reality of a debtor. This will involve the company possessing the asset having to provide for its depreciation and charging any interest implied in the lease payments as an expense in the profit and loss account.

In outline, the transactions in the finance company's accounts will be a mirror image of this. Amounts received as lease payments will have to be broken down between partial repayment of the loan and interest received with only the latter being shown as income in the profit and loss account. Such a proposed treatment begs two questions: what value should be placed on the lease payments as an asset and how much of the lease payments relates to interest?

The value of a lease

Both of these questions are related. Assume that the life of a lease also equals the asset's life and at the end of the lease the asset has no residual value. For all practical purposes, the lessee has gained an asset in exchange for future payments. The cost of the asset, however, will be less than these future payments as a payment in the future has a lower cost today. The cost today will therefore be the discounted present value of those payments and this is the approach required by SSAP 21.

This still leaves the discount rate unresolved. The discount rate will be the rate of interest effectively charged by the finance company, what SSAP 21 calls the *interest implicit in the lease*. Consequently, to find the cost to the lessee requires knowledge of the interest rate charged by the lessor. With no taxation, no grants and no residual value this is relatively straightforward as the lessee will know the approximate cost of the asset to the finance company and will already have information concerning the lease payment schedule. To demonstrate this consider the information given in Example 13.10.

Example 13.10

> Scarborough Ltd is a finance house. An asset costing £244,000 with a life of three years and no residual value is to be leased to Whitby Ltd for an annual payment of £100,000 payable in advance over the next three years.

The total interest paid by Whitby will be £56,000, made up of the total lease payments of £300,000 less the £244,000 cost of the asset being financed by the lessor. With Whitby owing more at the beginning of the life (or term) of the lease, earlier lease payments will contain more interest than later payments in a similar way to a domestic house mortgage.

Interest implicit in the lease

Had the example been expressed differently – had it given the payments and discount rate and required its cost today to be found – the solution would have been more straightforward. A simple discounted cashflow calculation would have produced the required answer. Being given the cashflows and their present value and having to solve for the implied discount rate is more difficult. Chapter 20 demonstrates an algorithm to solve for the discount rate. For the moment though, a trial and error approach will be used.

Whatever discount rate is being used, the initial lease payment will cost £100,000 as it is payable immediately. Put another way, the finance company is only advancing £144,000 as a loan. The cost today of the subsequent two payments, however, will vary depending on the discount rate used. For the sake of argument consider discount rates of 20 per cent and 30 per cent. The second payment will occur at the beginning of year 2 which is effectively in one year's time while the final payment will effectively be in two years' time. The discount factors for these two years at 20 per cent and 30 per cent will be:

	20%	30%
End of year 1	$\frac{1}{(1.20)^1} = 0.8333$	$\frac{1}{(1.30)^1} = 0.7692$
End of year 2	$\frac{1}{(1.20)^2} = 0.6944$	$\frac{1}{(1.30)^2} = 0.5917$

Applying these factors to the cashflow generated by the lease produces a present value of £252,770 when discounted at 20 per cent and £236,090 when discounted at 30 per cent. Neither give the current cost of £244,000. The present value at 20 per cent is too high while at 30 per cent it is too low, suggesting the true discount rate is somewhere in between. Continuing with the trial and error approach shows that the rate implicit in the lease is 25 per cent. The workings for these calculations are shown in Exhibit 13.17.

Exhibit 13.17 Interest rate implicit in a lease

End of year	NCF	20% factor	DCF	30% factor	DCF	25% factor	DCF
0	£100,000	1.0000	£100,000	1.0000	£100,000	1.0000	£100,000
1	£100,000	0.8333	£83,330	0.7692	£76,920	0.8000	£80,000
2	£100,000	0.6944	£69,440	0.5917	£59,170	0.6400	£64,000
Present value			£252,770		£236,090		£244,000

The lessor's accounts

In this simplified example the accounting treatment by both the lessor and the lessee can be developed. Consider first the position of Scarborough, the lessor, who has bought an asset costing £244,000 to lease to Whitby in exchange for £100,000 p.a. over the next three years. Exhibit 13.18 verifies that 25 per cent is the interest implicit in the lease while also identifying the amount of interest applicable to each year.

Exhibit 13.18 Interest charge in a lease

End of year	Detail	Amount
0	Cost of acquiring the asset	£244,000
0	Payment received	(£100,000)
0	Balance	£144,000
1	25% interest on amount outstanding	£36,000
1	Payment received	(£100,000)
1	Balance	£80,000
2	25% interest on amount outstanding	£20,000
2	Payment received	(£100,000)
2	Balance	nil

At the beginning of the lease, Whitby owes £144,000 as a result of the lease payments being in advance. To this is added £36,000 interest accrued by the end of the first year less the £100,000 received at the beginning of year 2/end of year 1. These transactions are repeated at the end of year 2, eliminating the amount implicitly owed by Whitby by the end of that year. The recording of these in the accounts of Scarborough, the finance company, are shown in Exhibit 13.19.

The first transaction shows the asset being purchased. As this is 'sold' to Whitby at cost via a leasing agreement, Scarborough exchanges the fixed asset for a debtor of the equivalent amount. With the first lease payment due immediately, the opening debtor balance is £144,000. By the end of the first year/beginning of the second year, the second £100,000 lease instalment is received, £36,000 of which represents interest and the balance a reduction in the amount owed by Whitby. As a result, the accounts at the end of year 1 – shown under the year 1 summary column – will report income from interest received of £36,000 and a debtor of £80,000. This process is repeated in the subsequent year, eliminating the debtor and showing income of £20,000 from interest received.

Exhibit 13.19 Accounting entries in the lessor's books

Detail (£000)	Asset purchased	Debtor created	1st lease receipt	Summary year 0	Interest	2nd lease receipt	Summary year 1	Interest	3rd lease receipt	Summary year 2
Fixed asset	+244	−244								
Debtor		+244	−100	+144	+36	−100	+80	+20	−100	nil
Interest received					−36			−36	−20		−20
Cash	−£244		+100			+100			+100	

The lessee's accounts

Having found the interest implicit in the lease, the recording of the leasing agreement can now be recorded in the books of Whitby. First it is necessary to *capitalise* the leased asset, that is to find the equivalent cost today of the lease payments. This involves a simple discounted cashflow calculation using the interest rate implicit in the lease, the workings for which are shown in Exhibit 13.20.

Exhibit 13.20 The capitalised value of a lease

End of year	NCF	25% factor	DCF
0	£100,000	1.0000	£100,000
1	£100,000	0.8000	£80,000
2	£100,000	0.6400	£64,000
Present value			£244,000

Having found the capitalised value of the lease, the leased asset will be recorded as a fixed asset of this amount with a corresponding amount as a creditor. The next stage is to determine the interest payable each year. In this particular example, the calculation will be identical to that for the lessor shown earlier in Exhibit 13.18. To complete the entries in Whitby's books, it is necessary to charge interest as an expense in the profit and loss account each year together with the depreciation provided on the fixed asset. Assuming straight line depreciation the required transactions are shown in Exhibit 13.21.

Exhibit 13.21 Accounting entries in the lessee's books

(£000)	Capitalise lease	1st lease payment	Summary year 0	Interest	2nd lease payment	Depreciation	Summary year 1	Interest	3rd lease payment	Depreciation	Summary year 2
Fixed asset	+244		+244			−81	+163			−81	+82
Creditor	−244	+100	−144	−36	+100		−80	−20	+100		nil
Interest			+36				+36	+20			+20
Depreciation						+81	+81			+81	+81
Cash		−100			−100				−100		

The opening balance sheet of Whitby will show a fixed asset of £244,000 and a creditor of £144,000. An extract is shown under summary year 0 in Exhibit 13.21. In the published accounts, the creditor would need to be broken down between that part repayable within one year and that part payable after one year.

As with the finance company, part of the second instalment on the lease relates to interest and part to the repayment of the implicit loan. Because the asset has been capitalised, depreciation has now to be provided and so at the end of year 1/beginnning of year 2 the fixed asset will be reported in the balance sheet at £163,000 along with the creditor of £80,000. In the profit and loss account there will be depreciation of £81,000 and interest payable of £36,000. These are shown within the summary year 1 column. A similar set of transactions take place in the next year, eliminating the creditor and, because the lease instalments are payable in advance, showing the asset as having one more year's life.

Additional complexities

In the real world, there is taxation. Indeed part of the growth in leasing in the UK originated because of the favourable capital allowances available throughout the 1970s. Taking account of the cashflows resulting from this makes the calculation of the interest implicit in the lease much more complicated. Further, the finance house might be guaranteed a residual amount by the supplier of the asset. These and other details may not be known to the lessee. SSAP 21 recognises this and suggests that the fair value of the asset – the price at which the asset could be acquired in an arm's length transaction – will 'often be a sufficiently close approximation to the present value of the...lease payments'. In other words, the market price which would have been paid had the asset been bought outright can be used as a substitute.

Disclosure requirements

SSAP 21 requires the finance lease to be reported in the lessee's accounts as an asset and as an obligation. Depreciation is then to be provided over the shorter of the lease term or the asset's useful life. Assets held under finance leases and the related obligations 'should be described in such a way as to be distinguishable from owned assets and debt'. In other words, the amount of assets held under finance leases and their depreciation have to be disclosed separately from other assets.

Similarly, obligations under finance leases have also to be disclosed separately from other obligations and liabilities. These obligations have then to be analysed between amounts payable in the next year, over the next two to five years and amounts payable thereafter.

Within the profit and loss account for the year it is necessary to disclose finance charges payable on leases and to show depreciation on leased assets separately from other assets.

The implication of these disclosures is that users can form an opinion of the likely commitments made by a company and so help to judge its future viability and profitability. SSAP 21, however, only applies to UK companies and although the FASB in the United States has a similar standard, many other countries do not. This is particularly relevant when considering accounts published in many of the continental European states. With their emphasis on legal and correct rather than true and fair, often only the lease payments will be recorded as an expense. French commercial law, for example, prevents the capitalisation of future lease rentals on the strictly legal grounds that the lessee is not the owner.

ACCOUNTING FOR PENSIONS

Leasing was not the only issue addressed by the Accounting Standards Committee that involved an understanding of compounding and discounting. In May 1988, the Committee also issued SSAP 24 Accounting for Pension Costs. Pensions involve setting aside funds now in order to make payments in the future. But what makes accounting for pension costs so complex is the large amounts involved and the long time delay between the original provision and the subsequent pension payment to a former employee.

Most pension schemes in the UK are funded ones, that is contributions are paid into a separate fund, usually administered by trustees, who then invest the funds in order to meet future pension payments. Within this, there are two types of pension possible. The payments into a *defined contribution* scheme are fixed and invested. Whatever amounts are generated from those contributions will then be available to pay pensions to former employees. The alternative is a *defined benefit* scheme where the benefits on retirement are specified, generally as a certain proportion of the former employee's average salary over the final years of employment. In the case of the defined contribution scheme, the immediate commitments are known but the future benefits uncertain. With the defined benefit scheme, the problem is reversed: the future pension is specified but this makes the necessary current contributions more difficult to determine. A defined benefit scheme involves estimates of (a) future remuneration levels, (b) future returns on investments made with the contributions, (c) the life expectancy of beneficiaries to the scheme and (d) the number of staff leaving the scheme and taking their contributions with them.

One way to look at pensions is to view them as deferred salaries and wages. Their provision is part of an organisation's cost of obtaining the services of employees. The cost of a pension scheme should therefore be treated in a similar way to salaries and wages by being charged to the profit and loss account in the periods when the organisation has the benefit of the employees' services. Until the issuing of SSAP 24, the charge in the profit and loss account to pensions was often the amount paid into the scheme in the particular period. This is still the case for a defined contribution scheme as the employer's liability is limited to the amount of the agreed contributions. Such treatment, however, is inadequate for a defined benefits scheme as there may be surpluses or deficits within the fund from time-to-time as a result of changes in the estimates identified above.

Actuarial valuations

Before discussing the accounting treatment of pension costs, it is useful to have an insight into the work undertaken by actuaries when valuing a pension fund and determining the necessary contributions. Example 13.11 brings out the issues.

This example has been kept deliberately oversimplified to reduce the tedium of calculation and to enable the process and issues to be highlighted. Pension contributions and subsequent payments, for instance, are generally made monthly while life expectancy is normally far in excess of two years. In addition, it is highly unlikely that a pension scheme will consist of only one employee. Where there are many employees, some will survive longer than others but, with a large number of employees, life expectancy, as an average figure, can be determined with a surprising degree of accuracy.

Example 13.11

Golden Age Ltd has one employee, Rebecca Preston, who has just joined the company. Rebecca plans to retire in three years' time. From statistical tables, her life expectancy beyond retirement age is two years. Her salary is currently £30,000 and this is expected to grow at 10 per cent p.a. The pension scheme provides for a pension equal to half her final salary. An actuary believes that funds invested can give an annual return of 25 per cent. Both the pension contribution, pension payments and any returns from investments can be assumed to be received and paid at the end of each year.

The first problem is to estimate Rebecca's final salary. With an expected compound growth of 10 per cent p.a., her final salary will be £39,930 and so her pension will be half that amount. Given that the first pension payment of £19,965 is due one year after retiring and given that funds invested can earn 25 per cent per year, it follows that at the beginning of her retirement, the pension fund does not need to have the full amount of the payment in its fund. Using 25 per cent discount tables, a payment of £19,965 at the end of year 1 can be satisfied by having £15,972 available at the beginning of the year as £15,972 grows to £19,965 when invested at 25 per cent per annum. Likewise, the payment at the end of the second year will require an even smaller amount at the commencement of Rebecca's retirement. From Exhibit 13.22, it can be seen that the total amount needed in the pension fund on her retirement is £28,750.

Exhibit 13.22 Determining the necessary pension contribution

Salary in three year's time = £30,000 × $(1.1)^3$ =	£39,930
50 per cent pension = £39,930 ÷ 2 =	£19,955
Capital sum required	
Pension payment end of year 1 = £19,965 × 0.800 =	£15,972
Pension payment end of year 2 = £19,965 × 0.640 =	£12,778
	£28,750
Capital value of salary if invested	
Salary year 1 = £30,000 × $(1.25)^2$ =	£46,875
Salary year 2 = £30,000 × $(1.25)^1$ =	£41,250
Salary year 3 = £30,000 =	£30,000
	£124,425
Per cent of salary required as pension contribution	
(£28,750 ÷ £124,425) × 100 =	23.1%

By the end of her employment, the total contributions, including any returns from their investment, need to be £28,750. Given the simplifying assumptions of the question, any contributions in Rebecca's first year of employment can be invested for a further two years at 25 per cent. Her contributions in her second year can be invested for a further one year while the contributions in her third year will be immediately available to pay the pension. If *all* her salary was invested in this way, the total of the investment on retirement would be £124,425. If half was invested, the capital sum would be £62, 214.50 while if only 10 per cent was invested, the capital sum would be £12,442.50. A 10 per cent contribution to the pension scheme is therefore insufficient while a 50 per cent contribution is too great. Recognising this, the percentage contribution can be found by dividing the required sum of £28,750 by the capital value available had all her salary been invested. From Exhibit 13.22, it can be seen that the necessary contribution is 23.1 per cent of salary.

Probably more important than the actual calculation is an awareness of the assumptions made. If returns from investments are less than 25 per cent or if salary growth is more than 10 per cent or if life expectancy is greater than two years then the value of the pension fund will be insufficient to meet the required payments based on final salary.

The accounting treatment of pensions

SSAP 24 recognises that the expense of a defined benefit pension scheme consists of two elements, the *regular cost* – the 23.1 per cent of Rebecca Preston's salary in Example 13.11 – and variations from that cost. If there were no variations, the accounting treatment would be straightforward. For Golden Age Ltd, the amount charged as pension expenses to the profit and loss account would simply be 23.1 per cent of salaries. It is the variations from regular cost that pose reporting difficulties.

Variations may arise because of what the standard calls *experience* surpluses and deficiencies – for example if the actual returns on investments to date are different from those originally planned they may arise from changes in the method the actuaries use to calculate the value of the pension fund or from a change in assumptions about the future; they may arise because of retroactive changes in benefits or conditions of membership; or they might change because of increases in pensions for which provision has not previously been made. The first two variations arise because the original assumptions inherent in the scheme have changed. The latter two arise because of conscious decisions to change the nature of the scheme.

From an accounting perspective, the issue is how to record these variations. There are three options: (a) to recognise that past assumptions were wrong and to treat any surplus or deficiency as a prior period adjustment through the reserves; (b) to charge any difference to the current period's profit and loss account; or (c) to spread any surplus or deficiency over some future period.

In the case of experience differences, any surplus or deficiency has arisen because of a failure to accurately estimate past expenses. There is, therefore, a strong case for treating any difference through the accumulated reserves. FRS 3, however, strictly limits the use of prior period adjustments to changes in accounting policies or the correction of fundamental errors. On that basis, the prior period adjustment is not available. With certain exceptions, SSAP 24 views any surplus or deficiency as arising from the normal difficulties involved in estimating accruals. Because of this, it requires any difference to be corrected by adjusting current and future pension expenses, in other words for any difference to be spread over the remaining service life of the employees. This will require future payments to be adjusted to the extent of any difference and so the concern of the statement is with matching.

Experience differences, revised assumptions and retroactive changes

The treatment of experience surpluses and deficiencies, the revision of actuarial assumptions and retroactive changes to the pension scheme are generally treated in a similar way, the main exceptions being if there has been a significant reduction in the number of employees in the scheme or where prudence requires any material deficiency to be recovered over a shorter period. This latter exception is restricted to any shortfall outside the normal actuarial assumptions and running of the scheme as for example if fraud has taken place within the pension fund. Example 13.12 demonstrates the accounting treatment of an experience deficiency.

Example 13.12

Whitehead plc operates a defined benefit scheme for its employees. The regular cost of the scheme is £10 million. On 1 January 19X7, an actuarial valuation shows there is a deficiency of £40 million in the pension fund. The actuaries employed by the scheme recommend that the deficit is eliminated by lump sum payments of £20 million in each of the next two years. The average remaining service life of employees in the scheme was five years.

For the next two years, Whitehead will have to make payments of £30 million, £10 million as the regular cost and £20 million as the payment to make up the deficiency. The £40 million deficiency, however, will be charged to the profit and loss account over the remaining service life of the employees. This will require an additional charge to the profit and loss account of £8 million in each of the five years to give a total pension expense of £18 million in each of the five years. The effect of this in the accounts of Whitehead are shown in Exhibit 13.23.

Exhibit 13.23 Accounting for a pension fund deficiency

Year (£m)	19X7 Payment	19X7 Charge	19X8 Payment	19X8 Charge	19X9 Payment	19X9 Charge	19X0 Payment	19X0 Charge	19X1 Payment	19X1 Charge	5 year total
Cash	−£30		−£30		−£10		−£10		−£10		−£90
Pension fund prepayment	+£30	−£18	+£30	−£18	+10	−£18	+£10	−£18	+£10	−£18	nil
Profit and loss account		+£18		+£18		+£18		+£18		+£18	+£90

Although the payment into the fund in the first year is £30 million, only £18 million is charged to the profit and loss account as the objective is to match the deficiency over the life of the remaining benefits from the employees. At the end of the first year, there will therefore be a prepayment of £12 million. By the end of the second year, this prepayment will have increased to £24 million. Over the following three years this prepayment is then eliminated as the charge to the profit and loss account is greater than the regular cost of £10 million paid into the scheme.

A similar approach is required if there is an experience surplus. The implications of this are demonstrated in Exhibit 13.24 which makes use of the data provided in Example 13.13.

Example 13.13

On 1 January 19X1, there is an experience surplus on the defined benefit scheme of Arden plc of £55 million. The regular cost is £20 million per annum. The actuaries recommend that no payment is paid into the scheme for the next two years and that subsequent payments should be reduced to £15 million per annum to eliminate the surplus. The average remaining service life of the employees is five years.

Exhibit 13.24 Accounting for a pension fund surplus

Year (£m)	19X1 Payment	19X1 Charge	19X2 Payment	19X2 Charge	19X3 Payment	19X3 Charge	19X4 Payment	19X4 Charge	19X5 Payment	19X5 Charge	5 year total
Cash	nil		nil		–£15		–£15		–£15		–£45
Pension fund accrual	nil	–£9	nil	–£9	+£15	–£9	+£15	–£9	+£15	–£9	nil
Profit and loss account		+£9		+£9		+£9		+£9		+£9	+£45

With a surplus of £55 million and a five-year average service life, the £20 million charge needs to be reduced by £55 million ÷ 5 years or £11 million per annum. The charge to the profit and loss account will therefore only be £9 million. The actuaries have recommended that payments into the fund be eliminated for two years – what is known as a contributions holiday – and for subsequent payments to be reduced. Combined, these revisions to the regular cost will eliminate the surplus. As Exhibit 13.24 demonstrates, the total payments into the scheme over the five years is £45 million and this equals the charge to the profit and loss account. Adding the £45 million charge to the profit surplus of £55 million totals £100 million, the amount required in regular contributions.

Reduction in the number of employees

Had the surplus in Example 13.13 arisen as a result of a reduction in the number of employees following the sale or termination of an operation, then FRS 3 requires that this be recognised immediately. The result would be to show an extraordinary gain in the first year of £55 million and the regular cost of £20 million as the pensions expense in the profit and loss account. Over the five years, the total effect will be the same, a net charge of £45 million but with £20 million as an expense in the subsequent years.

Discretionary pension increases

If discretionary pension increases are made on a regular basis, SSAP 24 prefers that they are incorporated into the actuarial calculations in the normal way. Failing that, the full capital value required to pay the pension should be provided for in the year when the pension is agreed and not in the years in which it is paid. Once again, this is SSAP 24 attempting to apply the matching concept. Recognising the obligation when paid as a pension fails the test of matching. A similar recording is necessary if an *ex gratia* pension is granted to an employee on retirement.

SUMMARY

This chapter has addressed five specific issues: the treatment of post balance sheet events, the implications of contingent liabilities, the role of taxation in company accounts, the accounting treatment of financial leases and the reporting of pension expenses. The discussion of post balance sheet events, contingent liabilities and financial leases lies at the heart of accounting. Such topics are concerned with asking the fundamental questions identified in the Accounting Standards Board's Statement of Principles: what are assets, what are liabilities and should they be recognised in financial statements?

The treatment of taxation, accounting for pensions and, in part, the reporting of financial leases, although also concerned with the identification and recognition of elements in financial statements, also address a more basic need in accounting, that of matching. All three depend for their value in the annual accounts on estimates about the future.

The tax charge in the profit and loss account and the tax liability in the balance sheet are not simply concerned to reflect the legal amount payable. Rather, with the use of deferred taxation, they attempt to reflect the matching of tax payable against the profits giving rise to that tax charge. As only partial provision is necessary, this inevitably involves significant judgements about the future. Both financial leases and pensions are also intimately tied up with the future because of the discounting and compounding necessary to determine the charge for the period in the profit and loss account.

To the extent that other countries do not have similar provisions, this makes the comparison of accounts between countries that much more difficult. Nevertheless, armed with the knowledge of the UK treatment, it is possible to analyse company accounts within the British context. This is the purpose of the next chapter.

TEST YOUR UNDERSTANDING

1 Differentiate adjusting events from non-adjusting events.

2 Pool and Derby plc has a 31 December year end. On 6 February 19X9, it suffered a fire at one of its locations, causing £30 million of uninsured damage. Although serious, the damage does not put the continued existence of the company in doubt. The fire should be reported as an expense in the profit and loss account for the year to 31 December 19X8 if it occurred:
    (a) before the annual accounts had been completed;
    (b) before the annual accounts had been published;
    (c) before the annual accounts had been approved by the shareholders;
    (d) before the annual accounts had been approved by the board of directors;
    (e) none of these.

3 Newport plc assembles and sells computers. By 30 September 19X4, its year end, the company became aware of a possible fault in the memory chip of all computers sold in the last six months although, so far, only six customers have complained. The company's warranty is limited to the replacement of faulty material and specifically excludes consequential losses. The company should:
   (a) estimate the likely cost and charge it as an expense to the accounts for the year ended 30 September 19X4;
   (b) estimate the likely cost and charge it as an expense to the accounts for the year ended 30 September 19X5;
   (c) attach a note to the accounts for 19X4 quantifying the possible cost;
   (d) ignore the potential expense.

4 Identify the two ways in which reported profit and taxable profit can differ.

5 The Inland Revenue disallows depreciation when calculating taxable profits. How does it allow for the cost of fixed assets?

6 What is meant by the deferral method and the liability method?

7 How does SSAP 15 treat deferred taxation?

8 Distinguish between the classical and imputation systems of taxation.

9 A UK company makes a dividend payment of £280,000. The value of the tax credit is 20 per cent although the basic rate of income tax is 25 per cent. Assuming the company has sufficient taxable profits, the advance corporation tax payable is:
   (a) £56,000;
   (b) £70,000;
   (c) £87,500.

10 Palmer plc has taxable profits of £500,000. Advance corporation tax is ¼. What is the maximum amount of ACT that can be offset against the total corporation tax charge?

11 What is meant by franked investment income?

12 Differentiate between operating leases and finance leases.

13 What is meant by the terms 'defined contribution' and 'defined benefit' in accounting for pension funds?

14 A company has a surplus on its pension fund. Under the provisions of SSAP 24, the surplus will be:
   (a) spread over the remaining service life of the employees in the scheme;
   (b) treated as a prior year adjustment via the reserves;
   (c) shown as part of the normal profit for the current period;
   (d) shown as an extraordinary item in the profit and loss account for the current period.

QUESTIONS

1 Taverner Protection plc was formed exactly one year ago. Its profit for the year to 30 April 19X4 was £2,800,000 after depreciation but before tax and before taking account of any dividends received. Depreciation for the current year was £800,000 although capital allowances were £2,000,000. This was the only difference between profit for taxation purposes and profit reported in the final accounts. Over the next four years, the directors estimate capital allowances and depreciation to be as follows:

Year ended 30 April	Capital allowances	Depreciation
19X5	£600,000	£1,000,000
19X6	£500,000	£1,000,000
19X7	£2,000,000	£1,200,000
19X8	£2,500,000	£1,600,000

Thereafter, capital allowances are likely to exceed depreciation charges into the foreseeable future because of a continuing policy of capital investment.

During 19X4, the company paid dividends of £2,100,000 and received dividends of £220,000. No further dividends are likely to be received or paid in the current year. Corporation tax is currently 33 per cent, income tax 25 per cent and advance corporation tax ¼.

Using the above information: (a) calculate the figure for corporation tax to appear in the final accounts, identifying its component parts; (b) reproduce the profit and loss account; and (c) show how taxation would appear in the balance sheet.

2   A company, whose year end is 31 December, agrees to lease a machine on 1 January for four years after which it has no residual value. The terms of the agreement are that the company will pay £10,000 each and every year, in advance, over the next four years. Had the company chosen to purchase the machine outright, its cost would have been £31,064. The policy of the company is to depreciate assets using the straight line method.

Making use of the discount factors reproduced below, calculate the interest rate implicit in the lease and show how all transactions, including depreciation, would be recorded in the balance sheet and profit and loss account in each of the four years on the assumption that the company is registered in the UK. (Taxation can be ignored.)

Discount factors

End of year	10%	15%	20%
1	0.9091	0.8696	0.8333
2	0.8264	0.7561	0.6944
3	0.7513	0.6575	0.5787
4	0.6830	0.5718	0.4823
5	0.6209	0.4972	0.4019

3* Larkin plc operates a defined benefit pension scheme for its employees. For 19X1, the regular cost was £40 million. During 19X2, it became clear that there was an experience surplus of £160 million. The actuaries recommend that no payment is paid into the scheme over the next two years and subsequent payments should be reduced to £30 million to eliminate the surplus. The average remaining service life of the employees is 10 years.

Show the effect of the above events on the balance sheet and profit and loss account of Larkin plc for the years 19X1 to 19X4 inclusive.

CHAPTER 14

Interpreting company accounts

Company accounts are both complex and voluminous. With so much data, there is a danger of users not being able to distinguish the essential from the superficial. To overcome this, data can be summarised and analysed. However, with so much judgement in financial reporting, it is often necessary for the user to make adjustments to the published information before carrying out the analysis. What these adjustments will be cannot be specified in advance: they depend on the needs of the user.

This chapter:

- Discusses the uses and limitations of traditional appraisal techniques, including the lack of standardised definitions

- Demonstrates how adjustments can be made to make the data more relevant to users' needs

- Identifies profitability, solvency, efficiency, financial risk, operating risk and market perceptions of the company as important elements in the interpretation of company performance

- Provides a worked example from a realistic set of company accounts

Modern day financial statements are complicated documents. This is partly due to advances in technology giving rise to expensive fixed assets and the difficulty of apportioning their cost to different accounting periods. Partly it is due to new forms of finance being developed such as the hybrid capital instruments and finance leases identified in earlier chapters. And partly it is due to the increasing complexity of the business world leading to takeovers, mergers and the need for group accounts.

Coupled with this has been the growing role of the state and other regulators in determining both the volume and content of disclosure. With so much detail there is a danger of a user suffering from *information overload*, the danger of having so much information that the essential cannot be separated from the superficial.

Possibly more serious than information overload, users may not be aware of the values implicit in any disclosure required by company law or accounting standards. A law which requires an asset to be shown at cost, for example, may be of little use in determining if a business has sufficient resources to continue in existence. With ownership separated from control, there is no automatic mechanism for correcting this problem, even assuming that owners are the only legitimate users of accounts. Appraising a modern company using financial statements is therefore an increasingly difficult task.

THE INFORMATION NEEDS OF USERS

The Accounting Standards Board's belief is that the objective of financial statements is 'to provide information about the financial position, performance and financial adaptability of an enterprise that is useful to a wide range of users in making economic decisions'. Information about an entity's financial position, both the resources it controls and how it is financed, is to be found in its balance sheet. The primary source of information about an enterprise's financial performance is likely to be its profit and loss account, backed up by an understanding from the cashflow statement of how that profit converts to cash. The cashflow statement, coupled with the balance sheet, is also likely to be a source for measuring a company's liquidity and solvency.

Information about a company's ability to adapt to changes in its environment can be gathered from all three accounting statements. The cashflow statement helps identify how cash is generated and absorbed. From this users can estimate the cashflow implications of any change in operations. The profit and loss account can give some indication of the breakdown of costs and so help a user to forecast changes in profits as a result of changes in the environment. Lastly, the balance sheet, by classifying assets and sources of finance, can give some idea of the flexibility within the enterprise. The more readily marketable are a company's assets, the easier it is to change those assets. Likewise, the more a company uses borrowings to finance its activities, the higher will be the unavoidable cash expenses it must meet before both declaring a profit and generating positive cashflows.

Areas of company performance

The Accounting Standards Board also suggested how users might use this knowledge. First, reliable and relevant information enables a user to *confirm* or correct previously held beliefs. This is the feedback or scorekeeping role of accounting information. Secondly, the information can have predictive value by helping the user to make forecasts about future levels of profitability, liquidity, resources, financial structure and financial adaptability.

Common sense suggests that users are concerned with at least four areas of a company's performance: its profitability, its solvency, its risk and how others perceive the company. But relevant information also depends on the choice of aspect or perspective of the user. Creditors are likely to place greater emphasis on a company's solvency. Their concern will be with realisable values. Profitability will only be of importance to the extent it suggests continuing future production and hence a continuing demand for the creditor's products. Shareholders, on the other hand, are likely to place greater emphasis on underlying profitability – which implies replacement costs – and how others perceive the company. If capital markets view the company favourably, its share price will improve giving shareholders two forms of return, dividends and capital gains.

Some users, however, will find little or nothing of help in financial statements. Rarely will mention be made of the impact on the environment from the company's operations while only limited information is likely to be provided about the management of human resources.

Segmental reporting

For those users who feel accounts may be of help, further difficulties await. Many companies make a whole range of products through a variety of subsidiaries located in various parts of the world. Identifying product and market profitability or risk may prove particularly difficult in such circumstances.

Company law and segmental reporting

The UK has gone some way to addressing this limitation. The 1985 Companies Act requires a segmental analysis where a company has more than one class of business and/or supplies more than one geographical market. However, where such disclosure is seriously prejudicial to the interest of the company – as in the defence industry – disclosure may be omitted. For all other companies, turnover and profit or loss before taxation should be disclosed by class of business activity while for geographical markets, only turnover is required to be disclosed. For listed companies, the UK stock exchange extends this latter requirement to include the contribution to trading results of operations carried on outside the UK and Ireland.

The benefits of such disclosures, however, are limited by their failure to address the issues of inter-group trading and the apportionment of common costs. One segment in the group might sell much of its production to another at cost, distorting the apparent profitability between segments. Similarly, group management has discretion to apportion joint costs in any way they think fit. A motor manufacturer, for example, may have a research and development unit in one country but manufacturing facilities in several others. How the research and development costs are apportioned between class or market segments involves judgement – albeit with a suspected tendency to load more costs to businesses in countries with higher rates of corporation tax.

SSAP 25 Segmental Reporting

SSAP 25 Segmental Reporting has extended the disclosure requirements of UK public limited companies and large private companies. For both different classes of business and different market segments, turnover has to distinguish between sales to external customers and other group segments. In addition the resulting operating profit before taxation, minority interests and extraordinary items also has to be disclosed for each segment, along with the net assets used. Normally the results should exclude interest payable and receivable with a similar exclusion of loans from the net assets of the segment as these tend to relate to group-wide activities. Common or shared costs and common assets should likewise be excluded from the segmental reporting.

This goes part of the way to overcoming some of the difficulties in interpreting the performance of large, complex business organisations. However, because the pricing policy of inter-group sales and purchases are not disclosed, SSAP 25 still poses difficulties in determining the underlying profitability of a segment where inter-group trading is a substantial part of revenues or costs. Similarly, although the exclusion of common costs prevents the deliberate distortion of profitability and assets employed in the segment, it nevertheless hides the use by segments of those common costs and assets, making the underlying profitability of the segment as an independent unit difficult to ascertain.

The need for comparisons

Data on its own is of only limited use. Evaluating data implies making comparisons. Logically, current data can be compared with past data, current data from other companies or some predefined standard.

Comparing current data with past data is not without its difficulties. Both current and previous results will be influenced by the accounting system used and accounting policies applied. Historical cost accounting systems will rarely reflect either the replacement cost of assets employed or their realisable value. Distortions resulting from this will be particularly high in times of inflation. To make matters even more confusing, some assets will be at their original cost, others at their net realisable value if below original cost while land and buildings may have been revalued at various stages in their life.

Similar distortions result from the application of particular accounting policies. The reducing balance method of depreciation, for example, charges most depreciation in the first year with each subsequent year being charged less and less. As a result profitability can appear to be improving without any underlying real change in performance. More than that, companies are not static. With the constant acquisition and disposal of products and subsidiaries, trends become less and less meaningful.

Difficulties also occur when using a cross-sectional analysis to make comparisons with other companies. For a comparison to be valid, like must be compared with like. Not only might another company have different accounting systems and policies, its structure may differ in substantial detail. Some brewers, for example, might restrict their activities simply to brewing. Some will also own outlets while others will own hotels, bookmakers and distribution networks. Simple comparisons therefore are fraught with difficulty. Even where companies appear substantially similar, there might be detailed manufacturing differences with one company perhaps making all the components of the finished product and another buying them in ready-made. Cost structures may also differ with one company perhaps renting premises and another owning them.

Predefined standards would appear to avoid some of these difficulties. However, a predefined standard implies a value determined in some absolute way. In the physical sciences such standards are common. The body temperature of a healthy human, for example, should be 98.4 degrees fahrenheit. In finance, such standards are much more difficult to develop and will often vary with the perspective of the user. What may be a satisfactory cash balance for a shareholder, for instance, may be less than ideal for a creditor.

None of this means that the appraisal of a company is a fruitless exercise. What it does mean is that extreme care is required in making comparisons. It also means that what might be a useful measure for one purpose may not be useful for another.

RATIO ANALYSIS

Absolute values on their own are of only limited use. To be told that a company owes £50,000 to its suppliers may at first appear disturbing. To be then told that cash resources total £80,000 puts the amount owed into perspective. Likewise, to be told that company A has made a profit of £50,000 and company B a profit of £60,000 suggests that B is the more successful company. However, if it was then found that A had achieved this result with an investment of £100,000 and B with an investment of £1,000,000 a totally different message is conveyed. Ratio analysis is concerned with putting financial results in perspective by expressing them in a relative form.

Limits of ratio analysis

It is, however, only an aid to a user and often needs to be supplemented by other information such as press reports on the individual company or information about current market conditions in which the company operates.

In developing ratios, three factors need to be borne in mind. First, the base data contains judgements as a result of the accounting system and policies used. Stock, for example, is likely to be valued at replacement cost under a current cost system of reporting. Under a historical cost system, it might be valued using FIFO or some other basis. For both systems, the company is assumed to be a going concern and so the value for stock may not be its value under a forced sale. Secondly, the data being used is past data and data which was valid only on the balance sheet date. Past data is not always a good guide to future activity while balance sheet data may not be representative. Thirdly, ratios are defined in different ways by different authors and analysts.

Lack of agreed definitions

Defining identical ratios in different ways is particularly confusing especially when ratios are presented in a prescriptive way with little explanation or justification. It is also increasingly important as more and more software becomes available which has either already calculated the ratios for a whole range of companies or enables ratios to be calculated from data provided by the user. Specific examples of different definitions are identified below when discussing individual ratios.

Often it is less a question of definitions being right or wrong and more a question of whether they are valid or invalid when viewed from a particular user's perspective. Profit for taxation purposes, for instance, is often significantly different from accounting profit and yet few would argue that one figure is right and the other wrong. For the tax authorities profit for taxation is the valid figure: for a shareholder, it is accounting profit. So it is with ratios: the suitability of their make up can only be appraised when the user's needs are taken into consideration.

Importance of accounting policies and notes to the accounts

With this in mind, a series of ratios can be developed which help to measure company profitability, solvency, risk and how the business is perceived by capital markets. At all times, however, two difficulties should be borne in mind: the effect of accounting policies on the resulting ratios and the possibility that data from the annual accounts may not necessarily be representative. The statement of accounting policies plus the notes to the accounts are at least as important as the accounting numbers themselves. Read intelligently, they often allow the user to amend the published data to make ratios more meaningful.

MEASURES OF PROFITABILITY

Company efficiency

Profitability is a measure of the efficiency of a company's performance, the financial outputs achieved from any given financial inputs. Other things being equal, the greater the value of the output from a given input, the greater the efficiency.

Immediately, however, there are objections to this definition. Some costs – such as environmental damage to the community – are excluded from the financial statements. Secondly, increased profits may not be due to increased efficiency but from the abuse of a company's monopoly position. Thirdly, companies might indulge in creative accounting by choosing policies which show the company in the most favourable light.

Little can be done about the first two objections. The last one, however, can be taken into account in principle by users replacing doubtful figures with more suitable ones of their own choosing. An expense shown as an exceptional item for instance can be added back to operating profit if users feel this gives a more meaningful figure. Regrettably other adjustments, such as those relating to foreign currency conversion, are much more difficult to make.

Use of year end data

Accepting the definition of efficiency, profit needs to be considered in terms of inputs to develop a valid measure of efficiency. An individual starting with cash of £100 invested in a savings scheme which realised £110 at the end of the year would view profit as £10 or 10 per cent on the original investment. This is consistent with the definition of efficiency. An input of £100 has generated an extra output of £10.

Unfortunately this is not the way it is traditionally measured when using financial ratios. Generally the profit for the year is measured against resources at the *end* of the year to give a return of £10/£110 or 9.1 per cent in this simple example. Alternatively, the average of the opening and closing resources for the year – £105 in this instance – is sometimes used as the base from which profit is measured.

This is not the only complexity found when using financial statements. Published accounts also show several measures of profit and several measures of resources.

Measures of profit and capital

Using the basic balance sheet equation developed in Chapter 2, there are three possible balance sheet formats to show resources employed. These are reproduced in Exhibit 14.1.

Exhibit 14.1 Resources employed

Balance sheet (a)		Balance sheet (b)		Balance sheet (c)	
Fixed assets	£x	Fixed assets	£x	Fixed assets	£x
Current assets	£x	Current assets	£x	Current assets	£x
		Less current liabilities	£x	Less current liabilities	£x
				Less long term liabilities	£x
	£x		£x		£x
Financed by:		Financed by:		Financed by:	
Shareholders' funds	£x	Shareholders' funds	£x	Shareholders' funds	£x
Long term liabilities	£x	Long term liabilities	£x		
Current liabilities	£x				
	£x		£x		£x

Balance sheet (a) shows all the financial resources – or capital employed – available to management in two alternative ways: by the total assets of the business and by the total sources of finance. It is therefore a useful base from which to measure the performance of management. It may not, however, give full credit to management if they are able to arrange for suppliers in the form of trade creditors to partly finance the business. Ultimately the suppliers will want paying and when this happens, the current assets will fall as cash is reduced, reducing the amount of assets under management control.

Deducting current liabilities from total assets identifies the net amount of assets under management control and, as balance sheet (b) shows, that is equivalent to the long term funds in the business. Which is the 'correct' base to use will depend on circumstances. If management has control over the level of creditors, it seems reasonable to use balance sheet (b) as the measure of resources. Objections to this treatment tend to centre on the composition of current liabilities. Legally an overdraft is repayable on demand and so it is a current liability. In reality, however, overdrafts are often a semi-permanent form of finance. If the user of accounts feels this is the case then either the overdraft should be transferred from current liabilities to long term liabilities for analysis purposes or balance sheet (a) should be used.

Balance sheet (c) takes a totally different perspective. It is concerned with the funds provided by shareholders and is similar to the format prescribed by the EU's Fourth Directive.

Whichever balance sheet is used, like needs to be compared with like and so the profit figure should be computed on a similar basis to capital employed when developing any profitability ratio. In the first two balance sheets, the sourcing of the company's long term funds between debt and equity was a strategic decision, separate from the day-to-day operating management. If the objective is to measure how well the operating management has performed, then the relevant profit is the profit from operations before paying *any* of the providers of finance. In effect, this is viewing profit as a fund generated by the operating management which is then used to reward *all* the providers of finance. Recognising this is of particular importance when making inter-company comparisons as Example 14.1 demonstrates.

Example 14.1

Company A is financed by £100,000 of shareholders' funds while company B is financed by £50,000 of shareholders' funds and £50,000 of 10 per cent loan stock. Both are in a similar business and both have a reported profit of £20,000 for the year after interest. Taxation can be ignored.

Both companies have £100,000 of long term funds and so both managements must have control over £100,000 of assets. Company A has made a net profit of £20,000. Company B's reported profit, however, is after paying £5,000 of interest. Its operating profit before rewarding the providers of finance must therefore be £25,000. From an *operational* view-point, company B appears the more efficient, generating a 25 per cent return on assets compared with only 20 per cent in company A. Further, both companies have earned £20,000 for their shareholders but as B's equity is only £50,000, it has achieved a 40 per cent return on shareholders' funds compared with only 20 per cent in A.

RETURN ON CAPITAL EMPLOYED

Relating profit from operations to resources controlled by management produces a ratio known as the *return on capital employed*. It is measuring in financial terms what the managers of an organisation have achieved with the resources under their control. Confusion sometimes exists over the phrase 'capital employed' when the ratio is then defined in terms of resources. An understanding of basic duality, however, resolves the problem as the total of assets or resources must equal the total of funds invested or capital employed. Example 14.1 has demonstrated this and outlined the importance of measuring like with like.

Difficulties of comparability

In the real world, ensuring comparability is extremely difficult. Under historical cost accounting, two otherwise similar firms could have purchased their assets at different times resulting in different balance sheet values for capital employed. They may choose different ways of recognising income, depreciating assets, valuing stock and accounting for subsidiaries, all of which would affect the capital employed and reported profits. Not all the ordinary profits might have been generated from core activities. Companies after all do make loans and investments. Equally, what might be an ordinary item in one company might be reported as an exceptional item in another.

No rules exist for handling these complexities. Given that the ratio is concerned with how well management has used the assets under its control, users have to form judgements as to what are the relevant assets and what are the relevant profits.

Sometimes it is possible to make meaningful adjustments. For example, one company might depreciate its fixtures and fittings over forty years where the norm is ten years. If the user wants to make a meaningful comparison between companies in that industry, it will be necessary to quadruple the depreciation charge in the profit and loss account and make a similar adjustment in the balance sheet. At other times, no meaningful adjustment will be possible, in which case this should be taken into account when appraising the results.

Defining capital employed

Exhibit 14.2 reproduces part of the final accounts for Morpeth plc. Before doing any analysis, however, it is first necessary to define capital employed. Assuming the objective of the exercise is to measure how well the managers have handled the resources in the business, irrespective from how it has been financed, then resources will either be defined as total assets – the £285 million of fixed assets plus the £87 million of current assets – or as net assets after deducting the current liabilities of £73 million to give total resources controlled of £299 million. As most managers are able to control the level of their current liabilities, the latter definition will be used. Capital employed will therefore be the £80 million of loans and the £219 million of shareholders' funds, in other words, the £299 million of long term funds used in the enterprise.

But even here, there is a further complexity. Within current liabilities is a bank overdraft. If the user thought this was a semi-permanent source of funds, then it might be better to deduct the amount from current liabilities and add it to the long term liabilities found under the heading of 'creditors: amounts falling due after more than one year'. Certainly this might be more meaningful if Morpeth plc was being compared with another company that had no overdraft but, instead, had a higher amount of long term loans.

Exhibit 14.2 Extract from the final accounts of Morpeth plc

Profit and loss account – year to 31 December 19X7		Balance sheet at 31 December 19X7	
	(£m)		*(£m)*
Turnover		Fixed assets	
Continuing operations	200	Intangible	90
Acquisitions	50	Tangible (note 2)	111
	250	Interest in associated undertakings	84
Discontinued operations	20 270		285
Cost of sales	(143)	Current assets	
Gross profit	127	Stocks (note 3)	47
Distribution costs	(56)	Debtors	28
Administration expenses	(24)	Cash and bank	12
Operating profit (note 1)	47		87
Exceptional gain from disposal of business	4	Creditors: amounts falling due within one year	
Income from interests in associated undertakings	19	Bank overdraft	20
Profit on ordinary activities before interest	70	Trade creditors	40
Interest payable	(20)	Corporation tax	8
Profit on ordinary activities before taxation	50	Dividends payable	5
Tax on profit on ordinary activities	(14)		73
Profit for the financial year	36	Net current assets	14
Dividends	(12)	Total assets less current liabilities	299
Retained profit	24	Creditors: amounts falling due after one year	
		10% loan repayable 31.12.19X9	80
			219
		Represented by:	
		60 million £1 ordinary shares	60
		Share premium account	47
		Revaluation reserve	28
		Retentions	54
			189
		30 million £1 10% preference shares	30
			219

Note 1	Continuing	Acquisitions	Discontinued	Total
Cost of sales	98	30	15	143
Net operating expenses				
Distribution costs	45	4	7	56
Administration expenses	17	3	4	24
	62	7	11	80

Note 2	Freehold land and buildings	Plant and machinery	Total
At 1.1 19X7	82	74	156
Additions	16	20	36
Disposals	(7)	(14)	(21)
Revaluations	9	—	9
At 31.12.19X7	100	80	180

Exhibit 14.2 (Continued)

Note 2 (continued)	Freehold land and buildings	Plant and machinery	Total
Depreciation			
At 1.1.19X7	30	39	69
Charge for year	2	8	10
Disposals	(3)	(7)	(10)
At 31.12.19X7	29	40	69

Note 3	Stocks	
	Raw materials	10
	Work in progress	17
	Finished stock	20

Note 4

Depreciation for the year is £10 million.

Deferred taxation of £5 million is included in the taxation charge for the year.

Interest of £4 million has been capitalised and included in tangible fixed assets.

Defining profit

Having defined the capital employed as the £299 million of long term funds in the business, the next stage is to identify the profits generated from these funds. The total profit for the financial year was £36 million. But this is both after tax and interest. As the objective is to measure the performance of the management separate from how the business has been financed, the profit figure needs to be before interest. The question then is whether profit should be before or after tax.

Once again, there is no right or wrong approach. If management has developed some particularly tax-efficient scheme which reduces the overall burden of taxation, it seems reasonable that it should be given credit for this when comparing profitability either over time or between companies. The contrary argument, which is the one preferred by most writers and analysts, is that the tax charge only partly relates to operating activity. Other factors include capital allowances and the amount of debt in the company – the interest from which is tax allowable – as well as tax rates, all of which are likely to vary from year to year. Including taxation therefore may be neither particularly useful in measuring management performance nor in forecasting the charge for future years.

With interest of £20 million and taxation of £14 million, the pre-tax, pre-interest profit will be £70 million. Is this then the figure against which to measure managers' performance? If it is, the return on capital employed will be:

$$\text{Return on capital employed} = \frac{\text{£70 million}}{\text{£299 million}} \times 100\% = 23.4\%$$

Associated undertakings and other income

There is, however, an immediate objection to this result. Included in the £70 million is an exceptional gain from the disposal of a business. If the objective is to measure the result of management's efforts, then it seems reasonable to exclude this figure – especially if the purpose of the exercise is to estimate likely performance in future years.

This argument can be carried further. Within the £70 million is not only the £4 million exceptional gain but also £19 million of profits from associated companies. Whether or not to exclude these depends on the purpose of the exercise. If it is merely to measure future performance of the company it might be acceptable to retain the profits in the calculation. However, if the ratio is being used to measure the direct results of management, then there is a strong case for excluding the associated undertakings as managers only have influence over those undertakings – not control.

Taking this as an approach, the normal or operating profit generated from the 'core business' must be the £47 million of operating profit. However, if the profits from associated undertakings are being excluded in determining the profit generated from the core business then the *resources* relating to those associated undertakings should also be excluded from the capital employed. The interest in associated undertakings stands at £84 million in the balance sheet and so deducting this from the net assets of £299 million gives a capital employed of £215 million. Where measuring the operating performance of management, the return on capital employed can now be defined as:

$$\text{Return on capital employed} = \frac{\text{Operating profit before taxation and interest}}{\text{Net operating assets}} \times 100\%$$

In the case of Morpeth, this will be:

$$\text{Return on capital employed} = \frac{£47 \text{ million}}{£215 \text{ million}} \times 100\% = 21.8\%$$

The return on capital employed and FRS 3

The danger, when faced with two different definitions of the same ratio is to believe one is right and the other is wrong. This is not necessarily so. Which one is to be preferred depends on the needs and perspective of the user. If the overall profitability generated from group resources is the issue, then the first definition might be preferred. If the user is more concerned with measuring the direct performance of managers, then the second definition eliminates the distortions introduced from associated activities.

The range of definitions for the return on capital employed ratio has been extended as a result of the introduction of the Accounting Standards Board's FRS 3, Reporting Financial Performance. For evaluating past performance, either of the two definitions of the return on capital employed might be of use in determining how well managers have performed. FRS 3, however, now allows an improvement to be made. As a measure of past efficiency, the disclosure requirements of FRS 3 enable the user to see that £13 million of current operating profit has been generated from acquisitions rather than existing activities. Certainly this is of importance if managers' remuneration is partly based on operating profits. In effect, performance may have been boosted by 'buying in' profits from the acquisitions.

Equally, FRS 3 enables an improvement to be made when forecasting future profits. Assume that the underlying performance of Morpeth will not change in the subsequent year and that the acquisitions took place half way through the current year. Turnover from continuing operations is likely to be £200 million – the same as this year. The turnover from the acquisitions, however, is likely to be twice what it was in the current year as the full effects of the acquisition are felt. (This assumes that sales are spread evenly throughout the year.) Following this argument through to all the expenses, it is possible to forecast operating profits next year of £66 million. The workings for this are shown in Exhibit 14.3.

Exhibit 14.3 The forecast profit

	Continuing activities	Acquired activities	Total activities
Turnover	200	100	300
Cost of sales	(98)	(60)	(158)
Distribution costs	(45)	(8)	(53)
Administration expenses	(17)	(6)	(23)
Forecast profit	40	26	66

RETURN ON SHAREHOLDERS' FUNDS

Instead of considering how well assets under management's control have been handled, a shareholder perspective might be considered. Ordinary shareholders, as the ultimate owners of the company, will be concerned with their overall return, however derived.

Returns to shareholders are only possible from profits after tax. The starting point will therefore be the profit on ordinary activities after taxation and the total of funds attributable to shareholders. From both the profit figure and the shareholders' funds must be deducted any amounts due to the preference shareholders. As the only income normally attributable to the preference shareholders is their dividend and the only capital obligation is normally limited to shares subscribed, it follows that the *return on ordinary shareholders' funds* is:

$$\frac{\text{Profits for the year after taxation less preference share dividends}}{\text{Ordinary shareholders' funds}}$$

Adjusting the data

Figures can then either be taken at their face value or adjustments made to eliminate the doubtful treatment of transactions. In terms of the annual accounts of Morpeth, it seems reasonable to exclude the exceptional gain from the disposal of the business as this is unlikely to recur. As the objective of this exercise is to determine the returns being made from the shareholders' funds rather than measuring the performance of managers, it seems reasonable to include any profits arising from associated undertakings. Had the consolidated accounts of Morpeth included a minority interest, then the profit figure would have been further reduced by the amount attributable to the minority interest while the shareholders' funds would also have been amended by the equity belonging to the minority equity shareholders.

The equity funds in Morpeth total £189 million. Although the profit for the year after taxation is £36 million, with 30 million 10 per cent preference shares the amount attributable to the preference shareholders is £3 million and so the profits attributable to the ordinary shareholders is £33 million. Deducting the distorting effect of the exceptional gain of £4 million gives a revised profit of £29 million. As a result, the return on shareholders' funds will be:

$$\text{Return on shareholders' funds} = \frac{£29 \text{ million}}{£189 \text{ million}} \times 100 = 15.3\%$$

LIMITATIONS TO THE RATIOS

Choice of definition

A simple figure for return on capital employed or return on shareholders' funds must never be accepted at its face value without information on its composition. For the return on capital employed, there are two possible bases, total assets or total assets less current liabilities. Having defined the overall base, there is then the question of whether associated undertakings should be included in both the profit and capital employed figures. Had the company made any other investments – such as a loan to another company, then, equally, a similar question would have arisen. Finally, further adjustments may be necessary to eliminate unrepresentative or one-off elements within the profit and loss account and balance sheet, all of which involves judgement on the part of the user.

Effect of the historical cost concept

One general difficulty is that most accounts are produced using the historical cost concept although sometimes with the inclusion of *ad hoc* revaluations of land and buildings. A company with old, depreciated assets is therefore likely to produce a better return on capital employed than one with newer, more expensive assets. In the latter case, not only will the assets employed be greater because of their higher price and limited accumulated depreciation but also profit will be reduced by higher depreciation charges.

The general problem of asset valuation is aggravated where a company acquires a subsidiary. If the goodwill on acquisition is immediately written off against reserves, capital employed will fall, automatically improving the return on capital employed ratio. Worse, the acquiring company might go further and select a low 'fair value' for the assets acquired. As a consequence goodwill written off will be even greater and, with lower asset values, future depreciation charged to the profit and loss account will be that much less.

Intangibles

Intangible assets include capitalised goodwill, patents, trademarks and a derivative of goodwill known as brands. Compared with tangible assets such as land and buildings and plant and machinery, it is very difficult to place a reliable value on these. Given the extreme subjectivity involved and given that some companies do not capitalise such assets, it might be better to eliminate intangible assets totally for ratio purposes, especially when making comparisons *between* companies. Had the intangibles been eliminated from the analysis of Morpeth, then the denominator for both the return on capital employed and the return on shareholders' funds would have been reduced by £90 million.

Changes in funds

Separate from the interpretation difficulties resulting from different accounting policies, there is the additional difficulty of interpreting results within a company when capital employed or shareholders' funds have substantially changed during the year.

If the change relates to a building up of assets ready for increased trading in a subsequent period, it seems unreasonable to load the measure of current performance with the increase in any year end asset values. Even if used to enhance current performance, the assets' effect on profitability will depend on when they were acquired, with little influence on profitability if purchased towards the end of the year but more influence if purchased earlier. Without further information, some analysts take a simple average of the opening and closing year asset values. However, this would only be strictly valid if the increase took place evenly over the year. Whether the average or year end capital employed is used, care is needed in interpreting the results.

Interpreting the ratios

Finally, there is the interpretation of the ratios themselves. Too often an increase in the return on capital employed or shareholders' funds is viewed as an improvement and a decrease as a deterioration. Mention has already been made of how the ratio can improve without any underlying change in performance. As time moves on, assets are depreciated and so their net book value falls. Short term, this reduces the capital base, resulting in an improved ratio even where profits have remained stable.

This is part of a wider problem. By emphasising returns relative to a capital base, a misleading picture can sometimes be painted. Consider a company currently making £50,000 profits from capital of £100,000 to give a healthy ratio of 50 per cent. Now assume a new proposal involves a capital outlay of a further £100,000 in exchange for additional profits of £40,000. If shareholders are content with a 30 per cent return from this particular company, undertaking the new proposal would benefit them. However, the revised return on capital employed will fall to £90,000/£200,000 or 45 per cent. Judging performance simply on the ratio, a company undertaking the new proposal will appear to show a deterioration in performance.

EXTENDING THE RETURN ON CAPITAL EMPLOYED

Despite these difficulties, the return on capital employed ratio can be of help in appraising the performance of a company when used intelligently. Changes in the ratio are traceable to two basic causes: changes in the sales or profit margin which measures profit per pound of sales, or changes in asset turnover – the intensity with which sales are generated from the asset base. Other things being equal, obtaining a higher margin per pound of sales will improve the capital employed ratio as would keeping the margin the same but achieving more sales from the same assets. An awareness of this allows the return on capital employed ratio to be deconstructed into two component parts.

The sales or profit margin ratio

Intuitively this ratio is measuring profitability per pound of sales. However, as with all other ratios, there is a problem in its formal definition. Given it is trying to measure management's ability to squeeze profits out of sales, it seems reasonable that the profits from associated companies should be excluded as these are unlikely to be under the direct control of management. For similar reasons, interest and investment income should also be excluded. Whether other operating income should be excluded can only be decided on the facts. If such income is an integral part of the operations of the group, it may be better to include it in the analysis. And given that the ratio is a breakdown of the return on capital employed, the relevant profit figure should be operating profit before interest and tax. With this in mind, the ratio becomes:

$$\text{Sales or profit margin ratio} = \frac{\text{Operating profit before interest and tax}}{\text{Turnover}} \times 100\%$$

The asset turnover ratio

The asset turnover ratio – or asset utilisation ratio as it is sometimes called – measures the intensity with which the assets are being used by relating the volume of sales to the assets used in their generation. The higher the ratio, the more intensive the assets are being used. As with the return on capital employed, judgement is necessary in deciding the value and contents of the asset base. Formally the ratio is:

$$\text{Asset turnover ratio} = \frac{\text{Turnover}}{\text{Capital employed}}$$

Multiplying the two ratios together results in the ratio for return on capital employed, i.e.

$$\frac{\text{Operating profit before interest and tax}}{\text{Turnover}} \times \frac{\text{Turnover}}{\text{Capital employed}} = \frac{\text{Operating profit before interest and tax}}{\text{Capital employed}}$$

Interpreting the results

This is a useful result as it provides an insight into how the profits are being generated. Using the data from Morpeth plc and excluding the associate undertakings, the sales margin was:

$$\text{Sales or profit margin ratio} = \frac{£47 \text{ million}}{£270 \text{ million}} \times 100\% = 17.4\%$$

while the asset turnover was:

$$\text{Asset turnover ratio} = \frac{£270 \text{ million}}{£215 \text{ million}} = 1.255 \text{ times}$$

Multiplying the two ratios gives 21.8 per cent, the return on capital employed. From this breakdown of the return on capital employed, it is clear that Morpeth is selling high margin but slow moving products.

In interpreting the ratios, no universal standards exist although patterns can be found within some industries. Supermarkets, for example, have traditionally had low margins but high asset turnover in compensation. In the engineering sector the reverse has tended to apply. Providing the base data for the ratios is reasonable, the two ratios can give a useful indicator of the source of a company's profits and a pointer to how profits might potentially be improved.

Forecasting future performance

A similar analysis is possible for Morpeth's next year of trading, given certain assumptions. Assuming no underlying growth, turnover from existing operations will remain at £200 million. Given the earlier assumption that the acquisition took place half way through the year, the turnover from that source in a full year will be £100 million. Forecast turnover next year will therefore be £300 million while Exhibit 14.3 has already demonstrated that the revised operating profit will be £66 million. Assuming the profit from associated undertakings does not change and that there is no change in the interest payable, then the forecast pre-tax profits will be the £66 million plus the £19 million from associated undertakings less £20 million of interest payable, a net figure of £65 million. Last year, the average tax rate was £14 million/£50 million or 28 per cent. If this is maintained, then after tax profits next year will be £46.8 million and, provided dividends are maintained at their current level, the retentions for the year will be £34.8 million. If retentions increase by this amount then so will the capital employed.

This analysis suggests a turnover next year of £300 million, an operating profit of £66 million and an increase in the capital employed of £34.8 million to give a total capital employed of £249.8 million. The prospective sale margin ratio will be 22 per cent, the asset turnover will be 1.2 times while the return on capital employed will be 26.4 per cent. From this analysis, it is clear that any improvement in the performance of Morpeth plc over the next year will be derived from improved margins rather than a more intensive use of assets.

WORKING CAPITAL CONTROL

The purpose of current assets

Fixed and current assets serve different purposes within a company. Plant and equipment and land and building are combined with labour to produce goods and services which will hopefully generate profits. Current assets are not part of that process. In an ideal world, there would be no stocks. Deliveries would take place just as they were required for production, eliminating the need for raw material stocks. Likewise, by scheduling production and sales to coincide, there would be no need for finished stocks. In such an ideal world there would be no need for the granting or receiving of credit and with production being timed to coincide with sales, the need for spare cash would be eliminated. The result would be neither current assets nor current liabilities.

The real world is not like that. Stock deliveries may be subject to delay. Production levels may not be fully known in advance and customer demand may be uncertain. Because of this, stocks have to be kept. Similarly, the business world would be chaotic if cash had to accompany every sale or purchase. Credit is therefore necessary. And given all these uncertainties, cash is essential to meet unplanned expenditure.

Current assets therefore serve a different purpose to fixed assets. Fixed assets are the essential profit-generating resources of a business. Current assets exist to *avoid losses* caused by bottlenecks and uncertainties. The management of current assets therefore has a different focus. It is concerned with minimising the funds tied up in stock, debtors and cash while ensuring sufficient of those resources are available to enable the day-to-day operations of the company to continue. One example of this is to be found with *just in time* stockkeeping where manufacturers strive to achieve the ideal scenario developed earlier. With just in time stockkeeping, manufacturers tie suppliers to strict deadlines for the delivery of previously scheduled materials, reducing, if not totally eliminating, the need for raw material stocks.

Working capital

This essential difference between fixed and current assets gives rise to the concept of *working* or *circulating capital.* Fixed assets will only change at discrete intervals as plant and machinery wear out or additional amounts are acquired to support more production.

Current assets and liabilities, however, are changing continuously as a result of day-to-day operations. Stock is acquired which gives rise to both an asset and a liability if purchased on credit. The stock is then consumed in production which gives rise to sales and the creation of debtors. The value of debtors then falls when they eventually pay, leading to an increase in cash. In turn, cash falls as creditors are paid, reducing the amount of current liabilities and so the cycle commences all over again. This process is describing the working or circulating capital of a company.

The meaning of working capital

The amount of working capital comprises stock plus debtors and cash less trade creditors, although it is often approximated to current assets less current liabilities. In this latter form a new insight into working capital can be derived from the balance sheet equation. Rearranging the balance sheet equation of:

Fixed assets + Current assets = Equity + Long term liabilities + Current liabilities

gives:

Equity + Long term liabilities = Fixed assets + Working capital

Expressed in this way, working capital is the amount of long term funds *tied up in short term operations*. Given that the providers of funds are looking for a return, and given that returns are only possible by producing and selling, the revised equation identifies the critical need to control working capital. The more funds tied up in working capital, the less is available to support the profit-generating activities of the business. Traditionally three ratios have been used to measure working capital efficiency: the average age of debtors, the average age of stock and the average age of creditors.

Average age of debtors

Probably the least contentious of the three ratios is the calculation of the average age of debtors. Consider a company which only sells on credit and assume its turnover for the year is £120,000 with debtors at the year end of £30,000. In effect, one-quarter of the sales for the year have not been converted to cash. Put another way, on average, it is taking the company three months to collect its debts. This is what is meant by the average age of debtors.

Clearly this is only an average. It could be that most of the debtors incurred in the last three months have paid and the reason for the high level of debtors is to be found in slow paying customers from earlier months of the year. Nevertheless, it gives a good indication of how well the company is managing its credit control policy.

The average age can be expressed in weeks, months or days depending on the user's preference. Although the detailed computation of the ratio varies, probably the easiest approach is to calculate sales per period and divide this into the value of trade debtors using the formula

$$\text{Average age of debtors} = \frac{\text{Trade debtors}}{\text{Credit sales per period}}$$

Example 14.2 demonstrates the calculation involved.

Example 14.2

> A company sells its products entirely on credit. During a six-month period, its turnover totalled £90,000 at the end of which its trade debtors stood at £30,000.

On average the company has had a credit sales turnover of £15,000 per month. With debtors of £30,000, the average time taken to collect debts will be two months.

Interpreting the average age of debtors ratio

Care is required in interpreting this ratio. First, published accounts do not differentiate between cash and credit sales and so there may be no alternative but to use total turnover even though this might distort the ratio. Secondly, the policy for recognising sales may vary from company to company even though the firm might be in the same sector. Some contracting companies, for example, recognise revenue as soon as work is completed while others wait until the work has been certified. Thirdly, a company might deliberately allow extended credit to customers as a sales device.

With these caveats in mind, the average age of debtors can be calculated for Morpeth plc. Assuming that all the debtors identified on the balance sheet are trade debtors – and with a real set of accounts the total figure would be broken down into the trade and non-trade elements – and assuming all the sales are on credit, monthly credit sales last year would have been £270 million/12 months or £22.5 million. As a result, the average age of debtors would have been:

$$\text{Average age of debtors} = \frac{£28 \text{ million}}{£22.5 \text{ million}} = 1.24 \text{ months}$$

This result can only be interpreted in the light of the industry within which Morpeth operates. If Morpeth was a supermarket chain – where practically all sales are for cash – then the figure would be disturbingly high. If, however, the normal credit terms in the industry allow customers two months to settle their debts then this suggests Morpeth is operating a fairly tight credit control policy.

A refinement to this analysis is possible as a result of the additional detail available since the introduction of FRS 3. If the discontinued operations ended six months ago, then the year end debtors are likely to only apply to continuing activities plus acquisitions. The turnover per month of the continuing operations would have been £200 million/12 months or £16.67 million per month. But if the acquisitions only occurred half way through the year, then sales per month would have been £50 million/6 months or £8.33 million per month. Combined, sales from these two sources would have been £25 million per month and so the average age of debtors can be revised to:

$$\text{Average age of debtors} = \frac{£28 \text{ million}}{£25 \text{ million}} = 1.12 \text{ months}$$

This slightly improved figure will have ramifications for next year. The less credit offered to debtors, the healthier will be the cash balance. This is just one further example of how FRS 3 can be used to improve forecasting company performance.

Average age of stock

A similar methodology allows the average of stock to be computed. Logically the process of sales causes debtors. The analogous process for stock is the cost of sales. If a retailer's cost of sales last month totalled £50,000 and the closing stock totalled £100,000, the retailer has sufficient stock to continue operating at the current level for two months. From this it is possible to develop a formula in a similar way to the one for the average age of debtors:

$$\text{Average age of stock} = \frac{\text{Closing stock}}{\text{Cost of sales per period}}$$

Sometimes it is suggested that the stock figure should be the average of the opening and closing stocks in order to obtain a more representative figure for the year as a whole. Such a view, however, is simplistic in that it assumes that the two year end figures produce the average for the year.

For some companies, the balance sheet value of stock is particularly sensitive to its chosen year end. A firework manufacturer, for example, is likely to have massive stocks in its balance sheet if its year end is two months before 5 November but practically no stocks if its year end is 5 November. Choosing the average of the opening and closing stock values would not reduce this distortion. An even stronger objection is that by including the opening figure, out-of-date values are being introduced.

Interpreting the average age of stock

The average age of stock ratio has to be treated with particular caution. Both the stock and the cost of sales are coloured by accounting policies such as FIFO or LIFO and the extent to which overheads are included. Rarely do annual accounts provide sufficient detail for the user to analyse the effect of these policies on stock valuations.

Secondly, stock levels often relate to future plans rather than past performance while the cost of sales figure is clearly a historical or backward looking piece of information. Account needs to be taken of this when interpreting the result.

Thirdly, sometimes the cost of sales will not be given in the accounts when the alternative profit and loss format is used. A surrogate figure then has to be used. Turnover would be one possibility although that includes not only costs but profit. The main alternative would be purchases but, although based on cost, it both excludes the labour and overhead component of the cost of sales while being based on a wider measure of activity than cost of sales.

Fourthly, the earlier choice of a retailer was disingenuous. For many companies, stocks will comprise raw materials and work-in-progress as well as finished stocks. Raw materials, by definition, will exclude labour and overheads. Work-in-progress and finished goods, however, will include an increasing proportion of them. Calculating a meaningful average age of stock is therefore fraught with difficulties. Including only finished stocks in the calculation would severely understate the funds tied up in stock by many companies. Equally, including raw materials and work-in-progress is not fully adding like with like.

The most sensible answer is probably to include all stocks but to treat the resulting ratio as merely a broad indicator. This is the way the ratio has been calculated for Morpeth plc. With the monthly cost of sales at £143 million/12 months or £11.92 million the average age of stock is:

$$\text{Average age of stock} = \frac{\text{£47 million}}{\text{£11.92 million}} = 3.94 \text{ months}$$

Whether this is excessive or not depends on the industry. If the company is a dairy, its average stock should be less than one day! If, however, it is a society jeweller and goldsmith, a normal ratio might be many months. Again, a refinement can be made to the above analysis by recognising that the year end stock will only represent continuing activities plus acquisitions. Referring to note 1 in Exhibit 14.2, the cost of sales for continuing operations came to £98 million and for acquired operations the figure was £30 million. Using the same assumptions as earlier, the monthly cost of sales for existing operations will be £98 million/12 months or £8.17 million while for acquired activities it will be £30 million/6 months or £5 million. On an annualised basis, therefore, the monthly cost of sales would have been £13.17 million to produce a revised average age of stock of:

$$\text{Average age of stock} = \frac{\text{£47 million}}{\text{£13.17 million}} = 3.57 \text{ months}$$

Average age of creditors

Trade creditors reduce the cost of financing working capital. The calculation of their average age will be analogous to the average age of debtors. Trade debtors were measured against credit sales, the trading flow from which they were generated. Creditors are generated as a result of purchases and so the average age of creditors can be found by

$$\text{Average age of creditors} = \frac{\text{Trade creditors}}{\text{Credit purchases per period}}$$

If a company's trade creditors are £20,000 and credit purchases over the last three months were £60,000, then creditors are, on average, equal to one month's purchases. In general, the greater the age of creditors, the less a company is having to use its own funds.

Superficially it would appear that the higher the ratio the better. This might not always be so. By using suppliers who allow large amounts of credit, the company may be paying more for its raw materials than otherwise necessary. Equally, a high average age of creditors might be less an indication of efficient working capital management and more a sign that the company is unable to pay its debts.

Interpreting the average age of creditors ratio

Accepting all of these interpretation difficulties, probably the greatest difficulty is a practical one: that the necessary data for the calculation of the ratio is generally not available from published accounts. Any figure for trade creditors is likely to include not only suppliers of raw materials but also wages and salaries as well as suppliers of power, telecommunications and rent and rates. Similarly the value of purchases for the period is rarely given, yet alone credit purchases. Often the only solution is to use surrogate data and treat the resulting ratio as very much a general indicator rather than an accurate statement.

Recognising this, the figure for Morpeth's trade creditors is shown as £40 million on its balance sheet. With no further disclosure, the figure has to be accepted on its face value even though it probably includes more than creditors relating to stock purchases.

An even greater difficulty is posed by attempting to find a surrogate for purchases during the period. The turnover figure should only be used as a last resort as by definition it comprises cost of sales plus gross profit. Creditors, however, are recorded at cost. Probably the 'least worst' figure to use is the cost of sales although it has to be recognised that part of the figure for creditors will relate to amounts recorded under distribution and administration expenses. With a cost of sales of £143 million, the monthly cost of sales will be £11.92 million to give an average age of creditors of:

$$\text{Average age of creditors} = \frac{\text{£40 million}}{\text{£11.92 million}} = 3.36 \text{ months}$$

This ratio can be revised to take account of the change in operations as a result of acquisitions and disposals. The cost of sales for continuing and acquired activities was found to be £13.17 million when analysing the average age of stock and so the revised average age of creditors will be:

$$\text{Average age of creditors} = \frac{\text{£40 million}}{\text{£13.17 million}} = 3.04 \text{ months}$$

The interpretation of either result – unlike that for the average of debtors – is made particularly difficult by the assumptions which had to be made. In the case of Morpeth, the distribution costs and administration expenses are large in relation to the cost of sales and so it is highly likely that a substantial amount of the creditors relate to transactions found under those two headings.

More than that, if Morpeth is a manufacturer then factory and machinery depreciation and production labour will have been included in the cost of sales. Depreciation involves no cash and hence no creditors while the latter will also probably not involve creditors if the year end date coincides with the payment date for salaries and wages. The denominator of the ratio therefore is likely to be an overstatement of the purchases per period and hence the ratio is likely to be an understatement. With this in mind, it would appear that Morpeth is being slow in paying its suppliers. However, the *significance* of this can only begin to be gauged by considering the solvency of the company.

LIQUIDITY AND SOLVENCY

Liquidity and solvency are not the same. Liquidity is concerned with the amount of assets held as cash or cash equivalents. Solvency is the ability to meet debts when due. It is therefore possible to be illiquid – have no cash funds – and yet still be solvent if, for example, cash inflows from debtors are timed to coincide with cash outflows required to pay creditors.

Solvency can be examined from a short term perspective, by comparing current obligations with available resources, and from a long term perspective where the concern is with meeting long term obligations such as loan stock or financial leases. Long term solvency is discussed later when assessing the risks faced within a company. For the moment, the emphasis is on short term considerations.

The current ratio

Traditional ratios have tended to fudge the difference between liquidity and solvency. One particular ratio which does this is the current or working capital ratio which expresses the current assets as a proportion of current liabilities, i.e.:

Current ratio = Current assets: Current liabilities

In effect, it is attempting to discover if there are sufficient short term resources within the company to meet short term liabilities. To demonstrate its workings consider the data given in Example 14.3.

If the creditors of Dover were to demand immediate payment, there would be insufficient cash available. This, however, is being ultra cautious. Debtors are only one stage removed from cash and will convert to cash within a short time. A similar argument can be applied to stock although the timings will be rather longer as it first has to be sold. On the face of it, the company has £100,000 of resources comprising stock, debtors and cash which, if not already cash, will soon turn into cash. Trade creditors, however, are £120,000 and so it would appear the company cannot meet its debts from liquid resources.

Example 14.3

Dover Ltd, a company with a turnover of £700,000, made a profit of £200,000 after charging depreciation of £100,000. Its balance sheet was as follows:

Shareholders' funds	£780,000	Fixed assets	£800,000
Trade creditors	£120,000	Stock	£60,000
		Debtors	£30,000
		Cash	£10,000
	£900,000		£900,000

Legal and technical insolvency

Although there is a difficulty, the company is not necessarily legally insolvent – that is a state wherein the debts could never be fully paid, no matter what the time period. Rather it is in a state which has been called *technical insolvency*. It cannot meet its debts immediately. Using the balance sheet data, the only way it can meet its debts is by selling off some of its fixed assets – the very assets which generate profit within a business. Whether this is viable depends on the realisable value of those fixed assets rather than their book values.

Dover has a current ratio of £100,000:£120,000 or 0.83:1. For a company to be able to pay its debts as they mature, it would appear from this analysis that the current ratio should be at least 1:1 although traditionally a figure of 2:1 has often been quoted as a desirable norm because of uncertainties in the valuation of the data. In particular, the value of stock contains uncertainties both because of the range of possible valuation methods and because of doubt as to the speed with which it can be turned into cash.

The quick ratio

Because of the uncertainties surrounding stock, an alternative stricter ratio has been developed known as the *quick ratio, liquidity ratio* or *acid test* and which excludes stock. Quick assets will be all assets which can be turned into cash within a very short period of time and includes marketable securities as well as debtors and cash. Formally the ratio is defined as:

Quick ratio = Debtors + Cash + Short term marketable securities : Current liabilities

In the case of Dover, the quick ratio is £40,000:£120,000 or 0.33:1. Received wisdom suggests that this ratio should be 1:1.

Limitations of the traditional ratios

Great care has to be taken in interpreting both liquidity ratios and especially in comparing them against the traditional norms, the logic for which have been lost in the mists of time. First, technology and new production methods are changing both the relative and absolute importance of components within the ratios. The growth of just in time stockkeeping, for example, has seen lower values of stocks required for any given level of trading. Secondly, for some companies such as supermarkets, stock may be a quicker asset than other companies' debtors. Thirdly, when simply applied, the ratios ignore timings. A loan repayable within 13 months, for example, will be classified as a long term liability, one repayable within 12 months as a current liability. Similarly, some current assets and liabilities are likely to convert to cash very quickly. Others, such as corporation tax, may not be payable for nine months while bank overdrafts might be a semi-permanent form of finance, in reality rarely repaid. In addition, only the current level of bank overdraft will appear on the balance sheet – rather than the size of the overall facility – and so a major source of liquidity is excluded from the ratios.

The ratios can also be influenced by window dressing in at least two ways. First the balance sheet data might not be representative. Once again, a firework manufacturer is a particularly good example. A balance sheet date shortly after 5 November will show very few current liabilities, very little stock and a large amount of cash.

Secondly, the ratios themselves are extremely sensitive to changes in the composition of working capital. Assume a company has current assets of £900,000 and current liabilities of £600,000 to give a current ratio of 1.5:1. Now assume half the current liabilities are paid. Nothing has really changed in the company and yet the ratio has now become £600,000:£300,000 or 2:1.

Income measures of solvency

Perhaps the major limitation of the ratios is their perspective. Essentially they are concerned with the availability of assets to meet debts. As such they emphasise the needs of creditors. The higher the ratios, the more secure will be the short term creditors. Shareholders, however, will view high ratios as signs of inefficiency as current assets do not generate profit.

In the real word most current liabilities are not met from a forced sale of assets. Instead they are met from future income generated in a similar way to individuals who pay their mortgage interest out of current salaries rather than wealth. Published accounts cannot show future income but what they can show is the past ability to generate profits and cash. Users can then make their own adjustments in the light of current circumstances.

Net current debt and the no credit interval

The choice is either to use data from the published cashflow statement as an estimate of the company's ability to generate cash or to use the reported profit figure adjusted to reflect cash generation.

Two measures are possible: the *net current debt* measure is concerned with how quickly a company can eliminate its current debt by trading, the other, sometimes known as the *no credit interval*, measures how long a company can keep producing without any inflow of funds. These are both defined below:

$$\text{Net current debt} = \frac{\text{Current liabilities} - \text{Quick assets}}{\text{Cash generated from operations per period}}$$

$$\text{No credit interval} = \frac{\text{Quick assets}}{\text{Operating outflow of cash per period}}$$

Calculating the net current debt

As an approximation, cash generated from operations can be defined as operating profits after tax plus depreciation and deferred taxation (both of which reduce profit but do not involve cashflows) less expenses capitalised. For Dover, the company in Example 14.3, the net current debt of immediate obligation less immediate resources is £80,000. It comprises the creditors of £120,000 less the cash and debtors of £40,000.

Without access to the cashflow statement, the cash generated from operations can be approximated to the profit of £200,000 plus the depreciation of £100,000 and so the measure of net current debt is:

$$\text{Net current debt} = \frac{£80,000}{£300,000}$$

On the basis of past performance, the company would take 80/300 of a year to generate sufficient funds to pay the amount owing to creditors which cannot be met from current resources. Multiplying 80/300 by 365 gives 97 days, the number of days of trading necessary to repay the net creditors.

Calculating the no credit interval

The no credit interval views the problem differently. It is concerned with how long the company can keep going without paying its creditors and without additional funds coming into the company. Currently it has £40,000 of quick assets to finance operations.

With a turnover of £700,000 and a profit of £200,000, annual expenses – assuming no exceptional items and other complexities – will be £500,000. Depreciation of £100,000, however, is included in this figure and so annual cash-based expenses will be £400,000. Applying this to the no credit interval ratio gives:

$$\text{No credit interval} = \frac{£40,000}{£400,000}$$

On the basis of the data given, the company has sufficient liquid resources to keep going for 36 days (40/400 × 365) without funds coming into the company. This does not seem unreasonable.

What is of more concern is the company taking 97 days to pay off net current debt. Within the limitations of the data, this suggests that the company is likely to be faced with difficulties if most creditors only allow 30 days' credit. Such conclusions, however, need to be treated with caution. Accounting data has been used rather than cashflows; the data used is past rather than current data; and stand-by facilities such as overdrafts have been excluded from the analysis. Nevertheless, used intelligently, both ratios are likely to be better measures of solvency as they emphasise flows and generating capacity rather than stocks of financial resources.

The liquidity of Morpeth plc

One difficulty in applying liquidity ratios to a real company is whether prepayments should be included in current assets for liquidity and solvency purposes. As they will not convert to cash and their realisable value may be extremely low, there is a good case for their exclusion. This is not a problem faced by Morpeth. With current assets of £87 million, current liabilities of £73 million and stocks of £47 million, the quick assets total £40 million. The resulting current and quick ratios for Morpeth are:

$$\text{Current ratio} = £87 \text{ million}: £73 \text{ million} = 1.19$$

$$\text{Quick ratio} = £40 \text{ million}: £73 \text{ million} = 0.55{:}1$$

One difficulty in calculating the net current debt concerns the treatment of bank overdrafts of £20 million recorded under current liabilities. *If* they are viewed as a semi-permanent form of finance, they need to be excluded from current liabilities for analysis purposes.

Treating the overdraft as a current liability, the net current debt is £33 million (£73 million − £40 million). To estimate how long it would take Morpeth to repay this amount requires an estimate of cash generated from operations. Without a cashflow statement, this involves making further assumptions.

It seems reasonable to exclude the exceptional gain from the figure as the aim of the exercise is to estimate the ability to generate *future* cash from *past* data. Equally it seems reasonable to exclude income from associated companies after tax as the group does not control their cashflows, any share of profit being used to increase the value of the associate in the balance sheet. To this must then be added depreciation charged for the year (given in note 4) and any increase in deferred taxation.

Taking all these into account, the estimated cash generated from operations over the year and the resulting net current debt will be:

Profit on ordinary activities after taxation		£36 million
Less exceptional gain	£4 million	
income from associates after taxation	£19 million	£23 million
		£13 million
Add depreciation	£10 million	
deferred taxation	£5 million	£15 million
Estimated cash generated		£28 million

$$\text{Net current debt} = \frac{£33 \text{ million}}{£28 \text{ million}} = 14 \text{ months}$$

Clearly the role of the bank and the treatment of the overdraft is critical in these circumstances. Even if the estimate of funds generated has erred on the side of caution, there is still grounds for concern about the short term liquidity of Morpeth.

Turning to the no credit interval, a somewhat different message is found. The operating outflows per annum can be approximated to the £143 million expenditure on the cost of sales, the £56 million distribution costs and the £24 million administration expenses less the £10 million depreciation charge, a total of £213 million. (This is only an approximation as some of these expenses might have been on credit.) With quick assets of £40 million, the no credit interval is found to be:

$$\text{No credit interval} = \frac{£40 \text{ million}}{£213 \text{ million}} = 2.2 \text{ months}$$

This suggests that the company could keep producing for a little over two months without any further support from short term creditors and without cash being derived from sales. On this measure, the company is reasonably liquid and solvent. If the bank overdraft was viewed as a long term source of finance then both the net current debt and the no credit interval ratios would have been that much healthier.

COMPANY RISKS

Problems of liquidity and solvency can result from two types of risk faced by companies. *Operating risk* is found to a greater or lesser extent in all companies. It is the risk inherent in the products and services provided by the company and the markets they serve.

The turnover and earnings of some industries are particularly susceptible to changes in consumers' spending power. Examples include package holidays and motor cars where a relatively small drop in consumer spending power leads to a large decrease in demand. At the other extreme are supermarkets which, in dealing with essentials, are more able to ride out any recession. To use a phrase beloved of economists, package holidays have a high income elasticity of demand.

The second type of risk faced by companies relates to how they are financed. The higher the level of debt finance, the greater the interest which has to be paid before a profit can be declared and so the greater the *finance risk*. The risk is not just in the variability of earnings available to shareholders as a result of these heavy commitments but also the possibility that the debts could bring a company down. Such risks are therefore an extension of the short term solvency difficulties already discussed.

MEASURING FINANCIAL RISK

As with the measurement of liquidity and solvency, financial risk can be measured either using balance sheet values – the more traditional approach – or by using earnings data. Using balance sheet data, ratios attempt to measure the proportion of a company's assets being financed by borrowings. To demonstrate this consider the balance sheet shown in Example 14.4.

Example 14.4

The financial position of Ashridge showed a profit of £60,000 for the current year. Its year end balance sheet was as follows:

Shareholders' funds	£600,000	Fixed assets	£800,000
10% loan stock	£300,000	Current assets	£200,000
Current liabilities	£100,000		
	£1,000,000		£1,000,000

Gearing or leverage

Most observers accept that the terms gearing or leverage are used to express the relationship of debt to equity. Beyond that, detailed definitions vary. Care is therefore necessary when attempting to interpret any previously calculated figure. With total assets of £1,000,000 and shareholders' funds of £600,000, the gearing or proportion of debt finance for Ashridge might be described as 40 per cent.

However, as gearing or leverage is more concerned with the relationship between the long term providers of funds and the long term resources within a company, it is probably better to consider the net assets in the company. Deducting current liabilities from total assets gives net assets of £900,000 and so gearing, using this measure, is 33 per cent. Expressing this as a ratio, gearing can be defined as:

$$\text{Gearing} = \frac{\text{Long term debt}}{\text{Net assets}} \quad \text{or} \quad \frac{\text{Long term debt}}{\text{Long term debt} + \text{Equity}} = \frac{£300,000}{£900,000}$$

To make matters even more confusing, similar data is often expressed in a slightly different form by expressing gearing as debt to equity, i.e.:

$$\text{Gearing} = \frac{\text{Long term debt}}{\text{Equity}} = \frac{£300,000}{£600,000} = 50\%$$

Both ratios always carry the same message as both ratios contain the same components. The first ratio shows that for every pound of debt there are net assets backing that up of £3. The second expresses this in a somewhat different fashion, that for every pound of debt there is an *extra* £2 of shareholders' funds supporting that debt. If debt were to increase, both ratios would increase.

Both ratios are therefore conveying the asset-backing for the debt and as such are security measures. Because of this, they are primarily of use to creditors, although if excessive gearing affects share prices or increases risk to the owners, they may equally be of interest to shareholders.

Limits to the amount of long term debt

Conventional wisdom suggests that no more than half of net assets should be financed by debt (a 100 per cent gearing ratio using the second definition). This presumably is to allow for uncertainties in balance sheet values and hopefully guarantee sufficient resources for debts to be repaid should the company face financial difficulties.

In exchange for this added security, providers of long term debt accept a lower (generally fixed) return in the form of interest. It is the shareholders who are the ultimate risk-takers in a company. They bear the cost of the interest payments and the resulting reduction in profits. They are also the beneficiaries when times are good and profits are high.

The reality, however, is that risk passes to the providers of debt if the gearing ratio becomes excessive. There is therefore a limit on the amount banks and other investors are prepared to lend to companies without demanding higher returns. Whether such ratios are the best measure of financial risk is open to question. What is not open to question is their limitations arising from the flexibility of accounting policies and the complex range of financial instruments available to modern companies.

Accounting policies and gearing

Ideally, to measure gearing as a security measure, assets should be valued at their real-isable value. This would then convey to creditors the real asset-backing for any loans made. Most published accounts, however, use the historical cost convention whereby assets are shown at their historical cost adjusted for depreciation and prudence. Others take advantage of the alternative accounting rules provided by the 1985 Companies Act and use replacement costs.

Irrespective of whether historical cost or replacement cost accounts are prepared, both assume that the company is a going concern and neither form of accounts necessarily reflect realisable values. As a generalisation, the more specific an asset, the less alterna-tive uses it has and the lower its realisable value on a forced sale. But even without this difficulty, balance sheet values will vary depending on the accounting policy chosen.

The treatment of goodwill

Recognising that balance sheet values partly depend on accounting policies begins to explain why some companies immediately write off goodwill on an acquisition while others choose to capitalise it. Eliminating goodwill in one fell swoop reduces the asset base and reduces the subsequent depreciation (or amortisation) of goodwill. As a result, profits will be higher both in absolute terms and as a measure of return on capital employed or shareholders' funds.

For a company with extensive debt, however, this reduction in the apparent asset base will increase its gearing ratio. It also goes part of the way to explaining why companies sometimes revalue their land and buildings. Revaluing assets, using replacement costs and capitalising goodwill on acquisitions all serve to increase the apparent asset base of a company and so reduce gearing.

The treatment of provisions and the minority interest

A second complexity in measuring gearing concerns the provision for liabilities and charges to be found on European balance sheets. Often the largest element within this will be deferred taxation. This will have been built up by charging more taxation to pre-vious profit and loss accounts than legally required by the Inland Revenue. Through time, it will be written back to compensate for periods when the actual tax charge will be greater.

It is therefore a reflection of an accounting policy rather than a legal charge owing to the Inland Revenue. In effect it attempts to smooth the tax charge over a period. Consequently it is not part of the long term debt of the company. Had no provision been made, retained profits would have been greater and so it seems reasonable to treat it as part of shareholders' funds for gearing purposes.

Less of a problem is the treatment of the minority interest in the balance sheet. The minority interest represents shareholders in subsidiaries who chose not to sell their shares when the subsidiaries were acquired by the group. As such, unless the group's behav-iour can be shown in a court of law to be oppressive, they cannot demand repayment. They are just as much equity shareholders as the ordinary shareholders in the group.

Convertible debentures and preference shares

The final significant difficulty in interpreting gearing ratios is the complexity of financial instruments. At its simplest, there is the question of whether overdrafts are in reality part of the long term debt of a company. More generally, companies sometimes issue convertible debentures, debentures which give the holders the right to exchange their loans on maturity for predetermined amounts of equity rather than a cash repayment.

Legally, the debentures remain debt until the holders choose to exercise their option. In reality, if the company is successful, capital markets will increasingly value the debentures as a way of acquiring additional equity. If this is how investors are treating the convertible debentures, it seems more reasonable to recognise this in calculating the amount of gearing by showing the securities as equity and eliminating the interest charge from the profit computation.

A second source of difficulty is the treatment of preference shares. Although, legally, part of the shareholders' funds of a company, preference shares have similarities to debt. This point has been reinforced by the Accounting Standards Board in FRS 4, Capital Instruments where shareholders' funds are broken down between equity interests and non-equity interests. The dividend is generally limited to a specific amount which has to be met before ordinary dividends can be paid. Because of this, preference share capital is sometimes included with the company's debt.

There are, however, two important differences. Preference share dividends do not have to be paid if a company makes no other distribution – unlike interest which has to be paid irrespective of profitability. Secondly, preference shareholders cannot force the sale of the company's assets if it defaults on the dividend. Preference shares therefore take on the appearance of debt when profits are high in that they are a fixed amount irrespective of profitability but the appearance of equity when times are more difficult. Because of this, and because gearing is predominantly concerned with security in the form of asset-backing, preference shares are more often treated as part of a company's non-debt funds in balance sheet ratios.

The gearing of Morpeth plc

With these considerations in mind, it is now possible to derive gearing ratios for Morpeth plc. The first decision concerns the treatment of the overdraft. Whether or not to treat this as part of the long term debt involves judgement.

The second decision concerns the treatment of intangibles. Certainly given the subjectivity involved and the fact that not all companies capitalise intangibles such as goodwill and brands, there is a strong case for excluding them when making inter-company comparisons.

The third decision concerns preference shares and whether or not they should be included as debt or shareholders' funds in the light of the pronouncements of FRS 4. There is no simple answer to any of these issues. It all depends on the purpose of the exercise and how the results will be used. But what is clear from this discussion is that it is wrong to accept any statement about a company's gearing without asking the basis and assumptions on which the ratio has been made. Because of this, caution is essential when interpreting the ready-made gearing ratios found in many surveys, newspaper reports and directories.[1]

Taking the ratios already introduced and merely using the raw data in the accounts, the net assets of Morpeth total £299 million and this is financed by £80 million of loans and £219 million of shareholder's funds. Immediately there are the two standard measures of gearing. Using these, the gearing of the company is:

$$\frac{\text{Long term debt}}{\text{Net assets}} = \frac{\text{Long term debt}}{\text{Long term debt + Shareholders' funds}} = \frac{£80 \text{ million}}{£299 \text{ million}} = 26.75\%$$

or

$$\frac{\text{Long term debt}}{\text{Shareholders' funds}} = \frac{£80 \text{ million}}{£219 \text{ million}} = 36.53\%$$

Beyond these calculations, however, are a range of other possible measures of gearing. The preference shares being non-equity could have been added to the debt to give a revised figure of £110 million leaving the funds belonging to the ordinary shareholders as a measure of the owners' stake in the company. This would involve revising the definitions above to read:

$$\frac{\text{Total fixed reward capital}}{\text{Net assets}} = \frac{\text{Total fixed interest securities + Non-equity shares}}{\text{Long term debt + Shareholders' funds}}$$

$$= \frac{£110 \text{ million}}{£299 \text{ million}} = 36.79\%$$

or

$$\frac{\text{Total fixed interest securities + Non-equity shares}}{\text{Equity}} = \frac{£110 \text{ million}}{£189 \text{ million}} = 58.20\%$$

Another adjustment would involve eliminating the intangibles from the net assets and shareholders' funds to make any ratio more comparable with companies that do not capitalise goodwill and brands. This would have the effect of increasing the measurement of gearing in all cases. Yet another refinement would be to view the bank overdraft as a long term source of debt. But equally, if the overdraft is included as debt, it could be argued that this indebtedness should be reduced by any cash balance in the current assets. As confusing as this makes the definition of gearing, all of these possible adjustments can be found in the many UK published directories and databases that provide financial ratios of companies. The message is clear: ready-prepared gearing measures must not be accepted on their face value without enquiring about their components.

Income measures of gearing

As with the traditional working capital ratios, the gearing ratio is more concerned with asset-backing for the debt and hence is more of a security measure for creditors. Of equal if not more importance to shareholders is whether the company can afford the servicing of the debt.

A popular measure to assess this is the *times interest earned* ratio. Ashridge, the company outlined in Example 14.4, showed a profit of £60,000 after paying interest. With £300,000 10 per cent loan stock, the interest would have been £30,000 and so the profit before interest was £90,000. It would therefore have been possible to pay interest three times over before making a loss to give a cover of 3.

Interest is an allowable expense for tax purposes and so the profit figure in the ratio should be the one before tax. Applying this to Morpeth and using the data in the accounts without any adjustments, interest payable is £20 million and the profit before interest is £70 million. Interest is therefore covered 3.5 times. This is the way the ratio is often calculated in many of the published figures for times interest earned. Despite this, it is not perfect. First, to obtain a more representative figure, the exceptional gain of £4 million might be excluded. Secondly, the company does not have full control over profits from associated undertakings. Thirdly, if a forecast figure is required, ideally the profit figure should exclude discontinued operations but include the annualised effect of acquisitions. Fourthly, the interest charged in the profit and loss account may not necessarily be the total interest payable in the period if some has been capitalised.

Exhibit 14.3 has demonstrated that the operating profit from the continuing and acquired operations is equivalent to an annualised £66 million. This amount already excludes any exceptional items. However, note 4 (Exhibit 14.2) shows £4 million of interest has been capitalised. As a result, the revised interest payable in the year was £24 million. Adding the £19 million profit from associated undertakings to the £66 million annualised operating profit gives a revised interest cover figure of 3.54.

By using an income measure of gearing and searching through the detailed notes, a more realistic picture has evolved. Such figures, however, need to be treated with caution. The profit figure is influenced by accounting conventions. Equally, interest is paid out of cash, not profit. And if the concern is with the effect of these fixed payments on the equity shareholders, a case can be made for including the cost of preference share dividends in the interest figure. Nevertheless, despite these problems, the ratio does give a new perspective on the debt burden of the company.

Gearing and profit forecasting

Both the balance sheet and income measures of gearing are primarily concerned with determining whether or not borrowing is excessive. An understanding of gearing, however, is also of help in forecasting. Because interest is payable whether or not a company makes profits, it is effectively a fixed cost. As such it serves to magnify the effect of changes in operating profit on the returns to shareholders. This is demonstrated in Example 14.5.

Example 14.5

Two companies are identical in all respects except for the way they are financed. Company A is financed entirely by 100,000 £1 ordinary shares whereas company B is financed by 50,000 £1 ordinary shares and £50,000 10 per cent debentures. Corporation tax is 50 per cent.

Profits before interest and tax are forecast at either (a) £5,000, (b) £10,000 or (c) £15,000.

Given this data, a user can forecast the return to the ordinary shareholders under the three possible scenarios. These are shown in Exhibit 14.4.

Exhibit 14.4 Gearing and earnings

	Company A			Company B		
Profit before interest and tax	£5,000	£10,000	£15,000	£5,000	£10,000	£15,000
Less interest				£5,000	£5,000	£5,000
Profit before tax	£5,000	£10,000	£15,000	nil	£5,000	£10,000
Tax at 50%	£2,500	£5,000	£7,500	nil	£2,500	£5,000
Profit after tax	£2,500	£5,000	£7,500	nil	£2,500	£5,000
Earnings per share (pence)	2.50	5.00	7.50	nil	5.00	10.00

In company A, a 50 per cent increase in operating profits from £10,000 to £15,000 results in a 50 per cent increase in the profits attributable to the ordinary shareholders. For company B, however, the effect is exaggerated with a similar 50 per cent increase in operating profits resulting in a doubling of the profits available to the shareholders. Equally dramatic, decreases in operating profit are magnified for shareholders in the company partly financed by debt. This is why taking on debt in a company's capital structure is known as gearing or leverage. Any percentage change in profits before interest and tax results in a greater percentage change in earnings after interest and tax.

MEASURING OPERATING RISK

In fact, the gearing effect on earnings is just one example of a more general phenomenon which helps investors forecast profits under different market conditions. Although an oversimplification, all elements making up the profit and loss account can be analysed in terms of their behaviour as turnover changes. A fuller explanation of this process is given in Chapter 17 but for the moment it is useful to consider the implications for forecasting company profitability.

Cost behaviour and price sensitivity

Other things being equal, a 20 per cent increase in demand for a company's products will lead to a 20 per cent increase in turnover. As a consequence, some costs – the variable or marginal costs introduced in Chapter 2 – will also increase by a similar amount while others, the fixed costs, will remain the same.

Care is required in carrying out this type of exercise. If the increased demand arises from a booming economy, it may well be that the increased volume is achievable without any decrease in prices. At other times, price reductions may be necessary to achieve the increased volume and so the effect on profit will be less dramatic. Similar assumptions apply to the treatment of the fixed and variable costs. Despite that, an understanding of a company's cost behaviour can give a useful insight into parts of its operating risk.

Some industries are insensitive to changes in wider economic activity. Water companies charging a fixed amount per household would be an obvious example. Customers have to have water. Only by moving to another area could a customer find an alternative supply. Water supply is therefore both income and price inelastic. Other industries are not so fortunate. Scheduled airlines, for example, are particularly sensitive to both changes in general economic activity and pricing policy. Consequently airlines face much greater operating risk than water companies.

Variable costs and operating risk

The extent of the operating risk for companies, however, is not simply the variability in demand which they face. Equally important is how companies are able to react to the varying demand and this is where an awareness of cost structures becomes important. A company which has high variable costs will tend to see these change in proportion to changes in sales activity. It is therefore more able to react to changing demand by changing its costs.

If, however, a company mainly faces fixed costs, its room for manoeuvre is limited in the short term. A 10 per cent decrease in demand for a particular newspaper will see newsagents decreasing their purchases by a similar percentage, reducing the damage caused to profitability by the decrease in demand. A cinema chain faced with a similar percentage decline has few if any costs it can reduce. It still has to provide the premises, it still has to provide the staff and it still has to provide the film whether one person watches the film or five hundred.

A similar analysis can be undertaken for other forms of income and expenditure. Interest received is more likely to change with changes in interest rates and surplus funds in the company rather than changes in activity. Royalties on the other hand are more likely to be associated with sales activity.

Interest payable under different levels of demand is less easy to estimate. If a company is faced with high variable costs, an increase in demand will probably lead to increased stock levels and increased debtors. To the extent that these have to be financed by short term borrowings, interest payable is likely to increase.

Changing turnover and profit

The effect of changing profits as demand changes is demonstrated in Example 14.6.

Example 14.6

Brighton Fun Ltd is a theme park which last year made a profit of £20,000 on a turnover of £100,000. Practically all of its costs are fixed costs. Warwick Toys Ltd also made the same profit from an identical turnover although its fixed costs were only £10,000.

Ignoring inflation and assuming no changes in costs, demand for both companies' products is likely to increase by 10 per cent next year.

Using this information, it is possible to estimate the future profitability of both companies. Brighton Fun's increased turnover will result in an increase in profits of an identical amount as all its costs are fixed costs. Warwick Toys, however, will only be able to increase its turnover by incurring additional variable costs. With a current profit of £20,000, total costs are £80,000 and so variable costs are currently £70,000. With a 10 per cent increase in turnover, variable costs will increase to £77,000.

The forecast profits arising from this are shown in Exhibit 14.5. A 10 per cent increase in Brighton Fun's turnover has led to a 50 per cent increase in its profit. Warwick Toys, however, has only experienced a 15 per cent increase in profits from a similar increase in turnover because of its low fixed costs.

Exhibit 14.5 Fixed costs and profitability

	Brighton Fun		Warwick Toys	
Forecast turnover		£110,000		£110,000
Less variable costs			£77,000	
fixed costs	£80,000	£80,000	£10,000	£87,000
Estimated profit		£30,000		£23,000

However attractive this appears to make Brighton Fun, there is a downside. A 30 per cent decrease in turnover will push Brighton Fun into a loss-making situation. Warwick Toys, however, will still be able to report a profit of £11,000. Other things being equal, the larger the absolute and relative amounts of fixed costs, the greater the variability in income and hence the greater the operating risk.

This has implications for company gearing. The greater the operating risk, the greater the variability in earnings and so the greater is the danger from using debt to finance a company. In assessing the risk from debt finance, users will be as concerned with the variability in earnings as with traditional measures of gearing.

The published accounts of Morpeth plc

Applying the analysis developed to published accounts, the user is immediately faced with a difficulty. The accounts do not show a breakdown between fixed and variable costs. The only option available is for the user to make assumptions. For the accounts of a retailer, this is relatively straightforward. Most of the reported cost of sales are likely to represent stock sold which is a variable cost.

When examining the accounts of manufacturing organisations, however, at least part of the cost of goods sold will represent depreciation and this is unlikely to vary with volume. Equally, the value placed on the cost of sales will vary depending on how stocks have been valued. For the other operating expenses of distribution and administration there may be little alternative but to make the simplifying assumption that they are all fixed costs. Although an oversimplification, it seems reasonable to assume that the cost of the accounting and personnel functions, for example, will not change greatly as turnover changes. With these difficulties in mind it is possible to estimate the effect of changes in turnover on the operating profit of Morpeth.

Assuming distribution costs and administration expenses are fixed costs, the only variable cost making up the trading profit will be the cost of sales. Exhibit 14.6 shows the likely changes to turnover and cost of sales from a 10 per cent increase in turnover.

Exhibit 14.6 Changing turnover and the effect on profit

	This year	10% increase
Annualised turnover	£300.0m	£30.0m
Estimated marginal cost of sales	£158.0m	£15.8m
Estimated increase in pre-tax profit		£14.2m

CREATIVE ACCOUNTING AND THE VALIDITY OF THE DATA

A ratio is only as good as the data on which it is based and yet the vast majority of the figures found in accounts are based on implicit or explicit assumptions. Sometimes these are embodied in law – as in the legal and correct approach found in many continental European countries. At other times, they will be based on managerial judgements or their interpretation of accounting standards. What is disturbing is the consistency with which many UK companies make use of such judgements to flatter their financial performance. None of them are illegal. All, however, tend to distort the reporting of the company's performance. This is what is meant by creative accounting.

As previous chapters have demonstrated, the Accounting Standards Board is increasingly tackling this important problem. FRS 3, for example, has tackled the tendency of companies to report favourable but irregular items as exceptional items above the line within 'normalised' profit and unfavourable transactions below that line. It is unlikely, however, that the ASB will completely eliminate the use of creative accounting. Because of this, any reader of accounts needs to be constantly aware of the small print and detail contained within financial statements and not just consider the 'headline' figures. This might involve users substituting their own accounting policies for those of the company by, for example, writing off intangibles such as goodwill. It might also involve users testing for the reasonableness of data in order to determine if the published information in the accounts is representative of the period's activities. Two particular tests are straightforward and easy to perform. These relate to the depreciation charge and the calculation of interest. Both are demonstrated in Example 14.7.

Example 14.7

Exeter plc and Bristol plc both operate in a similar industry. Extracts from their latest annual accounts are reproduced below.

	Exeter	Bristol
Extract from the profit and loss account:		
Profit on ordinary activities before interest	£20m	£20m
Interest payable	£6m	£3m
Profit on ordinary activities before taxation	£14m	£17m
Extract from the balance sheet:		
Net tangible assets (note 1)	£5m	£40m
Bank overdraft	£10m	£10m
Other debt: 10% loans in issue throughout the year	£20m	£20m
Note 1		
Plant and machinery at cost 1 January	£50m	£80m
Additions and disposals	nil	nil
Plant and machinery at cost 31 December	£50m	£80m
Depreciation balance 1 January	£40m	£24m
Charge for the year	£5m	£16m
Depreciation balance 31 December	£45m	£40m

Depreciation rates

A company's profits can be flattered by charging less depreciation. With some knowledge of the industry, however, it is possible to test for reasonableness. Exeter and Bristol are both in a similar industry and both appear to have the same profit on ordinary activities before interest. A reference to note 1, however, shows Exeter only charged £5 million of depreciation against profits for the year while Bristol charged £16 million. Neither company has disclosed whether these amounts have been calculated using the straight line or reducing balance methods of depreciation. Nevertheless, it is possible to develop a rough idea of their respective depreciation policies which can then be compared with their declared depreciation policies disclosed in the statement of accounting policies found in all UK published accounts.

To simplify matters, it has been assumed that both companies have only one class of fixed assets in the form of plant and machinery. At the year end, the plant and machinery at cost was £50 million in the accounts of Exeter. Depreciation for the year came to £5 million and so the depreciation rate appears to be 10 per cent per annum. In other words, the company is depreciating its fixed assets over ten years. Clearly this is only an approximation as the exact depreciation method is not known. Nevertheless, it is a useful figure. More than that, the average age of the fixed assets can also be approximated. With accumulated depreciation of £45 million at the year end, the conclusion must be that this represents nine years of the assets' lives which have been consumed. If nothing else, the message is clear: Exeter will soon have to incur substantial capital expenditure on replacing its fixed assets. Whether or not it is in a position to do this will depend on the strength of its cashflows from operations or its access to additional capital in the near future.

Even greater insight is possible by examining the accounts of Bristol. With depreciation for the year of £16 million and year end assets costing £80 million, Bristol is depreciating its assets at 20 per cent per annum. The company therefore is assuming the fixed assets have a five-year life. With accumulated depreciation of £40 million, Bristol's assets must have an average age of 2½ years. This certainly appears to be a more prudent policy than Exeter. Which policy is the more meaningful one can only be determined by knowledge of the industry. But if Bristol's policy is more reasonable then this suggests that Exeter is creating short term profits at the expense of its strategic, long term future.

Applying this analysis to Morpeth's plant and machinery, the company is depreciating those assets over ten years based on a depreciation charge of £8 million and a year end cost figure of £80 million. With accumulated year end depreciation of £40 million, the average age of the plant and machinery is five years.

Interest and borrowings

There is prima facie evidence that Exeter's borrowings in the balance sheet are not representative of its operations. At the year end, the company had £20 million 10 per cent loan outstanding plus an overdraft of £10 million. The interest on the loan would have been £2 million and with total interest payable in the year of £6 million, this leaves a balance of £4 million. If the only other source of borrowing was the overdraft, this suggests an interest rate of £4 million/£10 million or 40 per cent. The conclusion must be that either Exeter has an extortionate bank manager or, more likely, borrowings within the year were greater than the £10 million disclosed in the year end balance sheet. Taking a similar approach with Bristol, £2 million of the £3 million interest charge for the year relates to the 10 per cent loan. The balance of £1 million appears consistent with a £10 million pound overdraft.

Relating this analysis to Morpeth, there is an £80 million 10 per cent loan but interest payments of £20 million in the profit and loss account and £4 million capitalised. Of this £24 million, only £8 million relates to the loan, leaving a balance of £16 million. Assuming no other borrowings, this suggests that the reported overdraft at the year end understates the average overdraft for the year.

MARKET PERCEPTIONS OF THE COMPANY

Where a company has a stock exchange quotation, additional ratios are possible. Other things being equal, the lower the risk attached to a company's earnings and the greater their estimated growth the greater will be the value attached to those earnings by the market in the form of the share price. This is the logic behind the *price/earnings ratio*. Formally the P/E ratio is defined as:

$$\text{Price earnings ratio} = \frac{\text{Market price per share}}{\text{Earnings per share}}$$

A company with profits of £100,000 and 200,000 shares issued will have an earning per share of 50p. If the market price of each share is currently £5, then the P/E ratio will be 10.

Arithmetically the ratio is measuring the number of years it would take to repay the share's current value in earnings. Conceptually, it is doing something rather more: it is measuring the market's sentiment about those earnings. In principle, the higher the P/E ratio the greater the confidence the market has in those earnings, either in terms of their quality or growth potential.

Defining earnings

Critical to the ratio is the definition of earnings per share. SSAP 3 Earnings per Share originally defined earnings as the profit on ordinary activities after taxation and after deducting preference share dividends and profits attributable to the minority interest if the company is a group. It was therefore the profit on ordinary activities attributable to the ordinary shareholders before extraordinary items. FRS 3 has changed all this. The new standard defines ordinary activities so broadly that the occurrence of an extraordinary item should be a rarity. More importantly, the Accounting Standards Board, when issuing FRS 3, amended the definition of earnings originally found in SSAP 3. Now, the earnings figure is *after* extraordinary items. Earnings are now the profit (or in the case of a group the consolidated profit) of the period 'after tax, minority interests and extraordinary items and after deducting preference dividends and other appropriations in respect of preference shares'.

Taxation and dividend policy

For most companies the earnings figure is independent of its dividend policy, any advance corporation tax simply being used to reduce the mainstream tax. Where taxable profits are low relative to operating profits, however, some of the ACT may be disallowable and so the tax charge will be that much greater. Two possible definitions of after-tax earnings are then possible.

The nil and net basis

The nil basis calculates earnings on the *assumption* that no dividends have been paid. The corporation tax will then be the straightforward charge exclusive of any unrelieved ACT. The alternative is the net basis which shows the total tax charge including any unrelieved ACT. SSAP 3 requires the use of the net figure with the nil basis figure being shown if there is a material difference. Most companies will not have the problem of unrelieved ACT and so the nil and net bases will be the same, as Example 14.8 demonstrates.

Example 14.8

Scotland Ltd and Wales Ltd both have accounting profits of £80,000 and both plan to pay a dividend of £28,000. Scotland's taxable profit is also £80,000 while the taxable profit of Wales is only £20,000. Corporation tax can be assumed to be 33 per cent while advance corporation tax is ¼.

If it is assumed no dividend is payable – i.e. the nil basis – then earnings in both cases will simply be the £80,000 pre-tax profits less corporation tax of 33 per cent on taxable profits. For Scotland, the corporation tax will be £26,400 while for Wales it will be £6,600 to give after-tax earnings of £53,600 and £73,400 respectively.

Chapter 13 identified the rules for determining the maximum allowable advance corporation tax. For Scotland this will be £16,000 (20 per cent of £80,000) while for Wales it will be £4,000 (20 per cent of £20,000). For both companies, the ACT payable on the dividends will be ¼ of £28,000 or £7,000. Wales will therefore have disallowed ACT of £3,000. As a result, the net basis will produce the same after-tax earnings figure for Scotland but a reduced figure for Wales. Exhibit 14.7 shows the composition of the tax charge and net earnings figure for both companies.

Exhibit 14.7 The net basis of earnings

Scotland Ltd			Wales Ltd		
Operating profit before tax		£80,000	Operating profit before tax		£80,000
ACT	£7,000		Corporation tax	£6,600	
Mainstream	£19,400		ACT disallowed	£3,000	
Total taxation		£26,400			£9,600
After-tax earnings		£53,600			£70,400

The number of shares in issue

Having calculated the earnings figure for earnings per share, it is then necessary to calculate the number of shares. Where there has been no change in the number of shares in issue, this can simply be read from the accounts. Where there has been a change during the year, however, a weighted average of the number of shares in issue needs to be calculated. Earnings per share based on this weighted average is given in the accounts of all quoted companies.

Uses and limitations of P/E ratios

Many newspapers in the UK publish the price earnings ratios for companies. Accepting the ratio on its face value, however, is fraught with danger. First, the figure of earnings is based on accounting conventions and two otherwise identical companies can produce different earnings figures if, for example, they have different depreciation and stock valuation policies. More than that, some companies produce their accounts using some form of replacement cost accounting while many revalue assets such as land and buildings in their accounts.

Secondly, the ratio is not necessarily comparing like with like. The earnings figure is past data. The value of a share, however, will be based on investors' *future* expectations. As a result, peculiar P/E ratios are possible. For example, assume investors believe a company is capable of generating earnings per share of 50p but last year its earnings per share were reduced to 5p. Based on these future expectations, investors might value the shares at £5. The result is a not unreasonable *prospective* P/E ratio of 10. The reported P/E ratio, however, based on past earnings, will be 100. Equal difficulties of interpretation apply when a company is the subject of takeover rumours and its share price increases as a result.

Thirdly, as a result of FRS 3 requiring earnings to be effectively after all expenses – including many that would have been shown as extraordinary items in the past – earnings figures are likely to be more volatile. Because of this, crude P/E ratios derived simply from taking the earnings per share figure from the published accounts are also likely to be more volatile. This follows inevitably from the philosophy underlining FRS 3, that users should not concentrate on a single figure of short term results when appraising company performance. Two aspects of earnings are likely to gain prominence, normalised earnings (by adjusting for what the user believes to be extraordinary and exceptional items) and maintainable earnings – those attributable to the on-going business. This may well make earnings more meaningful. Unfortunately, it brings in greater judgement.

Nevertheless, providing a user is aware of these complexities, P/E ratios are a useful indication of how markets feel about a company and its performance. Sometimes their absolute value may be of interest. A P/E ratio in excess of 20 based on 'normal' profits implies either 20 years to pay back the current market price of the share in earnings or rapid growth. Whatever the reason, some investors would suggest the share was overvalued at this level. More likely, P/E ratios can be compared with other companies within the market sector once the user has made adjustments to the accounting data.

INTERPRETING COMPANY ACCOUNTS – A CASE STUDY

Before developing ratios for a company, the first stage has to be a check on the reasonableness of the data. If the base data is inadequate then any resulting ratio is unlikely to be of much use. Secondly, it is necessary to determine the perspective from which the accounts are being evaluated. Is the purpose to confirm or revise past beliefs or is it part of an attempt to forecast future performance? To derive maximum benefit from interpreting a set of company accounts, ratios need to be supplemented by other data. In particular, the cashflow statement may help to determine the quality of the reported profits, that is the extent to which the profits manifest themselves in cash.

The company and its results

The usefulness of ratio analysis and the interpretation of company accounts can be tested by making use of the appendix to this chapter which contains the annual report and accounts of a real company quoted on the London Stock Exchange. Briggs and Co. is involved in construction, property development and housing. Only the name of the company, the names of its associates and the names of its directors have been changed to maintain anonymity.

In the chairman's statement, in the summary of results and in the operating and financial review, there are three messages. The first is that there has been a significant change in performance from a loss before taxation of £22.043 million to a profit of £1.226 million. The second is that cash management has been particularly successful with year end cash balances increasing from £4.9 million to £10.7 million despite two acquisitions and additional land purchases. The third message is that the company has extremely low gearing. This success has been achieved despite a reduction in turnover from £296.026 million to £262.204 million.

Stockbrokers' evaluation

Certainly these messages appear to have been accepted by financially astute analysts. In a random sample of three major stockbrokers, all produced relatively favourable reports. None suggested that investors should move out of the shares in Briggs and Co. One even suggested that other investors should buy into the company. Particularly disturbing in all three reports was the uncritical acceptance and repetition of the information given in the chairman's statement and the operating and financial review. In the case of one report, this was then followed by a simple summary of the profit and loss account and balance sheet headings and values along with one or two ratios such as the sales margin and debt/equity ratios. Both of the other two reports drew readers' attention to the strong cash position with one mentioning that the pre-tax profits of £1.226 million 'came in ahead of our expectations'. All three reports then made some attempt to forecast future levels of profitability.

No detailed attempt was made by any of the reports to ask how the company had been able to significantly improve profitability over the year nor why there had been such an improvement in the cash balance. And not one of the reports drew attention to the decrease in shareholders' funds even though these figures were given in the summary following the chairman's report.

Adjusting the data

In order to begin to answer some of these queries, the starting point has to be a fuller understanding of the data. This might result in some figures being revised for analysis purposes. In other cases, it might simply develop a greater awareness of questionable accounting treatments that cannot be further quantified. The first step, therefore, simply involves reading through the annual report of Briggs and Co., identifying any contentious issues.

The operating and financial review

Starting with the operating and financial review, the first significant item is the contribution of £4 million profit from the property division. This has arisen from the sale of two properties, the supermarket site in Blackpool and the office scheme in Italy. Property organisations are unlike many enterprises. A food manufacturer or a supermarket will have sales and purchases continuously over the accounting period with sales being determined by what the many millions of consumers wish to buy. A property company, however, may only have two or three sales throughout the year and there is an element of discretion as to when to make the sale. For a supermarket with a 31 December year end, deferring sales from 31 December to 1 January will not substantially affect turnover or profit for either year. With a property company, because of the low volume of sales, bringing in a sale on the 31 December rather than 1 January may significantly influence both turnover and profits for any particular year. Because of this, the £4 million profits generated by the property division of Briggs may not be representative of either current or future performance in that division.

There is some evidence that this is what Briggs and Co. is doing with the sale of the supermarket site as its Construction division has reported that it has commenced work on the building of a superstore on the site it has sold. Had Briggs acquired the land and built the supermarket as a single transaction, profit taken from the land would have been deferred until the building had been completed.

Also in the review is mention of a shopping centre being developed as a joint venture in York. This is being financed by external borrowings of £15.2 million. However, because this enterprise is not a subsidiary, these borrowings will not appear in the balance sheet of Briggs and Co. Just taking the headline figures from the balance sheet would therefore understate the debt within the group structure.

If this borrowing is an obligation which fails to be disclosed in the accounts, equally, the UK trading and capital losses are an asset which is also not disclosed. Should Briggs generate future UK taxable profits, these will be available to offset the corporation tax charge.

Finally, there is an acknowledgement in the operating and financial review of Briggs having taken a pension contribution holiday. This will not affect reported profits but what it will do is adversely affect cashflows next year as contributions recommenced towards the year end.

Accounting policies

The accounting policies give some further insight into the information contained within the financial statements and notes. Goodwill on acquisition is written off against reserves, by-passing the profit and loss account and reducing the capital employed.

There seems to be two different policies for recognising turnover, the effect of which cannot be quantified. Turnover of the construction division appears to be based on *work carried out*, i.e. completed while other elements of turnover appear to be based on a more prudent basis of 'developments completed and *realised* and ... amounts of rents *receivable*'.

When undertaking the analysis of the company, it will be possible to approximate actual depreciation rates and compare them with the rates disclosed in the accounting policies. At this stage, what is more relevant is the failure of the company to provide depreciation on investment properties not occupied by the group. Certainly, this may be significant if inter-company comparisons were being undertaken. A similar comparison difficulty arises because Briggs and Co. classifies some investments as current assets. This will need to be recognised when calculating working capital ratios.

Notes to the accounts

Before analysing the financial statements, there might be further complexities buried in the detailed notes to the accounts. Because of this, the analysis of the financial statements will be left until last.

Information on directors and employees

Note 4 identifies that the directors were given bonuses this year 'based on financial results and specific key tasks'. Note 5 relates to employees. It expands on the contributions holiday identified earlier in the operating and financial review. Chapter 13 outlined the accounting treatment of pension holidays. Over previous years, (revised) amounts will have continued being charged to the profit and loss account but no payments would have been made. This has given rise to a creditor which will gradually be eliminated once contributions recommence. The implications for the future will therefore not be in terms of profit but cashflows on recommencing payments. These recommenced in November 19X7 and came to £175,000 or £87,500 per month. As an approximation, this will produce a cash outflow of £1,050,000 (£87,500 × 12 months) in a full year, an increase of £875,000 over the current year.

Tangible assets

Note 10 shows the composition of the £21.511 of tangible fixed assets outlined on the group balance sheet. This figure comprises total fixed assets at cost at the year end of £38,102 less accumulated depreciation at the year end of £16,591. Both the cost and depreciation values are then analysed by major classification of fixed asset along with information about additions and disposals during the year. Of particular importance is the depreciation charge for the year totalling £2.870 million and broken down between the charge for freehold properties, leasehold properties, plant and machinery and fixtures and fittings. The £2.870 million is also referred to in note 3 which shows the depreciation charge relating partly to owned assets and partly to assets held under finance leases. Exhibit 14.8 identifies the year end cost of each class of asset, the depreciation charged this year and the accumulated depreciation to date.

Exhibit 14.8 The depreciation policy of Briggs and Co.

(£000)	Freehold property	Leasehold property	Plant and machinery	Fixtures and fittings
Cost at 31 December 19X7	15,878	3,228	12,726	6,270
Accumulated depreciation	1,200	514	9,694	5,183
Net book value	14,678	2,714	3,032	1,087
Depreciation charge for the year	184	139	1,881	666
Depreciation rate	1.2%	4.3%	14.8%	10.6%
Life of assets	86 years	23 years	6.8 years	9.4 years
Average age of the assets	6.5 years	3.7 years	5.2 years	7.3 years

The depreciation rate has been found by dividing the depreciation charge for the year by the cost for each class of asset. The reciprocal of this gives the life of each class of asset. Dividing the accumulated depreciation by the cost of assets in existence at the year end identifies the proportion of the asset group already expensed. Multiplying this by the life of the asset enables the average age of each class of asset to be determined. For example, if an asset had a cost of £100, accumulated depreciation of £50 and a depreciation charge for the current year of £10, the depreciation rate is 10 per cent, the asset's life is 10 years and the age of the asset is 5 years.

Care has to be taken with this analysis. It assumes straight line depreciation rather than the reducing balance method and it also assumes no residual values. Equally, it ignores the complexities of assets being purchased part way through a year and not being charged with a full year's depreciation. Nevertheless, it is a useful 'ball park' figure to determine a company's depreciation policy.

The results contained in Exhibit 14.8 can be compared with the declared depreciation rates disclosed in the statement of accounting policies. One immediate difficulty is that the asset classifications used in note 10 are not identical with those declared in the accounting policies. Remember this is a real company quoted on the London Stock Exchange! First, the detailed notes do not disclose any information about motor cars which, according to the statement of accounting policies are depreciated at 20 per cent p.a. Secondly, the accounting policies refer to group occupied properties which would presumably include both freehold and long leasehold buildings but exclude investment properties within those headings.

Note (b) expands on this. Immediately there is a question mark over the validity of any revaluations of properties included in the book values as they have been revalued by an employee of the group. There is then the disclosure that had the accounts provided for depreciation on the properties not occupied by the group, the depreciation charge for the year would have been £773,000 this year and £621,000 in the previous year. Had this depreciation been incorporated within the accounts then an extra depreciation charge of £450,000, over and above the total of £323,000 already provided for properties, would have been necessary.

Fixed asset investments

Note 11(b) provides further information about the off balance sheet loans already discovered in the operating and financial review. Had Briggs and Co. owned 51 per cent of the shares in Median rather than 50 per cent, the whole of the £15.225 million of debt would have appeared on the group balance sheet.

Current assets and current liabilities

Note 14 identifies debtors relating to shared equity housing sales of £3.613 million. This amount arises from selling homes to house buyers who had insufficient funds to acquire the homes outright. In effect, the company is a part owner in those properties. Not only will these amounts not be immediately receivable – which is why they are disclosed as being amounts falling due after one year – there has to be a question mark over the financial strength of the debtors and their ability to repay the amounts owing in a depressed housing market.

Note 15 also discloses another anxiety. Briggs and Co. is including as an associate its investment in Dutch Builders BV despite only owning 15 per cent of the share capital. Although the directors justify this on the basis that the group exercises significant influence, there is no tangible evidence that this is so. The suspicion is that the Dutch company is highly profitable and by treating it as an associate, Briggs and Co. can bring in 15 per cent of profits within the group profit and loss account rather than merely dividends received had it been treated as a straightforward investment.

Within current liabilities, note 16 shows that Briggs and Co. is financing much of its activities by arranging for clients to pay in advance. For both the current and preceding years, the amount involved was in excess of £30 million. Also in current liabilities is the pension fund accrual. It is questionable whether this should be included in any working capital ratio as it is results from the standard treatment of pension contribution holidays which will gradually be reduced when payments recommence rather than through the traditional way of incurring liabilities.

Group reserves

Note 20 relating to group reserves begins to show why shareholders' funds have fallen. The company started the year with reserves of £56.826 million. However, after paying dividends for the year, there was a negative balance of £944,000 on the year's profit and loss account. In addition, £1.569 million of goodwill was written off in the year against reserves while £838,000 related to the difference on foreign currency translation.

Also in note 20 are the details of acquisitions made during the year. In total, Briggs and Co. acquired £958,000 of net assets from acquisitions but these only had a fair value of £28,000. Despite this, the company paid out £1.597 million to acquire those assets. Whatever the commercial benefits likely to arise from the acquisitions, what is clear is that, with only £28,000 of net assets, there is likely to be very little depreciation in future years to adversely affect future profitability.

Analysing the accounting data

Having identified the issues disclosed in the notes to the accounts, it is now possible to begin the analysis of the company's performance. This analysis will focus on the group profit and loss account and balance sheet, the group cashflow statement, the recognised gains and losses and the detailed make up of the profit and loss account as disclosed in notes 2 and 3. Simply taking the headline figures in the profit and loss account will give a distorted image of the results for both the current and preceding years. Instead, to identify underlying performance, use must be made of the additional disclosures in note 2.

Immediately, an apparent inconsistency is noticeable. In the profit and loss account for 19X6 there is an operating loss of £11.073 million on *continuing* operations resulting from £11.981 million in respect of major provisions and redundancy costs. There appears to be no similar expense for the current year. A detailed analysis of note 2, however, shows further redundancy costs of £475,000 treated as an ordinary expense of the current year. In addition, note 2 offers more information about the £11.981 provision in 19X6. This was made up of a £5,223,000 provision against commercial properties, a £5,101,000 provision against residential properties and £1,657,000 provision for redundancy costs. Making use of the data in note 2, Exhibit 14.9 shows the breakdown of operating profit disclosed in the profit and loss account.

Exhibit 14.9 The breakdown of operating profit

	Continuing	Exceptional	19X7	Continuing	Discontinued	Exceptional	19X6
Turnover	£262,204		£262,204	£293,196	£2,830		£296,026
Cost of sales	£242,406		£242,406	£274,629	£2,897	£10,324	£287,850
Gross profit	£19,798		£19,798	£18,567	(£67)	(£10,324)	£8,176
Administrative expenses	£20,874	£475	£21,349	£19,941	£297	£1,657	£21,895
Operating profit before share of associated company profits	(£1,076)	(£475)	(£1,551)	(£1,374)	(£364)	(£11,981)	(£13,719)
Associated profits	£2,802		£2,802	£2,282			£2,282
Operating profits	£1,726	(£475)	£1,251	£908	(£364)	(£11,981)	(£11,437)

Provisions, by their very nature, are difficult to quantify. In addition, there is an element of discretion in choosing when to recognise the loss in value on the relevant properties. To take a domestic analogy, a homeowner might have bought a house for £70,000 but its current value might only be £65,000. Should the loss be recognised against income for this year, next year or when sold? As no cash is involved, there is a choice. Because of this, the provisions and redundancy costs have been shown as exceptional items separate from the underlying and recurring operating expenses. In addition, the discontinued operations in 19X6 have also been shown separately. This allows the continuing operations of 19X6 to be directly compared with the continuing operations of 19X7.

Interpreting the profitability of Briggs and Co.

The result suggests that there has been barely any improvement in the operating performance of Briggs and Co. The main difference between the years' results from choosing to make large provisions in 19X6 rather than 19X7 (or any other year for that matter). In addition, had it not been for profits from associated companies, there would not have been an operating profit in 19X7. Finally, a second reason for the large losses in 19X6 was the £10.038 million loss on disposal of property fixed assets. No matter how real this item is, it is not a continuing one. The conclusion must therefore be that, despite the headline figures quoted in the summary of results, there has been no significant improvement in the underlying performance of the company.

This analysis can be carried further. Exhibit 14.10 merely compares disclosed expenses within the profit and loss accounts for both years from data given in note 3. What is immediately significant is that the charge for depreciation in 19X7 was £633,000 less than in the preceding year. Logically, this could have been due to a substantial disposal of fixed assets. Referring to note 10, however, total fixed assets were £39.548 million at the beginning of the year and £38.102 million at the year end – an insignificant difference.

With no discontinued operations in the current year and no reported losses on the disposal of fixed assets, the possibility that the depreciation charge has been revised to boost apparent profitability has to be considered. Some evidence that the directors are aware of the use of depreciation provisions to boost profits have already been identified. Had depreciation been provided on *all* properties, any extra charge of £450,000 would have been required for 19X7.

Exhibit 14.10 Analysis of disclosed expenses

	19X7	19X6	Difference
Depreciation			
Owned plant and equipment	£1,399	£1,988	£589
Owned properties	£323	£292	(£31)
Finance leased plant and equipment	£1,148	£1,223	£75
Total depreciation	£2,870	£3,503	£633

Cash management

A second major issue to be addressed is the cash management of the company. Once again, superficially, the company appears to be cash generative with year end cash balances increasing from £4.9 million to £10.7 million. This then raises the question of how representative these figures are. Already, mention has been made of an extra annual £875,000 outflow in subsequent years as a result of ending the pensions contribution holiday.

Turning to the cashflow statement, the cashflow from operations has fallen from £15.152 million in 19X6 to £7.892 million in 19X7. This reduction was then partially compensated for by much lower interest payments. Note 24 gives more detail to explain the cashflows. Immediately, it can be seen that a substantial explanation for the positive cashflows from operations in both years arises from the company running down its working capital, particularly its stocks and debtors. This may well be a sign of efficient management. However, given that Briggs and Co. is a building company, its stocks would comprise land to build on and this is not readily available at a moment's notice. By selling off land, it might well improve cashflows but, equally, it might restrict its operations in the future. Alternatively, the company will be faced with future substantial cash outflows when it becomes necessary to reacquire stocks of land.

Note 24 also suggests why interest payments have fallen. The company has redeemed obligations under finance leases and loans to the value of £864,000.

Finally, the analysis in Exhibit 14.8 suggests that both plant and machinery and fixtures and fittings are coming to the end of their useful lives. If these are to be replaced, it means that Briggs and Co. will have substantial cash outflows on their replacement in the near future. Alternatively, the company will have to enter into extensive leasing agreements to finance their replacement and this will have an adverse effect on the company's future gearing.

Evaluating the company

All of this suggests that the company is not performing as well as the chairman would like investors to believe. To quantify this, use can be made of the ratios developed earlier. The revised base data for these ratios is contained in Exhibit 14.11.

Exhibit 14.11 The adjusted data for Briggs and Co.

(£000)	19X7	19X6
Total assets less current liabilities	64,757	71,611
Less fixed asset investments	(1,241)	(361)
Less current asset investments	(1,119)	(279)
Less debtors falling due after one year	(3,809)	(5,688)
Capital employed in operations	58,588	65,283
Turnover of continuing operations	262,204	293,196
Operating cost of sales	242,406	274,629
Gross profit	19,798	18,567
Administrative expenses	20,874	19,941
Operating loss excluding associated profits	1,076	1,374
Debtors falling due within one year	36,121	43,374
Cash at bank and in hand	11,502	8,228
Quick assets	47,623	51,602
Stocks	64,694	70,319
Current operating assets	112,317	121,921
Creditors falling due within one year	75,240	80,767
Less pension fund accrual	(2,195)	(1,282)
Current liabilities	73,045	79,485
Debtors resulting from trading		
Trade debtors	19,542	11,985
Amounts recoverable on contracts	9,941	21,398
	29,483	33,383
Trade creditors	32,547	35,246
Shareholders' funds as per balance sheet	64,757	68,107
Creditors falling due after one year	nil	3,504
Less deferred taxation		(26)
Add off balance sheet finance (Median Ltd)	15,225	15,225
Debt finance	15,225	18,703

Return on capital employed

The capital employed in operations excludes investments in associated companies in order to determine the resources under the control of the day-to-day management of the company. In addition, the long term debtors are excluded as these are also not a resource necessary to generate current operations. Rather they are a consequence of past policies. Relating the capital employed in operations to the operating loss for both years results in a return on capital employed for the year of -1.84 per cent (19X6, -2.10 per cent), a negligible improvement on the previous year. Even this might be an overstatement because of the company's policy of not depreciating all of its properties and because there is some evidence of boosting performance by reducing other depreciation charges. In addition, Exhibit 14.8 suggests that the company is depreciating both its plant and machinery and fixtures and fittings towards the lower end of the ranges given in the accounting policies. This is particularly so for plant and machinery where Exhibit 14.8 suggests a life of 6.8 years. Many might feel this is too generous an assumption given the conditions to be found on building sites.

Two further refinements would have been to include the *value* of certain assets. Note 10 (b) shows the value of the freehold and leasehold properties at 31 December 19X7 came to £16.710 million. Their net book value – the amount they are reported in the accounts – totalled £17.392 million (£14.678 relating to freehold properties and £2.714 million relating to leasehold properties). Further, note 12 shows the replacement cost of builders plant and small tools exceeds the balance value by £3.575 million.

Further analysing the return on capital employed

These issues should be borne in mind when evaluating the sales margin and asset utilisation ratios such as the asset turnover. Using the data in Exhibit 14.11, the sales margin for the current year was -0.4 per cent (19X6, -0.4 per cent). With a capital employed in operations of £58.588 million and a turnover of £262.204 million, the asset turnover was 4.48 times (19X6, 4.49), again, suggesting no real improvement.

Working capital management

The directors of Briggs might legitimately argue that the lack of underlying improvement was due to the recession in the building industry – although this is not the message they are seeking to portray in the chairman's statement and the operating and financial review. But where they have room to manoeuvre is in maintaining strict controls over working capital. Even here, there does not seem to be any significant improvement.

Given the nature of the industry within which the company operates debtors arising from trading comprise the trade debtors plus amounts recoverable on contracts. For 19X7 these totalled £29.483 million. Set against turnover of £262.204 million, this gives an average age of 1.34 months (19X6, 1.37 months).

The average age of stocks for 19X7 is found by relating the £64.694 million of stocks to the cost of sales of continuing operations of £242.406 million to give an average age of

3.2 months (19X6, 3.1 months). Care has to be taken in interpreting this figure as stocks mainly comprise work-in-progress while the cost of sales relate to completed work. Because of this, it is likely that the ratios are an understatement of the amount of stock within the company. Perhaps more significant is the need for a standard against which to judge the ratios. A dairy would presumably hold stocks of little more than a day because of the nature of the business. Builders, however, are often working on developments which might take two years to complete. More than that, new land cannot be acquired at a moment's notice. Because of this, it could be argued that the levels of stock are perilously low.

The final major component of working capital is the creditors. Ideally, trade creditors should be measured against the purchases from which they originate but no such figure is disclosed in the accounts. Because of this, there is little alternative to using the cost of sales as a surrogate. With trade creditors in 19X7 of £32.547 million, their average age is 1.6 months (19X6, 1.54 months). Again, this is likely to be an understatement as the cost of sales will be made up of materials consumed, labour used and overheads allocated. Taking all three ratios together, there is no clear improvement between the two years.

Short term solvency

With current assets of £112.317 million and current liabilities of £73.045 million, the working capital ratio for 19X7 is 1.54:1 (19X6, 1.53:1) and with quick assets of £47.623 million the liquidity ratio or acid test is 0.65:1 (19X6, 0.65:1). Superficially, it appears that the company is not as liquid as it might appear when only considering the change in the cash balances.

Perhaps a better test would be to estimate the net current debt of the company, the number of days it would take to pay off the net debt from operations. Deducting the quick assets from current liabilities gives a net current debt for 19X7 of £25.422 million. In 19X7, however, the net cashflow from operations totalled £7.892 million which suggests it would take 38 months of trading at current levels to repay the net current debt! The equivalent figure for 19X6 was 22 months. Even allowing for the dividends received from associated companies of £2.00 million disclosed in the cashflow statement (19X6, £2.261 million), it would still take 30.8 months to repay the net current debt of 19X7. By focusing on cash balances, this significant deterioration in liquidity has been hidden.

Gearing

A superficial inspection of the balance sheet suggests that the company has no gearing in the current year. However, there is the £15.225 million of off balance sheet finance. Had Briggs owned one extra share, the shareholding would have been pushed over the critical 50 per cent level and the whole of the debt would have been incorporated within its balance sheet. In addition, there is the £250,000 of cumulative preference shares. Had profitability been high, these could legitimately be viewed as a fixed payment before paying the shareholders. However, with poor trading results, the dividends do not have to be paid and so, in these circumstances, it is more meaningful to treat them as part of the shareholders' funds.

A further issue is whether to include the bank loans and overdrafts found in the current liabilities as effectively long term borrowings and for these then to be reduced by the cash balance available to reduce those amounts. Again, given the poor state of the company, banks might well be viewing the loans and overdrafts as short term financing and so the preferred treatment is to concentrate on long term borrowings.

On that basis the total debt in 19X7 is £15.225 million. With shareholders' funds of £64.757 million, the debt to net assets or debt to debt plus shareholders' funds ratio for 19X7 will be 19 per cent (19X6, 21.4 per cent).

The breakeven point

The breakeven point for a company is that level of sales where there is neither profit nor loss. It is a particularly useful figure as, if a company is making a loss, it becomes a measure of the task involved in eliminating that loss. The subject is discussed in more detail in Chapter 17. Estimating the breakeven point from published accounts is fraught with difficulty as no analysis is given of fixed and variable costs. Equally, operating profits may not be totally representative where the operations include property sales. Despite this, it is possible to develop some idea of the task facing Briggs and Co. if it wants to generate operating profits.

One approach is to assume that the cost of sales is the only variable cost. However, for a construction company, this is likely to include at least some fixed costs such as depreciation. Ignoring this complexity for the moment, with a gross profit of £19.798 million and a turnover of £262.204 million, the contribution is 7.55 per cent. Assuming all the £20.874 million administrative expenses are fixed costs, the operating breakeven point will be £276.477 million. Consequently, Briggs and Co. needs to increase turnover by 5 per cent to breakeven.

Assuming the £2.547 million of depreciation on plant and equipment and fixtures and fittings disclosed in note 10 is included in the cost of sales, this would give a revised contribution of £22.345 million or 8.52 per cent. Adding this depreciation to the assumed administrative fixed costs gives a revised figure for fixed costs of £23.421 million and a revised breakeven turnover of £274.894 million, a 4.8 per cent increase.

Prospects for Briggs and Co.

Although a 4.8 or 5 per cent increase in turnover might not be a large increase, given the depressed state of the market, it might be difficult to achieve. The company also has a much more serious cash problem than at first appears. Added to this the average age of the operating fixed assets such as plant and machinery and it begins to appear that the company is not in good health to take account of any upturn in the economy. As a historical footnote, some three months after the accounts were published, Briggs and Co. had to have a large rights issue. What is even more disturbing than the poor state of health of the company is that three major stockbrokers failed to identify the worries discovered above.

SUMMARY

Many users of accounts wish to appraise a company's performance. Four areas have been identified: profitability, solvency, risk and market perspective. Ratios developed to measure performance can be divided into two groups. Traditional ratios are concerned more with balance sheet values and emphasise security. The more modern approach, particularly when applied to measures of solvency and risk, takes a different perspective – the ability to generate earnings and cash.

Three difficulties have been identified. Much of the data is past data and yet ratios are often used to forecast a company's future. Secondly, not all of the elements making up a ratio are available from published accounts. Consequently, there is little alternative but to develop surrogate measures and interpret the result with particular caution. Finally there are the assumptions implicit within all accounting numbers such as going concern and historical cost.

Ratios are only as reliable as the accounting numbers on which they are based. To make the best use of them involves at least as much attention being paid to the notes to the accounts as to actual financial data. Providing this is done, ratios can help to summarise and simplify the contents of financial reports. On their own, that is all they can do. However, by making comparisons with other companies or with previous results from the same company, it is possible to develop a greater meaning. Trends can be identified and unusual accounting policies discovered. This will still involve judgement by the user in their interpretation. Any single ratio is unlikely to be sufficient for that purpose. Instead the totality of ratios should be used to build up a general picture of the company and conclusions drawn from that.

REFERENCE

1 See for example Key Business Ratios, Dun and Bradstreet annually.

FURTHER READING

Bown D. and Laverick S. (1994) 'Measuring corporate performance', *Long range planning,* Vol. 27, No. 4.

Griffiths, I. (1987) *Creative Accounting,* Unwin.

Holmes, G. and Sugden, A. (1994) *Interpreting Company Reports and Accounts,* 5th edn, Woodhead-Faulkner.

Hussey, R. and Bishop, M. (1993) *Corporate Reports: A Guide for Preparers and Users,* Woodhead-Faulkner Ltd.

Pijper, T. (1993) *Creative Accounting,* Macmillan.

Samuels, J. M., Wilkes, F. M. and Brayshaw, R. E. (1990) *Management of Company Finance,* 5th edn, Chapman and Hall.

Smith, T. (1992) *Accounting for Growth,* Century Business.

TEST YOUR UNDERSTANDING

1 According to the Accounting Standards Board, how might users make use of the accounts of entities?

2 SSAP 25 is concerned with:
   (a) extraordinary items;
   (b) segmental reporting;
   (c) the reporting of turnover and operating expenses, broken down between continuing and acquired activities;
   (d) none of these.

3 Identify three limitations to ratio analysis.

4 The return on capital employed measures the return on assets. True or false?

5 How has FRS 3 helped users interpret company financial statements?

6 Identify two subdivisions of the return on capital employed.

7 How do current assets differ from fixed assets?

8 During a three-month period, a company had sales of £180,000. Debtors at the end of the period stood at £90,000. The average age of debtors is:
   (a) six months;
   (b) one month;
   (c) one and a half months;
   (d) none of these.

9 At the beginning of a 12-month period, a retailer has opening stocks of £40,000 and closing stocks of £60,000. The cost of sales for the year came to £220,000. Creditors at the commencement of the year stood at £20,000 and by the end of the year, this had risen to £35,000. The average age of creditors is:
   (a) 1.91 months;
   (b) 3.00 months;
   (c) 1.75 months;
   (d) none of these.

10 Solvency is the amount of readily available cash and cash equivalents. True or false?

11 Differentiate between financial risk and operating risk.

12 Why might some companies prefer to capitalise goodwill on an acquisition rather than write it off to reserves?

13 Are preference shares part of a company's debt for gearing purposes?

14 What is meant by creative accounting?

QUESTIONS

1 Burnup Tyres Ltd has recently joined the British Tyre Retailers Association and one of the association's services is to provide industry-wide ratios based on the accounts of member firms. The profit and loss account and balance sheet of Burnup Tyres for the current year is reproduced below. The loan is repayable in 13 months' time.

Balance sheet at end of current year			**Profit and loss account for the current year**		
		(£)			*(£)*
Fixed assets		66,000	Turnover		180,000
Depreciation		57,000	Cost of sales		120,000
		9,000	Gross profit		60,000
Current assets			Depreciation	3,000	
Stock *	87,000		Interest	3,000	
Debtors	30,000		Other expenses	45,000	
Cash	3,000		Net profit		9,000
	120,000				
Current liabilities					
Trade creditors	39,000	81,000			
		90,000			
Long term loan		30,000			
		60,000			
Ordinary share capital		10,000			
Reserves		50,000			
		60,000			

* Last year £90,000

The directors of Burnup Tyres wish to make use of the inter-firm comparisons provided by the association and have asked you to calculate likely ratios to help them compare their performance with other firms in the industry. They particularly request that you highlight any areas that should be brought to their attention.

2 Last year, your company considered acquiring Armley Bathroom Fittings Ltd but talks broke down over agreeing a fair price for its shares. One year later, your company has been approached by the directors of Armley Bathroom Fittings with a view to making a renewed bid.

Armley's directors feel that they have had a very successful subsequent year's trading. No dividends have been paid or proposed but the company managed to make a 40 per cent return on shareholders' funds and achieved an asset turnover – defined as sales over fixed assets plus current assets minus current liabilities – of six times. More than that, they were able to achieve such a respectable performance while ensuring a working capital ratio of 2:1 for the current year.

Because of the confidential nature of their enquiry, the directors feel unable to disclose the detailed final accounts although they inform you that the average age of debtors is four months, the average age of stock is three months and the average age of creditors is six months. No additional assets have been acquired and no disposals have taken place. Depreciation continues to be provided at 20 per cent on cost. Interest due on a long term loan which has been in existence for many years was also paid during the year. The only other information available to you is the previous year's balance sheet which formed the basis of the earlier discussions. This is reproduced below.

	(£)	(£)
Fixed assets		100,000
Depreciation		40,000
		60,000
Current assets		
Stock	60,000	
Debtors	80,000	
Cash	100,000	
	240,000	
Trade creditors	90,000	150,000
		210,000
10% long term loan		60,000
		150,000
Ordinary share capital		120,000
Reserves		30,000
		150,000

From the available information, reproduce as far as possible the final accounts of Armley Bathroom Fittings Ltd (taxation can be ignored).

3* Using the information extracted from the accounts of Lincoln Ltd which is reproduced below, evaluate the performance of the company over the year to 31 May 19X4 and for the year to 31 May 19X5 on the assumption that turnover is forecast to increase by 10 per cent.

Profit and loss account year to 31 May 19X4	Note	(£000)	(£000)
Turnover			
Continuing operations		300	
Acquisitions		150	
		450	
Discontinued operations		200	650
Cost of sales			(289)
Gross profit			361
Distribution costs			(131)
Administration expenses			(70)
Operating profit	(1)		160
Exceptional item gain from disposal of business			20
Interest payable			(58)
Income from interest in associated undertakings			40
Profit on ordinary activities before tax			162
Tax on profit on ordinary activities			(46)
Profit for the financial year			116
Dividends			(50)
Retained profit			66

Balance sheet at 31 May 19X4	Note	(£000)	(£000)
Fixed assets			
Intangible			97
Tangible	(2)		75
Interest in associated undertakings			236
			408
Current assets			
Stocks	(3)	127	
Debtors		39	
Cash and bank		1	
		167	
Creditors: amounts falling due within one year			
Bank overdraft		80	
Trade creditors		8	
Corporation tax		66	
Dividends payable		10	
		164	
Net current assets			3
Total assets less current liabilities			411
Creditors: amounts falling due after one year			
Loan repayable 31 June 19X5			(160)
			251
Represented by:			
80,000 £1 ordinary shares			80
Revaluation reserve			55
Retentions			96
			231
20,000 £1 10% preference shares			20
			251

Notes

1	Continuing	Acquisitions	Discontinued	Total
	(£000)	*(£000)*	*(£000)*	*(£000)*
Cost of sales	108	34	147	289
Net operating expenses	*(£000)*	*(£000)*	*(£000)*	*(£000)*
Distribution costs	70	21	40	131
Administration expenses	17	13	40	70
	87	34	80	201

The acquisitions were made three months before the year end while the disposal took place half way through the year.

2   Assets and accumulated depreciation

Assets	Freehold land and buildings (£000)	Plant and machinery (£000)	Total (£000)
At 1 June 19X3	45	60	105
Additions	12	23	35
Disposals	(10)	(17)	(27)
Revaluations	14	—	14
At 31 May 19X4	61	66	127
Depreciation	(£000)	(£000)	(£000)
At 1 June 19X3	24	39	63
Charge for year	2	6	8
Disposals	(7)	(12)	(19)
At 31 May 19X4	19	33	52

3   Stocks

	(£000)
Raw material	40
Work-in-progress	48
Finished stock	39

APPENDIX

BRIGGS AND CO.

CHAIRMAN'S STATEMENT

I am pleased to report that the group returned to profit during 19X7 with profits before tax of £1.2 million. Your directors are proposing a final dividend of 1.5p giving a maintained total for the year of 2.5p (19X6: 2.5p). Turnover was £262 million (19X6: £296 million). Trading profits in the Housing and Property divisions improved, largely offset, however, by losses in construction.

A continuing focus on cash management within the group resulted in an excellent improvement in net cash balances to £10.7 million at December 19X7 (19X6: £4.9 million). This cash position was achieved despite two small acquisitions and land purchases to support the increasing activity of the Homes division. The strength of the balance sheet has been a key component in winning construction work by maintaining client confidence.

In July, Cooper Limited was acquired and integrated into the UK Construction division. In August, Brigham Developments Limited was also acquired. Towards the end of the year, a joint venture, Knight Briggs Limited, was acquired with Knight Group plc to pursue commercial development opportunities on a forward funded basis. The group has also taken a 25 per cent stake in Gale plc.

The group purchased seven new housing sites in 19X7 and a further two subsequent to the year end providing a total of 440 units for immediate development. The cost of this investment was partly offset by the sale of some of the group's long term land bank of larger sites.

Provided corporate and consumer confidence strengthens further during 19X8 good progress should continue to be made in the UK property and housing businesses. Both these markets are showing higher levels of activity than in 19X7. Overcapacity in the UK building market and increasing cost pressures will however cause margins in the UK Construction division to be under continued pressure in 19X8 despite forecast improvements in the level of work available.

During 19X7 many demands were once again made on all those employed by the group and they have continued to meet the pressures and opportunities of the current trading conditions with enthusiasm and energy. I would like to express my appreciation and that of the board to them for their efforts.

James Merryweather
Chairman
28 March 19X8

SUMMARY OF RESULTS FOR THE YEAR ENDED 31 DECEMBER 19X7

	19X7 (£000)	19X6 (£000)
Turnover	262,204	296,026
Operating profit (loss)	1,251	(11,437)
Profit (loss) before taxation	1226	(22,043)
Profit (loss) after taxation	136	(21,342)
Net cash balances	10,741	4,966
Shareholders' funds	64,757	68,107
Dividends per ordinary share	2.5p	2.5p

EXTRACT FROM OPERATING AND FINANCIAL REVIEW FOR 19X7

CONSTRUCTION
In 19X7 construction turnover was £212.4 million (19X6: £250.8 million). This reduction reflected a selective tendering policy to avoid the worst extremes of the competitive tender market in the UK. The Construction division continues to win a broad range of work with the health leisure and retail sectors being particularly important. During the year a major new superstore for Triumph at Blackpool was also started.

PROPERTY
The Property divisions had a successful year, contributing £4 million to profits. The principal profit contributions came from the sale of a 12 acre site at Blackpool to Triumph supermarkets and from an office scheme in Italy.

HOUSING
The housing market began to recover in 19X7 with prices stabilising and volumes rising. The division achieved profits of £2.2 million with sales of 332 units compared to 262 in the previous year. The division started to buy new land early in 19X7 and has now secured nine sites, giving an additional 440 units for immediate development.

FINANCIAL REVIEW

The group's financial position remains strong and the board operates a policy of maintaining low gearing. This is particularly appropriate for a group whose principal businesses are cyclical with individual projects often involving significant risk.

Net cash balances increased from £4.9 million to £10.7 million. There was no particular seasonality behind the cashflows and both the Housing and Property divisions continued to be cash generative during the year. The Construction division absorbed cash partly due to its trading losses. £2.4 million was spent on acquisitions during the year.

During the course of the recession the group has sought to reduce housing and commercial property stocks commensurate with lower levels of activity. The group is now increasing its investment in housing as the economy recovers. The group has considerable working capital and bonding facilities and maintains a close relationship with its bankers and bondsmen.

The joint venture shopping centre development at York is financed by external borrowings amounting to £15.2 million. Subsequent to the year end an extension of this facility to 19X9 has been negotiated with no further recourse as to principal or interest. It is anticipated that the projects within Gale and Knight Briggs will be financed against the security of forward funding.

The results have been reported under Financial Reporting Standard No. 3. The detailed accounting practices to be applied by all businesses within the group are approved by the Audit Committee.

The tax charge for the current year is high mainly due to the level of profits earned in particular overseas locations. Considerable UK trading and capital losses are carried forward for offset against future taxable profits.

Details of the pension scheme and the latest valuation thereof are set out in note 5 of the accounts. For most of last year, the company benefited from a full contribution holiday but it resumed contributions in November 19X7 at a reduced rate.

FIVE YEAR REVIEW

	19X3 (£m)	19X4 (£m)	19X5 (£m)	19X6 (£m)	19X7 (£m)
Turnover					
Continuing operations	406	471	339	293	262
Discontinued operations	13	17	11	3	–
	419	488	350	296	262
	(£000)	(£000)	(£000)	(£000)	(£000)
Profit (loss) on ordinary activities before interest					
Continuing operations	25,645	12,246	(18,392)	(21,111)	1,215
Discontinued operations	181	(1)	(4,199)	(364)	–
	25,826	12,245	(22,591)	(21,475)	1,215
Net interest receivable (payable)	(2,155)	(4,345)	(2,748)	(568)	11
Taxation credit (charge)	(8,283)	(3,911)	5,616	701	(1,090)
Profit (loss) on ordinary activities after taxation	15,388	3,989	(19,723)	(21,342)	136
Earnings (loss) per ordinary share	45.5p	11.3p	(48.2)p	(48.4)p	0.3p
Dividends per ordinary share	20.0p	20.0p	9.0p	2.5p	2.5p

ACCOUNTING POLICIES

Basis of accounting
The accounts have been prepared in accordance with the requirements of the Companies Act 1985 using the historical cost basis of accounting modified to include the revaluation of certain assets and in accordance with applicable accounting standards.

Consolidation
The consolidated accounts comprise the accounts of the company and its subsidiaries all drawn up to 31 December. Purchases of companies are accounted for under the acquisition method. Goodwill arising on consolidation is written off to reserves.

Turnover
Turnover is the assessed value of construction and allied work carried out in the year, the sales value of developments completed and realised and the amounts of rents receivable, all net of VAT.

Long term contracts
Profit on long term contracts is recognised on a prudent basis as work is carried out and once the final outcome can be assessed with reasonable certainty. Full provision is made for all foreseeable losses.

Pensions
The group operates two pension schemes: a final salary scheme and a money purchase scheme. The scheme's funds are administered by trustees and are independent of the group's finances. The final salary scheme is fully funded and contributions are paid to the scheme in accordance with the rec-ommendations of independent actuaries to provide retirement benefits based on projected final salaries. The money purchase scheme is an insured scheme to which the company makes contribu-tions which are charged against the profits in the year in which they are payable. Company costs relating to the final salary scheme are charged to the profit and loss account so as to spread the cost of pensions over the working lives of employees who are members of the scheme.

Depreciation
This is provided under the straight line method at the following rates to write off the depreciable ele-ment of the cost or valuation of the group occupied freehold and leasehold properties and the cost of plant and equipment over their expected useful lives:

Group occupied properties	2%
Plant and machinery	12 ½% – 33 ⅓%
Motor cars	20%
Fixtures and fittings	10% – 20%

The same depreciation criteria are applied to assets acquired under finance leases as to those assets owned by the group.

The land upon which the group occupied properties stand is not depreciated nor is depreciation pro-vided for freehold and long leasehold investment properties not occupied by the group. In the opin-ion of the directors this departure from the requirements of the Companies Act 1985, which requires all properties to be depreciated, is necessary for the accounts to show a true and fair view in accor-dance with applicable accounting standards.

Leased assets

Leased assets are capitalised and obligations under finance leases are apportioned between finance charges and capital repayments in proportion to the balance of capital repayments outstanding. Costs of operating leases are charged to the profit and loss account as they are incurred.

Stocks

Commercial and residential developments are valued at the lower of cost and net realisable value. Builders' plant is valued annually on the basis of average cost price less a provision for obsolescence. Small tools and stocks are valued at the lower of cost and net realisable value.

Debtors

Amounts recoverable on contracts represent the excess of the value of work carried out over progress payments received or receivable. The value of such work is cost, which includes applicable overheads, plus any attributable profits, less any foreseeable losses.

Investments

The interest of the group in associated companies is stated at directors' valuation. The group's share of the results is included in the profit on ordinary activities before taxation based on audited accounts. Where the business of the associated company is the carrying out of individual construction contracts or property developments held for resale, the investment in that company is treated as a current asset.

Deferred taxation

Deferred taxation arising as a result of timing differences between the profit as computed for taxation purposes and that stated in the accounts is provided under the liability method. No provision is made for taxation on net surpluses arising from the revaluation of investment properties.

Foreign currencies

Balance sheets of overseas subsidiaries are translated into sterling at the rate of exchange ruling at 31 December each year: surpluses or deficits arising therefrom are taken directly into reserves. Trading profits or losses are converted at average rates prevailing during the accounting period. Realised gains or losses on exchange are included in the profit on ordinary activities before taxation.

GROUP PROFIT AND LOSS ACCOUNT
FOR THE YEAR ENDED 31 DECEMBER 19X7

	Note	19X7 (£000)	19X6 (£000)
Turnover			
Continuing operations		262,204	293,196
Discontinued operations		–	2,830
	1	262,204	296,026
Operating profit (loss)			
Continuing operations			
Ordinary trading		1,251	908
Major provisions and redundancy costs		–	(11.981)
		1,251	(11,073)
Discontinued operations		–	(364)
	2	1,251	(11,437)
Loss on disposals of property fixed assets		(36)	(10,038)

GROUP PROFIT AND LOSS ACCOUNT (CONTINUED)

	Note	19X7 (£000)	19X6 (£000)
Net interest receivable (payable)	6	11	(668)
Profit (loss) on ordinary activities before tax		1,226	(22,043)
Tax (charge) credit	7	(1,090)	701
Profit (loss) on ordinary activities after tax		136	(21,342)
Dividends	8	(1,080)	(1,115)
Retained loss		(944)	(22,457)
Earnings (loss) per ordinary share	9	0.3p	(48.4)p

Movements on reserves are detailed in note 20.

BALANCE SHEET AS AT 31 DECEMBER 19X7

	Note	19X7 (£000)	19X6 (£000)
Fixed assets			
Tangible assets	10	21,511	24,129
Investments	11	1,241	361
		22,752	24,490
Current assets			
Stocks	12	64,694	70,319
Debtors: amounts falling due within one year	13	36,121	43,374
Debtors: amounts falling due after one year	14	3,809	5,688
Investments	15	1,119	279
Cash at bank and in hand		11,502	8,228
		117,245	127,888
Creditors: amounts falling due within one year	16	75,240	80,767
Net current assets		42,005	47,121
Total assets less current liabilities		64,757	71,611
Creditors: Amounts falling due after one year	17	–	3,504
		64,757	68,107
Represented by:			
Capital and reserves:			
Called up share capital	19	11,281	11,281
Share premium account	20	25,152	25,151
Other reserves	20	52	62
Profit and loss account	20	28,272	31,623
		64,757	68,107

Approved by the board of directors on 28 March 19X4

James Merryweather
Alex Perth
Directors

GROUP CASHFLOW STATEMENT FOR THE YEAR ENDED 31 DECEMBER 19X7

	Note	19X7 (£000)	19X7 (£000)	19X6 (£000)	19X6 (£000)
Cashflow from operating activities	24(a)		7,892		15,152
Returns on investments and servicing of finance					
Interest received		606		803	
Interest paid		(492)		(1,460)	
Dividend received from an associated company		2,000		2,261	
Dividends paid		(1,093)	1,021	(1,777)	(173)
Tax refunded			542		8,442
Cash outflow from investing activities					
Additions to fixed assets		(2,673)		(3,926)	
Disposals of fixed assets		2,306		2,123	
Closure costs		–		(736)	
Purchase of subsidiaries	20	(1,572)		–	
Investments in current asset associated companies		(877)	(2,816)	–	(2,539)
Cash inflow before financing			6,639		20,882
Cash outflow from financing	24(d)		(864)		(3,278)
Net cash inflow	24(b)		5,775		17,604

STATEMENT OF TOTAL RECOGNISED GAINS AND LOSSES FOR THE YEAR ENDED 31 DECEMBER 19X7

	19X7 (£000)	19X6 (£000)
Profit (loss) for the financial year	136	(21,342)
Translation differences on foreign currency net investments	(838)	1,965
Total gains and losses recognised in the year	(702)	(19,377)

Note:
Historical cost profits and losses do not differ materially from those disclosed in the group profit and loss account

RECONCILIATION OF MOVEMENTS IN SHAREHOLDERS' FUNDS

	19X7 (£000)	19X6 (£000)
Profit (loss) for the financial year	136	(21,342)
Dividends	(1,080)	(1,115)
	(944)	(22,457)
Goodwill written off	(1,569)	–
Translation differences on foreign currency net investments	(838)	1,965
Proceeds of share options exercised	1	–
	(3,350)	(20,492)
Opening shareholders' funds	68,107	88,599
Closing shareholders' funds	64,757	68,107

NOTES ON THE ACCOUNTS

1 SEGMENTAL ANALYSIS

	Turnover		Profit (loss) before tax		Net assets	
	19X7	19X6	19X7	19X6	19X7	19X6
	(£000)	(£000)	(£000)	(£000)	(£000)	(£000)
Principal activities						
Construction	212,405	250,769	(2,083)	(2,925)	7,132	13,354
Property	17,849	13,361	4,003	(14,295)	37,760	33,201
Housing	31,950	29,066	2,251	(1,667)	19,865	21,552
	262,204	293,196	4,171	(18,887)	64,757	68,107
Discontinued operations	–	12,830	–	(364)	–	–
	262,204	296,026	4,171	(19,251)	64,757	68,107
Group and other costs			(2,945)	(2,792)		
			1,226	(22,043)		
Geographical areas						
United Kingdom	230,568	273,867	3,845	(18,543)	54,738	55,812
Rest of European Union	9,260	8,208	478	627	13,360	14,127
Elsewhere	22,376	11,121	(152)	(971)	(3,341)	(1,832)
	262,204	293,196	4,171	(18,887)	64,757	68,107
Discontinued operations	–	2,830	–	(364)	–	–
	262,204	296,026	4,171	(19,251)	64,757	68,107
Group and other costs			(2,945)	(2,792)		
			1,226	(22,043)		

Divisional trading results are stated after appropriate financing costs. The geographical analysis of turnover by destination is not materially different from the analysis by geographical origin shown above.

2 OPERATING PROFIT (LOSS)

		19X7		19X6
	(£000)	(£000)	(£000)	(£000)
Turnover				
Continuing operations	262,204		293,196	
Discontinued operations	–	262,204	2,830	296,026
Cost of sales				
Continuing operations				
Ordinary trading	(242,406)		(274,629)	
Major provisions	–		(10,324)	
Discontinued operations	–	(242,406)	(2,897)	(287,850)
Administrative expenses				
Continuing operations				
Ordinary trading	(20,874)		(19,941)	
Redundancy costs	(475)		(1,657)	
Discontinued operations	–	(21,349)	(297)	(21,895)
Share of associated company profits		2,802		2,282
Operating profit (loss)		1,251		(11,437)

Major provisions within cost of sales comprise commercial properties – £ nil (£5,223,000) and residential properties – £ nil (£5,101,000).

3 PROFIT AND LOSS ON ORDINARY ACTIVITIES BEFORE TAXATION

	19X7	19X6
	(£000)	(£000)
The profit (loss) is stated after crediting:		
Net rents receivable	1,104	1,659
Profit on disposal of fixed assets	284	256
and after charging:		
Depreciation on owned assets:		
Plant and equipment	1,399	1,988
Properties	323	292
Depreciation on plant and equipment assets held under finance leases	1,148	1,223
Auditors' remuneration	187	186
Fees payable to auditors for non-audit work in the UK	377	322
Finance charges payable on finance leases	152	275
Hire of plant on operating leases	1,182	1,317
Directors' emoluments (note 4)	749	790
Director's compensation for termination of service contract	209	–

Net rents receivable are shown after charging £551,000 (£674,000) payable for operating leases on land and buildings.

4 DIRECTORS' INFORMATION

	19X7	19X6
	(£000)	(£000)
(a) Remuneration (excluding pension contributions paid by the company)		
Chairman	50	68
Highest paid director	163	149

Other directors: Scale	19X7	19X6
	Numbers	Numbers
£5,001–£10,000	1	2
£10,001–£15,000	3	2
£90,001–£95,000	–	1
£105,001–£110,000	–	1
£110,001–£115,000	–	1
£115,001–£120,000	1	–
£130,001–£135,000	–	1
£135,001–£140,000	1	–
£140,001–£145,000	1	–
	7	8

The executive directors participate in a profit related bonus scheme. The performance related criteria based on financial results and specific key tasks are set by the Remuneration and Nominations Committee. Directors' emoluments in note 3 include £49,000 (£nil). In respect of bonuses, of which £nil (£nil) relates to the chairman and £14,000 (£nil) to the highest paid director. In addition to the remuneration shown above, pension contributions for the directors total £96,000 (£91,000) of which £15,000 (£nil) relates to the chairman and £18,000 (£17,000) to the highest paid director.

5 EMPLOYEE INFORMATION

	19X7 Numbers	19X6 Numbers
(a) The average number of persons, excluding the directors, employed by the group during the year is analysed below:		
Construction	1,102	1,286
Property	33	27
Housing	68	63
	1,203	1,376
(b) Group employment costs, excluding the directors:	(£000)	(£000)
Gross salaries and wages	22,538	25,155
Employers' national insurance contributions or foreign equivalents	1,972	2,221
Employers' pension costs under group schemes	1,210	1,105
	25,720	28,481

The group operates two pension schemes for eligible employees. The Staff Pension Scheme is a final salary scheme. The company pays contributions to the fund in order to provide security for existing pensions and the accrued benefits of current and former employees. The charge to the profit and loss account is such as to spread the cost of pensions over the working lives of employees who are members of the scheme and amounts to £1,032,000 (£801,000). The charge reflects the amortisation over 12 years of the funding surplus, which surplus has reduced between the actuarial valuations as at 5 April 19X5 and 5 April 19X7. The charge has been determined by qualified actuaries who are partners of a firm of consulting actuaries, and is based on the most recent actuarial valuation of the scheme, which took place as at 5 April 19X7 using the projected unit method. The most significant actuarial assumptions were that the rate of return on investments would be 9½ per cent p.a., the rate of increase in pay levels would be 7 per cent p.a. and the rate of pension increases would be 4 per cent p.a. Assets were valued assuming notional reinvestment in the FT-Actuaries All-Share Index with future dividends assumed to increase at 5 per cent p.a. in the long term, with an adjustment for short term dividend increase prospects. Following the results of the 19X7 valuation, company contributions which had been suspended since 19X4 because of the significant surpluses then available within the fund, were resumed with effect from November 19X7 and amounted to £175,000 (£nil) for the year. An amount of £2,195,000 (£1,282,000) which represents accumulated pension costs in excess of company contributions has been included in creditors.

The No. 2 Pension Scheme is a money purchase scheme and the company's contributions of £135,000 (£210,000) are charged to the profit and loss account in the year in which they are payable.

6 NET INTEREST RECEIVABLE (PAYABLE)

	19X7 (£000)	19X6 (£000)
Interest payable on:		
Bank loans and overdrafts wholly repayable within five years	(333)	(1,161)
All other loans	(177)	(293)
	(510)	(1,454)
Interest receivable	521	886
	11	(568)

7 TAXATION

Taxation (charge) credit on the profit (loss) on ordinary activities comprises

	19X7	19X6
UK corporation tax at the rate of 33% (33%) based on the taxable result for the year	(592)	1,593
Tax payable on associated company profits	(933)	(941)
Less relief for overseas taxation	1,273	688
	(252)	1,340
Overseas taxation	(838)	(639)
	(1,090)	701

8 DIVIDENDS

	19X7 (£000)	19X6 (£000)
On preference shares:		
4.9p paid per share (4.9p)	12	12
On ordinary shares:		
Interim paid 1.0p per share (1.0p)	419	441
Final proposed 1.5p per share (1.5p)	649	662
	1,080	1,115

9 EARNINGS PER SHARE

The earnings per ordinary share is calculated on the profit for the year before dividends on ordinary shares of £124,000 (loss £21,354,000) and 44,124,000 (44,124,000) being the weighted average number of ordinary shares in issue.

10 TANGIBLE ASSETS

	Properties freehold (£000)	Properties long leasehold (£000)	Plant and machinery (£000)	Fixtures and fittings (£000)	Total (£000)
(a) Group fixed assets before depreciation					
At 1 January 19X7					
Valuation	16,318	2,203	–	–	18,521
Cost	91	1,025	13,938	5,973	21,027
	16,409	3,228	13,938	5,973	39,548
Exchange adjustment	–	–	(2)	(7)	(9)
Additions	94	–	739	484	1,317
Disposals	(625)	–	(1,949)	(180)	(2,754)
At 31 December 19X7	15,878	3,228	12,726	6,270	38,102
Being					
Valuation	15,708	2,203	–	–	17,911
Cost	170	1,025	12,726	6,270	20,191
	15,878	3,228	12,726	6,270	38,102

10 TANGIBLE ASSETS (CONTINUED)

	Properties freehold (£000)	Properties long leasehold (£000)	Plant and machinery (£000)	Fixtures and fittings (£000)	Total (£000)
Depreciation					
At 1 January 19X7	1,016	375	9,372	4,656	15,419
Exchange adjustment	–	–	–	(3)	(3)
Charge for the year	184	139	1,881	666	2,870
Disposals	–	–	(1,559)	(136)	(1,695)
At 31 December 19X7	1,200	514	9,694	5,183	16,591
Net book value					
At 31 December 19X7	14,678	2,714	3,032	1,087	21,511
At 31 December 19X6	15,393	2,853	4,566	1,317	24,129

(b) The freehold and leasehold properties owned at 31 December 19X7 have been revalued to a net book value of £16,710,000. All properties have been incorporated at valuations made by a chartered surveyor who is an employee of the group on an open market basis at 31 December 19X7 (those in the group's occupation having been valued in their existing use). The historical cost of all group properties at 31 December 19X7 amounted to £19,277,000 (£20,468,000) against which depreciation of £773,000 (£621,000) would have been provided under SSAP 12.

(c) The net book value of fixed assets includes an amount of £1,470,000 (£2,756,000) in respect of plant and machinery and fixtures and fittings held under finance leases by the group.

11 FIXED ASSET INVESTMENTS

	Associated companies (£000)
(a) The group	
At 1 January 19X7	361
Additions	1,315
Disposals	(435)
At 31 December 19X7	1,241

(b) The group has an investment via a subsidiary in 50 per cent of the share capital of Median Limited, an associated company incorporated and operating in England. This company has a total issued share capital of £100 (£100) and bank borrowings totalling £15,225,000 (£15,225,000) at 31 December 19X7.

12 STOCKS

	19X7 (£000)	19X6 (£000)
Commercial developments	32,621	34,348
Residential developments	29,723	33,463
Net work-in-progress	62,344	67,811
Builders plant small tools and stocks	2,350	2,508
	64,694	70,319

The current replacement cost of builders' plant small tools and stocks exceeds the balance sheet value by £3,575,000 (£3,600,000).

13 DEBTORS: AMOUNTS FALLING DUE WITHIN ONE YEAR

	19X7 *(£000)*	*19X6* *(£000)*
Trade debtors	19,542	11,985
Amounts recoverable on contracts	9,941	21,398
Amounts owed by associated companies	3,055	4,237
Taxation recoverable	614	2,297
Prepayments and accrued income	1,855	3,111
Other debtors	1,114	346
	36,121	43,374

14 DEBTORS: AMOUNTS FALLING DUE AFTER ONE YEAR

	19X7 *(£000)*	*19X6* *(£000)*
Shared equity housing sales	3,613	5,282
Other	196	406
	3,809	5,688

15 CURRENT ASSET INVESTMENTS

	19X7	*19X6*
Associated companies	*(£000)*	*(£000)*
At 1 January 19X7	276	127
Additions at cost	977	–
Disposals at cost	(13)	–
Transfer to subsidiaries	–	(80)
Share of retained earnings	1,876	1,341
Distribution in the year	(2,000)	(2,261)
At 31 December 19X7	1,116	276
Quoted securities at 1 January 19X7 and 31 December 19X3	3	3
Total at 31 December 19X7	1,119	279

The quoted securities are shares in companies listed on the London Stock Exchange with a market value of £2,000 (£2,000).

	Proportion *of share capital* *owned by* *Briggs plc* *(%)*	*Country of* *incorporation* *and operation*	*Total* *issued* *ordinary* *shares* *(£000)*
Associated companies:			
UK Construction			
Loade Briggs Limited*	50	England	50
Gale plc	25	England	1
Knight Briggs Limited	50	England	–
Property Development			
Arrowpath Limited*	50	England	–
Verte (Espana) SL*	50	Spain	5
Dutch Builders BV*	15	Holland	12

*These shareholdings are owned by subsidiaries of Briggs plc

The directors have accounted for the interest in Dutch Builders BV as an associated undertaking on the basis that the group exercises significant influence in the affairs of that company.

16 CREDITORS: AMOUNTS FALLING DUE WITHIN ONE YEAR

	19X7 (£000)	19X6 (£000)
Bank loans and overdrafts	761	3,262
Obligations under finance leases	–	636
Payments received on account and advance payments	30,837	31,967
Trade creditors	32,547	35,246
Amounts owed to associated companies	2	–
Taxation on profits	208	152
Social security and other taxation	1,016	913
Dividends payable	649	662
Pension fund accrual (note 5)	2,195	1,282
Accruals and other creditors	7,025	6,647
	75,240	80,767

17 CREDITORS: AMOUNTS FALLING DUE AFTER ONE YEAR

	19X7 (£000)	19X6 (£000)
8% unsecured loan stock 19X9/X4	–	228
Obligations for deferred payments on sites	–	3,250
Taxation on profits	–	26
	–	3,504

The unsecured loan stock was redeemed in November 19X7.

18 PROVISIONS FOR LIABILITIES AND CHARGES

Full potential deferred taxation of £384,000 (£259,000) in relation to accelerated capital allowances and other timing differences has not been provided.

19 CALLED UP SHARE CAPITAL

	Authorised (£000)	Issued allotted and fully paid 19X7 (£000)	Issued allotted and fully paid 19X6 (£000)
4.9% (formerly 7%) cumulative preference shares of £1 each	250	250	250
Ordinary shares of 25p each	15,250	11,031	11,031
	15,500	11,281	11,281

20 GROUP RESERVES

	Share premium account (£000)	Other reserves (£000)	Profit & loss account (£000)	Total (£000)
At 1 January 19X7	25,151	52	31,623	56,826
Transfer from the profit and loss account	–	–	(944)	(944)
Goodwill written off	–	–	(1,569)	(1,569)
Translation difference on foreign currency net investments	–	–	(838)	(838)
Premium on share options exercised	1	–	–	1
At 31 December 19X7	25,152	52	28,272	53,476

The goodwill written off to reserves in 19X7 for subsidiaries acquired is as follows:

	Brigham (£000)	Cooper (£000)	Total (£000)
Book value of net assets acquired:			
Fixed assets	182	–	182
Current assets	718	558	1,276
Cash	–	66	66
	900	624	1,524
Creditors	–	(556)	(566)
	900	58	958
Fair value adjustments:			
Fixed assets	(125)	–	(125)
Current assets	(489)	(95)	(584)
Creditors	–	(221)	(221)
Fair value of net assets (liabilities) acquired	286	(258)	28
Purchase consideration	(1,570)	(27)	(1,597)
Goodwill	(1,284)	(265)	(1,569)

Cooper Limited was acquired on 23 July 19X7 and Brigham Developments limited was acquired on 9 August 19X7. The business of Cooper has been absorbed within other parts of the group and it is therefore not possible to identify its results for the period subsequent to acquisition. The Brigham loss before taxation for the period from the date of acquisition to 31 December 19X7 was £330,000.

The fair value adjustments have been made to align the accounting policies of the newly acquired subsidiaries with those of the group.

The net outflow of cash and cash equivalents in respect of the purchase of subsidiaries is as follows:

	(£000)
Purchase consideration	(1,597)
Cash recovered in 19X8	(41)
	(1,638)
Cash acquired	6
Net cash outflow in the year	(1,572)

21 COMMITMENTS FOR CAPITAL EXPENDITURE

Commitments contracted for at 31 December 19X7 but not provided for in these accounts were £695,000 (£156,000) .

22 COMMITMENTS FOR OPERATING LEASES

Commitments contracted for at 31 December 19X7 but not provided for in these accounts were £773,000 (£634,000) per annum. They all referred to land and buildings and fell into the following expiry bands: one year £49,000; two to five years £242,000; over five years £482,000.

23 CONTINGENT ITEMS

(a) The company
The company has guaranteed the bank overdrafts of subsidiary companies. The company has entered into guarantees and counter indemnities in respect of performance bonds in the normal course of business.

(b) The group
As is common in the construction industry, a number of disputes arise in the normal course of business some of which lead to litigation or arbitration proceedings. The directors make proper provision in the accounts when they consider that a liability exists.

24 CASHFLOW NOTES

	19X7 (£000)	19X6 (£000)
(a) Reconciliation of operating profit (loss) to cashflow from operating activities		
Operating profit (loss)	1,251	(11,437)
Share of associated company profits	(2,802)	(2,282)
Depreciation charges	2,870	3,503
Profit on sales of tangible fixed assets	(284)	(256)
Decrease in stocks	5,625	11,276
Decrease in debtors	7,790	2,354
(Decrease) increase in creditors	(5,729)	10,046
Currency translation of overseas accounts	(829)	1,948
Cashflow from operating activities	7,892	15,152
(b) Changes in cash and cash equivalents		
Balance at 1 January 19X7	4,966	(12,638)
Movement in the year	5,775	17,604
Balance at 31 December 1933	10,741	4,966
(c) Balances of cash and cash equivalents		
Cash at bank and in hand	11,502	8,228
Bank overdrafts	(761)	(3,262)
	10,741	4,966

(d) Changes in financing

Balance at 1 January 19X7	(864)	(4,142)
Movement in the year	864	3,278
Balance at 31 December 19X7	–	(864)

(e) Balances of sources of finance

Obligations under finance leases	–	(636)
Loan stock	–	(228)
	–	(864)

The cashflow impact of acquisitions is shown in note 20.

CHAPTER 15

Forecasting company failure

For shareholders, creditors and employees alike, probably the main concern will be whether a company will survive. As published accounts are often used to evaluate an enterprise's performance, it might reasonably be thought that the evaluation can be extended to measure the future viability of the organisation.

This chapter:

■ Identifies the difficulty of defining what is meant by company failure

■ Offers a qualitative approach to identifying companies likely to fail

■ Develops a rationale of company failure

■ Explains the logic underpinning quantitative approaches to the forecasting of company failure

■ Critically evaluates existing techniques for forecasting company failure

Will a company fail? This is the one big question omitted from the discussion of ratio analysis developed in Chapter 14. Immediately there is a semantic problem in defining what is meant by failure. Does it mean a company is insolvent? Does it mean calling in the liquidators? Or could it be something less such as a company being rescued by another company? Ignoring these problems for the moment, a working definition is possible by substituting financial distress for company failure. Financial distress can best be defined as 'severe liquidity problems that cannot be resolved without a sizeable re-scaling of the entity's operations or structure'.[1] It is what is colloquially known as financial difficulties. Normally a company in such difficulties would require a substantial restructuring such as a major injection of funds in order to survive in its present state.

Three approaches to the forecasting of company failure have been developed. The first two are essentially qualitative in nature. One involves the study of the root causes of failure. The second involves the identification of symptoms. Only in the third approach is the focus on quantitative data. Rather than building a logical case, it centres on what has been called brute empiricism – the combining of data from published accounts to develop financial indicators of a company's well-being. As such it appears a natural extension to the work developed in ratio analysis.

QUALITATIVE FEATURES OF COMPANY FAILURE

Root causes of failure

Many of the studies on fundamental causes and symptoms lie outside the narrow field of finance; they also vary in the rigour of their research. One author, for example, put company failures down to only one factor – greed.[2] Whether this is true or not, greed is both difficult to identify and measure. Another author, Bill Houston, identified two causes: commercial misjudgement leading to cash outflows, and the business cycle.[3] Again, it is obvious that more companies are likely to face financial difficulties in a recession than a boom and it is equally obvious that a major commercial mistake can lead to problems.

What is less obvious is how to identify such companies before the damage is done. To reduce the risk of company failure, Houston identifies areas where management must exercise particular care. These include adequate internal financial systems, attention to pricing policy, reliance on a single customer, the avoidance of overtrading – that is, attempting to support increasing levels of sales from an inadequate capital base – and major acquisition diversification and investment decisions. However valid these might be, many will only be known to internal management and no method is provided for quantifying their relative importance.

Attitudes and company survival

A different approach to forecasting failure was taken by Clutterbuck and Kernaghan.[4] They matched a sample of failed companies against a control group of non-failed companies in an attempt to identify attitudes which lead to company decline.

Their concern was with attitudes of management and employees towards controls, risk and the vision of the company. The authors identified five attitudes felt to be of importance for survival. Attitudes towards the (management) team included leadership styles, how staff perceived their roles and responsibilities and the quality and nature of communications. Attitudes towards customers, towards winning and losing and towards learning were also identified. Lastly Clutterbuck and Kernaghan identified attitudes towards investors. In particular, they felt that companies run by entrepreneurs appeared to collapse because of a failure to create working relationships with providers of finance.

From this they were able to produce a listing of failure indicators, although they did not differentiate between causes and symptoms. Areas identified included poor management, lack of planning, lack of financial control (particularly in the area of stock and credit control), over-reliance on one product or one customer, lack of reaction to economic and environmental change, inexperienced management (particularly in dealing with growth, acquisitions and international markets) and dissension within the management team. Other factors identified included inappropriate pricing, preoccupation with short term results, high cost structures and over-expansion, over-leverage and over-diversification.

In general, it is difficult to disagree with many of these factors although it is not clear whether they are underlying causes or only symptoms. Dissension in the management team might, for example, be at least a contributory cause of a company's failure. Equally, however, it might merely be a symptom of a greater but unidentified problem.

Qualitative characteristics

More significantly, the qualitative nature of many of the factors makes them difficult to identify and measure in an unambiguous way. One person's lack of planning, for instance, might be another person's flexibility. Because of this, the indicators are of only limited use as a forecasting mechanism. Having said that, Clutterbuck and Kernaghan do identify a totally subjective and scurrilous list of failure indicators which strikes a chord with anyone who has watched the recent history of UK corporate failures unfold. Factors they identify include:

- Personalised number plates
- Named car parking and executive washrooms
- Annual report showing the chairman leaving in a helicopter
- Fountain in the forecourt
- Fish tank in the boardroom
- New offices, opened by the Prime Minister
- Company yacht or aircraft
- Fast talking managing director
- Directors who use military titles
- Company matchboxes and other disposable promotions.

Company pathology

A less subjective list of causes of company failure is provided by the report *Company Pathology* published by a major UK stockbroker.[5] The report studies 45 quoted companies which appointed administrators or administrative receivers between 1989 and 1990. Some of the companies were fully quoted on the main stock exchange. Others were quoted on lesser markets then known as the unlisted securities market and the third market.

Six major contributory factors were identified in company collapses. Fast, aggressive expansion, whether organically or by acquisition, is likely to be an early warning, particularly if accompanied by sharp rises in debt – and especially short term debt. Secondly, some sectors such as property development appear to be inherently more risky than others. Thirdly, fully listed companies are less likely to fail than those quoted on secondary markets. As companies quoted on the secondary markets are smaller, younger and less well established, this is not particularly surprising. Fourthly, dominant personalities are often associated with companies which fall into difficulties, particularly where the chairman has a large shareholding and is also the chief executive. Fifthly, accounts normally show signs of impending difficulties but these are often disguised by creative accounting or the relegation of key information to the notes to the accounts. Finally, companies which do not appear to have financial advisers or do not disclose a long term relationship with a bank appear more vulnerable than those which have established such relationships.

What is interesting is that this survey does begin to identify factors which can be discovered by outside users even though the report does not separate causes from symptoms. Intuitively, it seems more likely that creative accounting is a symptom while a dominant personality is more likely to be a cause. A purist might argue that the findings are still subjective. What, for example, is meant by fast, aggressive expansion or a dominant personality? A pragmatist, however, might answer that such factors can be identified by users even though the factors might be difficult to fully define and measure. As evidence they might cite the late Mr Robert Maxwell and all of his alleged activities.

There are, however, stronger objections to such a listing of qualities found in failed companies. Having identified the characteristics of companies which fail, it is *illogical* to reverse the argument and suggest that all companies with those qualities will also fail. Secondly, there is no attempt to rank the relative importance of the factors identified. Thirdly, such listings do not offer a rationale as to why and how companies fail.

A RATIONALE AND RANKING OF COMPANY FAILURE

An attempt to explain the stages of financial distress and to rank the relative importance of different indicators has been made by Argenti.[6] Calling on evidence of past failures and discussions with operators in the field such as accountants and bankers, he believes that most failed companies follow a similar path and that causes of failure can be separated from symptoms.

The process which ultimately leads to failure can take five or more years and comprises three stages. The first stage identifies inherent defects in the company such as weakness in the company's management and an inability to change. This is then followed by a major mistake such as an ill thought-out attempt to diversify from which the company fails to recover. At this stage the course is probably set for failure. This is then followed by the appearance of both financial and non-financial symptoms of ensuing failure.

The inherent defects

Argenti identifies three areas of inherent corporate weakness, some of which are inter-related: the company's management, its accounting systems and the business's response to change.

One particular aspect of management he singles out is the dominant and domineering chief executive who is surrounded by unquestioning acolytes. Often the chief executive will also be the chairman. In the public perception he is viewed as 'the company'. Possibly related to this will be a weak board of directors with only limited business skills. Management skills below board level will also be limited with poor financial controls and direction.

So important is this last component that Argenti identifies it as a separate defect. Insufficient attention will be given to working capital management. Budgets and forecasts of profitability and cash may either not be adequate or not fully understood and used. Explanations for differences between performance and plan will not be fully investigated nor corrective action taken. Equally, real product costs may not be known nor their behaviour under changing conditions fully understood.

Finally, there is the company's failure to recognise change and the need to respond. Sometimes associated with an ageing board of directors, signs of a failure to recognise and respond to change include out-of-date products and production techniques, run-down factories, and insufficient attention to modern marketing techniques.

The mistakes

Argenti identified three mistakes associated with company failure, over-gearing, over-trading and emphasis on 'the big project'.

The implications of over-gearing have already been developed in the previous chapter. In times of expanding sales and profitability, the effect of gearing is to magnify profits attributable to shareholders. On a down turn, the reverse happens with the heavy fixed costs of servicing debt being unavoidable. Companies with an autocratic chief executive are alleged to be particularly prone to this problem, especially where financial advice is either limited or capable of being ignored.

Overtrading might well arise for similar reasons. An unwillingness to recognise that higher sales activity requires higher working capital and hence a higher capital base may well involve the company in taking on additional debt – especially short term debt – rather than equity. Debt can often be obtained without the full rigours of justifying the need for funds demanded when raising equity in the capital markets.

Lastly there is the 'big project' which is sufficiently large that if it fails, it brings down the rest of the company with it. The project can take a variety of forms. It could be a rush to diversify when the company suddenly awakens to the reality that it has an out-of-date product range. This might be reflected in an ill thought-out new product range or the takeover of other companies which often bear little relationship to the company's existing field of operations. In the construction industry it might be a single contract such as the building of a dam or a major highway on which the company's fortunes are entirely dependent. Alternatively, it might appear as a contingent liability, as when loans or other obligations are guaranteed in current or past subsidiaries.

The symptoms

Eventually the defects and the mistakes begin to manifest themselves. Four symptoms have been diagnosed by Argenti, two of which, deteriorating financial ratios and the development of creative accounting, relate to finance and accounting.

Financial signs begin to appear in the form of deteriorating financial ratios although these tend to occur relatively late in the process. Take, for example, a civil engineering contractor. In the early stages of a major project, interest might be being capitalised, disguising the true extent of the cost of borrowing. Later, as the lack of profitability in the project becomes clear, auditors are likely to disallow this treatment if the accounts are to show a true and fair view. The result is the 'times interest covered' ratio begins to fall drastically both as a result of the reduced profitability and the inability to capitalise further interest paid.

Hand in hand with this is the development of questionable accounting treatments of transactions. Attempts to boost profit by creative accounting can take many forms. Changing the depreciation policy is an obvious technique. Others are more sophisticated. A company might try to reduce its apparent debt by forming some kind of quasi-subsidiary which does not have to be consolidated. Alternatively a subsidiary may be converted into an associate and accounted for by using the equity method. Again, the result will be an apparent decrease in gearing.

The third symptom cannot be easily classified. It includes all the other non-financial signs of impending difficulties such as the freezing of capital expenditure and management salaries. Market share begins to fall significantly and there is a cutting back of essential overheads on service and quality control to boost short term profit and preserve cashflow. This is followed by the fourth and final symptom. Senior members of staff leave the company and rumours and writs begin to circulate. By this time, it is clear to even the most casual of observers that the company is in difficulties.

The weighting of indicators

Having developed a process of failure, Argenti went further and weighted the importance of the factors identified in financial failure in a form he called A scores. These are shown in Exhibit 15.1.

In developing an overall A score for a company, points should only be awarded by the user if the particular feature is confidently felt to exist. If the feature is absent a zero score should be recorded. No intermediate scores are allowed. Argenti believes that a score below 25 suggests a company is not in danger of failing. More points than that and the company is likely to fail within five years. He then goes beyond the overall total and suggests that a company with more than 10 points in the defects section is a warning that it might make a major mistake. Similarly, although the total points may be less than 25, more than 15 points for mistakes but less than 10 for defects implies that management is running the company at some risk.

Exhibit 15.1 Argenti's A Score

	Points score
DEFECTS	
Management:	
autocratic chief executive	8
chief executive is also chairman	4
unbalanced skill and knowledge on board	2
passive board	2
weak finance director	2
lack of professional managers below the board	1
Accounting systems:	
budgetary control	3
cashflow plans	3
costing systems	3
Response to change:	
products, processes, markets, employee practices, etc.	15
TOTAL POSSIBLE (Danger mark = 10)	43
MISTAKES	
Overtrading:	
expanding faster than cash funding	15
Gearing:	
bank overdrafts (loans) imprudently high	15
Big project:	
project failure jeopardising company	15
TOTAL POSSIBLE (Danger mark = 15)	45
SYMPTOMS	
Financial:	
deteriorating ratios	4
Creative accounting:	
signs of window dressing	4
Non-financial signs:	
declining quality, morale, market share, etc.	3
Terminal signs:	
writs, rumours, resignations	1
TOTAL POSSIBLE	12
TOTAL OVERALL POSSIBLE SCORE (Danger mark = 25)	100

Limitations to the Argenti analysis

Intuitively the scenario painted by Argenti is appealing. First, it does begin to offer an explanation for the failure of companies, unlike many of the other studies. Secondly, it attempts to weight the relative importance of the different stages making up the process of financial failure.

One difficulty, however, is that the three-stage process cannot be rigorously tested as features such as an autocratic chief executive or adequate accounting systems do not lend themselves to objective measurement. Having said that, the fault might lie with the poverty of scientific testing procedures rather than the analytical framework put forward by Argenti. Even though there is no unambiguous test of what makes an adequate accounting system, there is likely to be a consensus amongst accountants as to the desirable central features. Likewise, few people have difficulty in recognising an autocratic chief executive despite scientific method not yet being able to measure it in a value-free way.

There is, however, a greater criticism. Even if the features could be objectively measured, to show an association with failure would require a control group of non-failed companies to verify that the features were unique to failed companies. It also ignores the possibility that the path to financial failure might lie along a route other than that of defects, mistakes and symptoms.

In a later paper, Argenti[7] implicitly accepted this criticism by developing three profiles of failed companies. In the first case, a company never really takes off. It produces mediocre results before finally failing.

The second case is of a company which has initially spectacular growth in sales and profitability. Such companies tend to manufacture a single product which becomes fashionable. Just about all the accoutrements of recent yuppydom would fit this description. Unfortunately what is fashionable can equally quickly become unfashionable. The result can often be spectacular failure.

The third scenario put forward by Argenti is of a once solid company which goes into decline, possibly because the markets for its products have become saturated. This last scenario is the only one of the three which might reasonably be approximated with his earlier three-stage process of company failure. It is therefore not proven that all company failures follow the three-stage pattern of defects, mistakes and symptoms.

A further criticism is the lack of explanation and objectivity for the points awarded within the A scores. However intuitively reasonable they might at first appear, no proof is offered that an autocratic chief executive, for example, is eight times more critical than the lack of professional managers below board level. In addition to the subjectivity of measuring variables, it may well be that they are not independent. A lack of professional management below board level may, for example, directly result from the company having an autocratic chief executive.

Because of this, the additive nature of the A score lacks rigour. Consequently, Argenti's work, although an interesting contribution to the debate, cannot be shown to be an objective, foolproof tool for forecasting failure. At the most, it is a possible framework from which to begin evaluating companies.

STATISTICAL MODELLING – AN ALTERNATIVE APPROACH

Given the lack of any sound theory to *explain* financial failure, many authorities have returned to the data provided by financial statements to develop models for *forecasting* failure. This concern with ability to forecast rather than the wider concern to explain has been described as brute empiricism. It rejects the qualitative approach of Argenti and others as being subjective. Instead it uses financial ratios based on data taken from published accounts. As such the data is objective in the limited sense of being verifiable.

Univariate models

Some of the earliest work in this area was undertaken by Beaver[8] who used a univariate approach to predict financial failure. This involves the use of a single variable or financial ratio to predict failure. The assumptions are that the distribution of the variable for distressed firms will differ systematically from that in non-distressed firms and this difference can be used to predict future company failure. The technique involved can be demonstrated by using the data from Example 15.1.

Example 15.1

A particular industry is made up of ten companies. During one year, three companies found themselves in financial difficulties. The ratio of 'times interest earned' for all ten companies in the previous year along with their subsequent status is shown below.

Company	Ratio	Status
A	4.0	Non-failed
B	3.6	Non-failed
C	3.4	Non-failed
D	3.2	Non failed
E	2.8	Non-failed
F	1.6	Non failed
G	1.4	Failed
H	0.2	Failed
I	0.1	Non-failed
J	0.1	Failed

Ignoring the definitional problem of what is meant by financial difficulties and why the times interest earned ratio has been chosen, there appears to be a significant difference between the two groups. The average ratio for the failed group is 0.57 whereas for the non-failed group it is 2.67. (Using the student t test for small samples would verify that the difference is statistically significant.) Given this, the next stage is to develop a forecasting rule by determining a cut-off point for the classification.

Determining the cut-off point

Statistically, two types of error are possible. A Type I error would predict a failed company as a non-failed one. A Type II error would predict a non-failed company as having failed. There are therefore three possible cut-off points. One would minimise the total of Type I errors, the second the number of Type II errors, and the third the total number of errors. Suggesting that only firms with a ratio above 4.0 would survive ensures no Type I errors. Similarly using a ratio below 0.1 would prevent any Type II errors. This, however, is not particularly useful for forecasting.

Formally what is required is an analysis of the overall errors and the individual types of error at different cut-off points. Intuitively, however, the boundary between companies F and G seems an obvious starting point. Making the assumption that all firms with a ratio below 1.6 will fail would result in only one error, a Type II error which would wrongly predict company I as having failed. Making a stricter boundary – 2.8 for example – would increase the number of Type II errors without reducing the number of Type I errors. Reducing the boundary to below 1.4 would still leave a Type II error while introducing a Type I error in the form of company G. Continuing this analysis for all other possible boundaries, the boundary between companies F and G is the one which reduces the total number of errors.

Logically this is the cut-off point only if the objective is to minimise the total number of errors. For some users, however, the difference between a Type I and a Type II error will be significant. A bank, for example, if it wrongly classified a non-failed company as one likely to fail, would only lose the profit foregone on not making a loan. Classifying a company which fails as one which will not might mean the bank losing the full amount of money advanced. It is therefore more likely that a bank would be concerned with minimising the number of Type I rather than the overall total of errors.

The validation sample

Ignoring this difficulty, so far one sample of data (the estimation sample) has been used to develop a cut-off point. The next stage is then to test the cut-off point on a second group (the validation sample). This was the approach taken by Beaver. Using a paired sample design, he took 79 failed firms and matched each one with a non-failed firm from the same industry and with a similar asset size. The arithmetic mean of 30 financial ratios were calculated for the two different groups over the five years before failure.

In general there was a significant difference between the two groups for all ratios, a difference which became greater the nearer failure approached. Two ratios in particular, the cashflow to total debt ratio and the net income to total assets ratio, appear to show significant differences even five years before failure. Applying the analysis to individual firms, the cashflow to total debt ratios misclassified only 22 per cent of firms even five years before failure and within one year of failure this misclassification had fallen to 13 per cent. A similar result was found with the net income to total assets. Although showing a misclassification of 28 per cent five years before failure, the ratio closely matched the misclassification rate of the cashflow to total debt ratios over the final three years. What is of equal interest in Beaver's findings is the limited importance of the traditional solvency ratios.

Multivariate models

One limitation to the univariate approach is that a firm might be ranked as a prospective 'failure' under one ratio but a survivor using another. At the very least, this would involve a user having to make judgements about the relative importance of the different ratios.

A second difficulty is that it is easier for a company to distort a single ratio by creative accounting than a whole series of ratios. For example, a company might immediately write off all of the goodwill relating to an acquisition. If the possibility of failure is being judged by the single ratio of return on capital employed, such a policy will have the effect of improving the ratio. Using more than one ratio, however, may bring out negative aspects of the policy. Gearing, for example, will be adversely affected by the immediate writing off of goodwill.

A third limitation of the univariate approach is that not all the potentially useful data is being used when a single ratio is emphasised.

Multivariate models attempt to combine several financial variables within a single forecasting model. Models take many forms. They may be linear or non-linear. They may attempt to estimate the probability of failure or they may attempt to classify companies into one of two groups. Whichever the approach, choices have to be made about the ratios to be included and their relative importance or weighting.

Z SCORES AND DISCRIMINANT ANALYSIS

Discriminant analysis is the technique most often associated with multivariate modelling of company failure. It assumes a linear and additive relationship between several variables which enables the result to be expressed as a single figure known as the Z score. This can then be compared with a cut-off point to determine whether or not the company is likely to fail. The result is an equation of the form:

$$Z = aR_1 + bR_2$$

where R_1 and R_2 are financial ratios chosen for their ability to forecast financial failure and a and b are weights reflecting their relative importance. The most dramatic presentation of Z scores was presented by Taffler and Tisshaw.[9] They developed the idea of a solvency thermometer similar to the one reproduced in Exhibit 15.2.

Few could fail to be impressed with their findings. Of the 46 non-failed companies in their sample, the Z score thermometer accurately forecast every single one as being solvent. Of the 46 failed companies made up of the famous failures of the late 1960s and early 1970s, only one was incorrectly forecast. But even that was excusable as subsequent events showed.

The one error – shown as the one failed company within the solvent region of the thermometer – related to the collapse of Rolls Royce. However, all of its outstanding debts, including the debenture holders, were re-paid on liquidation along with a partial repayment to the equity holders. As such, Rolls Royce may not have really been insolvent in the first place.

The Z score within the solvency thermometer correctly forecast 96 per cent of the failed companies from their last published accounts even though only 22 per cent of the accounts had 'going concern' qualifications to their audit reports. Moreover, the model was able to predict 70 per cent of failures from the accounts of two year previous. As well as being accurate, the model is also claimed to be simple to apply. 'Its application ... requires no more than a set of draft accounts, a simple pocket calculator and ten minutes of ... time per company.'[10] Before examining the validity of the Z scores, it is useful to consider the intuitive make up of discriminant analysis although its detailed statistical rationale is outside the scope of this text.

Exhibit 15.2 The solvency thermometer

+ Z

Average solvent company

Failed
companies

Average insolvent company

– Z

(Adapted from Taffler, R. and Tisshaw, H. (1977), 'Going, Going, Gone – Four Factors which Predict', *Accountancy*, March, p. 51.)

The logic of discriminant analysis

Discriminant analysis can be demonstrated using a graphical approach if it is assumed there are only two variables in the analysis. In outline, the approach is not dissimilar to linear regression. Using linear regression, a company might for instance plot sales volume against a number of variables such as interest rates or unemployment to determine which is best for forecasting future demand. Assuming only two variables are used in the discriminant analysis, different pairings of ratios will be plotted for both failed and non-failed firms until the best fit is found.

A sample of failed firms will be matched with non-failed firms of similar size and industry. For the sake of argument, assume debtors/cash and stock/fixed assets are the first two ratios considered. The results will then be compared. Using a graphical approach, each pairing of ratios will be plotted together to give a single co-ordinate. A hypothetical set of results is shown in Exhibit 15.3 where failed firms are shown as a cross and non-failed firms as a circle.

No discernible pattern is evident from plotting debtors/cash against stock/fixed assets. The process therefore continues with other pairings of ratios until the best possible fit is found. Assume that the clearest pattern occurs when cash/net assets is plotted with the 'times interest earned' ratio. The hypothetical result is shown in Exhibit 15.4.

Here there is now a clear pattern with a definite boundary between failed and non-failed firms. As in Exhibit 15.4, rarely will the analysis eliminate all errors. Two failed and two non-failed firms have been wrongly classified. All that discriminant analysis can do is *minimise* the errors.

The relative importance of the two variables is given by the slope of the boundary and the task of discriminant analysis is to compute a formula for the boundary. Firms A and B actually lie on the boundary and so both are equally marginal even though the individual ratios show different characteristics. As such the value of their combined ratios will not only equal one another but also equal the cut-off point between failed and non-failed companies. To compute the cut-off Z value, assume the relevant ratios taken from their published accounts are as follows:

	Ratio 1 Cash/net assets	Ratio 2 Times interest earned
Firm A	0.8	1.0
Firm B	0.2	6.0

As both companies are equally marginal, it follows that:

$$0.8R_1 + 1.0R_2 = 0.2R_1 + 6.0R_2$$

where R_1 is the cash/net assets ratio and R_2 is the times interest earned ratio. Solving gives $0.6R_1 = 5R_2$ and so expressing both firms in terms of R_2 gives the following Z scores:

Firm A:	$0.8(8.33) + 1.0 = 7.67$
Firm B:	$0.2(8.33) + 6.0 = 7.67$

Consequently a firm with a Z score below 7.67 would be classified as one likely to fail while a firm with a Z score above this is likely to survive.

'Failure' methodology

One difficulty faced by all attempts to forecast failure is defining what is meant by the term. Simply relating it to companies which call in the receiver would omit those companies which avoid such a fate by merging with another company or rearranging its capital. No simple answer is possible. Care therefore has to be taken in interpreting the results of differing Z values.

Having defined what is meant by failure, the next stage involves statistical testing to ensure that any differences between failed and non-failed samples are due to differences in the population rather than random error.

Once this has been validated, the next stage is to apply the computed Z value to the original data from which it was derived. The forecasting power of this *estimation sample* should always be high as the Z value or discriminant function was derived from that original data. To complete the testing, a *validation sample* should be chosen. The computed Z value is then tested against this new data.

Exhibit 15.3 No relationship between the variables

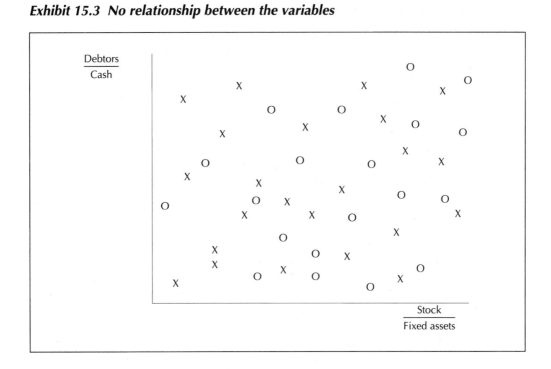

Exhibit 15.4 A relationship between the variables

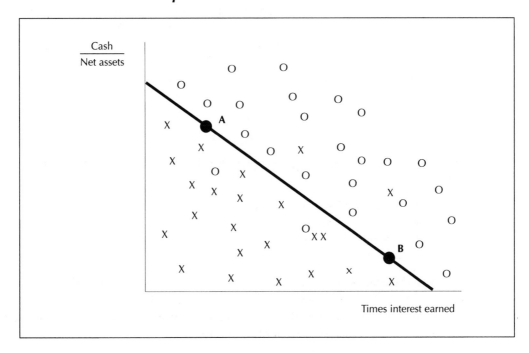

The findings from discriminant analysis

This was the approach taken by Altman,[11] one of the first observers to estimate Z values. As a result of the iterative process involved in discriminant analysis, he derived the following model:

$$Z = 1.2R_1 + 1.4R_2 + 3.3R_3 + 0.6R_4 + 1.0R_5$$

where:

R_1 = working capital/total assets
R_2 = retained earnings/total assets
R_3 = earnings before interest and tax/total assets
R_4 = market value of preference and ordinary shares/book value of total debt
R_5 = sales/total assets.

His sample comprised 33 US manufacturers that had filed for bankruptcy and these were paired with firms of similar size and industry which did not go bankrupt. He originally started with 22 ratios which were chosen on the basis of their popularity in the literature and their potential relevance to the field of study. By a process of iteration, these were whittled down to the five outlined above. When applied to the estimation sample, Altman found a 5 per cent misclassification.

He then used two validation samples: the first consisting of 25 bankrupt companies gave a 4 per cent error rate; the second, comprising 66 non-failed companies which had suffered 'temporary profitability difficulties,' predicted 52 out of the 66 as non-bankrupt. From his model, he was able to forecast that a company with a Z value above 3 would be safe. If, however, it fell below 1.8, it was a potential failure.

Taffler and Tisshaw omitted a validation sample when developing their solvency thermometer. This, they acknowledged when describing their model. 'The power of the model . . . indicates the results from applying the model to the 92 firms . . . The 99 per cent success rate will be noted.' Given that the solvency thermometer is describing the original data from which the Z value was developed, it is only to be expected that the success rate should be high. The Z model they developed and the ratios used were:

$$Z = C_0 + C_1R_1 + C_2R_2 + C_3R_3 + C_4R_4$$

where C_1 to C_4 are weightings given to ratios R_1 to R_4 and C_0 is a constant. The four ratios are:

R_1 = profit before tax/current liabilities
R_2 = current asset/total liabilities
R_3 = current liabilities/total assets
R_4 = the no-credit interval.

The no-credit interval was defined as immediate assets less current liabilities divided by operating costs excluding depreciation. Unfortunately, although Taffler and Tisshaw disclosed the ratios derived from the discriminant analysis, they did not disclose their coefficients and so their findings cannot be verified.

Limitations of Z scores

Much of the research undertaken on Z scores is of an *ex post* nature. To demonstrate the relevance of the scores requires *ex ante* predictions both about failures and timings. Further, there is only a meagre theoretical base for the inclusion of the variables. Altman, for example, partly chose his initial ratios because of their 'popularity in the literature'.

Adaptiveness of companies

The analysis takes the data as given and from that suggests the results are inevitable. Companies, however, consist of people and people are adaptive. They react to danger signals. On the other hand, if investors and others take note of the Z values and act on them, failure could become a self-fulfilling prophecy.

Benchmarks of success

A further problem is the standard or benchmark against which the model's success should be judged. Many models use a 50:50 relationship between failed and non-failed firms. *Random prediction* therefore will, on average, give a 50 per cent success rate. Equally the alternative *pure strategy* approach of accepting or rejecting all companies as failures will also give 50 per cent. However, both of these are naïve standards as they assume ignorance on the part of decision makers, namely that they cannot *judge* when a firm is more likely to go into liquidation.

Choosing a proportion other than 50:50 will change the benchmark against which the accuracy of the Z scores has to be measured. If 99 per cent of companies do not fail, then assuming no company fails will be correct 99 per cent of the time. Certainly there are far less failed than non-failed companies and so there is a danger that the individual characteristics of the model's failed companies will excessively affect the estimated discriminant function.

Some models try to avoid the problem of misclassification by developing a corridor rather than a boundary. Only if a company lies either side of this wide band would a forecast be made. Appealing as this is, the danger is that it merely segregates companies into three sections; the obviously healthy, the obviously distressed and the balance in the middle. And yet it is to the companies in the middle where human judgement is insufficient and where extra information would be of most benefit.

Other factors

The Z score methodology tends to concentrate on established firms using a paired sample design to match failed and non-failed companies. However, this excludes the three variables of age, industry and size. Failure may be signified by different ratios or different values of similar ratios between industries. The previous chapter, for example, highlighted the limited size of debtors and stock for supermarkets. Supporting this was the acknowledgement by Taffler and Tisshaw that a different Z value was derived for unquoted rather than quoted companies. If there are significant differences between quoted and unquoted companies, how much greater might the differences be between industries?

Finally, there is the validity of accounting numbers. Historical accounts convey costs which may not be current values. Similarly, creative accounting may attempt to disguise the underlying reality. Although there is tentative evidence that forecasting ability shows little difference whether reports are compiled under current purchasing power or historical cost accounting, the findings are not conclusive. Certainly, investors and analysts increasingly scrutinise accounts for unusual transactions and treatments. A failure to do the same for Z scores may well weaken their usefulness.

SUMMARY

The forecasting of company failure can be approached in two ways. The first looks at the common features found in failed companies. Argenti has expanded this by offering an explanation for failure. He describes a three-stage process of defects, mistakes and symptoms. The major limitations to this approach are the qualitative nature of many of the factors identified and the lack of evidence that all failures follow a similar process.

The alternative approach, particularly associated with Altman, is to not seek a hypothesis to explain failure but to concentrate on the forecasting ability of accounting numbers. By far the most popular technique used is discriminant analysis which results in a single Z score against which other companies can be measured. As appealing as it might be to summarise future solvency in a single figure, there are many difficulties with this approach, not least of which is that different sources produce different components and weightings for the Z scores.

With neither approach offering a full solution, the user is left with accepting aspects of both approaches. Certainly an understanding of the availability of cash is important, as is an understanding of the company's cost behaviour as circumstances change. Complementing this must be an awareness of the company's corporate strategy, its competitors, its relative cost structure, the ability of the firm to pass on cost increases, the stability of the industry and the quality of management. This must at some time manifest itself in financial data, some of which are more significant as indicators of solvency and well-being than others.

Finally, there are the external variables such as how potential investors see the company. Taking account of all these, there is no magic formula to indicate whether a company will succeed or fail. Rather, it involves the user coming to a judgement on the basis of both financial and non-financial information.

REFERENCES

1 Foster, G. (1986) *Financial Statement Analysis*, 2nd edn, p. 535, Prentice Hall.
2 Barmash, I. (1973) *Great Business Disasters*, Ballantine Books.
3 Houston, B. (1989) *Avoiding Adversity*, David & Charles.
4 Clutterbuck, D. and Kernaghan, S. (1990) *The Phoenix Factor: Lessons for Success from Management Failure*, Weidenfeld & Nicolson.
5 County NatWest Woodmac (1991) *Company Pathology*, Equity Briefing Paper 7.
6 Argenti, J. (1976) *Corporate Collapse*, McGraw-Hill. See also Argenti, J. (1977) 'Company Failure – Long Range Prediction is not Enough', *Accountancy*, August, and Argenti, J. (1983) 'Discerning the Cracks of Company Failure', *The Director*, October.

7 Argenti, J. (1977) 'Company Failure – Long Range Prediction is not Enough', *Accountancy*, August, pp. 46–52.

8 Beaver, W.H. (1966) 'Financial Ratios as Predictors of Failure, Empirical Research into Accounting' – supplement to *Journal of Accounting Research*, pp. 71–111.

9 Taffler, R. and Tisshaw, H. (1977) 'Going, Going Gone – Four Factors which Predict', *Accountancy*, March.

10 Ibid., p. 50.

11 Altman, I.E. (1968) 'Financial Ratios, Discriminant Analysis and the Prediction of Corporate Bankruptcy', *The Journal of Finance*, September, pp. 589–609.

FURTHER READING

Foster, G. (1989) *Financial Statement Analysis*, 2nd edn, Prentice Hall.

Argenti, J. (1976) *Corporate Collapse*, McGraw-Hill.

Koh, H.C. and Killough, L.N. (1990), 'The use of multiple discriminant analysis in the assessment of the going concern status of an audit client', *Journal of Business Finance and Accounting*, Spring, pp. 179–91.

TEST YOUR UNDERSTANDING

1 Identify three approaches to the study of company failure.
2 List Argenti's three areas of inherent corporate weakness.
3 List the three mistakes associated with company failure identified by Argenti.
4 What are Argenti's four symptoms of company failure?
5 What is an 'A' score?
6 What is meant by a univariate model of company failure?
7 Explain what is meant by a 'Z' score.

QUESTIONS

1 The model developed by Altman in 1968 to forecast company failures was as follows:

$$Z = 1.2R_1 + 1.4R_2 + 3.3R_3 + 0.64R_4 + 1.0R_5$$

where

R_1 = working capital/total assets
R_2 = retained earnings/total assets
R_3 = earnings before interest and tax/total assets
R_4 = market value of preference and ordinary shares/book value of total debt
R_5 = sales/total assets

In 1984*, Altman suggested that 'any firm with a Z score below 1.8 is considered to be a prime candidate for bankruptcy, and the lower the score, the higher the failure probability'. Using the accounts of Kingston and Thames plc reproduced below, estimate the Z score for the company and comment on your findings, identifying other data which might help in forecasting company failure.

Balance sheet at 31 December 19X3			**Profit and loss account for the year 19X3**	
		(£000)		*(£000)*
Fixed assets		6,000	Turnover	2,000
Stock	1,400		Earnings before interest and tax	300
Debtors	2,000		Interest	400
Cash	1,600		Loss before tax	(100)
	5,000		Corporation tax refundable	35
Trade creditors	800		Loss after tax	(65)
Other current liabilities	900 1,700	3,300		
		9,300		
Long term loans		4,000		
		5,300		
Ordinary share capital		4,000		
Profit and loss reserve		1,300		
		5,300		
Nominal value of ordinary shares		£1	Market value of ordinary shares	£6

*Altman, I. E. (1984) 'The Success of Business Failure Prediction Models: An Internation Survey', *Journal of Banking and Finance*, North-Holland Publishing Company.

2* Critically evaluate the validity of Z scores in forecasting company failure.

CHAPTER 16

Accounting within organisations

With so much emphasis on the external reporting aspects of accounting, it is easy to forget the origins of accounting as an aid to management. Indeed, there is an argument which suggests that accounting within organisations – management accounting – has lost its way, primarily because of the emphasis placed on the need of external reporting to shareholders and others.

This chapter:

■ Traces the evolution of management accounting and demonstrates how this was influenced by developments in other areas

■ Demonstrates the influence of technology in determining the way accounting data are collected and used

■ Discusses the validity of absorption costing and offers a rationale for its continued use

■ Summarises the debate over whether management accounting has lost its way

■ Addresses the issue of increasing overheads in organisations and identifies activity-based costing as being of potential benefit

With so many developments in company law and financial reporting, particularly over recent years, it is easy to lose sight of the origins of modern accounting. Accounting developed in the medieval ages before the extensive divorcing of ownership from control. The needs of the managers were the needs of the owners as often they were one and the same person and the focus of their needs was less on external reporting and more on accounting information as an aid to managing the organisation.

This internal use of accounting information would have been used to address at least three issues. One was the need to know how well the organisation was performing, the so-called scorekeeping role of accounting. A second use would have been to identify when things were going wrong, an attention directing role. The third use follows on from this and would have involved accessing the accounting information to aid decision making.

THE MEANING OF MANAGEMENT ACCOUNTING

The origins of management accounting

In medieval times, these needs would probably have been satisfied without the use of any formal system. Production was relatively simple and so problems – and their correction – were often self-evident. Businesses would have simply purchased the output from homeworkers and used the price paid to calculate profitability and measure efficiency. Scorekeeping was therefore a relatively simple matter. Any problems of production would have been the responsibility of the homeworkers, of interest to the business only if this caused difficulty with supplies or adversely affected profitability. Most decisions for the enterprise would have revolved around the price paid for the inputs and their likely selling price.

All this changed with the introduction of the factory system and the development of large business organisations. Homeworkers who had previously sold their output at market prices were now replaced by factory workers. As a result, market prices ceased to exist to measure profitability, to direct attention to difficulties or to help decision making. In their place were wages; but to measure the costs now required additional information about the productivity of the workers. Only then could efficiency be measured by comparing the unit costs with outside prices. Increasingly, even this was not viable as complex technology meant workers were often manufacturing intermediate products for which no outside market price existed.

No longer could the market mechanism in the form of independent homeworkers be relied on to provide output and known prices and costs. Instead, manufacturing had to be planned around the constraints imposed by the emerging new technology of the Industrial Revolution. This involved consciously considering the structure of the organisation within which production would take place and recognising for the first time a need for managers with responsibility for ensuring those plans were achieved.

Almost inevitably, these managers became distanced from the day-to-day operations as a result of the growth in size and complexity of the business. Personal observation to discover what was happening in the business was no longer possible and yet information was required by managers if they were to do their jobs properly. As a result, information gathering became formalised and one major source of this information was the data passing through the accounting system. These were the origins of what was to become known as management accounting.

Management control systems and management accounting

One difficulty in trying to define management accounting is that its scope is constantly changing. Nevertheless some insight can be gathered by considering the role of managers in an organisation. At its most general, management is responsible for the continuing survival of an enterprise. This managers do despite facing an uncertain world – of changing consumer tastes, changing markets, changing technology and changing employment practices – by developing systems of management control. Management control has been defined as 'the processes by which managers attempt to ensure their organisation adapts successfully to changes in its environment'.[1] Central to this is the development of an organisation structure and the gathering *and* use of information. Some of the information will be external to the firm – the plans of competitors for example – while other information will relate to its internal operations. Some information will be produced regularly as a result of formal systems while other will be *ad hoc* in nature.

Managers will need to plan. Plans, however, are not achieved on their own. Positive action is required to ensure they are both feasible and are achieved. This requires managers to coordinate and monitor activities. Should the results deviate from plan, corrective action is then necessary either to bring the results back to planned levels or to change those plans in the light of circumstances. Both of these involve managers in making new decisions.

The traditional uses of management accounting

None of this takes place in a vacuum. The organisation will require a structure and employees will need to be informed of objectives and motivated towards achieving those objectives. To achieve this, managers need information. Much of the raw data necessary will already be contained within the accounting system and so management accounting can be viewed as part – but only part – of the management control system of the organisation. Plans can be expressed in financial terms and compared with the actual results reported by the accounting system. The actual performance of individuals or departments can also be captured and used for monitoring and motivating by management. Similarly, existing cost data within the accounting system can be used by managers to help in making decisions.

The importance of the accounting system as part of the total management control system lies in its unique qualities. It is a readily accessible, extensive supply of verifiable data expressed in quantitative terms. Compared with other sources, it is hard data – unlike, for example, attempts to measure the morale of the workforce. It is also expressed in monetary terms which allows otherwise disparate activities within the organisation to be compared. In modern complex organisations, however, it serves two further purposes. By using monetary values, it provides a means for senior managers to evaluate activities from which they are far removed and about which they may only have limited technical knowledge. In addition, the use of money values allows the results of activities within the organisation to be aggregated, summarised and coordinated for the benefit of senior management. Finally, the importance of profitability for enterprises – or at least the concern for loss avoidance and survival – gives a special role to accounting information.

Management accounting, human behaviour and organisational structure

All of this is true. It is, however, only one aspect of management accounting. As painted, it suggests that the discipline is little more than a value-free, benign set of techniques, of help to management but which are independent of the organisation or the people in it. Conclusions about how management accounting is used in practice have to be tentative as, unlike financial accounting, much of the detail is not within the public domain. Nevertheless it is possible to picture management accounting playing a wider role.

One role might be to use the accounting information to monitor and motivate employees. Using accounting information in that way, however, can be counterproductive. Accounting reports do not capture all of the information. At its simplest, drawing the attention of employees to results which were below target when the fault was not of their making – perhaps because of constant machine breakdown – is unlikely to motivate better performance in the future and might even adversely affect it. The implication is that management accounting can affect human behaviour – although not always in the way assumed.

Not only might the use of management accounting affect behaviour, it is possible that it might actually influence the organisational structure. The need for information might *lead* to the organisational structure of the business being revised. By way of example, consider a company where all word processing is centralised. Estimating the cost for each user department will be fraught with difficulty. If this is an important element of cost, the organisation might be changed by closing down the central facility and attaching individual operators to specific user departments where costs can more accurately be collected.

This shows management accounting in a new light. As part of the management control system, it serves two functions. The first function is a form of financial planning and control, concerned with providing quantitative information, mainly in money terms, of plans, their results and any deviations. As such it borrows techniques from classical economic theory. This has been the traditional focus of management accounting.

The second function sees a more interactive role for management accounting. It is at least partially concerned with determining the organisational structure of the business and in modifying the behaviour of employees towards the goals of the enterprise. From this perspective, its base discipline is social psychology.

Management accounting defined

For many years, it has been the convention to identify separately the planning, coordinating, motivating, control and *ad hoc* decision-making roles of management. However, *all* of these involve decision making. Planning implies choosing between options and that requires the making of decisions. Coordination and control will often involve choosing from a whole range of possible methods while rarely will there be but a single organisational structure or method of motivation.

Common to all these roles is the need to choose between alternatives and the need for information to aid that choice. In most organisations, for reasons explained earlier, the accounting system is the major source of information. Management accounting can therefore be defined as the collection, analysis and interpretation of predominantly accounting data as an aid to management decision making in its widest sense.

MANAGEMENT ACCOUNTING FOUNDATIONS

Many of the management accounting techniques popular today were developed in the late nineteenth and early twentieth centuries. Their origins, however, can be traced back to an earlier need of industry to know the cost of products.

The development of cost accounting

With goods being manufactured within factories rather than being purchased ready-made from homeworkers, costs were no longer obvious. Existing bookkeeping systems would not have been capable of providing this information. Their main concern would have been simply to record financial transactions of amounts owed and owing – the traditional stewardship role of accounting. In all likelihood, early attempts to derive costs would have originated outside the formal (financial) accounting system, with separate records being kept of labour and material used in different parts of the factory. This would then have been related to physical work produced to derive unit costs. Through time, however, overheads became more significant and so these too would have been included in the product costings.

Keeping a separate system of cost information had one serious disadvantage. It involved a partial duplication of effort as much of the source data for the costing system was derived from the financial records of material purchased and labour hired. As a result, both the financial accounting and cost accounting systems became increasingly integrated.

The traditional explanation for the growth of management accounting techniques, and cost accounting in particular, relates to the need to set prices and value stocks. Many of the products being developed in those early years were oligopolistic or monopolistic in nature and so readily available market prices did not exist. Examples included the development of railway companies and water and sewerage companies. As has been shown in earlier chapters, governments were also increasingly regulating the external financial reporting of companies and so stock values were required to derive the cost of sales in annual accounts.

Johnson and Kaplan[2] in their important work, *Relevance Lost: The Rise and Fall of Management Accounting*, argue that management accounting had a much wider and active role. They argue that management accounting evolved to aid internal control in the organisation. In other words, internal accounting techniques did not simply grow as a response to the growth in size and complexity of business organisations, they actually facilitated their growth. This management accounting did by identifying the advantages of in-house production arising from the new technologies over the use of outside markets. Before discussing these accounting techniques, however, it is useful to consider the climate of thought then in existence as this will give some insight into how the techniques were applied and allow their use in today's changed society to be questioned.

The influence of other disciplines

Throughout the nineteenth century, problem-solving in science was dominated by what has been called the analytical method. This involved examining phenomena from the viewpoint of their constituent parts. By segmenting the whole into smaller and smaller parts, relationships between cause and effect could be determined and from these findings a better understanding of the total phenomenon was thought to be possible. Using such a methodology, Darwin developed his ideas on the origin of the species and the belief in the survival of the fittest.

Similar changes were happening in economics. The classical economic theory of the firm developed by the beginning of the twentieth century concerned itself with pricing and output decisions. The theory suggested that the output of the firm, and hence its profits, would increase just as long as the extra (or marginal) revenue was greater than the extra (or marginal) cost of providing that output. At the point where these equalled one another, no further increase in profit was possible and hence an optimal solution had been reached, a solution not only optimal for the firm but also optimal for the economy. Any firm not making a profit at this optimal point was, by definition, inefficient and market forces would ensure its failure. A second economic theory went on to highlight the advantages of the division of labour. By specialising, not only would the firm or individual be better off, but so would the economy as a whole.

Both economics and the physical sciences were sending out similar messages. Benefits and information could be derived from breaking down phenomena into smaller units. By identifying cause and effect, it would then be possible to prescribe a unique solution to achieve the desired outcomes. And in the choice of language to describe these outcomes – survival of the fittest and optimality – they were clearly felt to be superior. In this scheme of events, individuals counted for little. Only as part of the species were they of relevance to Darwin while classical economics viewed them as little more than units of resource, to be added or deleted in the search for optimality.

Early management theory

With such a dominant contemporary philosophy, it is perhaps not surprising that the early management thinkers developed similar ideas for business organisations. Early theories were universal in nature, prescribing a single ideal way of governing the organisation, independent of circumstances. Their concern with cause and effect was reflected in a very mechanistic view of the organisation. To be fair to the early writers, until the development of large business enterprises, it was only the state, the military and the church which were of sufficient size for their organisational structure to become an issue. Many of the early writers were ex-military personnel or ex-managers who, in passing on their experiences, attempted to generalise from their own individual experiences.

One particular writer, Frederick Taylor, had a profound effect not only on management thought but also on the design of management accounting systems. Taylor developed the idea of *scientific management* in the 1920s, based on his career which took him from being a labourer to chief engineer in a large US steel works. He claimed many things for his system: science, not rule of thumb; harmony, not discord; cooperation not individualism; the maximum output, in place of restricted output; and the development of people to their greatest efficiency and prosperity.[3] In fact it comprised what would be known today as work study.

By carefully scrutinising work and breaking it down into small, simple tasks – the division of labour – he believed the maximum productivity of workers, in 'harmony' with their machines, was possible. This would be achieved by applying standard equipment and specified methods of work to the task. The time allowed to perform the task would not be set by the operative but by 'experts' who had studied the task. All that then remained was for managers to match the worker to the task and train them in the prescribed methods.

Taylor's efforts were mainly focused on relatively simple tasks – hence his approach became known as the science of shoveling. Nevertheless, he believed the principles of scientific management could be universally applied to all kinds of business activity. Indeed other writers were addressing this very issue. As early as 1914, Fayol[4] had published a text in France offering general rules for the efficient administration of the firm and this was followed in the UK by Follett's[5] text *Creative Experience* in 1924.

Common to all such texts of the period was the belief that there was one single best way of organising the managerial and administrative structure and processes of the firm. Many of the ideas were borrowed from the way the military was then organised and were often presented as axioms with little justification or supporting evidence. Goals or objectives, for example, should be clear and unambiguous with only one source of authority, what Fayol called unity of command and unity of direction. Work should be divided – the division of labour once again. Responsibility should be attached to named units and individuals, and this responsibility should be commensurate with authority. The subordinates reporting to any manager should be limited to a particular number. The organisation should differentiate between those elements directly responsible for the achievement of objectives – line management – and those known as staff who merely acted as support.

These simplistic rules, independent of the circumstances, are the administrative equivalent of Taylor's scientific management. Common to both early administrative theory and scientific management was the belief in universal, prescriptive solutions, solutions where individuals are viewed as no more than inputs to the structure or process. One refinement to this, what McGregor[6] was later to call Theory X, suggested that people were essentially lazy and lacking in ambition, concerned with their own welfare rather than that of the organisation. Such people needed to be intensively supervised with stiff, often monetary, penalties being imposed to correct failure. No matter how naïve these ideas may appear today, what is important to remember is that many current management accounting techniques are based on just such beliefs.

THE COST ACCOUNTING FRAMEWORK

The need for costing information, as an aid in setting prices in the absence of markets and as part of the control mechanism for measuring efficiency, was the spur which encouraged the development of accounting for internal purposes. Early managers were faced with large-scale, complex technologies and manufacturing processes. These processes took basic raw materials such as wood and steel and converted the input into, often, equally complex final products. By breaking production down into smaller tasks, skilled craftworkers were required less and less. Instead, a whole army of semi-skilled workers were required. Nevertheless, no matter how sophisticated the plant and equipment, it was generally the speed of the workers which dictated the speed of production.

Influences on the design of cost accounting systems

Two influences were at work in choosing the organisational framework within which production should take place, the technology itself and the contemporary beliefs outlined earlier. Both guided the organisation of the business in the same direction. The breaking down of tasks into simpler sub-processes allowed less skilled labour to be used. At the same time, this enabled input expenses to be collected which could then be related to output from those sub-processes in order to determine the cost of that output. More than that, however, it enabled the effect of changes in input to be analysed and cause and effect to be determined.

The effect of these influences only served to reinforce the original beliefs. Knowledge of production techniques and costs were increasingly in the hands of the managers. Information, however, is power and so there was an increasing transfer of power from the workforce to the managers, reinforcing the belief that the workforce had no contribution to make to production other than as simple inputs to the process under the direction of management. The consequence of this was a need for even more managers such that ultimately managers themselves needed to be managed.

Cost centres, profit centres, investment centres and responsibility accounting

Collecting costs by product would be inadequate for control purposes as any deviation from planned cost would not be identifiable. Subdividing the manufacturing chain into smaller tasks or departments or processes overcomes this. For this to be effective, however, responsibility has to be allocated to individual operatives and managers. This is the basis for responsibility accounting, a feature identified by the early writers on administration.

Traditionally, responsibility accounting takes three forms: cost centres, profit centres and investment centres. Cost centres are where managers are held responsible for performing defined activities (outputs) within a defined cost (input). Monetary values are not associated with the output and so performance tends to be measured in terms of cost per unit produced. Profit centres relate to parts of the organisation where managers are held responsible for both revenues and costs and where performance is measured by profit generated. Investment centres are a stage beyond this. Performance is measured not just in terms of cost per unit or profitability but by relating profitability to the resources under the control of the managers. One particularly popular measure, the Return on Investment, is analogous to the Return on Capital Employed ratio of financial reporting.

The division of the business into responsibility centres – still evidenced in many management accounting systems today – was popularised by the works of Fayol. No matter how reasonable the division of the business into responsibility centres might at first appear, there are two particular dangers. The first is to hold managers responsible for costs they cannot control. The second danger is a desire to make all parts of the organisation responsibility centres – a further example of management accounting actually influencing the organisational structure. The fact is, some parts of a business can never be controlled by responsibility accounting either as cost centres, profit centres or investment centres.

Types of control

Three possible forms of organisational controls have been identified by Otley.[7] Where the relationship between inputs and outputs are well understood, *behaviour controls* are possible. Behaviour controls simply involve the giving of instructions. Because the means–end relationship is clear, the way of achieving the desired objective can easily be prescribed and the results measured, either by personal observation or via the accounting system. For example a 10 per cent increase in production by a car manufacturer should be reflected in a 10 per cent increase in the number of steering wheels used in production.

Where the means–end relationship is less well understood by senior management behaviour controls are no longer appropriate. How to achieve a particular objective has to be left to the discretion of the subordinate responsible whose performance will be measured using some form of *output controls* such as overall profit or Return on Investment. For other activities, however, it is often not possible to specify some overall financial target. Departments and managers faced with this situation can only be controlled by *input controls* by being allocated funds without requiring outputs to be measured. Examples would include research and development and the legal departments of businesses.

Strictly speaking, only behavioural controls are consistent with responsibility accounting. This is made clear by Drury[8] who states that the objective of responsibility accounting is to 'accumulate costs and revenues for each individual responsibility centre so that deviations . . . can be attributed to the person in charge'. In other words, he perceives responsibility accounting as identifying both inputs (costs) and outputs (revenues) and the *explanation* of any deviation.

This suggests there is a limit to the use of responsibility centres in businesses. Despite this, Otley[9] has drawn attention to the increasing pressure to create not just responsibility centres but profit centres. He cites the example of a car manufacturer whose production unit 'sold' output to its marketing division. According to the internal accounting system, production was profitable but marketing made a loss. In reality, however, it was the high production costs which were causing the losses but which were disguised by the artificial price charged to the marketing division. In effect the divisions were not profit centres but pseudo-profit centres.

This desire to create profit centres can partly be explained by the desire to break down complex processes into manageable, well-understood sub-units. There is, however, a greater force at work. By creating profit or pseudo-profit centres, senior managers are absolved from knowing the detailed cause–effect relationships of that unit. Instead performance and control can be measured by the single figure of profit or some derivation of that figure.

COST ACCOUNTING TECHNIQUES

In outline, cost accounting techniques follow the logic of manufacturing accounts developed in Chapter 3. Central to this was how production overheads should be treated in valuing stocks and hence deriving reported profit. For financial reporting purposes, SSAP 9 Stock and Long Term Contracts required an appropriate proportion of production overheads to be included in the closing stock valuations.

No matter how valid this might be for stewardship purposes and reporting to share-holders, it is likely to be inadequate for use by managers. Traditionally, their needs are for a more detailed breakdown of activities. In addition, they are likely to be concerned with *all* overheads, not just those relating to production. Perhaps even more important than this is the different focus of management and cost accounting. Financial account-ing is essentially backward looking and concerned with reporting to shareholders the results of the business using accounting concepts. Critical to this is the valuation of stock in determining the cost of sales. In effect, the cost of sales is simply the balancing figure after the stock values have been deducted from the cost of the inputs.

Internal accounting, however, is an aid to management. The management perspective is primarily forward looking and concerned with financial data to help in management control rather than financial reporting. Consequently, managers require detailed, up-to-date production information. There is therefore a difference in emphasis relative to finan-cial accounting. Stock valuations, while still of importance, are only of relevance to the extent they help in providing useful production information to management.

Technology and cost accounting

Immediately this need for more detailed information was recognised, it became clear that the way the information was collected would vary. Businesses operate in different tech-nologies. Housebuilding is different from the production of chocolate bars. In the former case, it is possible to collect costs by individual units produced – a technique known as *job costing* – and for profitability per unit to be calculated. Such an option is not a practi-cal proposition where chocolate bars are being produced in large numbers by the hour. Instead, the best that can be hoped for is to collect costs by each production run. This is known as *batch costing*.

Even this is not possible in some industries. Steel-making, for example, involves a con-tinuous operation of converting iron ore into steel. A similar problem is faced by many chemical companies where inputs enter a continuing process and may not reappear as a finished product until several days later. Determining the cost of the outputs is fraught with difficulty as there is no unique way of identifying those outputs with individual inputs. The only possibility might be initially to start up the plant and then close it down once a certain output has been achieved. This would, in effect, replicate the idea of batch costing. However, given the heavy costs of starting up and shutting down such plant, this is not a practical proposition. Some other way of determining cost has to be found. The method which has evolved is known as *process costing*.

Job costing, batch costing and process costing are the three major methods used by com-panies to classify costs for internal accounting purposes. Within these, there are many deriv-atives. A service industry, for example, may be able to collect costs by the job or the batch. To take but one example, consider a solicitor's office. The handling of a major claim might take several years and involve many members of staff. Under such circumstances, labour costs and other expenses can quite feasibly be collected for the individual claim. Collecting such detail for smaller tasks such as writing a single solicitor's letter on behalf of a client may not be practical. The *cost of costing* would be too great. Instead, a form of batch cost-ing might be used. All the costs of such small, one-off tasks could then be collected togeth-er and an average cost derived by dividing the costs by the number of letters written.

Marginal and absorption costing revisited

No matter whether job, batch or process costing is applied, a decision has to be made as to whether costs should be collected on a marginal or absorption costing basis. Despite all the problems outlined in Chapter 3 of associating fixed costs with units of production, most firms appear to use absorption costing in preference to marginal costing when collecting costs for internal purposes. The difficulties and dangers of using absorption costing are magnified when applied to internal accounting as a result of breaking down the business's activities into smaller and smaller units. In general, the more the business is subdivided, the greater will be the proportion of indirect costs associated with responsibility centres or departments.

All fixed overheads will generally be charged to their relevant account heading in the first place. At this stage they will all be direct costs. For some costs, the relevant account heading will be directly associated with a particular department or activity even though the costs may be fixed. Where this is possible, the procedure is known as *cost allocation*. The salary of a stores controller for instance can be directly allocated to running the stores. Other costs, however, may be shared between two or more cost centres in which case they will be indirect to those centres. Some method of *cost apportionment* is necessary to charge the costs to individual cost centres. Unfortunately there is no unambiguous way of dividing such costs. Factory rent for instance might initially be charged to the factory rent account as a direct cost of running the factory. However, associating the rent with production departments will turn the cost into an indirect expense of those departments. Sharing the rent on the basis of floor area might appear a reasonable solution. It might, however, not be a logical one. Some of the floor area might be more valuable than other parts. In a retail store, for example, the ground floor is often more valuable than the basement. Equally, some of the floor area might be surplus and not used by any of the departments.

Estimating overhead absorption rates

If we ignore these problems for the moment, the allocated and apportioned overheads have then to be associated with individual products in order to derive unit costs of help to management. This poses three further problems. Some cost centres – such as service departments – do not actually manufacture products. The answer is to apportion their costs in turn to producing departments.

This still leaves two further difficulties. In order to associate the overheads with units of production, both the amount of those overheads and the level of activity needs to be known. However, neither of these will be known for certain until the year end. The financial accounting solution of waiting until the year end will not be acceptable as managers require the information currently. In order to incorporate overheads in unit costs from the beginning of the year, there is no alternative but to estimate both the amount of the overheads and the production activity.

Even here there is yet another difficulty. Where a company is only making a single product, production activity can be measured as the number of units planned to be manufactured. Cost centres, however, are often used by more than one product. A company, for example, might plan to make 1,000 luxury coaches and 100,000 dustbins, both of which make use of the paintshop. Charging the cost of the paintshop to products on the basis of units would not produce particularly meaningful cost information.

The most popular answer has been to use some form of labour activity, either labour hours or labour costs, as traditionally labour input has dictated the amount of production. For example, each coach might involve two employees working for five hours in the paintshop while each dustbin might only require one employee spending six minutes carrying out the painting. The total time spent on coaches would therefore be 10,000 hours, the same time as required to paint the dustbins. Charging the costs of the paintshop on a 50:50 basis would therefore provide a better measure of the use being made of the facility by the two products.

Summarising, to estimate the overhead absorption rate per unit of activity – the so-called overhead recovery rate – involves five steps. The first step is to allocate overheads directly to cost centres for responsibility purposes. The (budgeted) overhead cost of any non-producing cost centres have then to be apportioned to those production departments which make use of their services. This ensures that all budgeted overhead is now associated with cost centres which are directly involved with the final product or service. Secondly, the basis of apportionment has to be chosen. Although there is no unambiguous method, the basis chosen should be the one with the closest cause–effect relationship to the costs being charged. This is often floor area for rent and rates and the number of machines for apportioning the cost of power. Thirdly, activity has to be estimated. Again, the activity chosen should be the one with the closest cause–effect relationship to the use of the overheads. Often this will be some form of labour measurement. On other occasions, other bases are possible such as machine hours. Fourthly, the overhead absorption rate has then to be calculated by dividing the budgeted or planned overheads by the planned activity. Finally, this is then used to charge overheads to production.

JOB AND BATCH COSTING

Job and batch costing share many similarities. Costs or inputs can be uniquely identified with outputs. The only difference is that costs can be traced to individual products under a job costing system whereas they are only traceable to a collection of units – the batch – under a batch costing system.

Some jobs and batches will not be repeated – for instance, the design of an office block by an architect or the printing of 30,000 booklets by a printer. Other jobs and batches might relate to continuous production. An aircraft manufacturer, for example, is likely to collect costs by each aircraft made even though the production run might be for several hundred units. Similarly, an electrical manufacturer might make, say, microwave cookers in batches of 2,000 but might continue to make such batches daily. Whether for one-off or high volume production, managers will be interested in costs for scorekeeping and for control purposes. In addition, where market prices are not readily available, they might also be interested in such costs to help in determining prices. Whether the costs produced by a job or batch costing system are of help to managers is another question which is returned to later.

More than one product but common overheads

Detailed costing systems are rarely required where a single product is manufactured. Under those circumstances, to derive the overhead absorption rate simply involves estimating overheads and planned activity. With only one product, activity can be measured in units while all of the overheads are uniquely associated with that product. The analysis becomes more complicated, however, when more than one product exists. Some overheads might relate to only one department; others might have to be apportioned. Units planned might not be a meaningful measure of activity and so some other measure has to be chosen. Many of the issues in job and batch costing can be identified by assuming more than one product but common overheads. This is the approach taken in Example 16.1.

Example 16.1

Meldreth and Manor Ltd manufacture two products, the Aston and the Brum. Details of their planned production over the next 12 months are as follows;

Product	Aston	Brum
Planned production units	400	800
Estimated labour hours per unit	1	2
Estimated machine hours per unit	6	2
Estimated labour rate per hour	£20	£5
Estimated material cost per unit	£16	£4

Production overheads are shared by both products and are forecast to be £24,000 for the year. For he sake of simplicity, labour can be assumed to be employed by the hour.

At the end of the twelve months, actual production was 380 units of the Aston and 750 units of the Brum. Actual production overheads came to £27,000 while all other costs were as planned.

As the two products share the same overhead facilities, the issue is restricted to calculating an overhead absorption rate to be applied in determining the full product costs, i.e. the total cost, including overheads. There are at least five possible measures of activity: labour hours, labour cost, machine hours, material cost or units of output. Exhibit 16.1 shows how each of these is calculated for production overhead.

Exhibit 16.1 Calculation of overhead absorption rates

Planned activity measure	Aston		Brum		Total	Production overhead absorption rate*
Production units		400		800	1,200 units	£20 per unit
Labour hours	(400 units × 1 hour)	400	(800 units × 2 hours)	1,600	2,000 hours	£12 per labour hour
Labour cost	(400 hours × £20)	£8,000	(1,600 hours × £5)	£8,000	£16,000	150% of labour cost
Machine hours	(400 units × 6 hours)	2,400	(800 units × 2 hours)	1,600	4,000 hours	£6 per machine hour
Material cost	(400 units × £16)	£6,400	(800 units × £4)	£3,200	£9,600	250% of material cost

* The £24,000 production overhead divided by the total activity measure.

The full product cost will vary depending on which overhead absorption rate is chosen. Given that the rate is attempting to measure the overhead resources consumed by the products, the rate which best measures that consumption should be the one chosen. As many overheads are time based, a rate relating to time may be the most appropriate. Within this, however, there are two measures of time: the labour hours and the machine hours. Where it is the machines which limit the extent of production, machine hours may be more appropriate than labour hours. Likewise, if labour hours dictate the use of the capacity represented by the overheads, a labour hour rate might be more appropriate.

Sometimes, however, even where labour is the appropriate choice, labour hours may be an inadequate measure of the use of the overheads. A managing director is likely to make more use of overheads than a humble factory floor worker. The MD might have a company car provided, an allocated car space, and individual secretarial back-up. Charging the same overheads per hour of the managing director's time would therefore not measure the use of the overheads. A similar argument can be applied when there is a substantial difference in the skills of employees. The Aston, for example, requires a much higher grade of labour than the Brum. An alternative therefore is to charge overheads not on labour hours but on labour cost. The implications of charging overheads using different bases is shown in Exhibit 16.2.

Exhibit 16.2 Possible overhead costs for each product

Absorption base	Aston		Brum	
Units		£20		£20
Labour hours	(1 hour × £12)	£12	(2 hours × £12)	£24
Labour cost	(1 hour × £20 × 150%)	£30	(2 hours × £5 × 150%)	£15
Machine hours	(6 hours × £6)	£36	(2 hours × £6)	£12
Material cost	(£16 × 250%)	£40	(£4 × 250%)	£10

The Aston requires one hour of labour at £20 plus material of £16, a manufacturing cost before charging overheads of £36. The Brum, although using two hours of labour, uses labour which only costs £5 per hour and so its total labour charge is £10. Adding materials of £4 to this, its manufacturing cost before charging overheads is £14. Depending on the base chosen, the production overheads would then range from £12 to £40 for the Aston and £10 to £24 for the Brum.

There is a second problem facing Meldreth and Manor. At the end of the year, both the actual overhead costs and the actual activity were different from planned. Overhead costs were required by management from day one of operations and yet the actual overheads and actual activity would only be known at the end of the year. It would be pointless revising all the costs of production. Unit costs were developed to help managers make decisions and those are now in the past. For financial accounting purposes, it is possible to amend any stocks unsold to take account of the revised data. More likely, the stocks will remain at their current values and any overheads not charged to production will simply be written off to the profit and loss account as an expense.

This is the way it is treated in Exhibit 16.3 which shows the outline accounting entries necessary to record all the transactions in the accounts of Meldreth and Manor. The assumption made is that overheads are charged on the basis of labour hours. As all other costs were as planned, the labour cost will be £15,100 and the material cost £9,080. (380 units of the Aston were produced. With labour of £20 per unit and material of £16 per unit, the total costs are labour £7,600 and materials £6,080. The Brum had a labour cost of £10 and a material cost of £4. 750 units will therefore have cost £7,500 for labour and £3,000 for materials.)

Exhibit 16.3 Accounting for overhead

(£)	Acquire materials, labour and overhead			Transfer to work-in-progress			Transfer to finished stock	Write off overhead underabsorbed
Cash	−15,100	−9,080	−27,000					
Labour	+15,100			−15,100				
Raw material stocks		+9,080			−9,080			
Overheads			+27,000			−22,560		−4,440
Aston work-in-progress				+7,600	+6,080	+4,560	−18,240	
Brum work-in-progress				+7,500	+3,000	+18,000	−28,500	
Aston finished stock							+18,240	
Brum finished stock							+28,500	
Overheads written off								+4,440

After the expenses of labour, material and overhead have been incurred, they are then transferred to their respective work-in-progress accounts. With overhead being absorbed on the basis of labour hours, the total overhead charged to Aston work-in-progress will be 380 units × £12, a total of £4,560. Similarly for the Brum. Each Brum is charged with £24 of overheads and so, with 750 units produced, the total overhead will be £18,000. £4,440 of overhead, however, has not been charged to the products. This is partly due to activity not being as high as planned and partly because overheads were underestimated. At the end of the year, there is nothing tangible to show for the overhead underabsorbed and so it has to be written off to the profit and loss account.

Before discussing the implications of absorption costing for management control, it is useful to consider a more complex batch costing problem and then consider process costing, as the treatment of overheads are equally relevant to both.

More than one product but differentiated overheads

Rarely will a company's products share overheads in the simplified way of Meldreth and Manor Limited. A retailer of cars, for example, generally also operates service bays, crash repair workshops and a paintshop as well as the car showrooms. Charging the expense of the car showrooms to the cost of running the service facility will not only exaggerate the cost of the servicing department, it will also provide misleading information if those costs are then used to determine prices.

Many businesses also face an additional complication. Some cost centres do not contribute directly to the production process. Examples include raw material and finished goods stores and maintenance departments. The ultimate objective is to charge overheads to products as, without any products, there would be no overheads – or any other costs for that matter.

Overhead absorption rates involve anticipated costs and anticipated activity. The first stage will therefore be to estimate overhead costs by department for responsibility purposes. The cost of service departments – departments which support the production departments but which do not manufacture anything themselves – will then need to be apportioned to the producing departments.

Activity measures used to carry out this task are often extremely crude. The likely number of raw material issues might be used to apportion the costs of a raw material stores for example. But the number of issues is only one factor in the cost of the stores. The physical size of the different stock items might be equally important. Some stock items will require greater security or more controlled conditions to prevent deterioration – all of which add to costs and which are not measured by using a simple apportionment base. Similarly, maintenance department costs might be apportioned on the number of machines, irrespective of their age and need for maintenance.

Once the service costs have been apportioned, the (planned) overheads of production departments are totalled and an absorption rate determined in a similar way to that developed for Meldreth and Manor. A similar procedure might take place for non-manufacturing overheads such as marketing and administration expenses if managers require full product costs as part of the management control process. The procedures involved are demonstrated in Example 16.2 where the analysis is restricted to manufacturing overhead.

Example 16.2

Eglin Engineering Ltd undertakes engineering work according to customer specifications. The factory consists of three production departments and two service departments responsible for stores and maintenance. Production departments A and B regularly require materials issued from store but department C is a finishing department which rarely, if ever, makes use of this facility.

Details of the five departments for the coming year as as follows:

Department	Supervisory salaries	Floor area	Number of machines	Store issues	Planned output labour hours
A	£50,000	40%	5	40%	9,000
B	£35,000	20%	3	55%	4,000
C	£40,000	20%	5	–	10,000
Maintenance	£72,000	15%	7	5%	
Stores	£35,000	5%	–	–	

Rent, rates and insurance for the factory is believed to be £100,000 for the coming year. The annual cost of power for the machines is estimated to be £80,000.

Exhibit 16.4 shows how costs are ultimately associated with production departments. The supervisory salaries are direct costs of the departments. Rent and power, however, apply to the factory as a whole and so some form of apportionment is required. In this particular example, floor area has been chosen as the basis for apportioning rent and rates while power has been apportioned on the number of machines.

Exhibit 16.4 Overhead absorption – service departments

Expense	Basis of apportionment	Production departments			Service departments		Total
		A	B	C	Maintenance	Stores	
Supervisory salaries	Direct	£50,000	£35,000	£40,000	£72,000	£35,000	£232,000
Rent, rates and insurance	Floor area	£40,000	£20,000	£20,000	£15,000	£5,000	£100,000
Power	Number of machines	£20,000	£12,000	£20,000	£28,000	–	£80,000
Subtotal		£110,000	£67,000	£80,000	£115,000	£40,000	£412,000
Apportion stores overheads	Per cent of issues	£16,000	£22,000	–	£2,000	–£40,000	–
Subtotal		£126,000	£89,000	£80,000	£117,000	–	£412,000
Apportion maintenance overhead	Number of machines	£45,000	£27,000	£45,000	–£117,000	–	–
TOTAL		£171,000	£116,000	£125,000	–	–	£412,000
Labour hours		9,000	4,000	10,000			
OVERHEAD ABSORPTION RATE		£19.00	£29.00	£12.50			

Having apportioned (planned) costs to the individual departments, the service department overheads need to be included in the producing department overheads in order to determine overhead absorption rates. As the stores provide a service to the maintenance department, the overheads of the stores are reapportioned to other departments before the reapportioning of the maintenance department.[10] In this particular example, the basis used is the percentage of stores issues. This might be the actual proportions of stock issues recorded last year, the result of a sample or merely an educated guess by management. The next stage is to carry out a similar exercise for all the overhead costs currently associated with the maintenance department. In the case of Eglin Engineering, the apportionment is based on the number of machines in the *production departments*. Finally, overhead absorption rates can be calculated for production departments. Using labour hours, these are £19.00 for department A, £29.00 for department B and £12.50 for department C.

Global and departmental absorption rates

One simplification practised in some businesses is to exclude the allocation and apportionment of overheads to departments. Instead, all overheads are pooled together and a single, company-wide or global absorption rate is calculated. This can be particularly distorting where not all products make the same use of all the overheads. With total overheads of £412,000 for Eglin Engineering and planned production of 23,000 labour hours, the global absorption rate becomes £17.91 per labour hour.

The implication of this can be shown by considering an individual job. Assume a customer of Eglin Engineering requires a job to be undertaken which involves five hours in department A and ten hours in department C. Using departmental rates, the production overhead element of the total cost will be £220, of which £95 relates to department A and

£125 to department C. With a global rate, however, the overhead charged will be £268.65 as a result of charging 15 hours of overheads at £17.91 per hour. In effect, the job is being partially charged with the high overheads of department B even though it makes no use of those facilities.

PROCESS COSTING

If job costing represents one extreme of production technology, process costing can be viewed as the other extreme. Job costing is characterised by individual, one-off products – often identified with individual customers – and requiring different inputs of labour, material and overheads for each job. Process costing on the other hand involves continuous production of more or less identical products. Unlike job costing, the technology often prevents inputs from being uniquely identified with outputs. Because of this, it is no longer possible unambiguously to identify costs with individual units of output.

The chemical and steel industries are classic examples of industries which use process costing. Common to both is a technology which sees measurable inputs entering complex plant, only to reappear some time later as either a finished product or as an intermediary product ready to enter a further process. Faced with such complexities, any unit cost calculated will be an average, found by dividing the input costs by the units output, in a similar way to batch costing. Unlike batch costing, however, work-in-progress is generally more significant. Because of the continuous nature of the technology, for any one period this will often be substantial. Unfortunately, the stock of work-in-progress may not be capable of physical identification. It will be located within the tanks and piping making up the plant, only physically identifiable when output in a finished or semi-finished state. Output for any period will therefore comprise work started and finished in the period plus work started in previous periods and completed in the current one.

Although not unique to process costing, a second difficulty often associated with process costing is a loss of part of the input. If the raw material input is in a liquid form, some of this may evaporate before the finished product is completed. On other occasions, the finished product may have to be extracted from a raw material with the balance merely being waste. As a result, whether estimating closing stocks for financial reporting or production costs for management control, process costing involves more significant complications than other costing systems.

The calculation of equivalent units

If the units in work-in-progress can be estimated, production costs per unit can be derived. This is made possible by developing *equivalent units*. Assume, for example, that an employee started a period by commencing work on 1,000 units and assume that, at the end of the period, the labour content is 50 per cent complete. Just because no units have been completed, it would be misleading to say the employee's production was nil. Instead of working on 1,000 units, the worker could have worked on only 500, in which case all 500 units would have been completely finished. This conversion of partly finished work into its equivalence of completed production enables both unit production costs and work-in-progress values to be determined. Example 16.3 demonstrates the necessary steps.

Example 16.3

Penny Lane is employed by Liverpool Chemicals where she is responsible for producing a particular brand of vitamin supplement. The process involves mixing raw materials with water which is then distilled to produce the supplement in bulk. Completed production is then transferred to the bottling plant, ready for sale to the general public.

At the beginning of a particular period, 80 litres were left in the distillation plant from the previous period. This was estimated to be 25 per cent complete. During the period, 200 litres were added. At the end of the period, 220 litres had been transferred to the bottling plant. No wastage or any other form of loss occurs and any inputs contained within the plant at the period end were estimated to be 40 per cent complete. Penny's wages for the period were £392.

At the beginning of the period, the process contained 80 litres, to which 200 litres were then added. With an output of 220 litres, 60 litres must have still been in the system at the period end on the assumption that there was no wastage. Of the 220 litres output, 80 would have related to the opening work-in-progress and 140 to production started and finished in the period.

The 80 litres of opening work-in-progress were 25 per cent complete and so required a further 75 per cent of work to finish, the *equivalent* of 60 litres being started and completed. An additional 140 litres were started and completed in the period while the 60 units of closing work-in-progress were 40 per cent complete. Armed with this, it is now possible to derive both Penny's production for the period and the average labour cost per unit. The detail is shown in Exhibit 16.5.

Exhibit 16.5 Equivalent production and unit labour cost

	Units worked	Percentage worked	Equivalent units
Opening work-in-progress completed	80	75%	60
Add work started and completed	140	100%	140
Add closing work-in-progress started but not completed	60	40%	24
Equivalent units produced			224
Labour cost			£392
Unit labour cost			**£1.75**

Estimating the cost of output and closing stocks

The use of equivalent units can be extended to both raw materials and overheads as well as labour. This enables not just the cost of outputs to be estimated but also the value of any closing stocks. For many processes, no further material is added other than that originally input. Consequently, the material element will be 100 per cent complete from the moment it enters the process. The passage of time plus the consumption of labour and overheads is all that is required to convert the raw materials into the finished product. Because of this, labour and overheads are often known as *conversion costs*.

Overheads are often charged on the basis of labour hours and involve all the allocation and apportionment procedures developed for job and batch costing. Many companies also make the simplifying assumption that labour and overheads in stocks are 50 per cent complete at the period end. The justification for this is based on the process being a continuous flow. Production just entering the process at the end of the period will effectively be only raw material. Production about to exit the process, however, is, for all practical purposes, 100 per cent complete. Assuming an even flow therefore, on average the work-in-progress will by 50 per cent complete as far as labour is concerned – and if overheads are absorbed on the basis of labour hours, they too will be 50 per cent complete. This is the approach taken in Example 16.4.

Example 16.4

> Guildford plc operates a process costing system for the manufacture of one of its products, the Supa. During the month of January, it adds 500 units of material to the process at a cost of £10,000. No further materials are added. Labour costs for the month relating to the production of the Supa came to £12,000 and overheads are absorbed on the basis of 150 per cent of labour cost. No losses take place in the production of the Supa.
>
> During the month 300 units were completed. The closing work-in-progress was 100 per cent complete in terms of materials and 50 per cent complete in terms of labour and overheads. There was no opening work-in-progress.

To value the cost of completed production and the work-in-progress requires equivalent units to be calculated for each element of cost. As the material element is 100 per cent complete as soon as it enters the process, the *material* equivalent units of production will be 500 and so, with material costs of £10,000, the average unit material cost will be £20. With 300 units completed in the period, 200 units must remain in work-in-progress. As the work-in-progress is 50 per cent complete, the equivalent units of labour and overhead *completed* must be 400. With total conversion costs of £30,000, the unit cost is £75.

With this information, the cost of finished production and the value of closing stock can be calculated. This is shown in Exhibit 16.6. The material element of closing stock is valued at £4,000, based on 200 units at a unit cost of £20. The labour and overhead, however, is only half complete and so that element is only equivalent to 100 units at a unit cost of £75.

The actual recording of this information in the accounts of Guildford plc would follow the format outlined earlier for batch and job costing. The materials, labour and overhead would initially be recorded in their own individual accounts. These would then be transferred out and brought together in the (process) work-in-progress account. In turn, the completed production would then be transferred from the work-in-progress account to a finished goods account, leaving a balance of £11,500 as the closing stock in the work-in-progress account.

*Exhibit 16.6 **The calculation of closing stock***

	Units worked	Percentage worked	Unit cost		Total cost
Work started and completed					
Material	300	100%	£20	£6,000	
Labour and overheads		100%	£75	£22,500	
Cost of finished stock				———	£28,500
Closing stock					
Material	200	100%	£20	£4,000	
Labour and overheads		50%	£75	£7,500	
					£11,500
				———	£40,000

Normal losses

The technology of many industries often results in raw material being lost as inputs are converted to final products. Tailoring, for example, involves cutting suit pieces from rolls of cloth. Because of the shape of the cut pieces, part of the material will be wasted. Companies which operate process technology are particularly susceptible to this form of loss, no matter how efficiently the plant is operated. Evaporation or shrinkage may be an inevitable consequence of the technology. This wastage – or *normal loss* as it is known – is as much a cost of production as labour or overheads.

In making a suit, for example, 10 per cent of the cloth may be wasted, no matter how well the pieces are cut. If the cloth cost £80 then £72 relates to the suit and £8 to the wastage. The wastage, however, arises directly from making the suit rather than any inefficiencies and so the £8 needs to be added to the £72 to calculate the material used.

In this simple example, it would have been sufficient to charge the £80 without uniquely identifying the normal loss. In practice, it is often necessary to show explicitly the normal loss. First, it allows any abnormal loss to be identified. Secondly, process costing often involves work-in-progress and so the loss may need to be shared between finished production and the work-in-progress. Depending at which stage of the process the loss takes place, a simple division of the normal loss may be inappropriate as work-in-progress will only be partially completed.

Where normal losses are assumed to occur at a particular point in the process, they must relate to all units which have reached that point. As a simplification, it is often assumed that normal losses take place at the point of final inspection, i.e. when the product leaves the process. If that is the case, the normal losses are assumed to be entirely attributable to the completed production. This is the approach taken in Example 16.5.

Example 16.5

Strathclyde plc manufactures plastic mouldings. At the beginning of April, 14,000 litres of material costing £21,000 were added to the process. Conversion costs – labour and overheads – totalled £24,000 for the month. There is a 10 per cent normal loss of inputs which occurs at the completion stage.

Output for the month totalled 9,000 litres and the work-in-progress related to 4,000 litres input at the beginning of April. Work-in-progress is 100 per cent complete in terms of materials and 50 per cent complete in terms of conversion costs. There were no opening stocks and no other losses.

If the normal loss is only recognised at the stage of completion, none will be associated with the work-in-progress. This is a reasonable assumption. It is similar to the earlier example of the tailor. There, wastage was only recognised when cutting began, not when the cloth was simply raw material stock. In other words, it is the *production of outputs* which causes the normal loss, not the inputs. With an output of 9,000 litres and a 10 per cent loss during manufacture, 10,000 litres of the original 14,000 litres must have been used to achieve the 9,000 litres of output. More than that, because the normal loss only takes place at the end of the process, each litre of normal loss will have consumed the same amount of materials and conversion costs as a litre of good production. The approach therefore is to calculate equivalent production – including the normal loss – and then to charge the cost of the normal loss to the good production.

Production, including the 1,000 litres lost, was fully complete in terms of materials and so the equivalent units of material will be 14,000 litres. With a cost of £21,000, the material cost per equivalent unit will be £1.50. Conversion costs relate to the 9,000 litres of good production, the 1,000 litres of normal loss and the 4,000 litres of work-in-progress 50 per cent complete – a closing stock equivalent to 2,000 litres. The £24,000 of conversion costs therefore related to the equivalent of 12,000 litres, to give a unit cost of £2.00. With this information, it is now possible to calculate both the cost of completed production and the value of the closing stock. The result is shown in Exhibit 16.7.

Exhibit 16.7 The cost of production and normal losses

	Units worked	Percentage worked	Unit cost		Total cost
Output – including normal loss					.
Material	10,000	100%	£1.50	£15,000	
Conversion costs		100%	£2.00	£20,000	
	10,000			———	£35,000
Less normal loss	1,000				
Good output	9,000				£35,000
Work-in-progress					
Material	4,000	100%	£1.50	£6,000	
Conversion costs		50%	£2.00	£4,000	
					£10,000
Cost of inputs					£45,000

Abnormal losses

Sometimes losses occur in a process which are not expected. A power surge, for example, could ruin part of the production. Unlike normal losses which are inherent in the production process, *abnormal losses* do not form part of the cost of production. They represent an inefficiency which, in some way, should be controllable by management. Put crudely, something has gone wrong. If the abnormal loss occurs at the end of the process, output is less than it should be. It is the equivalent of finished stock being destroyed and that gives a clue as to its treatment. Unlike normal losses which are an integral cost of production, abnormal losses are an expense to be borne by the business if costing data is to be meaningful. Equally, an abnormal gain represents additional income. To demonstrate the treatment of an abnormal loss, consider the data from Example 16.5 but now assume the output for the month was only 7,200 litres of good production. All other data remains the same.

With an input of 14,000 litres and a closing stock of 4,000 litres, 10,000 litres should have been applied to finished production and so, with a 10 per cent normal loss, output should have been 9,000 units at a cost of £35,000. There is therefore an abnormal loss of 1,800 litres which has to be borne by the company just as if it had originally been produced but then subsequently destroyed by accident. Where the loss occurs at the end of the process – as in the example of Strathclyde plc – the cost of the abnormal loss is calculated as though it were good production.

Exhibit 16.8 shows the implication for the company. In effect, the £35,000 cost of the forecast good output has been apportioned between the actual good output and the abnormal loss in proportion to the units involved. Of the £45,000 entered in the accounts as costs of production, £28,000 would be transferred as an asset to finished stock, £7,000 would be charged as an expense to the profit and loss account and £10,000 would remain in the production account as closing work-in-progress.

Exhibit 16.8 The cost of production and abnormal losses

	Units worked	Percentage worked	Unit cost		Total cost
Forecast output – including normal loss					
Material	10,000	100%	£1.50	£15,000	
Conversion costs		100%	£2.00	£20,000	
	10,000				£35,000
Less normal loss	1,000				
Forecast good output	9,000				£35,000
Less abnormal loss	1,800				£7,000
Actual good output	7,200				£28,000
Abnormal loss	1,800				£7,000
Work-in-progress					
Material	4,000	100%	£1.50	£6,000	
Conversion costs		50%	£2.00	£4,000	
					£10,000
Cost of inputs					£45,000

JOINT PRODUCTS AND BY-PRODUCTS

Sometimes a single manufacturing process will result in two or more products being manufactured simultaneously as an inevitable consequence of the production process. Where a product has little value and is not the main reason for manufacturing taking place, it is known as a by-product. However, where the process produces more than one product with relatively high sales values, they are known as joint products. Not only do joint products have higher sales values, they are also the dominant reason why manufacturing is undertaken. Refining crude oil, for example, produces not only petrol but also paraffin.

More than one product – the basic issue

In some ways, the issue is similar to the treatment of apportioned overheads. Some way has to be found to apportion the common costs to the different products. There is, however, a significant difference. Products which share overheads do not *have* to be produced. The interpretation of apportioned costs for decision making is dealt with in the next chapter. Nevertheless, if one of a range of products appears to be making a loss under absorption costing, it is possible to eliminate that product. In the long term, this might enable the level of overheads to be reduced. For example, if the overheads related to warehousing and one product appeared to be making a loss when using absorption costing, in the long term it might be possible to sell off the existing warehouse and replace it by a smaller, cheaper facility.

Such an option is not available to joint or by-products. Produce one and the other has to be manufactured. The revenue of by-products, being of relatively little value and incidental to the main purpose of production, is often used to reduce the cost of the inputs. It is analogous to buying a bottle of mineral water with a returnable deposit included in the price. The actual price of the mineral water is the selling price less the refund available when the bottle is returned. Where all the products from a process are significant, however, this would not provide meaningful data.

Accounting for joint products

Joint products are interdependent and share the same costs. Produce more of one and more of the other has to be produced. There is therefore no way that costs can be uniquely identified with individual products. Two basic methods have evolved to apportion the joint costs between the products. One involves a sharing on the basis of some physical measure of output such as litres, metres or kilograms. The other shares the joint costs on the basis of sales value. Both methods are demonstrated in Example 16.6.

Exhibit 16.9 shows production costs and reported profitability for the Alpha and Beta. With an output of 10,000 litres of Alpha and 15,000 litres of Beta, apportioning the costs on the basis of physical litres shows the cost of production as being £40,000 for Alpha and £60,000 for Beta. However, the sales value of 10,000 litres of Alpha is £60,000, the same as the sales value of the 15,000 litres of Beta. Using sales values to apportion production costs therefore results in identical costs of production for each product.

Example 16.6

Stockport Chemical manufactures two products, the Alpha and the Beta from a common process. During the month of June, the costs of inputs were £100,000. The output for the period comprised 10,000 litres of Alpha and 15,000 litres of Beta.

There were neither opening nor closing stocks of work-in-progress, no abnormal losses nor any opening stock of finished products. Sales for June totalled 8,000 litres of Alpha at £6 per litre and 12,000 litres of Beta at £4 per litre.

Exhibit 16.9 Joint product costs and profitability

	Physical units				Sales values			
	Alpha		Beta		Alpha		Beta	
	litres	£	litres	£	litres	£	litres	£
Cost of production	10,000	40,000	15,000	60,000	10,000	50,000	15,000	50,000
Less Closing stock	2,000	8,000	3,000	12,000	2,000	10,000	3,000	10,000
Cost of sales	8,000	32,000	12,000	48,000	8,000	40,000	12,000	40,000
Sales		48,000		48,000		48,000		48,000
Profit		16,000		nil		8,000		8,000

There are two implications to this. First, from a financial reporting perspective, the closing values of stock for each product will differ, depending on which base has been used to value the cost of production. Secondly, from a management perspective, the apparent profitability of the two products differs as the apportionment base changes. Apportioning costs – no matter how necessary for the final accounts – distorts the meaning for management purposes. The two products are not independent. Alpha cannot be produced without producing Beta. *From a managerial perspective, the focus has to be on the profitability of the process, not the individual products.* The only meaningful statement is that costs of £100,000 input to the process result in outputs with an ultimate sales value of £120,000 – and even this is only meaningful if the costs are direct to the process rather than a result of several apportionments. As Horngren states, 'no techniques for allocating joint-product costs should be used for judging the performance of product lines or for making managerial decisions'.[11]

Of the two techniques, the apportionment of the joint costs on the basis of sales revenue does least harm. If the process is profitable, the apportionment will show the individual products as being profitable, while if it is loss making, both of the products will report losses. Apportioning on the basis of some physical measure, however, can make some products appear profitable while others appear loss making. Given that the products are inextricably linked, individual costs are at best misleading.

THE VALIDITY OF ABSORPTION COSTING

Absorption costing and decision making

If apportioning costs to joint products can be misleading, a similar argument can be marshalled against absorption costing. Indeed the traditional academic view is that cost apportionment is a 'useless and wasteful exercise'.[12] According to this view, absorption costing distorts information. Including overheads in unit costs implies fixed costs behave in a similar way to variable costs. In reality, there is a crucial difference. Fixed costs – and overheads are predominantly fixed costs – are essentially time based while variable costs are volume based. The extra cost of producing one more unit is its marginal cost and this is likely to be of more help to managers in decision making than any figure which includes overheads.

From this follows other difficulties with absorption costing. First, as Example 3.9 of Chapter 3 showed, absorption costing can distort profits by carrying forward part of the fixed costs of production in stocks unsold. Secondly, because overhead rates are related to activity, overhead per unit will vary with the planned size of the activity. Thirdly, where more than one product is made, the amount of overhead charged to the different products will be at least partially dependent on the measure used for the activity – with unit overhead varying depending on whether machine hours, labour hours or some other measure has been used.

Absorption costing and financial reporting

For external financial reporting purposes, the effect of this is minimised by applying the concept of consistency and by the requirement of SSAP 9, Stocks and Long Term Contracts to base overheads on 'normal activity'. Chapter 7 demonstrated the implications of the 'normal activity' base. Rather than charging more overheads per unit if production is less than 'normal', overhead absorption based on normal activity writes off any shortfall due to lower volumes as an expense to the profit and loss account.

This may be acceptable for financial reporting purposes, where the concern is with *true and fair* and the need is to sum all the company's activities within a single representative figure of profit. It is also a less serious problem as most annual accounts are based on a 12-month time period. If the average age of stocks is three months, the distorting effect of overheads in stocks will be much less than for monthly management reports. In this example, stocks will only represent 25 per cent of production for annual accounting purposes but 300 per cent for monthly (management) reporting purposes.

The survival of absorption costing

The economic logic of marginal costing is difficult to refute. Producing one extra unit does not increase the level of overheads as these are, for the most part at least, fixed. Nevertheless, many firms still use absorption costing in their regular accounting reports to management. This is a humbling finding for any academic but one test of who is right and who is wrong – the managers or the academics – can be found in the discipline of economics itself. The classical theory of economics on which much of cost behaviour is based suggests that inefficient firms are driven out of markets. If absorption costing provides distorted information *and* managers act on this information, then their businesses should not survive as more efficient firms are able to charge lower prices. Firms using absorption costing, however, continue to exist. Therefore, either there must be impediments to competitors entering the market, the theory of cost behaviour must be wrong or managers are using absorption costing in ways not envisaged by classical economics.

Market impediments can partly explain the continuing use of absorption costing in some industries. Monopolies which provide essential goods such as the water industry cannot look to markets to give them selling prices. Given that customers cannot go elsewhere, charging a price based on absorption costing will ensure losses are avoided. Such industries often have government appointed regulators who, recognising that prices have to be sufficient to pay for both fixed and variable costs, allow the price to be set by including overheads. Perhaps the extreme example of this is the defence industry where the norm is to charge contracts on the basis of direct costs plus an agreed margin based on resources employed – a procedure known as 'cost-plus' pricing.

In competitive markets, however, prices are fixed by the powers of demand and supply and cost data is only one element in the equation. Under such circumstances, it is critical to know how costs behave and yet absorption pricing has been shown to distort this information. The answer to why firms still use absorption costing must therefore lie elsewhere.

One possibility is that the economic model of fixed and variable costs is over simplified. The economic theory of the firm from which much of accounting cost behaviour has been derived is silent about the time horizon. In the very short term, practically all costs are fixed. Even hiring labour by the hour results in labour being a fixed cost if the time horizon is one hour. Beyond that period, however, it becomes a variable cost. Consequently, the longer the time period, the more costs become variable. Taking a long term view, the cost of producing output is more than its marginal or variable cost. Fixed costs also need to be met.

Using this argument, absorption costing can be seen as an attempt to develop a representative cost of production. In effect, it becomes a ball park figure. For any given sales volume, selling prices have, on average and through time, to be above that cost if the company is to survive. Certainly this would help to explain the discomfort felt under a marginal costing regime when considering the Christmas cracker problem outlined in Chapter 3. Valuing the first six months' production at only its marginal cost resulted in a loss equal to the fixed costs for the period simply because *sales* only took place immediately prior to the Christmas period, rather than because of any inherent inefficiency.

Absorption costing and human behaviour

There is an even stronger argument to explain the survival of absorption costing. Much of the absorption costing debate has centred on its use for economic decision making. The concern has been about the *extra* costs and *extra* revenues from changing output levels. However, the traditional economic theory of the firm has little to say about the organisation of the business nor human behaviour within it. The need for coordination, motivation and control is never discussed and yet these are real issues of relevance to managers when operating a business. As soon as these are recognised, it is possible to develop a rationale for the continuing use of absorption costing.

The most powerful explanation why companies still use absorption costing has been put forward by Zimmerman.[13] He recognised that cost apportionment serves a variety of managerial roles. It helps to simplify complex organisational problems; it motivates decision makers; and it helps to coordinate decisions in decentralised organisations. Two particular uses were identified: as a constraint on managers' consumption of perquisites and as an approximation to 'difficult to observe' costs.

With the development of responsibility centres – and profit centres in particular – a great deal of discretion is delegated to managers. The larger and more complex the organisation, the less senior managers would know about the detailed operations of the centre. Without some form of control, there is a danger that funds might be used to acquire incidental benefits or perquisites such as the (unnecessary) refurbishment of offices or the acquisition of non-essential equipment. Apportionment is effectively a lump sum tax which reduces the profitability or increases the cost of responsibility centres and hence acts as a constraint on such discretionary expenditure. Bhirmani and Bromwich[14] have identified a similar phenomenon in Japanese management accounting. In some Japanese companies, the *influencing* role of management accounting dominates its *informing* function. Overheads were found to be allocated to labour in order to encourage managers to minimise its use. Any distortions caused were of little significance as the cost data was not being used as information but rather to influence.

The second explanation recognises that overheads are necessary to ensure production. Had the responsibility centre been an entirely independent activity it would have required the use of land and buildings, administration facilities and other overheads. Overhead apportionment is an attempt to approximate these costs. It is, however, only an approximation. As has been shown, methods for sharing overheads are often crude. Such crudity though can be justified if the cost of increased accuracy exceeds any benefits derived from the improvement. Despite the solution not being optimal, the argument does offer an explanation for the wide use of apportionments.

Many of the traditional justifications of absorption costing revolve around its effect on behaviour. One argument suggests that if managers in large, decentralised organisations are not made aware of overheads, they will tend to price output on the basis of the marginal costs known to themselves and this might lead to losses. In the economic theory of the firm, this line of reasoning is rejected. The theory assumes perfect knowledge and rationality by all participants, with prices being set by the forces of demand and supply. In the real world, however, organisations are complex and managers may well display ignorance of costs which originate outside their own area of responsibility. Secondly, readily available data relating to market prices may not be available. This is particularly true in low volume job or batch costing industries. In large, complex businesses, sales personnel, for example, often do not have detailed knowledge of costs or cost behaviour. Folklore suggests that giving marginal cost data to the salesforce results in many orders, all priced at fractionally above marginal cost!

A less controversial argument to explain the apportionment of overheads relates to services provided by a company. Where services to a responsibility centre are provided by an outside supplier, the manager is instantly aware of costs and is at liberty to change the supplier if dissatisfied. Providing the service centrally might be cheaper but it reduces the freedom of choice and discipline imposed by the market. Apportioning those service costs to individual responsibility centres provides a substitute for the market discipline. By being charged for those services, managers are not only made aware of the costs, they can begin to put pressure on the service if quality or price deteriorates. Although not as direct as dealings with outside suppliers, this does impose some discipline on the service providers, a discipline less likely to occur if the overheads were not brought to the attention of production managers by being apportioned.

Dysfunctional aspects of absorption costing

By using absorption costing to constrain managers' consumption of perquisites and as a way of disciplining the providers of central services, the accounting system is being used to modify behaviour towards the achievement of organisational goals. A rigid adherence to absorption costing, however, can result in just the opposite happening. Managers might carry out actions which are not in the best interests of the company.

One such dysfunctional aspect of apportionment relates to responsibility accounting. For responsibility to be effective, performance evaluation should reflect the responsibility centre's efforts and achievements. When overheads are shared between departments or where they represent a re-apportionment of a service department's overheads, production department managers are being judged on costs over which they have little or no control. This can affect a manager's performance in a variety of ways. At the one extreme, managers may waste time and effort trying to control the uncontrollable by constantly questioning the basis of the apportionment and putting pressure on service department managers. At the other extreme, they might choose to ignore *all* the accounting information on the basis that if the overhead figures are dubious then so will be the rest. Neither approach is likely to be in the best interests of the company.

A more immediate danger is that managers might use overheads in the wrong way, especially if overheads and other costs are used for pricing purposes. Consider a small, jobbing company. Assume its overheads are £100,000, its budgeted activity is 10,000 hours for the coming year and labour rates are £5.00 per hour. Overheads will be charged at the rate of £10.00 per labour hour or 200 per cent on labour cost. If the company bids for a job which involves materials of £4,000 and 1,000 labour hours, the minimum quotation must be £19,000 using absorption costing even before allowing for any profit. The danger in this approach becomes clear when market conditions change.

Assume for the sake of argument that there is a recession in the following year and that activity is likely to fall to only 8,000 hours. All other costs remain the same. Overhead will now be £12.50 per labour hour or 250 per cent of labour cost. Quoting for the same job one year later will result in a bid price of £21,500 and yet in a recession, market forces generally drive prices down. The likelihood is that, if the company continues to price on this basis, they will loose many of their bids. Consequently, planned activity will fall even further in subsequent periods which in turn forces up overhead rates even more. The result is a vicious circle which will end when the company goes into liquidation through failing to win any contracts. Using absorption costing under these circumstances is clearly dysfunctional. How this may be resolved is discussed in Chapter 17.

NEW PRODUCTION METHODS

Traditionally, the speed of labour has dictated the speed of production. Improving the efficiency of labour was therefore the key to increased production. For many years, this was reinforced by the attitudes and techniques of Taylor's scientific management and by the division of complex production into smaller functional units or responsibility centres. Arranging for all drilling, for example, to take place in a department restricted to that function enabled labour to specialise in the task of drilling – an example of the division of labour – and for allowable times to be determined by the principles of scientific management. Underpinning this was the internal accounting system. The development of separate responsibility centres enabled the accounting system to determine costs for each element making up production by the use of batch, job or process costing.

Absorption costing encouraged this focus on the efficiency of labour. Given the role of labour in determining the speed of production, labour hours or labour cost became the most popular measure of activity when apportioning overheads. The greater the throughput in any department, the lower the overheads per unit and the more efficient a manager appeared. This is therefore another potentially dysfunctional aspect of management accounting in general and absorption costing in particular. By measuring departmental efficiency in this way, individual managers are encouraged to produce higher volumes than necessary, irrespective of the consequences for other departments.

Traditional production flows

In fact this is just one part of a much wider problem. Costing techniques such as batch and process costing do not tell the whole story. Management face an uncertain demand for the resources under their control while production may involve convoluted flows. Take for instance the product shown in Exhibit 16.10. Its production may start in department A. From there, it might move to department D and then to departments E and B before returning to department D. Finally, it might be transferred to department C for completion.

Exhibit 16.10 Traditional production flows

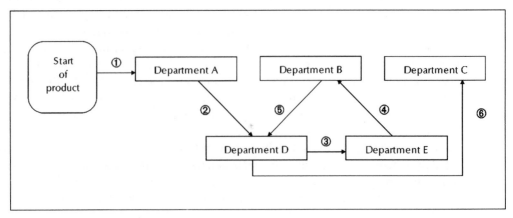

If the business manufactures several different products, production flows might be even more complex. This poses a conflict for managers. On the one hand, goods need to be available to satisfy customers' requirements. On the other hand, production has to be undertaken as efficiently as possible. With so many interdependencies between departments and jobs, rarely will the work flow smoothly on its own accord. Capacity might be available in one department but not another.

Any complicated production system faced with such uncertainties will have to build in slack if it wants to avoid such bottlenecks. Faced with the need to produce a particular job, one answer might be to take on additional labour. Another might be to temporarily stop work on existing jobs. Additional labour, however, would increase costs while stopping work would involve wasted time which could otherwise be used for production. Either way, the effect would be the same. Efficiency as measured by the *costing system* would fall for the departments concerned.

The solution which evolved was to build up stocks of work-in-progress between departments to reduce bottlenecks and to build up finished stocks at the end of production to meet customers' demands. Only once a sufficiently large amount of similar work was available would production commence in any particular department. Stocks became the slack or the buffer which made uninterrupted production possible. Once one batch was completed, a similar large batch of another product could then be worked. The result was high efficiency measured by the traditional accounting techniques of departmental unit costs.

However, by concentrating on cost centres and measuring the efficiency of throughput, the accounting system was failing to measure the overall efficiency of the organisation as a whole. Large amounts of work-in-progress might often be idle as they awaited the freeing of capacity in the next stage of production. Not only did this involve funds being tied up in the work-in-progress, it also involved extra overheads in the form of storage and clerical costs in its handling as the work-in-progress awaited transfer to subsequent stages of production. To use a modern phrase, the storing of the work-in-progress generated no 'added-value'. It was not part of the process of developing the (high value) finished product from the (low value) initial inputs of raw materials.

The new technology

For many years, the hidden stock costs were not a major problem. Firms only made a few products using a limited number of functional departments such as machining, painting and assembling. Production scheduling was then a relatively straightforward matter with few of the bottlenecks identified above and few work-in-progress buffer stocks. Job, batch and process costing systems were not only adequate as means of collecting data, they also reinforced the then dominant management philosophy of hierarchical structures and smaller, function-based responsibility centres.

With only a small number of functional departments, the difficulties of overhead apportionment were less significant. More than that, both the absolute and relative levels of overheads were often much lower than found today. Labour and materials comprised by far the largest element of unit cost. Because of that, it mattered less which activity measure was used to absorb overheads into unit product costs.

As early as the 1930s, this scenario was beginning to change, a change which has accelerated over the last twenty years. Huge, multinational companies began to dominate production, making a much wider range of products. Technology was also changing. Not only did it become much more complicated, it also involved much higher levels of capital investment in new plant and machinery. Increasingly, overheads became the major element in manufacturing cost with (direct) labour becoming less and less significant. As a result, the speed of the machines – rather than the speed of labour – dictated the pace of production. Labour therefore was no longer a reasonable measure of activity for charging overheads. Despite that, most accounting texts and many individual businesses still identified labour as the main base for absorbing overheads. With labour increasingly being replaced by machines, and the cost of the machines increasing the business's overheads, labour overhead recovery rates of several hundred per cent were not uncommon. Such rates might possibly be acceptable for *attaching* overheads to stocks for financial reporting purposes: they were, however, unlikely to be of help to managers. With so much overhead subsumed within a single figure, the cause–effect relationship of overheads to products had become lost.

'Just in time' production

The growing importance of advanced manufacturing technologies using computer-aided design, computer-aided manufacturing (CAD/CAM) and robotics saw a massive increase in what would traditionally be called fixed costs and a corresponding decrease in traditional variable costs. Workers were increasingly employed as sophisticated machine minders and so using labour as a measure of activity became increasingly inappropriate. This change in the role of labour meant that, even if the ideas of Taylor and Fayol had originally been of help in organisational design, they were less and less relevant to the newly evolving production methods of the 1980s and 1990s.

To take full advantage of the new technology required a different form of organisation. The origins of this can be traced back to the growth of Japanese manufacturing after the Second World War. Faced with few natural resources and a shortage of funds, the one resource Japanese companies had was a skilled and flexible workforce. This enabled the difficulties caused by the lack of funds and natural resources to be minimised. Culturally, the relationship of the employee with the company was different from that in the West. Employees tended to join a company for the whole of their working life, a particular example of the more general philosophy found in Japan of the valuing of the group or team over the individual. Not only did this encourage a flexibility in the workforce, it meant that, in a traditional sense, labour was very much a fixed cost.

To limit the disadvantage of lack of funds, the elimination of waste was critical – and waste was defined as anything which did not add value to the product as perceived by the customer. Storing work-in-progress or finished stock did not add to this value, nor did the costs of moving part-finished production from one department to another. Similarly, quality control before despatching goods to the customer did not add value. If quality could be built into the production process, not only might the quality control department be eliminated but the cost of warranty claims could also be minimised.

The way much of this waste was to be saved was by reorganising the structure of production. Instead of products flowing in batches through specialised, functional departments, manufacturing was organised around products and work cells. Products were organised into families which shared similar production requirements and routings. Functional departments were then eliminated and their resources shared out to individual production lines or cells, with each cell comprising a variety of different machines and a team of employees.

Exhibit 16.11 demonstrates the effect of this changed approach to production. By focusing on product groupings and cells within that, the output of the one cell became the immediate input of the next cell, eliminating the need for work-in-progress. The logic was even extended to raw materials by tying in suppliers to specific delivery schedules and demanding rigorous specifications which had to be exactly met. Deliveries would be timed to coincide with production needs and, because quality was agreed previously with the suppliers, the materials could immediately be issued to production without any detailed quality checks. Because of this scheduling of deliveries with production, the system became known as 'just in time' manufacturing or JIT.

Exhibit 16.11 'Just in time' production flows

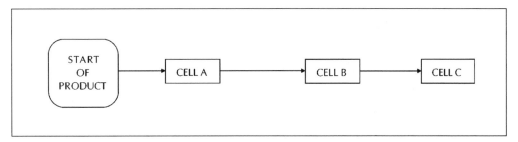

In 'just in time' manufacturing, specialised machines are no longer grouped together in a single functional department. Instead, each work cell might contain a variety of dissimilar machines. Each cell then produces a particular product or family of components. For this to work effectively, each worker needs to be flexible in terms of hours worked, be able to perform a variety of tasks and work as part of a team. It is this flexibility which provides the buffer otherwise provided by stocks in traditional processes. The result is a reversal of the traditional philosophy of production organisation.

Traditional methods reduce the complexity of tasks by increasing the complexity of production flows and emphasising specialisation and the division of labour. At the most, each department is only responsible for a small part of production and so overall production is identified with a large variety of subcomponents. Just in time manufacturing, however, increases the variety and complexity *within cells* but reduces both the complexity of work flows between cells and the number of subcomponents. More than that, without functional departments to be coordinated, JIT reduces the levels of management. The organisational structure becomes horizontal rather than hierarchical. As a result, managers become closer to production. However, JIT manufacturing, by emphasising the cell and the cell-team, makes individual outputs difficult to track, while concentrating on a wider range of tasks and products means the unit costs of traditional production can no longer be calculated.

RELEVANCE LOST

By the 1980s, it was clear that traditional methods of management accounting were inadequate to deal with the new technology and the organisational structure which flowed from that. Overheads were now much more significant, labour no longer dictated the pace of production and traditional functional responsibility centres were being replaced by work cells in many companies. Applying traditional management accounting techniques to JIT production could be dysfunctional.

Increasing production and reducing unit cost by one cost centre might not be in the interests of the company as a whole if this led to a build up of stocks or interfered with production flows. Sections of the business also become increasingly interdependent under JIT and so the apparent independence of cost centres is no longer appropriate. Under a traditional system, for example, the randomness of deliveries might pose problems for the goods received store. The problem might be solved by paying extra to suppliers to obtain timed deliveries. The effect, however, would be to increase the cost of the buying department, making it look less efficient when viewed in isolation. Taking the wider view found in JIT manufacturing, such suboptimisation difficulties are minimised.

Not only might traditional management accounting techniques be dysfunctional, they might also not be providing managers with the information they need under JIT. In one sense, cost information becomes less significant. Materials are subject to detailed specification and long term contracts which specify prices while direct labour becomes part of the overhead of the cell and no longer dictates the speed of production. As a result, unit costs are not likely to change from month to month. With managers being closer to production, they will often be aware of problems well before this is formally reported to them in the management accounting system. Their information needs therefore will be less concerned with costs and more with quality, lead times, flexibility and customer satisfaction. In another sense, however, costs became more significant. With increasing levels of overheads and fewer responsibility centres, their relationship with production was not clear.

These issues were crystallised by Johnson and Kaplan in their text, *Relevance Lost: The Rise and Fall of Management Accounting*.[15] They criticised the current state of management accounting on four grounds. The first two criticisms were that conventional management accounting does not meet the needs of today's manufacturing and business environment and that traditional product costing provides misleading information for management purposes. Both of these criticisms have been demonstrated in the earlier discussion on traditional management accounting methods and the new technology.

The third criticism offers a possible explanation for this failure of management accounting. Johnson and Kaplan believe that management accounting practices have become subservient to financial accounting practices. Chapter 7 has already described the rapid growth in legislation and other external regulation affecting financial reporting over the last 50 years. With the integration of management and financial accounting, it was perhaps inevitable that legal and other extra-statutory requirements would dominate when designing accounting systems. The suggestion is that accounting originally evolved as an aid to management but was hijacked by the imperative of financial reporting.

Their final criticism is one which is partly addressed in Chapter 20. They believe that the focus within management accounting on internal costs and activities is inadequate.

Years ago, this might have been sufficient as markets were less complex and not subject to such rapid change. To help today's managers make decisions requires information about the environment in which the business operates such as competitors' prices, products and plans. In other words, the focus of management accounting should be outward looking rather than inward looking.

ACTIVITY BASED COSTING

To remedy at least part of the first two criticisms, Cooper and Kaplan[16] developed the idea of activity based costing or ABC. Although particularly applicable to the new technology, ABC can be applied to all production processes, including service industries. Traditional accounting differentiates between fixed and variable costs in a simplistic way. By convention, direct labour, direct materials and power for machine time are viewed as variable costs. All other costs are treated as overheads. Overheads – predominantly fixed costs – are then allocated and apportioned to departments from where they are absorbed into individual products.

With increasing levels of overhead, one danger of this approach is to accept their level as given and not controllable. Often this is reinforced by presenting cost data per unit. Presenting data in this form, however, can be counterproductive 'because it tends to direct managers' attention to unit-level actions – to consider a price increase, for example, or to reduce labour, materials or machine-time processing. Some unit-level actions might be beneficial, but in many instances, there is little room for improvement.'[17] In other words, managers' attention is directed towards cost numbers rather than towards the resource-consuming activities which eventually cause costs.

Activities, cost drivers and transactions

All production, administration and marketing is made up of activities which consume resources. Examples include materials receipt and handling, assembly, and despatching goods to customers. The cost of those resources do not simply appear. They are incurred for a purpose. Something or someone must therefore be causing or *driving* those costs. Conventional short-run variable costs such as direct materials and direct labour are caused by the activity of production and driven by the number of units produced. Change production volume and labour and material costs will change.

Activity based costing extends this logic to overheads by analysing its components into activities and then identifying the forces which give rise to their cost. These forces are known as cost drivers. What drives costs are transactions. The number of goods received orders, for example, is the major transaction which drives the goods received department while the number of despatches is likely to be the major transaction driver for the goods despatched department.

Overhead cost drivers

Traditional short term variable costs should be charged to products in the normal way based on volume. This, however, is inappropriate for overheads. Nevertheless, many expenses accounted for as overheads are actually variable costs with very few expenses being true fixed costs.[18] Where they differ from conventional variable costs is in their timing and their measurement of activity.

Often there will be a timing delay between the reduction in the activity and the reduction in cost. Reducing the number of issues from stores will not immediately involve a reduction in the number of store personnel. In the longer term, however, numbers can be reduced and staff redeployed elsewhere.

This example also demonstrates the second difference from traditional short term variable costs. Although based on activity, the activity is not the volume of production but the number of stores issues. Cooper and Kaplan believe these long term variable costs are not driven by production volume but by product complexity and diversity. One of the best examples of this is the set up-costs of production. These costs derive from arranging and preparing the relevant machines suitable for the commencement of production. As such their total cost does not vary with volume but the number of production runs for different products. The greater the range of products and the smaller each production run, the greater the total set-up costs for any particular volume.

One difficulty with ABC is determining the appropriate cost drivers. Sometimes there might be more than one or the choice made may not fully explain the driver behind the activity's costs. The driver for the goods received store, for example, is often the number of deliveries received. Some deliveries, however, might consume more resources such as time and floor space than others. If this is felt to be a serious distortion, it is possible to have more than one cost driver in a similar way to telephone bills being divided between the cost of the line rental and the cost of calls made.

A second difficulty may lie in deriving transaction information. For some activities, volume data will be automatically generated by the accounting or production systems – the number of sales invoices issued for the sales department for instance or the number of production runs undertaken. For other activities, however, it may be necessary to undertake periodical sampling.

The final difficulty is that some overheads will not lend themselves to ABC analysis. Some head office expenses can rarely be related to transactions. Nevertheless, ABC does represent a genuine improvement on conventional treatments of overheads as Example 16.7 demonstrates.

Example 16.7

Buxton and Cheadle Engineering manufactures three products, the Exe, the Wye and the Zed. The Exe is produced on behalf of Derby plc which supplies the semi-finished product which Buxton and Cheadle complete on their behalf. No additional material is used in this task.

Planned overheads for the coming year total £255,000 and comprise production set-up costs of £150,000, the cost of the goods received department of £30,000 and the cost of the raw materials stores of £75,000. Labour costs are likely to be £8.00 per hour and overheads are currently absorbed on the basis of direct labour hours. Details of planned production are as follows:

Product	Exe	Wye	Zed
Budgeted production (units)	5,000	40,000	35,000
Batch size (units)	1,250	10,000	5,000
Unit material cost	nil	£40	£30
Direct labour hours per unit	1.0	0.625	2.0
Planned number of raw material deliveries received	8	4	8
Estimated number of material issues	20	10	20

By multiplying the planned production for each product by the labour hours per unit, the total planned labour hours can be obtained. For Exe, this is 5,000 hours, for Wye, 25,000 hours, and for Zed, 70,000 hours, a total of 100,000 hours. With total overheads of £255,000, the overhead absorption rate is £2.55 per labour hour. Exhibit 16.12 shows the resulting full product costs per unit.

Exhibit 16.12 Traditional absorption costing and product costs

Product	Exe £	Wye £	Zed £
Material	nil	40.00	30.00
Labour	8.00	5.00	16.00
Overhead	2.55	1.60	5.10
Unit full product cost	10.55	46.60	51.11

Traditional absorption costing, even with the refinement of departmental overhead rates, rarely reflects the extent to which individual products consume resources. By charging overheads to products on the basis of labour hours or some similar measure, cause–effect relationships are often ignored. Activity based costing seeks to remedy this defect. A glance at the data for Buxton and Cheadle, for example, shows that 5,000 units of Exe are to be produced in batches of 1,250. This means that plant and machinery will have to be set up four times to produce the planned volume. This is the same number of set-ups required for Wye even though the planned production volume is higher. Exe therefore is making the same demands on the set-up activity as Wye – an example of overhead costs being driven by complexity rather than production volume. When considering the costs of receiving and issuing materials, Exe generates twice as many transactions as Wye. Exe involves 8 deliveries of raw materials and 20 issues. For Wye, these figures are halved. Assuming these transactions are reasonable measures of resource usage or drivers, Exe is consuming more overhead resources than Wye.

The effect of this on product costs is shown in Exhibit 16.13 where it is assumed that the number of set-ups drive the set-up costs, the number of deliveries drive the cost of the goods received department and the number of issues drives the cost of the raw materials stores. The total number of set-ups are 15, four for Exe, four for Wye and seven for Zed. With set-up costs totalling £150,000, the cost per set-up is £10,000. Using a similar analysis, with 20 deliveries, the cost per delivery is £1,500, the same as the cost per issue assuming issue costs are £75,000 and the number of issues are 50.

Exhibit 16.13 Activity based costing and product costs

Product	Exe		Wye		Zed	
Set-up costs	(4 × £10,000)	£40,000	(4 × £10,000)	£40,000	(7 × £10,000)	£70,000
Material delivery costs	(8 × £1,500)	£12,000	(4 × £1,500)	£6,000	(8 × £1,500)	£12,000
Material issue costs	(20 × £1,500)	£30,000	(10 × £1,500)	£15,000	(20 × £1,500)	£30,000
		£82,000		£61,000		£112,000
Planned production		5,000		40,000		35,000
ABC unit overhead		£16.40		£1.52		£3.20
Materials		nil		£40.00		£30.00
Labour		£8.00		£5.00		£16.00
ABC unit full product cost		£24.40		£46.52		£49.20

The ABC analysis shows Exe is consuming a far higher proportion of Buxton and Cheadle's overheads as a result of its complexity. This explains a phenomenon found by Cooper and Kaplan.[19] Managers of a division were perplexed at winning business which their plant was not configured for but losing bids the plant could produce efficiently. The reason lay in the traditional use of overheads. The low volume work was being under-costed in terms of resources consumed while the high volume business was being over-costed.

How valid activity based costing is depends partly on the accurate identification of activity costs and the choice of appropriate drivers. It also depends on the ability, ultimately, to save costs if demands on activities are reduced. Cost savings will be related to the time period considered. In the case of Buxton and Cheadle, for example, if production of Exe was found to be no longer profitable, few overhead costs could be saved immediately. Within a short time, however, labour could be redeployed from material handling to other duties, although to save costs such as rent and rates might take much longer. Nevertheless, through time, even reductions in these costs might be possible by either finding smaller premises or using part of the existing premises for other purposes. Whether the costs saved will be in proportion to the amounts identified by the drivers will depend on the accuracy of the drivers.

The main advantage of activity based costing, however, may not come from its improvement to cost information. Long term, its major benefit might be its influence on management behaviour. By separating overheads into activities and then identifying drivers, ABC begins to highlight the forces behind overheads. As such, no longer need overheads be treated as a black hole which suck in costs but about which little is known. Instead, by identifying the causes of overheads, ABC allows their contribution to profitability to be questioned and recognises their controllability by management.

SUMMARY

This chapter has shown how much of management accounting evolved from a time when production was relatively simple. The way it evolved reflected the dominant views in society at that time. Production was broken down into smaller and smaller departments both to identify how costs behave and to ensure control by making managers responsible for those departments. Departments, however, are rarely independent and so, increasingly, costs in the form of overheads had to be apportioned between departments. At times, this could lead to dysfunctional behaviour by managers and sub-optimisation as their main concern was only for their own departments.

The growth in overheads was identified as causing particular difficulties because of the different behaviour of fixed and variable costs. Fixed costs are essentially time based whereas traditional variable costs change with changes in production volume. Because of this, there are strong academic arguments against the inclusion of overheads in product costs. Accounting, however, is not just about providing information, it is also about influencing behaviour and this offers a possible explanation for the continuing use of overheads.

With overheads becoming an increasing proportion of product costs, they could not simply be ignored nor was their absorption into products using some volume measure an appropriate treatment. Johnson and Kaplan suggested that, partly because of this, management accounting had lost its way. The suggested solution of activity based costing recognised that many overheads are not fixed but vary with activities other than volume. By identifying what drives overheads, cost information could once more be made relevant to the needs of managers.

REFERENCES

1 Emmanual, C., Otley, D. and Merchant, K., (1990) *Accounting for Management Control,* Chapman & Hall, Preface to 2nd edn.

2 Johnson, H. T. and Kaplan, R.S. (1987) *Relevance Lost: The Rise and Fall of Management Accounting,* Harvard University Press.

3 Taylor, F.W. (1947) *The Principles of Scientific Management,* Harper & Row, pp. 36–7.

4 Republished in the UK as Fayol, H. (1949) *General and Industrial Management,* Pitman.

5 Follett, M.P. (1924) *Creative Experience,* Longman and Green.

6 McGregor, D. (1965) *The Human Side of Enterprise,* McGraw-Hill.

7 Otley, D. (1987) *Accounting Control and Organisational Behaviour,* Heinemann, p. 10.

8 Drury, C. (1988) *Management and Cost Accounting,* 2nd edn, Van Nostrand Reinhold, p. 488.

9 Otley, D. (1987), op. cit., pp. 74–5.

10 See Horngren, C.T. and Foster, G. (1991) *Cost Accounting: A Managerial Emphasis,* 7th edn, Prentice Hall, pp. 468–74, for ways of apportioning costs where service department overheads are interrelated.

11 Horngren and Foster (1991), op. cit., p. 537.

12 Ahmed, M.N. and Scapens, R.W. (1991) 'Cost allocation theory and practice: the continuing debate', published in *Issues in Management Accounting,* Ashton, D., Hopper, T. and Scapens, R.W. (eds), Prentice Hall.

13 Zimmerman, J.L. (1979) 'The cost and benefits of cost allocation', *The Accounting Review,* July, pp. 504–21.

14 Bhirmani, A. and Bromwich, M. (1992) 'Management accounting: evolution in progress', published in *Management Accounting Handbook*, Drury, C. (ed.), Butterworth Heinemann.

15 Johnson and Kaplan (1927), op. cit.

16 Cooper, R. and Kaplan, R.S. (1987) 'How cost accounting systematically distorts product costs', in Bruns, W.J. and Kaplan, R.S. (ed.), *Accounting and Management: Field Study Perspectives*, Harvard Business School.

17 Cooper, R. and Kaplan, R.S. (1991) 'Profit priorities from activity-based costing', *Harvard Business Review*, May–June, p. 132.

18 See, for example, Cooper, R. (1987) 'The two-stage procedure in cost accounting', *Journal of Cost Management for the Manufacturing Industry*, Fall, pp. 39–45, for evidence of this.

19 Cooper and Kaplan (1991), op. cit., p. 132.

FURTHER READING

Ashton, D., Hopper, T. and Scapens, R.W. (1991) *Issues in Management Accounting*, Prentice Hall.

Emmanual, C., Otley, D. and Merchant, K. (1990) *Accounting for Management Control*, 2nd edn, Chapman & Hall.

Horngren, C.T. and Foster, G. (1991) *Cost Accounting: A Managerial Emphasis*, 7th edn, Prentice Hall.

Kaplan, R.S. and Atkinson, A.A. (1989) *Advanced Management Accounting*, 2nd edn, Prentice Hall.

TEST YOUR UNDERSTANDING

1 Differentiate between cost centres, profit centres and responsibility centres.

2 Explain the difference between behaviour controls, output controls and input controls.

3 What is meant by the term 'process costing'?

4 Equivalent units refer to:
- **(a)** a way of calculating job costs where each job is different from one another;
- **(b)** the average number of units in a batch;
- **(c)** a way of calculating production costs where part of the production is incomplete at the period end.

5 Distinguish between the accounting treatment of normal and abnormal losses.

6 Joint products:
- **(a)** use the same fixed costs and hence jointly share overheads with each other;
- **(b)** are two or more products which are the unavoidable outcome from a single input;
- **(c)** are products which both need to be produced if there is to be customer demand;
- **(d)** none of these.

7 Explain why absorption costing might be of help to an organisation despite it being a 'useless and wasteful exercise'.

8 List the four criticisms of management accounting highlighted in 'Relevance Lost'.

9 What is meant by activity based costing?

QUESTIONS

1 Hastings Ltd operates two machine departments, departments 1 and 2, and an assembly department, department 3. In addition, it has two service departments, a canteen and a maintenance unit. The forecast overheads of the production departments along with all the costs for the service departments are reproduced below.

Using the data and making explicit any assumptions, determine the budgeted overhead absorption rates for each production budget.

	Department 1 (£)	Department 2 (£)	Department 3 (£)	Canteen (£)	Maintenance (£)	Total (£)
Supervisory salaries	85,500	64,800	87,600	31,185	98,400	367,485
Materials	8,000	6,500	24,400	26,000		64,900
Rent and rates						18,000
Building insurance						4,000
Power						8,600
Heat and light						6,600
Machinery depreciation						60,000
Area square metres	10,000	18,000	40,000	2,000	10,000	80,000
Value of machinery	200,000	180,000	20,000			400,000
Power usage (%)	40	45	10		5	100
Direct labour hours	10,000	6,000	24,000			40,000
Machine usage	8,000	16,000				24,000

2 Caledonian-Sterling Ltd manufactures a coating used to protect the hulls of boats. At the beginning of January, there were no opening stocks of work-in-progress. During the month, 32,000 litres of material X costing £83,200 were added to the process and conversion costs came to £221,760. Evaporation, equivalent to 20 per cent of inputs completed, is identified at the end of the process.

At the end of the month, the closing work-in-process was 7,000 litres. This was 100 per cent complete in terms of materials and 20 per cent complete in terms of conversion costs. Completed output for the month totalled 18,000 litres.

Using the above information, estimate the absorption cost per litre of the coating for production completed in January, the cost of goods transferred to finished stock and the cost of the closing work-in-progress.

3 Speyside plc manufactures four products using the same plant and processes. Overhead costs are currently absorbed by products on a machine hour rate. For the period just ended, details of production volumes, costs and times were as follows:

Product	Volume	Material cost per unit	Direct labour hours per unit	Machine hours per unit	Labour cost per unit
A	500	£5.00	0.50	0.25	£3.00
B	5,000	£5.00	0.50	0.25	£3.00
C	600	£16.00	2.00	1.00	£12.00
D	7,000	£17.00	1.50	1.50	£9.00

Total production overhead for the period came to £59,879. An analysis of these overheads revealed the following information.

Factory overhead applicable to machine-oriented activity	£37,424
Set-up costs	£4,355
Cost of ordering materials	£1,920
Material handling costs	£7,580
Administration costs - spare parts	£8,600

However, a further investigation into the production overhead activities for the period identified the following totals.

Product	Number of set-ups	Number of material orders	Number of times material handled	Number of spare parts
A	1	1	2	2
B	6	4	10	5
C	2	1	3	1
D	8	4	12	4

Using the above information:
(a) estimate the unit overhead currently charged to each product;
(b) calculate an overhead cost per unit using activity based costing;
(c) briefly comment on the differences disclosed.

CHAPTER 17

Pricing and output decisions

Managers are not just concerned to know how well their organisation has performed. Of equal importance is an awareness of how well it might perform in different circumstances. Change costs, prices or the volume of business activity and a different profit will be reported.

This chapter:

- Identifies patterns of cost behaviour and differentiates between the accountant's and the economist's models of pricing and output decisions

- Develops the concept of contribution as an aid to decision making

- Examines the uses and limitations of cost–volume–profit analysis

- Considers the limitations of absorption costing data when making decisions

- Introduces the concept of shadow prices and opportunity cost as a framework for decision making

Using absorption costing when making decisions is fraught with difficulties. The amount of overhead charged will vary not only with the volume measure chosen but also its magnitude. Other things being equal, a doubling of volume will lead to a halving of overheads per unit. More than that, activity based costing has shown that traditional absorption measures fail to take account of the cause–effect relationship between costs and output. Consequently, some other approach is needed when considering pricing and output decisions.

If a business is concerned with profitability, it will need to focus on the components of profit. Three factors influence profitability: the organisation's cost structure, the prices it is able to charge for its output and the volume of that output. Change any one of the variables and profit will also change. An understanding of cost and price behaviour is therefore essential when making pricing and output decisions.

COST BEHAVIOUR AND THE TIME HORIZON

Unfortunately, the relationships between costs and profit are not simple. In particular, the relationships will vary depending on the time period chosen. The shorter the time period, the less control managers have over pricing and output. Take, for example, market traders selling fresh fruit on a Saturday and assume their stock cost £500. Because of its perishable nature, the fruit will not keep until Monday, the next day of trading. Having bought the fruit, it cannot be returned to the wholesaler if unsold nor kept for selling on a subsequent day. If none of the fruit is sold it will have to be thrown away with the traders standing the £500 cost. Equally, if all of the fruit is sold, the cost will also be £500. Therefore, taking a 24-hour time horizon, the cost of the fruit is a fixed cost.

Taking a longer time period, however, the cost of the fruit becomes a variable cost. If Saturdays are busier days, more stock will be bought to meet the increased demand. If trade on Mondays is lower, the traders will buy less fruit. On a weekly basis, the total cost of stock purchases will vary as demand varies and so it becomes a variable cost.

Another cost which market traders have to face is the rental of their stall. Traditionally it is a fixed cost. If no fruit is sold, the rental still has to be paid. But, taking a sufficiently long time horizon, even this becomes a variable or marginal cost. Within reason, the traders can sell more and more fruit from their single stall. There comes a stage, however, when it is no longer practicable to sell more and more stock from a single stall. Beyond that, another stall will be required to enable additional sales to take place. Fixed costs, therefore, are only fixed over the *relevant range*. In the case of the market traders, this relevant range will be the amount of stock they can display on their stall. More generally, for other businesses, it might relate to the number of machines or the floor space available.

THE ECONOMIST'S MODEL

The accountant's model of cost behaviour has been derived from the economist's theory of the firm. The time horizon chosen is sufficiently short term for some costs to be treated as fixed while others can be viewed as varying with output.

The economist's definition of marginal cost

Economists define marginal cost as the extra cost involved in producing one extra unit of output. As such it is a similar definition to the one used by the accountant, although in accounting it is more often known as variable cost. Where it differs is in the technical relationship between inputs and outputs. Consider, as an example, the operating of a restaurant. Trying to run it single handed would involve one person having to greet guests, take their order, cook their food, wait on them and staff the cash desk. Despite this, some customers would be served and so some 'production' would take place. Assume, for the sake of argument, that wages paid are £5 per hour and that, single handed, it is possible to serve one person per hour. Ignoring the cost of the food, the marginal cost of serving one customer is £5. Now consider doubling the number of staff to two. One employee could concentrate on the cooking and the other look after the customers. By specialising, the number of customers capable of being served – i.e. production – is likely to *more than* double.

As a result of doubling the number of staff to two, it might be possible to serve three customers per hour. By spending an additional £5 on labour, two *extra* customers can be served. The marginal cost of each of those two customers has now fallen to £2.50 each compared with £5 for the first customer. If a third member of staff is taken on, again at £5 per hour, an even more efficient sharing of tasks might be possible such that the restaurant can now handle an extra four customers. The marginal cost of each of the next four customers would have fallen to £1.25. Eventually, however, these reducing marginal costs will begin to flatten out. No further improvements through specialisation will be possible. A fourth member of staff, for example, might only be able to handle a further four customers, causing their unit marginal cost to remain constant at £1.25.

At some stage, with the same physical premises and equipment, ultimately the marginal costs will start increasing. Bottlenecks in the kitchen might begin to take place or the number of tables might be limited. A fifth employee might only be able to handle a further three customers and so their marginal cost will increase to £1.67 per customer. Although it is still possible to serve even more customers, this can only be achieved with less and less efficiency. A sixth employee may mean that the restaurant can only handle a further two customers to give a marginal cost for each of those two customers of £2.50 while taking on a seventh employee might mean that only one extra customer can be served at a marginal cost of £5. The implications of this are shown in Exhibit 17.1.

Exhibit 17.1 Average, marginal and total costs

Number of staff	Number of customers	Total cost	Average cost per customer	Marginal cost per customer
1	1	£5.00	£5.00	£5.00
2	3	£10.00	£3.33	£2.50
3	7	£15.00	£2.14	£1.25
4	11	£20.00	£1.82	£1.25
5	14	£25.00	£1.79	£1.67
6	16	£30.00	£1.88	£2.50
7	17	£35.00	£2.06	£5.00

Traditionally, economics has concentrated on unit marginal cost behaviour, showing marginal cost initially falling, then bottoming out and then increasing at an increasing rate. Theoretically, the assumption has been that inputs – the number of staff in this example – could be increased minutely to show how much extra input was required to achieve one extra unit of output. This is the basis for the smooth 'U' shaped marginal cost curve of economic texts.

The economist's total cost curves

Logically, however, the data could be presented in terms of total rather than unit marginal costs. This is how the data has been graphed in Exhibit 17.2. Generalising, the total of the variable or marginal costs[1] will increase as output increases. Initially, however, costs will increase at a slower rate than the increase in output to reflect the early cost savings from the efficient organisation of production. This is represented by the slope of the curve beginning to flatten out as production starts to increase. After a while, however, it is more difficult to obtain further efficiencies and so the slope of the total marginal cost curve rises at a more or less constant rate. Beyond that, increasing output is only possible by increasing disproportionately the amount of inputs. Consequently, the slope of the curve begins to increase at an increasing rate to reflect the difficulties of achieving higher output from a given amount of fixed costs.

To derive the economist's total cost curve, fixed costs need to be added to the total variable cost for any given level of output. Fixed costs, however, do not vary with output. They are payable even if production is nil. Consequently, they will be the same amount whatever the volume. Graphically they will be represented by a horizontal line, parallel to the volume axis. This is demonstrated in Exhibit 17.3 where the total variable costs have been added to the fixed costs, enabling the total cost to be estimated for any given level of output.

Exhibit 17.2 The economist's total marginal cost curve

Exhibit 17.3 The economist's total cost

Economist's total revenue

For most products, the lower the price, the greater the demand from customers. In terms of the restaurant example, setting the price of a fixed menu at £50 might only result in one customer per hour. Reducing it to £40, however, might encourage three customers to buy the menu. As a result, sales revenue or turnover will increase from £50 per hour to £120 per hour. Unfortunately, by setting the price at £40, although two extra customers are introduced, the one who was prepared to pay £50 is now able to purchase the same menu for the lower price of £40. This is inevitable unless some way is found of preventing the first customer from knowing about the reduction in prices. By reducing prices even further, more customers are likely to be enticed into the restaurant. The likely demand for meals at different prices and the effect on total revenue for the hypothetical restaurant is shown in Exhibit 17.4 where total revenue is found by multiplying price by the demand for meals at that price.

Exhibit 17.4 Demand, price and total revenue

Number of customers (demand)	Price (average revenue)	Total revenue (turnover)
1	£50	£50
3	£40	£120
7	£30	£210
14	£20	£280
16	£15	£240
17	£12	£204

Reducing prices causes the number of customers to increase. For a while, the total revenue also increases. Initially, a relatively small decrease in price results in a large increase in turnover. This increase in turnover comprises the revenue from the extra sales less the reduction in price gained by the original number of customers. At this stage, the extra revenue from new customers is far more significant than the decrease in revenue from charging less to the small number of existing customers who were prepared to pay more for their meals. As volume increases, however, subsequent price decreases have to be spread over more and more pre-existing customers. For a while this is still more than compensated for by extra revenue being generated by new customers. Turnover therefore continues to increase although at a slower and slower rate. Eventually, further price reductions actually cause total revenue to fall as the decrease in price given to existing customers more than offsets the gain in revenue from additional customers. By making the simplifying assumption of minute changes in price, total revenue for different levels of demand can be shown graphically. This is demonstrated in Exhibit 17.5.

Profit maximisation and optimal output

Superimposing the economist's total revenue curve on to the total cost curve, as shown in Exhibit 17.6, enables the optimal volume to be determined. This will be at point (a) where the difference between total revenue and total cost is at its greatest and hence profit will be at a maximum. With (a) being the required output to achieve maximum profit, the necessary unit price can be found by reading off the total revenue at the point and dividing by the volume. Assume, for example, that the optimal volume, (a), is 1,000 units and total revenue or turnover is £10,000. The price to be charged to achieve this output will be £10 per unit.

Exhibit 17.5 The economist's total revenue

Exhibit 17.6 Optimal output and profit

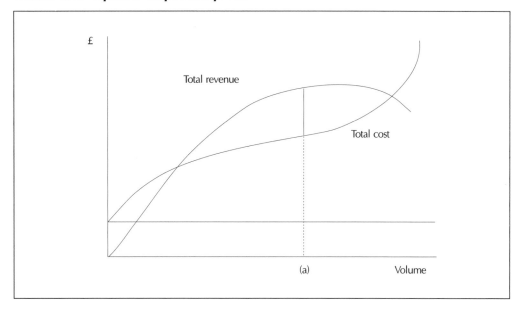

THE ACCOUNTANT'S MODEL

Accountant's variable costs

Many of the cost behaviour patterns found in the economist's model are accepted by accountants. Fixed costs, for example, are assumed to remain constant over the relevant range. There are, however, subtle differences. In the accounting model, the behaviour of variable or marginal costs is simplified. The relationship between inputs and outputs is assumed to be linear. If the output from one hour of labour is 10 units, then the output from two hours is assumed to be 20 units and the output from three hours is assumed to be 30 units. If labour rates are, say, £10 per hour, the labour cost of 10 units will then be £10, for 20 units, £20 and for 30 units, £30. A similar argument can be applied to materials and any other variable costs and so the marginal cost *per unit* is constant. Plotting the total marginal cost produces an increasing straight line graph of the form shown in Exhibit 17.7(a).

Graph (b) superimposes the accountant's total marginal cost curve on that of the economist, allowing both to be compared. The essential difference between the two relates to the extremes of exceedingly low and exceedingly high volumes. Rarely, if ever, do businesses operate at these extremes. Although theoretically possible, it is practically impossible for a car plant designed for 4,000 operatives, for example, to produce with only one worker. Similarly, although the plant might be capable of operating with perhaps 5,000 employees, only in theory would it be possible to operate with 20,000 workers. The extremes of the economist's curve are therefore of only theoretical interest. Practically, businesses will operate within these extremes – the volume levels identified as the relevant range in graph (b). Given all the practical difficulties of estimating the economist's marginal costs, the accountant's cost curve is a close approximation to the economist's cost curve over the relevant range.

Exhibit 17.7 The accountant's and economist's total marginal cost curves

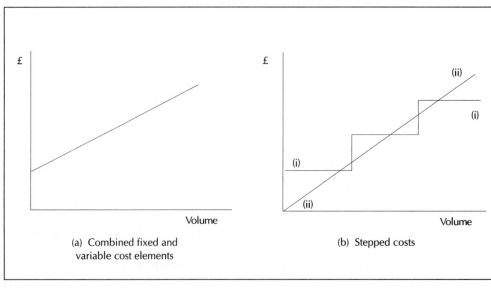

More complicated cost structures

Although the treatment of fixed costs by the accountant and the economist are similar, not all costs fall into the fixed or variable classifications. Some costs comprise both a fixed and variable element. One example is a telephone bill, part of which, the line rental, is fixed. Such costs, shown in part (a) of Exhibit 17.8, require their fixed and variable elements to be separated when determining total costs at various levels.

Exhibit 17.8 Other cost structures

Other costs have a more complicated mix. A supervisor, for instance, might be capable of overseeing the work of up to six employees. Within that range, the cost is fixed. Employing a seventh worker, however, will require an additional supervisor who will then be capable of supervising up to a further five employees before another supervisor is required. The cost of supervision is therefore a stepped cost. Depending on the accuracy and computation involved, stepped costs can either be shown as incremental increases in the form of line (i) in part (b) of Exhibit 17.8 or approximated as a variable cost by line (ii).

The accountant's total cost and total revenue curves

Ignoring the additional difficulties of complicated cost structures, the fixed and variable costs of accounting can be brought together to show total costs for any particular level of activity. Example 17.1 provides the data which enables this to be demonstrated.

Example 17.1

Gloucester Ltd manufacturers a single product known as the Severn. Fixed costs, including rent and rates, total £10,000 p.a. Each unit of the Severn sells for £15 and requires £6 of materials, £3 of direct labour and £1 of electricity per unit produced.

Even if no production takes place, there will be £10,000 of fixed costs incurred. Beyond that, each unit produced costs £10. Exhibit 17.9 shows costs, revenue and profit for Gloucester Ltd as the volume of activity changes. To simplify matters, only five output levels have been considered.

Exhibit 17.9 Output, costs, revenues and profits

Output units	Fixed cost	Total variable cost	Total cost	Total revenue	Profit/(loss)
nil	£10,000	nil	£10,000	nil	(£10,000)
1,000	£10,000	£10,000	£20,000	£15,000	(£5,000)
2,000	£10,000	£20,000	£30,000	£30,000	nil
3,000	£10,000	£30,000	£40,000	£45,000	£5,000
4,000	£10,000	£40,000	£50,000	£60,000	£10,000

No matter what the output level, fixed costs remain the same. Variable costs, however, vary directly with changes in volume. Turnover is also directly related to activity on the simplifying assumption that there are no stocks. A doubling of activity results in a doubling of turnover. These relationships are expressed graphically in Exhibit 17.10.

Exhibit 17.10 Output, costs and revenue graphs

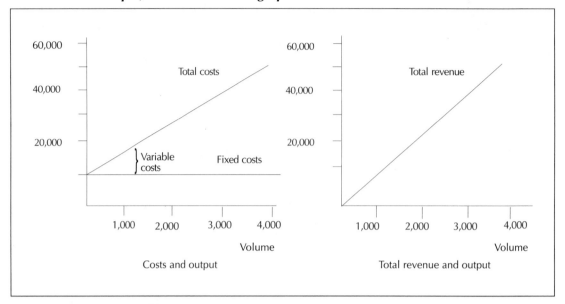

Profit and output decisions using the accountant's model

With the simplifying assumption of linearity, the accountant's total cost is not dissimilar to the equivalent curve derived by an economist. Where there is a substantial difference is in the representation of total revenue. The economist's model recognises that, other things being equal, increased demand can only be generated by decreasing prices. This ultimately results in total revenue reaching a maximum before starting to fall. The accountant's model, however, accepts the current price and simply multiplies this by different volumes to derive total revenue. Merging the accountant's total cost and total revenue curves shows, in Exhibit 17.11, the different levels of profitability at different output levels for Gloucester Ltd.

Total revenue is greater than total costs for all output levels beyond 2,000 units. Superficially, it appears that profit can continue to increase without limit by continually expanding output. As such, the accountant's approach to total revenue appears to lack the common sense of the economist's curve. This, however, is a misreading of the accountant's total revenue curve. It is not suggesting for one moment that output can continue to increase without having to reduce prices. Rather it is a specific example of the 'what if' analysis undertaken when using computer spreadsheets. What the accountant's total revenue curve is showing is that *if* the price of the Severn is £15 and *if* a sales volume of 3,000 units is achievable, then profit will be £5,000. Similarly, *if* the price can be held the same and *if* demand changes to 4,000 units, then profit will be £10,000.

Exhibit 17.11 Cost and revenue curves combined

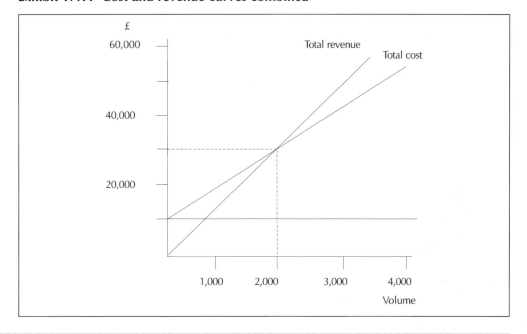

COST–VOLUME–PROFIT ANALYSIS AND 'WHAT IF' DECISIONS

The breakeven point and the margin of safety

Explaining costs in terms of their behaviour and their relationship to revenues rather than their function is known as *cost–volume–profit analysis*. Managers need to be aware that some costs vary with changes in output while others remain constant over the relevant range. Armed with this information, the impact on profit of changes in production can then be estimated. Of particular importance will be the minimum volume necessary before profits commence. This is known as the *breakeven point*. Either reading from the graph in Exhibit 17.11 or analysing the data in Exhibit 17.9, the breakeven point for Gloucester Ltd is found to be 2,000 units.

If the company's current output is 4,000 units, the volume of sales can fall by 2,000 units or 50 per cent before losses begin to be incurred. This relationship between the current output level and the breakeven point is known as the *margin of safety*. The greater the margin of safety, the more volume has to fall before losses are made.

'What if' analysis

Four variables determine the level of profitability: the unit price, the level of fixed costs, the marginal cost per unit and volume. Change any one variable and profit will also change. This understanding enables managers to model what will happen to profitability if a change takes place. Example 17.2 examines the effect of a change in just one variable, selling price, although the analysis could be extended to modelling the effect of changes in any of the other variables.

Example 17.2

> Temple Meadows Manufacturing is concerned about the profitability of one of its products, the Sower. Its current price is £700, at which price it sells 500 units per annum. The marginal cost per unit is estimated at £500 and its yearly fixed costs are £80,000. Harold Roy, the production manager, believes that increasing the price to £750 is feasible although annual demand might fall to 450 units.

With fixed costs of £80,000 and unit marginal costs of £500, the total cost for any level of activity can be read from the total cost curve in Exhibit 17.12. Currently, the Sower sells for £700. The total revenue from any given level of demand is shown by total revenue curve (a). From this, the breakeven point is calculated at 400 units and so, with current sales of 500, the margin of safety is 100 units or 20 per cent of current output. The current level of profitability can also be derived from the graph. It is represented by the difference between the total revenue and total cost curves at the 500 unit level. Alternatively it can be calculated arithmetically. With a selling price of £700 and demand at 500 units, total revenue will be £350,000. The unit variable cost is £500 and so total variable cost will be £250,000. With the only other cost being the fixed cost of £80,000, current profits must be £20,000.

Exhibit 17.12 The breakeven chart and 'what if' analysis

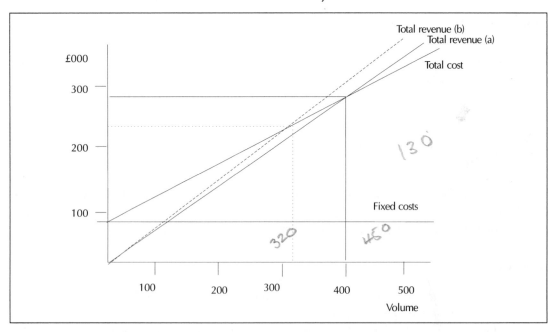

Having established the current operating position of Temple Meadows Manufacturing, it is now possible to evaluate the proposals put forward by Harold Roy. The effect of the proposed increase in price is to steepen the slope of the total revenue curve. Only at zero sales volume does it equal the old revenue curve. Beyond that, revenue will be 50/700ths greater for any output level. The revised total revenue is represented by curve (b) in Exhibit 17.12. With higher prices, less units need to be sold in order to breakeven. Reading from the graph, the breakeven point has been revised downwards to 320 units. If demand falls to 450 units, the margin of safety will be 130 units or 29 per cent. The resulting profit can once again be derived from the graphs or, alternatively, calculated. With 450 units planned to be sold at £750, total revenue will be £337,500. Total marginal costs will be £225,000 and so with fixed costs remaining at £80,000, forecast profit will be £32,500.

It therefore appears that Harold Roy's proposal is preferable to existing production and marketing plans. Not only do higher profits result but also the breakeven point falls while the margin of safety increases. However, the validity of the proposal is based on the validity of the assumptions – as with all 'what if' type calculations. Certainly it would be wrong to naïvely read from the graph that 500 units at the revised price is even more profitable. The revised total revenue curve was introduced only to show what turnover would be at different levels of output if the price changed to £750. It does not imply all those outputs are feasible. Indeed the question specifically restricts itself to Harold Roy's suggestion of 450 units and no more.

Cost behaviour and the contribution

One limitation to the graphical analysis of cost–volume–profit relationships results from the limitations of all graphs: their accuracy is constrained by the precision with which the graphs are drawn. The breakeven point – and other pertinent output levels – can more accurately be calculated by recognising the algebraic qualities of costs and revenues. In principle, all costs can either be classified as fixed or variable. Variable costs are assumed to vary with volume only. Double output and variable costs are doubled. As a simplification, issues such as quantity discounts resulting from higher volumes of raw materials or the payment of overtime rates are ignored – although they can quite easily be incorporated into the analysis. Likewise, fixed costs are assumed to vary with time only. Total costs therefore equal the sum of fixed and variable costs.

A useful concept in understanding cost behaviour is that of the *contribution*. Formally, the contribution is the difference between revenue and variable costs and can be expressed in total or per unit. In the case of Temple Meadows Manufacturing, the original unit contribution was £200 which is found by deducting the £500 unit variable cost from the £700 sales price. With a sales volume of 500 units, the total contribution was £100,000. This contribution is a kind of profit. It is the profit made before paying for fixed costs. As such it 'contributes' to the expense of the fixed costs. If the contribution is greater than the fixed costs, the result will be a (net) profit.

Cost–volume–profit relationships using physical values

With total costs made up of fixed and variable costs, profit will be the difference between turnover and total costs. This can be expressed in the form of an equation.

$$\text{Turnover} - \text{Total variable costs} - \text{Fixed costs} = \text{Profit} \qquad (17.1)$$

However, contribution is defined as turnover less total variable costs and so adding fixed costs to both sides of equation 17.1 enables a revised equation to be developed. This shows an alternative definition of contribution as fixed costs plus profit:

$$\text{Turnover} - \text{Total variable costs} = \text{Fixed costs} + \text{Profit} = \text{Contribution} \qquad (17.2)$$

Turnover, however, comprises the number of units sold multiplied by the selling price. Similarly, the total variable cost comprises the number of units sold multiplied by the unit variable cost on the assumption that there are no stocks. Common to both expressions is the number of units sold. Letting S equal the unit selling price, V equal the unit variable cost and Q equal the physical number of units sold, equation 17.2 can be rewritten as:

$$(S \times Q) - (V \times Q) = \text{Fixed costs} + \text{Profit} \qquad (17.3)$$

Q is common to both the terms on the left-hand side of the equation. Simplifying, equation 17.3 becomes:

$$Q(S - V) = \text{Fixed costs} + \text{Profit} \qquad (17.4)$$

However, $(S - V)$ is simply the unit selling price minus the unit variable cost, in other words the unit contribution. Dividing both sides of the equation by the unit contribution of $(S - V)$ gives a formula which not only allows the breakeven point to be derived but also the volume necessary for any other desired profit level. The result is equation 17.5:

$$Q = \frac{\text{Fixed costs} + \text{Profit}}{\text{Unit contribution}} \qquad (17.5)$$

The validity of the formula can be verified by using the earlier data relating to Temple Meadows Manufacturing. By definition, the breakeven point is where profit is nil. With an original selling price of £700 and a unit variable cost of £500, the unit contribution is £200. Applying this to fixed costs of £80,000 and the desired breakeven profit of nil enables the breakeven point to be found by solving for Q:

$$\text{Breakeven volume} = Q = \frac{£80,000 + £0}{£200} = 400 \text{ units}$$

Similarly, to calculate the volume necessary to produce a profit of £20,000, the desired profit is simply inserted into the formula shown as equation 17.5:

$$\text{Volume to achieve £20,000 profit} = \frac{£80,000 + £20,000}{£200} = 500 \text{ units}$$

Cost–volume–profit relationships using financial values

Sometimes, information about physical units will not be available. This is often the case when using data from published accounts. On other occasions, measuring output in units might not be appropriate. Engineering businesses which undertake one-off jobs of varying size and complexity, for example, are unlikely to measure activity by the number of units.

Providing some simplifying assumptions are made, a suitable alternative activity measure is turnover. Other things being equal, a doubling of turnover implies a doubling in activity. Unfortunately, things are not always equal. Inflation exists as well as specific price changes. Alternatively, in a multi-product firm, some products might have higher selling prices than others. Physically, the volume of production might remain the same but if more of the higher value products are sold, using turnover would imply an increase in activity. For a multi-product firm, the normal assumption is that the relative importance of the product mix remains the same unless additional information is available. Likewise, inflation and relative price changes are often assumed to be zero although approximate adjustments are possible. For instance, if inflation is currently 4 per cent per annum and a company has just announced a 4 per cent increase in turnover, much of the apparent increase is likely to have been caused by inflation.

Putting aside these complexities, it is possible to derive a formula, similar to the one for physical units, which enables breakeven and other relevant points to be determined in terms of sales values. Rather than considering the contribution per unit, the contribution can be expressed as a percentage of turnover. Both approaches are considered in Example 17.3.

Example 17.3

Stanley Worrell runs a small engineering works making a single product. Turnover for the current year is estimated to be £100,000 based on 1,000 units of production. At that level of output, variable costs are estimated at £40,000 and fixed costs at £12,000 to give an estimated profit of £48,000.

Given the data in the question, the unit selling price will be £100, unit variable cost will be £40 and so unit contribution will be £60. With fixed costs of £12,000, the breakeven point will be 200 units. Had physical data not been given, the only information would have been the turnover of £100,000, the variable costs of £40,000 and the fixed costs of £12,000. This gives a contribution of £60,000 or 60 per cent of sales. An awareness of this relationship allows the contribution for any level of sales to be calculated. Had sales been forecast at £50,000, providing selling prices do not change, the contribution would be £30,000. Contribution therefore can be found by multiplying turnover by the contribution percentage. Equally, however, equation 17.2 also showed contribution to equal fixed costs plus profit. Allowing C per cent to represent the contribution percentage and T the turnover, these relationships can be expressed in the form of an equation:

$$C\% \times T = \text{Fixed cost} + \text{profit} \qquad 17.6$$

Dividing both sides by C per cent results in a breakeven formula in monetary terms:

$$T = \frac{\text{Fixed cost} + \text{profit}}{C\%} \qquad 17.7$$

For Stanley Worrell, the breakeven turnover, T, is found by substituting his fixed costs, zero profit and contribution percentage into the formula:

$$\text{Breakeven turnover} = T = \frac{£12,000 + £0}{60\%} = £20,000$$

The breakeven turnover of £20,000 can be verified by taking the unit breakeven point of 200 units and multiplying by the selling price of £100. The result, a turnover of £20,000, agrees with the breakeven turnover calculated directly.

Calculating breakeven and other points using turnover rather than units is of particular use when appraising financial data. Although simplifying assumptions about inflation and the product mix have to be made, the findings can be of potential benefit to investors as Example 17.4 demonstrates.

Example 17.4

York and Minster last year reported profits of £200,000 on a turnover of £6,000,000. this year, their turnover increased to £7,000,000 which resulted in reported profits of £400,000. Next year, turnover is expected to be £7,750,000.

Despite the limited amount of data given for York and Minster, their breakeven point, level of fixed costs and prospective profit can be calculated if it is assumed there is no inflation, no changes in the product mix, no stocks, no changes in technology and no changes in accounting policies. With turnover last year of £6,000,000 and reported profits of £200,000, total costs must have been £5,800,000. Similarly, for the current year, total costs must have been £6,600,000. However, if fixed costs are the same in both years, the *increase* in costs must be entirely due to marginal or variable costs. This enables the contribution percentage to be determined. Turnover increased by £1,000,000, variable costs by £800,000 and so for every £100 of sales, marginal costs must be £80 to give a contribution of £20 or 20 per cent.

The contribution on last year's turnover of £6,000,000 must therefore have been £1,200,000. Profit, however, is after deducting fixed costs from the contribution and so with profits of £200,000, fixed costs must be £1,000,000. Using the current year's data, the contribution on a £7,000,000 turnover will be £1,400,000. Deducting from this figure the profit of £400,000 verifies the fixed costs as once more being £1,000,000. Having determined the fixed costs and the contribution percentage, the breakeven turnover can then be determined by use of the formula developed in equation 17.7:

$$\text{Breakeven turnover} = \frac{£1,000,000}{20\%} = £5,000,000$$

Similarly, the profit for the forthcoming year can be forecast on the assumption that turnover will increase to £7,750,000. At this level, with a 20 per cent contribution percentage, the total contribution will be £1,550,000 and so, after deducting the fixed costs of £1,000,000, the profit will be £550,000.

LIMITATIONS OF COST–VOLUME–PROFIT ANALYSIS

Some of the limitations of CVP analysis have already been identified. In the way the model has been presented, it has been assumed that costs are either fixed or variable in behaviour. This is an oversimplification. Quantity discounts have been ignored as have overtime payments and stepped fixed costs. All of these, however, can be incorporated in the model if desired. Including stepped fixed costs, for example, produces a discontinuous total cost curve similar to the one shown in Exhibit 17.13 – at the point where the fixed costs increase.

Exhibit 17.13 Stepped fixed costs and the total cost curve

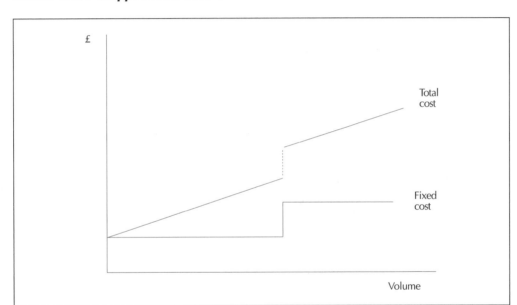

The model assumes technical relationships between inputs and outputs are given. Fatigue, boredom and other aspects of behaviour do not come into those relationships and yet in the real world, managers spend much of their time addressing these difficulties.

If used for a situation involving more than one product, the model's conclusions may not be valid. Altering the product mix by changing the proportion of outputs between products may change the overall contribution percentage if some products have higher margins than others.

Perhaps the CVP model's major limitation, however, is that the data may be influenced by accounting conventions. The variety of possible depreciation rates is one example. A more complex difficulty arises from stock valuations, especially under an absorption costing regime. By carrying forward overheads in stocks, the raw data might be inadequate for the model's purpose. Other things being equal, the lower the absolute values of stocks and the less stock amounts change between each period the less the distortion to the data from this source. Nevertheless, despite all these limitations, CVP analysis can be of considerable help to management when making pricing and output decisions.

COST BEHAVIOUR AND DECISION MAKING

Chapter 3 has already introduced the idea of direct costs. Direct costs are costs uniquely identified with a function, a responsibility centre or an activity. Eliminate the function, the responsibility centre or the activity and direct costs cease to exist. At the company level, all costs are direct. Close down the company and all costs are saved. Below that, however, costs increasingly become indirect by being shared between other functions, departments or activities. At the lowest level of organisation are individual units of production. At this level, direct costs are also variable costs. Alter output by one unit and variable costs will also change as a *direct* result of the the change in volume. All other costs are indirect, none of which will be saved by small changes in production.

In traditional accounting, indirect costs are often apportioned first to users and then to units of output. However, in the short term, eliminating part of the demand for indirect costs will not lead to any financial savings. Take for instance a factory which pays rent of £20,000 and manufactures several products. Eliminating one unit of output or even a whole product will still mean the factory having to pay rental of £20,000. Only if the rental was *direct* to the product could the rent be saved by closing down the product line.

Clearly, if the company is able to replace the eliminated product by another, the issue becomes more complicated. Similarly, in the longer term, a smaller factory at a lower rental can be acquired. Nevertheless, an understanding of cost behaviour is important for tactical or short term decision making.

To demonstrate the implications of cost behaviour on decision making, four scenarios will be outlined. The first considers whether to make a product in-house or acquire it from outside the organisation. The second investigates whether a product or segment should be deleted. The third looks at the implications of accepting an order below current selling prices while the fourth looks at joint products. In all of these, a major part of the decision will relate to the *change* in costs and revenues if the decision is undertaken.

The make or buy decision

From time to time, an organisation is faced with the opportunity either to produce goods or services in house or to place an outside contract for their supply. This is the situation faced by Essex City Council in Example 17.5.

Example 17.5

> Essex City Council has been quoted £7,000 to re-lay paving stones on the High Street. The council's own direct works department has quoted £8,000. The £8,000 has been arrived at by charging materials of £2,500, direct labour of £1,500, variable overheads of £500 and £3,500 of other overheads.

If the other overheads are merely an apportionment of costs such as the rent of the department and executive's salaries, then the total of these fixed costs will still have to be paid whether this job is undertaken internally or not. They are therefore irrelevant to the decision. The only extra costs which will be incurred if the job is undertaken internally relate to the materials, the labour (if a variable cost) and the variable overheads, a total of £4,500. It would therefore appear to be cheaper to accept the internal quotation. This assumes, however, that there is surplus capacity. If the department is working to full capacity, then undertaking the work internally might be achievable only by displacing more urgent or profitable work. Under these circumstances a fuller evaluation would be required.

Deleting a segment

Sometimes an organisation is faced with an apparently loss-making division, product or factory. Once more, the short term analysis should focus on what costs will be saved and what revenues lost if the decision goes ahead. This is the approach taken in Example 17.6.

Example 17.6

UK Trading plc is a retailer based in the North West and with two branches serviced from a central warehouse. The Board is considering the financial viability of the stores as a result of receiving the current period's management accounts. As in the previous three periods, the branch in Weston has once more reported losses. An outline of the accounts are reproduced below:

	Weston branch (£)	(£)	Easton branch (£)	(£)	Total (£)	(£)
Turnover		100,000		200,000		300,000
Cost of sales		50,000		100,000		150,000
Gross profit		50,000		100,000		150,000
Wages (fixed)	20,000		30,000		50,000	
Regional advertising	20,000		20,000		40,000	
Warehousing	14,000	54,000	28,000	78,000	42,000	132,000
Profit/(loss)		(4,000)		22,000		18,000

From the management accounts, it appears that the Weston branch is making a loss. The only *variable costs* are the cost of sales and so it currently makes a contribution of £50,000 to the business, represented by the gross profit. However, although a fixed cost, the wages are a direct cost of operating the branch and so these costs would be saved if the branch was closed down. The direct costs of running the branch are therefore £70,000 and from this a turnover of £100,000 is being generated. As the advertising and warehousing are merely apportioned costs, closing down the Weston branch will reduce overall company profitability by £30,000.

The gross profit of the company will then be the gross profit of the Easton branch. From this £100,000 gross profit must be deducted the wages of £30,000, the advertising of £40,000 and the warehousing of £42,000. As a result of closing the Weston branch, overall company profitability will fall by £30,000 from the current profit of £18,000 to a loss of £12,000.

Short term, this prospective loss might be reduced by moving from regional advertising to local advertising and this should be included in the analysis. But even with the current level of advertising, Weston would still make a profit if it was not for the apportioned warehousing charge. If it is not possible to close the warehouse down immediately or find some other use for the spare space, then the company will still be worse off financially from the planned closure. Short term therefore, unless the company can achieve savings in excess of £30,000 from advertising and warehousing, it would be unprofitable to close down the Weston branch.

Special selling prices

Ultimately, prices are determined by demand and supply and cost is only one element in that process. If goods are in short supply and demand is high, suppliers are in an advantageous bargaining position and can achieve higher prices. However, if they are faced with excess capacity and low demand then they may no longer have the power to sustain high prices. Competition will force prices down. In such circumstances, an awareness of cost behaviour is of particular importance as sometimes a company will be offered the opportunity of supplying goods or services below their current production cost. Example 17.7 considers just such a situation. Financially, what is of importance is the incremental cost and any incremental revenue arising from the proposal.

Example 17.7

Bradford and Huddersfield plc makes small domestic appliances. One product, the Blenda, is currently sold to retail outlets for £20 each. The company's budget for the current year, based on 10,000 units of production, is as follows:

Direct labour	£30,000
Direct material	£40,000
Variable overhead	£10,000
Fixed overhead	£80,000
	£160,000

All of the fixed overhead is a direct cost of Blenda production.

Argus Promotions, a mail-order company, has currently offered to buy 2,000 of the Blenda for £14 each which it will rename as the Blendrite before selling at a discount compared to current retail prices. As the unit cost is £16, the recommendation is that the offer should be rejected.

Even though the fixed overhead is direct to Blenda production, it is still a fixed cost. If there is spare capacity and if labour is a variable cost, then the incremental cost of producing an extra 2,000 units will be £16,000. Exhibit 17.14 shows how this amount has been derived. If Argus Promotions is prepared to pay £14 for each Blenda purchased, the additional revenue will be £28,000 and so company profitability will increase by £12,000.

Exhibit 17.14 Profitability of a special order

Direct labour	(2,000 units × £3)	£6,000
Direct materials	(2,000 units × £4)	£8,000
Variable overhead	(2,000 units × £1)	£2,000
Total incremental cost		£16,000
Incremental revenue		£28,000
Incremental profit		£12,000

However attractive this sort of analysis appears, there are dangers. Unless there is spare capacity, accepting the special order might displace more profitable work. More importantly, there might be hidden difficulties. The sales by Argus Distribution may be at the expense of sales through existing outlets. As these are more profitable than sales to Argus, the overall effect might be a reduction in Bradford and Huddersfield's profits. Another commercial consideration is the change in the product's image if consumers see it being discounted. This is the problem of product 'integrity' most often found with luxury goods such as expensive French perfumes. If price conveys an image of benefits and worth, reducing prices might lead to an overall *decrease* in demand as consumers now perceive the product as being less valuable.

A more immediate problem is the effect on relationships with existing customers if they discover that Argus Distribution is paying a lower price. They might, in turn, demand the lower price being offered to Argus. If this was to succeed and overall production remained at 10,000 units, then production of the Blenda would no longer be profitable. A similar result is possible if Argus place further orders. Having established a price, this will be uppermost in the minds of the Argus Distribution buyers resulting in a psychological resistance to any change.

Joint products

Accounting for joint products has already been considered in Chapter 16. From a decisional point of view, product profitability has little meaning as, if one product is produced, all other products also have to be produced. Rather than considering product profitability, the emphasis should be on the profitability of the process.

One complexity which arises from this relates to additional costs incurred by individual products after leaving the process. Sometimes, the output from the process is incomplete and additional costs have to be incurred by the separate products before being finally marketable. The stage at which products are separately identifiable is known as the *split-off point*. Beyond this point, further costs can be uniquely identified with products rather than just the process. These additional costs are direct to the particular product – unless, of course, they include an element of apportioned overhead.

A second complexity can occur at the split-off point. Sometimes, the output is marketable even though incomplete. Crude oil is an example of an unfinished output from a joint process which is readily marketable. Two decisions therefore have to be made. First, should additional processing take place beyond the split-off point? Secondly, is the joint process itself profitable? Both of these issues are considered in Example 17.8.

Example 17.8

Chelmsford Chemicals produce two products, the GTI and the XR3, from the same process. The cost of producing 30,000 litres of output is £120,000, made up of material, £40,000, labour, £10,000 and fixed overheads of £70,000. Of the 30,000 litres of output, two-thirds relate to GTI and one-third to XR3. In their unfinished state, immediately after leaving the joint process, GTI can be sold for £2 per litre while XR3 can be sold for £6 per litre. Currently Chelmsford Chemicals incurs extra direct costs to bring both products to their finished state. Details of the two products' profitability, extracted from the current period's management accounts, are shown below.

	GTI Production		XR3 Production	
Litres	20,000		10,000	
	(£)	(£)	(£)	(£)
Revenue		150,000		90,000
Process costs	80,000		40,000	
Separate processing costs	50,000	130,000	40,000	80,000
Operating profit		20,000		10,000

The first issue to resolve is whether the output from the process should be sold in its semi-finished state or processed further. To consider the financial aspects involves determining the extra costs and extra revenues from the further processing. The 20,000 litres of unfinished GTI can be sold for £2 per litre immediately it leaves the joint process, a total revenue of £40,000. Further processing therefore generates an additional £110,000 of turnover. With additional (direct) processing costs of £50,000, selling GTI production in its finished state results in an extra contribution of £60,000. It is therefore clearly profitable. The XR3, however, can be sold in its semi-finished state for £60,000 and so further processing only increases turnover by £30,000. To achieve this increase involves £40,000 of additional costs and so Chelmsford Chemicals would generate more profit if XR3 production was sold onto the market immediately after leaving the joint process.

The second issue is whether Chelmsford Chemicals should be undertaking the process in the first place. The charging of the joint process costs are in proportion to physical outputs. As such, individually they are irrelevant to decision making. What needs to be determined is the profitability of the process and this involves comparing the costs of the process with the revenue it generates.

As the semi-finished GTI and XR3 production can be bought or sold on the open market for £2 and £6 per litre respectively, the value of the process's output is £40,000 for the GTI and £60,000 for the XR3. With total joint processing costs of £120,000, operating the process appears unprofitable. Whether or not it is actually unprofitable will depend on the fixed overheads as all other costs are variable. If these fixed costs are merely an apportionment and represent resources which cannot be profitably used elsewhere, then the process is still generating a contribution of £50,000. Revenues at the split-off point total £100,000 but direct costs only total £40,000 for material and £10,000 labour. If, however, the fixed costs are *direct* to the process, then Chelmsford Chemicals should abandon the production of the joint products, to give a saving of £20,000. Production of the GTI could still take place as the semi-finished product can be purchased on the market for £40,000. Adding the further processing costs of £50,000 to the bought-in cost of £40,000 means that the output can be sold for £150,000 to give a profit of £60,000.

DECISION MAKING AND SCARCE RESOURCES

In a market economy, the price mechanism is used to share out scarce resources. Scarce in this sense is not necessarily measured in an absolute way but rather relative to demand. The higher the demand and the lower the supply, the greater will be the market price. Price therefore is a measure of scarcity. This has implications for businesses. Only if the sales value of production is greater than the (scarcity) cost of the resources consumed can a profit be said to have been made. Normally, the price paid is a sufficient measure of the inputs' scarcity value and so the decision rules developed so far in this chapter are sufficient.

At other times, however, they will be inadequate. The price paid will not fully reflect the scarcity value of the resource. A bottle of water – even expensive 'designer' French water – is likely only to cost 75p in the United Kingdom. A person shipwrecked on a desert island, with no fresh water other than the bottle purchased in the UK, is unlikely to measure the value of that bottle of water at 75p. In those circumstances, the price paid is clearly an inadequate measure of the water's worth or value. Firms are sometimes faced with a similar – albeit less extreme – situation. In the long term, markets will respond to shortages by increasing supply. Short term, however, there might be shortages which cannot be immediately overcome. Examples include temporary shortages of material, special grades of labour or even operating capacity or stores space. What is clear is that the price paid will be an inadequate measure of the resource's worth.

Decision making with one scarce resource

Faced with a shortage of resources, firms have to do what anyone else would do in those circumstances – make the most of those limited resources. Where there is only one scarce resource, the approach is relatively straightforward for a business. What will limit profitability will no longer be sales but the limited availability of the resource. Because of this, emphasising contribution per unit of output – no matter how useful on other occasions – may give misleading information. Businesses will therefore try to generate as much contribution from the *scarce resource* as possible. How this is done is demonstrated in Example 17.9.

Example 17.9

Preston Products manufactures two products, the Alpha and the Beta. Both products use the same skilled labour. Despite paying a labour rate of £10 per hour, the maximum number of labour hours available is likely to be limited to 800 per week for the foreseeable future. Details of product profitability are:

Product	Alpha	Beta
	(£)	(£)
Direct material	40	10
Direct labour	40	80
Variable overhead	20	20
Fixed overhead	10	20
Total cost	110	130
Unit profit	50	60
Selling price	160	190

Faced with this information, and assuming the fixed overheads merely represent an apportionment of shared resources, unit profitability is an invalid way of scheduling production to achieve maximum profitability. The superficial answer would be to judge each product on its contribution and, given only limited production is possible because of the scarcity of labour, produce as much as possible of the one with the highest contribution. With variable costs of £100 and a selling price of £160, the unit contribution of Alpha is £60. Beta's variable costs total £110 and so, with a unit selling price of £190, its contribution is £80. On that basis, producing Beta is preferable to producing Alpha.

Such an approach, however, is conceptually wrong. There is a shortage of labour and so the wages paid are an inadequate measure of the value of that labour. Given that labour is paid £10 per hour and that the labour costs of Alpha and Beta are £40 and £80 respectively, each Alpha requires four hours of labour while each Beta requires eight hours. With a total labour availability of 800 hours, Preston Products can either produce 200 units of Alpha or 100 units of Beta. As the Alpha has a unit contribution of £60, the company can generate a total contribution of £12,000 by only producing the Alpha. If, however, Preston Products concentrates production on the Beta, the maximum contribution will only be £8,000.

In the case of Preston Products, it is labour which restricts production and sales. Any resource which constrains production in this way is known as the *limiting factor*. Given that each unit of Alpha uses four hours of labour and has a contribution of £60, Alpha contributes £15 per labour hour. Beta, however, with a unit contribution of £80 and a need for eight labour hours per unit, contributes only £10 per labour hour. Calculating the contribution per unit of limiting factor is therefore a more direct way of determining the optimal production schedule necessary to maximise contribution.

Decision making with more than one scarce resource

In fact, the contribution per unit of limiting factor analysis is only one aspect of a more general approach to problem-solving known as linear programming. Linear programming is a mathematical technique for solving problems. It requires a clear objective, a choice between ways of achieving the objective, constraints on achieving the objective and linear relationships. In terms of Preston Products, the objective was to maximise contribution. The choice involved achieving this objective by either producing Alpha, Beta or a mix of both. The objective of maximising the contribution was constrained by the limited availability of labour. Within this, relationships were linear, that is they could be plotted as a straight line graph. Double or triple production of Alpha and the amount of labour required would double or triple. Similarly in terms of the contribution: a doubling of Alpha output would double the contribution made.

Preston Products' production and profitability were constrained by only one factor, the limited supply of labour. Because of that, the optimal decision could be found by concentrating production on the product which gave the highest contribution per unit of limiting factor. Where more than one resource is in limited supply, this approach may not give a unique solution. This is the difficulty faced by Hitchin HiTech Ltd in Example 17.10.

Example 17.10

Hitchin HiTech Ltd currently manufactures two products, the Exe and Wye. Product costings are as follows:

Product	Exe	Wye
	(£)	*(£)*
Direct labour	250	300
Direct material	500	1,000
Fixed overheads	100	200
Profit	100	100
Selling price	950	1,600

Both products use the same grade of labour and the same type of materials. Currently both are difficult to acquire. The labour rate is £5 per hour and Hitchin HiTech believe that no more than 3,000 hours are available per week. The material, which costs £100 per unit, is also in restricted supply. The company has been informed by the manufacturer of the material that no more than 400 units per week will be available for the foreseeable future.

If the labour rate is £5 per hour and Exe's unit labour cost is £250, each unit of Exe requires 50 hours of labour. For Wye, the labour hours per unit will be 60. Adding back the apportioned fixed overheads to profit gives the unit contribution. For Exe this will be £200 and for Wye it will be £300. Contribution per unit of labour therefore will be £4 per Exe and £5 per Wye. With only a limited availability of labour, Hitchin HiTech should concentrate on producing the Wye.

Labour, however, is not the only resource in short supply. With material costing £100 per unit and Exe having a material cost of £500, each unit of Exe requires five units of material. For Wye, the equivalent figure is ten units of material. Applying the contribution per limiting factor analysis to the materials, the figures for Exe and Wye will be £40 and £30 respectively. On this basis, Hitchin HiTech should concentrate its manufacturing on the Exe.

The company faces a conflict. On the one hand, the shortage of labour is suggesting that production should be concentrated on Wye. On the other, the material shortage suggests contribution will be maximised by only manufacturing units of the Exe. Linear programming was developed to solve this type of problem.

A graphical approach to linear programming

Linear programming is a complex mathematical technique. Starting from a feasible solution, i.e. one which may not be ideal but is capable of being achieved within the constraints imposed, it systematically moves to better and better solutions until the optimal solution is found. This it does by a series of steps known as iterations. Because of the amount of calculation and recalculation involved, the actual procedure is often left to a computer program. Nevertheless, providing there are only two variables – products Exe and Wye in the case of Hitchin HiTech – the technique can be shown graphically.

The first stage involves identifying what production is feasible. Hitchin HiTech is restricted to 3,000 labour hours per week. Each Exe requires 50 hours of labour and each Wye 60 hours. The company can therefore manufacture up to 60 units of Exe and no units of Wye, 50 units of Wye and no units of Exe or some in between combination of Exe and Wye. Assume the company initially concentrates production on Exe. By producing one less Exe, it will release 50 hours of labour, enabling it to produce 50/60ths of a unit of Wye. Producing two less units of Exe enables Hitchin HiTech to produce 1⅔ units of Wye. In other words, substituting production between the two products is a linear relationship. A similar argument can be applied to the material constraint. With only 400 units available per week, Hitchin HiTech can either produce a maximum of 80 units of Exe or 40 units of Wye or some level in between. This is shown graphically in Exhibit 17.15.

Exhibit 17.15 Production possibilities

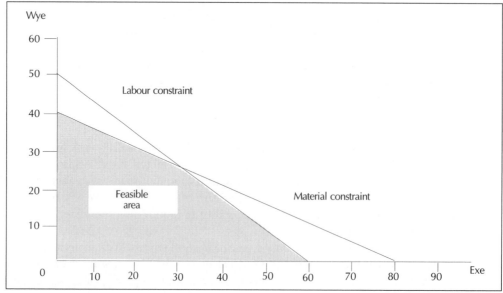

The graph identified as the labour constraint shows there is sufficient labour to produce 50 units of Exe and no Wye, 60 units of Wye and no Exe or any lesser combination. Any outputs to the left of the labour constraint – even down to producing no units of any product – are all *possible* production levels as far as labour is concerned. A similar analysis is possible in terms of material. There is sufficient material to produce up to either 40 units of Wye and no Exe or 80 units of Exe and no Wye. To produce either product, however, requires both materials and labour and so only where both are available is manufacturing possible. This is represented by the feasible area. Producing 45 units of Wye, for example, is not feasible as, although there is sufficient labour, there is insufficient material.

Having identified feasible production possibilities, Hitchin HiTech needs to determine the combination of output levels which will maximise its contribution. One possibility is to produce ten units of Wye. Not only is this possible, it is also profitable. With a unit contribution of £300, producing ten units of Wye will give a total contribution of £3,000. But this is not the only production level which would give Hitchin HiTech a £3,000 contribution. As each unit of Exe has a contribution of £200, producing 15 units of Exe would also generate a £3,000 contribution. This is also feasible. In fact there is a whole range of feasible production levels which would generate that level of contribution. For example, nine units of Wye and 1½ units of Exe or eight units of Wye and three units of Exe all give a £3,000 contribution. More generally, providing each unit reduction in Wye production is replaced by 1½ units of Exe, the contribution will remain the same. In other words, there is a linear relationship. All possible output levels which produce a £3,000 contribution are shown in Exhibit 17.16.

Exhibit 17.16 Equal contribution lines

A similar exercise is possible for other contribution levels. A £6,000 contribution is possible by producing 20 Wye, 30 Exe or some level in between while a £9,000 contribution is possible from producing 30 Wye or 45 Exe. These are plotted in Exhibit 17.16 as lines of equal contribution. What is noticeable is that all the lines have the same slope as a result, in this example, of needing to produce 1½ Exe to generate the same contribution as one unit of Wye.

The optimal solution

The further from the origin the equal contribution line, the greater the total contribution. This gives a clue as to how Hitchin HiTech should organise its production. It needs to achieve the highest possible contribution line consistent with the constraints of materials and labour represented by the feasible area. Superimposing the equal contribution lines on to the graph of the feasible area, Exhibit 17.17 identifies the production necessary to maximise contribution.

Exhibit 17.17 Optimal production

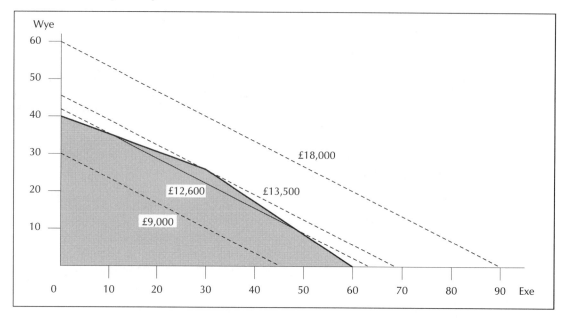

Producing 30 Wye or 45 Exe – or any combination in between – and generating a contribution of £9,000 is not the best Hitchin HiTech can achieve. Higher equal contribution lines are possible within the range of feasible production. Ideally, the company would prefer a contribution of £18,000 but it is unable to acquire sufficient material and labour to make this possible.

Producing 42 Wye or 63 Exe results in a total contribution of £12,600. Although both of these production levels lie outside the feasible area, nevertheless the company can still achieve that target by rearranging production. A whole range of production combinations are feasible, all represented by the solid part of the £12,600 equal contribution line where it lies within the feasible area. £12,600 therefore is not the maximum profitability of the company.

Extending the equal contribution line further while keeping its angle the same to reflect the relative unit profitability, the highest contribution possible is where the line just touches the feasible area. Only at that one point can the relevant contribution be achieved. Reading from the graph, the maximum contribution is achieved by producing 25 Wye and 30 Exe. The unit contribution for Wye and Exe is £300 and £200 respectively and so total contribution will be £13,500.

A mathematical expression of the linear programming problem

The issue facing Hitchin HiTech can be expressed mathematically. The objective of the company is to maximise its contribution. This it seeks to do by producing and selling units of the Exe and the Wye. Total contribution will be the number of Exe sold multiplied by the contribution of £200 plus the number of Wye sold multiplied by the contribution of £300. Letting X represent the number of Exe and Y the number of Wye, the objective of the firm can be expressed mathematically in the form of an equation known as the objective function:

$$\text{Maximise } 200X + 300Y$$

In effect the terms in the objective function are the equivalent of the slope of the equal contribution line and the desire to maximise the function is the equivalent of pushing the equal contribution line out as far as feasible.

As with the graphical presentation, there are limits to the possible size of the contribution. Restricting the amount of the contribution are the resource constraints. The maximum amount of labour is limited to 3,000 hours. For every Exe produced, 50 hours of labour is consumed while for every Wye it is 60 hours. The total labour hours consumed in production, however, cannot be more than 3,000. Again, letting X and Y represent the number of Exe and Wye produced, this also can be expressed mathematically as an inequality of the form:

$$50X + 60Y \leq 3,000$$

The left-hand side of the expression simply states that each Exe consumes 50 labour hours, each Wye consumes 60 hours and that the total hours consumed is found by multiplying the unit hours by the units produced. The right-hand side then specifies that the total labour hours consumed in production cannot be more than 3,000. The expression therefore represents a constraint on the objective of maximising contribution caused by the shortage of labour.

A similar inequality can be developed for the material constraint. The only other constraint – hardly necessary when solving the problem graphically, but critically important when using a computer program – is that production of Exe or Wye can never be less than zero. In other words, the problem is bounded by the axes of the graph and the material and labour constraints. If these constraints are not specified the computer program might otherwise suggest the best solution is to produce 500 of Exe and –200 of Wye! Bringing these constraints together, along with the objective function, the problem can be stated as:

Objective function: Maximise $200X + 300Y$

Subject to:

$50X + 60Y \leq 3,000$	(labour constraint)
$5X + 10Y \leq 400$	(material constraint)
$X, Y >= 0$	(non-negativity constraints)

Expressed in this way, more insight can be derived from the problem. Although the problem of Hitchin HiTech only involved two constraints, other constraints could have been introduced without invalidating the general findings. No matter how many constraints, the optimal solution will always be at a corner point. In the current example, this was at the intersection of the material and labour constraints. Producing at optimal capacity therefore means there is neither surplus labour nor surplus material. In other words, for the constraints whose intersection determines the optimal production, the inequalities become equalities. Having identified from the graph that labour and material are the relevant constraints, it is then possible to accurately solve for the optimal production plan. The optimal solution therefore is where:

$$50X+60Y= 3{,}000 \tag{17.8}$$

and:

$$5X + 10Y = 400 \tag{17.9}$$

The optimal production of Exe and Wye can be solved using simultaneous equations. Multiplying equation 17.9 by 10 gives:

$$50X + 100Y = 4{,}000 \tag{17.10}$$

Deducting equation 17.8 from equation 17.10 solves for the optimal number of Wye to be produced:

$$
\begin{aligned}
50X + 100Y &= 4{,}000 \\
50X + 60Y &= 3{,}000 \\
\hline
40Y &= 1{,}000
\end{aligned}
$$

The optimal production of Wye is therefore 25. Exe production can be found by substituting the figure of Wye output into either of the two equations. Substituting into equation 17.9 gives a value of 30 for the units of Exe to be produced:

$$
\begin{aligned}
5X + 10(25) &= 400 \\
5X &= 150 \\
X &= 30
\end{aligned}
$$

Entering these findings into the objective function shows the maximum contribution to be £13,500:

$$200X + 300Y = £200(30) + £300(25) = £13{,}500$$

Shadow prices and dual values

Whenever there is a shortage of a resource, the price paid will not fully reflect its value to the organisation. In effect, there is a scarcity value. This scarcity value is known as the *shadow price* or *dual value*. It can be measured by asking how worse off would a firm be if it was deprived of one unit of resource or, equivalently, how much better off it would be if resources increased by one unit.

Consider the problem faced by Hitchin HiTech. With only 3,000 hours of labour and only 400 units of material available, the optimal output is 30 units of Exe and 25 units of Wye. At this level of production, the contribution is £13,500. Assuming the supply of labour remains the same, what will happen to production and profitability if the company is deprived of one unit of material?

Graphically, the material constraint, shown in Exhibit 17.5, will move fractionally closer to the origin. Because the change is so small, a visual inspection shows the optimal production plan will still be where the labour and material constraints intersect. All labour and material will be fully used and so the inequalities, once again, become equalities. This enables the optimal plan to be derived. Equation 17.9, the material constraint, will now equal 399 because the availability of material has fallen by one. Equation 17.8, the labour constraint, remains the same. The solution which maximises contribution is where:

$$50X + 60Y = 3{,}000 \qquad\qquad (17.8)$$

and:

$$5X + 10Y = \ 399 \qquad\qquad (17.9 \text{ revised})$$

Again, multiplying equation 17.9 revised by 10 and deducting equation 17.8 from the result enables Wye production to be determined:

$$
\begin{aligned}
50X + 100Y &= 3{,}990 \\
50X + \ 60Y &= 3{,}000 \\
\hline
40Y &= \ \ 990
\end{aligned}
$$

Wye production will therefore be 24.75 units. Substituting this into either of the two equations shows Exe production to be 30.3 units. These findings can be entered into the objective function. The result is a revised contribution of £13,485. With an original contribution of £13,500, being deprived of one unit of material causes Hitchin HiTech to be worse-off by £15. This is the real cost to the company of being deprived of one unit of material and this is the shadow price or dual value of material. In passing, it should be noted that the reduction in the supply of material actually *increases* the production of Exe at the expense of Wye production. If nothing else, this should act as a warning against the all-too-often management reaction of 'cuts all round' when faced with a problem.

Had the supply of material *increased* by one unit, equation 17.8 would have still remained the same but the value of equation 17.9 would have increased to 401. Again, with such a small increase, it can be visually verified that optimal production will once more be at the intersection of the labour and material constraints. Solving for production of Exe and Wye gives 29.7 and 25.25 units respectively. At this level of production, the contribution is revised to £13,515 – an increase of £15 from acquiring one extra unit of material. In other words, the shadow price is the same whether materials increase or decrease by one unit.

A similar exercise is possible to determine the shadow price of labour. Material availability is held the same at 400 units but now labour is allowed to change by one hour. Decreasing labour availability by one hour to 2,999 hours, optimal production will be 29.95 Exe and 25.025 Wye. At this level of production, the contribution is £13,497.50, a decrease of £2.50. Similarly, increasing the supply of labour by one hour revises production to 30.05 Exe and 24.975 Wye while the contribution changes to £13,502.50 again a change of £2.50. The shadow price of labour therefore is £2.50.

The validity and limitations of linear programming and shadow prices

The validity of linear programming depends partly on whether its assumptions approximate reality. In particular, its assumptions of linearity and the division of costs into fixed and variable may not always be valid. As has already been demonstrated, the accountant's linear variable cost assumption is a simplification, although one often adequate for many areas of decision making. More important is the assumption of linearity of prices. Hitchin HiTech, for instance, accepts that the prices of Exe and Wye are given at £950 and £1,600 respectively. However, there is a clear shortage of materials and labour. If Hitchin HiTech is faced with shortages, so will other firms in the industry and so, by implication, there will also be a shortage of finished products such as the Exe and the Wye. Under those circumstances, the normal market reaction is to *increase* prices. Equally, suppliers are also likely to increase prices when there are shortages.

Other criticisms relate less to the technique itself and more to its practical use in some business situations. If linear programming is to give valid decisions, its base data must be accurate. If the cost data, for example, is invalid, then so might be the results. And for the results to be accurate, the constraints have to be exact. Hitchin HiTech's labour was assumed to be 3,000 hours, not *about* 3,000 hours. Change the availability of hours, and as has been shown when discussing shadow prices, the optimal plan also changes.

Generalising, one major difficulty of linear programming relates to the whole area of risk and uncertainty. Technically the linear programming model is determinist. It produces an exact plan from exact data. Introducing risk – such as, for example, assuming that some weeks the supply of material will be 10 per cent more or 10 per cent less than the norm – cannot easily be handled. All that can be practically done in these circumstances is to carry out a series of 'what if' calculations by remodelling the problem with the different assumptions and seeing how sensitive the problem is to changes in the constraints.

Another difficulty concerns those factors common to much of business life which are difficult to quantify such as the effect on customers of a failure to fully supply their needs. If these factors are quantifiable, they can be included in the model as a further constraint. In reality, however, they are difficult to measure with any degree of mathematical accuracy.

Linear programming also assumes both inputs and outputs are independent. If the Exe and the Wye were joint products, for example, the whole analysis would have been meaningless. A more subtle derivative of this problem, however, exists not where products are physically joined but where consumers only purchase a product if others are also available. Video disc players, for example, will only be purchased if video discs are also available. If these are the two products being modelled then a reduction in the output of one may well cause a reduction in demand – and hence output – for the other.

One criticism of linear programming which is rarely relevant is that the solution sometimes involves fractional units of production. If the optimal solution involves, say, producing 30.5 units per week, then taking a fortnightly time period often overcomes this problem. And if this is inadequate, a development of linear programming known as integer programming is available to resolve the difficulty.

All of the criticisms of linear programming apply equally to the use of shadow prices. There is, however, a further limitation on their use. Shadow prices are a marginal technique. They measure the value to the organisation of small changes in a scarce resource. Applying the findings to large changes might not be valid. Hitchin HiTech's shadow price for materials was £15. The real cost to the company of one less unit of material was £15 as this is the amount by which the contribution would fall. Equally, one extra unit would increase profitability by £15.

However, an extra 200 units will not increase the contribution by £3,000 as the company would meet the constraint of labour shortages before all the extra material could be used. With 600 units of material, there is sufficient material to produce 120 units of Exe and 60 units of Wye. But this is not feasible as the actual level of production will then be limited by the supply of labour which restricts production of Exe to 60 units and Wye to 50 units. Nevertheless, the concept of shadow prices or dual values is a useful one. Decisions tend to be taken by looking at the extra cost and extra revenue from a proposal and shadow prices are consistent with this approach. More than that, they show that accounting data might not always reflect the true cost of resources.

OPPORTUNITY COSTS

Accounting costs and expenses are based on transactions. In general therefore they represent the historical cost paid although sometimes this is overridden by the prudence concept. No matter how useful this might be for stewardship, at times it is less than adequate for decision making. Accounting costs might not show the true value of a decision. This is demonstrated in Example 17.11.

Example 17.11

Cardiff plc has in stock some material for which it has no further use. It originally cost £1,000. The company's marketing director, Hugh Jenkins, has identified a possible use for it. This involves incurring additional labour costs of £1,500 and then selling the completed product for £3,000.

If the material is not used in this way it can either be sold on the open market for £1,400 or used in another process where it could be substituted for material otherwise costing £1,200.

One way to look at the problem facing Cardiff is to analyse separately the three options. Exhibit 17.18 shows the implications of this.

Exhibit 17.18 Alternative opportunities

Option	Use elsewhere	Sell material	Make product	
Revenue/cost saving	£1,200	£1,400		£3,000
Labour cost			£1,500	
Material cost	£1,000	£1,000	£1,000	£2,500
	£200	£400		£500

Hugh Jenkins' suggestion is clearly the more profitable. But two issues arise from the analysis. First, in theory, all other possible uses for the material should be considered before making a decision. In the real world, this is often a practical impossibility. Secondly, it is not clear that making the product generates £500 profit.

Rather than be used to make the product, the material could either be used as a substitute elsewhere, in which case it would save Cardiff £200, or it could be sold on the open market, in which case it will generate a profit of £400. Clearly the best option is to sell the material on the open market for £1,400. This presumably is its market price, the price which would have to be paid if the material was acquired today. The £500 profit generated from making the product therefore comprises two elements, the £400 profit which would otherwise have been obtainable from a simple sale of the material plus the extra £100 profit which results from converting the material into a finished product.

Put another way, the 'real' cost of the material for making the product is £1,400. This is the most that could be derived from the material if used elsewhere. Consequently, only £100 profit is generated by making the product rather than selling the material on the open market. The £1,400 valuation of the material for decision purposes is known as its *opportunity cost*. Formally, opportunity cost can be defined as the value foregone by not using resources in their next best alternative use. In terms of Cardiff plc, the best option was to make the product. The next best option was to sell the material on the open market and therefore, by making the product, the company sacrifices or foregoes the opportunity of earning £1,400. This is Cardiff's opportunity cost of using the material for manufacture and verifies that only an extra £100 is generated from making the product rather than the next best alternative of selling the material.

Opportunity cost, by concentrating on the value of the *next best* alternative, effectively considers all options. Cardiff plc, for example, by accepting £1,400 as the material's opportunity cost, implicitly recognises the substitution possibility as being inferior. Secondly, by using opportunity costs, the profit or contribution measured is the extra profit which results from using the resources in the proposal under consideration rather than elsewhere.

Opportunity costs, deprival values, shadow prices and cost behaviour

Opportunity costs are similar to the deprival values of current cost accounting developed in Chapter 12. The question to ask is: if not used in the proposal under consideration, how worse off would the organisation be if deprived of the resource? Clearly, in the case of Cardiff, if deprived of the resource, the company is deprived of selling the material on the open market. It is therefore deprived of £1,400, the material's opportunity cost.

Opportunity costs are also related to the shadow prices or dual values of linear programming. In example 17.10, Hitchin HiTech's shadow price of material was £15 per unit. Being deprived of one unit caused Hitchin HiTech's contribution to fall by £15. This is sometimes called the *internal* opportunity cost of the resource. Being deprived of one unit, however, not only reduces contribution by £15, it also means the unit has to be replaced at a market price of £100. Market prices are sometimes referred to as the *external* opportunity cost. The total opportunity cost – the total loss if Hitchin HiTech is deprived of one unit of material – is therefore £115.

The idea of opportunity costs can be applied to the cost behaviour patterns developed earlier. Take, for instance, a company which has 20,000 square metres of floor space but only currently uses 15,000 square metres. If a new proposal uses an extra 1,000 square metres, there will be no opportunity cost. There is no extra rental to pay and so the *external* opportunity cost will be nil. Similarly, with spare capacity, production and sales – and hence contribution – are not constrained by floor area. Neither gaining nor losing an extra square metre of space will affect profitability and so the shadow price or *internal* opportunity cost will also be nil. Consequently, total opportunity cost is nil and so a charge for the 1,000 square metres of floor area should not enter the decision when considering a new proposal.

A similar approach can be taken with variable costs. Many variable costs are in plentiful supply and constant use by organisations. Using one unit will therefore simply involve a cash outlay or, equivalently, a reduction in stock which is made good by a cash outlay. The price or external opportunity cost is therefore a sufficient measure of resources consumed. Clearly, when resources are in short supply, they may also have a positive shadow price and this needs to be added to the price to derive the total opportunity cost.

The irrelevance of past costs

If a unit of stock which is in regular use by a company has been recorded in the accounts at £40 but its replacement cost is £60, using the book value to determine profitability might be misleading. The cost of using the item with a book value of £40 is £60 as that is the cost to replace the item. The original unit's opportunity cost and deprival value therefore is £60. Past costs are irrelevant. Even if past costs equal current costs, this does not automatically make them relevant to the decision. For example, a company might have paid £500 for some material which is also its current cost. If the company then finds it has no further use for the material, its only alternative use is sale on the open market. If this is, say, £400, then £400 is its opportunity cost or deprival value and not the £500 purchase price and replacement cost.

This issue of past costs is even more important in other areas of accounting. One area in particular merits special attention. Depreciation is an important fixed cost and yet it is often based on a wide range of assumptions. No matter how valid or acceptable this might be for financial reporting, it rarely, if ever, reflects the opportunity cost of the asset and so accounting depreciation is of dubious use in decision making. The irrelevance of past costs and the need for opportunity costs in decision making are brought together in Example 17.12.

Example 17.12

Stoke and Keele Ltd are asked to bid for a contract being awarded by Buxton plc. Its estimating department suggests the likely cost of the contract is £47,000. Buxton plc, however, has intimated that a figure nearer £30,000 is more likely to be successful. Detailed costings prepared by the estimating department are given below:

Note	Detail	Amount
1	Material A	£10,000
2	Material B	£9,000
3	Labour 500 hours × £6 per hour	£3,000
4	Overheads 500 hours × £40	£20,000
5	Depreciation of machinery	£1,000
6	Design work	£4,000
	Contract cost	£47,000

Notes:

1. The book value of material A is £10,000. It was purchased sometime ago for another contract although never used. Its replacement cost is £12,000. The company has no further use for the material although a competitor is prepared to offer £8,000 for it.
2. According to the accounting records, the FIFO cost of material B is £9,000. Had the stocks been valued on a LIFO basis, the cost would have been £10,500 although the current market price is £11,000. Material B is used on a regular basis within the company and its realisable value is currently £9,500.
3. The workforce of Stoke and Keele are guaranteed a working week and a trade union agreement specifies that three months' notice should be given of any short time working or redundancies. Currently the company estimates it has surplus labour equivalent to 300 hours per week.
4. Central overheads are charged on the basis of labour hours. The company's accountant particularly specifies that machine hours is an inappropriate method for charging overheads.
5. The depreciation of the machine is £25,000 per annum based on the straight line method. It is used for 2,500 hours each year and so is charged on the basis of £10 per machine hour. The machine is currently exclusively used to make the Double Whammy. Each Double Whammy used three hours of machine time and has a unit contribution of £60. The machine is currently being used to full capacity and Stoke and Keele believe the output of Double Whammies could at least double if it were not for the limitation of machine capacity.
6. The design work has already been completed. It comprises 200 hours at £10 per hour labour time with the balance representing design department general overheads.

Applying an opportunity costing analysis to the problem faced by Stoke and Keele suggests that the contract cost is overstated. Material A has only one other use, the sale to the competitor. The book value is a past cost and is irrelevant. Consequently, material A's opportunity cost is £8,000. Material B, however, is in regular use by the business. Using B in the contract will require its replacement and the cost of this – its opportunity cost – is £11,000.

With surplus labour of 300 hours per week, the contract can be completed without any extra labour cost providing it does not have to be finished within 500 working hours.

The labour is effectively a fixed cost with an opportunity cost of zero. Irrespective of the level of output, the labour cost will remain the same because of the guarantees given. Overheads are also irrelevant to the decision as they are merely an apportionment – again with a zero opportunity cost.

The cost of the machine, however, has been understated in the estimate. Each Double Whammy has a unit contribution of £60 or £20 per machine hour but sales are held back by the lack of machine availability. If the depreciation charged to the contract is £1,000 and if this is on the basis of £10 per hour, then the contract must make use of the machine for 100 hours. The cost therefore is £2,000 based on the lost contribution from producing less Double Whammies.

Finally, the design work is also irrelevant. It is a past cost. The money has been paid out and other than a few drawings and proposals, there is nothing to show for it. Undertaking or not undertaking the contract will not change that.

The implications of all these adjustments are shown in Exhibit 17.19. As a result of applying opportunity costs to the resources consumed, the contract cost is reduced to £21,000. However contrived the example might be, what it does demonstrate is that accounting data may be inadequate for decision purposes.

Exhibit 17.19 Opportunity costing and contract pricing

Material A	£8,000
Material B	£11,000
Labour	nil
Overheads	nil
Opportunity cost of machine	£2,000
Design work	nil
Revised contract cost	£21,000

SUMMARY

This chapter has looked at the use of costs to aid pricing and output decisions. Central to this has been an understanding of how costs behave as output changes. Some costs vary with changes in output. These are known as marginal or variable costs. Others – fixed costs – remain the same over a range of outputs. Absorption costing, by emphasising a representative figure based on 'normal' output, ignores these relationships and can distort decisions. By recognising the different aspects of cost behaviour, it is possible to derive the breakeven point and the profitability of other output levels for any enterprise as well as applying the findings to individual problem areas.

A particularly important aspect of decision making relates to situations where resources are in short supply. If only one resource is scarce, contribution per limiting factor can be used to choose an optimal production plan. Where there is more than one scarce resource, it may be necessary to use linear programming. This has been shown graphically and allowed the idea of shadow prices or dual values to be demonstrated. Effectively shadow prices or dual values are one element making up total opportunity cost. Together with market prices, they form total opportunity cost. Opportunity costs can then be used to identify the real cost of resources by expressing them in terms of their value in the next best alternative.

REFERENCE

1 Confusion sometimes exists between the terms marginal cost and variable cost. Anthony and Reece defined marginal costs as 'a term used in economics for what accountants call variable costs'. In other words, the terms are synonymous. This is the approach taken in this text (Anthony, R.N. and Reece, J.S., *Management Accounting: Text and Cases*, Richard D. Irwin Inc, 1975, p. 570).

FURTHER READING

Arnold, H. and Hope, T. (1983) *Accounting for Management Decisions*, Prentice Hall.
Horngren, C.T. and Foster, G. (1991) *Cost Accounting: A Managerial Emphasis*, 7th edn, Prentice Hall.
Kaplan, R.S. and Atkinson, A.A. (1989) *Advanced Management Accounting*, 2nd edn, Prentice Hall.

TEST YOUR UNDERSTANDING

1 Define what is meant by the relevant range.

2 Explain the difference between the economist's and the accountant's approach to marginal costs.

3 A company makes one product and has no opening or closing stocks. The selling price is £10 and the marginal cost per unit is £6. Fixed costs are £800 per period. The breakeven point is:
   (a) 80 units;
   (b) 133 units;
   (c) 200 units;
   (d) none of these.

4 Explain what is meant by the margin of safety.

5 Details relating to one product made by Bournmouth Ltd for the month of April 19X3 is as follows: sales £1,000,000, fixed costs £300,000, profit £200,000. The breakeven turnover is:
   (a) £500,000;
   (b) £600,000;
   (c) £700,000;
   (d) £800,000.

6 List the limitations of cost–volume–profit analysis.

7 What is another term for a shadow price?

8 Explain what is meant by opportunity cost.

9 Internal opportunity cost is:
- **(a)** the shadow price of a resource;
- **(b)** the benefits derived from using a resource internally;
- **(c)** the original cost of a resource;
- **(d)** the realisable value of a resource.

10 What is meant by linear programming?

11 A competitor of yours mentions that their turnover had increased by 25 per cent to £500,000 and that net profit before tax had increased by 40 per cent to £70,000 over a period of one month. Assuming that selling prices had remained constant and that no change had taken place in unit costs or the cost structure, estimate the fixed costs and breakeven point of the competitor.

QUESTIONS

1 The turnover and profit before tax of a division in your organisation is given below. From the data:
- **(a)** estimate the fixed and variable costs for February;
- **(b)** on the assumption that the price of the variable costs increased by 10 per cent, calculate the percentage increase in sales volume necessary to maintain profits at their February level.

Month	Jan	Feb
Turnover	£100,000	£120,000
Profit	£8,000	£12,000

2 Bolton and Burnley Ltd make two products, the Standard and the Supa which share the same production facilities, including labour. Factory overhead – all fixed – is charged to products on the basis of labour cost. Labour is currently costing £10 per hour and the plant is sufficient to handle 5,500 labour hours of production per four weeks. Each Standard takes one labour hour to make while each Supa takes two hours. The profitability of the two products for the last four weeks are detailed below.

		Standard (£)		Supa (£)
Sales		160,000		150,000
Materials	60,000		70,000	
Factory labour	20,000		30,000	
Factory overhead	44,000	124,000	66,000	166,000
Profit (loss)		36,000		(16,000)

The directors of the company are concerned with the losses being made by the Supa. Two independent options are being considered; the closing down of Supa production and the acceptance of a new regular order from Sandels plc. The order from Sandels would involve producing 1,000 units of an 'own label' version of the Standard per month. Sandel would be prepared to pay £50 for each Standard and promises to market the product under its own brand label.

Using the above information, advise the directors of Bolton and Burnley Ltd as to the appropriate courses of action, drawing their attention to any non-financial issues which they should also consider.

3 Bristol plc makes several products, two of which are the Alpha and the Beta. The unit selling price and costs for both are reproduced below. All are current costs.

Alpha		Beta	
Selling price	£100	Selling price	£102
Material X – 2 litres	£32	Material Y – 3 kilograms	£30
Labour – grade 1	£24	Labour – grade 2	£32
Overheads based on labour hours	£24	Overheads based on labour hours	£32
Unit profit	£20	Unit profit	£8

The contracts director of Bristol is considering whether to bid for a contract. Already the development department has spent 275 person-hours on preliminary work and this amount will double if a full bid is made. The charge-out rate for the development department is £330 per hour of which £90 relates to general overheads. However, the overhead component will double in the immediate future to allow for the department only working at 50 per cent capacity. In addition to these costs, the contract will require three types of material.

The contract calls for 1,000 kilograms of material A. Bristol currently has 1,500 kilograms in stock although the company has no further use for it. It originally cost £12 per kilogram but was subsequently written down to £6 per kilogram. The current purchase price is £8 while any surplus stock can be sold for £7 per kilogram.

Material B is also no longer used in the company. The contract requires 1,500 litres of which 600 litres is in stock. Originally this cost £19 per litre although the current purchase price is £24. If not used in the contract, material B could either be sold to a competitor for £15 per litre or used as a replacement for material X in the making of the Alpha. For each litre of material B used, Bristol could save purchasing one litre of material X.

Material C is used regularly by Bristol and 2,000 kilograms will be required by the contract. Bristol operates a first-in-first-out stock valuation system and the current stocks are 500 units at a unit cost of £6 purchased on 20 October 19X5 and 700 units costing £7.00 per unit purchased on 8 November 19X5. Additional supplies are available at a unit price of £8 and any surplus stocks can be sold for £7.75 each.

The contract calls for 2,000 hours of labour grade 2, the rate for which is £16 per hour. This includes a 100 per cent overhead recovery rate. Currently there is a severe shortage of this quality of labour. If the contract is won, Bristol will have to take employees away from producing the Beta.

The contract will also require the use of two machines for six months. These are special, heavy duty machines although they will be only required for light work on the contract. The depreciation charge per annum using the straight line method is £25,000 per machine. For the first three months of the contract, they would have no further use but for the second three months, Bristol has entered into an arrangement to rent them to another company for a total of £18,000. Less sophisticated machines suitable for use on the contract are available for hire at £2,000 per machine per month.

Bristol has a company-wide policy to add 120 per cent to all contract costs to cover general overheads.

Using the above data, estimate the minimum bid price which would not involve a loss for Bristol.

4* Stafford Ltd makes two products, the Amber and the Blue. It is currently considering expansion as it is unable to meet the demand for its current products and competitors are moving into the market offering similar products at similar prices.

Both products have to pass through departments 1 and 2. The maximum capacity of each department is 3,000 machine hours per week. In addition, both products make use of the same form of material which is currently available at £15 per metre. However, Stafford is having great difficulty acquiring more than 600 metres per week at this price. Both products also make use of a similar grade of labour, but this is in plentiful supply.

After passing through departments 1 and 2, both products are then finished in specialised departments unique to each product. The Amber uses department 3 which is capable of handling up to 30 Ambers per week while the Blue uses department 4. Department 4 has a capacity of 40 Blues per week.

The detailed costings of each product are reproduced below.

Amber	(£)	Blue	(£)
Selling price	2,850	Selling price	2,150
Materials	150	Materials	150
Labour	300	Labour	400
Overheads:		Overheads:	
Department 1 (50 hours)	500	Department 1 (60 hours)	600
Department 2 (75 hours)	900	Department 2 (40 hours)	480
Department 3	200	Department 4	150
Unit profit	800		370

The weekly direct cost of department 1 is £30,000 and for department 2, £36,000. For departments 3 and 4, the direct costs are £6,000 each per week.

The recommendation is that Blue production be abandoned and production concentrated on making as many Ambers as capacity allows.

Estimate the profit of Stafford if the recommendation is undertaken and advise the company as to any improvement possible.

CHAPTER 18

Accounting planning and control systems

Business activity does not simply happen. Planning is necessary and then plans have to be implemented. In all but the smallest organisations, this process has to be formalised. Sometimes, however, performance deviates from plan. Action will then be necessary to minimise any losses caused by the failure to achieve the objectives. Accounting has evolved two techniques to aid short term planning: budgetary control and standard costing.

This chapter:

■ Provides a framework within which planning can be considered

■ Shows how budgets are developed and identifies the technical interrelationships between the functions making up the budget

■ Explains the rationale of standard costing and applies this to sales, variable costs and fixed overheads

■ Demonstrates how traditional accounting information can be rearranged in the form of a more meaningful performance report

■ Provides worked examples of both budgets and standard costing

So far, the scorekeeping and short term decision making aspects of management accounting have been emphasised. Scorekeeping involves, amongst other things, calculating the cost or profitability of a job, batch or process. But for this to carry meaning for management, the result has to be compared with some standard. Having calculated the cost of a batch, for example, managers might implicitly compare that cost with the cost of a similar batch in the previous period or explicitly compare it with a technical estimate of cost derived prior to production. Of equal interest, given the need of the enterprise to survive, managers may attempt to compare their costs with those of any competitors.

Short term decision making also involves comparisons. By definition, a decision involves a choice between two or more courses of action. Considering the profitability of a segment involves at least two options – its closure or its continuance – while taking on a special order involves an even wider information search. The effect on existing and prospective customers and the possible reaction of competitors are just three factors which have to be taken into account. By comparing current activity against some alternative, the attention of managers is directed to possible improvements. This is part of the attention-directing role of management accounting.

MANAGEMENT ACCOUNTING AND MANAGEMENT CONTROL

Essential conditions for management control

Management accounting has already been identified as an important aspect of management control: those processes by which managers attempt to ensure their organisation adapts successfully to changes in its environment. Managers need to be constantly scanning the environment and comparing what the organisation is actually doing with what it needs to be doing in order to survive. But this implies the organisation has an objective or purpose – otherwise scanning the environment becomes little more than stargazing – and that current activity can be measured and compared with information coming from the environment. Traditionally, profit has often been assumed to be both the objective and the measure.

For effective management control, two further conditions have to be met. First, to change from 'what is' to 'what ought to be' requires an awareness of cause and effect. Here, a knowledge of cost behaviour is a necessary but not sufficient condition. The reaction of customers, competitors and employees as well as any long term implications are just some of the additional factors which need to be taken into account. Secondly, the organisation must have the ability to take any necessary corrective action. To be told that the enterprise can be successful if it cuts costs is not particularly helpful if those costs cannot be reduced. If any one of these conditions is missing – if the organisation has no objective, if current activities cannot be measured, if there is no predictive model of cause and effect, or if corrective action is not possible – then management control, in the form of successfully adapting to the environment, cannot be fully effective.

Forms of management control

Management control consists of a whole range of individual controls ranging from informal and qualitative personal observations to formal, quantitative and structured reports. All controls are concerned with attempting to make 'what is' equal to 'what ought to be'.

In other words, they compare actual performance against a standard in an attempt to move closer towards 'what ought to be'.

Moving from 'what is' to 'what ought to be' in an organisation is rarely a technical exercise. More often than not it involves influencing the behaviour of managers and workers. Some controls are in the form of rules and regulations – for example, requiring employees to complete time sheets or adhere to company-specified modes of dress. At the other extreme, social controls are more concerned with developing shared values and norms. Recruitment policy is an obvious example of the exercise of social controls.

Many controls, however, originate or are closely related to the internal accounting system, as this is often the only readily accessible, regular supply of verifiable, quantitative data. More than that, by being expressed in money terms, accounting provides information which is both understandable and comparable between different parts of the organisation. Actual results ('what is') can be compared with plans ('what ought to be') and, from this, managers can then take corrective action. This is the attention-directing role of management accounting.

ACCOUNTING CONTROLS AND SYSTEMS

Accounting control mechanisms

Two accounting control mechanisms in particular have evolved to help management identify differences between actual and planned results: budgetary planning and control, and standard costing. Both are concerned with establishing predetermined levels of performance and cost.

A budget is a quantitative, generally financial, expression of a plan of action for specific future periods and which relates to both the individual segments within an organisation as well as to the organisation as a whole. Most budgets are essentially short term – often for a period of one year. As such, many of the conditions faced by the organisation cannot be changed. The budget will therefore be developed on the basis of existing products, existing markets and existing resources – unless new products, markets or resources have already been planned for the budget period. Control is effected by comparing the budgetary plan against actual performance and highlighting any differences for corrective action.

Standard costing shares many of the assumptions of budgets but differs from budgeting in its focus. Budgets relate to a whole organisation, department or activity and generally relate to a specific time period. Standard costs, although also predetermined, relate to units of output. It is therefore possible to have a system of budgetary control without standard costing although the reverse is highly unlikely. For instance, it is possible to lay down a budget for the marketing department without the need for standard costs. Developing standard costs for a production department, however, almost inevitably involves the design of a budget.

Accounting and control systems

Both budgeting and standard costing share a concern with measuring actual results against a predetermined figure and a desire to remedy any deviation. Both also take place within the confines of the wider environment. As such, the concept of the control system developed in Chapter 6 provides a useful framework within which to evaluate their use and limitations. The basic model is reproduced as Exhibit 18.1. The input, process and output elements of the model represent the conversion of raw financial data into actual accounting results. The sensor is now the budget or standard which acts as a comparator. Any difference or *variance* from plan is fed back to management who are represented by the control device. Management then take any corrective action necessary to reduce an adverse error between the planned and actual results. There is therefore negative feedback.

Exhibit 18.1 Diagrammatic representation of a system

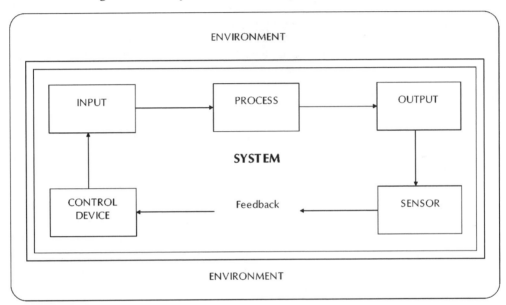

Interpreting feedback signals

The control system model is particularly useful for analysing the workings of an accounting control system. Not only does it identify the similarities with mechanical systems such as a central heating system, it also brings out critical differences. In the central heating example of Chapter 6, the error signal is clear and unambiguous while any necessary corrective action is automatic and exact. People, however, have to be motivated to respond to accounting variances and yet human behaviour is both complex and ill-understood. Managers might deliberately not carry out corrective action if they feel it will reflect badly on themselves, while any remedies available to make them act 'correctly' tend to be blunt and discretionary, such as the withholding of bonuses.

It may be that managers want to act 'correctly', but that the necessary corrective action is not known. This was less of a problem with a central heating system where the cause of the error signal is of little importance. If the temperature in the room falls, the answer is clear: increase the supply of fuel to the boiler. The reason for the fall in temperature is immaterial. In accounting systems, however, the reason for the variance can be critical. The same numerical variance can occur even though the cause of the variance might differ – and different causes often require different remedies.

As an example, consider a company which planned to spend £4,000 on materials for a particular job and assume the actual cost was £5,000. If this £1,000 variance arose because of a general price rise, the remedial action necessary may be to revise costings for subsequent periods. If, however, the error was caused by the buying department using a non-standard source of supply, then different corrective action is required to avoid a repetition. What the corrective action needs to be will depend on the circumstances. It might be that the buying department simply failed to use the existing supplier – in which case, a requirement that the buyer uses existing suppliers will bring the system back into control for subsequent periods. It might, however, be that the purchase was an emergency one, caused by the production department failing to inform the buyer of material requirements. In that case, the necessary corrective action lies with the production department who caused the error rather than the buying department against whom the error was reported.

Distorting feedback signals

The previous example demonstrates a third difficulty with accounting variances as error signals. The management accounting system is not producing a full signal. The error is being reported against the effect in the purchasing department rather than the cause in the production department. Sometimes this error signal is weakened by employees, including managers, introducing what has been called *noise* into the system. Noise is anything which distorts a signal. Crackling on the line is an example of noise in a telephone system. In accounting systems, noise can be produced by distorting either the reported data or the standard against which it is measured. Sometimes noise is created deliberately to make variances unclear. Managers might, for example, reduce essential expenses in order to reduce an adverse variance even though this has consequences for subsequent periods. Alternatively, they might inflate the standard against which they are measured in order to appear more successful at controlling expenses.

Further distortion is possible because of the timing and presentation of accounting variances by accountants. Unlike the central heating system where the error and response is immediate, accounting variances will usually only be formally reported at discrete intervals – perhaps in monthly management accounts. By then, it may be too late. Lower levels of management may well have corrected the error as a result of personal observation before the variance appears in the management accounts. Any correction to an already corrected error signal might, in itself, then produce further errors. In addition, as information is presented to higher and higher levels of management, that information is progressively summarised, often by accountants who may have different views as to what is and what is not relevant. As a result, senior management may only have a very imprecise view of any errors in the system.

Limitations of budgets and standards for control

Once the budget and standard costs have been set, actual performance is reported and differences identified. The danger is that budgets and standards are then 'set in stone', never to be altered until the next budget period. In Exhibit 18.1, the accounting system has become a closed system, reporting output against the desired condition represented by the sensor, irrespective of the environment within which the organisation *currently* operates. The budgets and standards may have been inappropriate in the first place or, even if originally valid, circumstances might have changed such that they are no longer appropriate. Whatever the reason, if the comparison is inappropriate, corrective action is also likely to be inappropriate.

A second limitation of budgets and standard costs for control is that errors are allowed to happen before corrective action is taken. This is the essential characteristic of all feedback models. Ideally, what is required is some form of *feedforward* mechanism. Rather than actual outputs being compared with some desired state, the environment can be searched for predictions of the future. These can then be compared with the desired state and steps taken to minimise any likely errors before they occur. Feedforward is therefore proactive whereas feedback is reactive. Its objective is to achieve control *before* any deviations from plan.

Planning and control

Traditionally, planning has been separated from control. Planning is the definition of objectives and the setting and agreeing of actions necessary to achieve those objectives. Control is then viewed as the activities necessary to see the plans implemented and objectives achieved. Much of the discussion, so far, has been about control in this traditional sense. If, however, management control comprises the processes by which managers ensure their organisation adapts successfully to changes in its environment, then traditional planning is also a form of control.

Planning budgets and standard costs involves a search of the environment to forecast, for example, consumer tastes, product demand, likely customers, input costs, and availability. These can then be compared with the outcomes desired by the organisation and plans developed. Should there be a significant error between the prospective and desired outcomes, plans can then be revised. In essence, this is feedforward control. To a greater or lesser extent, this process contains all of the necessary conditions for management control: an objective or objectives, measurement and comparison, a predictive model and the ability to take corrective action.

The only conceptual difference between traditional planning and control is in the form of the error messages, with planning using feedforward and control using feedback. In that sense a budget involves both feedback and feedforward. It involves feedforward when developing the plan and feedback when appraising actual performance against that plan.

The traditional planning aspects of budgets, however, are qualitatively different to the control aspects. In dealing with the future, cause and effect relationships may not be adequately known. Similarly, because it relates to the future, data will not be verifiable in the hard, accounting sense. Nevertheless, viewing traditional planning and control as part of the same process of management control rather than separate elements is more meaningful. Before discussing the ways accounting planning and control systems are used however, it is useful to have a fuller understanding of the mechanics of both budgeting and standard costing.

THE MECHANICS OF BUDGETING

The master budget

Planning a budget takes place within the guidelines or the objectives set by senior management. For business organisations, the overriding objective has traditionally been assumed to be profitability and survival. The budget will therefore be summarised in the form of a pro forma profit and loss account and balance sheet for the organisation, often with the addition of a forecast cashflow statement. Together, these are known as the *master budget*. Supporting these will be detailed budgets for individual segments making up the organisation. These are generally built up on the basis of organisational responsibility. Budgets will therefore be developed for the personnel, marketing, finance and production functions and within these may be further subdivisions, depending on the size and culture of the organisation.

The development of the master budget, however, will be constrained by the availability of resources, some of which are likely to be fixed for the budget period. Rarely, for instance, will it be possible to alter production capacity or change the whole range of products or services provided by the organisation within the short time period of the budget. The first stage in preparing a budget will therefore be to identify the factor or factors which limit the achievement of the objectives. In a commercial organisation, this is often the prospective level of sales, although it can be production capacity or the availability of other resources. In a not-for-profit organisation, it might be the availability of funding.

Having identified the main limiting factor, the actual preparation of the budget might identify further constraints. A company, for example, might initially identify sales volume as the major constraint. As a result of producing a budget on that basis, further limitations might be identified such as a lack of warehousing to meet the necessary production or a cash deficiency at some stage of the budget period. Consequently, the budget may have to be revised or further plans developed to overcome the difficulties discovered, a further example of feedforward. In theory therefore, budgeting is an iterative process although the time consuming nature of budgets in large organisations often limits the number of revisions possible. Once these difficulties have been resolved and managers accept responsibility for their individual budgets, the master budget is agreed. It then forms the plan for activities over the budget period.

Budgets and the conditions for control

Four conditions have been identified as being necessary for effective control.

1. Objectives need to exist, otherwise there is no goal to aim towards.
2. A predictive model of cause and effect has to exist.
3. Outputs must be measurable.
4. Corrective action must be possible.

All four factors are found in the planning stage of budgeting. The need for an objective and an example of feedforward corrective action have already been demonstrated, as has the quantification of outputs in the form of the master budget's prospective final accounts.

The only condition not so far outlined relates to the identification of cause and effect.

In the technical development of budgets, this is provided in two ways: a knowledge of cost behaviour as activity changes, and an understanding of the linkages between income, expenditure, cashflows and assets and liabilities developed from the earlier study of duality. Profit is not the only consideration; the effect on the organisation's cash balance will also be important.

Profit is rarely reflected as an increase in cash. Partly this is because depreciation does not involve cash and partly because the purchase of an asset involves a cash outflow without an immediate charge against the profit and loss account. There are other reasons why there is a difference, including shareholders providing more funds in the form of additional capital or withdrawing funds by way of dividends. A more pervasive reason, however, arises from timing differences. Production often takes place in advance of sales, causing costs to be incurred before a sale is made. Consequently, unit production for a period will rarely be the same as sales volume. Some production costs involve an immediate cash outlay while others will be partly funded by suppliers who grant credit. Similarly, when sales are made, these often result in the creation of a debtor rather than an immediate receipt of cash. Because of this, the cash budget is of particular importance as often it will identify a temporary cash shortage as a result of the planned activity.

The technical relationships between revenues, expenses, cash receipts and cash payments will vary from organisation to organisation. Nevertheless there is a general pattern which serves as a framework for developing budgets for particular organisations. These are brought out in Example 18.1.

Example 18.1

Nigel Newstart plans to market industrial vacuum cleaners with capital, in the form of cash, of £20,000 on 1 January. He will sell the cleaners for £200 each and allow two months' credit on all sales. The cleaners cost £120 each and the supplier will allow one month's credit. Nigel's only other expenses are rent and wages which total £2,000 per month. These are paid at the end of each month.

He believes he will sell 80 units in the first month and this will increase by 10 cleaners per month until sales reach 110 units, after which no further increase in volume is thought possible. Because of some uncertainty with supplies, he wishes stocks at each month end to be sufficient for a half month's trading. His only concern is whether the capital is sufficient for the first four months of operation.

The sales and purchase budgets

Although simplified, Example 18.1 brings out many of the issues of budgeting. Nigel will be interested not only in the profitability of the venture but also its liquidity. In addition, he will want details of purchases necessary to achieve the forecast level of sales. As sales appear to be the limiting factor, it is useful to analyse these to determine turnover, units sold and cash received. The sales for the first four months are shown in Exhibit 18.2. From these sales figures, it is also possible to derive the cash received. As two months' credit is allowed, it will only be in March that Nigel will receive the cash from the sales made in January. This pattern applies to all subsequent months and so, at the end of April, the debtors will represent the sales for March and April.

Also shown in Exhibit 18.2 is the purchases budget expressed in units and values along with a schedule of payment to creditors. The figures for purchases are found by rearranging the cost of sales equation from financial accounting:

$$\text{Opening Stock} + \text{Purchases} - \text{Closing Stock} = \text{Cost of Sales}$$

Rearranging gives:

$$\text{Purchases} = \text{Cost of Sales} + \text{Closing Stock} - \text{Opening Stock}$$

Nigel requires stocks at each month end to be sufficient for a further half month's trading. With sales of 90 units in February, the January closing stock must be 45 units and this will form the opening stock for February. All other stocks are found in a similar way. By April, sales volume has stabilised at 110 units and so May sales will also be 110 units, to give a closing stock in April of 55 units. With creditors allowing one month's credit, the January purchases will only be paid in February and so at the end of the first four months of trading, creditors will represent the cost of the purchases in April.

Exhibit 18.2 The sales and purchases budget

SALES BUDGET	January Units	(£)	February Units	(£)	March Units	(£)	April Units	(£)	Total (£)
Turnover	80	16,000	90	18,000	100	20,000	110	22,000	76,000
Cash received						16,000		18,000	34,000
Period end debtors									42,000

PURCHASES BUDGET	January Units	(£)	February Units	(£)	March Units	(£)	April Units	(£)	Total (£)
Cost of sales	80	9,600	90	10,800	100	12,000	110	13,200	45,600
Add closing stock	45	5,400	50	6,000	55	6,600	55	6,600	6,600
Less opening stock	0	0	45	5,400	50	6,000	55	6,600	0
Purchases required	125	15,000	95	11,400	105	12,600	110	13,200	52,200
Cash paid				15,000		11,400		12,600	39,000
Period end creditors									13,200

The budgeted profit and loss account and cashflow statement

The only other expenses facing Nigel are rent and wages of £2,000 per month. As these are paid currently, it is now possible to develop the monthly profit and loss and cashflow budgets. With the exception of the capital introduced and the wages paid, all the information necessary for both the budgeted profit and loss account and the budgeted cashflow statement is contained in the earlier workings. In practice, individual budgets would have been produced for both items. Given the simplicity of the question, however, it is not essential to show separate capital and expense budgets in this example. Nigel's budgeted profit and loss account and cashflow statement are shown in Exhibit 18.3.

Exhibit 18.3 The budgeted profit and loss account and cashflow forecast

PROFIT AND LOSS BUDGET	January (£)	February (£)	March (£)	April (£)	Total (£)
Turnover	16,000	18,000	20,000	22,000	76,000
Cost of sales	9,600	10,800	12,000	13,200	45,600
Gross profit	6,400	7,200	8,000	8,800	30,400
Rent and wages	2,000	2,000	2,000	2,000	8,000
Net profit	4,400	5,200	6,000	6,800	22,400

CASHFLOW BUDGET	January (£)	February (£)	March (£)	April (£)	Total (£)
Capital introduced	20,000				20,000
Receipts from debtors			16,000	18,000	34,000
Rent and wages	–2,000	–2,000	–2,000	–2,000	–8,000
Payment to creditors		–15,000	–11,400	–12,600	–39,000
Net cashflow	18,000	–17,000	2,600	3,400	7,000
Add opening cash balance		18,000	1,000	3,600	
Closing cash balance	18,000	1,000	3,600	7,000	7,000

The budgeted balance sheet

The data in the sales, purchases and cashflow budgets represents all of the transactions of the business. The budgeted profit and loss account merely summarises the revenue and expense elements. Consequently, by using the data from the sales, purchases and cash budgets, it is possible to record in outline all of the transactions and hence produce a budgeted balance sheet at the end of the four-month period. This is done in Exhibit 18.4. The budgeted data is recorded as if it represented actual transactions. As the objective is to derive a budgeted balance sheet rather than a historical record, the order in which the transactions are recorded is immaterial. Likewise, summary totals are sufficient rather than individual transactions. With this in mind, the total of budgeted sales derived from the sales budget is shown as a gaining of an asset of debtors and as an obligation to the owners in the profit and loss account. Purchases are then recorded as a gaining of stock and an incurring of creditors. These are the only two non-cash items.

As all the other transactions are cash-based, the transaction totals from the cash budget can be used to complete the recordings. Capital involves an increase in cash and an obligation to the owner for an equivalent amount. The heading of debtors represents cash received from debtors and a reduction in the amount they owe the business. Wages involve an outflow of cash and a corresponding benefit received which, because they are an expired cost, are charged to the profit and loss account. With the creditors being paid £39,000, cash is reduced by this amount along with an equivalent reduction in the amount owing to them. Finally, from the purchases budget, the cost of sales – the stock given up in order to make the sales – is seen to be £45,600. Deducting this from the asset of stock and charging to the line representing the profit and loss account completes the transactions. The result, in the final column, are the outstanding balances at the period end which then form the closing balance sheet.

Exhibit 18.4 Deriving the budgeted balance sheet

	Sales (£)	Purchases (£)	Capital (£)	Debtors (£)	Wages (£)	Creditors (£)	Cost of Sales (£)	Closing balance sheet (£)
Debtors	+76,000			−34,000				+42,000
Stock		+52,200					−45,600	+6,600
Cash			+20,000	+34,000	−8,000	−39,000		+7,000
								55,600
Creditors		−52,200				+39,000		−13,200
Profit and loss account	−76,000				+8,000		+45,600	−22,400
Capital			−20,000					−20,000
								55,600

If the budget showed a profit or balance sheet which was unacceptable to Nigel Newstart or if the budget had identified further constraints or bottlenecks, then revisions would be necessary. To be meaningful, however, the revisions would need to take account of the reality of the environment. Making unrealistic assumptions about the future simply produces an unrealistic budget.

BUDGETING – A WORKED EXAMPLE

The example of Nigel Newstart demonstrates the need for an objective and the need for cause and effect to be understood. In Nigel's case, the objective was assumed to be, at the minimum, survival. With a budgeted profit of £22,400 over four months and no liquidity problems, he appears to be achieving this objective if his assumptions can be believed.

The cause and effect relationships in budgets have also been demonstrated. Two forms of cost behaviour applied to Nigel's business: the fixed costs of rent and wages, and the variable cost of the goods sold. Other, more subtle, relationships were also identified such as the timing differences between sales and cash received from debtors and the linkages between cost of sales, purchases and cash paid to creditors. The understanding of the interrelationship between expenses, revenue, assets and liabilities caused by cost behaviour and timing differences is further developed in Example 18.2.

Example 18.2

Claude Monet Ltd currently makes a single product, the Giverny. Commencing 1 January, the selling price will be £60 each. The cost of material and labour for each Giverny from that date will be £14 and £10, respectively. For the purpose of this exercise, labour can be viewed as a variable cost. Prior to 1 January, the company's balance sheet was as follows:

	Cost (£)	Depreciation (£)	Net (£)
Fixed assets			
Factory machinery	300,000	240,000	60,000
Office equipment	60,000	36,000	24,000
	360,000	276,000	84,000
Current assets			
Raw material stock	11,000		
Finished stock	28,000	39,000	
Debtors		80,000	
Cash		1,000	
		120,000	
Current liabilities			
Trade creditors	11,000		
Dividends payable	10,000	21,000	99,000
			183,000
Financed by			
Ordinary share capital			60,000
Retained earnings			123,000
			183,000

The finished stock comprises 800 units of the Giverny while the raw material stock is sufficient to produce 1,000 units. Finished stock includes an appropriate proportion of factory overheads. Of the debtors, £38,000 relate to sales in November and £42,000 to sales in December. Monet's policy is to charge depreciation on all fixed assets at 20 per cent p.a. on the original cost.

For the coming year, factory rent and rates are likely to be £96,000 while those for the offices are likely to be £18,000. In both cases, rent is payable quarterly in advance, commencing 1 January. Selling and administration expenses will be £3,000 per month, payable by the end of each month and the proposed dividend will be paid sometime in January.

Production for the next twelve months is estimated to be 12,000 units of Giverny while estimated monthly sales for the first eight months are:

Month	January	February	March	April	May	June	July	August
Units	800	1,000	1,200	1,500	1,100	800	400	600

> All sales are on credit and debtors are allowed two months' credit. Production takes place the month before sales are required. Raw materials for production are acquired one month before production takes place. Suppliers allow one month's credit although wages are paid in the month they are incurred.
>
> Claude Monet Ltd has a six-month budget period, commencing 1 January.

Developing the sales and purchases budgets

Once again, it appears that selling volume is the factor which limits profitability. Given the unit selling price of £60 and the sales volume forecast, budgeted monthly sales revenue can be estimated. The result is shown in Exhibit 18.5. From the monthly turnover data, cash inflows from sales can then be derived. Given Monet's credit policy, cash from sales will only be received two months later. The company will therefore have to wait until March to receive cash from January's sales. However, as the company is already established, cash will be received in January and February from sales in the previous year. January should see the debtors relating to November's sales making payment while February should see cash being received from sales in December. The result is a total cash inflow from debtors over the six-month period of £350,000.

Exhibit 18.5 The sales and purchases budgets for Claude Monet

Sales Budget	January	February	March	April	May	June			Total
Units	800	1,000	1,200	1,500	1,100	800			6,400
Revenue (£)	48,000	60,000	72,000	90,000	66,000	48,000			384,000
Cash from sales (£)			48,000	60,000	72,000	90,000			270,000
Cash from debtors (£)	38,000	42,000							80,000
Total cash received									
from debtors	38,000	42,000	48,000	60,000	72,000	90,000			350,000
Purchases Budget	January	February	March	April	May	June	July	August	Total
Unit sales	800	1,000	1,200	1,500	1,100	800	400	600	
Unit production	1,000	1,200	1,500	1,100	800	400	600		
Unit purchases	1,200	1,500	1,100	800	400	600			5,600
Cost of purchases (£)	16,800	21,000	15,400	11,200	5,600	8,400			78,400
Payments (£)		16,800	21,000	15,400	11,200	5,600			70,000
Add payment to									
opening creditors (£)	11,000								11,000
Total cash paid (£)	11,000	16,800	21,000	15,400	11,200	5,600			81,000

A similar analysis can be undertaken for creditors by developing the purchases budget, which is also shown in Exhibit 18.5. Starting from unit sales, unit production can be derived by recognising that production takes place in the month prior to sales. Purchases, in turn, take place one month prior to production. Multiplying units purchased by the unit cost of £14 gives the monthly cost of purchases and from this can be derived the cash payments to suppliers. Payment takes place one month after the purchase. January, however, will see the creditors from December's purchases being paid and so the total payment to suppliers over the first six months will be £81,000.

Developing the production and selling and administration budgets

The only other two functions within Claude Monet Ltd are the production department and the selling and administration department. Of these, the production department is the more complicated. Unit monthly production will be equal to anticipated sales of the subsequent period. As purchases take place one month in advance of production, material used for production in February will equal the purchases in January. A similar pattern exists for subsequent months. Material purchased in June will be issued to production in July and hence will form the raw material stock at the end of the six-month budget period. Similarly, the material consumed in January will have been purchased in the previous month and is represented by the raw material stock in the opening balance sheet.

As the labour is assumed to be a variable cost, its total monthly cost can be calculated by multiplying monthly production by the unit cost of £10. Manufacturing overheads are more complex. Two expenses are involved, the depreciation of the factory machinery and the factory rent and rates of £96,000. Depreciation will be 20 per cent on cost, a total of £60,000 and so, with activity planned at 12,000 units, overhead per unit will be £8 for rent and £5 for depreciation. Multiplying these by units produced results in overheads absorbed per month. In order to help subsequent bookkeeping, the two elements of overhead are shown separately. The composition of the cost of production per month is shown in Exhibit 18.6.

Exhibit 18.6 The production and selling and administration budgets for Claude Monet

Production Budget	January	February	March	April	May	June	July	August	Total
Unit sales	800	1,000	1,200	1,500	1,100	800	400	600	
Unit production	1,000	1,200	1,500	1,100	800	400			6,000
Raw material (£)	11,000	16,800	21,000	15,400	11,200	5,600			81,000
Factory labour (£)	10,000	12,000	15,000	11,000	8,000	4,000			60,000
Overhead – rent (£)	8,000	9,600	12,000	8,800	6,400	3,200			48,000
Overhead – depreciation (£)	5,000	6,000	7,500	5,500	4,000	2,000			30,000
Total cost of production (£)	34,000	44,400	55,500	40,700	29,600	14,800			219,000

Selling and Administration budget	January	February	March	April	May	June	Total
Office rent (£)	1,500	1,500	1,500	1,500	1,500	1,500	9,000
Selling and administration expenses (£)	3,000	3,000	3,000	3,000	3,000	3,000	18,000
Depreciation (£)	1,000	1,000	1,000	1,000	1,000	1,000	6,000
Total cost of selling and administration (£)	5,500	5,500	5,500	5,500	5,500	5,500	33,000

By comparison, the selling and administration budget, which is also shown in Exhibit 18.6, is relatively straightforward. With the annual rental of the office costing £18,000, the monthly expense will be £1,500, while most of the selling and administration expenses are given in the example as £3,000 monthly. The only other expense will be depreciation, which is again at a rate of 20 per cent on cost. Total depreciation will therefore be £12,000 per annum or £1,000 per month.

The budgeted profit and loss account and cashflow statement

Having calculated the monthly cost of production, a budgeted profit and loss account can now be prepared. Turnover is simply taken from the sales budget. As production takes place one month ahead of sales, the cost of sales for February will equal January's cost of production. A similar pattern applies to subsequent months with the result that June's production will form the value of finished stock at the end of the six-month period. For January, the cost of sales will be equal to December's production, which is represented by the £28,000 stock of finished goods shown in the original balance sheet.

The only other expenses are those which relate to selling and administration. As there are no timing differences involved, these can simply be copied from the sales and administration budget to determine net monthly profit. The detail of the monthly budgeted profits is shown in Exhibit 18.7. Using other data from the individual budgets, a budgeted cashflow statement can be produced. This is also shown in Exhibit 18.7. The only cash inflow is from debtors, the details of which were derived in the sales budget. Payments to creditors were estimated in the purchases budget. Factory wages are paid currently

Exhibit 18.7 The budgeted profit and loss account and cashflow statement

Budgeted Profit and Loss Account	January (£)	February (£)	March (£)	April (£)	May (£)	June (£)	Total (£)
Turnover	48,000	60,000	72,000	90,000	66,000	48,000	384,000
Manufacturing cost of sales	28,000	34,000	44,400	55,500	40,700	29,600	232,200
Office rent	1,500	1,500	1,500	1,500	1,500	1,500	9,000
Selling and administration expenses	3,000	3,000	3,000	3,000	3,000	3,000	18,000
Office depreciation	1,000	1,000	1,000	1,000	1,000	1,000	6,000
Net profit	14,500	20,500	22,100	29,000	19,800	12,900	118,800

Cash Budget	January (£)	February (£)	March (£)	April (£)	May (£)	June (£)	Total (£)
Cash from debtors	38,000	42,000	48,000	60,000	72,000	90,000	350,000
Payment to creditors	–11,000	–16,800	–21,000	–15,400	–11,200	–5,600	–81,000
Factory wages	–10,000	–12,000	–15,000	–11,000	–8,000	–4,000	–60,000
Factory rent	–24,000			–24,000			–48,000
Office rent	–4,500			–4,500			–9,000
Selling and administration expenses	–3,000	–3,000	–3,000	–3,000	–3,000	–3,000	–18,000
Dividends	–10,000						–10,000
Net cashflow	–24,500	10,200	9,000	2,100	49,800	77,400	124,000
Add opening cash balance	1,000	–23,500	–13,300	–4,300	–2,200	47,600	1,000
Closing cash balance	–23,500	–13,300	–4,300	–2,200	47,600	125,000	125,000

and so can simply be taken from the production budget. For the same reason, the selling and administration expenses can be taken from the selling and administration budget. Rents, however, are paid quarterly in advance and so £24,000 for the factory and £4,500 for the offices will be paid on 1 January and 1 April. These amounts have already been charged to the profit and loss account, except they were matched with consumption following the accounting concept of accruals, rather than payment periods. Finally, the dividends proposed at the year end are to be paid in January.

The result is a forecast significant cash outflow in January, far higher than the opening cash balance. Even though subsequent months have positive cashflows, it is not until May that the cash deficiency is overcome. The budgetary exercise has therefore identified a potential difficulty. What the solution is will depend on circumstances. The obvious answer is to negotiate a short term overdraft facility with the bank. Failing that, revising budgeted sales downwards will reduce cash outflows on production and material purchases which will go part of the way to eliminating the cash deficiency. What is clear, however, is that by undertaking the budgetary process, a problem has been discovered before its occurrence and so avoiding action may be possible. This is an example of the feedforward control aspect of budgeting.

The budgeted balance sheet

To complete the master budget, a balance sheet at the end of the six months can be prepared. As with the earlier example of Nigel Newstart, all the necessary transactions have already been summarised in the individual functional budgets of sales, purchases, production and cashflows. These transactions are shown in Exhibit 18.8. With all sales taking place on credit, the £384,000 of sales estimated in the sales budget will cause debtors

Exhibit 18.8 Deriving the budgeted balance sheet of Claude Monet

(£)	Sales	Purchases	Cash rec'd from debtors	Cash paid to creditors	Other cash expenses	Work-in-progress	Transfer to finished stock	Cost of sales	Selling & admin. expenses	Closing balance sheet
Factory machinery	+60,000					−30,000				+30,000
Office equipment	+24,000								−6,000	+18,000
Finished stock	+28,000						+219,000	−232,200		+14,800
Raw material stock	+11,000	+78,400				−81,000				+8,400
Debtors	+80,000	+384,000	−350,000							+114,000
Cash	+1,000		+350,000	−81,000	−145,000					+125,000
Factory labour					+60,000	−60,000				
Factory rent and rates					+48,000	−48,000				
Office rent and rates					+9,000				−9,000	
Selling and admin. expenses					+18,000				−18,000	
Work-in-progress						+219,000	−219,000			
	204,000									310,200
Trade creditors	−11,000	−78,400		81,000						−8,400
Dividends payable	−10,000				10,000					
Ordinary share capital	−60,000									−60,000
Retained earnings	−123,000									−123,000
Profit this period		−384,000						232,200	33,000	−118,800
	204,000									310,200

to increase by that amount and for an equivalent amount to be credited to the profit and loss account. Purchases can then be recorded as an increase in stock and an increase in creditors. Other than depreciation, these are the only transactions not involving cash.

Analysing the cashflow statement will not only enable the closing debtors and creditors to be verified, it will also enable cash expenses to be recorded. The next two columns of Exhibit 18.8 show cash being received from debtors and cash paid to creditors. This is followed by cash expenditure of £145,000 representing all the other cash payments of the period identified in the cash budget. Raw material stock of £81,000 is then transferred to work-in-progress along with the cash expenses of labour and factory rent and rates and the non-cash expense of depreciation on the factory machinery. With no opening or closing work-in-progress, the total of £219,000 production is then transferred to finished stock. The £232,200 of finished stock consumed as cost of sales can be taken directly from the budgeted profit and loss account or individually calculated. Finally, the selling and administration expenses – including the depreciation of the office equipment – has to be charged to the profit and loss account. The result, in the final column, is the closing balance sheet which verifies the budgeted profit for the period as being £118,800.

FLEXIBLE BUDGETING

Reasons for budget differences

For planning to be effective, actual results have to be compared with plans, and variances identified. Arithmetically, variances between planned and actual performance can occur for three reasons:

1. the volume of activity can be different from planned;
2. unit selling prices can be different from those budgeted; and
3. actual costs can be different from planned.

To analyse further the variances in costs requires an understanding of cost behaviour. Fixed costs will not vary with volume of activity. Any change must therefore be due to changes in cost – for whatever reason. Changes in variable costs, however, can arise either because of cost differences compared with the budget or because actual usage was different from that planned. For example, the budget may have estimated that four hours of labour were required to produce one unit of output whereas actual labour hours were five per unit.

'Flexing' the budget

As we have seen, simply comparing actual and planned results will not identify the different immediate causes of variance. Fixed costs, for example, should remain the same, irrespective of any difference between planned and actual activity. Sales revenue and variable costs, however, are expected to change with changes in volume. Flexible budgeting has been developed to separate variances due to volume changes from other reasons such as different usage or different input prices.

For control purposes, the budget is re-cast, based on budgeted costs and revenues for the actual activity level achieved. By eliminating differences due to volume changes, factors more immediately under the control of management can then be identified. This process of 'flexing' the budget and the development of subsequent variances is demonstrated in Example 18.3. As Alfred Sisley only makes one product, activity can be measured in units. In a more complicated example, some other measure of activity such as labour hours may be necessary.

Example 18.3

Alfred Sisley Ltd makes a single product known as the Impression. Budgeted and actual results for the month of May are reproduced below along with variances produced by his bookkeeper.

	Budget (£)	Actual (£)	Variance* (£)	
Turnover	150,000	130,000	20,000	(A)
Direct material	30,000	25,000	5,000	(F)
Direct labour	50,000	39,000	11,000	(F)
Overheads – rent	10,000	9,000	1,000	(F)
Overheads – depreciation	20,000	14,000	6,000	(F)
Profit	40,000	43,000	3,000	(F)

* (A) = adverse, (F) = favourable variance

The budget was based on a sales volume of 100,000 units of the Impression although actual sales were only 80,000 units.

A variance is adverse if the actual data causes profit to be less than planned. Similarly, a variance is favourable if the actual data causes profit to be greater than planned. Favourable variances can therefore occur if revenue is greater than planned or expenses are less than planned. The simple variances produced by the bookkeeper, however, are misleading. Part of the labour and material variances, for example, are due to volume being lower than planned. As such, the variances are not particularly helpful for cost control purposes. Flexing the budget enables more meaningful variances to be produced. These are shown in Exhibit 18.9.

Exhibit 18.9 Flexible budgeting and variances

	Budget (£)	Flexed budget (£)	Actual (£)	Variance* (£)	
Turnover	150,000	120,000	130,000	10,000	(F)
Direct material	30,000	24,000	25,000	1,000	(A)
Direct labour	50,000	40,000	39,000	1,000	(F)
Overheads – rent	10,000	10,000	9,000	1,000	(F)
Overheads – depreciation	20,000	20,000	14,000	6,000	(F)
Profit	40,000	26,000	43,000	17,000	(F)

* (A) = adverse, (F) = favourable variance

Interpreting the variances

As actual volume was only 80 per cent of planned volume, turnover should also have been only 80 per cent of volume. With an actual turnover of £130,000, this is £10,000 more than expected on a sales volume of 80,000 units and so, given the actual volume, there is now a favourable variance. The selling price of the Impression was therefore higher than planned. As material and labour are assumed to be variable costs, these too should only have been 80 per cent of their budgeted amount. From the revised variances, material was £1,000 more than planned although this was compensated by labour being £1,000 less than planned.

Overheads are assumed to be entirely fixed. Consequently, they should not change even though volume changes. Any difference must simply be due to input prices being different from planned. Analysing the revised variances shows that rent is £1,000 below budget while depreciation is £6,000 less than planned. Overall therefore, the anticipated profit on a volume of 80,000 units should only have been £26,000 although there appears to be a favourable variance of £17,000.

What the flexible budget has done is to identify differences from budget caused by factors other than volume. What it has *not* done is identify the reasons for those differences. The higher unit selling price might be due to improved quality as a result of using more labour. Alternatively, the higher unit selling price might be the cause of the reduced volume.

For flexible budgeting to be meaningful as a control mechanism requires management to identify the causes of the differences and then to determine if the variances are under their control. If the adverse labour variance is due to inefficient use of labour, this can be remedied in subsequent periods. If it is due to, say, increased employers' contributions to social security as a result of government action then the cost cannot be brought back to budget.

One variance, the favourable change in the depreciation charge, requires particular attention. As depreciation is often a policy decision, a favourable variance in this may not reflect an improvement in efficiency. Indeed, it might be just the reverse with short term apparent gains being bought at a later cost of underprovision of depreciation. This is but one example of the more general problem of variances possibly being distorted by operating management in order to appear more successful. Although depreciation is perhaps an oversimplified example, it is representative of a more general problem. Certainly, there are expenses such as maintenance which provide managers with an element of discretion over their cost in any particular period and which may have longer term, dysfunctional aspects.

THE MECHANICS OF STANDARD COSTING

One other limitation of flexible budgeting is that it does not identify whether a variance was due to using a different volume of resources to that planned or whether the unit cost of those resources differed from their budgeted cost. Further analysis is therefore possible. By far the most common vehicle for analysing differences between budgeted and actual performance is standard costing. Standard costing involves predetermining the resources needed per unit of output and their cost. By multiplying this standard by actual activity, a standard cost for the activity can be determined against which to judge actual performance.

There are a whole variety of variances which can be calculated, all with their own apparently different formulae. At first then, the study of standard costing appears daunting. Nevertheless, the logic behind all standard costing variances is similar. Variances are concerned with analysing the difference between planned and actual activity and this difference can only result from four factors: volume being different from plan; selling prices being different from those budgeted; resources consumed being different from plan; or the cost of those resources being different from plan.

Price and usage variances

In discovering how standard cost variances are derived, it is useful initially to concentrate on manufacturing costs. The questions being asked will therefore be: *given* the actual output, how much should production have cost, how much did it cost and why was there a difference? In other words, the analysis involves breaking down the variance produced under flexible budgeting into differences caused by using non-standard amounts of a resource and differences resulting from input prices being different from planned. To demonstrate the logic and computation of variances, use will be made of the data in Example 18.4.

Example 18.4

Renior Ltd makes one particular product, the Cagnes, which requires 4 metres of wood per unit. The budgeted cost of the wood is £3 per metre and so the standard cost of wood per unit of Cagne produced is £12. In each of the first three weeks of one period, five units of the Cagne are manufactured. Details of material used in each of the three weeks are:

Week	Metres used	Cost per metre	Total cost
1	20	£4	£80
2	25	£3	£75
3	25	£4	£100

Each Cagne should use 4 metres of wood. Producing five units should therefore require 20 metres. With a unit cost of £3 per metre, the total material cost of production should be £60. This is the standard cost for a production level of five Cagnes.

In the first week, 20 metres were used but the unit price paid was £4 and so the actual cost was £80. The £20 adverse variance was entirely due to paying more for the materials. As such, it is known as a *price variance*. In the second week, the price paid for wood is equal to the price budgeted but more wood has been used than anticipated. The £15 variance from the standard cost of £60 arises from the excess use of wood and is therefore a *usage variance*. Both of these variances are demonstrated diagrammatically in Exhibit 18.10. In each case, the actual cost is represented by the total rectangle, the standard cost by the unshaded area and the variance by the shaded area. Exhibit 18.10 (a) represents week one's production and shows the reason for the variance as being due to paying £4 per metre for wood rather than £3 per metre. Week two's production is represented in Exhibit 18.10 (b). The shaded area represents the variance from standard due to using 5 metres more wood than planned.

Exhibit 18.10 Standard costing variances

(a) Price variance.

(b) Usage variance.

(c) Total variance.

The joint variance

Analysing week three's variance is more complicated. The excess cost of £1 per metre for the 20 metres of wood which *should* have been used is a pure price variance. Similarly, without the price variance, the pure usage variance as a result of using five metres more than planned would have been £15. This, however, only comes to £35 and yet, with a total cost for week 3 of £100, the total variance from standard is £40. The £5 discrepancy arises not only from using an extra five metres of wood but also from paying £1 per metre more for those extra metres. As such, the £5 is a joint variance and is represented by the heavier shading in Exhibit 18.10 (c).

Logically, the joint variance arises because there has been both a price and a usage variance. As such it cannot be uniquely identified with either cause. Reporting it as a joint variance, however, would be confusing and so the custom has developed of treating the joint variance as part of the price variance. This is not as arbitrary as it seems. If feedback controls are to be effective – and standard costing is a form of feedback – then the earlier error messages are reported, the sooner corrective action can be taken. As a practical measure, stock is often purchased in advance of production. Extracting the price variance at this early stage warns management of a change in input costs at the earliest possible opportunity, allowing corrective action to be taken. In so doing, however, the price variance relates to *all* material as no material has yet been issued to production. As a result, the joint variance is attached to the price variance.

Developing the standard costing formulae

The above treatment of the joint variance allows formulae to be developed to measure the extent of any price or usage variance. The total material variance is simply the difference between what the *actual* production should have cost and what it did cost. The price variance will then be the actual units of input used multiplied by any difference between the standard and actual unit price of the input. With any price differences accounted for, materials are now valued at how much they should have cost, their standard cost. The usage variance will therefore be the difference between the actual and planned units used for the particular production level multiplied by the standard cost of the unit of input. These relationships can be expressed in the form of formulae where AP represents actual price, SP, the standard price, AQ the actual quantity use and SQ the standard quantity for the particular production level.

$$\text{Total material variance} = (AP \times AQ) - (SP \times SQ)$$

$$\text{Material price variance} = (AP - SP) \times AQ$$

or, multiplying the terms in the brackets by AQ

$$(AP \times AQ) - (SP \times AQ)$$

$$\text{Material usage variance} = (AQ - SQ) \times SP$$

or, multiplying the terms in the brackets by SP

$$(SP \times AQ) - (SP \times SQ)$$

Adding the two variances together simplifies to the total variance:

$$(AP \times AQ) - (SP \times AQ) + (SP \times AQ) - (SP \times SQ) = (AP \times AQ) - (SP \times SQ)$$

Logically, variances are merely differences between actual and planned performance. As such, it makes no difference whether the first term in any equation is what should have occurred or what actually occurred. Taking the material price variance as an example, this could equally have been written as $(SP - AP) \times AQ$. What does matter is determining whether the variable is favourable or adverse and this simply involves applying common sense. If the price paid for inputs is more than planned or the material used is greater than budgeted, costs will be greater than anticipated and so, other things being equal, profit will be less. Any variance will therefore be adverse.

This can now be applied to the data for week 3 of Renoir Ltd. The actual price paid for the wood was £4 as against a standard or planned price of £3. To produce five Cagnes should have required 20 metres of wood whereas the actual amount of wood used was 25 metres. The result is a total variance of £40, a price variance of £25 and a usage variance of £15 which agrees with the diagrammatic representation of the variances. The full workings for the variances are shown below.

Total material variance $= (AP \times AQ) - (SP \times SQ) = (£4 \times 25 \text{ metres}) - (£3 \times 20 \text{ metres})$
$\qquad\qquad\qquad\qquad = £40 \text{ (adverse)}$

Material price variance $= (AP - SP) \times AQ = (£4 - £3) \times 25 \text{ metres} = £25 \text{ (adverse)}$

or, using the alternative formula

Material price variance $= (AP \times AQ) - (SP \times AQ) = (£4 \times 25 \text{ metres}) - (£3 \times 25 \text{ metres})$
$\qquad\qquad\qquad\qquad = £25 \text{ (adverse)}$

Material usage variance $= (AQ - SQ) \times SP = (25 \text{ metres} - 20 \text{ metres}) \times £3$
$\qquad\qquad\qquad\qquad = £15 \text{ (adverse)}$

or, using the alternative formula

Material usage variance $= (SP \times AQ) - (SP \times SQ) = (£3 \times 25 \text{ metres}) - (£3 \times 20 \text{ metres})$
$\qquad\qquad\qquad\qquad = £15 \text{ (adverse)}$

Recording and reporting variances

Implicit within standard costing is the belief in scientific management – that inputs can be exactly specified for outputs. Standard costing is also an example of *management by exception*. Faced with so many other calls on their time, managers only want information when things are not going according to plan. This is what is meant by management by exception. Standard costing only directs managers' attention to costs when they deviate from plan. A typical management report will therefore highlight these differences. Exhibit 18.11 demonstrates both a traditional management report and a standard costing management report for Cagne production.

Exhibit 18.11 Traditional and standard costing reports

Traditional Management Report Period X Week 3		Standard Costing Management Report Period X Week 3		
Production level	5 units	Production level	5 units	
Material cost	£100	Standard material cost	£60	
		Material price variance	£25	(A)
		Material usage variance	£15	(A)
		Actual material cost	£100	

Many organisations that use standard costing incorporate the technique within their financial accounting system. On the assumption that there are no other costs and that all of production is sold, the necessary transactions can be shown by using the data relating to Renoir Ltd. These are recorded in Exhibit 18.12.

The first transaction is the acquisition of the material in exchange for cash. Immediately, the price variance is extracted, giving an early warning to management and leaving the stock valued at its standard cost. Mechanically, the transaction is similar to reducing stock to the lower of cost or net realisable value, or writing off a bad debt in financial accounting. The £75 of stock is then issued to production. However, £15 of material is wasted and this is shown as a separate expense under the heading of material usage variance. Production is then transferred to finished stock at how much it should have cost and, upon being sold, is charged as the cost of sales to the profit and loss account. Also charged to the profit and loss account is the expense of the two variances. The result is a profit and loss account that corresponds to the earlier management report.

Exhibit 18.12 *Recording the variances*

	Transactions					Period end adjustments		
Material	+£100	−£25	−£75					
Cash	−£100							
Material price variance		+£25				−£25		
Material usage variance				+£15				−£15
Production			+£75	−£15	−£60			
Finished stock					+£60	−£60		
Profit and loss account						+£60	+£25	+£15

Other variable cost variances

Logically, all other variable costs share the same cost behaviour pattern as materials. Consequently, a variance relating to any variable cost can be broken down into its price and usage elements. Given the level of production, any difference between the planned and actual costs of labour or variable overheads such as power can only result from one or other of these two reasons. Either the amount of the resource is different from planned or the unit price paid is different.

Labour variances

Despite this, many texts continue to develop the formulae for labour and variable overhead variances as if they were in some way different. Part of the reason is a change in terminology when considering other variable costs. For labour, the price variance becomes the wage rate variance while the usage variance becomes the labour efficiency variance. But labour rate is merely another expression for the unit price of labour while efficiency merely measures the difference between the hours which should have been used and the hours which were actually used – in other words, a usage variance. The only possible explanation for this change in terminology to describe what is essentially the same phenomenon maybe lies in the belief that describing labour in terms of unit prices is socially unacceptable – perhaps the earliest example of the use of politically correct language!

Allowing SR to represent the standard hourly wage rate, AR the actual hourly wage rate, AH the actual hours worked and SH the number of hours which should have been worked to achieve the particular output, the labour variances can be expressed as formulae:

$$\text{Total labour variance} = (SH \times SR) - (AH \times AR)$$

$$\text{Wage rate variance} = (AR - SR) \times AH$$

$$\text{Labour efficiency variance} = (AH - SH) \times SR$$

By substituting Q (quantity) and P (price) for H and R, the formulae become the same as the price and usage variances for materials.

Variable overhead variances

Similar differences in terminology apply to variable overheads, where the price variance becomes the variable overhead expenditure variance and the usage variance becomes the variable overhead efficiency variance. To make matters worse, texts often use different language to define what are, in effect, similar variances. To take but one example, a leading text defines the variable overhead variances as:

Variable overhead expenditure variance =
(Budgeted variable overhead for actual input volume – actual variable overhead cost)

Variable overhead efficiency variance =
(Standard quantity of input hours for actual production – actual input hours) ×
variable overhead rate

Putting these formulae into plain English shows they are nothing more than the formulae developed for materials. The phrase 'budgeted variable overhead for actual input volume' in the variable overhead expenditure variance is the same as saying, given the variable overhead units used, how much should they have cost? In other words, it is the actual usage multiplied by the planned or budgeted unit price. Similarly, the second phrase 'actual variable overhead cost' is the same as actual unit price multiplied by actual usage. Using AP to represent actual price, SP to represent standard price and AQ to represent actual quantity, the variable overhead expenditure variance reduces to (SP × AQ) – (AP × AQ), which is the same as the price variance for materials.

The variable overhead efficiency variance can also be shown to be a simple usage variance. Variable overheads such as power are generally expressed as quantity per hour although they can be converted to cost per unit by estimating how many hours are necessary to produce one unit. The variable overhead rate is then simply the predetermined or standard price per unit of variable overhead. The phrase 'standard quantity of input hours for actual production' is the same as saying the number of hours which should have been used to achieve the production level – in other words the standard quantity – while actual input hours are equivalent to the actual quantity of those hours. Allowing AQ to represent actual quantity, the variable overhead efficiency variance therefore reduces to the usage variance of (SQ – AQ) × SP. To demonstrate the similarity between all three variable cost variances, consider Example 18.5.

Totalling the actual cost of material, wages and variable overheads shows the actual cost of production is £19,030. With production of 420 Wordsmiths and a standard cost of £46, the total production should have cost £19,320 and so, overall, there is a favourable variance of £290. Using the formulae and abbreviations developed earlier, the individual variances are calculated in Exhibit 18.13 and presented in the form of a report. What is of interest is the identical mechanics of all three price and usage variances.

Example 18.5

Bennet Ltd makes a variety of products. During the month of June, 420 units of one product, the Wordsmith, were produced. 1,700 units of material were consumed at a cost of £13,430, wages for 800 hours totalled £4,720 while variable overheads came to £880. The unit standard costs for the Wordsmith are as follows:

Direct material	4 units × £8	£32
Direct labour	2 hours × £6	£12
Variable overheads	2 hours × £1	£2
Total standard cost		£46

Exhibit 18.13 *Variable overhead variances and their reporting*

Bennett Ltd Management Report – Wordsmith Production for Month of June

Note			
	Standard cost of 420 units	£19,320	
1	Material price variance	£170	(F)
2	Material usage variance	£160	(A)
3	Wage rate variance	£80	(F)
4	Labour efficiency variance	£240	(F)
5	Variable overhead expenditure variance	£80	(A)
6	Variable overhead efficiency variance	£40	(F)
	Actual cost of production	£19,030	

1	Material price variance = (AP × AQ) – (SP × AQ) = £13,430 – (£8 × 1,700) =	£170	(F)
2	Material usage variance = (AQ – SQ) × SP = (1,700 – 1,680ᵃ) × £8 =	£160	(A)
3	Wage rate variance = (AR × AH) – (SR × AH) = £4,720 – (£6 × 800) =	£80	(F)
4	Labour efficiency variance = (AH – SH) × SR = (800 – 840ᵇ) × £6 =	£240	(F)
5	Variable overhead expenditure variance = (AR × AH) – (SR × AH) = £880 – (£1 × 800) =	£80	(A)
6	Variable overhead efficiency variance = (800 – 840ᶜ) × £1 =	£40	(F)

ᵃ420 Wordsmiths produced × 4 units of material = 1,680
ᵇ420 Wordsmiths produced × 2 hours of labour = 840
ᶜ420 Wordsmiths produced × 2 hours of variable overhead = 840

FIXED OVERHEAD VARIANCES

Absorption and marginal costing

Fixed overheads exhibit different cost behaviour to variable costs. The only way that more fixed overhead costs can be incurred is by paying more for the same resources. A company, for example, could budget for the rent on its factory to be £20,000. If the actual rent is £25,000, the adverse variance of £5,000 could only have arisen from the rent being greater than planned, not from using more rent – unless of course, additional floor space was hired during the year. Such a variance is known as the *fixed overhead expendi-*

ture (or spending) variance. Formally, it is the difference between budgeted and actual fixed overhead expenditure.

Companies which operate a standard marginal costing system would analyse fixed overheads no further than this. Under an absorption costing system however, the actual volume of output might be different from the normal level on which absorption rates were based. As such, at the period end, there is likely to be overhead under- or over-absorbed which is either debited or credited to the profit and loss account. A company might, for example, estimate the cost of fixed overheads for the coming year at £100,000 and estimate activity at 50,000 units. Assuming the actual fixed overheads were as estimated but only 40,000 units were produced, then only £80,000 of overheads would have been charged to production. The balance of £20,000, the overhead under-absorbed, would be written off to the profit and loss account as an expense.

The fixed overhead volume variance

In effect this £20,000 is a kind of variance and is used as such in standard costing where it is known as the *fixed overhead volume variance*. The fixed overhead volume variance, unlike the variable cost usage variances, does not measure how efficiently resources have been used in actual production. Efficiency relates the change in outputs to the change in inputs but fixed costs, by definition, do not vary with changes in output. Rather it measures the extent to which fixed overheads have been under- or over-absorbed as a result of production volumes being different from planned.

The fixed overhead volume variance is defined as the difference between actual and budgeted production, multiplied by the predetermined or standard overhead absorption rate. Allowing AP to stand for actual production, BP to stand for budgeted production and SR to stand for the standard overhead absorption rate, the volume variance can be expressed as a formula:

$$\text{Fixed overhead volume variance} = (AP - BP) \times SR$$

Production can, as usual, be expressed either in labour hours or units of production, although where several products are manufactured, often only the former is a meaningful measure of activity. Allowing SH to equal the (standard) hours of work produced and BH to equal the budgeted or planned hours, the volume variance expressed in hours becomes:

$$\text{Fixed overhead volume variance} = (SH - BH) \times SR$$

Subdividing the overhead volume variance

Where production is expressed in labour hours, a subdivision of the volume variance is possible. In theory, a plant could be run at full capacity and yet run so inefficiently that nothing is produced. Equally, it might be run below its physical capacity, but extremely efficiently. Relating the hours the plant was physically used to the budgeted hours measures the extent to which its capacity was used. Relating the hours of work produced to the actual hours it was physically used is a measure of the efficiency of the plant whilst in operation. By multiplying both measures by the overhead absorption rate, these can then be expressed in financial terms as a subdivision of the volume variance. The former is known as the fixed overhead capacity variance, the latter as the fixed overhead efficiency variance. Allowing AH to represent actual hours worked, the two formulae are:

$$\text{Fixed overhead capacity variance} = (AH - BH) \times SR$$

$$\text{Fixed overhead efficiency variance} = (SH - AH) \times SR$$

The fixed overhead efficiency variance is not a measure of the efficiency of the plant as such. Rather, it is a further measure of labour efficiency. The physical measure of the overhead efficiency variance is identical to what is measured by the labour efficiency variance. Both are relating the time budgeted for the physical production to the actual time taken. Indeed, as already shown, fixed costs cannot result in efficiency because of their fixed nature. Example 18.6 demonstrates the calculation of the fixed overhead efficiency variance and all the other fixed overhead variances.

Example 18.6

Derwent and Langham make a component for video recorders. Its trade name is the Eboracum. Each Eboracum is budgeted to take five hours to make. For the month of September, the company budgeted to work 20,000 hours and incur fixed overheads of £10,000.

At the end of the month, actual fixed overheads incurred totalled £14,000, actual units produced totalled 3,000, while 18,000 labour hours were actually worked.

With budgeted fixed overheads of £10,000 and actual fixed overheads of £14,000, the fixed overhead expenditure variance will be £4,000 (adverse). This still leaves budgeted overheads of £10,000 to explain. The budgeted output was 20,000 hours. As each Eboracum is budgeted to take five hours to make, budgeted production was 4,000 units and so the overhead per unit was £2.50. Only 3,000 Eboracums were produced and so only £7,500 of overheads were absorbed into production. The balance of £2,500 is the adverse fixed overhead volume variance which represents overheads under-absorbed as a result of output being less than planned.

Rather than measuring production in terms of units, labour hours could have been used. With an output of 3,000 units and each unit supposed to take five hours to make, the *standard* output is 15,000 hours. Similarly, with budgeted overheads of £10,000 and budgeted production of 20,000 hours, the overhead absorption rate expressed in hours is 50p per hour. This enables the fixed overhead volume variance to be expressed in hours:

$$\text{Fixed overhead volume variance} = (SH - BH) \times SR = (15,000 - 20,000) \times 50p$$
$$= \text{£2,500 (A)}$$

Using labour hours enables the volume variance to be subdivided to show how much was due to a failure to use capacity and how much was due to production taking longer than planned. As the workforce was only employed for 18,000 hours, 2,000 hours of capacity were not used. Given that fixed overheads are 50p per hour, the fixed overhead capacity variance can be expressed as £1,000 adverse. The effect on overheads absorbed as a result of the workforce only producing 15,000 hours of output for the 18,000 hours employed can also be expressed in financial terms using the 50p fixed overhead absorption rate. The result is a fixed overhead efficiency variance of £1,500 adverse. Together, both variances add up to the fixed overhead volume variance and can be expressed in terms of the formulae already developed:

$$\text{Fixed overhead capacity variance} = (\text{AH} - \text{BH}) \times \text{SR} = (18,000 - 20,000) \times 50\text{p}$$
$$= \text{£1,000 (A)}$$

$$\text{Fixed overhead efficiency variance} = (\text{SH} - \text{AH}) \times \text{SR} = (15,000 - 18,000) \times 50\text{p}$$
$$= \text{£1,500 (A)}$$

These relationships can be expressed diagrammatically. Exhibit 18.14 shows a graph of the fixed overheads being recovered as hours increase. The slope of the graph is 50p for each hour and so at 20,000 hours the overhead absorbed – the budgeted overhead – is £10,000. Reading off the hours actually produced – the standard hours – shows £7,500 was absorbed and so the volume variance can be seen to be £2,500 adverse. Plotting the 18,000 hours *actually worked* subdivides the £2,500 into the £1,000 capacity variance and the £1,500 efficiency variance.

Exhibit 18.14 Fixed overhead volume, capacity and efficiency variances

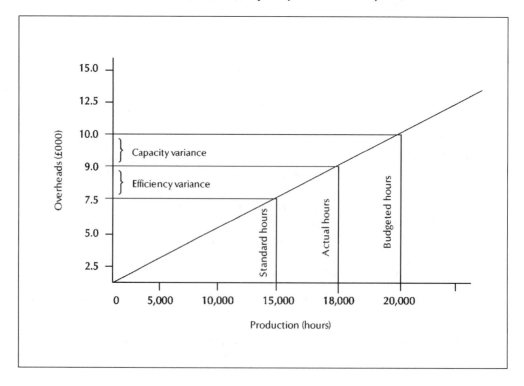

SALES VARIANCES

All of the cost variances had one thing in common. They were attempting to identify why costs differed from plan. Identifying a cost as being more than it should be, however, is equivalent to saying that profit is *less* than it should be. Given that profit is the assumed objective of the business, this seems a more meaningful way of interpreting the cost variances. As a variance is merely the difference between actual and planned data, it follows that planned data *plus* or *minus* any variances will equal the actual data. This is a second feature common to all variances. Together, this revised way of looking at variances enables the standard costing techniques to be applied to that part of the profit and loss account yet to be discussed, its turnover or sales revenue.

The sales price variance

Profit will be different from that budgeted if costs are not the same as planned, if selling prices are different from planned, or if the volume of sales is not the same as planned.

Consider a company which planned to sell 1,000 units for £20 each and assume it achieved this volume of sales without any cost variances. Actual and budgeted profit will be identical. Now assume the same conditions except that the selling price is £21. With costs and volume remaining the same, any difference in profit will be entirely due to the revised sales price. In this example, the extra profit will be £1 per unit sold, a total of £1,000. This is known as the *sales price variance* or the *sales margin price variance*. Allowing AS to equal the actual selling price, BS to equal the budgeted or standard selling price and AV to equal the actual sales volume, the formula for the sales price variance becomes:

$$\text{Sales price variance} = (AS - BS) \times AV$$

Unlike the price variance within the cost variances, the greater the difference between the planned and actual price, the more favourable is the variance. Applying the formula to the example, the variance is

$$\text{Sales price variance} = (£21 - £20) \times 1,000 = £1,000 \text{ (Favourable)}$$

The sales margin volume variance

The only other reason why actual profit might not be the same as budgeted profit is if the sales volume differs. Consider a business which planned to produce and sell 500 units at £10 each and whose marginal costs are £7 each. For the moment, assume there are no fixed costs. Now assume that all went according to plan except that actual sales and production were 550 units. The results are shown in Exhibit 18.15.

Although the marginal cost has increased by £350, there are no cost variances. Unit costs were according to plan. The only reason for the difference in total costs is because production volume is greater than budgeted. The increase in profit is entirely due to the change in sales volume. Each extra unit sold generated an extra £3 contribution and so with 50 extra units sold, the extra contribution resulting from the increase in sales is £150. This difference from budget is known as the *sales margin variance* or the *sales margin volume variance*. It shows the effect on profit or contribution of sales volume being different from budget. It also allows an exception report similar to the one shown in Exhibit 18.5 to be produced which immediately identifies why the budgeted profit was not the same as the actual profit.

Exhibit 18.15 Budgeted and actual profit statements

	Budgeted Profit and Loss Account	**Actual Profit and Loss Account**	**Standard Costing Profit Statement**	
Units	500	550	Budgeted contribution	£1,500
Turnover	£5,000	£5,500	Sales margin volume variance	£150 (F)
Marginal cost	£3,500	£3,850	Actual contribution	£1,650
Contribution	£1,500	£1,650		

Issues arising from sales variances

If the actual volume and the actual selling price is greater than budgeted, there is once again the problem of the joint variance. The traditional solution is to treat the joint variance as part of the sales price variance in a similar way to the material price variance.

A second difficulty, so far avoided, relates to the unit profitability in the sales margin volume variance. As part of the more general problem of all control models, signals should measure the extent of any error and be controllable. Other things being equal, the increase in profit from extra sales will be the extra revenue less the extra cost. With fixed costs being constant, the increase in profit will be the same as the increase in contribution. In other words, contribution measures the full strength of the error signal. In the sense that there is a cause and effect relationship between increased volume and increased variable costs, contribution is also controllable.

Absorption costing, including standard absorption costing, might therefore distort any error signal by appearing to reduce unit profitability to the extent of the unit fixed overheads and by implying that fixed overheads vary with activity. Despite this, perhaps for behavioural reasons outlined in Chapter 16, unit standard profit is often used for measuring the sales margin volume variance. As a result, it is possible to define the sales margin volume variance in two ways, one for standard marginal costing and one for standard absorption costing. Letting BV represent budgeted sales volume, AV the actual sales volume, and SM the standard or budgeted contribution for marginal costing or the standard or budgeted unit profit for absorption costing, the formula for the sales margin volume variance becomes:

$$\text{Sales margin volume variance} = (AV - BV) \times SM$$

There is a third issue which arises from the use of sales variances. Economics teaches that, other things being equal, the higher the price, the lower the demand. The sales price and sales margin volume variances are therefore often interlinked. This brings into question, the usefulness of separating the two variances.

In addition, if variances are to be viewed as error signals – to bring the system back into control – for those error signals to be meaningful, they have to be controllable.

Otherwise, at the least, they are a waste of time and effort. This difficulty applies to all variances, but particularly to sales variances. Some companies, for example, might be price takers, accepting whatever price the market gives. Similarly, the volume of sales may be under the control of consumers rather than the business although, under some circumstances, sales can possibly be gained at the expense of competitors.

PERFORMANCE REPORTS

The use and meaning of standard costs, budgets and variances is discussed later. Before considering them, it is useful to bring all the variances together and compare how reports would appear under a traditional accounting system, standard marginal costing and standard absorption costing. Example 18.7 provides the necessary data.

Example 18.7

Woodhouse-Lane plc manufactures the Shipley, a popular hi-fi accessory. In 19X3, it planned to manufacture and sell 10,000 units. Details of the standard cost data and the budgeted and actual profit and loss accounts are as follows:

Standard Cost Data		Profit Statement for the Year		
	(£)		Budget (£)	Actual (£)
Selling price	62	Turnover	620,000	617,500
Material 2 litres × £7	14	Material	140,000	120,000
Labour 3 hours × £6	18	Labour	180,000	159,500
Variable overhead	6	Variable overhead	60,000	60,900
Fixed overhead	9	Fixed overhead absorbed	90,000	85,500
		Overhead under-absorbed		6,500
Unit cost	47	Total cost	470,000	432,400
Unit profit	15	Profit for the year	150,000	185,100

Actual sales and production during 19X3 totalled 9,500 units. 20,000 litres of materials were used in production and 29,000 labour hours were worked. Both fixed and variable overheads are charged to production on the basis of labour hours.

Variable cost variances

Using the data of Woodhouse-Lane plc, the traditional variable cost variances can be calculated. Standard quantities will be based on the actual activity of 9,500 units of the Shipley. Any savings in standard costs arising from activity being 500 units below budget is automatically taken into account as a result of calculating the sales margin volume variance. The sales margin is the standard price less the standard unit cost. This is then multiplied by any change in physical volume to derive the sales margin volume variance. Adjusting for a change in volume via the sales margin volume variance therefore not only takes account of the reduced turnover but also the reduced standard costs caused by the lower volume. With this in mind, the variable cost variances are reproduced below in Exhibit 18.16 using the abbreviations developed earlier. The most convenient formula has been used in all cases. For the price variance this is often the expression $(AP \times AQ) - (SP \times AQ)$ as $(AP \times AQ)$ equals the actual cost and this is already given in the actual profit and loss account for Woodhouse-Lane plc.

Exhibit 18.16 Variable cost variances

Variance	Workings	Amount	
Material price =	$(AP \times AQ) - (SP \times AQ) = £120,000 - (£7 \times 20,000 \text{ litres}) =$	£20,000	(F)
Material usage =	$(AQ - SQ) \times SP = (20,000 \text{ litres} - \{2 \text{ litres} \times 9,500 \text{ units}\}) \times £7 =$	£7,000	(A)
Wage rate =	$(AR \times AH) - (SR \times AH) = £159,500 - (£6 \times 29,000 \text{ hours}) =$	£14,500	(F)
Labour efficiency =	$(AH - SH) \times SR = 29,000 \text{ hours} - \{3 \text{ hours} \times 9,500 \text{ units}\}) \times £6 =$	£3,000	(A)
Variable overhead expenditure =	$(AP \times AQ) - (SP \times AQ) = £60,900 - (£2 \times 29,000 \text{ hours}) =$	£2,900	(A)
Variable overhead efficiency =	$(AQ - SQ) \times SP = (29,000 \text{ hours} - 28,500 \text{ hours}) \times £2 =$	£1,000	(A)

Fixed overhead variances

The variable costs are charged to production on the basis of labour hours and so with three hours of labour, there will also be three hours of variable overheads at £2 per hour. Turning to the fixed overheads, the treatment will vary depending on whether marginal or absorption costing is being practised. With budgeted fixed overheads of £90,000 and actual fixed overheads of £92,000 – made up of those absorbed into production and those written off as an expense at the period end – both approaches will report a fixed overhead expenditure variance of £2,000 (Adverse). No further analysis takes place if standard marginal costing is in operation. If standard absorption costing is being used, however, further analysis is possible. Two solutions to the fixed overhead volume variance are given in Exhibit 18.17. The first is based on units of production. The second is based on hours of production. By converting units of production to hours, a further subdivision between capacity and efficiency is possible. If this refinement is undertaken, the standard overhead absorption rate of £9 per unit has to be converted to £3, its equivalent expressed in hours.

Exhibit 18.17 Fixed overhead variances

Variance	Workings	Amount	
Expenditure =	Budgeted – Actual fixed overhead = £90,000 – £92,000	£2,000	(A)
Volume =	$(AP - BP) \times SR = (9,500 \text{ units} - 10,000 \text{ units}) \times £9 \text{ per unit} =$	£4,500	(A)
Alternatively, volume =	$(SH - BH) \times SR = (28,500 \text{ hours} - 30,000 \text{ hours}) \times £3 \text{ per hour} =$	£4,500	(A)
Capacity =	$(AH - BH) \times SR = (29,000 \text{ hours} - 30,000 \text{ hours}) \times £3 =$	£3,000	(A)
Efficiency =	$(SH - AH) \times SR = (\{9,500 \text{ units} \times 3 \text{ hours}\} - 29,000 \text{ hours}) \times £3 \text{ per hour} =$	£1,500	(A)

Sales variances

The final variances relate to turnover. Irrespective of whether marginal or absorption costing is used, the sales price variance will be the same as it simply measures the difference between budgeted and actual selling prices, multiplied by actual activity. Physically, the sales margin volume variance will also be the same. It will be the difference between planned and actual sales volume. Expressed in financial terms, however, there will be a difference. Under absorption costing, the margin used will be the standard unit profit of £15. With marginal costing, the emphasis is on contribution and so adding back the unit fixed costs of £9 gives a standard unit contribution of £24. Both approaches are shown in Exhibit 18.18, where the actual selling price of £65 was found by dividing the actual sales volume of 9,500 units into the actual turnover of £617,500.

Exhibit 18.18 Sales variances

Variance	Workings	Amount	
Sales price =	(AS – BS) × AV = (£65 – £62) × 9,500 units =	£28,000	(F)
Sales margin volume (marginal costing) =	(AV – BV) × SM = (9,500 units – 10,000 units) × £24 =	£12,000	(A)
Sales margin volume (absorption) =	(AV – BV) × SM = (9,500 units – 10,000 units) × £15 =	£7,500	(A)

Reporting the variances

Having calculated all the variances, the actual profit and loss account of Woodhouse-Lane plc can be re-cast in standard costing terms. Both a marginal costing and absorption costing approach is shown in Exhibit 18.19. The standard costing statements recognise that variances are simply the difference between planned and actual performance and so, starting from the budgeted profit and adjusting for variances, the final result must be the actual profit.

Exhibit 18.19 The standard costing profit reports

Woodhouse–Lane plc Standard Costing Statements – Year 19X3				
	Standard marginal costing		Standard absorption costing	
	(£)	(£)	(£)	(£)
Budgeted profit		150,000		150,000
Sales price variance	28,500 (F)		28,500 (F)	
Sales margin volume variance	12,000 (A)		7,500 (A)	
Material price variance	20,000 (F)		20,000 (F)	
Material usage variance	7,000 (A)		7,000 (A)	
Wage rate variance	14,500 (F)		14,500 (F)	
Labour efficiency variance	3,000 (A)		3,000 (A)	
Variable overhead expenditure variance	2,900 (A)		2,900 (A)	
Variable overhead efficiency variance	1,000 (A)		1,000 (A)	
Fixed overhead expenditure variance	2,000 (A)		2,000 (A)	
Fixed overhead capacity variance			3,000 (A)	
Fixed overhead efficiency variance		35,100 (F)	1,500 (A)	35,100 (F)
Actual profit		185,100		185,100

In this example, because there are no stocks, the overall profit under both absorption and marginal costing must be the same, as all income and all expenditure will have been charged to the profit and loss account, irrespective of the costing method. The only difference between the two statements will relate to the sales margin volume variance and the two fixed overhead variances under absorption costing which combine to make up the fixed overhead volume variance. As the standard sales margin is less under absorption costing because of the element of fixed costs, the adverse sales margin volume variance will also appear less significant. This is, however, balanced by the charging of the overhead under-absorbed within the fixed overhead capacity and efficiency variances as a result of volume being less than planned. Standard marginal costing, by using the standard contribution as the margin and by charging all of the fixed costs to the profit and loss account as a period expense, addresses this reduction in profits as a result of lower volume in a more direct manner. As such, it shows a more meaningful cause–effect relationship. Directly arising from selling 500 less units, profit decreased by £12,000.

SUMMARY

This chapter has been concerned with the attention-directing role of management accounting. It has further demonstrated that management accounting is an important and integral part of the management control process. Four conditions were identified for control: an objective must exist; current activity must be measurable and comparable; cause and effect needs to be identifiable; and corrective action must be possible. The systems control model was then re-introduced. Although a useful model to demonstrate the workings of accounting systems, it is not a perfect analogy as accounting feedback signals are neither automatic nor unambiguous.

The two major accounting control systems of budgets and standard costing were introduced. Both depend on predetermined performance measures against which to compare actual performance. Budgeting, however, is time-based whereas the focus of standard costing is on the individual unit.

The approach taken to describe both budgeting and standard costing was essentially mechanistic. This allowed the causal relationships to be identified. What was not discussed is the use made of budgets and standard costing in practice. This is the subject of Chapter 19.

FURTHER READING

Horngren, C.T. and Foster, G. (1991) *Cost Accounting: A Managerial Emphasis*, Prentice Hall.
Arnold, J. and Hope, T. (1983) *Accounting for Managerial Decisions*, Prentice Hall.

TEST YOUR UNDERSTANDING

1 Identify the four prerequisites for successful management control.

2 Negative feedback is:
   (a) the distorting of information when reporting back to managers;
   (b) the reporting of adverse information;
   (c) increasing adverse variances;
   (d) increasing positive variances;
   (e) the acting on a variance to reduce subsequent deviations from plan.

3 What is meant by the term 'noise' and how does it occur in accounting systems?

4 Explain the meaning of the term 'master budget'?

5 Flexible budgeting refers to:
   (a) revising budgetary data to show what the budget would have been had it been based on the activity which actually occurred;
   (b) a non-dogmatic, participative approach to setting budgets by managers;
   (c) a non-dogmatic, participative approach to interpreting variances by managers;
   (e) none of these.

6 What is the essential difference between budgeting and standard costing?

7 A company produces nine units of product X in a four-week period. The standard material cost per unit is 7 litres at a price of £8 per litre. The actual material consumed in making product X is 65 litres costing £533 in total. The material price variance for the period is:
   (a) £29 favourable;
   (b) £29 adverse;
   (c) £12.60 favourable;
   (d) £12.60 adverse;
   (e) £13 favourable;
   (f) £13 adverse.

8 What is the joint variance?

9 How do fixed overhead variances differ from variable cost variances such as material and labour?

10 A company operates a standard marginal costing system. The standard selling price of product Y is £30 per unit. The standard marginal costs are £8 for labour and £12 for materials. The actual cost of labour for a unit of Y was £9 and for material, £14. The planned sales volume was 2,000 units of Y while the actual volume was 2,400 units at a selling price of £31. The sales volume variance is:
   (a) £400 favourable;
   (b) £2,400 favourable;
   (c) £4,000 favourable;
   (d) £2,000 favourable;
   (e) £12,400 favourable;
   (f) £3,200 favourable.

QUESTIONS

1 Sheffield Ltd is an engineering company producing a single product. It works a 50 week year and the sales forecast for the next 50 weeks is 1,263,220 units made up as follows:

Week	1	2	3	4	Subsequent weeks
Unit sales	17,640	19,600	25,480	28,420	25,480

A similar pattern and volume of sales is anticipated next year. Because of the technical nature of the product, production has to take place one week prior to sale. In addition, there is a 2 per cent wastage which is only discovered on completion. This wastage has no monetary value.

The production workforce is employed by the week at a cost of £270,000 and is able to produce up to 27,000 units before taking account of wastage. Any production over this figure can only be achieved by paying overtime, the cost for which is estimated to be £15 per unit produced. The material component of each unit is £3.50. The budgeted overhead for the 50 weeks is estimated at £7,734,000 and is charged to production on the basis of the number of units produced.

(a) On the assumption that all production takes place one week before sale, prepare a production budget for each of the first three weeks showing the physical units to be produced and the total and unit cost of production.

(b) Making use of the data in the question, prepare a revised production schedule which will maximise cost savings.

2 Butterworth and Maunders Ltd makes several products. Details of the budgeted and actual results of one product, the Blenheim, is reproduced below. Each Blenheim was budgeted to use three metres of material and two hours of labour. Both fixed and variable overhead are charged to production on the basis of labour hours and there was no opening or closing stock of any form. Actual material used totalled 24,960 metres and 14,820 labour hours were worked.

Profit statement for the year

	Budget	Actual
Units produced and sold	8,000	7,800
Turnover	£440,000	£468,000
Materials	(£144,000)	(£124,800)
Labour	(£128,000)	(£121,524)
Variable overhead	(£32,000)	(£26,676)
Fixed overhead	(£40,000)	(£42,000)
Profit	£96,000	£153,000

From the above data, produce a statement reconciling the budgeted profit to the actual profit using standard absorption costing variances.

3* Halifax Ltd makes a single product, the Porter. Over the next twelve months, the company plans to produce 1,500 units. Detailed sales for the first eight months, based on a selling price of £140.00, are as follows:

Month	January	February	March	April	May	June	July	August
Units	100	120	130	140	130	120	100	80

The unit material cost of each Porter will be £20 while labour cost per unit is estimated at £8. Rent and rates for the year are forecast to be £12,000 and these are payable quarterly in advance, beginning 1 January. Heat, light and power, forecast at £6,000 for the year, is payable quarterly in arrears at the end of March, June, September and December. The directors of Halifax Ltd believe that 50 per cent of the rent and rates and 50 per cent of the light heat and power relate to manufacturing with the balance being attributable to administration and distribution. In addition, administration and distribution will incur salaries of £57,600 for the year as well as other expenses of £38,400 p.a. Factory overheads are absorbed into production on the basis of estimated yearly production. Any overheads under- or over-absorbed at the end of six month are charged or credited to the profit and loss account for internal reporting purposes. The company's balance sheet at 31 December was as follows:

	Cost	Depreciation to date	Net book value
	(£)	(£)	(£)
Fixed assets			
Factory plant and machinery	150,000	90,000	60,000
Office equipment	42,000	16,800	25,200
	192,000	106,800	85,200
Current assets			
Stocks		6,700	
Debtors		5,360	
Cash		8,600	
		20,660	
Current liabilities			
Trade creditors	4,400		
Corporation tax payable	8,200		
Dividends payable	2,000	14,600	6,060
			91,260
Financed by			
Ordinary share capital			40,000
Retained earnings			51,260
			91,260

The factory machinery is depreciated at 10 per cent p.a straight line while the office equipment is depreciated on a similar basis at 20 per cent p.a. This policy is likely to continue throughout the forthcoming year. The creditors comprise £2,000 incurred in November and £2,400 incurred in December, the latter being represented by raw materials within the figure of stocks on the balance sheet sufficient for January's budgeted production. There is currently no work-in-progress, nor is there any planned in the foreseeable future. Production in any one month is equal to estimated sales in the subsequent month while, because of delivery difficulties, purchase of raw materials take place one month prior to use. Trade creditors allow two months to pay.

All sales are on credit with half of the debtors paying one month after the month when the sale takes place and the balance paying in the subsequent month. At the end of December, £1,600 of the debtors relate to November sales and the balance to sales in December.

Factory wages are paid monthly at the end of the month in which they are incurred, as are office salaries and expenses. The dividends are payable at the end of February while the corporation tax is payable at the end of June.

Using the above information, produce sales, purchases, production and cash budgets for Halifax Ltd for each of the first six months of the forthcoming year and a profit and loss account and balance sheet at the period end.

4* Budgetary controls have been likened to a system of thermostatic control. In what ways is the analogy inappropriate?

CHAPTER 19

Accounting, organisations and behaviour

A great many advantages are claimed for budgets and standard costing. Allegedly, they aid the planning and controlling processes; they motivate; and they provide a system to authorise expenditure in large organisations. Often these claims are presented as self-evident. In fact little is known about planning and control processes in organisations because much information is not in the public domain. What evidence there is, however, suggests that budgeting and standard costing are not the straightforward technical devices they appear to be.

This chapter:

- Examines the traditional role of budgets and the influence on their design of the universal solution approach of the early management thinkers

- Considers an alternative, contingency framework which recognises that there is no single 'one best way' of developing and using budgets

- Discusses the changing nature of budgets if objectives are unclear and/or there exists uncertainty over outcomes

- Surveys some of the motivational literature from organisational behaviour theory and relates this to the accounting context

S tandard costing and budgeting have many features in common. Both can be used as part of the management control system to identify deviations from plan. Almost inevitably, if a business operates a standard costing system, it will also operate a budgeting system. Considering how budgets are used in organisations will therefore also address the issue of how standard costing is used.

THE TRADITIONAL ROLES OF BUDGETS

As accounting information is often the only quantifiable measure of an organisation's performance, budgets derived from it are used for various purposes. Seven possible functions of budgets have been identified. Budgets can be used to aid planning, to coordinate activities, to assist control, to communicate information, to motivate managers, to evaluate performance and to authorise actions.

Planning, coordinating and controlling

The role of budgets in planning, coordinating and controlling has already been demonstrated. Planning forces managers to acknowledge the existence of the often uncontrollable environment – at least at the planning stage – and to best arrange those activities which are controllable in order to achieve objectives. For planning to be meaningful requires a predictive model of cause and effect. The very process of planning highlights interrelationships between the organisation's departments. Any bottlenecks or other difficulties can be identified and, at least in theory, revisions made to the plan. This is the coordinating role of budgets. In the conventional sense, control is then the reporting back of variances and the remedying of any errors by management.

Budgets and management performance

Budgets provide a target for managers to achieve. As such, it is sometimes argued that budgets are a motivating device. Certainly, budgets are likely to influence the behaviour of managers. Unfortunately, this is not always in the way anticipated by their designers. Budgets are also used to evaluate the performance of those managers, with financial and other rewards sometimes being associated with a good performance relative to budget. As performance evaluation and motivation are such important aspects of budgets – aspects which are often understated when considering the mechanical complexities of budgets – they are considered separately later.

Budgets as authority

Finally, there is the authorising role of budgets which limits how much a department can spend. This quasi-legal function is most often found in the public sector but it can also be found elsewhere. It is associated with responsibility accounting but more particularly with segments where the only possible controls are the input controls outlined in Chapter 16. Input controls are used where there is no clear cause–effect relationship, behavioural control nor any meaningful way of measuring outputs. The legal department and the research and development department are examples where input controls are often the only controls which can be applied and where budgets primarily serve an authorising function.

CAUSES OF VARIANCES

Bromwich[1] has identified five general reasons why variances occur. The first, inefficiency in operation, implies that reasonable standards have not been met because of some failing of management. The second arises if the plan or standards were originally incorrect or became incorrect by environmental changes. Reporting of such variances may require plans to be revised rather than attempting to change actual performance in subsequent periods. As such the variance is serving an educational role.

Unfortunately, traditional variances will not always identify environmental change. A purchasing department may have acquired 1,000 units of raw materials for £8 each. If the unit standard cost had earlier been set at £10, there is a favourable price variance of £2,000. If, however, the market price at *the time of purchase* was only £7, the reported variance is distorting reality. Given the circumstances, the cost of the material should have only been £7,000.

The £2,000 favourable price variance can be subdivided. The first part, known as the *planning variance*, is £3,000 favourable and represents the error in the forecast. It is found by deducting the revised standard from the original standard. The £8,000 actual cost can then be compared with the revised standard of £7,000. The resulting £1,000 adverse variance is known as the *operating variance*. It represents the 'true' variance when measured against the best performance achievable in the circumstances. Combined, the two variances sum back to the traditional price variance of £2,000 favourable. All variances – both price and usage – can be subdivided in this way. Although presenting a more meaningful error signal, the major difficulty is that managers are likely to define the revised standard as equalling the actual price or usage achieved and so eliminate any operating variance!

The third way a variance can occur is if there is poor communication of standards and budgetary goals, while the fourth way an error can occur is by the actions of another department. The sales department, for example, could introduce a rush order which causes the production department to incur overtime payments. Although shown as an adverse wage rate variance against the production department, the real cause lies with the sales department.

Finally, a variance can occur through random fluctuations. Standards are often only averages. In addition, clerical errors in financial records can distort the reporting of actual results although these are likely to be corrected in subsequent periods. Whatever the reason, taking one period with another, these errors should average out so that no corrective action is required. One difficulty, however, is determining whether an error is merely random or an early warning of something more significant.

SETTING STANDARDS OF PERFORMANCE

The measurement of standards

Affecting the size of reported variances will be the basis on which standards or budgets are set. Five possible measures have been identified. One option is to use historical data, although this reinforces inefficiencies from previous periods. Another possibility is to use similar standards from other functions, but this assumes such comparisons exist. A third approach is to estimate standards in advance via work study and other techniques of the scientific management era. For some tasks this is viable. However, not only might the exercise be expensive, it also requires a detailed understanding of cause and effect relationships. Causality might be determinable for simple tasks. For more complex ones it will be much more difficult.

Ex post standards of the form used in planning and operating variances are a further possibility. However, as already pointed out, it is difficult to apply hindsight fairly. In addition, if being used for motivation, the standard needs to be known in advance. Lastly, the standard could be the performance necessary to achieve the objective of the business or department. The main criticism of such a measure is that it might not be achievable and so variances will always be adverse.

Managers and management

Beyond these technical problems of standard measurement is a wider issue. Many of the assumptions underpinning budgets and standard costing can be traced back to the ideas of Taylor and Fayol: the division of organisations into (apparently) independent sub-units, the simplistic identification of cause and effect, and the belief in universal, 'one best way' solutions. In the real world, organisational activity is complex and can rarely be summarised in a single set of variances. Trade-offs have to be made – for example, between quality and quantity or long term versus short term costs – and this involves judgement. Many tasks are interdependent and require cooperation between departments. Measuring such departments *as though they were independent* – and that is what standard costing and budgeting tend to do – may encourage managers to only concern themselves with their own function, at the expense of the company as a whole.

Management's role is to establish plans, monitor actual performance and take any necessary corrective action to bring performance back to plan. However, there is a difference between management as a function and managers as members of the organisation. The work of managers is complex and varied and often involves both discretion and judgement. Evaluating their individual performance will therefore also involve judgement. As individuals, they are not impartial and value-free but are in the organisation as part of the problem and part of the solution. They are the people most likely to know what is possible when designing budgets but, in the knowledge they will be held accountable, they may be less than forthcoming when setting their own budget targets.

CONTINGENCY THEORY

Limitations of traditional theories

None of these issues are addressed within the mechanics of budgeting and standard costing, with their implicit acceptance of the ideas of Taylor and Fayol and their belief in universal, 'one best way' solutions. Organisations comprise people and yet the traditional organisational theories view them as little more than additional factors of production. The traditional theories view the organisation as a closed system with a clear objective, a full understanding of cause and effect, the ability to unambiguously measure plans and actual performance, and the ability to take corrective action. Responsibility centres are established and, using the hierarchical organisational structure, authority and responsibility is assigned to individuals who are held accountable for the achievement of specific tasks. By assuming the organisation is a closed system with all the conditions for control in place, rationality appears to rule. With accounting as a subset of the management control system, accounting controls follow a similar pattern. Budgets and standard costing are viewed as programmable, that is they are assumed to have a clear objective and well-defined relationships between inputs and outputs which allow unambiguous solutions to be determined. This was the approach developed in Chapter 18.

Organisations, however, are not homogeneous. They face different environments and different technologies and there is increasing anecdotal and empirical evidence that accounting control systems vary with the circumstances in which the organisation operates. Burns and Stalker,[2] for instance, suggest that the traditional mechanistic structure is more appropriate to stable organisations facing known production technologies and an unchanging market. This is less appropriate for organisations in a dynamic technological environment where controls – including accounting controls – need to be less formal and more flexible.

As an example, consider a dairy making milk deliveries. With established customers, regular demand and an established production technology, cause and effect is clear and a 'correct way' of production and selling will have been established. There is no need to be constantly searching the environment for changes in technology or changes in customers and their tastes. As such, a closed system approach might be adequate. Budgets can be accurately established for production costs, selling prices and sales volume for each delivery round and managers held accountable for these in the traditional way. Now consider a 'pop' music record company. Detailed forecasts of sales volumes are impossible as consumer tastes vary greatly over relatively short time periods. Groups and singers currently popular may be replaced by others within six months. There is a need therefore to be constantly searching the environment. Applying rigid controls in such circumstances might not be particularly helpful. For example, promotional expenses for each recording can only be determined when likely consumer response is more accurately known, that is, once additional information from the environment has been received. Such information may not be available at the start of the budgeting exercise. In such a changing world, holding managers responsible for budgets agreed several months earlier might not be particularly helpful in achieving organisational objectives.

Modern theories of organisation

Modern theories of organisation recognise these differences. They take an open systems approach by relating organisational structure to the wider environment in which the organisation operates. Only by successfully adapting to that environment can the organisation survive. This is often a two-way process with the organisation not only being influenced by the environment but also, in turn, helping to shape it. Launching a new product, for example, changes the tastes of consumers and so changes the environment. Modern organisational theories therefore relate the design of organisations and their accounting systems to the specific circumstances faced by the enterprise, with the appropriate system being *contingent* on those circumstances.

This has given rise to an approach to organisational design known as *contingency theory*. In fact, no coherent theory has yet developed, only a series of insights. Nevertheless, its general conclusion is valid: that to achieve management control requires different structures in different circumstances and that universal approaches are inappropriate. Where it has so far failed is in developing a prescription to identify the optimal structure and features necessary for any particular organisation.

Contingency theory and management accounting

Applied to management accounting, contingency theory attempts to match the design of the accounting system with the circumstances of the organisation. Although there is no coherent theory to explain the character of different accounting systems, several factors have been identified which influence their design. One factor, technology, has long been recognised by accountants. Chapter 16, for instance, identified job, batch and process costing as three major ways of determining costs according to the technology of the organisation. Technology, however, goes beyond this to include the interdependence of departments. There is some evidence, for instance, that budgets are applied less rigidly where there is a great deal of interdependence between departments.

A second feature is the external environment. This was brought out in the earlier comparison of a dairy and a record producer. Factors influencing environmental uncertainty include, the rate of change in the industry, the number of products manufactured by the enterprise and the hostility of competitors. Intuitively, the greater the uncertainty, the less rigid budgets should be. Indeed success might more reasonably be measured by management's ability to react to the changes in the environment rather than its ability to adhere to, perhaps, out-of-date budgets.

From an accounting point of view, the organisational structure itself may be a contingent variable. Its size, interdependence of departments, the extent of decentralisation and the availability of resources are all possible influences on the design and use of budgets and standards. Other things being equal, the larger the size of the organisation, the more formal is the budgeting process. In a very small firm, the budget may be no more than ideas in the managing director's head. This might even be preferable to a formal system, with the budget being constantly adapted as new information from the environment is recognised by the managing director. Such informality is not possible with larger organisations, if only because the managing director would not have full knowledge of all the detailed cause–effect relationships within the enterprise. To take another example of an organisational factor, if a business is faced with resource constraints, the budget focus will be less on sales volume and more on making the maximum possible use of those resources.

Although it is possible to identify a whole variety of other different contingent variables, the only other variable regularly identified in the literature is that of culture. Culture is the shared values and beliefs of a group of people. Organisations consist of people and so management control, including budgets and standard costing, are concerned with influencing their behaviour. Control systems incompatible with an organisation's value system are likely to be met by resistance from managers and subordinates alike, who may be motivated to defeat the purpose of those controls.

UNCERTAINTY OVER OBJECTIVES AND UNCERTAINTY OVER CAUSALITY

Organisations comprise groups of individuals who bring with them their own value systems and beliefs. In addition, the organisation faces the wider, external environment which, although managers might not be fully able to monitor or understand it, affects the well-being of the organisation. To make sense of all this potential confusion, budgets and standard costing superimpose a sense of rationality by assuming objectives and causality are known. With the objectives of the managers perhaps differing from the objectives of the organisation, with organisational objectives possibly being uncertain because of uncertainties in the environment and with cause–effect relationships not being fully understood, there is a constant tension in organisations between the rational, closed system approach and the uncertain, open systems approach. Within this are two issues faced by the accounting system. Its technical features may be inappropriate for the organisation or the way it is used may not be appropriate – the very point identified by Johnson and Kaplan as 'relevance lost'. This is particularly apposite when considering their complaint that management accounting has become subservient to financial accounting.

Earl and Hopwood[3] recognised that not all budgets are the programmable, rational exercises of traditional theory. Because of lack of clear objectives or because of an inability to identify results with cause and effect, budgets and other accounting controls may not be programmable but rather involve judgement and values by the participants. As a result, there are four possible scenarios a firm can face. These are identified in Exhibit 19.1.

Exhibit 19.1 Uncertainty and accounting control systems

| | | Relative uncertainty over objectives | |
		Certain	Uncertain
Relative uncertainty over results	Certain	Computation *Answer machine*	Bargaining *Ammunition machine*
	Uncertain	Judgemental *Learning machine*	Inspirational *Rationalisation machine*

Certainty of objectives

If a company is operating in a stable and known environment and has considerable past experience, there will be relative certainty not only about objectives but also about any results which will follow from proposals. This enables budgeting to be a rational, mathematical or programmable exercise. Exhibit 19.1 identifies this style as computational. Budgets become 'answer machines' which introduce structure into decision making in the light of agreed objectives and hence assist integration and coordination by following logical rules. This is the way budgets and standard costing were treated in Chapter 18.

Where objectives are clear but the consequences of actions are not foreseeable, decisions (i.e. budgets) are the result of judgement with organisational participants subjectively evaluating the range of possible outcomes in the light of an agreed objective. Judgemental decision making involves acknowledging the uncertainties of outcomes and learning from them. Participants should not be searching for a particular answer – as in the 'answer machine' scenario – but exploring the problems and implication of the assumptions before reaching a judgement, perhaps with the help of 'what-if' analysis on a spreadsheet.

Uncertainty of objectives

If objectives are uncertain but the consequences of actions are clear, the rationale for action becomes political rather than programmable, as participants in the budget process seek to further their own objectives. The budgetary process is therefore characterised by bargaining and compromise. Here, budgets become ammunition to articulate and promote particular ends.

Finally, there is the situation where neither objectives nor causality are clear. Decision making becomes even less clear than in the previous case – hence Hopwood's use of the term 'inspirational'. In an inspirational environment, accounting control mechanisms are used to justify and legitimise actions taken. Budgets become a 'rationalisation machine' where actions are decided upon and data is then manipulated to meet the pre-set parameters. Budgets can also then be used to justify decisions which would otherwise be more difficult, a process of sanitising whereby proposals can be turned down without being evaluated with the explanation that 'it's not in the budget'. The recognition that budgets can be used as rationalisation machines, because objectives and results are uncertain, also provides an explanation for the 'cuts all round' policy so often used in organisations at a time of retrenchment even though the effect on individual projects might be dysfunctional.

What is clear from the work of Earl and Hopwood is that budgets are used in ways other than those specified in traditional accounting textbooks, where the emphasis is on budgets as answer machines. As soon as the conventional model of budgets is rejected, accounting information becomes a valuable resource. It can serve to constrain and influence behaviour in a political context, it can facilitate the exercise of judgement and it can legitimise what has been done and what might be done. Perhaps therefore uncertainties about objectives and uncertainties about outcomes should be identified as contingent variables – although practically this would be difficult to do because of the lack of any empirical measure or readily available evidence to enable organisations to be so classified.

BUDGETS, MOTIVATION AND PERFORMANCE APPRAISAL

Irrespective of whether the budgeting process is computational, bargaining, judgemental or inspirational, once the budget is accepted, it has then to be achieved. Results, however, do not just happen. They need the active participation and support of the individuals who make up the organisation.

Factors influencing performance

An individual's performance will depend on three factors: (a) the amount of effort expended; (b) the ability of the individual; and (c) uncontrollable factors such as luck or misfortune which change the complexity of the individual's tasks. The ability of individuals depends on their aptitude, their training and their experience. Uncontrollable factors, by definition, cannot be analysed further. This leaves effort, the amount of physical or mental power exerted by an individual in pursuit of a goal.

Motivation

For the good of the enterprise, individual effort needs to be directed towards organisational goals. The merging of individual goals with the goals of the organisation is known as goal congruence and can be defined as the extent to which an individual shares the goals and aspirations of senior management. Motivation is therefore the amount of an individual's energy that is directed towards the achieving of organisational goals. It is not the same as performance. Performance also requires ability and, at times, luck. Nevertheless, motivation is an important part of performance as it can be directly influenced by the accounting system.

Developments in motivation theory have tended to follow the changing approaches found in organisational theory. Theories of motivation fall into two broad categories, content theories and process theories.

CONTENT THEORIES OF MOTIVATION

Content theories are concerned with identifying the specific factors which result in high motivation, independent of the individuals concerned or the organisation in which they operate. Perhaps the most extreme example of this was Taylor's theory of scientific management, which identified motivation as paying employees to do the job and dismissing them if they failed after their training.

Maslow's hierarchy of needs

A less extreme, but still universal, theory of motivation was put forward by Maslow[4] when he developed his hierarchy of needs, reproduced in Exhibit 19.2. The most basic needs are physiological and include the need for food and drink, and air to breath. Next are safety and security needs such as housing, clothing and freedom from anxiety. This is then followed by belonging needs such as love and affection and the need to be accepted by one's peers. These first three needs are deficiency needs which have to be satisfied if the individual is to be comfortable.

The next two needs are fundamentally different. They are concerned with personal growth and development. Esteem needs include a positive self-image and respect by others. The final hierarchy of needs, once all the others have been achieved, were termed self-actualisation needs. They include realising one's full potential and becoming all that one is capable of being.

Maslow suggested that lower needs must be satisfied before higher needs can have any motivational impact and that once a need is met, it ceases to be a motivator. Motivation should therefore be aimed at needs that are recognised by the individual but not yet achieved. As appealing as the theory might appear, it suffers from several deficiencies. Some motivating factors cannot be uniquely identified with a particular hierarchy. Being paid a bonus, for example, could be seen as both a physiological need, an esteem need or even as a contribution towards self-actualisation needs. More significantly, research has shown that not all five levels of need are always present, the actual hierarchy does not always conform with the one proposed by Maslow and the need structure is more dynamic, unstable and variable than the theory suggests.[5]

Exhibit 19.2 Maslow's hierarchy of needs

Motivation-hygiene factors

A more specific theory of motivation was developed by Herzberg[6] who interviewed 200 accountants and engineers in the USA. They were asked to recall times when they felt especially satisfied and motivated by their jobs and times when they felt especially dissatisfied and demotivated. Herzberg found two different sets of factors were identified with two kinds of feelings about work. For example, a person who identified low pay as a cause of dissatisfaction would not necessarily identify high pay as a cause of satisfaction and motivation. From this he was able to conclude that the dissatisfying factors – what he chose to call hygiene factors – could adversely affect performance by their presence but their absence would not positively motivate improved performance. Hygiene factors included supervision, pay, working conditions, company policies and interpersonal relationships. Only those factors which positively contributed towards satisfaction were likely to motivate individuals. Satisfying or motivating factors included achievement, recognition, responsibility and advancement. Improve these and motivation would increase.

Several criticisms of Herzberg's work have been advanced. Other researchers, using a different research methodology have not been able to replicate the two-factor classification. Accountants and engineers may not be a representative sample. The theory is a universal one which ignores differences between individuals. Subsequent research has shown contradictions with, for example, pay appearing as a hygiene factor in some studies but as a motivating factor in others. Other research has shown that reactions to Herzberg's factors vary with an individual's age and position in the organisation. Finally, the theory does not define the relationship between satisfaction and motivation.[6]

The theories of Maslow and Herzberg are very similar, with the first three of Maslow's hierarchies approximating to Herzberg's hygiene factors. Both theories emphasise the general needs of individuals and categorise factors or contents which motivate behaviour. However, they focus on only a few aspects of the total relationship between individuals and the organisation. Their greatest weakness is that they say very little about the process of motivation. For example, two people might be equally motivated by esteem needs and yet may pursue totally different paths to satisfy those needs.

PROCESS THEORIES OF MOTIVATION

Content theories describe the causes of motivated behaviour by identifying needs. Process theories, however, describe the processes which give rise to motivated behaviour by predicting how individuals satisfy those needs. Three theories will be outlined: equity theory, expectancy theory and goal setting theory.

Equity theory

Equity theory assumes individuals compare themselves with others and want to be treated fairly. This comparison might be with another colleague in the same work group or some other part of the organisation or even a composite of other members of the organisation. As a result of this comparison, individuals either feel equity (fairness) or inequity (unfair treatment). The comparison is based on input/outcome ratios. Inputs are the contributions made to the organisation by the individual such as qualifications, effort and loyalty. Outcomes are what the individual receives in return such as pay, status and intrinsic rewards. Both inputs and outcomes are therefore based partly on objective data and partly on perceptions. If an individual's ratio is different from the one being compared, there is inequity.

If the ratio of inputs to outcomes generates a feeling of equity, the status quo is maintained and the individual will continue contributing the same level of output. If the ratios are different, however, there is inequity and the individual is motivated to reduce the difference. This might be by changing inputs – working less hard – or attempting to change outcomes by asking for more salary or some other benefit. Alternatively, individuals can change their perceptions of themselves by believing they are working less or more hard than first thought. Equally, they might change their views of the inputs or outcomes of the person being compared. A more complex reaction would be to change the person being used as a comparison in order to provide a more acceptable comparison. Finally, if none of these bring equity, the individual might exit the situation by transferring to another department or even finding alternative employment.

Expectancy theory

Expectancy theory is more complex than equity theory. It suggests that motivation is related to how much an individual wants an outcome and the likelihood of that outcome. A recent graduate might see an advertisement for a job as a professor in her discipline. Despite desperately wanting the job, she will not apply as she recognises there is no chance of her being offered it. Another job offers £1.50 per hour, no experience necessary. Again she does not apply even though she is likely to be offered it. In the first case, she wanted the job but recognised the chances of getting it were nil. In the second case, she knew she was likely to be offered the job but did not want it. Only if she wanted a particular job and thought there was a reasonable chance of obtaining it would she apply. This is the basis of expectancy theory.

In performing a task, there are three elements. The first is the effort made. The second is the actual performance and the third is the outcome from performing that task. Linking these are two steps. The first, the *effort to performance expectancy*, is the perceived likelihood that effort will lead to performance. On a scale of zero to one, one is a strong belief that the desired performance will follow from the effort. A score of zero suggests that the person feels the task cannot be accomplished, no matter what the effort.

The second linkage is the *performance to outcome expectancy*, that is the probability that achieving performance will lead to a particular outcome. The particular outcome might be a salary increase. A firm belief that high performance will lead to a salary increase might score one. A belief that no matter what the performance, there will be no salary increase, will score zero.

Outcomes are anything which might possibly result from performance. The term *valence* is used to describe the attractiveness of any outcome for a particular individual. A salary increase, a promotion or any other form of recognition have positive valences. Stress, fatigue or less free time all have negative valences. The intensity of all these valences will vary from person to person. Take as an example a 10 per cent increase in salary. This may be a strong positive valence for someone who is desperately short of money but only slightly positive for someone with sufficient funds who would prefer shorter working hours.

The expectancy model gives a considerable insight into whether motivated behaviour is possible. To achieve motivated behaviour there must first be a strong belief that effort will lead to the achievement of performance. Second, the belief that performance leads to outcomes must also be high. Third, the sum of all the valences or perceived psychological benefits of the potential outcomes from performance must be positive. If effort does not lead to performance or if performance does not lead to outcome or if the net value of the valences is negative, motivation will not happen. People will not exhibit motivated behaviour unless they value the expected rewards, they believe effort will lead to performance and that performance will lead to the desired rewards.

Goal setting theory

The importance of setting goals as a way of influencing behaviour has long been recognised. Only recently, however, has the belief been tested and analysed.[7] Goal setting theory is concerned with the processes by which people set goals and then strive to achieve them. As with expectancy theory, there are three elements in performing a task: the goal-directed effort, the performance of the task and the satisfaction gained from its achievement – what would be called the valence in expectancy theory. Central to the theory are two concepts: *goal difficulty* and *goal specificity*.

Goal difficulty is concerned with the extent to which a goal is challenging and the amount of effort required. Its general conclusion is that people work to achieve goals and, up to a point, the harder the goal, the harder people will work in order to achieve it. A goal, however, must not be so difficult that it is unattainable, otherwise disillusionment might result. Goals, therefore, must be realistic but difficult. This link between motivation and difficult goals can be reinforced by acknowledging achievement and the giving of rewards. Supporting this is the concept of goal specificity which relates to the definition of the targeted performance. For goals to be achieved, they need to be specific and unambiguous, and preferably measurable in some verifiable, quantitative way. For instance, asking managers to 'do their best' is unlikely to be as effective as setting a target of a 5 per cent increase in sales volume.

On their own, goal difficulty and specificity are insufficient. Two other conditions are necessary: *goal acceptance* and *goal commitment*. Goal acceptance is the degree to which individuals internalise or accept the organisational goal as their own. Goal commitment is the strength of commitment to seeing the goal achieved. Factors which influence goal acceptance and commitment include the setting of challenging but achievable targets and the belief that achievement will lead to rewards. With all four factors in place, there is the potential for performance.

Actual performance, however, will require three further conditions. The first one, the ability to do the task, has already been identified as a major element in performance. A second condition, often assumed although less often made explicit, is organisational support. Put crudely, without the tools to do the job, ability and motivation come to nothing. Finally, there is the satisfaction from completing the task. Satisfaction can take two forms, extrinsic rewards such as bonuses and intrinsic rewards such as the feeling derived from a job well done. These form a feedback, influencing motivation in subsequent periods.

ACCOUNTING CONTROLS AND MOTIVATION

The findings from theories of motivation need to be treated with caution. Some have only been derived from experiments, often under artificial conditions. The generality of their application therefore has constantly to be questioned. Others have been treated to more substantial field trials. None, on their own, give a complete explanation of human motivation. What is clear, however, is that the traditional content theories, with their prescriptions based on allegedly universal listings of needs, are inadequate, as they do not recognise that individual needs differ nor do they set those needs in an organisational context.

The more modern process theories are based on individual choice; that individuals differ in the importance they attach to rewards and that this may require different motivational devices according to the circumstances. This realism, however, is bought at a cost. None of the theories give a full, detailed explanation of motivation. Rather each of them gives a different insight into the totality of motivation. What is clear from all of them is that motivation is contingent on a variety of factors and these factors will vary between individuals and organisations. Equally clear – especially from a study of expectancy theory – is that budgets *per se* rarely motivate. It is individuals' *reactions* to budgets which determine if they act as a motivator.

Budgets as targets

One extensive investigation of the use of budgets by managers was undertaken by Hofstede.[8] His findings are generally supportive of the process theories. He found that budgets were only motivational if internalised and that, up to a point, more demanding budgets are not only seen as more relevant but are also likely to produce better results. This is consistent with the goal setting theory outlined earlier. The budget which motivates the best performance therefore will be set at a higher level than is likely to be achieved. If, however, budgetary targets were felt to be unattainable, then there was a distinct likelihood that they would produce worse results. This is shown diagrammatically in Exhibit 19.3.

Exhibit 19.3 Budget difficulty and performance

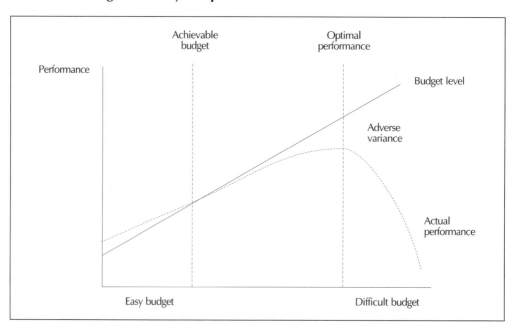

Up to a point, as the budget becomes more difficult, actual performance increases. At some stage, however, the individual recognises the impossibility of the task (expectancy theory) and performance deteriorates rapidly. To motivate individuals to perform as well as possible therefore requires setting budgets which cannot be achieved! This has three implications. First, there is a potential conflict between budgets for financial planning, where the concern is for accuracy of the forecasts, and budgets for motivation where the concern is with maximising motivation and improving performance. In the latter case, small adverse variances of the form shown in Exhibit 19.3 should be the norm. Secondly, if small adverse variances are healthy, the attitude of those evaluating the variances becomes critical. Thirdly, individual managers are likely to be motivated by different levels of difficulty.

Budgets for performance appraisal

Rewards, whether described as outcomes, valences or satisfaction, were identified in the three process theories as being an important element of motivation. Individuals also have their own goals which may not be the same as organisational goals. This poses a difficulty. Organisational goals have to be translated into desirable performance measurements. Although goals and performance measures might be similar, rarely will they be identical. Often goals will be expressed qualitatively but then have to be quantified for performance measures. A company, for instance, might have as a goal to be the largest firm in its industry. This might then be translated into a performance measure of 20 per cent sales growth for the current period.

Without some system of tying personal objectives into group objectives, individuals are likely to concentrate on achieving personal goals. The effect of this is shown in Exhibit 19.4. The objectives of the enterprise are represented by the circle A. It is impossible to quantify all the objectives as performance measures and even those which are quantified may only be an approximation to the real objectives. This is represented by the only partial overlapping of the performance measures, circle B, and the true objectives, circle A. Superimposed on both are the manager's personal goals. The objective of motivation and reward systems is to push these personal objectives closer towards the desirable performance of circle B. Organisational performance, however, will only be improved to the extent that the performance measures are a good approximation to the organisational objectives.

Exhibit 19.4 Objectives and performance standards

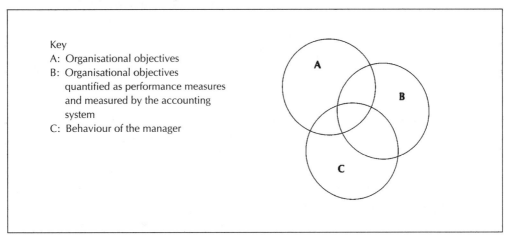

Key
A: Organisational objectives
B: Organisational objectives
   quantified as performance measures
   and measured by the accounting
   system
C: Behaviour of the manager

Bias in budgets

If the aim of a reward system is to encourage motivated behaviour, then it is that behaviour which should be measured. There are, however, difficulties in specifying and measuring behaviour and so the tendency is to monitor and reward results. This can lead to bias being introduced into the budgetary process. Managers might try to make budget standards easier in good years by building in slack[9] or manipulating the actual results to show more favourable variances. Alternatively, performance might be achieved in undesirable ways by, for example, failing to replace plant when necessary because of the increased depreciation charge.

In terms of Exhibit 19.4, introducing bias by manipulating either targets or actual results reduces the need of managers to amend their own personal objectives in favour of those required by the company. Paradoxically, Otley[10] found that managers facing tough trading conditions biased their budgets in the opposite direction by setting budgets unlikely to be achieved. The explanation possibly lay in the gain from promising good performance outweighing the later consequences of failure to meet agreed targets.

The extent of bias in budgeting is difficult to measure. It is not the sort of information publicly disclosed. Otley,[11] however, felt it is a less significant problem than sometimes suggested, partly because superiors have some knowledge of the area of operations undertaken by subordinates. This, however, still leaves the problem that motivation encourages the achievement of the performance measure and this may not necessarily be the same as the organisation's objectives. All measures of performance, therefore, are to a greater or lesser extent imperfect.

BUDGETS FOR FINANCIAL PLANNING

The danger of bias has ramifications for the financial planning and coordinating aspects of budgeting, where distortions may feed back to cashflows and profit forecasts. There is, however, a further danger. In large organisations, budgets become more and more summarised as they move up the organisational hierarchy. Despite giving the appearance of being objective and doubt-free, budgets are nothing of the sort. Although expressed as a single figure, a variety of other figures could have been used if different assumptions had been made. Exactly what budgeted data is measuring might vary from department to department. One department might budget for what can be easily achieved, another for what is most likely, while another might budget for what can be achieved on average. If the range of possible outcomes are skewed, the last two will not be identical.

Consider an example of four sales managers who operate in different markets for the same firm and who all estimate budgeted activity on the basis of the most likely outcome – a not unreasonable assumption. Although the markets are independent, to simplify matters, assume that in each one there is a 75 per cent chance of a sales revenue of £100,000 and a 25 per cent chance that turnover will only be £50,000. The total budget, on which the organisation will plan, will be £400,000. If the probability of the alternative sales levels are accurate, however, on average, one of those managers will only achieve a sales level of £50,000. The result is that, even without any deliberate bias of the numbers, the organisation's budget will be wrong by £50,000. To avoid this, average data should be used for financial planning and this only reinforces the belief that budgets for financial planning are not necessarily appropriate for motivating purposes.

MANAGERS AND BUDGETS

What is clear from this is that the use of budgets is far more complex than the rational models suggest. First, difficulties in specifying desirable behaviour lead to results being emphasised even though these may be only an approximation of the underlying objectives. Secondly, budgets based on financial planning criteria may not be appropriate for motivating improved performance. Thirdly, the process of budgeting may lead to bias and distortions being introduced. How managers use budgets is therefore critical. Unfortunately, little is known about how they do actually use budgets, although some insight is gained from considering the results of experiments and field studies which have taken place.

Budgets and management style

Hopwood[12] observed the use of budgets in a manufacturing division of a large company where there was a great deal of interdependence between departments. Two styles of budget use were of particular significance. A rigid, mechanical use of budget and accounting data to evaluate performance – what Hopwood called a budget constrained style – focused on achieving the budget on a short term basis. He concluded that where accounting information was an inadequate measure of performance, using a budget constrained style led to a variety of dysfunctional consequences such as job-related tension, poor inter-colleague relationships and the distorting of accounting information. In comparison, a more flexible approach within the same organisation – what Hopwood called a profit conscious style – involved a manager's performance being judged more widely, often with additional information other than the budget. Here rewards were still possible even though the budget might not be achieved, providing there was good reason for the failure. Few of the dysfunctional aspects identified with the budget constrained style were found when using the profit conscious style even though both styles were associated with a high involvement in cost awareness.

A later study by Otley[13] looked at a company with independent profit centres, some of which used a rigid style, but did not find the problems identified by Hopwood. Management style varied, with those in favourable environments operating a rigid style and those in a less favourable environment being evaluated more flexibly. This suggests that management style in using budgets is significantly influenced by the environment. It is also consistent with the earlier work which identified different uses of budgets as uncertainty over objectives and uncertainty over results varied. In effect, the favourable environment approximated the answer machine use of budgets, where cause and effect could more easily be identified. Under these circumstance, variances are more easily attributable directly to management. This conclusion has been borne out by Hirst[14] who found that medium to high reliance on accounting data will minimise dysfunctional behaviour where task uncertainty is low.

Participation in budget setting

Budgets can be built up as a result of edicts from an autocratic chief executive giving instructions to subordinates – the so-called 'top down' approach to budgets. At the other extreme is a 'bottom up' approach, where much lower levels of management make proposals that are then incorporated into the master budget. Both approaches are to be found in business. Rarely, however, is the bottom up approach found without some constraints imposed by the organisation. In theory both approaches are an iterative process, with amendments being made when potential budgeted performance is not found to match organisational objectives. How realistic this is as a description of the budgetary process is open to question. Budgets are such complicated phenomena in large organisations that time prevents many alterations.

Somewhere in between the two extremes is participation – the ability of managers to influence the content of their budgets as a result of the budgetary exercise rather than merely having the information communicated to them. Hofstede[8] has suggested that participation improves managers attitudes towards the budgetary process and reduces dysfunctional aspects. Managers then see the budget standard as being more relevant. Participation also affects performance because of the improved communication which it brings.

These are the reasons often put forward for encouraging participation in budgeting. Unfortunately, the evidence that participation improves performance is, at the best, conflicting. Logically, the equity, expectancy and goal theories all offer an explanation why participation does not automatically result in improved performance. For participation to result in improved performance requires that the organisational goals be internalised by the manager and that goal commitment be high. In addition, a high performance to expectancy score and positive valences are also necessary.

The evidence in support of participation is patchy and by no means universal. Indeed Bryan and Locke[15] found a negative association between performance and participation. Bruns and Waterhouse,[16] however, found that managers in decentralised organisations had more influence as a result of participation in the budget process than colleagues in centralised organisations where participation was viewed as being less appropriate. The suggestion from these findings is that participation might be partly contingent on organisational structure.

Another contingent variable identified by Brownwell[17] was the personality of the manager. Brownwell used the concept of the locus of control – the degree to which people accept personal responsibility for what happens to them. An external locus of control implies events are unrelated to the individual and beyond his or her personal control. An internal locus of control, however, suggests an individual has a belief in his or her own destiny. Brownwell demonstrated that people with an internal locus of control performed best and learned more quickly when they participated in the budgetary process whereas those with an external locus of control were happier having targets set for them. Personality, therefore, also appears to be a contingent variable in determining the benefits of participation within the organisation.

SUMMARY

The message coming through from all these research studies is that the traditional model of the budget is an inadequate description of its use in organisations. Equally, it is not self-evident that all the alleged advantages of budgets are achieved in practice. Only where budgets operate in an environment with clear objectives and clear causal relationships – where they are effectively answering machines – do they approximate their textbook description. Even there, a conflict arises between the use of budgets for financial planning and their use as a motivating and performance evaluation measure.

Contingency theory has demonstrated that budgets have to be tailored to the circumstances of the organisation. Even as a technical operation therefore, they will differ from organisation to organisation, both in their build up via cost centres and their detail. Used as a motivating device, modern motivation theories suggest budgets will only perform that role when they relate to the needs of individuals. No universal prescription is available for budgetary design. Managers develop and use budgets in different ways. What is clear is that the way budgets are used and whether the process is improved by participation is contingent on circumstances. In some ways this is a depressing conclusion as no immediate solution to budget design and use is available. However, it does have positive aspects. The traditional model of budgets with clear objectives, cause and effect identified and unambiguous actual performance measures has been shown to appear only rarely in the real world. This alone is a useful discovery. It demonstrates that the process of budgetary planning and control is an extremely complex one, bound up in the psychology of individuals rather than a technically complicated but mechanical application of basic economic principles.

REFERENCES

1 Bromwich, M. (1980) Standard Costing for Planning and Control, in *Topics in Management Accounting*, Arnold, J., Carsberg, B. and Scapens, R. (eds), Philip Allan Publishers Ltd.

2 Burns, T. and Stalker, G.M. (1961) *The Management of Innovation*, Tavistock Institute.

3 Earl, M.J. and Hopwood, A.G. (1981) From Management Information to Information Management, in *The Information Systems Environment*, Lucas, H.C. *et al.* (eds), North-Holland.

4 Maslow, A. (1954) *Motivation and Personality*, Harper and Row.

5 *See* Griffin, R.W. and Moorhead, G. (1986) *Organisational Behaviour*, Houghton Mifflin, for a more extensive review of criticisms.

6 Herzberg, F., Mausner, B. and Snyderman, B. (1959) *The Motivation to Work*, Wiley.

7 This summary of goal setting theory is based extensively on the work undertaken by Edwin Locke. See for example, Edwin Locke, Towards a Theory of Task Performance and Incentives, *Organizational Behaviour and Human Performance*, **3**, 1968, pp. 157–89 and Gary P. Latham and Edwin Locke, Goal Setting – A Motivational Technique That Works, *Organizational Dynamics*, Autumn 1979, pp. 68–80.

8 Hofstede, G.H. (1969) *The Game of Budgetary Control*, Tavistock Institute.

9 Schiff, M. and Lewin, A.T. (1970) The Impact of People on Budgets, *The Accounting Review*, pp. 259–68.

10 Otley, D.T. (1978) Budget Use and Managerial Performance, *Journal of Accounting Research*, **16**, pp. 122–49.

11 Otley, D.T. (1987) *Accounting Control and Organisational Behaviour*, Heinemann, p. 54.

12 Hopwood, A.G. (1976) *Accounting and Human Behaviour*, Prentice Hall.

13 Otley, D.T. (1978) Budget Use and Managerial Performance, *Journal of Accounting Research*, **16**, pp. 122–49.

14 Hirst, M.K. (1981) Accounting Information and the Evaluation of Subordinate Performance, *The Accounting Review*, pp. 771–84.

15 Bryan, J.F. and Locke, E.A. (1967) Goal Setting as a Means of Increasing Motivation, *Journal of Applied Psychology*, June, pp. 264–7.

16 Bruns, W.J. and Waterhouse, J.H. (1975) Budgetary Control and Organisational Structure, *Journal of Accounting Research*, Autumn, pp. 177–203.

17 Brownwell, P. (1981) Participation in Budgeting, Locus of Control and Organisational Effectiveness, *The Accounting Review*, October, pp. 944–58.

FURTHER READING

Emmanuel, C., Otley, D. and Merchant, K. (1990) *Accounting for Management Control*, 2nd edn, Chapman & Hall.

Griffin, R.W. and Moorhead, G. (1986) *Organisational Behaviour*, Houghton Mifflin.

Hopwood, A.G. (1976) *Accounting and Human Behaviour*, Prentice Hall.

Macintosh, N. B. (1994) *Management Accounting and Control Systems*, John Wiley and Sons.

Otley, D.T. (1987) *Accounting Control and Organisational Behaviour*, Heinemann.

Puxty, A. G. (1993) *The Social and Organisational Context of Management Accounting*, Academic Press.

TEST YOUR UNDERSTANDING

1 Identify the five traditional roles for budgeting.

2 List the possible reasons why accounting variances occur.

3 What is meant by contingency theory in accounting?

4 If an organisation is uncertain of its objectives and uncertain of the cause and effect of its actions, budgeting becomes:
    (a) an answer machine;
    (b) a rationalisation machine;
    (c) an ammunition machine;
    (d) a learning machine.

5 Identify three factors which influence an individual's performance in an organisation.

6 What is meant by motivation?

7 Explain what is meant by, and give two examples of, content theories of motivation.

8 Give three examples of process theories of motivation.

9 Explain why there may be a logical inconsistency between using budgets as planning devices and using them to motivate performance.

QUESTIONS

1 Grosvenor Ltd has introduced a new product, the Square. The material standard cost per Square is £80, comprising 5 metres of material X at £16 per metre. Just before production commenced, Grosvenor became aware of a proposed EU directive requiring an enhanced material, material X2 and this was introduced into the first month's production. To make each Square requires 6 metres of X2 and the planned unit cost is £18. Total production for the first period was 200 Squares. Material consumed in the first period was 1,100 metres costing £18,700.

Calculate both the traditional material variances and revised figures, differentiating between planning and operating variances.

2* 'A budget is a quantitative expression of a plan of action and an aid to co-ordination and implementation. . . .When administered intelligently, budgets (a) compel planning, (b) provide performance criteria and (c) promote communication and co-ordination.' (Horngren, C. and Foster, G. *Cost Accounting: A Managerial Emphasis*, Prentice Hall International, 7th edn, 1991, pp. 172–3.)

Discuss, the extent to which this is an adequate description of budgeting in organisations, highlighting and debating any inadequacies in Horngren and Foster's definition of budgeting.

3* In modern organisations, managers are often judged on budget performance. Do budgets motivate managers to achieve organisational objectives?

CHAPTER 20

Strategic management accounting and the capital budgeting decision

Until recently, the focus of management accounting texts has been on short term operational matters with any planning and control restricted to conventional short term budgeting. The one exception to this has been the capital budgeting decision involving the financial appraisal of long term investments. Over the last few years, however, partly because of the growth of business strategy as a separate discipline, increasing interest has been shown in a more strategic approach to management accounting. Although still in its early days, strategic management accounting is identifying limitations within traditional management accounting and giving new insight into the components making up the information for capital budgeting.

This chapter:

- Provides an introduction to the discipline of business strategy and identifies the implications for management accounting

- Considers traditional methods of appraising the investment in long term assets

- Develops an alternative approach, using discounted cashflows

- Critically appraises the validity of the DCF model and its limitations

- Discusses the treatment of investment projects where there is a shortage of funds or where the investment proposal is a risky one

Management control has been defined as the processes by which managers attempt to ensure their organisation adapts successfully to changes in its environment. Within this, management accounting has been shown to play a significant role as a major, if not the major, source of information. There are, however, at least three elements making up the totality of management control. Anthony[1] identified these three elements as being task (or operational) control, management control *per se*, and strategic planning.

Task control is performed by first-line supervisors who handle issues as they occur. The focus is on the single, immediate task where cost data is specific, directly related to the problem and where causality is clear. Such costs are known as engineered costs, that is they reflect a clear-cut relationship between inputs and outputs based on the technology being used. In car manufacture, steering wheels are an example of an engineered cost, with one being required for each car produced. A knowledge of such technical relationships enables information to be generated immediately. For instance, a supervisor can determine instantly how many labour hours were wasted in producing a faulty product caused by a machine mis-setting. Often, the solution to the error is equally obvious. The source of knowledge to both identify and correct the error is an understanding of the technology.

What Anthony called management control has a different focus. Rather than being the concern of first-line supervisors, it is more likely to be of relevance to both senior and middle managers and reflects the activities of the whole organisation. The accounting control systems of budgets and standard costing are the primary examples of this form of management control. The data tends to be internal and historical, often produced by the management accounting system. Its relevant time period is likely to be monthly and, as was shown in Chapter 19, its source discipline is often social psychology. The costs will also differ from those for task control with many having an element of discretion and judgement about them, unlike engineered costs. The marketing budget and the research and development budget are two such examples.

There is a third layer of the management control process known as strategic planning, which is undertaken by only the most senior of managers, aided by staff specialists. Strategic planning is concerned with where the organisation wants to go and with scanning the environment to see whether this is possible. The time horizon is several years and therefore all aspects of the organisation's activities will be variable – unlike in budgeting where the organisation often has to accept its existing products, its existing resources and its existing cost structures. Once the plan is accepted, however, costs are not only significant, they are also committed, as for example, when a business decides to set up a new factory. To make this kind of decision also requires information. Rarely, however, will it be available from the accounting system. Instead, the necessary information will relate to the environment and be based on the future. Such information is essentially economic in nature.

Although an oversimplification – partly because there are linkages between all three elements of management control – this is nevertheless a useful classification which highlights the different qualities of the long term decisions faced by an organisation. Strategic planning, or corporate strategy, is a discipline on its own. One area, however, is of particular relevance to management accounting. Once a strategic decision has been made, it will often involve substantial funds and commit the organisation for many years. Some way, therefore, has to be found of financially evaluating all the options available.

STRATEGIC DECISION MAKING

There are three levels from which to analyse strategic decision making. First, corporate strategy is concerned with asking what type of business the organisation should be in and the allocation of resources to the organisation's various segments. Secondly, competitive or business strategy relates to how the business should compete in a particular product or geographical market, while thirdly operating strategy relates the role of the various functions within the organisation – such as finance and marketing – to both corporate and business strategy.

Characteristics of strategic decisions

Strategic decisions are concerned with the *scope* of the organisation's activities: its product range and whether it should be integrating itself backwards towards the sources of supply or forwards into the distribution networks for its products. Strategic decisions are concerned with identifying the organisation's boundaries. They are also concerned with matching the organisation's activities with the continually changing environment within which it operates. Not only does the organisation have to satisfy the changing needs of customers it also has to achieve this in the face of actions by competitors.

There is, however, a second area of matching, that of matching the business's activities with its resource availability. Strategic decisions have major resource implications. They can include moving into new markets, changing product ranges, opening or closing factories or changing the production technology – including the way materials are sourced or final products distributed. As a result, strategic decisions generally set off a wave of other, smaller decisions which affect lower levels of decision making. These are likely to be both organisational and financial. Building a new factory and changing the product range, for instance, will have major ramifications for the annual budgets both in terms of profitability and cashflow.

The environment and resource availability are not the only factors affecting strategic decision making. Also of importance are the values, beliefs and expectations of those with power in the organisation. The word *mission* is often used to describe in more detail these attitudes. A company's mission statement, for instance, will consider the organisation's position and role in society.

What is clear from all this is that strategic decisions are both complex and affect the long term direction of the company. They often involve: (i) a high degree of uncertainty as a result of planning for the far distant future; (ii) an integrated approach, using the skills of most of the functional specialisms in the organisation; and (iii) major structural change. The objective is to secure a sustainable competitive advantage over other companies in the same industry either in the form of lower costs, superior quality or more efficient distribution.

Stages of strategic management

Strategic management is concerned with the development of an appropriate strategy and its application within the organisation. Although interrelated, three stages can be identified: strategic analysis, strategic choice and strategic implementation.

Strategic analysis is concerned with perceived changes in the environment, the resource availability within the business, the cultural values of senior managers and the views of owners. It involves scanning the environment for both threats and opportunities and analysing the company's resources for strengths and weaknesses.

Strategic choice is concerned with the generation of long term strategic options such as whether to compete directly with competitors or rather focus on a niche market. It is concerned with identifying where growth is to come from: from developing a greater share of existing markets or the development of new markets or products; from internal growth or growth by the acquisition of other businesses. Central to this is the role seen for research and development and the danger of technological obsolescence. Given the financial costs involved and the opportunity cost of a wrong decision, studying the feasibility and evaluating the possible options is critical. Selecting a strategy, however, is rarely a clear-cut decision as often it is based on views of the future and views of where the company wants to be within that future.

Finally, there is strategic implementation, which involves the development of the necessary organisational structure and ensuring the availability of resources. It can involve the closing down of factories and the building of new ones; the acquisition of new plant and machinery to enable new or improved production to take place; and the choice of new distribution methods. This is the stage where strategy interfaces with budgets and other accounting control systems developed in the previous two chapters. Techniques which can help evaluate strategic choice is the subject of this chapter.

STRATEGY EVALUATION

Some insight into strategy evaluation can be gained by considering three of the many concepts which have developed since the 1950s to match strategic options to the organisation's environment and its resource capability. These are the product life cycle, the experience curve and the product portfolio.

The product life cycle

Bringing a new product to the market may have involved many years of research and development and the consumption of many millions of pounds of resources. Once launched, however, the pattern of sales and profitability tends to follow a regular pattern. This pattern is demonstrated in Exhibit 20.1.

Initially, sales volume will be low and prices high as potential customers become aware of the product. Early customers are innovators – people who are prepared to change their customary needs and experiment with new products. Given that the product is new, the business will face very few competitors. As awareness of the product develops, sales and profitability begin to increase at an increasing rate and this attracts the interest of competitors. In this growth stage, prices begin to fall. The company's product strategy will therefore be to maintain, if not to increase, its share of the market to maintain overall profitability. This it can do by identifying the characteristics of its product which are not found in those of competitors.

Exhibit 20.1 The product life cycle

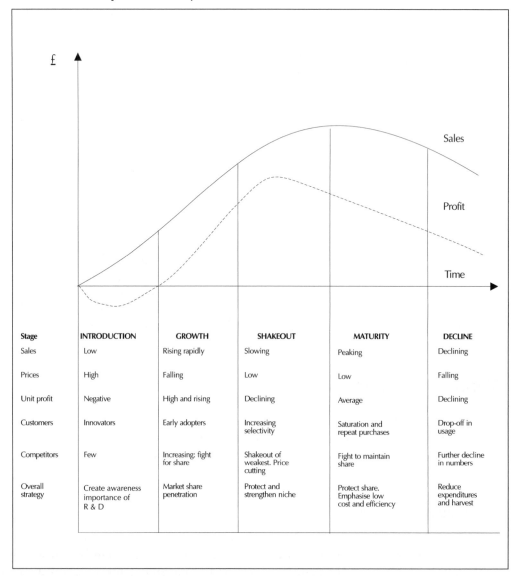

Stage	INTRODUCTION	GROWTH	SHAKEOUT	MATURITY	DECLINE
Sales	Low	Rising rapidly	Slowing	Peaking	Declining
Prices	High	Falling	Low	Low	Falling
Unit profit	Negative	High and rising	Declining	Average	Declining
Customers	Innovators	Early adopters	Increasing selectivity	Saturation and repeat purchases	Drop-off in usage
Competitors	Few	Increasing: fight for share	Shakeout of weakest. Price cutting	Fight to maintain share	Further decline in numbers
Overall strategy	Create awareness importance of R & D	Market share penetration	Protect and strengthen niche	Protect share. Emphasise low cost and efficiency	Reduce expenditures and harvest

There then follows a third stage which involves a shakeout of the weakest competitors. Sales growth begins to tail off, with prices and unit profitability being particularly hard hit by the increasing competition and fight for survival. This stage is then followed by sales peaking. The product has reached its maturity stage where there will be fewer new customers and where, increasingly, sales will be achieved by repeat purchases. Products with the lowest costs are the ones most likely to survive. Finally, there is the decline stage of the product with a decreasing volume of sales and further reduction in competitors. Although unit profitability is still falling, the product may still be profitable as there are fewer competitors and no longer a need for further research and development.

The learning curve

Additional insight into the profitability of a product can be gained by considering what happens to costs as the total number of units produced increases. Cost savings are often possible with increased volume. The phenomenon first came to prominence during the Second World War when aircraft manufacturers found a regular pattern of savings in labour hours as production increased. Applied to these savings in labour hours (and labour costs), it became known as the learning curve. The first time a unit or batch is produced, employees will be working in unfamiliar territory. As the volume of output increases, workers become more familiar with the tasks. Not only do they become less hesitant, they might also find more convenient ways of carrying out their tasks. Hours taken to perform a particular operation are therefore likely to fall with the result that labour costs will also fall. The potential for such savings will be at their greatest in the early stages of production. As volume increases, further savings, although possible, will be less and less significant. There is an intuitive logic to this, as anyone who has tried wallpapering a ceiling will testify. The largest savings in time will be identified almost immediately. Subsequent time savings will come from further, more subtle efficiencies and will generally be less significant.

Study of this phenomenon revealed a regular pattern. For each doubling of total production, the average hours taken to produce those units fell at a constant rate. Although the rate varied from product to product, what was significant was how constant the rate remained for any particular product. Example 20.1 demonstrates the mechanics of the learning curve. An 80 per cent learning curve is assumed, that is for every doubling of cumulative production, the average time taken for all units produced to date falls to 80 per cent of the average time for the previous cumulative level of production.

Example 20.1

> Richmond Ltd is about to commence work on a new product called the Thames which has been estimated to take 1,000 labour hours to produce. From previous experience, the company believes that an 80 per cent learning curve is applicable.

The first unit produced will take 1,000 hours. Doubling output involves producing one more unit. The average time taken to produce both of those units will fall to 80 per cent of the time required to produce the original batch of one unit, an average of 800 hours. The total time taken for both units will therefore be 1,600 hours and so the time taken to produce the second batch of one unit will be 600 hours.

If cumulative production was to double yet again, to a total of four units, the learning curve would suggest that the average time taken per unit to produce all four units will be only 80 per cent of the previous average time of cumulative production. As the previous average time per unit of cumulative production was 800 hours, the average time for producing a total of four units should fall to 640 hours. This gives a total of 2,560 hours. Deducting from this figure the time estimated to produce the first two units suggests that it will take 960 hours to produce the second two units. The time taken for each unit in that third batch will therefore be 480 hours.

Exhibit 20.2 Hours taken and the learning experience

Batch size	Cumulative production	Average hours per unit of cumulative production	Total hours taken for cumulative production	Total hours taken to produce batch	Average hours taken per unit per batch
(a)	(b)	(c)	(d = b × c)	(e)	(f = e ÷ a)
1	1	1,000.00	1,000	1,000	1,000
1	2	800.00	1,600	600	600
2	4	640.00	2,560	960	480
4	8	512.00	4,096	1,536	384
8	16	409.60	6,554	2,458	307
16	32	327.68	10,486	3,932	246
32	64	262.14	16,777	6,291	197
64	128	209.71	26,843	10,066	157

The effect on hours taken to produce a unit as cumulative production continues to double is demonstrated in Exhibit 20.2. For both average hours per unit of cumulative production and average hours per unit for each batch, the effect is initially dramatic. As further doublings of production take place, however, the reductions become less and less significant. This is because the 80 per cent applies to a smaller number each time and because each stage requires a further doubling of output. In theory, the reduction in average hours continues *ad infinitum*. In practice, there comes a stage when no further reductions are possible and a steady state of constant hours per unit comes into existence. The effect of graphing the learning curve data is shown in Exhibit 20.3.

Exhibit 20.3 The learning curve

The experience curve

The concept of the learning curve can be applied to other areas of cost such as marketing, distribution and manufacturing expenses in general. This broader approach is known as the experience curve. Although taking on a similar shape to the learning curve, it comprises at least three elements. The first component is the learning curve experience outlined above. A second element is increasing specialisation made possible by increased production which also brings increased efficiencies. Related to this is the third influence, that of scale. The unit capital costs required to finance additional activity falls as activity increases. This not only applies to manufacturing costs where the effect of volume on fixed costs is well known, but also to other areas such as distribution and marketing.

The product portfolio matrix

An awareness of the product life cycle and the experience curve suggests ways in which businesses can gain a competitive advantage. So far, however, little has been said about the cash implications for an organisation. While a product is being developed, there is likely to be severe negative cashflow as a result of high research and development costs and heavy capital expenditure on plant, equipment and factories. This negative cashflow is likely to continue through to the introduction stage because of heavy promotional expenditure and the expense of establishing distribution channels and other facilities. As the product moves into its growth phase, cashflow might either be negative or positive, depending on circumstances. If production can be dramatically increased, either by increasing market share at the expense of competitors or by rapid market growth, the experience curve suggests that cost savings might be considerable. In its turn this can have a beneficial effect on cashflow.

The Boston Consulting Group developed the idea of the product portfolio matrix as a way of evaluating the cash consuming and cash generating tendencies of both products and companies. The product portfolio matrix is a two-factor analysis concerned with a product's – or company's – relative market share and the growth of that market. Relative market share is an indication of profitability and cash generating capacity. The greater the market share, the greater the cash which might be generated. Growth, however, is a measure of cash absorption. Other things being equal, the greater the growth, the more cash a product will consume. This enables the four scenarios reproduced in Exhibit 20.4 to be considered.

Exhibit 20.4 The product portfolio matrix

		Market share	
		HIGH	LOW
Market growth	**HIGH**	**Star** Cash generator or absorber	**Wildcat** Cash absorber
	LOW	**Cash Cow** Large cash generator	**Dog** Modest cash generator or absorber

The scenario identified as a cash cow is one of high market share and low market growth. With market dominance, unit costs will be low relative to other competitors as a result of the experience curve. With only limited growth, new investment is likely to be small. As a result, positive cashflow is likely to be large.

Where a product has both a high market share and a high market growth, the *potential* for positive cashflow is also large. Because of this, such products are identified as stars. They may not, however, necessarily be current cash generators. If there is high growth, cash currently being received from debtors will be less than current levels of sales. As a result, increasing levels of debtors are having to be financed. This will be partly offset by credit granted by suppliers. However, this is unlikely to be sufficient if there are severe timing delays between the purchase of raw materials, their incorporation in production and their sale. Larger and larger levels of production and stock are having to be financed based on future growth in sales. Whether a star is a cash generator or not will therefore depend on the speed with which debtors pay, the credit granted by suppliers, the growth in sales (and hence stock costs), the profit margins being achieved and the nature of the costs. Where costs are fixed – or better still, where costs such as depreciation do not involve any cash outlay – there will be no increase in cash outflow resulting from the growth in sales activity.

The third quadrant, identified as the wildcat, shows a product with only a limited share of the market but with high growth potential. With only a limited share of the market, the product will not be benefiting from the reduced costs of the experience curve. At the same time, high growth is likely to involve more cash being tied up in financing sales and the need to continually invest to stay in the market. The options open to the company are therefore to either attempt to move the product into a star position or withdraw. This is the position identified as 'shakeout' in the product life cycle.

Finally, there is the product which only has a low market share and a low market growth. From such a base, market dominance is likely to be unacceptably expensive when related to the possible returns. Where a product can accurately be described as a dog, the best policy may well be to withdraw from the market as it reflects a failure to capture the leadership position in the growth stage.

STRATEGIC MANAGEMENT AND MANAGEMENT ACCOUNTING

What is clear from this brief outline of business strategy is that survival and profitability are related to external environmental factors such as market share and market growth. Central to this are the needs of the customer and the position of competitors. To be successful, a firm must both satisfy customer needs and maintain a competitive advantage over existing and potential competitors.[2]

The benefits generated by a product need to be both sufficient to retain existing customers and to win new ones in markets where there are rivals. Competitive advantage is not simply based on price but additional factors such as lower product cost, higher quality, superior delivery times and good after-sales support. Each product is not a homogeneous whole but a series of separate characteristics offered to the consumer. It is these attributes which actually constitute the product. In effect, the demand for a product is a derived demand stemming from the demand for its underlying qualities such as reliability, operating performance and warranties. To sustain a competitive advantage requires the identification of the qualities valued by customers, their costs to the business, and the costs of competitors.

Traditional management accounting

Management accounting, with its internal focus, rarely provides this information. Often, the only external information is the level of sales achieved. Traditional accounting systems tend to associate costs with products and responsibility centres rather than with the various benefits provided to customers. And, as has been demonstrated in earlier chapters, too often the emphasis is on variable costs. Overheads are then attached to products in some arbitrary way. Not only is this dangerous because of the increasing importance of overheads, but also because many of those overheads such as marketing, research and development, quality control and after-sales service are closely related to the achieving of the business strategy.

Strategic management accounting – a framework

The development of strategic management accounting is at an early stage. Nevertheless, it is possible to identify an outline framework. Initially, the activities which create consumer value such as quality and operating performance need to be identified. The next stage is to identify costs and other resources associated with these benefits and to determine their cost drivers. In business strategy, the ultimate cost drivers are the benefits provided to customers by products. Customers are prepared to pay for these benefits. If customers, for example, are prepared to pay a higher price for reliability, this is the cost driver not only for quality control but also for the more sophisticated and expensive equipment and work practices necessary to achieve built-in quality.

Conventional cost systems say little about the cost aspects of those strategic success factors which a firm must sustain if it is to survive. Therefore there is a need to determine the cost of the company's strategic activities. The cost of most strategic activities cannot be deduced from existing accounting reports. One reason is because such costs are often subsumed within enterprise-wide overheads. A second reason is that the cost of strategic activities often crosses the formal responsibility accounting structure. But a third reason relates to the conventions of financial accounting. Many costs incurred in a particular period are charged to the profit and loss account as period costs even though they may well be related to other stages of the product life cycle. An extensive advertising campaign for instance may be charged to an initial period even though it is critical to subsequent stages.

Finally, there are the dysfunctional aspects which result from the performance measurement aspect of management accounting. Most values attached to products by consumers are difficult to quantify. The ability to immediately respond to a customer order is one example. This implies having surplus capacity as a strategic decision and yet this may adversely affect a manager's immediate performance. Nowhere is this more critical than when considering the investment in long term assets such as plant and machinery. Faced with two pieces of equipment, the one more expensive but offering greater flexibility and long term savings in operating costs in later periods, the danger is for the manager to choose the cheaper alternative. Most of the benefits of the more expensive machine might either relate to future periods or be intangible ones such as greater flexibility. Consequently, such benefits will not appear as part of the manager's formal appraisal of performance. To overcome this, strategic management accounting needs to report in some way the costs of the entire product life cycle, allowing future savings to be offset against any higher immediate expense. Costs to be included in the strategic cost analysis will therefore need to be both actual and planned costs.

CAPITAL BUDGETING

Although strategic management accounting is in its infancy, there is one area of traditional management accounting which has always interfaced with business strategy. Strategic decisions generally involve substantial funds which commit the organisation for many years. At its simplest, a firm might be concerned with the purchase of new equipment to continue existing production. Alternatively, the issue might be much more complex, for example, when the development of a new product requires a whole new infrastructure of factories, equipment, workforce and distribution channels. Whatever the type of proposal, two steps are essential: funds need to be made available, and the viability of the options needs to be evaluated. This is the area of capital budgeting or, as it is sometimes known, the capital investment decision.

Sources of finance

The source of finance may be internal to the company. One advantage of having a product which is a cash cow is that it provides funding for the development of other products which will hopefully become stars. Sometimes, however, it will be necessary to raise funds from other sources. If the company has a stock exchange quotation, it is possible to raise additional funds by either issuing additional equity or additional debt in the form of loans or debentures. Companies without a stock exchange quotation may either borrow from banks or specialised financial institutions or raise funds from existing shareholders.

Irrespective of the source, investors will want to be repaid. For new shareholders, this will be in the form of dividends and, hopefully, a rising share price. For the providers of debt capital, it will not only be the interest on but also the repayment of the original loan. In their long term plans and annual budgets therefore, companies will have to take account of these payments using mechanical procedures similar to those for the other forms of budgeting described in Chapter 18.

Components of the investment decision

For the remainder of this chapter, the emphasis will be on techniques to evaluate the capital budgeting or investment decision. The proposal might relate to the acquisition or replacement of fixed assets such as plant and machinery or land and buildings. It might be concerned with appraising the planned benefits of research and development expenditure or a major promotional campaign. It might even be the acquisition of another business. Common to all of these is a substantial initial outlay, hopefully followed by benefits in later years. These benefits need not be additional profit; they could be cost savings. Whatever their form, investment decisions are often difficult to reverse once made. In addition, because they are concerned with benefits which might only manifest themselves in the distant future, there is generally a high degree of uncertainty about those potential benefits.

Ideally, some way has to be found of appraising the investment proposal. This will involve an estimation of costs and benefits, and then their comparison against some desired standard. Two other features also need to be considered. Any proposal needs to fit into the total strategy of the company. It is no good a manager showing that operating a string of bingo halls is profitable if the company is striving to become a major airline. Apart from the image problem, it diverts managers' focus away from where the company wants to be.

Secondly, the riskiness of the proposal needs to be considered. In the literature, it is usual to differentiate between risk and uncertainty. Risk is where there is more than one possible outcome but where all outcomes and their likelihood are known. A simple example is tossing a coin. Despite having more than one outcome, the number of outcomes – heads or tails – is known, as are their respective probabilities of 0.5. Uncertainty is anything less than this, such as not being able to ascertain all possible outcomes or not being able to estimate likelihoods where outcomes are known. However, for the purpose of this chapter, the terms will be used interchangeably.

TRADITIONAL INVESTMENT APPRAISAL TECHNIQUES

The accounting rate of return

When appraising the past performance of a business, it is normal to relate profitability to some form of capital base to derive the return on capital employed. This is then compared with some desired standard for appraisal purposes. Investment decisions can be appraised using a similar approach, where the likely future benefits are expressed as a proportion of the capital outlay. When expressed in this way, the result is known as the accounting rate of return. Example 20.2 demonstrates the mechanics.

Dividing the total profits by the number of years gives an average profit of £28,000 for machine A and £25,000 for machine B. This profit can then be expressed as a percentage of the capital cost. The result is a 22.4 per cent return for A and a 20.8 per cent return for B. Using the accounting rate of return, machine A appears to be the preferred choice.

$$\text{Rate of return (machine A)} = \frac{£28,000}{£125,000} \times 100\% = 22.4\%$$

$$\text{Rate of return (machine B)} = \frac{£25,000}{£120,000} \times 100\% = 20.8\%$$

One immediate objection to this analysis is the treatment of capital employed. At the commencement of the asset's life, the capital employed will be the initial cost. At the end of its life, the machine will be fully depreciated and so the capital employed will be zero.

On average therefore, the capital employed *throughout* its life will only be half the original cost if depreciation is provided on a straight line basis. Consequently, the average capital employed for machine A will only be £62,500 and for machine B, £60,000. The effect of substituting these figures in the denominators of the previous equations is to double the rate of return for both machines although, in fairness, this does not alter their respective rankings.

Example 20.2

Oxford plc is considering the acquisition of a new machine to make plastic mouldings. Two machines are currently available, both equally suitable in terms of quality but with different costs. Machine A costs £125,000 and machine B costs £120,000. Both machines are depreciated using the straight line method and neither has any residual value. Based on similar anticipated sales levels, the estimated yearly profits are as follows:

Year	Machine A	Machine B
1	£10,000	£40,000
2	£20,000	£40,000
3	£20,000	£30,000
4	£40,000	£20,000
5	£50,000	£10,000
6		£10,000
Total	£140,000	£150,000
Average profit per year	£28,000	£25,000

This difficulty is only part of a more general problem with the rate of return calculation. There is no single definition for either the numerator or the denominator. Being told that a proposal offers a 40 per cent return therefore is meaningless without disclosing the basis on which the elements are valued. This applies with even more force to the figure for profit. Profit will be based on accounting conventions. It might even include a proportion of company-wide overheads. If this is the case, the *extra* profit as a result of the proposals will be understated by the reapportioning of overheads which would occur whether or not the proposal is undertaken.

Distorting the data is possible by using the average profit. If proposal B was abandoned after the end of year 5, its total profit would be £140,000 – the same as for machine A – and hence its annual yearly profit would increase to £28,000 per annum. With a smaller initial outlay, machine B would then give a higher rate of return.

There is, however, a more general objection to the rate of return when evaluating the capital budgeting decision. Profit is a nebulous term which is influenced by accounting conventions. Proposals will only be undertaken if the organisation is better off as a result of making the investment and this begs the question as to what is meant by the term 'better off'. Ignoring intrinsic factors such as image and any 'feel good' factor, an organisation will be better off if it has more resources after undertaking the investment than before. Ultimately, resources are measurable in cash as, in a market economy, it is cash which provides the command over the acquisition of resources. What should be being measured therefore, is the extent to which any proposal generates cash. More than that, the timing of the cashflow is equally important. The earlier cash is received, the sooner it can be used productively elsewhere if only by earning interest in a bank deposit account. This 'time value of money' is totally ignored by the rate of return calculation.

The payback period

The payback period is the number of years it takes for an investment's initial outlay to be recovered from benefits received. Ideally, these benefits should be measured in cash for the same reasons outlined when criticising the rate of return ratio. In that sense, the payback period is the time it takes for the proposal to pay for itself. Sometimes, however, cashflows may not be available and so profit might be used as a surrogate. If this is the case, the profit figure must be *before* depreciation, otherwise there will be double counting. Depreciation is merely an allocation of cost and the purpose of the exercise is to determine how long it takes for funds to be generated to meet that cost. The result will be a revised profit figure comprising revenue from sales less all of the expenses directly relating to the investment other than depreciation.

Using the data for Oxford plc given in Example 20.2, the profit figures first need to be adjusted to eliminate depreciation. Machine A cost £125,000. With a five-year life and straight line depreciation, the annual depreciation is £25,000. For machine B, with a six-year life, the depreciation is £20,000 per annum. The revised profit figures are shown in Exhibit 20.5.

Exhibit 20.5 The payback period – amending the profit figures

Year	Machine A	Machine B
1	£35,000	£60,000
2	£45,000	£60,000
3	£45,000	£50,000
4	£65,000	£40,000
5	£75,000	£30,000
6	£30,000	

From Exhibit 20.5, it is now possible to calculate the payback period for both machines A and B. Machine A will have generated £35,000 by the end of the first year. With an initial outlay of £125,000, £90,000 of the original investment will not yet have been recovered. By the end of year two, a further £45,000 will have been received, leaving the amount outstanding also at £45,000. The cashflow of year 3 is just sufficient to meet this amount and so the payback period is three years. A similar analysis for machine B shows it pays for itself within two years.

Had the payback period been between two year ends, the normal procedure is to *pro rata* the amount still outstanding. For example, if a machine had cost £80,000 and the cashflows were £50,000 for year 1 and £90,000 for year 2, then the payback point is somewhere between year 1 and year 2. At the end of year 1, £30,000 of the original outlay has yet to be recovered. With a cash inflow of £90,000 in the second year, the asset will have paid for itself one third of the way through the second year and so the payback period will be one year and four months. In effect, the payback period is a kind of breakeven point. It specifies how long a proposal needs to continue before the initial (fixed) cost of the outlay has been met.

The one immediate advantage of the payback period is its simplicity and intuitive appeal. As a concept it is easy to understand. It does, however, suffer from two limitations. First, it ignores benefits in those years beyond the payback period. For machine A, years 4 and 5 are ignored while for machine B, no account is taken of the benefits in years 3 to 6. Secondly, it ignores the timings of benefits within the payback period. For instance, two proposals might each have the same cost of, say, £100,000. The first one might have cashflows of £90,000 in year 1 and £10,000 in year 2. The second proposal might have the cashflows reversed and yet both proposals show a two-year payback. Indeed, this is merely a particular example of a wider issue, that the payback period ignores the time value of money.

Despite these limitations, the payback period continues to be used in practice. There are two possible explanations for its continuing popularity. First, it may be being used as a measure of risk. For many proposals, the further into the future are potential benefits, the less certain they are likely to be. Most people can guess their income for the following month. They might even be able to estimate their income in one year's time. Attempting to estimate their income in five years' time, however, is unlikely to be particularly accurate or meaningful because of so many imponderables. Knowing that a proposal pays for itself in a relatively short period reduces this difficulty.

Secondly, if an organisation has only limited funds, it might find itself with more potentially profitable proposals **than** available resources. Such a situation is known as capital rationing. A proposal which quickly pays back its initial cost helps to reduce any capital shortages in subsequent periods and so might be preferred to an apparently more profitable proposal which has a much longer payback period.

Although there are theoretically superior techniques for handling both risk and capital rationing, they are much more complex. Not only do they require a much more sophisticated awareness of mathematics, they also require much more detailed information than that necessary to calculate the payback period. The payback period might therefore be being used as a crude measure of both risk and availability of funds.

DISCOUNTED CASHFLOW AND THE INVESTMENT DECISION

A further technique for appraising long term investments has already been introduced in Chapter 6 although in a different context. When measuring economic income, the value of an asset was shown to be dependent on its future benefits. With benefits expressed in cashflows, the greater the benefits, the greater the value of the asset. More than that, by discounting future cashflows to their equivalent value in today's pounds, the time value of money was expressly taken into account. Receiving £100 at the end of year 3, for instance, was shown to have less value than the same amount received one year earlier. At the least, the earlier amount could be invested in a bank to generate interest while waiting for the £100 at the end of year 3 to be realised.

Net present values

Applying discounted cashflows (DCF) to an investment appraisal, the value of the cash inflows can be translated into their equivalent amount today to give the *present value of the inflows*. The difference between this and the initial outlay is known as the *net present value*. If the net present value (NPV) is positive, the benefits expressed in today's terms exceed the outlay and so undertaking the proposal is worthwhile. Before discussing the assumptions and validity of this, it is useful to recall the mechanics of DCF. These are demonstrated in Example 20.3.

Example 20.3

Pembroke Ltd is planning to acquire a machine for £16,000 to produce a car accessory. The machine will have a life of three years, after which it has no residual value. The company uses a 25 per cent discount rate. Estimated cash inflows and outflows for the three years are as follows:

Year	Cash inflows	Cash outflows	Net cashflow
1	£8,000	£3,000	£5,000
2	£20,000	£10,625	£9,375
3	£30,000	£14,375	£15,625

To simplify matters, cashflows are normally assumed to arise at the year end. At a discount rate of 25 per cent, today's value of year 1's cashflow is found by multiplying the amount by $1/(1.25)^1$. Similarly, year 2's cashflow will be multiplied by $1/(1.25)^2$ and year 3's by $1/(1.25)^3$. This results in discount factors of 0.800, 0.640 and 0.512 for years 1 to 3, respectively. The application of these factors to Pembroke's net cashflows is shown in Exhibit 20.6.

Exhibit 20.6 The net present value of a proposal

End of year	Net cashflow	Discount factor	Discounted cashflow
1	£5,000	0.800	£4,000
2	£9,375	0.640	£6,000
3	£15,625	0.512	£8,000
Present value of inflows			£18,000
Cost			£16,000
Net present value			£2,000

The assumptions of the DCF model

In effect, Pembroke is giving up £16,000 today to receive the equivalent of £18,000 today. The company is therefore £2,000 better off. It does not actually receive £18,000 today. Rather it plans to receive larger individual amounts over the next three years but these are *equivalent* to £18,000 today. In essence, the problem is similar to paying out pounds sterling and receiving in exchange, say, French francs. To appraise such a proposal requires either all money to be converted to French francs or pounds sterling. Logically, it makes no difference whether the appraisal is in the foreign or the home currency. Practically, however, a UK-based company is more familiar with the magnitude of money expressed in pounds sterling and so using the home currency carries more meaning. So it is with discounted cashflow. Logically, all the cashflows could have been shown in values at the end of year 3 or any other year for that matter. By expressing the value of the proposal in pounds today, the extent of the benefit is easier to comprehend.

A more immediate concern is likely to be that money received today is certain, whereas money to be received in the future is uncertain. Equally, if there is a shortage of funds, money today is to be preferred to money in the future. As an analogy, a person stranded in the desert would much rather have a bottle of water today than a whole case in six months' time. Given the assumptions of the DCF model, however, these criticisms are not valid[3]. The model assumes perfect competition, including perfect knowledge. Consequently, if a company estimates cashflows for any subsequent period, these can be verified in a similar way to past transactions. In its basic form, the model therefore assumes away risk and uncertainty. As a result of these assumptions, there will be no difference between loans, other borrowings or equity.

In the real world, shareholders demand a higher return than lenders because their investment is more risky. Lenders receive interest irrespective of whether or not profits have been made. In addition, the loans are often secured on the company's assets. Shareholders, however, are always last in the line for their dividends and the extent of these are based on the discretion of the directors. Assuming away risk eliminates the essential difference between debt finance and equity. As a result, the return required by providers of finance will be the same irrespective from where it is sourced.

Two further conditions are necessary before the full implications of the model can be considered. First, perfect competition assumes there are many buyers and sellers – or borrowers and lenders in the case of capital markets. Consequently, there will not be any capital rationing. With perfect knowledge, lenders will be able to verify the certainty of the cash inflows from their loans. Should one source prefer not to lend, a borrower can simply obtain funds from elsewhere. Secondly, perfect competition assumes that there are no transaction costs. Even assuming away risk, interest rates vary in the real world depending on whether a person is borrowing or lending. Banks and other financial intermediaries have to rent accommodation and employ staff as well as aim to make a profit. These represent the transaction costs of finance and explain why there is a difference between borrowing and lending rates. In the basic DCF model, they are assumed not to exist.

Implications of the DCF model

Given the model's assumptions of no risk, no transaction costs and no capital rationing, all investors and borrowers will face a single, market-determined, interest rate. Under these conditions, all a business needs to know is whether the net present value is positive or not. If it is, the proposal is profitable and should be undertaken. Lack of funds is no obstacle as borrowing is possible.

One real-world, practical problem concerns the payment of dividends. Because shareholders are rarely familiar with the detailed operations of a company, they look to their dividend to convey a message about the company's viability. Any failure by a company to pay a dividend is often taken by investors to be a warning of severe difficulties. Even without this difficulty, investors might be relying on dividends to provide them with an income. Dividend policy is therefore a real concern for senior managers who have to ensure cash is available to meet such payments.

How an investment proposal is financed and whether the timing of its cashflows meet the need of the firm's dividend policy are unimportant within the confines of the DCF model. The model enables the viability of the investment proposal to be evaluated independently of the financing and dividend decisions. This is known as the separation theorem. To verify this conclusion, the data relating to Pembroke Ltd in Example 20.3 will be used.

Exhibit 20.7 shows both the financing and dividend implications for Pembroke. Initially, consider what would happen to Pembroke Ltd if it had no funds. With no transaction costs and complete certainty, the borrowing and lending rates will equal one another. Likewise, with complete certainty, there is no risk and so the return required from loans or other borrowings will be the same as that required by shareholders. The company can therefore borrow funds at the assumed market rate of 25 per cent. The implications of this are considered in the column headed 'Year 3 Amount'.

Exhibit 20.7 The independence of the financing and dividend decisions

End of year	Dividend paid: Details	Year 3 Amount	Year 1 Amount
0	Borrow	(£16,000.00)	(£16,000.00)
1	Interest at 25%	(£4,000.00)	(£4,000.00)
1	Pay dividend		(£2,500.00)
1	Add net cashflow	£5,000.00	£5,000.00
1	Balance	(£15,000.00)	(£17,500.00)
2	Interest at 25%	(£3,750.00)	(£4,375.00)
2	Add net cashflow	£9,375.00	£9,375.00
2	Balance	(£9,375.00)	(£12,500.00)
3	Interest at 25%	(£2,343.75)	(£3,125.00)
3	Add net cashflow	£15,625.00	£15,625.00
3	Balance	£3,906.25	nil

With an interest rate of 25 per cent, borrowing £16,000 at the end of year 0/beginning of year 1 results in an interest charge of £4,000 for the year. The amount outstanding will therefore be £20,000, but this will be reduced by the cash inflow at the year end of £5,000. Pembroke therefore starts year 2 owing £15,000 to the providers of finance. Interest at 25 per cent per annum for the second year totals £3,750 while the net cashflow of £9,375 is used to offset the amount owed. For year 3, the interest will be 25 per cent on the amount outstanding at the beginning of that year, a total of £2,343.75. At the end of the year, however, there is a net cash inflow of £15,625 and so, at the end of year 3, Pembroke will have a surplus of £3,906.25. In effect, the proposal reduces to a single cash inflow of £3,906.25 at the end of year 3. To find the present value of the £3,906.25 simply involves applying the 25 per cent discount factor for year 3 to the figure. Multiplying £3,906.25 by 0.512 gives a present value of £2,000 which is the value found in the normal DCF calculation. Within the confines of the model's assumptions therefore, how the proposal is financed is a mere detail.

The same data can be used to demonstrate that the model also treats the dividend decision as a mere detail. Continuing with the assumption of borrowing funds, Pembroke could pay a dividend of £3,906.25 at the end of year 3. If this was not suitable it could pay the dividend in some other time period. The company has a project which has a net present value of £2,000. If it wished, it could pay that amount immediately as a dividend rather than waiting until year 3. To do this, it would have to borrow the £2,000. At an interest rate of 25 per cent per annum, the £2,000 loan will grow to £3,906.25 at the end of year 3 and, as can be seen from Exhibit 20.7, this debt can be repaid by the funds generated by the project at that time. By multiplying the £2,000 by the expression $(1.25)^n$, the dividend at the end of any year can be calculated. Assuming the dividend is desired to be paid out at the end of year 1, the maximum amount payable is £2,500. This is verified in the final column of Exhibit 20.7.

One difficulty sometimes experienced with using the DCF model relates to the way calculations such as that shown in Exhibit 20.6 are presented. Superficially it appears as though the providers of finance are not receiving their return as all the adjustments are to the inflows rather than the initial amount invested. Using the data from Pembroke, newcomers to the DCF model might want to charge interest for the use of the £16,000 invested. This, however, would be wrong. Remember, the objective of the exercise is to compare like with like by putting all cash amounts on a comparable footing. This can be achieved by either discounting the cash inflows and expressing the net benefit in pounds today or compounding the investment and expressing the net benefit in terms of pounds at the end of the project.

With borrowing rates equal to lending rates, investors are looking for a 25 per cent compound rate of interest. An investment of £16,000 now should therefore grow to £31,250 at the end of year 3. This can be compared with the cash generated by the project by the end of year 3. Any cash received before that time will not be left idle but will be invested at 25 per cent per annum as borrowing rates equal lending rates. The £5,000 cash received in year 1 will therefore be invested for a further two years to give a value at the end of year 3 of £7,812.50. Similarly, the £9,375 cash received at the end of year 2 will be invested for a further year to grow to £11,718.75. Adding these to the £15,625.00 generated in year 3 gives a total cash generated of £35,156.25 at the end of the project. This is known as the terminal value. The composition of the terminal value is shown in Exhibit 20.8.

Deducting the £31,250 which investors require after three years from the terminal value leaves a net surplus of £3,906.25 and, as has already been shown, this is equivalent to £2,000 today. This demonstrates that investors' needs are taken into account in the DCF model. It also further demonstrates that, given the assumptions of the model, the only figure of any importance is the net present value. All other data is irrelevant, including the initial outlay, as the mechanics of DCF reduces all cashflows to their equivalent value today. In effect, the proposal facing Pembroke is an outlay of £16,000 now in exchange for an inflow which is equivalent to £18,000 now. As these relate to the same time period, the initial outlay is irrelevant. All that matters is the net amount, the net present value. The NPV decision rule for investment decisions, therefore, is to undertake all proposals with a positive NPV.

Exhibit 20.8 The terminal value of an investment

End of year	Net cashflow (a)	Compounding factor (b)	Terminal value (a × b)
1	£5,000.00	$(1.25)^2$	£7,812.50
2	£9,375.00	$(1.25)^1$	£11,718.75
3	£15,625.00	$(1.25)^0$	£15,625.00
Terminal value			£35,156.25
Investment	£16,000	$(1.25)^3$	£31,250.00
Surplus			£3,906.25

Tables of discount factors

Before discussing an alternative way of evaluating the investment decision, there is a way of speeding DCF calculations. Rather than determining the discount factor each time by using $1/(1+r)^n$, use can be made of tables where the factors have already been calculated for various discount rates and various years. These are provided in the Appendix at the end of this chapter. The 25 per cent discount column, for instance, shows that the appropriate factor for a cashflow at the end of one year is 0.800, for year 2, 0.640 and for year 3, 0.512. The factor for any other rate or year can be determined by identifying the appropriate rate and year and reading the factor. Had discount rates been 10 per cent and a cashflow related to year 4 for instance, the appropriate factor is seen to be 0.683. Although only accurate to three decimal places, the factors should be sufficient for most purposes.

THE INTERNAL RATE OF RETURN

Net present values and the discount rate

A glance at the discount tables shows that for any single year, the value of the factor falls as the discount rate increases. At a rate of 10 per cent for instance, £1,000 at the end of year 1 is worth the equivalent of £909 today whereas at a 50 per cent discount rate it is only worth the equivalent of £667. This loss in value as discount rates increase is magnified the further into the future is the cashflow. Had the £1,000 related to the end of year 10, its present value at 10 per cent would have fallen to £386 but at 50 per cent this would have fallen even further to £17. The reason for this substantial difference in later years is due to the discount factor being raised to the power of the number of years. This can be considered further by appraising the proposal faced by Hastings plc in Example 20.4.

Example 20.4

Hastings plc is considering a proposal which will cost £12,303. As a result of this capital expenditure, net cashflows at the end of year 1 are forecast to be £5,000; at the end of year 2, £7,000; at the end of year 3, £4,000; and at the end of year 4, £2,000.

The effect on the value of the proposal as discount rates vary is shown in Exhibit 20.9, where the 10 per cent, 15 per cent, 20 per cent and 25 per cent discount factors have been used. As the discount rate increases, so the present value of the cash inflows fall. This is particularly noticeable in the later years of the project's cashflows.

Exhibit 20.9 Net present values and changing discount rates

End of year	NCF	10% factor	DCF (£)	15% factor	DCF (£)	20% factor	DCF (£)	25% factor	DCF (£)
1	5,000	0.909	4,545	0.870	4,350	0.833	4,165	0.800	4,000
2	7,000	0.826	5,782	0.756	5,292	0.694	4,858	0.640	4,480
3	4,000	0.751	3,004	0.658	2,632	0.579	2,316	0.512	2,048
4	2,000	0.683	1,366	0.572	1,144	0.482	964	0.410	820
			14,697		13,418		12,303		11,348
Cost			12,303		12,303		12,303		12,303
NPV			2,394		1,115		0		(955)

The internal rate of return rule

In the case of Hastings plc, the net present value falls to zero at 20 per cent. Beyond that, NPVs are negative. If Hastings faced a discount rate – or cost of capital as it is often called – beyond 20 per cent, the proposal would no longer be worthwhile. The value of the inflows in today's pounds would be less than the initial outflow.

As discount rates increase, at some stage – 20 per cent for Hastings – the net present value will fall to zero. This phenomenon of NPVs decreasing as discount rates increase allows an alternative decision rule to be developed for the evaluation of capital expenditure. The discount rate which reduces a proposal's NPV to zero is known as the *internal rate of return or yield*. Instead of determining the NPV at the organisation's cost of capital, the cost of capital can be compared with the internal rate of return. Assume, for example, that Hasting plc's cost of capital is 10 per cent. At 10 per cent, the proposal has a net present value of £2,394. Given the cashflows of Hastings, it follows that if the proposal has a positive NPV when discounted at the cost of capital, the IRR must be greater, as it has been defined as the discount rate which reduces the NPV to zero. The internal rate of return rule therefore is to accept a project if the IRR is greater than the cost of capital. Applying this to Hastings, the IRR is 20 per cent, the cost of capital is 10 per cent, and so the proposal is worthwhile.

Developing the internal rate of return

One difficulty with the internal rate of return involves its calculation. Had Hasting's IRR not been known, it would have been necessary to determine it. This involves solving for the discount rate which reduces the NPV to zero or, equivalently, solving for the discount rate which reduces the present value of the inflows to the value of the initial outlay. Using the data for Hastings and allowing r to equal the IRR discount rate, the problem is reduced to:

$$\left(5,000 \times \frac{1}{(1+r)^1}\right) + \left(7,000 \times \frac{1}{(1+r)^2}\right) + \left(4,000 \times \frac{1}{(1+r)^3}\right) + \left(2,000 \times \frac{1}{(1+r)^4}\right) = 12,303$$

Although expressing the IRR in an equation form is straightforward, solving for r is made difficult by the terms being raised to different powers. An approximate solution, however, can be found by taking two discount rates, one where the NPV is likely to be positive, the other where it is likely to be negative and then approximating the internal rate of return by a process known as *linear interpolation*. The approach is demonstrated in Exhibit 20.10 which graphs the net present value of Hasting's proposal at varying discount rates. The graph is curvilinear because the denominator of the discount factor is raised to the power of the year for each cashflow. Choosing 10 per cent and 25 per cent as the low and high discount rates, interpolation assumes there is a linear relationship between the two discount rates and their NPVs. Linear interpolation will therefore calculate the point shown as the estimated IRR in Exhibit 20.10.

Exhibit 20.10 Estimating the internal rate of return

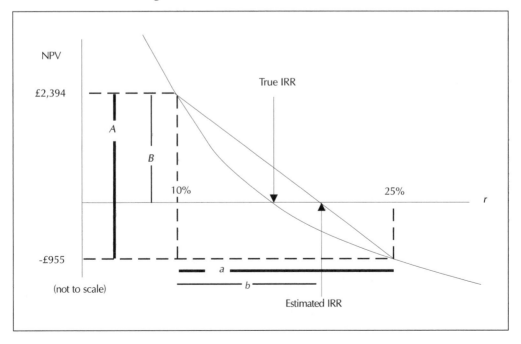

In effect, the range from 10 per cent to 25 per cent forms the base of a right-angled tri-angle whose vertical measurement is from £2,394 (the NPV at 10 per cent) to –£955 (the NPV at 25 per cent). Its height, measured as the range from –£955 to +£2,394, will there-fore be £3,349. The base of the triangle is represented by a and the perpendicular by A. This perpendicular is intersected by the axis representing the various discount rates. In geometry, it can be shown that the relationship of B to A is the same as b to a. This enables the estimated IRR to be calculated. At 10 per cent, the net present value is still positive. The approximated internal rate of return will therefore be 10 per cent plus a proportion of the range from 10 per cent to 25 per cent, that is a proportion of 15 per cent. This pro-portion is found by using the relationship of B to A to estimate b to a. For Hastings, this will be £2,394/£3,349. The computed IRR will therefore be:

$$\text{Computed IRR} = 10\% + \left(\frac{2,349}{3,349} \times 15\%\right) = 20.7\%$$

NPV AND IRR COMPARED

The project being considered by Hastings consisted of an outflow followed by an inflow. In addition, the implicit assumption was that the proposal was independent of any other possible investments, that is undertaking the current proposal does not preclude the acceptance of other proposals. Where both of these conditions are met, the NPV and IRR rules give identical decisions. If the net present value is positive, the proposal should be undertaken. Likewise, if the internal rate of return is greater than the cost of capital, the proposal is also worthwhile. Given the assumptions of the DCF model, these are mere-ly two different ways of expressing the same phenomenon. The rule therefore is to accept *all* proposals with a positive NPV or an internal rate of return greater than the cost of capital.

Sometimes there is a desire to relate the net present value of a proposal to its initial outlay. Given the assumptions of the model, however, this would be wrong. The process of discounting has translated the cash inflows into their equivalent value today. For Hastings plc, the present value of the inflows when discounted at its 10 per cent cost of capital equals £14,697. Its initial outlay is £12,303. The proposal therefore reduces the decision to paying out £12,303 immediately in exchange for the equivalent of £14,697 immediately and this is equivalent to paying out nothing now to immediately gain £2,394. That the cash inflows will not be immediately receivable has been taken account of in the process of discounting.

Consider, for example, two proposals. Project A involves an immediate outlay of £100 in exchange for inflows with a present value of £190, while project B costs £100,000 although the present value of its inflows are £100,100. Forced to choose between the two propos-als, there is a natural tendency to prefer A because of its lower initial cost. Within the con-fines of the model, however, this would be wrong. There is no risk and so any possibility of losing the initial outlay can be ignored. Secondly, the process of discounting has been shown to take account of the interest demanded on the investment. Given the need to choose, the answer is to accept the project with the highest NPV. Accepting B will provide the investor with the equivalent of £10 more today than undertaking project A.

Mutually exclusive projects

Recognising this conclusion helps overcome a possible conflict between the NPV and IRR rules where projects are mutually exclusive. Mutually exclusive projects occur where undertaking one proposal precludes the acceptance of all others. A company, for example, might be planning to offer photocopying services to the public. Several machines may be suitable, all profitable in their own right, and yet only one will be required. Using discounted cashflow to analyse the worth of the proposals may give different rankings, depending on whether the NPV or IRR technique is used. This difficulty is demonstrated in Example 20.5.

Example 20.5

> Winchester plc is considering acquiring a machine to produce parts for the motor industry. Two machines are available, the Delta and the Sigma. Details of estimated cashflows from their purchase are given below. No machine has any residual value.
>
> The Delta will result in net cashflows of £4 million in year 1, £2 million in year 2, £1 million in year 3 and £500,000 in the subsequent two years. Its capital cost will be £4,843,000.
>
> The Sigma will result in net cashflows of £1 million in the first two years and £4 million in the following three years. Its purchase price is £7,590,000.
>
> Winchester's cost of capital is 10 per cent and cashflows can be assumed to occur at the end of each year.

Exhibit 20.11 shows the workings necessary to derive the net present values and the internal rates of return. As both proposals are positive when discounted at 10 per cent, this can also serve as the low discount rate to obtain a positive NPV. The rate chosen to achieve a negative discount rate is 40 per cent. On the basis of the net present value rule, Sigma is preferred as its NPV is £2,365. Using the internal rate of return rule, however, the Delta is the better choice with an IRR of 35 per cent. There is therefore a conflict. Exhibit 20.12 graphs the net present values of each machine at different discount rates and identifies the issues involved.

If it was possible to invest in both proposals, the conflict would not have occurred. Whichever decision rule is used, both projects are identified as being worthwhile. Even with mutually exclusive projects, there would have been no conflict had the cost of capital been above 13 per cent. Below this figure, however, there is a conflict. The reason lies in the timing of the cashflows, with Sigma having most of its inflows in later years. The higher the discount rate, the lower will be any present value and, because the discount formula involves a raising to the power of the number of years, this will be disproportionately so the later the year being considered. Consequently, projects with cashflows mainly in later years will require relatively small increases in discount rates to reduce their NPV to zero, that is they are likely to suffer from lower internal rates of return. This is what has happened with Sigma. With Delta having most of its cashflows in earlier years, a much greater increase in discount rates is necessary before its NPV is reduced to zero and so it has a higher internal rate of return. With a relatively low cost of capital, projects with later cashflows are less penalised and so it is possible to have conflicting results between the net present value and the internal rate of return.

Exhibit 20.11 The net present value and internal rate of return compared

	\multicolumn{10}{c}{Investment proposal}									
	\multicolumn{5}{c}{DELTA}					\multicolumn{5}{c}{SIGMA}				
End of year	*NCF (£000)*	*10% factor*	*DCF (£000)*	*40% factor*	*DCF (£000)*	*NCF (£000)*	*10% factor*	*DCF (£000)*	*40% factor*	*DCF (£000)*
1	4,000	0.909	3,636	0.714	2,856	1,000	0.909	909	0.714	714
2	2,000	0.826	1,652	0.510	1,020	1,000	0.826	826	0.510	510
3	1,000	0.751	751	0.364	364	4,000	0.751	3,004	0.364	1,456
4	500	0.683	342	0.260	130	4,000	0.683	2,732	0.260	1,040
5	500	0.621	311	0.186	93	4,000	0.621	2,484	0.186	744
PV of inflows			6,692		4,463			9,955		4,464
Cost			4,843		4,843			7,590		7,590
NPV			1,849		(380)			2,365		(3,126)

$$\text{IRR(Delta)} = 10\% + \left(\frac{1849}{2229} \times 30\%\right) = 35\% \qquad \text{IRR(Sigma)} = 10\% + \left(\frac{2365}{5491} \times 30\%\right) = 22\%$$

Exhibit 20.12 VPV vs. IRR

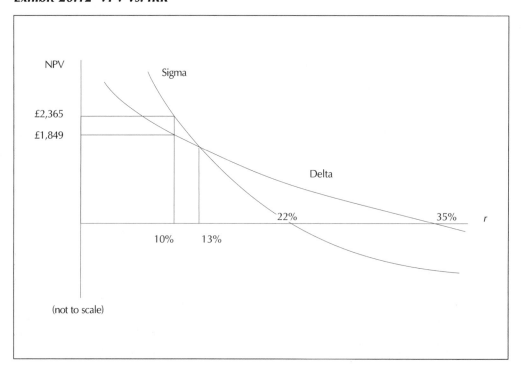

Given the assumptions of the DCF model, the choice is to accept the project with the highest NPV. The reason is that, if accurately estimated, the cost of capital is an opportunity cost which takes account of the real cost of finance. As a result, the net present value represents the increase in wealth in today's pounds from undertaking the proposal, a wealth which is generated from the income stream of the proposal. Put crudely, the issue facing Winchester plc is whether the company would prefer the equivalent of £1,849 today or £2,365. Given a choice has to be made, and given no risk, Sigma is the preferred proposal.

Multiple rates of return

A second limitation of the internal rate of return is that it is possible, under certain circumstances, to have more than one answer. This is demonstrated in Example 20.6.

Example 20.6

Windsor Ltd is considering investing in a machine which will cost £5,206. At the end of the first year there will be a net cash inflow of £14,014 although at the end of the second year the cashflow is a negative one of £11,000. Finally, year 3 brings a further cash inflow of £2,020.

The proposal facing Windsor Ltd has two internal rates of return, 15 per cent and 25 per cent. This is demonstrated in Exhibit 20.13. The reason for this peculiarity is the negative cashflow in year 2. A normal project, that is one with an outflow followed by inflows,

Exhibit 20.13 Multiple rates of return

End of year	NCF (£)	15% factor	DCF (£)	25% factor	DCF (£)
1	14,014	0.870	12,192	0.800	11,211
2	(11,000)	0.756	(8,315)	0.640	(7,039)
3	2,020	0.658	1,329	0.512	1,034
			5,206		5,206
Cost			5,206		5,206
NPV			nil		nil

has a lower net present value the higher the discount rate. A loan has the reverse characteristics. A loan involves an inflow followed by outflows. With a very low discount rate, the loan will have a net present cost, that is, even when measured in today's pounds, the repayments will be greater than the initial advance. As discount rates increase, however, it is possible for the value today of the repayments in later years to fall below the initial advance and for the loan to have a positive net present value. In effect, the proposal facing Windsor has elements of both a loan and a normal investment. The initial outlay followed by the cash inflow of year 1 takes on the appearance of a normal investment while the cash inflow of year 1 followed by the cash outflow of year 2 takes on the appearance of a loan. As discount rates change, the relative importance of these two features change and so the proposal's profile varies between that of a normal investment and a loan. As a result, more than one IRR is possible.

Further criticisms of the internal rate of return

There are two further criticisms sometimes made of the internal rate of return. The first is that it ignores the scale of a proposal by expressing the decision as a percentage to be measured against the cost of capital. Consider two projects, one costing £10,000 and producing a net cashflow of £12,500 at the end of year 1, the other costing £1,000 and generating a cash inflow of £1,250 also at the end of year 1. Assume further that the cost of capital is 10 per cent. Both proposals give a 25 per cent internal rate of return and so, using the IRR decision rule, a company would be indifferent between the two projects. However, at any cost of capital below this figure, the larger project generates the higher net present value. This criticism is only valid if the projects are mutually exclusive. If they are totally independent, the decision should be to undertake both projects as both are worthwhile when discounted at the 10 per cent cost of capital. The internal rate of return rule also comes to this conclusion as both proposals have an internal rate of return greater than the cost of capital.

The second criticism sometimes made of the internal rate of return relates to the reinvestment assumption. It has been argued that for the internal rate of return to be accurate, surplus funds have to be reinvested at that rate of return. To consider the validity of this objection, the data in Example 20.7 will be used.

Example 20.7

> Reading plc is considering investing in new plant and equipment which will generate £10,000 in the first year and £1,000 in each of the two subsequent years. The cost of the plant and equipment will be £9,600.

The internal rate of return of the proposal is 20.5 per cent, the workings for which are shown in Exhibit 20.14. The danger is to read the IRR of 20.5 per cent as being a measure of the absolute benefits over the three years on the funds invested in the project, in other words, to compare it with an investment of 20.5 per cent in a bank deposit. To demonstrate this, assume that surplus funds can only be reinvested at 10 per cent – either in other proposals or on deposit in a bank. Starting with the cashflow generated in year 1, this can be invested at 10 per cent p.a. At the end of the three years, Reading will have a total cash balance of £14,200 from making the investment. The make up of this is shown in Exhibit 20.15. The project has been redefined as an outflow of £9,600 in exchange for a single inflow of £14,200 at the end of year 3. This represents an IRR of only 14 per cent, not the 20.5 per cent shown by the original calculation. This is the basis for the reinvestment criticism.

Exhibit 20.14 The internal rate of return

End of year	NCF (£)	10% factor	DCF factor	25% factor	DCF (£)
1	10,000	0.909	9,090	0.800	8,000
2	1,000	0.826	826	0.640	640
3	1,000	0.751	751	0.512	512
			10,667		9,152
Cost			9,600		9,600
NPV			1,067		(448)

$$\text{IRR} = 10\% + \left(\frac{1067}{1525} \times 15\%\right) = 20.5\%$$

Exhibit 20.15 The reinvestment assumption

End of year	Detail	Amount (£)
1	Net cashflow	10,000
2	10% interest	1,000
2	Net cashflow	1,000
2	Balance	12,000
3	10% interest	1,200
3	Net cashflow	1,000
3	Balance	14,200

As valid as this criticism might be, it is not necessarily a criticism of the internal rate of return as a simple decision rule. The decision rule states that if the internal rate of return is greater than the cost of capital, the project should be undertaken. The extent of the IRR does not come into the rule other than as a comparison with the cost of capital. Providing the project is independent and has normal cashflows, the IRR rule gives the correct decision. Where it may possibly be misleading is if users try to read into it a measure of the scale of the benefits, by, for example, believing that an internal rate of return of 40 per cent is better than an IRR of 38 per cent. Even this is not automatically misleading. If the funding for the proposal is financed in the form of an overdraft and if the project's cashflows are used to repay the overdraft, the IRR is a particularly useful measure. For normal investments, it signifies the extent to which finance charges can increase before the net present value becomes negative.

Conclusions of the DCF model

For normal investments – those with an outflow followed by inflows – both the net present value and the internal rate of return rules give identical decisions where projects are independent. Given the assumptions of the model, if the NPV is positive or the IRR greater than the cost of capital, the proposal is worthwhile, although only the net present value gives a measure of the scale of the benefits derived from the investment. Where projects are mutually exclusive or where they involve abnormal cashflows, there are potential difficulties with the internal rate of return. For these reasons, the net present value is felt to be superior.

Missing from the model, however, are real-world problems such as capital rationing, risk and taxation. These form a substantial part of a body of knowledge known as financial management. As such, a detailed treatment is outside the scope of this text. Nevertheless, some insight can be gained by relaxing the assumptions of the model and considering, in outline, the issues raised. This forms the basis for the rest of this chapter.

CAPITAL RATIONING

Capital rationing occurs whenever an organisation has more worthwhile projects than funds available. Sometimes this occurs artificially, as when a parent company restricts the supply of funds to a subsidiary. At other times, it may arise from the financial system. Companies which operate in countries with less-developed capital markets and exchange control may find they cannot access the markets for funds, despite having profitable projects. Capital rationing can, however, occur in even the most sophisticated of markets if the providers of finance choose to disbelieve the cashflow forecasts of potential borrowers.

A variety of proposals have been put forward to handle capital rationing.[4] Most are extremely complex and all have deficiencies of one sort or another. Probably the most successful approach uses the technique of linear programming introduced in Chapter 17. Linear programming concerns itself with the allocation of scarce resources, the issue faced by any organisation with capital rationing. Without going into the detail, linear programming offers an explanation for why a company might reject proposals with a higher NPV in favour of proposals with a lower NPV. If a project has a lower net present value but a large, early positive cashflow, the value of the cashflow to the organisation may be much greater than its discounted present value. Because of their early timing, the cashflows are more than just part of the return on the investment. They actually help to overcome the shortage of funds. In so doing, further worthwhile projects can then be undertaken.

INTRODUCTION TO RISK

In an uncertain environment, a company will not be sure that interest rates today will apply tomorrow or that a forecast of cashflows will in fact be realised. This casts further doubt on the neat conclusions of the basic DCF model and begins to explain why a company may prefer a project with a lower NPV if there is less risk attached to it. Given the existence of risk, companies can take account of this in one of two ways: by amending the discount rate or amending the cashflows.

Security prices, risk and return

Most companies obtain their finance from a variety of sources: the issue of ordinary and preference shares, the issue of loans and the use of overdraft facilities. To survive long term, a company must meet the aspirations of its investors. For a quoted company, any failure to meet shareholders' needs will result in members selling their shares. In turn this will depress the share price and make the company susceptible to a takeover bid. The discount rate for a company will therefore be one which satisfies the needs of investors.

For a shareholder, the required return will be based on three factors: market interest rates, the financial risk of the company, and its operating risk. Market interest rates will set the minimum desired return and can be approximated by the interest payable on short-dated government stock. This is probably the nearest to a risk-free investment possible, although it is not totally free of risk. Despite holders being guaranteed both the interest and repayment, there is still an element of risk from inflation by being repaid in a depreciated currency.

In addition, shareholders will require an extra return because of the risks inherent in the company. These originate from two sources. Operating risk is the variability in returns from the industry and technology within which the business operates. A company with high fixed costs and fickle demand is likely to see much greater variability in earnings than a company with regular demand or high variable costs. With a regular demand, earnings are likely to remain steady irrespective of the cost structure. In the face of changing demand, a company with a high proportion of variable costs has greater flexibility and can reduce its expenses more easily to meet any fall in demand. Financial risk relates to the amount of debt in a company. The greater the amount of debt, the higher are interest payments. As these have to be paid irrespective of profitability, this poses an additional risk for shareholders, not only in the form of more variability in earnings from the fixed interest payments, but also from the possibility that the providers of debt finance could also cause the company to be liquidated if their trust deeds were breached.

The cost of capital by source

For companies with a stock exchange quotation for their shares, the three factors of market interest rates, financial risk and operating risk will determine their share price. To demonstrate this, consider a company which issued £1, 6 per cent preference shares at their face value when market interest rates were at 5 per cent. If the shares were then priced at £1 on the stock exchange, it means that investors are content with a 6 per cent annual return from their investment, a 1 per cent premium to cover financial and operating risk.

Had investors only wanted a 3 per cent return, the shares would have been a bargain. Other investors would have rushed in to buy the shares. Market forces would then have driven the share price up to £2 as, at that price, the 6p dividend per share would provide the shareholders with their 3 per cent required return. A similar analysis is possible to demonstrate the effect of interest rate changes. If the shares originally traded at their £1 issue price but interest rates doubled to 10 per cent, the preference share price will fall. A new investor will be unwilling to accept a dividend of 6p when a relatively risk-free investment will provide 10p for every pound invested.

This analysis enables the return required by shareholders to be determined. The required return is found by relating the benefits of the share to the price investors are prepared to pay for those benefits in the form of its market price. In the case of preference shares this will be

$$k_p = \frac{D}{P}$$

where k_p is the required return or cost of capital for preference shares, D is the dividend and P is the share price. This logic applies equally to loan stock and debentures, although the required return is likely to be less because of their greater security. Allowing I to equal the interest payments and k_d the required return for the providers of debt finance, the formula becomes

$$k_d = \frac{I}{P}$$

The required return for ordinary shareholders follows a similar argument. There is, however, an additional complexity. Ordinary shareholders do not just receive the current level of dividends. Hopefully, there will be a growth in the dividends through time and this will lead to an increase in the share price. Where growth is assumed to be a constant percentage, g, the formula for the required return of equity shareholders, k_e, can be shown to be

$$k_e = \frac{D}{P} + g$$

The weighted average cost of capital

This awareness of the relationship between share prices and the required return allows a company to calculate its cost of capital, the discount rate which will provide the returns demanded by the providers of its finance. Assume a company is financed by 50 per cent loans and 50 per cent ordinary shares. The loan holders may require, say, a 6 per cent return while the shareholders might require a 10 per cent return. With half of the funds needing to obtain a 6 per cent return and half requiring a 10 per cent return, achieving an overall return of 8 per cent will be sufficient to pay the necessary returns to the two sources of finance. This approach to determining the required return is known as the *weighted average cost of capital*. The data in Example 20.8 can be used to show how it is calculated.

Example 20.8

Paisley plc is financed 40 per cent by loans, 10 per cent by £1 preference shares and 50 per cent by £1 ordinary shares. The loans currently pay £8 interest per £100 subscribed and the interest on the preference shares is 6 per cent. It is anticipated that the next ordinary dividend will be 20 per cent. Dividend growth is thought to be 5 per cent per annum.

The current market price of the debt is £80 per £100 nominal. Preference shares are currently trading at 50p each while the market price of the ordinary shares is 200p.

With the market price of the loan stock at only £80 and interest per annum of £8, investors in Paisley's loans are looking for a 10 per cent return. Similarly, with a preference share dividend of 6p and a market price of 50p, preferences shareholders require a 12 per cent return. Applying the market price of the ordinary shares to the planned dividend and taking into account the growth factor, the required return on ordinary shares is

$$k_e = \frac{20p}{200p} + .05 = 0.15$$

Weighting these individual required returns by their proportions gives Paisley a 12.7 per cent weighted average cost of capital. If it is able to achieve this overall return on all its capital investments, it will be able to provide the individual sources of finance with their particular required returns. Exhibit 20.16 shows how the weighted average cost of capital has been derived. Subsumed within the individual required returns are investors' views on the risks currently faced by Paisley plc. Providing any new proposal is of a similar risk profile to the company's existing investments and providing there is no change in its capital structure, the 12.7 per cent weighted average cost of capital can be used as the discount rate. No further adjustment is necessary because risk, as perceived by the providers of funds, has already been taken into account when determining the price of shares and loans – and these are then incorporated within the weighted average cost of capital.

Exhibit 20.16 The weighted average cost of capital

Source of finance	Cost of capital	Proportion	Weighted cost
Loans	10%	0.4	4.0%
Preference shares	12%	0.1	1.2%
Ordinary shares	15%	0.5	7.5%
Weighted average cost of capital			12.7%

Measuring the risk of an individual proposal: adjusting the discount rate

A problem occurs when a business is considering a proposal outside its normal range of capital investments. A supermarket chain, for instance, has a particular weighted average cost of capital because investors perceive the company's risk as coming from the selling of food. As such, the risk is relatively slight. If, however, the company decided to move into the operating of casinos, it would be inappropriate to apply the current weighted average cost of capital. This only measures how investors feel about the current risk and returns from supermarkets. Casino operation is a much more risky proposition. The discount rate to be used is the one appropriate to that level of risk in the same way that the (lower) weighted average cost of capital is appropriate for the analysis of other supermarket investments.

What is needed is some way of determining the risk investors perceive is inherent in casino operations. Ideally, this could be determined if there currently exist other casino companies with stock exchange quotations. The supermarket could then simply estimate their costs of capital. Rarely, however, is this possible. What tends to happen in companies is for more risky projects to be discounted at a higher discount rate. Unfortunately, the choice is often subjective and, as has previously been demonstrated, a slight error in the discount rate can significantly alter net present values, especially if many of the cashflows relate to later years.

Measuring the risk of an individual proposal: adjusting the cashflows

An alternative treatment would be for the company to estimate the riskiness of the cashflows from the proposal and make adjustments to these. Risk and uncertainty occur because more than one outcome is possible. If these are known and their likelihoods can also be estimated, probability theory can be used.

Consider a company which is proposing to invest £1,000 now for a single cash inflow at the end of one year. It is uncertain what the value of the cash inflow is but estimates that there is a 50 per cent chance of it being £800 and a 50 per cent chance of it being £2,000. If the cashflows and probabilities are accurately estimated and if the company could undertake the project *many times*, then half of the investments will return an £800 cashflow and half a £2,000 cashflow. On average, each investment is guaranteed to return £1,400 for certain. If the investment can be undertaken many times therefore, the appropriate cashflow for DCF purposes is £1,400.

Unfortunately, most firms do not carry out the same investment many times. However, this does not matter. Even where each project is a one-off, providing there are many projects, it can be shown that using the average of the cashflows is still the appropriate figure. Although its proof is statistically quite complex, there is an intuitive logic for this conclusion. In effect, it is an extension of the 'swings and roundabouts' argument, with any above average results being at least partially balanced by below average results from other projects. The greater the number of projects, the more the above and below average results will balance one another. Consequently, the average or *expected value* of the cashflows will be a sufficient measure for investment appraisal purposes. This is demonstrated in Example 20.9.

Example 20.9

Portsmouth Ltd is considering an investment which will cost £90,000 now and will generate cashflows over the next two years. Its weighted average cost of capital is 30 per cent, although the company estimates the risk-free rate as being 15 per cent. Estimates of the likely cashflows and their probabilities are as follows:

Year 1		Year 2	
Probability	*Net cashflow*	*Probability*	*Net cashflow*
0.3	£50,000	0.2	£30,000
0.4	£70,000	0.3	£40,000
0.3	£80,000	0.5	£60,000

The first stage is to determine the expected cashflows for each year. For year 1 this will be (0.3 × £50,000) + (0.4 × £70,000) + (0.3 × £80,000), a total expected cashflow of £67,000. Using a similar logic, the expected cashflow for year 2 is £48,000. From there onwards, the capital investment appraisal follows the normal pattern – but with one exception. By using expected values, the cashflows have already been adjusted for risk. The discount rate to be used is therefore the risk-free rate and not Portsmouth's weighted average cost of capital. The full appraisal is shown in Exhibit 20.17.

Exhibit 20.17 Expected net present value

End of year	Expected NCF	Discount factor	Discounted cashflow
1	£67,000	0.870	£58,290
2	£48,000	0.756	£36,288
			£94,578
Cost			£90,000
Expected net present value			£4,578

Where a company has insufficient projects to eliminate risk, then risk has to be explicitly taken into account. As risk involves the variability of returns, the standard deviation is often suggested as a measure of risk. However, even that will not provide the full answer because investors' *reactions* to risk are of equal importance. These problems will not be considered further as one practical difficulty has already been identified. In the real world, it is difficult enough forecasting a single figure several years ahead. Forecasting a whole range, along with their probabilities, is often a practical impossibility.

Sensitivity analysis

An investment proposal is made up of several variables: the discount rate, its estimated life, its cost and the amount of the net cashflows. In turn, the net cashflows comprise other variables such as unit price, volume, variable costs and fixed costs. Given the real-world uncertainties which surround all of these, it is useful to know how vulnerable the proposal is to changes in any of the variables. This is the function of sensitivity analysis. To demonstrate its use, the data in Example 20.10 will be used.

Example 20.10

> Chester Ltd has received an application from one of its divisional managers to acquire a machine for £50,000 to manufacture silk scarves over the next four years. Annual sales are likely to be 1,000 units at a selling price of £50. The marginal cost of a scarf is believed to be £20 and, in addition, fixed costs per annum of £10,000 will be incurred. Chester's cost of capital is 14 per cent.

With a selling price of £50 and a marginal cost of £20, the unit contribution will be £30 and so the annual contribution will be £30,000. Deducting the fixed costs of £10,000 from this – assumed all to be cash expenses – leaves an annual net cashflow of £20,000. The resulting investment appraisal is shown in Exhibit 20.18.

Exhibit 20.18 Net present value and sensitivity analysis

End of year	Net cashflow	Discount factor	Discounted cashflow
1	£20,000	0.877	£17,540
2	£20,000	0.769	£15,380
3	£20,000	0.675	£13,500
4	£20,000	0.592	£11,840
			£58,260
Cost			£50,000
Net present value			£8,260

The easiest variable to test for sensitivity is the initial outlay of £50,000. With a net present value of £8,260, the initial outlay would have to increase to £58,260 before the proposal was no longer worthwhile, a 16.52 per cent increase. The sensitivity of the discount rate is also relatively straightforward. To find how much this can increase before the NPV becomes negative simply involves calculating the internal rate of return. This is found to be 22 per cent. A third element of the project is its life. The present value of the cash inflows of years 1 to 3 inclusive is £46,420, £3,580 less than the initial cost. Therefore, only if the project continues into year 4 will it break even. As year 4 brings in £11,840 of present value and as the project is £3,580 short of breaking even at the end of year 3, breakeven takes place 3,580/11,840 into year 4. Only if the project continues beyond three years four months will it be viable. This sensitising on the project's life is more generally known as the discounted payback period.

Sensitising on other variables becomes a little more complex. Consider, for example, the breakeven sales volume. With a unit contribution of £30 and annual fixed costs of £10,000, annual cashflow will be (£30X – £10,000) where X is the desired volume of sales. For year 1, the present value of the cashflow will be 0.877(£30X – £10,000). By multiplying the term (£30X – £10,000) by each year's discount factor, the present value of the inflows can be determined. As the objective is to determine the breakeven sales volume, the present value of the inflows must equal the initial outlay to ensure a net present value of nil. This can be expressed as an equation:

$$0.877(£30X - £10,000) + 0.769(£30X - £10,000) + 0.675(£30X - £10,000)$$
$$+ 0.592(£30X - £10,000) = £50,000$$

As all the terms in the brackets are identical, this reduces to

$$2.913(£30X - £10,000) = £50,000$$

Solving for X, the breakeven sales volume is 905 units. Sensitising on fixed costs, variable costs or selling prices all involve terms within the brackets and so all that is necessary is to substitute X for the variable which is being sensitised. For fixed costs, this will be

$$2.913(£30,000 - X) = £50,000$$

With X now representing fixed costs, these can increase to £12,836 before the project is no longer worthwhile. Solving for the breakeven contribution allows the breakeven unit variable cost and selling price to be determined. The total contribution will be the 1,000 units produced multiplied by X, the unit contribution. Solving for X in the following equation gives the breakeven unit contribution.

$$2.913(\pounds1,000X - \pounds10,000) = \pounds50,000$$

The result is a breakeven unit contribution of £27.16. As selling price less unit variable costs equal contribution, unit variable costs plus contribution must equal selling price. With unit variable costs of £20.00, the selling price can therefore fall to £47.16. Equally, with a selling price of £50 and a breakeven contribution of £27.16, unit variable costs can increase to £22.84 before the viability of the project is called into question.

Sensitivity analysis has an intuitive appeal, an appeal similar to the breakeven analysis of marginal costing and pricing and output decisions. Having identified the variables, managers should focus on those to which the NPV is most sensitive. Sensitivity, however, is not without its criticisms. First, it involves isolating one variable at a time. Allowing several to vary may be more realistic; it is also much more complex. Secondly, sensitivity is not the same as probability. For example, in the case of Chester, if prices were to fall by only 5.68 per cent, the proposal would no longer be viable. If, however, the company has entered into a fixed price contract, then there is no *likelihood* of the price reduction happening and so the project's extreme sensitivity to a reduction in prices is irrelevant when attempting to measure risk.

TAXATION AND THE CAPITAL INVESTMENT DECISION

One further real-world issue, ignored in the basic model, is the role of taxation in capital budgeting. Dividends are paid out of after-tax income and so the worth of any investment proposal should also be considered in after-tax terms. The treatment of taxation varies in detail from one country to another and from one year to the next. Nevertheless, there are some common features.

First, tax will have to be paid on the profits generated by any capital investment. Secondly, the depreciation charge applied in the financial accounts and that allowed by the tax authorities (known as capital allowances in the UK) are unlikely to be the same. Depreciation itself does not come into capital budgeting as it is an allocation of cost rather than a cash expense. To the extent that the tax authorities allow some kind of depreciation, however, it is relevant as the tax charge will be reduced. In the UK, most capital allowances are calculated at a constant rate on the reducing balance in a similar way to reducing balance depreciation. Thirdly, there is likely to be a delay between the tax being calculated and actually being paid. For UK limited companies, corporation tax is payable nine months after the accounting year end, although for investment appraisal purposes, this is approximated to 12 months. Fourthly, when an asset comes to the end of its life or is disposed of, there is either a balancing allowance or a balancing charge for tax purposes. For example, if an asset cost £100,000 and, at the end of its life, the tax authorities had allowed £80,000 of that as an expense, in the final year the balance of £20,000 will be allowable.

As a result of all these factors, the net cashflow of an investment appraisal will comprise two elements. The first is the normal operating cashflows used so far – the cash receipts from sales less any payments to suppliers and employees. The second is the cash payments to the taxation authorities based on the project's profitability. Before estimating the net present value therefore, it is necessary to determine the corporation tax payable and its timings. These can then be deducted from the operating net cashflows, allowing the proposal's net present value to be calculated. The mechanics involved will be demonstrated by using the data in Example 20.11.

Example 20.11

Peacehaven Ltd has a 25 per cent cost of capital. It is currently considering the acquisition of a machine for £80,000 which will increase profits before tax and depreciation by £60,000 over the next three years. After that time the machine will be worthless. At each year end there will be no trade debtors or trade creditors and so the profit before tax and depreciation will also be the net cashflow before taxation for each year.

Capital allowances are likely to be 25 per cent on the reducing balance, while corporation tax is estimated at 40 per cent, payable one year in arrears.

The first step is to estimate the effect of taxation. The capital allowance in the first year will be 25 per cent of £80,000, a total of £20,000. In the second year, it will be 25 per cent on the written down value of £60,000, a total of £15,000. This leaves a written down value of £45,000 at the commencement of year 3. As the life of the machine is only three years, the capital allowance for year 3 will be a balancing allowance equal to this amount. The calculation of the tax payable and the year of payment is shown in Exhibit 20.19. In each year, the profit before depreciation and tax is reduced by the amount of the capital allowance to give the taxable profit. From this, the actual tax payable is calculated by applying the 40 per cent corporation tax rate to the taxable profit. Strictly, the amount will then be payable nine months later but, for the purposes of this exercise, this is approximated to twelve months. Having calculated the tax payable and the due date, these payments can then be used to reduce the net cashflows from operating. Applying the discount factors in the normal way results in a net present value of £15,204 for Peacehaven's proposal. This is shown in Exhibit 20.20.

Exhibit 20.19 The tax computation

Year	Profit before tax and depreciation (a)	Capital allowance (b)	Taxable profit (a – b = c)	Tax payable 40% × (c)	Payable in year
1	£60,000	£20,000	£40,000	£16,000	2
2	£60,000	£15,000	£45,000	£18,000	3
3	£60,000	£45,000	£15,000	£6,000	4

Exhibit 20.20 Discounted cashflow and taxation

End of year	Operating NCF	Tax paid	NCF	Discount factor	DCF
1	£60,000		£60,000	0.800	£48,000
2	£60,000	(£16,000)	£44,000	0.640	£28,160
3	£60,000	(£18,000)	£42,000	0.512	£21,504
4		(£6,000)	(£6,000)	0.410	(£2,460)
					£95,204
Cost					£80,000
Net present value					£15,204

SUMMARY

Much of management accounting focuses on the short term, with budgets and standard costs being the major control mechanisms. This chapter has been concerned with widening that focus and considering the broader, strategic implications. This has allowed profitability to be seen differently. Not only is product profitability at least partially based on its current stage within the product life cycle, it is also dependent on the product's market position and market growth. Awareness of such relationships are likely to be increasingly important to management accounting in the future. Success for an enterprise is likely to come from recognising the elements of its products which give benefits to customers. To derive profitability, the management accounting system needs to be able to determine the cost of providing these benefits. Currently, with costs predominantly collected on a responsibility basis and with an inadequate treatment of overheads, management accounting is failing to provide this information. However, if the concepts of business strategy are valid, businesses will increasingly depend on such information for their success.

One difficulty with the development of strategic management accounting is that it may involve data other than from the current period. Whatever the limitation of this, the role of capital budgeting within the management accounting framework has shown that such difficulties are not insurmountable. Indeed, capital budgeting is at the interface of management accounting and business strategy.

Several approaches to capital budgeting were considered. The theoretically superior method is based on discounted cashflow as this takes account of the time value of money. The model was developed using a theoretical approach. This was deliberate as it enabled its validity to be questioned and the effect of relaxing some of the assumptions to be evaluated. Two particular problems were then considered in outline: capital rationing and the treatment of risk. Much of the theoretical treatment of risk revolves around probability theory and this assumes not only that all outcomes can be determined but also that their probabilities can be estimated. Given the real-world difficulties of this, a practical alternative to measuring risk is to carry out sensitivity analysis.

REFERENCES

1 Anthony, R. A. (1988) *The Management Control Function*, Harvard Business School Press.
2 See Porter, M. E. (1985) *Competitive Strategy: Creating and Sustaining Superior Performance*, The Free Press.
3 In effect, what follows is a numerical expression of the model developed by Hirschleifer, J. (1958) 'On the Theory of the Optimal Investment Decision', *Journal of Political Economy*, August.
4 See for example Samuels, J. M., Wilkes, F. M. and Brayshaw, R. E. (1990) *Management of Company Finance*, Chapman & Hall, Chapter 6.

FURTHER READING

Bromwich, M. (1976) *The Economics of Capital Budgeting*, Penguin.
Bromwich, M. (1992) 'Strategic Management Accounting' in *Management Accounting Handbook*, ed. Drury, C., Butterworth Heinemann.
Johnson, G. and Scholes, K. (1993) *Exploring Corporate Strategy*, Prentice Hall. 3rd edn.
Lumby, S. (1988) *Investment Appraisal and Financing Decisions*, Chapman & Hall.
Samuels, J. M., Wilkes, F. M. and Brayshaw, R. E. (1990) *Management of Company Finance*, Chapman & Hall.
Ward, K. (1992) *Strategic Management Accounting*, Butterworth Heinemann.

TEST YOUR UNDERSTANDING

1 In the three elements identified by Anthony as making up the totality of management control, engineered costs are mainly associated with:
 (a) task or operational control;
 (b) management control *per se*;
 (c) strategic planning;
 (d) none of these.

2 A product has the following characteristics: low prices, a slowing down in sales volume, declining unit profit, increasing selectivity amongst customers and price cutting. At what stage is it in the product life cycle?

3 What phenomenon is identified with the learning curve?

4 A product has high market share and low market growth. In terms of the product-portfolio matrix, it is known as:
 (a) a star;
 (b) a cash cow;
 (c) a wild cat;
 (d) a dog.

5 What is meant by the time value of money and does it depend on there being risk and/or inflation?

6 Without risk or inflation, the net present value of a project represents:
 (a) the net profit from the project;
 (b) the value, in today's pounds, of the inflows from the project;

(c) the increased value in today's pounds attributable to the investor from undertaking the project;

(d) the net amount of cash receivable in the first year.

7 What is meant by the internal rate of return?

8 A company has to choose one of two machines to produce a new product. Both are equally suitable for the proposed task. Machine A costs £150,000, has a net present value of £78,000 and an internal rate of return of 20 per cent. Machine B costs £89,000, has a net present value of £48,000 but an internal rate of return of 24 per cent. Assuming no risk and an adequate supply of funds, which machine should be acquired?

9 What is meant by capital rationing and what is its implication for capital investment appraisal?

10 A share with a nominal value of 50p pays a dividend of 20p each and every year. Investors believe that this will continue into the future. Investors are currently looking for a 10 per cent return. Estimate the market price of the share.

QUESTIONS

1 Nene plc manufactures parts for the aircraft industry. One part is a valve which requires a great deal of skilled labour. The first batch of valves comprised 10 units and took 900 hours to complete. Nene has now been offered the possibility of further sequential contracts as follows:

Contract number	Size in units
2	10
3	20
4	40
5	80

Estimate the average time taken to produce a unit for each contract on the assumption that a 90 per cent learning curve exists.

2 Powell Power plc has been invited to bid for a contract to supply the navigational equipment for a soon to be launched aircraft. The contract will last four years and requires 10 navigational systems to be delivered in each of those years. Building 10 systems in the first year will require 350,000 hours of skilled labour at a rate of £14 per hour. In addition, materials will cost £2.8 million per 10 systems and direct overheads £900,000 per year.

The contract involves stage payments from the aircraft manufacturer, £8 million immediately the contract commences, the same amount at the end of year 2 and £14 million on completion at the end of the fourth year. Powell Power's cost of capital is 20 per cent and for appraisal purposes, it can be assumed that all expenditure takes place at the end of each relevant year.

Recommend whether Powell Power should bid for the contract assuming:

(a) no learning curve phenomenon exists;

(b) there is an 80 per cent learning curve.

The learning curve factors have already been calculated as follows:

Batch number	Batch size	Cumulative size	Learning factor
1	100%	100%	1.0000
2	100%	200%	0.8000
3	100%	300%	0.7021
4	100%	400%	0.6400

3 Dundee and Sterling Ltd is considering the replacement of a milling machine as the current machine is coming to the end of its useful life. Because of the specific nature of both the existing and proposed machines, neither will have a residual value at any time. Details of the proposal are as follows:

Sales and production per annum (units)	10,000
Turnover per annum	£300,000
Annual material and labour	£140,000
Annual overheads	£20,000
Straight line depreciation over 5 years	£100,000
Annual profit	£40,000

The machine would be used to make a single product, the costs for which are included in the above appraisal. The annual overheads represent the cost of the product line manager whose time is spent exclusively on that product. No debtors or creditors are planned at the end of each year. The recommendation to the board is that the project should be rejected as it fails to meet the 10 per cent minimum return demanded by its parent company.

Evaluate the implications for the company of the above proposal and determine the sales level in units and the discount rate at which the board would be indifferent between renewing or not renewing the machine.

4* Richmond Ltd is considering which of two mutually exclusive projects it should undertake. The finance director thinks that the project with the higher net present value should be chosen whereas the managing director thinks that the one with the higher internal rate of return should be undertaken especially as both projects have the same initial outlay and length of life. The company anticipates a cost of capital of 10 per cent and the net after-tax cashflows of the project are as follows:

End of year	Project A (£000)	Project B (£000)
0	(200)	(200)
1	35	218
2	80	10
3	90	10
4	75	4
5	20	3

You are required to:

    (a) calculate the net present value and internal rate of return of each project;
    (b) recommend, with reasons, which project you would undertake (if either);
    (c) explain the inconsistency in ranking of the projects in view of the directors' remarks;
    (d) identify the cost of capital at which your recommendation in (b) would be reversed.

APPENDIX:

STRATEGIC MANAGEMENT ACCOUNTING AND THE CAPITAL BUDGETING DECISION

Discount rate	5	6	7	8	9	10	11	12	13	14	15	16	17	18	19	20	25	30	35	40	50
End of year																					
1	0.952	0.943	0.935	0.926	0.917	0.909	0.901	0.893	0.885	0.877	0.870	0.862	0.855	0.847	0.840	0.833	0.800	0.769	0.741	0.714	0.667
2	0.907	0.890	0.873	0.857	0.842	0.826	0.812	0.797	0.783	0.769	0.756	0.743	0.731	0.718	0.706	0.694	0.640	0.592	0.549	0.510	0.444
3	0.864	0.840	0.816	0.794	0.772	0.751	0.731	0.712	0.693	0.675	0.658	0.641	0.624	0.609	0.593	0.579	0.512	0.455	0.406	0.364	0.296
4	0.823	0.792	0.763	0.735	0.708	0.683	0.659	0.636	0.613	0.592	0.572	0.552	0.534	0.516	0.499	0.482	0.410	0.350	0.301	0.260	0.198
5	0.784	0.747	0.713	0.681	0.650	0.621	0.593	0.567	0.543	0.519	0.497	0.476	0.456	0.437	0.419	0.402	0.328	0.269	0.223	0.186	0.132
6	0.746	0.705	0.666	0.630	0.596	0.564	0.535	0.507	0.480	0.456	0.432	0.410	0.390	0.370	0.352	0.335	0.262	0.207	0.165	0.133	0.088
7	0.711	0.665	0.623	0.583	0.547	0.513	0.482	0.452	0.425	0.400	0.376	0.354	0.333	0.314	0.296	0.279	0.210	0.159	0.122	0.095	0.059
8	0.677	0.627	0.582	0.540	0.502	0.467	0.434	0.404	0.376	0.351	0.327	0.305	0.285	0.266	0.249	0.233	0.168	0.123	0.091	0.068	0.039
9	0.645	0.592	0.544	0.500	0.460	0.424	0.391	0.361	0.333	0.308	0.284	0.263	0.243	0.225	0.209	0.194	0.134	0.094	0.067	0.048	0.026
10	0.614	0.558	0.508	0.463	0.422	0.386	0.352	0.322	0.295	0.270	0.247	0.227	0.208	0.191	0.176	0.162	0.107	0.073	0.050	0.035	0.017
11	0.585	0.527	0.475	0.429	0.388	0.350	0.317	0.287	0.261	0.237	0.215	0.195	0.178	0.162	0.148	0.135	0.086	0.056	0.037	0.025	0.012
12	0.557	0.497	0.444	0.397	0.356	0.319	0.286	0.257	0.231	0.208	0.187	0.168	0.152	0.137	0.124	0.112	0.069	0.043	0.027	0.018	0.008
13	0.530	0.469	0.415	0.368	0.326	0.290	0.258	0.229	0.204	0.182	0.163	0.145	0.130	0.116	0.104	0.093	0.055	0.033	0.020	0.013	0.005
14	0.505	0.442	0.388	0.340	0.299	0.263	0.232	0.205	0.181	0.160	0.141	0.125	0.111	0.099	0.088	0.078	0.044	0.025	0.015	0.009	0.003
15	0.481	0.417	0.362	0.315	0.275	0.239	0.209	0.183	0.160	0.140	0.123	0.108	0.095	0.084	0.074	0.065	0.035	0.020	0.011	0.006	0.002
16	0.458	0.394	0.339	0.292	0.252	0.218	0.188	0.163	0.141	0.123	0.107	0.093	0.081	0.071	0.062	0.054	0.028	0.015	0.008	0.005	0.002
17	0.436	0.371	0.317	0.270	0.231	0.198	0.170	0.146	0.125	0.108	0.093	0.080	0.069	0.060	0.052	0.045	0.023	0.012	0.006	0.003	0.001
18	0.416	0.350	0.296	0.250	0.212	0.180	0.153	0.130	0.111	0.095	0.081	0.069	0.059	0.051	0.044	0.038	0.018	0.009	0.005	0.002	0.001
19	0.396	0.331	0.277	0.232	0.194	0.164	0.138	0.116	0.098	0.083	0.070	0.060	0.051	0.043	0.037	0.031	0.014	0.007	0.003	0.002	0.000
20	0.377	0.312	0.258	0.215	0.178	0.149	0.124	0.104	0.087	0.073	0.061	0.051	0.043	0.037	0.031	0.026	0.012	0.005	0.002	0.001	0.000
25	0.295	0.233	0.184	0.146	0.116	0.092	0.074	0.059	0.047	0.038	0.030	0.024	0.020	0.016	0.013	0.010	0.004	0.001	0.001	0.000	0.000
30	0.231	0.174	0.131	0.099	0.075	0.057	0.044	0.033	0.026	0.020	0.015	0.012	0.009	0.007	0.005	0.004	0.001	0.000	0.000	0.000	0.000
35	0.181	0.130	0.094	0.068	0.049	0.036	0.026	0.019	0.014	0.010	0.008	0.006	0.004	0.003	0.002	0.002	0.000	0.000	0.000	0.000	0.000
40	0.142	0.097	0.067	0.046	0.032	0.022	0.015	0.011	0.008	0.005	0.004	0.003	0.002	0.001	0.001	0.001	0.000	0.000	0.000	0.000	0.000

Discount factors

CHAPTER 21

Divisional performance and transfer pricing

The modern business enterprise is increasingly large and complex, often selling a variety of goods and services in many different markets. To be successful, companies need to have in place an appropriate organisational structure and this has accounting implications. If accounting is to help monitor the immediate past and provide a guide to future performance, then the accounting system needs to reflect that organisational structure.

This chapter:

- Discusses the concepts of centralisation, decentralisation and divisionalisation

- Identifies the prerequisite for successful divisionalisation

- Develops the return on investment and residual income as measures of divisional performance

- Outlines the difficulties in setting an appropriate transfer price where there is inter-divisional trading

The modern, large business will often sell a wide variety of goods or services in many different markets. If the enterprise is to be successful, it must have in place an appropriate organisational structure to handle the resulting complexities which will satisfy both the needs of the consumers in those markets and the stakeholders within the firm. This has implications for accounting. If accounting information is to be meaningful it must reflect the physical flows of inputs and outputs and the organisational structure. Only then can it be of help to management in monitoring the recent past and acting as a guide to future decisions.

At the extremes, an organisational structure can either be centralised or decentralised. Within this spectrum is found a particularly popular form of organisation known as divisionalisation. This is the subject matter of this final chapter. It has deliberately been left until the last as the subject brings together many of the ideas developed in earlier chapters. In particular, there will be a continuing tension between the ideas of neo-classical economics outlined in Chapters 17 and 18 and the findings from the more modern study of organisational behaviour introduced in Chapter 19.

CENTRALISATION, DECENTRALISATION AND DIVISIONALISATION

A centralised enterprise is one where decisions are made at relatively high levels within the organisation. Decentralised organisations are where discretion and authority to make important decisions are delegated to lower levels of management. Decentralisation can be either functional or federal.

Functional decentralisation

Functional decentralisation involves dividing the organisation into its component parts based on primary tasks or functions such as production, finance, marketing and personnel. As such it represents the traditional economic idea of division of labour. Central management is responsible for establishing pricing policies, the product-mix and output levels. Functional managers are then responsible for meeting targets within these constraints. Often, these targets are expressed in physical terms with an added requirement to minimise costs. For example, a manager of an electricity generating power station might be responsible for achieving a certain output of electricity each period but not with establishing a selling price nor determining how the output might be marketed. Even the purchasing of raw materials might be handled centrally. As a consequence, the power station manager is responsible for meeting a physical target at least cost rather than achieving a particular level of profitability.

Federal decentralisation

Federal decentralisation is conceptually quite different. It involves dividing the organisation into quasi-autonomous sub-units. This is often made on the basis of different product groupings but it can be based on different types of market such as industrial and private customers or different geographical areas. These sub-units are known as *divisions*. Sometimes these divisions are separate legal entities of the form introduced in Chapter 9. At other times they will merely be organisational segments within the one legal entity.

Unlike the managers operating in a functionally decentralised environment, divisional managers can often be responsible for determining manufacturing methods, the sourcing of materials, the setting of prices and the choice of markets. Not only will they be responsible for these and other similar decisions, their success is also likely to be substantially judged by some measure of the profit generated by their decisions.

Divisionalisation defined

A division has been defined as an organisational unit 'headed by a person fully responsible for the profitability of its operations, including planning, production, financial and accounting activities ... [and usually with] ... its own sales force'.[1] However valid this might be as a definition, it says nothing about decentralisation within the division. It might be, for example, that *within* the division, control is extremely centralised. As a result, it is wrong to assume that divisionalisation is synonymous with decentralisation. Further, it is silent about how profitability should be measured.

THE DIVISIONAL FRAMEWORK

Arguments for divisionalisation

Organisational needs – a contingency theory response

Divisionalisation can be seen as a response to the increasing complexity of business organisations resulting not only from the increased size of enterprises but also the greater range of products and the wider geographical spread of markets. This increasing complexity and diversity means product and marketing expertise becomes more localised, making informed decisions by central management more difficult. Because of this, it can be argued that divisionalisation enhances the quality and speed of decision making as local decision makers are more familiar with the issues. In turn this facilitates further diversification by providing a mechanism for effective organisation.

It can also be argued that the devolving of decision making improves the motivation of divisional management by making their jobs more challenging and giving them greater freedom. However, as the evidence presented in Chapter 19 demonstrates, this is not necessarily an automatic consequence of devolving power. Divisions can also be used as training grounds for future senior management.

Viewed in this light, a divisional structure often becomes the most appropriate response to the modern-day conditions faced by multi-product firms operating in diverse markets. In other words, it is a contingency theory response to the environment originally identified in Chapter 19.

Efficient allocation of resources

The organisational perspective may well explain why multi-product enterprises divisionalise but what it does not explain is why the enterprises became multi-product in the first place. Divisions do not just happen. They are consciously developed or acquired. And, given their popularity, there has to be some powerful force encouraging their development.

The alternative to a division is a stand alone, independent firm. To explain divisions therefore involves identifying the main advantage a division has over an independent firm. Predominantly, this advantage is lower transaction costs.[2] A company will develop a hierarchy of divisions when it is more economical to arrange activities and transactions through that structure than through markets. Managers may be able to obtain detailed information at a much lower cost from a division than through independent business units operating in markets. With this access to low cost detailed information, they are able to monitor performance and efficiency more effectively than markets. In addition, because they have access to detailed information, managers may be more effective than markets in the form of shareholders in making any necessary adjustments. For example, independent business units are often only closed down when they become insolvent. Group management, by having detailed knowledge and regular monitoring, may be able to anticipate the demise of a division and either take corrective action or close the business unit down at an earlier, less costly stage.

Efficient transmission of information

The danger with so much low cost information in an organisation is information overload. This is particularly true of centralised organisations. However, a divisionalised structure, by at least devolving power down to the divisional level, overcomes this by eliminating the need for the centre to have excessive, detailed, operational data.

Reduction in suboptimal behaviour

Divisional managers do not always act in the best interests of shareholders. By freeing central management from day-to-day operational problems, suboptimal behaviour by divisional managers can be reduced. Central management is able to concentrate on the strategic issues and to monitor the performance of divisions. In addition, a climate of co-operation can be encouraged between the divisions rather than the opportunistic behaviour sometimes found in market-oriented transactions.

Arguments against divisionalisation

Suboptimisation

While minimising some aspects of suboptimisation, divisionalisation can encourage other forms of the problem. By giving divisional management more freedom, the opportunity for suboptimisation is increased. First, a division might increase its profits by undertaking activities which reduce the profits for the organisation as a whole. Secondly, and resulting from this, a climate of conflict between managers might develop. Thirdly, *if* markets are efficient, they are likely to provide a better mechanism for judging strategic decisions than the second guesses of central management.

Extra explicit costs

If divisionalisation gives complete freedom to divisional managers – and autonomy at least at divisional director level is central to the concept of divisionalisation – there can be extra explicit costs for each division. Each division, for instance, may choose to have its own separate accounting system, its own separate human resource management team and its own separate purchasing system. This is not only likely to increase the explicit costs of running those systems, it may also lead to duplication and coordination difficulties.

Interdependencies

More than that, divisionalisation for its own sake may be counterproductive. This is particularly so if there are interdependencies between divisions. With interdependencies, group objectives cannot be broken down into self-standing independent divisional objectives.

Equally, corporate resources may be complementary. In this case, the potential for economies of scale may be reduced by divisionalisation. Indeed, attempting to manage these interdependencies as independent divisions may actually result in increased costs. In effect, divisionalisation would have become pseudo-divisionalisation.

Prerequisites for successful divisionalisation

Divisional independence

Ideally each division should be independent of all the others – although if taken to its logical conclusion this destroys the idea that divisions are an integral part of the total enterprise.

Minimising suboptimal behaviour

At its simplest, minimising suboptimal behaviour implies that no division should be allowed to make profits at the expense of the organisation as a whole. But if there is suboptimal behaviour, this implies that there is also optimal behaviour and that the enterprise has unambiguous and consistent goals. In reality, goals can be multiple, conflicting and ambiguous, questioning the operational meaning of optimality.

Performance measurement

Any measure of performance should be as independent as possible of the efficiencies and managerial decisions of other parts of the organisation. For example, overheads in one division should not increase because of decreased activity in another division. In addition the measure should not be capable of being manipulated by divisional managers –

as when overheads are carried forward to another period by the building up of period end stocks.

Organisational structure and types of decision making

Strategic decision making which impinges on the profile of the enterprise should be made by central, corporate management but with a high level of autonomy within the divisions for operating decisions. However, to make this effective requires four controls. First, it requires an incentive system involving both monetary and non-monetary rewards to bring the interests of divisional managers in line with the interests of the enterprise as a whole. Secondly, there has to be suitable accounting measures against which to monitor and evaluate the performance of both the divisions and their managers. Thirdly, there is a need for an allocation system which guides resources to the most profitable options as determined by the corporate management of the enterprise rather than allowing the resources to be retained in the divisions. (But this then may have an effect on motivation by taking away the devolved freedom to the divisions which is the central characteristic of divisionalisation.) Fourthly, the enterprise requires an appropriate organisational structure within which to operate and achieve the other controls.

A discussion of detailed organisational structures and reward systems is outside the scope of this text although some of the issues involved have been identified in earlier chapters. Rather, the focus will be on discussing appropriate performance measurements and the difficulty of measuring that performance when there is a particular form of interdependency – where one division sells to another.

OBJECTIVES OF DIVISIONAL PERFORMANCE MEASUREMENT

Divisional performance measurement serves three purposes. First, it helps central management to measure the efficiency of each division as an economic entity. Secondly, it helps them measure the efficiency of divisional managers in running their divisions. This is not the same as the first objective. A manager might have been placed in a problem division to remedy those problems. This, the manager might have successfully achieved even though the subsequent performance of the division might initially be below that of other divisions. Finally, it should guide divisional managers towards the correct decisions they have to make within their own divisions.

Responsibility accounting

If managers are to be held accountable for their performance, they must have clearly defined areas of responsibility over which they can exercise control. Chapter 16 introduced the concept of responsibility accounting and the associated ideas of cost centres, profit centres and investment centres. Just as the flow of accounting information should track the physical flows of production and sales within an organisation, so should responsibility accounting parallel the organisational structure of the enterprise if responsibility accounting is to be effective. What this structure will be will depend on a variety of contingencies such as technology, uncertainties within markets and management styles.

Responsibility accounting within functional and federal decentralisation

With no responsibility for profits, a manager in a functionally decentralised organisation can only be viewed as a cost centre. However, if an organisation is federally decentralised, a divisional manager can be viewed either as a profit centre or an investment centre. Profit centres are concerned with achieving optimal levels of profit and are more appropriate to situations where capital expenditure is outside the control of the divisional manager. Investment centres are an extension of profit centres and relate profit to the resources invested in the division. An investment centre is where the managers can, to a significant extent, influence the size of the investment base.

Both measures involve determining profit. Profit centres in their purest form are where the outputs of a division have a well-established market price and where the managers of the divisions are free to sell that output to whom ever they choose. Many divisions, however, are forced to sell their output to other divisions either because corporate management prevents sales to outsiders or because the product is an intermediate product, only of value to another division within the enterprise. Because of this, it may be more appropriate to view such divisions as pseudo-profit centres.

As will be seen later, one great difficulty is determining the price at which any intermediate product is transferred between divisions. The higher the transfer price, the greater the apparent profitability of the producing division and the lower the profitability of the purchasing division. More than that, the purchasing division might try to minimise this disadvantage in its own interests even though the overall effect on the enterprise will be negative.

The prevalence of profit and investment centres

There is only limited evidence of the extent to which profit and investment centres are used, mainly because such information is not automatically in the public domain – unlike the published financial accounts of companies. One survey of companies in the USA showed that 13 per cent operated profit centres, 82 per cent operated investment centres and 5 per cent had neither.[3] An earlier UK-based study found 40.5 per cent of respondents had profit centres and 38 per cent had investment centres with 20.5 per cent reporting neither structure.[4] What these figures do not show is the degree of autonomy within the different structures. An investigation by Ezzamel and Hilton[5] found close supervision by central management of capital expenditure but much greater discretion by divisional managers in operating decisions such as setting prices, choosing output levels and determining purchasing policies.

IDENTIFYING THE RELEVANT PERFORMANCE MEASURE

Three reasons have already been advanced for measuring the performance of a division: the efficiency of the division as an economic entity, the performance of the divisional managers and an aid to divisional management in making correct decisions. A single figure of profit is unlikely to serve equally well all three objectives.

Managerial performance

If the objective is to measure the performance of divisional management then only items directly controllable by those managers should be included. If the divisional management is free to choose its customers then all the resulting revenue should be included. From this must then be deducted all the expenses under the control of the divisional management. This would not only include marginal costs but also any fixed costs directly controlled by the division. An example of the latter would be buildings insurance where the management has the freedom to find the most appropriate and least costly policy.

Services provided by the centre such as legal services and corporate advertising can only be controlled at source and not where charged. If these have been apportioned to the divisions, then logically they should be excluded in measuring the performance of the managers.

Divisional performance

Any resulting profit might well be a useful measure of the effectiveness of divisional management. It is unlikely, however, to be an accurate measure of the economic performance of the division. Had the division been a totally independent unit, it most likely would have had to incur other expenses such as the legal services and corporate advertising identified earlier which are currently met by the centre. A revised profit base is therefore necessary in order to measure economic performance of the division.

Unfortunately, this then introduces the vexed problem of apportioning essentially indivisible central costs. One possible solution is to make these central services profit centres in themselves, charging out their services to user divisions as consumed. As appealing as this may be, it can lead to increased costs of divisionalisation and, if the divisions are forced to use those services, a reduction in the main quality of divisionalisation, the autonomy of the divisions.

Performance measurement in practice

Despite the logical need for separate performance measures as a prerequisite for effective responsibility accounting, it appears that central management sometimes uses the same measures to evaluate both divisional management and divisional performance. According to one survey,[6] the uncontrollable aspects of a division which managers have been held responsible for included uncontrollable but relevant expenses such as interest and central administration, economic conditions such as the point in the business cycle and even acts of nature such as accidents. The justification appeared to be to force divisional managers to pay attention to interest charges and central expenses, to take action to minimise adverse economic conditions and to attempt to minimise acts of nature such as accidents.

The profit base used for evaluation also appears to vary between companies.[7] Some use the net profit as determined by traditional financial accounting concepts, some controllable profit, some net profit before tax and others the net profit before tax and interest either before or after central expenses. Yet others use a refinement of the net profit, the residual income – a concept discussed below.

Measurement of divisional profit

Despite this, Emmanuel, Otley and Merchant[8] feel that there is broad agreement that controllable profit or controllable contribution is an appropriate measure of performance for profit centre managers. Drawing on the work of earlier writers they suggest the composition of the measures should be as shown in Exhibit 21.1.

Exhibit 21.1 Divisional profit

	(£)
Sales to outside customers	X
Internal sales	X
	X
Less variable cost of goods sold and variable divisional expenses	X
Controllable contribution	X
Less controllable divisional overhead *	X
Controllable profit	X

* Excludes depreciation as this directly results from capital investments over which the division has no control

Where Emmanuel *et al* feel there is less agreement is in the treatment of investment centres. Two measures have been identified for measuring the performance of divisions treated as investment centres, return on investment and residual income.

RETURN ON INVESTMENT

The return on investment measure of divisional performance relates the profitability of the division to the resources employed in that division and expresses this as a percentage. For example, a division might have reported a profit of £300,000 while controlling resources of £1,000,000. The return on investment will therefore be 30 per cent. This can then be compared with some standard such as a budgeted or target return. Mechanically, it is similar to the *return on capital employed* ratio introduced in Chapter 14 when interpreting company accounts. As such, it is capable of further analysis by making use of subsidiary ratios such as the sales margin and asset turnover ratios. This is one of the major justifications for using the return on investment as a measure of performance.

Unlike a single figure of profit, the ratio is a relative measure, relating profit to the resources required to generate that profit. Because the return on investment is conceptually similar to the return on capital employed and uses similar data and values, it can help divisional management to see the effect of their actions on company-wide performance.

Determining profit

Critical to any ratio is the make up of its component parts. Using the controllable profit identified earlier as a starting point, Emmanuel *et al* identify three other bases for measuring profit. These are shown in Exhibit 21.2.

Exhibit 21.2 Alternative profit measures

	(£)
Controllable profit	X
Less depreciation on divisional fixed assets	X
non-controllable divisional overheads	X
Traceable profit	X
Less allocated central expenses	X
Net profit	X
Less taxation on divisional profit	X
Net profit after tax	X

Determining the level of investment

Apart from choosing the definition of profits, it is also necessary to determine the value of the denominator. This will be influenced by two factors, the resources included in the denominator and the value placed on those resources. Clearly, like should be compared with like and so if interest, for example, is excluded from the profit measure then the loans giving rise to that interest should be excluded from any measure of resources. This mirrors the difficulties identified in Chapter 14 when attempting to measure company performance. In particular, it is necessary to determine whether assets financed by current liabilities should be included or not.

Equally important, however, is the value placed on the resources included in the denominator. Probably the most significant issue is to determine the value placed on the fixed assets. In principle, these can be their gross book value, that is before deducting accumulated depreciation, their net book value or some measure of current cost such as their replacement cost. This issue is returned to below.

The return on investment and dysfunctional behaviour

One of the problems with the return on investment ratio is that it is capable of generating dysfunctional behaviour on the part of divisional management, it is capable of being manipulated and it can send out distorted signals. This encouragement of dysfunctional behaviour is demonstrated in Example 21.1 where managers are being judged primarily by the return on investment.

Example 21.1

> A company currently has a target return on investment of 20 per cent and uses this to appraise the performance of managers.
>
> Division A is currently achieving a 30 per cent return on investments of £6 million and is currently considering the implication of investing £2 million. This would cause its annual profits to increase by £500,000 per annum.

If the managers of division A were to undertake this proposal, the combined profits will be £2.3 million and the revised level of investment will be £8 million to give a return on capital employed of 28.75 per cent. If they are being judged by the return on investment achieved – and particularly if their remuneration were tied into this measure – then they are likely to reject the proposal even though, on its own, it offers a 25 per cent return.

The return on investment can also be distorted by managers. This is demonstrated in Example 21.2.

Example 21.2

> The Western division of Boston plc consists of two groups of assets. The first group is valued at £2 million and generates profits of £600,000. The second group is valued at £1 million and generates profits of £240,000. Central management has set a minimum target return on assets of 20 per cent and pays a bonus to the divisional management if they are able to improve on this figure.

With combined profits of £840,000 and assets of £3 million, the Western division is currently achieving a 28 per cent return on investments. If, however, the division was to dispose of the second group of assets, its return would improve to 30 per cent. As a result, the division will appear to have improved its performance even though the company as a whole would be worse-off from the disposal of the second group of assets.

In this example, the managers increased their return on investment at the expense of the company as a whole by disposing of assets. Equally it is possible for a division to increase its assets and its return on investments while making the company worse-off. This is particularly true when a division increases its return on investment by taking on excessive risk, to the disadvantage of other stakeholders in the wider company. During 1994, for instance, a trader employed by Barings, an old-established merchant bank, was being judged by his performance in generating profits on specialised financial instruments. On that basis he was performing extremely well and this was reflected in his remuneration. However, these profits were bought at the expense of undertaking extremely risky investments such that in 1995 the Bank was brought down and had to be rescued by outsiders.

The return on investment and accounting policies

By focusing on the return on investment, there is also a danger that management will attempt to distort information in order for their performance to appear in a better light. Under an absorption costing system, for example, reported profit for any single period can be increased by simply producing more, causing more overheads to be carried forward in the value of stock.

This is part of the more general problem that the return on investment is coloured by accounting policies. One possible way round this is for the centre to impose uniform accounting policies on the divisions but this is done at the expense of autonomy which is held to be a central feature of divisionalisation. In addition, it does not stop managers manipulating discretionary expenses such as research and training.

But it is possible for distorted signals to be generated even without this conscious manipulation if assets are valued at their net book value, particularly if the reducing balance method of depreciation is being used. With no real improvement in profitability, reported profit will increase period by period simply because the depreciation charge per period is falling. This will then be reinforced in the return on investment ratio as the denominator will be falling with the accumulated depreciation to date reducing the net book value of the assets. This in turn can lead to incorrect decision making with managers holding on to out-of-date assets, possibly putting the division at a competitive disadvantage against other producers.

One answer to this is to use replacement costs although this is only rarely found in practice, partly because of the costs involved and partly because of unfamiliarity with the measure amongst many operating management. An easily obtained alternative to the net book value is the gross book value but even here there might be dysfunctional aspects as managers might be encouraged to replace assets even when not strictly necessary if there is no change in their original cost.

RESIDUAL INCOME

Even without these difficulties, there is a case for believing that the return on investment often sends out an inappropriate measure of performance. To understand why, it is necessary to introduce a popular alternative measure known as residual income. The return on investment measure attempts to take into account the capital implications of a division by expressing them as the denominator in the ratio.

Residual income also attempts to take the cost of capital into account. However, it does so in a different way, by deducting a charge for the capital from whichever variant of profit is used. Residual income represents the 'excess of ... earnings over the cost of capital and is therefore a measure of performance for investment centres'[9]. The residual income measure is an attempt to overcome some of the limitations associated with the return on investment ratio although it still suffers from the problems arising from the use of accounting concepts, from the content and values attached to the divisional assets and from the different definitions of divisional profit. Residual income can be defined as:

Residual income = divisional profit – (cost of funds × divisional investment)

For example, a division might have a capital base of £40,000,000 and a profit of £9,000,000. Assuming that the cost of funds – the cost of capital of Chapter 20 – is 10 per cent, it follows that the capital charge is £4,000,000 and so the residual income is £5,000,000.

The residual income is an absolute figure. Because the division's capital base has been taken account of in the form of an expense, there is no need to express the result as a ratio. In *that* sense it is similar to the net present value rule of capital budgeting. It is not, however, identical to the net present value rule, partly because it does not use cashflows, partly because it only relates to one period and partly because the capital base might be based on accounting conventions such as accumulated depreciation. Further, it does not take into account the timings of the elements making up residual income.

Residual income and dysfunctional behaviour

Despite these limitations, residual income can reduce some of the dysfunctional aspects found in the return on investment. This is demonstrated by making use of the data given earlier in Examples 21.1 and 21.2.

In Example 21.1, assume the target return of 20 per cent is the division's cost of capital. The residual income before the proposed investment will therefore be £600,000, comprising the £1.8 million reported profit less the capital charge of £6 million × 20 per cent. The residual income generated from the new proposal will be the prospective profit of £500,000 less the capital charge of 20 per cent of £2 million, a net gain of £100,000 and so the division is likely to undertake the proposal.

The dysfunctional aspects identified in Example 21.2 are also eliminated when residual income is used. With an investment base of £2 million, the capital charge for the first group of assets will be £400,000 assuming the target return is the cost of capital. The result will be a residual income of £200,000. For the second group of assets, the residual income will be £40,000 after the capital charge of £200,000. Disposing of the second group of assets will therefore see the Western division's overall residual income fall by £40,000.

The validity of residual income

Residual income does appear to be a better measure than the return on investment. Not only is it a measure of performance, it also helps to correctly guide divisional decisions as the two examples above demonstrate. No profitable projects would be avoided, unlike the return on investment ratio. It also focuses divisional management's attention on the need to cover their capital costs. More than that, risk can explicitly be taken into account by charging different costs of capital dependent on the risk profile of different projects within divisions.

However, the technique is not without its detractors. Although the detailed arguments are outside the scope of this text[10], there is an intuitive argument which suggests that imputing a capital charge in the calculation of divisional performance is not economically sound. In summary the argument is that the cost of capital *should* be used for evaluating any proposed or *ex ante* capital expenditure – as when undertaking the kind of investment appraisal demonstrated in Chapter 20. Once committed, however, the decision has been made and so the objective is to make the best use of the committed resources and this involves determining the costs of production and the revenues generated at different output levels. Introducing a capital charge into this may distort performance.

LIMITATIONS OF THE RETURN ON INVESTMENT AND RESIDUAL INCOME

In practice, both measures suffer from organisations attempting to reduce to a single figure the performance of a division, the performance of the divisional management and a guide to future decisions. The criticisms of both measures fall into two groupings, the technical and the strategic.

Technical limitations

Neither measure avoids short-run measurement difficulties. Both allow managers to exploit the limitations of traditional accounting measures to report profits different from 'real' profits. Sometimes this is through the misvaluing of assets as when excessive depreciation is charged to a period or when costs are carried forward to another period in closing stock valuations. At other times, it is through reducing current expenditure which will have adverse consequences for future periods as when research and development is cut back.

Both measures are essentially backward looking and yet, to guide managerial decisions, a future perspective is required. More than that, a single time period is inappropriate. Managers might choose options which boost immediate profit even though, when longer term cashflows are allowed for, such decisions are not in the best interests of the organisation as a whole.

The return on investment ratio and residual income can be further criticised for their failure to capture operational suboptimal behaviour. Because accounting records are mainly based on historical transactions, they fail to capture within a division's performance the dysfunctional consequences of its actions on other parts of the organisation.

Strategic limitations

More generally, divisions operate in a changing and increasingly uncertain environment. Both their survival and that of the company as a whole depends on gaining and maintaining a strategic advantage. As such, their concerns should be with where their products are in relationship to the product portfolio mix and the product life cycle outlined in Chapter 20. Their concerns should be with product leadership, quality, delivery and innovation. None of these will be adequately reflected in either the short term return on investment or residual income measures. Johnson and Kaplan[11], for instance, argue for a greater use of non-financial indicators and that these non-financial indicators should be driven by corporate strategy needs.

These key figures would identify manufacturing, marketing and research and development successes. Assume, for example, that quality is the chosen route to gain competitive advantage over other companies. Non-financial indicators should be developed which reflect both internal failures such as reworkings, machine breakdowns and defects, and external failures such as warranty expenses and customer complaints.

TRANSFER PRICING

Despite the need for other, non-financial measures of divisional performance, it has been shown that many companies still emphasise short term financial measures such as return on investment or residual income. Given this, a particular problem arises where one division sells to another. The price at which goods or services are exchanged – known as the transfer price – takes on a significance. The higher the transfer price, the more profitable will appear the division making the sale and the less profitable will appear the division making the purchase.

To give an extreme example, assume just two divisions, the manufacturing division which produces the product and the marketing division which sells it. The manufacturing division might set a transfer price above the current market price. The result initially is for the manufacturing division to appear extremely efficient and the marketing department to appear equally inefficient. Apart from the effect on the morale of the marketing division, dysfunctional behaviour is possible if that division attempts to minimise its disadvantage – perhaps by buying the item for resale from outside at the expense of company-wide profitability.

Desirable qualities in a transfer price

Ideally a valid transfer pricing system should generate information which enables managers to make valid decisions for the benefit of the company as a whole. Conceptually, this suggests that the system should optimise company-wide profitability. More realistically, it suggests that no division should be able to report an increase in profit at the expense of company-wide profits. In addition, it should provide a reasonable measure of the division's managerial performance and it should maintain the advantages of divisionalisation, especially the autonomy of the division.

As will be seen, except in the simplest of cases, no such system exists with all these three qualities. Nevertheless, a useful insight into the problem and the issues involved can be developed by considering a range of scenarios. To identify the issues involved it will be assumed that a company has only two divisions, a manufacturing division which produces an intermediate product and a marketing or retail division which completes the product and undertakes the final sale to the customer.

READILY IDENTIFIABLE MARKET PRICES

Where there exists a current market price for the output of the manufacturing division, that price may be a valid transfer price to the marketing division. The market price will represent both the value of the output of the manufacturing division and the 'real' cost of any of that output consumed by the marketing division. As such, it provides a valid base for subsequent measurement of managerial and divisional performance. For this to be valid, however, there needs to exist a perfectly competitive market for the goods or services being transferred. Conditions necessary for a perfectly competitive market include a homogeneous product, many buyers and sellers, freedom of entry and exit to the market and no transaction costs.

Unfortunately, these conditions are rarely found in practice. Often there will not be an external market for the intermediate good. A division, for example, producing part-finished castings which ultimately form part of a motor car has no external demand for its output. Even when there is an external demand for the intermediate product, there is likely to be cost savings from selling to another division. The manufacturing division, for instance, may well have lower selling and transport costs when output is sold to another division rather than to the external market. As a result, the enterprise as a whole will be faced with at least three prices, the price the marketing division faces when buying externally, the price the manufacturing division can sell externally and the price the manufacturing division can sell to the marketing division which will optimise the profitability of the company as a whole.

Without entering into the complex theoretical issues involved in resolving this problem, the possible implications are clear.[12] Depending on the choice of transfer price, divisions can be made to look more or less profitable. And faced with a transfer price which it finds unacceptable, divisional management is likely to take avoiding action to improve its reported performance. The implications of this are brought out in Example 21.3.

Example 21.3

Axelby plc is a divisionalised company. One of its divisions is the print room which is responsible for all in-house printing within the company. The average volume of printing per four-week period is 500,000 pages. The print room incurs the following fixed costs in each period: rental of equipment £3,000; salaries £1,000; other fixed costs £2,000. The marginal cost of printing is 2.5p per page. The net assets of the print room total £195,000 and it has a target return on investment of 10 per cent. It uses this target return to set transfer prices.

Division X currently requires 50,000 pages to be printed per period. The managing director of that division is unhappy about the current transfer price and has received an outside quotation for the printing to be done at a cost of 3.8p per page.

With an investment of £195,000, the print room needs to earn a profit of £19,500 each year. With 52 weeks in a year, there are 13 four-week periods and so the target profit per period is £1,500. Fixed costs per period are £6,000 and so the print room needs to earn a contribution of £7,500 per period to achieve the target return. With a volume of 500,000 pages, the contribution per page must be 1.5p. Adding this to the marginal cost of 2.5p per page gives a transfer price of 4p per page. This enables the proposal to be considered from both a divisional and company-wide perspective. The workings are shown in Exhibit 21.3.

Exhibit 21.3 Transfer pricing and overall profitability

Division X		Company	
External price (3.8p × 50,000)	£1,900	External price (3.8p × 50,000)	£1,900
Internal price (4.0p × 50,000)	£2,000	Savings (2.5p × 50,000)	£1,250
Saving	£100	Loss	£650

If Division X arranges for its printing to be produced by an outside supplier, it will increase its profits by £100 per four-week period. However, from a company-wide perspective, the only savings will be the marginal cost of the printing and so the group-wide effect of Division X's decision is to reduce profit by £650 per period. This demonstrates the possibilities of suboptimisation under divisionalisation.

Long term, it might be argued that Division X has highlighted a way of improving group performance by finding a cheaper source of printing. However, given the data in the question, even this is unlikely. With a current volume of 500,000 pages the marginal cost will be £12,500 per period. Adding the fixed costs of £6,000 to this gives a total cost of £18,500 and so the total unit cost will only be 3.7p. If the fixed costs of the print room are only apportioned costs, even this figure might be an overstatement of the true cost.

All of this assumes that the price quoted by the outside supplier is a 'true' market price. In reality, there can be market imperfections. For instance, the price quoted might be a loss leader to entice Division X away from the in-house facility. Alternatively, it might be an attempt by the outside supplier to make use of temporary spare capacity. In either case, the price quoted may not be sustainable in the future.

INTERMEDIATE PRODUCTS WITH NO MARKET PRICE

The situation where the intermediate product has no external market has been developed in the literature of neo-classical economics.[13] The economist's total cost curve has already been outlined in Chapter 17. At some stage, this curve begins to produce a steadily increasing *marginal* cost as output increases. Other things being equal, to increase volume, selling prices have to be reduced. Output will therefore continue to increase as long as the extra (or *marginal*) revenue is greater than the extra (or *marginal*) cost. Where they just equal one another, no further increase in profitability is possible.

If profit is maximised at the point where marginal cost equals marginal revenue, this gives a clue to determining the optimal transfer price. If there are just two divisions – the manufacturing and marketing divisions outlined earlier – then the company-wide marginal cost will comprise the marginal cost of the manufacturing division plus the marginal cost of the marketing division. Where this combined marginal cost equals marginal revenue will be the optimal output of the company as a whole.

This can be expressed in the form of an equation. Letting MC^1 represent the marginal cost of the manufacturing division, MC^2 the marginal cost of the marketing division and MR the marginal revenue, the optimal, company-wide output will be where

$$MR = (MC^1 + MC^2)$$

The implications of this result for transfer pricing is demonstrated in Example 21.4.

Example 21.4

> Pam Parke Producers plc has two divisions, a manufacturing division and a marketing division. The manufacturing division's marginal cost is £3,000 per unit and fixed costs are £10,000 per period. The only costs of the marketing division are marginal costs of £1,000 per unit sold. The marketing director believes that if the selling price is £12,000, only one unit could be sold but for every reduction in price of £1,000, sales volume will increase by one extra unit.

With sales of only one unit both total and marginal revenue will be £12,000. Doubling sales will involve a reduction in selling price to £11,000 to give total revenue of £22,000 and hence an increase in – or *marginal* revenue of – £10,000. Exhibit 21.4 shows the effect on marginal revenue as sales volume increases. TR represents total revenue and MR, marginal revenue.

If the equation is to hold true, profit will be maximised when the combined unit marginal cost of £4,000 equals marginal revenue of the same amount. A marginal revenue of £4,000 is generated at an output level of five units and so this will be the optimal output where profits are maximised. In Exhibit 21.4, TC^1 is the total cost of the manufacturing division and MC^1 the resulting marginal cost. TC^2 is the total cost of the marketing division and MC^2 the marginal cost of that division. From these detailed workings of costs and revenues, it can be verified that profit is indeed at a maximum of £10,000 when output is five units.

Exhibit 21.4 Transfer prices and the intermediate product

Units	TC^1 (£)	MC^1 (£)	TC^2 (£)	MC^2 (£)	Combined TC (£)	Combined MC (£)	Selling price (£)	TR (£)	MR (£)	Profit (£)
1	13,000	3,000	1,000	1,000	14,000	4,000	12,000	12,000	12,000	(2,000)
2	16,000	3,000	2,000	1,000	18,000	4,000	11,000	22,000	10,000	4,000
3	19,000	3,000	3,000	1,000	22,000	4,000	10,000	30,000	8,000	8,000
4	22,000	3,000	4,000	1,000	26,000	4,000	9,000	36,000	6,000	10,000
5	25,000	3,000	5,000	1,000	30,000	4,000	8,000	40,000	4,000	10,000
6	28,000	3,000	6,000	1,000	34,000	4,000	7,000	42,000	2,000	8,000
7	31,000	3,000	7,000	1,000	38,000	4,000	6,000	42,000	0	4,000
8	34,000	3,000	8,000	1,000	42,000	4,000	5,000	40,000	(2,000)	(2,000)
9	37,000	3,000	9,000	1,000	46,000	4,000	4,000	36,000	(4,000)	(10,000)

Transfer pricing and profitability

Consider now what would happen at different transfer prices. First assume that the transfer price was set at £7,000. If the marketing division had to pay this amount, it would be faced with a combined marginal cost of £8,000 when its own marginal cost of £1,000 per unit is included. Faced with this, the division would restrict sales volume to only three units as that is the volume at which the combined marginal costs equal the marginal revenue. Equally, had the transfer price been set at only £1,000, the marketing division would have been faced with a combined marginal cost of £2,000 and so would have increased output to six units even though this would have reduced overall company profitability. Only when the transfer price is set at such a level that the combined marginal cost of the marketing division equals the sum of the individual marginal costs is output at an optimum and profit maximised. (In the example, profit could also be maximised at an output of four units. The reason for this is the limitations imposed by only considering discrete units. Had the firm been able to make and sell less than whole units, the optimal solution would have been in between four and five units.)

The optimal transfer price

To achieve maximum profits requires the manufacturing unit to sell its output at its marginal cost to the marketing division. Given the assumption of constant marginal costs of £3,000 per unit, not only will the manufacturing division never make a profit, it will always report a loss because of the fixed cost element. There is therefore no incentive for the manufacturing division to achieve the company-wide optimum. Whether using residual income or return on investment, the manufacturing division will always appear to be failing and the marketing division succeeding. There is therefore a conflict between the transfer price for decision making and the use of divisional performance as a motivation and evaluation technique.

One solution sometimes proposed is for the centre to impose the transfer price on the manufacturing division but this breaks one of the most powerful reasons for divisionalisation, that of autonomy. Another solution suggested is for there to be a two-part transfer fee comprising a fixed element to compensate for any losses by the manufacturing division plus a charge per unit based on marginal cost. This will still ensure optimality as a fixed cost has no effect on marginal costs.

Unfortunately, by failing to tie in profit to units produced, the incentive element is destroyed. In fact there may well be a positive disincentive for the manufacturing division to produce more if this involves increased stocks. Increasing stocks will increase the investment level within the division and so reduce both the return on investment and residual income. But by far the most limiting of the criticisms of the economist's approach is the assumption of total knowledge about selling prices and costs and rational behaviour. With all these predetermined, the profit figure is bound to follow and so there is no need to measure managerial or divisional performance. As such, it is an inappropriate measure for determining actual, *ex post* managerial performance in a real world of risk and uncertainty.

OPPORTUNITY COST TRANSFER PRICES

Underpinning the discussion so far has been the economist's concept of opportunity cost. The opportunity cost of any action is the cost involved in committing resources to their next best alternative. Where there is a readily available market price, the next best alternative to selling to another division is to sell to external customers. Under such a scenario, market price represents the opportunity cost for both the divisions involved in the transaction. Similarly, where there is no external market, the next best alternative to selling a unit to another division would be not to produce that unit. In other words, the costs saved – the marginal cost – is the opportunity cost.

The manufacturing division, however, might be faced with outside possibilities even though these do not include selling the current intermediate product externally. There is always the option for the manufacturing division to produce an entirely separate product which could be sold on the external market. Hence, the opportunity cost, the true cost, of trading with the marketing division, is the profit foregone by not making the next best alternative product.

It is possible to build up complex mathematical models of opportunity costs using the linear programming approach outlined in Chapter 15. There are, however, three objections to the opportunity cost approach apart from its complexity and understandability for divisional management. They are that the data is difficult to derive, it involves imposing a centralised solution and it treats the division as a stand-alone, independent entity – and yet often the division was created because it was not a stand-alone activity but rather an integral part of the manufacturing and marketing process of a company.

COST BASED PRICING

The theoretical ideal transfer price has significant behavioural limitations. Perhaps because of this, some companies determine transfer prices on the basis either of cost or cost plus a mark up. Including overheads in the cost can ensure the manufacturing division does not make a loss – but as was demonstrated earlier – this may produce a suboptimal solution for the enterprise as a whole.

There is also a danger that such a system might encourage inefficiencies. If the manufacturing division simply recharges to the marketing division, there is no incentive to minimise costs and without a profit incentive there is nothing to encourage management to invest in new, cost saving equipment. Indeed, if the transfer price is based on cost plus a margin, there is a positive advantage in the manufacturing division being inefficient as this enables a higher margin to be charged. Because of this, some form of standard cost might be preferred, but only if the standard is an appropriate one.

NEGOTIATED TRANSFER PRICES

If a cost plus system is in operation, this begs the question as to who sets the 'plus' in cost plus. If it is the centre, there is a reduction in divisional autonomy. If it is not the centre, then the transfer price will have to be as a result of negotiation between the divisions concerned. There is some evidence that negotiated transfer prices can help to resolve conflicts between divisions and avoid the dysfunctional aspects of a centrally imposed transfer price.[14]

The need for a negotiated transfer price only occurs if there is no clear market derived price. Equally, however, for negotiation to be meaningful, each manager needs to have *some* idea of the likely transfer price. Negotiated prices are therefore likely to be most appropriate where managers operate in competitive markets but where there are imperfections. This enables both managers to have some idea of market price but also allows peripheral negotiations to take account of conditions unique to the two divisions such as lower transport costs and the lack of selling expenses.

This is not to say that negotiated transfer prices are not without their limitations. It can still lead to suboptimal decisions. The need to negotiate can lead to conflict between divisions. The process is time consuming and the outcome depends partly on the negotiating skills of the respective managers. Despite this, these disadvantages might be outweighed by the motivational and behavioural advantages.

TRANSFER PRICING IN PRACTICE

There are two tensions in transfer pricing, the search for a theoretically valid transfer price and the need to minimise dysfunctional behaviour. Despite the powerful logic supporting the marginal costing approach to determining transfer prices, marginal costing is rarely used in practice. It is full cost and cost plus transfer prices which are more likely to be found in practice.[15]

Perhaps the reason for this lies in the role of transfer pricing within the divisionalised firm. Transfer pricing was not introduced into firms as an independent tool to aid managers make decisions. Rather, it is a subsidiary by-product of decentralisation which, in turn, involves the delegation of power to lower levels of management who are responsible for outcomes from the resources they control. Decentralisation is concerned with improving managerial decisions, encouraging management development and enhancing motivation. Divisional autonomy is therefore a prerequisite for decentralised management. In other words, the behavioural dimension is central to divisionalisation and this is missing from the economist's marginalist approach.

SUMMARY

Divisionalisation is such a complex issue that this chapter could only begin to touch on the issues involved. Nevertheless the reasons for the growth in divisionalised organisations are clear. These relate to the increasing size of the modern organisation, product diversity, market diversity and interdependence between markets and products. The driving force must be the generation of economies when a business unit is part of a larger group rather than an independent, separate firm and the central feature has to be autonomy – at least at divisional board level.

Mechanisms then have to be put in place to ensure the potential gains from divisionalisation are achieved. Two mechanisms have been considered in this chapter. The first was a performance evaluation system. Two *ex post* measures of performance have been identified, the return on investment and residual income. Both have limitations – including the ability to be manipulated and a short term time horizon – and so in evaluating a division's performance, it may also be necessary to consider non-financial factors. The second mechanism was, in effect, a surrogate for the external market by determining transfer prices. Two tensions permeated the discussion, the economist's marginalist approach to resource allocation and the wider behaviouralist perspective to managing an organisation in an uncertain but rapidly changing environment.

REFERENCES

1 Solomons D. (1965) *Divisional Performance: Measurement and Control,* Financial Executives Research Foundation, p. 3.
2 See Williamson O. E. (1970) *Corporate Control and Business Behaviour*, Prentice Hall and (1975) *Markets and Hierarchies: Analysis and AntiTrust Implications*, Free Press.
3 Vancil R. F. (1979) *Decentralisation: Ambiguity by Design*, Unwin.
4 Tomkins C. (1973) *Financial Planning in Divisionalised Companies*, Haymarket.
5 Ezzamel M. A. and Hilton K. (1980) 'Divisionalisation in British industry: a preliminary study', *Accounting and Business Research*, Spring, pp. 197–214.
6 Merchant K. (1989) *Rewarding Results: Motivating Profit Centre Managers*, Harvard Business School Press.
7 Tomkins C. (1973) *Financial Planning in Divisionalised Companies*, Haymarket.
8 Emmanuel C., Otley D. and Merchant K. (1990) *Accounting for Management Control,* 2nd edn, p. 242.
9 Ezzamel M. (1992) *Business Unit and Divisional Performance Measurement*, Academic Press.
10 See Ezzamel M. (1992) *Business Unit and Divisional Performance Measurement*, Academic Press, pp. 31–7 for a summary of the cost of capital debate and the issues involved.
11 Johnson H. T. and Kaplan R. S. (1987) *Relevance Lost: The rise and fall of Management Accounting*, Harvard Business School Press.
12 For a theoretical discussion, see Emmanuel C. and Mehafdi M. (1994) *Transfer Pricing*, Academic Press.
13 The seminal work in this area was begun by Hirshleifer J. (1956) in 'Economics of the divisional firm', *Journal of Business*.
14 Watson D. J. H. and Baumler J. V. (1975) 'Transfer pricing: a behavioural context', *The Accounting Review* [July].
15 See Emmanuel C. and Mehafdi M. (1994) *Transfer Pricing*, Academic Press for a comprehensive review of the empirical findings.

FURTHER READING

Emmanuel C. and Mehafdi M. (1994) *Transfer Pricing*, Academic Press.
Emmanuel C., Otley D. and Merchant K. (1990) *Accounting for Management Control* ,Chapman & Hall, 2nd edn.
Ezzamel M. (1992) *Business Unit and Divisional Performance Measurement*, Academic Press.
Solomons D. (1965) *Divisional Performance: Measurement and Control*, Financial Executives Research Foundation.
Tomkins C. (1973) *Financial Planning in Divisionalised Companies*, Haymarket.
Vancil R. (1979) *Decentralisation: Ambiguity by Design*, Irwin.

TEST YOUR UNDERSTANDING

1 Explain the difference between functional decentralisation and federal decentralisation.

2 A company can either form or acquire a division or it can carry out transactions such as the acquiring of inputs with independent firms. What is the main argument in favour of forming divisions?

3 Identify three arguments against divisionalisation.

4 What are the reasons for measuring divisional performance?

5 Identify two ways the performance of an investment centre can be measured.

6 What are the ideal qualities in a transfer price?

7 List six possible bases for transfer pricing.

QUESTIONS

1 Alpha and Beta are two divisions within Megacorp plc. Their profit and loss accounts and balance sheets for the year to 31 December 19X6 are as follows:

	Alpha (£000)	Beta (£000)
Turnover	53,000	43,000
Sale of fixed assets		2,400
Total revenue	53,000	45,400
Direct labour	6,400	8,200
Direct material	23,530	12,100
Depreciation	4,000	2,800
Divisional overheads	4,100	5,800
Apportioned central overheads	870	590
Total expenses	38,900	29,490
Net book value of fixed assets	10,000	12,000
Stock	8,300	1,400
Trade debtors	5,200	1,800
Bank	2,900	(3,100)
Trade creditors	(2,900)	(2,400)
Net assets	23,500	9,700

The central management of Megacorp are considering ways of measuring division-al performance. Three suggestions have been put forward as a suitable measure; resid-ual income based on the company's cost of capital of 15 per cent, return on capital employed and controllable profit. This latter measure views the purchase and control of fixed assets as a central management responsibility and focuses on those revenue aspects of the division which are controllable by divisional management.

Using data from the divisional accounts to 31 December 19X6, calculate the three proposed measures for Alpha and Beta. You should state explicitly any assumptions or reservations you have about the data used in your calculations.

2* Explain the advantages and disadvantages of the three measures proposed by Megacorp for performance appraisal and identify any further measures needed for the effective appraisal of divisional performance.

3 Gransden plc has two divisions, the manufacturing division makes an intermediate product, the only use for which is as a component in the Fox, a small, battery powered portable alarm. The alarm is finished and marketed to supermarkets through Gransden's distribution division.

Currently, the manufacturing division is faced with fixed costs of £2,000 per day plus a variable cost of £2.125 per unit. The division's policy is to add a 100 per cent mark up to the variable cost of production. The distribution division is faced with fixed costs of £1,000 per day and is able to complete and market up to 1,500 units at no extra cost beyond that. For production above 1,500 units, however, it incurs additional variable costs of £2.00 per unit.

Market research suggests the Fox is sensitive to changes in selling price to the super-markets. The likely sales volume at different selling prices is as follows:

Sales units	Price per unit
1,000	7.75
2,000	7.50
3,000	7.25
4,000	7.00
5,000	6.75
6,000	6.50
7,000	6.25
8,000	6.00
9,000	5.75
10,000	5.50

(a) Determine the sales volume and profitability by division under the existing policies on the assumption that where two prices give the same profit, the higher volume is chosen to increase market penetration.

(b) Show the resulting sales volume and divisional profits which maximises group prof-itability.

4* Outline the main objectives of a transfer pricing system. Using one method of transfer pricing with which you are familiar, identify the benefits and limitations of the method.

SOLUTIONS

CHAPTER 1

Outline solutions

1. Money measurement, entity, periodicity, cost attachment, duality, matching.

2. Luca Pacioli documented the idea of duality or double-entry bookkeeping which enabled more complex accounting records of assets, liabilities, capital, income and expenses to be kept.

3. (c)

4. Both an asset and an expense are benefits acquired by an entity. An expense is a benefit consumed by the period end. An asset is a benefit which has not yet been fully consumed.

5. A balance sheet shows the resources in existence at the balance sheet date and how these have been financed. As these are two different aspects of the same transactions, they must balance given the accounting concept of cost attachment.

6. A business can be financed by the owners or by borrowings. Equity represents the amount owing by the business to the owner(s) and comprises capital introduced plus any profits retained in the business but owing by the business to them. Liabilities are the amounts owing to third parties as a result of earlier transactions.

7. (b)

8. The profit and loss account, the balance sheet and the cashflow statement.

9. Net assets is the total of all assets less the total of all liabilities. It is equivalent to the total of the equity in an enterprise.

10. (c)

11. Stewardship, scorekeeping, forecasting, influencing behaviour, decision making.

Solution 1

	Capital	Shop	Stock	Sales	Sales	Stock	Sales	Wages	Sales	Stock	Wages
				Transactions					*Adjustments*		
Cash	+60	−40	−12	+20	+10	−6	+15	−4			
Capital	−60										
Shop		+40									
Stock			+12			+6				−18	
Sales				−20	−10		−15		+45		
Wages								+4			−4
Profit and loss									−45	+18	+4

Income for April		Balance sheet at 30 April		Cashflow statement for month of April		
Sales	£45,000	Assets		Net cash inflow from operations		£23,000
Stock used	£18,000	Cash	£43,000			
Wages	£18,000	Shop	£40,000	Investing activities – shop		£40,000
Profit	£23,000		£83,000			
		Financed by		Net cashflow before financing		(£17,000)
		Capital	£60,000	Financing – capital	£60,000	
		Retained profit	£23,000	Net cash inflow from financing		£60,000
			£83,000	Increase in cash		£43,000

Solution 2

		Transactions						Adjustments		
	Capital	Rent	Stock	Sales	Wages	Sales		Rent	Stock	Wages
Cash	+20	−3	−6	+9	−4					
Capital	−20									
Rent		+3						−3		
Stock			+6						−6	
Sales				−9		+9				
Wages					+4					−4
Profit and loss						−9		+3	+6	+4

Income for August		Balance sheet at 31 August		Cashflow statement for month of August		
Sales	£9,000	Assets		Net cash outflow from operations		£4,000
Stock used	£6,000	Cash	£16,000			
Rent	£3,000		£16,000	Net cash outflow before financing		£4,000
Wages	£4,000					
Loss	£4,000	Financed by		Financing – capital	£20,000	
		Capital	£20,000	Net cash inflow from financing		£20,000
		Loss	(£4,000)	Increase in cash		£16,000
			£16,000			

CHAPTER 2

Outline solutions

1. (b)

2. (c)

3. Reserve accounting refers to expenses – and possibly income – being recorded in any of the accounts making up the equity of the enterprise other than the profit and loss account. Whichever treatment is undertaken, the overall effect on the equity in the balance sheet will be the same. The danger of reserve accounting is that users will not notice the adjustment to equity via the reserves rather than its direct reporting in the profit and loss account. Its only justification is when a transaction is so unusual that recording it in the profit and loss account might itself distort accounting information.

4. The statement of total recognised gains and losses.

5. (a)

6. When there is objective evidence of a right to receive cash and where the receipt of the cash is reasonably certain.

7. The concept of 'going concern' assumes that the enterprise has a continuing existence. Because of this, the concept allows simple valuation rules to be developed based on the cost and matching concepts.

8. (b)

9. Sometimes, there is more than one way to record a transaction. A sale, for example, could possibly be recognised when the contract is agreed or when the cash is received. The various possibilities are known as accounting bases. An enterprise must then choose one and this becomes its accounting policy.

10. (d)

11. Fixed assets are assets held for long term use in a business. Current assets are assets which are constantly changing as a direct result of trading. Current liabilities are liabilities which arise from trading. They, too, are constantly changing as trading takes place.

12. (b)

Solution 1

		(a)	(b)	(c)	(d)	(e)	(f)	(g)	(h)	(i)	(j)	(k)	(l)	(m)	(n)	(o)	(p)	(q)	(r)
Premises	+30.0																		+30.0
Vehicles	+20.0																		+20.0
Stock	+2.4			+1.9				+1.2					−3.1					+2.4
Debtors	+2.9	+4.1	−1.8				+4.4			−6.2									+3.4
Rent prepaid	+0.6				+1.2											−0.8			+1.0
Cash and bank	+3.8		+1.8	−0.7		−1.2	−1.4				−2.7	+6.2	−5.1						+0.7
Creditors	−4.2			+0.7	−1.9					−1.2			+5.1						−1.5
Electricity accrued	−0.7						+1.4										−1.0		−0.3
Capital	−28.0																		−28.0
Retentions	−26.8																	−0.9	27.7
Sales		−4.1					−4.4						+8.5						0.0
Wages										+2.7					−2.7				0.0
Profit and loss														−8.5	+3.1	+2.7	+0.8	+1.0	+0.9	0.0

Period end adjustments:
(l) Transfer of sales to the profit and loss account
(m) Cost of sales
(n) Wages charged to the profit and loss account
(o) Rent charged to the profit and loss account at £200 per week
(p) Electricity charged to the profit and loss account
(q) Net profit transferred to retentions
(r) Unexpired balances at period end

Trading and profit and loss account **for four weeks ended 28 March 19X7**			**Balance sheet** **at 28 March 19X7**			
		(£)		*(£)*	*(£)*	*(£)*
Turnover		8,500	**Assets**			
Cost of sales		3,100	*Fixed assets*			
Gross profit		5,400	Premises			30,000
Overheads			Vehicles			20,000
Wages	2,700					50,000
Rent	800		*Current assets*			
Electricity	1,000	4,500	Stock	2,400		
Net profit		900	Debtors	3,400		
			Prepayment	1,000		
			Cash and bank	700	7,500	
			Current liabilities			
			Creditors	1,500		
			Accrual	300	1,800	5,700
						55,700
			Financed by			
			Owner's capital			28,000
			Retentions			27,700
						55,700

Solution 2

(a) Kevin's Hardware Shop has no long term liabilities and so, on that basis, the equity at the beginning and end of the six-month period is as follows:

Net assets	*1 July*	*31 December*
Premises	£80,000	£80,000
Fixtures and fittings	£30,000	£44,000
Stock	£65,000	£73,000
Debtors	£34,000	£42,000
Cash	£4,500	£6,000
	£213,500	£245,000
Less creditors	£51,000	£13,500
= Equity	£162,500	£231,500

The income for a period can be found by using the expression

$$Y_1 = W_1 - W_0 \pm D_1$$

On that basis, and allowing for Kevin's extra £40,000 of capital introduced, income for the six-month period is

$$Y_1 = (£231,500 - £162,500) - £40,000 = £29,000$$

(b) *Reasons why profit is not the same as cash*
Sales on credit
Purchases on credit
Assets purchased but not charged to the profit and loss account in their entirety, e.g. fixed assets and closing stock
Paying in additional capital
Withdrawing capital – drawings for a sole trader
Borrowing or redeeming a loan – only the interest appears as an expense in the profit and loss account.

CHAPTER 3

Outline solutions

1. False. Only if there is no partnership agreement or if the agreement is silent on some matter will the Partnership Act take effect.

2. (c)

3. (b)

4. (f)

5. (b)

6. False. Loans can be redeemed as, in law, they are not part of the capital. Ordinary shares can also be redeemed providing there is an equivalent increase in the permanent capital of the company by the issue of additional shares, by the transfer of revenue reserves to a capital redemption reserve fund or by the issuing of bonus shares from revenue reserves.

7. Limited companies pay corporation tax and this is a charge on the company. Directors are employees of the company and hence their salaries are an expense of the company in a similar way to the wages of other employees. Capital has a specific legal meaning and hence retained profits should be kept totally separate from share capital.

8. A reserve does not affect the profit for the period. It is either an appropriation of profit or – like the share premium account – it originates outside the profit and loss account. Provisions are a charge to the profit and loss account for known or likely expenses, the amount of which cannot be accurately estimated.

9. There is no legal definition of a revenue reserve. The creation of such a reserve is merely a statement of intent by the current directors and can generally be reversed if required.

10. Share premium account, the capital redemption reserve fund and the asset revaluation reserve. They are not available for distribution as dividends.

11. False. Depreciation is an allocation of cost – an attempt to charge the cost of an asset over its useful life. The net book value is the original cost less accumulated depreciation to date. Original cost does not necessarily reflect market value. Neither does accumulated depreciation necessarily reflect the loss in value. Because of this net book value would only reflect market values by coincidence.

12. (c)

13. Marginal costing treats production fixed costs as being time based and so charges them to the time period to which they related. Absorption costing includes production fixed costs in the

cost of production. Consequently, if some of the production remains unsold, part of the production fixed costs are carried forward in the closing stock figure, to be charged to a subsequent time period.

14. The conflict is between matching and prudence. Prudence suggests that profit should only be recognised on the completion of the contract. Matching takes the view that profit is earned throughout the life of the contract.

Solution 1

	Opening balance	(a) Pre-payment	(b) Accrual	(c) Purchases	(d) Sales	(e) Debtors	(f) Creditors	(g) Drawings Amanda	(h) Drawings Barry	(i) Electricity	(j) Rates	Summary
Premises	+65											+65
Fixtures & fittings	+15											+15
Stocks	+18			+60								+78
Debtors	+19				+90	-60						+49
Prepayments	+2	-2										
Cash/bank	+36					+60	-51	-8	-12	-15	-9	+1
Creditors	-10			-60			+51					-19
Accruals	-5		+5									
Loan – Amanda	-50											-50
Capital – Amanda	-50											-50
Capital – Barry	-30											-30
Current – Amanda	-20											-20
Current – Barry	+10											+10
Electricity			-5							+15		+10
Rates		+2									+9	+11
Sales					-90							-90
Drawings – Amanda								+8				+8
Drawings – Barry									+12			+12

	Summary	Pre-payment	Accrual	Turn-over	Cost of sales	Elect-ricity	Rates	Loan interest	Approp-riation	Salary	Interest capital a/c	Interest current a/c	Division of profit	Transfer drawings	Closing balance
Premises	+65														+65
Fixtures & fittings	+15														+15
Stocks	+78				-47										+31
Debtors	+49														+49
Prepayments		+4													+4
Cash/bank	+1														+1
Creditors	-19														-19
Accruals			-6												-6
Loan – Amanda	-50														-50
Capital – Amanda	-50														-50
Capital – Barry	-30														-30
Current – Amanda	-20							-4			-5	-2	+5	+8	-18
Current – Barry	+10									-17	-3	+1	+5	+12	+8
Electricity	+10		+6			-16									0
Rates	+11	-4					-7								0
Sales	-90			+90											0
Drawings – Amanda	+8													-8	0
Drawings – Barry	+12													-12	0
Profit and loss				-90	+47	+16	+7	+4	+16						0
Appropriation									-16	+17	+8	+1	-10		0

Trading and profit and loss account for the year ended 30 June				
Turnover				£90,000
Cost of sales				£47,000
Gross profit				£43,000
Power			£16,000	
Rates			£7,000	
Loan interest			£4,000	£27,000
Net profit				£16,000
Appropriation				
Salary	Amanda		£17,000	
Interest on capital:	Amanda	£5,000		
	Barry	£3,000	£8,000	
Current account interest:	Amanda	£2,000		
	Barry	(£1,000)	£1,000	
Division of loss	Amanda	(£5,000)		
	Barry	(£5,000)	(£10,000)	£16,000

Balance sheet at 30 June				
Fixed assets				
Premises				£65,000
Fixtures and fittings				£15,000
				£80,000
Current assets				
Stock			£31,000	
Debtors and prepayments			£53,000	
Cash/bank			£1,000	
			£85,000	
Current liabilities				
Creditors and accruals			£25,000	£60,000
				£140,000
Less long term loan	Amanda			£50,000
				£90,000
Financed by				
Owners capital	Amanda		£50,000	
	Barry		£30,000	£80,000
Current accounts	Amanda		£18,000	
	Barry		(£8,000)	£10,000
				£90,000

Solution 3

	Opening balance sheet	Redemption of preference shares	Capital redemption reserve fund	Issue ordinary shares at a premium	Revalue fixed assets	Closing balance sheet
Fixed assets	+£200,000				+£300,000	+£500,000
Net current assets	+£600,000	–£100,000		+£200,000		+£700,000
	£800,000					£1,200,000
Financed by:						
Ordinary shares	–£200,000			–£100,000		–£300,000
Preference shares	–£100,000	+£100,000				
Retentions	–£500,000		+£100,000			–£400,000
Capital redemption reserve			–£100,000			–£100,000
Share premium				–£100,000		–£100,000
Revaluation reserve					–£300,000	–£300,000
	£800,000					£1,200,000

Solution 4

Calculating depreciation involves four stages: estimating the cost of an asset, its life, the asset's residual value, and then choosing an appropriate method of charging the depreciation over that life. The object is to charge the full cost of the asset over its useful life. Depreciation is therefore an allocation of cost, not an attempt to measure the loss in value for any single period. However, just because an asset is fully depreciated, does not mean that it is worthless. Errors might have occurred in originally estimating its effective life.

Depreciation does not automatically ensure cash is available at the end of an asset's life. With rising prices, total depreciation is unlikely to equal the replacement cost of an asset. Secondly, depreciation is a provision. By charging depreciation to the profit and loss account, profit is reduced and resources kept back in the business. However, as accounts are based on the accruals concept, this may not manifest itself as an increase in cash but rather an increase in overall assets. The logic is similar to that used to explain why profit is not the same as the increase in cash.

Solution 5

Straight line depreciation will be (£10,000 – £625)/4 or £2,343.75 each year. Making use of the formula for the reducing balance, the rate is found to be 50 per cent. The depreciation charge per annum and the net book values are shown below.

Year	Detail	Straight line	Reducing balance
now	Cost	£10,000	£10,000
1	Depreciation	£2,344	£5,000
1	Net book value	£7,656	£5,000
2	Depreciation	£2,344	£2,500
2	Net book value	£5,312	£2,500
3	Depreciation	£2,344	£1,250
3	Net book value	£2,968	£1,250
4	Depreciation	£2,343	£625
4	Net book value	£625	£625

CHAPTER 4

Outline solutions

1. Debit refers to the gaining aspect of a transaction or value received. Credit refers to the value given up or obligation increased.

2. The bank account statement reflects the company's account in the books of the bank. If the company has £100 lodged with the bank, this is an asset in the company's accounts. In the accounts of the bank, however, the £100 is owing to the company and so is a credit balance.

3. The trial balance is a prima facie evidence that transactions have been correctly recorded. It cannot recognise errors caused by (a) total omission of a transaction, (b) compensating errors or (c) mispostings.

4. Day books separate the trading activities of a business from the recording of those activities in the accounts. Not only is this more efficient in that the transactions can be entered into the accounts at a more convenient time by specialist staff, it also improves control and reduces the risk of fraud by making more than one person responsible for the recording of a total transaction.

5. Most transactions generate evidence such as invoices to support their recording. Some transactions will not be able to provide evidence. Often this is because of the implementation of a company policy such as when to write-off a debt as bad or how much to charge as depreciation. The journal is the permanent record to support these transactions.

Solution 3

	Debit	Credit	Turn-over	Cost of sales	Heat & light	Rates	Admin-istration	Depreciation Cars	Depreciation Fittings	Bad debt pro-vision	Loan inter-est	Direc-tors fees	Debt written off	Wages	Office salaries	Trans-fer	Balance
Purchases	+610			−470													+140
Sales		−900	+900														0
Vehicles at cost	+160																+160
Provision for vehicle depreciation		−48						−32									−80
Opening stock	+160			−160													0
Trade debtors	+80																+80
Trade creditors		−52															−52
8% loan stock		−100															−100
Directors' fees	+12											−12					0
Bad debts written off	+2												−2				0
Loan interest paid	+4										−8						−4
Share premium account		−40															−40
Profit and loss account balance		−57														−83	−140
Wages	+35													−35			0
Rates	+3					−2											+1
Heating and lighting	+6				−8												−2
Office salaries	+48														−48		0
Administration expenses	+38						−36										+2
Freehold property	+350																+350
Ordinary share capital		−400															−400
Fittings	+30																+30
Provision for depreciation – fittings		−6							−3								−9
Provision for bad debts		−3								−1							−4
Bank	+68																+68
Profit and loss a/c – this year			−900	+630	+8	+2	+36	+32	+3	+1	+8	+12	+2	+35	+48	+83	0
	1,606	−1,606															0

Note: Accrual of loan interest.

<table>
<tr><td colspan="3">Trading and profit and loss account
– year ended 30 September 19X5</td></tr>
<tr><td></td><td></td><td>(£)</td></tr>
<tr><td>Turnover</td><td></td><td>900,000</td></tr>
<tr><td>Cost of sales</td><td></td><td>630,000</td></tr>
<tr><td>Gross profit</td><td></td><td>270,000</td></tr>
<tr><td>Operating expenses</td><td></td><td></td></tr>
<tr><td>Wages</td><td>35,000</td><td></td></tr>
<tr><td>Rates</td><td>2,000</td><td></td></tr>
<tr><td>Heat and lighting</td><td>8,000</td><td>45,000</td></tr>
<tr><td>Administration expenses</td><td></td><td></td></tr>
<tr><td>Office salaries</td><td>48,000</td><td></td></tr>
<tr><td>Administration expenses</td><td>36,000</td><td></td></tr>
<tr><td>Bad debts written off</td><td>2,000</td><td></td></tr>
<tr><td>Increase in bad debt provision</td><td>1,000</td><td></td></tr>
<tr><td>Depreciation – fittings</td><td>3,000</td><td></td></tr>
<tr><td>Depreciation – vehicles</td><td>32,000</td><td></td></tr>
<tr><td>Directors' fees</td><td>12,000</td><td></td></tr>
<tr><td>Loan interest</td><td>8,000</td><td>142,000</td></tr>
<tr><td></td><td></td><td>187,000</td></tr>
<tr><td>Net profit</td><td></td><td>83,000</td></tr>
</table>

Balance sheet at
30 September 19X5

Fixed assets	Cost	Accumulated depreciation	Net book value
Freehold property	350,000		350,000
Vehicles	160,000	80,000	80,000
Furniture and fittings	30,000	9,000	21,000
	540,000	89,000	451,000

Current assets			
Stock		140,000	
Debtors	80,000		
Less provision for bad debts	4,000	76,000	
Prepayment			
Administration expenses	2,000		
Rates	1,000	3,000	
Bank		68,000	
		287,000	

Current liabilities				
Creditors		52,000		
Accruals				
Loan interest	4,000			
Heat and light	2,000	6,000	58,000	229,000
				680,000
Long term loan				100,000
				580,000

Financed by	
Ordinary share capital	400,000
Share premium account	40,000
Profit and loss reserve	140,000
	580,000

Solution 4

Given that the information on both balance sheets is valid and making use of the data from the bank statement, it is possible to partially recreate some of the detailed accounts. In the workings below, data subsequently derived from original information is shown in italics.

Creditors				Stock			
Bank	£3,500	Opening balance	£200	Opening balance	£400	Closing balance	£200
Closing balance	£500	∴ stock =	£3,800	Creditors (see stock) £3,800		∴ cost of sales	£4,000
	£4,000		£4,000		£4,200		£4,200

If the cost of sales is £4,000 then sales should have been £6,000 as selling price is 150 per cent of cost. This enables the debtors account to be recreated and from this an estimate of cash received calculated.

Debtors			
Opening balance	£300	Closing balance	£200
Estimated sales	£6,000	∴ estimated cash =	£6,100
	£6,300		£6,300

As the bank statement shows only £5,100 being received from debtors, it appears that £1,000 cash is missing.

CHAPTER 5

Outline solutions

1. Hardware refers to the physical equipment such as the computer itself, its disk drives, its monitor and its printer. Software is the program or set of instructions represented or stored magnetically in the machine which enables it to perform its tasks. There are two forms of software; the operating system and applications software.

2. Data is the unstructured raw material for producing information. Information is the output from that data in a form relevant to the user's needs. Information can include the collating, filtering, arranging, summarising and reporting of data.

3. Source documents are the evidence which allows recording to take place. They include sales and invoices, journal entries, and day books.

4. (a) More precise than literal account names. (b) Facilitates classification.

5. The 673411 account code comprises a real code of 67341 plus the final check digit of 1. Transposing the first two digits will give a check digit other than 1 and hence the code will be rejected. The check digit for a real code of 76341 will be 0. This is made up as $7 \times 5 = 35$; $6 \times 4 = 24$; $3 \times 3 = 9$; $4 \times 2 = 8$; $1 \times 1 = 1$. The total of 77 gives a check digit of 0 and so 763411 is an invalid code.

6. Just as there are check digits to reduce human errors, so other checks can be built in to reject possibly invalid transactions. A reasonableness check is one example. This involves writing into the program a range outside of which transactions will be rejected. One example might be to only allow a weekly wage to no more than £800 and no less than £60 without further verification if a company only employs full-time staff.

Solution 1

Similarity of both systems with input, process and output.

Limited number of different types of procedure although high volume of data.

Neither system *requires* judgement once accounting policies and treatment have been agreed – i.e. essentially mechanical.

Higher capital cost of computer systems for both hardware and software – but note cost of training for manual systems.

Computer systems follow program instructions exactly without fatigue, etc.

Possibility of automatic generation of entries when computerised.

Ease with which computer records can be destroyed – e.g. DEL *.* in MSDOS – therefore need for additional security.

Extensive damage possible to computer systems *if* there is a hardware or software fault.

Need for backups at all times.

Lack of flexibility and need to compromise when buying ready-made software packages.

Changing a computerised system is often much more expensive and complex than changing parts of a manual system.

Solution 2

Decreasing cost of both hardware and software.

Ease of generating additional information once the data has been captured.

Improved accuracy especially where there are validity and reasonableness checks and where transactions are produced automatically.

Speed of production – e.g. some systems will produce an invoice, update stock records and record the basic accounting transactions from keying in a single set of data.

Little or no understanding of bookkeeping required by the operative.

CHAPTER 6

Outline solutions

1. A conceptual framework is a comprehensive set of generally accepted beliefs and values which provide a reference point to identify how events and transactions should be measured and disclosed to others.

2. To provide information about the financial position, performance and financial adaptability of an enterprise that is useful to a wide range of users in making economic decisions.

3. Threshold quality: materiality.

   Primary characteristics: relevance and reliability.

   Secondary characteristics: comparability and understandability.

4. False. The ASB defines assets as 'rights or other access to future economic benefits controlled by an entity as a result of a past transaction or event'. Ownership is not mentioned.

5. The Statement of Total Recognised Gains and Losses is necessary to highlight the total gains recognised by an entity in an accounting period. The ASB's Chapters 3 and 4 identified the elements which comprise the financial accounts and the issues involved in whether or not these elements should be recognised. Gains should be recognised but only those which have been realised should be reported in the profit and loss account. Other gains must be reported via the reserves. The new primary statement brings all these gains together in a single statement.

6. Both measures are concerned with income and wealth and both treat period end wealth as equal to the opening wealth plus income generated, assuming no capital injections of withdrawals. For financial reporting purposes, the accountant views an entity's wealth as being the adjusted historical cost of the net assets. From this base, income is then generated. The perspective is essentially backward looking. The economist views the process differently. Assets only have value because of the benefits which will flow from their acquisition and so wealth is the value of those benefits with income being the residue flowing from that.

7. Under economic income, a windfall gain enhances future income generating capacity. Reporting the whole of the gain in a single period is therefore misleading. Despite this, windfall gains and losses are normally reported in total when they happen in financial reporting. Because of this, it is normal to disclose such gains or losses in financial reports.

8. Input or entry values are concerned with the possible values to be attached to assets on acquisition. Output or exit values are concerned with valuing assets on their value should they leave

the entity. Historical cost is an example of an entry value, realisable value an example of an exit value.

9. Replacement cost accounting is concerned with maintaining the operating capacity of an entity by only recognising profit once sufficient resources have been held back in order to maintain the current levels of activity. Realisable value accounting has a different focus. It is concerned with showing on the balance sheet values which would be realised if the assets were sold. In essence, it is measuring the opportunity cost of those resources. As such, it is concerned with helping users to decide whether or not the entity should continue in its existing form.

10. Backlog depreciation is an adjustment which often has to be made when preparing accounts under the replacement cost convention. Where an asset's replacement cost increases, additional depreciation over the historical amount needs to be provided in each year. If replacement costs are increasing each year, however, the additional depreciation in previous years is unlikely to be adequate. To overcome this backlog depreciation has to be provided.

Solution 1

Users of financial reports are generally defined as those who lack the authority to prescribe the financial information they want from an enterprise and therefore must use the information that management communicates to them. Because of this, management is excluded. The corporate report identified the following as users of financial reports: (a) the equity investor group; (b) the loan creditor group; (c) the employee group; (d) the analyst-advisor group; (e) government; and (f) the public. A case can be made out for excluding governments as they have the power to enforce disclosure by passing legislation.

Some of the users and their possible needs are:

Shareholders: profit, risk, growth.

Short term creditors: solvency and realisable value of assets.

Loan stock holders: solvency, long term sustainability and risk of the business, extent of debt.

Employees: sustainability of the business, investment, including where located.

Neighbourhood: environmental issues, commitment to locality.

Government: tax charge, investments and their location – home or abroad, employment generation.

Analyst-advisor group: future profitability and risk.

Within this list are potential conflicts – disclosing realisable values might benefit creditors but potentially reduce the share price to the disadvantage of the owners. Despite this, the ASB presumption is that, in satisfying the needs of shareholders, other users' needs are also satisfied.

A case can also be made for differentiating between users' needs and rights. As shareholders pay for the audit via reduced profits, it might be argued that their needs are more legitimate than those of other users. However, to the extent that the audit fee is tax allowable and to the extent that it might possibly be passed on in higher prices, ultimately it may not be borne by those shareholders.

Traditional financial accounting has a historical or backward-looking focus. Many of the needs of users, however, are forward looking with their concern with future decisions. Traditionally, the emphasis has been on maintaining financial capital in nominal terms and yet both shareholders and employees might be equally concerned with the long term sustaining of operating capacity.

Solution 2

Balance sheets end of year 2

(£000)	Historical cost	Replacement cost	Realisable value
Fixed assets	160	200	160
Depreciation	64	80	80
Net book value	96	120	80
Stock	27	30	42
Cash	157	157	157
	280	307	279
Capital	150	150	150
Retained profit	130	103	129
Replacement cost reserve	—	54	—
	280	307	279

Replacement cost reserve (£000)

Fixed assets year 1	20
Stock year 1	8
Fixed assets year 2	20
Stock year 2	10
Backlog depreciation year 2	(4)
	54

Profit and loss accounts

(£000)	Historical cost			Replacement cost			Realisable value		
	Year 1	Year 2	Total	Year 1	Year 2	Total	Year 1	Year 2	Total
Turnover	84	105	189	84	105	189	84	105	189
Cost of sales	48	61	109	54	70	124	38	56	94
Gross profit	36	44	80	30	35	65	46	49	95
Depreciation	32	32	64	36	40	76	50	30	80
Net profit/(loss)	4	12	16	(6)	(5)	(11)	(4)	19	15

Solution 3

Economists' ideal income

End of year 0			End of year 1			End of year 2			End of year 3		
NCF	$\frac{1}{(1+r)^n}$	DCF	NCF	$\frac{1}{(1+r)^n}$	DCF	NCF	$\frac{1}{(1+r)^n}$	DCF	NCF	$\frac{1}{(1+r)^n}$	DCF
330,000	0.800	264,000	330,000	1.000	330,000	330,000	1.250	412,500	412,500	1.250	515,625
330,000	0.640	211,200	330,000	0.800	264,000	330,000	1.000	330,000	330,000	1.250	412,500
330,000	0.512	168,960	330,000	0.640	211,200	330,000	0.800	264,000	330,000	1.000	330,000

	End of year 0	End of year 1	End of year 2	End of year 3
Closing wealth	644,160	805,200	1,006,500	1,258,125
Opening wealth	240,000	644,160	805,200	1,006,500
Income	*404,160	161,040	201,300	251,625

* Windfall gain at commencement of business.

(£)	Historical cost accounting			Realisable value accounting		
	Year 1	Year 2	Year 3	Year 1	Year 2	Year 3
Turnover	530,000	530,000	530,000	530,000	530,000	530,000
Expenses	(200,000)	(200,000)	(200,000)	(200,000)	(200,000)	(200,000)
Depreciation	(80,000)	(80,000)	(80,000)	(140,000)	(90,000)	(10,000)
Interest		82,500	185,625		82,500	185,625
Profit	250,000	332,500	435,625	190,000	322,500	505,625

CHAPTER 7

Outline solutions

1. (c)

2. Cost of an additional report is negligible. Producing one extra report does not reduce availability to others. 'Lumpiness' argument applies, i.e. cannot produce marginal differences to suit all individuals except at disproportionate cost.

3. Corporate governance is concerned with how companies are managed and their relationships with their stakeholders. It is an issue because of the privileged position of senior management within an organisation who have access to information denied to others and are able, at least partially, to determine what information is disclosed.

4. There are two approaches to corporate governance. The one found in the UK is concerned with the relationship of directors to their shareholders and is manifested in the Cadbury Code. In the Code, the emphasis is on the appointment of non-executive directors to play an independent role separate from the executive directors. The second approach, primarily found in Germany, takes a more strategic, longer term, wider perspective of stakeholders. Governance is achieved by having two boards, the management board and the supervisory council.

5. Public good aspect of accounting; agency problem; need to consider stakeholders other than shareholders.

6. (d) True and fair is an evolving and dynamic concept, not defined in any Act of Parliament but rather interpreted by the practices and views of accountants. True and fair relates to freedom from intentional bias, the disclosure of all material facts and the reporting of the substance of transactions.

7. (a) Additional information about existing accounting elements; (b) disclosure of new areas of accounting information; (c) the choice of valuation methods; (d) the presentation of accounting information.

8. False. Although the 1989 Act recognised accounting standards in law for the first time, the Act also provided for the true and fair override.

9. (a)

10 (b)

11. Neither. Research expenditure must be charged as an expense as it occurs. Development expenditure then *may* be capitalised and matched against future revenues.

12. (a) Lack of a conceptual framework; (b) excessive flexibility in standards; (c) failure to sufficiently involve non-accountants; (d) excessive delay in introducing standards; (e) no mechanism for dealing with emerging issues; (f) no statutory backing.

13. (e) Accounting standards are developed by the Accounting Standards Board.

Solution 1

There are two options allowable under SSAP 12. The net book value at the end of the first year is £240,000. In the first option, the £240,000 can be charged to the profit and loss account in equal instalments over the rest of its life. This would give an annual charge of £80,000 per annum (£240,000/3 years).

Had the life been accurately estimated at the beginning, the annual charge would have been £75,000. The alternative treatment is therefore to charge the underprovision of £15,000 to year 2's revised depreciation, a total of £90,000 and then to charge £75,000 in each of the subsequent years.

CHAPTER 8

Outline solutions

1. (a) Legal systems, (b) role of the private investor – stock exchange vs. banking finance, (c) role of taxation, (d) the role, extent and development of the accounting profession, (e) role of theory – Netherlands, (f) accidents of history – French accounting plan.

2. In France and Germany, there is uniform accounting which is prescriptive even to the level of individual recordings. These legally backed accounting requirements also apply to unincorporated businesses. In the UK, there is no law governing the accounting requirements of partnerships and sole traders. The focus of accounting law within the Companies Acts and the quasi-law of the Accounting Standards Board is on the content and values within published financial statements with entities being free to choose how the detailed recording is undertaken.

3. (a) Simplifies work of other agents such as auditors and tax inspectors; (b) it reduces the need for accounting by standardising the accounting systems and prescribing treatments which reduce the need for judgement; (c) because of uniformity and the number of entities regulated, it allows suitable software to be developed at very low prices; (d) facilitates the transferability and flexibility of accounting staff who are trained to a single system; (e) assists and simplifies the collection of national statistics. The main disadvantages relate to its rigidity and limited scope for judgement.

4. (b)

5. False. Small companies in the UK do not have to publish a profit and loss account. To be classified as a small company, the entity has to meet two out of the three conditions identified in Exhibit 8.3. In addition, from 1994, a limited company, with certain exceptions, does not have to be audited if it has an annual turnover of no more than £90,000 and gross assets of less than £1.4 million.

6. Expenditure can be classified by function, broken down into cost of sales, distribution costs and administration expenses. Alternatively, expenditure can be classified by expenditure type such as wages, materials, etc.

7. As a result of the Fourth Directive, liabilities are now analysed between those due for repayment within 12 months and those due for repayment beyond that time.

8. SSAP 6 was attempting to differentiate recurring and regular items of income and expenditure from those which would rarely occur or which, although regular, were abnormal in their amount. The objective was to produce a figure of normalised profit. It was replaced by FRS 3 because of the abuses possible resulting from the different treatments of exceptional and extraordinary profits.

9. The profit and loss account now gives more information with major headings broken down between continuing, discontinued and acquired activities. In addition, extraordinary items have been so closely defined that they are highly unlikely to occur.

10. Capital instruments refer to all the many forms of long term finance. FRS 4 was introduced as a result of the increasing use of hybrid securities which were in between pure debt and pure equity. In the balance sheet, the temptation was for instruments to be reported as shareholders' funds even though they might have features of debt in order to appear to reduce the debt burden. Similarly, in the profit and loss account, the danger was to report only the (generally much reduced) legal interest payments of the current period without recognising other costs such as premiums on redemption.

Solution 1

Profit and loss account for year ended 31 December 19X8

	(£000)
Turnover	7,482
Cost of sales	3,805
Gross profit	3,677
Distribution costs	(441)
Administration costs	(825)
Other operating income	47
Interest payable and similar charges	(112)
Profit on ordinary activities before taxation	2,346
Tax on profit on ordinary activities	(800)
Profit for the financial year	1,546
Dividends proposed	(400)
Retained profits for the year	1,146
Profits retained 1 January	621
Profits retained 31 December	1,767

Balance sheet at 31 December 19X8

	(£000)	(£000)	(£000)
Fixed assets			
Intangible assets			1,290
Tangible assets			2,331
			3,621
Current assets			
Stocks		2,050	
Debtors		2,127	
Cash at bank and in hand		819	
		4,996	
Creditors: amounts falling due within one year			
Loan	248		
Trade creditors	362		
Other creditors including taxation and social security	1,200	1,810	
Net current assets			3,186
			6,807
Creditors: amounts falling due after more than one year			
8% debentures			1,000
			5,807
Capital and reserves			
Called up share capital			2,000
Share premium account			500
			2,500
Other reserves			
Capital redemption reserve		700	
General reserve		840	1,540
Profit and loss account			1,767
			5,807

Notes to the accounts

1. **Accounting policies:** the accounts have been prepared under the historical cost concept. Depreciation is provided on fixed assets at rates estimated to write-off their cost over their useful lives at rates between 10 per cent and 25 per cent per annum. Stocks are valued at the lower of cost or net realisable value and include an appropriate proportion of overheads. Turnover represents amounts invoiced, net of VAT, for goods supplied.

2. **Interest payable:** interest payable entirely relates to loans, overdrafts and borrowings repayable within five years.

3. **Profit on ordinary activities before taxation** is after charging wages and salaries of £2,414,000, social security costs of £57,000, pensions of £348,000, depreciation of £541,000, auditors' remuneration of £98,000, directors' fees of £80,000 and directors' other emoluments of £292,000. The chairman's emoluments were £110,000. The emoluments of the highest paid director were £130,000 and one other director received emoluments within the band £50,001– £55,000.

4. **Movement on fixed assets**

Fixed assets at cost	Factory machinery	Office equipment	Vehicles	Total
At 1 January	£2,000,000	£400,000	£84,000	£2,484,000
Additions	£800,000			£800,000
At 31 December	£2,800,000	£400,000	£84,000	£3,284,000
Depreciation at 1 January	£200,000	£160,000	£52,000	£412,000
Charge for year	£480,000	£40,000	£21,000	£541,000
Depreciation at 31 December	£680,000	£200,000	£73,000	£953,000
Net book value 1 January	£1,800,000	£240,000	£32,000	£2,072,000
Net book value 31 December	£2,120,000	£200,000	£11,000	£2,331,000

5. **Stocks:** stocks consist of raw materials £100,000, work-in-progress £862,000 and finished goods £1,088,000.

6. **Debtors and trade creditors:** debtors entirely consist of trade debtors. Other creditors including taxation comprise dividends proposed of £400,000 and corporation tax payable of £800,000.

7. **Called-up share capital:** the authorised share capital of the company is 5,000,000 £1 ordinary shares of which 2,000,000 have been issued fully paid.

Solution 2

Gransden plc profit and loss account – year ended 31 December 19X6

	19X6 (£m)	19X6 (£m)	19X5 as restated (£m)	19X5 as restated (£m)
Turnover				
Continuing operations	340		346	
Acquisitions	40		—	
	380		346	
Discontinued	20		24	
	—	400	—	370
Cost of sales		310		281
Gross profit		90		89
Distribution costs		12		10
Administration expenses		24		20
Operating profit				
Continuing operations	43		54	
Acquisitions	10		—	
	53		54	
Discontinued operations	1	54	5	59
Exceptional item		6		—
Profit on ordinary activities before interest		60		59
Interest payable		12		12
Profit on ordinary activities before taxation		48		47
Taxation on profit of ordinary activities		16		17
Profit for the financial year		32		30
Dividends		12		8
Retained profit for the financial year		20		22

Note to the profit and loss account

	Continuing operations 19X6 (£m)	Discontinued operations 19X6 (£m)	Total 19X6 (£m)	Continuing operations 19X5 (£m)	Discontinued operations 19X5 (£m)	Total 19X5 (£m)
Cost of sales	296	14	310	266	15	281
Net operating expenses						
Distribution costs	10	2	12	8	2	10
Administration expenses	21	3	24	18	2	20
	31	5	36	26	4	30

The total figure for continuing operations in 19X6 include the following amounts relating to acquisitions: cost of sales £18 million, distribution costs £5 million and administration expenses £7 million.

Statement of total recognised gains and losses

	19X6 (£m)	19X5 (£m)
Profit for the financial year	32	30
Unrealised surplus on revaluation of freehold properties	6	—
	38	30

Note of historical cost profit and loss

	19X6 (£m)	19X5 (£m)
Reported profit on ordinary activities before taxation	48	47
Difference between historical cost depreciation charge and the actual depreciation charge for the year calculated on the revalued amount	5	—
Historical cost profit on ordinary activities before taxation	53	47

Reconciliation of movements in shareholders' funds

		19X6 (£m)	19X5 (£m)
Profit for the financial year		32	30
Dividends		(12)	(8)
		20	22
Other recognised gains and losses		100	
New share capital subscribed:			
Ordinary shares issued	£40,000,000		
Share premium	£80,000,000	120	—
Net addition to shareholders' funds		240	22
Opening shareholders' funds		600	578
Closing shareholders' funds		840	600

CHAPTER 9

Outline solutions

1. (c)

2. (b)

3. Pre-acquisition reserves along with share capital and other reserves are the claims within a subsidiary's accounts on the assets of the subsidiary. As such, they are netted out against the investment in the subsidiary within the parent's accounts on consolidation. Because of this, they are not available for distribution by the group. Post-acquisition reserves, providing they are not capital reserves, represent retained profits of the group and as such are available for distribution.

4. (a) and (b)

5. Pre-acquisition write downs refer to the reduction in the fair value of the assets in a new subsidiary as a result of them being incorporated into the parent's operations. Examples include stock write downs and the provision for redundancies if the parent intends to close part of the subsidiary's operations. This reduces the value of the net assets and increases the goodwill which can then be written off against reserves, so enabling major expenses to bypass the profit and loss account. FRS 7 attempts to prevent this abuse by viewing fair value through the eyes of the seller without taking account of what the purchaser intends to do with the assets.

6. Merger accounting may be applied where there is a genuine marriage of two equal companies. Acquisition accounting is where one company takes over another. Merger accounting offers two distinct advantages. No assets have to be revalued – and hence possibly improving future *reported* performance – and all reserves are available for distribution. Acquisition accounting requires the assets of the subsidiary being revalued and results in pre-acquisition reserves being eliminated. Because of the advantages of merger accounting, it is often preferable to treat a combination as a merger. As a result, both EU law and the UK ASB have tried to restrict its use to genuine mergers.

7. (e)

8. An associated undertaking arises where an entity has an interest in another sufficient to give it influence but not control. If the investment can be viewed as an associated undertaking, the parent is able to bring in its share of the profits from the associate and not just the amount of dividends received.

9. FRS 6 is concerned with laying down criteria for allowing merger accounting. These are so stringent that merger accounting will only be rarely used in the future.

10. Off balance sheet finance refers to the possibility of a company obtaining debt finance but not having to show it as a liability. One example is a sale with a repurchase option when, in reality, the sale is effectively a loan. FRS 5 Reporting the substance of transactions addresses many of these abuses.

11. (a)

12. No. The 1989 Companies Act also recognised accounting standards. Since that Act, FRS 2 Accounting for subsidiary undertakings has been introduced. This takes the view that subsidiaries should only be excluded under exceptional circumstances. Neither expense nor delay are reasons for excluding subsidiaries. However, the standard *requires* subsidiaries to be excluded where there are severe long term restrictions.

Solution 1

100% Subsidiary

(£000)	Peacock plc (a)	(b)	(c)	Wiseman plc (d)	(e)	(f)	(g)	(h)	Consolidation (i)	(j)	(k)	(l)
Fixed assets	+290		+290	+80	+20	+100	+390			+390		+390
Investment in Wiseman		+200	+200				+200	−160	−40			
Goodwill									+40	+40	−40	
Stock	+40		+40	+14		+14	+54			+54		+54
Debtors	+25		+25	+18		+18	+43			+43		+43
Cash	+240	−200	+40	+44		+44	+84			+84		+84
Creditors	−40		−40	−16		−16	−56			−56		−56
	555		555	140		160	715			555		515
£1 ordinary shares	−340		−340	−100		−100	−440	+100		−340		−340
Revaluation reserve					−20	−20	−20	+20				
Reserves	−215		−215	−40		−40	−255	+40		−215	+40	−175
	555		555	140		160	715			555		515

Key: (a) original balance sheet of Peacock; (b) purchase of Wiseman; (c) revised balance sheet of Peacock; (d) original balance sheet of Wiseman; (e) revaluation of assets of subsidiary; (f) revised balance sheet of Wiseman; (g) aggregation of the two balance sheets; (h) matching of investment with shareholders' funds acquired in Wiseman; (i) balance equals goodwill; (j) final balance sheet if goodwill *not* written off; (k) writing off of goodwill against reserves; (l) final balance sheet if goodwill written off.

75% Subsidiary

(£000)	Peacock plc (a)	(b)	(c)	Wiseman plc (d)	(e)	(f)	(g)	(h)	Consolidation (i)	(j)	(k)	(l)	(m)
Fixed assets	+290		+290	+80	+20	+100	+390				+390		+390
Investment in Wiseman		+150	+150				+150	−120	−30				
Goodwill									+30		+30	−30	
Stock	+40		+40	+14		+14	+54				+54		+54
Debtors	+25		+25	+18		+18	+43				+43		+43
Cash	+240	−150	+90	+44		+44	+134				+134		+134
Creditors	−40		−40	−16		−16	−56				−56		−56
	555		555	140		160	715				595		565
£1 ordinary shares	−340		−340	−100		−100	−440	+75		+25	−340		−340
Revaluation reserve					−20	−20	−20	+15		+5			
Reserves	−215		−215	−40		−40	−255	+30		+10	−215	+30	−185
Minority interest										−40	−40		−40
	555		555	140		160	715				595		565

Key: (a) original balance sheet of Peacock; (b) purchase of 75% of Wiseman; (c) revised balance sheet of Peacock; (d) original balance sheet of Wiseman; (e) revaluation of assets of subsidiary; (f) revised balance sheet of Wiseman; (g) aggregation of the two balance sheets; (h) matching of investment with 75% of shareholders' funds acquired in Wiseman; (i) balance equals goodwill; (j) identification of minority interest; (k) final balance sheet if goodwill *not* written off; (l) writing off of goodwill against reserves; (m) final balance sheet if goodwill written off.

Solution 2

(£000)	Devon	Kingsbridge	(a)		(b)	(c)	(d)	(e)	(f)	(g)
Fixed assets	+150	+80	+30	+110	+260				+260	+260
Investment in Kingsbridge	+120				+120	−99	−21			
Goodwill							+21		+21 −21	
Stock	+10	+27		+27	+37				+37	+37
Debtors	+25	+14		+14	+39				+39	+39
Cash	+15	+20		+20	+35				+35	+35
Creditors	−10	−11		−11	−21				−21	−21
	310	130		160	470				371	350
£1 ordinary shares	−140	−60		−60	−200	+54		+6	−140	−140
Reserves	−70	−20		−20	−90	+18		+2	−70 +21	−49
Revaluation reserve			−30	−30	−30	+27		+3		
£1 preference shares	−100	−50		−50	−150			+50	−100	−100
Minority interest								−61	−61	−61
	310	130		160	470				371	350

The columns under Consolidation are (b) (c) (d) (e) (f) (g).

Key: (a) revaluation of assets of Kingsbridge; (b) aggregation of the two balance sheets; (c) matching of investment with shareholders' funds acquired; (d) balance equals goodwill; (e) identification of minority interest; (f) final balance sheet if goodwill *not* written off; (g) final balance sheet if goodwill written off.

Note: treatment of preference shareholders in Kingsbridge as part of the minority interest.

CHAPTER 10

Outline solutions

1. (b)

2. (c)

3. (d)

4. (a)

5. Currency conversion relates to the exchange rate used to record transactions in foreign currency within the detailed accounting records of the home company. Currency translation refers to the adjustments necessary to show the accounts of an overseas subsidiary in the home currency.

6. Both apply to foreign subsidiaries and branches. The temporal method uses the exchange rate existing at the time of acquisition or revaluation for non-monetary assets and the closing rate for monetary elements. The closing rate method uses the closing rate for all assets and liabilities.

7. Net investment is a concept developed in SSAP 20 to justify the closing rate method. It views a subsidiary as essentially being an investment where the detailed breakdown between asset headings is of little significance.

8. For the closing rate/net investment method, any exchange difference on conversion is treated as a change in the reserves. Under the temporal method, any difference is accounted for via the profit and loss account.

9. (b)

Solution 1

(£000)	Parent (£)	(a) (£)	(b) (£)	Subsidiary FF	Rate	(£)	Consolidation (c) (£)	(d)	(e)	(f)
Goodwill									+18		+18
Investment	+90	+10	+100				+90	−72	−18	
Net assets	+4,500		+4,500	+1,170	9	+130	+4,630			+4,630
	4,590		4,600	1,170		130	4,720			4,648
Share capital	−2,000		−2,000	−400	10	−40	−2,040	+40		−2,000
Reserves	−2,540		−2,540	−320	10	−32	−2,572	+32		−2,540
Profit this year				−450	9	−50	−50		+2	−48
Loan	−50	−10	−60				−50		−10	−60
Gain on exchange						−8	−8		+8	
	4,590		4,600	1,170		130	4,720			−4,648

Notes:

(a) sterling value of loan at year end is DM150,000/2.5 = £60,000 and so conversion loss is £10,000. Value of investment at beginning of year = £90,000 × 10FF = FF900,000. Sterling value at year end = FF900,000/9 = £100,000 to give a conversion gain of £10,000.

(b) shows the balance sheet of the company at the year end after taking account of the translation differences.

(c) represents the aggregation of Guildhall's balance sheet with that of the subsidiary.

(d) represents the netting out of the equity acquired in exchange for the purchase price to leave (e) as the goodwill.

(f) introduces the translation loss on the loan which would normally be charged to the profit and loss account. This is partially offset by the translation gain and so only the net £2,000 is charged to the group profit and loss account.

Solution 2

At the time of acquisition, the exchange rate stood at $10:£1 and so the pre-acquisition reserves are treated in a similar way to the share capital acquired. Net assets at the beginning of the year ($648,900) equal net assets at the end of the year ($774,900) less profit for the year ($126,000). Opening fixed assets ($756,000) comprise their current value ($630,000) plus depreciation for the year ($126,000). Given this and no change to loans or the issued share capital, the balance must be the total of debtors plus cash less trade creditors and these are all converted at the same rate irrespective of the method used. With net assets of $648,900 and with the share capital and pre-acquisition reserves known, the balance must be retentions at the beginning of the year.

Consolidated profit and loss account

Temporal	(£)	(£)	Closing rate/net investment	(£)	(£)
Turnover		207,000	Turnover		218,000
Cost of sales		(120,000)	Cost of sales		(126,000)
Gross profit		87,000	Gross profit		92,000
Depreciation	17,600		Depreciation	23,000	
Other expenses	10,900	(28,500)	Other expenses	11,400	(34,400)
Exchange gain		1,100	Net profit		57,600
Net profit		59,600			

Consolidated balance sheet

Temporal	(£)	(£)	Closing rate/net investment	(£)	(£)
Net fixed assets		150,000	Net fixed assets		177,000
Goodwill		60,000	Goodwill		60,000
Debtors	70,000		Debtors	70,000	
Cash	20,000		Cash	20,000	
	90,000			90,000	
Less creditors	30,000	60,000	Less creditors	30,000	60,000
		270,000			297,000
Less loan		20,000	Less loan		20,000
		250,000			277,000
Financed by			Financed by		
Ordinary share capital		100,000	Ordinary share capital		100,000
Retentions		150,000	Retentions		177,000
		250,000			277,000

CHAPTER 11

Outline solutions

1. (a)

2. Cash, working capital, funds in general.

3. Cashflows can be derived by applying duality and deriving the effect of cash transactions on the other accounts concerned.

4. Cash plus cash equivalents. Cash refers to cash in hand plus bank and similar deposits repayable on demand. Cash equivalents are short term, highly liquid investments convertible into known amounts of cash without notice and were within three months of maturity when acquired less advances from banks repayable within three months from the date of advance.

5. (d)

6. The gross approach derives the cashflows from a direct summarising of the cash account. The net approach involves analysing the effect of cash movements on the other accounts.

7. Net cashflow from operating activities; net cashflow from returns on investment and servicing of finance; net cashflow from investing activities; net cashflow from financing.

8. Free cashflow is a suggested revision to the net cashflow before financing. It differentiates between investing for the maintenance of operating capacity and investing to enhance the strategic operations of the entity.

Solution 1

FRS 1 cashflow statement for the year ended.......

		(£000)
Net cash inflows from operating activities		40
Returns on investments and servicing of finance		
Dividends paid	30	
Net cash outflows from servicing finance	—	(30)
Corporation tax paid	50	
Tax paid	—	(50)
Investment activities		
Payments to acquire tangible fixed assets	400	
Net cash outflow from investing activities		(400)
Net cash outflow before financing		(440)
Financing		
Issue of loan	400	
Net cash outflow from financing	—	400
Decrease in cash and cash equivalents		(40)
Reconciliation of operating profit to net cashflow from operating activities		
Operating profit		270
Depreciation charges		40
Decrease in stocks		50
Increase in debtors		(200)
Decrease in creditors		(120)
		40

Solution 2

FRS 1 cashflow statement for the year ended....

		(£000)
Net cash inflows from operating activities		147
Returns on investments and servicing of finance		
Interest paid	22	
Dividend paid	10	
Net cash outflows from servicing finance	—	(32)
Corporation tax paid	50	
Tax paid	—	(50)
Investment activities		
Payments to acquire tangible fixed assets	630	
Receipts from sale of tangible fixed assets	(230)	(400)
Net cash outflow from investing activities	——	——
Net cash outflow before financing		(335)
Financing		
Issue of ordinary share capital	125	
Issue of loan	220	
Repayment of loan	(400)	
Expenses in connection with share issue	(60)	
Net cash outflow from financing	——	(115)
Decrease in cash and cash equivalents		(450)

Reconciliation of operating profit to net cashflow from operating activities

Operating profit	235
Depreciation charges	90
Profit on sale of asset	(40)
Increase in stocks	(80)
Increase in debtors	(100)
Decrease in creditors	(40)
Interest payments	22
Issue expenses	60
Net cash inflow from operating activities	147

CHAPTER 12

Outline solutions

1. (c)

2. (a)

3. (c)

4. Debatable. It is often argued that CPP accounting overstates the profitability of highly geared companies because of the gain from having a monetary liability in the form of the loan. However, if markets are aware of high inflation, interest rates will be higher and so any gain is likely to be balanced by a higher interest charge.

5. (d)

6. Deprival value is the loss an entity would suffer if it was deprived of an asset. Historical cost, except by coincidence, is irrelevant. At the most, the loss would be the cost of replacement. However, it can be below that figure. If the asset is not to be replaced then the loss would be the higher of the asset's economic value or realisable value.

7. (e)

8. The cost of sales adjustment, the monetary working capital adjustment, the depreciation adjustment, the gearing adjustment.

9. Under current cost accounting, the historical cost depreciation in the profit and loss account will need to be supplemented to take account of current costs. Provisions for current cost depreciation in previous periods, although adequate at the time, will be insufficient if prices are continuing to rise. Back-log depreciation is the amount required to bring the total of accumulated current cost depreciation up to the costs applicable to the balance sheet date.

Solution 1

Balance sheet	HC 19X2 (£000)	HC 19X3 (£000)	Index	CPP 19X2 (£000)	Index	CPP 19X3 (£000)
Fixed assets	600	600	140/70	1,200	140/70	1,200
Depreciation	300	330	140/70	600	140/70	660
	300	270		600		540
Stock	40	50	140/110	51	140/130	54
Debtors	60	70	140/120	70	140/140	70
Cash	20	70	140/120	23	140/140	70
Creditors	(50)	(70)	140/120	(58)	140/140	(70)
	370	390		686		664
Financed by						
Share capital	300	300	140/70	600	140/70	600
Retentions	70	90	Balance	86	Balance	64
	370	390		686		664

Profit and loss account	HC (£000)		Index		CPP (£000)
Turnover		195	140/126		217
Opening stocks	40		140/110	51	
Purchases*	140		140/126	156	
Closing stocks	(50)		140/130	(54)	
Cost of sales	___	130		___	153
Gross profit		65			64
Depreciation		30	140/70		60
Other expenses		15	140/126		17
Net profit/(loss)		20			(13)

	HC (£000)		Index		CPP (£000)
Opening CPP net monetary assets		30	140/120	35	
Increase		40	140/126	44	
Closing CPP net monetary assets				79	
Actual closing net monetary assets				70	
Loss from holding net monetary assets					(9)
Total CPP loss				___	(22)

Movement on reserves

Reserves at end of year		64
Reserves at beginning of the year		86
Total loss as per balance sheet		(22)

* Purchases = Cost of sales +closing stock – opening stock

Solution 2

Workings (£000)

Stocks	HC	Index	CC	Debtors	HC	Index	CC
Opening stock	60.0	600/480	75.0	Opening balance	60.0	600/500	72.0
Purchases	500.0		500.0	Closing balance	110.0	600/687.5	96.0
Closing stock	–100.0	600/625	–96.0	Increase	50.0		24.0
Cost of sales	460.0		479.0	**Creditors**			
Cost of sales adjustment			**19.0**	Opening balance	30.0	600/500	36.0
				Closing balance	55.0	600/687.5	48.0
Depreciation	80.0	500/250	160.0	Increase	25.0		12.0
Depreciation adjustment			**80.0**	**Working Capital adjustment**	26.0 –13.0 =		**13.0**

Balance sheet adjustments	HC	Index	CC	Difference		HC	Index	CC
Fixed assets	800.0	540/250	1728.0	928.0	Stock	100.0	687.5/625	110.0
Depreciation	240.0	540/250	518.4	278.4	Adjustment			**10.0**
Less depreciation adjustment				80.0				
Back-log depreciation				**198.4**				

Gearing adjustment

Last year's equity	HC	Index	CC	Net Borrowings	Loan	Cash	Net
Fixed assets	800.0	400/250	1,280.0	Opening balance	400.0	200.0	200.0
Less depreciation	(160.0)	400/250	(256.0)	Closing balance	400.0	275.0	125.0
Stocks	60.0	500/480	62.5	Average for year			162.5
Debtors	60.0		60.0				
Creditors	(30.0)		(30.0)				
Cash	200.0		200.0				
Loan	(400.0)		(400.0)				
Shareholders' funds	530.0		916.5				
Closing Shareholders' funds			1,249.6				
Average for year			1,083.0				

Gearing = 162.5/(162.5 + 1083.0) = 13%

Gearing Adjustment = 13% × (19.0 + 80.0 + 13.0) = 14.6

Current cost reserve

Cost of sales adjustment	19.0
Monetary working capital	13.0
Revaluation of fixed assets	928.0
Back-log depreciation	(198.4)
Revaluation of closing stock	10.0
	771.6
Less gearing adjustment	14.6
Balance	757.0

Current cost profit and loss account
Year ended 30 September 19X8

	(£)
Turnover	800.0
Cost of sales	(460.0)
Gross profit	340.0
Depreciation	(80.0)
Other expenses	(200.0)
Net profit	60.0
Current cost adjustments	
Cost of sales	(19.0)
Depreciation	(80.0)
Monetary working capital	(13.0)
Gearing	14.6
Current cost operating loss	(37.4)

Current cost balance sheet at
30 September 19X8

	(£)	(£)
Fixed assets		1,728.0
Less depreciation		518.4
		1,209.6
Current assets		
Stocks	110.0	
Debtors	110.0	
Cash	275.0	
	495.0	
Less creditors	55.0	440.0
		1,649.6
Less loan		400.0
		1,249.6
Financed by		
Ordinary share capital		300.0
Retentions		192.6
Current cost reserve		757.0
		1,249.6

CHAPTER 13

Outline solutions

1. Adjusting events are events after the balance sheet date which give new insight into events which existed at the balance sheet date. Non-adjusting events are events which relate to conditions which did not exist on the balance sheet date.

2. (e) The fire is a non-adjusting event which should be disclosed by way of a note in the published accounts.

3. This is a contingent liability and its treatment depends on whether the cost of replacing all the faulty chips is (i) probable and quantifiable, (ii) possible or (iii) remote. Although these terms are not defined, it seems likely that the cost of replacing the chips will have to be met. As this is quantifiable, the answer appears to be (a).

4. Differences can arise from permanent difference as when an expense is allowed in one calculation but not the other and from timing differences when the expense is allowed in both profit figures but in different accounting periods.

5. Some fixed assets are not allowable against tax. Others – such as plant and machinery – are given capital allowances, normally based on the reducing balance.

6. Both are approaches to deferred taxation. The deferral method views the deferred tax as originating in the year of the originating timing difference. As such, the liability remains the same even when tax rates change. The liability method views the deferred tax as being an amount payable at the rate of tax existing when the reversal takes place. Given the best estimate of a future tax rate is the current one, this means that the liability should be maintained at the current tax rate.

7. SSAP 15 only requires the provision for deferred taxation to the extent that the liability would probably crystallise. With its focus on future liabilities, the liability method of deferred taxation is to be used.

8. The classical system involves a corporation being taxed on its profits. Any subsequent distribution is then taxed as income on the recipient. This is achieved by the company withholding tax at the basic rate of income tax from distributions and paying over the total amount to the authorities. The imputation system attempts to avoid this double taxation. Dividends are now paid as a net amount with the company paying an advance payment of corporation tax equivalent to the tax credit. With certain exceptions, this amount is then available to be offset against the total corporation tax charge.

9. (b)

10. £100,000

11. Franked investment income is mainly dividends received on shares held by a company. SSAP 8 requires these dividends to be grossed up and the increase to be shown as part of the total tax charge in the profit and loss account.

12. Both types of lease involve the use of an asset. Operating leases are essentially short term where the lease period is substantially less than the asset's economic life and where the legal owner retains most of the risk and rewards derived from ownership. Financial leases are where the user has the use of the asset for a substantial part of its economic life and takes on the risks and rewards which would otherwise accrue to the legal owner.

13. A defined contribution pension is where the payments into a fund are known but where the final pension payments depend on how well the fund has performed. A defined benefit scheme is where the final pension is known. As a result, contributions will vary to reflect the changing value of the pension fund and the changing future demands on it to pay the agreed pensions.

14. (a)

Solution 1

Reversals of £400,000 take place in 19X4 and £500,000 in19X5. Beyond that there are further originating differences and so deferred taxation need only be provided on the £900,000 of reversals rather than the £1,200,000 difference of the current year. With corporation tax at 33 per cent, the deferred taxation to be provided in the current year will be £297,000.

Corporation tax computation

Profit after depreciation but before corporation tax	£2,800,000
Add back depreciation	£800,000
	£3,600,000
Less capital allowances	(£2,000,000)
Profit for corporation tax purposes	· £1,600,000
Corporation tax at 33%	£528,000
Maximum ACT allowable = £1,600,000 × 20%	£320,000

Extract from the profit and loss account for 19X4		**Extract from the balance sheet of 19X4**	
	(£000)		*(£000)*
Operating profit before corporation tax	2,800	Current assets	
Dividends received	275	ACT recoverable*	150
Profit on ordinary activities before taxation	3,075		
Tax on profits on ordinary activities (note 1)	880	Current liabilities	
Profit for the year after taxation	2,195	ACT payable	470
Dividends paid	2,100		
Retentions for the year	95	Provision for liabilities and charges	
		Deferred taxation	
		Opening balance	nil
Note 1 Taxation for 19X4		In respect of capital allowances	297
Corporation tax at 33%	528	Closing balance	297
Deferred tax	297		
Tax on franked investment income	55	* If not recoverable within 12 months,	
	880	available for offset against deferred taxation.	

Solution 2

Schedule of interest payments		
End of year	*Detail*	*(£)*
	Cost	31,064
0	Repayment	10,000
	Balance	21,064
1	Interest	4,213
		25,277
1	Repayment	10,000
	Balance	15,277
2	Interest	3,055
		18,332
	Repayment	10,000
	Balance	8,332
3	Interest	1,666
	Balance	9,998
	Repayment	10,000
	Balance *	2

Interest rate implicit in the lease = 20%

End of year	*NCF*	*Factor*	*DCF*
0	£10,000	1.0000	£10,000
1	£10,000	0.8333	£8,333
2	£10,000	0.6944	£6,944
3	£10,000	0.5787	£5,787
Present value of lease payments			£31,064

Extract from balance sheet: end of	*Year 1*	*Year 2*	*Year 3*	*Year 4*
Fixed assets (leased)	£31,064	£31,064	£31,064	£31,064
Depreciation	£7,766	£15,532	£23,298	£31,064
Net book value	£23,298	£15,532	£7,766	nil
Obligations under finance leases	£25,277	£18,332	*£10,000	nil
Extract from the profit and loss account				
Interest	£4,213	£3,055	*£1,668	
Depreciation	£7,766	£7,766	£7,766	£7,766
	£11,979	£10,821	£9,434	£7,766

* Rounding error of £2 added to final year interest.

CHAPTER 14

Outline solutions

1. Users may use financial reports to confirm or correct previously held beliefs and use them as an aid to predicting future performance.

2. (b)

3. Base data may contain judgements, mainly dependent on past data; no prescribed definitions of the ratios.

4. True – although the definition of assets may be either gross or net. The apparent inconsistency arises from net assets equalling capital employed as a result of the application of duality.

5. Identifies continuing, acquired and discontinued activities. Also reduced likelihood of extra-ordinary items.

6. Return on sales (sales margin) and asset turnover.

7. Fixed assets are part of a company's infrastructure enabling profits to be generated. Current assets exist to avoid losses.

8. (c)

9. (c)

10. False. Solvency is the ability to pay debts when due. Liquidity is a measure of the extent to which assets are held in the form of cash and cash equivalents.

11. Financial risk arises from the use of debt in a company's capital structure. Because of the resulting interest having to be paid irrespective of profitability or cashflows, taking on debt finance increases the risk of an entity. Operating risk arises from the products and markets the company operates in. There are two aspects: the variability in demand as a result of changes in the wider economy and the ability to avoid the worst excesses of a recession by having a cost structure mainly comprising variable costs.

12. By capitalising goodwill, a company's net assets appears greater and so its gearing will appear smaller.

13. With increasing profits, preference shares take on many of the features of debt as they are both a fixed expense and an expense which has to be met before the equity shareholders can be given a return. However, in times of decreasing profits, the preference dividend does not have to be paid, provided no dividend is paid to the ordinary shareholders. In this case, preference shares have features more commonly associated with equity shares.

14. Creative accounting refers to accounting measures undertaken by the directors of companies in order to enhance the apparent performance and strength of their company. Examples include the capitalisation of interest and the choice of lower depreciation rates. Although not illegal, creative accounting distorts information.

Solution 1

Return on shareholders' funds	$\dfrac{9,000}{60,000}$	= 15%	Return on capital employed	$\dfrac{12,000}{90,000}$	= 13⅓%
Asset turnover	$\dfrac{180,000}{90,000}$	= 2	Net profit margin	$\dfrac{12,000}{180,000}$	= 6⅔%
Gross profit percentage	$\dfrac{60,000}{180,000}$	= 33⅓%	Working capital ratio	120:39	= 3:1
Liquidity ratio/acid test	33:39	= 0.85:1	Average age of debtors	$\dfrac{30,000}{15,000}$	= 2 m
Average age of stock	$\dfrac{87,000}{10,000}$	= 8.7 m	Average age of creditors	$\dfrac{39,000}{9,750}$	= 4 m
Gearing (debt/equity)	$\dfrac{30,000}{60,000}$	= 50%	Gearing (debt/debt + equity)	$\dfrac{30,000}{90,000}$	= 33⅓%
Life of fixed assets	$\dfrac{66,000}{3,000}$	= 22 years	Remaining life of fixed assets	$\dfrac{9,000 \times 22}{66,000}$	= 3 years
Net current debt	$\dfrac{6,000}{12,000}$	= 6 m	No credit interval	$\dfrac{33,000}{168,000}$	= 2.4 m

Assuming the only variable cost is the cost of sales, the fixed operating costs will be £48,000 and the contribution percentage, 33.33 per cent. The breakeven point will be £48,000/0.333 = £144,000.

Items requiring attention

High stock levels; age of fixed assets – if all machinery then a low depreciation rate; need for renewal soon (effect on cashflow); long term loan due for renewal giving misleadingly assuring liquidity measures. Other issues: lack of a standard against which to interpret the ratios; lack of information about the accounting policies.

Solution 2

Balance sheet – this year		*(£)*	*Profit and loss account – this year*		*(£)*
Fixed assets		100,000	Turnover		1,860,000
Depreciation		60,000	Cost of sales		800,000
		40,000	Gross profit		1,060,000
Current assets			Depreciation	20,000	
Stock	200,000		Interest	6,000	
Debtors	620,000		Other expenses	934,000	960,000
Cash	(280,000)		Net profit		100,000
	540,000				
Creditors	270,000	270,000			
		310,000			
10% loan		60,000			
		250,000			
Ordinary share capital		120,000			
Reserves		130,000			
		250,000			

Workings

(a) Opening shareholders' funds given at £150,000 and so, with no dividends, closing shareholders' funds will be £150,000 plus the net profit. Letting NP represent the current year's net profit and recognising that the return on shareholders' funds is 40 per cent, the actual profit can be found by solving for NP in the expression $NP/(150,000 + NP) = 40\%$ to give a net profit of £100,000. (b) Depreciation can be calculated as 20% × £100,000 and interest as 10% × £60,000. (c) If the net profit for the year is £100,000, then year end shareholders' funds will be £250,000. With a long term loan of £60,000, the capital employed in the business will be £310,000 and – using duality – the total of fixed assets plus current assets minus current liabilities will also equal this figure. Given an asset turnover of six, sales turnover will be £1,860,000 and given an average age of debtors of four months, the year end debtors will equal £620,000. (d) Fixed assets plus current assets minus current liabilities equals £310,000. With the net book value of the fixed assets equalling £60,000 after providing £20,000 depreciation this year, the working capital must equal £270,000. As the working capital ratio is 2:1, current assets must equal £540,000 and current liabilities – only trade creditors in this example –£270,000. (e) As the average age of the £270,000 of trade creditors is six months, purchases must have been £540,000 during the year. From this, it is possible to derive the cost of sales. The cost of sales is defined as opening stock plus purchases minus closing stock. Although the closing stock is not given, its average age is known to be three months and so cost of sales = £60,000 + £540,000 – [3/12 cost of sales] = £800,000. This enables the gross profit to be calculated and the closing stock figure of £200,000 found by calculating 3/12 of the cost of sales. The only figures missing are the cash on the balance sheet and the other expenses in the profit and loss account. These are the balancing items.

CHAPTER 15

Outline solutions

1. The study of root causes, the identification of symptoms, brute empiricism.

2. Company's management, its accounting system and the business's response to change.

3. Over gearing, overtrading, emphasis on 'the big project'.

4. Deteriorating financial ratios, creative accounting, non-financial signs and terminal signs.

5. A numerical weighting given to the signs of defects, mistakes and symptoms by Argenti.

6. The use of a single variable or financial ratio to predict failure.

7. A 'Z' score represents the sum of the values and weightings of those accounting ratios which have been identified as differing between failed and non-failed firms. The combination of ratios and weightings used is the one which gives the best prediction of the boundary between failed and non-failed firms.

Solution 1

Workings

Number of ordinary shares = 4,000,000   Market value ∴ £24,000,000

$R_1 =$	Working capital/total assets* =	$3300/11000 = 0.3000 ∴ 1.2R_1 = 0.3600$
$R_2 =$	Retained earnings/total assets =	$1300/11000 = 0.1182 ∴ 1.4R_2 = 0.1655$
$R_3 =$	Earnings before interest and tax/total assets =	$300/11000 = 0.0273 ∴ 3.3R_3 = 0.0901$
$R_4 =$	Market value of preference shares and ordinary shares/book value of debt =	$24000/4000 = 6.0000 ∴ 0.6R_4 = 3.6000$
$R_5 =$	Sales/total assets=	$2000/11000 = 0.1818 ∴ 1.0R_5 = 0.1818$
		Z score = 4.3974

* Fixed assets of £6,000,000 and current assets of £5,000,000

Kingston and Thames plc has made a loss for the period after tax and interest. Despite that, the information is not directly used in the Z score. R_3 is merely concerned with earnings before interest and tax. Only in R_2, which measures after-tax and interest retained earnings against total assets, does current profitability enter the Z score – and even then its importance is watered down by the inclusion of previous years' retentions. In other words, the ratio is giving the same strength to current data as past data despite past performance being, at best, an uncertain guide to future performance.

Secondly, all of the ratios except R_4 use total assets as the denominator. The book value of total assets, however, is dependent on accounting conventions. Assume, for example, that the fixed assets were revalued at the end of the year in question. The effect would be to reduce the value of all the elements making up the Z score except R_4. If investors are efficient, however, and can see through the accounting numbers to the underlying value of the business of Kingston and Thames, then such an accounting change should not affect the value of the company's shares and therefore not effect R_4. This is part of a more general criticism that most of the numerators and denominators are influenced by accounting conventions for their valuation. It might be that Kingston and Thames mainly trade through subsidiaries in countries with 'soft' currencies and strict exchange controls. On the balance sheet, the cash balances of the subsidiaries will have been translated at the official exchange rate to derive their sterling equivalent even though there might be no way of converting these amounts into sterling.

Probably the greatest criticism in this particular example, however, is the major influence of the market value of the equity within R_4 on the ultimate Z score. In essence, this is a non-accounting figure and yet the rationale of Z scores relates to the ability of accounting numbers to forecast company failure.

A more general criticism of Z scores is that the variables are mainly firm oriented and yet '… there is considerable evidence that failure rates in the economy are correlated with macro-economic variables such as interest rate changes and unemployment rate changes' (Foster G., *Financial Statement Analysis,* 2nd edn, Prentice Hall International, 1986). This raises the possibility that multivariate models including macro-economic aggregates would improve the predictive ability of Z score models.

CHAPTER 16

Outline solutions

1. Cost centres are units of the organisation where costs can and are meaningfully collected. They can be departments, products or an activity. Managers are then held responsible for performing defined outputs within defined costs. A profit centre is where the output can and is measured in financial terms, allowing a profit to be determined. Investment centres go beyond this and give managers responsibility for the capital employed.

2. Behaviour controls are where there is a clear cause and effect – as when cost behaviour is clearly known – and so control is exercised if the actual result is equal to the calculated result. Where this means-end relationship is less well understood, control is exercised by considering overall performance using measures such as the return on capital employed. Input controls apply to responsibility centres where it is difficult to determine cause and effect and where output controls are not possible.

3. Process costing refers to situations where production is continuous and where it is not possible to clearly and uniquely identify work-in-progress from completed production.

4. (c)

5. Normal losses are inevitable. They form part of the cost of production and hence part of the cost of sales and closing stock. Abnormal losses, by definition, should not occur in the ordinary course of events. If they occur, they do not add any value and so should not be included in closing stock valuations.

6. (b)

7. Absorption costing has been justified because of its effect on managerial behaviour. It may be an approximation to 'difficult to observe costs' and it may reduce dysfunctional behaviour by reducing a manager's consumption of perquisites. In addition, it makes managers aware that they are consuming overheads.

8. (i) Failure of management accounting to meet the needs of modern business environments; (ii) traditional product costing provided misleading information for management; (iii) management accounting driven by the needs of financial accounting and external reporting; (iv) focus on internal costs and activities.

9. Activity based costing recognises that many overheads are, in reality, variable costs but subject to timing delays and not necessarily variable with the volume of production. ABC is concerned with identifying what causes these costs by identifying cost-drivers for each major heading of overhead. The end result is that it is easier to identify products or other cost centres which are consuming the overheads.

Solution 1

Overhead	Basis	Department 1	Department 2	Department 3	Canteen	Maintenance	Total
Salaries	direct	85,500	64,800	87,600	31,185	98,400	367,485
Materials	direct	8,000	6,500	24,400	26,000		64,900
Rent and rates	area	2,250	4,050	9,000	450	2,250	18,000
Insurance	area	500	900	2,000	100	500	4,000
Power	estimate	3,440	3,870	860	0	430	8,600
Heat and light	area	825	1,485	3,300	165	825	6,600
Depreciation	machine cost	30,000	27,000	3,000			60,000
		130,515	108,605	130,160	57,900	102,405	529,585
Canteen	labour hours	14,475	8,685	34,740	(57,900)		0
Maintenance	machine hours	34,135	68,270			(102,405)	0
		179,125	185,560	164,900	0	0	529,585
Overhead absorption rates		£22.39 machine hour	£11.60 machine hour	£6.87 labour hour			

Solution 2

Input	Cost	Equivalent units	Unit cost
Material	£83,200	32,000 litres	£2.60
Conversion costs	£221,760	26,400 litres	£8.40

	Units worked	Percentage worked	Unit cost		Total cost
Forecast output – including normal loss					
Material	25,000	100%	£2.60	£65,000	
conversion costs		100%	£8.40	£210,000	
	25,000				£275,000
Normal loss	5,000				
Forecast good output	20,000		£13.75		£275,000
Actual output	18,000		£13.75		£247,500
Abnormal loss	2,000		£13.75		£27,500
Work-in-progress					
Material	7,000	100%	£2.60	£18,200	
Conversion costs		20%	£8.40	£11,760	£29,960
Cost of inputs					£304,960

Solution 3

Overhead absorption rate

Total overheads $= \dfrac{£59,879}{} = £4.80$ per machine hour

Total machine hours $= (125 + 1,250 + 600 + 10,500) = 12,475$ hours

Overhead per unit	Product A		Product B		Product C		Product D	
	(hours)	*(£)*	*(hours)*	*(£)*	*(hours)*	*(£)*	*(hours)*	*(£)*
Overhead @ £4.80 per hour	125	600	1,250	6,000	600	2,880	10,500	50,400
Units produced		500		5,000		600		7,000
Overhead per unit		£1.20		£1.20		£4.80		£7.20

Overhead cost		Cost driver	Units of activity	Cost per unit of activity
Machine oriented overhead	£37,424	Machine hours	12,475	£3.00
Set-up costs	£4,355	Number of set-ups	17	£256.18
Material ordering costs	£1,920	Number of material orders	10	£192.00
Material handling costs	£7,580	Number of times material handled	27	£280.74
Spare parts administration	£8,600	Number of spare parts consumed	12	£716.67

ABC Overhead cost	Unit cost	Product A		Product B		Product C		Product D	
		Units of activity	*(£)*	Units of activity	*(£)*	Units of activity	*(£)*	Units of activity	*(£)*
Machine costs	£3.00	125	375.00	1,250	3,750.00	600	1,800.00	10,500	31,500.00
Set-up costs	£256.18	1	256.18	6	1,537.08	2	512.36	8	2,049.44
Material ordering	£192.00	1	192.00	4	768.00	1	192.00	4	768.00
Material handling	£280.74	2	561.48	10	2,807.40	3	842.22	12	3,368.88
Spare parts	£716.67	2	1,433.34	5	3,583.35	1	716.67	4	2,866.68
			2,818.00		12,445.83		4,063.25		40,553.00
Units produced			500		5,000		600		7,000
ABC overhead per unit			£5.64		£2.49		£6.77		£5.79

Although almost 40 per cent of the overhead cost of Speyside relates to non-machine activity, the traditional method of charging overheads using machine hours has failed to reflect this. Product D is a high volume product. Under the traditional system, it has been charged for overheads which relate to the product complexity of the other products.

CHAPTER 17

Outline solutions

1. The relevant range refers to the range of output levels possible with the current amount of fixed costs.

2. The economist views unit marginal costs as initially decreasing, then increasing at an increasing rate. The accountant views marginal cost per unit as a constant.

3. (c)

4. The margin of safety is the difference between any given output level and the breakeven point. It can either be expressed in units, turnover or a percentage.

5. (b)

6. Ignores factors such as quantity discounts and needs to alter prices to achieve different levels of sales volume – although these can be incorporated in the model; assumes simple technical relationships and takes no account of behavioural issues; difficult to apply with any accuracy to a multi-product problem; data may be influenced by accounting conventions – especially closing stocks.

7. Dual value or internal opportunity cost.

8. The value foregone by not using resources in the next best alternative use.

9. (a)

10. Linear programming is a mathematical technique which identifies an optimal solution when there are conflicting constraints. Both the objective and the constraints are assumed to be linear and the optimal solution is found by a series of iterations.

11. Fixed costs £30,000, breakeven turnover £150,000.

Solution 1

Change in turnover	£20,000		
Change in profit	£4,000		
Contribution percentage = £4,000/£20,000 = 20%			

Turnover	£120,000	Contribution	£24,000
Contribution	£24,000	Profit	£12,000
Variable costs	£96,000	Fixed costs	£12,000

Revised variable costs = £96,000 × 110% = £105,600	
Contribution	£24,000
Revised turnover	£129,600
Original turnover	£120,000
Increase	£9,600 = 8%

Solution 2

	Standard (£)		Supa (£)		Total (£)
Sales		160,000		150,000	310,000
Materials	60,000		70,000		130,000
Factory labour	20,000	80,000	30,000	100,000	50,000 180,000
Contribution		80,000		50,000	130,000
Fixed costs					110,000
Net profit					20,000

Abandon Supa production

Abandoning the Supa will result in a loss of £30,000 made up of the £80,000 contribution from the Standard less the (fixed) factory overhead of £110,000. Assuming production facilities could not be more profitably used by making other products, the continuing production of the Supa is recommended.

Acceptance of the Sandels order

With labour costing £10 per hour, total production is currently 5,000 hours of which 2,000 relates to producing the Standard. Each Standard takes one labour hour to produce while each Supa takes two hours to give production of 2,000 Standard and 1,500 Supa units. Unit contributions are £40.00 (£80,000/2,000) for the Standard and £33.33 (£50,000/1,500) for the Supa.

Accepting the special order appears to generate a contribution of £10 per unit, an overall increase in contribution of £10,000 but the company only has 500 surplus hours of production and so the extra 500 hours can only be achieved by cutting back existing production. The contribution per unit of labour is £40.00 (£40/1 hour) for each Standard and £16.67 (£33.33/2 hours) for each Supa. There is therefore an opportunity cost of lost contribution which will result from accepting the order. This is minimised by reducing production of the Supa. Accepting the order will result in a loss of contribution from Supa production of 500 × £16.67, a total of £8,335. Consequently, the net increase in contribution will only be £1,665 per period.

The wider issues

Effect on existing customers resulting from cut back in Supa production; existing customers moving to own-label product or demanding similar price reductions; effect on Bolton and Burnley if Sandels requires a greater number of units – each unit over and above the 500 hours of surplus capacity involves giving up £16.67 contribution from the Supa to gain £10 contribution from the Sandels order; effect on prices of existing models if Sandels plans to sell below the prices of Bolton and Burnley.

Solution 3

CONTRACT COSTING

Expenditure			(£)
Development department costs			Nil
Material A	1,000 kg @ £7		7,000
Material B	600 @ £16	£9,600	
	900 @ £24	£21,600	31,200
Material C	2,000 @ £8		16,000
Labour	2,000 @ £18		36,000
Machinery	2 machines × 3 months × £2,000		12,000
General overheads			nil
Minimum bid price			102,200

CHAPTER 18

Outline solutions

1. (a) objective; (b) ability to measure activities; (c) predictive model of cause and effect; (d) corrective action possible.

2. (e)

3. Noise is anything which distorts a signal. In accounting it can involve distorting the actual results, distorting the standard against which they are measured or by interfering with the reporting of a variance.

4. The master budget generally refers to the budgeted profit and loss account, budgeted balance sheet and, sometimes, the budgeted cashflow statement.

5. (a)

6. Budgeting is essentially time based, standard costing is unit based.

7. (f)

8. Variances arise from either consuming more or less of a resource than planned or paying more or less than planned. Where both the price paid and amount used is greater than standard, a joint variance can occur. It represents the excess price paid for the excess resource consumed. As such it is neither a pure price nor a pure usage variance. Conventionally, the joint variance is included in the price variance.

9. Variable cost variances can be broken down into price and usage. Fixed costs, by definition, do not vary with volume and so the only true variance must be because expenditure is different from planned. Any attempt to calculate a usage variance – or volume variance as it is known – for fixed overheads involves measuring the extent to which overheads fail to be absorbed into production.

10. (c)

Solution 1

(a)	Week 1	Week 2	Week 3	Week 4
Sales	17,640	19,600	25,480	28,420
Good production	19,600	25,480	28,420	
Loss = 2/98 × good production	400	520	580	
Total production	20,000	26,000	29,000	

Over the 50 week period, good production equals sales volume = 1,263,220. Gross production required will be 1,263,220 × (100/98) = 1,289,000 units and with production overheads of £7,734,000, overhead per unit will be £6.

	Week 1	Week 2	Week 3	Total
Total production	20,000	26,000	29,000	75,000
Good production	19,600	25,480	28,420	73,500
	(£)	*(£)*	*(£)*	*(£)*
Weekly paid labour	270,000	270,000	270,000	810,000
Overtime			30,000	30,000
Total labour	270,000	270,000	300,000	840,000
Material	70,000	91,000	101,500	262,500
Production overhead	120,000	156,000	174,000	450,000
Production cost	460,000	517,000	575,500	1,552,500
Unit cost (based on good production)	£23.47	£20.29	£20.25	£21.12

(b)

Units	Week 1	Week 2	Week 3
Planned production	20,000	26,000	29,000
Maximum production	27,000	27,000	27,000
(Over)/under capacity	(7,000)	(1,000)	2,000
Change in production	1,000	1,000	(2,000)
Revised production	21,000	27,000	27,000

Savings in overtime of £30,000.

Solution 2

Blenheim performance report: period ended ....

Budgeted profit			£96,000
Sales			
Price variance	£39,000	(F)	
Margin volume variance	£2,400	(A)	£36,600 (F)
Material			
Price variance	£24,960	(F)	
Usage variance	£9,360	(A)	£15,600 (F)
Labour			
Rate variance	£2,964	(A)	
Efficiency variance	£6,240	(F)	£3,276 (F)
Variable overhead			
Expenditure variance	£2,964	(F)	
Efficiency variance	£1,560	(F)	£4,524 (F)
Fixed overhead			
Expenditure variance	£2,000	(A)	
Capacity variance	£2,950	(A)	
Efficiency variance	£1,950	(F)	£3,000 (A)
Actual profit			£153,000

CHAPTER 19

Outline solutions

1. Planning, coordinating, controlling, motivating, authorising.

2. Variations in efficiency, incorrect or changed standards, poor communication of standards, random fluctuations.

3. Contingency theory as applied to accounting suggests that there is no single, prescriptive ideal accounting control system. Instead the most effective structure will depend on a variety of conditions such as the technology within which the business operates, the instability of the external environment and the culture of the organisation.

4. (b)

5. Amount of effort, individual's ability and luck or misfortune.

6. The amount of an individual's energy which is directed towards the achieving or organisational goals.

7. Content theories attempt to identify the specific factors in an individual which result in high motivation. Examples include Maslow's hierarchy of needs and Herzberg's motivation-hygiene factors.

8. Equity theory, expectancy theory, goal setting theory.

9. Planning budgets are concerned with the most accurate possible forecast to help in determining whether objectives will be met and to identify possible coordination problems. From the work by Hofstede, however, the best motivating budget is one which is unlikely to be achieved in full.

Solution 1

Traditional variances
Price	£1,100	(A)
Usage	£1,600	(A)
Total	£2,700	(A)

Revised variances
Planning
Price	£2,400	(A)
Usage	£3,200	(A)

Operating
Price	£1,100	(F)
Usage	£1,800	(F)
	£2,700	(A)

CHAPTER 20

Outline solutions

1. (a)

2. Shakeout.

3. For each doubling of production, the average time taken to produce the cumulative units falls at a constant rate.

4. (b)

5. Even without inflation or risk, money invested today will grow to a larger amount over any given future period. This is because there are borrowers who prefer money now and are prepared to pay a price – interest – for the privilege. This, in turn, entices lenders to defer the immediate use of cash in exchange for the reward represented by the interest. Without risk or inflation, the time value of money is represented by the interest rate implicit in borrowing or lending. Even if an individual or entity does not need to borrow, there is still a time value of money as the opportunity cost of investing is the loss of interest the money would have earned elsewhere.

6. (c)

7. It is the discount rate which, when applied to the cashflows of a proposal, reduces their net present value to zero.

8. Machine A has the highest net present value, the value of the proposal in terms of today's pounds and so is to be preferred. The initial outlay is irrelevant as this is deducted from the present value of the inflows in determining the net present value.

9. Several assumptions underpin the net present value rule including the availability of funds. Within these assumptions, the rule suggests that all proposals with non-negative net present values should be undertaken. Capital rationing, however, is a state where there are insufficient funds to undertake all financially beneficial projects. Because of this, the net present value rule can begin to break down. It may be preferable to undertake a project with a lower NPV than another if the chosen project brings in earlier cashflows and so reducing the rationing problem.

10. £2.

Solution 1

Contract number	Batch size	Cumulative production	Learning factor	Cumulative data Average hours	Cumulative data Total hours	Batch data Total hours	Batch data Average hours
1	10	10	1.0000	90.000	900.00	900.00	90.00
2	10	20	0.9000	81.000	1620.00	720.00	72.00
3	20	40	0.8100	72.900	2916.00	1296.00	64.80
4	40	80	0.7290	65.610	5248.80	2332.80	58.32
5	80	160	0.6561	59.049	9447.84	4199.04	52.49

Solution 2

Learning curve data					Batch data	
Batch		Cumulative	Learning	Average	Total	Total
number	Size	production	factor	hours	hours	hours
1	10	10	1.0000	35,000.0	350,000	350,000
2	10	20	0.8000	28,000.0	560,000	210,000
3	10	30	0.7021	24,573.6	737,208	177,208
4	10	40	0.6400	22,400.0	896,000	158,792

(columns 3–5 grouped under **Cumulative data**)

Investment appraisal – no learning experience

Annual costs	(£)	End of year	Payments (£)	Receipts (£)	NCF (£)	Factor	DCF (£)
Labour	4,900,000	0		8,000,000	8,000,000	1.000	8,000,000
Materials	2,800,000	1	8,600,000		(8,600,000)	0.833	(7,163,800)
Overheads	900,000	2	8,600,000	8,000,000	(600,000)	0.694	(416,400)
	8,600,000	3	8,600,000		(8,600,000)	0.579	(4,979,400)
		4	8,600,000	14,000,000	5,400,000	0.482	2,602,800
		Net present value					(1,956,800)

Learning curve costs

	Year 1	Year 2	Year 3	Year 4
Labour hours	350,000	210,000	177,208	158,792
	(£)	(£)	(£)	(£)
Labour cost	4,900,000	2,940,000	2,480,912	2,223,088
Material	2,800,000	2,800,000	2,800,000	2,800,000
Overheads	900,000	900,000	900,000	900,000
	8,600,000	6,640,000	6,180,912	5,923,088

Investment appraisal – learning experience

End of year	Payments (£)	Receipts (£)	NCF (£)	Factor	DCF (£)
0		8,000,000	8,000,000	1.000	8,000,000
1	8,600,000		(8,600,000)	0.833	(7,163,800)
2	6,640,000	8,000,000	1,360,000	0.694	943,840
3	6,180,912		(6,180,912)	0.579	(3,578,748)
4	5,923,088	14,000,000	8,076,912	0.482	3,893,072
					2,094,364

Solution 3

End of year	Net cashflow (£)	10% DCF factor	Discounted cashflow (£)
1	140,000	0.909	127,260
2	140,000	0.826	115,640
3	140,000	0.751	105,140
4	140,000	0.683	95,620
5	140,000	0.621	86,940
			530,600

Cost = 5 years × £100,000 depreciation p.a.   500,000
Net present value   30,600

At the company's cost of capital of 10 per cent, the project is viable with an NPV of £30,600. Presumably, the original proposal had used the accounting rate of return, relating the accounting profit of £40,000 to the initial outlay of £500,000, a ratio of 8 per cent.

What is missing from the analysis is a measure of the sensitivity to change of the variables making up the proposal. Two variables are considered in the question, the level of sales and the discount rate.

Internal rate of return = 12.73%
Breakeven sales volume = 8,370 units per annum

CHAPTER 21

Outline solutions

1. Functional decentralisation breaks the organisation down into sub-units based on function such as accounting and production. Federal decentralisation is concerned with dividing the organisation into quasi-autonomous parts, often based on products or markets.

2. The lowering of transaction costs.

3. Suboptimisation, extra explicit costs and the existence of interdependencies making divisionalisation counterproductive.

4. Helps measure the efficiency of a division as an economic entity; helps measure the efficiency of divisional managers; helps guide divisional managers towards correct decisions.

5. Return on investment and residual income.

6. The transfer price should optimise organisation-wide profitability; it should provide a reasonable measure of the division's managerial performance; and it should maintain the autonomy of the division.

7. Cost, cost plus, the economist's model of marginal cost equalling marginal revenue, market price, opportunity cost, negotiated transfer price.

Solution 1

	Alpha (£000)	Beta (£000)
Turnover	53,000	43,000
Direct labour	6,400	8,200
Direct material	23,530	12,100
Divisional overheads	4,100	5,800
Controllable profit	18,970	16,900
Total revenue	53,000	45,400
Total expenses	38,900	29,490
Profit	14,100	15,910
Capital employed	23,500	9,700
Return on capital employed (%)	60.00	164.02
Turnover	53,000	43,000
Direct labour	6,400	8,200
Direct material	23,530	12,100
Divisional overheads	4,100	5,800
Profit	18,970	16,900
Interest on net assets @ 15%	3,525	1,455
Residual income	15,445	15,445

Assumptions and reservations:

Controllable profit has excluded depreciation as this directly arises from decisions of central management. For similar reasons the profit on the sale of fixed assets and central overheads has been excluded. However, this does not address the issue of one division making more use of those central services than another.

Return on capital employed has taken the data simply from the accounts and this is the main problem as the accounts are, presumably, based on historical cost data. Assuming straight line depreciation and no residual values, the fixed assets of Alpha have an estimated 2.5 years to run before being completely written off. For Beta, the corresponding figure is 4.3 years. Without the original cost of the fixed assets, it is not possible to identify if depreciation rates *per se* are different. Even so, with different lives left, it is possible that the assets were purchased at different times. One further issue is that Beta, by having a large overdraft, has effectively reduced its capital employed. To overcome this, net assets might be before any form of short or long term debt finance.

Residual income has excluded depreciation as this might be viewed as double counting when the cost of financing assets is included. Two general issues arise: the use of the same interest charge irrespective of any possible difference in the risk of the divisions and the imputed rate of interest on assets based on net book values in the case of the fixed assets.

Solution 3

Volume units	Price (£)	Turnover (£)	Distribution costs (£)	Transfer costs (£)	Total cost (£)	Profit (£)
1,000	7.75	7,750	1,000	6,250	7,250	500
2,000	7.50	15,000	2,000	10,500	12,500	2,500
3,000	7.25	21,750	4,000	14,750	18,750	3,000
4,000	**7.00**	**28,000**	**6,000**	**19,000**	**25,000**	**3,000**
5,000	6.75	33,750	8,000	23,250	31,250	2,500
6,000	6.50	39,000	10,000	27,500	37,500	1,500
7,000	6.25	43,750	12,000	31,750	43,750	0
8,000	6.00	48,000	14,000	36,000	50,000	(2,000)
9,000	5.75	51,750	16,000	40,250	56,250	(4,500)
10,000	5.50	55,000	18,000	44,500	62,500	(7,500)

Volume = 4,000 units	Distribution (£)	Manufacturing (£)	Group (£)
Turnover	28,000	19,000	28,000
Costs	25,000	10,500	16,500
Divisional profit	3,000	8,500	11,500

Volume units	Price (£)	Turnover (£)	Distribution costs (£)	Manufacturing costs (£)	Total cost (£)	Profit (£)
1,000	7,750	7,750	1,000	4,125	5,125	2,625
2,000	7,500	15,000	2,000	6,250	8,250	6,750
3,000	7,250	21,750	4,000	8,375	12,375	9,375
4,000	7,000	28,000	6,000	10,500	16,500	11,500
5,000	6,750	33,750	8,000	12,625	20,625	13,125
6,000	6,500	39,000	10,000	14,750	24,750	14,250
7,000	6,250	43,750	12,000	16,875	28,875	14,875
8,000	**6,000**	**48,000**	**14,000**	**19,000**	**33,000**	**15,000**
9,000	5,750	51,750	16,000	21,125	37,125	14,625
10,000	5,500	55,000	18,000	23,250	41,250	13,750

Volume = 8,000 units	Distribution (£)	Manufacturing (£)	Group (£)
Turnover	48,000	19,000	48,000
Costs	33,000	19,000	33,000
Divisional profit	15,000	nil	15,000

INDEX

Accounting in the
Business Environment